B

Fodor's 99

New England

D1092487

The complete guide, thoroughly up-to-date

Packed with details that will make your trip

The must-see sights, off and on the beaten path

What to see, what to skip

Mix-and-match vacation itineraries

City strolls, countryside adventures

Smart lodging and dining options

Essential local do's and taboos

Transportation tips, distances and directions

Key contacts, savvy travel tips

When to go, what to pack

Clear, accurate, easy-to-use maps

Books to read, videos to watch, background essays

Fodor's Travel Publications, Inc.
New York • Toronto • London • Sydney • Auckland
www.fodors.com

Fodor's New England

EDITOR: Daniel Mangin

Contributors: Michelle Bodak Acri, Stephanie Adler, Dorothy Antczak, Anne Peracca Bijur, David Brown, Anthony Chase, Chris Cochrane, Andrew Collins, Laura Cronin, Richard Dworkin, Fawn Fitter, Paula J. Flanders, Carolyn Heller, David Laskin, Matthew Lore, Robert Nadeau, Hilary M. Nangle, Alan W. Petrucelli, Seth Rolbein, Kirsten C. Sadler, Helayne Schiff, Stephanie Schorow, M. T. Schwartzman (Gold Guide editor), Michelle Seaton, Anne Stuart, Nancy van Itallie, K. D. Weaver.
Creative Director: Fabrizio La Rocca
Associate Art Director: Guido Caroti
Photo Researcher: Jolie Novak
Cartographer: David Lindroth
Cover Photograph: Kevin Galvin
Text Design: Between the Covers

Copyright

Special Sales

Fodor's Travel Publications are available at special discounts for bulk purchases for sales promotions or premiums. Special editions, including personalized covers, excerpts of existing guides, and corporate imprints, can be created in large quantities for special needs. For more information, contact your local bookseller or write to Special Markets, Fodor's Travel Publications, 201 East 50th Street, New York, NY 10022. Inquiries from Canada should be directed to your local Canadian bookseller or sent to Random House of Canada, Ltd., Marketing Department, 2775 Matheson Boulevard East, Mississauga, Ontario L4W 4P7. Inquiries from the United Kingdom should be sent to Fodor's Travel Publications, 20 Vauxhall Bridge Road, London SW1V 2SA, England.

PRINTED IN THE UNITED STATES OF AMERICA

10 9 8 7 6 5 4 3 2 1

CONTENTS

Maps

ON THE ROAD WITH FODOR'S

WHEN I PLAN A VACATION, the first thing I do is cast around among my friends and colleagues to find someone who's just been where I'm going. That's because there's no substitute for a recommendation from a good friend who knows your tastes, your budget, and your circumstances, someone who's just been there. Unfortunately, such friends are few and far between. So it's nice to know that there's *Fodor's New England '99*.

In the first place, this book won't stay home when you hit the road. It will accompany you every step of the way, steering you away from wrong turns and wrong choices and never expecting a thing in return. It includes a full-color map from Rand McNally, the world's largest commercial mapmaker. Most important, it's written and assiduously updated by the kind of people you *would* hit up for travel tips if you knew them. They're as choosy as your pickiest friend, except they've probably seen a lot more of New England. In these pages, they don't send you chasing down every town and sight in New England but have instead selected the best ones, the ones that are worthy of your time and money. To make it easy for you to put it all together in the time you have, they've created short, medium, and long itineraries and, in cities, neighborhood walks that you can mix and match in a snap. Just tear out the map at the perforation, and join us on the road in New England.

About Our Writers

Our success in helping to make your trip the best of all possible vacations is a credit to the hard work of our extraordinary contributors.

Michelle Bodak Acri, who updated the Connecticut chapter, has lived in the Nutmeg State for 29 years, the last seven of them working as an editor for *Connecticut* magazine. She never tires of sharing Connecticut's glories with the uninitiated.

Rhode Island updater **K. D. Weaver,** a transplant to the state from Maine, is the editor of the weekly *Block Island Times* and a stringer for the Associated Press. He is a graduate of Bennington College and the Columbia School of Journalism.

Boston exploring updater **Stephanie Schorow,** a former Associated Press reporter, is the assistant lifestyles editor for the *Boston Herald*. **Robert Nadeau** writes a dining column for the *Boston Phoenix*. After 14 years of hosting visiting friends and family, **Fawn Fitter** learned where to put them up and where to take them out—knowledge put to good use updating our Lodging and Nightlife chapters. **Kirsten Sadler,** who covered the North Shore and western Massachusetts, has lived in the state since 1986. Eastham resident **Alan W. Petrucelli** updated our coverage of the Upper and Mid Cape and Martha's Vineyard. **Dorothy Antczak,** a freelance writer and editor who lives in Provincetown, updated the Lower Cape and Nantucket sections.

Vermont updater **Anne Peracca Bijur** grew up in Connecticut but was drawn to Vermont for its quality of life and skiing. Anne, who is earning a master's degree in Natural Resource Planning, is a contributor to the *Encyclopedia of the Environment*.

Originally from Maine, **Paula J. Flanders** writes travel features for several New England newspapers and teaches writing at the University of New Hampshire's Department of Continuing Education.

Hilary M. Nangle is travel editor for a daily newspaper in Maine and writes regularly about travel, food, and skiing for publications in the United States and Canada.

Connections

We're pleased that the American Society of Travel Agents continues to endorse Fodor's as its guidebook of choice. ASTA is the world's largest and most influential travel trade association, operating in more than 170 countries, with 27,000 members pledged to adhere to a strict code of ethics reflecting the Society's motto, "Integrity in Travel." ASTA shares Fodor's devotion to providing smart, honest travel information and advice to travelers, and we've long recommended that our readers—even those who have guidebooks and traveling friends—consult ASTA member agents for the experience and professionalism they bring to your vacation planning.

On the Web, check out Fodor's site (http://www.fodors.com) for information on major destinations around the world and travel-savvy interactive features that are replete with hot links to complementary on-line resources.

How to Use This Book

Organization

Up front is the **Gold Guide,** an easy-to-use section arranged alphabetically by topic. Under each listing you'll find tips and information that will help you accomplish what you need to in New England. You'll also find addresses and telephone numbers of organizations and companies that offer destination-related services and detailed information and publications.

The first chapter in the guide, Destination: New England, helps get you in the mood for your trip. New and Noteworthy cues you in on trends and happenings, What's Where gets you oriented, Pleasures and Pastimes describes the activities and sights that make New England unique, Fodor's Choice showcases our top picks, and Festivals and Seasonal Events alerts you to special events.

Chapters in *Fodor's New England '99* are arranged by state, from south to north. Each state chapter is divided by geographical area; within each area, towns are covered in logical geographical order, and attractive stretches of road and minor points of interest between them are indicated by the designation *En Route.* And within town sections, all restaurants and lodgings are grouped together.

To help you decide what to visit in the time you have, all chapters begin with our recommended itineraries. The A to Z sections in each chapter provide tips for getting to and getting around the destinations covered and provide contacts and resources.

At the end of the book you'll find Portraits, an essay about Cape Cod, followed by suggestions for pretrip research, from recommended reading and audiotapes to movies on tape that use New England as a backdrop.

Icons and Symbols

★   Our special recommendation
✕   Restaurant
🏠   Lodging establishment
✕🏠   Lodging establishment whose restaurant warrants a special trip
△   Campground
ℭ   Good for kids (rubber duck)
☞   Sends you to another section of the guide for more information
✉   Address
☎   Telephone number
◷   Opening and closing times
💰   Admission prices (those we give apply to adults; substantially reduced fees are almost always available for children, students, and senior citizens)

Numbers in white and black circles ③ ❸ that appear on the maps, in the margins, and within the tours correspond to one another.

Hotel Facilities

Unless otherwise noted, assume that the rooms in the lodgings reviewed have private baths and that the rates include no meals. If a lodging serves breakfast, we specify whether it's full or Continental in the italicized service information at the end of the review; if more than breakfast is served we specify whether the lodging operates on the **Modified American Plan** (MAP, with breakfast and dinner daily), or the **Full American Plan** (FAP, with all meals).

Restaurant Reservations and Dress Codes

Reservations are always a good idea; we mention them only when they're essential or are not accepted. Book as far ahead as you can, and reconfirm as soon as you arrive. Unless otherwise noted, the restaurants listed are open daily for lunch and dinner. We mention dress only when men are required to wear a jacket or a jacket and tie.

Credit Cards

The following abbreviations are used: **AE,** American Express; **D,** Discover; **DC,** Diners Club; **MC,** MasterCard; and **V,** Visa.

Don't Forget to Write

You can use this book in the confidence that all prices and opening times are based on information supplied to us at press time; Fodor's cannot accept responsibility for any errors. Time inevitably brings changes, so always confirm information when it matters—especially if you're making a detour to visit a specific place.

Were the restaurants we recommended as described? Did our hotel picks exceed your expectations? Did you find a museum we recommended a waste of time? Keeping a travel guide fresh and up-to-date is a big job, and we welcome your feedback, positive and negative. If you have complaints, we'll look into them and revise our entries when the facts warrant it. If you've discovered a special place that we haven't included, we'll pass the information along to our correspondents and have them check it out. So send us your thoughts via e-mail at editors@fodors.com (specifying the name of the book on the subject line) or on paper in care of the New England editor at Fodor's, 201 East 50th Street, New York, New York 10022. In the meantime, have a wonderful trip!

Karen Cure

Karen Cure
Editorial Director

New England

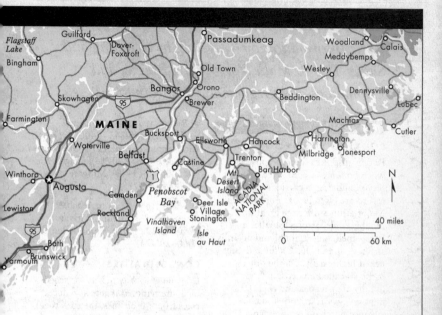

Flagstaff Lake
Bingham
Guilford
Dover-Foxcroft
Passadumkeag
Woodland
Calais
Meddybemps
Wesley
Dennysville
Old Town
Skowhegan
Bangor
Orono
Beddington
Lubec
Brewer
Machias
Cutler
Farmington
MAINE
Bucksport
Ellsworth
Hancock
Harrington
Waterville
Trenton
Milbridge
Jonesport
Belfast
Castine
Bar Harbor
Winthrop
Augusta
Penobscot Bay
Mt. Desert Island
ACADIA NATIONAL PARK
N
Camden
Deer Isle
Village
Lewiston
Rockland
Vinalhaven Island
Stonington
Isle au Haut
0   40 miles
0   60 km
Bath
Brunswick
Yarmouth

ATLANTIC OCEAN

NEW BRUNSWICK
0   40 miles
0   60 km
St. Lawrence River
CANADA
Fort Kent
Van Buren
Allagash
Fort Fairfield
QUEBEC
Ashland
Presque Isle
Chamberlain Lake
11
Houlton
Patten
Island Falls
Seboomook
Rockwood
Moosehead Lake
Danforth
Provincetown
Jackman
Greenville
MAINE
95
Topsfield
Cod
Chatham
West Forks
Milo
Lincoln
Springfield
Stratton
Guilford
Dover-Foxcroft
Howland
Woodland
Nantucket
Rangeley
Dexter
Old Town
Wesley
Newport
Bangor
Brewer
Beddington

SMART TRAVEL TIPS A TO Z

*Basic Information on Traveling in New England,
Savvy Tips to Make Your Trip a Breeze, and
Companies and Organizations to Contact*

AIR TRAVEL

BOOKING YOUR FLIGHT

Price is just one factor to consider when booking a flight: Frequency of service and even a carrier's safety record are often just as important. Major airlines offer the greatest number of departures. Smaller airlines—including regional and no-frills airlines—usually have a limited number of flights daily. On the other hand, so-called low-cost airlines usually are cheaper, and their fares impose fewer restrictions, such as advance-purchase requirements. Safety-wise, low-cost carriers as a group have a good history—about equal to that of major carriers.

When you book, **look for nonstop flights** and **remember that "direct" flights stop at least once.** Try to **avoid connecting flights,** which require a change of plane. Two airlines may jointly operate a connecting flight, so ask if your airline operates every segment—you may find that your preferred carrier flies you only part of the way.

Ask your airline if it offers electronic ticketing, which eliminates all paperwork. There's no ticket to pick up or misplace. You go directly to the gate and give the agent your confirmation number—a real blessing if you've lost your ticket or made last-minute changes in travel plans. There's no worry about waiting in line at the airport while precious minutes tick by.

CARRIERS

➤ MAJOR AIRLINES: **American** (☎ 800/433–7300). **Continental** (☎ 800/525–0280). **Delta** (☎ 800/221–1212). **Northwest** (☎ 800/225–2525). **Southwest** (☎ 800/435–9792). **TWA** (☎ 800/221–2000). **United** (☎ 800/241–6522). **US Airways** (☎ 800/428–4322).

➤ REGIONAL AIRLINES: **Business Express** (☎ 800/345–3400). **Cape Air/Nantucket Airlines** (☎ 508/790–3122 or 800/352–0714). **Colgan Air** (☎ 800/272–5488). **Midway** (☎ 800/446–4392).

➤ FROM THE U.K.: **American** (☎ 0345/789–789). **British Airways** (☎ 0345/222–111). **Virgin Atlantic** (☎ 01293/747–747).

CONSOLIDATORS

Consolidators buy tickets for scheduled international flights at reduced rates from the airlines, then sell them at prices that beat the best fare available directly from the airlines, usually without restrictions. Sometimes you can even get your money back if you need to return the ticket. Carefully read the fine print detailing penalties for changes and cancellations, and **confirm your consolidator reservation with the airline.**

➤ CONSOLIDATORS: **Cheap Tickets** (☎ 800/377–1000). **Discount Travel Network** (☎ 800/576–1600). **Unitravel** (☎ 800/325–2222). **Up & Away Travel** (☎ 212/889–2345). **World Travel Network** (☎ 800/409–6753).

CUTTING COSTS

The least-expensive airfares to New England are priced for round-trip travel and usually must be purchased in advance. It's smart to **call a number of airlines, and when you are quoted a good price, book it on the spot**—the same fare may not be available the next day. Airlines generally allow you to change your return date for a fee. If you don't use your ticket, you can apply the cost toward the purchase of a new ticket, again for a small charge. However, most low-fare tickets are nonrefundable. To get the lowest airfare, **check different routings.** Compare prices of flights to and from different airports if your destination or home city has more than one gateway. Also, price off-peak flights, which may be significantly less expensive.

When flying within the U.S., **plan to stay over a Saturday night** and **travel during the middle of the week** to get the lowest fare. These low fares are usually priced for round-trip travel and are nonrefundable. You can, however, change your return date for a fee ($75 on most major airlines).

Travel agents, especially those who specialize in finding the lowest fares (☞ Discounts & Deals, *below*), can be especially helpful when booking a plane ticket. When you're quoted a price, **ask your agent if the price is likely to get any lower.** Good agents know the seasonal fluctuations of airfares and can usually anticipate a sale or fare war. However, waiting can be risky: The fare could go *up* as seats become scarce, and you may wait so long that your preferred flight sells out. A wait-and-see strategy works best if your plans are flexible. If you must arrive and depart on certain dates, don't delay.

CHECK IN & BOARDING

Airlines routinely overbook planes, assuming that not everyone with a ticket will show up, but sometimes everyone does. When that happens, airlines ask for volunteers to give up their seats. In return these volunteers usually get a certificate for a free flight and are rebooked on the next flight out. If there are not enough volunteers, the airline must choose who will be denied boarding. The first to get bumped are passengers who checked in late and those flying on discounted tickets, so **get to the gate and check in as early as possible** especially during peak periods.

Although the trend on international flights is to drop reconfirmation requirements, many airlines still ask you to reconfirm each leg of your international itinerary. Failure to do so may result in your reservation being canceled.

Always **bring a government-issued photo ID to the airport.** You may be asked to show it before you are allowed to check in.

ENJOYING THE FLIGHT

For better service, **fly smaller or regional carriers,** which often have higher passenger-satisfaction ratings. Sometimes you'll find leather seats, more legroom, and better food.

For more legroom, **request an emergency-aisle seat.** Don't sit in the row in front of the emergency aisle or in front of a bulkhead, where seats may not recline.

If you don't like airline food, **ask for special meals when booking.** These can be vegetarian, low-cholesterol, or kosher, for example.

FLYING TIMES

Flying time to Boston is 1 hour from New York, 2 hours and 15 minutes from Chicago, 6 hours from Los Angeles, 4 hours from Dallas, and 8 hours from London.

HOW TO COMPLAIN

If your baggage goes astray or your flight goes awry, complain right away. Most carriers require that you **file a claim immediately.**

➤ AIRLINE COMPLAINTS: U.S. Department of Transportation **Aviation Consumer Protection Division** (✉ C-75, Room 4107, Washington, DC 20590, ☎ 202/366–2220). **Federal Aviation Administration Consumer Hotline** (☎ 800/322–7873).

AIRPORTS

A major gateway to New England is Boston's **Logan International Airport,** the largest airport in New England. **Bradley International Airport,** in Windsor Locks, Connecticut, 12 mi north of Hartford, is convenient to southern Massachusetts and all of Connecticut. **Theodore Francis Green State Airport,** just outside Providence, Rhode Island, is another major airport. Additional New England airports served by major carriers include those in Manchester, New Hampshire; Portland and Bangor, Maine; Burlington, Vermont; and Hyannis and Worcester, Massachusetts.

➤ AIRPORT INFORMATION: **Logan International Airport** (✉ Exit 24 off Rte. 93 N, East Boston, MA, ☎ 800/ 235–6426). **Bradley International Airport** (✉ Rte. 20; take Exit 40 off

I–91, Windsor Locks, CT, ☎ 860/292–2000). **Theodore Francis Green State Airport** (✉ Rte. 1, Warwick, RI, ☎ 401/737–4000).

BIKE TRAVEL

BIKES IN FLIGHT

Most airlines will accommodate bikes as luggage, provided they are dismantled and put into a box. Call to see if your airline sells bike boxes (about $5; bike bags are at least $100) although you can often pick them up free at bike shops. International travelers can sometimes substitute a bike for a piece of checked luggage for free; otherwise, it will cost about $100. Domestic and Canadian airlines charge a $25–$50 fee.

BOAT & FERRY TRAVEL

See the A to Z sections at the end of Chapters 2 through 7.

BUS TRAVEL

All New England states have bus service; fares are cheap and buses normally run on schedule, although service can be infrequent and travel time can be long due to traffic and frequent stops.

➤ BUS LINES: **Bonanza** (☎ 800/556–3815). **Concord Trailways** (☎ 800/639–3317). **Greyhound Lines** (☎ 800/231–2222). **Peter Pan Bus Lines** (☎ 800/237–8747). **Vermont Transit** (☎ 802/864–6811 or 800/451–3292).

CAMERAS & COMPUTERS

EQUIPMENT PRECAUTIONS

Always **keep your film, tape, or computer disks out of the sun.** Carry an extra supply of batteries, and **be prepared to turn on your camera, camcorder, or laptop** to prove to security personnel that the device is real. Always **ask for hand inspection of film,** which becomes clouded after successive exposure to airport X-ray machines, and **keep videotapes and computer disks away from metal detectors.**

ONLINE ON THE ROAD

Checking your e-mail or surfing the Web can sometimes be done in the business centers of major hotels, which usually charge an hourly rate. Web access is also available at many fax and copy centers, many of which are open 24 hours and on weekends. In major cities look for cyber cafés, where tabletop computers allow you to log on while sipping coffee or listening to live jazz. Whether you have e-mail at home or not, you can **arrange to have a free temporary e-mail address** from several services, including one available at www.hotmail.com (the site explains how to apply for an address).

TRAVEL PHOTOGRAPHY

➤ PHOTO HELP: **Kodak Information Center** (☎ 800/242–2424). **Kodak Guide to Shooting Great Travel Pictures,** available in bookstores or from Fodor's Travel Publications (☎ 800/533–6478; $16.50 plus $4 shipping).

CAR RENTAL

Rates in Boston begin at $31 a day and $149 a week for an economy car with air-conditioning, an automatic transmission, and unlimited mileage. This does not include tax on car rentals, which is 5%.

➤ MAJOR AGENCIES: **Alamo** (☎ 800/327–9633, 0800/272–2000 in the U.K.). **Avis** (☎ 800/331–1212, 800/879–2847 in Canada, 008/225–533 in Australia). **Budget** (☎ 800/527–0700, 0800/181181 in the U.K.). **Dollar** (☎ 800/800–4000; 0990/565656 in the U.K., where it is known as Eurodollar). **Hertz** (☎ 800/654–3131, 800/263–0600 in Canada, 0345/555888 in the U.K., 03/9222–2523 in Australia, 03/358–6777 in New Zealand). **National InterRent** (☎ 800/227–7368; 0345/222525 in the U.K., where it is known as Europcar InterRent).

CUTTING COSTS

To get the best deal, **book through a travel agent who is willing to shop around.** When pricing cars, **ask about the location of the rental lot.** Some off-airport locations offer lower rates, and their lots are only minutes from the terminal via complimentary shuttle. You also may want to **price local car-rental companies,** whose rates may be lower still, although their service and maintenance may not be as good as those of a name-brand agency. Remember to ask about required deposits, cancellation penalties, and drop-off charges if you're planning to pick up the car in one city and leave it in another.

Also **ask your travel agent about a company's customer-service record.** How has the company responded to late plane arrivals and vehicle mishaps? Are there often lines at the rental counter? If you're traveling during a holiday period, does a confirmed reservation guarantee you a car?

Be sure to **look into wholesalers,** companies that do not own fleets but rent in bulk from those that do and often offer better rates than traditional car-rental operations. Prices are best during off-peak periods.

➤ RENTAL WHOLESALERS: **Auto Europe** (☎ 207/842–2000 or 800/223–5555, FAX 800–235–6321). **Kemwel Holiday Autos** (☎ 914/835–5555 or 800/678–0678, FAX 914/835–5126).

INSURANCE

When driving a rented car you are generally responsible for any damage to or loss of the vehicle. You also are liable for any property damage or personal injury that you may cause while driving. Before you rent, **see what coverage you already have** under the terms of your personal auto-insurance policy and credit cards.

For about $15 to $20 per day, rental companies sell protection, known as a collision- or loss-damage waiver (CDW or LDW), that eliminates your liability for damage to the car; it's always optional and should never be automatically added to your bill.

In Massachusetts, the car-rental company must pay for damage to third parties up to a preset legal limit. Once that limit is reached, your personal auto or other liability insurance kicks in. However, **make sure you have enough coverage to pay for the car.** If you do not have auto insurance or an umbrella policy that covers damage to third parties, purchasing liability insurance and a CDW or LDW is highly recommended.

REQUIREMENTS

You must be 21 to rent a car, and rates may be higher if you're under

25. You'll pay extra for child seats (about $3 per day), which are compulsory for children under five, and for additional drivers (about $2 per day). Non–U.S. residents will need a reservation voucher, a passport, a driver's license, and a travel policy that covers each driver in order to pick up a car.

SURCHARGES

Before you pick up a car in one city and leave it in another, **ask about drop-off charges or one-way service fees,** which can be substantial. Note, too, that some rental agencies charge extra if you return the car before the time specified in your contract. To avoid a hefty refueling fee, **fill the tank just before you turn in the car,** but be aware that gas stations near the rental outlet may overcharge.

CAR TRAVEL

Because public transportation is spotty or completely lacking in the outer reaches of New England, a car is the most convenient means of transportation.

GASOLINE

Self-service gas stations are the norm in New England, though in some of the less populated regions you'll find stations with one or two pumps and a friendly attendant who provides full service (pumping your gas, checking your tires and oil, washing your windows). At press time, rates for unleaded gas at self-service stations in New England were about $1.09 per gallon; rates at full-service stations ranged from 30¢ to 50¢ more.

ROAD MAPS

Each of the states in New England makes available, free on request, a map that has directories, mileage, and other useful information—contact the state offices of tourism (☞ Visitor Information, *below*; in Maine contact the Maine Publicity Bureau). Jimapco produces detailed maps of Massachusetts. Hagstrom sells maps of Connecticut. Rand McNally prints a detailed map of Rhode Island. Delorme publishes topographical maps of Maine, New Hampshire, and Vermont that include most back roads and many outdoor recreation

THE GOLD GUIDE / SMART TRAVEL TIPS

sites. The maps are widely available in the state.

RULES OF THE ROAD

The speed limit in much of New England is 65 miles per hour (55 in more populated areas). In New England, drivers can turn right at a red light providing they come to a full stop and check to see that the intersection is clear first.

CHILDREN & TRAVEL

CHILDREN IN NEW ENGLAND

In New England, there's no shortage of things to do with children. Major museums have children's sections, and there are children's museums in cities large and small. Children love the roadside attractions found in many tourist areas, and miniature golf courses are easy to come by. Attractions such as beaches and boat rides, parks and planetariums, lighthouses and llama treks are fun for youngsters as are special events, such as crafts fairs and food festivals.

Be sure to plan ahead and **involve your youngsters** as you outline your trip. When packing, include things to keep them busy en route. On sightseeing days try to schedule activities of special interest to your children. If you are renting a car don't forget to **arrange for a car seat** when you reserve.

➤ LOCAL INFORMATION: Consult Fodor's lively by-parents, for-parents *Where Should We Take the Kids? Northeast* (available in bookstores, or ☎ 800/533–6478; $16).

➤ DISCOUNT PASS: The **American Lung Association's** (☎ 800/458–6472) "Children's Fun Pass" costs $15 annually and gives a child free admission to 100 of northern New England's top attractions, including ski areas, with the purchase of an adult admission.

DINING

You don't have to stick with fast food. Asking around will turn up family-oriented restaurants that specialize in pizza or pasta and come equipped with Trivial Pursuit cards, pull toys, fish tanks, and other families traveling with children. A New England–based restaurant chain known for its legendary ice cream desserts, Friendly's, is particularly family-friendly: In some, you'll find crayons on the tables and a rack of children's books not far from the stack of booster seats. Like many other restaurants in the region, Friendly's has a children's menu and special deals for families.

FLYING

If your children are two or older, **ask about children's airfares.** As a general rule, infants under two not occupying a seat fly at greatly reduced fares or even for free.

In general the adult baggage allowance applies to children paying half or more of the adult fare. When booking, **ask about carry-on allowances for those traveling with infants.** In general, for babies charged 10% of the adult fare you are allowed one carry-on bag and a collapsible stroller, which may have to be checked; you may be limited to less if the flight is full.

Experts agree that it's a good idea to use safety seats aloft for children weighing less than 40 pounds. Airlines, however, can set their own policies: U.S. carriers allow FAA–approved models but usually require that you buy a ticket, even if your child would otherwise ride free, since the seats must be strapped into regular seats. Airline rules vary, so it's important to **check your airline's policy about using safety seats during takeoff and landing.** Safety seats cannot obstruct the movement of other passengers in the row, so get an appropriate seat assignment as early as possible.

When making your reservation, **request children's meals or a free-standing bassinet** if you need them; the latter are available only to those seated at the bulkhead, where there's enough legroom. Remember, however, that bulkhead seats may not have their own overhead bins, and there's no storage space in front of you—a major inconvenience.

GROUP TRAVEL

When planning to take your kids on a tour, look for companies that specialize in family travel.

➤ FAMILY-FRIENDLY TOUR OPERATORS: **Families Welcome!** (✉ 92 N. Main St., Ashland, OR 97520, ☎ 541/482–6121 or 800/326–0724, FAX 541/482–0660).

LODGING

Chain hotels and motels welcome children, and New England has many family-oriented resorts with lively children's programs. You'll also find farms that accept guests and that are lots of fun for children; the Vermont Travel Division (☞ Visitor Information, *below*) publishes a directory. Rental houses and apartments abound, particularly around ski areas; off-season, these can be economical as well as comfortable touring bases. Some country inns, especially those with a quiet, romantic atmosphere and those furnished with antiques, are less enthusiastic about small fries, so **be up front about your traveling companions** when you reserve.

Most hotels allow children under a certain age to stay in their parents' room at no extra charge; others charge them as extra adults. Be sure to **ask about the cutoff age.**

CONSUMER PROTECTION

Whenever possible, **pay with a major credit card** so you can cancel payment or get reimbursed if there's a problem, provided that you can provide documentation. This is the best way to pay, whether you're buying travel arrangements before your trip or shopping at your destination.

If you're doing business with a particular company for the first time, **contact your local Better Business Bureau and the attorney general's offices** in your state and the company's home state, as well. Have any complaints been filed?

Finally, if you're buying a package or tour, always **consider travel insurance** that includes default coverage (☞ Insurance, *below*).

➤ LOCAL BBBS: **Council of Better Business Bureaus** (✉ 4200 Wilson Blvd., Suite 800, Arlington, VA 22203, ☎ 703/276–0100, FAX 703/525–8277).

CUSTOMS & DUTIES

When shopping, **keep receipts** for all of your purchases. Upon reentering the country, **be ready to show customs officials what you've bought.** If you feel a duty is incorrect, appeal the assessment. If you object to the way your clearance was handled, get the inspector's badge number. In either case, first ask to see a supervisor, then write to the appropriate authorities, beginning with the port director at your point of entry.

IN AUSTRALIA

Australian residents who are 18 or older may bring back $A400 worth of souvenirs and gifts (including jewelry), 250 cigarettes or 250 grams of tobacco, and 1,125 ml of alcohol (including wine, beer, and spirits). Residents under 18 may bring back $A200 worth of goods.

➤ INFORMATION: **Australian Customs Service** (Regional Director, ✉ Box 8, Sydney, NSW 2001, ☎ 02/9213–2000, FAX 02/9213–4000).

IN CANADA

Canadian residents who have been out of Canada for at least seven days may bring in C$500 worth of goods duty-free. If you've been away less than seven days but more than 48 hours, the duty-free allowance drops to C$200; if your trip lasts 24–48 hours, the allowance is C$50. You may not pool allowances with family members. Goods claimed under the C$500 exemption may follow you by mail; those claimed under the lesser exemptions must accompany you. Alcohol and tobacco products may be included in the 7-day and 48-hour exemptions but not in the 24-hour exemption. If you meet the age requirements of the province or territory through which you reenter Canada, you may bring in, duty-free, 1.14 liters (40 imperial ounces) of wine or liquor *or* 24 12-ounce cans or bottles of beer or ale. If you are 16 or older you may bring in, duty-free, 200 cigarettes and 50 cigars.

You may send an unlimited number of gifts worth up to C$60 each duty-free to Canada. Label the package UNSOLICITED GIFT—VALUE UNDER $60. Alcohol and tobacco are excluded.

THE GOLD GUIDE / SMART TRAVEL TIPS

➤ INFORMATION: **Revenue Canada** (✉ 2265 St. Laurent Blvd. S, Ottawa, Ontario K1G 4K3, ☎ 613/993–0534, 800/461–9999 in Canada).

IN NEW ZEALAND

Although greeted with a "Haere Mai" ("Welcome to New Zealand"), homeward-bound residents with goods to declare must present themselves for inspection. If you're 17 or older, you may bring back $700 worth of souvenirs and gifts. Your duty-free allowance also includes 4.5 liters of wine or beer; one 1,125-ml bottle of spirits; and either 200 cigarettes, 250 grams of tobacco, 50 cigars, or a combo of all three up to 250 grams.

➤ INFORMATION: **New Zealand Customs** (Custom House, ✉ Box 29, 50 Anzac Ave., Auckland, New Zealand, ☎ 09/359–6655, ☎ 09/309–2978).

IN THE U.K.

From countries outside the EU, including the United States, you may import, duty-free, 200 cigarettes or 50 cigars; 1 liter of spirits or 2 liters of fortified or sparkling wine or liqueurs; 2 liters of still table wine; 60 milliliters of perfume; 250 milliliters of toilet water; plus £136 worth of other goods, including gifts and souvenirs.

➤ INFORMATION: **HM Customs and Excise** (Dorset House, ✉ Stamford St., London SE1 9NG, ☎ 0171/202–4227).

IN THE U.S.

Non–U.S. residents ages 21 and older may import into the United States 200 cigarettes or 50 cigars or 2 kilograms of tobacco, 1 liter of alcohol, and gifts worth $100. Prohibited items include meat products, seeds, plants, and fruits.

➤ INFORMATION: **U.S. Customs Service** (Inquiries, ✉ Box 7407, Washington, DC 20044, ☎ 202/927–6724; complaints, Office of Regulations and Rulings, ✉ 1301 Constitution Ave. NW, Washington, DC 20229; registration of equipment, Resource Management, ✉ 1301 Constitution Ave. NW, Washington DC 20229, ☎ 202/927–0540).

DISABILITIES & ACCESSIBILITY

ACCESS IN NEW ENGLAND

In Boston, many sidewalks are brick or cobblestone and may be uneven or sloping; many have curbs cut at one end and not the other. To make matters worse, Boston drivers are notorious for running yellow lights and ignoring pedestrians. Back Bay has flat, well-paved streets; older Beacon Hill is steep and difficult; Quincy Market's cobblestone and brick malls are crisscrossed with smooth, tarred paths. The downtown financial district and Chinatown are accessible, while areas such as South Boston and the Italian North End may prove more problematic for people who use wheelchairs. In Cape Cod, a number of towns such as Wellfleet, Hyannis, and Chatham have wide streets with curb cuts; and the Cape Cod National Seashore has several accessible trails. In Kennebunkport, as in many of Maine's coastal towns south of Portland, travelers with mobility impairments will have to cope with crowds as well as with narrow, uneven steps and sporadic curb cuts. L.L. Bean's outlet in Freeport is fully accessible, and Acadia National Park has some 50 accessible mi of carriage roads that are closed to motor vehicles. In New Hampshire, many of Franconia Notch's natural attractions are accessible.

➤ LOCAL RESOURCES: **Massachusetts Bay Transportation Authority** (✉ MBTA, Office for Transportation Access, 10 Boylston Pl., Boston 02116, ☎ 617/222–5123, TTY 617/222–5415) has a brochure, "MBTA: Access," that outlines Boston's transportation options. **Cape Cod Chamber of Commerce** (✉ Rtes. 6 and 132, Hyannis 02601, ☎ 508/362–3225 or 888/332–2732) has two publications with accessibility ratings: "Visitor's Guide" and "Accommodations Directory." The **Cape Cod National Seashore** (✉ South Wellfleet 02663, ☎ 508/349–3785) publishes "Cape Cod National Seashore Accessibility." The **New Hampshire Office of Vacation Travel** (☎ 603/271–2343) puts out "New Hampshire Guide Book," which includes accessibility ratings for lodgings and restaurants.

MAKING RESERVATIONS

When discussing accessibility with an operator or reservations agent, **ask hard questions.** Are there any stairs, inside *or* out? Are there grab bars next to the toilet *and* in the shower/tub? How wide is the doorway to the room? To the bathroom? For the most extensive facilities meeting the latest legal specifications, **opt for newer accommodations,** which are more likely to have been designed with access in mind. Older buildings or ships may have more limited facilities. Be sure to **discuss your needs before booking.**

➤ COMPLAINTS: **Disability Rights Section** (U.S. Department of Justice, Civil Rights Division, ⊠ Box 66738, Washington, DC 20035–6738, ☎ 202/514–0301 or 800/514–0301, TTY 202/514–0383 or 800/514–0383, FAX 202/307–1198) for general complaints. **Aviation Consumer Protection Division** (☞ Air Travel, *above*) for airline-related problems. **Civil Rights Office** (U.S. Department of Transportation, Departmental Office of Civil Rights, S-30, ⊠ 400 7th St. SW, Room 10215, Washington, DC 20590, ☎ 202/366–4648, FAX 202/366–9371) for problems with surface transportation.

TRAVEL AGENCIES & TOUR OPERATORS

As a whole, the travel industry has become more aware of the needs of travelers with disabilities. In the U.S., the Americans with Disabilities Act requires that travel firms serve the needs of all travelers. Note, though, that some agencies and operators specialize in making travel arrangements for individuals and groups with disabilities.

➤ TRAVELERS WITH MOBILITY PROBLEMS: **Access Adventures** (⊠ 206 Chestnut Ridge Rd., Rochester, NY 14624, ☎ 716/889–9096), run by a former physical-rehabilitation counselor. **CareVacations** (⊠ 5019 49th Ave., Suite 102, Leduc, Alberta T9E 6T5, ☎ 403/986–6404, 800/648–1116 in Canada) has group tours and is especially helpful with cruise vacations. **Flying Wheels Travel** (⊠ Box 382, 143 W. Bridge St., Owatonna, MN 55060, ☎ 507/451–5005 or 800/535–6790, FAX 507/451–1685), a travel agency specializing in customized tours and itineraries worldwide. **Hinsdale Travel Service** (⊠ 201 E. Ogden Ave., Suite 100, Hinsdale, IL 60521, ☎ 630/325–1335), a travel agency that benefits from the advice of wheelchair traveler Janice Perkins.

➤ TRAVELERS WITH DEVELOPMENTAL DISABILITIES: **Sprout** (⊠ 893 Amsterdam Ave., New York, NY 10025, ☎ 212/222–9575 or 888/222–9575, FAX 212/222–9768).

DISCOUNTS & DEALS

Be a smart shopper and **compare all your options** before making any choice. A plane ticket bought with a promotional coupon may not be cheaper than the least expensive fare from a discount ticket agency. For high-price travel purchases, such as packages or tours, keep in mind that what you get is just as important as what you save. Just because something is cheap doesn't mean it's a bargain.

CLUBS & COUPONS

Many companies sell discounts in the form of travel clubs and coupon books, but these cost money. You must use participating advertisers to get a deal, and only after you recoup the initial membership cost or book price do you begin to save. If you plan to use the club or coupons frequently, you may save considerably. Before signing up, find out what discounts you get for free.

➤ DISCOUNT CLUBS: **Entertainment Travel Editions** (⊠ 2125 Butterfield Rd., Troy, MI 48084, ☎ 800/445–4137; $20–$51, depending on destination). **Great American Traveler** (⊠ Box 27965, Salt Lake City, UT 84127, ☎ 801/974–3033 or 800/548–2812; $49.95 per year). **Moment's Notice Discount Travel Club** (⊠ 7301 New Utrecht Ave., Brooklyn, NY 11204, ☎ 718/234–6295; $25 per year, single or family). **Privilege Card International** (⊠ 237 E. Front St., Youngstown, OH 44503, ☎ 330/746–5211 or 800/236–9732; $74.95 per year). **Sears's Mature Outlook** (⊠ Box 9390, Des Moines, IA 50306, ☎ 800/336–6330; $19.95

per year). **Travelers Advantage** (CUC Travel Service, ✉ 3033 S. Parker Rd., Suite 1000, Aurora, CO 80014, ☎ 800/548–1116 or 800/648–4037; $59.95 per year, single or family). **Worldwide Discount Travel Club** (✉ 1674 Meridian Ave., Miami Beach, FL 33139, ☎ 305/534–2082; $50 per year family, $40 single).

CREDIT-CARD BENEFITS

When you use your credit card to make travel purchases you may get free travel-accident insurance, collision-damage insurance, and medical or legal assistance, depending on the card and the bank that issued it. American Express, MasterCard, and Visa provide one or more of these services, so **get a copy of your credit card's travel-benefits policy.** If you are a member of an auto club, always **ask hotel and car-rental reservations agents about auto-club discounts.** Some clubs offer additional discounts on tours, cruises, and admission to attractions.

DISCOUNT RESERVATIONS

To save money, **look into discount-reservations services** with toll-free numbers, which use their buying power to get a better price on hotels, airline tickets, even car rentals. When booking a room, always **call the hotel's local toll-free number** (if one is available) rather than the central reservations number—you'll often get a better price. Always ask about special packages or corporate rates.

When shopping for the best deal on hotels and car rentals, **look for guaranteed exchange rates,** which protect you against a falling dollar. With your rate locked in, you won't pay more, even if the price goes up in the local currency.

➤ AIRLINE TICKETS: ☎ **800/FLY–4–LESS.** ☎ **800/FLY–ASAP.**

➤ HOTEL ROOMS: **Central Reservation Service (CRS)** (☎ 800/548–3311).**RMC Travel** (☎ 800/245–5738).**Steigenberger Reservation Service** (☎ 800/223–5652).

PACKAGE DEALS

Packages and guided tours can save you money, but don't confuse the two. When you buy a package, your travel remains independent, just as though you had planned and booked the trip yourself. Fly/drive packages, which combine airfare and car rental, are often a good deal.

GAY & LESBIAN TRAVEL

➤ GAY- AND LESBIAN-FRIENDLY TRAVEL AGENCIES: **Corniche Travel** (✉ 8721 Sunset Blvd., Suite 200, West Hollywood, CA 90069, ☎ 310/854–6000 or 800/429–8747, FAX 310/659–7441). **Islanders Kennedy Travel** (✉ 183 W. 10th St., New York, NY 10014, ☎ 212/242–3222 or 800/988–1181, FAX 212/929–8530). **Now Voyager** (✉ 4406 18th St., San Francisco, CA 94114, ☎ 415/626–1169 or 800/255–6951, FAX 415/626–8626). **Yellowbrick Road** (✉ 1500 W. Balmoral Ave., Chicago, IL 60640, ☎ 773/561–1800 or 800/642–2488, FAX 773/561–4497). **Skylink Travel and Tour** (✉ 3577 Moorland Ave., Santa Rosa, CA 95407, ☎ 707/585–8355 or 800/225–5759, FAX 707/584–5637), specializing in lesbian travel.

HEALTH

MEDICAL PLANS

No one plans to get sick while traveling, but it happens, so **consider signing up with a medical-assistance company.** Members get doctor referrals, emergency evacuation or repatriation, 24-hour telephone hot lines for medical consultation, cash for emergencies, and other personal assistance. Coverage varies by plan, so **review the benefits of each carefully.**

➤ MEDICAL-ASSISTANCE COMPANIES: **International SOS Assistance** (✉ 8 Neshaminy Interplex, Suite 207, Trevose, PA 19053, ☎ 215/245–4707 or 800/523–6586, FAX 215/244–9617; ✉ 12 Chemin Riant-bosson, 1217 Meyrin 1, Geneva, Switzerland, ☎ 4122/785–6464, FAX 4122/785–6424; ✉ 10 Anson Rd., 14-07/08 International Plaza, Singapore, 079903, ☎ 65/226–3936, FAX 65/226–3937).

LYME DISEASE

Use insect repellent; outbreaks of Lyme disease all over the East Coast make it imperative (even in urban areas) that you protect yourself from ticks from early spring through summer. To prevent bites, **wear light-colored clothing and tuck pant legs into socks.** Look for black ticks about the size of a pin head around hairlines and the warmest parts of the body. If you have been bitten, **consult a physician, especially if you see the telltale bull's-eye bite pattern.** Influenza-like symptoms often accompany a Lyme infection. Early treatment is imperative.

HOLIDAYS

Major national holidays include: New Year's Day (Jan. 1); Martin Luther King, Jr. Day (third Mon. in Jan.); President's Day (third Mon. in Feb.); Memorial Day (last Mon. in May); Independence Day (July 4); Labor Day (first Mon. in Sept.); Thanksgiving Day (fourth Thurs. in Nov.); Christmas Eve and Day (Dec. 24–25); and New Year's Eve (Dec. 31).

INSURANCE

Travel insurance is the best way to **protect yourself against financial loss.** The most useful plan is a comprehensive policy that includes coverage for trip cancellation and interruption, default, trip delay, and medical expenses (with a waiver for preexisting conditions).

Without insurance, you will lose all or most of your money if you cancel your trip, regardless of the reason. Default insurance covers you if your tour operator, airline, or cruise line goes out of business. Trip-delay covers unforeseen expenses that you may incur due to bad weather or mechanical delays. It's important to compare the fine print regarding trip-delay coverage when comparing policies.

For overseas travel, one of the most important components of travel insurance is its medical coverage. Supplemental health insurance will pick up the cost of your medical bills should you get sick or injured while traveling. Residents of the United Kingdom can buy an annual travel-insurance policy valid for most vacations taken during the year in which the coverage is purchased. If you are pregnant or have a preexisting condition, make sure you're covered. British citizens should buy extra medical coverage when traveling overseas, according to the Association of British Insurers. Australian travelers should buy travel insurance, including extra medical coverage, whenever they go abroad, according to the Insurance Council of Australia.

Always **buy travel insurance directly from the insurance company;** if you buy it from a cruise line, airline, or tour operator that goes out of business, you probably will not be covered for the agency or operator's default, a major risk. Before you make any purchase, **review your existing health and home-owner's policies** to find out whether they cover expenses incurred while traveling.

➤ TRAVEL INSURERS: In the U.S., **Access America** (✉ 6600 W. Broad St., Richmond, VA 23230, ☎ 804/285–3300 or 800/284–8300). **Travel Guard International** (✉ 1145 Clark St., Stevens Point, WI 54481, ☎ 715/345–0505 or 800/826–1300). In Canada, **Mutual of Omaha** (Travel Division, ✉ 500 University Ave., Toronto, Ontario M5G 1V8, ☎ 416/598–4083, 800/268–8825 in Canada).

➤ INSURANCE INFORMATION: In the U.K., **Association of British Insurers** (✉ 51 Gresham St., London EC2V 7HQ, ☎ 0171/600–3333). In Australia, the **Insurance Council of Australia** (☎ 613/9614–1077, FAX 613/9614–7924).

LODGING

Hotel and motel chains provide standard rooms and amenities in major cities and at or near traditional vacation destinations. At small inns, where each room is different and amenities vary in number and quality, price isn't always a reliable indicator; fortunately, when you call to make reservations, most hosts will be happy to give all manner of details about their properties, down to the color scheme of the handmade quilts—so **ask all your questions before you book.** At small inns, **don't expect a telephone, TV, or honor bar in your room;** you may even have to share a bathroom.

APARTMENT & VILLA RENTALS

If you want a home base that's roomy enough for a family and comes with cooking facilities, **consider a furnished**

rental. These can save you money, especially if you're traveling with a large group of people. Home-exchange directories list rentals (often second homes owned by prospective house swappers), and some services search for a house or apartment for you (even a castle if that's your fancy) and handle the paperwork. Some send an illustrated catalog; others send photographs only of specific properties, sometimes at a charge. Up-front registration fees may apply.

➤ RENTAL AGENTS: **Property Rentals International** (✉ 1008 Mansfield Crossing Rd., Richmond, VA 23236, ☎ 804/378–6054 or 800/220–3332, ℻ 804/379–2073).**Rent-a-Home International** (✉ 7200 34th Ave. NW, Seattle, WA 98117, ☎ 206/789–9377 or 800/488–7368, ℻ 206/789–9379).**Hideaways International** (✉ 767 Islington St., Portsmouth, NH 03801, ☎ 603/430–4433 or 800/843–4433, ℻ 603/430–4444; membership $99) is a club for travelers who arrange rentals among themselves.

B&BS

Most inns offer breakfast—hence the name bed-and-breakfast—yet this formula varies, too; at one B&B you may be served muffins and coffee, at another a multicourse feast with fresh flowers on the table. Many inns prohibit smoking, which is a fire hazard in older buildings, and some of the inns with antiques or other expensive furnishings do not allow children. Almost all say no to pets.

➤ RESERVATION SERVICES: *See* Contacts and Resources *in* the A to Z sections at the end of Chapters 2 through 7.

CAMPING

The state offices of tourism (☞ Visitor Information, *below*; in Maine contact the Maine Publicity Bureau) supply information about privately operated campgrounds and ones in parks run by state agencies and the federal government.

HOME EXCHANGES

If you would like to exchange your home for someone else's, **join a home-exchange organization,** which will send you its updated listings of available exchanges for a year and will include your own listing in at least one of them. It's up to you to make specific arrangements.

➤ EXCHANGE CLUBS: **HomeLink International** (✉ Box 650, Key West, FL 33041, ☎ 305/294–7766 or 800/638–3841, ℻ 305/294–1148; $83 per year).

HOSTELS

No matter what your age, you can **save on lodging costs by staying at hostels.** In some 5,000 locations in more than 70 countries around the world, Hostelling International (HI), the umbrella group for a number of national youth hostel associations, offers single-sex, dorm-style beds and, at many hostels, "couples" rooms and family accommodations. Membership in any HI national hostel association, open to travelers of all ages, allows you to stay in HI-affiliated hostels at member rates (one-year membership is about $25 for adults; hostels run about $10–$25 per night). Members also have priority if the hostel is full; they're eligible for discounts around the world, even on rail and bus travel in some countries.

➤ HOSTEL ORGANIZATIONS: **Hostelling International—American Youth Hostels** (✉ 733 15th St. NW, Suite 840, Washington, DC 20005, ☎ 202/783–6161, ℻ 202/783–6171). **Hostelling International—Canada** (✉ 400-205 Catherine St., Ottawa, Ontario K2P 1C3, ☎ 613/237–7884, ℻ 613/237–7868). **Youth Hostel Association of England and Wales** (Trevelyan House, ✉ 8 St. Stephen's Hill, St. Albans, Hertfordshire AL1 2DY, ☎ 01727/855215 or 01727/845047, ℻ 01727/844126); membership in the U.S. $25, in Canada C$26.75, in the U.K. £9.30).

HOTELS

Hotel chains are amply represented in New England. Some of the large chains, such as Holiday Inn, Hilton, Hyatt, Marriott, and Ramada, operate all-suites, budget, business-oriented, or luxury resorts, often variations on the parent corporation's name (Courtyard by Marriott, for example). Though some chain hotels may have a standardized look to them, this "cookie-cutter" approach also means that you can rely on the same level of comfort and efficiency at all properties in a well-managed chain, and at a chain's premier properties—its so-called flagship hotels—the decor and services may be outstanding.

Most hotels will hold your reservation until 6 PM; **call ahead if you plan to arrive late.** Some will hold a late reservation for you if you reserve with a credit-card number.

When you call to make a reservation, **ask all the necessary questions up front.** If you are arriving with a car, ask if the hotel has a parking lot or covered garage and whether there is an extra fee for parking. If you like to eat your meals in, ask if the hotel has a restaurant or whether it has room service (most do, but not necessarily 24 hours a day—and be forewarned that it can be expensive). Most hotels and motels have in-room TVs, often with cable movies, but verify this if you like to watch TV. If you want an in-room crib for your child, there will probably be an additional charge.

➤ TOLL-FREE NUMBERS: **Best Western** (☎ 800/528–1234). **Budgetel Inns** (☎ 800/301–0400). **Clarion** (☎ 800/252–7466). **Comfort Inn** (☎ 800/228–5150). **Days Inn** (☎ 800/325–2525). **Doubletree and Red Lion Hotels** (☎ 800/528–0444). **Embassy Suites** (☎ 800/362–2779). **Hilton** (☎ 800/445–8667). **Holiday Inn** (☎ 800/465–4329). **Howard Johnson** (☎ 800/654–4656). **Hyatt Hotels& Resorts** (☎ 800/233–1234). **Inter-Continental** (☎ 800/327–0200). **Le Meridien** (☎ 800/543–4300). **Marriott** (☎ 800/228–9290). **Omni** (☎ 800/843–6664). **Quality Inn** (☎ 800/228–5151). **Radisson** (☎ 800/333–3333). **Ramada** (☎ 800/228–2828). **Renaissance Hotels & Resorts** (☎ 800/468–3571). **Ritz-Carlton** (☎ 800/241–3333). **Sheraton** (☎ 800/325–3535). **Westin Hotels & Resorts** (☎ 800/228–3000). **Wyndham Hotels & Resorts** (☎ 800/822–4200).

MOTELS

➤ TOLL-FREE NUMBERS: **Budget Hosts Inns** (☎ 800/283–4678). **Econo Lodge** (☎ 800/553–2666). **Motel 6** (☎ 800/466–8356). **Super 8** (☎ 800/848–8888).

MONEY

CREDIT & DEBIT CARDS

Should you use a credit card or a debit card when traveling? Both have benefits. A credit card allows you to delay payment and gives you certain rights as a consumer (☞ Consumer Protection, *above*). A debit card, also known as a check card, deducts funds directly from your checking account and helps you stay within your budget. When you want to rent a car, though, you may still need an old-fashioned credit card. Although you can always *pay* for your car with a debit card, some agencies will not allow you to *reserve* a car with a debit card.

Otherwise, the two types of plastic are virtually the same. Both will get you cash advances at ATMs worldwide if your card is properly programmed with your personal identification number (PIN).

➤ ATM LOCATIONS: **Cirrus** (☎ 800/424–7787). **Plus** (☎ 800/843–7587) for locations in the U.S. and Canada, or visit your local bank.

➤ REPORTING LOST CARDS: To report lost or stolen credit cards, call the following toll-free numbers: **American Express** (☎ 800/327–2177); **Discover Card** (☎ 800/347–2683); **Diners Club** (☎ 800/234–6377); **Master Card** (☎ 800/307–7309); and **Visa** (☎ 800/847–2911).

EXCHANGING MONEY

For the most favorable rates, **change money through banks.** Although fees charged for ATM transactions may be higher abroad than at home, Cirrus and Plus exchange rates are excellent, because they are based on wholesale rates offered only by major banks. You won't do as well at exchange booths in airports or rail and bus stations, in hotels, in restaurants, or in stores, although you may find their hours more convenient. To avoid lines at airport exchange booths, **get ~~of local currency before you lea~~ home.**

➤ EXCHANGE SERVICES: **Chase Currency To Go** (☎ 800/935–9935; 935–9935 in NY, NJ, and CT). **International Currency Express** (☎ 888/842–0880 on the East Coast, 888/278–6628 on the West Coast). **Thomas Cook Currency Services** (☎ 800/287–7362 for telephone orders and retail locations).

TRAVELER'S CHECKS

Do you need traveler's checks? It depends on where you're headed. If you're going to rural areas and small towns, go with cash; traveler's checks are best used in cities. Lost or stolen checks can usually be replaced within 24 hours. To ensure a speedy refund, buy your own traveler's checks— don't let someone else pay for them: Irregularities like this can cause delays. The person who bought the checks should make the call to request a refund.

NATIONAL PARKS

Look into discount passes to **save money on park entrance fees.** The Golden Eagle Pass ($50) gets you and your companions free admission to all parks for one year. (Camping and parking are extra). Both the Golden Age Passport ($10), for those 62 and older, and the Golden Access Passport (free), for travelers with disabilities, entitle holders to free entry to all national parks, plus 50% off fees for the use of many park facilities and services. You must show proof of age and of U.S. citizenship or permanent residency (such as a U.S. passport, driver's license, or birth certificate) and, if requesting Golden Access, proof of disability. All three passes are available at all national park entrances where entrance fees are charged. Golden Eagle and Golden Access passes are also available by mail.

➤ PASSES BY MAIL: **National Park Service** (National Capitol Area Office, ✉ 1100 Ohio Dr. SW, Washington, DC 20242).

OUTDOOR ACTIVITIES & SPORTS

Biking, fishing, and hiking are popular in New England. Biking trails are plentiful; freshwater-lake fishing, surf-casting, deep-sea fishing, angling, and trout fishing are available; and for hikers, New England has many miles of the famous Appalachian Trail. Ask state information offices (☞ Visitor Information, *below*) about sporting opportunities.

➤ BIKING: **Maine Sport Outdoor School** (✉ Rte. 1, Rockport, 04856, ☎ 207/236–8797 or 800/722–0826). **Vermont Bicycle Touring** (✉ Box 711, Bristol, 05443, ☎ 802/453–4811 or 800/245–3868).

➤ FISHING: **Connecticut's Department of Environmental Protection** (✉ Fisheries Division, 79 Elm St., Hartford 06106, ☎ 860/424–3474). **Maine Department of Inland Fisheries and Wildlife** (✉ 284 State St., State House Station 41, Augusta, ME 04333, ☎ 207/287–8000). **Massachusetts Division of Fisheries and Wildlife** (✉ 100 Cambridge St., Room 1902, Boston, MA 02202, ☎ 617/727–3151). **New Hampshire Fish and Game Department,** Information and Education Division (✉ 2 Hazen Dr., Concord, NH 03301, ☎ 603/271–3211). Rhode Island's **Department of Environmental Management, Division of Fish and Wildlife** (✉ 4808 Tower Hill Rd., Wakefield, RI 02879, ☎ 401/789–3094). **Vermont Fish and Wildlife Department** (✉ 103 S. Main St., Waterbury, VT 05676, ☎ 802/241–3700).

➤ HIKING: **Green Mountain Club** (✉ Box 650, Rte. 100, Waterbury, VT 05677, ☎ 802/244–7037). **Appalachian Mountain Club** (✉ Box 298, Gorham, NH 03581, ☎ 603/466–2725, ext.116). **White Mountains National Forest** (✉ 719 North Main St., Laconia, NH 03246, ☎ 603/528–8721). **Audubon Society of New Hampshire** (✉ 3 Silk Farm Rd., Concord, NH 03301, ☎ 603/224–9909).

PACKING

LUGGAGE

How many carry-on bags you can bring with you is up to the airline. Many have begun to allow only one bag, either systemwide or on certain flights; some airlines allow you to board with two bags. Gate agents will take excess baggage—including bags they deem oversize—from you as you board and add it to checked luggage. To avoid this situation, make sure that everything you carry aboard will fit under your seat. Also, get to the gate early and request a seat at the back of the plane; you'll probably board first, while the overhead bins are still empty. Because big, bulky baggage attracts the attention of gate agents and flight attendants on a busy flight, make sure your carry-on is really a carry-on. Finally, a carry-on that's long and narrow is more likely to remain unnoticed than one that's wide and squarish.

If you are flying internationally, note that baggage allowances may be determined not by piece but by weight—generally 88 pounds (40 kilograms) in first class, 66 pounds (30 kilograms) in business class, and 44 pounds (20 kilograms) in economy.

Airline liability for baggage is limited to $1,250 per person on flights within the United States. On international flights it amounts to $9.07 per pound or $20 per kilogram for checked baggage (roughly $640 per 70-pound bag) and $400 per passenger for unchecked baggage. You can buy additional coverage at check-in for about $10 per $1,000 of coverage, but it excludes a rather extensive list of items, shown on your airline ticket.

Before departure, **itemize your bags' contents** and their worth, and label the bags with your name, address, and phone number. (If you use your home address, cover it so that potential thieves can't see it readily.) Inside each bag, **pack a copy of your itinerary.** At check-in, **make sure that each bag is correctly tagged** with the destination airport's three-letter code. If your bags arrive damaged or fail to arrive at all, file a written report with the airline before leaving the airport.

PACKING LIST

The principal rule on weather in New England is that there are no rules. A cold, foggy morning can and often does become a bright, 60-degree afternoon. A summer breeze can suddenly turn chilly, and rain often appears with little warning. Thus, the best advice on how to dress is to **layer your clothing** so that you can peel off or add garments as needed for comfort. Showers are frequent, so **pack a raincoat and umbrella.** Even in summer you should bring long pants, a sweater or two, and a waterproof windbreaker, for evenings are often chilly and sea spray can make things cool.

Casual sportswear—walking shoes and jeans—will take you almost everywhere, but swimsuits and bare feet will not: Shirts and shoes are required attire at even the most casual venues. Dress in restaurants is generally casual, except at some of the distinguished restaurants of Boston, Newport, Maine coast towns such as Kennebunkport, a number of inns in the Berkshires, and in Litchfield and Fairfield counties in Connecticut.

In summer, **bring a hat and sunscreen.** Remember also to **pack insect repellent**; to prevent Lyme disease you'll need to guard against ticks from early spring through the summer (☞ Health, *above*).

In your carry-on luggage **bring an extra pair of eyeglasses or contact lenses** and **enough of any medication you take** to last the entire trip. You may also want your doctor to write a spare prescription using the drug's generic name, since brand names may vary from country to country. **Never put prescription drugs or valuables in luggage to be checked.** To avoid customs delays, carry medications in their original packaging. And don't forget to copy down and carry addresses of offices that handle refunds of lost traveler's checks.

PASSPORTS & VISAS

When traveling internationally, **carry a passport even if you don't need one** (it's always the best form of ID), and make **two photocopies of the data page** (one for someone at home and another for you, carried separately from your passport). If you lose your passport, promptly call the nearest embassy or consulate and the local police.

➤ U.K. CITIZENS: U.S. Embassy Visa Information Line (☎ 01891/200–

290; calls cost 49p per minute, 39p per minute cheap rate), for U.S. visa information. **U.S. Embassy Visa Branch** (⊠ 5 Upper Grosvenor St., London W1A 2JB), for U.S. visa information; send a self-addressed, stamped envelope. Write the **U.S. Consulate General** (Queen's House, ⊠ Queen St., Belfast BTI 6EO) if you live in Northern Ireland.

PASSPORT OFFICES

The best time to apply for a passport or to renew is during the fall and winter. Before any trip, be sure to check your passport's expiration date and, if necessary, renew it as soon as possible. (Some countries won't allow you to enter on a passport that's due to expire in six months or less.)

➤ AUSTRALIAN CITIZENS: **Australian Passport Office** (☎ 131–232).

➤ NEW ZEALAND CITIZENS: **New Zealand Passport Office** (☎ 04/494–0700 for information on how to apply, 0800/727–776 for information on applications already submitted).

➤ U.K. CITIZENS: **London Passport Office** (☎ 0990/21010), for fees and documentation requirements and to request an emergency passport.

SENIOR-CITIZEN TRAVEL

To qualify for age-related discounts, **mention your senior-citizen status up front** when booking hotel reservations (not when checking out) and before you're seated in restaurants (not when paying the bill). Note that discounts may be limited to certain menus, days, or hours. When renting a car, **ask about promotional car-rental discounts,** which can be cheaper than senior-citizen rates.

➤ EDUCATIONAL PROGRAMS: **Elderhostel** (⊠ 75 Federal St., 3rd floor, Boston, MA 02110, ☎ 617/426–8056).

STUDENT TRAVEL

➤ STUDENT IDs & SERVICES: **Council on International Educational Exchange** (CIEE, ⊠ 205 E. 42nd St., 14th floor, New York, NY 10017, ☎ 212/822–2600 or 888/268–6245, FAX 212/822–2699), for mail orders only, in the United States. **Travel Cuts** (⊠ 187 College St., Toronto, Ontario

M5T 1P7, ☎ 416/979–2406 or 800/667–2887) in Canada.

➤ STUDENT TOURS: **Contiki Holidays** (⊠ 300 Plaza Alicante, Suite 900, Garden Grove, CA 92840, ☎ 714/740–0808 or 800/266–8454, FAX 714/740–2034).

TAXES

Sales taxes in New England are as follows: Connecticut 6%; Maine 6%; Massachusetts 5%; Rhode Island 7%; Vermont 5%. No sales tax is charged in New Hampshire. Some states and municipalities levy an additional tax (from 1% to 10%) on lodging or restaurant meals.

TELEPHONES

COUNTRY CODES

The country code for the United States is 1.

DIRECTORY & OPERATOR INFORMATION

To reach an operator in New England, dial 0. To reach directory assistance information, dial the area code and 555–1212. Within the area code dial 411.

INTERNATIONAL CALLS

Dial 011, followed by the country code, the city code, and the phone number. The country code for Australia is 61; New Zealand, 64; and the United Kingdom, 44. To reach Canada, dial 1+ area code + number.

LONG-DISTANCE CALLS

Competitive long-distance carriers make calling within the United States relatively convenient and let you avoid hotel surcharges. By dialing an 800 number, you can get connected to the long-distance company of your choice.

➤ LONG-DISTANCE CARRIERS: **AT&T** (☎ 800/225–5288). **MCI** (☎ 800/888–8000). **Sprint** (☎ 800/366–2255).

PUBLIC PHONES

A local call on a public pay telephone throughout most of New England costs 25¢.

TIPPING

At restaurants, a 15% tip is standard for waiters; up to 20% may be expected at more expensive establishments. The same goes for taxi drivers, bartenders, and hairdressers. Coat-check operators usually expect $1; bellhops and porters should get 50¢ to $1 per bag; hotel maids in upscale hotels should get about $1 per day of your stay. On package tours, conductors and drivers usually get $10 per day from the group as a whole; check whether this has already been figured into your cost. For local sightseeing tours, you may individually tip the driver-guide $1 if he or she has been helpful or informative. Ushers in theaters do not expect tips.

TOUR OPERATORS

Buying a prepackaged tour or independent vacation can make your trip to New England less expensive and more hassle-free. Because everything is prearranged, you'll spend less time planning.

Operators that handle several hundred thousand travelers per year can use their purchasing power to give you a good price. Their high volume may also indicate financial stability. But some small companies provide more personalized service; because they tend to specialize, they may also be more knowledgeable about a given area.

BOOKING WITH AN AGENT

Travel agents are excellent resources. In fact, large operators accept bookings made only through travel agents. But it's a good idea to **collect brochures from several agencies,** because some agents' suggestions may be influenced by relationships with tour and package firms that reward them for volume sales. If you have a special interest, **find an agent with expertise in that area**; ASTA (☞ Travel Agencies, *below*) has a database of specialists worldwide.

Make sure your travel agent knows the accommodations and other services. Ask about the hotel's location, room size, beds, and whether it has a pool, room service, or programs for children, if you care about these. Has your agent been there in person or sent others you can contact?

Do some homework on your own, too: Local tourism boards can provide information about lesser-known and small-niche operators, some of which may sell only direct.

BUYER BEWARE

Each year consumers are stranded or lose their money when tour operators—even very large ones with excellent reputations—go out of business. So **check out the operator.** Find out how long the company has been in business, and ask several travel agents about its reputation. If the package or tour you are considering is priced lower than in your wildest dreams, **be skeptical.** Try to **book with a company that has a consumer-protection program.** If the operator has such a program, you'll find information about it in the company's brochure. If the operator you are considering does not offer some kind of consumer protection, then ask for references from satisfied customers.

In the U.S., members of the National Tour Association and United States Tour Operators Association are required to set aside funds to cover your payments and travel arrangements in case the company defaults. It's also a good idea to choose a company that participates in the American Society of Travel Agent's Tour Operator Program (TOP). This gives you a forum if there are any disputes between you and your tour operator; ASTA will act as mediator.

➤ TOUR-OPERATOR RECOMMENDATIONS: **American Society of Travel Agents** (☞ Travel Agencies, *below*). **National Tour Association** (NTA, ⊠ 546 E. Main St., Lexington, KY 40508, ☎ 606/226–4444 or 800/755–8687). **United States Tour Operators Association** (USTOA, ⊠ 342 Madison Ave., Suite 1522, New York, NY 10173, ☎ 212/599–6599 or 800/468–7862, FAX 212/599–6744).

COSTS

The more your package or tour includes, the better you can predict the ultimate cost of your vacation. Make sure you know exactly what is covered, and **beware of hidden costs.**

THE GOLD GUIDE / SMART TRAVEL TIPS

Are taxes, tips, and service charges included? Transfers and baggage handling? Entertainment and excursions? These can add up.

Prices for packages and tours are usually quoted per person, based on two sharing a room. If traveling solo, you may be required to pay the full double-occupancy rate. Some operators eliminate this surcharge if you agree to be matched with a roommate of the same sex, even if one is not found by departure time.

TRAIN TRAVEL

OPTIONS

State-run, national, and international train service are options in New England: Massachusetts's MBTA connects Boston with outlying areas on the north and south shores of the state; Amtrak offers frequent daily service along its Northeast Corridor route from Washington and New York to Boston and Vermont.

➤ TRAIN SCHEDULES: **Amtrak** (☎ 800/ 872–7245). **Massachusetts Bay Transportation Authority** (☎ 617/ 722–5000).

TRAVEL AGENCIES

A good travel agent puts your needs first. Look for an agency that has been in business at least five years, emphasizes customer service, and has someone on staff who specializes in your destination. In addition, **make sure the agency belongs to a professional trade organization,** such as ASTA in the United States. If your travel agency is also acting as your tour operator, *see* Buyer Beware *in* Tour Operators, *above*).

➤ LOCAL AGENT REFERRALS: **American Society of Travel Agents** (ASTA, ☎ 800/965–2782 24-hr hot line, FAX 703/684–8319). **Association of Canadian Travel Agents** (✉ Suite 201, 1729 Bank St., Ottawa, Ontario K1V 7Z5, ☎ 613/521–0474, FAX 613/ 521–0805). **Association of British Travel Agents** (✉ 55–57 Newman St., London W1P 4AH, ☎ 0171/ 637–2444, FAX 0171/637–0713). **Australian Federation of Travel Agents** (☎ 02/9264–3299). **Travel Agents' Association of New Zealand** (☎ 04/499–0104).

TRAVEL GEAR

Travel catalogs specialize in useful items, such as compact alarm clocks and travel irons, that can **save space when packing.**

➤ CATALOGS: **Magellan's** (☎ 800/ 962–4943, FAX 805/568–5406). **Orvis Travel** (☎ 800/541–3541, FAX 540/ 343–7053). **TravelSmith** (☎ 800/ 950–1600, FAX 800/950–1656).

U.S. GOVERNMENT

Government agencies can be an excellent source of inexpensive travel information. When planning your trip, **find out what government materials are available.**

➤ PAMPHLETS: **Consumer Information Center** (✉ Consumer Information Catalogue, Pueblo, CO 81009, ☎ 719/948–3334 or 888/878–3256) for a free catalog that includes travel titles.

VISITOR INFORMATION

TOURIST INFORMATION

➤ IN NEW ENGLAND: **Connecticut Department of Tourism** (✉ 505 Hudson St., Hartford, CT 06106, ☎ 860/270–8081 or 800/282–6863). **Maine Publicity Bureau** (✉ Box 2300, 325-B Water St., Hallowell, ME 04347, ☎ 207/623–0363 or 800/533–9595 for brochures). **Massachusetts Office of Travel and Tourism** (✉ 100 Cambridge St., Boston, MA 02202, ☎ 617/727– 3201 or 800/447–6277 for brochures). **New Hampshire Office of Travel and Tourism** (✉ Box 1856, Concord, NH 03302, ☎ 603/271– 2343, 800/258–3608 for seasonal events, 800/386–4664 for brochures). **Rhode Island Department of Economic Development, Tourism Division** (✉ 1 West Exchange St., Providence, RI 02903, ☎ 401/222– 2601 or 800/556–2484 for brochures). **Vermont Department of Tourism and Marketing** (✉ 134 State St., Montpelier, VT 05602, ☎ 802/ 828–3237 or 800/837–6668 for brochures). **Vermont Chamber of Commerce, Department of Travel and Tourism** (✉ Box 37, Montpelier, VT 05602, ☎ 802/223–3443).

➤ IN THE U.K.: **Discover New England** (✉ Admail 4 International,

Greatness La., Sevenoaks TN14 5BQ,
☎ 01732/742777).

WEB SITES

Connecticut: The site of the Connecticut State Tourism Office (http://www.state.ct.us/tourism/) is easy to navigate; from the home page you can access a vacation planner, an events calendar, and links to lodging, transport, outdoors, and regional-tourism sites.

Maine: The comprehensive Maine State Government site (http://www.state.me.us/) has two notable links: "Office of Tourism" brings you to www.visitmaine.com, which has an events calendar, links to local and regional chambers of commerce, and sightseeing, lodging, and dining information; "State Parks" provides details about park fees, facilities, and regulations.

Massachusetts: The site of the Massachusetts Office of Travel and Tourism (http://www.mass-vacation.com/) is a good trip-planning resource. "What to See and Do" has a useful beach finder and in the fall a weekly foliage report. Boston.com (http://www.boston.com/), home of the *Boston Globe* online, has news and feature articles, ample travel information, and links to towns throughout Massachusetts via "Your Town." The site for Boston's arts and entertainment weekly, the *Boston Phoenix* (http://www.bostonphoenix.com/), has nightlife, movie, restaurant, and fine and performing arts listings. There are links to the *Providence Phoenix* and the *Worcester Phoenix* sites. The frequently updated site of the Cape Cod Information Center (http://www.allcapecod.com/) carries events information and has useful town directories with weather, sightseeing, lodging, and dining entries.

New Hampshire: The resources on the New Hampshire Office of Travel and Tourism Development site (http://www.visitnh.gov/) can be explored by region or activity. Regional sections have links to local chamber of commerce web sites.

Rhode Island: The official site of the Rhode Island Tourism Division

(http://www.visitrhodeisland.com/) is attractive (if slow because of the heavy graphics), and has a vacation planner and events calendars. There are useful links to sites via "Attractions" in the trip planner.

Vermont: Though somewhat poorly designed, the Vermont Department of Travel and Tourism (http://www.travel-vermont.com/) site can help you find just about any kind of information; follow "The Links to Vermont" from the home page.

General Interest: A must-visit for anyone interested in the greener side of travel, the Great Outdoor Recreation Page (http://www.gorp.com/) is arranged into three easily navigated categories: attractions, activities, and locations; within most of the "locations" are links to the state parks office. Another helpful resource is the National Park Service site (http://www.nps.gov/), which lists all the national parks and has extensive historical, cultural, and environmental information.

➤ CONNECTICUT

http://www.state.ct.us/tourism/

➤ MAINE

http://www.state.me.us/

➤ MASSACHUSETTS

http://www.mass-vacation.com/;
http://www.boston.com/;
http://www.bostonphoenix.com/;
http://www.allcapecod.com/

➤ NEW HAMPSHIRE

http://www.visitnh.gov/

➤ RHODE ISLAND

http://www.visitrhodeisland.com/

➤ VERMONT

http://www.travel-vermont.com/

➤ GENERAL INTEREST

http://www.gorp.com/;
http://www.nps.gov/

WHEN TO GO

All six New England states are largely year-round destinations. But you might want to **stay away during mud season in April and black-fly season in the last two weeks of May.** Many smaller museums and attractions are open only from Memorial Day to mid-October, at other times by appointment only.

Memorial Day is the start of the migration to the beaches and the mountains, and summer begins in earnest on July 4. Those who are driving to Cape Cod in July or August should know that Friday and Sunday are the days weekenders clog the overburdened Route 6; a better time to visit the beach areas and the islands may be after Labor Day.

Fall is the most colorful season in New England, a time when many inns and hotels are booked months in advance by foliage-viewing visitors. The first scarlet and gold colors emerge in mid-September in northern areas; "peak" color occurs at different times from year to year. Generally, it's best to **visit the northern reaches in early October and move southward as the month progresses.**

All leaves are off the trees by Halloween, and hotel rates fall as the leaves do, dropping significantly until ski season begins. November and early December are hunting season in much of New England; those who venture into the woods then should wear bright orange clothing.

Winter is the time for downhill and cross-country skiing. New England's major ski resorts, having seen dark days in years when snowfall was meager, now have snowmaking equipment.

In spring, despite mud season, maple sugaring goes on in Maine, New Hampshire, and Vermont, and the fragrant scent of lilacs is never far behind.

CLIMATE

HARTFORD, CT

Jan.	36F	2C	May	70F	21C	Sept.	74F	23C
	20	– 7		47	8		52	11
Feb.	38F	3C	June	81F	27C	Oct.	65F	18C
	20	– 7		56	13		43	6
Mar.	45F	7C	July	85F	29C	Nov.	52F	11C
	27	– 3		63	17		32	0
Apr.	59F	15C	Aug.	83F	28C	Dec.	38F	3C
	38	3		61	16		22	– 6

BOSTON, MA

Jan.	36F	2C	May	67F	19C	Sept.	72F	22C
	20	– 7		49	9		56	13
Feb.	38F	3C	June	76F	24C	Oct.	63F	17C
	22	– 6		58	14		47	8
Mar.	43F	6C	July	81F	27C	Nov.	49F	9C
	29	– 2		63	17		36	2
Apr.	54F	12C	Aug.	79F	26C	Dec.	40F	4C
	38	3		63	17		25	– 4

BURLINGTON, VT

Jan.	29F	– 2C	May	67F	19C	Sept.	74F	23C
	11	–12		45	7		50	10
Feb.	31F	– 1C	June	77F	25C	Oct.	59F	15C
	11	–12		56	13		40	4
Mar.	40F	4C	July	83F	28C	Nov.	45F	7C
	22	– 6		59	15		31	– 1
Apr.	54F	12C	Aug.	79F	26C	Dec.	31F	– 1C
	34	1		58	14		16	– 9

PORTLAND, ME

Jan.	31F	− 1C	May	61F	16C	Sept.	68F	20C
	16	− 9		47	8		52	11
Feb.	32F	0C	June	72F	22C	Oct.	58F	14C
	16	− 9		54	15		43	6
Mar.	40F	4C	July	76F	24C	Nov.	45F	7C
	27	− 3		61	16		32	0
Apr.	50F	10C	Aug.	74F	23C	Dec.	34F	1C
	36	2		59	15		22	− 6

➤ Forecasts: WEATHER CHANNEL CONNECTION (☎ 900/932−8437), 95¢ PER MINUTE FROM A TOUCH-TONE PHONE.

THE GOLD GUIDE / SMART TRAVEL TIPS

1 Destination: New England

A NEW ENGLAND PAUL REVERE WOULD RECOGNIZE

JUST 20 YEARS after the Declaration of Independence, the Reverend Timothy Dwight, President of Yale College and grandson of the fiery Puritan preacher Jonathan Edwards, set out on the first of a series of annual rambles through his native New England. In his journal, Dwight declared, "A succession of New England villages, composed of neat houses, surrounding neat schoolhouses and churches, adorned with gardens, meadows, and orchards, and exhibiting the universally easy circumstances of the inhabitants, is . . . one of the most delightful prospects which this world can afford." Two hundred years after Dwight's first tour, the graceful small towns he described remain intact: Clapboard farmhouses, weather-beaten barns, lovely old churches, and some of the nation's best schools still line the rural routes in all six New England states.

The difference from Dwight's day to our own is that a whole world of cities and suburbs has grown up around these rural villages. New England's first cities—Portland, Boston, Providence, Newport, New London, New Haven—began as harbor towns. In the 17th century, English Puritans, fleeing religious persecution and civil war, were the first Europeans to make their fortunes in these harbors. Merchants, fishermen, and shipbuilders from all over the world thrived here in the years before the American Revolution.

Even as their cities expanded, New Englanders protected their natural resources. The most famous pioneer of conservation and outdoor recreation is poet and naturalist Henry David Thoreau, who led the way in the 1840s with his famous pilgrimages to Walden Pond in Massachusetts and Mount Katahdin in Maine. In the years after the Civil War, New Englanders flocked to the mountains and the seashore seeking relief from the pressures of city life. Nature lovers and amateur mountaineers cut hiking trails and built rustic shelters in the White Mountains of New Hampshire; Massachusetts families camped and tramped in the rolling Berkshire hills; in Maine, Harvard president Charles W. Eliot and his fellow "rusticators" conserved craggy cliffs, rocky beaches, and pine forests for future generations by donating land to establish Acadia National Park. By 1910, Vermont hikers had begun work on the 265-mi "Long Trail," which connects the Green Mountain summits from Canada to the Massachusetts border. During the Great Depression, conservationists rescued the trail from highway planners who would have paved this favorite mountain footpath.

New England's tangle of turnpikes and highways originated with the area's first inhabitants. The Pocumtucks, Nehantics, Nipmucks, Wampanoags, Pequots, Mohegans, Kennebecs, Penobscots, and Narragansetts created footpaths with skills that modern engineers might envy. This vast trail network extended over rolling hills, through dense woodlands, along riverbanks and the Atlantic coast. The Mohawk Trail—Route 2 on your Massachusetts road map—ran east to west through the Deerfield and Connecticut River valleys to the Hudson River. Seasonal feasts and athletic competitions were held along this route for hundreds of years.

Like well-worn Indian byways, the familiar ingredients of the New England diet have been around since before the *Mayflower*: clams, cranberries, pumpkins, corn, squash, beans, blueberries, cod, and lobster. Clambakes and baked beans were also Native American specialties.

Another New England specialty is education: There are 65 institutions of higher learning in the greater Boston area alone. Dedication to the life of the mind is fostered at Harvard, Yale, and hundreds of excellent secondary schools, colleges, and universities throughout the region.

When it comes to weather, variety is New England's great virtue: All four seasons get full play here. September and October are dazzling as the dying leaves turn color. Foliage enthusiasts take to the rural roads and country inns to observe the way in which warm sunny days and cool autumn nights work together to paint the treetops crimson and gold. Winter usually brings plenty of snow, but if Mother Nature fails to satisfy skiers, resort owners rely on high-tech Yankee know-how (in the form of snow-making devices) to make up the difference. Spring brings crocuses, muddy boots, and maple syrup—sugaring begins when the days are warm and the nights are still below freezing. Summer is the season to enjoy New England's lakes, beaches, and ocean resorts, from Cape Cod to Bar Harbor. Although they may not agree on matters of state, both George Bush and Bill Clinton concede that New England is a great place for a summer vacation: President Clinton is a regular guest on Martha's Vineyard and former president Bush is a longtime summer resident of Kennebunkport, Maine.

THE STREETS OF BOSTON, New England's largest city, provide a crash course in the early political history of the United States. The red line of the Freedom Trail begins at Boston Common, America's oldest public park, and winds past a dozen Revolutionary-era memorials, including the Granary Burial Ground where the victims of the Boston Massacre were laid to rest; Faneuil Hall, the meeting house and marketplace that earned the name "the Cradle of Liberty"; Old North Church, immortalized in Longfellow's poem "Paul Revere's Ride"; and the obelisk commemorating the Battle of Bunker Hill. Monuments to 18th-century glory stand alongside glass office towers in the busy financial district; and in the North End, the house where midnight rider Paul Revere lived is just around the corner from some of the best Italian restaurants in town.

The story of the preservation of Boston's most elegant neighborhood gives us clues about the New England character that we know incompletely from novels, films, and history books. The Boston Brahmin, the ingenious Yankee, the doom-laden Puritan, and the straitlaced reformer have contributed as much to our sense of the place as have New England's snug harbors, salty sea air, stone walls, and pine forests. In 1947, Beacon Hill matrons, dressed in felt hats and furs, conducted a sit-in to save the brick sidewalks of this

historic neighborhood, whose noteworthy architectural elements include its gaslights, cast-iron fences, and sturdy brownstones. With true New England spirit, these earnest women let their opinions be known. Such a polished group of protesters was impossible to resist. Tradition was properly preserved.

These days prominent people with roots in New England are a diverse crowd. The traditional monikers—Yankee, Puritan, and Brahmin—no longer quite fit. New England luminaries include culinary icon Julia Child; actors and philanthropists Paul Newman and Joanne Woodward; actresses Glenn Close, Meg Ryan, and Geena Davis; actor James Spader; disco diva Donna Summer; rockers Aerosmith and Talking Heads; *Star Trek*'s Mr. Spock, Leonard Nimoy; media exec Sumner Redstone; Supreme Court Justice David Souter; conservative pundit John McLaughlin; novelist John Irving; and talk show host Conan O'Brien.

Despite two hundred years of growth and change—and several large cities notwithstanding—the Reverend Dwight would still recognize his beloved New England. And he'd be delighted you've decided to visit.

— Laura E. Cronin

NEW AND NOTEWORTHY

Connecticut

Connecticut may not be a hotbed of professional sports activity, but minor league teams it does have. Newcomers the Beast of New Haven and the Hartford Wolf Pack play in the American Hockey League. The New Haven Ravens, the Norwich Navigators, and the New Britain Rock Cats are Double-A affiliates of major league baseball, and the new Bridgeport Bluefish belong to the independent Atlantic baseball league. The women of the professional-level American Basketball League's New England Blizzard play at the Hartford Civic Center.

Sea lions and dolphins and whales—oh my! The Mystic Marinelife Aquarium, already home to 6,000 specimens and 50 live exhibits of sea life, is scheduled to complete a $50-million expansion project in the spring of '99. New attractions will include the world's largest outdoor beluga whale habitat and the Institute for Exploration, headed by the world-renowned ocean explorer Dr. Robert Ballard.

Rhode Island

T. F. Green Airport in Warwick continues to grow; the renovated facility has lured many Boston-based travelers away from their own city's Logan International Airport. Historically popular with society's elite, Newport was without a luxury hotel until the recent opening of Vanderbilt Hall. Well-preserved Block Island continues to grow in popularity as a summer destination; new restaurants and spiffed-up lodgings have made visiting here more appealing than ever.

Massachusetts

Downtown Boston's massive multiyear construction project, known locally as the Big Dig, continues apace. When completed, the elevated Central Artery that bisects the downtown area will be redirected underground, and the city center will be reunited with the North End and the waterfront. In the meantime, traffic delays and street closings abound. Allow extra time when traveling in this area. Efforts also continue to spiff and spruce up the Freedom Trail, whose sites are now identified by distinctive medallions—colorful banners help guide you en route.

As you plan your trip to Boston, Cape Cod, or the Berkshires in 1999, book your hotel or B&B room as far in advance as you can. Boston has one of the highest lodging occupancy rates of any city in the nation, and the two other areas are as popular as ever. Peak times of year when rooms can be particularly hard to come by are the graduation months of May and June and the fall-foliage season.

Main Street in Hyannis is gradually becoming a more attractive place for an afternoon stroll. A design improvement plan has been responsible for rose plantings, a gazebo beside the post office, and signs that are more complementary to the surroundings. "Walkway to the Sea," a flower-lined promenade designed by Ben Thompson, the architect responsible for Boston's Faneuil Hall Marketplace, should be finished by the beginning of 1999. The path will connect Main Street with the harbor.

The art scene on Martha's Vineyard has blossomed, with more than 35 galleries displaying the work of internationally recognized artists and photographers. Weekly openings are eagerly awaited social events, where guests can nibble, sip, and meet-and-greet the men and women behind the works. The Granary Gallery in Chilmark still carries the late photographer Alfred Eisenstaedt's work, and the breathtaking photography of Peter Simon (Carly's brother) can be viewed at his gallery at the Feast of Chilmark restaurant.

Vermont

Marsh-Billings National Historic Park, the first national park devoted to conservation history and land stewardship, opened in Woodstock on 500 acres of land donated by the Rockefeller family. This wooded park contains hiking trails, an operational farm and museum, and the Billings mansion. Frederick Billings created the estate in the late 19th century to provide a model of conservation in a region suffering from deforestation and overgrazing.

Several land transactions have occurred in the world of skiing. Bolton was bought by a young entrepreneur with plans to upgrade facilities without compromising the resort's family-friendly image. Jay Peak has new Canadian owners; international flair and glade skiing will remain this resort's strengths. And plans are underway to connect the Killington and Pico resorts.

New Hampshire

Skiers in New Hampshire have also benefited from resort improvements, most notably at Attitash Bear Peak, which recently added several new trails, not to mention the slope-side, full-service Grand Summit Hotel. Visitors continue to venture to northern New Hampshire in hopes of seeing moose, so Dixville Notch State Park has added a moose observation platform to help visitors willing to wait for one of the gangly creatures to venture into the vicinity. The popularity of snowshoeing and kayaking has grown immensely in the late 1990s in New Hampshire. Many inns and resorts have added snowshoeing to their lineup of activities and guided kayak trips can be arranged along the Seacoast and in the Lakes Region.

Maine

Getting into and around Maine will be easier as soon as two road projects are completed, hopefully before the end of 1999: the widening of the Maine Turnpike to three lanes from Kittery to Portland and the building of a new bridge on Route 1 between Bath and Woolwich. Also expected to be in operation before the year 2000 is the 18-hole golf course Robert Trent Jones Jr. designed for the Sunday River Ski Resort.

WHAT'S WHERE

Connecticut

Southwestern Connecticut, the richest part of the richest state, is home to commuters, celebrities, and others who seek privacy and rusticity and proximity to New York City. Far less touristy than other parts of the state, the Connecticut River valley is a stretch of small river villages and uncrowded state parks punctuated by a few small cities and one large one: Hartford. The Litchfield Hills have grand old inns, rolling farmlands, and plenty of forests and rivers, making it a popular retreat for New Yorkers. The Quiet Corner, a string of sparsely populated towns in the northeast known chiefly for their antiquing potential, is also becoming a weekend escape from New York City. New Haven is home to Yale and several fine museums. Along the southeastern coast lie quiet shoreline villages, and, a bit inland, Foxwoods Casino draws droves of gamblers to the Mashantucket Pequots' reservation in Ledyard.

Rhode Island

Wedged between Connecticut and Massachusetts and occupying a mere 48 mi × 37 mi, Rhode Island is the smallest of the 50 states. Providence, the state capital, is in the northeast portion of the state. To the southeast is Newport, the state's other well-known city and one of the great sailing capitals of the world. The area known as South County contains coastal towns along Route 1, rolling farmland, sparsely populated beaches, and wilderness; it's just a short ferry ride from the South County town of Galilee to scenic Block Island. The Blackstone Valley, in the northern portion of the state, was the cradle of the Industrial Revolution in the United States. The region, which includes the towns of Pawtucket, Woonsocket, and Slatersville, is beginning to blossom as a tourist destination.

Massachusetts

Much of what makes Massachusetts famous is in the eastern part of the state: academically endowed Boston, the historic South Shore town of Plymouth, chic Martha's Vineyard, scenic Cape Cod, and cozy Nantucket; witch-obsessed Salem and the port town of Gloucester are on the North Shore, which extends past grimy docklands to the picturesque Cape Ann region. But the western reaches of the state hold attractions as well: The Pioneer Valley is a string of historic settlements, and the Berkshires, in the western end of the state, live up to the storybook image of rural New England.

Vermont

Southern Vermont has farms, freshly starched New England towns, quiet back roads, bustling ski resorts, and strip-mall sprawl. Central Vermont's trademarks include famed marble quarries, just north of Rutland, and large dairy herds and pastures that create the quilted patchwork of the Champlain Valley. The heart of the area is the Green Mountains, and the surrounding wilderness of the Green Mountain National Forest. Both the state's largest city (Burlington) and the nation's smallest state capital (Montpelier) are in northern Vermont, as are some of the most rural and remote areas of New England. Much of the state's logging, dairy farming, and skiing takes place here. With Montréal only an hour from the border, the Canadian influence is strong, and Canadian accents and currency common.

New Hampshire

Portsmouth, the star of New Hampshire's 18-mi coastline, has great shopping, restaurants, music, and theater, and one of the best historic districts in the nation. Exeter is New Hampshire's enclave of Revolutionary War history. The lakes region, rich with historic landmarks, also has good restaurants, several golf courses, hiking trails, and antiquing. People come to the White Mountains to hike and climb, to photograph the dramatic vistas and the vibrant sea of foliage, and to ski. Western and central New Hampshire have managed to keep the water slides and the outlet malls at bay. The lures here include Lake Sunapee and Mt. Monadnock, the second-most-climbed mountain in the world.

Maine

Maine is by far the largest state in New England. At its extremes it measures 300 mi by 200 mi; all other New England states could fit within its perimeters. Due to overdevelopment, Maine's southernmost coastal towns won't give you the rugged, "down-east" experience, but the Kennebunks will: classic townscapes, rocky shorelines punctuated by sandy beaches, quaint downtown districts. Augusta, the state's capital, is inland a bit on I–95. Purists hold that the Maine coast begins at Penobscot Bay, where the vistas over the water are wider and bluer, the shore a jumble of granite boulders. Acadia National Park is Maine's principal tourist attraction; Bar Harbor is one of the park's gateway towns. Bangor is north of Penobscot Bay on the Penobscot River. The vast North Woods region is a destination for outdoors enthusiasts.

PLEASURES AND PASTIMES

Beaches

Long, wide beaches edge the New England coast from southern Maine to southern Connecticut; the most popular are on Cape Cod, Martha's Vineyard, Nantucket, and the shore areas north and south of Boston; on Maine's York County coast; Block Island Sound in Rhode Island; and the coastal region of New Hampshire. Many are maintained by state and local governments and have lifeguards on duty; they may have picnic facilities, rest rooms, changing facilities, and concession stands. Depending on the locale, you may need a parking sticker to use the lot. The waters are at their warmest in August, though they're cold even at the height of summer along much of the Maine coast. Inland,

there are small lake beaches, most notably in New Hampshire and Vermont.

Biking

Cape Cod has miles of bike trails, some paralleling the National Seashore, most on level terrain. On either side of the Cape Cod Canal is an easy 7-mi straight trail with views of the canal traffic. Other favorite areas for bicycling are the Massachusetts Berkshires, the New Hampshire lakes region, and Vermont's Northeast Kingdom. Nantucket, Martha's Vineyard, and Block Island can be thoroughly explored by bicycle. Biking in Maine is especially scenic in and around Kennebunkport, Camden, Deer Isle, and the Schoodic Peninsula. The carriage paths in Acadia National Park are ideal. Sunday River Ski Resort operates a mountain bike park during the summer months.

Boating

In most lakeside and coastal resorts, sailboats and powerboats can be rented at a local marina. Newport, Rhode Island, and Maine's Penobscot Bay are famous sailing areas. Lakes in New Hampshire and Vermont are splendid for all kinds of boating. The Connecticut River in the Pioneer Valley and the Housatonic River in the Berkshires are popular for canoeing. In Massachusetts, Gloucester and Newburyport are traditional fishing ports, and Essex is known for saltwater and freshwater canoeing.

Dining

Seafood is king throughout New England. Clams, quahogs, lobster, and scrod are prepared here in an infinite number of ways, some fancy and expensive, others simple and moderately priced. One of the best ways to enjoy seafood is in the rough—off paper plates on a picnic table at a clam boil or clambake—or at one of the many shacklike eating places along the coast, where you can smell the salt air.

Among the quintessentially New England dishes served at inland resorts and inns are Indian pudding, clam chowder, fried clams, and cranberry anything. You can also find multicultural variations on themes, such as Portuguese *chouriço* (a spicy red sausage that transforms a clam boil into something heavenly) and the mincemeat pie made with pork in the tradition of the

French Canadians who populate the northern regions.

Fishing

Anglers will find sport aplenty throughout the region—surf-casting along the shore, deep-sea fishing in the Atlantic on party and charter boats, fishing for trout in rivers, and angling for bass, landlocked salmon, and other fish in freshwater lakes. Maine's Moosehead and Rangeley Lakes regions are draws for serious fisherfolk. Sporting goods stores and bait-and-tackle shops are reliable sources for licenses—necessary in fresh waters—and for leads to the nearest hot spots.

Hiking

Probably the most famous trails are the 255-mi Long Trail, which runs north–south through the center of Vermont, and the Maine-to-Georgia Appalachian Trail, which runs through New England on both private and public land. You'll find good hiking in many state parks throughout the region.

National and State Parks and Forests

National and state parks offer a broad range of visitor facilities, including campgrounds, picnic grounds, hiking trails, boating, and ranger programs. State forests are usually somewhat less developed. For more information on any of these, contact the state tourism offices or parks departments (☞ Contacts and Resources, at the end of each state's chapter).

CONNECTICUT➤ The Litchfield Hills have a strong concentration of wilderness areas, of which the best include Kent Falls State Park, Mt. Tom, Dennis Hill, Haystack Mountain, Campbell Falls, Housatonic Meadows, and Burr Pond. Elsewhere in the state, Rocky Neck State Park in Niantic has one of the finest beaches on Long Island Sound; Wadsworth Falls, near Wesleyan University, also has a beautiful waterfall and 285 acres of forest; and Dinosaur State Park, north of Middletown in Rocky Hill, has dinosaur tracks dating from the Jurassic period. There's excellent hiking and picnicking at Gillette Castle State Park, an outrageous hilltop castle on 117 acres.

RHODE ISLAND➤ With 19 preserves, state parks, beaches, and forest areas, including Charlestown's Burlingame State Park

and Ninigret National Wildlife Refuge, South County is a region that respects the concept of wilderness. Fifteen state parks in Rhode Island permit camping.

MASSACHUSETTS➤ Cape Cod National Seashore, a 40-mi stretch of the Cape between Eastham and Provincetown, offers excellent swimming, bike riding, bird-watching, and nature walks. Parks in Lowell, Gardner, North Adams, Holyoke, Lawrence, Lynn, Roxbury, and Fall River, which commemorate the Industrial Revolution, have been created as part of the Urban Heritage State Park Program for Economic Revitalization.

VERMONT➤ The 275,000-acre Green Mountain National Forest extends south from the center of the state to the Massachusetts border. Hikers treasure the miles of trails; canoeists work its white waters; and campers and anglers find plenty to keep them happy. Among the most popular spots are the Falls of Lana and Silver Lake near Middlebury; Hapgood Pond between Manchester and Peru; and Chittenden Brook near Rochester.

NEW HAMPSHIRE➤ The White Mountain National Forest covers 770,000 acres of northern New Hampshire. New Hampshire parklands vary widely, even within a region. Major recreation parks are at Franconia Notch, Crawford Notch, and Mt. Sunapee. Rhododendron State Park (Monadnock) has a singular collection of wild rhododendrons; Mt. Washington Park (White Mountains) is on top of the highest mountain in the Northeast.

MAINE➤ Acadia National Park, which preserves fine stretches of shoreline and high mountains, covers much of Mount Desert Island and more than half of Isle au Haut and Schoodic Point on the mainland. Baxter State Park comprises more than 200,000 acres of wilderness surrounding Katahdin, Maine's highest mountain. Hiking and moose-watching are major activities. The Allagash Wilderness Waterway is a 92-mi corridor of lakes and rivers surrounded by vast commercial forest property.

Shopping

Antiques, crafts, maple syrup and sugar, fresh produce, and clothing and housewares lure shoppers to New England's factory outlet stores, flea markets, shopping malls, bazaars, yard sales, country stores, and farmers' markets. Connecticut sales tax is 6%; Rhode Island, 7%; Massachusetts, 5% (except clothing purchases under $150, which are not taxed); Vermont, 5%; and Maine, 6%. New Hampshire has no sales tax.

ANTIQUES> Best bets for antiquing in Connecticut include Route 7, Deep River, New Preston and Putnam, Woodbury and Southbury, and the area of West Cornwall just over the covered bridge. Antiques stores are plentiful in Newport but are a specialty of Rhode Island's South County: The best places to browse are Wickford, Charlestown, and Watch Hill. In Massachusetts, there's a large concentration of antiques stores on the North Shore around Essex, but there are also plenty in Salem and Cape Ann. Also try the Berkshires around Great Barrington, South Egremont, and Sheffield. Particularly in the Monadnock region, dealers abound in barns and home stores strung along back roads—along Route 119, from Fitzwilliam to Hinsdale; Route 101, from Marlborough to Wilton; and in the towns of Hopkinton, Hollis, and Amherst. In the Seacoast region, the stretch of Route 4 between Barrington and Concord is another mecca. In Maine, antiques shops are clustered in Wiscasset and Searsport and along Route 1 between Kittery and Scarborough.

CRAFTS> Try Washington Street in South Norwalk, Connecticut, and in Massachusetts, Boston, Cape Cod, and the Berkshires. In Vermont, Burlington and Putney are crafts centers. On Maine's Deer isle, Haystack Mountain School of Crafts attracts internationally renowned craftspeople to its summer institute. The Schoodic Peninsula is home to many skilled artisans. Passamaquoddy Indian baskets can be found in Eastport.

OUTLET STORES> In Connecticut, try Clinton, Westbrook, and Mystic; in Massachusetts, the area around New Bedford; in Maine, shop along the coast in Kittery, Freeport, and Ellsworth; in New Hampshire, North Conway; and in Vermont, Manchester. In Rhode Island's Blackstone Valley, dozens of clothing and manufacturing outlets are actually inside factory walls.

PRODUCE> Opportunities abound for obtaining fresh farm produce from the source; some farms allow you to pick your own strawberries, raspberries, blueberries, and apples. October in Maine is prime time for pumpkins and potatoes. There are maple-syrup producers who demonstrate the process to visitors, most noticeably in Vermont. Maple syrup is available in different grades; light amber is the most refined; many Vermonters prefer grade C, the richest in flavor and the one most often used in cooking. A sugarhouse can be the most or the least expensive place to shop, depending on how tourist-oriented it is. Small grocery stores are often a good source of less-expensive syrup.

Skiing

The softly rounded peaks of New England have been attracting skiers for a full century.

LIFT TICKETS> A good bet is that the bigger and more famous the resort, the higher the price of a lift ticket. A single-day, weekend-holiday adult lift ticket always has the highest price; astute skiers look for off-site purchase locations, senior discounts and junior pricing, and package rates, multiple days, stretch weekends (a weekend that usually includes a Monday or Friday), frequent-skier programs, and season-ticket plans to save their skiing dollars. Some independently owned areas are bona fide bargains for skiers who don't require the glamour and glitz of the high-profile resorts.

LODGING> Most ski areas described in this book have a variety of accommodations—lodges, condominiums, hotels, motels, inns, bed-and-breakfasts—close to or at a short distance from the action. For stays of three days or more, a package rate may be the best way to go. Packages vary in composition, price, and availability throughout the season; their components may include a room, meals, lift tickets, ski lessons, rental equipment, transfers to the mountain, parties, races, and use of a sports center, tips, and taxes.

TRAIL RATING> Ski areas have devised standards for rating and marking trails and slopes that offer fairly accurate guides. Trails are rated Easier (green circle), More Difficult (blue square), Most Difficult (black diamond), and Expert (double diamond). Keep in mind that trail difficulty is measured relative to that of other trails *at the same ski area*, not to those of an area down the road, in another state, or in another part of the country; a black-diamond trail at one area may rate only a blue square at a neighboring area. Yet the trail-marking system throughout New England is remarkably consistent and reliable.

EQUIPMENT RENTAL AND LESSONS➤ Rental equipment is available at all ski areas, at ski shops around resorts, and even in cities far from ski areas. Shop personnel will advise customers on the appropriate equipment and how to operate it. Within the United States, the Professional Ski Instructors of America (PSIA) have devised a progressive teaching system that is used with relatively little variation at many schools (though not the ones at the New England resorts run by the American Skiing Company). This allows skiers to have more fulfilling lessons at ski schools in different ski areas. Some ski schools have adopted the PSIA teaching system for children, and many also use SKIwee, which awards progress cards and applies other standardized teaching approaches.

CHILD CARE➤ Nurseries can be found at virtually all ski areas and often accept children from ages six weeks to six years. Parents must usually supply formula and diapers for infants; reservations are advised.

GREAT ITINERARIES

Scenic Coastal Tour

From southwestern Connecticut through Rhode Island and Massachusetts to Maine, New England's coastline is a picturesque succession of rocky headlands, sand-rimmed coves, and small towns built around shipbuilding, fishing, and other seaside trades.

DURATION➤ 4–9 days

1–2 DAYS➤ Travel through such classic Connecticut towns as Old Lyme and Mystic, passing through Rhode Island's South County to end up in Newport, with its magnificent turn-of-the-century mansions open for tours.

1–3 DAYS➤ Spend a day in Boston, then head for one of the resort towns of Cape Cod.

1 DAY➤ Head north through such historic North Shore fishing towns as Marblehead, Gloucester, and Rockport; visit sea captains' mansions in Newburyport.

1–3 DAYS➤ Swing through the Kennebunks and Portland to the small towns and islands around Penobscot Bay.

Historical Preservations

Though they appear to be villages that time forgot, many of New England's meticulously preserved hamlets are the products of years of research and painstaking restoration. Tour escorts in these places are likely to be immensely learned; the costumed interpreters at some sites may make you feel like you've just stepped out of a time machine.

DURATION➤ 6 days

2 DAYS➤ From a base in Boston, venture south on Route 3 to Plimouth Plantation for a glimpse into the lives of the first Puritan settlers. Then refresh your sense of Colonial history by following the Freedom Trail, a route of fine historic sites in the middle of busy modern Boston.

1 DAY➤ Head west on the Massachusetts Turnpike to Old Sturbridge Village, which re-creates life in a prosperous farm town of the 1830s.

1 DAY➤ Interstate 395 will take you south to Mystic, Connecticut, and Mystic Seaport, a large, lively restoration that focuses on the whaling and shipbuilding industries of the 19th century.

1 DAY➤ A half-day's drive to Hartford and then up I–91 into western Massachusetts will take you to Old Deerfield, a tranquil pre-Revolutionary settlement preserved as a National Historic District.

1 DAY➤ Take either the Massachusetts Turnpike or the more scenic Mohawk Trail (Route 2) west, then take Route 7 to Hancock, Massachusetts, where the Hancock Shaker Village sheds light on a way of life that has always stood apart from America's mainstream.

College Towns

As one of the first settled areas in the United States, New England was the site of some of the nation's first colleges and universities, which enshrined in the American imagination an image of imposing ivy-

New England Ski Areas

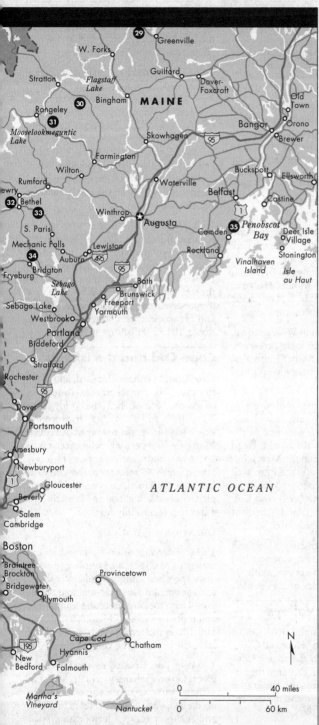

clad buildings on green, shady campuses. College towns have an added attraction in that they usually contain excellent bookstores and museums, inexpensive restaurants, and casual street life.

DURATION➤ 5–10 days

1–3 DAYS➤ In the greater Boston area, visit the Cambridge campuses of Harvard University and the Massachusetts Institute of Technology and the busy urban campus of Boston University. Head to the suburbs to visit Tufts University (Medford), Brandeis University (Waltham), Boston College (Newton), or Wellesley College (Wellesley).

1–2 DAYS➤ Drive west to the five-college region of the Pioneer Valley, where you can visit Amherst College, Hampshire College, and the University of Massachusetts in Amherst; Mount Holyoke College in the village of South Hadley; and Smith College in Northampton.

1–2 DAYS➤ Head west to Williamstown, home of Williams College, in the Berkshires. Then swing north on Route 7 into Vermont to Bennington, where you'll find Bennington College.

1–2 DAYS➤ Travel east on Route 9 to Keene State College, in Keene, New Hampshire, a well-kept town with one of the widest main streets in the world. Head southeast through Worcester, Massachusetts, where Holy Cross is the most well known of several colleges, and on to Providence, Rhode Island, where Brown University and the Rhode Island School of Design share a fine hillside site.

1 DAY➤ A westward drive along I-95 will take you to New Haven, Connecticut, the home of Yale University, with its Gothic-style quadrangles of gray stone.

Mountains and Valleys

This circuit takes in some of the most spectacular parts of the White and Green mountains, along with the upper Connecticut River valley. In this area the antiques hunting is exemplary, the traffic often almost nonexistent, and the scenery right out of Currier & Ives.

DURATION➤ 3–7 days

1–3 DAYS➤ From the New Hampshire coast, head northwest to Wolfeboro, perhaps detouring to explore the Lake Winnipesaukee area. Take Route 16 north to Conway, then follow Route 112 west along the Kancamagus Pass through the White Mountains to the Vermont border.

1–2 DAYS➤ Head south on Route 10 along the Connecticut River, past scenic Hanover, New Hampshire, home of Dartmouth College. At White River Junction, cross into Vermont. You may want to follow Route 4 through Woodstock to Killington, and then travel along Route 100 and I-89 to complete the loop back to White River Junction. Otherwise, simply proceed south along I-91, with stops at Putney and Brattleboro.

1–2 DAYS➤ Take Route 119 east to Rhododendron State Park in Fitzwilliam, New Hampshire. Nearby is Mt. Monadnock, the most-climbed mountain in the United States; in Jaffrey take the trail to the top. Dawdle along back roads to visit the preserved villages of Harrisville, Dublin, and Hancock, then continue east along Route 101 to return to the coast.

Cape Cod and the Islands

Cape Cod, Martha's Vineyard, and Nantucket are favorite resort areas in and out of season. Because the Cape is only some 70 mi from end to end, day trips from a single base are easily managed. A visit to Martha's Vineyard or Nantucket takes about two hours each way from Hyannis (and it's only 45 minutes to the Vineyard from Woods Hole), so you may want to plan to stay overnight on an island, though a day trip is certainly feasible.

DURATION➤ 7–8 days

1 DAY➤ Drive east on Route 6A to experience old Cape Cod, sampling some of the Cape's best antiques and crafts shops and looking into historic sites and museums. Here, too, are charming restaurants and intimate bed-and-breakfasts. Scargo Hill Tower in Dennis yields views of the lake, the bay, and the village below.

1 DAY➤ Take Route 6 east to Provincetown. Go on a whale-watching excursion in the morning, spend the afternoon browsing the shops and galleries of the main street, and at sunset go for a Jeep or horseback ride through the dunes of the Province Lands. Visit one of Provincetown's fine restaurants—or drive south to Chatham for dinner and theater.

1 DAY➤ Take Route 6 to the Salt Pond Visitor Center in Eastham and choose your activity: swimming or surf-fishing at Coast Guard or Nauset Light Beach, wandering the bike path, taking a self-guided nature walk, or joining in one of the National Seashore programs. On the way there, peek into some of the galleries or crafts shops in Wellfleet.

4–5 DAYS➤ From Hyannis, take a ferry to either Martha's Vineyard or Nantucket. If you choose the Vineyard, visit the Camp Meeting Grounds and the old carousel in Oak Bluffs, then head for the sunset at Gay Head Cliffs before returning on the evening ferry; if you stay over, explore a nature preserve or the historic streets of Edgartown the next day. In Nantucket, you might explore the Whaling Museum, the mansions, and the shops; if you stay over, bike or take a bus to 'Sconset for a stroll around this village of rose-covered cottages and perhaps a swim at a fairly uncrowded beach.

FODOR'S CHOICE

Dining

★ **The Golden Lamb Buttery, Brooklyn, CT.** This is Connecticut's most unusual—and magical—dining experience. Eating here is a social and gastronomical event. $$$$

★ **Abbott's Lobster in the Rough, Noank, CT.** This unassuming seaside lobster shack with a magnificent view serves some of the state's best lobster, mussels, crab, and clams. $$

★ **White Barn Inn, Kennebunkport, ME.** Considered by many to be Maine's best restaurant, the White Barn Inn combines fine dining with unblemished service in a rustic setting. $$$$

★ **Round Pond Lobster, Round Pond, ME.** For lobster-in-the-rough, you can't beat this dockside takeout with views over Round Pond Harbor. Order the lobster dinner, settle in at a picnic table with the beverages you've brought with you, and wait for your number to be called. $

★ **Biba, Boston, MA.** Boston's favorite place to see and be seen serves gutsy fare that mixes flavors from five continents. $$$$

★ **Blantyre, Lenox, MA.** If you choose to dine on the French cuisine served here, set aside several hours and put on your evening clothes—a meal here is truly an event. $$$$

★ **Chillingsworth, Brewster, MA.** The chefs at this dramatic spot prepare award-winning French and nouvelle cuisine; the wine cellar here is extensive. $$$$

★ **Lambert's Cove Country Inn, West Tisbury, MA.** This romantic gourmet restaurant that serves Continental cuisine is in a 1790 farmhouse surrounded by pine woods and an apple orchard. $$$

★ **Balsams Grand Resort Hotel, Dixville Notch, NH.** The summer buffet lunch here is heaped upon a 100-ft-long table; stunning dinners might include chilled strawberry soup spiked with Grand Marnier and poached fillet of salmon with caviar sauce. $$$$

★ **Al Forno, Providence, RI.** The Italian dishes served at one of New England's best restaurants make the most of the region's fresh produce. $$$$

Lodging

★ **Boulders Inn, New Preston, CT.** This idyllic and prestigious inn on Lake Waramaug has panoramic views and a window-lined, stone-wall dining room. $$$$

★ **Manor House, Norfolk, CT.** Among the house's remarkable features are 20 stained-glass windows designed by Louis Tiffany. $$$–$$$$

★ **Lodge at Moosehead Lake, Greenville, ME.** This lumber baron's mansion overlooking Moosehead Lake is as close as it gets to luxury in the North Woods. All rooms have whirlpool baths, fireplaces, and hand-carved four-poster beds; most have lake views. $$$$

★ **Ullikana Bed and Breakfast, Bar Harbor, ME.** Hidden within this staid Tudor mansion tucked behind Bar Harbor's Maine Street is a riot of color and art. Fireplaces, private decks, water views, and gourmet breakfasts make it a real treat. $$$$

★ **Blantyre, Lenox, MA.** The lavishly decorated rooms in the main house at Blantyre have hand-carved four-poster beds, overstuffed chaise longues, chintz chairs, boudoirs, walk-in closets, and Victorian bathrooms. $$$$

Charlotte Inn, Edgartown, MA. Rooms here, in one of the finest inns in New England, are smartly furnished, and the landscaped grounds include an English garden. $$$$

The Ritz-Carlton, Boston, MA. In the old Yankee manner, this perennial favorite still stands for luxury combined with understatement. Coveted rooms and suites have fireplaces and views of the Public Garden across the street. $$$$

Captain's House Inn, Chatham, MA. Preserved architectural details, tasteful decor, and delicious baked goods help to create an overall feeling of warmth and quiet comfort here. $$$–$$$$

Harbor Light Inn, Marblehead, MA. If you were to describe the ideal New England inn, it might resemble the Harbor Light. Stately antiques are arranged in rooms with floral wallpaper or period color paint, like Wedgwood blue or Federal red. $$$–$$$$

Historic Merrell Inn, South Lee, MA. Built as a stagecoach stopover around 1794, this inn has an authentic, unfussy style. $$–$$$

Newbury Guest House, Boston, MA. This redbrick and brownstone row house is always full, because it's expertly managed, well furnished, and ideally located on Boston's most fashionable shopping street. $–$$

Manor on Golden Pond, Holderness, NH. The 23 rooms in this English manor, the only inn on exclusive Squam Lake, are filled with luxurious touches. $$$$

Snowvillage Inn, Snowville, NH. The operators of this 18-room inn take guests on gourmet-picnic hikes. Rooms are named after authors; the nicest, with 12 windows that look out over the Presidential Mountain Range, is a tribute to Robert Frost. $–$$$

Weekapaug Inn, Weekapaug, RI. On a peninsula surrounded by the tidal waters of Winnapaug Pond, this all-inclusive retreat has a wholesome atmosphere. $$$$

The Inn at Shelburne Farms, Shelburne, VT. This is storybook land: A Tudor-style inn built for William Seward and Lila Vanderbilt Webb that sits on the edge of Lake Champlain and has views of the Adirondack Mountains. $$$–$$$$

West Mountain Inn, Arlington, VT. This former farmhouse of the 1840s has a llama ranch on the property and sits on 150 acres that provide glorious views. $$$–$$$$

Ski Resorts

Smugglers' Notch, VT, for learning to ski. With an 1,150-ft vertical, Morse Mountain at Smuggler's is great for beginners.

Jay Peak, VT, for the international ambience. Because of its proximity to Québec, Jay Peak, which receives the most natural snow of any ski area in the East, attracts many Montréalers.

Mad River Glen, VT, for challenging terrain. The apt motto at this area owned by a cooperative of skiers is "Ski It If You Can."

Sugarbush, VT, for an overall great place to ski. Sugarbush has beginner runs, intermediate cruisers, and formidable steeps; there's a with-it attitude, but nearly everyone will feel comfortable here.

Attitash Bear Peak, NH, for innovative ticketing and special events. There's always something happening at Attitash—from demo days to race camps.

Big Squaw Mountain, ME, for scenic wilderness views. A down-home, laid-back atmosphere prevails at Squaw, which overlooks Moosehead Lake and distant Mt. Katahdin. This is no frills, big mountain skiing at bargain basement prices.

Sugarloaf, ME, for the East's only above-tree-line skiing. With a vertical of 2,820 ft, Sugarloaf is taller than any other New England ski peak except Killington.

Sunday River, ME, for great snow from November into May. The trademarks of the flagship of the American Skiing Company empire are good snowmaking and reliable grooming.

Sights

Long Island Sound from the tip of Water Street in Stonington Village, CT. Wander past the historic buildings, which line the town green and border both sides of Water Street, to the imposing Old Lighthouse Museum, which you can climb for a spectacular view.

⭐ **The mansions of Bellevue Avenue, Newport, RI.** Magnificent mansions with pillars, mosaics, and marble are set on grounds with fountains, formal gardens, and broad lawns that roll to the ocean.

⭐ **Bright purple cranberries floating on the flooded bogs just before the fall harvest on Cape Cod and Nantucket.** Cape Cod's Rail Trail passes salt marshes, cranberry bogs, and ponds. On Nantucket, visit the 205-acre Windswept Cranberry Bog.

⭐ **The candy-color Victorian cottages of the Oak Bluffs Camp Ground on Martha's Vineyard.** More than 300 Carpenter Gothic Victorian cottages, gaily painted in pastels and trimmed in lacy filigree, are tightly packed on a warren of streets.

⭐ **Nantucket, whose cobblestone streets and antique houses evoke whaling days.** Settled in the mid-17th century, Nantucket has a town center that remains remarkably unchanged, thanks to a strict building code.

⭐ **The view from Appalachian Gap on Route 17, VT.** Views from the top and on the way down this panoramic mountain pass near the quiet town of Bristol are a just reward for the challenging drive.

⭐ **Early October on the Kancamagus Highway between Lincoln and Conway, NH.** This 34-mi trek with classic White Mountains vistas erupts into fiery color each fall.

⭐ **Sunrise from the top of Cadillac Mountain on Mt. Desert Island, ME; sunset over Moosehead Lake from the Lily Bay Road in Greenville, ME.** From the summit of Cadillac Mountain you have a 360° view of the ocean, islands, jagged coastline, woods, and lakes; Lily Bay Road passes through Greenville, the largest town on Moosehead Lake, as well as outposts with populations of "not many."

⭐ **Yacht-filled Camden Harbor, ME, from the summit of Mt. Battie.** Mt. Battie may not be very tall, but it has a lovely vista over Camden Harbor, which shelters the nation's largest fleet of windjammers.

FESTIVALS AND SEASONAL EVENTS

WINTER

DECEMBER➤ The **reenactment of the Boston Tea Party** takes place on the *Beaver II* in Boston Harbor. In Arlington (VT), the **St. Lucia Pageant** is a "Festival of Lights" that celebrates the winter solstice. Christmas celebrations are plentiful throughout New England: In **Nantucket** (RI), the first weekend of the month sees an early Christmas celebration with elaborate decorations, costumed carolers, theatrical performances, art exhibits, and a tour of historic homes. In **Newport** (RI), several Bellevue Avenue mansions open for the holidays, and there are crafts fairs, holiday concerts, and candlelight tours of Colonial homes throughout the month. At **Mystic Seaport** (CT), costumed guides escort visitors to holiday activities. **Old Saybrook** (CT) has a Christmas Torchlight Parade and Muster of Ancient Fife and Drum Corps, which ends with a carol sing at the Church Green. Historic **Strawbery Banke** (NH) has a Christmas Stroll, with carolers, through nine historic homes decorated for the season. **Christmas Prelude** in Kennebunkport (ME) celebrates winter with concerts, caroling, and special events. The final day of the year is observed with festivals, entertainment, and food in many locations during **First Night Celebrations.** Some of the major cities hosting such events are Portland (ME), Burlington (VT), Providence (RI), Boston, and, in Connecticut, Danbury, Hartford, and Norwalk.

JANUARY➤ Stowe's (VT) **Winter Carnival** heats up around mid-month; it's among the country's oldest such celebrations. Brookfield (VT) holds its **Ice Harvest Festival,** one of New England's largest. The weeklong **Winter Carnival** in Jackson (NH) includes ski races, ice sculptures, and parades.

FEBRUARY➤ On tap at the **Brattleboro Winter Carnival,** held on weekends throughout the month, are jazz concerts and an ice fishing derby. The **Mad River Valley Winter Carnival** (VT) is a week of winter festivities, including dogsled races and a masquerade ball; Burlington's **Vermont Mozart Festival** showcases the Winter Chamber Music Series. The **New England Boat Show** is held in Boston's Bayside Expo Center.

SPRING

MARCH➤ This is a boon time for **maple-sugaring festivals and events:** Throughout the month and into April, the sugarhouses of Maine, New Hampshire, Massachusetts, and Vermont demonstrate procedures from maple-tree tapping to sap boiling. During **Maine Maple Sunday** Maine sugarhouses open for tours and tastings. At Sunday River (ME), you can warm up after a morning of skiing at the annual **Eat the Heat Chili Cookoff.** Maine's Moosehead Lake has a renowned **Ice-Fishing Derby,** and Rangeley's **New England Sled Dog Races** attract more than 100 teams from throughout the Northeast and Canada. Stratton Mountain (VT) hosts the **U.S. Open Snowboarding Championships.** March 17 is traditionally a major event in Boston: Its **St. Patrick's Day Parade** is one of the nation's largest.

APRIL➤ During **Reggae Weekend** at Sugarloaf/ USA (ME), Caribbean reggae bands play outdoors and inside throughout the weekend. During Sunday River's annual **Bust 'n' Burn Mogul Competition,** professional and amateur bump skiers test their mettle on the notorious White Heat trail's man-eating moguls. Early blooms are the draw of Bristol's (RI) **Annual Spring Bulb Display,** which takes place at Blithewolde Gardens and Arboretum, and of Nantucket's **Daffodil Festival,** which celebrates spring with a flower show, elaborate shop-window displays, and a procession of antique cars along roadsides bursting with daffodils. You can gorge on sea grub at Boothbay Harbor's (ME) **Fishermen's Festival,** held on the third weekend in April. Dedicated runners draw huge crowds to the **Boston Marathon,** run each year on Patriot's Day (the Monday nearest April 19).

MAY➤ You know all those Holsteins you see grazing in fields alongside Vermont's windy roads? Well, the Enosburg Falls **Vermont Dairy Festival** is just the place to celebrate the delicious fruits (or cheeses, rather) of their labor. If you want to see a moose, visit Greenville (ME) during **Moose-Mainea**, which runs from mid-May to mid-June. Events include moose safaris, mountain bike and canoe races, a parade and a family fun day. Rhode Island's **May breakfasts** have been a tradition since 1867: Johnnycakes and other native dishes are served statewide at bird sanctuaries, churches, grange halls, yacht clubs, schools, and veterans' posts. **Lobsterfest** kicks off Mystic Seaport's (CT) summer of festivities with live entertainment and plenty of good food. Holyoke's (MA) **Shad Fishing Derby** is said to be the largest freshwater fishing derby in North America.

SUMMER

JUNE➤ In Vermont, you can listen to jazz at Burlington's **Discover Jazz Festival** or folk at Warren's **Ben & Jerry's One World One Heart Festival,** which is held at Sugarbush. **Jacob's Pillow Dance Festival** at Becket (MA) in the Berkshires hosts performers of various dance traditions from June to September. The spring thaw calls for a number of boating celebrations, including the

Vermont Canoe and Kayak Festival at Waterbury State Park; the **Yale–Harvard Regatta** along New London's (CT) Thames River, the oldest intercollegiate athletic event in the country; the **Boothbay Harbor Windjammer Days,** which starts the high season for Maine's boating set; and the **Blessing of the Fleet** in Provincetown, which culminates a weekend of festivities—a quahog feed, a public dance, a crafts show, a parade. Young ones are the stars of Somerworth's (NH) **International Children's Festival,** where games, activities, and crafts keep everybody busy. **A Taste of Hartford** lets you eat your way through the capital city while enjoying outdoor music, dance, comedy, and magic. Nothing is sweeter than a fresh Maine strawberry, and during the **Strawberry Festival** in Wiscasset you can get your fill of strawberry shortcake and other goodies. You can visit Providence's (RI) stately homes, some by candlelight, on one of the **Providence Preservation Society's tours.** Major **crafts and antiques fairs** are held in Farmington (CT) and Springfield (MA).

JULY➤ **Fourth of July** parties and parades occur throughout New England; Bristol's (RI) parade is the nation's senior Independence Day parade; and concerts, family entertainment, an art show, a parade, and fireworks are held in Bath (ME). Later in the month, Exeter (NH) holds a **Revolutionary War Festival** at the American Independence Museum with battle

reenactments, period crafts and antiques, and a visit from George Washington himself. And the **Mashpee Powwow** (MA) brings together Native Americans from North and South America for three days of dance contests, drumming, a fireball game, and a clambake; Native American food and crafts are sold. Some of the better music festivals include the **Marlboro Music Festival** of classical music, held at Marlboro College (VT); Newport's (RI) **Music Festival,** which brings together celebrated musicians for two weeks of concerts in Newport mansions; the **Bar Harbor Festival** (ME), which hosts classical, jazz, and popular music concerts into August; the **Bowdoin Summer Music Festival** (ME), a six-week series of chamber music concerts; and the **Tanglewood Music Festival** at Lenox (MA), which shifts into high gear with performances by the Boston Symphony Orchestra and a slew of major entertainers. Shoppers can rummage through major **antiques fairs** in Wolfeboro (NH) and Dorset (VT), or simply admire the furnishings of homes during **Open House Tours** in Litchfield (CT) and Camden (ME). Boaters and the men and women who love them flock to the **Sail Festival** at the City Pier in New London (CT) to watch sail races, outdoor concerts, fireworks, and the Ugliest Dog Contest. In nearby Mystic, vintage powerboats and sailboats are on view at the **Antique and Classic Boat Rendezvous.** The **Yarmouth Clam Festival** (ME) is more than a seafood celebration—expect fireworks, a parade, continuous entertainment, and a crafts show throughout the three-day event. Two of the region's most popular **country fairs** are held in Bangor (ME) and on Cape Cod in Barnstable (MA).

AUGUST➤ The music festivals continue—in Newport (RI) with **Ben & Jerry's Newport Folk Festival** and **JVC's Jazz Festival** and in Essex (CT) with the **Great Connecticut Traditional Jazz Festival.** Stowe (VT) hosts a popular **Antique and Classic Car Rally.** Popular arts, crafts, and antiques festivals include the **Southern Vermont Crafts Fair** in Manchester (VT), the **Outdoor Arts Festival** in Mystic (CT), the **Maine Antiques Festival** in Union, and the **Fair of the League of New Hampshire Craftsmen** at Mt. Sunapee State Park in Newbury. There's a **Lobster Festival** in Rockland (ME) and a **Blueberry Festival** in Rangeley Lake (ME) . Most summers find a **major air show** with precision teams, acrobat and stunt pilots, and military planes both flying and on display at the Brunswick (ME) Naval Air Station. Also in Brunswick is **The Maine Festival,** a four-day celebration of Maine arts. A few general summer fairs include the **Woodstock Fair** (CT), which has livestock shows, Colonial crafts, puppet shows, and food; the **Hyannis Street Festival** (MA), a three-day weekend of Main Street shopping, food, and entertainment; and the **Martha's Vineyard Agricultural Fair** (MA), which includes contests, animal shows, a carnival, and evening entertainment.

AUTUMN

SEPTEMBER➤ New England's dozens of Labor Day fairs include the **Vermont State Fair** in Rutland, with agricultural exhibits and entertainment; the **Providence Waterfront Festival** (RI), a weekend of arts, crafts, ethnic foods, musical entertainment, and boat races; the **International Seaplane Fly-In Weekend,** which sets Moosehead Lake (ME) buzzing; and the **Champlain Valley Exposition,** a Burlington (VT) event with all the features of a large county fair. Foot stomping and guitar strumming are the activities of choice at several musical events: the **Cajun & Bluegrass Music-Dance-Food Festival** at Stepping Stone Ranch in Escoheag (RI), the **National Traditional Old-Time Fiddler's Contest** in Barre (VT), the **Bluegrass Festival** in Brunswick (ME), and the **Rockport Folk Festival** in Rockport (ME). In Stratton (VT), artists and performers gather for the **Stratton Arts Festival.** One of the best and oldest **antiques shows** in New England occurs in New Haven (CT). Providence (RI) shows off its diversity during its **Annual Heritage Festival.**

Agricultural fairs not to be missed are the **Common Ground Country Fair** in Windsor (ME), an organic farmer's delight; the **Deerfield Fair** (NH), one of New England's oldest; and the **Eastern States**

Exposition in Springfield (MA), New England's largest. The six small Vermont towns of Walden, Cabot, Plainfield, Peacham, Barnet, and Groton host the weeklong **Northeast Kingdom Fall Foliage Festival** (VT). Crafts, entertainment, and buckets of fried scallops are served up at the **Bourne Scallopfest** in Buzzards Bay (MA). For the **Martha's Vineyard Striped Bass and Bluefish Derby,** from mid-September to mid-October, locals drop everything to cast their lines in search of a prize-winning whopper. The weekend-long **Eastport Salmon Festival** (ME) hosts entertainers and crafts artists. At the **Annual Seafood Festival** in Hampton Beach, you can sample the seafood specialties of more than 50 local restaurants, dance to live bands, and watch fireworks explode over the ocean.

OCTOBER➤ The **Fryeburg Fair** (ME) presents agricultural exhibits, harness racing, an iron-skillet-throwing contest, and a pig scramble. The **Nantucket Cranberry Harvest** is a three-day celebration including bog and inn tours and a crafts fair.

NOVEMBER➤ In Vermont there are two major events in this otherwise quiet month: The **International Film Festival** presents films dealing with environmental, human rights, and political issues for a week in Burlington, and the **Bradford Wild Game Supper** draws thousands to taste large and small game animals and birds.

2 Connecticut

Southwestern Connecticut is home to commuters, celebrities, and others who enjoy its privacy and convenience to New York City. Far less touristy than other parts of the state, the Connecticut River valley is a stretch of small river villages punctuated by a few small cities. The Litchfield Hills have grand old inns and rolling farmlands. New Haven is home to Yale and several fine museums, and along the southeastern coast are quiet shoreline villages. A string of sparsely populated towns in the northeast composes the Quiet Corner.

By Andrew
Collins

Updated by
Michelle
Bodak Acri

CONNECTICUT HAS VERY FEW SIDEWALKS. Except for a dozen midsize metropolises, Connecticut's towns and villages exist without those concrete emblems of urbanity—the brackets that crisscross much of America at right angles, defying nature's alluvial and undulating boundaries: the rivers and ridges, mountains and meadows. In this densely populated place—only three states have more residents per square mile—visitors are often taken aback by the seeming wealth of space and the seeming distance and inaccessibility between the homes of neighbors.

A glorious elm-shaded town green anchors nearly every Connecticut town—a throwback to a forgotten era but evidence that today's "Nutmeggers" still hold dear the commodity of elbowroom and the rich and verdant gifts of nature. Zoning laws in most towns forbid abutting edifices—at least in residential neighborhoods—and 2-acre zoning is the norm in many counties.

This is not to say Connecticut Yankees are unfriendly, or even aloof. Connecticut is a state of decidedly civilized and proper persons. But behind what you may find a somewhat frosty veneer often glows a hospitable, if not garrulous, soul. Ask for directions, and you may be informed not only how to get where you're going, but also told about a complicated but scenic shortcut, the description of which is executed with hand gestures, furrowed brows, and ponderous gazes.

People in Connecticut are inventive, particular, and quirky: History has seen the manufacture of locks, clocks, guns, hats, submarines, bicycle spokes, and numerous tools and mechanisms. A historic example of an innovative scheme is that clever whittlers once passed off to unsuspecting buyers wood fashioned to resemble nutmeg, then a high-priced item.

The aforementioned stereotypes apply mostly to the state's natives—and this fraction of the population is dwindling rapidly. Remember the state motto: "He who transplanted still sustains." Outsiders move here, often to build or renovate their dream house in the sticks, and as elsewhere, locals generally resent the throngs of city dwellers invading the countryside like locusts. Urban sprawl starts in the southwest corner and fans out a little farther every year. Hillside after hillside is taken, stripped of its flora and fauna, and developed. And even with all those zoning laws, things are getting crowded. Some newer developments even have sidewalks. The immigration is not without its financial advantages, but most natives would gladly trade wealth—which many already have—for privacy.

Connecticut is the richest state in the country. A troublesome aspect of this wealth is its uneven distribution. From the top of Yale University's ivory-like Harkness Tower, you can look in no direction without seeing evidence of a deeply troubled city, New Haven, too much of which trudges along below the poverty level. Winding country roads flow arterially from Connecticut's struggling cities into prosperous satellite communities. The notions of ethnic integration and urban renewal are hotly discussed at town meetings these days, as residents find ways to keep Connecticut a desirable gateway to New England.

Pleasures and Pastimes

Antiquing

Although you'll find everything from chic boutiques to vast outlet malls in Connecticut, the state is an antiquer's paradise. The Litchfield

Hills region, in the state's northwest corner, is the heart of antiques country. In the Quiet Corner, east of the Litchfield Hills, are several hundred dealers and complexes. Mystic, Old Saybrook, and other towns south along the coast are filled with markets, galleries, and shops, many specializing in antique prints, maps, books, and collectibles.

Dining

Call it the fennel factor. Or the arugula influx. Or the prosciutto preponderance. However you wish to characterize it, southern New England has witnessed a gastronomic revolution in recent years. Preparation and ingredients now reflect the culinary trends of nearby Manhattan and Boston. And though a few traditional favorites remain, such as New England clam chowder, Yankee pot roast, and grilled haddock, Grand Marnier is now favored on ice cream over hot fudge sauce, sliced duck is wrapped in phyllo and served with a ginger-plum sauce (the rich, gooey orange glaze decidedly absent), and everything from lavender to fresh figs is being used to season and complement dishes. Dining in the cities is highly international: Indian, Vietnamese, Thai, Malaysian, and Japanese restaurants, even Spanish tapas bars. Nutmeggers are also going a tad decadent; designer martinis are quite the rage, cigar bars and swanky brew pubs have popped up all around the state—heck, even caviar is making a comeback. The one drawback of this turn toward sophistication is that finding an under-$10 dinner entrée is proving increasingly difficult.

CATEGORY	COST*
$$$$	over $40
$$$	$25–$40
$$	$15–$25
$	under $15

*average cost of a three-course dinner, per person, excluding drinks, service, and 6% sales tax

Fishing

Connecticut teems with possibilities for anglers, from deep-sea fishing in coastal waters to fly-fishing in the state's many streams. Try the Litchfield Hills region for freshwater fish: If you're just a beginner, don't fret, you'll be catching trout or bass in the Housatonic River in no time. Southeastern Connecticut is the charter- and party-boat capital of New England. Charter fishing boats take passengers out on Long Island Sound for half-day, full-day, and overnight trips.

Lodging

Connecticut has plenty of business-oriented chain hotels and low-budget motels, but the state's unusual inns, resorts, bed-and-breakfasts, and country hotels are far more atmospheric. You'll pay dearly for rooms in summer on the coast and in autumn in the hills, where thousands peek at the peaking foliage. The rates are lowest in winter, but so are the temperatures, making spring the best time for bargain seekers to visit.

CATEGORY	COST*
$$$$	over $170
$$$	$120–$170
$$	$70–$120
$	under $70

*All prices are for a standard double room during peak season, with no meals unless noted, and excluding service charge and 12% state lodging tax.

State Parks

Sixty percent of Connecticut is forest land, some of it under the jurisdiction of the state parks division, which also manages several beaches on the southern shoreline. Many parks have campgrounds. Trails meander through most of the parks—the hiking is especially spectacular around the cool, clear water at Lake Waramaug State Park and the 200-ft-high waterfall at Kent Falls State Park. At Gillette Castle State Park in East Haddam there are several trails, some on former railroad beds. Some state parks have no entrance fees year-round. At others the fee varies, depending on the time of year, day of the week, and whether or not your car bears a Connecticut license plate.

Exploring Connecticut

Southwestern Connecticut contains the wealthy coastal communities. Moving east along the coast (in most states you usually travel north or south along the coast, but in Connecticut you actually travel east or west), you'll come to New Haven and the southeastern coast, which is broken by many small bays and inlets. The Quiet Corner, bordered by Rhode Island to the east and Massachusetts to the north, contains rolling hills and tranquil countryside. To the west is the fertile farmland of the Connecticut River valley and the state's capital, Hartford. In the middle and northwestern parts of the state is the Litchfield Hills area, covered with miles of forests, lakes, and rivers.

Numbers in the text and in the margin correspond to numbers on the maps: Southwestern Connecticut, Connecticut River Valley, Downtown Hartford, Litchfield Hills, the Quiet Corner, and Southeastern Connecticut.

Great Itineraries

IF YOU HAVE 1 DAY

Begin in **New Preston** ㉟, and then head for Lake Waramaug. In **West Cornwall** ㊳ have a look at the state's largest covered bridge. Working your way north, stop in **Lakeville** ㊵ and **Salisbury** ㊶ (a good place to stop for lunch). Spend a couple of hours in **Litchfield** ㊼, where you can tour historic houses before heading south via **Bethlehem** ㊾ to **Woodbury** (51) to visit the town's churches and antiques shops.

IF YOU HAVE 3 DAYS

Greenwich ①, a wealthy community with grand homes and great restaurants, makes a good starting point. From here head to **Stamford** ②, where you can visit the Whitney Museum of American Art at Champion or go malling across the street. East along the coast is **Norwalk** ③, whose SoNo commercial district and Maritime Aquarium are popular attractions. Have dinner in **Westport** ⑩, and end your first day in **Ridgefield** ⑥. After touring Ridgefield the next morning, head for **New Preston** ㉟. From here drive north via **West Cornwall** ㊳ to **Norfolk** ㊸. Then it's on to **Litchfield** ㊼, where you may want to conclude your day. If not, travel a little farther south to charming **Washington** ㊿. Begin day three in **Woodbury** (51) and then head to **New Haven** (54). Near the Yale University campus are many great shops and restaurants.

IF YOU HAVE 5 DAYS

Spend the morning of your first day in **Hartford** ㉒–㉙ and the early part of the afternoon in **West Hartford** ㉚ before heading to **Farmington** ㉛, which has two excellent house museums, and **Simsbury** ㉜, where you can visit Massacoh Plantation. Spend the night in either town. On your second day, head west to **Woodbury** (51), stopping in **Litchfield** ㊼ and **Kent** ㊱. Stay the night in **Washington** ㊿ or **Ridgefield** ⑥. Begin your third day in southwestern Connecticut in **Greenwich** ①, followed by stops in **Stamford** ②, **Westport** ⑩, and **Bridgeport** ⑫. Spend the remainder of your day in **New Haven** (54). Start your fourth day in **Essex** ⑭ and visit the Connecticut River Museum. At Gillette Castle

Connecticut

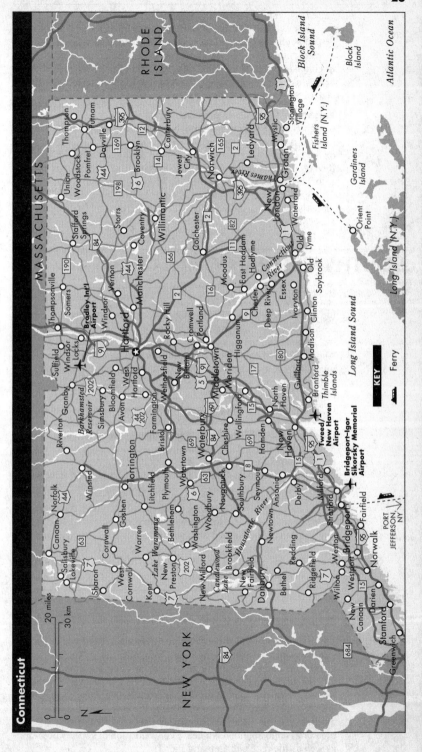

State Park in **East Haddam** ⑰ you can tour the hilltop estate built by the actor William Gillette. From here, backtrack to the coastal town of **Old Saybrook** ㉘ and then cross the river to ⌖ **Old Lyme** ㉙, a former art colony. On the fifth day, continue touring the coast, starting in either **New London** ㉑ or **Groton** ㉓ and heading east toward **Mystic** ㉔. Take time to visit Mystic Seaport before heading to the little village of **Stonington** ㉕.

When to Tour Connecticut

Connecticut is lovely year-round, but fall and spring are the best times to visit. A drive in fall along the rolling hills of the state's back roads or the Merritt Parkway (which has been designated a National Scenic Byway) is a memorable experience. Leaves of yellow, orange, and red color the fall landscape, but the state blooms in springtime, too—town greens are painted with daffodils and tulips, and blooming trees punctuate the rich green countryside. The scent of flower blossoms is in the air, especially in Fairfield, which holds an annual Dogwood Festival. Many attractions that are closed in winter reopen in March or April.

SOUTHWESTERN CONNECTICUT

A mere 50 mi from midtown Manhattan, southwestern Connecticut is a rich swirl of old New England and new New York. Encompassing all of Fairfield County, this region consistently reports the highest cost of living and most expensive homes of any community in the country. Its bedroom towns are home primarily to white-collar executives; some still make the nearly two-hour dash to and from Gotham, but most enjoy a more civilized morning drive to Stamford, which is reputed to have more corporate headquarters per square mile than any other U.S. city. Strict zoning has preserved a certain privacy and rusticity uncommon in other such densely populated areas, and numerous celebrities—Paul Newman, David Letterman, Michael Bolton, Diana Ross, and Mel Gibson, among them—live in Fairfield County. The combination of drivers, winding roads, and heavily wooded countryside has resulted in at least one major problem: According to a survey in central Fairfield County, nearly 50% of area drivers have struck a deer.

Venture away from the wealthy communities, and you'll discover cities in different stages of urban renewal: Stamford, Norwalk, Bridgeport, and Danbury. These four have some of the region's best cultural and shopping opportunities, but the economic disparity between Connecticut's tony towns and troubled cities is perhaps nowhere more visible than in Fairfield County.

Greenwich

❶ *28 mi northeast of New York City, 64 mi southwest of Hartford.*

You'll have no trouble believing that Greenwich is one of the wealthiest towns in the United States when you drive along Route 1 (which goes by the names West Putnam Avenue, East Putnam Avenue, and the Post Road, among others), where the streets are lined with ritzy car dealers, Euro-chic clothing shops, and other posh businesses. **Greenwich Avenue,** which runs perpendicular to the Post Road and ends, under a different name, at a viewpoint where people often drop a line into the Long Island Sound, has a heavy concentration of swanky boutiques as well as the requisite Gap and Pier 1.

You'll probably want to start your visit to Greenwich by buying a Ferrari or Aston Martin at **Miller Motor Cars** (✉ 275 and 342 W. Putnam

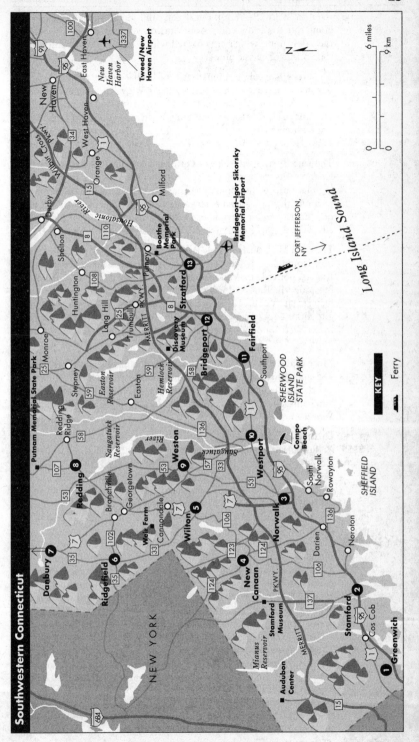

Southwestern Connecticut

Ave., ☎ 203/629–8830). But if you can't plunk down $150,000 (the going rate for a low-end Aston Martin), you can inspect the walls of the sales room, which are covered with a terrific collection of sepiatone prints of classic autos.

☞ The **Bruce Museum** is a must-visit for both kids and adults. A section devoted to environmental history has a wigwam, a spectacular mineral collection, a marine touch tank, and a 16th-century-era woodland diorama. There's also a small but worthwhile collection of American Impressionist paintings. ⊠ *1 Museum Dr. (Exit 3 off I–95),* ☎ *203/ 869–0376.* ⊡ *$3.50, free on Tues.* ⊙ *Tues.–Sat. 10–5, Sun. 1–5.*

The small, barn-red **Putnam Cottage,** built in 1690 and operated as Knapp's Tavern during the Revolutionary War, was a frequent meeting place of Revolutionary War hero General Israel Putnam. You can meander through a lush herb garden and examine the cottage's Colonial furnishings and prominent fieldstone fireplaces. ⊠ *243 E. Putnam Ave./Rte. 1,* ☎ *203/869–9697.* ⊡ *$2.* ⊙ *Wed., Fri., Sun. 1–4.*

The circa 1732 **Bush–Holley House,** a handsome central-chimney saltbox, contains a wonderful collection of artworks by sculptor John Rogers, potter Leon Volkmar, and painters Childe Hassam, Elmer Livingstone MacRae, and John Twachtman. The visitor center, set in the historic site's circa 1805 storehouse, holds exhibition galleries and a gift shop. ⊠ *39 Strickland Rd.,* ☎ *203/869–6899.* ⊡ *$6.* ⊙ *Jan.– Mar., Wed. noon–4, Sat. 11–4, Sun. 1–4; Apr.–Dec., Wed.–Fri. noon–4, Sat. 11–4, Sun. 1–4.*

More than 1,000 species of flora and fauna have been recorded at the 485-acre **Audubon Center** in northern Greenwich, where exhibits survey the local environment and 8 mi of trails meander through woods and fields. ⊠ *613 Riversville Rd.,* ☎ *203/869–5272.* ⊡ *$3.* ⊙ *Tues.– Sun. 9–5.*

Dining and Lodging

$$$$ ✕ **Restaurant Jean-Louis.** Roses, Villeroy & Boch china, and white table-
★ cloths with lace underskirts complement this restaurant's world-class cuisine. Specialties include quail-and-vegetable ragout with foie-gras sauce, scallopini of salmon on a bed of wilted red cabbage with an Italian parsley coulis, and, for dessert, lemon and pear gratin. ⊠ *61 Lewis St.,* ☎ *203/622–8450. Jacket. AE, D, DC, MC, V. Closed Sun. No lunch Sat.–Thurs.*

$$$–$$$$ ✕ **The Ivy.** The chef at this restaurant describes the cuisine as "Talyfornian"—a mix of robust Italy and health-conscious California with a few variations on those themes. Among the appetizers are a potato pancake topped with goat cheese and meaty slices of Portobello mushroom; for an entrée try the risotto of the day, flavored with anything from rabbit to salmon, or the pan-roasted veal with a stuffing of artichoke, spinach, and fontina cheese. ⊠ *554 Old Post Rd., No. 3,* ☎ *203/661–3200. AE, D, DC, MC, V. No lunch weekends.*

$$$ ✕ **64 Greenwich Avenue.** With a country-yet-contemporary American decor and superbly presented nouvelle American cuisine, 64 Greenwich has flair to spare. A tasty small plate (as appetizers are called here) of roasted Prince Edward Island mussels may be followed by New York Black Angus sirloin or perhaps medallions of veal with crabmeat. Don't miss the desserts, especially the crème brûlée. ⊠ *64 Greenwich Ave.,* ☎ *203/861–6400. AE, DC, MC, V.*

$$–$$$ ✕ **Pasta Vera.** The plain white dining space of this small shop-cum-restaurant hardly hints at the many splendid variations on simple pasta. Try the wild-mushroom ravioli or the popular Siciliana (sautéed eggplant, fresh tomatoes, and mozzarella). Fettuccine, linguine, and angel hair pasta are available with 18 different preparations. ⊠ *48 Green-wich Ave.*, ☎ *203/661–9705. Reservations not accepted. AE, MC, V.*

$$$–$$$$ ✕⚏ **Homestead Inn.** In a posh residential neighborhood not far from the water, this enormous Italianate wood-frame house has a cupola, ornate bracketed eaves, and an enclosed wraparound Victorian porch. Rooms are decorated individually with antiques and period repro-ductions. For all its architectural fine points, though, the Homestead is becoming better known for the up-to-the-minute fine French cuisine prepared by chef-owner Thomas Henkelmann. The menu, which changes seasonally, might include Atlantic black sea bass with a veal-based black truffle sauce or seared Hudson Valley duck foie gras jazzed up with a puff-pastry base and cap, and sea scallops. Reservations are essential for dinner, for which a jacket is required. ⊠ *420 Field Point Rd., 06830,* ☎ FAX *203/869–7500. 17 rooms, 6 suites. Restaurant, meet-ing rooms. AE, DC, MC, V.*

$$$–$$$$ ⚏ **Hyatt Regency Greenwich.** The Hyatt's vast but comfortable atrium
★ contains a flourishing lawn and abundant flora. The rooms are spa-cious, with modern furnishings and many amenities, including modem-compatible telephones. The pleasant Winfield's restaurant serves interesting renditions of classic dishes. ⊠ *1800 E. Putnam Ave., 06870,* ☎ *203/637–1234,* FAX *203/637–2940. 349 rooms, 4 suites. 2 restau-rants, bar, in-room modem lines, indoor pool, sauna, health club, busi-ness services, meeting rooms. AE, D, DC, MC, V.*

$$ ⚏ **Greenwich Harbor Inn.** Rooms at this informal harborside inn have soft colors, floral bedspreads, and reproductions of 18th-century an-tiques. More like an upscale chain property than an inn, the hotel is within walking distance of the railroad station and the Greenwich Av-enue boutiques. ⊠ *500 Steamboat Rd., 06830,* ☎ *203/661–9800,* FAX *203/629–4431. 94 rooms, 2 suites. Restaurant, pub, dock. AE, DC, MC, V.*

$$ ⚏ **Stanton House Inn.** The original structure of this Federal-style man-sion, within walking distance of downtown, was built in 1840. In 1899, under architect Stanford White's supervision, the house was enlarged. The interior has been carefully decorated with a mixture of antiques and reproductions; two rooms have fireplaces. ⊠ *76 Maple Ave., 06830,* ☎ *203/869–2110,* FAX *203/629–2116. 24 rooms, 2 share bath. Pool. Continental breakfast. AE, D, MC, V. No smoking.*

Stamford

❷ *6 mi northeast of Greenwich, 38 mi southwest of New Haven, 33 mi northeast of New York City.*

Glitzy office buildings, chain hotels, and major department stores are among the new landmarks in revitalized Stamford, the most dynamic city on the southwestern shore. Restaurants, nightclubs, and shops line Atlantic and lower Summer streets, these businesses poised to harness the region's affluence and satisfy the desire of suburbanites to spend an exciting night on the town without having to brave New York City.

The primary focus of the **Whitney Museum of American Art at Cham-pion,** a facility affiliated with the Whitney Museum in New York City, is 20th-century American painting and photography. Past exhibits have included works by Edward Hopper, Alexander Calder, and Geor-gia O'Keeffe. Free gallery talks are held on Tuesday, Thursday, and Sat-urday at 12:30. ⊠ *Atlantic St. and Tresser Blvd.,* ☎ *203/358–7630.* ⚏ *Free.* ⊙ *Tues.–Sat. 11–5. Closed Sun. and Mon.*

One of the country's most unusual houses of worship is the fish-shape **First Presbyterian Church,** which contains beautiful stained-glass win-dows and an enormous mechanical-action pipe organ. ⊠ *1101 Bed-*

ford St., ☎ 203/324–9522. ⊙ Sept.–June, weekdays 9–5; July–Aug.,
weekdays 9–3.

🐄 Oxen, sheep, pigs, and other animals roam the 118-acre **Stamford Mu-**
seum and Nature Center, a New England-style farmstead with many
nature trails for humans to wander. Kids can climb into the large birds'
nests at Nature's Playground, which also has a tree house and plenty
of slides. Exhibits survey natural history, art, Americana, and Native
American life. Two enjoyable times to come are during spring harvest
and maple-sugaring season—call for exact dates. ⊠ *39 Scofieldtown*
Rd./Rte. 137, ☎ 203/322–1646. ☞ Grounds $5, planetarium an ad-
ditional $2, observatory $3 (but no grounds fee). ⊙ Grounds Mon.–
Sat. 9–5, Sun. 1–5; farm daily 9–5; planetarium shows Sun. 3 PM;
observatory Fri. 8–10 PM.

The 64-acre **Bartlett Arboretum,** owned by the University of Connecticut, holds natural woodlands, cultivated gardens, marked ecology trails, a swamp walk, and a pond. The wildflower garden is
stunning in the spring. ⊠ *151 Brookdale Rd., off High Ridge Rd. (Exit*
35 Merritt Pkwy.), ☎ 203/322–6971. ☞ Free. ⊙ Grounds daily
8:30–dusk; visitor center Mon.–Fri. 8:30–4

Dining and Lodging

$$$–$$$$ ✕ **Amadeus.** One of a dozen great restaurants along its stretch of
Summer Street, Amadeus leads the pack. The dining room overflows
with dried-flower arrangements, and lavishly framed prints dot the walls.
The fare is Continental with a Viennese flair: Try the Mediterranean
fish and shellfish soup, followed by the trademark Vienna schnitzel,
served with golden panfried potatoes. ⊠ *201 Summer St., ☎ 203/348–*
7775. AE, D, DC, MC, V. No lunch weekends.

$$$ ✕ **Kathleen's.** Behind a striking facade of black with cornflower-blue
trim lurks this wonderful, uncharacteristically quiet little eatery that
serves hearty interpretations of regional American cuisine: pan-seared
yellowfin tuna with white- and black-bean sauces, veal with country
ham stuffing, and many pastas. Save room for the apple pie or Kathleen's famous chocolate cake. This restaurant is within walking distance of downtown clubs, theaters, and shopping. ⊠ *25 Bank St., ☎*
203/323–7785. AE, DC, MC, V. No lunch weekends.

$$–$$$ ✕ **La Hacienda.** The decor of this restaurant is more upscale Mexican
★ than Americanized south-of-the-border—there are no streamers here.
The imaginative and authentic cuisine includes chicken mole and *tacos*
pibil, a Yucatán specialty consisting of shredded pork marinated in a
delicious roasted-tomato salsa. ⊠ *222 Summer St., ☎ 203/324–0577.*
AE, DC, MC, V. No lunch Sun.

$$–$$$$ 🏨 **Stamford Sheraton.** The driveway leading to the ultramodern en-
trance of this downtown luxury hotel should prepare you for the dra-
matic atrium lobby, whose main feature is a brass-and-glass-enclosed
gazebo. The attractive rooms have contemporary furnishings and spa-
cious bathrooms. ⊠ *1 First Stamford Pl., 06902, ☎ 203/967–2222,*
FAX 203/967–3475. 451 rooms, 23 suites. Restaurant, indoor pool, 2
tennis courts, health club, meeting rooms. AE, D, DC, MC, V.

$$–$$$ 🏨 **Stamford Marriott Hotel.** The Marriott stands out for its up-to-date
facilities and convenience to trains and airport buses. Furnishings
throughout are modern and comfortable, if unmemorable. The busy
lobby is a favorite meeting place of the city's movers and shakers. ⊠
2 Stamford Forum, 06901, ☎ 203/357–9555, FAX 203/358–0157.
500 rooms, 7 suites. Restaurant, bar, coffee shop, indoor-outdoor
pool, barbershop, beauty salon, health club, jogging, racquetball, car
rental. AE, D, DC, MC, V.

Nightlife and the Arts

NIGHTLIFE

For alternative dance music try the **Art Bar** (⌧ 84 W. Park Pl., ☎ 203/973–0300), which is gay and lesbian on Sunday night. **Connecticut Shade Cigar Lounge & Boutique** (⌧ 211 Summer St., ☎ 203/353–1245) is the place for a cigar or premium single-malt Scotch. At the **Terrace Club** (⌧ 1938 W. Main St., ☎ 203/961–9770) you can dance to everything from ballroom and country western to Top 40 and disco. **Tigin Pub** (⌧ 175 Bedford St., ☎ 203/353–8444), has the feel of an Irish pub.

Noelle Spa for Beauty & Wellness (⌧ 1100 High Ridge Rd., ☎ 203/322–3445) is open late on Tuesday and Thursday for facials, massages, body wraps, and other healthful regimens.

THE ARTS

The **Stamford Center for the Arts** (☎ 203/325–4466) presents everything from one-act plays and comedy shows to musicals and film festivals. Performances are held at the Rich Forum (⌧ 307 Atlantic St.) and the Palace Theatre (⌧ 61 Atlantic St.). The Stamford Symphony Orchestra (☎ 203/325–1407) and the Connecticut Grand Opera and Orchestra (☎ 203/327–2867) perform at the Palace.

Outdoor Activities and Sports

The greens fee at the 18-hole, par-72 **Sterling Farms Golf Course** (⌧ 1349 Newfield Ave., ☎ 203/461–9090) ranges from $28 to $35; an optional cart costs $10.

Shopping

The **Stamford Town Center** (⌧ 100 Greyrock Pl., ☎ 203/356–9700) houses 130 chiefly upscale shops, including Saks Fifth Avenue, Talbot's, and Tommy Hilfiger. Northern Stamford's **United House Wrecking** (⌧ 535 Hope St., ☎ 203/348–5371) sells acres of architectural artifacts, decorative accessories, antiques, nautical items, lawn and garden furnishings, and other less valuable but unusual items.

Norwalk

❸ *14 mi northeast of Stamford, 42 mi northeast of New York City, 16 mi southwest of Bridgeport.*

Norwalk is the home of Yankee Doodle Dandies: In 1756, Colonel Thomas Fitch threw together a motley crew of Norwalk soldiers and led them off to fight at Fort Crailo, near Albany, New York. Supposedly, Norwalk's women gathered feathers for the men to wear as plumes in their caps in an effort to give them some appearance of military decorum. Upon the arrival of these foppish warriors, one of the British officers sarcastically dubbed them "macaronies"—slang for dandies. The saying caught on, and so did the song.

In the 19th century, Norwalk became a major New England port and manufactured pottery, clocks, watches, shingle nails, and paper. It later fell into a state of neglect, in which it has remained for much of this century. During the past decade, however, Norwalk's coastal business district has been the focus of a major redevelopment project.

Art galleries, restaurants, and trendy boutiques have blossomed on and around Washington Street; the stretch is now known as the **SoNo** (short for South Norwalk) commercial district.

★ ☺ The cornerstone of the SoNo district is the **Maritime Aquarium at Norwalk,** a 5-acre waterfront center that brings to life the ecology and history of Long Island Sound. A huge aquarium competes for attention with marine vessels like the 56-ft oyster sloop *Hope,* and there's an

IMAX theater. Although not as popular as Mystic Seaport, the Maritime Center is one of the state's most worthwhile attractions—especially for families. ⊠ *10 N. Water St.,* ☎ *203/852–0700.* ⊡ *Aquarium $7.75, IMAX theater $6.50, combined $12.* ⊙ *Daily 10–5 (July–Labor Day, until 6).*

Restoration continues at the **Lockwood-Mathews Mansion Museum,** an ornate tribute to Victorian decorating. It's hard not to be impressed by the octagonal rotunda and 50 rooms of gilt, fresco, marble, woodwork, and etched glass. ⊠ *295 West Ave.,* ☎ *203/838–1434.* ⊡ *$5.* ⊙ *Mar.–early-Jan., Tues.–Fri. 11–2, Sun. 1–4, Sat. 1–4 for special exhibitions; Jan.–Mar. by appointment.*

The 3-acre park at the **Sheffield Island Lighthouse** is a prime spot for a picnic. The 1868 lighthouse has four levels and 10 rooms to explore. ⊠ *Ferry service from Hope Dock (corner of Washington and North Sts.),* ☎ *203/838–9444 for ferry and lighthouse.* ⊡ *$10 round-trip ferry service and lighthouse tour; $4 tour only.* ⊙ *Ferry: Memorial Day–mid-June, weekends 10, 12:30, and 3; mid-June–Labor Day, daily 9:30 and 1:30, weekends 10, 12:30, and 3. Lighthouse open when ferry is docked. Closed Labor Day–Memorial Day.*

Dining and Lodging

$$$ ✕ **Meson Galicia.** The inventive tapas served in this restored trolley barn in downtown Norwalk electrify the taste buds. Ingredients include sweetbreads, capers, asparagus, chorizo . . . the list goes on. Come with an empty stomach and an open mind, and let the enthusiastic staff spoil you. The paella is a must-try. ⊠ *10 Wall St.,* ☎ *203/866–8800. AE, D, DC, MC, V. Closed Mon. No lunch weekends.*

$$–$$$ ✕ **Côte d'Azur.** Dining is by candlelight at this neighborhood bistro with rustic furnishings and yellow walls. Past delicacies on the seasonally changing menu have included marinated braised rabbit, crayfish, and broiled monkfish served with an artichoke-potato puree. ⊠ *86 Washington St.,* ☎ *203/855–8900. MC, V. Closed Sun.–Mon.*

$$ ✕⊡ **Silvermine Tavern.** The cozy rooms at this inn, one of the state's ★   best values, are furnished with hooked rugs and antiques along with some modern touches. The large, low-ceiling dining rooms ($$–$$$; closed on Tuesday) are romantic, with an eclectic Colonial decor; many tables overlook a waterfall. Traditional New England favorites receive modern accents—roast duckling, for instance, is served with maple mashed sweet potatoes and a peach reduction. Attending Sunday brunch here is a local tradition. ⊠ *194 Perry Ave., 06850,* ☎ *203/ 847–4558,* ℻ *203/847–9171. 10 rooms, 1 suite. Restaurant. Continental breakfast. AE, DC, MC, V.*

Nightlife and the Arts

Some good bars can be found in the SoNo district of South Norwalk. **Barcelona** (⊠ 63 N. Main St., ☎ 203/899–0088), a wine bar, is a hot spot for Spanish tapas. Brewing memorabilia adorns the **Brewhouse** (⊠ 13 Marshall St., ☎ 203/853–9110). The **Fairfield Orchestra** (☎ 203/831–6020) performs at the Norwalk Concert Hall (⊠ 125 East Ave.). Its offshoot, the **Orchestra of the Old Fairfield Academy,** performs music of the Baroque and other classical periods.

Outdoor Activities and Sports

For charters, rentals, lessons, or even advice on buying a boat, contact the **Sound Sailing Center** (⊠ 160 Water St., ☎ 203/838–1110).

Shopping

Stew Leonard's (⊠ 100 Westport Ave., ☎ 203/847–7213), the self-proclaimed "Disneyland of Supermarkets," has a petting zoo, animated characters wandering the aisles, scrumptious chocolate chip cookies, and free samples. When in Danbury, stop by the location at 99 Federal Road. Along **Washington Street** in South Norwalk (SoNo) are some excellent galleries and crafts dealers.

New Canaan

❹ *5 mi northwest of Norwalk, 33 mi southwest of New Haven.*

So rich and elegant is the landscape in New Canaan that you may want to pick up a local street map and spend the afternoon driving around the estate-studded countryside. Or you might prefer lingering on **Main Street,** which is loaded with upscale shops.

The **New Canaan Historical Society** operates several buildings on its property, including a town house, the John Rogers Sculpture Studio, a Colonial schoolhouse, a tool museum, a print shop, an 1845 pharmacy, and a restored Georgian Colonial home. ⊠ *13 Oenoke Ridge,* ☎ *203/966–1776.* ☑ *Donation suggested.* ☉ *Main building Tues.– Sat. 10–noon and 2–4; other buildings Wed.–Thurs. and Sun. 2–4.*

The **New Canaan Nature Center** comprises more than 40 acres of woods and habitats. You can take part in the hands-on natural science exhibits at the Discovery Center in the main building or walk along the many nature trails. Demonstrations take place in fall at the cider house and in spring at the maple sugar shed (reservations required). ⊠ *144 Oenoke Ridge,* ☎ *203/966–9577.* ☑ *Donation suggested for museum.* ☉ *Grounds daily dawn–dusk, museum Mon.–Sat. 9–4.*

Lodging

$$$ ▦ **Maples Inn.** This yellow clapboard structure a short drive from downtown has 13 gables, most of which are veiled by a canopy of aged maples. Bedrooms are furnished with antiques and queen-size canopy beds. Mahogany chests, gilt frames, and brass lamps gleam from energetic polishing. The Mural Room, whose walls are painted with images of New Canaan in each of the four seasons, is an ideal locale for breakfast. ⊠ *179 Oenoke Ridge, 06840,* ☎ *203/966–2927,* ℻ *203/966– 5003. 10 rooms with bath, 3 suites, 10 apartments. Continental breakfast. AE, MC, V.*

Wilton

❺ *6 mi east of New Canaan, 35 mi southwest of New Haven.*

★ Dapper, wooded Wilton is home to **Weir Farm,** a National Historic Site dedicated to the legacy of painter J. Alden Weir. The property's 60 wooded acres include hiking paths, picnic areas, and a restored rose and perennial garden. Tours of Weir's studio and sculptor Mahonri Young's studio are conducted, and you can take a self-guided walk past Weir's painting sites. ⊠ *735 Nod Hill Rd.,* ☎ *203/834– 1896.* ☑ *Free.* ☉ *Grounds daily dawn–dusk, visitor center Wed.– Sun. 8:30–5.*

The forest and wetlands of 146-acre **Woodcock Nature Center** (⊠ 56 Deer Run Rd., ☎ 203/762–7280) straddle Wilton and Ridgefield. Activities here include botany walks, birding and geology lectures, and hikes on 2 mi of trails and swamp boardwalk.

Dining

$$$ ✕ **Mediterranean Grill.** The owners of Norwalk's Meson Galicia run this stylish dining room in an otherwise dull shopping center. Like Meson Galicia, Mediterranean is a tribute to things Spanish—trendy Spanish, that is. Appetizers range from a sweet-onion tart with assorted wild mushrooms to grilled baby squid with a bell-pepper vinaigrette. Ex-

pertly prepared dishes from other Mediterranean lands include ones from Morocco, Greece, and Italy. ⊠ *Wilton Center, 5 River Rd.,* ☎ *203/762–8484. AE, D, DC, MC, V. Closed Mon. No lunch weekends.*

Nightlife and the Arts

The **Wilton Playshop** (⊠ Lovers La., ☎ 203/762–7629), which dates from 1937, presents five major productions a year, from musicals to mysteries.

Shopping

Antiques sheds and boutiques can be found along and off Route 7. **Cannondale Village** (⊠ Off Rte. 7, ☎ 203/762–2233), a pre–Civil War farm village, holds a complex of antiques shops, restaurants, and galleries.

Ridgefield

❻ *8 mi north of Wilton, 43 mi west of New Haven.*

In Ridgefield, you'll find a rustic Connecticut atmosphere within an hour of Manhattan. The town center, which you approach from Wilton on Route 33, is a largely residential sweep of lawns and majestic homes.

The **Aldrich Museum of Contemporary Art** presents changing exhibitions of cutting-edge work rivaling that of any small collection in New York and has an outstanding 2-acre sculpture garden. ⊠ *258 Main St.,* ☎ *203/438–4519.* ☑ *$5.* ☉ *Tues.–Thurs. and Sat.–Sun. 12–5, Fri. 12–8. Closed Mon.*

A British cannonball is lodged in the wall of the **Keeler Tavern Museum,** a historic inn and the former home of the late architect Cass Gilbert. Furniture and Revolutionary War memorabilia fill the museum, where tours given by guides dressed in Colonial costumes conduct tours. ⊠ *132 Main St.,* ☎ *203/438–5485.* ☑ *$4.* ☉ *Feb.–Dec., Wed. and weekends 1–4. Closed Jan. and Mon.–Tues., Thurs.–Fri.*

Dining and Lodging

$$$ ✕▥ **Stonehenge Inn & Restaurant.** The manicured lawns and bright white-clapboard buildings of Stonehenge are visible just off Route 7. The inn's tasteful rooms are a mix of Waverly and Schumacher; the gem of a restaurant ($$$–$$$$) is run by Christian Bertrand, whose previous stops include Lutèce in Manhattan. An eye-catching appetizer of a lobster medallion with warm artichoke, a poached egg, and coral vinaigrette and an entrée of sautéed sea scallops and fresh pasta in a light sauternes sauce with Indian curry are two good bets on the French-accented menu. ⊠ *Stonehenge Rd. off Rte. 7, 06877,* ☎ *203/438–6511,* ℻ *203/438–2478. 14 rooms, 2 suites. Restaurant. Continental breakfast. AE, MC, V.*

$$–$$$ ✕▥ **The Elms Inn.** The best rooms at this inn are in the frame house built by a Colonial cabinetmaker in 1760; antiques and reproductions furnish all the rooms. Chef Brendan Walsh presents fine new American cuisine in the restaurant ($$$–$$$$)—pan-roasted Maryland crab cakes with three-pepper relish, and maple–thyme grilled loin of venison, and the like. ⊠ *500 Main St., 06877,* ☎ ℻ *203/438–2541. 20 rooms, 4 suites. Restaurant, pub, meeting rooms. Continental breakfast. AE, DC, MC, V.*

Outdoor Activities and Sports

The **Mountain Workshop** (⊠ 17 Catoonah St., ☎ 203/438–3640) conducts one-day to two-week programs in rock climbing, caving, canoeing, biking, and hiking throughout northwestern Connecticut.

The greens fee at the 18-hole, par-71 **Ridgefield Golf Course** (⊠ 545 Ridgebury Rd., ☎ 203/748–7008) is $40; an optional cart costs $24.

Shopping

The **Hay Day Market** (⊠ 21 Governor St., ☎ 203/431–4400) stocks hard-to-find fresh produce, jams, cheeses, sauces, baked goods, flowers, and much more. Other locations are in Greenwich (☎ 203/637–7600), Westport (☎ 203/254–5200), and New Canaan (☎ 203/972–8200).

Danbury

7 *9 mi north of Ridgefield, 20 mi northwest of Bridgeport.*

A middle-class slice of suburbia, Danbury was the hat capital of America for nearly 200 years—until the mid-1950s. Rumors persist that the term "mad as a hatter" originated here. Hat makers suffered widely from the injurious effects of mercury poisoning, a fact that is said to explain the resultant "madness" of veteran hatters.

The **Military Museum of Southern New England** exhibits an impressive collection of U.S. and allied forces memorabilia from World War II, plus 19 tanks dating from the war to the present. ⊠ *125 Park Ave.,* ☎ *203/790–9277.* ⊡ *$4.* ☉ *Tues.–Sat. 10–5, Sun. noon–5. Closed Mon.*

☻ A station built in 1903 for the New Haven Railroad houses the **Danbury Railway Museum.** Amid the train yard are 20 or so examples of freight and passenger railroad stock, including a restored 1944 caboose, a 1948 Alco locomotive, and an operating locomotive turntable. Museum exhibits include vintage American Flyer model trains. ⊠ *White St. and Patriot Dr.,* ☎ *203/778–8337.* ⊡ *$3.* ☉ *Wed.–Sun. 10–4 and by appointment.*

Dining and Lodging

$$$$ ✕ **Ondine.** Drifts of flowers, soft lighting, hand-written menus, and waitstaff in white jackets make every meal at Ondine feel like a celebration. The five-course prix-fixe traditional French menu, updated once a week, might include medallions of venison with a hunter's sauce made of blackberries or fresh salmon with a horseradish crust served with a parsley sauce. The Grand Marnier soufflé is the signature dessert. ⊠ *67 Pembroke Rd.,* ☎ *203/746–4900. AE, D, DC, MC, V. Closed Mon. No lunch.*

Outdoor Activities and Sports

Golf Digest has rated the 18-hole, par-72 **Richter Park Golf Course** (⊠ 100 Aunt Hack Rd., ☎ 203/792–2550) one of the top 25 public courses in the country. The greens fee is $44; an optional cart costs $23.

Shopping

The **Danbury Fair Mall** (⊠ Rte. 7 and I–84, ☎ 203/743–3247) has more than 225 shops.

Redding

8 *11 mi east of Danbury, 35 mi southwest of Waterbury.*

Redding was the home of Mark Twain's estate, Stormfield. Little has changed since Twain described the area as "one of the loveliest spots in America."

In the winter of 1778–79, three brigades of Continental Army soldiers under the command of General Israel Putnam made their winter encampment at the site of **Putnam Memorial State Park,** then known as "Connecticut's Valley Forge." Superb for hiking, picnicking, and cross-country skiing, the park has a small history museum. ⊠ *Rtes. 58 and 107, West Redding,* ☎ *203/938–2285.* ⊠ *Donation suggested.* ☉ *Grounds 8 AM–dusk; museum Memorial Day–Labor Day, Fri., Sat., and holidays 10–5.*

En Route From Redding to Weston, take Route 53 south along the picturesque Saugatuck Reservoir.

Weston

❾ *6 mi south of Redding, 36 mi southwest of New Haven.*

Erica Jong, Keith Richards, Christopher Plummer, and other artists and entertainers have homes in heavily wooded Weston.

Dining

$$$ ✕ **Cobb's Mill Inn.** It's hard to take your eyes off the ducks and swans frolicking in the waterfall outside this former mill and inn that is now a charming restaurant. But the Continental cuisine also warrants your attention. Start with the pheasant pistachio pâté and follow with the Mediterranean mixed grill, a flavorful combination of grilled chicken, shrimp, sausage, roasted red peppers, and mushrooms. The menu is heavy on red meat dishes, but lighter fare includes grilled swordfish and shrimp *l'Arlesienne* (shrimp sautéed in garlic butter with cherry tomatoes, leeks, white wine, and Pernod). The Sunday brunch is a good deal. ⊠ *12 Old Mill Rd., off Rte. 57,* ☎ *203/227–7221. AE, D, DC, MC, V. No lunch Mon. or Sat.*

Outdoor Activities and Sports

The 1,746 acres of woodlands, wetlands, and rock ledges at the **Nature Conservancy's Devil's Den Preserve** (⊠ 33 Pent Rd., ☎ 203/226–4991) include 20 mi of hiking trails. Trail maps are available in the parking lot registration area, and guided walks take place year-round. There are no rest rooms.

Westport

❿ *7 mi south of Weston, 47 mi northeast of New York City.*

Westport, an artists' mecca since the turn of the century, continues to attract creative types. Despite commuters and corporations, Westport remains more arty and cultured than its neighbors: If the rest of Fairfield County is stylistically five years behind Manhattan, Westport lags by just five months. Paul Newman and Joanne Woodward have their main residence here, as does America's homemaking and entertaining guru, Martha Stewart.

Hiking trails traverse the 62-acre **Nature Center for Environmental Activities,** a peaceful sanctuary of woods, fields, streams, and wetlands. The indoor attractions include a natural-history museum, an Aquarium Room, a live Animal Hall, and a Discovery Room with hands-on exhibits. ⊠ *10 Woodside La.,* ☎ *203/227–7253.* ⊠ *Donations requested.* ☉ *Grounds dawn–dusk; Nature Center building Mon.–Sat. 9–5, Sun. 1–4.*

Summer visitors to Westport congregate at **Sherwood Island State Park** (⊠ I–95, Exit 18, ☎ 203/226–6983), which has a 1½-mi sweep of sandy beach, two water's-edge picnic groves, an environmental-protection museum with artifacts from the parks and forestry divisions, and several food concessions. The museum and concessions are open seasonally.

Dining and Lodging

$$$–$$$$ ✕ **Splash.** Cutting-edge Pacific Rim cuisine at a white-clapboard coun-
★ try club? That's right. The funky made-for-sharing dishes prepared by
the chefs at Splash include "Baang" chicken salad with shreds of white
meat tossed with Asian vegetables and sesame oil; lobster-coconut
soup; medallions of monkfish perfumed with lemongrass; and sword-
fish with a sake-ginger-lime sauce. ✉ *The Inn At Longshore, 260
Compo Rd. S,* ☎ *203/454–7798. AE, D, DC, MC, V. Closed Mon.
No lunch Sun.*

$$$ ✕ **Cafe Christina.** The outstanding variations on American-Mediter-
★ ranean cuisine produced at this café are among the reasons Westport
rivals Greenwich as Connecticut's culinary capital. You might start with
baked polenta or an arugula-and-Portobello mushroom risotto fritter.
The entrées, which change every few weeks, always include seafood
and filling pasta dishes. In a former library, Cafe Christina has faux
columns and other trompe l'oeil touches. ✉ *1 Main St.,* ☎ *203/221–
7950. Reservations essential on weekends. AE, DC, MC, V.*

$$$ ✕ **Tavern on Main.** This intimate restaurant takes the tavern concept
★ to a new level—fresh flowers and soft music included. In winter the
glow of fireplaces reaches every table, and in summer a terrace with
an awning beckons. The gourmet comfort food includes starters like
lobster-and-shrimp rolls and a robust clam chowder with bacon.
Among the entrées of note are the potato-wrapped sea bass on a bed
of Swiss chard and the roast duckling with star anise sauce, caramelized
pears, and crisp baby vegetables on a bed of grains and dried fruit.
All the desserts are made in-house; the apple pie with cinnamon ice
cream is a blue-ribbon winner. ✉ *146 Main St.,* ☎ *203/221–7222.
AE, MC, V.*

$$$$ ✕▥ **Inn at National Hall.** Each whimsically exotic room in this tow-
★ ering Italianate redbrick is a study in innovative restoration, wall-
stenciling, and decorative painting (including magnificent hand-painted
trompe l'oeil designs). The furniture collection is exceptional. The
rooms and suites are magnificent—some have sleeping lofts and 18-ft
windows overlooking the Saugatuck River. With its Corinthian columns
and tasseled curtain swags, the Restaurant at National Hall ($$$–$$$$;
reservations essential for dinner) serves a seasonally changing menu
of creative Continental dishes. ✉ *2 Post Rd. W, 06880,* ☎ *203/221–
1351 or 800/628–4255; 203/221–7572 for restaurant,* FAX *203/221–
0276. 8 rooms, 7 suites. Restaurant, refrigerators, in-room VCRs,
meeting room. Continental breakfast. AE, DC, MC, V.*

$$$$ ▥ **Cotswold Inn.** Honeymooners often nest at this cottage in the heart
of downtown Westport's chic shopping area. Though the steep gabled
roof and stone porches recall England's Cotswolds region, the rooms,
more museumlike than homey, capture the essence of 18th-century Con-
necticut, with reproduction Chippendale and Queen Anne furnishings—
highboys, mule chests, wing chairs. Two rooms have canopy beds; the
suite has a fireplace. ✉ *76 Myrtle Ave., 06880,* ☎ *203/226–3766,* FAX
203/221–0098. 3 rooms, 1 suite. Continental breakfast. AE, MC, V.

$$–$$$ ▥ **Westport Inn.** Bedrooms in this upscale motor lodge have attrac-
tive contemporary furniture. Rooms surrounding the large indoor pool
are set back nicely and are slightly larger than the rest. Several excel-
lent restaurants are within walking distance. ✉ *1595 Post Rd. E,
06880,* ☎ *203/259–5236 or 800/446–8997,* FAX *203/254–8439. 114
rooms, 2 suites. Restaurant, bar, indoor pool, hot tub, sauna, health
club. AE, D, DC, MC, V.*

Nightlife and the Arts

The **Levitt Pavilion for the Performing Arts** (✉ Jesup Rd., ☎ 203/221–
4422) sponsors an excellent series of summer concerts, most of them

free, that range from jazz to classical, folk-rock to blues. The **Westport Playhouse** (⊠ 25 Powers Ct., ☎ 203/227–4177) presents six productions each summer in a converted barn.

Shopping

J. Crew, Ann Taylor, Coach, Laura Ashley, Brooks Brothers, and other fashionable shops have made **Main Street** in Westport the outdoor equivalent of the upscale Stamford Town Center.

Fairfield

⑪ *9 mi east of Westport, 33 mi south of Waterbury.*

Fairfield, a town that was settled well before Westport, still has many old Dutch and postmedieval English Colonials on a network of quaint, winding roads north of Route 1.

Each May the Greenfield Hill historic area hosts the annual **Dogwood Festival** (☎ 203/259–5596), which has been going strong for more than six decades. The **Quick Center for the Arts** (⊠ Fairfield University, N. Benson Rd., ☎ 203/254–4010) hosts children's theater performances and runs a summer performing-arts series for children.

The **Connecticut Audubon Society** (⊠ 2325 Burr St., ☎ 203/259–6305) maintains a 160-acre wildlife sanctuary that includes 6 mi of rugged hiking trails and special walks for people with visual impairments and mobility problems.

The **Birdcraft Museum** (⊠ 314 Unquowa Rd., ☎ 203/259–0416), also operated by the Connecticut Audubon Society, has a children's activity corner, 6 acres of trails, and a pond that attracts waterfowl during their spring and fall migrations.

Dining

$ ✕ **Rawley's Hot Dogs.** The hot dogs at this drive-in are deep-fried in vegetable oil, then grilled for just a few secs—a recipe the stand has been following since it opened in 1946. Martha "It's a good thing" Stewart is among the regulars here. Her favorite? A cheesedog with the works. ⊠ *1886 Post Rd.,* ☎ *203/259–9023. No credit cards. Closed Sun.*

Bridgeport

⑫ *5 mi east of Fairfield, 28 mi south of Waterbury, 63 mi west of New London.*

Bridgeport, a city that has fallen on hard times, is unsafe at night and unappealing by day. Civic leaders are, however, hard at work making improvements, and the city does contain several worthwhile attractions.

Exhibits at the **Barnum Museum,** associated with past resident and former mayor P. T. Barnum, depict the career of the great showman, who presented performers like General Tom Thumb and Jenny Lind, the Swedish Nightingale. You can tour a scaled-down model of Barnum's legendary five-ring circus. ⊠ *820 Main St.,* ☎ *203/331–1104.* 🎫 *$5.* ☉ *Tues.–Sat. 10–4:30, Sun. noon–4:30.*

♻ The indoor walk-through South American rain forest at the 30-acre **Beardsley Park and Zoological Gardens** itself justifies a visit. Also at in the park, which is north of downtown Bridgeport, are a carousel museum, a working carousel, and a New England farmyard. ⊠ *1875 Noble Ave.,* ☎ *203/394–6565.* 🎫 *$5.* ☉ *Daily 9–4.*

Captain's Cove on historic Black Rock Harbor, is the home port of the HMS *Rose*—a replica of a Revolutionary War frigate and the largest

ICE CREAM, YOU SCREAM

DOZENS OF EXTRAORDINARY ICE-CREAM SHOPS IN CONNECTICUT produce hundreds of homemade flavors. Here are some favorite stops:

Timothy's (✉ 2974 Fairfield Ave., Bridgeport, ☎ 203/366–7496) still makes its ice cream using an old-fashioned salt-and-ice freezer stationed in the shop's front window. Kahlua chip, peach, and Black Rock (French vanilla with chocolate-covered almonds) are noteworthy varieties, and you can customize your flavors with Timothy's renowned assortment of mixin's. The shop is closed on Monday from November to March.

Those in the know in Monroe swear there is no better place in the world to enjoy an ice-cream cone than on the Victorian front porch of **Dr. Mike's Ice Cream** (✉ 444 Main St., ☎ 203/452–0499; also in Bethel at ✉ 158 Greenwood Ave., ☎ 203/792–4388). Chocolate lace is the flavor locals clamor for. The shop is closed on Monday from November to February.

The two **Shady Glen** (✉ 840 E. Middle Turnpike., ☎ 860/649–4245; ✉ 360 W. Middle Turnpike., ☎ 860/643–0511) shops in Manchester are known for their a unique chocolate chip, malts, and seasonal varieties like black cherry, peach, Dutch apple, and pumpkin.

Stosh's Ice Cream (✉ 38 Main St., Kent, ☎ 860/927–4495) shares space with an antiques dealer in the restored Kent Railroad Station. The top flavors here include turtle (pecans, chocolate and caramel), Havana banana (pureed bananas with a caramel swirl), and the very rich Chocolate Chocolate. The shop is open daily from April to October.

Dave Redente, owner of **Peaches 'N Cream** (✉ Rte. 202, Litchfield, ☎ 860/496–7536), says he likes to "keep things as traditional as possible" at his shop, and that means using fresh, natural ingredients. His peach, blueberry and red raspberry ice creams, made with fresh fruits, are top summer sellers.

Ashley's Ice Cream (✉ 2100 Dixwell Ave., Hamden, ☎ 203/288–7497) has been a tradition in Greater New Haven since 1979. Among Ashley's repertoire of 150 flavors are sweet cream, coffee Oreo, and bittersweet chocolate. Ashley's sundae-to-end-all-sundaes, the Downside Watson, includes seven scoops, nine toppings, and two bananas served on a Frisbee. Ashley's has additional locations in New Haven, Branford, Guilford, and Fairfield.

One of the many attractions of downtown Mystic is **Mystic Drawbridge Ice Cream** (✉ 2 W. Main St., ☎ 860/572–7978). This location, which has handsome wood floors and an antique soda fountain, has been the site of an ice-cream shop almost continuously since the 1700s. At least 30 flavors of ice cream are available daily—Mystic Mud is the flavor of choice. Additional shops are in Old Mystic and Groton.

The University of Connecticut's **Dairy Bar** (✉ Rte. 195, Storrs, ☎ 860/486–2634), part of the school of agriculture, has been a campus institution for more than 40 years. The Oreo cookie, chocolate chip, and Jonathan's Supreme (named for the Husky mascot) are the flavors to try, either by themselves or sandwiched between the Dairy Bar's gigantic chocolate-chip cookies.

wooden tall ship in action today—and the Lightship #112 *Nantucket*. Band concerts take place on Sunday afternoon in summer. The boardwalk holds two dozen shops and a casual restaurant. ⊠ *1 Bostwick Ave. (I–95, Exit 26),* ☎ *203/335–1433.* ☒ *Free to cove, $2 to tour lightship, $5 to tour frigate (when it's in port).* ☉ *Tours on the hr Memorial Day–Labor Day, weekends noon–4.*

The draws at the **Discovery Museum and Wonder Workshop** include its eclectic collection of art from the Renaissance to contemporary times, a planetarium, several hands-on science exhibits, a computer-art exhibit, the *Challenger* learning center (which has a simulated space flight), and a children's museum. The Wonder Workshop schedules storytelling, arts-and-crafts, science, and other programs. ⊠ *4450 Park Ave.,* ☎ *203/372–3521.* ☒ *$6.* ☉ *Tues.–Sat. 10–5, Sun. noon–5.*

Sports
The **Bridgeport Bluefish** (⊠ Harbor Yard, 500 Main St., off I–95, ☎ 203/333–1608) is a team in the Atlantic League of Professional Baseball.

Stratford

⑱ *3 mi east of Bridgeport; 15 mi southwest of New Haven.*

Stratford, named after the English town Stratford-upon-Avon, has more than 150 historic homes, many of which are on Long Island Sound. The Academy Hill neighborhood, near the intersection of Main (Route 113) and Academy Hill streets, is a good area to stroll.

Boothe Memorial Park & Museum, a 32-acre complex with several unusual buildings, includes a blacksmith shop, carriage and tool barns, and a museum that traces the history of the trolley. Also on the grounds are a beautiful rose garden and a children's playground. ⊠ *Main St., Putney,* ☎ *203/381–2046.* ☒ *Free.* ☉ *Park daily dawn–dusk. Museum June–Oct., Tues.–Fri. 11–1, weekends 1–4; closed Nov.–May.*

Shopping
About 200 dealers show their wares at the **Stratford Antique Center** (⊠ 400 Honeyspot Rd., ☎ 203/378–7754).

Southwestern Connecticut A to Z

Arriving and Departing

BY BUS
Bonanza Bus Lines (☎ 800/556–3815) provides service to Danbury from Hartford, New York, and Providence. **Peter Pan Bus Lines** (☎ 800/343–9999) stops in Bridgeport en route from Hartford, Boston, Providence, and New York.

BY CAR
The main routes into southwestern Connecticut are Route 15 (called the Merritt Parkway in this area) and I–95.

BY PLANE
Bridgeport–Igor Sikorsky Memorial Airport (⊠ 1000 Great Meadow Rd., Exit 30 off I–95, ☎ 203/576–7498), 4 mi south of Stratford, is served by US Airways Express (☎ 800/428–4322).

BY TRAIN
Amtrak (☎ 800/872–7245) stops in Stamford and Bridgeport. **Metro-North Railroad** (☎ 800/638–7646; 212/532–4900 from New York City) trains stop in Greenwich, Stamford, Norwalk, New Canaan, Wilton, Danbury, Redding, Westport, Fairfield, Bridgeport, Stratford.

Getting Around

BY BUS

Connecticut Transit buses (☎ 203/327–7433) stop in Greenwich, Stamford, and Norwalk. The Greater Bridgeport Transit District's **People Movers** (☎ 203/333–3031) provide bus transportation throughout Bridgeport, Stratford, and Fairfield. **Norwalk Transit** provides bus service in Norwalk (☎ 203/852–0000) and Westport (☎ 203/226–0422).

BY CAR

The Merritt Parkway and I–95 are the region's main arteries; both are subject to harrowing rush-hour snarls. Greenwich, Stamford, Norwalk, Westport, Fairfield, Bridgeport, and Stratford are on or just off I–95. From I–95 or the Merritt Parkway take Route 124 north to New Canaan; Route 7 north to Wilton or Danbury; Routes 7 and 33 north to Ridgefield; Route 53 north to Weston; and Route 58 north to Redding.

Contacts and Resources

EMERGENCIES

Norwalk Hospital (✉ 34 Maple St., Norwalk, ☎ 203/852–2000).

24-HOUR PHARMACY

CVS Pharmacy (✉ 235 Main St., Norwalk, ☎ 203/847–6057).

VISITOR INFORMATION

Housatonic Valley Tourism District (✉ 30 Main St., Danbury 06810, ☎ 203/743–0546 or 800/841–4488). **Coastal Fairfield County Convention and Visitors Bureau** (✉ The Gate Lodge–Mathews Park, 297 West Ave., Norwalk 06850, ☎ 203/899–2799 or 800/866–7925).

THE CONNECTICUT RIVER VALLEY

Westward expansion in the New World began along the meandering Connecticut River. Dutch explorer Adrian Block first checked things out in 1614, and in 1633 a trading post was set up in what is now Hartford. Within five years, throngs of restive Massachusetts Bay colonists had settled in this fertile valley. What followed was more than three centuries of barque building, shad hauling, and river trading with ports as far away as the West Indies and the Mediterranean.

Less touristy than the coast and northwest hills, the Connecticut River valley is a swath of small villages and uncrowded state parks punctuated by a few small cities and a large one: Hartford. To the south of Hartford, with the exception of industrial Middletown, genuinely quaint hamlets vie for a share of Connecticut's tourist crop with antiques shops, scenic drives, and trendy restaurants.

Essex Area

14 *29 mi east of New Haven.*

Essex looks much as it did in the mid-19th century, at the height of its shipbuilding prosperity. So important to a young America was Essex's boat manufacturing that the British burned more than 40 ships here during the War of 1812. Gone are the days of steady trade with the West Indies, when the aroma of imported rum, molasses, and spices hung in the air. Whitewashed houses—many the former roosts of sea captains—line Main Street, whose shops sell clothing, antiques, paintings and prints, and sweets.

In addition to pre-Colonial artifacts and displays, the **Connecticut River Museum** has a full-size reproduction of the world's first submarine, the *American Turtle*; the original was built by David Bushnell in 1775. ✉

Steamboat Dock, 67 Main St., ☎ *860/767–8269.* 🖾 *$4.* ☉ *Tues.– Sun. 10–5.*

The **Valley Railroad** travels alongside the Connecticut River and through the lower valley; if you wish to continue, a-riverboat can take you up the river. The train trip lasts an hour; the riverboat ride, 90 minutes. ⊠ *Exit 3 off Rte. 9,* ☎ *860/767–0103.* 🖾 *Train fare $10; combined train–boat fare $15.* ☉ *Call for schedule.*

Dining and Lodging

$$–$$$ ✕ **Steve's Centerbrook Café.** Latticework and gingerbread trim are among the architectural accents of the Victorian house that holds this bright café. The culinary accents lean toward the ornate as well, especially in the few classic French dishes. Also on the menu are creative pastas, main-dish salads, and grilled chicken, fish, and steaks. ⊠ *78 Main St., Centerbrook,* ☎ *860/767–1277. AE, MC, V. Closed Mon. No lunch.*

$$ ✕🏠 **Griswold Inn.** Two-plus centuries of catering to changing tastes at what's billed as America's oldest inn has resulted in a kaleidoscope of decor—some Colonial, a touch of Federal, a little Victorian, and just as much modern (air-conditioning, phones, but no in-room TVs) as is necessary to meet present-day expectations. The chefs at the restaurant ($$–$$$) prepare country-style and gourmet dishes—try the famous 1776 sausages, which come with sauerkraut and German potato salad, or the risotto croquettes. The Tap Room, built in 1738 as a schoolhouse, is ideal for after-dinner drinks: A potbelly stove keeps things cozy, and there's nightly entertainment. The English Hunt Breakfast, a feast of muffins, eggs, fresh cod, creamed chipped beef, and smoked bacon, is a Sunday event. ⊠ *36 Main St., 06426,* ☎ *860/767–1776,* FAX *860/767–0481. 18 rooms, 12 suites. Dining room, bar, air-conditioning. Continental breakfast. AE, MC, V.*

$$–$$$ 🏠 **Riverwind.** All the guest rooms at this splendid inn have antique furnishings, collectibles, and touches of stenciling. One room has a country-pine bed and a painted headboard; another holds a carved oak bed; a third contains an 18th-century bird's-eye maple four-poster with a canopy. In the 18th-century-style keeping room that was added onto the original building a few years ago, there's a huge stone cooking fireplace, where hot cider and rum are mulled all winter. Co-owner Barbara Barlow serves a hearty country breakfast of Smithfield ham, her own baked goods, and several casseroles. Freshly brewed tea and coffee and home-baked cookies are always on hand. ⊠ *209 Main St., Deep River, 06417,* ☎ *860/526–2014. 7 rooms, 1 suite. Full breakfast. AE, MC, V. 2-night minimum weekends mid–Apr.–Dec.*

Ivoryton

⑮   *4 mi west of Essex.*

Ivoryton was named for its steady import of elephant tusks from Kenya and Zanzibar during the 19th century—piano keys were Ivoryton's leading export during this time. At one time, the Comstock-Cheney piano manufacturers processed so much ivory that Japan regularly purchased Ivoryton's surplus, using the scraps to make souvenirs. The Depression closed the lid on Ivoryton's pianos, and what remains is a sleepy, shady hamlet.

The **Museum of Fifers and Drummers,** said to be the only one of its kind in the world, contains martial sheet music, instruments, and uniforms chronicling America's history of parades, from the Revolutionary War to the present. Performances take place on Tuesday night in summer. ⊠ *62 N. Main St.,* ☎ *860/767–2237.* 🖾 *$2.* ☉ *June–Sept.,*

Connecticut River Valley

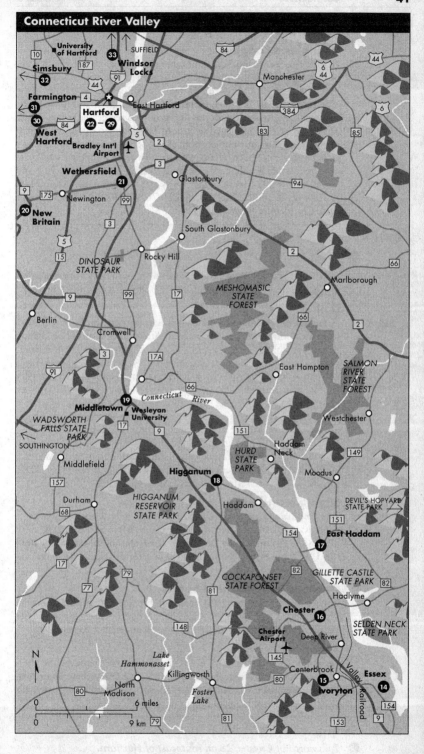

weekends 2–5 or by appointment. Closed 3rd weekend in July and 4th weekend in Aug.

Dining and Lodging

$$$　✕🏠 **Copper Beech Inn.** A magnificent copper beech tree shades the imposing main building of this Victorian inn. The four rooms in the main house have an old-fashioned feel, right down to the claw-foot tubs; the nine rooms in the Carriage House are more modern and have decks. Seven acres of wooded grounds and groomed terraced gardens create an atmosphere of privileged seclusion. The distinctive country-French menu in the romantic dining room ($$$–$$$$; reservations essential; jacket and tie; no lunch) changes seasonally. Specials might include the inn's renowned bouillabaisse or lamb roasted with an herb crust and served with white beans. Dinner starts at 1 PM on Sunday. ✉ *46 Main St., 06442,* ☎ *860/767–0330,* FAX *860/767–7840. 13 rooms. Restaurant. Continental breakfast. AE, DC, MC, V.*

Chester

⓰ *5 mi north of Ivoryton, 24 mi northwest of New London.*

Arty Chester has a quaint Main Street lined with tony antiques shops and boutiques—shopping is a favorite pastime in this upscale town.

Dining

$$$–$$$$　✕ **Restaurant du Village.** A black wrought-iron gate beckons you away from the antiquaries of Chester's Main Street, and an off-white awning draws you through the door of this classic little Colonial storefront, painted in historic Newport blue and adorned with flower boxes. Here you can sample exquisite classic French cuisine—escargots in puff pastry, filet mignon—while recapping the day's shopping coups. ✉ *59 Main St.,* ☎ *860/526–5301. AE, MC, V. Closed Mon.–Tues. No lunch.*

$$$　✕ **Fiddler's.** The specialties at this fine fish house are the rich bouillabaisse and the lobster with a sauce of peaches, peach brandy, shallots, mushrooms, and cream. Blond bentwood chairs, lacy stenciling on the walls, prints of famous schooners, and the amber glow of oil lamps lend the place a gentrified air. ✉ *4 Water St.,* ☎ *860/526–3210. DC, MC, V. Closed Mon. No lunch Sun.*

Nightlife and the Arts

The **Goodspeed at Chester** group presents new works or works in progress at the Norma Terris Theatre (✉ N. Main St./Rte. 82, ☎ 860/873–8668) from April to December. The **National Theatre of the Deaf** (✉ 5 W. Main St., ☎ 860/526–4971) performs in sign language and the spoken word.

Outdoor Activities and Sports

You can take a ride in a 1941 Stearman biplane at **Chester Airport** (✉ Winthrop Rd., ☎ 860/526–4321), which also operates plane and helicopter sightseeing rides over the lower Connecticut River valley.

Shopping

Ceramica (✉ 36 Main St., ☎ 800/782–1238) carries hand-painted Italian tableware and decorative accessories. The **Connecticut River Artisans** (✉ 4 Water St., ☎ 860/526–5575), a crafts cooperative, sells one-of-a-kind works, including pottery, jewelry, and folk art.

East Haddam

⓱ *7 mi north of Chester, 28 mi southeast of Hartford.*

Fishing, shipping, and musket-making were the chief enterprises at East Haddam, the only town in the state that occupies both banks of the Connecticut River.

★   **Gillette Castle State Park** holds the outrageous 24-room oak-and-field-stone hilltop castle built by the eccentric actor and dramatist William Gillette between 1914 and 1919; he modeled it after the medieval castles of the Rhineland. You can tour the castle and hike on trails near the remains of the 3-mi private railroad that chugged about the property until the owner's death in 1937. Gillette, who was born in Hartford, wrote two famous Civil War plays and was beloved for his play *Sherlock Holmes* (he performed the title role). In his will, Gillette demanded that the castle not fall into the hands of "some blithering saphead who has no conception of where he is or with what surrounded." To that end, the castle and 200-acre grounds were designated a state park that's an excellent spot for hiking and picnicking. ⊠ *67 River Rd., off Rte. 82,* ☎ *860/526–2336.* ⌑ *Castle $4; grounds free.* ☉ *Hrs were in flux at press time; call ahead.*

★   The upper floors of the 1876 Victorian gingerbread **Goodspeed Opera House** have served as a venue for theatrical performances for more than 100 years. From 1960 to 1963 the Goodspeed underwent a restoration that included the stage area, the Victorian bar, the sitting room, and the drinking parlor. More than 14 Goodspeed productions have gone on to Broadway, including *Annie* and *Man of La Mancha.* The performance season runs from April to December. ⊠ *Rte. 82,* ☎ *860/ 873–8668.* ⌑ *Tour $2.* ☉ *Tours Memorial Day–Columbus Day; call for times.*

St. Stephen's Church is listed in the *Guinness Book of World Records* as having the oldest bell in the United States. Crafted in Spain in the year 815, the bell is believed to have been taken from a monastery by Napoléon and used for ballast in a ship. A Captain Andrews from East Haddam discovered it in Florida and brought it back to his hometown, where it now sits in the belfry of St. Stephen's, a small stone Episcopal church with cedar shingles. The church was built in 1794 and was moved to its present site in 1890. ⊠ *Main St./Rte. 149,* ☎ *860/873– 9547.* ☉ *Call for hrs.*

The **Nathan Hale Schoolhouse,** where the patriot of grade-school textbooks taught from 1773 to 1774, displays some of his possessions and other items of local history. ⊠ *Rte. 149 (rear of St. Stephen's Church),* ☎ *860/873–9547.* ⌑ *Donation suggested.* ☉ *Memorial Day–Labor Day, weekends 2–4.*

Sixty-foot cascades flow down Chapman Falls at the 860-acre **Devil's Hopyard State Park.** The park's campground is near the falls. ⊠ *366 Hopyard Rd., 3 mi north of junction of Rtes. 82 and 156,* ☎ *860/873– 8566. 21 sites.* ⌑ *Day use free; campsites $9.* ☉ *Park daily 8 AM–dusk. Campground daily Memorial Day–Labor Day and weekends mid-Apr.– Memorial Day; no camping rest yr.*

Lodging

$$ ▦ **Bishopsgate Inn.** Around the bend from the landmark Goodspeed Opera House, this 1818 Colonial inn contains cozy and inviting rooms furnished with period reproductions, a smattering of antiques, and fluffy featherbeds. Four rooms have fireplaces, and one has a sauna. You can order elaborate candlelight dinners served in your room. ⊠ *Box 290, 7 Norwich Rd./Rte. 82, 06423,* ☎ *860/873–1677,* 𝔽𝔸𝕏 *860/873–3898. 5 rooms, 1 suite. Full breakfast. MC, V.*

Outdoor Activities and Sports

Allegra Farm (⊠ *Rte. 82 and Petticoat La.,* ☎ *860/873–9658*) operates carriage, sleigh, and hay rides and displays antique carriages.

Higganum

⑱ *15 mi north of East Haddam.*

Higganum's name is a variation on the Native American word *higganumpus* (fishing place). Indeed, it was the home for many years to several important shad fisheries.

The three formal herb gardens—a knot garden of interlocking hedges, a typical 18th-century geometric garden with central sundial, and a topiary garden—at the **Sundial Herb Garden** surround an 18th-century farmhouse. An 18th-century barn serves as a formal tearoom and a shop where you'll find herbs, books, and gourmet items. Sunday afternoon teas and special programs take place throughout the year. ⊠ *59 Hidden Lake Rd. (6 mi from Higganum Center; head south on Rte. 81, turn right on Brault Hill Rd., and right again when road ends),* ☎ *860/345–4290.* ⌨ *$1.* ☉ *Jan.–late-Nov. weekends 10–5 (except last 2 weekends of Oct.); late Nov.–Dec. 24, daily 10–5.*

Camping

⚠ **Nelson's Family Campground.** A 2-acre pond, a pool, two playgrounds, a recreation hall, boccie, tennis, volleyball, and planned activities keep the folks at this camping area's wooded and field sites busy. ⊠ *71 Mott Hill Rd., East Hampton,* ☎ *860/267–4561.* ⌨ *$26. 300 sites. Coin laundry, electric hook-ups, fire rings, flush toilets, showers, water. Closed Columbus Day–mid-Apr.*

Middletown

⑲ *14 mi north of Higganum, 24 mi northeast of New Haven.*

Middletown, once a bustling river city, was named for its location halfway between Hartford and Long Island Sound (it's also halfway between New York City and Boston). The wealthiest town in the state from about 1750 to 1800, Middletown had been in decline for more than a century before recently being chosen to take part in the National Trust for Historic Preservation's "Main Street Program." A multiyear rehabilitation project will hopefully revitalize the downtown area.

The imposing campus of Wesleyan University, founded here in 1831, is traversed by **High Street,** which Charles Dickens once called "the loveliest Main Street in America"—even though Middletown's actual Main Street runs parallel to it a few blocks east. High Street is an architecturally eclectic thoroughfare. Note the massive, fluted Corinthian columns of the Greek Revival Russell House (circa 1828) at the corner of Washington Street, across from the pink Mediterranean-style Davison Arts Center, built just 15 years later; farther on are gingerbreads, towering brownstones, Tudors, and Queen Annes. A few hundred yards up on Church Street, which intersects High Street, is the Olin Library. The 1928 structure, Wesleyan University's library, was designed by Henry Bacon, the architect of the Lincoln Memorial.

The Federal **General Mansfield House** has 18th- and 19th-century decorative arts, Civil War memorabilia and firearms, and local artifacts. ⊠ *151 Main St.,* ☎ *860/346–0746.* ⌨ *$2.* ☉ *Sun. 2–4:30, Mon. 1–4, and by appointment.*

Dinosaurs once roamed in the vicinity of **Dinosaur State Park,** north of Middletown. Tracks dating from the Jurassic period, 200 million years ago, are preserved here under a giant geodesic dome. From May to October you can make plaster casts of tracks on a special area of the property. (Call ahead to learn what materials you will need.) A newly renovated exhibit center with interactive displays interprets the dinosaurs, geology, and paleontology of the Connecticut River valley region. A great place for hiking, the park has nature trails that run through woods, along a ridge, and through swamps on a boardwalk. ⊠ *West St., east of I–91's Exit 23, Rocky Hill,* ☎ *860/529–8423.* ☜ *$2.* ☉ *Exhibits Tues.–Sun. 9–4:30; trails daily 9–4.*

You can pick your own fruits and vegetables at **Lyman Orchards** (⊠ Rtes. 147 and 157, Middlefield, ☎ 860/349–3673), just south of Middletown, from June to October—berries, peaches, pears, apples, even sweet corn.

Dining

$ ✕ **O'Rourke's Diner.** For a university town, Middletown has surprisingly few worthy eateries. The food served at this stainless-steel-and-glass-brick diner is a cut above that at any of the "real" restaurants. You'll find the expected diner fare, along with a tasty Irish stew, corned-beef hash, and regional delicacies like steamed cheeseburgers (not served on weekends); it's all unusually good. The weekend breakfast menu is extensive. The diner opens at 4:30 AM. ⊠ *728 Main St.,* ☎ *860/346–6101. No credit cards. No dinner.*

Nightlife and the Arts

Wesleyan University's **Center for the Arts** (⊠ Between Washington Terr. and Wyllys Ave., ☎ 860/685–3355) frequently hosts concerts, theater, films, and art exhibits. At last count, **Eli Cannon's** (⊠ 695 Main St., ☎ 860/347–3547) had 26 beers on tap and more than 100 bottled selections.

Outdoor Activities and Sports

Lyman Orchards Golf Club (⊠ Rte. 157, Middlefield, ☎ 860/349–8055) has two 18-hole championship courses. The greens fee at both the par-72 course designed by Robert Trent Jones and par-71 course designed by Gary Player ranges between $32 and $40. At the Jones course an optional cart costs $12; the greens fee for the Player course includes the cost of the mandatory cart.

Dinosaurs from the Cretaceous Period—tyrannosaurus, triceratops, even stegosaurus—are your playing partners at the **Prehistoric Golf** (⊠ Portland-Cobalt Rd./Rte. 66, Portland, ☎ 860/342–3517) miniature golf course; a round of 18 holes costs $2.

Shopping

Tours of the **Wesleyan Potters** (⊠ 350 S. Main St., ☎ 860/347–5925) pottery and weaving studios can be arranged in advance; all the products—jewelry, clothing, baskets, pottery, weavings, and more—are for sale.

Skiing

Powder Ridge. The trails here drop straight down from the 500-ft-high ridge for which this ski area is named. Half the 15 trails are designed for intermediate skiers, the others split between beginner trails and expert Black Diamonds; all of the trails are lighted for night skiing. One quad lift, two doubles, and a handle tow cover the mountain. Special features include a new snowtubing area, a snowboard park, an alpine park, a full-service restaurant, and ski instruction for children ages 4 and up. ⊠ *99 Powder Hill Rd., Middlefield, 06455,* ☎ *860/349–3454 or 800/622–3321 for conditions.*

New Britain

⓪ *13 mi northwest of Middletown, 10 mi southwest of Hartford.*

New Britain got its start as a manufacturing center producing sleigh bells. From these modest beginnings, it soon became known as "Hardware City," distributing builders' tools, ball bearings, locks, and other such items. No longer a factory town, New Britain is home to the Central Connecticut State College campus and a thriving performing arts community.

Among the 3,000 works at the **Museum of American Art** are murals by Thomas Hart Benton, western bronzes by Solon Borglum, and the Sanford Low Memorial collection of American Illustration. ⊠ *56 Lexington St.,* ☎ *860/229–0257.* ☞ *$3; free Sat. 10–12.* ◷ *Tues.–Fri. 1–5, Sat. 10–5, Sun. noon–5.*

Outdoor Activities and Sports
The **New Britain Rock Cats,** the Double-A affiliate of the Minnesota Twins, play at New Britain Stadium (⊠ Willow Brook Park, S. Main St., ☎ 860/224–8383)

Wethersfield

① *7 mi northeast of New Britain, 32 mi northeast of New Haven.*

Wethersfield, a vast Hartford suburb, dates from 1634. As was the case throughout early Connecticut, the Native Americans indigenous to these lands fought the arriving English with a vengeance; here their struggles culminated in the 1637 Wethersfield Massacre, when Pequot Indians killed nine settlers. Three years later, the citizens held a public election, America's first defiance of British rule, for which they were fined five British pounds.

The Joseph Webb House, Silas Deane House, and Isaac Stevens House, all built in the mid- to late 1700s, form one of the state's best historic house museums, the **Webb-Deane-Stevens Museum.** The structures, well-preserved examples of Georgian architecture, reflect their owners' lifestyles as, respectively, a merchant, a diplomat, and a tradesman. The Webb House was the site of the strategy conference between George Washington and the French general Jean-Baptiste Rochambeau that led to the British defeat at Yorktown. ⊠ *211 Main St. (Exit 26 off I–91),* ☎ *860/529–0612.* ☞ *$8.* ◷ *May–Oct., Wed.–Mon. 10–4; Nov.–Apr., weekends 10–4.*

Comstock Ferre & Co. (⊠ 263 Main St., ☎ 860/571–6590), founded in 1820, is the country's oldest continuously operating seed company. In a chestnut post-and-beam building, a National Historic Landmark that dates to the late 1700s, Comstock Ferre sells more than 800 varieties of seeds and 3,000 varieties of perennials.

Dining
$$$ ✕ **Ruth's Chris Steak House.** Every steak at this branch of the national chain is served sizzling hot and dripping with flavorful butter. Heat from an 1,800° oven seals in the juices. ⊠ *2513 Berlin Turnpike, Newington,* ☎ *860/666–2202. AE, D, DC, MC, V. No lunch.*

Hartford

4 mi north of Wethersfield, 45 mi northwest of New London, 81 mi northeast of Stamford.

America's insurance industry was born in Hartford in 1810—largely in an effort to protect the Connecticut River valley's tremendously important shipping interests. Throughout the 19th century, insurance companies expanded their coverage to include fires, accidents, life, and (in 1898) automobiles. Through the years, Hartford industries have included the inspection and packing of the northern river valley's once prominent tobacco industry and the manufacture of everything from bedsprings to artificial limbs to pool tables to coffins. Hartford's distinctive office towers and a lively downtown make what is actually an ever-expanding suburban development seem more urban.

㉒ The Federal **Old State House,** a building with an elaborate cupola and roof balustrade, was designed by Charles Bulfinch, architect of the U.S. Capitol. The Great Senate Room, where everyone from Abraham Lincoln to George Bush has spoken, contains a Gilbert Stuart portrait of George Washington that remains in its commissioned location. ⊠ *800 Main St.,* ☎ *860/522–6766.* ☞ *Free.* ☉ *Weekdays 10–4, Sat. 11–4.*

The hallmark of Hartford's skyline, the 527-ft-high **Travelers Insurance Tower,** was once the tallest building in New England. Capped by a pyramidal roof and gold-leafed cupola, it looms over the Old State House. Tours of the tower include a climb of 72 steps. ⊠ *1 Tower Sq.,* ☎ *860/ 277–0111.* ☞ *Free.* ☉ *Tours, weather permitting, mid-May–early-Oct., weekdays on the ½ hr 10–2:30.*

★ ㉓ The 50,000 artworks and artifacts at the **Wadsworth Atheneum,** first public art museum in the country, span 5,000 years and include paintings from the Hudson River School, the Impressionists, and 20th-century painters. Also of note are the many pilgrim-era furnishings and the impressive holdings of the Fleet Gallery of African-American Art. The Museum Café is an ideal spot for lunch. ⊠ *600 Main St.,* ☎ *860/ 278–2670.* ☞ *$7; free Sat. 11–noon and all-day Thurs.* ☉ *Tues.–Sun. 11–5 (1st Thurs. of some months until 8).*

㉔ The **Center Church,** built in 1807 (the parish itself dates from 1632) and patterned after London's Church of St. Martin-in-the-Fields, was founded by Thomas Hooker. Five of the stained-glass windows were created by Louis Tiffany. The Ancient Burying Ground, in the churchyard, is filled with granite and brownstone headstones, some dating from the 1600s. ⊠ *Main and Gold Sts.,* ☎ *860/249–5631.* ☉ *Mid-Apr.–mid-Dec., Wed.–Fri. 11–2 and by appointment.*

㉕ The **Butler-McCook Homestead** was built in 1782 and occupied continuously by the same family until 1971. Its furnishings show the evolution of American taste over time. There's an extensive collection of East Asian artifacts, Victorian-era toys, and a restored Victorian garden. ⊠ *396 Main St.,* ☎ *860/522–1806 or 860/247–8996.* ☞ *$4.* ☉ *Mid-May–mid-Oct., Tues., Thurs., and Sun. noon–4.*

Bushnell Park, which fans out from the State Capitol building, was the first public space in the country with natural landscaping instead of a traditional village-green configuration. The park was created by the firm of Frederick Law Olmsted, the Hartford landscape architect who with Calvert Vaux designed New York City's Central Park. Amid Bushnell's 40 acres are 150 varieties of trees as well as landmarks like a 1914 Stein & Goldstein carousel and the 100-ft-tall, 30-ft-wide medieval-style Soldiers and Sailors Memorial Arch, dedicated to Civil War soldiers.

㉖ Rising above Bushnell Park and visible citywide is the grandiose **State Capitol,** a colossal edifice composed of wholly disparate architectural elements. Built in 1879 of marble and granite—to a tune of $2.5 million—this gilt-dome wonder is replete with crockets, finials, and pointed arches. It houses the governor's office and legislative chambers and dis-

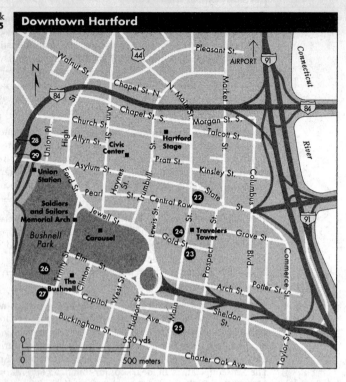

Downtown Hartford

plays historic statuary, flags, and furnishings. ⊠ *210 Capitol Ave.,* ☎
860/240–0222. 🎦 *Free.* 🕙 *Weekdays 9–3; tours weekdays 9:15–1:15
on the hr year-round and Sat. 10:15–2:15 on the hr Apr.–Oct.*

㉗ The **Museum of Connecticut History** exhibits artifacts of Connecticut military, industrial, and political history, including the state's original Colonial charter and a vast assemblage of Samuel Colt firearms—the so-called
Arm of Law and Order was first manufactured in Hartford. ⊠ *231 Capitol Ave.,* ☎ *860/566–3056.* 🎦 *Free.* 🕙 *Weekdays 9:30–4.*

Nook Farm, a late-19th-century neighborhood, was home to several
prominent families. Samuel Langhorne Clemens, better known as
Mark Twain, built his Stick-style Victorian mansion here in 1874.
㉘ During his residency at the **Mark Twain House,** he published seven major
novels, including *Tom Sawyer, Huckleberry Finn,* and *The Prince and
the Pauper.* Personal memorabilia and original furnishings are on display. Described on the one-hour guided tours of the house are its spectacular architecture and interior and Twain's personal and family life.
⊠ *351 Farmington Ave., at Forest St.,* ☎ *860/493–6411.* 🎦 *$7.50.*
🕙 *Memorial Day–mid-Oct. and Dec., Mon.–Sat. 9:30–5, Sun. 11–
5, last tour at 4; mid-Oct.–Nov. and Jan.–Memorial Day Mon., Wed.–
Sat. 9:30–5, Sun. 12–5, last tour at 4; closed Tues.*

㉙ The **Harriet Beecher Stowe House,** a Victorian Gothic cottage that was
erected in 1871, stands as a tribute to the author of one of 19th-cen-
tury America's most popular novels, *Uncle Tom's Cabin.* Inside are
her personal writing table and effects, several of her paintings, a period pinewood kitchen, and a terrarium of native ferns, mosses, and
wildflowers. ⊠ *71 Forest St.,* ☎ *860/525–9317.* 🎦 *$6.50.* 🕙 *Memo-
rial Day–Columbus Day and Dec. Mon.–Sat. 9:30–4, Sun. noon–
4; mid-Oct.–Nov. and Jan.–Memorial Day Tues.–Sat. 9:30–4, Sun.
noon–4.*

Dining and Lodging

$$$$ ✕ **Cavey's.** It takes 20 minutes to get here from Hartford, but the drive is worth it. Downstairs is a formal French restaurant decorated with priceless antiques; the cuisine is classic all the way. Upstairs is a casual Italian dining room with Palladian windows, rush-seated wooden chairs, and contemporary art. Although both menus change seasonally, Cavey's French restaurant can be counted on for exemplary rack of lamb and cassoulet. Fresh pastas and veal are the stars upstairs. ⊠ *45 E. Center St., Manchester,* ☎ *860/643–2751. AE, MC, V. Closed Sun.–Mon. No lunch downstairs.*

$$$–$$$$ ✕ **Max Downtown.** The latest of restaurateur Richard Rosenthal's culinary creations, upscale Max Downtown serves cuisine from around the world—everything from Portobello mushroom napoleon and steamed miso-sake–glazed Chilean sea bass to aged New York strip steak and grilled veal loin chop. A separate cigar bar serves classic port and single-malt liquor. ⊠ *CityPlace, 185 Asylum St.,* ☎ *860/522–2530. Reservations essential. AE, DC, MC, V. No lunch weekends.*

$$$–$$$$ ✕ **The Savannah.** The dining experience at this chic eatery is truly eclectic: Dishes combine French, Spanish, Asian, and southern influences. Favorites include an appetizer of ravioli filled with a puree of sweet potato and topped with chive butter sauce and a touch of nutmeg and an entrée of tuna crusted with sesame seeds and served with warm curried bananas and papayas in a salad infused with cinnamon. ⊠ *391 Main St.,* ☎ *860/278–2020. AE, DC, MC, V. Closed Sun. No lunch Sat.–Tues.*

$$$ ✕ **Civic Café.** Spacious, hip, and smartly designed, Civic Café recalls restaurants in New York or San Francisco. Sashimi-style tuna with a black-sesame vinaigrette and Black Angus steak with fried oysters are two choices on the fusion menu. There are cappuccino and raw bars and a Wednesday-night Martini Club. Care for a banana-nut-flavored "Monkey" martini? ⊠ *150 Trumbull St.,* ☎ *860/493–7412. AE, D, DC, MC, V. Closed Sun. No lunch Sat.*

$ ✕ **First and Last Tavern.** What looks to be a simple neighborhood joint
★ south of downtown is actually one of the state's most hallowed pizza parlors. The long, old-fashioned wooden bar in one room is jammed most evenings with suburbia-bound daily-grinders shaking off their suits; the main dining room is just as noisy, its brick outer wall covered with the requisite array of celebrity photos. The pie toppings are refreshingly untrendy. ⊠ *939 Maple Ave.,* ☎ *860/956–6000. Reservations not accepted. AE, D, DC, MC, V. No lunch Sun.*

$$$$ 🏨 **Goodwin Hotel.** Connecticut's only truly grand city hotel looks a
★ little odd in the downtown business district—the Civic Center dwarfs the ornate dark red structure, a registered historic landmark built in 1881. Despite the hotel's stately exterior, its rooms are nondescript but are large and tastefully decorated and have Italian marble baths. The clubby, mahogany-panel Pierpont's Restaurant serves commendable new American fare. ⊠ *1 Haynes St., 06103,* ☎ *860/246–7500 or 800/922–5006,* 𝔽𝔸𝕏 *860/247–4576. 124 rooms, 11 suites. Restaurant, exercise room, meeting rooms. AE, D, DC, MC, V.*

$$$ 🏨 **Sheraton-Hartford Hotel.** At 15 stories, this is the city's largest hotel. It's not sumptuous, but there are touches of elegance, such as the street-level lobby abloom with fresh flowers. Connected to the Civic Center by an enclosed bridge, it's within walking distance of the downtown area. ⊠ *315 Trumbull St. (at the Civic Center Plaza), 06103,* ☎ *860/728–5151,* 𝔽𝔸𝕏 *860/240–7247. 389 rooms, 8 suites. Restaurant, bar, indoor pool, health club. AE, D, DC, MC, V.*

$ 🏨 **Ramada Inn Capitol Hill.** Adjacent to Bushnell Park, the Ramada has an unobstructed view of the Capitol. Ask for a room in front—the ones facing the rear overlook the train station around the corner, a parking lot, and a busy highway. The restaurant serves steaks, hamburgers, and other traditional American fare. ⊠ *440 Asylum St., 06103,* ☎ *860/246–6591,* FAX *860/728–1382. 96 rooms. Restaurant. Continental breakfast weekdays. AE, D, DC, MC, V.*

Nightlife and the Arts

NIGHTLIFE

The **Arch Street Tavern** (⊠ 85 Arch St., ☎ 860/246–7610) hosts local rock bands. For barbecue and blues head to **Black-eyed Sally's** (⊠ 350 Asylum St., ☎ 860/278–7427). **Bourbon Street North** (⊠ 70 Union Pl., ☎ 860/525–1014) has a large dance floor; the music ranges from pop to alternative. Arch Ale and Bacchus Ale are two popular beers (among three dozen) on tap at the **Hartford Brewery** (⊠ 35 Pearl St., ☎ 860/246–2337). **Mozzicato–De Pasquale's Bakery, Pastry Shop & Caffe** (⊠ 329 Franklin Ave., ☎ 860/296–0426) serves up late-night Italian pastries in the bakery and espresso, cappuccino, gelato, and pizza, in the café, which has a full bar.

THE ARTS

The Tony Award–winning **Hartford Stage Company** (⊠ 50 Church St., ☎ 860/527–5151) turns out future Broadway hits, innovative productions of the classics, and new plays. **Theatreworks** (⊠ 233 Pearl St., ☎ 860/527–7838), the Hartford equivalent of Off-Broadway, presents experimental new dramas.

The Bushnell (⊠ 166 Capitol Ave., ☎ 860/246–6807) hosts the Hartford Ballet (☎ 860/525–9396), the Hartford Symphony (☎ 860/244–2999), and tours of major musicals. **Hartford Conservatory** (⊠ 834 Asylum Ave., ☎ 860/246–2588) presents musical performances, with an emphasis on traditional works. **Real Art Ways** (⊠ 56 Arbor St., ☎ 860/232–1006) presents mostly modern and experimental recitals. The mammoth **Meadows Music Theater** (⊠ 63 Savitt Way, ☎ 860/548–7370) hosts nationally known acts.

Outdoor Activities and Sports

The **Hartford Wolf Pack** (☎ 860/246–7825) of the American Hockey League plays at the 16,500-seat Civic Center (⊠ 1 Civic Center Plaza). The **New England Blizzard** (☎ 860/522–4667), a team in the women's American Basketball League, plays at the Civic Center.

Shopping

The **Civic Center** (⊠ 1 Civic Center Plaza, ☎ 860/275–6100) has more than 60 shops. The art deco–style **Pavilion** (⊠ State House Sq., ☎ 860/241–0100) has 25 shops.

Skiing

Mt. Southington. This mountain, an easy drive from Hartford, has 14 trails off the 425 ft of vertical range split equally between basic beginner, intermediate, and advanced. All trails are lit for night skiing and are serviced by one triple chairlift, one double, two T-bars, 1 J-bar, and a handle tow. There are also a halfpipe and terrain park for snowboarders. The ski school (with 150 instructors) includes a popular SKIwee program for kids from 4 to 12 years old. The Mountain Room provides respite for skiers and snowboarders alike. ⊠ *396 Mount Vernon Rd., 06489,* ☎ *860/628–0954 or 860/628–7669 for conditions.*

West Hartford

③⓪ *5 mi west of Hartford, 33 mi northeast of Woodbury.*

Almost every square inch of West Hartford is developed and landscaped. Not as white-bread as much of the suburbs, the city holds many ethnic communities—grocery stores here stock Japanese pickled cabbage, Indian spices, and other ingredients from around the world. The languages you might hear include Russian and Spanish.

★ ☾ A life-size walk-through replica of a 60-ft sperm whale greets patrons of the **Science Center of Connecticut,** whose attractions include an aquarium with a tank you can reach into, a minizoo, and a planetarium. The Kids Factory teaches kids about magnetics, motion, optics, sound, and light through colorful hands-on exhibits. "Mathmagical" toys in the lower exhibit hall include a giant bubble maker, a hands-on weather station, and "Kaleidovision"—a 30-ft by 9-ft walk-in kaleidoscope. ⊠ *950 Trout Brook Dr.,* ☎ *860/231–2824.* ⊡ *Science Center $6; laser and planetarium shows $3.* ☉ *Tues.–Wed. and Fri.–Sat. 10–5, Thurs. 10–8, Sun. noon–5. Closed Mon. Sept.–June, except holidays.*

The **Noah Webster House and Museum** is the birthplace of the famed author of the *American Dictionary*. The 18th-century farmhouse contains Webster memorabilia and period furnishings. ⊠ *227 S. Main St.,* ☎ *860/521–5362.* ⊡ *$5.* ☉ *Sept.–June, daily 1–4; July–Aug., Mon.–Tues. and Thurs.–Fri. 10–4, weekends 1–4.*

The **Museum of American Political Life** houses rare political materials and memorabilia—buttons, posters, bumper stickers, and pamphlets—from the campaigns of U.S. presidents from George Washington to the present. A small section is devoted to memorabilia from the women's rights and temperance movements. ⊠ *University of Hartford, 200 Bloomfield Ave.,* ☎ *860/768–4090.* ⊡ *Donation suggested.* ☉ *Sept.–May, Tues.–Fri. 11–4, Sat.–Sun. noon–4. Closed Sun. June–Aug.*

Dining

$$ ✗ **Butterfly Chinese Restaurant.** The piano entertainment suggests that this is not your ordinary order-by-number Chinese restaurant; indeed, the food is authentic, the staff gracious and outgoing. Among the 140 mostly Cantonese (some Szechuan) entrées are Peking duck and shrimp with walnuts. ⊠ *831 Farmington Ave.,* ☎ *860/236–2816. AE, MC, V.*

Farmington

③① *5 mi southwest of West Hartford, 67 mi northeast of New Canaan.*

Busy Farmington, incorporated in 1645, is a classic river town with lovely estates, a perfectly preserved main street, and the prestigious **Miss Porter's School** (60 Main St.), the late Jacqueline Kennedy Onassis's alma mater. Antiques shops can be found near the intersection of Routes 4 and 10, along with some excellent house museums.

★ The **Hill-Stead Museum** was converted from a private home into a museum by its unusual owner, Theodate Pope, the woman who helped Stanford White design it. A Colonial Revival farmhouse, it contains a superb collection of Impressionist art. Monet haystacks hang at each end of the drawing room, and Manet's *The Guitar Player* hangs in the middle. ⊠ *35 Mountain Rd.,* ☎ *860/677–4787.* ⊡ *$6.* ☉ *May–Oct., Tues.–Sun. 10–5; Nov.–Apr., Tues.–Sun. 11–4.*

The **Stanley-Whitman House** has been a museum since the 1930s. The house, which was built in 1720, has a massive central chimney, an overhanging second story, and superlative 18th-century furnishings. ⊠ *37 High St.,* ☎ *860/677–9222.* ⊡ *$5.* ☉ *Nov.–Apr., Sun. noon–4 and by appointment; May–Oct., Wed.–Sun. noon–4.*

Dining and Lodging

$$$ ✕ **Ann Howard's Apricots.** A white Colonial with dozens of windows looking out over gardens and the Farmington River holds the area's best eatery. Fine new American cuisine—like the inventive warm lamb and spinach salad and the grilled sirloin with brandied mushrooms—is presented in the quiet and cozy formal dining room; less expensive fare is available in the convivial pub. ⊠ *1593 Farmington Ave.,* ☎ *860/ 673–5903. AE, DC, MC, V. No lunch Sun.*

$$ ▥ **Barney House.** This 1832 mansion on a quiet street is set amid 4½ acres of formal gardens. Owned and operated by the University of Connecticut Foundation as a conference center, Barney House accepts overnight guests by reservation. Many antiques furnish the large rooms, all of which have ornately papered walls, lead-glass bookcases, fetching bed quilts, and substantial bathrooms with modern plumbing. ⊠ *11 Mountain Spring Rd., 06032,* ☎ *860/674–2796,* FAX *860/677–7259. 7 rooms. Tennis court. Continental breakfast. AE, MC, V. No smoking, no pets.*

$$ ▥ **Farmington Inn.** This modern alternative to the Barney House has an ill-chosen white-painted brick exterior, but the rooms are generous in size and appointed tastefully with antiques and reproductions. Much nicer than a chain hotel, it's very close to Miss Porter's and area museums. ⊠ *827 Farmington Ave., 06032,* ☎ *860/677–2821 or 800/648– 9804,* FAX *860/677–8332. 59 rooms, 13 suites. Business services, meeting rooms. Continental breakfast. AE, D, DC, MC, V.*

Shopping

A glitzy new wing of the 140-shop **Westfarms Mall** (⊠ I–84, Exit 40, ☎ 860/561–3024) includes Nordstrom, April Cornell, Williams-Sonoma, and Restoration Hardware.

Simsbury

㉜ *12 mi north of Farmington; from Farmington, follow Rte. 10 through Avon.*

With its Colonial-style shopping centers, smattering of antiques shops, and proliferation of insurance-industry executives, Simsbury closely resembles the tony bedroom communities of Fairfield County.

Visit the **Massacoh Plantation,** and you'll learn about the 300-year, largely agrarian history of Simsbury, which was settled in 1640 and incorporated in 1670. Included on the property are a Victorian carriage house (circa 1880), a 1795 cottage and herb garden, a 1740 schoolhouse, and the highlight, the period-furnished 1771 Colonial home of sea captain Elijah Phelps. You can only view the houses on a tour, but the highly strollable grounds are accessible all the time. ⊠ *800 Hopmeadow St.,* ☎ *860/658–2500.* ☞ *$5.* ⊙ *Tours May–Oct., daily 1–4 (last tour at 2:30); grounds open year-round.*

The **Old New-Gate Prison and Copper Mine** was the country's first chartered copper mine (in 1707) and later (in 1773) Connecticut's first Colonial prison. Tours of the underground mine (where temperatures rarely top 55 degrees) are a great way to chill out in summer. There are hiking trails and a picnic area. ⊠ *Newgate Rd., East Granby,* ☎ *860/653– 3563 or 860/566–3005.* ☞ *$3.* ⊙ *Mid-May–Oct., Wed.–Sun. 10–4:30.*

Climb 1 mi from the parking lot at **Talcott Mountain** to the 165-ft Heublein Tower, a former private home, and you'll be rewarded with views of four states. ⊠ *Rte. 185,* ☎ *860/242–1158.* ☞ *Free.* ⊙ *Tower late Apr.–Labor Day, Thurs.–Sun. 10–5; Labor Day–late Oct., daily 10–5.*

Lodging

$$$ 🏨 **Avon Old Farms Hotel.** This 20-acre compound of redbrick Georgian-style buildings is set into the Avon countryside at the foot of Talcott Mountain, about midway between Farmington and Simsbury. An immense place that caters largely to business travelers, it has quietly elegant rooms. ✉ *Rtes. 10 and 44, 06001,* ☎ *860/677–1651,* FAX *860/677–0364. 164 rooms. Restaurant, pub, outdoor pool, meeting rooms. AE, D, DC, MC, V.*

$$$ 🏨 **Simsbury 1820 House.** The rooms at this inn perched on a hillside contain a judicious mix of antiques and modern furnishings. Each of the rooms and suites in the main house has a special feature—a decorative fireplace or balcony, a patio, a wet bar, a dormer with a cozy window seat. Under the porte cochere and across the parking lot is a former carriage house with 11 rooms; the split-level Executive Suite here has a private patio, entrance, and Jacuzzi. ✉ *731 Hopmeadow St., 06070,* ☎ *860/658–7658 or 800/879–1820,* FAX *860/651–0724. 29 rooms, 3 suites. Continental breakfast. AE, D, DC, MC, V.*

Shopping

Arts Exclusive Gallery (✉ 690 Hopmeadow St., ☎ 860/651–5824) represents 35 contemporary artists. The **Farmington Valley Arts Center** (✉ 25 Arts Center La., Avon, ☎ 860/678–1867) shows the works of nationally known artists.

Windsor Locks

③ *13 mi northeast of Simsbury, 94 mi northeast of Greenwich, 48 mi northeast of New Haven, 56 mi northwest of New London.*

Windsor Locks was named for the locks of a canal built to bypass falls in the Connecticut River in 1833; in 1844 the canal closed to make way for a railroad line.

★ The 80 aircraft at the **New England Air Museum** include flying machines that date from 1909. The World War II–era P-47 Thunderbolt and B-29 Superfortress are on display, along with other vintage fighters and bombers. ✉ *Next to Bradley International Airport, off Rte. 75,* ☎ *860/623–3305.* 🎫 *$6.50.* ☉ *Daily 10–5.*

The **Connecticut Trolley Museum** holds more than 50 trolleys and operates a 3-mi round-trip antique-trolley ride. A special "Electric Sleigh" ride runs each Christmas, during which the trolley rolls through a colorful tunnel of Christmas lights. ✉ *58 North Rd., East Windsor,* ☎ *860/627–6540.* 🎫 *$6.* ☉ *Mar.–Memorial Day and Labor Day–Dec., Sat. 10–5, Sun. noon–5; Memorial Day–Labor Day, daily 10–5. Closed Jan.–Feb.*

The **Hatheway House,** 7 mi north of Windsor Locks, is one of the finest architectural specimens in New England. The walls of its neoclassical north wing (1794) still wear their original 18th-century French hand-blocked wallpaper. The double-front doors and gambrel roof of the main house (1761) were typical accoutrements of Connecticut River valley homes. An ornate picket fence fronts the property. ✉ *55 S. Main St. (take Rte. 75 north from Windsor Locks), Suffield,* ☎ *860/668–0055 or 860/247–8996.* 🎫 *$4.* ☉ *Mid-May–June and Sept.–mid-Oct., Wed. and weekends 1–4; July–Aug., Wed.–Sun. 1–4.*

Connecticut River Valley A to Z

Arriving and Departing

BY BUS AND TRAIN

Hartford's renovated **Union Station** (✉ 1 Union Pl.) is the main terminus for Amtrak (☎ 800/872–7245) trains and Greyhound (☎ 800/

231–2222) and Peter Pan Bus Lines (☎ 800/237–8747) buses. Bus and train service is available to most major northeastern cities.

BY CAR

Interstates 84 and 91, Route 2, Route 202, and Route 44 intersect in Hartford.

BY PLANE

Bradley International Airport (⊠ Rte. 20; take Exit 40 off I–91, ☎ 860/627–3000), 12 mi north of Hartford, is served by American, Continental, Delta, Midway, Northwest, TWA, United, and US Airways. *See* Airline Travel *in* the Gold Guide for airline phone numbers.

Getting Around

BY BUS

Connecticut Transit (☎ 860/525–9181) provides bus service throughout the greater Hartford area. The fare varies according to destination.

BY CAR

The major road through the valley is Route 9, which extends from south of Hartford at I–91 to I–95 at Old Saybrook. Essex, Ivorytown, Chester, Higganum, Middletown, and New Britain are all on or near Route 9; Westerfield is east of Route 9 on Route 175. From just below Deep River to just above Higganum, Route 154 loops east of Route 9; head east from Route 154 on Route 151 to reach East Haddam. Farmington is west of Hartford on Route 4. To reach Simsbury head west from Hartford on Route 202/44 and north on Route 202. To reach Windsor Locks, take I–91 north from Hartford and head north on Route 159.

Contacts and Resources

EMERGENCIES

Hartford Hospital (⊠ 80 Seymour St., ☎ 860/545–5555). **Middlesex Hospital** (⊠ 28 Crescent St., Middletown, ☎ 860/347–9471).

GUIDED TOURS

Heritage Trails (☎ 860/677–8867) operates daily city tours of Hartford and candlelight dinner tours of Farmington and sells self-guided driving tours on tape for $9.95.

LATE-NIGHT PHARMACIES

CVS (⊠ 1099 New Britain Ave., West Hartford, ☎ 860/236–6181). **Community Pharmacy** (⊠ 197 Main St., Deep River, ☎ 860/526–5379).

VISITOR INFORMATION

Connecticut River Valley and Shoreline Visitors Council (⊠ 393 Main St., Middletown 06457, ☎ 860/347–0028 or 800/486–3346). **Greater Hartford Tourism District** (⊠ 234 Murphy Rd., Hartford 06114, ☎ 860/244–8181 or 800/793–4480). **Central Connecticut Tourism District** (⊠ 1 Grove St., Suite 310, New Britain 06053, ☎ 860/225–3901). **Connecticut's North Central Tourism Bureau** (⊠ 111 Hazard Ave., Enfield 06082, ☎ 860/763–2578 or 800/248–8283).

THE LITCHFIELD HILLS

Two scenic highways, I–84 and Route 8, form the southern and eastern boundaries of the Litchfield Hills region. New York, to the west, and Massachusetts, to the north, complete the rectangle. Here in the foothills of the Berkshires is some of the most spectacular and unspoiled scenery in Connecticut. Grand old inns are plentiful, as are sophisticated eateries. Rolling farmlands abut thick forests, and trails traverse the state parks and forests. Two rivers, the Housatonic and the Farmington, attract anglers and canoeing enthusiasts, and the state's three largest natural lakes, the Waramaug, Bantam, and Twin, are here.

Sweeping town greens and stately homes anchor Litchfield, New Milford, and Sharon. Kent, New Preston, and Woodbury draw avid antiquers, and Washington, Salisbury, and Norfolk provide a glimpse into New England village life as it might have existed two centuries ago.

Favorite roads for admiring fall foliage are Route 7, from New Milford through Kent and West Cornwall to Canaan; Routes 41 to 4 from Salisbury through Lakeville, Sharon, Cornwall Bridge, and Goshen to Torrington; and Routes 47 to 202 to 341 from Woodbury through Washington, New Preston, Lake Waramaug, and Warren to Kent.

Numbers in the margin correspond to points of interest on the Litchfield Hills map.

New Milford

③④ *28 mi east of Waterbury.*

New Milford is a practical starting point to begin a tour of the Litchfield Hills. It was also a starting point for a young cobbler named Roger Sherman, who, in 1743, opened his shop where Main and Church streets meet. A Declaration of Independence signatory, Sherman also helped draft the Constitution and the Articles of Confederation.

Up to its junction with Route 67, the combined Route 7/202 is a dull stretch of shopping centers and consistently ugly storefronts. But where the road crosses the Housatonic River, you'll find old shops, galleries, and eateries all within a short stroll of New Milford green—one of the longest in New England.

OFF THE BEATEN PATH **THE SILO –** New Yorkers who miss Zabar's and Balducci's feel right at home in this silo and barn packed with objets de cookery and crafts; the array of gourmet goodies and sauces is unbelievable. The founder and music director of the New York Pops, Skitch Henderson, and his wife, Ruth, own and operate this bazaar, where several dozen classes taught by culinary superstars are given between March and December. ⊠ *44 Upland Rd., 4 mi north of the New Milford town green on Rte. 202,* ☎ *860/355-0300.* ☉ *Apr.–Dec., daily 10–5; Jan.–Mar., Tues.–Sun. 10–5.*

Dining and Lodging

$$–$$$ ★ ✕ **Bistro Café.** Copper pots hang about and vintage black-and-white photos adorn the walls of this café in a redbrick corner building. The well-crafted regional American dishes change weekly—tender grilled swordfish with whipped potatoes, veggies, and a chive aioli one week, oven-roasted duck with pecans and cranberry coulis the next. For something new and different, sample buffalo, moose, antelope, kangaroo, alligator, or northern black bear—they're all farm-raised and low in cholesterol. Upstairs is a taproom where you can relax with a bottle of wine or feast from the same menu as downstairs. The dessert list is frighteningly long. ⊠ *31 Bank St.,* ☎ *860/355–3266. AE, MC, V.*

$$ ★ ▥ **Homestead Inn.** High on a hill overlooking New Milford's town green, the Homestead was built in 1853 and opened as an inn in 1928. Life is casual here, and the owners, Rolf and Peggy Hammer, are always game for a leisurely chat. Breakfast is served in a cheery living room, where you can sit by the fire or admire the Steinway piano. The eight rooms in the main house have more personality than those in the motel-style structure next door. ⊠ *5 Elm St., 06776,* ☎ *860/354–4080,* ℻ *860/354–7046. 14 rooms. Continental breakfast. AE, D, DC, MC, V.*

Outdoor Activities and Sports
Black Duck Boat Works (⊠ 143 West St., ☏ 860/350–5170) at the headwaters of Lake Lillinonah (also known as the Housatonic River) rents canoes, kayaks, rowing vessels, and electric launches.

New Preston

③⑤ *4 mi north of New Milford.*

The crossroads village of New Preston, perched above a 40-ft waterfall on the Aspetuck River, has a little town center that's packed with antiques shops specializing in everything from 18th-century furnishings to painted furniture from the Southwest.

Lake Waramaug, north of New Preston on Route 45, is an area that reminds many of Austria and Switzerland. If you drive the 8-mi perimeter of the lake, named for Chief Waramaug, one of the most revered figures in Connecticut's Native American history, you'll see beautiful inns—many of which serve delicious Continental food—and homes. The state park of the same name, at the northwest tip, is an idyllic 75-acre spread, great for picnicking and lakeside camping.

The popular **Hopkins Vineyard** overlooks Lake Waramaug. More than 13 varieties of wine are produced here, from sparkling to dessert. A weathered red barn houses a gift shop and a tasting room, and there's a picnic area. The wine bar serves a fine cheese and pâté board. ⊠ *Hopkins Rd.,* ☏ *860/868–7954.* 🎟 *Free.* ☉ *Jan.–Apr., Fri.–Sat. 10–5, Sun. 11–5; May–Dec., Mon.–Sat. 10–5, Sun. 11–5.*

Dining and Lodging

$ ★ **✕ Black Bear Coffee Roasters.** Bright and airy, with exposed beams, plank flooring, and iron café tables, Black Bear sells delicious coffee roasted on the premises and creative soups, salads, sandwiches (the Maryland crab cake is a showstopper), and desserts (from scones to a chocolate-cherry tart). ⊠ *239 New Milford Turnpike/Rte. 202, Marble Dale (1 mi west of New Preston),* ☏ *860/868–1446. MC, V. Closed Tues.–Wed. No dinner.*

$$$$ ★ **✕🛏 Boulders Inn.** The most idyllic and prestigious of the inns along Lake Waramaug opened in 1940 but still looks like the private home it was a century ago. Apart from the main house, a carriage house and several guest houses command panoramic views of the countryside and the lake. The rooms, four with double whirlpool baths, contain Victorian antiques and wood-burning fireplaces. The exquisite menu at the window-lined, stone-wall dining room changes seasonally but might include sautéed jumbo shrimp with sun-dried tomatoes, julienne fennel and leeks, and a cognac butter sauce. ⊠ *E. Shore Rd./Rte. 45, 06777,* ☏ *860/868–0541 or 800/552–6853,* 📠 *860/868–1925. 15 rooms, 2 suites. Restaurant, lake, tennis court, boating. MAP. AE, MC, V.*

$$$–$$$$ ★ **✕🛏 Birches Inn.** One of the area's poshest inns, the Birches is something of a Lake Waramaug institution. Antiques and reproductions decorate the rooms; three on the waterfront have private decks. Executive chef Frederic Faveau presides over the lakeview dining room. His signature dishes include roasted garlic custard, roasted red beet tartar, and grilled marinated leg of lamb with Parmesan polenta, sautéed mustard greens, and a roasted garlic sauce. ⊠ *233 West Shore Rd., 06777,* ☏ *860/868–1735,* 📠 *860/868–1815. 8 rooms. Restaurant. Continental breakfast. AE, D, DC, MC, V. Closed Tues.–Wed. No lunch.*

$–$$ ★ **✕🛏 Hopkins Inn.** A grand 1847 Victorian that sits on a hill overlooking Lake Waramaug, the Hopkins is one of the best bargains in the Hills. Most rooms have plain white bedspreads, simple antiques, and pastel

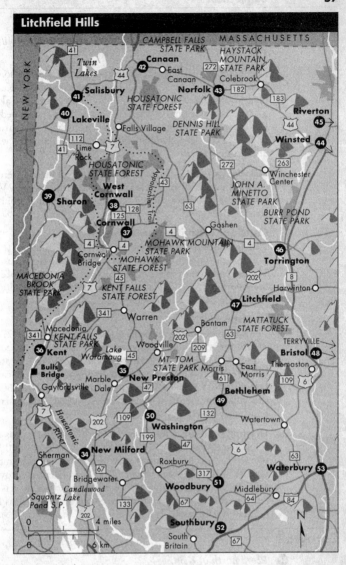

Litchfield Hills

floral wallpaper. In winter, the whole inn smells of burning firewood; year-round, it is redolent of the aromas coming from the rambling dining rooms, which serve outstanding Swiss and Austrian dishes—calves' brains in black butter, Wiener schnitzel, sweetbreads Viennese. When the weather is kind, you can dine on the terrace and view the lake. ⊠ *22 Hopkins Rd. (1 mi off Rte. 45), 06777,* ☎ *860/868–7295,* ℻ *860/ 868–7464. 8 rooms with bath, 2 rooms share bath, 1 room with hall bath, 2 apartments. Restaurant. AE, MC, V. Closed Jan.–late Mar.*

Shopping

More than a dozen shops with art, antiques, and related items can be found within walking distance of downtown New Preston. **J. Seitz & Co.** (⊠ 9 E. Shore Rd., ☎ 860/868–0119) sells southwestern antiques and reproduction painted furniture. **Ray Boas, Bookseller** (⊠ 6 Church St., ☎ 860/868–9596) stocks thousands of antiquarian and out-of-print books. **The Trumpeteer** (⊠ 5 Main St., ☎ 860/868–9090) specializes in English antiques and eccentricities with a masculine touch.

Kent

 12 mi northwest of New Preston; reached from New Milford on Rte. 7 or from New Preston on Rte. 341.

Kent has the area's greatest concentration of art galleries, some nationally renowned. Home to a prep school of the same name, Kent once held many ironworks. The Schaghticoke Indian Reservation is also here. During the Revolutionary War, 100 Schaghticokes helped defend the Colonies: They transmitted messages of army intelligence from the Litchfield Hills to Long Island Sound, along the hilltops, by way of shouts and drum beats.

Bulls Bridge (⊠ Rte. 7, south of Kent), one of three covered bridges in Connecticut, is open to cars. But be careful: George Washington's horse is said to have slipped on a rotted plank and tumbled into the roaring river.

Outdoor Activities and Sports

The **Appalachian Trail's** longest riverwalk, off Route 341, is the almost 8-mi hike from Kent to Cornwall Bridge along the Housatonic River. The early-season trout fishing is superb at 2,300-acre **Macedonia Brook State Park** (⊠ Macedonia Brook Rd. off Rte. 341, ☎ 860/927–3238), where you can also hike and cross-country ski.

Shopping

The **Bachelier-Cardonsky Gallery** (⊠ Main St., ☎ 860/927–3129), one of the foremost galleries in the Northeast, exhibits contemporary works. The **Paris–New York–Kent Gallery** (⊠ Kent Station, off Rte. 7, ☎ 860/927–4152) shows contemporary works by local and world-famous artists. **Pauline's Place** (⊠ 79 N. Main St., ☎ 860/927–4475) specializes in Victorian, Georgian, Art Deco, Edwardian, and contemporary jewelry.

En Route Heading north from Kent toward Cornwall, you'll pass the entrance to 275-acre **Kent Falls State Park** (⊠ Rte. 7, ☎ 860/927–3238), where you can hike a short way to one of the most impressive waterfalls in the state and picnic in the lush hemlock grove above the falls. The fee to use the park on weekends and holidays is $5 for Connecticut residents and $8 for nonresidents; admission is free on non-holiday weekdays.

Cornwall

 12 mi north of Kent.

Among the virgin pines and thick forest in Cornwall, fleeting pockets of civilization came and went throughout the 18th and 19th centuries. Starvation and cold took the lives of most who settled here in the eerily named communities of Mast Swamp, Wildcat, Great Hollow, Crooked Esses, and Ballyhack.

Mohawk Mountain State Park (⊠ 1 mi south of Cornwall off Rte. 4, ☎ 860/927–3238) is a great spot for a picnic. The view at the top of 1,683-ft Mohawk Mountain is breathtaking; the hike up is 2½ mi long.

Skiing

Mohawk Mountain. Mohawk's 23 trails, ranged down 640 vertical ft, include plenty of intermediate terrain, with a few trails for beginners and a few steeper sections toward the top of the mountain. Trails are serviced by one triple lift and four doubles and are lit for night skiing except on Sunday. The base lodge has munchies and a retail shop, and the Pine Lodge, halfway up the slope, has an outdoor patio. Mohawk's SKIwee program is for kids from age 5 to 12. There are facilities for ice-skating and snowboarding. ⊠ *46 Great Hollow Rd., off Rte. 4, 06753,* ☎ *860/672–6100; 860/672–6464 for conditions.*

West Cornwall

❸❽ *3 mi northwest of Cornwall.*

Connecticut's most romantic covered bridge, the wooden, barn-red, one-lane **Cornwall Bridge,** is not in the town of the same name, but several miles up Route 7 in West Cornwall. The Cornwall Bridge was built in 1841 and has since carried travelers into West Cornwall, the site of a few notable crafts shops and restaurants. The bridge, which won national recognition for its superb restoration, incorporates strut techniques that were copied by bridge builders around the country.

Outdoor Activities and Sports

Clarke Outdoors (⊠ Rte. 7, ☎ 860/672–6365) rents canoes and kayaks and operates 10-mi trips from Falls Village to Housatonic Meadows State Park. **Housatonic Anglers** (⊠ Rte. 7, ☎ 860/672–4457), which operates half- and full-day tours, provides fly-fishing instruction for trout and bass on the Housatonic and its tributaries. **Housatonic River Outfitters** (⊠ Rte. 128, ☎ 860/672–1010) operates a full-service flyshop and guided trips of the rivers and lakes of the region and gives classes in fly-fishing and casting.

Shopping

Cornwall Bridge Pottery Store (⊠ Rte. 128, ☎ 860/672–6545) sells its own pottery, glass by Simon Pearce, and Shaker-style furniture. **Ian Ingersoll Cabinetmakers** (⊠ Main St. by the Cornwall Bridge, ☎ 860/ 672–6334) stocks reproduction Shaker-style reproduction furniture.

Sharon

❸❾ *17 mi west of Cornwall, 24 mi northwest of Litchfield.*

The well-preserved Colonial town of Sharon was a manufacturing center during Colonial times. Munitions, oxbows, wooden mousetraps—all sorts of things were made here. An attempt in later years to introduce the silkworm failed because of New England's unwelcoming climate, but the mulberry trees that were planted as part of the experiment still line Main Street. Perhaps the strangest sight in town is the elaborate **Hotchkiss Clock Tower,** which looms above the intersection of Routes 4 and 41. It was built in 1885 of native gray granite as a memorial to town son Benjamin Berkeley Hotchkiss, the inventor of the Hotchkiss explosive shell.

With many trails and nature walks, the **Sharon Audubon Center,** a 758-acre sanctuary for many types of birds, is one of the best places to hike in Connecticut. On-site are an exhibit center, a gift shop, and a library. ⊠ *325 Cornwall Bridge Rd.,* ☎ *860/364–0520.* ☞ *$3.* ☉ *Mon.–Sat. 9–5, Sun. 1–5; trails dawn–dusk.*

Camping

⚠ **Housatonic Meadows State Park.** Tall pine trees near the Housatonic River shade the campsites here. Fly-fishers consider this 2-mi stretch of the river among the best places to practice their sport in New England. ⊠ *Rte. 7, Cornwall Bridge,* ☎ *860/672–6772 or 860/927–3238.* ☞ *$10. 95 sites. Pit toilets, water (hand pump). No credit cards.* ☉ *Park year-round. Campground closed Jan.–mid-Apr.*

Lakeville

 9 mi north of Sharon.

You can usually spot an original Colonial home in Lakeville by looking for the grapevine design cut into the frieze above the front door. It's the apparent trademark of the builder of the town's first homes. The lake of Lakeville is **Lake Wononscopomuc.** As you drive along Route 44 or 41, you'll catch glimpses of the lake's sparkling waters—the closest you're likely to get because most of its shoreline is private property.

The holdings of the **Holley House Museum,** which chronicle 18th- and 19th-century life, include a 1768 ironmaster's home whose 1808 Classical Revival Wing contains family furnishings, Colonial portraits, and a Holley Manufacturing Co. pocketknife exhibit. "From Corsets to Freedom" is a popular hands-on 1870s kitchen exhibit demonstrating the debate between women's rights versus "women's sphere" in the home. Living History tours are conducted. Admission also includes the on-site **Salisbury Cannon Museum,** where hands-on exhibits and activities survey the contributions of area residents and the local iron industry to the American Revolution. ⊠ *15 Millerton Rd./Rte. 44,* ☎ *860/435–2878.* 🖼 *$3.*☉ *Mid-June–mid-Oct., weekends 12–4.*

From mid-June to mid-September, **Music Mountain** (⊠ Falls Village, ☎ 860/824–7126) presents chamber music concerts on Sunday afternoon and jazz concerts on Saturday night.

Outdoor Activities and Sports

Auto racing at renowned **Lime Rock Park** (⊠ Rte. 112, ☎ 860/435–2571 or 860/435–0896) takes place on Saturday and holiday Mondays from late April to mid-October; amphitheater-style lawn seating allows for great views all around. **Rustling Wind Stables** (⊠ Mountain Rd., Falls Village, ☎ 860/824–7634) gives lessons, takes riders along the beautiful trails of Canaan Mountain, and operates pony rides for the kids.

Salisbury

 6 mi north of Lakeville.

Salisbury, were it not for the obsolescence of its ironworks, might today be the largest city in Connecticut. Instead, it settles for having both the state's highest mountain, Bear Mountain (2,355 ft), and its highest point, the shoulder of Mt. Frissel (2,380 ft)—whose peak is in Massachusetts. There's a spot on Mt. Frissel where if the urge strikes you (as it does many) you can stretch your limbs across the Connecticut, Massachusetts, and New York borders.

Iron was discovered here in 1732, and for the next century, the slopes of Salisbury's Mt. Riga produced the finest iron in America—Swiss and Russian immigrants, and later Hessian deserters from the British army, worked the great furnaces. These mysterious people inbred and lived in tiny hillside cabins in these parts until well into the 20th century, long after the last forge cast a glow in 1847. "Raggies," as they were known, are cloaked in a legend of black magic and suspicion and are believed to be responsible for various mishaps and ghostly sightings. As for the ironworks, the spread of rail transport opened up better and more accessible sources of ore, the region's lumber supply was eventually depleted, and the introduction of the Bessemer process of steel manufacturing—partially invented by Salisbury native Alexander Holley—reduced the demand for iron products. Most signs of cinder heaps and slag dumps are long gone, replaced by grand summer homes and gardens.

Harney & Sons Fine Teas supplies its high-quality Darjeeling, Earl Grey, Keemun, and other blends to some of the world's best hotels and restaurants. At the tasting room you can sample some of the 100 varieties, and there's a gift shop. If you call ahead you might even be able to schedule a tour, led by founder John Harney himself, of the factory where the tea is blended and packaged. ⊠ *11 Brook St.,* ☎ *860/435–5050.* ⛳ *Free.* ☉ *Mon.–Sat. 10–5.*

Dining and Lodging

$$$$ ✕⊞ **Under Mountain Inn.** The nearest neighbors of this white-clapboard farmhouse are the horses grazing in the field across the road. Antiques, knickknacks, and objets d'art fill every space; chess and checkers games are set up by the fireplace. The hospitality has a pronounced British flavor (there's a British video lounge and "The Pub"—a faithful replica of a typical English taproom); dinner, too, recalls Britain with authentic game dishes and hearty steak-and-kidney pie. The restaurant (reservations essential) is open to the public on Friday and Saturday. ⊠ *482 Under Mountain Rd./Rte. 41, 06068,* ☎ *860/435–0242,* FAX *860/435–2379. 7 rooms. Restaurant, pub, hiking. MAP. MC, V.*

$$–$$$ ✕⊞ **White Hart Inn.** With its fresh coat of white paint and broad front
★ porch, the White Hart, which has welcomed travelers since the 1860s, stands out on Salisbury's village green. The rooms and suites have excellent Colonial-reproduction furniture, good reading lamps, and modern bathrooms. The upholstery, bedspreads, and curtains are done in contrasting colors and patterns—a lively stripe here, a floral splash there, and maybe a colorful ribbon to tie it all together. Several rooms on the eastern side have private entrances, and a few steps away in the 1815 Gideon Smith House, similar rooms and suites are available on two levels. Dining in any of the White Hart's three restaurants—the bright and sunny Garden Room, the tavernlike Tap Room, or the elegant American Grill—is a pleasure. Dishes at the grill include braised lamb shank with mushroom-barley risotto and Tuscan grilled vegetables with mushroom polenta, black olives, and parsley-basil pesto. ⊠ *The Village Green, 06068,* ☎ *860/435–0030,* FAX *860/435–0040. 22 rooms, 3 suites. 3 restaurants, meeting rooms. AE, DC, MC, V.*

Shopping

The **Salisbury Antiques Center** (⊠ 46 Library St., off Rte. 44, ☎ 860/435–0424) carries a varied selection of American and English pieces. The **Village Store** (⊠ Main St./Rte.44, ☎ 860/435–9459) stocks high-quality sportswear, bikes, cross-country skis, hiking boots, and maps; you can rent cross-country skis, snowshoes, and bikes here.

Canaan

㊷ *10 mi northeast of Salisbury, 84 mi northeast of Stamford, 42 mi northwest of Hartford.*

Canaan is one of the more developed towns in the Litchfield region: It has a McDonald's. Canaan was the site of some important late-18th-century industry, including a gun-barrel factory and a paper mill, and was also the home of Captain Gershom Hewitt, who is credited with securing the plans of Fort Ticonderoga for Ethan Allen.

Canaan Union Station was built in 1871 as a train station and now houses a pub-style restaurant and a few shops.

Camping

⛺ **Lone Oak Campsites.** This family campground has two pools, a hot tub, a store-deli, and a lounge with a full bar. On weekends live entertainment and activities take place. ⊠ *Rte. 44, East Canaan,* ☎ *860/824–7051.* ⛳ *$27. 500 sites, 1 cabin, 6 trailers. Coin laundry, elec-*

tric hook-ups, fire rings, flush toilets, showers, water. Closed mid-Oct.–mid-Apr. 2-night minimum stay for trailers and cabin; 2-night minimum stay in-season for sites.

Dining

$$$ ✕ **Cannery Café.** The eggshell-color walls of this storefront American
★   bistro are painted with a pattern of gleaming gold stars; elegant brass
fixtures reflect the muted lighting. All is crisp and clean, the service
chatty but refined. Pistachio-crusted salmon and sautéed lamb with straw
potato cakes headline the menu. Sunday brunch is a favorite with locals. ⊠ *85 Main St. (Rtes. 44 and 7),* ☎ *860/824–7333. AE, DC, MC,
V. Closed Tues. (and Wed. in winter). No lunch.*

$ ✕ **Collin's Diner.** There's no denying that this 1942 O'Mahony diner,
★   inspired by the jazzy railroad dining cars of the '20s and '30s, is a classic beauty. Although locals count on Collin's for traditional diner fare,
the nightly specials are the biggest draw—on Friday there's baked
stuffed shrimp, on Saturday a meaty two-inch cut of prime rib. ⊠ *Rte.
44,* ☎ *860/824–7040. No credit cards.* ⊙ *Daily 5:30–5, Wed. 5:30–
1. Call for extended summer hrs.*

Shopping

The **Connecticut Woodcarvers Gallery** (⊠ Rte. 44, East Canaan, ☎ 860/
824–0883) sells the work of woodcarver Joseph Cieslowski, whose
unique relief carvings embellish clocks, mirrors, and decorative panels. Carved pieces by other artists are also for sale.

Norfolk

43 *12 mi east of Canaan, 59 mi north of New Haven.*

Norfolk, thanks to its severe climate and terrain, is one of the best-preserved villages in the Northeast. Notable industrialists have been
summering here for two centuries, and many enormous homesteads
still exist. At the junction of Routes 272 and 44 is the striking town
green. At its southern corner is a fountain—designed by Augustus
Saint-Gaudens and executed by Stanford White—a memorial to Joseph
Battell, who turned Norfolk into a major trading center.

You can purchase most of what you see at **Hillside Gardens,** one of the
foremost nurseries and perennial gardens in the Northeast. The 5 acres
of gardens, surrounded by a stone walls, glow from May to September with daffodils, lilies, foxgloves, chrysanthemums, and ornamental grasses. ⊠ *515 Litchfield Rd./Rte. 272, 2½ mi south of town green,*
☎ *860/542–5345.* ☒ *Free.* ⊙ *May–mid-Sept., daily 9–5.*

Dr. Frederick Dennis lavishly entertained guests, among them President Howard Taft and several Connecticut governors, in the stone pavilion at the summit of what is now **Dennis Hill State Park.** You can picnic
on the park's lush grounds, which are adjacent to Hillside Gardens,
or take a hike. ⊠ *Rte. 272,* ☎ *860/482–1817.* ☒ *Free.* ⊙ *8 AM–dusk.*

Dining and Lodging

$$–$$$ ✕ **The Pub.** Bottles of trendy beers line the shelves of this down-to-earth
★   restaurant on the ground floor of a redbrick Victorian near the town
green. Burgers, pizzas, and other cheap grub are on the menu, which
also lists strip steak and lamb curry. This place is a real melting pot.
⊠ *Rte. 44,* ☎ *860/542–5716. AE, MC, V. Closed Mon.*

$$$$ 🏠 **Greenwoods Gate.** The cheerful George Shumaker, a former Hilton
★   executive with a penchant for playing cupid, runs Connecticut's foremost romantic hideaway. Every room holds countless amenities, from
chocolates and cognac to soaps, fresh flowers, and powders to board
games with titles like "Romantic Liasons"; champagne or a deep mas-

sage are available with notice. Starched white linens cover the beds of the four suites (the Levi Thompson is the most interesting). George prepares a huge breakfast—a spread of muffins and fresh fruit followed by a hearty hot meal—and lays out snacks and afternoon wine and cheese. ⊠ *105 Greenwoods Rd. E/Rte. 44, 06058,* ☎ *860/542–5439,* FAX *860/542–5897. 4 suites. Full breakfast. No credit cards. No smoking, no pets. 2-night minimum weekends.*

$$$–$$$$ 🏠 **Manor House.** The architect of London's subway system built and
★ designed this unusual Bavarian Tudor residence that opened for business in 1898. Among the house's remarkable features are its characterful bibelots, mirrors, carpets, antique beds, and prints—not to mention the 20 stained-glass windows designed by Louis Tiffany. The vast Spofford Room has windows on three sides, a king-size canopy bed with a cheery fireplace opposite, and a balcony. The intimate Lincoln Room has an antique double sleigh bed, a white fainting couch, and a working fireplace—along with the best view of the neighboring landscape. But the Balcony Room has the most remarkable feature— a private wood-panel elevator (added in 1939). It also has a private deck. This inn is not suitable for young children. ⊠ *Box 447, Maple Ave., 06058,* ☎ FAX *860/542–5690. 7 rooms, 1 suite. Full breakfast. AE, D, DC, MC, V.*

Nightlife and the Arts

The **Norfolk Chamber Music Festival** (☎ 860/542–3000), at the Music Shed on the Ellen Battell Stoeckel Estate at the northwest corner of the Norfolk green, presents world-renowned artists and ensembles on Friday and Saturday summer evenings. Students from the Yale School of Music perform on Thursday evening and Saturday morning. The festival also sponsors the Indian Summer series in October and November. Early arrivals can stroll or picnic on the 250-acre grounds or visit the art gallery.

Outdoor Activities and Sports

The birding is superb at **Campbell Falls State Park** (⊠ Old Spaulding Rd. off Rte. 272, ☎ 860/482–1817), where you can also hike. Easy to challenging trails crisscross **Haystack Mountain State Park** (⊠ Rte. 272, ☎ 860/482–1817). **Loon Meadow Farm** (⊠ Loon Meadow Dr., ☎ 860/542–6085) operates horse-drawn sleigh, hay, and carriage rides.

Shopping

Norfolk Artisans Guild (⊠ Greenwoods Rd. E, ☎ 860/542–5487) carries local crafts—from hand-painted pillows to hand-crafted baskets.

Winsted

❹ *9 southeast of Norfolk, 28 mi north of Waterbury, 25 mi northwest of Hartford.*

With its rows of old homes and businesses seemingly untouched since the 1940s, Winsted still looks a bit like the set of a Frank Capra movie. Though it's far less fashionable than nearby Norfolk, the town, which was devastated by a major flood in 1955, is still worth a brief stop. You can drive around the hills and alongside the reservoirs, hoping to glimpse the notorious "Winsted Wild Man," who has been described during sightings that span a couple centuries as possessing everything from cloven feet to an upright, hairy, 8-ft, 300-pound frame. Authorities explain away these stories as black bear sightings, but you never know.

Most of the several hundred hanging and standing lamps at the **Kerosene Lamp Museum,** which occupies a former country store, date from 1852 to 1880. ⊠ *100 Old Waterbury Turnpike/Rte. 263, Win-*

chester Center (4 mi west of Winsted), ☎ *860/379–2612.* ⊡ *Free.* ☉ *Daily 9:30–4.*

Camping

⚠ **White Pines Campsites.** There are wooded sites and swimming, hiking, and fishing on the premises of this campground, which also has a pool, a game room, a snack bar, and a rec hall. ⊠ *232 Old North Rd.,* ☎ *860/379–0124.* ⊡ *$26. 206 sites. Electric hook-ups, fire rings, flush toilets, showers, water. Closed mid-Oct.–mid-Apr.*

Nightlife

The **Gilson Café and Cinema** (⊠ 354 Main St., ☎ 860/379–6069), a refurbished Art Deco movie house, serves food and drinks unobtrusively during movies, every evening except Monday. You must be 21 or older for most shows.

Outdoor Activities and Sports

Main Stream Canoe Corp. (⊠ Rte. 44, New Hartford, ☎ 860/693–6791) rents and sells canoes and conducts flat-water and white-water day trips on the Farmington River. Moonlight trips take place on summer evenings. **North American Canoe Tours** (⊠ Satan's Kingdom State Recreation Area, Rte. 44, New Hartford, ☎ 860/739–0791) rents tubes and flotation devices for exhilarating self-guided tours along the Farmington River. The company is open for business from Memorial Day to June on weekends and daily from June to Labor Day.

Shopping

Folkcraft Instruments (⊠ Corner of High and Wheeler Sts., ☎ 860/379–9857) crafts harps and psalteries on the premises.

Skiing

Ski Sundown. This area has some neat touches—a sundeck on the top of the mountain and a Senior Spree social club for skiers 55 and older—as well as excellent facilities and equipment. The vertical drop is 625 ft. Of the 15 trails, 8 are for beginners, 4 for intermediates, and 3 for advanced skiers. All are lit at night and serviced by three triple chairs and one double. Terrain features are set up on the mountain; lessons are available for ages 4 and up. ⊠ *Ratlum Rd., New Hartford, 06057,* ☎ *860/379–9851; 860/379–7669 for conditions.*

Riverton

🚃 *6 mi north of Winsted.*

Almost every New Englander has sat in a Hitchcock chair. Riverton, formerly Hitchcockville, is where Lambert Hitchcock built the first one in 1826. The Farmington and Still rivers meet in this tiny hamlet. It's one of the more unspoiled regions in the Hills, great for hiking and driving.

The **Hitchcock Museum** is in the gray granite Union Church; the nearby Hitchcock Factory Store, which sells first-quality merchandise at outlet prices and also has a seconds department, is open year-round. ⊠ *Rte. 20,* ☎ *860/379–4826.* ⊡ *Donation suggested.* ☉ *By appointment only.*

Lodging

$$ 🏨 **Old Riverton Inn.** This historic inn, built in 1796 and overlooking the west branch of the Farmington River and the Hitchcock Chair Factory, is a peaceful weekend retreat. Rooms are small—except for the fireplace suite—and the decorating, which includes Hitchcock furnishings, is for the most part ordinary, but the inn always delivers warm hospitality. The inviting dining room serves traditional New England fare—the stuffed pork chops are local favorites. ⊠ *Rte. 20, 06065,* ☎ *860/379–8678 or 800/378–1796,* FAX *860/379–1006. 11 rooms, 1 suite. Restaurant. AE, D, DC, MC, V.*

Outdoor Activities and Sports

American Legion & People's State Forests (☎ 860/379–2469) border the west bank and the east bank, respectively, of this West Branch of the Farmington River—a stretch that has been designated a National Wild and Scenic River. Superb hiking, fishing, tubing, and canoeing can be had on each bank.

Torrington

46 *14 mi south of Riverton.*

Torrington is birthplace of abolitionist John Brown. Also born here was Gail Borden, who developed the first successful method for the production of evaporated milk. Torrington's pines were for years used for shipbuilding, and its factories produced brass kettles, needles, pins, and bicycle spokes.

The **Hotchkiss-Fyler House,** a 16-room century-old Queen Anne structure with a slate and brick exterior, is one of the better house museums in Connecticut. The design high points include hand-stenciled walls and intricate mahogany woodwork and ornamental plaster. European porcelains, American and British glass, and paintings by Winfield S. Clime are on display. If you'll be arriving around noon on a weekday, call ahead; the house sometimes closes briefly at lunchtime. ⊠ *192 Main St.,* ☎ *860/482–8260.* ⊡ *$2.* ☉ *Tours Apr.–Oct. and last 2 wks of Dec., Tues.–Fri. 10–4, Sat. noon–4.*

OFF THE BEATEN PATH

GOSHEN – Once a dairy farming center, this town 5 mi west of Torrington hosts one of the best agricultural fairs in the Northeast on Labor Day weekend. It's also the home of **Nodine's Smokehouse** (⊠ Rte. 63, ☎ 860/491–4009), known statewide for smoked meats with just the right blend of hickory and hardwood flavors.

Nightlife and the Arts

The **Warner Theatre** (⊠ 68 Main St., ☎ 860/489–7180), an Art Deco former movie palace, presents live Broadway musicals, ballet, and concerts by touring pop, classical, and country musicians. The Warner's **Studio Theatre** (⊠ 69 Main St.) is a small dinner theater that presents children's and cabaret-style shows.

Outdoor Activities and Sports

The lures at 88-acre **Burr Pond State Park** (⊠ Burr Mountain Rd./Rte. 8, ☎ 860/482–1817) include canoe rentals, crystal-clear swimming areas, hiking paths, and wheelchair-accessible picnic grounds.

Litchfield

47 *5 mi south of Torrington, 48 mi north of Bridgeport, 34 mi west of Hartford.*

Everything in Litchfield, the wealthiest and most noteworthy town in the Litchfield Hills, seems to exist on a larger scale than in neighboring burgs, especially the impressive **Litchfield Green** and the white Colonials that line the broad elm-shaded streets. Harriet Beecher Stowe and Henry Ward Stowe were born and raised in Litchfield, and many famous Americans earned their law degrees here. During the infamous Stove Wars of the late 18th century, worshipers vehemently debated the burning issue of whether a church would retain its sanctity if heated by a stove. By 1790, with a population exceeding 20,000, Litchfield had become the third most populous town in America.

The **Tapping Reeve House** held the Litchfield Law School, which was founded in 1773. Aaron Burr, Horace Mann, John C. Calhoun, and Noah Webster are among the prominent graduates of America's first law school—six U.S. cabinet members, 26 U.S. senators, more than 100 members of Congress, and dozens of Supreme Court justices, governors, and college presidents are among the school's alumni. A recent renovation of the house included the installation of interpretive exhibits about the school and its graduates. ⊠ *82 South St.,* ☎ *860/567–4501.* ⊡ *$5 (includes Litchfield Historical Society Museum).* ☉ *Mid-May–mid-Oct., Tues.–Sat 11–5, Sun. 1–5.*

The well-organized galleries at the **Litchfield Historical Society Museum** display decorative arts, paintings, and antique furnishings. There's also an extensive reference library, where you can find information about the town's many historic buildings, including the Sheldon Tavern (where George Washington slept on several occasions) and the Pierce Academy, America's first school for girls. ⊠ *7 South St., at Rtes. 63 and 118,* ☎ *860/567–4501.* ⊡ *$5 (includes Tapping Reeve House).* ☉ *Mid-Apr.–mid-Nov., Tues.–Sat. 11–5, Sun. 1–5.*

A stroll through the grounds of **White Flower Farm** is nearly always a pleasure. The farm is the home base of a mail-order operation that sells perennials and bulbs to gardeners throughout the United States. ⊠ *Rte. 63 (3 mi south of Litchfield),* ☎ *860/567–8789.* ⊡ *Free.* ☉ *Nov.–Mar., daily 10–5; Apr.–Oct., daily 9–6.*

Haight Vineyard and Winery flourishes despite the area's severe climate. Stop in for vineyard walks, winery tours, and tastings. ⊠ *Chestnut Hill Rd./Rte. 118 (1 mi east of Litchfield),* ☎ *860/567–4045.* ⊡ *Free.* ☉ *Mon.–Sat. 10:30–5, Sun. noon–5.*

The Catholic Montfort Missionaries built and operate the **Lourdes of Litchfield Shrine,** a 35-acre complex a short drive from the village green that contains a replica of the famous grotto at Lourdes, France. During pilgrimage season, from mid-May to October, outdoor Mass is held daily except Monday at 11:30 AM; Holy Hour is at 3. Picnickers are welcome at any time. ⊠ *Rte. 118,* ☎ *860/567–1041.* ☉ *Grounds year-round dawn–dusk.*

The **White Memorial Foundation** is Connecticut's largest nature center and wildlife sanctuary. The 4,000-acre sanctuary contains fishing areas, bird-watching platforms, two self-guided nature trails, several boardwalks, and 35 mi of hiking, cross-country skiing, and horseback-riding trails. The main conservation center houses natural-history exhibits and a gift shop. ⊠ *Rte. 202 (2 mi west of village green),* ☎ *860/567–0857.* ⊡ *Grounds free; conservation center $2.* ☉ *Grounds 24 hrs; conservation center spring–fall, Mon.–Sat. 9–5, Sun. noon–5; winter, weekdays 8:30–4:30, Sat. 9–4:30, Sun. noon–4.*

The chief attractions at **Topsmead State Forest** are a Tudor-style cottage built by architect Henry Dana Jr. and a 40-acre wildflower preserve. The forest holds picnic grounds, hiking trails, and cross-country skiing areas. ⊠ *Buell Rd. off E. Litchfield Rd.,* ☎ *860/567–5694.* ⊡ *Free.* ☉ *8 AM–dusk.*

Dining and Lodging

$$$ ✕ **West Street Grill.** Many of Connecticut's up-and-coming chefs have
★   gotten their starts cooking for the glamorous patrons of this urbane dining room on Litchfield's historic green. Imaginative grilled fish, steak, poultry, and lamb dishes are served with fresh vegetables and pasta or

risotto. The grilled Parmesan aioli bread is superb. ⊠ *43 West St./Rte. 202,* ☎ *860/567–3885. AE, MC, V.*

$$–$$$ ✕ **Village Restaurant.** The folks who run this storefront eatery in a red-brick town house serve food as tasty as any in town—inexpensive pub grub in one room, updated New England cuisine in the other. Whether you order burgers or homemade ravioli, you'll get plenty to eat. ⊠ *25 West St.,* ☎ *860/567–8307. AE, MC, V.*

$$$ ✕▣ **Tollgate Hill Inn and Restaurant.** The Tollgate, formerly a stage-coach stop, retains a romantic tavern atmosphere. The menu, however, is contemporary: The walnut-crusted roast rack of lamb with apple-dried cherry chutney is one good choice. Vibrant Colonial prints and comfortable period furnishings decorate the guest rooms, which are in the main building, a nearby schoolhouse, and a modern building; many have working fireplaces. ⊠ *Rte. 202 (2½ mi east of Litchfield Center), 06759,* ☎ *860/567–4545,* ℻ *860/567–8397. 15 rooms, 5 suites. Restaurant. Continental breakfast. AE, D, DC, MC, V.*

Outdoor Activities and Sports

Lee's Riding Stables (⊠ 57 E. Litchfield Rd., ☎ 860/567–0785) conducts trail and pony rides. At **Mt. Tom State Park** (⊠ Rte. 202, ☎ 860/868–2592), you can boat, hike, and fish in summer and ice-skate in winter. The view from atop the mountain is outstanding.

Shopping

Black Swan Antiques (⊠ 17 Litchfield Commons, Rte. 202, ☎ 860/567–4429) carries 17th- and 18th-century English and Continental country furniture. **Carretta Glass Studio** (⊠ 513 Maple St., ☎ 860/567–4851) sells remarkable glass sculptures and works that are made on the premises. The **P.S. Gallery** (⊠ 41 West St., ☎ 860/567–1059) is an excellent fine-arts gallery. **Susan Wakeen Dolls** (⊠ 425 Bantam Rd., ☎ 860/567–0007) stocks limited-edition and play dolls.

Bristol

㊽ *17 mi southeast of Litchfield.*

There were some 275 clock makers in and around Bristol during the late 1800s—it is said that by the end of the 19th century just about every household in America told time to a Connecticut clock. Eli Terry (for which nearby Terryville is named) first mass-produced clocks in the mid-19th century. Seth Thomas (for which nearby Thomaston is named) learned under Terry and carried on the tradition.

☏ **Lake Compounce,** which opened in 1846, is the oldest continuously operating amusement park in the country. New owners have doubled the number of rides and attractions at the 325-acre facility; these include an antique carousel, a classic wooden roller coaster, and a white-water raft ride. There are also picnic areas, a beach, and a water playground with slides, spray fountains, and a wave pool. ⊠ *Rte. 229 N, I–84 Exit 31,* ☎ *860/583–3631.* ☜ *$19.95 rides and general admission; $4.95 general admission.* ☉ *Memorial Day–late Sept., call for hrs.*

You can see examples of more than 1,800 New England–made clocks and watches at the **American Clock and Watch Museum,** one of the most interesting and charming museums in the state. Try to arrive on the hour, when 300 clocks strike in close succession. ⊠ *100 Maple St., south of Rte. 6,* ☎ *860/583–6070.* ☜ *$3.50.* ☉ *Apr.–Nov., daily 10–5.*

★ The **Carousel Museum of New England** displays carousel art, much of it full-size pieces, in the Coney Island, Country Fair, and Philadelphia styles. Miniature carousels are also on display, and there's an antique carving shop where volunteers occasionally demonstrate the craft. ⊠

95 Riverside Ave., ☎ 860/585–5411. 🖾 $4. ☉ Apr.–Nov., Mon.–Sat. 10–5, Sun. noon–5; Dec.–Mar., Thurs.–Sat. 10–5, Sun. noon–5.

Lodging

$$ 🏨 **Chimney Crest Manor.** All the rooms in this impressive circa-1930 Tudor mansion have spectacular views of the Farmington Valley. The 40-ft-long Garden Suite, in what was the mansion's ballroom, has gleaming hardwood floors, a fireplace, a queen-size canopy bed, its own kitchen, and tile walls with a dazzling sunflower motif. The Manor View Suite has a Thermo-Spa. Breakfast, which might include yogurt pancakes or yummy strawberry bread, is served on fine china in the formal dining room or, more casually, on the grand fieldstone patio. You can lounge in the cherry-panel library, the bright Spanish-tile sunroom, or by a fireplace in the main salon. 🖂 5 Founders Dr., 06010, ☎ 860/582–4219, FAX 860/584–5903. 2 rooms, 4 suites. Full breakfast. MC, V.

Bethlehem

㊾ 16 mi west of Bristol.

Come Christmas, Bethlehem is the most popular town in Connecticut. Cynics say that towns such as Canaan, Goshen, and Bethlehem were named primarily with the hope of attracting prospective residents and not truly out of religious deference. In any case, the local post office has its hands full postmarking the 220,000 pieces of holiday greetings mailed from Bethlehem every December.

The **Bethlehem Christmas Town Festival** (☎ 203/266–5702), which takes place in early December, draws quite a crowd. Year-round, the **Christmas Shop** (🖂 18 East St., ☎ 203/266–7048) hawks the trimmings and trappings that make for happy holidays.

The **Abbey of Regina Laudis** operates a shop that sells fine handcrafts, honey, cheese, herbs, beauty products, and more, all prepared by the abbey's Benedictine nuns. An 18th-century Neopolitan crèche with 80 hand-painted Baroque porcelain figures is on view from March to December. 🖂 Flanders Rd., ☎ 203/266–7637. ☉ Mon.–Tues. and Thurs.–Sun. 10–4.

Washington

㊿ 11 mi west of Bethlehem.

The beautiful buildings of the Gunnery prep school mingle with stately Colonials and churches in Washington, one of the best-preserved Colonial towns in Connecticut. The Mayflower Inn, south of the Gunnery on Route 47, attracts an exclusive clientele. Washington, which was settled in 1734, became in 1779 the first town in the United States to be named for George Washington.

Dining and Lodging

$$ ✕ **G.W. Tavern.** The walls of the main dining room here are covered with a mural depicting the surrounding countryside as it used to be. The cuisine, too, is reminiscent of once-upon-a-time: meat loaf, chicken potpie, roast beef with Yorkshire pudding. A stone terrace for warm-weather dining overlooks the Shepaug River where Bee Brook joins in. 🖂 20 Bee Brook Rd., ☎ 860/868–6633. AE, D, DC, MC, V. Closed Mon. No lunch weekends.

$$$$ ✕🏨 **Mayflower Inn.** Though the most expensive suites at this inn cost
★ as much as $580 a night, the Mayflower is always booked months in advance. And with good reason. The inn's 28 impeccably groomed acres are replete with running streams, rambling stone walls, and rare spec-

imen trees. Each of the rooms is an individual work of art with fine antiques, 18th- and 19th-century art, and four-poster canopy beds. The colossal baths have mahogany wainscoting, much marble, and handsome Belgian tapestries on the floors. At the restaurant ($$$–$$$$), chef Thomas Moran prepares mouthwatering cuisine like roast Muscovy duck breast on a barley, wheatberry, and vegetable risotto. ⊠ *118 Woodbury Rd./Rte. 47, 06793,* ☎ *860/868–9466,* ℻ *860/868–1497. 17 rooms, 8 suites. Restaurant, pool, tennis courts, health club, meeting rooms. AE, MC, V.*

En Route   The **Institute for American Studies,** between Roxbury and Washington, is an excellent and thoughtfully arranged collection of exhibits and displays that details the history of the state's Native Americans. Highlights include a replicated longhouse and nature trails. The Institute is at the end of a forested residential road (just follow the signs from Route 199). ⊠ *Curtis Rd. off Rte. 199,* ☎ *860/868–0518.* 🎦 *$4.* ☉ *Jan.–Mar., Wed.–Sat. 10–5, Sun. noon–5; Apr.–Dec., Mon.– Sat. 10–5, Sun. noon–5.*

Woodbury

⑤   *12 mi east of Bridgewater.*

There may very well be more antiques shops in the quickly growing town of Woodbury than in all the towns in the rest of the Litchfield Hills combined. Five magnificent **churches** and the Greek Revival **King Solomon's Temple,** formerly a Masonic lodge, line Route 6; they represent some of the finest-preserved examples of Colonial religious architecture in New England.

The **Glebe House** is the large gambrel-roofed Colonial in which Dr. Samuel Seabury was elected America's first Episcopal bishop in 1783. It holds an excellent collection of antiques. Horticulturist Gertrude Jekyll designed the historic garden here. ⊠ *Hollow Rd.,* ☎ *203/263–2855.* 🎦 *$4.* ☉ *Apr.–Nov., Wed.–Sun. 1–4, Dec.–Mar. by appointment.*

Dining and Lodging

$$$ ✕ **Good News Café.** Carole Peck is a kitchenhold name in these parts,
★   and her decision to open a restaurant in Woodbury was met with cheers. The emphasis is on healthful, innovative fare: venison filet mignon with a horseradish crust in grilled onions and snowpeas with a cabernet-cherry sauce; wok-seared shrimp with new potatoes, grilled green beans, and a garlic aioli. You can drop by for cappuccino and munchies in a separate room decorated with fascinating vintage radios. ⊠ *694 Main St. S,* ☎ *203/266–4663. AE, MC, V. Closed Tues.*

$ ✕ **Charcoal Chef.** Sprung straight from the 1950s, this eatery with knotty pine paneling is the real thing. Feast on charcoal-broiled halibut, chicken, steaks, or burgers served with a baked potato or fries and coleslaw. The bartender pours generous drinks. ⊠ *670 Main St. N (Rte. 6 on the way to Watertown),* ☎ *203/263–2538. No credit cards.*

$–$$$ 🎦 **Curtis House.** Connecticut's oldest inn (1754), at the foot of Woodbury's antiques row, may also be its cheapest; some rooms are even under $50. The inn has seen dozens of alterations and renovations over the years, including a complete $400 overhaul in 1900, but the floorboards still creak like whoopie cushions, and the TVs in some rooms look to be from the Ed Sullivan era. A fireplace roars downstairs, where the restaurant serves filling dishes in the steak-and-potato genre. ⊠ *506 Main St./Rte. 6, 06798,* ☎ *203/263–2101. 12 rooms with bath, 6 rooms share baths. Restaurant. D, MC, V.*

$$ 🎦 **Tucker Hill Inn.** Susan Cebelenski runs this B&B in her 1923 Colo-
★   nial-style clapboard home, which has spacious rooms with cable TV

and VCRs and country-style furnishings. The location is great—about 40 minutes from both New Haven and Hartford. ⊠ *96 Tucker Hill Rd., Middlebury 06762,* ☎ *203/758–8334,* FAX *203/598–0652. 2 rooms with bath, 2 rooms share bath. Full breakfast. AE, MC, V.*

Shopping

British Country Antiques (⊠ 50 Main St. N, ☎ 203/263–5100) imports polished pine and country furniture from England and France. **Country Loft Antiques** (⊠ 557 Main St. S, ☎ 203/266–4500) sells 18th- and 19th-century European furniture and accessories. **David Dunton** (⊠ Rte. 132 off Rte. 47, ☎ 203/263–5355) is a respected dealer of formal American Federal furniture. **Mill House Antiques** (⊠ 1068 Main St. N, ☎ 203/263–3446) carries formal and country English and French furniture and has the state's largest collection of Welsh dressers. **Monique Shay** (⊠ 920 Main St. S, ☎ 203/263–3186) stocks French-Canadian country antiques. At the **Woodbury Pewterers** (⊠ 860 Main St. S., ☎ 203/263–2668) factory store you'll find discounts on fine reproductions of Early American tankards, Revere bowls, candlesticks, and more.

Skiing

Woodbury Ski Area. This ski area with a 300-ft vertical drop has 18 downhill trails of varying difficulty that are serviced by a double chairlift, three rope tows, a handle tow, and a T-bar. About two-thirds of the 20 km (12 mi) of cross-country trails are groomed, and 2 km (1 mi) are lighted and covered by snowmaking when necessary. There's an extensive snowboard and alpine park, a skateboard and in-line skating park, and a special area for sledding and tubing serviced by two lifts and three tows. Ski parties are held on Friday and Saturday nights in the base lodge; lessons are given for adults and for children ages 2 and up. ⊠ *Rte. 47, Woodbury 06798,* ☎ *203/263–2203.*

Southbury

52 *6 mi south of Woodbury, 36 mi south of Winsted, 18 mi northwest of New Haven.*

Southbury, a former agricultural community with well-preserved Colonial homes and many antiques shops, has been heavily developed. Like New Milford to the west, the town acts as the bridge between southern Connecticut's modern suburbia and the Litchfield Hills' pre-20th-century charm.

Lodging

$$$ 🏨 **Heritage Inn.** You may be disappointed if you come here expecting to find a quaint country inn—the rooms and public areas have a contrived rusticity about them. Still, as far as resorts go, the Heritage has plenty to offer, and its several meal plans are good values. ⊠ *Heritage Village, 06488,* ☎ *203/264–8200 or 800/932–3466,* FAX *203/264–5035. 160 rooms, 3 suites. Restaurant, bar, 18-hole and 9-hole golf course, 3 tennis courts, recreation room. AE, D, DC, MC, V.*

Outdoor Activities and Sports

G.E.M. Morgans (⊠ 75 N. Poverty Rd., ☎ 203/264–6196) conducts hay and carriage rides using registered Morgan horses. **Steppin' Up Balloons** (☎ 203/264–0013) operates flights above the Litchfield Hills.

Waterbury

53 *15 mi northeast of Southbury, 28 mi southwest of Hartford, 28 mi north of Bridgeport.*

Waterbury may well be one of America's gloomiest cities, but civic leaders have plans to remedy that. Many of the several dozen important buildings in the historic downtown district date back to the days when the city was the cradle of the brass industry in the United States. The dramatic 240-ft **Clock Tower** (389 Meadow St.) was modeled after the city hall tower in Siena, Italy.

Stop by the **Waterbury Region Convention and Visitors Bureau** (✉ 21 Church St., ☎ 203/597–9527) to pick up literature that contains a detailed and fascinating self-guided walking tour of the downtown area.

The **Mattatuck Museum** has a fine collection of 19th- and 20th-century Connecticut art and memorabilia documenting the state's industrial history. ✉ *144 W. Main St.,* ☎ *203/753–0381.* ▨ *Free.* ☯ *Tues.–Sat. 10–5; Sept.–mid-June, also Sun. noon–5.*

Dining and Lodging

$$$ ✕ **Carmen Anthony Steak House.** A worthy re-creation of the steak
★ houses of old, Carmen Anthony has rich wood paneling, handsome oil paintings on the walls, and white linen on the tables. You can order Delmonico, filet mignon, porterhouse, and other steaks; the popular "Italian" steaks are served on a bed of rotini pasta. ✉ *496 Chase Ave.,* ☎ *203/757–3040. AE, D, DC, MC, V. No lunch.*

$$$ ✕ **Diorio Restaurant and Bar.** The dining room at Diorio, a Waterbury
★ tradition for more than a half-century, retains its original mahogany bankers' booth, marble brass bar, high tin ceilings, exposed brick, and white-tile floors. The dishes here are expertly prepared, from the juicy shrimp scampi to the dozens of pasta, chicken, veal, steak, and seafood plates. ✉ *231 Bank St.,* ☎ *203/754–5111. AE, DC, MC, V. Closed Sun. No lunch Sat.*

$$–$$$ ✕▨ **House on the Hill.** Owner-innkeeper Marianne Vandenburgh's fanciful B&B is surrounded by lush gardens in a historic hillside neighborhood. The three-story 1888 Victorian has a glorious exterior color scheme of teal, sage-green, red, and ivory. The accommodations here are furnished in a welcoming blend of antiques and nostalgia. ✉ *92 Woodbury Terr., 06710,* ☎ *203/757–9901. 4 suites. No credit cards. Closed Dec. 15–Jan. 15.*

Nightlife and the Arts

Seven Angels Theatre (✉ Hamilton Park Pavilion, Plank Rd., ☎ 203/757–4676) presents top-rate plays, musicals, children's theater, cabaret concerts, and youth programs.

Outdoor Activities and Sports

Watershed Balloons (☎ 860/274–2010) operates flights over the Litchfield Hills.

Shopping

Howland-Hughes (✉ 120 Bank St., ☎ 203/753–4121) is stocked entirely with items made in Connecticut, from Wiffle balls to Pez candies, fine pottery to glassware.

Litchfield Hills A to Z

Arriving and Departing

BY BUS

Bonanza Bus Lines (☎ 800/556–3815) operates daily buses between New York City's Port Authority terminal and Southbury.

BY CAR

Route 44 west and Route 6 south are the most direct routes from Hartford to the Litchfield Hills. To get here from New York, take I–684 to I–84, from which the roads off Exits 7 to 18 head northward into the Hills.

BY PLANE
The nearest airport to the Litchfield Hills region is Hartford's **Bradley International Airport** (☞ Connecticut River Valley A to Z, *above*).

Getting Around

BY BUS
There is no local bus service in the Litchfield Hills.

BY CAR
Route 7 winds from New Milford through Kent, Cornwall Bridge, Cornwall, and West Cornwall to Canaan. Sharon is west of Route 7 on Route 4; continue north from Sharon on Route 41 to get to Lakeville and Salisbury. Route 44 heading east from Salisbury passes through Canaan, Norfolk, and Winsted. Route 63 travels southeast from South Canaan through Litchfield to Waterbury; at Watertown head west from Route 63 on Route 6 and north on Route 61 to get to Bethlehem. Southbury is at the junction of Route 6 and I–84. Route 8, the main north–south road through the eastern part of the Litchfield Hills, passes through Winsted, Torrington, and Waterbury; Bristol is east of Route 8 off Route 6, and Riverton is east of Route 8 on Route 20.

Contacts and Resources

EMERGENCIES
New Milford Hospital (✉ 21 Elm St., ☎ 860/355–2611). **Sharon Hospital** (✉ 50 Hospital Hill Rd., ☎ 860/364–4141).

24-HOUR PHARMACY
CVS (✉ 627 Farmington Ave., Bristol, ☎ 860/583–8351).

VISITOR INFORMATION
Litchfield Hills Travel Council (✉ Box 968, Litchfield 06759, ☎ 860/567–4506).

NEW HAVEN AND THE SOUTHEASTERN COAST

As you drive northeast along I–95, culturally rich New Haven is the final urban obstacle between southwestern Connecticut's overdeveloped coast and southeastern Connecticut's quieter shoreline villages. The remainder of the jagged coast, which stretches all the way to the Rhode Island border, consists of small coastal villages, quiet hamlets, and undisturbed beaches—the only interruptions along this mostly undeveloped seashore are the industry and piers of New London and Groton. Mystic, Stonington, Old Saybrook, and Guilford are havens for fans of antiques and boutiques. North of Groton, near the town of Ledyard, the Mashantucket Pequots Reservation owns and operates the Foxwoods casino. The Mohegan Indians run the Mohegan Sun casino in Uncasville.

Some call southeastern Connecticut the charter- and party-boat capital of New England. Charter fishing boats take passengers for half-day, full-day, and some overnight trips at fees from $20 to $35 per person; tuna-fishing trips may cost as much as $100 a day. Charter companies in the towns covered below are listed in the Outdoor Activities and Sports sections.

Numbers in the margin correspond to points of interest on the Southeastern Connecticut map.

New Haven

🛈 *46 mi northeast of Greenwich, 36 mi south of Hartford, 59 mi southeast of Norfolk.*

New Haven is a city of extremes. The historic district surrounding Yale University and the shops, museums, theaters, and restaurants on nearby **Chapel Street** prosper, but roughly 20% of the city's residents live below the poverty level. The areas away from the campus and city common can be unsafe at night.

New Haven is a manufacturing center dating from the 19th century, but the city owes its fame to Elihu Yale. In 1718, Yale who had amassed a fortune as a trader, enabled the Collegiate School, founded in 1701,
★ to settle in New Haven, where it changed its name to **Yale University** to honor its benefactor. The university's knowledgeable guides conduct one-hour walking tours that include Connecticut Hall in the Old Campus, which counts Nathan Hale, William Howard Taft, and Noah Webster among its past residents. ✉ *149 Elm St.,* ☎ *203/432–2300.* ☾ *Tours weekdays at 10:30 and 2, weekends at 1:30. Tours start from 149 Elm St. on north side of New Haven Green.*

James Gamble Rogers, an American architect, designed many buildings for Yale, his alma mater, including the **Sterling Memorial Library** (✉ 120 High St., ☎ 203/432–2798), which he built to be "a cathedral of knowledge and a temple of learning." This is evident in the major interior area, which resembles a Gothic cathedral. The **Beinecke Rare Book and Manuscript Library** (✉ 121 Wall St., ☎ 203/432–2977) houses major collections, including a Gutenberg Bible, illuminated manuscripts, and original Audubon bird prints.

The **Yale University Art Gallery,** the country's oldest college art museum (it opened in 1832), contains American, African, and Near and Far Eastern art, as well as Renaissance paintings and European art of the 20th century. There's a remarkable reconstruction of a Mithraic shrine here. ✉ *1111 Chapel St.,* ☎ *203/432–0600.* ▦ *Free.* ☾ *Tues.– Sat. 10–5, Sun. 1–6.*

☉ The **Peabody Museum of Natural History** opened in 1876; with more than 9 million specimens, it's one of the largest natural history museums in the nation. Some of the best exhibits survey dinosaurs, meteorites, and Andean, Mesoamerican, and Pacific cultures. ✉ *170 Whitney Ave.,* ☎ *203/432–5050.* ▦ *$5.* ☾ *Mon.–Sat. 10–4:45, Sun. noon–4:45.*

The **Yale Center for British Art** has the most comprehensive collection of British art outside of Britain. The center's skylit galleries, designed by Louis I. Kahn, contain works by Constable, Hogarth, Gainsborough, Reynolds, and Turner, to name but a few. You'll also find rare books and paintings documenting English history. Most of the museum closed in 1998 for structural and cosmetic improvements, but the facility is scheduled to be back in full operation in 1999. ✉ *1080 Chapel St.,* ☎ *203/432–2800.* ▦ *Free.* ☾ *Tues.–Sat. 10–5, Sun. noon–5.*

The most notable example of the Yale campus's neo-Gothic architecture is the **Harkness Tower** (✉ High St.), built between 1917 and 1921, which was modeled on St. Botolph's Tower in Boston, England. The university's famous motto, inscribed on Memorial Gate near the Tower, is sometimes described as the world's greatest anticlimax: "For God, for country, and for Yale." Bordered on one side by the Yale campus, the **New Haven Green** (✉ between Church and College Sts.) is a fine example of urban planning. As early as 1638, village elders set aside the 16-acre plot as a town common. Three early 19th-century churches— the Gothic-style **Trinity Episcopal Church,** the Georgian-style **Center Congregational Church,** and the predominantly Federal **United Church**— contribute to its present appeal.

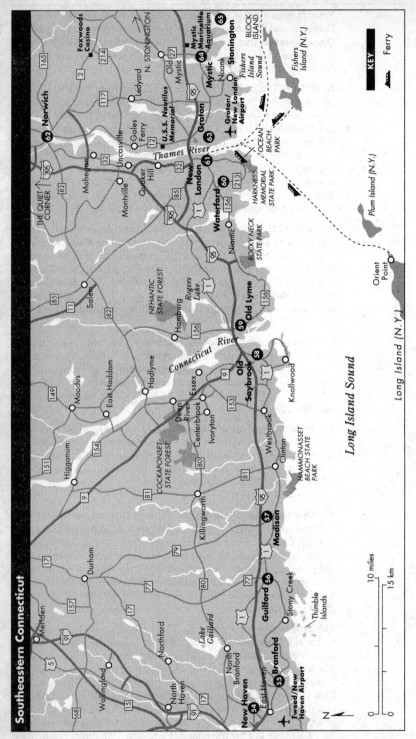

74

Southeastern Connecticut

KEY
⚓ Ferry

Long Island Sound

Long Island (N.Y.)

Orient Point

Plum Island (N.Y.)

Fishers Island (N.Y.)

BLOCK ISLAND

Fishers Island Sound

OCEAN BEACH PARK

65 Mystic Marinelife Aquarium
64 Mystic
Stonington
N. Stonington
Old Mystic
Noank
Foxwoods Casino

63 Groton/New London Airport
61 New London
60 Waterford
59 Old Lyme
58 Old Saybrook
57 Madison
56 Guilford
55 Branford
54 New Haven

62 Norwich

U.S.S. Nautilus Memorial
Ledyard
Gales Ferry
Uncasville
Quaker Hill
Mohegan
Montville
Salem
Hamburg
Moodus
East Haddam
Hadlyme
Higganum
Deep River
Essex
Ivoryton
Centerbrook
Westbrook
Clinton
Knollwood
Killingworth
Durham
Northford
North Branford
North Haven
Wallingford
Meriden
East Haven

Thames River
Connecticut River

HARKNESS MEMORIAL STATE PARK
ROCKY NECK STATE PARK
NEHANTIC STATE FOREST
Rogers Lake
COCKAPONSET STATE FOREST
HAMMONASSET BEACH STATE PARK
Lake Gaillard
Stony Creek
Thimble Islands
Tweed/New Haven Airport

THE QUIET CORNER ↑

Niantic

Rivers Lake

10 miles
15 km

N

Dining and Lodging

$$$ ✕ **Caffé Adulis.** High ceilings and exposed brick lend this trendy Ethiopian restaurant a comfortable, contemporary feel. The house specialty is shrimp *barka* (shrimp in a tomato-basil sauce with unsweetened coconut, dates, Parmesan cheese, and a touch of light cream). Another worthy northeast African entrée is *tibsies,* a fajita-like affair. There are several vegetarian dishes, including fragrant stews and fresh greens. ✉ *228 College St.,* ☎ *203/777–5081. Reservations not accepted. AE, MC, V. No lunch Sun.–Wed.*

$$$ ✕ **Union League Café.** Creative twists enliven this café's seasonally changing country-French menu. Among the past dishes are the lobster and bay-scallop terrine and the roasted Norwegian salmon with chanterelles and cranberry butter. The menu is prix fixe on Sunday. ✉ *1032 Chapel St.,* ☎ *203/562–4299. AE, MC, V. No lunch weekends.*

$$–$$$ ✕ **Pika Tapas Café.** Chic and colorful, this cosmopolitan café serves
★ delicate Spanish hors d'oeuvres meant for sharing; each region in Spain is well represented on the menu. *Gambas al ajilo* (shrimp sautéed in a pungent good-to-the-last-drop garlic sauce) and a Portobello mushroom on garlic toast are among the popular tapas. A few salads and entrées— the paella is a standout—are also prepared. ✉ *39 High St.,* ☎ *203/ 865–1933. AE, MC, V. No lunch Sun.*

$ ✕ **Frank Pepe's.** Does this place serve the best pizza in the world, as
★ some reviewers claim? If it doesn't, it comes darn close. Pizza is the only thing prepared here—try the famous white-clam pie, and you won't be disappointed. Expect to wait an hour or more for a table—or, on weekend evenings, come after 10. The Spot (☎ 203/865–7602), right behind the restaurant, is owned by Pepe's and is usually open when Pepe's is not. ✉ *157 Wooster St.,* ☎ *203/865–5762. Reservations not accepted. No credit cards. Closed Tues. No lunch Mon. and Wed.–Thurs.*

$ ✕ **Louis' Lunch.** This All-American luncheonette on the National Register of Historic Places claims to be the birthplace of the hamburger in America. The first-rate burgers are cooked in an old-fashioned, upright broiler and served with either a slice of tomato or cheese on two slices of toast. (Don't even think about asking for ketchup.) ✉ *263 Crown St.,* ☎ *203/562–5507. No credit cards. Closed Sun.–Mon. No dinner.*

$$$ 🏠 **Three Chimneys Inn.** This 1870 Victorian mansion is one of the classi-
★ est small inns in the state. Rooms have posh Georgian furnishings: mahogany four-poster beds, oversize armoires, Chippendale desks, and luxurious Oriental rugs. Three rooms have fireplaces. ✉ *1201 Chapel St., 06511,* ☎ *203/789–1201,* 𝖥𝖠𝖷 *203/776–7363. 10 rooms. Business services, meeting rooms. Full breakfast. AE, MC, V.*

$$ 🏠 **New Haven Hotel.** A quiet hotel in the heart of the city, the New Haven has the feel of a small, exclusive hotel. But the amenities are those of a large facility. The freshly decorated rooms are comfortable and modern, and the restaurant serves innovative American cuisine. ✉ *229 George St., 06510,* ☎ *203/498–3100,* 𝖥𝖠𝖷 *203/498–3190. 92 rooms. Restaurant, bar, indoor lap pool, hot tub, business services, meeting rooms. AE, D, DC, MC, V.*

Nightlife and the Arts

NIGHTLIFE

BAR (✉ Crown St. at College St., ☎ 203/495–1111) is a cross between a nightclub, a brick-oven pizzeria, and a brew pub. **Daily Caffe** (✉ 316 Elm St., ☎ 203/776–5063) serves up late-night espresso, cappuccino, and live music to an artsy crowd. **Richter's** (✉ 990 Chapel St., ☎ 203/ 777–0400) is famous for its half-yard glasses of beer. Alternative and traditional rock bands play at **Toad's Place** (✉ 300 York St., ☎ 203/ 624–8263).

THE ARTS

The **Long Wharf Theatre** (⊠ 222 Sargent Dr., ☎ 203/787–4282) presents works by new writers and imaginative revivals of neglected classics. The **Shubert Performing Arts Center** (⊠ 247 College St., ☎ 203/562–5666) hosts musicals and dramas, usually following a run in the Big Apple, and also opera. The highly professional **Yale Repertory Theatre** (⊠ Chapel and York Sts., ☎ 203/432–1234) mounts world premieres and is known for its fresh interpretations of the classics.

The century-old **New Haven Symphony Orchestra** (☎ 203/865–0831) plays at Yale University's Woolsey Hall (⊠ College and Grove Sts.). The orchestra's Young People's Concerts series—the country's leading music program for children—is in its seventh decade. The **Oakdale Theatre** (⊠ 95 S. Turnpike Rd./Rte. 150, ☎ 203/265–1501) in Wallingford, 18 mi north of New Haven, presents nationally known theatrical and musical performances. **Yale School of Music** (☎ 203/432–4157) presents an impressive roster of performers, from classical to jazz; most events take place in the Morse Recital Hall in Sprague Memorial Hall (⊠ College and Wall Sts.).

Outdoor Activities and Sports

A public beach, nature trails, and a stunning antique carousel in a century-old beach pavilion are attractions of the 88-acre **Lighthouse Point Park** (⊠ Lighthouse Rd. off Rte. 337, ☎ 203/946–8005), in southeastern New Haven.

The **New Haven Ravens** (☎ 800/728–3671), the AA affiliate of the Colorado Rockies, play home games at Yale Field (⊠ Rte. 34/Derby Ave.).

The **Beast of New Haven** (☎ 203/777–7878), an American Hockey League team, plays at the New Haven Coliseum (⊠ S. Orange St. at George St., ☎ 203/772–4200).

Shopping

Chapel Street near the town green has a pleasing assortment of shops and eateries. **Arethusa Book Shop** (⊠ 87 Audubon St., ☎ 203/624–1848) carries a huge selection of out-of-print and used books, including first editions. Here you can pick up a handy guide to the many new and used bookstores in this university town.

En Route The oldest rapid-transit car and the world's first electric freight locomotive are among classic trolleys on display at the **Shoreline Trolley Museum.** Admission includes a 3-mi round-trip ride aboard a vintage trolley. ⊠ *17 River St., East Haven (midway between New Haven and Branford),* ☎ *203/467–6927.* ☞ *$5.* ⊙ *Memorial Day–Labor Day, daily 11–5; May, Sept.–Oct., and Dec., weekends 11–5; Apr. and Nov., Sun. 11–5.*

Branford

⑤⑤ *8 mi east of New Haven.*

The town of Branford, founded in 1644, was a prosperous port and the site of a saltworks that during the Revolutionary War provided salt to preserve food for the Continental Army. The small Branford village of Stony Creek, with a few tackle shops, a general store, and a marina, is the departure point for cruises to the **Thimble Islands.** This group of 365 tiny islands was named for its abundance of thimbleberries, which are similar to gooseberries. Legend has it that Captain Kidd buried pirate gold on one island. Two sightseeing vessels vie for your patronage, the *Volsunga IV* (☎ 203/481–3345 or 203/488–9978) and the *Sea Mist II* (☎ 203/488–8905). Both depart from Stony Creek Dock, at the end of Thimble Island Road, from May to Columbus Day.

Dining

$$ **✕ Le Petit Café.** The prix-fixe menu at this 15-table café focuses on
★ country dishes from southern France. For $21.50 you get fresh bread
and pâté, a tray of five or six appetizers (perhaps grilled leeks or sea-
weed salad), soup, an entrée (such as roast lamb or salmon au poivre),
and a dessert. Chef Roy Ip, the former sous chef at Raoul's in Man-
hattan, who recently bought the café, is working hard to maintain its
tradition of excellence. ⊠ *225 Montowese St.,* ☎ *203/483–9791.*
Reservations essential. MC, V. Closed Mon.–Tues. No lunch.

Shopping

Branford Craft Village (⊠ 779 E. Main St., ☎ 203/488–4689), on the
150-year-old, 85-acre Bittersweet Farm, contains a dozen crafts shops
and studios, an herbery, a barnyard petting zoo, an antiques shop, and
a small café. The village is closed Monday.

Guilford

56 *5 mi east of Stony Creek, 37 mi west of New London.*

The **Henry Whitfield State Museum** is the oldest house in the state and
the oldest stone house in New England. It was built by the Reverend
Henry Whitfield, an English minister who settled here in 1639. The
furnishings in the medieval-style building were made between the 17th
and 19th centuries. The visitors center contains two exhibition galleries
and a gift shop. ⊠ *248 Old Whitfield St.,* ☎ *203/453–2457.* ☜ *$3.*
☉ *Feb.–mid-Dec., Wed.–Sun. 10–4:30; mid-Dec.–Jan. by appoint-
ment.*

Dining

$$–$$$ **✕ Quattro's.** The two owner-chefs at Quattro's are Ecuadoran but
★ trained in the Italian style. Their menu includes familiar dishes such as
spaghetti and meatballs, but it's with the daily specials these pros really
cut loose. Look for delicacies like the smoky bacon-wrapped scallops
served over a bed of lobster sauce and the filet mignon topped with fresh
spinach, sautéed shrimp, and cognac sauce. ⊠ *1500 Boston Post Rd.,*
☎ *203/453–6575. Reservations essential. AE, D, DC, MC, V.*

Shopping

The **Guilford Handcrafts Center** (⊠ 411 Church St., ☎ 203/453–
5947) sponsors three major crafts exhibitions a year and has a shop.

Madison

57 *5 mi east of Guilford, 62 mi northeast of Greenwich.*

Coastal Madison has an understated charm. Ice-cream parlors, antiques
stores, and quirky gift boutiques prosper along Route 1, the town's
main street.

Hammonasset Beach State Park, the largest of the state's shoreline sanc-
tuaries, has a 2-mi beach, and a popular 550-site campground. ⊠ *I–
95, Exit 62,* ☎ *203/245–2785 for park; 203/245–1817 for campground.*
☜ *Park $5–$12 Apr.–Sept., free Oct.–Mar. Campground $12 year-
round.* ☉ *Park daily 8 AM–dusk.*

Dining, Lodging, and Camping

$$$–$$$$ **✕☰ Inn at Café Lafayette.** Skylights, painted murals, and handcrafted
woodwork are among the design accents at this airy hostelry in an
1830s converted church. The rooms may be small for the price, but
the decoration is immaculate, with beautiful fabrics and reproduction
17th- and 18th-century antique furniture. The modern marble baths
have telephones. Many local ingredients are used in the nouvelle

American cuisine prepared at the restaurant. ⊠ *725 Boston Post Rd.,*
06443, ☎ *203/245–7773,* ℻ *203/245–6256. 5 rooms. Restaurant,*
bar, business services. Continental breakfast. AE, DC, MC, V.

$ ⚠ **Riverdale Farm Campsite.** A rec hall, an adult lounge, a pond and
a river for swimming and fishing, and courts for tennis, basketball, and
shuffleboard are among the draws of this campground. There are
wooded and open campsites, and trailer and cabin rentals are available. ⊠ *111 River Rd., Clinton,* ☎ *860/669–5388.* ⌑ *$25. 222 sites,*
3 trailers, 1 cabin. Coin laundry, electric hook-ups, fireplaces, flush toi-
lets, showers, water. Closed Nov.–mid-Apr.

Shopping

The **Clayhouse** (⊠ 749 Boston Post Rd., ☎ 203/318–0399) is a fine
paint-your-own ceramic studio. **R. J. Julia Booksellers** (⊠ 768 Boston
Post Rd., ☎ 203/245–3959) is a past *Publishers Weekly* bookseller
of the year designee.

En Route The big-name discount stores at **Clinton Crossing Premium Outlets** (⊠
I–95, Exit 63, ☎ 860/664–0700) include Off 5th-Saks Fifth Avenue,
Donna Karan, and Lenox. Represented at **Westbrook Factory Stores** (⊠
I–95, Exit 65, ☎ 860/399–8656) are Carter's, Springmaid/Wamsutta,
Oneida, J. Crew, and Clifford & Wills.

Old Saybrook

⊕ *9 mi east of Madison, 29 mi east of New Haven.*

Old Saybrook, once a lively shipbuilding and fishing town, bustles with
summer vacationers.

Dining and Lodging

$$–$$$ ✕ **Aleia's.** The Old Saybrook Aleia's, a recent transplant from West-
★ brook, is as light, bright, and bountiful as the Italian countryside. Raf-
fia, silk flowers, and hand-painted plates from Capri decorate the
walls, and trompe l'oeil fruits, vegetables, and herbs adorn the table-
tops. Chef-owner Kimberly Snow takes a contemporary approach to
Italian cuisine by applying nouvelle touches to her mother's tried-and-
true recipes. ⊠ *1687 Boston Post Rd. ,* ☎ *860/399–5050. AE, MC,*
V. Closed Mon. No lunch.

$$ ✕ **Café Routier.** Duck-leg ragout in a rich red-wine sauce, fried oys-
★ ters with a chipotle remoulade, and steak au poivre with potatoes
Dauphinois are among the dishes served at this classy café. White
tablecloths and candlelight provide a fitting atmosphere in which to
enjoy the snappy French and American cuisine. ⊠ *1080 Boston Post*
Rd., ☎ *860/388–6270. AE, D, DC, MC, V. Closed Sun.–Mon. No*
lunch.

$$$$ ✕⌂ **Saybrook Point Inn & Spa.** Rooms at the Saybrook are furnished
with traditional British reproductions and Impressionist- and classi-
cal-style art. The health club and pools overlook the inn's marina and
the Connecticut River. The Terra Mar Grille serves stylish northern Ital-
ian cuisine, including Dijon-and-pistachio-crusted lamb with pear
compote. ⊠ *2 Bridge St., 06475,* ☎ *860/395–2000,* ℻ *860/388–1504.*
55 rooms, 7 suites. Restaurant, indoor pool, outdoor pool, spa, health
club, meeting rooms. AE, D, DC, MC, V.

$$$–$$$$ ✕⌂ **Water's Edge Inn & Resort.** With its spectacular setting on Long
★ Island Sound, this traditional weathered gray-shingle compound in West-
brook is one of the Connecticut shore's premier resorts. The main build-
ing has warm and bright public rooms furnished with antiques and
reproductions, and its upstairs bedrooms, with wall-to-wall carpeting
and clean, modern bathrooms, afford priceless views of the sound. Suites
in the surrounding outbuildings are not as nicely kept and lack the fine

views. ✉ *1525 Boston Post Rd., Westbrook, 06498,* ☎ *860/399–5901 or 800/222–5901,* ⟨FAX⟩ *860/399–6172. 100 rooms and suites. Restaurant, bar, indoor and outdoor pools, spa, health club, tennis courts, volleyball, beach, meeting rooms. AE, D, DC, MC, V.*

Outdoor Activities and Sports

Colvin Yachts (✉ Hammock Rd. S, Westbrook–Old Saybrook, ☎ 860/399–9300) rents and charters boats (sailboat rentals start at about $150 per day). Deep-sea fishing and private charter boats, whose rentals range from $400 for a half day to $500 and up for a full day, are available at **Sea Sprite Charters** (✉ 113 Harbor Pkwy., Clinton, ☎ 860/669–9613). Charters leave from Old Saybrook Point.

Shopping

More than 120 dealers operate out of the **Essex-Saybrook Antiques Village** (✉ 345 Middlesex Turnpike, ☎ 860/388–0689). **North Cove Outfitters** (✉ 75 Main St., ☎ 860/388–6585) is Connecticut's version of L.L. Bean. **Saybrook Country Barn** (✉ 2 Main St., ☎ 860/388–0891) has everything country, from tiger-maple dining-room tables to hand-painted pottery.

Old Lyme

⑤⑨ *4 mi east of Old Saybrook, 40 mi south of Hartford.*

Old Lyme, on the other side of the Connecticut River from Old Saybrook, is renowned among art lovers throughout the world for its history as America's foremost Impressionist art colony.

Central to Old Lyme's artistic reputation is the **Florence Griswold Museum,** the former home of a great patron of the arts. Willard Metcalfe, Clark Voorhees, and Childe Hassam were part of an art colony that occupied the 1817 late-Georgian mansion. Many of their works are displayed in revolving exhibits, along with 19th-century furnishings and decorative items. The studio of William Chadwick is open seasonally. ✉ *96 Lyme St.,* ☎ *860/434–5542.* 💵 *$4.* 🕐 *Jan.–May, Wed.–Sun. 1–5; June–Dec., Tues.–Sat. 10–5, Sun. 1–5.*

The **Lyme Academy of Fine Arts** is in a Federal home built in 1817. It has a popular gallery with works by contemporary artists, including the academy's students and faculty. ✉ *84 Lyme St.,* ☎ *860/434–5232.* 💵 *$2 donation suggested.* 🕐 *Tues.–Sat. 10–4, Sun. 1–4.*

Dining and Lodging

$$–$$$ ✕🏨 **Bee & Thistle Inn.** Behind a weathered stone wall in the Old Lyme
★ historic district is a two-story 1756 Colonial house on 5½ acres of broad lawns, towering trees, blooming flowers in a formal garden, and herbaceous borders. The scale of rooms throughout is deliberately small and inviting, with fireplaces in the downstairs parlors and dining rooms and light and airy curtains in the multipaned guest room windows. Most rooms have canopy or four-poster beds with old quilts and afghans. Breakfast can be brought to your room before or after a morning soak in an herbal bath (scented soap provided). Downstairs you might encounter a harpist one evening or take high tea late on a winter afternoon. Fireplaces and candlelight create a romantic atmosphere in the restaurant ($$$–$$$$; closed on Tuesday and the first three weeks in January), where classic American cuisine—grilled free-range chicken, filet mignon, crab cakes—is served with style. ✉ *100 Lyme St., 06371,* ☎ *860/434–1667 or 800/622–4946,* ⟨FAX⟩ *860/434–3402. 11 rooms, 1 cottage. Restaurant. AE, DC, MC, V.*

$$–$$$ ✕🏨 **Old Lyme Inn.** A gray clapboard 1850s farmhouse with blue shutters is the centerpiece of this dining and lodging establishment in the

heart of Old Lyme's historic district. Behind the ornate iron fence, tree-shaded lawn, and banistered front porch are spacious guest rooms impeccably decorated with antiques and contemporary furnishings. When she isn't busy working for the local art academy or the Connecticut River Museum, innkeeper Diana Field Atwood is lifting pot lids in the kitchen for whiffs of the gourmet American dishes prepared by her chef for the always-busy dining rooms. Diana collects local art, some of which is displayed in the cozy ground-floor common rooms. ⊠ *85 Lyme St. (just north of I–95), 06371,* ☎ *860/434–2600 or 800/434–5352,* FAX *860/434–5352. 5 rooms, 8 suites. Restaurant. Continental breakfast. AE, D, DC, MC, V.*

Waterford and Niantic

60 *13 mi east of Old Lyme (Waterford).*

Harkness Memorial State Park, the former summer estate of Edward Stephen Harkness, a silent partner in Standard Oil, encompasses formal gardens, picnic areas, a beach for strolling and fishing (but not swimming), and the Italian villa–style mansion, Eolia. Classical, pop, and jazz talents perform at the Summer Music at Harkness (☎ 800/969–3400) festival in July and August (tickets range from $10 to $65). ⊠ *275 Great Neck Rd./Rte. 213,* ☎ *860/443–5725.* ☞ *Memorial Day–Labor Day $4–$8; free rest of year.* ☉ *8 AM–dusk.*

Among the attributes of **Rocky Neck State Park** are its picnic facilities, saltwater fishing, and historic stone and wood pavilion, which was built in the 1930s. The park's mile-long crescent-shape strand is one of the finest beaches on Long Island Sound. ⊠ *Rte. 156, Niantic,* ☎ *860/739–5471.* ☞ *Apr.–Sept. $5–$12; free Oct.–Mar.* ☉ *8 AM–dusk.*

☾ The **Children's Museum of Southeastern Connecticut,** about a mile from Waterford, is an excellent museum that uses a hands-on approach to engage kids in the fields of science, math, and current events. ⊠ *409 Main St., Niantic,* ☎ *860/691–1255.* ☞ *$3.50.* ☉ *Mon.–Sat. 9:30–4:30, Fri. until 8, Sun. noon–4.*

Outdoor Activities and Sports

Captain John's Dock (☎ 860/443–7259) operates sightseeing cruises in search of whales, seals, or eagles aboard the 100-ft-long *Sunbeam Express.* Naturalists from Mystic Aquarium accompany the boat.

New London

61 *3 mi east of Waterford, 46 mi east of New Haven.*

New London is home to the **U.S. Coast Guard Academy,** whose 100-acre cluster of redbrick buildings includes a museum and visitors' pavilion with a gift shop. The three-masted training bark, the USCGC **Eagle,** may be boarded when in port. ⊠ *15 Mohegan Ave.,* ☎ *860/444–8270.* ☞ *Free.* ☉ *Academy daily 9–5; museum weekdays 9–4:30, Sat. 10–4:30, Sun. noon–5.*

The **Lyman Allyn Art Museum,** at the southern end of the Connecticut College campus, displays a small collection of art and antiques dating from the 18th and 19th centuries. You can also see decorative arts from Africa, India, China, and Japan, as well as the museum's dolls, dollhouses, miniature furniture, and toys, housed in the adjacent Deshon–Allyn House. ⊠ *625 Williams St.,* ☎ *860/443–2545.* ☞ *$3.* ☉ *Tues.–Sat. 10–5, Sun. 1–5.*

The **Monte Cristo Cottage,** the boyhood home of Nobel Prize–winning playwright Eugene O'Neill, was named for the literary count, his actor-father's greatest role. The setting figures in two of O'Neill's landmark plays, *Ah, Wilderness!* and *Long Day's Journey into Night.* ⊠ *325 Pequot Ave.,* ☎ *860/443–0051.* ⊡ *$4.* ⊙ *Memorial Day–Oct., Tues.– Sat. 10–5, Sun. 1–5.*

The beach at **Ocean Beach Park** (⊠ 1225 Ocean Ave., ☎ 860/447– 3031) is ½-mi long. Also here are an Olympic-size outdoor pool (with a triple water slide), a miniature golf course, a video arcade, a board-walk, and a picnic area.

Dining and Lodging

$ ✕ **Recovery Room.** It's a favorite game of Connecticut pizza parlors to declare "We're as good as Pepe's"—a reference to the famed New Haven eatery. But this white Colonial storefront eatery, presided over by the friendly Cash family, lives up to its claim. Plenty of "boutique" toppings are available, but don't ruin a great pizza with too many fla-vors. Perfection is realized by the three-cheese 'za with grated Parme-san, Romano, and Gorgonzola. ⊠ *445 Ocean Ave.,* ☎ *860/443–2619. MC, V. No lunch weekends.*

$$$ ⊡ **Radisson Hotel.** The rooms have nondescript furnishings but are quiet and spacious at this downtown property that's convenient to State Street, I–95, and the Amtrak station. ⊠ *35 Gov. Winthrop Blvd., 06320,* ☎ *860/443–7000,* ℻ *860/443–1239. 116 rooms, 4 suites. Restaurant, bar, indoor pool. AE, D, DC, MC, V.*

Nightlife and the Arts

The **El 'n' Gee Club** (⊠ 86 Golden St., ☎ 860/437–3800) presents heavy metal, reggae, and other local and national bands. The **Garde Arts Cen-ter** (⊠ 325 State St., ☎ 860/444–6766) hosts the Eastern Connecti-cut Symphony Orchestra, a theater series, innovative dance programs, and other events. Connecticut College's **Palmer Auditorium** (⊠ Mo-hegan Ave., ☎ 860/439–2787) presents dance and theater programs.

Outdoor Activities and Sports

Burr's Yacht Haven (☎ 860/443–8457) charters private fishing boats.

Norwich Area

㊿   *15 mi north of New London, 37 mi southeast of Hartford.*

Outstanding Georgian and Victorian structures surround the triangu-lar town green in Norwich, and more can be found downtown by the river. The Connecticut Trust for Historic Preservation and the state De-partment of Economic Development are renovating this former mill town—here's hoping for a prosperous rebound.

The **Slater Memorial Museum & Converse Art Gallery** on the grounds of the Norwich Free Academy has the largest plaster-cast collection of classical statues in the country, including *Winged Victory, Venus de Milo,* and Michelangelo's *Pietà.* ⊠ *108 Crescent St.,* ☎ *860/887–2505* or *860/887–2506.* ⊡ *$2.* ⊙ *Sept.–June, Tues.–Fri. 9–4, weekends 1– 4; July–Aug., Tues.–Sun. 1–4.*

On the Mashantucket Pequot Indian Reservation, 15 mi from Norwich near Ledyard, **Foxwoods Casino** is the state's first—and the world's largest—gambling operation. The skylit Colonial-style compound draws more than 55,000 visitors daily to its 5,500 slot machines, 3,500-seat high-stakes bingo parlor, poker rooms, keno station, smoke-free gam-ing area, theater, and Race Book room. This complex includes the Grand Pequot Tower, the Great Cedar Hotel, and Two Trees Inn, which have more than 1,400 rooms combined, a retail concourse, a food court, and 25 restaurants. A large game room and arcade and a movie theater in-the-round keep the kids entertained, along with Turbo Ride, which has specially engineered seats that simulate takeoffs and G-force pressure. ⊠ *Rte. 2, Mashantucket,* ☎ *860/885–3000 or 800/752–9244; 800/369–9663 for hotel reservations.* ⊙ *24 hrs.*

The Mohegan Indians, known as the Wolf People, opened Connecticut's second casino, the **Mohegan Sun,** which has 3,000 slot machines, 180 gaming tables, bingo, a theater, "Kids Quest" family entertainment complex, and, among 20 food-and-beverage suppliers, three fine-dining restaurants. Free entertainment, including nationally known acts, is presented nightly in the Wolf Den. ⊠ *Mohegan Sun Blvd. off Rte. 395, Uncasville,* ☎ *860/848–5682.*

The small **Tantaquidgeon Indian Museum** is run by Gladys Tantaquidgeon, a direct descendent of Uncas, former chief of the Mohegan Nation. Here you'll find examples of native artisanry such as baskets, bowls, and tools from the Mohegans and other tribes around the country. Gladys can direct you to other Indian sites of interest in the area, including a burial ground and a place of worship. ⊠ *Rte. 32, Uncasville,* ☎ *860/848–9145.* ⊡ *Donation suggested.* ⊙ *May–Oct., Tues.–Sun., 10–3.*

Lodging

$$$$ ✕⊞ **Grand Pequot Tower.** Foxwoods' newest hotel is an imposing 17 stories. Mere steps from the gaming floors, and the expansive showpiece contains deluxe rooms and suites. ⊠ *Box 3777, Rte. 2, Mashantucket 06339,* ☎ *800/369–9663. 750 rooms, 75 suites. 4 restaurants, 2 bars, room service, indoor pool, beauty salon, health club, shops, meeting rooms. AE, D, DC, MC, V.*

$$$–$$$$ ⊞ **Norwich Inn and Spa.** This posh Georgian-style inn is on 40 acres on a bluff a few hundred yards from the Thames River. Many treatments and fitness classes are offered in the newly renovated facility, which now encompasses more than 25,000 square ft. The American contemporary spa cuisine served at the inn goes well beyond carrot and celery sticks. ⊠ *607 W. Thames St./Rte. 32, 06360,* ☎ *860/886–2401 or 800/275–4772,* ℻ *860/886–4492. 65 rooms, 70 villas. Restaurant, indoor pool, spa, golf, health club. AE, DC, MC, V.*

Sports

The **Norwich Navigators** (☎ 800/644–2867), the AA affiliate of the New York Yankees, play at Senator Thomas J. Dodd Stadium (⊠ 14 Stott Rd.).

Groton

⑥³ *15 mi south of Norwich, 6 mi south of Ledyard.*

The world's first nuclear-powered submarine, the *Historic Ship Nautilus,* launched from Groton in 1954, is permanently berthed at the **Submarine Force Museum;** you're welcome to climb aboard. The adjacent museum contains submarine memorabilia, artifacts, and displays, including working periscopes and controls. The museum is outside the entrance to the submarine base. ⊠ *Crystal Lake Rd.,* ☎ *860/449–3174 or 860/449–3558.* ⊡ *Free.* ⊙ *Mid-May–mid-Oct., Wed.–Mon. 9–5, Tues. 1–5; late Oct.–early May, Wed.–Mon. 9–4.*

Fort Griswold Battlefield State Park contains the remnants of a Revolutionary fort. Historic displays at the museum here mark the site of the massacre of American defenders by Benedict Arnold's British troops in 1781. A sweeping view of the shoreline can be had from the top of the Groton monument. ⊠ *Monument St. and Park Ave.,* ☎ *860/445–1729.* ⊙ *Park year-round, daily 8 AM–dusk. Museum and monument*

Memorial Day–Labor Day, daily 10–5 . Closed Labor Day–Memorial Day.

Outdoor Activities and Sports

The **Hel-Cat II** (⊠ 181 Thames St., ☎ 860/445–5991) is a party fishing boat.

Mystic

64 *8 mi east of Groton.*

The town of Mystic has tried with dedication (if also with excessive commercialism) to recapture the spirit of the 18th and 19th centuries. Downtown Mystic has an interesting collection of boutiques and galleries.

★ ☺ Some people think the name of the town is **Mystic Seaport,** and it very well might be, given the popularity of the 17-acre museum that goes by that name. The nation's largest maritime museum, Mystic Seaport has authentic 19th-century sailing vessels you can board, a maritime village with historic homes, working craftspeople who give demonstrations, shops, restaurants, art exhibits, special events, and seasonal steamboat cruises and small-boat rentals. ⊠ *75 Greenmanville Ave.,* ☎ *860/572–0711.* ▨ *$16.* ☉ *May–Oct., daily 9–5; Nov.–Apr., daily 9–4.*

☺ Mystic's branch of the **Carousel Museum of New England** displays carousel art and operates a contemporary carousel. ⊠ *193 Greenmanville Ave.,* ☎ *860/536–7862.* ▨ *$4.* ☉ *Apr.–Nov., Mon.–Sat. 10–5, Sun. noon–5; Dec.–Mar., Thurs.–Sat. 10–5, Sun. noon–5.*

☺ Sea lions and dolphins and whales—oh, my! The **Mystic Marinelife Aquarium,** with more than 6,000 specimens and 50 live exhibits of sea life, includes Seal Island, a 2½-acre outdoor exhibit, which shows off seals and sea lions from around the world, the Marine Theater where dolphins perform, and the beloved Penguin Pavilion. The aquarium is scheduled to complete its $50 million expansion in the spring 1999. Exhibits will include the world's largest outdoor beluga whale habitat (with a 750,000-gallon pool). The Institute for Exploration, headed by world-renowned ocean explorer Dr. Robert Ballard, will use high-tech exhibits to allow visitors an almost-first-hand view of the ocean depths. ⊠ *55 Coogan Blvd.,* ☎ *860/536–3323 or 860/536–9631.* ▨ *$13.* ☉ *Daily 9–5.*

Dining and Lodging

$$ ✕ **Abbott's Lobster in the Rough.** If you want some of the state's best
★ lobster, mussels, crab, or clams on the half shell, grab a bottle of wine and slip down to this unassuming seaside lobster shack in sleepy Noank. Seating is outdoors or on the dock, where the views are magnificent. ⊠ *117 Pearl St., Noank,* ☎ *860/536–7719. AE, MC, V. BYOB. Closed Columbus Day–1st Fri. in May and weekdays Labor Day–Columbus Day.*

$–$$ ✕ **Mystic Pizza.** It's hard to say who benefited most from the success of the 1988 sleeper film *Mystic Pizza:* then-budding actress Julia Roberts or the pizza parlor on which the film is based (though no scenes were filmed here). This joint, which is often teeming with customers in summer, does serve other dishes but is best known for its inexpensive pizza, garlic bread, and grinders. ⊠ *56 W. Main St.,* ☎ *860/536–3700. D, MC, V.*

$ ✕ **Kitchen Little.** A great place for breakfast, this offbeat restaurant serves up delicious eggs dishes, including the Portuguese Fisherman—scrambled eggs, chorizo, linguiça, onions, peppers, and jalapeño cheese. The clam chowder, fried scallops, and lobster roll are sure bets for lunch.

This spot is small, so anticipate a wait (it's worth it). ⊠ *Rte. 27,* ☎ *860/536–2122. No credit cards. No lunch Sat.–Sun.*

$$$–$$$$ ✕⚏ **Inn at Mystic.** The highlight of this inn, which sprawls over 15 hill-
★   top acres and overlooks picturesque Pequotsepos Cove, is the five-bed-
room Georgian Colonial mansion in which Lauren Bacall and Humphrey
Bogart honeymooned. Almost as impressive are the rambling four-bed-
room gatehouse and the unusually attractive motor lodge. The convivial,
sun-filled Floodtide Restaurant specializes in New England fare. Brun-
chaholics flock here on Sunday. ⊠ *Rtes. 1 and 27, 06355,* ☎ *860/536–
9604 or 800/237–2415,* 𝔽𝔸𝕏 *860/572–1635. 68 rooms. Restaurant,
pool, tennis courts, dock, boating. AE, D, DC, MC, V.*

$$–$$$ ✕⚏ **Whaler's Inn and Motor Court.** A perfect compromise between a
chain motel and a country inn, this complex with public rooms that
contain lovely antiques is one block from the Mystic River and down-
town. Guest rooms are decorated in a Victorian style with quilts and
reproduction four-poster beds. The restaurant, Bravo Bravo, serves nou-
velle Italian food: The fettuccine comes with grilled scallops, roasted
apples, sun-dried tomatoes, and a Gorgonzola cream sauce. The bagel
shop here is terrific. ⊠ *20 E. Main St., 06355,* ☎ *860/536–1506 or
800/243–2588,* 𝔽𝔸𝕏 *860/572–1250. 41 rooms. 2 restaurants, outdoor
café, meeting rooms. AE, MC, V.*

$$$$ ⚏ **Steamboat Inn.** The rooms at this inn are named after famous Mys-
tic schooners, but it's hardly a creaky old establishment—many of the
rooms look as though they're posing for the cover of *House Beauti-
ful.* Six have wood-burning fireplaces, all have whirlpool baths, and
most have dramatic river views. Despite the inn's busy downtown lo-
cation (within earshot of the eerie hoot of the Bascule Drawbridge and
the chatter of tourists), its rooms are the most luxurious and roman-
tic in town. ⊠ *73 Steamboat Wharf, off W. Main St., 06355,* ☎ *860/
536–8300,* 𝔽𝔸𝕏 *860/536–9528. 10 rooms. Continental breakfast. AE,
D, MC, V.*

Outdoor Activities and Sports
Private charter boats depart from **Noank Village Boatyard** (⊠ 38 Bay-
side Ave., ☎ 860/536–1770). **Shaffer's Boat Livery** (⊠ 106 Mason's
Island Rd., ☎ 860/536–8713) rents small outboard skiffs.

Shopping
Finer Line Gallery (⊠ 48 W. Main St., ☎ 860/536–8339) exhibits nau-
tical and other prints. At the **Mystic Factory Outlets** (⊠ Coogan Blvd.),
nearly two dozen stores discount famous-name clothing and other
merchandise. **Olde Mistick Village** (⊠ I–95, Exit 90, ☎ 860/536–1641),
a re-creation of what an American village might have looked like in
the early 1700s, is at once hokey and picturesque. The stores here sell
crafts, clothing, souvenirs, and food. **Qué Lindo** (⊠ 3 Pearl St., ☎ 860/
536–1109), stocks extraordinary Spanish and Sicilian pottery.
Tradewinds Gallery (⊠ 20 W. Main St., ☎ 860/536–0119) represents
some New England artists but specializes in antique maps and prints.

Stonington

⑥⑤ *7 mi east of Mystic, 57 mi east of New Haven.*

The memorable village of Stonington pokes into Fishers Island Sound.
A quiet fishing community clustered around white-spired churches, Ston-
ington is far less commercial than Mystic. Historic buildings line the
town green and border both sides of Water Street up to the imposing
Old Lighthouse Museum.

The **Old Lighthouse Museum** was built in 1823. Seventeen years later
it was moved to higher ground, where it remains today, displaying a

wealth of shipping, whaling, and early village artifacts. Climb to the top of the tower for a spectacular view of Long Island Sound and three states. ⊠ *7 Water St.,* ☎ *860/535–1440.* 🖼 *$4.* ☾ *July–Aug., daily 10–5; May–June and Sept.–Oct., Tues.–Sun. 10–5, or by appointment.*

The **Stonington Vineyards,** a small coastal winery, has grown premium vinifera, including chardonnay and French hybrid grape varieties, since 1979. Picnicking on the grounds is encouraged. ⊠ *Taugwonk Rd.,* ☎ *860/535–1222.* 🖼 *Free.* ☾ *Daily 11–5; tours at 2.*

Dining and Lodging

$$ ✕🖼 **Randall's Ordinary.** The waiters dress in Colonial garb at this inn
★ famed for its open-hearth cooking. Arrive by 7 PM (reservations essential for dinner), and watch the preparations before sitting down at rustic wood tables. The prix-fixe menu ($$$) changes daily; choices might include out-of-this-world Nantucket scallops or loin of pork. The 17th-century John Randall House provides simple accommodations, but all rooms have modern baths with whirlpools and showers. The barn houses irregular guest rooms, all with authentic early-Colonial decor. ⊠ *Box 243, Rte. 2, North Stonington 06359,* ☎ *860/599–4540,* 🗚 *860/599–3308. 14 rooms, 1 suite. Restaurant. Continental breakfast. AE, MC, V.*

$$$–$$$$ 🖼 **Antiques & Accommodations.** The British influence is evident in the
★ Georgian formality of this Victorian country home, built about 1861. Exquisite furniture and accessories, many of them for sale, decorate the rooms. An 1820 house has similarly furnished suites. Aromatic candles and fresh flowers create an inviting atmosphere. Breakfast is a grand four-course affair served on fine china. ⊠ *32 Main St., North Stonington 06359,* ☎ *860/535–1736 or 800/554–7829. 3 rooms, 2 suites. Full breakfast. MC, V.*

Outdoor Activities and Sports

Dodson Boat Yard (⊠ 194 Water St., ☎ 860/535–1507) rents and charters power boats and sailboats.

New Haven and the Southeastern Coast A to Z

Arriving and Departing

BY BUS

Peter Pan (☎ 800/237–8747) buses service New Haven from Boston, Hartford, and New York. **Prime Time Shuttle** (☎ 800/733–8267) provides shuttle service between New Haven and La Guardia and John F. Kennedy airports in New York City.

BY CAR

Interstate 95 and Route 1, which run mostly parallel but sometimes intertwine, are the main routes to and through southeastern Connecticut; the two roads intersect with I–91 (coming south from Hartford) in New Haven.

BY FERRY

From New London, **Cross Sound Ferry** (☎ 860/443–5281) operates year-round passenger and car service to and from Orient Point, Long Island, New York. **Fishers Island Ferry** (☎ 860/443–6851) has passenger and car service to and from Fishers Island, New York. **Interstate Navigation** (☎ 401/783–4613) operates passenger and car service to and from Block Island, Rhode Island, from June to early September.

BY PLANE

Tweed/New Haven Airport (⊠ Burr St. off I–95, ☎ 203/946–8283), 5 mi southeast of the city, is served by US Airways Express (☎ 800/428–4322).

Amtrak (☎ 800/872–7245) trains make stops in New Haven, New London, and Mystic. **Metro-North Railroad** (☎ 800/638–7646; 212/532–4900 from New York City) stops in New Haven.

Getting Around

BY BUS

Connecticut Transit (☎ 203/624–0151) provides local bus service in New Haven and surrounding towns; there is also service to and from Tweed/New Haven Airport.

BY CAR

Most of the southeastern Connecticut towns described above are on or just off I–95 and Route 1. Interstate 395 branches north from I–95 to Norwich.

BY TAXI

Metro Taxi (☎ 203/777–7777) serves New Haven and environs.

BY TRAIN

The Connecticut Department of Transportation's **Shore Line East** (☎ 860/594–2000; 800/255–7133 in Connecticut) operates commuter rail service (weekdays, westbound in the morning, eastbound in the evening) connecting New Haven, Branford, Guilford, Madison, Clinton, Westbrook, Old Saybrook, and New London.

Contacts and Resources

EMERGENCIES

Lawrence & Memorial Hospital (✉ 365 Montauk Ave., New London, ☎ 860/442–0711). **Yale–New Haven Hospital** (✉ 20 York St., ☎ 203/688–2000).

LATE-NIGHT PHARMACY

CVS (✉ 1168 Whalley Ave., New Haven, ☎ 203/389–4714) is open until 10 on weeknights, 9 on weekends.

VISITOR INFORMATION

Connecticut River Valley and Shoreline Visitors Council (✉ 393 Main St., Middletown 06457, ☎ 860/347–0028 or 800/486–3346). **Connecticut's Mystic and More** (✉ Box 89, 470 Bank St., New London 06320, ☎ 860/444–2206 or 800/863–6569). **Greater New Haven Convention and Visitors District** (✉ 1 Long Wharf Dr., Suite 7, New Haven 06511, ☎ 203/777–8550 or 800/332–7829).

THE QUIET CORNER

Few visitors to Connecticut experience the old-fashioned ways of the state's "Quiet Corner," a vast patch of sparsely populated towns that looks today much as Litchfield County did in 1980. The Quiet Corner has a reclusive allure: People used to leave New York City for the Litchfield Hills; now many are leaving for northeastern Connecticut, where the stretch of Route 169 from Brooklyn past Woodstock is one of 14 roads in the country to be named a National Scenic Byway.

The cultural capital of the Quiet Corner is Putnam, a small mill city on the Quinebaug River whose formerly industrial town center has been transformed into a year-round antiques mart. Smaller jewels in and around the Putnam area are Brooklyn, Pomfret, Thompson, and Woodstock—four towns where authentic Colonial homesteads still seem to outnumber the contemporary, charmless clones that are springing up rapidly across the state.

The Quiet Corner

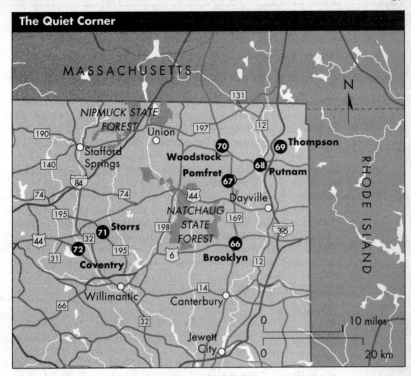

Brooklyn

66 *45 mi east of Hartford.*

The village of Brooklyn bears no resemblance to the more famous borough that carries the same name. White picket fences and beautifully restored Colonial homes are the norm here.

The **New England Center for Contemporary Art** is a four-story pre-Revolutionary barn that hosts exhibitions of 20th-century art. ⊠ *Rte. 169,* ☎ *860/774–8899.* ⊡ *Free .* ☉ *April–Nov., Tues.–Sun. 1–5. Closed Dec.–Mar.*

Dining

$$$$ ✕ **Golden Lamb Buttery.** Connecticut's most unusual and magical din-
★ ing experience has achieved almost legendary status. Eating here is far more than a chance to enjoy good food: It's a social and gastronomical event. There is one seating each for lunch and dinner in this converted barn. Owners Bob and Virginia "Jimmie" Booth have a vintage Jaguar roadster and a hay wagon that guests can ride in before dinner (a musician accompanies you). Choose from one of three daily soups and four entrées, which might include duck à l'orange or panfried beef tenderloin. ⊠ *Wolf Den and Bush Hill Rds. (off Rte. 169),* ☎ *860/ 774–4423. Reservations essential. No credit cards. Closed Jan.–late May and Sun.–Mon. No dinner Tues.–Thurs.*

Pomfret

67 *6 mi north of Brooklyn.*

Pomfret, one of the grandest towns in the region, was once known as the inland Newport. The hilltop campus of the Pomfret School offers some of Connecticut's loveliest views.

Sharpe Hill Vineyard, one of the state's newest wineries, is centered around an 18th-century-style barn in the hills of Pomfret. Tours and tastings are given, and from May to October you can nibble on smoked salmon and fruit and cheese in the European-style wine garden. ⊠ *108 Wade Rd.,* ☎ *860/974–3549.* 🎫 *Free.* ☉ *Fri.–Sun. 11–5.*

Dining and Lodging

$$ ✕ **Vanilla Bean Café.** A perfect stop for lunch, this tan Colonial-style barn serves salads and hearty sandwiches in an informal dining room. Dinner entrées such as lobster ravioli and roast pork with winter vegetables are served until 8. From May to October, fare from the outside grill is served on the patio until 9; the indoor grill is fired up for burgers year-round. Breakfast is served on weekends. ⊠ *450 Deerfield Rd. (Rtes. 44, 97, and 169),* ☎ *860/928–1562. No credit cards. No dinner Mon.–Tues.*

$$ 🏠 **Karinn Bed and Breakfast.** Grand Victorian furnishings and a hospitable manager, Karen Schirack, make this 100-year-old inn near Pomfret's town center the nicest of the area's many moderately priced B&Bs. The antiques-filled rooms were once part of Miss Vinton's School for Girls. Ricotta cheese pie and Belgian waffles are two dishes on the long breakfast menu. ⊠ *330 Pomfret St., 06258,* ☎ *860/928–5492. 4 rooms. Full breakfast. No credit cards.*

Shopping

Majilly (⊠ 56 Babbitt Hill Rd., ☎ 860/974–3714), an upscale line of hand-painted ceramic giftware crafted in Deruta, Italy, is based in a 150-year-old Pomfret barn. Open by appointment from April to December, the outlet sells still-gorgeous seconds at 50% to 70% off the retail prices. **Martha's Herbary** (⊠ 589 Pomfret St./Rte. 169, ☎ 860/928–0009), set in a 1780 home, is a combination herb-theme gift shop, garden, and learning center. Classes in the demonstration kitchen cover everything from cooking with herbs to making herbal facial masks.

Putnam

🚍 *10 mi northeast of Pomfret.*

Ambitious antiques dealers have reinvented Putnam, a mill town 30 mi west of Providence that became neglected after the Depression. Putnam's downtown, with more than 10 antiques shops, is the heart of the Quiet Corner's antiques trade. The first weekend in November is **Antiquing Weekend,** when nearly two dozen area shops offer discounts and give workshops.

Dining

$$$ ✕ **Vine Bistro.** This stylish trattoria-bistro is *the* place to go for a break from antiquing. Don't miss the eggplant rollatini (thinly sliced eggplant rolled with ricotta, mozzarella, Parmesan, and sun-dried tomatoes with a marinara sauce), a starter; you can follow with the house special: Chicken D'Vine (sautéed chicken breast with artichoke hearts, tomatoes, black olives, and mushrooms). ⊠ *85 Main St.,* ☎ *860/928–1660. Reservations essential for dinner. AE, MC, V. Closed Mon.*

Shopping

The three-level, 20,000-square-ft **Antiques Marketplace** (⊠ 109 Main St., ☎ 860/928–0442) houses nearly 200 dealers. The 30,000-square-ft **Putnam Antique Exchange** (⊠ 75–83 Main St., ☎ 860/928–1905) stocks 18th-century to Art Deco–era paintings, stained glass, architectural elements, and fine furnishings.

Thompson

69 *7 mi north of Putnam, 50 mi north of Groton.*

Thompson, like Pomfret, has 19th-century estates and restored Colonial homes. One particularly impressive stretch is along Route 200, from Thompson Center to where it crosses I–395.

Dining and Lodging

$$$ ✕ **White Horse at Vernon Stiles Inn.** The tavern inside this rambling white Colonial will give you an inkling of what such places in New England were like 150 years ago. The food spans generations, though, with traditional favorites like the New York sirloin with a peppercorn-cognac cream sauce and bolder new American platters such as curried oatmeal oysters on a bed of black-pepper linguine tossed with roasted corn and red peppers in a whole-grain mustard sauce. The bakery serves a light lunch. ✉ *351 Thompson Rd. (Rtes. 193 and 200),* ☎ *860/923–9571. AE, DC, MC, V. Closed Tues.*

$$ 🏨 **Lord Thompson Manor.** You may feel like you've landed in En-
★ gland's Devonshire countryside when you reach the end of the ½-mi winding driveway that leads to this stunning B&B. The 30-room mansion has African marble fireplaces and parquet floors; Frederick Law Olmsted laid out the sprawling grounds. ✉ *Box 428, Rte. 200, 06277,* ☎ *860/923–3886,* FAX *860/923–9310. 3 rooms, 4 suites. Meeting rooms. Full breakfast. AE, DC, MC, V.*

Woodstock

70 *10 mi west of Thompson.*

The landscape of this enchanting town is splendid in every season—the gently rolling hills seem to stretch for miles. **Roseland Cottage** is probably the region's most notable historic home. The rose-hued board-and-batten Gothic Revival home was built in 1846 by New York publisher and merchant Henry Bowen. The pride of its grounds is an 1850s boxwood parterre garden that four presidents—Ulysses S. Grant, Rutherford B. Hayes, Benjamin Harrison, and William McKinley—have visited. The neighboring barn contains what may be the oldest indoor bowling alley in the country. An hour-long stroll around the grounds is one of several dozen walks held during the Quiet Corner's **Walking Weekend** each Columbus Day weekend. ✉ *Rte. 169,* ☎ *860/928–4074.* 🎫 *$4.* ☉ *June–mid-Oct., Wed.–Sun. 11–5. Tours on the hr, last one at 4.*

Dining and Lodging

$$–$$$ ✕🏨 **Inn at Woodstock Hill.** This inn on a hill overlooking the countryside has sumptuous rooms with antiques, four-poster beds, fireplaces, pitched ceilings, and timber beams. The restaurant ($$$; reservations essential) next door serves excellent Continental and American shrimp, veal, and chicken dishes. ✉ *94 Plaine Hill Rd., South Woodstock 06267,* ☎ *860/928–0528,* FAX *860/928–3236. 22 rooms. Restaurant, meeting rooms. D, MC, V.*

Shopping

The **Christmas Barn** (✉ 835 Rte. 169, ☎ 860/928–7652) has 12 rooms of country and Christmas goods. **Scranton's Shops** (✉ 300 Rte. 169, ☎ 860/928–3738) sells antiques and the wares of 90 local artisans. **Windy Acres Florist** (✉ Rte. 171, ☎ 860/928–0554) overflows with fresh and dried floral arrangements, baskets, pottery, and other collectibles.

Storrs

71 *25 mi southwest of Woodstock.*

The majority of the rolling hillside and farmland of Storrs is occupied by the 4,400 acres and 12,000 students of the **University of Connecticut** (UConn). Many cultural programs, sporting events, and other happenings take place here. University Parking Services and the Student Union supply campus maps.

Hand puppets, rod puppets, body puppets, shadow puppets, marionettes—the **Ballard Institute and Museum of Puppetry** has more than 2,000 puppets in its extraordinary collection. Half of them were created by Frank Ballard, a master of puppetry who established the country's first complete undergraduate and graduate degree program in puppetry at UConn more than three decades ago. Exhibits change seasonally. If you're lucky you might even catch Scooter from "The Muppet Show" on display. ✉ *Univ. of Connecticut Depot Campus, 6 Bourn Place, U-212 ,* ☎ *860/486–4605.* ☞ *Free.* ☷ *Mid-Apr.–mid-Nov., Fri. 10–5, Sat.–Sun. 12–5.*

The **William Benton Museum of Art** presents fine-arts exhibitions. The museum's permanent collection includes European and American paintings, drawings, prints, and sculptures from the 16th century to the present. ✉ *Univ. of Connecticut, 245 Glenbrook Rd.,* ☎ *860/486–4520.* ☞ *Free.* ☷ *Tues.–Fri. 10–4:30, Sat.–Sun. 1–4:30. Closed between exhibitions.*

Talk about diversity! The **University of Connecticut Greenhouses** are internationally acclaimed for their more than 3,000 different kinds of plants, from 900 varieties of exotic orchids to banana plants to a redwood tree. ✉ *Univ. of Connecticut, 75 N. Eagleville Rd.,* ☎ *860/486–4052.* ☞ *Free.* ☷ *Mon.– Fri. 8–4. Organized tours given weekends in Mar. and Apr.*

Nightlife and the Arts

The **Jorgenson Auditorium** (✉ Univ. of Connecticut, 2132 Hillside Rd., ☎ 860/486–4226) presents music, dance, and theater programs. **Mansfield Drive-In** (✉ Rtes. 31 and 32, Mansfield, ☎ 860/423–4441), with three big screens, is one of the state's few remaining drive-in theaters.

Shopping

The **Eastern Connecticut Flea Market** (✉ Mansfield Drive-In, Rtes. 31 and 32, Mansfield, ☎ 860/456–2578), with more than 150 vendors, unfolds on Sunday from the first weekend of spring until Thanksgiving weekend.

Coventry

72 *5 mi southwest of Storrs.*

Coventry is the birthplace of the Revolutionary War hero Captain Nathan Hale, who was hanged as a spy by the British in 1776. It was Hale who spoke the immortal last words, "I only regret that I have but one life to lose for my country."

The **Nathan Hale Homestead** was rebuilt by Deacon Richard Hale, Nathan's father, in 1776. Ten Hale children, six of whom served in the Revolutionary War, were raised here. Family artifacts are on exhibit in the completely furnished house. The grounds include a corncrib and an 18th-century barn. ✉ *2299 South St.,* ☎ *860/742–6917.* ☞ *$4.* ☷ *Mid-May–mid-Oct., daily 1–5.*

Coventry's **Caprilands Herb Farm** (⊠ 534 Silver St., ☎ 860/742–7244) draws thousands of visitors annually to 38 gardens that hold more than 300 varieties of herbs. There's a noon luncheon lecture program, and tea is held on the weekends (phone for reservations).

Quiet Corner A to Z

Arriving and Departing
BY CAR

You'll need a car to reach and to explore the Quiet Corner. Many Nutmeggers live their entire lives without even noticing I–395, let alone driving on it, but this is the main highway connecting Worcester, Massachusetts, with New London—and it passes right through the Quiet Corner. From Hartford take I–84 east to Route 44 east, and from Providence, Rhode Island, take either Route 44 or 6 west.

Getting Around
BY CAR

All the towns in the Quiet Corner are on or just off historic Route 169.

Contacts and Resources
Northeast Connecticut Visitors District (⊠ Box 598, Putnam 06260, ☎ 860/928–1228).

CONNECTICUT A TO Z

Arriving and Departing

By Bus
Bonanza Bus Lines (☎ 800/556–3815) connects Hartford, Farmington, Southbury, Waterbury, Manchester, and Danbury with Boston and New York. **Greyhound** (☎ 800/231–2222) links Connecticut with most major cities in the United States. **Peter Pan Bus Lines** (☎ 800/237–8747) serves the eastern seaboard, including many New England cities.

By Car
From New York City head north on I–95, which hugs the Connecticut shoreline into Rhode Island or, to reach the Litchfield Hills and Hartford, head north on I–684, then east on I–84. From Springfield, Massachusetts go south on I–91, which bisects I–84 in Hartford and I–95 in New Haven. From Boston take I–95 south through Providence or take the Massachusetts Turnpike west to I–84. Interstate 395 runs north–south from southeastern Connecticut to Massachusetts.

By Plane
Many people visiting Connecticut fly into New York City's **John F. Kennedy International Airport** (☎ 718/244–4444) or **LaGuardia Airport** (☎ 718/533–3400), both of which are served by many major carriers. Another option is **Bradley International Airport** (⊠ Rte. 20; take Exit 40 off I–91), ☎ 860/627–3000), 12 mi north of Hartford (☞ Connecticut River Valley A to Z, *above*, for a list of carriers that service the airport).

AIRPORT TRANSFERS

The **Airport Connection** (☎ 860/627–3400) has scheduled service from Bradley to Hartford's Union Station, as well as door-to-door service. **Connecticut Limo** (☎ 800/472–5466) operates bus and van service between Connecticut and the New York airports and to and from Bradley International Airport. **Prime Time Shuttle** (☎ 800/733–8267) serves New Haven and Fairfield counties and the greater Danbury area with service to and from both New York airports.

By Train

Amtrak (☎ 800/872–7245) runs from New York to Boston, stopping in Stamford, Bridgeport, and New Haven before heading either north to Hartford or east to Mystic. **Metro-North Railroad** (☎ 800/638–7646; 212/532–4900 from New York City) stops locally between Greenwich and New Haven, and a few trains head inland to New Canaan, Danbury, and Waterbury.

Getting Around

By Bus

See By Bus *in* the regional A to Z sections, *above,* for intrastate bus information.

By Car

The interstates are the quickest routes between many points in Connecticut, but they are busy and ugly. If time allows, skip them in favor of the historic Merritt Parkway (Route 15), which winds between Greenwich and Middletown; Routes 7 and 8, extending between I–95 and the Litchfield Hills; Route 9, which heads south from Hartford through the Connecticut River valley to Old Saybrook; and scenic Route 169, which meanders through the Quiet Corner. Maps are available free from the **Connecticut Department of Tourism** (☞ Visitor Information, *below*).

Contacts and Resources

B&B Reservation Services

B&B, Ltd. (☎ 203/469–3260). **Covered Bridge B&B Reservation Service** (☎ 860/542–5944). **Nutmeg B&B Agency** (☎ 860/236–6698).

Guided Tours

Classics Limited (⌧ 855 Ridge Rd., Wethersfield 06109, ☎ 860/563–0848) conducts individual and group tours throughout Connecticut and southern New England by private car, limousine, van, and coach.

Visitor Information

Connecticut Department of Tourism (⌧ 505 Hudson St., Hartford 06106, ☎ 800/282–6863 for brochure). **State Parks Division Bureau of Outdoor Recreation** (⌧ 79 Elm St., Hartford 06106, ☎ 860/424–3200).

3 Rhode Island

From the Block Island coast, you can peruse much of southern Rhode Island. To the northwest lie the beaches of South County. The vague outline in the opposite direction is Newport, the city of mansions and Colonial homes. From Newport Harbor it's a 30-mile trip up Narragansett Bay to the state's capital, Providence; 20 miles farther north is the Blackstone Valley, birthplace of the American Industrial Revolution. With such history and natural beauty, it's no wonder Rhode Island is a premier New England destination.

Revised and
updated by
K. D. Weaver

RHODE ISLAND, which shares with New Jersey the distinction of being one of the two most densely populated states in the Union, has one other characteristic in common with the Garden State: All too often it is a place people pass through on their way to somewhere else. The culprit in both cases is I–95, but for Rhode Island the problem is compounded by its size, 48 mi × 37 mi. Just about everyone knows Rhode Island is the smallest of the 50 states. What is less known is how much American history is packed within its borders: The state holds 20% of the country's National Historic Landmarks and has more restored Colonial and Victorian buildings than anywhere else in the United States.

To experience Rhode Island as an end rather than a means, stay off the interstate and even Route 1. If you travel instead on city streets and blacktop roads, you'll discover a place where changes in landscape and character come abruptly. The 5 mi or so of Route 1 above Wickford, for example, are as crass and tacky a stretch of modern strip-mall Americana as you're likely to find anywhere. But if you turn off the highway on a discreetly marked drive in North Kingstown, you'll pass through a grove of trees and enter the 17th-century world of Smith's Castle, a beautifully preserved saltbox plantation house on the quiet shore of an arm of Narragansett Bay. Little appears to have changed here since Richard Smith built his "castle" after buying the surrounding property from Rhode Island's founder, Roger Williams, in 1651. Three miles south of here, at Route 1A, the scene changes once again: The bayside town of Wickford is the kind of almost-too-perfect, salty New England period piece that is usually conjured up only in books and movies. In fact, this was John Updike's model for the New England of his novel *The Witches of Eastwick*.

So there it is: a run of tawdry highway development, a restored relic of a house that was once the seat of a 17,000-acre plantation, and a picture-perfect seacoast town that suggested the locale for a novel of contemporary witchcraft. Pick the Rhode Island you want—your other choices include the 2,600-acre Great Swamp south of Kingston, the Victorian shore resort of Watch Hill, the mansions of Newport, and exquisitely desolate Block Island—all of them just a short detour off the main highways.

Pleasures and Pastimes

Beaches

Rhode Island has 400 mi of shoreline with more than 100 salt- and freshwater beaches. Almost all the ocean beaches around the resort communities of Narragansett, Watch Hill, Newport, and Block Island are open to the public. Deep sands blanket most Rhode Island beaches, and their water is clear and clean—in some places, the water takes on the turquoise color of the Caribbean Sea. There's a beautiful view of Newport's harbor from the beach at Fort Adams State Park; nearby Middletown has a long beach adjacent to a bird sanctuary; and Jamestown's Mackerel Cove Beach is sheltered from heavy surf. With naturally occurring white sands and a rock reef to the north that's ideal for snorkeling, Mansion Beach—the northernmost section of Block Island's 2-mi-long Crescent Beach—is one of the most splendid coastal stretches in New England.

Boating

It should come as no surprise that a place nicknamed the Ocean State would attract multitudes of boaters. With a well-sheltered harbor,

Rhode Island

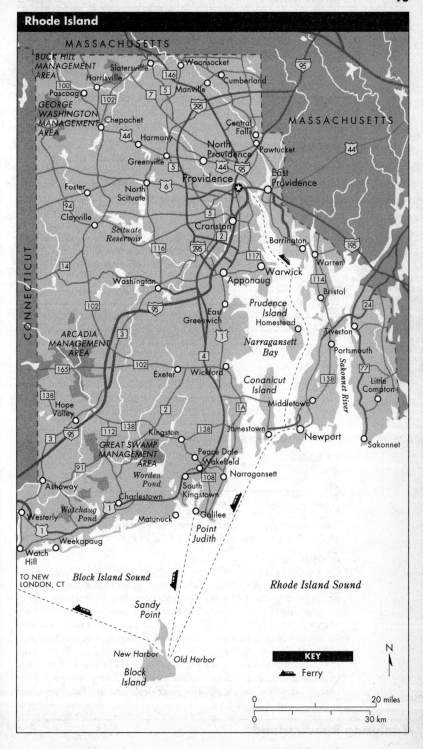

Newport prospered from shipbuilding and overseas trade, and even today boating is the city's second-largest industry after tourism. Point Judith Pond, which is close to deep Atlantic waters, harbors New England's largest commercial fishing fleet and nearly four dozen sport-fishing charter boats. Block Island's Great Salt Pond is New England's busiest summertime harbor. At the head of the Narragansett Bay, an impressive riverfront park, Waterplace, is a recently built destination for small powerboats, canoes, and kayaks. Many tidal rivers and salt ponds in South County are ideal for peaceful kayaking and canoeing.

Dining

The regional fare prepared in Rhode Island includes johnnycakes, a corn-cake–like affair cooked on a griddle, and the native clam, the quahog (pronounced *ko*-hog), which is served stuffed, fried, in chowder, and even in pie. "Shore dinners" consist of clam chowder, steamers, clam cakes, sausage, corn-on-the-cob, lobster, watermelon, and Indian pudding (a steamed pudding made with cornmeal and molasses). The Federal Hill neighborhood in Providence holds some superlative Italian restaurants, and the culinary offerings in a few of the city's several dozen other restaurants rival those in Boston's finest eateries.

CATEGORY	COST*
$$$$	over $35
$$$	$25–$35
$$	$15–$25
$	under $15

average cost of a three-course dinner, per person, excluding drinks, service, and 7% sales tax.

Lodging

The major chain hotels are represented in Rhode Island, but the state's many smaller bed-and-breakfasts and other inns offer a more down-home experience. Rates are very much seasonal; in Newport, for example, winter rates are often half those of summer.

CATEGORY	COST*
$$$$	over $150
$$$	$100–$150
$$	$60–$100
$	under $60

All prices are for a standard double room during peak season, with no meals unless noted, and excluding 12% hotel and sales taxes.

Shopping

Newport is a shopper's—but not a bargain hunter's—city. You can find antiques, traditional clothing, and marine supplies in abundance. Antiques are a specialty of South County; more than 30 stores are within an hour's drive of each other. The best places to browse are Wickford, Charlestown, and Watch Hill. Providence has a full range of stores. Its ethnic communities produce specialties like Italian groceries and Hmong (Laotian) clothing, and its student population ensures a variety of secondhand boutiques and funky shops. The Blackstone Valley contains myriad outlet stores; unlike suburban "factory outlets," these places, often low on decor, offer great deals and are usually a short walk from the factory floor.

Exploring Rhode Island

Great Itineraries

Numbers in the text and in the margin correspond to numbers on the maps: Central Providence, the Blackstone Valley, Block Island, South

*County and Newport County, Downtown Newport, and Greater
Newport.*

IF YOU HAVE 3 DAYS

Spend a day and a half in the city of ☷ **Newport** ⑩–㉔, then make the
40-minute drive north to ☷ **Providence** ①–⑰. Though this city's attractions are less packaged than Newport's, they include sophisticated
restaurants, historic districts, and a new downtown park.

IF YOU HAVE 5 DAYS

Spend your first three days in ☷ **Newport** ⑩–㉔ and ☷ **Providence** ①–
⑰, then take two days to explore the South County. With pristine beaches
and restaurants and inns, South County encourages a take-it-as-it-goes
attitude that's just right for summer and fall touring. Shop and soak
up the turn-of-the-century elegance of ☷ **Watch Hill** ㉓, and then spend
a day beaching it in **Charlestown** ㉕ or **South Kingstown** ㉖ (try **Misquamicut** if you prefer beaches with a carnival atmosphere). ☷ **Narragansett** ㉗, which has great beaches and numerous B&Bs, is one option
for a second South County night—or you might board a ferry for a
day trip to unspoiled **Block Island** ㉙–㊳.

When to Tour Rhode Island

The best time to visit Rhode Island is between May and October.
Newport hosts several high-profile music festivals in the summer, Providence is at its prettiest, and Block Island and the beach towns of
South County are in full swing (though not nearly as crowded as Newport). Because of the foliage, the light traffic, and the often gorgeous
weather, October is a great time to come to Rhode Island.

PROVIDENCE

*50 mi south of Boston, 30 mi north of Newport, 190 mi north of New
York City.*

Roger Williams founded Providence in October 1635 as a refuge for
freethinkers and religious dissenters. Providence remains a community
that embraces independent thinking in business, the arts, and aca-
demia. Brown University, Rhode Island School of Design (RISD), and
Trinity Square Repertory Company are major forces in New England's
intellectual and cultural life.

The decline of Providence's two main industries, textiles and costume
jewelry (the city was once the nation's chief producer of glittering
baubles), precipitated a severe population exodus in the 1940s and '50s.
The 1990s began with a statewide banking crisis, but New England's
third-largest city (behind Boston and Worcester) is again proudly shining: Unsightly railroad tracks have been put underground, dilapidated
neighborhoods are being rejuvenated, and a convention center and a
downtown riverfront park have opened in the last few years. The city,
home to the Johnson and Wales University Culinary Institute, is also
developing into something of a culinary hotbed.

Meanwhile, an emerging community of creative types—encouraged by
a state referendum exempting Providence-based artists from income
taxes—is heightening the charm of the downtown. A shopping mall is
under construction here, and an ice rink is planned for the city's central plaza. Such incentives and large-scale changes in infrastructure have
piqued the interest of city planners nationwide. One of the principals
in Providence's transformation, its personable mayor of 15 years, Vincent "Buddy" Cianci, has become a sought-after authority on rejuve-
nating American cities.

Surrounding the center city are some strollable neighborhoods: Fox Point's gentrifying Wickenden Street, Federal Hill's Italian section, the historically Yankee East Side, and young and hip College Hill.

A Good Walk

Begin at the **Rhode Island State House** ①, whose south portico looks down over the city of Providence and Narragansett Bay. Engraved here is a passage from the Royal Charter of 1663: "To hold forth a lively experiment that a most flourishing civil state may stand and best be maintained with full liberty in religious concernments." After touring the capitol, proceed to Smith Street, at the north end of the State House grounds. Follow the road east to **Roger Williams National Memorial** ②. **Benefit Street** ③ is one block east (up the hill). Walk south on the historic street to the **Museum of Art, Rhode Island School of Design** ④ and the **Providence Athenaeum** ⑤. Head east (away from the Providence River) on College Street and north (to the left) on Prospect Street to reach the **John Hay Library** ⑥. The **Brown University** ⑦ campus is across the street. Walk east on Waterman Street; you can enter the grounds at Brown Street. After you've toured the campus, continue east three blocks on Waterman Street. Turn left (north) on Hope Street and the stately **Governor Henry Lippit House Museum** ⑧ will be on your right. Head south four blocks on Hope Street to Benevolent Street and turn left. The **Museum of Rhode Island History at Aldrich House** ⑨ will be on your right. Return to Hope Street, walk one block north to George Street. Head west (toward the Providence River) five blocks to the magnificent **First Unitarian Church of Providence** ⑩. The **John Brown House** ⑪ is two blocks south of here. From the Brown house, walk one block downhill on Power Street and turn right on South Main Street. Proceed north until you reach the **Market House** ⑫ and, one block farther north, the **First Baptist Church in America** ⑬. Turn left at Steeple Street (also called Thomas Street), and you will shortly reach **Waterplace Park and Riverwalk** ⑭.

The **Rhode Island Black Heritage Society** ⑮, **Federal Hill** ⑯, and **Wickenden Street** ⑰ are best visited via car or taxi.

TIMING

The timing of the walk from the state house to Waterplace Park will vary greatly depending on how much time you spend at each sight. If you stop for a half hour at most sights and an hour at the RISD Museum of Art, the tour will take a full day.

Sights to See

❸ **Benefit Street.** The centerpiece of any visit to Providence is the "Mile of History," where a bumpy cobblestone sidewalk passes a row of early Federal and 19th-century candy-color houses crammed shoulder-to-shoulder on a steep hill overlooking downtown Providence. Romantic Benefit Street is a reminder of the wealth brought to Rhode Island in Colonial times through the triangular trade of slaves, rum, and molasses. Much of Providence beyond Benefit Street was brought back into fashion in the 1980s by Bostonians looking for cheaper real estate, even though the investment meant enduring an hour-long commute. The Providence Preservation Society (✉ 21 Meeting St., at Benefit St., ☎ 401/831–7440) conducts guided tours from Memorial Day to Labor Day and has maps and pamphlets with self-guided tours.

❼ **Brown University.** The nation's seventh-oldest college was founded in 1764. The Ivy League institution has more than 40 academic departments, including a school of medicine. Gothic and Beaux Arts struc-

Central Providence

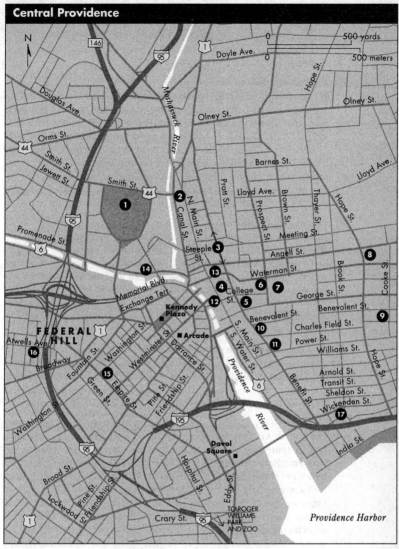

tures dominate the campus, which has been designated a National Historic Landmark. University tours leave from the admissions office, in the Corliss-Brackett House (⊠ 45 Prospect St., ☎ 401/863–2378 or 401/863–2703). Thayer Street is the campus's principal commercial thoroughfare.

⑯ Federal Hill. You're as likely to hear Italian as English in this neighborhood that is vital to Providence's culture and sense of self. You might for a moment even imagine you've time-traveled to a small Italian town. The stripe down the middle of Atwells Avenue is repainted each year in red, white, and green, and a huge *pigna* (pinecone), an Italian symbol of abundance and quality, hangs on an arch soaring over the street. Hardware shops sell boccie sets and the corner store sells china statues of saints, but the "Avenue," as locals call it, isn't cutesy. The St. Joseph's and Columbus Day celebrations, with music, food stands, and parades, are not to be missed.

⑬ First Baptist Church in America. This historic house of worship was built in 1775 for a congregation established in 1638 by Roger Williams and his fellow Puritan dissenters. The church, one of the finest examples of Georgian architecture in the United States, has a carved wood interior, a Waterford crystal chandelier, and graceful but austere Ionic columns. ⊠ *75 N. Main St.,* ☎ *401/751–2266.* ≊ *Free; donations appreciated.* ⊙ *Memorial Day–Columbus Day, weekdays 9:30–3:30, Sun. service at 11, guided tour at 12:15; July–Aug., Sun. service at 9:30, guided tour at 10:45.*

⑩ First Unitarian Church of Providence. This Romanesque house of worship made of Rhode Island granite was built in 1816. Its steeple houses a 2,500-pound bell, the largest ever cast in Paul Revere's foundry. ⊠ *1 Benevolent St. (corner of Benefit St.),* ☎ *401/421–7970.* ≊ *Free.* ⊙ *Guided tours by appointment; Sun. service at 10:30.*

❽ Governor Henry Lippit House Museum. The two-term Rhode Island governor made his fortune selling textiles to both armies of the Civil War, and he spared no expense in building his home, an immaculate Renaissance Revival mansion. The floor of the billiard room is made with nine types of inlaid wood; the ceilings are intricately hand-painted (some look convincingly like tiger maple—*faux bois,* or fake wood, was an expensive fad at the time), and the neoclassical chandeliers are cast in bronze. The home was fitted with central heating and electricity, quite an extravagance in 1863. ⊠ *199 Hope St.,* ☎ *401/453–0688.* ≊ *$6.* ⊙ *Apr.–Dec., Tues.–Fri. 11–3; Jan.–Mar. and weekends by appointment only.*

★ ⑪ John Brown House. John Quincy Adams called this house "the most magnificent and elegant private mansion that I have ever seen on this continent." George Washington and other historical figures also visited the house. Designed by Joseph Brown for his brother in 1786, the three-story Georgian mansion has elaborate woodwork and is filled with decorative art, furniture, silver, and items from the China trade, which is how John Brown made his fortune. In addition to opening trade with China, John Brown is famous for his role in the burning of the British customs ship *Gaspee.* He was also a slave trader: His abolitionist brother, Moses, brought charges against him for illegally engaging in the buying and selling of human lives. Across the street and open to the public only on Friday from 1 to 4, is the Nightingale House, built by Brown's chief rival in the China trade. ⊠ *52 Power St.,* ☎ *401/331–8575.* ≊ *$6.* ⊙ *Mar.–Dec., Tues.–Sat. 10–5, Sun. noon–4; Jan.–Feb., Mon.–Thurs. by appointment, Fri.–Sat. 10–5, Sun. noon–4.*

⑥ John Hay Library. Built in 1910 and named for Abraham Lincoln's secretary, "the Hay" houses 11,000 items related to the 16th president. The noncirculating library also stores American drama and poetry collections, 500,000 pieces of American sheet music, the Webster Knight Stamp Collection, the letters of horror and science-fiction writer H. P. Lovecraft, military prints, and a world-class collection of toy soldiers. ⊠ *20 Prospect St.,* ☎ *401/863–2146.* 🎟 *Free.* ☉ *Weekdays 9–5.*

⑫ Market House. Designed by Joseph Brown and owned by Rhode Island School of Design, this brick structure was central to Colonial Providence's trading economy. Tea was burned here in March 1775, and the upper floors were used as barracks for French soldiers during the Revolutionary War. From 1832 to 1878, Market House served as the seat of city government. A plaque shows the height reached by floodwaters during the Great Hurricane of 1938. The building is not open to the public. ⊠ *Market Sq., S. Main St.*

④ Museum of Art, Rhode Island School of Design. This small college museum is amazingly comprehensive. Many of the exhibitions, which change annually, are of textiles, a long-standing Rhode Island industry. The museum's permanent holdings include the Abby Aldrich Rockefeller collection of Japanese prints, Paul Revere silver, 18th-century porcelain, and French Impressionist paintings. Popular with children are the 10-ft statue of Buddha and the Egyptian mummy from the Ptolemaic period (circa 300 BC). The admission fee includes the adjoining **Pendleton House,** a replica of an early 19th-century Providence house. ⊠ *224 Benefit St.,* ☎ *401/454–6500.* 🎟 *$5; free Sat.* ☉ *Wed.–Sun. 10–5, Fri. 10–8.*

⑨ Museum of Rhode Island History at Aldrich House. The Federal-style Aldrich House, built in 1822, was given to the Rhode Island Historical Society in 1974 by the heirs of New York financier Winthrop W. Aldrich. The first comprehensive museum about Rhode Island history, it presents rotating exhibits. ⊠ *110 Benevolent St.,* ☎ *401/331–8575.* 🎟 *$2.* ☉ *Tues.–Fri. 9–5, Sun. noon–4; until 9 PM 3rd Thurs. of each month.*

★ **⑤ Providence Athenaeum.** The Athenaeum was the center of the intellectual life of old Providence. Established in 1753 and housed in a granite 1838 Greek Revival structure, this is among the oldest lending libraries in the world. Here Edgar Allan Poe, visiting Providence to lecture at Brown, met and courted Sarah Helen Whitman, who was said to be the inspiration for his poem "Annabel Lee." The library holds Rhode Island art and artifacts, an original set of elephant folio *Birds of America* prints by John J. Audubon, and one of the world's best collections of travel literature. ⊠ *251 Benefit St.,* ☎ *401/421–6970.* 🎟 *Free.* ☉ *June–Labor Day, weekdays 8:30–5:30 (until 8:30 Wed. in summer); Labor Day–May, weekdays 8:30–5:30, Sat. 9:30–5:30, Sun. 1–5.*

⑮ Rhode Island Black Heritage Society. The historical photographs, taped interviews, and other artifacts at this museum across the street from the Trinity Square Repertory Company chronicle the contributions of African Americans to Rhode Island life, beginning with the days of slave trading (until its abolition, slavery was a key element in Rhode Island's economy). Also examined is the present-day experience—education, political integration, and new immigration from Africa, the Caribbean, and elsewhere. ⊠ *202 Washington St., 2nd floor,* ☎ *401/751–3490 or 800/335–3490.* 🎟 *Donation requested.* ☉ *Weekdays 10–4:30, Sat. 10–2.*

① Rhode Island State House. Rhode Island's awe-inspiring capitol, erected in 1900, has the first unsupported marble dome in the United States (and the fourth largest in the world), which was modeled on St. Peter's Basilica in Rome. The ornate white Georgian marble exterior is topped by the gilded statue *Independent Man.* The interior's focal point is a full-length portrait of George Washington by Rhode Islander Gilbert Stuart, the same artist who created the likeness on the $1 bill. You'll also see the original parchment charter granted by King Charles to the colony of Rhode Island in 1663 and military accoutrements of Nathaniel Greene, Washington's second-in-command during the Revolutionary War. Booklets are available for self-guided tours. A gift shop is located on the basement level. ⊠ *82 Smith St.,* ☎ *401/222–2357.* ☉ *Weekdays 8:30–4:30; guided tours at 10 and 11.*

② **Roger Williams National Memorial.** Roger Williams contributed so significantly to the development of the concepts that underpin the Declaration of Independence and the Constitution that the National Park Service dedicated a 4.5-acre park to his memory. Displays offer a quick course in the life and times of Rhode Island's founder, who wrote the first-ever book on the language of North American Indians. ⊠ *282 N. Main St.,* ☎ *401/785–9450.* ⊠ *Free.* ☉ *Daily 9–4:30.*

OFF THE
BEATEN PATH

ROGER WILLIAMS PARK AND ZOO – This beautiful 430-acre Victorian park is immensely popular. You can have a picnic, feed the ducks in the lakes, ride a pony, or rent a paddleboat or miniature speedboat. At Carousel Village, kids can ride the vintage carousel or a miniature train. There's also the Museum of Natural History and the Cormack Planetarium, and the Tennis Center has Rhode Island's only public clay courts. More than 900 animals of 150 different species live at the zoo. Among the attractions are the Tropical Rainforest Pavilion, the African Plains exhibit, and an open-air aviary. To get here, take I–95 south to Route 1 south (Elmwood Avenue); the park entrance will be the first left turn. ⊠ *Elmwood Ave.,* ☎ *401/785-3510 for zoo, 401/785-9450 for park.* ⊠ *$3.50.* ☉ *Zoo daily 9–5 (until 4 in winter), museum daily 10–5.*

⑭ **Waterplace Park and Riverwalk.** A key component of Providence's revitalization effort, Waterplace Park was completed in 1997. The 4-acre tract with Venetian-style footbridges, cobblestone walkways, and an amphitheater encircling a tidal pond has won national and international design awards. The Riverwalk passes the junction of three rivers—the Woonasquatucket, Providence, and Moshassock—a nexus of the shipping trade during the city's early years. On sunny summer days the park draws pedestrians, boaters, artists, and performers. The amphitheater hosts free concerts and plays. Inquire about upcoming events at the visitor information center, in the clock tower. ⊠ *Boat House Clock Tower, 2 American Express Way,* ☎ *401/751–1177.* ☉ *Mon.–Sat. 10–4.*

⑰ **Wickenden Street.** The main artery in the Fox Point district, a working-class Portuguese neighborhood that is undergoing gentrification, Wickenden Street is chockablock with antiques stores, galleries, and trendy cafés. Professors, artists, and students are among the newer residents here. Many of the houses along Wickenden, Transit, Gano, and nearby streets are still painted the pastel colors of Portuguese homes, and locals still sit out on their stoops on hot summer evenings.

Dining

American

$$$–$$$$ ✕ **Capital Grille.** Dry-aged beef is the star, but lobster and fish are also on the menu at the cavernous Capital Grille. The mashed potatoes, cottage fries, and Caesar salads are served in portions that will sate even the heartiest appetite. Leather, brass, mahogany, oil portraits, a mounted

wooden canoe, and Bloomberg News ticking away in the barroom lend this establishment the feel of an opulent men's club. ⊠ *1 Cookson Pl.,* ☎ *401/521–5600. AE, D, DC, MC, V. No lunch weekends.*

American/Casual

$$–$$$ ✕ **Union Station Brewery.** The historic brick building that houses this brew pub was once the freight house for the Providence Train Station. You can wash down a tasty chipotle-glazed pork quesadilla, an old-fashioned chicken potpie, or ale-battered fish-and-chips with a pint of Providence cream ale or one of several other fine beers brewed here. ⊠ *36 Exchange Terr.,* ☎ *401/274–2739. AE, DC, D, MC, V.*

Contemporary

$$$–$$$$ ✕ **Al Forno.** The owners of Al Forno, George Germon and Johanne ★ Killeen, wrote an acclaimed book on the art of food, and their restaurant cemented the city's reputation as a culinary center in New England. Try a wood-grilled pizza as an appetizer, followed by roasted clams and spicy sausage served in a tomato broth or charcoal-seared tournedos of beef with mashed potatoes (called "dirty steak" by regulars) and onion rings. Your made-to-order dessert could be crepes with apricot puree and crème anglaise or a fresh cranberry tart with walnuts and brown sugar. ⊠ *577 S. Main St.,* ☎ *401/273–9760. Reservations not accepted. AE, MC, DC, V. Closed Sun.–Mon. No lunch.*

$$$–$$$$ ✕ **The Gatehouse.** A redbrick cottage houses this much-praised restau- ★ rant, where the views of the Seekonk River and the classy decor (which includes works from owner Henry Kate's art collection) complement the New Orleans–influenced New England cuisine. Chef Steven Marsella, who trained under Louisiana's Frank Brigtsen and Emeril Lagasse, prepares dishes that might include slow-roasted duck with sautéed vegetables, served with spiced pumpkin gravy and accompanied by cranberry wild rice, butternut squash puree, and spaghetti squash. ⊠ *4 Richmond Sq.,* ☎ *401/521–9229. Reservations essential on weekends. AE, DC, MC, V. No lunch Sat. Brunch served Sun.*

$$–$$$$ ✕ **Rue de l'Espoir.** The eclectic new American offerings change often at this homey longtime Providence favorite. Tempting appetizers might include chicken-and-cashew spring rolls and grilled chili rellenos, followed by an entrée of roast pork crusted with mustard and pepper. The pastas are particularly creative. Breakfast is served on weekdays, brunch on weekends. ⊠ *99 Hope St.,* ☎ *401/751–8890. AE, D, DC, MC, V. Closed Mon.*

French

$$–$$$$ ✕ **Pot au Feu.** As night falls, business-driven downtown Providence clears ★ out, and this bastion of French country cuisine lights up. For a quarter century the chefs at Pot au Feu have worked to perfect the basics, like pâté du foie gras, beef bourguignon, and potatoes au gratin, and the restaurant has gained notice for its distinctive list of French wines. The dining experience is more casual at the downstairs Bistro than at the upstairs Salon. ⊠ *44 Custom House St.,* ☎ *401/273–8953. AE, DC, MC, V. Salon closed Sun.–Mon.*

Indian

$–$$ ✕ **India.** Mango chicken curry and swordfish kabobs are two of the inexpensive entrées at this downtown restaurant filled with Oriental rugs, colorful paintings, and large plants. India is known for its wide freshly made breads, including paratha, wheat bread cooked on a grill and stuffed with various fillings. ⊠ *123 Dorrance St.,* ☎ *401/278–2000. AE, MC, V.*

Italian

$$$–$$$$ ✕ **L'Epicureo.** One of Providence's most refined restaurants began life as half of a Federal Hill butcher shop called Joe's Quality. Joe's daugh-

ter Rozann and son-in-law Tom Buckner transformed the former market into an Italian bistro that has won high marks for its wood-grilled steaks, veal chops, and pasta dishes like fettuccine tossed with arugula, garlic, and lemon. ⊠ *238 Atwells Ave.,* ☎ *401/454–8430. AE, D, DC, MC, V. Closed Sun.–Mon. No lunch.*

$$–$$$$ ✕ **Camille's Roman Garden.** Perhaps the most classic of the Italian eateries on Federal Hill, the second oldest family-run restaurant in the United States serves traditional fare like veal scallopini and shrimp scampi. Black-tie service and reproductions of early Renaissance murals in the massive dining room (which was a speakeasy in the 1920s) impart an air of sophistication. ⊠ *71 Bradford St.,* ☎ *401/751–4812. AE, DC, MC, V. Closed Sun. July–Aug.*

$–$$ ✕ **Angelo's Civita Farnese.** On Federal Hill in the heart of Little Italy, lively (even boisterous) Angelo's is a family-run place with Old World charm. Locals come here for good-size portions of fresh and simply prepared pasta. ⊠ *141 Atwells Ave.,* ☎ *401/621–8171. Reservations not accepted. No credit cards.*

Japanese

$–$$$ ✕ **Tokyo Restaurant.** New carpeting and a fresh coat of paint may be in order at Tokyo, but the Japanese cuisine served here is the best in the state. Choose traditional or American seating—or take a stool at the sushi bar, where local fish like tuna, mackerel, and eel are prepared alongside red snapper and fish from points beyond. The designer rolls include beef, squid, duck or seaweed. ⊠ *123 Wickenden St.,* ☎ *401/ 331–5330. AE, D, MC, V.*

Lodging

$$$$ 🛏 **Westin Hotel.** The multiturreted 25-story Westin towers over Providence's compact downtown, connected by a skywalk to the city's gleaming convention center. The redbrick hotel's Agora restaurant has an award-winning wine cellar. ⊠ *1 W. Exchange St., 02903,* ☎ *401/ 598–8000 or 800/937–8461,* ℻ *401/598–8200. 363 rooms. 2 restaurants, 2 bars, pool, hot tub, health club, meeting rooms, parking (fee). AE, D, DC, MC, V.*

$$$–$$$$ 🛏 **Marriott Hotel.** The Marriott may lack the old-fashioned grandeur of a property like the Providence Biltmore, but the hotel has all the modern conveniences. Tones of peach and green grace the good-size rooms. The Blue Fin Grille restaurant specializes in local seafood prepared with a French flair. ⊠ *Charles and Orms Sts. near Exit 23 off I–95, 02904,* ☎ *401/272–2400 or 800/937–7768,* ℻ *401/273– 2686. 345 rooms, 6 suites. Restaurant, indoor and outdoor pools, sauna, health club, meeting rooms, free parking. AE, D, DC, MC, V.*

$$$ 🛏 **Old Court Bed & Breakfast.** This three-story Italianate inn on historic Benefit Street was built in 1863 as a rectory. Antique furniture, richly colored wallpaper, and memorabilia throughout the house reflect the best of 19th-century style. The rooms have high ceilings and chandeliers; most have nonworking marble fireplaces and some have views of the state house and downtown. ⊠ *144 Benefit St., 02903,* ☎ *401/751–2002. 10 rooms, 1 suite. Free parking. Continental breakfast. AE, D, MC, V.*

$$$ 🛏 **Providence Biltmore.** The Biltmore, completed in 1922, has a sleek
★ Art Deco exterior, an external glass elevator with delightful views of Providence, a grand ballroom, and an interesting history. The personal attentiveness of its staff (there is a European-style concierge system), the downtown location, and modern amenities make this hotel one of the city's best. ⊠ *Kennedy Plaza, Dorrance and Washington Sts., 02903,* ☎ *401/421–0700 or 800/294–7209,* ℻ *401/455–3040. 87*

rooms, 157 suites. Restaurant, café, health club, meeting rooms, parking (fee). AE, D, DC, MC, V.

$$$ ⊞ **State House Inn.** The beautifully restored rooms of this classy inn
★   convenient to the state house are furnished with Shaker- or Colonial-
style pieces, and a few have working fireplaces. Some rooms in the 1880s
Colonial Revival home are on the small side, but that's the only draw-
back to this inviting B&B, where smoking is not permitted. ⊠ 43 Jew-
ett St., 02903, ☎ 401/785–1235. 10 rooms. Free parking. Full breakfast.
AE, D, MC, V.

$$–$$$ ⊞ **Days Hotel on the Harbor.** Despite its small lobby (modern, with
marble floors and ficus trees), this plain but comfortable hotel has an
open feel. Guest rooms have contemporary furnishings in pastel col-
ors. Half the rooms have harbor views; the other half overlook speed-
ing traffic on I–95. A few rooms have whirlpool baths. ⊠ 220 India
St., 02903, ☎ 401/272–5577, FAX 401/272–5577. 136 rooms. Restau-
rant, hot tub, exercise room, meeting rooms, airport shuttle, free park-
ing. AE, D, DC, MC, V.

$$ ⊞ **C. C. Ledbetter's.** The unmarked somber green exterior of innkeeper
C. C. Ledbetter's mansard-roof 1770 home gives few hints of the vibrancy
within—lively art, photographs, quilts, and a shrewd blend of contemporary furnishings and antiques fill the place. The rooms at this B&B
across from the John Brown House are priced well below the competition, making it a favorite of the parents of Brown University students.
⊠ 326 Benefit St., 02903, ☎ FAX 401/351–4699. 1 room with bath, 4
rooms share 2 baths. Free parking. Continental breakfast. AE, V.

Nightlife and the Arts

For events listings consult the daily *Providence Journal Bulletin* and
the weekly *Providence Phoenix* (free in restaurants and bookstores).
Brown University and RISD often present free lectures and performances.

Nightlife

BARS

The **Hot Club** (⊠ 575 S. Water St., ☎ 401/861–9007) is a fashionable
waterside bar. **Oliver's** (⊠ 83 Benevolent St., ☎ 401/272–8795), a popular hangout for Brown students that serves good pub food, has three
pool tables. **Snookers** (⊠ 145 Clifford St., ☎ 401/351–7665) is a stylish
billiard hall in the Jewelry District; through a double doorway at the
rear of the billiard room is a '50s-style lounge where food is served.

MUSIC CLUBS

AS220 (⊠ 111 Empire St., ☎ 401/831–9327) is a gallery and performance space; the musical styles run the gamut from techno-pop, hip-
hop, and jazz to traditional Hmong folk music and dance. **The Call** (⊠
15 Elbow St., ☎ 401/751–2255), a large blues bar, hosts top local groups
like Roomful of Blues. Country-western is the theme at **Desperado's
Contemporary Country Night Club** (⊠ 180 Pine St., ☎ 401/751–
4263), where you can take line-dancing lessons. **Gerardo's** (⊠ 1
Franklin Sq., ☎ 401/274–5560) is a popular gay and lesbian disco.
The Living Room (⊠ 23 Rathbone St., ☎ 401/521–5200) presents live
entertainment nightly, often by prominent local blues musicians. **Lupo's
Heartbreak Hotel** (⊠ 239 Westminster St., ☎ 401/272–5876), a road-
house-style nightclub, books local and international talents. A pink Cadil-
lac is part of the decor at the '50s-theme **Sh-Booms** (⊠ 108 N. Main
St., ☎ 401/751–1200), which plays dance music from the past.

The Arts

FILM

The **Cable Car Cinema** (⊠ 204 S. Main St., ☎ 401/272–3970) is on
the musty side, but the theater books a fine slate of alternative and for-

eign flicks. There are couches rather than seats. Street performers entertain prior to most shows.

MUSIC

Rock bands and country acts occasionally perform at the 14,500-seat **Providence Civic Center** (⌂ 1 LaSalle Sq., ☎ 401/331–6700). The **Providence Performing Arts Center** (⌂ 220 Weybosset St., ☎ 401/421–2787), a 3,200-seat hall that opened in 1928, hosts touring Broadway shows, concerts, and other large-scale happenings. Its lavish interior contains painted frescoes, Art Deco chandeliers, bronze moldings, and marble floors. The **Rhode Island Philharmonic** (☎ 401/831–3123) presents 10 concerts at Veterans Memorial Auditorium between October and May. **Veterans Memorial Auditorium** (⌂ 69 Brownell St., ☎ 401/222–3150) hosts concerts, children's theater, and ballet.

THEATER

Alias Stage (⌂ 31 Elbow St., ☎ 401/831–2919), an ambitious offshoot of Trinity Square Repertory (☞ *below*), presents original works. **Brown University** (⌂ Leeds Theatre, 77 Waterman St., ☎ 401/863–2838) mounts productions of contemporary, sometimes avant-garde, works as well as classics. **New Gate Theatre** (⌂ 134 Mathewson St., ☎ 401/421–9680) specializes in new plays, but also stages Broadway musicals and a popular Christmas cabaret. The **Trinity Square Repertory Company** (⌂ 201 Washington St., ☎ 401/351–4242) presents plays in the renovated Majestic movie house. The varied season generally includes classics, foreign plays, and new works.

Outdoor Activities and Sports

Basketball

The **Providence College Friars** play Big East basketball at the Providence Civic Center (⌂ 1 LaSalle Sq., ☎ 401/331–6700 for event information, 401/331–2211 for tickets).

Biking

The best biking in the Providence area is along the 14½-mi **East Bay Bicycle Path,** which hugs the Narragansett Bay shore from India Point Park, through four towns, to Independence Park in Bristol. **Esta's Too** (⌂ 257 Thayer St., ☎ 401/831–2651), which rents bicycles, is near the path.

Boating

Prime boating areas include the Providence River, the Seekonk River, and Narragansett Bay. **Baer's River Workshop** (⌂ 222 S. Water St., ☎ 401/453–1633) rents canoes and kayaks from April to October and conducts guided tours of Providence's waterfront. The **Narragansett Boat Club** (⌂ River Rd., ☎ 401/272–1838) has information about local boating.

Football

The **Brown Bears** (☎ 401/863–2773) of Brown University play at Brown Stadium (⌂ Elmgrove and Sessions Sts.).

Golf

The 18-hole, par-72 **Triggs Memorial Golf Course** (⌂ 1533 Chalkstone Ave., ☎ 401/521–8460) has lengthy fairways. The greens fee ranges from $25 to $30; an optional cart costs $23.

Hockey

The **Providence Bruins** (☎ 401/331–6700), a farm team of the Boston Bruins, play at the Civic Center. The **Brown Bears** (☎ 401/863–2773) play high-energy hockey at Meehan Auditorium (⌂ 235 Hope St.).

Jogging

Three-mile, tree-lined Blackstone Boulevard is a good place to run.

Shopping

Antiques

Wickenden Street contains many antiques stores and several art galleries. **The Cat's Pajamas** (⊠ 227 Wickenden St., ☎ 401/751–8440) specializes in 20th-century jewelry, linens, housewares, accessories, and small furnishings. **CAV** (⊠ 14 Imperial Pl., ☎ 401/751–9164) is a restaurant, bar, and coffeehouse in a revamped factory space where fine rugs, tapestries, prints, portraits, and antiques are sold. **Tilden-Thurber** (⊠ 292 Westminster St., ☎ 401/272–3200) carries high-end Colonial- and Victorian-era furniture, antiques, and estate jewelry.

Art

The **Alaimo Gallery** (⊠ 301 Wickenden St., ☎ 401/421–5360) specializes in ephemeral items: hand-colored engravings, magazine and playbill covers, political cartoons, antique prints, book plates, antique posters, and box labels. **JRS Fine Art** (⊠ 218 Wickenden St., ☎ 401/331–4380) sells works by national, regional, and Rhode Island artists. **The Peaceable Kingdom** (⊠ 116 Ives St., ☎ 401/351–3472) stocks folk art. The store's strengths include Native American jewelry and crafts, Haitian paintings, Oriental rugs, kilims, and Hmong story cloths. (Rhode Island has a sizable Hmong community, and Joan Ritchie, the owner of the store, has written about the cloths made by these people from Laos.)

Foods

Roma Gourmet Foods (⊠ 310 Atwells Ave., ☎ 401/331–8620) on Federal Hill sells homemade pasta, bread, pizza, pastries, and meats and cheeses. Across the street is **Tony's Colonial** (⊠ 311 Atwells Ave., ☎ 401/621–86750), a superb Italian grocery and deli with a wide assortment of freshly prepared foods.

Mall

America's first shopping mall is the **Arcade** (⊠ 65 Weybosset St., ☎ 401/598–1199), built in 1828. A National Historic Landmark, this graceful Greek Revival building has three tiers of shops and restaurants. Expect the unusual at **Copacetic Rudely Elegant Jewelry** (⊠ The Arcade, 65 Weybosset St., ☎ 401/273–0470), which sells the work of more than 130 diverse artists. **The Game Keeper** (⊠ The Arcade, 65 Weybosset St., ☎ 401/351–0362) sells board games, puzzles, and gadgets.

Maps

The Map Center (⊠ 671 N. Main St., ☎ 401/421–2184) carries maps of all types and nautical charts.

Providence A to Z

Arriving and Departing

See Arriving and Departing *in* Rhode Island A to Z, at the end of this chapter.

Getting Around

BY BUS

RIPTA (Rhode Island Public Transportation Authority; ☎ 401/781–9400; 800/244–0444 in RI) buses run around town and to T. F. Green State Airport; the main terminal is in Kennedy Plaza (⊠ Washington and Dorrance Sts.). The fares range from $1 to $3.

BY CAR

Overnight parking is not allowed on Providence's streets, and during the day it can be difficult to find curbside parking, especially downtown and on Federal and College hills. The Westin Hotel (☞ *above*), in downtown, has a large parking garage. Right turns are permitted on red lights after stopping. To get from T. F. Green Airport to downtown Providence, take I–95 north to Exit 22.

BY TAXI

Fares are $1.20 at the flag drop, then $2 per mi. The ride from the airport takes about 15 minutes and costs about $25. Try **Airport Taxi** (☎ 401/737–2868), **Checker Cab** (☎ 401/273–2222), **Economy Cab** (☎ 401/944–6700), or **Yellow Cab** (☎ 401/941–1122).

Contacts and Resources

EMERGENCIES

Rhode Island Hospital (✉ 593 Eddy St., ☎ 401/444–4000).

GUIDED TOURS

Providence Preservation Society (✉ 21 Meeting St., ☎ 401/831–7440) publishes a walking-tour guidebook ($2.50) to historic Benefit Street and operates tours of stunning private homes on the second weekend in June.

24-HOUR PHARMACY

Brooks Pharmacy (✉ 1200 N. Main St., ☎ 401/272–3048).

VISITOR INFORMATION

Greater Providence Convention and Visitors Bureau (✉ 1 W. Exchange St., 02903, ☎ 401/274–1636).

THE BLACKSTONE VALLEY

The 45-mi-long Blackstone River runs from Worcester, Massachusetts, to Pawtucket, Rhode Island, where its power was harnessed in 1790, setting off America's Industrial Revolution. Along the river and its tributaries are many old mill towns separated by woods and farmland. Pawtucket and Woonsocket grew into large cities in the 1800s when a system of canals, and later railroads, became distribution channels for local industry, which attracted a steady flow of French, Irish, and Eastern European immigrants.

The region is named for William Blackstone, who in 1628 became the first European to settle in Boston. In 1635, having grown weary of the ways of the Puritan settlers who had become his neighbors, this Anglican clergyman built a new home in wilderness that is now called Rhode Island. Called "the sage of the wilderness," Blackstone was known for traveling atop a docile white bull. It may never be known, however, if he was a 17th-century Thoreau or Emerson—his cabin and his writings were destroyed in 1675, during the year-long King Philip's War, a devastating conflict between white settlers and Native Americans.

The United States Park Service recently designated the Blackstone Valley a National Heritage Corridor. A planned bike path will run from Worcester to the Narragansett Bay, and a prominent new museum in Woonsocket relates the region's history through multimedia exhibits. But the work to make the valley a significant tourist destination is just beginning. Signage is lacking, and accommodations can be difficult to find. Luckily, the hotels and inns of Providence are a short drive away, making the Blackstone Valley an excellent day trip.

Pawtucket

18 *5 mi north of Providence.*

In Algonkian, "petuket" (similar to standard Rhode Island pronunciation of the city's name, accent on the second syllable) means "water

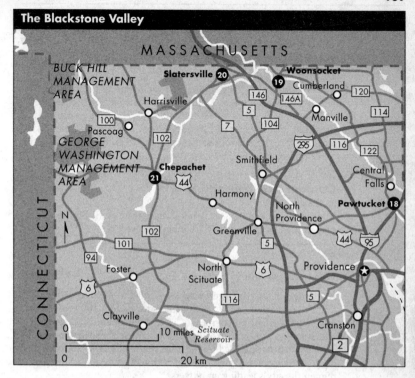

The Blackstone Valley

MASSACHUSETTS

BUCK HILL MANAGEMENT AREA

GEORGE WASHINGTON MANAGEMENT AREA

CONNECTICUT

Slatersville 20 · Woonsocket 19 · Cumberland · 120

Harrisville · 146 · 146A · Manville · 114

100 · Pascoag · 5 · 104 · 295 · 116 · 122

102 · 7 · Smithfield · Central Falls

Chepachet 21 · 44 · Harmony · North Providence · Pawtucket 18

102 · Greenville · 5 · 44 · 95

94 · 101 · 5

Foster · 6 · North Scituate · 6 · Providence

116 · 5

Clayville · Scituate Reservoir · Cranston · 2

0 — 10 miles

0 — 20 km

falls." A small village was established at the falls in 1670 by Joseph Jenks Jr., who considered the area a prime spot for an iron forge. Using the ready supply of timber and iron ore, his company manufactured plows, anchors, and scythes. When Samuel Slater arrived 120 years later, he was delighted to find a corps of skilled mechanics ready to assist him in his dream of organizing America's first factory system. Many of Pawtucket's older buildings were torn down as part of urban renewal projects in the 1970s, though significant portions of the city's history have been preserved.

In 1793, Samuel Slater and two Providence merchants built the first factory in America to produce cotton yarn from water-powered machines. The yellow clapboard **Slater Mill Historic Site** houses classrooms, a theater, and machinery illustrating the conversion of raw cotton to finished cloth. A 16,000-pound waterwheel powers an operational 19th-century machine shop; it and the adjacent 1758 Sylvanus Brown House, furnished according to an inventory taken in 1824, are open to the public. ⊠ 727 Roosevelt Ave., ☎ 401/725–8638. ☜ $6. ☉ June–Nov., Tues.–Sat. 10–5, Sun. 1–5; Mar.–May and Nov.–mid-Dec., weekends 1–5. Guided tours given daily; call for times.

Slater Memorial Park stretches along Ten Mile River. Within this stately park are picnic tables, tennis courts, playgrounds, a river walk, and two historic sites. Eight generations of Daggetts lived in the **Daggett House**, Pawtucket's oldest home, which was built in 1685 to replace an earlier home destroyed during the King Philip's War. Among the 17th-century antiques on display are bedspreads owned by Samuel Slater. The **Loof Carousel** was built by Charles I. D. Loof. The carousel's 42 horses, three dogs, lion, camel, and giraffe are the earliest examples of the Danish immigrant's work. ⊠ Newport Ave./Rte. 1A, ☎ 401/728–0500 for park information, 401/722–2631 for Daggett House. ☜ Free *for park and carousel; $2 for Daggett House.* ☉ *Park daily dawn–dusk; Daggett House June–Sept., daily 2–5; carousel July–Labor Day, daily 10–5, late-Apr.–June and Labor Day–Columbus Day, weekends 10– 5. Closed Columbus Day–late-Apr.*

Dining

$–$$ **Modern Diner.** This 1941 Sterling Streamline eatery—a classic from the heyday of the stainless steel diner—was the first diner to be listed on the National Register of Historic Places. The food—especially the breakfast menu—is worthy of notice, too. The modern takes on classic diner fare include lobster Benedict and French toast with custard sauce and berries. ⊠ *364 East Ave.,* ☎ *401/726–8390. MC, V. No dinner.*

Outdoor Activities and Sports

BASEBALL

The **Pawtucket Red Sox,** the Triple-A farm team of the Boston Red Sox, play at McCoy Stadium (⊠ 1 Columbus Ave., ☎ 401/724–7300).

Woonsocket

⑲ *15 mi north of Providence.*

Rhode Island's sixth-largest city was settled in the late 17th century, home to a sawmill and Quaker farmers for its first 100 years. A steep hill on the northern end of the city looks down on the Blackstone River, which makes a dozen turns in its 5-mi course through Woonsocket. The river's flow spawned textile mills that made Woonsocket a thriving community in the 19th and early 20th century. Manufacturing plants remain the city's leading employers.

☖ Multimedia and more traditional exhibits at the **Museum of Work and Culture** examine the lives of American factory workers and owners during the Industrial Revolution. The genesis of the textile-workers' union is described, as are the events that led to the National Textile Strike of 1934. A model of the triple decker (a three-family tenement building) demonstrates the practicality behind what was once the region's preeminent style of home. Youngsters are often fascinated by presentations about child labor. ⊠ *42 S. Main St.,* ☎ *401/769–9675.* ▢ *$5.* ☉ *Weekdays 9:30–4, Sat. 10–5, Sun. 1–5.*

Dining and Lodging

$ ✕ **Ye Olde English Fish & Chips.** Fresh fried fish and potatoes have been served at this statewide institution for eons. The decor is simple—wood paneling and booths—so it must be the inexpensive and consistently excellent food, served in red plastic baskets, that has kept folks returning to this joint since 1922. ⊠ *Market Sq., S. Main St.,* ☎ *401/762–3637. No credit cards. Closed Sun.–Mon.*

$$ ▣ **The Pilsbury House.** Stately Prospect Street stretches along the crest of the steep ridge north of the Blackstone River; its mansions, like the mansard-roof Pilsbury House, were built by wealthy mill owners in the late 1800s. The common room has a baby grand piano, a parquet floor, and a fireplace with a maple hearth. The two guest rooms on the second floor are furnished in Victorian style, with antiques, plants, high beds, and fringed lamp shades. The third-floor suite has a more rustic-country decor. ⊠ *341 Prospect St., 02895,* ☎ *401/766–7983 or 800/205–4112. 3 rooms. Full breakfast. AE, D, DC, MC, V.*

Nightlife

The impressive entertainment lineup at **Chan's Fine Oriental Dining** (⊠ 267 Main St., ☎ 401/765–1900) includes blues, jazz, and folk performers. Reservations are required; ticket prices range from $10 to $18.

Shopping

Storefront renovations and public improvement of the road and sidewalks have made for much better shopping along Main Street in Woonsocket. **Main Street Antiques** (⊠ 32 Main St., ☎ 401/762–0805) is a good place to start your browsing.

Slatersville

⓴ *3 mi west of Woonsocket.*

Samuel Slater's brother, John, purchased a small sawmill and blacksmith shop along the Branch River and turned the area, now part of North Smithfield township, into America's first planned city, Slatersville. With their factory well removed from population centers, Slater and his partners built homes, a green, a Congregational church, and a general store for their workers. The village, west of the junction of Routes 102 and 146, has been well preserved, and though it does not cater to tourists, it is a fine place for for an afternoon stroll.

Dining

$ ✕ **Wright's Farm Restaurant.** Chicken Family Style—all-you-can-eat bread, salad, roasted chicken, pasta, and potatoes—a northern Rhode Island tradition, was born of a Woonsocket social club's need to feed many people as efficiently as possible. More than a dozen restaurants in the Blackstone Valley serve this food combo; Wright's Farm, the largest, dishes up 300 tons of chicken each year. Excluding drinks, the meals cost $8 per person. ⊠ *84 Inman Rd., west of Slatersville off Rte. 102, Burrillville,* ☎ *401/769–2856. No credit cards. Closed Mon.–Tues. No lunch.*

Chepachet

㉑ *20 mi northwest of Providence.*

Antiques shops and other businesses line Main Street in the village of Chepachet, at the intersection of Routes 44 and 102 in the township of Glocester. The setting feels so much out of a storybook that you might find it jolting to see paved roads and automobiles upon exiting emporiums like the **Brown & Hopkins Country Store** (⊠ 1197 Main St., ☎ 401/568–4830). Established in 1809, B&H has been in operation for longer than any other country store in America. Crafts, penny candy, a deli, antiques, and a potbellied stove await visitors.

Dining

$$–$$$ ✕ **The Stagecoach Tavern.** Formerly a stagecoach stop between Providence and Hartford, this establishment serves hearty meat dishes and pastas at reasonable prices. Locals hang out at the casual bar. ⊠ *1157 Main St.,* ☎ *401/568–2275. AE, D, DC, MC, V.*

OFF THE **BUCK HILL MANAGEMENT AREA** – Tucked away in the remote northwest
BEATEN PATH corner of the state, 7 mi from Chepachet, this area supports waterfowl, songbirds, deer, pheasant, owls, foxes, and wild turkeys. Hiking trails traverse the preserve and cross into Connecticut and Massachusetts. ⊠ *Buck Hill Rd. off Rte. 100 or Wallum Lake Rd.,* ☎ *401/789–0281.* 🎫 *Free.* ⊙ *Daily, from ½ hr before sunrise to ½ hr after sunset.*

Blackstone Valley A to Z

Arriving and Departing

BY BUS

Rhode Island Public Transit Authority (☎ 401/781–9400; 800/244–0444 in RI) buses travel from Providence's Kennedy Plaza (⊠ Washington and Dorrance Sts.) to the Blackstone Valley.

BY CAR

The easiest way to explore the Blackstone Valley is by car. A good map is helpful, as signage satisfying tourists' needs is not yet in place. Call the Northern Rhode Island Chamber of Commerce (☞ *below*) for a map, or pick up *Street Atlas Rhode Island,* available at most gas stations.

Pawtucket is north of Providence on I–95. To reach Woonsocket, take Route 146 northwest from Providence and head north at Route 99; from Woonsocket, take Route 146A west to Route 102 to get to Slatersville. Chepachet is southwest of Slatersville on Route 102 and west of Providence on Route 44.

Getting Around
See Arriving and Departing, *above.*

Contacts and Resources
The **Blackstone Valley Tourism Council** (✉ 171 Main St., Pawtucket 02860, ☎ 401/724–2200 or 800/454–2882). **Northern Rhode Island Chamber of Commerce** (✉ 6 Blackstone Valley Pl., Suite 105, Lincoln 02865, ☎ 401/334–1000).

SOUTH COUNTY

When the principal interstate traffic shifted from Route 1 to I–95, coastal Rhode Island—known within the state as South County—largely escaped the advance of malls and tract-housing developments that overtook other, more accessible areas. With 19 preserves and state parks encompassing beaches, forests, and swamps, South County is a region that respects the concept of wilderness.

Westerly

㉒ *50 mi from Providence, 100 mi from Boston, 140 mi from New York City.*

The village of Westerly is a busy little railway town that grew up in the late 19th century around a major station on what is now the New York–Boston Amtrak corridor. The 30-square-mi community of 15 villages has since sprawled out along Route 1. Victorian and Greek Revival mansions line many streets off the town center, which borders Connecticut and the Pawcatuck River. During the Industrial Revolution and into the 1950s, Westerly was distinguished for its flawless blue granite, from which monuments throughout the country were made.

Watch Hill and Misquamicut are two summer communities generally recognized without mention of their township. Gaming developments in North Stonington and Ledyard, Connecticut, are slowly changing Westerly's economic climate. Many residents work in the casinos, and gambling vacationers are discovering that Westerly's B&Bs provide pleasant alternatives to casino hotels.

Wilcox Park (✉ 71½ High St., ☎ 401/596–8590), designed in 1898 by Warren Manning, an associate of Frederick Law Olmsted and Calvert Vaux, is an 18-acre park in the heart of town with a garden designed so that people with visual and other impairments can identify—by taste, touch, and smell—carnations, mint, chives, thyme, bay leaves, and geraniums.

Dining and Lodging

$$$$ ✕▥ **Weekapaug Inn.** Weekapaug is a picturesque coastal village 6 mi
★   from Westerly center and 3 mi from Misquamicut Beach. This inn, with a peaked roof and huge wraparound porch, sits on a peninsula sur-

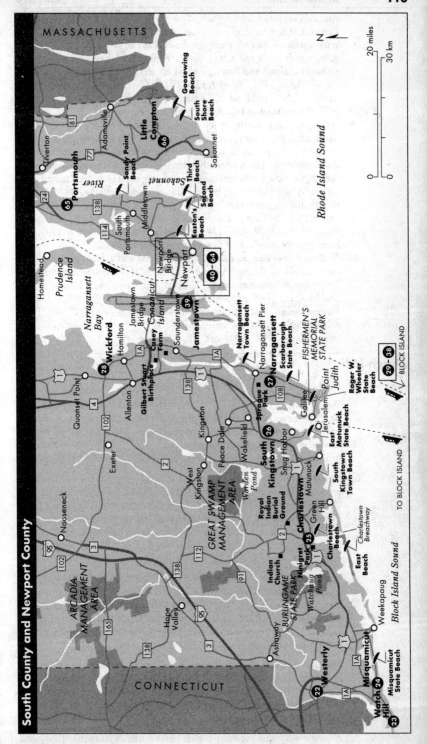

rounded on three sides by salty Quonochontaug Pond. The rooms are cheerful, if not particularly remarkable; most are big and bright, with wide windows that have impressive views. The standards at the restaurant, which has a full-time baker, are high: Each new daily menu emphasizes seafood and lists four to six entrées. ✉ *25 Spring Ave., 02891,* ☎ *401/322–0301,* FAX *401/322–1016. 55 rooms. Restaurant. MAP available. No credit cards. Closed Nov.–June.*

\$\$–\$\$\$ ✕🖫 ★ **Shelter Harbor Inn.** About 6 mi east of downtown in a quiet rural setting not far from the beach, this inn has many rooms with fireplaces and decks. The rooms are furnished with a combination of Victorian antiques and reproduction pieces; bedspreads and curtains are in muted floral patterns. The frequently changing menu at the excellent restaurant might include smoked scallops and cappellini or pecan-crusted duck breast. A bowl of warm, buttery Indian pudding makes a solid finish to any dinner. Breakfast is good every day, but Sunday brunch is legendary. ✉ *10 Wagner Rd., off Rte. 1, 02891,* ☎ *401/322–8883 or 800/468–8883,* FAX *401/322–7907. 23 rooms. Restaurant, hot tub, croquet, paddle tennis. Full breakfast. AE, D, DC, MC, V.*

\$\$ 🖫 **Grandview Bed and Breakfast.** Relaxed and affordable, this B&B on a rise above Route 1A has comfortable, if nondescript, rooms (the front ones have ocean views). The common room has a TV with VCR. Breakfast is served on the porch in summer. ✉ *212 Shore Rd., Dunn's Corner (between Misquamicut and Weekapaug), 02891,* ☎ *401/596–6384 or 800/447–6384,* FAX *401/596–6384. 5 rooms with bath, 4 rooms share 2 baths. Full breakfast. AE, MC, V.*

Watch Hill

★ ㉓ *5 mi south of downtown Westerly.*

Watch Hill, a Victorian-era resort village, contains miles of beautiful beaches. Long before the first Europeans showed up, southern Rhode Island was inhabited by the Narragansett, a powerful Native American tribe. The Niantics, ruled by Chief Ninigret in the 1630s, were one branch of the tribe. A **statue of Ninigret** stands watch over Bay Street.

🌀 **Flying Horse Carousel,** at the beach end of Bay Street, is the oldest merry-go-round in America. It was built by the Charles W. F. Dare Co. of New York in about 1867. The horses, suspended from above, swing out when in motion. Each is hand-carved from a single piece of wood and embellished with real horse hair, a leather saddle, and agate eyes. Adults are not permitted to ride the carousel. ✉ *Bay St.* 🎟 *50¢.* ☉ *Mid-June–Labor Day, weekdays 1–9, weekends and holidays 11–9.*

The immensity of the **Ocean House** (✉ 2 Bluff Ave., ☎ 401/348–8161), a yellow-clapboard Victorian building, will just about take your breath away. Built by George Nash in 1868, this was one of the grand hotels that helped earn Watch Hill its fame as a 19th-century resort. Though the place is a bit down at the heels these days, its views of the Atlantic remain unparalleled.

The **U.S. Coast Guard Light Station** has great views of the ocean and of Fishers Island, New York. The tiny museum contains exhibits about the light. Parking is for the elderly only; everyone else must walk from lots at the beach. ✉ *Lighthouse Rd.,* ☎ *no phone.* 🎟 *Free.* ☉ *May–Sept., Tues. and Thurs. 1–3.*

A long sandy spit between Watch Hill's Little Narragansett Bay and the ocean, **Napatree Point** is a protected conservation area (great for a stroll) teeming with wildlife. Napatree has no admission fee, no phone, and no parking, but there's a fee lot nearby.

Dining and Lodging

$$-$$$$ ✕ **Olympia Tea Room.** A step back in time, this small restaurant that opened in 1916 has varnished wood booths and a soda fountain—try a marshmallow sundae or an orangeade—behind a long marble counter. Mussels steamed in white wine are on the dinner menu. The "world famous Avondale swan" dessert is a fantasy of ice cream, whipped cream, chocolate sauce, and puff pastry. ⊠ *30 Bay St.,* ☎ *401/348–8211. Reservations not accepted. AE, MC, V. Closed Dec.–Easter.*

$$$$ 🏨 **Ocean House.** This grand old lady has one of the best seaside porches in New England. Casual, relaxing, and quiet, the inn has a reassuring if faded elegance. The furniture could best be described as maple eclectic. Ask for a room with an ocean view. Splintery stairs lead to an excellent private beach. ⊠ *2 Bluff Ave., 02891,* ☎ *401/348–8161. 59 rooms. Restaurant, lounge, beach. Full breakfast; MAP available. MC, V. Closed Sept.–June.*

Shopping

Bay Street is a good place to shop for jewelry, summer clothing, and antiques. The **Book and Tackle Shop** (⊠ 7 Bay St., ☎ 401/596–0700) buys, sells, and appraises old and rare books, prints, autographs, and photographs. **Puffins of Watch Hill** (⊠ 60 Bay St., ☎ 401/596–1770) carries fine American crafts, collectibles, pottery, jewelry, and gifts.

Misquamicut

㉔ *2 mi east of Watch Hill.*

Strip motels jostle for attention in Misquamicut, where a giant water slide, a carousel, miniature golf, a game arcade, children's rides, batting cages, and fast-food stands attract visitors by the hundreds to **Atlantic Beach Park** (⊠ Atlantic Ave., ☎ 401/322–9298). The mile-long beach is accessible year-round, but the amusements are open only between Memorial Day and Labor Day.

Dining and Lodging

$$-$$$ ✕ **Paddy's Seafood Restaurant.** The food is good and the portions are generous at this no-frills, family-style beachside restaurant. Lobster, scrod, stuffed shrimp, grilled tuna, and other seafood plates rule the menu, but you can also order pastas and salads. ⊠ *159 Atlantic Ave., Misquamicut Beach,* ☎ *401/596–2610. AE, D, MC, V. Closed Jan.–Apr. and Tues.–Wed., Oct.–Apr.*

$$$-$$$$ 🏨 **Breezeway Motel.** The Bellone family takes great pride in its business and offers a variety of accommodations: villas with fireplaces and hot tubs, suites, efficiencies, and standard rooms. The grounds hold a swing set, shuffleboard, and floodlighted fountains. ⊠ *70 Winnapaug Rd. (Box 1368), 02891,* ☎ *401/348–8953 or 800/462–8872,* ℻ *401/596–3207. 47 rooms, 9 suites, 2 villas. Refrigerators, pool, recreation room. Continental breakfast. AE, D, DC, MC, V. Closed Nov.–May.*

Nightlife

The **Windjammer** (⊠ Atlantic Ave., Misquamicut Beach, ☎ 401/322–9298) hosts dancing to rock bands in a room that holds 1,500.

Charlestown

㉕ *10 mi east of Misquamicut.*

Charlestown stretches along the Old Post Road (Route 1A). Route 1 bisects the village, whose 37 square mi contain parks, the the largest saltwater marsh in the state, 4 mi of pristine beaches, and many oceanfront motels, summer chalets, and cabins.

The 2,100-acre **Burlingame State Park** (⊠ 75 Burlingame Park Rd., ☎ 401/322–7337 or 401/322–7994) has nature trails, picnic and swimming areas, and campgrounds. There's boating and fishing on Watchaug Pond. **Ninigret Park** (⊠ Park La. off Rte. 1A, ☎ 401/364–1222) is a 172-acre park with picnic grounds, ball fields, a bike path, tennis courts, nature trails, and a spring-fed pond; also here is the **Frosty Drew Observatory and Nature Center** (☎ 401/364–9508), which presents nature and astronomy programs on Friday evening. **Ninigret National Wildlife Refuge** (⊠ Rte. 1A, ☎ 401/364–9124) consists of two stretches of beachlands and marshes, plus the abandoned naval air station on Ninigret Pond, where there are 9 mi of trails over 400 acres of diverse upland and wetland habitats—including grasslands, shrublands, wooded swamps, and freshwater ponds.

Many Narragansetts still live in the Charlestown area, but their sites are unmarked and easy to miss. The **Royal Indian Burial Ground,** resting place of sachems (chiefs), is on the left side of Narrow Lane north of Route 1. You'll recognize it by the tall fences, but there's no sign and it's not open for visits except during the annual Narragansett meeting, usually the second Sunday in August, when tribal members from around the nation convene for costumed dancing and rituals.

The two beaches in Charlestown have calm, warm waters that make them popular with families. Both beaches have parking, a snack bar, and rest rooms. **Charlestown Town Beach** (⊠ Charlestown Beach Rd.) ends at a beachway that is part of Ninigret National Wildlife Refuge (☞ *above*). Glorious **East Beach** (⊠ East Beach Rd.), composed of 3½ mi of dunes backed by the crystal-clear waters of Ninigret Pond, is a 2-mi hike from the beachway at Charlestown Town Beach. Parking is available at the end of East Beach Road.

Dining and Lodging

$$–$$$ ✕▤ **The General Stanton Inn.** For helping pay the ransom of an Indian princess in 1655, the Narragansetts rewarded Thomas Stanton with the land where this inn stands. Stanton, a trader from England, first ran it as a schoolhouse for African American and Native American children. Since the 18th century, it has provided dining and lodging in an authentic Colonial atmosphere. The rooms have low ceilings, uneven floorboards, small windows, and period antiques and wallpapers. The dining rooms in the restaurant ($–$$) have brick fireplaces, beams, and wooden floors. Traditional New England fare—steaks, lobster, scrod, rack of lamb—is prepared. ⊠ *Old Post Rd./Rte. 1A, 02813,* ☎ *401/364–0100,* FAX *401/364–5021. 16 rooms. Restaurant, bar. Full breakfast. AE, MC, V. Restaurant closed Nov.–Apr.*

Outdoor Activities and Sports

BOATING

Narragansett Kayak Co. (⊠ 2144 Matunuck Schoolhouse Rd., ☎ 401/364–2000) rents canoes and kayaks. **Ocean House Marina** (⊠ 60 Town Dock Rd. , ☎ 401/364–6060), at the Cross Mills Exit off Route 1, is a full-service marina with boat rentals and fishing supplies.

Shopping

Artists Guild and Gallery (⊠ 5429 Post Rd./Rte. 1, ☎ 401/322–0506) exhibits 19th- and 20th-century art. **Fox Run Country Antiques** (⊠ Rtes. 1 and 2, Crossland Park, ☎ 401/364–3160 or 401/377–2581 for appointments) sells jewelry, lighting devices, Orientalia, antiques, china, and glassware.

The **Fantastic Umbrella Factory** (⊠ 4920 Old Post Rd., off Rte. 1, ☎ 401/364–6616) comprises four rustic shops and a barn built around a wild garden where peacocks, pheasants, and chickens parade. For sale in the backyard bazaar are hardy perennials and unusual daylilies, greeting cards, kites, crafts, tapestries, incense, and blown-glass jewelry. There is also an art gallery, a greenhouse, and a café that serves organic foods.

South Kingstown

26 *2 mi east of Charlestown, 6 mi west of Point Judith Pond.*

The 55-square-mi town of South Kingstown encompasses Wakefield, Snug Harbor, Matunuck, Green Hill, Kingston, and 10 other villages. At the old **Washington County Jail,** built in 1792 in Wakefield, the largest South Kingstown village, you can view jail cells, rooms from the Colonial period, a Colonial garden, and changing exhibits that depict South County life during the last 300 years. ⊠ *1348 Kingstown Rd.,* ☎ *401/ 783–1328.* 🎦 *Free.* ☉ *May–Oct., Tues., Thurs., and Sat. 1–4.*

Crabs, mussels, and starfish populate the rock reef that extends to the right of **Matunuck Beach.** Southward, the reef gives way to a sandy bottom. When the ocean is calm, you can walk on the reef and explore its tidal pools. On the dunes sits a popular roadhouse, **The Ocean Mist** (⊠ 145 Matunuck Beach Rd., ☎ 401/782–3740), which hosts musicians nightly in summer.

East Matunuck State Beach (⊠ Succotash Rd.) is popular with the college crowd for its white sand and picnic areas. **Roy Carpenter's Beach** (⊠ Matunuck Beach Rd.) is part of a cottage-colony of seasonal renters but is open to the public for a fee. **South Kingstown Town Beach** (⊠ Matunuck Beach Rd.) draws many families.

Dining and Lodging

$–$$ ✕ **Mews Tavern.** The food at this cheery tavern is consistently excellent. Rhode Islanders consider this the best place in the state to get a hamburger (buy one, get one free on Thursday night), but you can also order seafood. ⊠ *465 Main St.,* ☎ *401/783–9370. Reservations not accepted. AE, D, MC, V.*

$$–$$$ ✕🏨 **Larchwood Inn.** This 168-year-old country inn with a Scottish flavor is set in a grove of larch trees. The dining room ($–$$) is open for three meals daily—a winner for dinner is the halibut stuffed with scallops. Ask for a table near the fireplace in winter or a patio spot under the trees in summer. Rooms at the inn, a favored home away from home for Block Islanders who miss the last ferry to the island, range from suites with grand views to smaller, back-of-the-house affairs. ⊠ *521 Main St., Wakefield 02879,* ☎ *401/783–5454,* 𝔽𝔸𝕏 *401/783–1800. 18 rooms. Restaurant. AE, D, DC, MC, V. No lunch Sun.*

$$–$$$ 🏨 **Admiral Dewey Inn.** Victorian antiques furnish the rooms of this inn that was built in 1898 as a seaside hotel—it's across the road from Matunuck Beach—and is now on the National Register of Historic Places. Some rooms have views of the ocean, others are tucked cozily under the eaves. Smoking is permitted only on the wraparound veranda, which is filled with old-fashioned rocking chairs. ⊠ *668 Matunuck Beach Rd., 02881,* ☎ *401/783–2090. 8 rooms with bath, 2 rooms share bath. Continental breakfast. MC, V.*

Nightlife and the Arts

Ocean Mist (⊠ 145 Matunuck Beach Rd., ☎ 401/782–3740) is a distinctive beachfront barroom with music nightly in summer and on weekends off-season. The hard-drinking crowd at this hangout of the South County's younger generation can be as rough-hewn as the building. The barn-style **Theatre-by-the-Sea** (⊠ Cards Pond Rd. off Rte. 1, ☎ 401/782–8587), built in 1933 and listed on the National Register of Historic Places, presents musicals and plays in summer.

Outdoor Activities and Sports

FISHING

The well-stocked **Gil's Custom Tackle** (⊠ 101 Main St., Wakefield, ☎ 401/783–1370) sells recreational fishing gear. **Snug Harbor Marina** (⊠ 410 Gooseberry Rd., Wakefield, ☎ 401/783–7766) sells bait, rents kayaks, and arranges fishing charters. At Snug Harbor it is not uncommon to see on the docks giant tuna and shark weighing more than 300 pounds.

HIKING

Great Swamp (⊠ Great Neck Rd. near West Kingston, ☎ 401/789–0281), a temporary home to migrating waterfowl, has a network of trails.

WATER SPORTS

The Watershed (⊠ 396 Main St., Wakefield, ☎ 401/789–3399) rents surfboards, Windsurfers, body boards, and wet suits. Owner Peter Pan gives lessons at nearby Narragansett Town Beach.

Shopping

ANTIQUES

Dove and Distaff Antiques (⊠ 365 Main St., Wakefield, ☎ 401/783–5714) is a good spot for Early American furniture. **Peter Pots Authentic Americana** (⊠ 494 Glen Rock Rd., West Kingston, ☎ 401/783–2350) sells stoneware, period furniture, and collectibles.

ART GALLERIES

Hera Gallery (⊠ 327 Main St., Wakefield, ☎ 401/789–1488), a women's art cooperative, exhibits the work of emerging local artists.

Narragansett

㉗ *2 mi east of South Kingstown.*

The town of Narragansett is on the peninsula east of Point Judith Pond and the Pettaquamscutt River. Its 16 villages include Galilee, Jerusalem, Bonnett Shores, and Narragansett Pier.

Narragansett Pier, the beach community often called simply the Pier, was named for an amusement wharf that no longer exists. The Pier, now populated by summertime "cottagers," college students, and commuting professionals, was in the late 1800s a posh resort linked by rail to New York and Boston. The well-to-do traveled here from these cities and from Providence, New Bedford, and beyond. Many of them headed for the Narragansett Pier Casino, which had a bowling alley, billiard tables, tennis courts, a rifle gallery, a theater, and a ballroom. The grand edifice burned to the ground in 1900. Only the **Towers** (⊠ Rte. 1, ☎ 401/783–7121), the grand stone entrance to the former casino, remain. Along Ocean Road, from Point Judith to Narragansett Pier, are most of the mansions built during Narragansett's golden age.

The village of **Galilee** is a busy, workaday fishing port from which whale-watching excursions, fishing trips, and the **Block Island Ferry** (⊠ Galilee State Pier, Point Judith, ☎ 401/783–4613) depart. The occasionally pungent smell of seafood will lead you to the area's fine restaurants and markets. From the port it's a short drive to the **Point Judith Lighthouse** (⊠ 1460 Ocean Rd., ☎ 401/789–0444) and a beautiful ocean view. The lighthouse is open from dawn to dusk. The highlight of **Sprague Park** (⊠ Kingstown Rd. and Strathmore St.) is the Narragansett Indian Monument. Sculptor Peter Toth created the 5-ton, 23-ft monument from the trunk of a giant Douglas fir, working with hammer and chisel 12 hours a day for two months, after which he applied 100 coats of preservative.

⟲ **Adventureland in Narragansett** has bumper boats, miniature golf, batting cages, and a go-cart track. ⊠ *Rte. 108,* ☎ *401/789–0030.* ☞ *Combination tickets $1.50–$9.50.* ☉ *Mid-June–Labor Day, daily 10–10; Labor Day–Oct. and mid-Apr.–May, weekends 10–10.*

⟲ The seven buildings of the **South County Museum** house 20,000 artifacts dating from 1800 to 1933. Exhibits include a country kitchen, a carpentry shop, a cobbler's shop, a tack shop, a working print shop, and an antique carriage collection. ⊠ *Canonchet Farm, Anne Hoxie La. off Rte. 1A,* ☎ *401/783–5400.* ☞ *$3.50.* ☉ *May–Oct., Wed.–Sun. 11–4.*

Beaches

Popular **Narragansett Town Beach** (⊠ Rte. 1A) is within walking distance of many hotels and guest houses. Its pavilion has changing rooms, showers, and concessions. **Roger W. Wheeler State Beach** (⊠ Sand Hill Cove Rd., Galilee) has a new pavilion; the beach, sheltered from ocean swells, has picnic areas and a playground. **Scarborough State Beach** (⊠ Ocean Rd.), considered by many the jewel of Ocean State beaches, has a pavilion with showers and concessions. On weekends, teenagers and college students blanket the sands.

Dining and Lodging

$$$–$$$$ ✕ **Basil's.** Within walking distance of Narragansett Beach, Basil's serves
★ French and Continental cuisine in an intimate setting. Dark floral wallpaper and fresh flowers decorate the small dining room. The specialty is veal topped with a light cream-and-mushroom sauce; other dishes include fish and duck à l'orange. ⊠ *22 Kingstown Rd.,* ☎ *401/789–3743. AE, DC, MC, V. Closed Mon. and Oct.–June Tues. No lunch.*

$$$ ✕ **Coast Guard House.** This restaurant, which dates from 1888 and was a lifesaving station for 50 years, displays interesting photos of Narragansett Pier and the Casino. Candles light the tables and picture windows on three sides allow views of the ocean. The fare is American—seafood, pasta, veal, steak, and lamb. The upstairs lounge hosts entertainers and has a DJ on Friday and Saturday night. ⊠ *40 Ocean Rd.,* ☎ *401/789–0700. AE, D, DC, MC, V.*

$$–$$$ ✕ **Spain Restaurant.** South County's only true Spanish restaurant is appropriately dark and atmospheric. The appetizers include shrimp in garlic sauce, stuffed mushrooms, and Spanish sausages; lobster, steak, and paella are among the main courses. ⊠ *1144 Ocean Rd.,* ☎ *401/783–9770. AE, D, DC, MC, V.*

$–$$$ ✕ **Aunt Carrie's.** This tremendously popular family-owned restaurant has been serving up Rhode Island shore dinners, clam cakes and chowder, and fried seafood for more than 60 years. At the height of the season the lines can be long; one alternative is to order from the take-out window and picnic on the grounds of the nearby lighthouse. Try the enormous but light clam cakes or the squid burger served on homemade bread—squid is the chief product of the largest fish-packing house in Galilee, credited with bringing fried calamari to menus across the country. ⊠ *Rte. 108 and Ocean Rd., Point Judith,* ☎ *401/783–7930. Reservations not accepted. MC, V. Closed Mon–Thurs. in Sept. and May, and Labor Day–Memorial Day.*

$–$$$ ✕ **George's of Galilee.** The lines at George's on summer nights baffle local residents, who assume the cause must be the restaurant's location on a spit of land in a busy fishing harbor rather than the atmosphere (frantic and noisy) or the food (much better can be found elsewhere in Galilee). Yet it's hard to argue with success, and this place has been a "must" for tourists since 1948. The restaurant serves several chowders and hosts barbecues on the beach on summer weekends. ⊠ *Port of Galilee,* ☎ *401/783–2306. Reservations not accepted. D, MC, V. Closed Nov.–Dec. and weekdays Jan.–Feb.*

$$$–$$$$ 🏠 **Stone Lea.** McKim, Mead and White, the architectural firm responsible for the State House and other Rhode Island landmarks, designed this dignified shingle-covered house that has views across Narragansett Bay to Newport, Jamestown, Tiverton, and Block Island. In a section of private homes called Millionaire's Mile, this B&B is replete with rotundas, bay windows, carved wood paneling, and other accents (like the grand-piano staircase that rises from the parquet floor of the foyer). The Block Island room and the three other large rooms are worth the extra cost. Breakfast here is almost as substantial as the home, which is built on a foundation of Rhode Island granite. ⊠ *40 Newton Ave., 02882,* ☎ *401/783–8237,* ℻ *401/792–8237. 7 rooms. Full breakfast. AE, MC, V.*

$$ 🏠 **The Richards.** Imposing and magnificent, this mansion has a broodingly Gothic mystique that is almost the antithesis of a summer house. French windows in the wood-panel common rooms downstairs open up to views of a lush landscape. A grand swamp oak is the centerpiece of a handsome garden. A fire crackles in the library fireplace on chilly afternoons. Some rooms have 19th-century English antiques, floral-upholstered furniture, and fireplaces. Breakfast consists of main courses like eggs Florentine and oven pancakes and fresh fruit and baked goods. ⊠ *144 Gibson Ave., 02882,* ☎ *401/789–7746. 2 rooms with bath, 2 rooms share bath, 1 2-bedroom suite. Full breakfast. No credit cards.*

Outdoor Activities and Sports

FISHING

The **Frances Fleet** (⊠ 2 State St., ☎ 401/783–4988 or 800/662–2824) operates day and overnight fishing trips. Narragansett-based charter boats include the *Persuader* (☎ 401/783–5644), *Prowler* (☎ 401/783–8487), and *Reel Time* (☎ 401/783–0049). **Maridee Canvas–Bait & Tackle** (⊠ 120 Knowlesway Ext., ☎ 401/789–5190) stocks supplies and provides helpful advice.

WHALE-WATCHING

Whale-watching excursions aboard the *Lady Frances* (⊠ Frances Fleet, 2 State St., Point Judith, ☎ 401/783–4988 or 800/662–2824) depart at 1 PM and return at 6 PM. The fare is $30. The trips operate daily except Sunday from July to Labor Day.

En Route   Off Route 1A between Narragansett and Wickford are two historic sights in beautiful locations. The **Silas Casey Farm** still functions much as it has since the 18th century. The farmhouse contains original furniture, prints, paintings, and 300 years of political and military documents. Nearly 30 mi of stone walls surround the 360-acre farmstead. ⊠ *Boston Neck Rd., Saunderstown,* ☎ *401/295–1030.* 🎫 *$3.* 🕐 *June–Oct., Tues., Thurs., Sat. 1–5. Closed Nov.–May and June–Oct., Sun., Mon., Wed., Fri.*

On a country road and along little Mattatuxet River is the **Gilbert Stuart Birthplace.** Built in 1751, this was the home of America's foremost portraitist of George Washington. The adjacent 18th-century snuff mill was the first in America. ⊠ *815 Gilbert Stuart Rd., Saunderstown,* ☎ *401/294–3001.* 🎫 *$3.* 🕐 *Apr.–Oct., Thurs.–Mon. 11–4. Closed Nov.–Mar. and Tues.–Wed. year-round.*

Wickford

★ ㉘   *10 mi north of Narragansett Pier, 15 mi south of Providence.*

The Colonial village of Wickford—in the town of North Kingstown— has a little harbor, dozens of 18th- and 19th-century homes, and antiques and curiosity shops. **Old Narragansett Church,** now called St. Paul's, was built in 1707. It's one of the oldest Episcopal churches in America. ⊠ *55 Main St.,* ☎ *401/294–4357.* ⊘ *Mid-June–Labor Day, Fri. 11–5, Sat. 10–5, Sun. for worship, and by appointment.*

Smith's Castle, built in 1678 by Richard Smith Jr., was the site of many orations by Roger Williams. This is one of the first military burial grounds (open during daylight hours) in the country: Interred in a marked mass grave are 40 colonists killed in the Great Swamp battle. ⊠ *55 Richard Smith Dr., 1 mi north of Wickford,* ☎ *401/294–3521.* ☞ *$3.* ⊘ *May and Sept., Fri.–Sun. noon–4; June–Aug., Thurs.–Mon. noon–4. Castle tours by appointment Oct.–Apr.*

Shopping
ANTIQUES
Mentor Antiques (⊠ 7512 Post Rd., ☎ 401/294–9412) receives monthly shipments of English furniture—mahogany, pine, and oak. **Wickford Antiques Center I** (⊠ 16 Main St., ☎ 401/295–2966) sells wooden kitchen utensils and crocks, country furniture, china, glass, linens, and jewelry. **Wickford Antiques Center II** (⊠ 93 Brown St., ☎ 401/295–2966) carries antique furniture from many periods and fine art.

CRAFTS
Needlepoint pillows, Florentine leather books, lamps, and woven throws are a few of the gifts and home furnishings you'll find at **Askham & Telham Inc.** (⊠ 12 Main St., ☎ 401/295–0891).

South County A to Z

Arriving and Departing
BY BUS
RIPTA (Rhode Island Public Transportation Authority; ☎ 401/781–9400; 800/244–0444 in RI) provides service from Providence and Warwick to Kingston, Wakefield, Narragansett, and Galilee.

BY CAR
Interstate 95 passes 10 mi north of Westerly before heading inland toward Providence. Routes 1 and 1A follow the coastline along Narragansett Bay and are the primary routes through the South County resort towns.

BY PLANE
Westerly Airport (⊠ Airport Rd., 2 mi south of Westerly off Rte. 1, ☎ 401/596–2460) is served by **New England Airlines** (☎ 401/596–2460 or 800/243–2460), which flies from Westerly to Block Island and operates charter flights.

BY TRAIN
Amtrak (☎ 800/872–7245) trains stop in Westerly and Kingston.

Getting Around
See Arriving and Departing, *above.*

Contacts and Resources
EMERGENCIES
South County Hospital (⊠ 100 Kenyon Ave., Wakefield, ☎ 401/782–8000). **Westerly Hospital** (⊠ 25 Wells St., Westerly, ☎ 401/596–6000).

24-HOUR PHARMACY
CVS Pharmacy (⊠ Granite Shopping Center, 114 Granite St., Westerly, ☎ 401/596–0306).

VISITOR INFORMATION
The state operates a visitor information center off I–95 at the Connecticut border. **Charlestown Chamber of Commerce** (⊠ 4945 Old Post

Rd., 02813, ☎ 401/364–3878). **Greater Westerly Chamber of Commerce** (✉ 74 Post Rd., Westerly, 02891, ☎ 401/596–7761 or 800/732–7636). **Narragansett Chamber of Commerce** (✉ The Towers, Rte. 1A, 02882, ☎ 401/783–7121). **South County Tourism Council** (✉ 4808 Tower Hill Rd., Wakefield 02879, ☎ 401/789–4422 or 800/548–4662).

BLOCK ISLAND

12 mi south of Galilee.

Tourists have been visiting Block Island, 12 mi off Rhode Island's southern coast, since the 19th century. Despite the many people who come here each summer, and thanks to the efforts of local conservationists, the island's beauty has been preserved; its 365 freshwater ponds support more than 150 species of migrating birds.

The original inhabitants of the island were Native Americans who called it Manisses, or Isle of the Little God. Since the eloquent Native American name was abandoned, the island has had many names. In 1524, the explorer Giovanni da Verrazano named it Louisa, after the mother of French King Francis I; however, the king's wife, Claudia, died soon after Verrazano's return, and the island was renamed Claudia's. Following a visit in 1614 by the Dutch explorer Adrian Block, the island was given the name Adrian's Eyelant, and later Block Island. In 1661 the island was settled by farmers and fishermen from Massachusetts Bay Colony. They developed their own specialized fishing boats, "double enders"—and gave Block Island a second name, the Town of New Shoreham, when it became part of the colony of Rhode Island in 1672.

Block Island is a laid-back community. Phone numbers are exchanged by the last four digits (466 is the prefix), and you can dine at any of the island's establishments in shorts and a T-shirt. The heaviest tourist activity takes place between May and Columbus Day—at other times, most restaurants, inns, stores, and visitor services close down.

Block Island has two harbors, Old Harbor and New Harbor. Approaching Block Island by sea from New London, Newport, or Point Judith, you'll see Old Harbor and its group of Victorian hotels. The Old Harbor area is the island's only village—most of the inns, shops, and restaurants are here, and it's a short walk from the ferry landing to any hotel and to most of the interesting sights.

With the exception of a short strip called Moped Alley (actually Weldon's Way), where tourists test-drive mopeds, there's not a bad walk on all of Block Island. But the West Side loop is gorgeous.

㉙ Three docks, two hotels, and four restaurants huddled in the southeast corner of the Great Salt Pond make up the **New Harbor** commercial area. The harbor itself (also called Great Salt Pond) shelters as many as 800 boats on busy weekends, hosts sail races and fishing tournaments, and is the landing point for two ferries that run from Long Island to Block Island. From Payne's Dock you can look across the harbor to see a spit of land called Beane Point; owned by the U.S. Fish and Wildlife Service, this area is so important to migrating birds that it is off-limits to hikers.

㉚ One-half mile west on West Side Road from New Harbor is the **Island Cemetery,** which has held the remains of island residents since the 1700s. At this well-maintained graveyard you can spot the names of long-standing Block Island families (Ball, Rose, Champlin) and enjoy views of the Great Salt Pond, the North Light, and the Rhode Island Coast; on a clear day, the Jamestown–Newport Bridge will be visible to the east.

Block Island

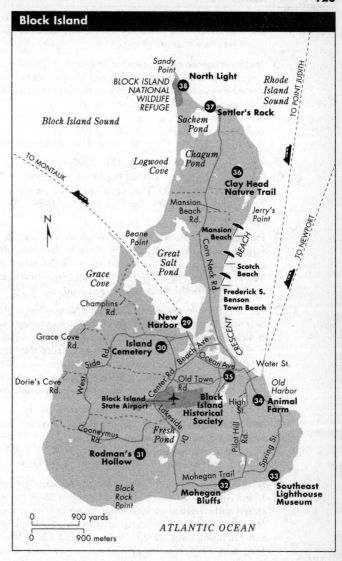

Sandy
Point
BLOCK ISLAND
NATIONAL
WILDLIFE
REFUGE

North Light
38
37
Settler's Rock

*Rhode
Island
Sound*

TO POINT JUDITH

Block Island Sound

*Sachem
Pond*

*Chagum
Pond*

*Logwood
Cove*

TO MONTAUK

36
**Clay Head
Nature Trail**

Mansion
Beach
Rd.

*Jerry's
Point*

N

*Beane
Point*

**Mansion
Beach**

Corn Neck Rd.

BEACH

*Great
Salt
Pond*

**Scotch
Beach**

*Grace
Cove*

Champlins
Rd.

**Frederick S.
Benson
Town Beach**

**New
Harbor** 29

CRESCENT

TO NEWPORT

Grace Cove
Rd.

**Island
Cemetery** 30

Beach Ave.

Ocean Ave.

Water St.

Side Rd.

West Rd.

Center Rd.

Old Town
Rd.

35

*Old
Harbor*

Dorie's Cove
Rd.

**Block Island
State Airport**

**Block
Island
Historical
Society**

High St.

34 **Animal
Farm**

Cooneymus
Rd.

Lakeside Dr.

*Fresh
Pond*

Pilot Hill Rd.

Spring St.

**Rodman's
Hollow** 31

*Black
Rock
Point*

Mohegan Trail

32

33 **Southeast
Lighthouse
Museum**

**Mohegan
Bluffs**

0   900 yards

0   900 meters

ATLANTIC OCEAN

Continuing west, you'll pass a horse farm and some small ponds. You get to the beach by turning right on Dorie's Cove Road or Cooneymus Beach Road; both dead-end at the island's tranquil west shore. One mile down, peaceful West Side Road jogs left and turns into Cooneymus Road. On your right ½ mi farther is a deep ravine.

★ ③① **Rodman's Hollow** is a fine example of a glacial outwash basin. This was the first piece of property purchased in the island's quarter-century-long tradition of land conservation, an effort that has succeeded in saving 25% of the island from development. At Rodman's you can descend along winding paths to the ocean, where you can hike the coastline, lie on beaches at the foot of sand and clay cliffs, or swim, if the waters are calm.

The 200-ft cliffs along Mohegan Trail, the island's southernmost road, ③② are called **Mohegan Bluffs**—so named for an Indian battle in which the local Manisses pinned down an attacking band of Mohegans at the base of the cliffs. From **Payne Overlook**, west of the Southeast Lighthouse

Museum, you can see to Montauk Island, New York, and beyond. Winds and fog can make the bluffs an exhilarating experience. An intimidating set of stairs leads down to the beach.

㉝ **Southeast Lighthouse Museum** is a "rescued" 1873 redbrick beacon with gingerbread detail. For 120 years, erosion ate away at the bluffs, until the lighthouse sat precariously close to the edge of a 200-ft drop-off. An inspired grassroots movement raised the funds necessary to move the structure away from the precipice in 1993. The lighthouse, a National Historic Landmark, has a small museum. ⊠ *Mohegan Trail*, ☎ *401/466–5009.* 🖃 *$5.* ☉ *Memorial Day–Labor Day, daily 10–4.*

㉞ The owners of the 1661 Inn and Hotel Manisses (☞ Dining and Lodging *below*) run a small **Animal Farm** with a collection of llamas, emus, sheep, goats, and ducks. The animals happily coexist in a meadow next to the hotel. ⊠ *Off Spring or High St.*, ☎ *401/466–2063.* 🖃 *Free.* ☉ *Daily dawn–dusk.*

㉟ Exhibits at the **Block Island Historical Society** describe the island's farming and maritime pasts. Many original pieces furnish the society's headquarters, an 1850 mansard-roof home that's well worth a visit. ⊠ *Old Town Rd.*, ☎ *401/466–2481 or 401/466–5009.* 🖃 *$2.* ☉ *July–Aug., daily 10–4; June and Sept., weekends 10–4.*

★ **㊱** *Outside* magazine hailed the **Clay Head Nature Trail** as Rhode Island's best hike. The trail meanders past Clay Head Swamp and along 150-ft-high oceanside cliffs. Songbirds chirp and flowers bloom along the paths that lead into the interior—an area called the Maze. The trailhead is at the end of a dirt road that begins at Corn Neck Road, just past Mansion Beach Road; it is recognizable by a simple white-post marker. Trail maps are available at the **Nature Conservancy** (⊠ Ocean Ave., ☎ 401/466–2129).

㊲ **Settler's Rock,** on the spit of land between Sachem Pond and Cow Beach, is an inauspicious monument that lists the names of the original settlers and marks the spot where they landed in 1661. A 1-mi hike over sandy terrain will get you to the somber North Light.

★ **㊳** **North Light,** a granite lighthouse on the northernmost tip of the Block Island National Wildlife Refuge, was built in 1867. In 1993, it was restored and reopened as a maritime museum. The protected area is a temporary home to American oystercatchers, piping plovers, and other rare migrating birds. ☎ *401/466–3200.* 🖃 *$2.* ☉ *Mid-June–Labor Day, daily 10–4, weather permitting. Closed Labor Day–mid-June.*

Beaches

The 2½-mi **Crescent Beach** runs from Old Harbor to Jerry's Point. **Frederick J. Benson Town Beach,** a family beach less than 1 mi down Corn Neck Road, has a beach pavilion, parking, showers, and lifeguards. Farther north there are fewer rocks to impede wading, but the surf is heavier and there are no lifeguards. Young summer workers congregate ½ mi north of Town Beach at **Scotch Beach** to play volleyball, surf, and sun themselves. **Mansion Beach,** off Mansion Beach Road south of Jerry's Point, has deep white sand and is easily one of New England's most beautiful beaches. In the morning, you may spot deer on the dunes.

Dining and Lodging

$$$–$$$$ ✕ **Eli's.** In summer there's always a wait at Block Island's favorite restau-
★ rant, but the food is worth your patience. Pastas are the menu's mainstays, but the kitchen makes profound excursions into local seafood, Asian dishes, and steaks like the Carpetbagger, a 12-ounce filet mignon filled

with lobster, mozzarella, roasted garlic, sun-dried tomatoes, and fresh basil, topped with a béarnaise sauce. ⊠ *Chapel St.,* ☎ *401/466–5230. Reservations not accepted. MC, V. Closed Tues.–Wed. in winter.*

$$$–$$$$ ✕ **Highview Inn Eatery.** One of the better places to dine on Block Island, this restaurant in an 1880s country inn is well worth the ½-mi walk from town. The service is excellent, as is the Mediterranean fare with Caribbean and American influences. Murals in the dining room detail island life in the 1940s. ⊠ *Connecticut Ave.,* ☎ *401/466–5912. AE, MC, V. Closed Nov.–June.*

$$–$$$ ✕ **Finn's.** A Block Island institution, Finn's serves reliable fried and broiled seafood, and prepares a wonderful smoked bluefish pâté. For lunch try the Workman's Special platter—a burger, coleslaw, and french fries. You can eat inside, out on the deck, or get food to go. Finn's raw bar is on an upstairs deck that overlooks Old Harbor. ⊠ *Ferry Landing,* ☎ *401/466–2473. Reservations not accepted. AE, MC, V. Closed mid-Oct.–May.*

$ ✕ **The BeacHead.** The food at the BeacHead—especially the Rhode Island clam chowder—is very good, the price is right, and you won't feel like a tourist at this locals' hangout. Play pool, catch up on town gossip, or sit at the bar and stare out at the sea. The menu and service are unpretentious; burgers are served on paper plates with potato chips, pickles, and a smile. ⊠ *Corn Neck Rd.,* ☎ *401/466–2249. Reservations not accepted. No credit cards.*

$$$–$$$$ ✕▥ **Atlantic Inn.** Bravely facing the elements on a hill above the ocean,
★ this long, white, classic Victorian resort has big windows, high ceilings, and a sweeping staircase. Most of the oak and maple furnishings in the rooms are original to the building. And then there are the views: Isolated from the hubbub of the Old Harbor area, you can perch on a hillside and contemplate the shape of the island or the sparkle of nearby ocean. Each morning, the inn's pastry chef prepares a buffet breakfast with fresh-baked goods. The restaurant ($$$$; reservations essential; no lunch; closed from November to April), at which President Clinton dined in 1997, serves four-course, prix-fixe meals. The inn welcomes children. ⊠ *Box 1788, High St., 02807,* ☎ *401/466–5883 or 800/224–7422,* ℻ *401/466–5678. 21 rooms. Restaurant, tennis courts, croquet, playground, meeting rooms. Continental breakfast. D, MC, V. Closed Nov.–Easter.*

$$$–$$$$ ✕▥ **Hotel Manisses.** The chef at the island's premier restaurant for American cuisine uses herbs and vegetables from the hotel's garden and locally caught seafood to prepare superb dishes like littleneck clams Dijonnaise. The desserts, concocted by a talented pastry chef, are also delicious. Period furnishings and knickknacks fill the rooms in the 1872 mansion, some of which were named after shipwrecks; because of the antiques, the hotel is not suitable for children. The extras here include picnic baskets, an animal farm, island tours, afternoon wine and hors d'oeuvres in a parlor overlooking the garden, and many rooms with whirlpool baths. ⊠ *1 Spring St., 02807,* ☎ *401/466–2421 or 800/626–4773,* ℻ *401/466–3162. 17 rooms. Restaurant, fans. Full breakfast. AE, MC, V. Restaurant closed Nov.–Mar.*

$$$–$$$$ ▥ **Barrington Inn.** When a former Welcome Wagon hostess decides to open a B&B, you can bet she'll do things right. Owners Howard and Joan Ballard run a tidy, inviting place. They enjoy helping you plan your days; the breakfast table is commonly called "command central." Meticulously clean, precisely arranged, and thoroughly soundproofed, the Barrington Inn, which has unusual views of Trims Pond, Great Salt Pond, and Crescent Beach, is not recommended for families with children. Three of the rooms have private decks (there's also a large common deck). ⊠ *Box 397, Beach Ave., 02807,* ☎ *401/466–5510,* ℻ *401/466–5880. 6 rooms, 2 apartments. Continental breakfast. D, MC, V.*

$$$–$$$$ ☒ **Blue Dory Inn.** This Old Harbor district inn has been a guest house
  ★ since its construction in 1898. Thanks to Ann Loedy, the dynamic
     owner-manager, things in the main building and the three small shin-
     gle-and-clapboard outbuildings run efficiently. Though not large, the
     rooms are tastefully appointed, and each has either an ocean or a har-
     bor view. Couples looking for a romantic hideaway often enjoy the
     Tea House, which has a porch overlooking Crescent Beach. An ex-
     panded Continental breakfast is served each morning in a homey
     kitchen that faces the ocean. ☒ *Box 488, Dodge St., 02807, ☎ 401/*
     466–2254 or 800/992–7290. 11 rooms, 4 cottages, 3 suites. Conti-
     nental breakfast. AE, MC, V.

$$$–$$$$ ☒ **1661 Inn and Guest House.** If your island vacation fantasy includes
  ★ lounging in bed while gazing at swans in the marshes that overlook
     the blue Atlantic, come to the 1661. Even if your room doesn't face
     the water, you can loll on the inn's expansive deck or curl up in a chair
     on the gently sloping oceanside lawn; from both spots you'll enjoy the
     panorama of the water below. The room decor reflects the innkeep-
     ers' attention to detail: Floral wallpaper in one room matches the col-
     ors of the hand-painted tiles atop its antique bureau, and another
     room has a collection of handmade wooden model ships. The ample
     breakfast buffet might consist of fresh bluefish, corned-beef hash,
     Boston baked beans, sausage, Belgian waffles, roast potatoes, French
     toast, scrambled eggs, hot and cold cereal, fruit juices, and fresh
     muffins. ☒ *Spring St., 02807, ☎ 401/466–2421 or 800/626–4773,*
     FAX *401/466–2858. 21 rooms, 19 with bath. Playground. Full break-*
     fast. AE, MC, V. Closed mid-Nov.–mid-Apr.

$$–$$$ ☒ **Surf Hotel.** A stone's throw from the ferry dock, in the heart of the
     Old Harbor area and near Crescent Beach, the Surf seems to have
     changed little over the years; in fact, it's not hard to imagine what the
     hotel must have been like when it first opened in 1876. Dimly lit hall-
     ways take you to small rooms furnished with a jumble of antique fur-
     niture and odds and ends. The rooms have sinks but share toilets and
     baths, but the many return guests don't seem to mind sharing. ☒
     Dodge St. (Box C), 02807, ☎ 401/466–2241. 38 rooms, 3 with bath.
     Breakfast room. Continental breakfast. MC, V. Closed mid-Oct.–Apr.

Nightlife

Check the *Block Island Times* for band listings. **Captain Nick's Rock
and Roll Bar** (☒ 34 Ocean Ave., ☎ 401/466–5670), a fortress of sum-
mertime debauchery, has four bars and two decks on two floors. In
season, bands play nightly. A 360-degree mural that depicts Block Is-
land in the 1940s covers the walls at atmospheric **Club Soda** (☒ 35
Connecticut Ave., ☎ 401/466–5397). The man who painted the mural
was paid in whiskey. **McGovern's Yellow Kittens Tavern** (☒ Corn Neck
Rd., ☎ 401/466–5855), established in 1876, hosts reggae, rock, and
R&B bands every night in season.

Outdoor Activities and Sports

Boating

Block Island Boat Basin (☒ West Side Rd., New Harbor, ☎ 401/466–
2631) is the island's best-stocked ship's store. **New Harbor Kayak** (☒
Ocean Ave., New Harbor, ☎ 401/466–2890) rents kayaks. **Oceans &
Ponds** (☒ Ocean and Connecticut Aves., ☎ 401/466–5131) rents
kayaks and books charter-boat trips.

Fishing

Most of Rhode Island's record fish were caught on Block Island.
From almost any beach, skilled anglers can land tautog and bass. Bonito

and fluke are often hooked in the New Harbor channel. **Oceans & Ponds** (✉ Ocean and Connecticut Aves., ☎ 401/466–5131) sells tackle and fishing gear, operates charter trips, and provides guide services. **Twin Maples** (✉ Beach Ave., ☎ 401/466–5547) is the island's only bait shop. Shellfishing licenses may be obtained at the town hall, on Old Town Road.

Hiking

The Greenway, a well-maintained trail system, meanders across the island, but some of the best hikes are along the beaches. You can hike around the entire island in about eight hours. There are only two interruptions: Water crosses the shoreline at the New Harbor Channel; you'll have to cross 100 yards of pavement. Trail maps for the Greenway are available at the **Chamber of Commerce** (✉ High St., ☎ 401/466–2982) and the **Nature Conservancy** (✉ Ocean Ave. near Payne's Dock, ☎ 401/466–2129). The Nature Conservancy conducts nature walks; call for times or check the local papers.

Water Sports

Island Outfitters (✉ Ocean Ave., ☎ 401/466–5502) rents wet suits, spearguns, and scuba gear. PADI-certification diving courses are given weekly, and beach gear and bathing suits are for sale. **Para-sailing on Block Island** (✉ Old Harbor Basin, ☎ 401/466–2474) also rents jet boats.

Shopping

Art and Crafts

Red Herring (✉ The Shoreline, Water St., 2nd Floor, ☎ 401/466–2540) sells distinctive folk art and crafts—pottery, jewelry, home furnishings. **Scarlet Begonia** (✉ Dodge St., ☎ 401/466–5024) carries unusual jewelry and crafts, including place mats and handmade quilts. **Spring Street Gallery** (✉ Spring St., ☎ 401/466–5374) shows and sells hand-knit baby clothing, stained glass, serigraphs, and other work by island artists and artisans.

Block Island A to Z

Arriving and Departing

BY CAR AND FERRY

Interstate Navigation Co. (✉ Galilee State Pier, Narragansett, ☎ 401/783–4613) operates ferry service from Galilee, a one-hour trip, for $16.30 round trip. Make auto reservations well ahead. Foot passengers cannot make reservations; you should arrive 45 minutes ahead in high season—the boats do fill up. Ferries run daily from Memorial Day to October from Providence's India Street Pier to Newport's Fort Adams State Park, and to Block Island, and then return along the same route in the afternoon.

Nelseco Navigation (✉ 2 Ferry Rd., New London, CT, ☎ 860/442–7891) operates an auto ferry from New London, Connecticut, in summer. Reservations are advised for the two-hour trip. One-way fares from New London are $15 per adult and $28 per vehicle.

Viking Ferry Lines (☎ 516/668–5709) operates passenger and bicycle service from Montauk, Long Island, from mid-May to mid-October. The trip, which takes 1¾ hours, costs $16 each way, plus $3 per bicycle.

BY PLANE

Block Island Airport (✉ Center Rd., ☎ 401/466–5511) is served by a few small airlines. **Action Air** (☎ 203/448–1646 or 800/243–8623) flies in from Groton, Connecticut, between June and October. **Block**

Island Airlines (☎ 401/466–5400) operates charter flights throughout New England. **New England Airlines** (☎ 401/466–5881 or 800/243–2460) flies from Westerly to Block Island and operates charter flights.

Getting Around

BY BICYCLE AND MOPED

The best way to explore the island is by bicycle (about $15 a day to rent) or moped (about $40). Most of the rental places below are open through October and have child seats for bikes: **Block Island Boat Basin** (☎ 401/466–2631); **Esta's at Old Harbor** (☎ 401/466–2651); **Moped Man** (☎ 401/466–5011); **Old Harbor Bike Shop** (☎ 401/466–2029); and **Sea Crest Inn** (☎ 401/466–2882), bikes only.

BY CAR

Corn Neck Road runs north to Settler's Rock from the old Harbor. West Side Road loops west from New Harbor; to return to the area take Cooneymus Road east and Lakeside Drive, Center Road, and Beach Avenue north. If you need to rent a car, try **Block Island Car Rental** (☎ 401/466–2297).

BY TAXI

Taxis are plentiful at the Old Harbor and New Harbor ferry landings. The island's dispatch services include **Minuteman Taxi** (☎ 401/782–5826) and **Wolfie's Taxi** (☎ 401/466–5550).

Contacts and Resources

HOME RENTALS

Inns and hotels on Block Island are booked well in advance for weekends in July and August. Many visitors to the island rent homes for a week or more. These rental homes can also be a good value. Many, however, are booked solid by April. **Block Island Realty** (✉ Chapel St., ☎ 401/466–54260) and **Sullivan Real Estate** (✉ Water St., ☎ 401/466–5521) handle rentals.

VISITOR INFORMATION

Block Island Chamber of Commerce (✉ Drawer D, Water St., 02807, ☎ 401/466–2982).

NEWPORT COUNTY

Perched gloriously on the southern tip of Aquidneck Island and bounded on three sides by water, Newport is one of the great sailing cities of the world and the host to world-class jazz, blues, folk, and classical music festivals. Newport County encompasses all of Newport, plus Conanicut Island, also known as Jamestown, and the portion of Rhode Island east of Newport that abuts Massachusetts. The most-visited city in this last region is Little Compton.

Jamestown

39 *25 mi south of Providence, 3 mi west of Newport.* The east and west passages of Narragansett Bay encompass the 9-mi-long, 1-mi-wide landmass that goes by the names Jamestown and Conanicut Island. Valuable as a military outpost in days gone by, the island presented an impediment to commercial cross-bay shipping.

In 1940 the Jamestown Bridge linked the island to western Rhode Island, and in 1969 the Newport Bridge completed the cross-bay route, connecting Newport to the entire South County. Summer residents have come to Jamestown since the 1880s, but never to the same extent as in Watch Hill, Narragansett, or Newport. The locals' "We're not a T-shirt town" attitude has resulted in a relatively low number of tourists, even in July and August, making this a peaceful alternative to the hustle and bustle of nearby Newport and South County.

The conditions range from tranquil to harrowing at **Beavertail State Park,** which straddles the southern tip of Conanicut Island. The currents and surf here are famously deadly during rough seas and high winds; but on a clear, calm day, the park's craggy shoreline seems intended for sunning, hiking, and climbing. The **Beavertail Lighthouse Museum,** in what was the lighthouse keeper's quarters, has displays about Rhode Island's lighthouses. ⊠ *Beavertail Rd.,* ☎ *401/423–3270.* ⊡ *Free.* ☉ *June–Labor Day, daily 10–4. Closed Labor Day–May.*

Thomas Carr Watson's family had worked the **Watson Farm** for 190 years before he bequeathed it to Society for the Preservation of New England Antiquities when he died in 1979. The 285-acre spread, whose mission includes educating the public about agrarian history, has 2 mi of trails along Jamestown's southwestern shore with amazing views of Narragansett Bay and North Kingstown. If you're lucky, you'll spot a fox among the many critters on land. ⊠ *455 North Rd.,* ☎ *401/423–0005.* ⊡ *$3.* ☉ *June–mid-Oct., Tues., Thurs., Sun 1–5. Closed mid-Oct.–May.*

The English-designed **Jamestown Windmill,** built in 1789, ground corn for nearly 100 years—and it still works. Mills like this one were once common in Rhode Island. ⊠ *North Rd., east of Watson Farm,* ☎ *no phone.* ⊡ *Free.* ☉ *Mid-June–Sept., weekends 1–4.*

A working 1859 hand tub and a horse-drawn steam pump are among the holdings of the **Jamestown Fire Department Memorial Museum,** an informal display of firefighting equipment in a garage that once housed the fire company. ⊠ *50 Narragansett Ave.,* ☎ *401/423–0062.* ⊡ *Free.* ☉ *Daily 7–3; inquire next door at Fire Department if door is locked.*

Fort Wetherill State Park, an outcropping of stone cliffs at the southeastern peninsula, has been a picnic destination since the 1800s. There's great swimming at the small cove here. ⊠ *Ocean St.,* ☎ *401/423–1771.* ⊡ *Free.* ☉ *Daily, dawn–dusk.*

The **Jamestown and Newport Ferry Co.** stops in Newport at Bowen's Landing and Long Wharf, and will stop on request at Fort Adams or Goat Island. The 26-ft passenger ferry departs on its half-hour voyage from Ferry Wharf about every 1½ hours, from 9 AM to 10 PM (11:30 PM on weekends). The last run leaves from Newport at 10:30 PM (midnight on weekends). The ferry operates from Memorial Day to mid-October. ⊠ *Ferry Wharf,* ☎ *401/423–9900.* ⊡ *About $6.*

Mackerel Cove Beach (⊠ *Beavertail Rd.*) is sandy and highly sheltered from the currents of Narragansett Bay. Parking costs $10 for non-residents.

Dining and Lodging

$$$–$$$$ ✕ **Trattoria Simpatico.** A jazz trio plays on sunny weekends at Jamestown's signature restaurant, while patrons dine alfresco under a 275-year-old copper beech tree. An herb garden, fieldstone walls, and white linen complete the picture. You can munch on the splendid appetizers and salads, taste pasta dishes cooked northern Italian style, or try meats prepared with a Continental flair. A recent memorable appetizer: crispy-skin duck confit with deep-fried fettuccine, truffle oil, savoy cabbage, and onion marmalade. ⊠ *13 Narragansett Ave.,* ☎ *401/423–3731. Reservations essential on summer weekends. AE, D, MC, V. No lunch weekdays Labor Day–Memorial Day, no lunch weekends Memorial Day–Labor Day.*

$$–$$$ ✕ **Jamestown Oyster Bar.** Whether you're ordering clam chowder and a dollar draft or grilled swordfish and a martini, you'll feel right at home here. Oysters are kept on ice behind the bar, whose tenders pour fine microbrews and wines. The burgers are locally renowned, but for something more delicate, try one of the seafood specials listed on the chalkboard. ⊠ *22 Narragansett Ave.,* ☎ *401/423–3380. Reservations not accepted. AE, MC, V. No lunch weekdays.*

$ ✕ **East Ferry Market and Deli.** Year-rounders and summer residents frequent this standby that's open daily from 6 AM to 5 PM for coffees, salads, and specialty sandwiches. There are tables inside and out; grab one on the patio if you can. ⊠ *47 Conanicus Ave.,* ☎ *401/423–1592. No credit cards.*

$$$$ ▦ **Bay Voyage.** In 1889 this Victorian inn was shipped to its current location from Newport and named in honor of its trip. The inn's one-bedroom suites, furnished in floral prints and pastels, have been sold as time shares, which makes availability tight in summer months. The view and the facilities make staying here a memorable experience; the restaurant is known for its Sunday brunch. ⊠ *150 Conanicus Ave., 02835,* ☎ *401/423–2100,* ⅎ⅀ *401/423–3209. 32 suites. Restaurant, bar, air-conditioning, kitchenettes, outdoor pool, indoor hot tub, sauna, exercise room. AE, D, DC, MC, V.*

$$ ▦ **East Bay B&B.** If Karen Montoya's three rooms aren't booked, you can get a great deal at her humble B&B. The circa-1896 Victorian is peaceful day and night, even though it's a block from Jamestown's two main streets and bustling wharf. The original trim and bullnose molding are all in great shape, as is the formal living room, which has a fireplace and Oriental rugs. ⊠ *14 Union St., 02835,* ☎ *401/423–2715. 1 room with bath, 2 rooms share bath. Continental breakfast. No credit cards.*

Outdoor Activities and Sports

DIVING AND KAYAKING

Ocean State Scuba (⊠ 79 N. Main Rd., ☎ 401/423–1662 or 800/933–3483) rents kayaks and diving equipment.

GOLF

Jamestown Country Club (⊠ 245 Conanicus Ave., ☎ 401/423–9930) has a nine-hole course. The greens fee is $11; a second round costs $5.

Newport

The Golden Age of Newport ran from roughly 1720 to the 1770s, when products like cheese, clocks, and furniture as well as livestock and the slave trade put the city on a par with Charleston, South Carolina; the two cities trailed only Boston as centers of New World maritime commerce. In the mid-1700s, Newport was home to the best shipbuilders in North America. Their small, swift, and reliable slave ships were the stars of the triangle trade (rum to Africa for slaves; slaves to the West Indies for molasses; molasses and slaves back to America, where the molasses was made into rum). This unsavory but reliable scheme guaranteed investors a 20% return on their money and earned Newport the distinction of being the largest slave-trading port in the North. Ironically, in 1774, progressive Rhode Island became the first colony to outlaw trading in slaves.

In the 19th century, Newport became a summer playground for the wealthiest families in America. These riches were not made in Rhode Island but imported by the titans of the Gilded Age and translated into the fabulous "cottages" overlooking the Atlantic. Newport's mansions served as proving grounds for the country's best young architects.

Richard Upjohn, Richard Morris Hunt, and firms like McKim, Mead and White have left a legacy of remarkable homes.

Recreational sailing, a huge industry in Newport, convincingly melds the attributes of two eras: the conspicuous consumption of the Gilded Age and the nautical expertise of the Colonial era. Tan and garish young sailors often fill Newport bars and restaurants, where they talk of wind, waves, and expensive yachts. For those not arriving by water, a sailboat tour of the harbor is a great way to get your feet wet.

Downtown

30 mi from Providence, 80 mi from Boston.

More than 200 pre-Revolutionary buildings (mostly private residences) remain in Newport, more than any other city in the country. Most of these national treasures are in the neighborhood known as the Point. Hunter House, the start of the tour, is here.

A GOOD WALK

Numbers in the text correspond to numbers in the margin and on the Downtown Newport map.

The ideal first sight in a walking tour of Newport is the Colonial-era **Hunter House** ㊵. Walk north from Hunter House on Washington Street. At Van Zandt Avenue, turn right and proceed to the **Common Burial Ground** ㊶. Aptly named Farewell Street crosses the cemetery, then heads southeast. At the Marlborough Street intersection you'll stumble past the country's oldest bar and restaurant, the **White Horse Tavern** ㊷. Across Farewell Street stands **Friends Meeting House** ㊸. To the east, Marlborough intersects Spring Street and Broadway; ahead on your right you'll see the **Wanton-Lyman-Hazard House** ㊹, the oldest home in Newport. Follow Spring Street three short blocks south to Washington Street, which heads west into Washington Square. Over your left shoulder is the imposing **Colony House** ㊺. At the bottom of Washington Square is the **Brick Market** ㊻, which houses the **Museum of Newport History.** Walk two blocks up Touro Street (on the south side of the square); **Touro Synagogue** ㊼ will be on your left. Next door is the **Newport Historical Society** ㊽. Cross the road and follow High Street one block; then turn right on Church Street to see the immaculate **Trinity Church** ㊾. Proceed east on Church Street. Across Bellevue Avenue are the four pillars of **Redwood Library** ㊿. The **Newport Art Museum and Art Association** (51) is one block south. You can walk south on Bellevue Avenue and cross Memorial Boulevard to visit the remnants of the Gilded Age—the mansions that compose the bulk of the Greater Newport Walk. It's best to do the Colonial walk over one day, and the Bellevue Avenue section the following day; either way, you should be mighty hungry by dinner.

TIMING: The Colonial section of the walk covers 2½ mi. If you spend time inside each building, it should take about 4½ hours to reach Bellevue Avenue. A good stopping point on the Colonial tour is the Brick Market. Newport in summer can be exasperating, its streets jammed with visitors, the traffic slowed by the procession of sight-seeing buses (3.5 million people visit the city each year). Yet the quality of Newport's sights and arts festivals persuades many people to brave the crowds. In fall and spring, you can explore the city without having to stand in long lines.

SIGHTS TO SEE

㊻ **Brick Market.** The market building once used for slave trading houses the **Museum of Newport History.** Multimedia exhibits explore the city's social and economic influences, and antiques like James Franklin's print-

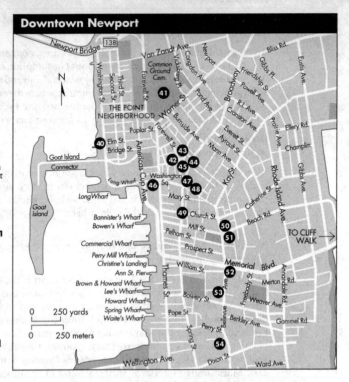

Downtown Newport

ing press inspire the imagination. Built in 1760 and designed by Peter Harrison, who was also responsible for the Touro Synagogue and the Redwood Library, the building served as a theater and a town hall. ⊠ *Thames St.,* ☎ *401/841–8770.* 🔳 *$5.* ☉ *Mon. and Wed.–Sat. 10–5, Sun. 1–5.*

45 **Colony House.** This redbrick structure above downtown Washington Square was the place where, on May 4, 1776, Rhode Island and Providence Plantations became the first colony to renounce British authority. The same year, from the balcony of this building, the Declaration of Independence was read to Newporters. In 1781, George Washington met here with French commander Count Rochambeau to plan the Battle of Yorktown, which led to the end of the Revolutionary War. The Colony House appears in the film *Amistad.* ⊠ *Washington Sq.,* ☎ *401/846–2980.* ☉ *Tours by appointment.*

41 **Common Burial Ground.** Farewell Street is lined with historic cemeteries; the many tombstones at this 17th-century graveyard are fine examples of Colonial stone carving, much of it the work of John Stevens.

43 **Friends Meeting House.** Built in 1699, this is the oldest Quaker meeting house in America. With its wide-plank floors, simple benches, balcony, and beam ceiling (considered lofty by Colonial standards), this two-story shingle structure reflects the quiet reserve and steadfast faith of Colonial Quakers. ⊠ *29 Farewell St.,* ☎ *401/846–0813.* 🔳 *$5.* ☉ *Tours by appointment.*

★ **40** **Hunter House.** The French admiral Charles Louis d'Arsac de Ternay used this 1748 home on the banks of the Narragansett Bay as his Revolutionary War headquarters. The carved pineapple over the doorway was a symbol of welcome throughout Colonial America; a fresh pineapple placed out front signaled an invitation to neighbors to visit a returned seaman or to look over a shop's new stock. The elliptical arch in the central hall is a typical Newport detail. Pieces made by Newport artisans Townsend and Goddard furnish much of the house. ⊠ *54 Washington St.,* ☎ *401/847–7516.* ⬚ *$6.50.* ☉ *Late Mar.–Apr., weekends 10–5; May–Oct., daily 10–5 Closed Nov.–late Mar.*

51 **Newport Art Museum and Art Association.** Richard Morris Hunt designed the Stick-style Victorian building that houses this community-supported center for the arts. The galleries exhibit contemporary works by New England artists. ⊠ *76 Bellevue Ave.,* ☎ *401/848–8200.* ⬚ *$4.* ☉ *Memorial Day–Labor Day, daily 10–5; Labor Day–Memorial Day, Tues.–Sat. 10–4, Sun. 1–5.*

48 **Newport Historical Society.** The historical society's small museum contains Newport memorabilia, furniture, and maritime items. The museum and the Gateway Center are departure points for walking tours of Newport; call for times. ⊠ *82 Touro St.,* ☎ *401/846–0813.* ⬚ *Free.* ☉ *Tues.–Fri. 9:30–4:30, Sat. 9:30–noon (to 4:30 in summer).*

50 **Redwood Library.** Peter Harrison designed the nation's oldest library in continuous use, a magnificent structure that, though made of wood, mimics the look of a Roman temple—the original exterior paint was mixed with sand to resemble stone. The library's paintings include works by Gilbert Stuart, Rembrandt Peale, and other important Early American artists. ⊠ *50 Bellevue Ave.,* ☎ *401/847–0292.* ⬚ *Free.* ☉ *Mon.– Sat. 9:30–5:30.*

47 **Touro Synagogue.** Jews, like Quakers and Baptists, were attracted by Rhode Island's religious tolerance; they arrived from Amsterdam and Lisbon as early as 1650. The oldest surviving synagogue in the United States, this house of worship, designed by Peter Harrison, was dedicated in 1763. Although simple on the outside, the Georgian building has an elaborate interior. Its classical style influenced Thomas Jefferson in the building of Monticello and the University of Virginia. ⊠ *85 Touro St.,* ☎ *401/847–4794.* ⬚ *Free.* ☉ *July 4 weekend–Labor Day, Sun.–Fri. 10–5; Memorial Day weekend–July 4 weekend and Labor Day–Columbus Day, Sun. 11–3 and Mon.–Fri. 1–3; Columbus Day– Memorial Day weekend Sun. 1–3 and Mon.–Fri. for 2 PM tour only; guided tours year-round on the ½ hr.*

49 **Trinity Church.** This Colonial beauty was built in 1724 and modeled after London churches designed by Sir Christopher Wren. A special feature of the interior is the three-tier wineglass pulpit, the only one of its kind in America. The lighting, woodwork, and conspicuous history make attending services here an unforgettable experience. ⊠ *Queen Anne Sq.,* ☎ *401/846–0660.* ⬚ *Free.* ☉ *June–Oct., daily 10–4; Nov.–May, daily 10–1. Services at 8 and 10; off-season at 8 and 10:30.*

44 **Wanton-Lyman-Hazard House.** Newport's oldest residence dates from the mid-17th century. The dark-red building was site of the city's Stamp Act riot of 1765—after the British Parliament levied a tax on most printed material, the Sons of Liberty stormed the house, which was occupied by the English stamp master. The home was later a center of social life for 5,000 French troops who moved into the city when an occupying British army left for New York City in 1779. The house contains period artifacts, and there's a colonial garden. ⊠ *17 Broadway,* ☎ *401/846–0813.* ⬚ *$4.* ☉ *By appointment.*

42 **White Horse Tavern.** William Mayes, the father of a successful and notorious pirate, received a tavern license in 1687, which makes this building, built in 1673, the oldest tavern in America. Its gambrel roof, low dark-beam ceilings, cavernous fireplace, and uneven plank floors epitomize Newport's Colonial charm (☞ Dining, *below*). ⊠ *Marlborough and Farewell Sts.,* ☎ *401/849–3600.*

Greater Newport

The homes built during the Gilded Age are almost obscenely grand, laden with ornate rococo detail and designed with a determined one-up-manship. The **Preservation Society of Newport County** (☎ 401/847–1000) maintains 12 mansions, some of which are described below. Guided tours are given of each; you can purchase a combination ticket at any of the properties for a substantial discount. The hours and days the houses are open during the off-season are subject to change, so it's wise to call ahead. Chateau-sur-Mer, the Elms, and in some years the Marble House or the Breakers, are decorated for Christmas and usually open for tours daily from Thanksgiving Day to Christmas Day.

A GOOD TOUR
Numbers in the text correspond to numbers in the margin and on the Downtown Newport and Greater Newport maps.

At the corner of Memorial and Bellevue is the **International Tennis Hall of Fame Museum at the Newport Casino** ⑫, birthplace of the U.S. Open. Catercorner from Newport Casino is **Kingscote** ⑬, the first "cottage" along this walking tour. **The Elms** ⑭ is two blocks south. Three blocks farther is **Chateau-sur-Mer** ⑮. **Rosecliff** ⑯ is four more blocks in the same direction. **Astors' Beechwood** ⑰ and the **Marble House** ⑱ are on the same side of this lengthy block of palaces. Farther down, on the corner of Lakeview and Bellevue, is **Belcourt Castle** ⑲. Beyond this mansion, Bellevue Avenue turns 90 degrees west and dead-ends at what most consider the end of the **Cliff Walk** ⑳. From here you can stroll along the Rhode Island Sound and prepare to treat your eyes to Newport's most renowned mansion, **The Breakers** ㉑, which can be reached from the Cliff Walk by heading west on Ruggles Avenue and north on Ochre Point Avenue.

You'll need a car to visit three sights. The **Museum of Yachting** ㉒ is at **Fort Adams State Park.** From downtown Newport, drive south on Thames Street to Wellington Avenue. Turn right and follow Wellington to the bend where Wellington becomes Halidon Avenue. Turn right on Harrison Avenue. One mile to the right is the entrance to the park; the museum is at the end of Fort Adams Road. To reach **Hammersmith Farm** ㉓, turn right as you exit the park; the entrance is 300 yards down on the right. To get back to town, you can follow Ocean Drive to Bellevue Avenue. To reach the **Naval War College Museum** ㉔, at the intersection with Memorial Boulevard, turn left; Memorial becomes America's Cup Avenue. At the cemetery, turn left on Farewell Street. Farewell runs into Bridge Access Road, where you will veer left to reach to Connell Highway traffic circle. Exit at the west end of the circle on Training Station Road. A small bridge will take you to Coasters Harbor Island. Park at the naval base entrance and walk two blocks along the same road to the museum, which is on a hill to your right.

TIMING: It's best to tour two or three mansions and see the others only from the outside. To avoid long lines on summer days, go early or choose the less-popular but still amazing mansions—The Elms, Kingscote, and Belcourt Castle. It's under 2 mi from Kingscote to Belcourt—the first and last mansions on Bellevue Avenue. Plan on spending one hour at each mansion. The Cliff Walk is 3½ mi long. Seeing the Tennis Hall of Fame, three mansions, walking the length of Bellevue Avenue, and returning via the Cliff Walk takes five or six hours. The driving portion of the tour is about 11 mi long. You could easily spend an hour at each of the sights on the drive.

Greater Newport

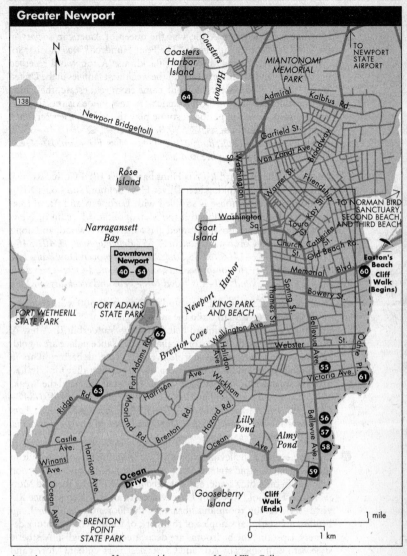

N

Coasters Harbor Island

Coasters Harbor

MIANTONOMI MEMORIAL PARK

TO NEWPORT STATE AIRPORT

138

Newport Bridge (toll)

Admiral

Kalbtus Rd.

64

Garfield St.

Van Zandt Ave.

Broadway

Warren St.

Friendship

Rose Island

Washington St.

Kay St.

TO NORMAN BIRD SANCTUARY, SECOND BEACH, AND THIRD BEACH

Washington Sq.

Touro St.

Narragansett Bay

Goat Island

Church St.

Catherine St.

Old Beach Rd.

Easton's Beach

Cliff Walk (Begins)

60

Downtown Newport

40 — 54

Newport Harbor

Memorial Blvd.

Bowery St.

Spring St.

Thames St.

Bellevue Ave.

FORT WETHERILL STATE PARK

FORT ADAMS STATE PARK

Brenton Cove

KING PARK AND BEACH

Brenton Cove

Wellington Ave.

Webster St.

Ogbe Pl.

62

Fort Adams Rd.

Halidon Ave.

Victoria Ave.

55

61

Ridge Rd.

63

Moorland Rd.

Harrison Ave.

Wickham Rd.

Hazard Rd.

Lilly Pond

Almy Pond

56

57

58

Castle Ave.

Brenton Rd.

Ocean Ave.

Bellevue Ave.

59

Winans Ave.

Harrison Ave.

Ocean Drive

Ocean Ave.

BRENTON POINT STATE PARK

Gooseberry Island

Cliff Walk (Ends)

0   1 mile

0   1 km

Astors' Beechwood, **57**

Belcourt Castle, **59**

The Breakers, **61**

Chateau-sur-Mer, **55**

Cliff Walk, **60**

Hammersmith Farm, **63**

Marble House, **58**

Museum of Yachting, **62**

Naval War College Museum, **64**

Rosecliff, **56**

SIGHTS TO SEE

➐ Astors' Beechwood. The original mistress of this oceanfront mansion, Caroline Schermerhorn Astor, was the queen of American society in the late 19th century; her list of "The Four Hundred" was the first social register. Her husband, William Backhouse Astor, was a reserved businessman and a member of one of the wealthiest families in the United States (much of the Astors' fortune came from real estate, the China trade, and fur trading in North America). As they guide visitors through the mansion, actors in period costume play the family, their servants, and their household guests. ⊠ *580 Bellevue Ave.,* ☎ *401/846–3772.* ⌨ *$8.75.* ☼ *May–Sept., daily 10–5; Dec.–May, Fri.–Sun. 10–4; call about Christmas-season hrs and events.*

➒ Belcourt Castle. Richard Morris Hunt based this 1894 Gothic Revival mansion, built for banking heir Oliver H. P. Belmont, on Louis XIII's hunting lodge. The house is so filled with European and Asian treasures that locals have dubbed it the Metropolitan Museum of Newport. Sip tea and admire the stained glass and carved wood, and don't miss the Golden Coronation Coach. ⊠ *657 Bellevue Ave.,* ☎ *401/846–0669 or 401/849–1566.* ⌨ *$6.50.* ☼ *Apr.–Memorial Day, daily 10–5; Memorial Day to Columbus Day, daily 9–5; mid-Oct.–Dec. daily 10–4. Mar. weekends 10–4. Closed Jan.–Feb. and weekdays in Mar.*

★ ➏ The Breakers. It's easy to understand why it took 2,500 workers in the early 1890s two years to build the most magnificent Newport palace, the 70-room home of railroad heir Cornelius Vanderbilt II. A few of the marvels within the four-story Italian Renaissance palace are a gold-ceiling music room, a blue marble fireplace, rose alabaster pillars in the dining room, and a porch with a mosaic ceiling that took Italian artisans six months, lying on their backs, to install. To build the Breakers today would cost $400 million. ⊠ *Ochre Point Ave.,* ☎ *401/847–6544.* ⌨ *$10.* ☼ *May–Oct., daily 10–5; Nov., weekends 10–4.; Apr., weekdays 10–4. Closed Dec. (most yrs) and Jan.–Mar., Apr. weekends, Nov. weekdays.*

➎ Chateau-sur-Mer. Bellevue Avenue's first stone mansion was built in the Victorian Gothic style in 1852 for William S. Wetmore, a tycoon involved in the China trade, and enlarged in the 1870s by Richard Morris Hunt. The Gold Room by Leon Marcotte and the Renaissance Revival–style dining room and library by the Florentine sculptor Luigi Frullini are sterling examples of the work of leading 19th-century designers. Upstairs, the bedrooms are decorated in the English Aesthetic style with wallpapers by Arts and Crafts designers William Morris and William Burges. In December, the house is decorated for a Victorian Christmas. ⊠ *Bellevue Ave. at Shepard Ave.,* ☎ *401/847–1000.* ⌨ *$6.50.* ☼ *May–Sept., daily 10–5; Oct.–mid-Nov., weekends 10–4. Thanksgiving–Dec. 25, daily 10–4; Jan.–Mar., weekends 10–4. Apr., weekdays 10–4. Closed weekdays Oct.–mid-Nov and Jan.–Mar.*

★ ➏ Cliff Walk. Easton's Beach (also called First Beach) is the beginning of this 3-mi path that runs south along Newport's cliffs to Bailey's Beach. The promenade affords views of sumptuous mansions on one side and the rocky coastline on the other. The Cliff Walk can be accessed from any road running east off Bellevue Avenue. The unpaved sections can be difficult for small children or people with mobility problems.

➍ The Elms. In designing this graceful 48-room French neoclassical mansion, architect Horace Trumbauer paid homage to the style, fountains, broad lawn, and formal gardens of the Château d'Asnières near Paris. The Elms was built for Edward Julius Berwind, a bituminous-coal baron, in 1899. The well-nurtured trees throughout the 12-acre backyard are labeled, providing an exemplary botany lesson. ✉ *Bellevue Ave.,* ☎ *401/842–0546.* 🎟 *$7.* ☉ *May–Oct., daily 10–5; 1st 2 wks of Nov. and Thanksgiving Day–Dec. 25, daily 10–4; Jan.–Apr., weekends 10–4. Closed mid-Nov.–Thanksgiving Day and weekdays Jan.–Mar.*

★ 63 **Hammersmith Farm.** This elaborate country estate was the childhood summer home of Jacqueline Bouvier Kennedy Onassis, the site of her wedding to John F. Kennedy, and a summer White House during the Kennedy Administration. It is the only working farm in Newport. Loaded with Bouvier and Kennedy memorabilia, the house is so comfortable that it seems as though its owners have temporarily stepped out of its rooms. The gardens, with breathtaking views of Narragansett Bay, were designed by Frederick Law Olmsted. The friendly guides at the farm are well informed. ✉ *Ocean Dr. near Ft. Adams,* ☎ *401/846–7346.* 🎟 *$8.50.* ☉ *Memorial Day–Labor Day, daily 10–7; Mar.–Memorial Day and Labor Day–mid-Nov., daily 10–5; special openings around Christmas. Closed mid-Nov.–Feb. except for special openings.*

52 **International Tennis Hall of Fame Museum at the Newport Casino.** The photographs, memorabilia, and multimedia exhibits at the Hall of Fame provide a definitive chronicle of the game's greatest moments and characters. Newport Casino is an ideal location for the museum. The magnificent shingle-style social club was designed by Stanford White and built in 1880 for publisher James Gordon Bennett Jr., who quit the nearby men's club, the Newport Reading Room, after a polo player—at Bennett's behest—rode a horse into the building and was subsequently banned. Bennett further retaliated by commissioning the Casino, which has 13 grass courts and one court-tennis facility (court tennis is the 13th-century precursor to modern tennis). The Casino quickly became the social and recreational hot spot of the Gilded Age. ✉ *194 Bellevue Ave.,* ☎ *401/849–3990.* 🎟 *$8.* ☉ *Daily 9:30–5.*

53 **Kingscote.** This Victorian mansion was designed by Richard Upjohn for George Noble Jones, a Savannah, Georgia, plantation owner. (Newport was popular with southerners before the Civil War.) Decorated with antique furniture, glass, and Asian art, it contains a number of Tiffany windows. ✉ *Bowery St., off Bellevue Ave,* ☎ *401/847–1000.* 🎟 *$6.50.* ☉ *May–Sept., daily 10–5; Apr. and Oct., weekends 10–4. Closed Nov.–Mar. and weekdays in Apr. and Oct.*

58 **Marble House.** Perhaps the most opulent Newport mansion, the Marble House, with its extravagant gold ballroom, was the gift of William Vanderbilt to his wife, Alva, in 1892. Alva divorced William in 1895 and married Oliver Perry Belmont to become the lady of Belcourt Castle. When Oliver died in 1908, she returned to Marble House. Mrs. Belmont was involved with the suffragist movement and spent much of her time campaigning for women's rights. The Chinese teahouse behind the estate was built in 1913. ✉ *Bellevue Ave.,* ☎ *401/847–1000.* 🎟 *$6.* ☉ *Apr.–Oct., daily 10–5; Jan.–Mar., weekends 10–4. Closed Nov. and (most yrs) Dec. and weekdays Jan.–Mar.*

62 **Museum of Yachting.** The museum has four galleries: Mansions and Yachts, Small Craft, America's Cup, and the Hall of Fame for Single-handed Sailors. In summer months, eight classic wooden yachts constitute a floating exhibition. ✉ *Ft. Adams Park, Ocean Dr.,* ☎ *401/847–1018.* 🎟 *$3.* ☉ *May–Oct., daily 10–5.*

64 **Naval War College Museum.** The Naval War College, the oldest school of its kind in the world, represents the pinnacle of education in the U.S. Navy. The museum's exhibits analyze the history of naval warfare and tactics and trace the history of the navy in Narragansett Bay. ✉

Founders Hall, Gate 1, Naval Education and Training Center, ☎ *401/841–4052.* 🎫 *Free.* ۞ *Daily 10–4.*

OFF THE
BEATEN PATH

NORMAN BIRD SANCTUARY – The 450-acre preserve has nature trails, guided tours, and a small natural history museum. From Bellevue Avenue, turn east on Memorial Boulevard (Route 138A), pass First Beach, then turn right on Purgatory Road. Make another right on Hanging Rock Road. From here, signs will lead you to a left turn on Third Beach Road. ⊠ *583 Third Beach Rd., Middletown,* ☎ *401/846-2577.* 🎫 *$4.* ۞ *Tues.–Sun. 9–5; Memorial Day–Labor Day, daily 9–5.*

56 **Rosecliff.** Newport's most romantic mansion was built for Mrs. Hermann Oelrichs in 1902; her father had amassed a fortune from Nevada silver mines. Stanford White modeled the palace after the Grand Trianon at Versailles. Rosecliff has 40 rooms, including the Court of Love, and a heart-shape staircase. Its grand ballroom has appeared in several movies, including *True Lies* and the 1974 version of *The Great Gatsby.* ⊠ *Bellevue Ave.,* ☎ *401/847–5793.* 🎫 *$6.* ۞ *Apr.–Oct., daily 10–5. Closed Nov.–Mar.*

Beaches

Easton's Beach (⊠ Memorial Blvd.), also known as First Beach, is popular for its carousel. **Fort Adams State Park** (⊠ Ocean Dr.), a small beach with a picnic area and lifeguards during the summer, has beautiful views of Newport Harbor. **Sachuest Beach,** or Second Beach, east of First Beach in the Sachuest Point area of Middletown, is a beautiful sandy area adjacent to the Norman Bird Sanctuary. Dunes and a campground make it popular with young travelers and surfers. **Third Beach,** also in the Sachuest Point area of Middletown, is on the Sakonnet River. It has a boat ramp and is a favorite of windsurfers.

Dining and Lodging

$$$$ ✕ **Asterix & Obelix.** Danish chef John Bach-Sorensen makes fine dining as fun and colorful as the madcap French cartoon strip after which this eatery was named. An auto repair garage before Sorensen—winner of the Culinary World Cup in 1986—took it over, the restaurant's concrete floor has been painted to look like it's been covered with expensive tiling. The garage doors can be opened or closed depending on the weather. Asian twists enliven Mediterranean fare with strong French influences. Carefully selected wines, brandies, and aperitifs enhance the flavors. Sunday brunch is served year-round. ⊠ *599 Thames St.,* ☎ *401/841–8833. AE, D, DC, MC, V. No lunch Oct.–Apr.*

$$$$ ✕ **The Black Pearl.** Tourists and yachters flock to this dignified converted dock shanty, where award-winning clam chowder is sold by the quart. Dining is in the casual tavern or the formal Commodore's Room. The latter serves an appetizer of black-and-blue tuna with red-pepper sauce. The French and American entrées include duck breast with green peppercorn sauce and swordfish with Dutch pepper butter. ⊠ *Bannister's Wharf,* ☎ *401/846–5264. Commodore Room: Reservations essential. Jacket required. AE, MC, V.*

$$$$ ✕ **Clarke Cooke House.** Waiters in tuxedos and the richly patterned pillows on wood chairs and booths underscore this restaurant's luxurious Colonial atmosphere. Formal dining is on the upper level, in a partially enclosed room with a timber-beam ceiling, dark green latticework, and water views; there's open-air dining in warm weather. The refined Mediterranean menu incorporates local seafood; specials often include game dishes. ⊠ *Bannister's Wharf,* ☎ *401/849–2900. Reservations essential on summer weekends. Jacket required upstairs. AE, D, DC, MC, V.*

$$$$ ✕ **La Petite Auberge.** The colorful owner-chef of La Petite Auberge, who once worked for General Charles de Gaulle, prepares delicacies like trout with almonds, duck flambé with orange sauce, and medallions of beef with goose-liver pâté. The setting for his exquisite cooking is a series of intimate rooms inside a Colonial house. In summer, dinner is served in the courtyard. ⊠ *19 Charles St.,* ☎ *401/849–6669. AE, MC, V.*

$$$$ ✕ **Restaurant Bouchard.** Many of the dishes at this upscale yet homey restaurant are modern, regional takes on French cuisine: Sautéed local cod, for instance, is topped with fresh Maine crab and asparagus, then finished with a light beurre blanc. ⊠ *505 Thames St.,* ☎ *401/846–0123. AE, D, MC, V.*

$$$$ ✕ **White Horse Tavern.** The nation's oldest operating tavern, once a
★ meeting house for Colonial Rhode Island's General Assembly, offers intimate dining with black-tie service, a top-notch wine cellar, and consistently excellent food. The tavern serves suave American cuisine, including local seafood and beef Wellington, along with exotic entrées like cashew-encrusted venison tenderloin topped with an apple-cider demi-glace. ⊠ *Marlborough and Farewell Sts.,* ☎ *401/849–3600. Reservations essential. Jacket required. AE, D, DC, MC, V. No lunch Tues. and Wed.*

$$$ ✕ **Pronto.** Outstanding jazz and new Italian cuisine prepared with a European flair lure locals and tourists to cozy, funky, chandelier-bedecked Pronto. The beef carpaccio appetizer is the best in town; rack of lamb and farfalle pasta with shiitake mushrooms, kalamata olives, and chèvre are among the entrées. ⊠ *464 Thames St.,* ☎ *401/847–5251. AE, MC, V.*

$$$ ✕ **Scales & Shells.** Busy, sometimes noisy, but always excellent, this
★ restaurant serves as many as 15 types of superbly fresh wood-grilled fish—the cooks occasionally send your waitperson to your table with your future dinner in tow so you'll know exactly how fresh it is. Similar offerings are available in a more formal setting upstairs at Upscales. ⊠ *527 Thames St.,* ☎ *401/848–9378. Reservations not accepted downstairs. No credit cards.*

$$–$$$ ✕ **The Mooring.** The seafood chowder at this family-oriented restau-
★ rant won the local cook-off so many times the contest's officials removed it from further competition. In fine weather you can dine on the enclosed patio overlooking the yachts moored in the harbor; on chilly winter evenings take advantage of the open fire in the sunken interior room. The prices are reasonable at the Mooring, and there's plenty of parking. ⊠ *Sayer's Wharf,* ☎ *401/846–2260. AE, D, DC, MC, V.*

$$ ✕ **Puerini's.** The aroma of garlic and basil greets you as soon as you enter this laid-back neighborhood restaurant. Lace curtains hang in the windows, and black-and-white photographs of Italy cover the soft-pink walls. The long and intriguing menu includes green noodles with chicken in marsala wine sauce, tortellini with seafood, and cavatelli with four cheeses. ⊠ *24 Memorial Blvd.,* ☎ *401/847–5506. Reservations not accepted. MC, V. Closed Mon. in winter. No lunch.*

$ ✕ **Ocean Coffee Roasters.** Known to locals as Wave Café, this nonchalant diner draws locals aplenty for fresh-roasted coffee and fresh-baked muffins and bagels, salads, and homemade Italian soups. Breakfast is served until 2 PM. ⊠ *22 Washington Sq.,* ☎ *401/846–6060. Reservations not accepted. MC, V.*

$$$$ ✕🏨 **Vanderbilt Hall.** A former YMCA building donated to Newport by the Vanderbilt family in 1909 has been converted into the city's most sophisticated inn and restaurant. A butler greets arriving guests, a musician solos nightly at the grand piano in the center of the home, and there's a classy billiard room. Room 35 has a king-size bed and three windows with views of Newport Harbor and Trinity Church; suites have office space and sitting rooms. All the rooms have bathrobes and are decorated with antiques. The butler serves canapés and cocktails in the common room while patrons peruse the options for dinner: classic Continental cuisine served on Wedgwood china at tables set with silver. A fire crackles in the somber dining room, where a veteran and meticulous waitstaff tends to your needs. ⊠ *41 Mary St., 02840, ☎ 401/846–6200, FAX 401/846–0701. 30 rooms, 10 suites. Dining room, pool, spa, billiards. Continental breakfast available. AE, DC, MC, V.*

$$$$ ★ 🏠 **Cliffside Inn.** Grandeur and comfort come in equal supply at this swank Victorian home on a tree-lined street near the Cliff Walk. The wide front porch has a view of the lawn, and the rooms—all with Victorian antiques, some with bay windows—are light and airy. The Governor's Suite (named for Governor Thomas Swann, of Maryland, who built the home in 1880) has a two-sided fireplace, a whirlpool bath, a four-poster king-size bed, and a brass birdcage shower. Seven other rooms also have whirlpool baths; 10 have working fireplaces. ⊠ *2 Seaview Ave., 02840, ☎ 401/847–1811 or 800/845–1811. 15 rooms. Air-conditioning. Full breakfast. AE, D, DC, MC, V.*

$$$$ 🏠 **Elm Tree Cottage.** William Ralph Emerson (Ralph Waldo's cousin) designed the incomparable Elm Tree, a shingle-style house. This 1882 architectural treasure has massive guest rooms (most with fireplaces) furnished with English antiques and decorated by owner Priscilla Malone, an interior designer. Guests rave about her creative breakfasts, which are served on linen-bedecked tables. ⊠ *336 Gibbs Ave., 02840, ☎ 401/849–1610 or 800/882–3356, FAX 401/849–2084. 5 rooms, 1 suite. Lounge, air-conditioning, beach access. Full breakfast. AE, MC, V. No smoking; 2-night minimum weekends, 3-night minimum holiday weekends.*

$$$$ ★ 🏠 **Francis Malbone House.** The design of this stately painted-brick house is attributed to Peter Harrison, the architect responsible for the Touro Synagogue and the Redwood Library. A lavish inn with period reproduction furnishings, the 1760 structure was tastefully doubled in size in the mid-1990s. All new rooms have whirlpool tubs and fireplaces. The rooms in the main house are all in corners (with two windows) and look out over the courtyard, which has a fountain, or across the street to the harbor. Fifteen rooms have working fireplaces. The suite, on the ground floor, has its own entrances from Thames Street and the garden. ⊠ *392 Thames St., 02840, ☎ 401/846–0392 or 800/846–0392. 17 rooms, 1 suite. Full breakfast. AE, MC, V.*

$$$$ ★ 🏠 **Castle Hill Inn and Resort.** Much of the furniture at this inn is original to the structure, a summer home built in 1874 on a cliff at the mouth of the Narragansett Bay. Views over the bay are enthralling, and the public areas have tremendous charm. The inn, 3 mi from the center of Newport, is famous for its Sunday brunches. On Sunday afternoons, the lawn is crowded with people enjoying cocktails. ⊠ *Ocean Dr., 02840, ☎ 401/849–3800. 18 rooms with bath, 3 share bath. Restaurant, 3 beaches. Full breakfast. AE, D, MC, V. Restaurant closed Nov.–Mar.*

$$$$ 🏠 **Newport Islander Doubletree Hotel.** On Goat Island across from the Colonial Point District, the Doubletree has great views of the harbor and Newport Bridge. Most rooms have water views. There's free parking, and although the hotel is a 15-minute walk to Newport's center, bike and moped rentals are nearby. All rooms have oak furnishings and multicolor jewel-tone fabrics. ⊠ *Goat Island, 02840, ☎ 401/849–2600, FAX 401/846–8342. 269 rooms. Restaurant, indoor and outdoor pools, beauty salon, sauna, tennis, health club, racquetball, boating, meeting rooms. AE, D, DC, MC, V.*

$$$$ 🏠 **Newport Marriott.** This luxury hotel on the harbor at Long Wharf has an atrium lobby with marble floors and a gazebo. Rooms that don't border the atrium overlook the city or the waterfront. Fifth-floor rooms facing the harbor have sliding French windows that open onto large decks. Rates vary greatly according to season and location (harbor-view rooms cost more). ⊠ *25 America's Cup Ave., 02840,* ☎ *401/849–1000 or 800/228–9290,* FAX *401/849–3422. 317 rooms, 7 suites. Restaurant, bar, indoor pool, hot tub, sauna, health club, racquetball, meeting rooms, parking (fee). AE, D, DC, MC, V.*

$$$ 🏨 **Inntowne.** This small town-house hotel is in the center of Newport, 1½ blocks from the harbor. The neatly appointed rooms are decorated in a floral motif. Light sleepers may prefer rooms on the upper floors, which let in less traffic noise. The staff members greet you warmly on your arrival and are on hand throughout the day to give sightseeing advice. ⊠ *6 Mary St., 02840,* ☎ *401/846–9200 or 800/457–7803,* FAX *401/846–1534. 26 rooms. Air-conditioning, free parking. Continental breakfast. AE, MC, V.*

$$$ 🏨 **Ivy Lodge.** The only B&B in the mansion district, this grand (though
★ small by Newport's standards) Victorian has gables and a Gothic turret. Designed by Stanford White, the home has 11 fireplaces, large and lovely rooms, a spacious dining room, window seats, and two common rooms. The defining feature is a Gothic-style 33-ft-high oak entryway with a three-story turned baluster staircase and a dangling wrought-iron chandelier. Summer guests congregate on the wraparound front porch, which has wicker chairs. ⊠ *12 Clay St., 02840,* ☎ *401/849–6865. 8 rooms. Parking. Full breakfast. AE, MC, V.*

$$–$$$ 🏨 **Admiral Benbow Inn.** Listed on the National Register of Historic Places, this tidy 1855 Victorian is ideally situated on Newport's tranquil Historic Hill, between Bellevue Avenue and Thames Street. Maple and pine trees shade the front yard. Period antiques decorate the rooms, each of which has either an antique brass or hand-carved wood bed. Two rooms have fireplaces, and one has a private deck with a view of Newport Harbor. Kitchen facilities are available. ⊠ *93 Pelham St., 02840,* ☎ *401/846–4256. 15 rooms. Parking. Continental breakfast. AE, D, MC, V.*

$ 🏨 **Harbor Base Pineapple Inn.** This basic motel is the least expensive lodging in Newport. All rooms contain two double beds; some also have kitchenettes. Close to the naval base and jai alai, it's a five-minute drive from downtown. Renovations planned for 1999 will likely lead to a rate increase. ⊠ *372 Coddington Hwy., 02840,* ☎ *401/847–2600. 48 rooms. AE, D, DC, MC, V.*

Nightlife and the Arts

Detailed events calendars can also be found in *Newport This Week* and the *Newport Daily News.*

NIGHTLIFE

For a sampling of Newport's lively nightlife, you need only stroll down **Thames Street** after dark. The **Candy Store** (⊠ Bannister's Wharf, ☎ 401/849–2900) in the Clarke Cooke House restaurant is a snazzy place for a drink. **Newport Blues Café** (⊠ 286 Thames St., ☎ 401/841–5510) hosts great blues performers. **One Pelham East** (⊠ 270 Thames St., ☎ 401/847–9460) draws a young crowd for progressive rock, reggae, and R&B. **Thames Street Station** (⊠ 337 America's Cup Ave., ☎ 401/849–9480) plays high-energy dance music and videos and books rock bands from Thursday to Monday in summer.

THE ARTS

Murder-mystery plays are performed on Thursday evening from June to October at 8 PM at the **Astors' Beechwood** (⊠ 580 Bellevue Ave., ☎ 401/846–3772). **Newport Children's Theatre** (⊠ Box 144, ☎ 401/848–0266) mounts several productions each year. **Newport Playhouse**

& Cabaret (✉ 102 Connell Hwy., ☎ 401/848–7529) stages comedies and musicals; dinner packages are available.

Outdoor Activities and Sports

BIKING

Ten Speed Spokes (✉ 18 Elm St., ☎ 401/847–5609) rents bikes for $25 per day. The 12-mi swing down Bellevue Avenue, along Ocean Drive and back, is a great route to ride your rented wheels.

BOATING

Adventure Sports Rentals (✉ The Inn at Long Wharf, America's Cup Ave., ☎ 401/849–4820) rents waverunners, sailboats, kayaks, and canoes. **Newport Yacht Services Worldwide** (✉ 580 Thames St., ☎ 401/846–7720) charters yachts. **Oldport Marine Services** (✉ Sayer's Wharf, ☎ 401/847–9109) operates harbor tours and daily and weekly crewed yacht charters, rents moorings, and provides launch services. **Sail Newport** (✉ Ft. Adams State Park, ☎ 401/846–1983) rents sailboats by the hour.

DIVING

Newport Diving Center (✉ 550 Thames St., ☎ 401/847–9293) operates charter dive trips, refills Nitrox, conducts PADI training and certification, and offers rentals, sales, and service.

FISHING

Beachfront Bait Shop (✉ 103 Wellington Ave., ☎ 401/849–4665) stocks gear and tackle. **Fishin' Off** (✉ American Shipyard, Goat Island Causeway, ☎ 401/849–9642) runs charter fishing trips on a 36-ft Trojan. The **Saltwater Edge** (✉ 561 Thames St., ☎ 401/842–0062) sells fly-fishing tackle, gives lessons, and conducts guided trips.

HORSEBACK RIDING

Surprise Valley Farm (✉ 200 Harrison Ave., ☎ 401/847–2660) operates trail rides and hay rides on a gorgeous ranch near Ocean Drive.

JAI ALAI

Newport Jai Alai (✉ 150 Admiral Kalbfus Rd., ☎ 401/849–5000) has its season from March to mid-September.

Shopping

Many of Newport's arts and antiques shops are on Thames Street; others are on Spring Street, Franklin Street, and at Bowen's and Bannister's wharves. The Brick Market area—between Thames Street and America's Cup Avenue—has more than 40 shops.

ANTIQUES

Aardvark Antiques (✉ 475 Thames St., ☎ 401/849–7233) carries architectural pieces, such as mantels, doors, and stained glass; the nearby yard sells unique fountains and garden statuary. The 125 dealers at **The Armory** (✉ 365 Thames St., ☎ 401/848–2398), a vast 19th-century structure, carry antiques, china, and estate jewelry. **John Gidley House** (✉ 22 Franklin St., ☎ 401/846–8303) sells Continental furnishings from the 18th and 19th centuries. **The Nautical Nook** (✉ 86 Spring St., ☎ 401/846–6810) stocks unusual nautical-theme antiques and collectibles: maps, navigational instruments, model boats, and ships in bottles.

ART

ARTifacts (✉ 105 Spring St., ☎ 401/848–2222) sells hand-painted wood, glass, and faux marble. **MacDowell Pottery** (✉ 140 Spring St., ☎ 401/846–6313) is a studio and shop where you can purchase the wares of many New England potters. The delicate and dramatic blown-glass gifts sold at **Thames Glass** (✉ 688 Thames St., ☎ 401/846–0576) are designed by Matthew Buechner and created in the adjacent studio.

William Vareika Fine Arts (⊠ 212 Bellevue Ave., ☎ 401/849–6149) exhibits and sells American paintings and prints from the 18th to the 20th century.

BOOKS

Anchor & Dolphin Books (⊠ 30 Franklin St., ☎ 401/846–6890) specializes in books on garden history, architecture, and design. The **Armchair Sailor** (⊠ 543 Thames St., ☎ 401/847–4252) stocks marine and travel books, charts, and maps.

CLOTHING

Explorer's Club (⊠ 104 Spring St., ☎ 401/846–8465) specializes in quality outdoor sportswear with British and American labels. **JT's Ship Chandlery** (⊠ 364 Thames St., ☎ 401/846–7256) is a major supplier of clothing, marine hardware, and equipment. **Michael Hayes** (⊠ 204 Bellevue Ave., ☎ 401/846–3090) sells upscale clothing for men, women, and children. **Tropical Gangsters** (⊠ 375 Thames St., ☎ 401/847–9113) stocks hip clothing for men and women.

CRAFTS

Kelly & Gillis (⊠ 29 America's Cup Ave., ☎ 401/849–7380) carries offbeat and artsy American crafts.

Portsmouth

⑥⑤ *4 mi north of Newport.*

� Half the fun of a trip to Portsmouth is a ride on the **Old Colony & Newport Railway,** which follows an 8-mi route along Narragansett Bay from Newport to Portsmouth's Green Animals Topiary Gardens (☞ *below*). The vintage diesel train and two century-old coaches make three-hour round-trips, with a 1¼-hour stop at the gardens. ⊠ *19 America's Cup Ave.,* ☎ *401/624–6951.* 🎫 *$6.* ◷ *May–Oct.*

Green Animals Topiary Gardens is on a Victorian estate that has a remarkable toy collection and a plant shop. The gardens are filled with plants sculpted to look like an elephant, a camel, a giraffe, and even a teddy bear. ⊠ *Cory La. off Rte. 114,* ☎ *401/847–1000.* 🎫 *$6.50.* ◷ *May–Oct., daily 10–5. Closed Nov.–Mar.*

� Portsmouth's **Sandy Point Beach** is a choice spot for families and beginning windsurfers because of the calm surf along the Sakonnet River.

En Route Route 77, the main thoroughfare to Little Compton, passes through **Tiverton Four Corners**, a great place to stretch your legs and catch your first breath of East Bay air. **Provender** (⊠ 3883 Main Rd., ☎ 401/624–8096), in a former general store and post office, is a gourmet foods store, coffee shop, and bakery. Across the street fronting Provender is the stout building where the delicious **Gray's Ice Cream** (☎ 401/624–4500) is produced and sold. Also within walking distance are a half dozen galleries and gift shops.

Little Compton

⑥⑥ *19 mi from Portsmouth; 23 mi from Newport.*

The rolling estates, picture-perfect homes, farmlands, woods, and gentle western shoreline make Little Compton one of the Ocean State's prettiest areas. Little Compton and Tiverton were part of the Massachusetts Colony until 1747—to this day, residents here often have more roots in Massachusetts than in Rhode Island. Little Compton celebrated its 300th birthday in 1975, but locals said they hoped no one would come to the party. "Keep Little Compton little" is a popular sentiment, but considering the town's remoteness and its steep land prices, there may not be all that much to worry about.

Little Compton Commons (Meetinghouse Lane) is the epitome of a New England town square. As white as the clouds above, the spire of the Georgian-style United Congregational Church rises over the tops of adjacent oak trees. Within the triangular lawn is a cemetery with Colonial headstones, among them that of Elizabeth Padobie, said to be the first white girl born in New England. Surrounding the green is a rock wall and all the elements of small community: town hall, a community center, the police station, and the school. You will find town squares only in a few northern Rhode Island towns, ones that were once a part of Massachusetts Bay Colony; Rhode Islanders, adamant about separating church and state, did not favor this layout.

The **Wilbur House** is a neatly kept timepiece of Rhode Island living. The 1680 home was occupied by eight generations of Wilburs—the first of which included 11 children born between 1690 and 1712. The Common Room is 17th century; the bedrooms 18th and 19th; the kitchen 19th; and the living room 18th. In the barn museum is a one-horse shay, an oxcart, and a buggy and coach. ⊠ *548 W. Main Rd.,* ☎ *401/635– 4559.* ☞ *$4.* ☉ *Mid-June–mid-Sept., Wed.–Sun. 2–5; mid-Sept.–early Oct., weekends 2–5. Closed rest of yr.*

Sakonnet Point, a surreal spit of land, reaches out toward three tiny islands. The point begins where Route 77 ends. The ½-mi hike to the tip of Sakonnet Point passes tidal pools, a beach composed of tiny stone, and outcroppings that recall the surface of the moon. Parking is sometimes available in the lot adjacent to Sakonnet Harbor.

Tours and tastings are free of charge at **Sakonnet Vineyard** (⊠ 162 W. Main Rd., ☎ 401/635–8486), New England's largest winery. A few of its brands are well known, including Eye of the Storm, which was born of compromise: A power outage caused by a hurricane forced the wine makers to blend finished wine with what was in the vats.

Dining and Lodging

$$–$$$ ✕ **Abraham Manchester's.** Little Compton's former general store houses a restaurant with a basic menu of chicken, steak, seafood, and pasta. Antiques adorn the walls of the bar and dining room, enhancing the feel of history (the banter of locals will bring you up to the present). Take time to cross the street and look for the Rhode Island Red Monument (actually a plaque in the ground)—this community developed the famous Rhode Island Red breed of chicken. ⊠ *Main Rd.,* ☎ *401/635–2700. MC, V.*

$ ✕ **Commons Lunch.** Across from the church on the town square, this unpretentious old-Yankee restaurant opens daily at 5 AM. The food may not be spectacular, but it's reliable and priced to move. The menu is greasy-spoon standard, along with Rhode Island favorites like cabinets (milk shakes). ⊠ *South of Commons Rd.,* ☎ *401/635–4388. No credit cards. No dinner.*

$$ ☷ **The Roost.** A former farmhouse amid the fields of Sakonnet Vineyards is an intimate B&B that's remote yet accessible to rural pleasures like hiking, biking, and main-street shopping. The smartly furnished rooms all have private baths. Call well ahead for stays on summer weekends. ⊠ *170 W. Main Rd., 02837,* ☎ *401/635–8486,* ☏ *401/635– 2101. 3 rooms. Continental breakfast. MC, V.*

Outdoor Activities and Sports

FISHING

The 38-ft boat **Oceaneer** (⊠ Sakonnet Point Marina, ☎ 401/635–4292) can accommodate up to six people on chartered fishing trips.

HIKING

Wilbur Woods (✉ Swamp Rd.), a 30-acre hollow with picnic tables and a waterfall, is a good place for a casual hike. A trail winds along and over Dundery Brook.

Newport County A to Z

Arriving and Departing

BY BOAT

Interstate Navigation Co. (✉ Fort Adams State Park, ☏ 401/783–4613) operates passenger ferry service from Providence and Block Island to Newport.

BY BUS

RIPTA (Rhode Island Public Transportation Authority; ☏ 401/847–0209; 800/244–0444 in RI) buses leave from Providence throughout the day for Newport and also serve the city from other Rhode Island destinations.

BY CAR

From Providence take I–95 east into Massachusetts and head south on Route 24. From South County take Route 1 north to Route 138 east. From Boston take I–93 south to Route 24 south.

BY PLANE

Newport State Airport (☏ 401/848–7086) is 3 mi northeast of Newport. Charter companies fly from here to T. F. Green State Airport in Warwick, Rhode Island. **Cozy Cab** (☏ 401/846–2500) runs a shuttle service ($15) between the airport and Newport's visitors bureau.

Getting Around

BY BOAT

The **Jamestown and Newport Ferry Co.** (☏ 401/423–9900) runs a passenger ferry about every 1½ hours from Newport's Bowen's Landing and Long Wharf (and on request Fort Adams and Goat Island) to Jamestown's Ferry Wharf. The ferry operates from Memorial Day to mid-October. **Old Port Marine Company** (☏ 401/847–9109)) operates a water-taxi service for boaters in Newport Harbor.

BY BUS

See Arriving and Departing, *above.*

BY CAR

With the exception of Ocean Drive, Newport is a walker's city. In summer, traffic thickens, and the narrow one-way streets can constitute an unbearable maze. Once you're in town, it's worth parking in a pay lot—try one at the Gateway Information Center at 23 America's Cup Avenue—and leave your car behind while you visit in-town sights.

Contacts and Resources

EMERGENCIES

Newport Hospital (✉ Friendship St., ☏ 401/846–6400).

GUIDED TOURS

More than a dozen yacht companies operate tours of Narragansett Bay and Newport Harbor. Outings usually last just two hours and cost about $25 per person. **Flyer** (☏ 401/848–2100), a 57-ft catamaran, departs from Long Wharf. **Madeline** (☏ 401/847–0298), a 72-ft schooner, departs from Bannister's Wharf. **RumRunner II** (☏ 401/847–0299), a vintage 1929 motor yacht, once carried "hooch." **The Spirit of Newport** (☏ 401/849–3575), a 200-passenger multideck ship, departs for tours of Narragansett Bay and Newport Harbor from the Newport Harbor Hotel, on America's Cup Avenue, from May to mid-October.

Viking Bus and Boat Tours of Newport (⊠ Gateway Center, 23 America's Cup Ave., ☎ 401/847–6921) conducts Newport tours in air-conditioned buses from April to October. One-hour boat tours of Narragansett Bay operate from mid-May to Columbus Day weekend.

Newport on Foot (☎ 401/846–5391), led by guide extraordinaire Anita Raphael, organizes fascinating 1- to 2-mi walks through Colonial Newport. The **Newport Historical Society** (⊠ 82 Touro St., ☎ 401/846–0813) sponsors similar walking tours on Saturday from May to November.

24-HOUR PHARMACY
Brooks Pharmacy (⊠ 268 Bellevue Ave., ☎ 401/849–4600).

VISITOR INFORMATION
Newport County Convention and Visitors Bureau (⊠ Gateway Information Center, 23 America's Cup Ave., ☎ 401/849–8048 or 800/326–6030) has parking, rest rooms, and a gift shop. This spacious tourist center shows an orientation film and provides maps and advice.

RHODE ISLAND A TO Z

Arriving and Departing

By Bus
Bonanza Bus Lines (☎ 800/556–3815), **Greyhound Lines** (☎ 800/231–2222), and **Peter Pan Bus Lines** (☎ 800/237–8747) serve the **Providence Bus Terminal** (⊠ Bonanza Way, off Exit 25 from I–95, ☎ 401/751–8800). A shuttle service connects the terminal with Kennedy Plaza (⊠ Washington and Dorrance Sts.) in downtown Providence, where you can board the local public transit buses. Bonanza runs a bus from Boston's Logan Airport to Providence.

By Car
Interstate 95, which cuts diagonally across the state, is the fastest route to Providence from Boston, coastal Connecticut, and New York City. Interstate 195 links Providence with New Bedford and Cape Cod. Route 146 links Providence with Worcester and I–90. Route 1 follows much of the Rhode Island coast east from Connecticut before turning north to Providence. The detailed *Street Atlas Rhode Island,* published by Arrow Map, Inc., is available at many bookstores.

By Plane
T. F. Green State Airport (⊠ Rte. 1, Warwick, ☎ 401/737–4000) has scheduled daily flights by several major airlines, including American, Continental/Northwest, Southwest, United, and US Airways, with additional service by regional carriers. The main regional airports in Rhode Island are in Westerly (☞ South County A to Z, *above*) and Block Island (☞ Block Island A to Z, *above*).

By Train
Amtrak (☎ 800/872–7245) service between New York City and Boston makes stops at Westerly, Kingston, and Providence's **Union Station** (⊠ 100 Gaspee St., ☎ 401/331–2291). The **MBTA commuter rail service** (☎ 617/722–3200) connects Boston and Providence during weekday morning and evening rush hours for about half the cost of an Amtrak ride.

Getting Around

By Bus
RIPTA (Rhode Island Public Transportation Authority; ☎ 401/781–9400; 800/244–0444 in RI) buses crisscross the state.

By Car

Interstate 95 is the fastest route to the cities in southern and eastern Rhode Island. Route 1 travels more or less parallel to I–95, though closer to the coast. Route 146 passes through the northeastern portion of the Blackstone Valley. Route 44 travels west from Providence toward Connecticut. Route 138 heads east from Route 1 to Jamestown, Newport, and Little Compton.

Contacts and Resources

Guided Tours

Stumpf Balloons (☎ 401/253–0111) conducts fall-foliage tours of Rhode Island by balloon.

Hiking

One of the best trail guides for the region is the *AMC Massachusetts and Rhode Island Trail Guide,* available at local outdoors shops or from the **Appalachian Mountain Club** (✉ 5 Joy St., Boston, MA 02114, ☎ 617/523–0636). The **Rhode Island Audubon Society** (✉ 12 Sanderson Rd., Smithfield 02917, ☎ 401/949–5454) leads interesting hikes and field expeditions.

Reservation Service

Bed and Breakfast of Rhode Island, Inc. (✉ Box 3291, Newport 02840, ☎ 401/849–1298).

Visitor Information

Rhode Island Office of Tourism (✉ 1 W. Exchange St., Providence 02903, ☎ 401/789–0281 or 800/556–2484).

4 Massachusetts

Only a half dozen states are smaller than Massachusetts, but few have influenced American life more profoundly. Generations of Bay State merchants, industrialists, and computer executives have charted the course of the country's economy; Massachusetts writers, artists, and academics have enriched American culture; and from the meeting house to the White House, the state's politicians, philosophers, and pundits have fueled national debates.

MASSACHUSETTS SEABOARD TOWNS—from Newburyport to Provincetown—were built before the Revolution, during the heyday of American shipping. These coastal villages evoke a bygone world of clipper ships, robust fishermen, and sturdy sailors bound for distant Cathay. Lowell, on the Merrimack River, was the first American city to be planned around manufacturing. This textile town introduced the rest of the nation to the routines of the Industrial Revolution. In our own time, the high-tech firms of the greater Boston area helped to launch the information age, and the Massachusetts Institute of Technology (MIT) and Harvard supplied intellectual heft to deliver it to the wider world.

The Massachusetts town meeting set the tone for politics in the 13 original colonies. A century later, Boston was a hotbed of rebellion—Samuel Adams and James Otis, the "Sons of Liberty," started a war with words, inciting action against British colonial policies with patriotic pamphlets and fiery speeches at Faneuil Hall. Twentieth-century heirs to Adams include Boston's flashy midcentury mayor James Michael Curley; Thomas "Tip" O'Neill, the late Speaker of the House; and, of course, the Kennedys. In 1961, the young senator from the Boston suburb of Brookline, John Fitzgerald Kennedy, became president of the United States. JFK's service to Massachusetts was family tradition: In the years before World War I, Kennedy's grandfather, John "Honey Fitz" Fitzgerald, served in Congress and as mayor of Boston. But political families are nothing new here—Massachusetts is the only state that has sent both a father and a son—John Adams and John Quincy Adams—to the White House.

Massachusetts has an extensive system of parks, protected forests, beaches, and nature preserves. Like medieval pilgrims, readers of *Walden* come to Concord to visit the place where Henry David Thoreau wrote his prophetic essay. Thoreau's disciples can be found hiking to the top of the state's highest peak, Mt. Greylock, shopping for organic produce in an unpretentious college burg like Williamstown, or strolling the beaches of Martha's Vineyard and Nantucket. For those who prefer the hills to the ocean, the rolling Berkshire terrain defines the landscape from North Adams to Great Barrington in the western part of the state. A favorite vacation spot since the 19th century, when eastern aristocrats built grand summer residences, the Berkshires has been described as an inland Newport. This area attracts vacationers seeking superb scenery and food and an active cultural scene.

The list of Bay State writers, artists, and musicians who have shaped American culture is long indeed. The state has produced great poets in every generation: Anne Bradstreet, Phillis Wheatley, Emily Dickinson, Henry Wadsworth Longfellow, William Cullen Bryant, e.e. cummings, Robert Lowell, Elizabeth Bishop, Sylvia Plath, and Anne Sexton. Massachusetts writers include Louisa May Alcott, author of the enduring classic *Little Women*; Nathaniel Hawthorne, who re-created the Salem of his Puritan ancestors in *The Scarlet Letter*; Herman Melville, who wrote *Moby Dick* in a house at the foot of Mt. Greylock; Eugene O'Neill, whose early plays were produced at a makeshift theater in Provincetown on Cape Cod; Lowell native Jack Kerouac, author of *On the Road*; and John Cheever, chronicler of suburban angst. Painters Winslow Homer and James McNeill Whistler both hailed from the Commonwealth. Norman Rockwell, the quintessential American illustrator, lived and worked in Stockbridge. Celebrated composer and Boston native Leonard Bernstein was the first American to conduct the New York Philharmonic. Joan Baez got her start singing in Harvard Square, and contemporary Boston singer-songwriter Tracy Chapman picked up the beat with folk songs for the new age.

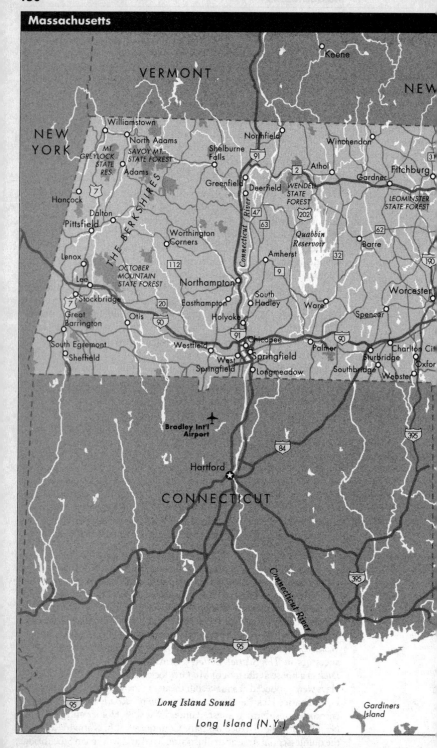

Keene

VERMONT

NEW

Williamstown

NEW YORK

North Adams

MT GREYLOCK STATE RES.

SAVOY MT. STATE FOREST

Shelburne Falls

Northfield

Winchendon

91

Athol

2

Gardner

Fitchburg

31

Adams

Greenfield

Deerfield

WENDELL STATE FOREST

LEOMINSTER STATE FOREST

Hancock

THE BERKSHIRES

47

63

202

Quabbin Reservoir

Barre

62

Dalton

Pittsfield

Worthington Corners

Amherst

32

190

Lenox

112

Connecticut River

9

Lee

OCTOBER MOUNTAIN STATE FOREST

Northampton

South Hadley

Ware

Worcester

7

Stockbridge

20

Easthampton

Spencer

Great Barrington

Otis

90

Holyoke

Sturbridge

Charlton Ci

South Egremont

Westfield

91

Chicopee

Palmer

Southbridge

Oxfor

Sheffield

West Springfield

Springfield

90

Webster

Longmeadow

Bradley Int'l Airport

395

84

Hartford

CONNECTICUT

395

Connecticut River

95

95

Long Island Sound

Gardiners Island

Long Island (N.Y.)

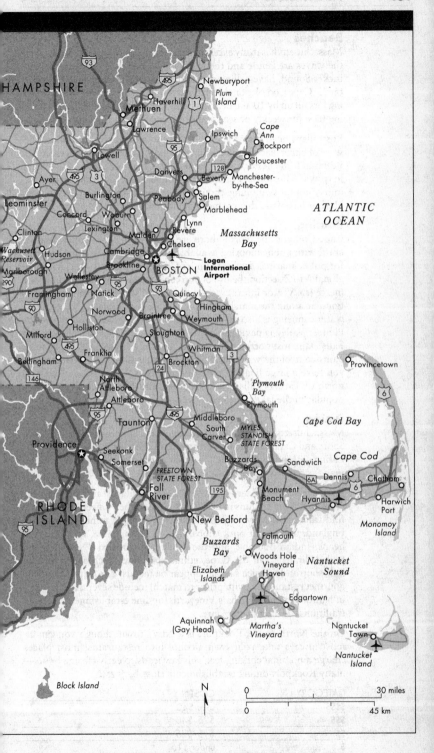

Pleasures and Pastimes

Beaches

Massachusetts has many excellent beaches, especially on Cape Cod, where the waves are gentle and the water cool. Southside beaches, on Nantucket Sound, have rolling surf and are warmer. Open-ocean beaches on the Cape Cod National Seashore are cold and have serious surf. Parking lots fill up by 10 AM. Beaches not restricted to residents charge parking fees; for weekly or seasonal passes, contact the local town hall.

Bostonians head for wide sweeps of sand along the North Shore (beware of biting blackflies in late May and early June), among them Singing Beach in Manchester, Plum Island in Newburyport, and Crane Beach in Ipswich. Boston city beaches are not particularly attractive and definitely not for swimming, though the ongoing rehabilitation of Boston Harbor has made them somewhat cleaner.

Boating

Cape Cod and the North Shore are centers for ocean-going pleasure craft, with public mooring available in many towns—phone numbers for public marinas are listed under Contacts and Resources in the regional A to Z sections below, or you can contact local chambers of commerce (☞ Visitor Information in the A to Z sections). Sea kayaking is popular along the marshy coastline of the North Shore, where freshwater canoeing is also an option. Inland, the Connecticut River in the Pioneer Valley is navigable by all types of craft between the Turners Falls Dam, just north of Greenfield, and the Holyoke Dam. The large dams control the water level daily, so you will notice a tidal effect; if you have a large boat, beware of sandbanks. Canoes can also travel north of Turners Falls beyond the Vermont border; canoeing is also popular in the lakes and small rivers of the Berkshires.

Dining

Massachusetts invented the fried clam, which appears on many North Shore and Cape Cod menus. Creamy clam chowder is another specialty. Eating seafood "in the rough"—from paper plates in shacklike buildings—is a revered local custom.

Boston restaurants serve New England standards and cutting-edge cuisine. At country inns in the Berkshires and the Pioneer Valley you'll find traditional New England "dinners" strongly reminiscent of old England: double-cut pork chops, rack of lamb, game, Boston baked beans, Indian pudding, and the dubiously glorified "New England boiled dinner." On the Cape, ethnic specialties such as Portuguese kale soup and linguiça sausage appear on menus. The Cape's first-rate gourmet restaurants (with prices to match) include several in Brewster; in Nantucket and Martha's Vineyard, top-line establishments prepare traditional and innovative fare.

On the North Shore, Rockport is a "dry" town, though you can almost always take your own alcohol into restaurants; most places charge a nominal corking fee. This law leads to early closing hours—many Rockport dining establishments close by 9 PM.

CATEGORY	COST*
$$$$	over $40
$$$	$25–$40
$$	$15–$25
$	under $15

*average cost of a three-course dinner, per person, excluding drinks, service, and 5% sales tax

Fishing

Deep-sea fishing trips depart from Boston, Cape Cod, and the South and North shores; surf casting is popular on the North Shore. The rivers, lakes, and streams of the Pioneer Valley and Berkshire County abound with fish—bass, pike, and perch, to name but a few. Stocked trout waters include the Hoosic River (south branch) near Cheshire; the Green River around Great Barrington; Notch Brook and the Hoosic River (north branch) near North Adams; Goose Pond and Hop Brook around Lee; and the Williams River around West Stockbridge.

Lodging

The signature accommodation outside Boston is the country inn; in the Berkshires, where magnificent mansions have been converted into lodgings, the inns reach a very grand scale indeed. Less extravagant and less expensive are bed-and-breakfast establishments, many of them in private homes. On Cape Cod, inns are plentiful, and rental homes and condominiums are available for long-term stays.

CATEGORY	BOSTON, THE CAPE, AND THE ISLANDS*	OTHER AREAS*
$$$$	over $150	over $100
$$$	$95–$150	$70–$100
$$	$70–$95	$40–$70
$	under $70	under $40

All prices are for a standard double room during peak season and do not include tax or gratuities. Some inns add a 15% service charge. The state tax on lodging is 5.7%; individual towns can impose an additional tax of up to 10%.

Shopping

Boston has many high-quality shops, especially in the Newbury Street and Beacon Hill neighborhoods, and most suburban communities have at least a couple of main-street stores selling old furniture and collectibles. Antiques can be found on the South Shore in Plymouth and Essex; on the North Shore in Newburyport, Marblehead, and elsewhere; in the northern towns of the Pioneer Valley (especially in Amherst or along the Mohawk Trail); and just about everywhere in the Berkshires, with particularly rich hunting grounds around Sheffield and Great Barrington. On Cape Cod, Provincetown and Wellfleet are centers for fine arts and crafts. Bookstores, gift shops, jewelers, and clothing boutiques line Main Street in Hyannis. Chatham's Main Street is a pretty, upscale shopping area.

Whale-Watching

In summer and fall, boats leave Boston, Cape Cod, and Cape Ann two or more times a day to observe the whales feeding a few miles offshore. It's rare not to have the extraordinary experience of seeing several whales, most of them extremely close up.

Exploring Massachusetts

Boston has the museums, the history, the shopping, and the traffic; Cape Cod and the North and South shores have beaches, more history, more shopping, and plenty of traffic. In the Berkshires and the Pioneer Valley you'll find centuries-old towns, antiques shopping, green hills, and a little less traffic. There's beauty to be discovered after the tourists have gone, wandering through snowy fields or braving the elements on a deserted winter beach, followed by a hot cider at the hearth of a local inn.

Numbers in the text and in the margin correspond to numbers on the maps: Cape Cod, Martha's Vineyard, Nantucket, the North Shore, the Pioneer Valley, and the Berkshires.

Great Itineraries

IF YOU HAVE 3 DAYS

Spend two days touring ⊡ **Boston.** On the third day either swing west on Route 2 and tour **Lexington** and **Concord** or north on Route 1A and east on Route 129 to **Marblehead** ㉘. Explore Marblehead and have lunch there before heading west on Route 114 and north on Route 1A to **Salem** ㉙.

IF YOU HAVE 7 DAYS TO SPEND ON THE CAPE

Head south from Boston (take I–93 to Route 3 to Route 6). Have lunch in **Sandwich** ① and tour the town before continuing on Route 6 to ⊡ **Chatham** ⑪, where you'll stay the night (have dinner and stroll Main Street in the evening). On morning two drive to **Orleans** ⑫ and spend the day at **Nauset Beach.** On day three continue on Route 6 to ⊡ **Provincetown** ⑯, stopping briefly in **Wellfleet** ⑭ to tour the galleries and detouring east off Route 6 to **Cahoon Hollow Beach.** After dinner take a walk down **Commercial Street.** On morning four head to **Race Point Beach,** go on a whale-watching cruise, or take a dune-buggy tour. On day five take Route 6 to **Hyannis** ⑥, where you can catch the ferry to ⊡ **Martha's Vineyard** ⑰–㉓.

IF YOU HAVE 7 OR 8 DAYS

Follow the three-day itinerary above, and spend your third night in **Salem** ㉙. On day four take the Massachusetts Turnpike (I–90) out of Boston and make a half-day stop at **Old Sturbridge Village** ㊻. Afterward, continue west on I–90 and north on I–91, stopping briefly in **Northampton** ㊷ before heading to ⊡ **Deerfield** ㊵, where you'll spend the night and day five. On day six head to the Berkshires—from Deerfield head north on I–91 to Greenfield, where you'll take Route 2 west to ⊡ **Williamstown** ㊽. On the morning of day seven tour the **Sterling and Francine Clark Art Institute** in Williamstown. Route 7 south takes you through **Pittsfield** ㊿; detour west on Route 20 to **Hancock Shaker Village** before heading on to ⊡ **Lenox** ㉜, where you'll spend the night. On day eight, visit Edith Wharton's **The Mount,** in Lenox, and the Norman Rockwell Museum, in **Stockbridge** ㉟. If you're visiting in summer take a picnic to an evening concert at **Tanglewood.**

When to Tour Massachusetts

Fall is the best time to visit western Massachusetts, and it's the perfect season to see Boston as well. Everyone else knows this, so make reservations for fall visits well ahead. Summer is ideal for visits to the Cape and the beaches. Bostonians often find their city to be too hot and humid in July and August, but if you're visiting from points south, the cool evening coastal breezes might strike you as downright refreshing. Many towns save their best for Christmas—lobster boats parade around Gloucester harbor adorned with lights, inns open their doors for goodies and caroling, shops serve eggnog, and tree-lighting ceremonies are often magical moments. The off-season is the perfect time to try cross-country skiing, take a walk on a stormy beach, or spend a night by the fire, tucked under a quilt catching up on Hawthorne or Poe.

BOSTON

Updated by
Stephanie
Schorow,
Fawn Fitter,
and Robert
Nadeau

New England's largest and most important city and the cradle of American independence, Boston is more than 360 years old, far older than the republic its residents helped to create. The city's most famous buildings are not merely civic landmarks but national icons; its local heroes are known to the nation: the Adamses, Reveres, and Hancocks, who live at the crossroads of history and myth.

At the same time, Boston is a contemporary center of high finance and higher technology, a place of granite and glass towers rising along what once were rutted village lanes. Its many students, artists, academics, and young professionals has made the town a haven for the arts, international cinema, late-night bookstores, Asian food, alternative music, and unconventional politics.

Best of all, Boston is meant for walking. Most of its historical and architectural attractions are in compact areas. Its varied and distinctive neighborhoods reveal their character to visitors who take the time to stroll through them. Should you need to make short or long hops between neighborhoods, the "T"—the safe and easy-to-ride trains of the Massachusetts Bay Transportation Authority (MBTA; ☞ Getting Around *in* Boston A to Z, *below,* for more information)—covers the city.

Beacon Hill and Boston Common

Contender for the "Most Beautiful" award among the city's neighborhoods and the hallowed address of many literary lights, Beacon Hill is Boston at its most Bostonian. As if with a flick of a Wellsian time-machine, the redbrick elegance of its narrow, cobbled streets transports visitors back to the 19th century. From the gold-topped splendor of the State House to the neoclassical panache of its mansions, Beacon Hill exudes power, prestige, and a calm yet palpable undercurrent of history.

Beacon Hill is bounded by Cambridge Street to the north, Beacon Street to the south, the Charles River Esplanade to the west, and Bowdoin Street to the east. In contrast to Beacon Hill, the Boston Common, the country's oldest public park, has a far more egalitarian feel. Beginning with its use as public land for cattle grazing, the Common has always accommodated the needs and desires of Bostonians. The public hangings once held there, however, have gone the way of the Puritans.

Numbers in the text and in the margin correspond to numbers on the Boston map.

A Good Walk

Stock up on brochures at the **Visitor Information Booth** on Tremont Street before heading into the **Boston Common** ① to see Frog Pond and the Central Burying Ground. Head back to **Beacon Street** near the corner of Park Street to reach Augustus Saint-Gaudens' **Robert Gould Shaw Memorial,** a commemoration of Boston's Civil War unit of free blacks. Walk past the **Park Street Church** ② and the **Old Granary Burial Ground** ③, the final resting place of some of Boston's most illustrious figures. Return to Beacon, turn left, and you'll arrive at the **Boston Athenaeum** ④. Retrace your steps to the neoclassical **State House** ⑤. Continue down Beacon for about six blocks to another classic, the **Bull & Finch Pub** ⑥, the bar in the *Cheers* TV show. Continue ahead two blocks to Arlington Street and, to your right, the footbridge that leads to the **Esplanade** ⑦. (The **Museum of Science** ⑧, best visited by car or T, is north of the Esplanade across the Charles River.) A pedestrian overpass (at the Charles/Massachusetts General Hospital T stop) connects the Esplanade with **Charles Street.** Head south on Charles, east on **Chestnut Street,** and north on Willow. This will land you at photogenic **Acorn Street.** Continue on Willow across **Mt. Vernon Street** to **Louisburg Square** ⑨. Turn east (to the right) on Pinckney Street and follow it to Joy Street: Two blocks north on Smith Court are the **African Meeting House** ⑩ and the **Museum of Afro American History and Abiel Smith School** ⑪. You can pick up a brochure here for the **Black Heritage Trail** (you can also pick one up at the Shaw memorial).

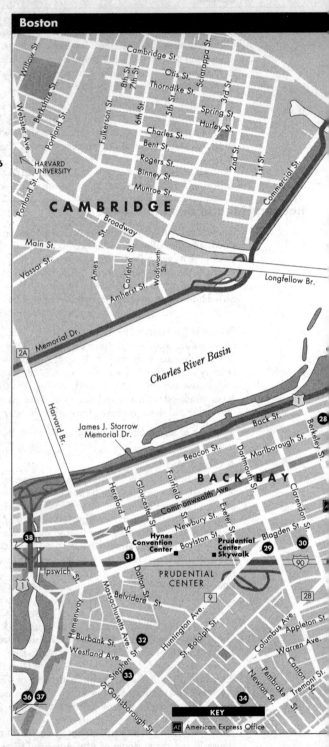

Boston

KEY

AE American Express Office

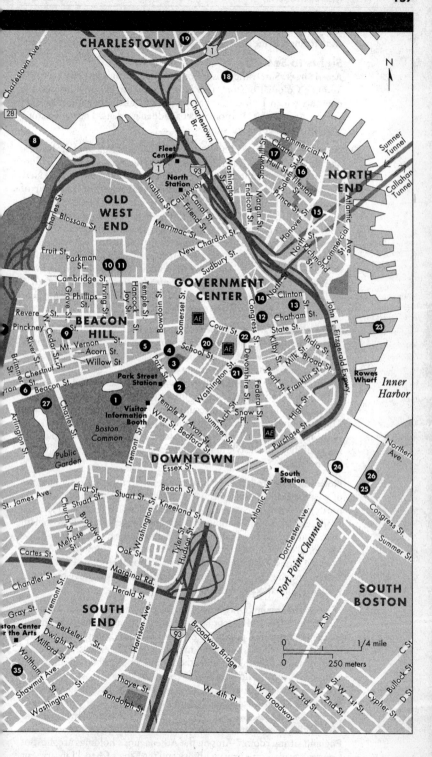

TIMING

Allow yourself the better part of a day for this walk, particularly if you want to linger in the Common or in the antiques shops on Charles Street.

Sights to See

Acorn Street. Surely the most photographed street in the city, Acorn is Ye Olde Colonial Boston at its best. Almost toylike row houses line one side, which 19th-century artisans once called home; on the other are the doors to Mt. Vernon Street's hidden gardens. The cobblestone street is rough going for some.

① **African Meeting House.** Built in 1806 and the centerpiece of the historic Smith Court African-American community, the African Meeting House is the oldest black church building in the United States. In 1832 the New England Anti-Slavery Society was formed here under the leadership of William Lloyd Garrison. A gallery on the first floor has changing exhibitions. Plans are underway for a major renovation of the meeting house after renovations are completed at the nearby Abiel Smith School. The five residences on **Smith Court** are typical of black Bostonian homes of the 1800s, including Number 3, the 1799 clapboard house where William C. Nell, America's first published black historian, lived. ✉ *8 Smith Ct. (off Joy St. between Cambridge and Myrtle Sts.).* ☎ *617/ 742–1854.* ☜ *$5 donation suggested.* ☉ *Memorial Day–Labor Day, daily 10–4; rest of yr, weekdays 10–4. T stop: Park St.*

Beacon Street. One of the city's most famous thoroughfares, Beacon Street epitomizes Boston. From the magnificent State House to the stately patrician mansions, the street is lined with architectural treasures. The **Boston Athenaeum** (☞ *below*) is on this street as are the **Appleton Mansions**, at Nos. 39 and 40. Only a few buildings have panes like those of the mansions: Sunlight on the imperfections in a shipment of glass sent to Boston around 1820 resulted in an amethystine mauve shade. The mansions are not open to the public. Farther along, you'll find some of the most important buildings of Charles Bulfinch—the ultimate designer of the Federal style in America—and dozens of elegant bowfront row houses.

Black Heritage Trail. The mention of Beacon Hill conjures up images of wealthy Boston Brahmins; yet until the end of the 19th century, its north side was home to many free blacks. The 1.6-mi Black Heritage Trail celebrates that community, stitching together 14 Beacon Hill sites. Tours guided by National Park Service rangers meet at the Shaw Memorial on the Beacon Street side of the Boston Common; the African Meeting House (☞ *above*), the Boston National Historic Park Visitor Center, and the Visitors Information Center (☞ *below*) have brochures with self-guided walking tours.

④ **Boston Athenaeum.** Only 1,049 proprietary shares exist for membership in this cathedral of scholarship, and most have been passed down for generations. The public is permitted to walk through the first and second floors, to marvel at the marble busts, the exquisite porcelain vases, lush oil paintings, and leather-bound books of this Brahmin institution. A second-floor gallery presents art shows, most with a literary bent. A guided tour affords one of the most marvelous sights in the world of Boston academe, the fifth-floor Reading Room. In the words of critic David McCord, it "combines the best elements of the Bodleian, Monticello, the frigate *Constitution*, a greenhouse, and an old New England sitting room." Among the Athenaeum's holdings are most of George Washington's private library and the King's Chapel Library sent from England by William and Mary in 1698. ✉ *10½ Beacon St.,* ☎ *617/227–0270.* ☜ *Free.* ☉ *Weekdays 9–5:30; Sept.–May also Sat.*

9–4. Free guided tours Tues. and Thurs. at 3, by appointment 24 hrs ahead. Closed Bunker Hill Day (June 17). T stop: Park St.

❶ Boston Common. The oldest public park in the United States is the largest and undoubtedly the most famous of the town commons around which New England settlements were traditionally arranged. As old as the city around it (it dates from 1634), the Common contains intriguing sights. The **Central Burying Ground** is the final resting place of Tories and Patriots, as well as many British casualties of the Battle of Bunker Hill. On the Beacon Street side of the Common sits the splendidly restored **Robert Gould Shaw Memorial,** executed in deep-relief bronze by Augustus Saint-Gaudens in 1897. It honors the 54th Massachusetts Regiment, led by the young Robert Gould Shaw, the first Civil War unit made up of free blacks. Their stirring saga inspired the 1989 movie *Glory.*

❻ Bull & Finch Pub. If when you come upon this pub, you find yourself humming the words, ". . . where everybody knows your name," there's a reason: It's the watering hole that inspired the long-running NBC sitcom *Cheers.* There's a yellow *Cheers* flag (and often a long line of tourists) outside. The interior, however, has merely a passing resemblance to its TV counterpart. ✉ *84 Beacon St.,* ☎ *617/227–9605. T stop: Arlington.*

Charles Street. With few exceptions, Beacon Hill lacks commercial development, but the section of Charles Street north of Boston Common more than makes up for it. Antiques shops, bookstores, small restaurants, and flower shops vie for attention, but tastefully: Even the 7-Eleven storefront conforms to the prevailing Colonial aesthetic. The contemporary activity would present a curious sight to the elder Oliver Wendell Holmes, the publisher James T. Fields (of the famed Bostonian firm of Ticknor & Fields), and many others who lived here when the neighborhood belonged to establishment literati. Charles Street sparkles at dusk from gas-fueled lamps, making it a romantic place for an evening stroll.

Chestnut Street. Delicacy and grace characterize virtually every structure along this street, from the fanlights above the entryways to the wrought-iron boot scrapers on the steps. The **Swan Houses,** at Nos. 13, 15, and 17, have Adam-style entrances, marble columnnettes, and recessed arches commissioned from Charles Bulfinch.

❼ Esplanade. At the northern end of Charles Street is one of several footbridges crossing Storrow Drive to the Esplanade, which stretches along the Charles River. The scenic patch of green is a great place to jog, picnic, and watch the sailboats along the river. For the almost nightly entertainment in the summer, Bostonians haul chairs and blankets to the lawn in front of the **Hatch Memorial Shell.**

Freedom Trail. A 3-mi tour of the sites of the American Revolution, the Freedom Trail is a crash course in history. There are 16 sites beginning at the Boston Common and ending at the Bunker Hill Monument in Charlestown; depending on how many are visited in depth, the walk can take from an aerobic 90 minutes to a leisurely half day. Trail walks led by National Park Service rangers take place from mid-April to November and begin at the Boston National Historic Park Visitor Center (☞ *below*); self-guided tour maps are available here and at the Visitor Information Center on Boston Common (☞ *below*).

❾ Louisburg Square. One of the quaintest corners in a neighborhood that epitomizes quaint, Louisburg Square is the very heart of Beacon Hill. Its houses—many built in the 1840s—have seen their share of famous tenants, including the Alcotts at No. 10 (Louisa May died here, on the day of her father's funeral). In 1852 the popular Swedish singer Jenny Lind was married in the parlor of No. 20, the residence of Samuel Ward, brother of Julia Ward Howe.

Mt. Vernon Street. Some of Beacon Hill's most distinguished addresses are on Mt. Vernon Street, whose houses rise tall from the pavement. The street even has a freestanding mansion, the Second Harrison Gray Otis House, at No. 87. Henry James once wrote that this was "the only respectable street in America" (he lived with his brother William at No. 131 in the 1860s).

⓫ Museum of Afro American History and Abiel Smith School. Ever since Crispus Attucks became one of the legendary victims of the Boston Massacre of 1770, the African-American community of Boston has played an important part in the city's history. Throughout the 19th century, abolition became the cause célèbre for Boston's intellectual elite, and during that time the black community thrived in neighborhoods like Smith Court and Joy Street. The museum was founded in 1964 to promote this history. Its headquarters occupy the 1830s Abiel Smith School, the first public grammar school for black children in Boston. The building was closed in late 1997 for a two-year renovation project that will create new space for the museum and for exhibits about the struggle for equal education in Boston. The museum is temporarily relocating to 78 Mount Fort Street in Brookline. ⊠ *46 Joy St.,* ☎ *617/742–1854. T stop: Park St.*

⑧ Museum of Science. With 15-ft lightning bolts in the Theater of Electricity and a 20-ft-high T. Rex model, this is just the place to ignite any child's Jurassic spark. The museum, astride the Charles River Dam, has a restaurant, a gift shop, a planetarium, and a theater you can visit separately. The **Charles Hayden Planetarium,** with its sophisticated multi-image system, produces exciting programs on astronomical discoveries. The **Mugar Omni Theater** has a four-story domed screen (27,000 watts of power drive the 84 loudspeakers). ⊠ *Science Park at the Charles River Dam,* ☎ *617/723–2500; 617/523–6664 for planetarium and theater.* ▧ *Museum $9, planetarium and theater $7.50 each; reduced price combination tickets available for museum, planetarium, and Omni Theater.* ☉ *Sat.–Thurs. 9–5, Fri. 9–9; extended hrs July 5–Sept. 5. T stop: Science Park.*

③ Old Granary Burial Ground. "It is a fine thing to die in Boston," A. C. Lyons once remarked—alluding to Boston's cemeteries, among the most picturesque and historic in America. If you found a resting place at the Old Granary, just to the right of Park Street Church, chances are your headstone would have been eloquently ornamented and your neighbors would have been mighty eloquent, too: Samuel Adams, John Hancock, Paul Revere, and "Mother" Goose. ⊠ *Tremont St. near Bosworth St.* ☉ *Daily 8–4:30. T stop: Park St.*

② Park Street Church. If the Congregationalist Park Street Church, which was designed by Peter Banner and completed in 1810, could talk, what a joyful noise it would make. Samuel Smith's hymn "America" debuted here on July 4, 1831; two years earlier, William Lloyd Garrison began his long public campaign for the abolition of slavery. The church—called "the most impressive mass of brick and mortar in America" by Henry James—is earmarked by its steeple, considered by many critics to be the most beautiful in New England. ⊠ *1 Park St., at Tremont St.,* ☎ *617/523–3383.* ☉ *Tours July–Aug., Tues.–Sat. 9:30–3:30; Sun. services at 9, 10:45, and 5:30 Sept.–June; 10:45 and 5:30 July–Labor Day. T stop: Park St.*

⑤ **State House.** Charles Bulfinch's magnificent State House, one of the greatest works of classical architecture in America, is so striking that it hardly suffers for having been appendaged in three directions by bureaucrats and lesser architects. The neoclassical design is poised between Georgian and Federal; its finest features are the delicate Corinthian columns of the portico, the graceful pediment and window arches, and the vast yet visually weightless dome. The dome is sheathed in copper from the foundry of Paul Revere. ⊠ *Beacon and Park Sts.,* ☎ *617/727–3676.* 🎟 *Free.* ☉ *Tours weekdays 10–4, last tour at 3:30. T stop: Park St.*

Visitor Information Center. You can pick up pamphlets, flyers, maps, and coupons at this kiosk, which is between the Park Street and Boylston mass-transit stations. ⊠ *Boston Common, Tremont St. near West St.,* ☎ *617/536–4100 or 888/733–2678 for recorded information.* ☉ *Mon.–Sat. 8:30–5, Sun. 9–5.*

Government Center and the North End

Government Center is the section of town Bostonians love to hate. Not only does it house that which they cannot fight—City Hall—but it also holds some of the bleakest architecture since the advent of poured concrete. The sweeping brick plaza aside City Hall and the twin towers of the John F. Kennedy Federal Office Building begins at the junction where Cambridge Street becomes Tremont Street.

Separating the Government Center area from the North End is the Fitzgerald Expressway, which will eventually be replaced with an underground highway in a massive construction project dubbed "The Big Dig" by locals. In the meantime, calling the area a mess is putting it mildly. Driver alert: The rerouting of traffic and constant reconfiguration of one-way streets have changed what was once a conquerable maze into a nearly impenetrable puzzle. Trust no maps.

Opposite the pedestrian tunnel beneath the Fitzgerald Expressway is the North End, the oldest neighborhood in Boston and one of the oldest in the New World. People walked these narrow byways when Shakespeare was not yet 20 years buried and Louis XIV was new to the throne of France. In the 17th century the North End *was* Boston—much of the rest of the peninsula was still underwater or had yet to be cleared.

Today's North End is almost entirely a creation of the late 19th century, when brick tenements began to fill up with European immigrants—first the Irish, then Eastern European Jews, then the Portuguese, and finally the Italians. For more than 60 years the North End attracted an Italian population base. There are dozens of Italian restaurants here, along with Italian groceries, bakeries, churches, social clubs, and cafés.

Numbers in the text and in the margin correspond to numbers on the Boston map.

A Good Walk

The stark expanse of Boston's City Hall Plaza introduces visitors to the urban renewal age, but across Congress Street is **Faneuil Hall** ⑫, a site of political speechmaking since Revolutionary times. Just beyond that is **Quincy Market** ⑬, where shop-till-you-droppers can sample a profusion of international taste treats. For more Bostonian fare, walk back toward Congress Street to the **Blackstone Block** ⑭ and the city's oldest restaurant, the **Union Oyster House,** for some oysters and ale. Around the corner to the north on Blackstone Street are the open-air stalls of **Haymarket,** always aflutter with activity on Friday and Saturday. To sample Italian goodies, make your way through a pedestrian tunnel underneath the Fitzgerald Highway and enter the North End at Salem Street. Follow to Parmenter Street, turn right, and continue past Hanover Street, one of the North End's main thoroughfares; here Parmenter becomes Richmond Street. At North Street, turn left, following the Freedom Trail, to the **Paul Revere House** ⑮. Take Prince Street to Hanover Street, then continue on Hanover to St. Stephen's, the only remaining church designed by Charles Bulfinch. Directly across the street is the Prado, or Paul Revere Mall, dominated by a statue of the patriot and hero. At the end of the mall is the **Old North Church** ⑯, of "One if by land, two if by sea" fame. Continue following the Freedom Trail to Hull Street and **Copp's Hill Burying Ground** ⑰, the resting place of many Revolutionary War heroes.

TIMING

You can explore Faneuil Hall and Quincy Market in about an hour, more if you linger in the food stalls or shop. Give yourself another two to three hours to stroll through the North End. Finish the day with an Italian meal or at least a cappuccino.

Sights to See

⑭ **Blackstone Block.** For decades the butcher trade dominated the city's oldest commercial block. Today, the block is Boston at its time-machine best, with more than three centuries of architecture on view. The centerpiece of the block is the **Union Oyster House** (☞ Dining, *below*), whose patrons have included Daniel Webster and John F. Kennedy.

⑰ **Copp's Hill Burying Ground.** An ancient and melancholy air hovers over this Colonial-era burial ground like a fine mist. Many headstones were chipped by practice shots fired by British soldiers during the occupation of Boston, and a number of musketball pockmarks can still be seen. ⊠ *Snowhill St.* ☉ *Daily 9–4. T stop: Haymarket.*

⑫ **Faneuil Hall.** Faneuil Hall was erected in 1742 to serve as a place for town meetings and a public market. Inside are the great mural *Webster's Reply to Hayne,* Gilbert Stuart's portrait of Washington at Dorchester Heights, and, on the top floors, the headquarters and museum of the Ancient and Honorable Artillery Company of Massachusetts, the oldest militia in the nation (1638). ⊠ *Faneuil Hall Sq.* ▨ *Free.* ☉ *Daily 9–5. T stop: Government Center or Aquarium.*

Haymarket. Centered on the relentlessly picturesque Blackstone Block, this exuberant maze of a marketplace is packed with loudly self-promoting vendors of fruit and vegetables who fill Marshall and Blackstone streets on Friday and Saturday from 7 AM until mid-afternoon.

⑯ **Old North Church.** This church is famous not only for its status as the oldest in Boston (1723) but for the two lanterns that glimmered from its steeple on the night of April 18, 1775. This is Christ Church, or the Old North, where a middle-aged silversmith named Paul Revere and a young sexton named Robert Newman managed that night to signal the departure by water to Lexington and Concord of the British regulars. (Longfellow's poem aside, the lanterns were not a signal *to* Revere but *from* him to the citizens of Charlestown across the harbor.) The church was designed by William Price from a study of Christopher Wren's London churches. ⊠ *193 Salem St.,* ☎ *617/523–6676.* ☉ *Daily 9–5; Sun. services at 9, 11, and 4. T stop: Haymarket.*

☾ ⑮ **Paul Revere House.** It is an interesting coincidence that the oldest house standing in one of the oldest sections of Boston should also have been the home of Paul Revere, patriot activist and silversmith. And it *is* a coincidence, since many homes of famous Bostonians have burned or been demolished over the years. It was saved from oblivion in 1905 and restored, lovingly though not quite authentically, to an approximation of its original 17th-century appearance. The house was built nearly a hundred years before Revere's 1775 midnight ride through Middlesex County. Few of Revere's furnishings are on display, but just gazing at Paul's own toddy-warmer brings the great man alive. Many special events are scheduled here through the year for children. ☒ *19 North Sq.,* ☎ *617/523–1676.* ☞ *$2.50.* ☉ *Daily 9:30–4:15; mid-Apr.– Oct. until 5:15. Closed Mon., Jan.–Mar. T stop: Haymarket.*

🔞 **Quincy Market.** Also known as Faneuil Hall Marketplace, this pioneer effort at urban recycling set the tone for many similar projects throughout America. The market consists of three block-long annexes: Quincy, North, and South markets, each 535 ft long, built to the 1826 design of Alexander Parris. Abundance and variety have been the watchwords of Quincy Market since its reopening in 1976. Some people consider it hopelessly commercial; 50,000 or so visitors a day rather enjoy the extravaganza. At the east end of Quincy Market, **Marketplace Center** has tempting boutiques and food shops. ☒ *Off State St.,* ☎ *617/ 338–2323.* ☉ *Mon.–Sat. 10–9, Sun. noon–6. Restaurants and bars generally open daily 11 AM–2 AM; food stalls open earlier. T stop: Haymarket, Government Center, State St., or Aquarium.*

Charlestown

Charlestown was a thriving settlement a year before Colonials headed across the Charles River to found Boston proper. The district lures visitors with two of the most visible—and vertical—monuments in Boston's history: the Bunker Hill Monument and the USS *Constitution.*

To get to Charlestown, you can take Bus 93 from Haymarket Square, Boston, which stops three blocks from the Navy Yard entrance. A more interesting way to get here is to take the MBTA water shuttle from Long Wharf in downtown Boston, which runs every 15 or 30 minutes year-round.

Numbers in the text and in the margin correspond to numbers on the Boston map.

A Good Walk

Charlestown can be reached by foot via the Charlestown Bridge. From Copp's Hill Burial Ground, follow Hull Street to Commercial Street, and turn left to reach the bridge. The Charlestown Navy Yard will be on your right after you alight from the bridge. Ahead is the **USS Constitution** ⑱ museum and visitor center. From here, you can follow the red line of the Freedom Trail to the **Bunker Hill Monument** ⑲.

TIMING

Give yourself two or three hours for a Charlestown walk; the lengthy stroll across the Charlestown Bridge calls for endurance in cold weather. Many save Charlestown's stretch of the Freedom Trail for a second-day outing. You can save backtracking the historic route by taking the MBTA water shuttle that ferries back and forth between the navy yard and Long Wharf.

Sights to See

⑲ **Bunker Hill Monument.** British troops sustained heavy losses on June 17, 1775 at the Battle of Bunker Hill—one of the earliest major confrontations of the Revolutionary War. Most of the battle took place on Breed's Hill, which is where the monument, erected in 1842, stands. The famous war cry "Don't fire until you see the whites of their eyes" may not have been uttered by American colonel William Prescott, but if he did shout it, he was quoting an old Prussian command. No matter. The Americans employed a deadly delayed-action strategy and proved

themselves worthy fighters—though they lost the battle, the engage-
ment made clear that the British could be challenged. The monument's
zenith is reached by a flight of 294 steps. There is no elevator, but the
views from the observatory are worth the arduous climb. In the lodge
at the base, dioramas tell the story of the battle; and ranger programs
are conducted hourly. On June 17, the battle is reenacted on the hill
in a quite splendid production. ⊠ *Main St. to Monument St., then straight
uphill,* ☎ *617/242–5641.* ⊠ *Free.* ☉ *Lodge daily 9–5, monument daily
9–4:30. T stop: Community College.*

A multimedia presentation, **"Whites of Their Eyes,"** is shown in the
Bunker Hill Pavilion near the navy yard entrance. ⊠ *55 Constitution
Rd.,* ☎ *617/241–7576.* ⊠ *$3.* ☉ *Apr.–Nov. 9:30–4; June–Aug.
9:30–5; shows every ½ hr.*

⑱　USS Constitution. Better known as "Old Ironsides," the two-centuries-
old USS *Constitution* is docked at the **Charlestown Navy Yard.** The
oldest commissioned ship in the U.S. fleet, it's a battlewagon of the old
school, of the days of "wooden ships and iron men"—when she and
her crew of 200 asserted the sovereignty of an improbable new nation.
Her principal service was in the War of 1812. Of her 42 engagements,
her record was 42–0. Once a year, on July 4, she is towed out into
Boston harbor. ⊠ *Constitution Wharf,* ☎ *617/426–1812 museum, 617/
242–5670 ship.* ⊠ Constitution *free; museum $4.* ☉ *Museum: sum-
mer, daily 9–5; winter daily 9–4. Ship: daily 9:30–sunset; 20-min tours,
last at 3:30 PM. T stop: Haymarket; then MBTA Bus 92 or 93 to
Charlestown City Sq. Or take the MBTA water shuttle from Long Wharf.*

Downtown Boston

The financial district—what Bostonians usually refer to as "downtown"—may seem off the beaten track for visitors who are concen-
trating on following the Freedom Trail, yet there is much to see in a
walk of an hour or two. There is little logic to the streets here; they
were, after all, village lanes that only now happen to be lined with 40-
story office towers. The area may be confusing, but it is mercifully small.

Downtown is home to some of Boston's most idiosyncratic neighborhoods. The old Leather District directly abuts Chinatown, which is also
bordered by the Theater District (and the buildings of the Tufts New
England Medical Center), farther west; to the south, the red light of
the once brazen and now decaying Combat Zone flickers weakly.

*Numbers in the text and in the margin correspond to numbers on the
Boston map.*

A Good Walk

After viewing the dramatic interior of **King's Chapel** ⑳ at the corner
of Tremont (that's *Tre*-mont, not *Tree*-mont), visit the burying ground
next door. Walk south on School Street, past the Globe Corner Bookstore, to Washington Street; turn right to see the **Old South Meeting
House** ㉑, which seethed with revolutionary fervor in the 1770s. Retrace your steps on Washington and continue toward Court Street to
get to the **Old State House** ㉒. In a traffic island in front is a circle of
stones that marks the site of the Boston Massacre, a 1770 riot in
which five townspeople were killed by British troops. Follow State Street
east to the harbor and the **New England Aquarium** ㉓, on Central
Wharf. From here you can walk south to **Rowes Wharf,** Boston's most
glamorous waterfront development. Continue on Atlantic Avenue—
most likely a solid wall of traffic due to construction of an underground
central artery highway nearby—to Congress Street, and then turn left
onto the bridge to reach the *Beaver II* ㉔, a faithful re-creation of the

Boston MBTA (the "T")

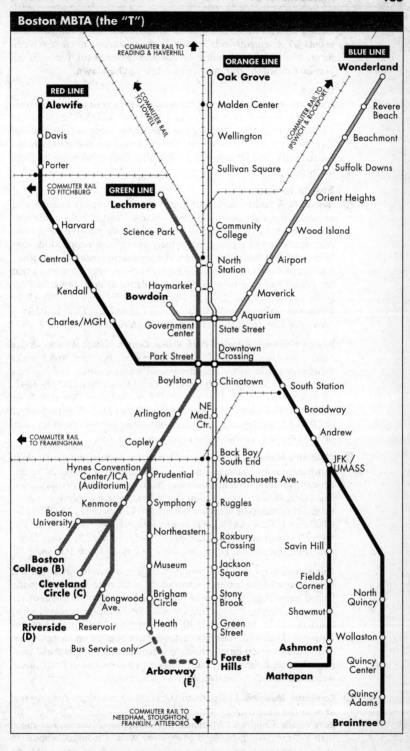

hapless British ship that was carrying tea in 1773. Continue over the Congress Street Bridge to the **Children's Museum** ㉕ and **Computer Museum** ㉖, conveniently side by side. If you're starting to crave refreshment, cross back to Atlantic Avenue and continue south past South Station toward the distinctive gate marking **Chinatown.**

TIMING

If you are traveling with small children, you may wish to limit this walk to the area around the New England Aquarium and the Computer and Children's museums. (In fact, you'll probably want to spend two or three hours just in the museums). Otherwise budget about three hours for the walk, and be prepared for the often cool wind coming off the harbor.

Sights to See

㉔ *Beaver II.* A faithful replica of one of the ships forcibly boarded and unloaded the night Boston Harbor became a teapot bobs in the Fort Point Channel at the Congress Street Bridge. Visitors receive a complimentary cup of tea, and when there are enough people, kids may be pressed into donning feathers and war paint to reenact the tea drop. The site of the actual Boston Tea Party—a revolt over a tax on tea that the British had levied—is marked by a plaque at Pearl Street and Atlantic Avenue. ⊠ *Congress St. Bridge,* ☎ *617/338–1773.* ☞ *$7.* ☺ *Memorial Day–Labor Day, daily 9–6; Labor Day–Dec. and Mar.– Memorial Day, daily 9–5. T stop: South Station.*

Boston National Historical Park Visitor Center. National Park Service ranger–led tours of the Freedom Trail leave from the center, which stocks brochures about many attractions and walking tours and has rest rooms. ⊠ *15 State St., near the Old State House,* ☎ *617/242–5642.* ☞ *Free.* ☺ *Late June–Labor Day, daily 9–6; Labor Day–late June, daily 9–5. Tours mid-Apr.–late June and Labor Day–Nov., weekdays at 10 and 2, weekends at 10, 11, 2, and 3; late June–Labor Day daily at 10, 11, 12, 1, 2, and 3. No tours Dec.–mid-Apr.*

☺ ㉕ **Children's Museum.** Hands-on exhibits at this popular museum include computers, video cameras, and displays designed to help children understand cultural diversity, their own bodies, the nature of disabilities, and more. Don't miss Grandmother's Attic, where children can dress up in old clothing. ⊠ *Museum Wharf, 300 Congress St.,* ☎ *617/426– 6500 or 617/426–8855 for recorded information.* ☞ *$7; $1 on Fri. 5–9.* ☺ *Mid-June–Labor Day, daily 10–5, Fri. until 9; Labor Day– mid-June, Tues.–Sun. 10–5, Fri. until 9. T stop: South Station.*

Chinatown. Boston's Chinatown may be geographically small, but it is home to one of the larger concentrations of Chinese-Americans in the United States. Beginning in the 1870s, Chinese immigrants began to trickle in, many setting up tents in Ping On Alley. Immigration increased when restrictions were lifted after 1940. In recent years, Vietnamese, Korean-Japanese, Thai, and Malaysian eateries have popped up alongside the many Chinese restaurants—most along Beach and Tyler streets and Harrison Avenue. A three-story pagoda-style arch at the end of Beach Street welcomes visitors to the district. *T stop: Chinatown.*

☺ ㉖ **Computer Museum.** Learn about the thinking machines running our lives in this user-friendly setting kids and adults enjoy. Conveniently next to the Children's Museum, the Computer Museum has more than 170 exhibits, including the two-story Walk-Through Computer™ and a software gallery with the newest games. ⊠ *300 Congress St.,* ☎ *617/426–2800; 617/423–6758 for talking computer.* ☞ *$7; ½ price Sun. 3–5.* ☺ *Sept.–mid-June, Tues.–Sun. 10–5; mid-June–Aug., daily 10–6. T stop: South Station.*

㉑ King's Chapel. Somber yet dramatic, King's Chapel looms over the corner of Tremont and School streets. The distinctive shape of the 1754 structure was not achieved entirely by design; for lack of funds it was never topped with the steeple that architect Peter Harrison had planned. The interior is a masterpiece of elegant proportion and Georgian calm. The chapel's bell is Paul Revere's largest and, in his judgment, his sweetest-sounding. Take the path to the right from the entrance of the **King's Chapel Burying Ground,** the oldest cemetery in the city. On the left is the gravestone (1704) of Elizabeth Pain, the model for Hester Prynne in Hawthorne's *The Scarlet Letter.* Elsewhere, you'll find the graves of the first Massachusetts governor, John Winthrop, and several generations of his descendants. ⊠ *58 Tremont St., at School St.,* ☎ *617/ 227–2155.* ☉ *Mid-June–Labor Day, Mon., Fri., Sat. 9:30–4, Tues., Wed. 9:30–11, Sun. 1–3; Labor Day–mid-Nov., Mon., Fri., Sat. 10– 2; mid-Nov.–mid-Apr., Sat. 10–2; mid-Apr.–mid-June, Mon., Fri., Sat. 10–2. Year-round music program Tues. 12:15–1. Services on Sun. at 11, Wed. at 12:15. T stop: Park St. or Government Center.*

㉓ New England Aquarium. This perennially popular attraction has added a 17,400-square-ft West Wing—with barking seals outside to welcome visitors—to its already astounding main facility. Inside the main building are specimens of more than 2,000 species of marine life from penguins to jellyfish, many of which make their homes in a four-story ocean reef tank. Don't miss feeding time, a fascinating procedure that lasts nearly an hour. Educational programs, like the "Science at Sea" cruise, take place year-round. Sea lion shows are held aboard Discovery, a floating marine mammal pavilion; and whale-watch cruises ($24) leave from the aquarium's dock from April to October. ⊠ *Central Wharf, between Central and Milk Sts.,* ☎ *617/973–5200 or 617/ 973–5277 for whale-watching information.* ☏ *$11.* ☉ *Memorial Day–Labor Day, Mon., Tues., Fri. 9–6; Wed., Thurs. 9–8; weekends and holidays 9–7. Labor Day–Memorial Day, Mon–Fri. 9–5; weekends and holidays 9–6. T Stop: Aquarium.*

㉑ Old South Meeting House. Some of the fieriest pre-Revolutionary town meetings were held at Old South, culminating in the tumultuous gathering of December 16, 1773, convened by Samuel Adams to address the question of dutiable tea that activists wanted returned to England. This was also the congregation of Phillis Wheately, the first published African-American poet. A permanent exhibition, "Voices of Protest," celebrates Old South as a forum for free speech from Revolutionary days to the present. ⊠ *310 Washington St.,* ☎ *617/482–6439.* ☏ *$3.* ☉ *Apr.–Oct., daily 9:30–5; Nov.–Mar., daily 10–4. T stop: State or Downtown Crossing.*

㉒ Old State House. A brightly gilded lion and unicorn, symbols of British imperial power, adorn the State Street gable of this landmark structure. This was the seat of the Colonial government from 1713 until the Revolution, and after the evacuation of the British from Boston in 1776 it served the independent Commonwealth until its replacement on Beacon Hill was completed. The permanent collection traces Boston's Revolutionary War history. ⊠ *206 Washington St.,* ☎ *617/720–3290.* ☏ *$3.* ☉ *Daily 9:30–5. T stop: State.*

Rowes Wharf. This 15-story Skidmore, Owings, and Merrill extravaganza is the site of the Boston Harbor Hotel and the Rowes Wharf Restaurant. Great views of Boston Harbor and the luxurious yachts parked in the marina can be had from under the complex's gateway six-story arch. Water shuttles pull up here from Logan Airport—the most spectacular way to enter the city. *T Stop: Aquarium.*

The Back Bay

In the folklore of American neighborhoods, the Back Bay stands with New York's Park Avenue and San Francisco's Nob Hill as a symbol of propriety and high social standing. The main east–west streets—Beacon Street, Marlborough Street, Commonwealth Avenue, Newbury Street, and Boylston Street—are bisected by eight streets named in alphabetical order from Arlington to Hereford.

Numbers in the text and in the margin correspond to numbers on the Boston map.

A Good Walk

A walk through the Back Bay properly begins with the **Public Garden** ㉗, the oldest botanical garden in the United States. Wander its paths to the corner of Commonwealth Avenue and Arlington Street. Walk up Arlington to Beacon Street and turn left to visit the **Gibson House** ㉘ museum. Follow Beacon to Berkeley and turn left to return to Commonwealth Avenue. Stroll the avenue to Clarendon, turn left and head into **Copley Square** ㉙, where you will find **Trinity Church,** the Boston Public Library, and the **John Hancock Tower** ㉚. From Copley Square, you can walk west on Dartmouth to **Newbury Street** and its posh boutiques. For a dose of the avant-garde turn left on Hereford Street and right on Boylston and drop into the **Institute of Contemporary Art** ㉛. From there, proceed one block farther on Boylston Street to Massachusetts Avenue. Turn left to reach the **Christian Science Church** ㉜ and **Symphony Hall** ㉝.

TIMING

The Public Garden is such a delight in the spring and summer that you should give yourself at least a hour to explore it if this is when you're visiting. Distances between sights are a bit longer here than in other parts of the city, so allow one or two hours for a walk down Newbury Street. The Museum of Contemporary Art and the Christian Science Church can each be explored in a hour.

Sights to See

Boylston Street. This broad thoroughfare is the southern commercial spine of the Back Bay. It holds interesting shops and restaurants, the Hynes Convention Center, and an F.A.O. Schwarz store with a huge teddy bear sculpture on the sidewalk in front.

㉜ **Christian Science Church.** The world headquarters of the Christian Science faith has an Old World basilica and a sleek office complex designed by I. M. Pei. This church was established here by Mary Baker Eddy in 1879. Mrs. Eddy's original granite First Church of Christ, Scientist (1894), has since been enveloped by a domed Renaissance basilica, added to the site in 1906. In the publishing society's lobby is the fascinating **Mapparium,** a huge stained-glass globe that allows visitors to traverse its 30-ft diameter via a glass bridge. The 670-ft reflecting pool is a splendid sight on a hot summer day. ⊠ *175 Huntington Ave.,* ☎ *617/450–3790.* ☉ *Mother church Mon.–Sat. 10–4, Sun. 11:15–2, free 30-min tours; Mon. only original edifice open for tours; Sun. services at 10 AM and 7 PM; Mapparium. Mon.–Sat. 10–4. T stop: Prudential.*

㉙ **Copley Square.** For thousands of folks in April, a glimpse of this square is a welcome sight; this is where Boston Marathon runners end their 26-mi race. The Boston Public Library, the Copley Plaza Hotel, and Trinity Church border the square. Copley Place, an upscale glass and brass urban mall, comprises two major hotels, shops, restaurants, and offices attractively grouped around bright, open indoor spaces. The John Hancock Tower looms over all. *T stop: Copley.*

㉘ Gibson House. One of the first Back Bay residences (1859), the Gibson House has been preserved with all its Victorian fixtures and furniture intact; a Gibson scion lived here until the 1950s and left things as they had always been. ✉ *137 Beacon St.,* ☎ *617/267–6338.* ✇ *$5.* ☉ *Tours May–Oct., Wed.–Sun. at 1, 2, and 3; Nov.–Apr., weekends at 1, 2, and 3. T stop: Arlington.*

㉛ Institute of Contemporary Art. Multimedia art, installations, film and video series, and other events take place in this cutting-edge institution inside a 19th-century police station and firehouse. ✉ *955 Boylston St.,* ☎ *617/266–5152.* ✇ *$5.25; free Thurs. 5–9.* ☉ *Wed.–Sun. noon–5, Thurs. noon–9. Tours weekends at 1 and 3. T stop: ICA/Hynes Convention Center.*

㉚ John Hancock Tower. The tallest building in New England is a stark and graceful reflective blue rhomboid tower designed by I. M. Pei. The 60th-floor observatory is one of the best vantage points in the city, and the "Boston 1775" exhibit shows what the city looked like before the great hill-leveling and landfill operations commenced in 1854. ✉ *Observatory ticket office, Trinity Pl. and St. James Ave.,* ☎ *617/247–1977 or 617/572–6429.* ✇ *$4.25.* ☉ *Mon.–Sat. 9 AM–10 PM, Sun. 9–5. T stop: Copley.*

Newbury Street. The eight blocks of Newbury Street have been compared to New York's Fifth Avenue, and certainly this is Boston's poshest shopping mecca. But here the pricey boutiques are more intimate than grand, and people actually live above the trendy restaurants and hair salons. Toward the Massachusetts Avenue end, cafés proliferate and the stores get funkier.

Prudential Center Skywalk. The 50th-floor observatory atop the Prudential Center affords spectacular vistas of Boston, Cambridge, and the suburbs to the west and south—on clear days, you can even see Cape Cod. There are chairs for sitting and noisy interactive exhibits on Boston's history that ease the bite of the admission ticket. ✉ *800 Boylston St.,* ☎ *617/859–0648.* ✇ *$4.* ☉ *Daily 10–10. T stop, Prudential.*

㉗ Public Garden. The Public Garden is the oldest botanical garden in the United States. The park's pond has been famous since 1877 for its foot pedal–powered **swan boats,** which make leisurely cruises in warm months. They were invented by Robert Paget, who was inspired by the popularity of swan boats made fashionable by Wagner's opera *Lohengrin.* Paget descendants still run the boats. Follow the kids quack-quacking along the pathway between the pond and the park entrance at Charles and Beacon streets to the *Make Way for Ducklings* bronze statues. Jack, Kack, Lack, Mack, Nack, Ouack, Pack, and Quack compose Mrs. Mallard's pack—made famous in the 1941 classic children's story (set along Beacon Street and within the Public Garden). ☎ *617/635–4505.* ✇ *Swan boats $1.50.* ☉ *Public Garden dawn–10 PM; swan boats mid-Apr.–late Sept., daily 10–4. Not recommended for strolling after dark. T stop: Arlington.*

㉝ Symphony Hall. The home of the Boston Symphony Orchestra since 1900, the hall was designed by the architectural firm McKim, Mead & White, but the acoustics, rather than the exterior design, make this a special place for performers and concertgoers. ✉ *301 Massachusetts Ave.,* ☎ *617/266–1492 or 800/274–8499.* ☉ *Tours by appointment with volunteer office (call 1 wk ahead). T stop: Symphony.*

Trinity Church. In his 1877 masterpiece, architect Henry Hobson Richardson brought his Romanesque Revival style to maturity; all the aesthetic elements for which he was famous—bold masonry, careful

arrangement of masses, sumptuously carved interior woodwork—
come together magnificently. The church remains the centerpiece of Copley Square. ⊠ *206 Clarendon St.,* ☎ *617/536–0944.* ⊙ *Daily 8–6; Sun. services at 8, 11, and 6. T stop: Copley.*

The South End

History has come full circle in the South End. Once a fashionable neighborhood created with landfill in the mid-19th century, it was deserted by the well-to-do for the Back Bay toward the end of the century. Solidly back in fashion, today it is a polyglot of upscale eateries and ethnic enclaves of redbrick row houses in refurbished splendor or elegant decay. The Back Bay is French-inspired, but the South End's architectural roots are English, the houses continuing the pattern established on Beacon Hill (in a uniformly bowfront style), though aspiring to a much more florid standard of decoration.

There is a substantial Latino and black presence in the South End, particularly along Columbus Avenue and Massachusetts Avenue, which marks the beginning of the predominantly black neighborhood of Roxbury. Harrison Avenue and Washington Street at the north side of the South End lead to Chinatown, and consequently there is a growing Asian influence. Along East Berkeley Street, neighbors have created a lush community garden. Many lesbians and gay men live in the South End.

Numbers in the text and in the margin correspond to numbers on the Boston map.

A Good Walk

From the Back Bay, walk down Massachusetts Avenue to Columbus Avenue; turn left and follow it to **Rutland Square** ㉞ on your right. Cross to Tremont and continue on Tremont and turn right at **Union Park** ㉟. Walk south through the park to Shawmut Street, which holds a mixture of ethnic outlets and retail spaces. Walk east along Shawmut to East Berkeley Street, and then turn left (to the north) and head back to Tremont. On Tremont Street, near Clarendon Street, is the **Boston Center for the Arts.** After a break at one of the many trendy restaurants and shops along Tremont Street, retrace your steps on Tremont to Arlington and traverse walkway over the Massachusetts Turnpike to reach **Bay Village,** on your right.

TIMING

You can walk through the South End in two to three hours. It's a good option on a pleasant day; go elsewhere in inclement weather, as most of what you'll see here is outdoors.

Sights to See

Bay Village. This neighborhood is a pocket of early 19th-century brick row houses that appears to be almost a toylike replication of Beacon Hill. Edgar Allan Poe once lived here. It seems improbable that so fine and serene a neighborhood can exist in the shadow of busy Park Square—a 1950s developer might easily have leveled these blocks in an afternoon—yet here it is, another Boston surprise. To get here, follow Columbus Avenue almost into Park Square, turn right on Arlington Street, then left onto one of the narrow streets of this neighborhood.

Boston Center for the Arts. Of Boston's multiple arts organizations, the city-sponsored arts and culture complex is the one that is closest "to the people." Here you can see the work of budding playwrights, view exhibits on Haitian folk art, or walk through an installation commemorating World AIDS Day. The BCA houses three small theaters, the Mills Gallery, and studio space for some 60 artists. The mélange that is the BCA represents a huge leap from the original purpose of the **Cyclorama Building,** which was built by William Blackall in 1884 to house a 400-by-50-ft circular painting of the Battle of Gettysburg. After the painting was sent to Pennsylvania, the building was used as a boxing ring, a bicycle ring, and a garage (during which time Alfred Champion invented the spark plug here). ⊠ *539 Tremont St.,* ☎ *617/ 426–5000 or 617/426–7700; 617/426–8835 Mills Galleries.* ⬛ *Free.* ☉ *Weekdays 9–5; Mills Galleries Wed.–Sun. 1–4, Thurs.–Sat. 7 PM– 9 PM. T stop: Back Bay.*

③④ ③⑤ **Rutland Square** (between Columbus Avenue and Tremont Street) and **Union Park** (between Tremont Street and Shawmut Avenue) are elliptical, shady havens, bordered by rows of bowhouses. Both reflect a time during which the South End was the most prestigious Boston address.

The Fens

The marshland known as the Back Bay Fens gave this section of Boston its name, but two quirky institutions give it its character: Fenway Park, where hope for another World Series pennant springs eternal, and the Isabella Stewart Gardner Museum, the legacy of a bon vivant Brahmin. Kenmore Square, a favorite haunt for college students, adds a bit of funky flavor to the mix.

The Fens mark the beginning of Boston's Emerald Necklace, a loosely connected chain of parks designed by Frederick Law Olmsted that extends along the Fenway, Riverway, and Jamaicaway to Jamaica Pond, the Arnold Arboretum, and Franklin Park.

Numbers in the text and in the margin correspond to numbers on the Boston map.

A Good Walk

The attractions in the Fens are best visited separately. The **Museum of Fine Arts** ㊱, between Huntington Avenue and the Fenway, and the **Isabella Stewart Gardner Museum** ㊲ are just around the corner from each other. **Kenmore Square** is at the west end of Commonwealth Avenue, not far from **Fenway Park** ㊳.

TIMING
The Green Line of the MBTA stops near the attractions on this tour. The Gardner is much smaller than the MFA, but each can take up an afternoon if you take a break at their cafés.

Sights to See

㊳ Fenway Park. Fenway may be one of the smallest parks in the major leagues (capacity 34,000), but it is one of the most loved. Since its construction in 1912, there has been no shortage of heroics: Babe Ruth pitched here when the place was new; Ted Williams and Carl Yastrzemski had epic careers here. ⊠ *4 Yawkey Way,* ☎ *617/267–8661; 617/267– 1700 for tickets. T stop: Fenway.*

㊲ Isabella Stewart Gardner Museum. A spirited young society woman named Isabella Stewart came from New York in 1860 to marry John Lowell Gardner. When it came time to create a permanent home for the Old Master paintings and Medici treasures she and her husband had acquired in Europe, she decided to build the Venetian palazzo of her dreams along Commonwealth Avenue. The complex stands as a monument to one woman's extraordinary taste.

Despite the loss of a few masterpieces in a daring 1990 robbery, there is much to see: a trove of spectacular paintings—including masterpieces like Titian's *Rape of Europa*, Giorgione's *Christ Bearing the Cross*, Piero della Francesca's *Hercules*, and John Singer Sargent's *El Jaleo*—rooms bought outright from great European houses, Spanish leather panels, Renaissance hooded fireplaces, and Gothic tapestries. An intimate restaurant overlooks the courtyard, and in the spring and summer tables and chairs spill outside. To fully conjure up the spirit of days past, attend one of the concerts held in the elegant Music Room. ⊠ *280 The Fenway,* ☎ *617/566–1401; 617/566–1088 for café.* ⊠ *$10; concert and galleries $15; free admission to café and gift shop.* ⊗ *Museum Tues.– Sun. 11–5; weekend concerts at 1:30. T stop: Museum.*

Kenmore Square. Kenmore Square is home to fast-food parlors, rock-and-roll clubs, an abundance of university students, and an enormous sign advertising Citgo gasoline. The red, white, and blue neon sign put up in 1965 is so thoroughly identified with the area that historic preservationists have fought, successfully, to save it—proof that Bostonians are an open-minded lot who do not insist that their landmarks be identified with the American Revolution. ⊠ *Intersection of Commonwealth Ave., Brookline Ave., and Beacon St. T stop: Kenmore Sq.*

㊱ Museum of Fine Arts. The MFA's holdings of American art surpass those of all but two or three U.S. museums. There are more than 50 works by John Singleton Copley, Colonial Boston's most celebrated portraitist; plus major paintings by Winslow Homer, John Singer Sargent, and Edward Hopper. Other artists represented include Mary Cassatt, Georgia O'Keeffe, and Berthe Morisot.

The museum also has a sublime collection of French Impressionists— 38 Monets, the largest collection of his work outside France—plus renowned collections of Asian, Egyptian, and Nubian art. The museum's West Wing presents changing exhibits of contemporary arts, prints and photographs. The museum has a gift shop, a good restaurant, and a cafeteria; in the newly re-opened **Fraser Court,** a charming oasis of green trees and statuary, beverages are served on the terrace from April to October. On the Fenway Park side of the museum, the **Tenshin-En Garden,** the "Garden in the Heart of Heaven," allows visitors to experience landscape as a work of art (daily except Monday from April to October). A combination of Japanese and American trees and shrubs fuses the concept of the Japanese garden with elements of the New England landscape. ⊠ *465 Huntington Ave.,* ☎ *617/267–9300.* ⊠ *$10; voluntary admission Wed. 4–9:45, children under 17 with adult free.* ⊗ *Entire museum: Mon.–Fri., 10–5, weekends 10–6, Wed. until 10; West Wing only: Thurs. and Fri. until 10 with admission reduced by $2. 1-hr tours available weekdays. T stop: Museum.*

Cambridge

Pronounced with either prideful satisfaction or a smirk, the nickname "The People's Republic of Cambridge" sums up this independent city of 95,000 west of Boston. Cambridge not only houses two of the country's greatest educational institutions—Harvard University and the Massachusetts Institute of Technology—it has a long history as a haven for freethinkers, writers, activists, and iconoclasts of every stamp. Once a center for publishing, Cambridge has become a high-tech mecca; more than a few MIT students launched software companies even before they graduated. The more than 30,000 students in Cambridge ensure a cornucopia of cafés, record stores, music clubs, street-chic boutiques, and bookstores that stay open until the wee hours.

Cambridge is easily reached on the Red Line train. The Harvard Square area is notorious for limited parking. If you insist on driving into

Cambridge, you may want to avoid the local circling ritual by pulling into a garage.

Numbers in the text and in the margin correspond to numbers on the Cambridge map.

A Good Walk

Begin your tour in **Harvard Square** ① near the T station entrance. Enter **Harvard Yard** for a look at one of the country's premier educational institutions: **Harvard University** ②. Just past Memorial Hall (ask any student for directions) is Kirkland Street; turn right and follow it to Divinity Avenue and turn left. At 11 Divinity, you'll find an entrance to the extensive complex of the **Harvard Museums of Cultural and Natural History** ③. It's about a 15-minute walk to Harvard's **Fogg Museum** ④, on Quincy Street, and **Arthur M. Sackler Museum** ⑤, on Broadway. The **Longfellow National Historic Site** ⑥ is a 15-minute walk west of Harvard Square on Brattle Street.

In good weather, you can walk along Massachusetts Avenue through the bustle and ethnic diversity of urban Central Square and into the warehouse-like openness of the Kendall Square area, where the campus of the **Massachusetts Institute of Technology** ⑦ dominates the neighborhood. If the weather is poor, take the T Red Line heading inbound from Harvard Square two stops to Kendall Square.

TIMING

Budget at least two hours to explore Harvard Square, plus at least three more if you plan to go to either Harvard's cultural and history museums or the art museums. The walk down Massachusetts Avenue to MIT will take an additional 30 to 45 minutes, and you could easily spend an hour or two on the MIT campus admiring its architecture and visiting its museum or List gallery.

Sights to See

❺ **Arthur M. Sackler Museum.** The richness of the Orient and artistic treasures of the ancient Greeks, Egyptians, and Romans fill three of the four floors of this modern structure. The permanent collection includes Chinese, Japanese, Buddhist, Indian, and Islamic works. The fee for the Sackler gains you entrance to the Fogg Museum. ⊠ *485 Broadway,* ☎ *617/495–9400.* ☞ *$5, free Sat. 10–noon and after 4:30.* ☼ *Mon.–Sat. 10–5, Sun. 1–5.*

❹ **Fogg Art Museum.** Harvard's most famous art museum owns 80,000 works of art from every major period and from every corner of the world. Behind Harvard Yard on Quincy Street, the Fogg was founded in 1895; its collection focuses primarily on European, American, and Far Eastern works, with notable 19th-century French Impressionist and medieval Italian paintings. A ticket to the Fogg is good for admission to the Arthur M. Sackler Museum (☞ *above*) and the **Busch–Reisinger Museum** (☎ 617/495–9400), in the Werner Otto Hall, entered through the Fogg. From the serenity of the Fogg's Old Masters, you step into the jarring and mesmerizing world of German Expressionists and other 20th-century artists. ⊠ *32 Quincy St.,* ☎ *617/495–9400.* ☞ *$5; free Sat. 10–noon.* ☼ *Mon.–Sat. 10–5, Sun. 1–5.*

❸ **Harvard Museums of Cultural and Natural History.** Many museums promise something for every member of the family; the Harvard museum complex actually delivers. There are four museums here; one fee admits you to all of them. The glass flowers in the **Botanical Museum** (⊠ 26 Oxford St., ☎ 617/495–3045) were created as teaching tools. The **Peabody Museum of Archaeology and Ethnology** (⊠ 11 Divinity Ave., ☎ 617/495–2248) holds one of the world's most outstanding

Cambridge

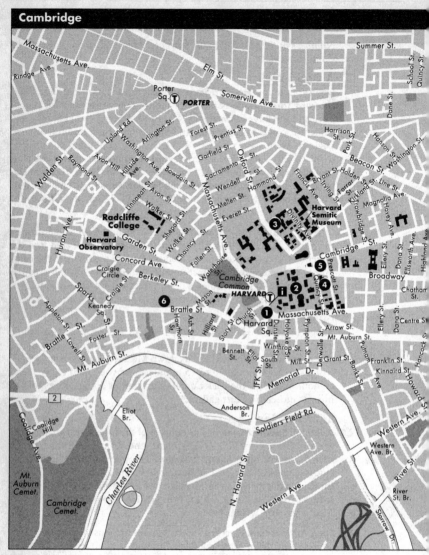

Arthur M. Sackler Museum, **5**

Fogg Art Museum, **4**

Harvard Museums of Cultural and Natural History, **3**

Harvard Square, **1**

Harvard University, **2**

Longfellow National Historic Site, **6**

Massachusetts Institute of Technology, **7**

anthropological collections; exhibits focus on Native American and Central and South American cultures. The **Museum of Comparative Zoology** (✉ 26 Oxford St., ☎ 617/495–3045) traces the evolution of animals (including dinosaurs) and humans. Oversize garnets and crystals are among the holdings of the **Mineralogical and Geological Museum** (✉ 24 Oxford St., ☎ 617/495–4758), which also has an extensive collection of meteorites. 🎫 *$4; free Sat. 9–11.* ⊙ *Mon.–Sat. 9–4:30, Sun. 1–4:30. T stop: Harvard Sq.*

Harvard Semitic Museum. This institution serves as an exhibit space for Egyptian and ancient Middle East artifacts and as a center for archaeological exploration. Here you can discover how the pyramids were excavated, not just what was discovered inside. Rotating exhibits treat varied subjects, such as the history of writing. The building also houses the Department of Near Eastern Languages and Civilization—the permanent exhibit space upstairs serves as a classroom. ✉ *6 Divinity Ave.,* ☎ *617/495–4631.* 🎫 *Free.* ⊙ *Weekdays 10–4, Sun. 1–4. T stop: Harvard Sq.*

❶ Harvard Square. Gaggles of students, street musicians, people hawking the paper *Spare Change* (as well as asking for some), end-of-the-world preachers, and political-cause proponents make for a nonstop pedestrian flow at this most celebrated of Cambridge crossroads. Not a square at all, Harvard Square is where Massachusetts Avenue (locally, Mass Ave.), coming from Boston, turns and widens into a triangle broad enough to accommodate a brick peninsula (beneath which the MBTA station is located). Sharing the peninsula is the Out-of-Town newsstand, a local institution that occupies the restored 1928 kiosk that used to be the entrance to the MBTA station. Harvard Square is walled on two sides by banks, restaurants, and shops, and on the third by Harvard University. The **Cambridge Visitor Information Booth** (☎ 617/497–1630), just outside T station entrance, is a volunteer-staffed kiosk with maps and brochures in several languages. The booth is open from 9 to 5 (Sunday from 1 to 5), and has maps for historic and literary walking tours of the city, and an excellent guide to the bookstores in the square and beyond.

❷ Harvard University. In 1636 the Great and General Court of the Massachusetts Bay Colony established the country's first college here. Named in 1638 for John Harvard, a young Charlestown clergyman who died that year, leaving the college his entire library and half his estate, Harvard remained the only college in the New World until 1693, by which time it was firmly established as a respected center of learning. Students run the **Harvard University Information Office,** which has maps of the university area. You can take a free hour-long walking tour of Harvard Yard. ✉ *Holyoke Center, 1350 Massachusetts Ave.,* ☎ *617/495–1573.* ⊙ *During the academic year, weekdays at 10 and 2, Sat. at 2; mid-June–Aug., Mon.–Sat. at 10, 11:15, 2, and 3:15, Sun. at 1:30 and 3. T stop: Harvard Sq.*

List Visual Arts Center. Founded by Albert and Vera List, pioneer collectors of modern art, this MIT center has three galleries showcasing exhibitions of cutting-edge art and mixed media that often challenge conventional ideas about culture. Be prepared to murmur: "Interesting, but is it art?" ✉ *Weisner Bldg., 20 Ames St.,* ☎ *617/253–4680.* 🎫 *Free.* ⊙ *Oct.–June, Tues.–Thurs. noon–6, Fri. noon–8, weekends 12–6. Closed July–Sept. T stop: Kendall Sq.*

❻ Longfellow National Historic Site. Once home to Henry Wadsworth Longfellow—the poet whose stirring renditions of "Miles Standish," "The Village Blacksmith," "Evangeline," "Hiawatha," and "Paul Revere's Midnight Ride" thrilled 19th-century America—this elegant mansion was a wedding gift for the poet in 1843. He filled it with the exuberant spirit of his own work and that of his literary circle, which included Emerson, Thoreau, and Holmes. ⊠ *105 Brattle St., ¼ mi from the Cambridge Information Booth,* ☎ *617/876–4491.* ☜ *$2.* ☉ *Mid-Mar.–May and Nov.–mid-Dec., Wed.–Fri. noon–4:30, Sat.–Sun. 10–4:30; June–Oct., Wed.–Sun. 10–4:30 for guided tours only; last tour departs at 4. Gardens open year-round for a self-guided tour. T stop: Harvard Sq.*

❼ Massachusetts Institute of Technology. MIT, at Kendall Square, occupies 135 acres 1½ mi southeast of Harvard, bordering the Charles River. The West Campus has some extraordinary buildings: The Kresge Auditorium, designed by Eero Saarinen with a curving roof and unusual thrust, rests on three, instead of four, points; the nondenominational MIT Chapel is a circular Saarinen design. Free campus tours leave from the **MIT Information Center** (⊠ Building 7, 77 Massachusetts Ave., ☎ 617/253–4795) on weekdays at 10 and 2. The center is open on weekdays from 9 to 5.

MIT Museum. A place where art and science meet, the MIT Museum showcases photos, paintings, and scientific instruments and memorabilia. A popular ongoing exhibit is the "Hall of Hacks," a look at the pranks MIT students have played over the years. The museum has an extensive collection of alluring holograms, including the "Light Forest Gallery"—a holographic room filled with the sights and sounds of the rain forest. ⊠ *265 Massachusetts Ave.,* ☎ *617/253–4444.* ☜ *$3.* ☉ *Tues.–Fri. 10–5, weekends noon–5. Closed Mon. and holidays. T stop: Kendall Sq.*

Radcliffe College. More than just the "female" half of Harvard, Radcliffe continues to redefine its mission in a time of coeducation. Its lovely and serene yard is the heart of the college, founded in 1879 "to furnish instruction and the opportunities of collegiate life to women and to promote their higher education." An independent corporation within Harvard University, Radcliffe maintains its own physical plant, including the Agassiz Theater. The college also sponsors events, programs, and workshops devoted to women's issues. ⊠ *10 Garden St. T stop: Kendall Sq.*

Dining

Back Bay/Beacon Hill

CONTEMPORARY

$$$$ ✕ **Ambrosia.** Chef Tony Ambrose likes his flavors vivid and his platters tall, from an ostrich meat appetizer to "grilled lamb rack and saddle on a crisp potato layered with Morbier cheese and served with a caper eggplant vinaigrette." Take down the French decorations, and the food is haute Yankee, based on native ingredients. The decor is designer-chic: burnished woods, floor-to-ceiling glass windows, an ever-changing arrangement of modern art on the walls. ⊠ *116 Huntington Ave.,* ☎ *617/247–2400. Reservations essential. AE, MC, V. No lunch weekends.*

$$$$ ✕ **Biba.** Arguably Boston's best restaurant, and surely one of the most
★ original and high-casual restaurants in America, Biba is a place to see and be seen. The menu encourages inventive combinations, unusual cuts and produce, haute comfort food, and big postmodern desserts. Take your time, and don't settle for the "classic lobster pizza" if something like "crusted ocean perch" is available. The wine list is an adventure. ⊠ *272 Boylston St.,* ☎ *617/426–7878. Reservations essential. D, DC, MC, V.*

Boston Dining and Lodging

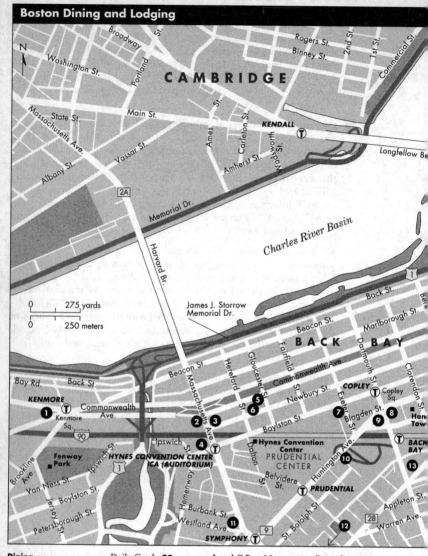

Dining

Ambrosia, **10**
Aujourd'hui, **19**
Baja Mexican Cantina, **13**
Biba, **20**
Brew Moon, **38**
Cena, **11**
Chau Chow, **36**

Daily Catch, **25**
Grill 23, **16**
Hamersley's Bistro, **14**
Jae's Café, **12**
Jimmy's Harborside, **34**
Julien, **31**
Lala Rokh, **22**

Legal C Bar, **18**
Legal Sea Foods, **17**
Les Zygomates, **35**
L'Espalier, **5**
Miyako, **6**
Montien, **37**
Mucho Gusto Café, **4**
Olives, **23**

Pomodoro, **24**
Ritz-Carlton Dining Room, **21**
Rowes Wharf Restaurant, **32**
Sonsie, **3**
Tatsukichi-Boston, **29**
Turner Fisheries, **9**
Union Oyster House, **27**

Massachusetts

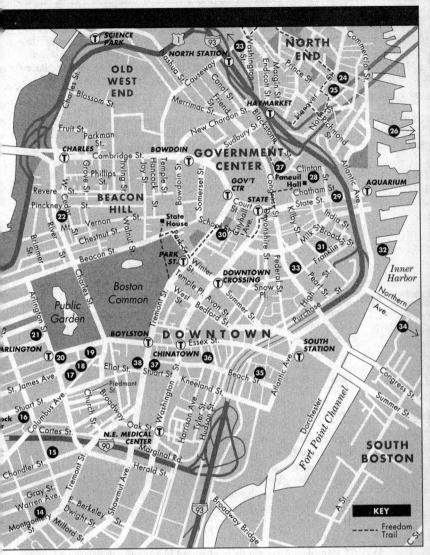

Lodging

Boston Harbor Hotel
at Rowes Wharf, **32**

Chandler Inn, **15**

Eliot Hotel, **2**

Fairmont Copley
Plaza, **8**

Four Seasons, **19**

Harborside Hyatt
Conference Center
and Hotel, **26**

Hotel Buckminster, **1**

Le Meridien
Hotel, **33**

Lenox Hotel, **7**

Omni Parker
House, **30**

Regal Bostonian, **28**

Ritz-Carlton, **21**

$$ ✕ **Brew Moon.** Instead of the usual industrial decor of a brew pub, the flagship of this minichain looks like a California Zen health food palace and has rather flashy food, although with an emphasis on the salty and peppery morsels that call out for beer. Save room for serious desserts. Also in Harvard Square, Cambridge. ⊠ *115 Stuart St., Back Bay,* ☎ *617/742–5225.* ⊠ *Cambridge: 50 Church St., Harvard Square,* ☎ *617/499–2739. AE, DC, MC, V.*

$$ ✕ **Cena.** Red hot, Cena (pronounced like Latin, "kay-nah") has captured the Symphony crowd with a bistro menu of world-beat flavors that quietly drops red meat and barely mentions chicken and cheese. ⊠ *14 Westland Ave.,* ☎ *617/262–1485. Reservations essential. AE, D, MC, V.*

$$ ✕ **Sonsie.** Café society blossoms along Newbury Street, particularly at the elegant Sonsie, where much of the clientele either sips coffee up front or angles for places at the bar. The restaurant, which opens at 7 AM, is famous for breakfasts that extend well into the afternoon. During warm weather months, the entire front of Sonsie becomes an open-air café looking out on upper Newbury Street. The dishes on the menu are basic bistro with an American twist, such as a pan-seared fish sandwich with spicy tartar sauce. ⊠ *327 Newbury St.,* ☎ *617/351–2500. AE, MC, V.*

CONTINENTAL

$$$$ ✕ **Ritz-Carlton Dining Room.** Traditional in the best sense of the word, the restaurant at the Ritz has a subtly modern menu that still includes classic rack of lamb, roast beef hash, broiled scrod, and seasonal Yankee favorites such as shad roe in May and June. The true glory of the Ritz is the service, aristocratic in its detail, democratically offered to all. Second-floor windows provide a commanding view of the Public Garden. ⊠ *15 Arlington St.,* ☎ *617/536–5700, ext. 6286. Reservations essential. Jacket and tie. AE, D, DC, MC, V.*

CUBAN

$$ ✕ **Mucho Gusto Cafe.** On a bohemian block full of jazz students from Berklee College sits this hospitable Cuban restaurant with an *I Love Lucy* decor (most of it for sale) and terrific food. The kitchen excels at black-bean soup, eggplant salad, french-fried onions, and Cuban sandwiches. The coffee makes you want to get up and dance to the old mambos that are always playing. ⊠ *1124 Boylston St.,* ☎ *617/236–1020. Reservations not accepted for fewer than 5. No credit cards. No lunch Mon.–Wed.*

FRENCH

$$$$ ✕ **L'Espalier.** An elegantly modernized Victorian Back Bay town house
★ is the setting for what some critics consider Boston's best restaurant. Chef-owner Frank McClelland creates an intoxicating blend of new French and newer American cuisine. You can simplify the opulent menu by choosing a prix fixe tasting menu, such as the innovative vegetarian *dégustation.* ⊠ *30 Gloucester St.,* ☎ *617/262–3023. Reservations essential. Jacket and tie. AE, D, DC, MC, V. Closed Sun. No lunch.*

JAPANESE

$$ ✕ **Miyako.** A very competitive sushi bar amid many at this end of Back Bay, this little spot also offers estimable hot dishes, including *age shumai* (shrimp fritters), *hamachi teriyaki* (yellowtail teriyaki), and *age dashi* (fried bean curd). Ask for one of the tatami rooms if you have a big party. ⊠ *279A Newbury St.,* ☎ *617/236–0222. AE, DC, MC, V.*

PERSIAN

$$$ ✕ **Lala Rokh.** This is one of the best western Asian restaurants in the
★ United States, a beautifully detailed and delicious fantasia upon Persian food and art. The food includes exotically flavored specialties, and

dishes as familiar (but superb here) as eggplant puree, pilaf, kebabs, *fesanjoon* (the classic pomegranate-walnut sauce), and lamb stews. ⊠ *97 Mount Vernon St.,* ☎ *617/720–5511. AE, DC, MC, V. No lunch.*

SEAFOOD

$$$ ✕ **Legal C Bar** What a headline: "Staid Legal Sea Foods Backs Haitian Chef Novilus Petit-Frère in Caribbean Restaurant!" This offshoot of famed Legal Seafoods (☞ *below*) serves the same superb fried calamari or wood-grilled scallops as the original, but also turns out tropical side dishes, impeccable conch fritters, Bermuda fish chowder, and acra (St. Lucia-style codfish cakes). The rum drinks are great, too. ⊠ *27 Columbus Ave.,* ☎ *617/426–5566. Reservations not accepted. AE, D, DC, MC, V.*

$$$ ✕ **Legal Sea Foods.** What began as a tiny restaurant upstairs over a
★ Cambridge fish market has grown to important regional status. The hallmark, as always, is extra-fresh seafood. Once puritanically simple preparations have loosened up to include Chinese and French sauces, and wood-grilling is now the preparation of choice. The smoked bluefish pâté is one of the finest appetizers anywhere. Dishes come to the table in whatever order they come out of the kitchen, as freshness is held to be more important than the order of courses. ⊠ *35 Columbus Ave., Park Sq.,* ☎ *617/426–4444.* ⊠ *Cambridge: 5 Cambridge Center, Kendall Sq.,* ☎ *617/864–3400.* ⊠ *Logan Airport: Terminal C,* ☎ *617/569–4622. Reservations not accepted. AE, D, DC, MC, V.*

$$$ ✕ **Turner Fisheries of Boston.** On the first floor of the Westin Hotel in Copley Square, Turner Fisheries is second only to Legal Sea Foods (☞ *above*) in its traditional appeal and has outstripped it in trimmings and service. Turner broils, grills, bakes, fries, and steams everything in the ocean, but also applies classic and modern sauces, vegetables, and pasta with panache. Any meal should begin with the creamy chowder. ⊠ *10 Huntington Ave.,* ☎ *617/424–7425. Reservations essential. AE, D, DC, MC, V.*

STEAK

$$$ ✕ **Grill 23.** Dark paneling, comically oversized flatware, and waiters in white jackets lend this steak house a men's-club ambience. The rotisserie tenderloin with Roquefort mashed potatoes is a winner, as is the meat loaf with mashed potatoes and truffle oil. Seafood actually outsells beef by a narrow margin; roasted monkfish with caramelized golden beets is one option. ⊠ *161 Berkeley St.,* ☎ *617/542–2255. Reservations essential. Jacket and tie. AE, D, DC, MC, V. No lunch.*

Cambridge

CONTEMPORARY

$$$$ ✕ **Salamander.** Entrées at this superb restaurant are generous and ap-
★ petizers are eccentric and flavorful, often Asian influenced. Favorites are the wood-grilled squid with coconut sauce and the pepper tenderloin over a ragout of wild mushrooms. For dessert, the banana wontons are deliciously indescribable. Best of all, the service is extremely well paced. Salamander's wines by the glass are perhaps the best in town. ⊠ *1 Atheneum St.,* ☎ *617/225–2121. Reservations essential. AE, D, DC, MC, V. Closed Sun.*

$$$$ ✕ **Union Square Bistro.** Chef David Smoke McCluskey's "native nou-
★ velle" cuisine emphasizes American foodstuffs and game, prepared with a nod to his Native American heritage. Recent dishes have included venison with pemmican sauce made of black cherries and venison jerky, roast pumpkin and hazelnut soup, and sweet corn and walnut pudding with an Indian berry cream. Brunch is served on Sunday. ⊠ *16 Bow St., Union Sq., Somerville,* ☎ *617/628–3344. Reservations essential. AE, D, DC, MC, V.*

Cambridge Dining and Lodging

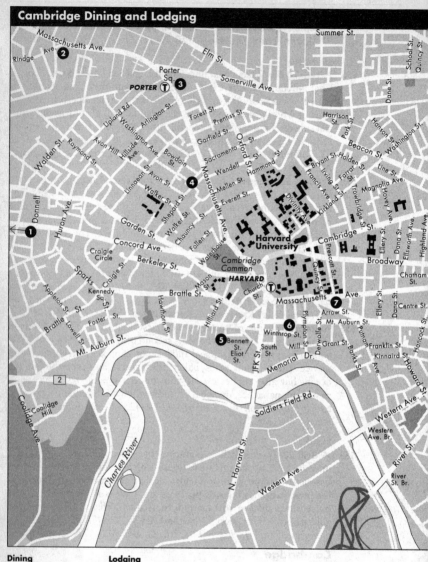

Dining

Blue Room, **11**

Chez Henri, **4**

Cottonwood Café, **3**

East Coast Grill, **9**

Green Street Grill, **14**

Salamander, **13**

Sandrine's Bistro, **6**

Sunset Café, **10**

Union Square
Bistro, **8**

Lodging

A Cambridge House
Bed and Breakfast, **2**

The Charles Hotel, **5**

Inn at Harvard, **7**

Royal Sonesta
Hotel, **12**

Susse Chalet Inn, **1**

$$$ ✕ **Blue Room.** Hip, funky, and totally Cambridge, the Blue Room has brightly colored furnishings, a friendly staff, and counters where you can meet other diners while you eat. Convivial owner-chef Steve Johnson blends a whole world of ethnic cuisines, with an emphasis on Mediterranean small plates. At peak hours noise level can become rather loud. Brunch is served on Sunday. ⊠ *1 Kendall Sq.,* ☏ *617/494–9034. AE, D, DC, MC, V. No lunch Mon.–Sat.*

$$$ ✕ **East Coast Grill.** Owner-chef-author Chris Schlesinger built his na-
★   tional reputation on grilling and red-hot condiments, but is now an-
gling to make his establishment one of the top fish restaurants in town. Spices and condiments are more restrained, and Schlesinger has compiled a selection of wines bold and flavorful enough to share a table with the still highly spiced food. The dining space is completely informal. Brunch is served on Sunday. ⊠ *1271 Cambridge St.,* ☏ *617/491–6568. AE, D, MC, V. No lunch.*

$$$ ✕ **Green Street Grill.** Caribbean-born co-owner-chef John Levins is one
★   of the living masters of mixing hot spices with other distinctive flavors. A recent example: "Punished conch meat finished in sugarcane, curry, coconut milk, Myers's rum, grated cassava and lots of hot chili peppers." But expect an entirely different—and elaborate—preparation with Caribbean grouper or Muscovy duck. ⊠ *280 Green St.,* ☏ *617/876–1655. AE, MC, V. No lunch.*

$$ ✕ **Cottonwood Café.** This is Tex-Mex pushed to the next dimension.
★   The atmosphere is Nuevo-Wave-o, with exotic architectural touches and rustic southwestern details. Best of all is the Snake Bite appetizer: deep-fried jalapeños stuffed with shrimp and cheese—impossible to resist yet nearly too spicy-hot to eat. ⊠ *1815 Massachusetts Ave.,* ☏ *617/661–7440.* ⊠ *Back Bay: 222 Berkeley St.,* ☏ *617/247–2225. Reservations essential. AE, D, DC, MC, V.*

FRENCH

$$$ ✕ **Sandrine's Bistro.** Chef-owner Raymond Ost goes to his Alsatian
★   roots for flavors easy and intense, but this is a bistro only in the way that little palace at Versailles was a country house. One hit is the flammekuche, the Alsatian onion pizza, but much else is haute cuisine, like the trout Napoleon. ⊠ *8 Holyoke St.,* ☏ *617/497–5300. AE, DC, MC, V. Closed Sun.*

FRENCH/CUBAN

$$$ ✕ **Chez Henri.** French–Cuban cuisine may sound like a weird combination, but it works for this comfortable restaurant. The dinner menu gets serious with duck tamale with ancho chili, a fancy paella, and truly French desserts. Brunch is served on Sunday. Turnovers, fritters, and grilled three-pork Cuban sandwiches are served in the bar. ⊠ *1 Shepard St.,* ☏ *617/354–8980. Reservations not accepted. AE, DC, MC, V. No lunch.*

PORTUGUESE

$$ ✕ **Sunset Café.** Specialties at this lively café include kale soup thick-
★   ened with potatoes, *mariscada a chefe* (a great seafood combination in a casserole with fine spices) and shrimp Ana María (panfried shrimp in seafood stock). The bargain-priced wines on the list include some of the best Dão reds available outside Portugal. ⊠ *851 Cambridge St.,* ☏ *617/547–2938. AE, D, DC, MC, V.*

Charlestown

MEDITERRANEAN

$$$ ✕ **Olives.** This bistro sets the local standards for grilled pizza, piled-
★   on platters of delicious things, "vertical food," and smart signature offerings like the open-face roast lamb sandwich. The crowded seating, noise, long lines, and abrupt service only add to the legend. Come early

or late—or be prepared for an extended wait: Reservations are taken only for groups of six or more at 5:30 or 8:30 PM, and there are few nearby alternatives. ✉ *10 City Sq.,* ☎ *617/242–1999. AE, DC, MC, V. Closed Sun., Mon. No lunch.*

Chinatown

CHINESE

$$ ✕ **Chau Chow.** *Chau Chow* is the word for people from Swatow in
★ China's Fujian province, and they are folks who are known for their wonderful seafood. Try the clams in black bean sauce, steamed sea bass, gray sole with its fried fins, or any dish with their famous ginger sauce. Chau Chow has expanded to a larger storefront called Grand Chau Chow across the street. Seating at old Chau Chow is very tight. ✉ *50 Beach St.,* ☎ *617/426–6266. No credit cards.*

Downtown

CONTEMPORARY

$$$$ ✕ **Aujourd'hui.** The formula for Aujourd'hui's success has been to speak softly and attract a discreet crowd. The food reflects an inventive approach to regional ingredients and new American cuisine. Some entrées, such as rack of Colorado meadow lamb with layered potato and lasagna, can be extremely rich, but the seasonal menu also offers "alternative cuisine" and vegetarian choices. Window tables overlook the Public Garden. ✉ *Four Seasons Hotel, 200 Boylston St.,* ☎ *617/351–2071. Reservations essential. Jacket required. AE, DC, MC, V.*

FRENCH

$$$$ ✕ **Julien.** The handsomest dining room in the city serves some of the
★ best French food in Boston. Julien is a favorite of French business travelers and Boston Francophiles who enjoy the detail of a great Parisian restaurant in their own hometown. The menu marries modern French cuisine and native New England ingredients. ✉ *Hotel Meridien, 250 Franklin St.,* ☎ *617/451–1900, ext. 7120. Reservations essential. Jacket and tie. AE, D, DC, MC, V. Closed Sun. No lunch Sat.*

$$$ ✕ **Les Zygomates.** *Zygomates,* in French, are the muscles on the
★ human face that make you smile—and this combination wine bar/bistro will certainly do that. In a world of culinary overstatement, Les Zygomates serves up classic French bistro fare that dares to be simple and simply delicious. The restaurant offers prix-fixe menus at both lunch and dinner. Pan-seared catfish with house vinaigrette and roasted rabbit leg stuffed with vegetables typify the taste. ✉ *129 South St.,* ☎ *617/542–5108. Reservations essential. AE, DC, MC, V. No lunch weekends.*

JAPANESE

$$ ✕ **Tatsukichi-Boston.** Sushi and sashimi are specialties, as are potcooked dinners and *kushiagi* (deep-fried kabobs). Meals are served in a modern Japanese setting with Western or tatami room seating. Upstairs is a karaoke lounge that's popular with Japanese business travelers and tourists. ✉ *189 State St.,* ☎ *617/720–2468. AE, D, DC, MC, V. No lunch weekends.*

THAI

$$ ✕ **Montien.** A favorite with theatergoers, Montien serves Southeast Asian classics like *pla sarm ros* (spicy whole fish) and *pad thai* (noodles with shrimp, tofu, and peanut sauce) as well as dishes seldom seen on Thai menus: *kat thuong-tong* (chicken tartlets with corn and coriander) and cupid wings (stuffed boneless chicken wings). ✉ *63 Stuart St.,* ☎ *617/ 338–5600. AE, D, DC, MC, V. No lunch weekends.*

Faneuil Hall

AMERICAN

$$–$$$ ✕ **Union Oyster House.** At Boston's oldest continuing restaurant (it was established in 1826), it's best to have what Daniel Webster had—oysters on the half shell at the ground-floor raw bar, which is the oldest part of the restaurant, and still the best. The rooms at the top of the narrow staircase are very Ye Olde New England. Uncomfortably small tables and chairs tend to undermine the simple, decent, but expensive food. There is valet parking after 6 PM. ⊠ *41 Union St.,* ☎ *617/227–2750. AE, D, DC, MC, V.*

North End

ITALIAN

$$ ✕ **Pomodoro.** The dishes at this tiny gem of a trattoria, where there's
★ often a wait, include white beans with various pastas, roasted vegetables, and a fine salad of field greens. The walls are decorated with lacquered cutlery, and the wine list is exceptional. The best choice could well be the clam and tomato stew with herbed flat bread—don't forget to enjoy it with a bottle of Vernaccia. ⊠ *319 Hanover St.,* ☎ *617/367–4348. No credit cards.*

SEAFOOD

$$ ✕ **Daily Catch.** Shoulder-crowding small, this storefront restaurant spe-
★ cializes in calamari dishes, lobster *fra diavolo* (in spicy marinara sauce), and linguine with clam sauce. You've just got to love this place—for the noise, the intimacy, and above all, the food. ⊠ *323 Hanover St.,* ☎ *617/523–8567. Reservations not accepted. No credit cards.*

South End

CONTEMPORARY

$$$ ✕ **Hamersley's Bistro.** Gordon Hamersley has earned national renown
★ for dishes like his grilled mushroom-and-garlic sandwich and a cassoulet of duck confit, pork, and garlic sausage. His place has a full bar, a café area with 10 tables for walk-ins, and a larger dining room that's a little more formal and decorative than the bar and café, though nowhere near stuffy. ⊠ *553 Tremont St.,* ☎ *617/423–2700. D, MC, V.*

MEXICAN

$$ ✕ **Baja Mexican Cantina.** Anything-but-traditional Mexican food is served in a postmodern Southwest decor. Start with a margarita made from your choice of premium tequilas. All the Cal-Mex food that follows is quite good, with lots of vegetarian options. If you're health-conscious, go for the salads, relatively low-fat burritos, or the lean hamburger served in a tortilla. ⊠ *111 Dartmouth St.,* ☎ *617/262–7575. AE, D, DC, MC, V.*

PAN-ASIAN

$$ ✕ **Jae's Café.** Jae's fusion cuisine attracts a young, happening crowd for sushi, dishes served in hot-stone pots, and rice noodles served with shrimp and dusted with sugar. The main dining room is adorned with a big fish tank, while outside a garden beckons (seating there is forbidden by their license). In the summer, there's lots of sidewalk seating. ⊠ *520 Columbus Ave.,* ☎ *617/338–8586. AE, DC, MC, V.*

Waterfront

CONTEMPORARY

$$$ ✕ **Rowes Wharf Restaurant.** Chef Daniel Bruce creates scintillating mod-
★ ern menus between the field trips on which he takes his staff to hunt wild mushrooms—his personal passion. Sautéed local wild mushrooms over stone-ground polenta is his signature composition. The Maine lobster sausage over lemon pasta has intense flavors and unforgettable essences of the sea. The restaurant has Boston's most extensive list of

American wines. ✉ *70 Rowes Wharf,* ☎ *617/439–3995. Reservations essential. Jacket required. AE, D, DC, MC, V.*

SEAFOOD

$$$ ✕ **Jimmy's Harborside.** The fish chowder here is fresh and bright-tasting, and seasonal fish specials simply broiled or fried are excellent. You will fish through a lot of cream sauce to find the traditional finnan haddie, however. The wine list is almost all-American, with oversized bottles a specialty. ✉ *242 Northern Ave.,* ☎ *617/423–1000. Reservations essential. AE, DC, MC, V. No lunch Sun.*

Lodging

If your biggest dilemma is deciding whether to spend $300 per night on old-fashioned elegance or extravagant modernity, you've come to the right city. The bulk of Boston's accommodations are not cheap; however, visitors with limited cash will find choices among the smaller, older establishments, the modern motels, or—perhaps the best option (if you can take early morning small talk)—the bed-and-breakfast inn.

Back Bay

$$$$ ⊞ **Fairmont Copley Plaza.** The public spaces of this 1912 landmark
★ recall an era long gone, with high gilded and painted ceilings, mosaic floors, marble pillars, and crystal chandeliers; the guest rooms have custom furniture from Italy, elegant marble bathrooms, and fax machines. One of the restaurants, called the Oak Room to match its mahogany-paneled twin in New York's Plaza Hotel, has a dance floor and a raw bar. Despite the imposing Victorian surroundings, the atmosphere is utterly gracious and welcoming, thanks to the multilingual staff. Children under 18 stay free in their parents' room, and pets are welcome. ✉ *138 St. James Ave., 02116,* ☎ *617/267–5300 or 800/527–4727,* Ⅲ *617/247–6681. 379 rooms, 51 suites. 2 restaurants, 2 bars, in-room modem lines, minibars, no-smoking floors, room service, barbershop, beauty salon, exercise room, baby-sitting, laundry service and dry cleaning, concierge, business services, parking (fee). AE, D, DC, MC, V.*

$$$$ ⊞ **Four Seasons.** The only hotel in Boston other than the Ritz-Carl-
★ ton to overlook the Public Garden is also, to the Ritz's chagrin, the only five-star hotel in the city. The Four Seasons is famed for luxurious personal service of the sort demanded by celebrities and heads of state. It has huge rooms with king-size beds, 24-hour concierge and room service, and a fully equipped health club on the eighth floor with whirlpool, sauna, and heated 51-ft swimming pool. The Bristol Lounge serves high tea daily at 3 PM. Pets are welcome. ✉ *200 Boylston St., 02116,* ☎ *617/338–4400 or 800/332–3442,* Ⅲ *617/423–0154. 216 rooms, 72 suites. 2 restaurants, in-room modem lines, in-room safes, minibars, no-smoking floors, room service, indoor pool, health club, baby-sitting, laundry service and dry cleaning, concierge, business services, parking (fee). AE, D, DC, MC, V.*

$$$$ ⊞ **Ritz-Carlton.** Despite the attractions of the upstart Four Seasons, many
★ visitors to Boston would never dream of staying anywhere but the Ritz, thanks to its unmatched location, dignified elegance, and fierce devotion to its guests' comfort and privacy. Suites in the older section have parlors with working fireplaces and wonderful views of the Public Garden. The three top floors cost extra but have butler service and a private club with complimentary food and drinks, newspapers, and games. Public rooms include the elegant café, the sedate bar, and The Lounge. Small pets are welcome. ✉ *Arlington and Newbury Sts., 02117,* ☎ *617/536–5700 or 800/241–3333,* Ⅲ *617/536–1335. 236 rooms, 42 suites. Restaurant, bar, lobby lounge, in-room safes, no-smoking rooms,*

refrigerators, room service, beauty salon, exercise room, baby-sitting, laundry service, concierge, parking (fee). AE, D, DC, MC, V.

$$$–$$$$ **🏨 Eliot Hotel.** The luxurious suites at the Eliot have Italian marble bath-
   ★   rooms, two cable-equipped televisions, and tasteful pastel-hued decor.
            The airy restaurant, Clio, has been garnering rave reviews for its serene
            ambience and contemporary French-American cuisine. The Eliot is steps
            from Newbury Street and a short walk to Kenmore Square. Children
            under 16 stay free in their parents' room. ✉ 370 Commonwealth
            Ave., 02215, ☎ 617/267–1607 or 800/443–5468, ℻ 617/536–9114.
            95 suites. Restaurant, in-room modem lines, minibars, no-smoking
            rooms, room service, baby-sitting, laundry service and dry cleaning,
            concierge, valet parking (fee). AE, D, DC, MC, V.

$$$–$$$$ **🏨 Lenox Hotel.** The soundproof guest rooms at the Lenox contain cus-
   ★   tom-made traditional furnishings, spacious walk-in closets, and mar-
            ble baths; some of the corner rooms have working fireplaces. The
            Samuel Adams Brew House and the popular bistro Anago are both wor-
            thy stops. Children under 18 stay free in their parents' room. ✉ 710
            Boylston St., 02116, ☎ 617/536–5300 or 800/225–7676, ℻ 617/236–
            0351. 209 rooms, 3 suites. 2 restaurants, bar, in-room modem lines,
            no-smoking floor, room service, exercise room, baby-sitting, dry clean-
            ing, concierge, parking (fee). AE, D, DC, MC, V.

$–$$ **🏨 Chandler Inn.** This cozy little hotel with economical rates and a friendly
            staff is one of the best bargains in the city. Located an overpass away
            from the Back Bay, at the end of one of the South End's prettiest
            streets, it's an easy walk to the T, the Amtrak station, Newbury Street's
            boutiques, or any of Tremont Street's trendy restaurants. Rooms are
            small but comfortable. Small pets are welcome. ✉ 26 Chandler St.,
            02115, ☎ 617/482–3450, ℻ 617/542–3428. 56 rooms. Restaurant
            (Sat., Sun. only), bar. AE, D, DC, MC, V.

Cambridge

$$$$ **🏨 Charles Hotel.** You can't stay much closer to the center of Harvard
   ★   Square than at this first-class hotel adjacent to the Kennedy School of
            Government. Guest rooms, which were all renovated in 1998, are
            equipped with terry robes, quilted down comforters, and Bose radios;
            suites have fireplaces. Both restaurants are excellent, and the Regat-
            tabar attracts world-class musicians. ✉ 1 Bennett St., 02138, ☎ 617/
            864–1200 or 800/882–1818, ℻ 617/864–5715. 296 rooms, 44 suites.
            2 restaurants, bar, in-room modem lines, in-room safes, minibars, no-
            smoking rooms, room service, pool, spa, health club, nightclub, baby-
            sitting, laundry service and dry cleaning, concierge, business services,
            parking (fee). AE, DC, MC, V.

$$$$ **🏨 Inn at Harvard.** Doubletree Hotels operates this understated four-
   ★   story property for Harvard University. Original 17th- and 18th-century
            sketches, on loan from the nearby Fogg Art Museum, and contempo-
            rary watercolors decorate the rooms, many of which have tiny balconies;
            most rooms have oversize windows with views of Harvard Square or
            Harvard Yard. Guests are granted access to the Cambridge YMCA in
            Central Square. ✉ 1201 Massachusetts Ave., 02138, ☎ 617/491–
            2222 or 800/458–5886, ℻ 617/491–6520. 109 rooms, 4 suites. Restau-
            rant, in-room modem lines, no-smoking floors, room service, dry
            cleaning, business services, parking (fee). AE, D, DC, MC, V.

$$$–$$$$ **🏨 Royal Sonesta Hotel.** The views of Beacon Hill across the Charles
   ★   River are superb from this 10-floor building, which is near the Mu-
            seum of Science and adjacent to the CambridgeSide Galleria. Impres-
            sive modern artworks are displayed throughout the hotel. Some suites
            have kitchenettes. Children under 18 stay free in their parents' room,
            and the hotel offers family excursion packages that include boat rides,
            ice cream, and bicycles. ✉ 5 Cambridge Pkwy., 02142, ☎ 617/491–

3600 or 800/766–3782, FAX *617/661–5956. 400 rooms, 26 suites. 2 restaurants, 2 bars, in-room modem lines, in-room safes, minibars, no-smoking rooms, room service, indoor-outdoor pool, spa, health club, bicycles, laundry service and dry cleaning, business services, parking (fee). AE, DC, MC, V.*

$$–$$$$ 🏨 **A Cambridge House Bed and Breakfast.** This Greek Revival Cambridge House home is on busy Massachusetts Avenue but set well back from the road. The B&B is a haven of peace and otherworldliness, with richly carved cherry paneling, a grand mahogany fireplace, elegant Victorian antiques, and polished wood floors overlaid with Oriental rugs. Harvard Square is a distant walk, but public transportation is nearby. ⊠ *2218 Massachusetts Ave., 02140,* ☎ *617/491–6300 or 800/232–9989,* FAX *617/868–2848. 16 rooms (4 share baths). Parking (free). Full breakfast. No pets. No smoking. MC, V.*

$ 🏨 **Susse Chalet Inn.** This is a typical Susse Chalet operation: clean, economical, and spare. A 10-minute drive from Harvard Square, it is isolated from most shopping and attractions but within walking distance of the Red Line terminus, offering T access to Boston and Cambridge sights. All rooms have color TV and air-conditioning. ⊠ *211 Concord Turnpike, 02140,* ☎ *617/661–7800 or 800/524–2538,* FAX *617/868–8153. 78 rooms. In-room modem lines, no-smoking rooms, coin laundry, dry cleaning, free parking. Continental breakfast. AE, D, DC, MC, V.*

Downtown

$$$$ 🏨 **Boston Harbor Hotel at Rowes Wharf.** Everything here is done on
★ a grand scale, starting with the dramatic entrance through an 80-ft archway. Guest rooms—decorated in shades of mauve, green, and cream—have either city or water views, and some have balconies. The Rowes Wharf Restaurant specializes in seafood and American cuisine and hosts a spectacular Sunday brunch. The hotel is within walking distance of Faneuil Hall, the North End, the New England Aquarium, and the Financial District. Small pets are welcome. ⊠ *70 Rowes Wharf, 02110,* ☎ *617/439–7000 or 800/752–7077,* FAX *617/345–6799. 230 rooms, 26 suites. 2 restaurants, bar, outdoor café, no-smoking rooms, room service, indoor lap pool, beauty salons, spa, health club, concierge, business services, valet parking. AE, D, DC, MC, V.*

$$$$ 🏨 **Le Meridien Hotel.** Once the Federal Reserve Building, this 1922 Re-
★ naissance Revival landmark in the center of the Financial District still exudes an almost intimidating aura of money and power. Most rooms, including some cleverly designed bilevel, skylighted suites, have queen-size or king-size beds; all have a small sitting area. Some pets are permitted. ⊠ *250 Franklin St., 02110,* ☎ *617/451–1900 or 800/543–4300,* FAX *617/423–2844. 326 rooms, 17 suites. 2 restaurants, 2 bars, in-room modem lines, minibars, no-smoking floors, room service, indoor pool, health club, laundry service and dry cleaning, concierge, parking (fee). AE, D, DC, MC, V.*

$$$$ 🏨 **Regal Bostonian.** Every room at this small luxury hotel receives fresh-
★ cut flowers daily. Seasons, the hotel's rooftop restaurant, overlooks Quincy Market. The Bostonian is adjacent to Government Center and the Financial District and just an underpass away from the North End. Request a room facing away from the street if you'd rather not awaken to the bustle of Quincy Market at dawn. Children under 12 stay free in their parents' room. Some pets are allowed. ⊠ *Faneuil Hall Marketplace, 02109,* ☎ *617/523–3600 or 800/222–8888,* FAX *617/523–2454. 152 rooms, 11 suites. Restaurant, lobby lounge, in-room modem lines, no-smoking rooms, room service, laundry service and dry cleaning, concierge, valet parking. AE, D, DC, MC, V.*

$$–$$$$ 🏨 **Omni Parker House.** The oldest continuously operating hotel in America is known for two things: Parker House rolls and Boston cream pie, both of which were invented here. Eighty percent of the smallish, quaint rooms are nonsmoking. Much-needed renovations were underway at press time. Appropriately, this historic hotel stands opposite old City Hall, near Government Center, and right on the Freedom Trail. ⊠ *60 School St., 02108,* ☎ *617/227–8600 or 800/843–6664,* ℻ *617/742–5729. 552 rooms, 26 suites. Restaurant, lounge, in-room modem lines, room service, exercise room, baby-sitting, concierge, business services, valet parking (fee). AE, D, DC, MC, V.*

Kenmore Square

$–$$ 🏨 **Hotel Buckminster.** An economical and tastefully decorated European-style inn two blocks from Fenway Park, the Buckminster has maids but no bellhops, and breakfast is by room service only. Though there's no restaurant in the hotel, the ground floor of the building houses a branch of the Pizzeria Uno chain as well as an excellent sushi restaurant, and Kenmore Square itself offers a wide range of cuisines. Small pets are welcome. ⊠ *645 Beacon St., 02215,* ☎ *617/236–7050 or 800/727–2825,* ℻ *617/236–0068. 120 rooms. AE, D, DC, MC, V.*

Logan Airport

$$$–$$$$ 🏨 **Harborside Hyatt Conference Center and Hotel.** It's easy to get anywhere from the Hyatt, which operates its own shuttle to all Logan Airport terminals and the Airport T stop; guests get a discount on the water shuttle that runs between the airport and downtown. All floors but one are nonsmoking, and all rooms are soundproofed. ⊠ *101 Harborside Dr., 02128,* ☎ *617/568–1234 or 800/233–1234,* ℻ *617/567–8856. 270 rooms, 11 suites. Restaurant, bar, in-room modem lines, room service, indoor pool, sauna, exercise room, laundry service and dry cleaning, concierge, business services, parking (fee). AE, D, DC, MC, V.*

Nightlife and the Arts

Nightlife

Good sources of information are the *Boston Globe* Calendar section and the weekly listings of the *Boston Phoenix* (both published on Thursday). The Friday Music and Sunday Arts sections in the *Boston Globe* also contain recommendations for the week's top events. *Boston* magazine's "On the Town" feature provides a somewhat less detailed but useful monthly overview.

BARS AND LOUNGES

Boston Beer Works (⊠ 61 Brookline Ave., ☎ 617/536–2337) brews up regular and seasonal brews for a crowd that's largely students, young adults, and fans from nearby Fenway Park.

Bull & Finch Pub (⊠ 84 Beacon St., at Hampshire House, ☎ 617/227–9605) was dismantled in England, shipped to Boston, and reassembled here, an obvious success. This place was the inspiration for the TV series *Cheers.* An international crowd of tourists and students often lines up out the door.

Mercury Bar (⊠ 116 Boylston St., ☎ 617/482–7799), popular among well-heeled young professionals and theatergoers, has a sleek 100-ft bar facing a row of raised, semicircular booths and a more private dining room off to the side. Bar patrons can order from the extensive tapas menu.

Punch Bar (⊠ Sheraton Hotel & Towers, 39 Dalton St., ☎ 617/236–2000) is considered one of the country's best cigar bars. Scotch and imported beers are served at this hangout that has an air of retro, ever-so-British manliness.

The Spot (✉ 1270 Boylston St., ☎ 617/424–7747) is that new hybrid in the bar world: It's a straight *and* a gay bar. On Monday the crowd is gay male; Friday sees gay men and lesbians; and on Thursday, Saturday, and Sunday the bar attracts a straight crowd. During good weather, everyone comes to enjoy the un-Bostonian roof deck.

Top of the Hub (✉ Prudential Center, ☎ 617/536–1775) has a wonderful view of the entire city, which along with the sounds of hip jazz makes the drinks at the 52nd-floor lounge worth the steep prices.

BLUES/R&B/FOLK CLUBS

Club Passim (✉ 47 Palmer St., ☎ 617/492–7679), formerly Passim's, is one of the country's most famous venues for live folk music. The spare, light basement room has tables close together, with wait service, and a separate coffee bar/restaurant counter.

House of Blues (✉ 96 Winthrop St., Cambridge, ☎ 617/491–2583) is co-owned by Dan Aykroyd and the late John Belushi's wife, Judy, plus other celebrity investors. Live music begins at 10 PM; on Sunday there's a gospel brunch. The cover charge varies.

Marketplace Café (✉ 300 Faneuil Hall, ☎ 617/227–9660) is a "no cover" treasure in the North Market building amid the bustle of Faneuil Hall. It has a blues/jazz format, with music every night from 9; nouvelle American cuisine is served.

CAFÉS AND COFFEEHOUSES

Caffé Vittoria (✉ 296 Hanover St., ☎ 617/227–7606) is the biggest and the best of the North End cafés, with gleaming espresso machines going nonstop. Many Italian-restaurant patrons head here for dessert and coffee after dining elsewhere.

Daily Grind (✉ 168 Cambridge St., ☎ 617/367–3233) is a welcome bit of funkiness on the edge of Beacon Hill that serves well-prepared coffee drinks, fresh pastries, and sandwiches and other lunch fare, all at low prices. It's open on weeknights until 8 (6 in winter) and weekends until 4 PM. No credit cards.

Roasters (✉ 85 Newbury St., ☎ 617/867–9967) has outdoor seating for sunny days. A huge bay window allows maximum people-watching while you sip coffee roasted on the premises. Roasters is open till 10 PM from Sunday to Thursday and 11 PM on Friday and Saturday.

COMEDY

Comedy Connection (✉ Faneuil Hall Marketplace, ☎ 617/248–9700) books local and nationally known acts seven nights a week, with a cover charge.

Nick's Comedy Stop (✉ 100 Warrenton St., ☎ 617/482–0930) presents local comics every night except Monday; occasionally a well-known comedian pops in. Reservations are advised on weekends; the cover charge varies.

DANCE CLUBS

Axis (✉ 13 Lansdowne St., ☎ 617/262–2424), near Kenmore Square, has high-energy disco and a giant dance floor. Friday is "X Night," starring DJs from alternative radio station WFNX. At Sunday's "Gay Night," Axis and neighboring mega-club Avalon let dancers circulate between the two for one cover charge. Some nights are 18+; others are over-21 only. The cover charge varies.

International (✉ 184 High St., ☎ 617/542–4747) is a multifaceted club in the ordinarily staid Financial District. Wednesdays are jazz nights, Thursdays are "Soul International," with soul, acid jazz, and house music. Fridays feature dance hits of the '70s, and Saturdays are "Tribe," with two DJs improvising with two percussionists. Cover charge.

Karma Club (✉ 11 Lansdowne St., Kenmore Square, ☎ 617/421–9678) is an exotic fantasyland with incense, carved temple doors from Asia, and an immense stone Buddha who watches the proceedings with a beatific smile from Thursday to Sunday.

Man-Ray (✉ 21 Brookline Street, Cambridge, ☎ 617/864–0400) is the home of Boston's underground scene, where the Gothic, glam, and alternatively lifestyled go for long nights of industrial, house, techno, disco, and trance music. Friday night is "Fetish Night." You needn't participate in the staged spankings—just don't stare. Wear black. The club is closed on Monday and Tuesday.

Roxy (✉ 279 Tremont St., Theater District, ☎ 617/338–7699) is the biggest nightclub in Boston. On Thursday night the club caters to an upscale African-American crowd. International students take over on Friday. Saturday is popular with sports stars and celebrities, who congregate in the club's VIP room.

GAY AND LESBIAN CLUBS

Axis (☞ Dance Clubs, *above*).

Buzz (✉ 67 Stuart St., ☎ 617/267–8969), one of the city's trendiest gay clubs, stands just where the South End gives way to the Theater District. Bump and grind with the wall-to-wall hardbodies on the dance floor, or simply savor the sights from the bar. Saturday is the hottest night.

Club Café (✉ 209 Columbus Ave., ☎ 617/536–0966) is one of the smartest spots in town for gay men and lesbians. The front end of the bar area, popular with suits after work, is the most mixed gay/lesbian. The video bar in back is open only from Thursday to Sunday. An upscale new-American restaurant is part of the package.

Napoleon Club (✉ 52 Piedmont St., ☎ 617/338–7547), the city's oldest gay bar, is a former speakeasy with three separate, quietly elegant sections, each with its own piano. The crowd tends to be well-dressed, over 30, and uninhibited about crooning show tunes and ballads. Liza Minnelli has actually been here (and how the queens did swoon that night). The top floor is Josephine's, a tiny dance floor open only on weekends.

The Spot (☞ Bars and Lounges, *above*).

JAZZ

Regattabar (✉ Charles Hotel, Bennett and Eliot Sts., Cambridge, ☎ 617/864–1200; 617/876–7777 for tickets) headlines top names in jazz. Even when there's no entertainment, the club is a pleasant (if expensive) place for a drink. It's closed on Sunday and Monday.

Ryles (✉ 212 Hampshire St., Cambridge, ☎ 617/876–9330) is one of the best places for new music and musicians, with a different group playing on each floor. There's a cover charge, and reservations are not accepted.

Turner Fisheries Bar (✉ Westin Hotel, 10 Huntington Ave., ☎ 617/262–9600, ext. 7425) hosts a jazz pianist between Sunday and Wednesday; from Thursday to Saturday the Debra Mann Trio backs varying soloists and plays till 1 AM. The sleek but comfortable room is hung with modern art and adjacent to a handsome oyster bar. There's no cover charge.

Wally's (⊠ 427 Massachusetts Ave., South End, ☎ 617/424–1408) is a racially integrated bar with a loyal clientele hooked on jazz and blues. The performers are mostly locals; there's no cover charge.

ROCK CLUBS

Avalon (⊠ 15 Lansdowne St., ☎ 617/262–2424) is one of two clubs in this building outside Kenmore Square. Avalon hosts concerts by alternative, rock, and dance acts, then turns into a dance club. Sunday is gay night when next-door Axis and Avalon combine forces and permit dancers to circulate between the two clubs. Concert show times vary; Ticketmaster (☞ *below*) sells advance tickets. Closing at 2 AM each night, the dance club opens at 10:30 PM on Thursday, 9:30 PM on Friday and Saturday, and 9 PM on Sunday, with cover charge.

Causeway (⊠ 65 Causeway St., North Station, ☎ 617/367–4958) is one of the most authentic rock bars in town, housed in a tiny room barely identifiable from the street. One of the pierced doormen will be your guide upstairs—all you have to do is ask. This is often a great place to celebrity-spot after a rock show at the FleetCenter.

Mama Kin (⊠ 36 Lansdowne St., ☎ 617/536–210) is jointly owned by members of the Boston-based rock group Aerosmith and a local impresario. The long, narrow club room, in gothic black and red, has a stage at one end, a CD jukebox, and a custom-built bar with the names of Aerosmith's hit songs inscribed in gold.

The Paradise (⊠ 967 Commonwealth Ave., ☎ 617/254–3939) is a small club known for having hosted big-name talent such as Matthew Sweet, Soul Coughing, and the Finn Brothers. National and local rock, jazz, folk, blues, alternative, and country acts all take their turn here. Tickets may be purchased in advance at Ticketmaster (☞ *below*) or at the box office.

SINGLES

Avenue C (⊠ 5 Boylston Place, Back Bay, ☎ 617/423–3832) caters to the older members of Generation X with a music mix heavy on hits from the 1980s.

Frogg Lane Bar and Grille (⊠ Faneuil Hall Marketplace, ☎ 617/720–0610) is a popular spot with tourists and singles. The jukebox is very loud. The club is open from Sunday to Thursday until 11 and on Friday and Saturday until 12:30.

Il Panino (⊠ 295 Franklin St., ☎ 617/338–1000) attracts a mature, upscale crowd. The first two floors in this five-floor complex offer informal and formal dining, the third has a jazz bar, and the top two are dance floors. There's no cover charge.

The Arts

Bostix is Boston's official entertainment information center and the city's largest ticket agency. It is a full-price Ticketmaster outlet, and, beginning at 11 AM, sells half-price tickets for same-day performances; the "menu board" in front of the booth announces the available events. Only cash and traveler's checks are accepted. People often begin queuing up well before the agency opens. ⊠ *Faneuil Hall Marketplace,* ☎ *617/723–5181 recorded message.* ☉ *Tues.–Sat. 10–6, Sun. 11–4.* ⊠ *Copley Sq. near corner of Boylston and Dartmouth Sts.* ☉ *Mon.–Sat. 10–6, Sun. 11–4.*

Out of Town Tickets and Sports Charge (☎ 617/497–1118), in the Harvard Square T station, is open on weekdays between 9 and 6 and on Saturday from 9 to 1; the service takes major credit cards.

Ticketmaster (☎ 617/931–2000 or 617/931–2787) allows phone charges to major credit cards on weekdays from 9 AM to 10 PM and on weekends from 9 to 8. The service also has outlets in local stores.

DANCE

Boston Ballet (✉ 19 Clarendon St., ☎ 617/695–6950), the city's premier dance company, performs at the Wang Center for the Performing Arts and the Shubert Theater. **Dance Umbrella** (✉ 380 Green St., Cambridge, ☎ 617/492–7578) presents contemporary dance.

FILM

The **Brattle Theater** (✉ 40 Brattle St., Cambridge, ☎ 617/876–6837) is a small downstairs cinema catering to classic-movie buffs and fans of new foreign and independent films. **Harvard Film Archive** (✉ Carpenter Center for the Visual Arts, 24 Quincy St., Cambridge, ☎ 617/495–4700) screens the works of directors not usually shown at commercial cinemas; there are two or more programs daily in the comfortable downstairs theater.

MUSIC

Berklee Performance Center (✉ 136 Massachusetts Ave., ☎ 617/266–1400 or 617/266–7455 for recorded information) is best known for its jazz programs. **Harborlights** (✉ Fan Pier off Northern Ave., ☎ 617/737–6100 or 443–0161) presents top pop, R&B, and country artists in a picturesque white tent on the waterfront. **Hatch Memorial Shell** (✉ off Storrow Dr. at Embankment, ☎ 617/727–9548) is a jewel of an acoustic shell where the Boston Pops perform their famous free summer concerts. **Jordan Hall at the New England Conservatory** (✉ 30 Gainsborough St., ☎ 617/536–2412) is one of the world's acoustic treasures, ideal for chamber music yet large enough to accommodate a full orchestra. The hall is home to the Boston Philharmonic. **Kresge Auditorium** (✉ 77 Massachusetts Ave., Cambridge, ☎ 617/253–2826 or 617/253–4003) is MIT's hall for pop and classical concerts. **Pickman Recital Hall** (✉ 27 Garden St., Cambridge, ☎ 617/876–0956, ext. 991) is Longy School of Music's excellent acoustical setting for smaller ensembles and recitals. **Symphony Hall** (✉ 301 Massachusetts Ave., ☎ 617/266–1492 or 800/274–8499), one of the world's most perfect acoustical settings, is home to the Boston Symphony Orchestra and the Boston Pops.

OPERA

The **Boston Lyric Opera Company** (✉ 114 State St., ☎ 617/542–6772) presents three productions each season.

THEATER

The **Boston Center for the Arts** (✉ 539 Tremont St., ☎ 617/426–7700) houses more than a dozen quirky low-budget troupes in four spaces. **Emerson Majestic Theatre** (✉ 219 Tremont St., ☎ 617/578–8727), at Emerson College, is a 1903 Beaux Arts building that hosts everything from avant-garde dance to drama to classical concerts. The **Huntington Theatre Company** (✉ 264 Huntington Ave., ☎ 617/266–0800), under the auspices of Boston University, is Boston's largest professional resident theater company, performing five plays annually, a mix of established 20th-century plays and classics. The **Loeb Drama Center** (✉ 64 Brattle St., ☎ 617/495–2668) has two theaters, the main one an experimental stage. This is the home of the American Repertory Theater, which produces classic and experimental works.

Outdoor Activities and Sports

Participant Sports

Most public recreational facilities, including the many skating rinks and tennis courts, are operated by the **Metropolitan District Commission** (✉ 20 Somerset St., ☎ 617/727–5114, ext. 555).

BIKING

The **Dr. Paul Dudley White Bikeway,** approximately 18 mi long, runs along both sides of the Charles River. The **Bicycle Workshop** (✉ 259 Massachusetts Ave., Cambridge, ☎ 617/876–6555) rents bicycles, fixes flat tires (while you wait), and delivers bicycles to your hotel.

BILLIARDS

Flat Top Johnny's (✉ 1 Kendall Square, Cambridge, ☎ 617/494–9565) is the hippest billiards hall around. Members of Boston's better local bands often hang out here on their nights off. **Jillian's Billiard Club** (✉ 145 Ipswich St., ☎ 617/437–0300) is a semiposh joint with the atmosphere of an English gentleman's library. The 56-table pool hall also has three bars, a café, darts, shuffleboard, table tennis, a motion simulator, and more than 200 high-tech games.

JOGGING

Both sides of the Charles River are popular with joggers. Many hotels have printed maps of nearby routes.

PHYSICAL FITNESS

The extensive facilities of the **Greater Boston YMCA** (✉ 316 Huntington Ave., ☎ 617/536–7800) are open for $5 per day (for up to two weeks) to members of other YMCAs in the Boston area; if you have out-of-state YMCA membership, you can use the Boston Y free for up to a week. Nonmembers pay $10 per day or $65 for one month. The site has pools, squash, racquetball courts, cardiovascular equipment, free weights, aerobics, track, and sauna.

ROLLERBLADING

From May to October, **Memorial Drive** on the Cambridge side of the Charles River is closed to auto traffic on Sunday from 11 AM to 7 PM. On the Boston side of the river, the **Esplanade** area offers some excellent skating opportunities. **Beacon Hill Skate Shop** (✉ 135 Charles St. S, off Tremont St., ☎ 617/482–7400) rents blades for $5 per hour or $15 per day (you need a credit card for deposit) year-round.

Spectator Sports

The **Boston Bruins** (☎ 617/624–1000; 617/931–2000 for Ticketmaster) of the National Hockey League hit the ice at the FleetCenter (✉ Causeway St. at Haverhill St.). The **Boston Celtics** (☎ 617/624–1000; 617/931–2000 for Ticketmaster) of the National Basketball Association shoot their hoops at the FleetCenter. The **Boston Red Sox** (☎ 617/267–1700 for tickets) play American League baseball at Fenway Park (✉ 4 Yawkey Way). The **New England Patriots** (☎ 800/543–1776) of the National Football League play their games at Foxboro Stadium in Foxboro, 45 minutes south of the city.

Every Patriot's Day (the Monday closest to April 19), fans gather along the Hopkinton-to-Boston route of the **Boston Marathon** to cheer the more than 12,000 runners from all over the world. The race ends near Copley Square in the Back Bay. For information, call the Boston Athletic Association (☎ 617/236–1652).

Shopping

Boston's shops and stores are generally open from Monday to Saturday between 9:30 and 7. Some stores, particularly those in malls or tourist areas, are open on Sunday from noon until 5. The state sales tax of 5% does not apply to clothing or food (except food bought in restaurants and for clothing purchases of more than $300). Boston's two daily newspapers, the *Globe* and the *Herald,* are the best places to learn about sales.

Shopping Districts

Most of Boston's stores and shops are in the area bounded by Quincy Market, the Back Bay, downtown, and Copley Square. There are few outlet stores in the area, but there are plenty of bargains, particularly in the world-famous Filene's Basement and Chinatown's fabric district.

BOSTON

Charles Street in Beacon Hill attracts antiques and boutique lovers; some of the city's prettiest shops are here. (River Street, parallel to Charles and near the intersection with Chestnut, is also an excellent source for antiques.) **Copley Place** (⊠ 100 Huntington Ave., ☎ 617/375–4400), an indoor shopping mall that connects the Westin and Marriott hotels in Back Bay, is a blend of the elegant, the glitzy, and the often overpriced. Prices in the shops on the second level tend to be a bit lower. **Downtown Crossing,** Boston's downtown shopping area, has a festival feeling year-round in its usually crowded pedestrian mall. The city's two largest department stores, Macy's and Filene's (with the famous Filene's Basement beneath it), are here. **Faneuil Hall Marketplace** (☎ 617/338–2323) has dozens of specialty shops, pushcarts with a variety of wares, street performers, and one of the area's great food experiences, Quincy Market. Friday and Saturday are the days to walk through **Haymarket,** a jumble of outdoor fruit and vegetable vendors, meat markets, and fishmongers. **Newbury Street** contains stylish clothing and jewelry boutiques and au courant art galleries. Toward Massachusetts Avenue, Newbury Street gets funkier with hip clothing stores, ice-cream shops, music stores, bookstores, and Tower Music and Video.

CAMBRIDGE

CambridgeSide Galleria (⊠ 100 CambridgeSide Pl., ☎ 617/621–8666) is a three-story mall in East Cambridge, accessible from the Green Line Lechmere T stop and a shuttle from the Kendall T stop. Filene's and Sears anchor the center. **Harvard Square** comprises just a few blocks but holds more than 150 stores selling clothes, books and records, furnishings, and a surprising range of specialty items.

Department Stores

Filene's (⊠ 426 Washington St., ☎ 617/357–2100; ⊠ CambridgeSide Galleria, Cambridge, ☎ 617/621–3800) carries name-brand and designer-label men's and women's formal, casual, and career clothing. Furs, jewelry, shoes, and cosmetics are found at the Downtown Crossing store. **Filene's Basement** (⊠ 426 Washington St., ☎ 617/542–2011) has spawned suburban outlets, but this is the only branch where items are automatically reduced in price according to the number of days they've been on the rack. **Loehmann's** (⊠ 385 Washington St., ☎ 617/338–7177), the off-price clothing store, is near Filene's. **Macy's** (⊠ 450 Washington St., ☎ 617/357–3000) carries men's and women's clothing, including top designers, as well as housewares, furniture, and cosmetics. Like Filene's, it has direct access to the Downtown Crossing T station. **Neiman Marcus** (⊠ 5 Copley Pl., ☎ 617/536–3660), the flashy Texas retailer, has three levels of high fashion, Steuben glass, and gadgetry. **Saks Fifth Avenue** (⊠ 1 Ring Rd., Prudential Center, ☎ 617/262–8500) offers top-of-the-line clothing, from more traditional styles to avant-garde apparel, plus accessories and cosmetics.

Specialty Stores

ANTIQUES

Autrefois Antiques (⊠ 125 Newbury St., ☎ 617/424–8823) stocks ivory, silver, Chinese lamps and vases, and country-French and some Italian 18th- and 19th-century antiques and furniture. The dealers at the **Boston Antique Co-op** (⊠ 119 Charles St., ☎ 617/227–9810 or 227–9811) sell everything from furniture to jewelry. **Cambridge Antique Mar-**

ket (✉ 201 Msgr. O'Brian Highway, ☎ 617/868–9655), off the beaten track, has four floors of dealers, some with reasonably priced items.

CLOTHING

Alan Bilzerian (✉ 34 Newbury St., ☎ 617/536–1001) is the place to go for the most avant-garde and au courant men's and women's clothing in Boston. **Jasmine** (✉ 329 Newbury St., ☎ 617/437–8466; ✉ 37A Brattle St., Cambridge, ☎ 617/354–6043) has the work of current designers from New York and Los Angeles. The Cambridge store includes the Sola and Sola Men shoe boutiques. **Louis, Boston** (✉ 234 Berkeley St., ☎ 617/262–6100) is the city's ultrapricey clothing store for men and women.

JEWELRY

Shreve, Crump & Low (✉ 330 Boylston St., ☎ 617/267–9100) sells the finest jewelry, china, crystal, and silver and has an extensive collection of clocks and watches.

Side Trip: Lexington and Concord

Lexington

To reach Lexington by car from Boston, cross the Charles River at the Massachusetts Avenue Bridge and continue on Massachusetts Avenue through Cambridge, passing Harvard Square and then Porter Square. Cross the Fresh Pond Parkway into Arlington and continue through Arlington Center.

The **MBTA** (☎ 617/722–3200) operates buses to Lexington and Boston's western suburbs from the Alewife and Harvard Square stations in Cambridge. You can also catch buses along Massachusetts Ave. The trip takes about one hour.

The events of the American Revolution are very much a part of present-day Lexington. The town comes alive each Patriot's Day (the Monday nearest April 19) when groups of costume-clad "Minutemen" participate in re-created battle maneuvers, "Paul Revere" reenacts his midnight ride, and the town turns out for a parade, pancake breakfasts, and other celebrations.

Minuteman Captain John Parker assembled his men out on **Battle Green,** a 2-acre, triangular piece of land, to await the arrival of the British, who were marching from Boston toward Concord to "teach rebels a lesson." Parker's role is commemorated in Henry Hudson Kitson's renowned sculpture, the **Minuteman Statue,** which stands at the tip of the green, facing downtown Lexington. Because it's in a traffic island, it's a bit hard to pose for photos. A shot rang out from an unknown source—what Lexingtonians call "the shot heard 'round the world," although those in Concord claim the shot for their own.

The **visitor center** has a diorama of the 1775 clash on the green, plus a gift shop. ✉ *1875 Massachusetts Ave.,* ☎ *781/862–1450.* ☉ *Mid-Apr.–Oct., daily 9–5; Nov.–mid-Apr., generally weekdays 10–3, weekends 10–4.*

On the east side of the Green is **Buckman Tavern,** built in 1690, where the Minutemen gathered on the morning of April 19, 1775. A 40-minute tour takes in the tavern's seven rooms. ✉ *1 Bedford St.,* ☎ *781/862–5598.* 🎟 *$3.* ☉ *Mid-Apr.–Oct., Mon.–Sat. 10–5, Sun. 1–5. Special hrs and tours during winter holidays.*

As April 19 dragged on, British forces met far fiercer resistance in Concord. Dazed and demoralized after the battle at Old North Bridge (☞ Concord, *below*), the British backtracked and regrouped at the **Munroe**

Tavern (built in 1695) while the Munroe family hid in nearby woods; then the troops retreated to Boston. The tavern is 1 mi east of Lexington Common. ⊠ *1332 Massachusetts Ave.,* ☎ *781/674–9238.* 🎟 *$3; Lexington Historical Society offers a combination ticket for admission to Munroe Tavern, Buckman Tavern, and Hancock-Clarke House.* ⊙ *Mid-Apr.–Oct., Mon.–Sat. 10–5, Sun. 1–5.*

★ The **Museum of Our National Heritage** displays items and artifacts from all facets of American life, putting them in social and political context. The "Lexington Alarm'd" exhibit illustrates Revolutionary-era life through everyday household objects. ⊠ *33 Marrett Rd.,* ☎ *781/861–6559.* 🎟 *Free; donation suggested.* ⊙ *Mon.–Sat. 10–5, Sun. noon–5.*

Minute Man National Historical Park Visitor Center is part of the 800-acre Minute Man National Historical Park that extends into Lexington, Concord, and Lincoln. The center's exhibits and film focus on the Revolutionary War. ⊠ *Rte. 2A, ½ mi west of Rte. 128,* ☎ *781/862–7753.* ⊙ *Mid-Apr.–Oct., daily 9–5; Oct.–mid-Apr. contact North Bridge Visitor Center, 174 Liberty St., Concord, 781/369–6993.*

DINING

$ **Bertucci's.** Part of a popular chain, this Italian restaurant offers good food, reasonable prices, a large menu, and a family-friendly atmosphere. Specialties include ravioli, calzones, and a wide assortment of brick-oven baked pizzas. ⊠ *1777 Massachusetts Ave.,* ☎ *781/860–9000. AE, D, MC, V.*

Concord

To reach Concord from Lexington, take Routes 4 and 225 through Bedford and Route 62 west to Concord; or backtrack on Massachusetts Avenue to pick up Route 2A west at the Museum of Our National Heritage. The latter route is a longer but charming drive that takes you through parts of Minute Man National Historical Park. Stop off at the point where Revere's midnight ride ended with his capture by the British; it's marked with a boulder and plaque. Route 2A also takes you past the Minute Man Visitor Center. To reach Concord or Lincoln by car, take Route 2 out of Boston, or take I–90 (the Massachusetts Turnpike) to I–95 north, and exit at Route 2, heading west.

While the initial Revolutionary War sorties were in Lexington, word of the American losses spread rapidly to surrounding towns: When the British marched into Concord, more than 400 Minutemen were waiting. A marker set in the stone wall along Liberty Street, behind the Old North Bridge Visitors Center, announces: "On this field the Minutemen and militia formed before marching down to the fight at the bridge."

At the **Old North Bridge,** ½ mi from Concord center, the Concord Minutemen turned the tables on the British in the morning hours of April 19, 1775. The Americans did not fire first, but when two of their own fell dead from a Redcoat volley, Major John Buttrick of Concord roared, "Fire, fellow soldiers, for God's sake, fire." The Minutemen released volley after volley, and the Redcoats fled. Daniel Chester French's statue *The Minuteman* (1875) honors the country's first freedom fighters.

Of the confrontation, the essayist and poet Ralph Waldo Emerson wrote in 1837: "By the rude bridge that arched the flood/Their flag to April's breeze unfurled/Here once the embattled farmers stood/And fired the shot heard round the world." (The lines are inscribed at the foot of *The Minuteman* statue.) Hence, Concord claims the right to the "shot," believing that native son Emerson was, of course, referring to the North Bridge standoff. Park Service officials skirt the issue, saying the shot could refer to the battle on Lexington Green, when the very first shot rang out from an unknown source, or to Concord when Minutemen held back the Redcoats in the revolution's first major battle, or even to the Boston Massacre. What's important is Emerson's vision that here began the modern world's first experiment in democracy.

The Reverend William Emerson, the grandfather of Ralph Waldo Emerson, watched rebels and Redcoats battle from behind his home, the **Old Manse,** on Monument Street, within sight of the Old North Bridge. The house, built in 1770, was occupied by the family except for a period of 3½ years, when renter Nathaniel Hawthorne lived and wrote short stories here. The furnishings date from the late 18th century. ⊠ *Monument St.,* ☎ *978/369–3909.* ▨ *$5.* ☉ *Mid-Apr.–Oct., Mon.–Sat. 10–5, Sun. and holidays, noon–5.*

The **Wright Tavern** (⊠ 2 Lexington Rd.), built in 1747, served as headquarters first for the Minutemen, then the British, then both on April 19. It is closed to the public.

The **Jonathan Ball House,** built in 1753, was a station on the underground railroad for runaway slaves during the Civil War. Ask to see the secret room. The house hosts art exhibits, and its garden and waterfall are refreshing sights. ⊠ *Art Association, 37 Lexington Rd.,* ☎ *978/369–2578.* ▨ *Free.* ☉ *Tues.–Sat. 10–4:30, Sun. 2–4:30.*

Ralph Waldo Emerson lived in the Old Manse between 1834 and 1835 before moving to what is known as the **Ralph Waldo Emerson House,** where he resided until his death in 1882. Here he wrote the *Essays* ("To be great is to be misunderstood"; "A foolish consistency is the hobgoblin of little minds"). Except for Emerson's study, now at the nearby Concord Museum (☞ *below*), the Emerson House furnishings have been preserved as the writer left them, down to his hat resting on the newel post. ⊠ *28 Cambridge Turnpike, on Rte. 2A,* ☎ *978/369–2236.* ▨ *$4.50.* ☉ *Mid-Apr.–late Oct., Thurs.–Sat. 10–4:30, Sun. 2–4:30.*

The original contents of Emerson's private study are in the **Concord Museum,** just east of the town center. In a 1930 Colonial Revival structure, the museum houses 15 period rooms, ranging in decor from Colonial to Empire. It has the world's largest collection of Thoreau artifacts, including furnishings from the Walden Pond cabin, as well as a diorama of the Old North Bridge battle, Native American artifacts, and one of two lanterns hung at Boston's Old North Church on the night of April 18, 1775. ⊠ *200 Lexington Rd./Rte. 2A,* ☎ *978/ 369–9763.* ▨ *$6.* ☉ *Apr.–Dec., Mon.–Sat. 9–5, Sun. noon–5.; Jan.– Mar., generally Mon.–Sat. 10–4, Sun. noon–4.*

The dark rusty-brown exterior of Louisa May Alcott's family home, **Orchard House,** poses a sharp contrast to the light, wit, and energy so much in evidence inside. Named for the apple orchard that once surrounded it, Orchard House was home for the Alcott family from 1857 to 1877. Here Louisa wrote *Little Women,* based on her life with her three sisters. Many of the original furnishings remain in the house. Portraits and watercolors by May Alcott (the model for Amy) abound; in her room you can see where she sketched figures on the walls—the Alcotts encouraged such creativity. ⊠ *399 Lexington Rd.,* ☎ *978/369–4118.* ▨ *$5.50.* ☉ *Apr.–Oct., Mon.–Sat. 10–4:30, Sun. 1–4:30; Nov.–Mar., weekdays 11–3, Sat. 10–4:30, Sun. 1–4:30. Closed Jan. 1–15.*

Nathaniel Hawthorne lived at the Old Manse in 1842–1845, working on stories and sketches; he then moved to Salem (where he wrote *The Scarlet Letter*) and later to Lenox (*The House of the Seven Gables*). In 1852 he returned to Concord, bought a rambling structure called **The**

Wayside, and lived here until his death in 1864. The subsequent owner, Margaret Sidney (author of *Five Little Peppers and How They Grew*), kept Hawthorne's tower-study intact—to the fascination of visitors today. Prior to Hawthorne's ownership, the Alcotts lived here, from 1845 to 1848. ⊠ *455 Lexington Rd./Rte. 2A,* ☎ *978/369–6975.* ☜ *$4.* ☻ *Mid-Apr.–Oct., daily except Wed., 10–5 . Guided tours until 4:30.*

A Concord curiosity, the yard of the privately owned **Grapevine Cottage** has the original Concord grapevine, the grape that the Welch's jams and jellies company made famous. In 1983, Welch's moved its corporate headquarters from New York to Concord to bring the company "back to its roots." A plaque on the fence tells how Ephraim Wales Bull began cultivating the Concord grape. ⊠ *491 Lexington Rd.* ☻ *Not open to the public.*

Each Memorial Day, Louisa May Alcott's grave in the nearby **Sleepy Hollow Cemetery** (⊠ entrance on Rte. 62 West) is decorated in commemoration of her death. Like Emerson, Thoreau, and Hawthorne, Alcott is buried in a section of the cemetery known as **Author's Ridge.** ⊠ *Bedford St.,* ☎ *978/371–6299.* ☻ *Generally, weekdays 7–dusk.*

A trip to Concord can also include a pilgrimage to **Walden Pond,** Henry David Thoreau's most famous residence. Here, in 1845, at age 28, Thoreau moved into a one-room cabin—built for $28.12½ cents—on the shore of this 100-ft-deep kettle hole, formed 12,000 years ago by the retreat of the New England glacier. Living alone over the next two years, Thoreau discovered the benefits of solitude and the beauties of nature. Thoreau later published *Walden* (1854), a collection of essays on observations he made while living here. The site of that first cabin is staked out in stone. A full-size, authentically furnished replica of the cabin stands about ½ mi from the original site, near the Walden Pond State Reservation parking lot. Even when the cabin is closed, you can peek through its windows. Now, as in Thoreau's time, the pond is a delightful summertime spot for swimming, fishing, and rowing, and there's hiking in the nearby woods. ⊠ *Rte. 126; from Concord take Main St. west from Monument Sq., turn left on Walden St., cross over Rte. 2 onto Rte. 126, and head south ½ mi to entrance (on left),* ☎ *978/369–3254.* ☜ *Free; parking across road from pond $2 per vehicle.* ☻ *Daily until approximately ½ hr after sunset.*

DINING

$–$$ ✗ **Walden Grille.** In an old brick firehouse, Walden Grille prepares contemporary dishes including fresh seafood. ⊠ *24 Walden St.* ☎ *978/ 371–2233. AE, D, DC, MC, V.*

Side Trip: Plymouth

If you have time to visit just one South Shore destination, make it Plymouth, a historic seaside town of narrow streets and clapboard mansions. Plymouth, 41 mi south of Boston, is known across the nation as "America's hometown" because of the 102 weary Pilgrims who disembarked here in December 1620.

MBTA (☎ 617/722–3200 or 800/392–6100) commuter rail service is available to Plymouth. **Plymouth & Brockton Street Railway** (☎ 508/ 746–0378) links Plymouth and the South Shore to Boston with frequent service. To get to Plymouth by car, take the Southeast Expressway I–93 south to Route 3 toward Cape Cod; exits 6 and 4 lead to downtown Plymouth and Plimoth Plantation, respectively.

The 1640 **Sparrow House** is Plymouth's oldest structure. ⊠ *42 Summer St.,* ☎ *508/747–1240.* ☜ *$1.50.* ☻ *Thurs.–Tues. 10–5.*

The 1749 **Spooner House,** home to the same family for 200 years, has guided tours, historic recipes, and a garden. ⊠ *27 North St.,* ☎ *508/746–0012.* ☐ *Donation.* ⊗ *June–mid-Aug., Thurs.–Sat 10–3:30 or 4.*

★ ☾ Over the entrance of the **Plimoth Plantation** is the caution: "You are now entering 1627." Believe it. Against the backdrop of the Atlantic Ocean, a Pilgrim village has been painstakingly re-created, from the thatched roofs, cramped quarters, and open fireplaces to the long-horned livestock. Throw away your preconception of white collars and funny hats; through ongoing research, the Plimouth staff has developed a portrait of the Pilgrims richer and more complex than the dour folk in elementary school textbooks. Listen to the quaint accents and mannerism of the "residents," who never break out of character. Feel free to engage them in conversation about their life, but expect only curious looks if you ask about anything that happened later than 1627.

Elsewhere on the plantation is **Hobbamock's Homestead,** where descendants of the Wampanoag Indians re-create the life of a Native American who chose to live near the newcomers. In the **Carriage House Craft Center** visitors may see such items created using the techniques of 17th-century English craftsmanship—that is, what the Pilgrims might have imported. (You can also buy samples.) At the **Nye Barn,** youngsters can see goats, cows, pigs, and chickens bred from 17th-century gene pools or bred to represent animals raised in the original plantation. The visitor center has gift shops, a cafeteria, and multimedia presentations. ⊠ *Warren Ave./Rte. 3A,* ☎ *508/746–1622.* ☐ *$18.50 (includes entry to Mayflower II); plantation only: $15.* ⊗ *Apr.–Nov., daily 9–5.*

One of the country's oldest public museums, the **Pilgrim Hall Museum,** established in 1824, transports visitors back to the time before the Pilgrims' landing, with items carried by those weary travelers to the New World. Included are a carved chest, a remarkably well-preserved wicker cradle, Miles Standish's sword, John Alden's Bible, Native American artifacts, and the remains of the *Sparrow-Hawk,* a 17th-century sailing ship that was wrecked in 1626. ⊠ *75 Court St./Rte. 3A,* ☎ *508/746–1620.* ☐ *$5.* ⊗ *Daily 9:30–4:30. Closed Jan.*

From the Pilgrim Hall Museum, it's a short walk to the harbor and the **Mayflower II,** an exact replica of the 1620 *Mayflower.* Like Plimoth Plantation, the ship is staffed by Pilgrims and hearty mates in period dress. ⊠ *State Pier,* ☎ *508/746–1622.* ☐ *$5.75 or as part of Plimoth Plantation fee.* ⊗ *Apr.–Nov., daily 9–5 (until 7 in July and Aug.).*

A few dozen yards from the *Mayflower II* is **Plymouth Rock,** popularly believed to have been the Pilgrims' stepping stone when they left the ship. Given the stone's unimpressive appearance—many visitors are dismayed that it's little more than a boulder—and dubious authenticity (as explained on a nearby plaque), the grand canopy overhead seems a trifle ostentatious. For a more traditional view of the Pilgrims, visit the **Plymouth National Wax Museum,** on the top of Cole's Hill. It contains 26 scenes with 180 life-size models that tell the Pilgrims' story. ⊠ *16 Carver St.,* ☎ *508/746–6468.* ☐ *$5.* ⊗ *Mar.–May, Nov., daily 9–5; June, Sept.–Oct., daily 9–7; July–Aug., daily 9–9.*

Imagine an entire museum devoted to a Thanksgiving side dish. But **Cranberry World,** operated by the Ocean Spray juice company, is amazingly popular. After learning how the state's local crop is grown, harvested, and processed, you can sip juices and sample products made from *Vaccinium macrocarpon* (the Latin name for cranberries). In October, you can see harvesting techniques and attend local cranberry fes-

tivals. ⊠ *225 Water St.,* ☎ *508/747–2350.* ⬛ *Free.* ☉ *May–Nov.,*
daily 9:30–5.

Dining

$$–$$$ ✕ **Bert's Cove.** This local landmark just off the entrance to Plymouth
Beach has great ocean views. The entrées include veal medallions, sirloin steak, risotto, and fresh seafood. ⊠ *Warren Ave., Rte. 3A.* ☎ *508/*
746–3330. AE, D, MC, V.

$$ ✕ **Iguana's.** A good spot for lunch or late-night dining, Iguana's serves
fajitas, burritos, and other Mexican-southwestern fare, plus burgers,
sandwiches, and chicken, steak, and rib dishes. The place has a bar, a
patio, ocean views—and a live iguana. ⊠ *Village Landing Marketplace,*
170 Water St., ☎ *508/747–4000. AE, DC, MC, V.*

Boston A to Z

Arriving and Departing

BY BUS

South Station (⊠ Atlantic Ave. and Summer St., ☎ 617/345–7451) is
the depot for most of the major bus companies that serve Boston. For
a list, *see* Massachusetts A to Z, at the end of this chapter.

BY CAR

Interstate 95 (which is the same as Route 128 in some parts) skirts the
western edge of Boston. Interstate 93 connects Boston to the north and
New Hampshire; the highway runs through the city as the Fitzgerald
Expressway. This section of I–93 is scheduled to be turned into an un-
derground highway as part of the massive Central Artery Project; ex-
pect construction and delays here well into 2000. Interstate 90 enters
the city from the west. Route 9, which travels roughly parallel to I–
90, passes through Brookline on its way into the the city. Route 2 en-
ters Cambridge from the northwest.

BY PLANE

Logan International Airport (⊠ Rte. 93 N, Exit 24, ☎ 617/561–1800
or 800/235–6426 for 24-hr information about parking and the ground
transportation options) receives flights from most major domestic air-
lines and some carriers from outside the United States. *See* Air Travel
in the Gold Guide for airline numbers. If you are driving from Logan
to downtown, take the Sumner Tunnel; if that's not passable, try Route
1A north to Route 16, then to the Tobin Bridge and into Boston.

Cabs can be hired outside each terminal. Fares to and from down-
town average about $20, including tip, via the most-direct route, the
Sumner Tunnel, assuming no major traffic jams. The Ted Williams Tun-
nel, for taxis and commercial use only, connects the airport to South
Boston. Call **Massport** (☎ 617/561–1751) for information. The **Air-
port Water Shuttle** (☎ 800/235–6426) crosses Boston Harbor in
about seven minutes, running between Logan Airport and Rowes
Wharf (a free shuttle bus operates between the ferry dock and airline
terminals). The **MBTA Blue Line** (617/222–3200 or 800/392–6100) sub-
way to Airport Station is one of the fastest ways to reach downtown
from the airport. Shuttle bus 22 runs between Terminals A and B and
the subway. Shuttle bus 33 goes to the subway from Terminals C, D,
and E. **US Shuttle** (☎ 617/894–3100) provides door-to-door van ser-
vice 24 hours a day between the airport and Boston, Cambridge, and
many suburban destinations. Call and request a pickup when your flight
arrives. To go to the airport, call for reservations 24 to 48 hours in
advance. Sample one-way fares are $8 to downtown or the Back Bay,
$15.50 to Cambridge.

BY TRAIN

Amtrak (☎ 617/482–3660 or 800/872–7245) Northeast Corridor trains from New York, Washington, D.C., and elsewhere stop at South Station and Back Bay Station. South Station is the eastern terminus of Amtrak's *Lake Shore Limited,* which travels daily between Boston and Chicago by way of Albany, Rochester, Buffalo, and Cleveland.

Getting Around

Massachusetts Bay Transportation Authority (MBTA; 617/222–3200 or 800/392–6100, TTY 617/722–5146) dispenses information on bus, subway, and train routes; schedules; fares; and other matters including wheelchair access around the clock. MBTA visitor passes are available for unlimited travel on city buses and subways for one-, three-, and seven-day periods (fares: $5, $9, and $18 respectively). Buy passes at the following MBTA stations: Airport, South Station, North Station, Back Bay, Government Center, and Harvard Square. Passes are also sold at the Boston Common Information Kiosk and at some hotels.

BY BUS

MBTA (☎ 617/222–3200) bus routes crisscross the metropolitan area and travel farther into suburbia than subway and trolley lines. Some suburban schedules are designed primarily for commuters. Current local fares are 60¢ for adults, 30¢ children from age 5 to 11; you must pay an extra fare for longer suburban trips. **Smart Traveler** (☎ 617/374–1234) provides service updates.

BY CAR

Boston is not an easy city to drive in. It's important to have a map with you. If you must bring a car, keep to the main thoroughfares and park in lots—no matter how expensive—rather than on the street, which is a tricky business. Some neighborhoods have residents-only rules, with just a handful of two-hour visitor's spaces; others have meters (25¢ for 15 minutes, one or two hours maximum). Major public lots are at Government Center and Quincy Market, beneath Boston Common (entrance on Charles Street), beneath Post Office Square, at the Prudential Center, at Copley Place, and off Clarendon Street near the John Hancock Tower. Smaller lots are scattered throughout downtown. Most are expensive; the few city-run garages are a bargain at about $6 to $10 per day.

BY SUBWAY OR TROLLEY

The MBTA (☞ *above*)—or "T," for short—operates subways, elevated trains, and trolleys along four different lines. Trains operate from about 5:30 AM to about 12:30 AM. Current T fares are 85¢ for adults, 40¢ for children from ages 5 to 11. An extra fare is required heading inbound from distant Green and Red Line stops. The **Red Line** originates at Braintree and Mattapan to the south; the routes join near South Boston and proceed to suburban Arlington. The **Green Line,** a combined underground and elevated surface line, uses trolleys that operate underground in the central city. It originates at Cambridge's Lechmere, heads south and divides into four routes; these end at Boston College (Commonwealth Avenue), Cleveland Circle (Beacon Street), Riverside, and Heath Street (Huntington Avenue). Buses connect Heath Street to the old Arborway terminus. The **Blue Line** runs on weekdays from Bowdoin Square and on weeknights and weekends from Government Center to the Wonderland Racetrack in Revere, north of Boston. The **Orange Line** runs from Oak Grove in north suburban Malden to Forest Hills near the Arnold Arboretum. Park Street Station (on the Common) and State Street are the major downtown transfer points.

BY TAXI

Cabs are not easily hailed on the street; if you need to get somewhere in a hurry, use a hotel taxi stand or telephone for a cab. Taxis charge about $1.90 per mi, with a $1.50 base charge; one-way streets often make circuitous routes necessary and increase your cost. Companies offering 24-hour service include **Boston Cab Association** (☎ 617/262–2227); **Checker** (☎ 617/536–7000); **Green Cab Association** (☎ 617/628–0600); **Independent Taxi Operators Association** (ITOA; ☎ 617/426–8700); and **Yellow Cab** (☎ 617/547–3000). In Cambridge try **Ambassador Brattle Cab** (☎ 617/492–1100) or **Cambridge Taxi** (☎ 617/547–3000).

Contacts and Resources

BED AND BREAKFAST RESERVATION SERVICE

A Bed and Breakfast Reservation Agency of Boston (✉ 47 Commercial Wharf, 02110, ☎ 617/720–3540, 800/248–9262, or 0800/895128 in the U.K.) can book a variety of accommodations ranging from historic B&Bs to modern condominiums.

EMERGENCIES

Police, fire, ambulance (☎ 911). **Massachusetts General Hospital** (☎ 617/726–2000). **Dental emergency** (☎ 508/651–3521). **Poison control** (☎ 617/232–2120).

GUIDED TOURS

ORIENTATION TOURS: The red **Beantown Trolley** (✉ Transportation Bldg., 14 Charles St. S, ☎ 617/236–2148) has 17 sightseeing stops; the cost is $18. Trolleys run every 20 minutes from 9 AM to 4 PM. From March to November **Brush Hill/Gray Line** (✉ Transportation Bldg., 14 Charles St. S, ☎ 617/236–2148) picks up passengers from hotels for 3½-hour Boston–Cambridge tours. Other tours are available to Plymouth, Plimoth Plantation, Cape Cod, Salem and Marblehead, New Hampshire, and Newport. Reservations are required for all tours. The blue trolleys of **Minuteman Tours** (✉ 329 W. 2nd St., South Boston, 02127, ☎ 617/269–7010) run every 20 minutes from 9 AM to 4 PM from May to October; tours cost $15, or $18 with a visit to the Tea Party ship. The orange and green **Old Town Trolley** (✉ 329 W. 2nd St., South Boston, 02127, ☎ 617/269–7010) runs every 10 minutes from 9 AM to 4:30 PM, for $20; in summer only the company operates tours of Cambridge.

WALKING TOURS: The **Black Heritage Trail** (☎ 617/742–5415 or 617/742–1854), a self-guided walk, explores Boston's 19th-century black community, passing 14 sites of historic importance. The 2½-mi **Freedom Trail** (☎ 617/242–5642) follows a red line past 16 of Boston's most important historic sites. For more information about the Black Heritage and Freedom trails, *see* Beacon Hill and Boston Common, *above*. The nonprofit **Historic Neighborhoods Foundation** (✉ 99 Bedford St., ☎ 617/426–1885) covers the North End, Chinatown, Beacon Hill, the waterfront, and other urban areas on 90-minute guided walks from Wednesday to Saturday between April and November. Tours range from $5 to $15. The **Society for the Preservation of New England Antiquities** (SPNEA; ✉ 141 Cambridge St., ☎ 617/227–3956) conducts a walking tour of Beacon Hill that focuses on the neighborhood as it was in the early 1800s. The tour takes place between May and October on Saturday at 3 PM, with an added 10 AM tour in October. The cost is $10. The **Women's Heritage Trail** (☎ 617/522–2872) celebrates more than 80 accomplished women on four self-guided walks. The Old State House (✉ 206 Washington St.) and the Boston National Historic Park Service Visitor Center (✉ 15 State St.) sell maps for $5.

The volunteers of **Boston by Foot** (✉ 77 N. Washington St., ☎ 617/367–2345 or 617/367–3766 for recorded information) conduct guided 90-minute walks daily from May to October. Highlights include an underground tour on Sunday, frequent Freedom Trail and Beacon Hill tours, and tours of the waterfront and the North End. Most tours cost $8; no reservations are required.

WATER TOURS: Boston Harbor Cruises (✉ 1 Long Wharf, ☎ 617/227–4321) runs harbor tours and other cruises (including whale-watching; prices vary) from mid-April to October. The **Charles Riverboat Co.** (☎ 617/621–3001) offers a 55-minute narrated tour of the Charles River Basin. Tours depart from the CambridgeSide Galleria in East Cambridge on the hour from noon to 5 daily from June to August and on weekends in April, May, and September; the fare is $8. **Massachusetts Bay Lines** (✉ 60 Rowes Wharf, ☎ 617/542–8000) operates evening cruises with rock, blues, or reggae music and dancing, concessions, and cash bar, as well as daily harbor tours ($8) and sunset cruises.

Boston Duck Tours (✉ 790 Boylston St., Plaza Level, ☎ 617/723–3825) conducts 80-minute city tours on World War II-era amphibious landing vehicles. Tours begin and end at the Huntington Avenue entrance to the Prudential Center, at 101 Huntington Avenue. From April to November, tours leave every half hour from 9 AM till dark; the fare is $19. Tickets are sold inside the Prudential Center from 9 to 8 daily (9 to 6 on Sundays); some tickets are available up to two days in advance. Weekend tours often sell out early.

LATE-NIGHT PHARMACIES

CVS (✉ 155 Charles St., ☎ 617/523–4372). **CVS** (✉ Porter Square Shopping Plaza, White St. at Massachusetts Ave., Cambridge, ☎ 617/876–5519).

VISITOR INFORMATION

The **Boston Common Information Kiosk** (✉ Tremont St., where the Freedom Trail begins, ☎ 617/426–3115) is open from Monday to Saturday between 8:30 and 5 and on Sunday between 9 and 5). The **Boston Welcome Center** (✉ 140 Tremont St., Boston 02111, ☎ 617/451–2227) is open from Sunday to Thursday between 9 and 5 and on Friday and Saturday between 9 and 6 for most of the year; it's open until 7 except Sunday during the summer. **Greater Boston Convention and Visitors Bureau** (✉ 2 Copley Pl., Suite 105, Boston 02116, ☎ 617/536–4100 or 800/888–5515) has brochures and information.

CAPE COD

Updated by Dorothy Antczak and Alan W. Petrucelli

Dining updated by Seth Rolbein

A Patti Page song from the 1950s promises that "If you're fond of sand dunes and salty air, quaint little villages here and there, you're sure to fall in love with old Cape Cod." The tourism boom since the '50s has certainly proved her right. So popular has the Cape become that today parts of it have lost the charm that brought everyone here in the first place. Still, much of the area remains compellingly beautiful and unspoiled. Even at the height of the season, there won't be crowds at the less-traveled nature preserves and historic villages. In the off-season, many beaches are dream material for solitary walkers, and life returns to a small-town hum.

Separated from the Massachusetts mainland by the 17.4-mi Cape Cod Canal—at 480 ft, the world's widest sea-level canal—and linked to it by three bridges, the Cape is always likened in shape to an outstretched arm bent at the elbow, its Provincetown fist turned back toward the

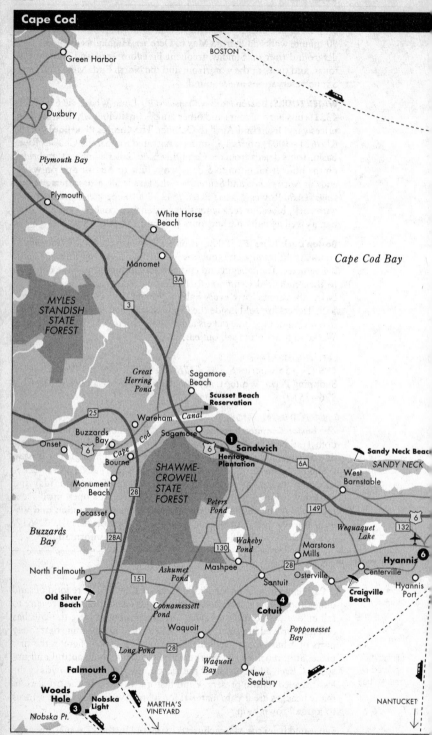

BOSTON

Green Harbor

Duxbury

Plymouth Bay

Plymouth

White Horse
Beach

Manomet

3A

Cape Cod Bay

3

MYLES
STANDISH
STATE
FOREST

*Great
Herring
Pond*

Sagamore
Beach

**Scusset Beach
Reservation**

25

Wareham

Canal

Buzzards
Bay

Cod

Sagamore

1

Sandwich

Sandy Neck Beach

Onset

6

Cape

Bourne

SHAWME-
CROWELL
STATE
FOREST

6

**Heritage
Plantation**

6A

SANDY NECK

West
Barnstable

Monument
Beach

28

*Peters
Pond*

149

*Wequaquet
Lake*

132

Pocasset

*Buzzards
Bay*

28A

*Ashumet
Pond*

130

*Wakeby
Pond*

Mashpee

Marstons
Mills

28

Osterville

Hyannis

6

North Falmouth

151

Santuit

Centerville

Hyannis
Port

**Old Silver
Beach**

*Coonamessett
Pond*

4

Cotuit

**Craigville
Beach**

Waquoit

*Popponesset
Bay*

Long Pond

28

*Waquoit
Bay*

New
Seaburg

NANTUCKET

Falmouth

2

**Woods
Hole**

3

**Nobska
Light**

Nobska Pt.

MARTHA'S
VINEYARD

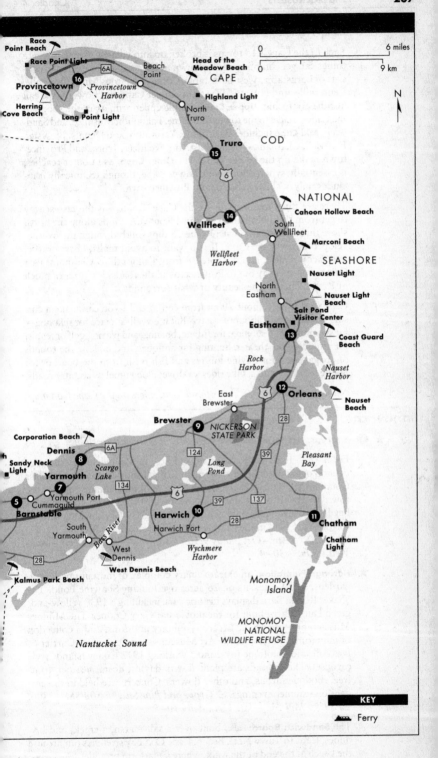

Race
Point Beach
■ Race Point Light
Provincetown
16
Provincetown Harbor
6A
Beach
Point
Head of the
Meadow Beach
CAPE
Herring
Cove Beach
Long Point Light
■ Highland Light
North Truro
Truro
15
COD
6
NATIONAL
Cahoon Hollow Beach
Wellfleet
14
South
Wellfleet
Marconi Beach
Wellfleet
Harbor
SEASHORE
Nauset Light
North
Eastham
Nauset Light
Beach
Salt Pond
Visitor Center
Eastham
13
Coast Guard
Beach
Rock
Harbor
Nauset
Harbor
East
Brewster
12
Orleans
Nauset
Beach
Brewster
9
NICKERSON
STATE PARK
28
Corporation Beach
Pleasant
Bay
Dennis
6A
124
39
Sandy Neck
Light
8
Scargo
Lake
Long
Pond
Yarmouth
7
134
6
39
137
5
Yarmouth Port
Barnstable
Cummaquid
Harwich
10
Chatham
11
South
Yarmouth
Bass River
Harwich Port
28
Chatham
Light
28
West
Dennis
Wychmere
Harbor
Kalmus Park Beach
West Dennis Beach
Monomoy
Island
MONOMOY
NATIONAL
WILDLIFE REFUGE
Nantucket Sound

0   6 miles
0   9 km
N

KEY
⛴ Ferry

mainland. The Cape "winds around to face itself" is how the writer Philip Hamburger has put it.

Each of the Cape's 15 towns is broken up into villages, which is where things can get complicated. The town of Barnstable, for example, consists of Barnstable, West Barnstable, Cotuit, Marstons Mills, Osterville, Centerville, and Hyannis. The terms Upper Cape and Lower Cape can also be confusing. **Upper Cape**—think upper arm, as in the shape of the Cape—refers to the towns of Bourne, Falmouth, Mashpee, and Sandwich. **Mid Cape** includes Barnstable, Yarmouth, and Dennis. Brewster, Harwich, Chatham, Orleans, Eastham, Wellfleet, Truro, and Provincetown make up the **Lower Cape.** The **Outer Cape,** as in outer reaches, is essentially synonymous with Lower Cape, though technically it includes only Wellfleet, Truro, and Provincetown.

There are three major roads on the Cape. Route 6 is the fastest way to get from the mainland to Orleans. Route 6A winds along the north shore through scenic towns; Route 28 dips south through the overdeveloped parts of the Cape. If you want to avoid malls, heavy traffic, and tacky motels, avoid Route 28 from Falmouth to Chatham. Past Orleans on the way out to Provincetown, the roadside clutter of much of Route 6 masks the beauty of what surrounds it.

Cape Cod is only about 70 mi from end to end—you can make a cursory circuit of it in about two days. But it is really a place for relaxing— for swimming and sunning; for fishing, boating, and playing golf or tennis; for attending the theater, hunting for antiques, and making the rounds of art galleries; for buying lobster and fish fresh from the boat; or for taking leisurely walks, bike rides, or drives along timeless country roads.

Numbers in the margin correspond to numbers on the Cape Cod map.

Sandwich

★ ❶   *3 mi east of the Sagamore Bridge, 11 mi west of Barnstable.*

From 1825 until 1888, the main industry in Sandwich was the production of vividly colored glass, made in the Boston and Sandwich Glass Company's factory. The **Sandwich Glass Museum** contains relics of the town's early history, a diorama showing how the factory looked in its heyday, and examples of blown and pressed glass. Glassmaking demonstrations are held in the summer. ⊠ *129 Main St.,* ☎ *508/888–0251.* 🎟 *$3.50.* ⊙ *Apr.–Oct., daily 9:30–4:30; Nov.–Dec. and Feb.–Mar., Wed.–Sun. 9:30–4.*

★   **Heritage Plantation,** an extraordinary complex of museum buildings, gardens, and a café, sits on 76 acres overlooking Shawme Pond. The Shaker Round Barn displays historic cars, including a 1930 yellow-and-green Duesenberg built for the movie star Gary Cooper. The Military Museum houses antique firearms, military uniforms, and a collection of miniature soldiers. At the Art Museum are an extensive Currier & Ives collection, antique toys, and a working 1912 Coney Island–style carousel. The grounds are planted with daylily, hosta, heather, fruit-tree, rhododendrons, and other flowers. Concerts are held in the gardens on summer evenings. ⊠ *Grove and Pine Sts.,* ☎ *508/888–3300.* 🎟 *$9.* ⊙ *Mid-May–late Oct., daily 10–5.*

The **Sandwich Boardwalk,** built over a salt marsh, a creek, and low dunes, leads to Town Neck Beach. Cape Cod Bay stretches out around the beach at the end of the walk, where a platform provides fine views, especially at sunset. From town cross Route 6A on Jarves Street, and at its end turn left and then right on the mile-plus trip to the boardwalk parking lot.

Dining, Lodging, and Camping

$$$–$$$$ ✕⊞ **Dan'l Webster Inn.** Built in 1971 on the site of a 17th-century inn, the Dan'l Webster is a contemporary hotel with old New England friendliness and hospitality. Chef's specials at the restaurant ($$$), which change monthly, might include striped bass crusted with cashews and macadamia nuts and accompanied by mango sauce. Seating is in four intimate dining rooms, a garden room, or the less formal tavern, which serves casual fare. Lodgings are in the main inn and wings or in two nearby historic houses with four suites each. All rooms have floral fabrics, reproduction mahogany and cherry furnishings, and some antiques. Some suites have fireplaces or whirlpools, and one has a baby grand piano. ⊠ *149 Main St., 02563,* ☎ *508/888–3622 or 800/444–3566,* FAX *508/888–5156. 47 rooms, 9 suites. 2 restaurants, bar, air-conditioning, no-smoking rooms, room service, pool. AE, D, DC, MC, V.*

$$$ ⊞ **Sandwich Lodge & Resort.** Set amid 10 rolling acres, this glorified motel has suites and efficiencies with gleaming kitchens; some of the accommodations have two-person whirlpool tubs. ⊠ *Box 1038, 54 Rte. 6A, 02653,* ☎ *508/888–2275 or 800/282–5353,* FAX *508/888–8102. 41 rooms, 17 suites, 5 efficiencies. Restaurant, bar, no-smoking rooms, indoor-outdoor pool, hot tub, shuffleboard, volleyball, recreation room. Continental breakfast. AE, D, MC, V.*

$$–$$$ ⊞ **Summer House.** The antique furniture, hand-stitched quilts, painted hardwood floors, and airy fabrics at this 1835 Greek Revival inn conjure the breezy feeling of an old-fashioned summer home. ⊠ *158 Main St., 02563,* ☎ *508/888–4991 or 800/241–3609. 5 rooms share 4 baths. Bicycles. Full breakfast. No smoking. AE, D, MC, V.*

$$ ⊞ **Inn at Sandwich Center.** Directly across from the Sandwich Glass Museum, this house is listed on the National Register of Historic Places. All the rooms have Laura Ashley comforters and bedding, hooked rugs, and bathrobes. ⊠ *118 Tupper Rd., 02563,* ☎ *508/888–6958 or 800/249–6949,* FAX *508/833–2770. 5 rooms. Continental breakfast. No smoking. AE, D, MC, V.*

$$ ⊞ **Wingscorton Farm.** This enchanting oasis is a working farm. The main house, built in 1756, has three second-floor suites, each with a fireplace, braided rugs, and wainscoting. Also on the property are a detached cottage and a converted stone carriage house. Traditional clambakes are prepared year-round by visiting members of the Wampanoag tribe. A private bay beach is a five-minute walk away. ⊠ *11 Wing Blvd., 02537,* ☎ *508/888–0534. 4 suites, 1 carriage house, 1 2-bedroom cottage. Full breakfast. AE, MC, V.*

$ ⚠ **Shawme-Crowell State Forest.** Open-air campfires are allowed at the 285 wooded tent and RV campsites here, and campers have free access to Scusset Beach. ⊠ *Rte. 130, 02563,* ☎ *508/888–0351.*

Nightlife and the Arts

Atmospheric **Bobby Byrne's Pub** (⊠ Rte. 6A, ☎ 508/888–6088) is a good place to stop for a drink. **Town band concerts** (⊠ Henry T. Wing Elementary School, Rte. 130, ☎ 508/888–5281) are held on Thursday at 7:30 PM from late June to late August.

Shopping

Brown Jug (⊠ 155 Main St., at Jarves St., ☎ 508/833–1088) specializes in antique glass and Staffordshire china. **Horsefeathers** (⊠ 454 Rte. 6A, E. Sandwich, ☎ 508/888–5298) sells antique linens, lace, and vintage baby and children's clothing. **Titcomb's Bookshop** (⊠ 432 Rte. 6A, E. Sandwich, ☎ 508/888–2331) stocks used, rare, and new books, including many Cape and nautical titles.

OFF THE BEATEN PATH	**ROUTE 6A** – If you're heading to Orleans and you're not in a hurry, take this lovely road that heads east from Sandwich, passing through the oldest settlements on the Cape. Part of the Old King's Highway historic district, this stretch is protected from development. In autumn the foliage along the road is bright—maples with their feet wet in ponds and marshes put on a good display. Along 6A east of Sandwich center, you can stop to watch the harvesting of cranberries in flooded bogs.

Falmouth

➋ *15 mi south of the Bourne Bridge, 4 mi north of Woods Hole.*

Falmouth, the Cape's second-largest town, was settled in 1660. The **Falmouth Historical Society** conducts free walking tours in season and maintains two museums. The 1790 **Julia Wood House** retains wonderful architectural details—a widow's walk, wide-board floors, lead-glass windows. The smaller **Conant House,** a 1724 half Cape next door, has military memorabilia, whaling items, sailors' valentines, and a genealogical and historical research library. ✉ *Palmer Ave.,* ☎ *508/548–4857.* 🎫 *$3.* ☉ *Mid-June–mid-Sept., Wed.–Sun. 2–5, Fri. by appointment rest of year.*

Old Silver Beach, a long crescent of white sand, is especially good for small children because a sandbar keeps it shallow at one end and creates tidal pools full of crabs and minnows. There are lifeguards, rest rooms, showers, and a snack bar. ✉ *Off Quaker Rd.*

Dining and Lodging

$$$–$$$$
★ ✕ **Regatta of Falmouth-by-the-Sea.** The menu constantly evolves at this restaurant with beautiful views of Nantucket Sound and Martha's Vineyard. Continental and Asian influences turn up in dishes like seared center-cut black and white sesame encrusted swordfish steak with wasabe vinaigrette and marinated cucumber noodles. ✉ *217 Clinton Ave., Falmouth Harbor,* ☎ *508/548–5400. AE, MC, V. Closed Oct.– Memorial Day. No lunch Sat.*

$–$$ ✕ **Quarterdeck Restaurant.** Part bar, part restaurant—but all Cape Cod—this spot is across the street from Falmouth's town hall, so the lunch talk tends to focus on local politics. The stained glass is not old and authentic, but the huge whaling harpoons are. Hearty sandwiches like Reubens and grilled chorizo are on the menu, along with nightly entrées that might include striped bass with a lemon-pepper-polenta crust served with roasted-red-pepper mashed potatoes. ✉ *164 Main St.,* ☎ *508/548–9900. AE, D, DC, MC, V.*

$$$–$$$$ 🏨 **Inn on the Sound.** Nearly every room at this tranquil inn on a bluff faces the Vineyard Sound. The furnishings are casual and simple. Common areas include the art-laden living room, a breakfast room, and a deck with stunning views. ✉ *313 Grand Ave., Falmouth Heights 02540,* ☎ *508/457–9666 or 800/564–9668,* 📠 *508/457–9631. 10 rooms. Beach. Full breakfast. No smoking. AE, D, MC, V.*

$$$–$$$$
★ 🏨 **Wildflower Inn.** The innkeepers here call their decorating style "old made new again": Tables are constructed from early 1900s pedal sewing machine bases, and the living room's sideboard was a '20s electric stove. The somewhat whimsical decor continues in the guest rooms, one of which has a safari theme. The five-course breakfast might include sunflower crepes or calendula corn muffins. ✉ *167 Palmer Ave., 02540,* ☎ 📠 *508/548–9524 or 800/294–5459. 5 rooms, 1 cottage. Air-conditioning. Full breakfast. No smoking. AE, MC, V.*

$$$–$$$$
★ 🏨 **Coonamessett Inn.** With plenty of art, wood, and hanging plants all around, this is one of the best and oldest inn-restaurants on the Cape.

One- or two-bedroom suites are in five buildings around a broad lawn that spills down to a wooded pond. Rooms are casually decorated, with bleached wood or pine paneling and New England antiques or reproductions. ✉ *311 Gifford St., at Jones Rd., 02540,* ☎ *508/548–2300,* 📠 *508/540–9831. 25 suites, 1 cottage. Restaurant, bar. Continental breakfast. AE, MC, V.*

$$$ 🏨 **Admiralty Inn.** Some rooms at this motel outside Falmouth center have whirlpool tubs, and the town house suites have cathedral ceilings, two baths, a loft, and a living room. There is beach access. Children under 12 stay free. ✉ *51 Teaticket Hwy./Rte. 28, 02540,* ☎ *508/548–4240,* 📠 *508/457–0535. 70 rooms, 28 suites. Restaurant, bar, indoor-outdoor pools, hot tub, children's programs, playground. AE, D, DC, MC, V.*

$$$ 🏨 **Mostly Hall.** Looking very much like a private estate, this imposing
★ 1849 house has a wraparound porch and a dramatic widow's walk. Accommodations are in corner rooms, with reading areas, antiques and canopy beds, and leafy views through shuttered casement windows. Adirondack chairs are set around lush gardens in the backyard. ✉ *27 Main St., 02540,* ☎ *508/548–3786 or 800/682–0565,* 📠 *508/457–1572. 6 rooms. Air-conditioning, bicycles, library. Full breakfast. No smoking. AE, D, MC, V. Closed Jan.*

Nightlife and the Arts

On Thursday evenings the **Nimrod Inn** (✉ 100 Dillingham Ave., ☎ 508/540–4132) presents the 16-piece Stage Door Canteen Band. **Town band concerts** (✉ Marina Park, Scranton Ave., ☎ 508/548–8500 or 800/526–8532) take place on summer Thursdays at 8 PM.

Outdoor Activities and Sports

BIKING

The **Shining Sea Trail** is an easy 3½-mi route between Locust Street in Falmouth and the Woods Hole ferry parking lot.

FISHING

The Cape Cod Canal is a good place to fish; the Army Corps of Engineers operates a **canal fishing hot line** (☎ 508/759–5991). Freshwater ponds are good for perch, pickerel, and trout; the required license is available at **Eastman's Sport & Tackle** (✉ 150 Main St., ☎ 508/548–6900).

TENNIS

Falmouth Sports Center (✉ 33 Highfield Dr., ☎ 508/548–7433) has three all-weather and six indoor tennis courts, plus racquetball courts and a health club.

Woods Hole

❸ *4 mi southwest of Falmouth, 19 mi south of the Bourne Bridge.*

Woods Hole is home to several major scientific institutions: the Woods Hole Oceanographic Institution (WHOI), the Marine Biological Laboratory (MBL), the National Marine Fisheries Service, and the U.S. Geological Survey's Branch of Marine Geology. The WHOI is the largest independent private oceanographic laboratory in the world. Its staff led the successful U.S.–French search for the *Titanic* (found about 400 mi off Newfoundland) in 1985. Although the Oceanographic Institution (✉ 86 Water St.) is not open to the public, you can learn about it at the small **WHOI Exhibit Center.** ✉ *15 School St.,* ☎ *508/289–2663.* 🎟 *$2.* ☉ *Memorial Day–Labor Day, Mon.– Sat. 10–4:30, Sun. noon–4:30; Apr. and Nov., Fri.–Sat. 10–4:30, Sun. noon–4:30; May, Sept., and Oct., Tues.–Sat. 10–4:30, Sun. noon–4:30.*

The **Marine Biological Laboratory** (✉ 7 MBL St., ☎ 508/548–3705) is closed to the public, but retired scientists conduct free 1½-hour tours during the summer. Make reservations one week ahead.

★ ☺ The exhibition tanks at the **National Marine Fisheries Service Aquarium** contain regional fish and shellfish. You can see things up close through magnifying glasses. Several hands-on pools hold banded lobsters, crabs, snails, sea stars, and other creatures. The star attractions are two harbor seals, which can be seen in the outdoor pool near the entrance. ✉ *Albatross and Water Sts.,* ☎ *508/495–2267.* 🎫 *Free.* ☻ *Late June–mid-Sept., daily 10–4; mid-Sept.–late June, weekdays 10–4.*

Dining

$$ ✕ **Fish Monger's Café.** The ambitious contemporary menu at this
★ restaurant on the Sound includes a light fried calamari appetizer with a hot-pepper sauce and many grilled seafood dishes with tropical fruit sauces—the mango and cilantro sauce over grilled salmon is particularly delectable. ✉ *25 Water St.,* ☎ *508/540–5376. Reservations not accepted. AE, MC, V. Closed Dec.–mid-Feb. and Tues. off-season.*

Cotuit

❹ *12 mi east of Falmouth.*

★ The **Cahoon Museum of American Art** is in a 1775 Georgian Colonial farmhouse that was once a tavern and an overnight way station for travelers on the Hyannis-Sandwich Stagecoach line. Its several rooms display American primitive paintings by Ralph and Martha Cahoon along with other 19th- and early 20th-century art. ✉ *4676 Rte. 28,* ☎ *508/428–7581.* 🎫 *Free.* ☻ *Mar.–Jan., Tues.–Sat. 10–4.*

Dining and Lodging

$$ ✕ **The Flume.** Indian artifacts adorn the dining room of the Flume, owned
★ for 25 years by author and Wampanoag elder Earl Mills. The menu concentrates on New England staples; the chowder is among the best on the Cape. ✉ *Lake Ave. off Rte. 130, Mashpee,* ☎ *508/477–1456. MC, V. Closed Thanksgiving–Easter. No lunch Columbus Day–Thanksgiving.*

$$$$ ✕▥ **New Seabury Resort and Conference Center.** This self-contained
★ resort community on a 2,000-acre point surrounded by Nantucket Sound contains furnished apartments—available for overnight stays or longer—in some of its 13 villages. Among the amenities are fine waterfront dining ($$$–$$$$), a restaurant overlooking the fairways ($$–$$$), and a private beach. The resort's golf courses are open to the public from September to May. ✉ *Box 549, Rock Landing Rd., Mashpee 02649,* ☎ *508/477–9400 or 800/999–9033,* ℻ *508/477–9790. 167 1- or 2-bedroom units. 5 restaurants, 2 pools, 2 18-hole golf courses, miniature golf, 16 tennis courts, health club, jogging, soccer, beach, windsurfing, boating, jet skiing, bicycles, pro shops. AE, DC, MC, V.*

Barnstable

❺ *16 mi east of Sandwich.*

Hovering above Barnstable Harbor and the 4,000-acre **Great Salt
★ Marsh, Sandy Neck Beach** stretches 6 mi across a peninsula that ends at **Sandy Neck Light.** The beach is one of the Cape's most beautiful—dunes, sand, and sea spread east, west, and north. The lighthouse, a few feet from the eroding shoreline at the tip of the neck, has been out of commission since 1952. The main beach at Sandy Neck has lifeguards, a snack bar, rest rooms, and showers. ✉ *Sandy Neck Rd. off Rte. 6A,*

W. Barnstable. ⌾ *$10 parking fee, Memorial Day–Labor Day.* ☉ *Daily 9–9, but staffed only until 5 PM.*

Lodging

$$$–$$$$
★

🏠 **Beechwood Inn.** This yellow and pale-green 1853 Queen Anne is trimmed with gingerbread, wrapped by a wide porch with a glider swing, and shaded by beech trees. The parlor is pure mahogany-and-red-velvet Victorian; the guest rooms are decorated with antiques in lighter, earlier Victorian styles. ✉ *2839 Main St./Rte. 6A, 02630,* ☎ *508/362–6618 or 800/609–6618,* ℻ *508/362–0298. 6 rooms. Refrigerators, bicycles. Full breakfast. No smoking. AE, MC, V.*

$$–$$$$

🏠 **Acworth Inn.** The large rooms at this 1860 house on the National Register of Historic Places are decorated in pastels, designer linens, and hand-painted furniture. One breakfast specialty is the innkeeper's cranberry granola with homegrown fresh fruit or the creamy cinnamon rolls. ✉ *Box 256, 4352 Main St./Rte. 6A, Cummaquid 02637,* ☎ *508/362–3330 or 800/362–6363,* ℻ *508/375–0304. 4 rooms, 1 suite. Bicycles. Full breakfast. No smoking. AE, D, MC, V.*

$$$
★

🏠 **Heaven on High.** Deanna and Gib Katten's haven is indeed heaven, nestled on a hill on one of the Cape's oldest roads. The decor, light and breezy, combines California beach house style and Cape Cod comfort. ✉ *Box 346, 70 High St., 02668,* ☎ *508/362–4441 or 800/362–4044,* ℻ *508/362–4465. 3 rooms. Air-conditioning. Full breakfast. No smoking. MC, V.*

Shopping

Black's Handweaving Shop (✉ 597 Main St./Rte. 6A, ☎ 508/362–3955) is a barnlike shop with working looms. **Salt & Chestnut** (✉ 651 Main St./Rte. 6A, ☎ 508/362–6085) sells antique and custom-designed weather vanes.

Hyannis

❻ *11 mi east of Mashpee, 23 mi east of the Bourne Bridge.*

Perhaps best known for its association with the Kennedy clan, Hyannis is the Cape's year-round commercial hub.

The enlarged and annotated photographs at the **John F. Kennedy Hyannis Museum** document JFK's Cape years (1934–63). ✉ *Old Town Hall, 397 Main St.,* ☎ *508/790–3077.* ⌾ *$3.* ☉ *Mid-Apr.–mid-Oct., Mon.–Sat. 10–4, Sun. 1–4; Mar.–mid-Apr. and mid-Oct.–Dec., Wed.–Sat., 10–4. Closed Jan.–Feb.*

Hyannis Port, 1½ mi south of Hyannis, was a mecca for Americans during the Kennedy presidency, when the **Kennedy Compound** became the summer White House. The Kennedy mystique is such that tourists still seek it out.

Kalmus Park Beach (✉ south end, Ocean St., Hyannis Port) is a wide beach with a section for windsurfers and a sheltered area for children. It has a snack bar, rest rooms, showers, and lifeguards.

Dining and Lodging

$$$–$$$$
★

✕ **The Paddock.** For 29 years, the Paddock has been synonymous with excellent formal dining—in the authentically Victorian main dining room or the breezy old-style-wicker summer porch. Steak au poivre with five varieties of crushed peppercorns is but one of the many traditional yet innovative preparations. You can't go wrong with any of the local seafood dishes or appetizers from the raw bar. Manhattans are the drink of choice in the lounge, where musicians perform in the evening. ✉ *W. Main St. rotary next to Melody Tent,* ☎ *508/775–7677. AE, DC, MC, V. Closed mid-Nov.–Mar.*

$$–$$$ ✕ **Roadhouse Café.** Candlelight flickers off the white linen tablecloths
★ and dark wood wainscoting at this stylish café. The calamari appetizer
is a chef's favorite, and the codfish chowder is a hit with locals. In the
casual bistro and the handsome mahogany bar, you can order from a
lighter menu of pizzas and sandwiches. All the desserts are made on
the premises—the tiramisu is one of several well worth the calories.
⊠ *488 South St.,* ☎ *508/775–2386. AE, D, DC, MC, V. No lunch.*

$$ ✕ **Harry's.** Harry's feels as though it's been transplanted from New
★ Orleans, and serves accordingly—Cajun and Creole dishes (including
meal-size sandwiches, blackened local fish, and a stupendous jamba-
laya), with great spices and sizable portions. Blues musicians perform
on Friday and Saturday night. ⊠ *700 Main St.,* ☎ *508/778–4188. Reser-
vations not accepted. AE, DC, MC, V.*

$–$$ ✕ **Baxter's Fish N' Chips.** The delicious fried clams here are served with
homemade tartar sauce. Picnic tables make it possible for you to lose
no time in the sun while you dine on lobster, burgers, or delicacies from
the excellent raw bar. ⊠ *Pleasant St.,* ☎ *508/775–4490. Reservations
not accepted. AE, MC, V. Closed weekdays Labor Day–Columbus Day
and entirely Columbus Day–Apr.*

$$$–$$$$ ⊞ **Breakwaters.** If you were staying any closer to the water, you'd be
★ *in* the water—that's how close these charming weathered gray-shin-
gle cottages are to Nantucket Sound. The one-, two-, and three-bed-
room condos, rented by the day or week, offer all the comforts of home.
The units have one or two bathrooms; kitchens with microwaves, cof-
feemakers, refrigerators, toasters, and stoves; and a deck or patio with
a grill—and most have water views. An added plus: daily (except Sun-
day) maid service. ⊠ *Box 118, Sea St. Beach, 02601,* ☎ FAX *508/775–
6831. 18 cottages (weekly rentals in season). Refrigerators, pool,
beach, baby-sitting. No credit cards. Closed mid-Oct.–Apr.*

$–$$ ⊞ **Sea Breeze Inn.** The rooms at this cedar-shingle seaside B&B have
★ antique or canopied beds and are decorated with well-chosen antiques.
Innkeeper Patricia Gibney's breakfasts, served in the dining room or
the gazebo, are worth rising early for. The nicest of the three detached
cottages is the three-bedroom Rose Garden, which has two baths, a
TV room, a fireplace, and a washer and dryer. ⊠ *397 Sea St., 02601,*
☎ *508/771–7213,* FAX *508/862–0663. 14 rooms, 3 cottages. Air-conditioning, no-smoking rooms. Continental breakfast. AE, D, MC, V.*

Nightlife and the Arts

The **Cape Cod Melody Tent** (⊠ 21 W. Main St., ☎ 508/775–9100) presents music and stand-up comedy. **Duval Street Station** (⊠ 477 Yarmouth
Rd., ☎ 508/771–7511) is the Upper and Mid Cape's only gay club.
The Prodigal Son (⊠ 10 Ocean St., ☎ 508/771–1337) hosts live music
most nights, with special events year-round, such as an acoustic folk
music series on Sunday and spoken-word nights midweek. Weekends
bring performances of up-and-coming rock, blues, and jazz bands. **Town
band concerts** (⊠ Village Green, Main St., ☎ 508/362–5230) take place
at 7:30 PM on Wednesday in July and August.

Shopping

Cape Cod Mall (⊠ Rtes. 132 and 28, ☎ 508/771–0200) has 90 shops,
a food court, and a movie complex.

Yarmouth

❼ *21 mi east of the Sagamore Bridge, 4 mi west of Dennis.*

For a peek into the past, stop at **Hallet's,** a country drugstore preserved
as it was in 1889, when the current owner's grandfather, Thacher Hallet, opened it. ⊠ *Rte. 6A,* ☎ *508/362–3362.* ⌑ *Free.* ☉ *Call for hrs.*

★ ☾ One of Yarmouth's most beautiful spots is Bass Hole, which stretches from Homer's Dock Road to the salt marsh. **Bass Hole Boardwalk** extends over a marshy creek. The 2.4-mi **Callery-Darling nature trails** meander through salt marshes, vegetated wetlands, and upland woods. Gray's Beach is a little crescent of sand with calm waters. ⊠ *Trail entrance on Center St. near the Gray's Beach parking lot.*

☾ An entertaining and educational stop for kids, **ZooQuarium** has sea lion shows, wandering peacocks, a petting zoo with native wildlife, pony rides in summer, aquariums, educational programs, and the Children's Discovery Center. ⊠ *674 Rte. 28, W. Yarmouth,* ☎ *508/775–8883.* ☞ *$7.50.* ☉ *Mid-Feb.–June and Sept.–late Nov., daily 9:30–5; July–Aug., Mon.–Thurs. 9:30–8, Fri.–Sun. 9:30–5.*

NEED A
BREAK?

The **19th Century Mercantile** is a wonderful trip to the past—an old-fashioned store that sells new merchandise with an old-time flair, such as Grandpa's Pine Tar Shampoo, sarsaparilla, and Vinolia, the brand of soap used on the *Titanic*. ⊠ *2 N. Main St.,* ☎ *508/398–1888.*

Dining and Lodging

$$–$$$ ✕ **Inaho.** Yuji Watanabe's sushi and sashimi is artistically presented,
★   and his tempura is fluffy and light. Given the authentic ambience, attention to detail, and remarkably high quality, if you dine here you might forget you're still on old Cape Cod. ⊠ *157 Main St./Rte. 6A,* ☎ *508/ 362–5522. MC, V. Closed Mon. No lunch.*

$–$$ ✕ **Jack's Outback.** Tough to find, tough to forget, this eccentric little
★   serve-yourself-pretty-much-anything-you-want joint goes by the motto "Good food, lousy service." Solid breakfasts give way to thick burgers, and traditional favorites like Yankee pot roast. Jack's has no liquor license, and you can't BYOB. ⊠ *161 Main St.,* ☎ *508/362–6690. Reservations not accepted. No credit cards. No dinner.*

$$$–$$$$ 🏨 **Wedgewood Inn.** This handsome 1812 Greek Revival building,
★   white with black shutters and fan ornaments on the facade, is on the National Register of Historic Places. Inside, the sophisticated country decor is a mix of fine Colonial antiques, Oriental rugs, handcrafted cherry pencil-post beds, antique quilts, and wide-board floors. ⊠ *83 Main St./ Rte. 6A, 02675,* ☎ *508/362–5157 or 508/362–9178,* 𝔽𝔸𝕏 *(508/ 362-5851. 4 rooms with bath, 5 suites. Air-conditioning. Full breakfast. No smoking in common areas. AE, DC, MC, V.*

$$–$$$ 🏨 **Village Inn.** Many of the guests who stay here say it's just like stay-
★   ing at grandmother's—provided, of course, that grandmother maintains the kind of clean, snug rooms found in Esther Hickey's 1795 sea captain's house. The rooms, which have floors with wide pine planks, are lessons in history: The Provincetown Room, for instance, served as the house's schoolroom; the original (now unused) light fixtures are still in place. Room sizes and amenities fluctuate; avoid the Wellfleet Room, which is as big as the oyster that bears its name. (Even the tub is half-size.) The Brewster, Truro, and Hyannis rooms connect to make one large space. The large first-floor Yarmouth Room has its own library, bathroom with fireplace, and private entrance. The common rooms have as many books as some public libraries. ⊠ *Box 1, 92 Main St., Yarmouth Port, 02675,* ☎ *508/362–3182. 10 rooms. Full breakfast. No smoking. MC, V.*

$ 🏨 **Americana Holiday Motel.** If you want (or need) the convenience
★   of staying on Route 28, this family-owned motel is a good choice. Rooms in the rear Pine Grove section overlook serene sea pines. ⊠ *99 Rte. 28, W. Yarmouth 02673,* ☎ *508/775–5511 or 800/445–4497,* 𝔽𝔸𝕏 *508/ 790–0597. 149 rooms, 4 suites. Coffee shop, air-conditioning, refrigerators, 1 indoor pool, 2 outdoor pools, hot tub, sauna, putting green,*

shuffleboard, video games, playground. Continental breakfast (off-season only). AE, D, DC, MC, V. Closed Nov.–Mar.

Nightlife and the Arts

The 90-member **Cape Cod Symphony Orchestra** (⊠ Higgins-Crowell Rd., ☎ 508/362–1111) gives classical and children's concerts from October to May.

Shopping

Cummaquid Fine Arts (⊠ 4275 Rte. 6A, Cummaquid, ☎ 508/362–2593) has works by Cape Cod and New England artists, and decorative antiques. **Parnassus Book Service** (⊠ Rte. 6A, ☎ 508/362–6420), in an 1840 former general store, specializes in Cape Cod, maritime, and antiquarian books. **Peach Tree Designs** (⊠ 173 Rte. 6A, ☎ 508/362–8317) carries home furnishings accessories made by local craftspeople.

Dennis

8 *7 mi west of Brewster, 5 mi north of Dennisport.*

Hundreds of sea captains lived in Dennis when fishing, salt making, and shipbuilding were the main industries. The elegant houses they constructed—now museums and B&Bs—still line the streets.

The holdings of the **Cape Museum of Fine Arts** include more than 850 works by Cape-associated artists. The museum hosts film festivals, lectures, and art classes. ⊠ *60 Hope La.,* ☎ *508/385–4477.* ☞ *$3.* ☯ *Late-May–Nov., Mon.–Sat. 10–5, Sun. 1–5; Dec.–mid-May, Tues.–Sat. 10–5, Sun. 1–5.*

West Dennis Beach (⊠ Davis Beach Rd.), which has bathhouses, lifeguards, a playground, and food concessions, is long and wide; it's one of the best beaches on the south shore.

Dining and Lodging

$$–$$$ ✕ **Gina's by the Sea.** Some places are less than the sum of their parts;
★ Gina's is more. In a funky old building tucked into a sand dune, the aroma of fine northern Italian cooking blends with a fresh breeze off the bay. Look for lots of fresh pasta and seafood. The bar gets crowded and loud, and is often fun. ⊠ *134 Taunton Ave.,* ☎ *508/385–3213. Reservations not accepted. AE, MC, V. Closed Dec.–Mar. and Mon.–Wed. Oct.–Nov. No lunch.*

$$–$$$ ✕ **Scargo Café.** Because the Cape Playhouse is right across the street, this café with a neocolonial feel. is a favorite haunt before and after shows. Try the mussels Ferdinand, a plate of farm-raised mussels with a buttery Pernod sauce over pasta. ⊠ *799 Rte. 6A,* ☎ *508/385–8200. AE, D, MC, V.*

$$–$$$ ☷ **Four Chimneys Inn.** Russell and Kathy Tomasetti have transformed
★ their three-story, four-chimney 1881 Queen Anne gem into a relaxing getaway in the heart of the Mid Cape. The eight rooms are tastefully furnished and have views of either Scargo Lake or of the surrounding woods and gardens. ⊠ *946 Main St./Rte. 6A, 02638.* ☎ *508/385–6317 or 800/874–5502,* FAX *508/385–6285. 7 rooms, 1 suite. Continental breakfast. AE, D, MC. V. Closed late Oct.–late Apr.*

$$–$$$ ☷ **Isaiah Hall B&B Inn.** Lilacs and pink roses trail the white fence out-
★ side this 1857 Greek Revival farmhouse on the bay side. Guest rooms are decorated with antiques, floral-print wallpapers, quilts, and Oriental carpets. In the carriage house, rooms have stenciled white walls and knotty pine, and some have small balconies overlooking gardens. ⊠ *152 Whig St., 02638,* ☎ *508/385–9928 or 800/736–0160,* FAX *508/385–5879. 9 rooms, 1 suite. Picnic area, air-conditioning, badminton, croquet. Continental breakfast. No smoking. AE, MC, V. Closed mid-Oct.–mid-Apr.*

Nightlife and the Arts

For Broadway-style shows and children's plays, attend a production at the **Cape Playhouse** (✉ Main St./Rte. 6A, ☎ 508/385–3911), the most renowned summer theater in the country. The **Reel Art Cinema** (☎ 508/385–4477) at the Cape Museum of Fine Arts (☞ *above*) shows avant garde, classic, art, and independent films from Thursday to Sunday between September and April.

Outdoor Activities and Sports

See Cape Cod Rail Trail *in* Cape Cod A to Z, below.

Shopping

Scargo Pottery (✉ Dr. Lord's Rd. S, off Rte. 6A, ☎ 508/385–3894) is in a pine forest, where potter Harry Holl's unusual wares sit on tree stumps and hang from branches. Inside are the workshop and kiln; viewing is encouraged.

Brewster

❾ *6 mi north of Chatham, 5 mi west of Orleans.*

Brewster is the perfect place to learn about the natural history of the Cape: The area contains conservation lands, state parks, forests, freshwater ponds, and brackish marshes.

For nature enthusiasts, a visit to the **Cape Cod Museum of Natural History** is a must-see. In the museum and on the grounds are a library, nature and marine exhibits, and trails through 80 acres of forest and marshland rich in birds and wildlife. The exhibit hall upstairs has a display of aerial photographs documenting the process by which the Chatham sandbar split in two. Knowledgeable guides conduct field walks. ✉ *869 Main St./Rte. 6A,* ☎ *508/896–3867 or 800/479–3867 in MA.* ⌑ *$5.* ☉ *Mon.–Sat. 9:30–4:30, Sun. 11–4:30.*

The **Brewster Store** is a local landmark. Built in 1852, it is a typical New England general store providing essentials like the daily papers, penny candy, and benches out front for conversation. ✉ *1935 Main St./Rte. 6A, at Rte. 124,* ☎ *508/896–3744.*

The 1,961 acres of **Nickerson State Park** consist of oak, pitch pine, hemlock, and spruce forest dotted with freshwater kettle ponds formed by glacial action. Recreational opportunities include fishing, boating, biking along 8 mi of trails, cross-country skiing, and bird-watching. ✉ *Rte. 6A,* ☎ *508/896–3491.*

Flax Pond in Nickerson State Park has picnic areas, a bathhouse, and water-sports rentals.

Dining, Lodging, and Camping

$$$$ ✕ **Chillingsworth.** This crown jewel of Cape restaurants is extremely
★ formal, terribly pricey, and completely upscale. The classic French menu and wine cellar continue to win award after award. The seven-course table d'hôte menu ($40–$56) includes an assortment of appetizers, entrées—like super-rich risotto, roast lobster, or grilled venison—and "amusements." At dinner, a modest bistro menu is served in the Garden Room, a patio-like area in the front of the restaurant. ✉ *2449 Main St./Rte. 6A,* ☎ *508/896–3640. Reservations essential. AE, DC, MC, V. Closed Mon. mid-June–Thanksgiving; closed some weekdays Memorial Day–mid-June and mid-Oct.–Thanksgiving; closed entirely Thanksgiving–Memorial Day.*

$$$$ ✕ **High Brewster.** The restored Colonial farmhouse of this country inn
★ has low ceilings and exposed ceiling beams, and it overlooks a picture-perfect landscape. The five-course prix-fixe regional American menu

changes frequently. Longtime dinner highlights include squash soup, grilled duck breast with a black-currant reduction, and apple-cranberry crisp. ⊠ *964 Satucket Rd.,* ☎ *508/896–3636 and 800/203–2634. Reservations essential. AE, MC, V. Closed Dec.–Mar.; call for weekday hrs off-season. No lunch.*

$$$$ 🏨 **Ocean Edge.** This self-contained resort with superior sports facilities is almost like a town. Concerts, tournaments, clambakes, and other activities are scheduled throughout the summer. The modern accommodations range from oversize hotel rooms to luxurious condominiums in the woods. ⊠ *2907 Main St./Rte. 6A, 02631,* ☎ *508/896–9000 or 800/343–6074,* FAX *508/896–9123. 170 condominium units, 90 hotel rooms. 3 restaurants, pub, room service, 2 indoor pools, 4 outdoor pools, ponds, saunas, driving range, golf privileges, putting greens, 11 tennis courts, basketball, exercise room, beach, bicycles, children's programs, concierge. MAP. AE, D, DC, MC, V.*

$$$–$$$$ 🏨 **Captain Freeman Inn.** The opulent details at this 1866 Victorian
★   include a marble fireplace, herringbone-inlay flooring, ornate Italian ceiling medallions, and 12-ft ceilings. Guest rooms have hardwood floors, antiques, and eyelet spreads. ⊠ *15 Breakwater Rd., 02631,* ☎ *508/896–7481 or 800/843–4664,* FAX *508/896–5618. 12 rooms. Pool, badminton, croquet, bicycles. Full breakfast. No smoking. AE, MC, V.*

$$–$$$ 🏨 **Old Sea Pines Inn.** Fronted by a white-column portico, the Old
★   Sea Pines evokes the summer estates of an earlier time. A sweeping staircase leads to rooms decorated with framed old photographs and antique furnishings. Rooms in a newer building are sparsely but well decorated. The shared-bath rooms are *very* small but a steal in summer. ⊠ *Box 1070, 2553 Main St./Rte. 6A, 02631,* ☎ *508/896–6114,* FAX *508/896–7387. 22 rooms, 5 with shared bath; 3 suites. Restaurant. Full breakfast. No smoking. AE, D, DC, MC, V. Closed Jan.–Mar.*

$ ⛺ **Nickerson State Park.** Some of the popular sites at this 2,000 acre-park are right on the edges of ponds. The facilities include showers, bathrooms, barbecue areas, and a store. ⊠ *3488 Main St./Rte. 6A, E. Brewster 02631,* ☎ *508/896–3491; 508/896–4615 for reservations,* FAX *508/896–3103. 418 sites.* 🏕 *$6–$7. No credit cards.* ☼ *Open mid-Oct.–mid-Apr. to self-contained campers only.*

Outdoor Activities and Sports

Captain's Golf Course (⊠ 1000 Freeman's Way, ☎ 508/896–5100) is a great 18-hole, par-72 public course with a greens fee ranging from $20 to $45; rental carts are not available. The **Cape Cod Rail Trail Bikeway** (☞ Cape Cod A to Z *below*) cuts through Brewster at Long Pond Road, Underpass Road, Millstone Road, and other points. **Jack's Boat Rentals** (⊠ Nickerson State Park, Flax Pond, Rte. 6A, ☎ 508/896–8556) rents canoes, kayaks, Seacycles, Sunfish, pedal boats, and sailboards. **Ocean Edge Golf Course** (⊠ Villagers Dr. off Rte. 137, ☎ 508/896–5911), an 18-hole, par-72 course winding around five ponds, has a greens fee that ranges from $25 to $59. Carts, mandatory at certain times, cost $14.

Shopping

Kemp Pottery (⊠ 258 Main St./Rte. 6A, W. Brewster, ☎ 508/385–5782) has functional and decorative stoneware and porcelain. **Kingsland Manor** (⊠ 440 Main St./ Rte. 6A, ☎ 508/385–9741) sells everything "from tin to Tiffany." **The Spectrum** (⊠ 369 Main St./Rte. 6A, ☎ 508/385–3322) purveys American arts and crafts. **Sydenstricker Galleries** (⊠ 490 Main St./Rte. 6A, ☎ 508/385–3272) is a working glass studio.

Harwich

10 *3 mi east of Dennisport, 1 mi south of Brewster.*

Originally known as Setucket, Harwich separated from Brewster in 1694 and was renamed after the famous seaport in England. Like other townships on the Cape, Harwich is actually a cluster of seven small villages, including Harwich Port. Three naturally sheltered harbors make the town, like its English namesake, a popular spot for boaters. Wychmere Harbor is particularly beautiful. Each September Harwich holds a Cranberry Festival to celebrate the importance of this indigenous berry.

Once a private school, the pillared 1844 Greek Revival building of **Brooks Academy** now houses the museum of the **Harwich Historical Society.** In addition to a large photo-history collection and exhibits on artist Charles Cahoon (grandson of Alvin), the socio-technological history of the cranberry culture, and shoemaking, the museum displays antique clothing and textiles, china and glass, fans, toys, and much more. There is also an extensive genealogical collection for researchers. On the grounds is a powder house that was used to store gunpowder during the Revolutionary War, as well as a restored 1872 outhouse. ⊠ *80 Parallel St.,* ☎ *508/432–8089.* ⌂ *Donations accepted.* ☉ *June–mid-Oct., Thurs.–Sun. 1–4.*

Dining and Lodging

$$$ ✕ **Cape Sea Grill.** Though some find this place stuffy, the food is first-rate. The best main dishes are Chatham cod and the swordfish wrapped in apple-wood–smoked bacon. Spanish-style paella takes its cue from a version that originates in the mountains of Spain, where toasted pasta thickened with bread, parsley, and almonds takes the place of the traditional rice. The Twin Brûlée dessert sampler changes now and then—pray for the espresso and vanilla combo. The wine list is excellent, but decidedly upscale. ⊠ *31 Sea St., Harwich Port,* ☎ *508/432–4745. AE, MC, V. Closed Jan.–Mar., and some evenings after Columbus Day. No lunch.*

$$$$ ☶ **Augustus Snow House.** This grand Victorian is the epitome of ele-
★ gance. The stately dining room is the setting for the three-course breakfast, with dishes like baked pears in a raspberry-cream sauce. Up a wide staircase, the rooms, which all have fireplaces, are decorated with Victorian-print wallpapers, luxurious carpets, and fine antiques and reproduction furnishings. ⊠ *528 Main St., Harwich Port 02646,* ☎ *508/430–0528 or 800/320–0528.* ℻ *508/432-7995. 5 rooms. Air-conditioning. Full breakfast. AE, D, MC, V.*

Nightlife and the Arts

Town band concerts in Harwich take place in summer on Tuesday at 7:30 PM in Brooks Park (⊠ Main St., ☎ 508/432–1600).

Outdoor Activities and Sports

Cape Water Sports (⊠ Rte. 28, Harwich Port, ☎ 508/432–7079) rents Sunfish, Hobie Cats, Lasers, powerboats, sailboards, day sailers, and canoes. Fishing trips are operated from spring to fall on the *Golden Eagle* (⊠ Wychmere Harbor, Harwich Port, ☎ 508/432–5611).

Cranberry Valley Golf Course (⊠ 183 Oak St., ☎ 508/430–7560) has a championship 18-hole, par-72 layout. The greens fee is $45; an optional cart costs $20.

Chatham

11 *5 mi east of Harwich, 1 mi west of Orleans.*

At the bent elbow of the Cape, Chatham has all the charm of a quiet seaside resort, with relatively little commercialism. And it *is* charming:

gray-shingled houses with tidy awnings and cheerful flower gardens, an attractive Main Street with crafts and antiques stores alongside homey coffee shops, and a five-and-ten. There is none of Provincetown's flash, but Chatham is not overly quaint—it's well-to-do without being ostentatious, casual and fun but refined, and never tacky.

The view from **Chatham Light**—of the harbor, the offshore sandbars, and the ocean beyond—justifies the crowds that gather to share it. When fog shrouds the area, pierced with darting beams from the beacon, the feel is dreamlike. Coin-operated telescopes allow a close look at the famous Chatham Break, the result of a fierce 1987 nor'easter that blasted a channel through a barrier beach just off the coast. ✉ *Main St.*

Monomoy National Wildlife Refuge is a 2,750-acre preserve including the Monomoy Islands, a fragile, 9-mi-long barrier-beach area south of Chatham. A paradise for bird-watchers, the island is an important stop along the North Atlantic Flyway for migratory waterfowl and shore birds. The Massachusetts Audubon Society in South Wellfleet conducts tours of the island. The **Monomoy National Wildlife Refuge headquarters,** on Morris Island, has a visitor center (☎ 508/945–0594), open daily from 8 to 5, where you can pick up pamphlets.

Harding's Beach, west of Chatham center, is open to the public and charges daily parking fees to nonresidents in season.

Dining and Lodging

$$–$$$ ✕ **Christian's/Upstairs at Christian's.** Two solid dining establishments inhabit this house on Main Street. Downstairs, an Old Cape/country-French motif prevails in the decor and on the menu: Boneless roast duck with raspberry sauce, lobster, scallops, and shrimp over pasta. Upstairs is casual and great for families with a movie theme, a seafood-based menu, and a mahogany-panel piano bar. ✉ *443 Main St.,* ☎ *508/945–3362. AE, D, MC, V. No lunch.*

$$–$$$ ✕ **Vining's Bistro.** Chatham's restaurants tend to serve conservative fare,
★ but the cuisine at this bistro is among the most inventive in the area. The wood grill, where the chef employs zesty spices from all over the globe, is the center of attention. A spicy pasta with andouille sausage, spit-roasted Jamaican chicken, and the Portobello mushroom sandwich are among the best dishes here. ✉ *595 Main St.,* ☎ *508/945–5033. Reservations not accepted. AE, D, MC, V. Closed mid-Jan.–Apr.*

$$ ✕ **Chatham Squire.** What was a bar scene and not much more has
★ evolved into an excellent dining experience. The fish served here is as good as it gets, and the kitchen continues to innovate without forgetting its Cape roots. The Squire is not as inexpensive as it was (or as its exterior implies), but it is much finer. ✉ *487 Main St.,* ☎ *508/945–0945. Reservations not accepted. AE, D. MC, V.*

$$$$ ▦ **Queen Anne Inn.** Built in 1840 as a wedding present for the daugh-
★ ter of a famous clipper-ship captain, this grand structure has large rooms furnished in a casual yet elegant style. Some have working fireplaces, private balconies, and hot tubs. Lingering and lounging are encouraged—around the large pool, on the veranda, in front of the fireplace in the sitting room, and in the plush parlor. ✉ *70 Queen Anne Rd., 02633,* ☎ *508/945–0394 or 800/545–4667,* ℻ *508/945–4884. 31 rooms. Restaurant, bar, air-conditioning, heated outdoor pool, spa, 3 tennis courts. AE, D, MC, V.*

$$$$ ▦ **Wequassett Inn.** This exquisite resort offers accommodations in 20
★ villas along a bay and on 22 acres of woods. Luxurious dining, attentive service, evening entertainment, and plenty of sunning and sporting opportunities are among the draws. The rooms, some of which have won design awards, are decorated in typical New England style in white pine, fir, and white wicker. ✉ *Pleasant Bay Rd., 02633,* ☎ *508/432–*

5400 or 800/225–7125, FAX 508/432–5032. 102 rooms, 2 suites. Restaurant, grill, piano bar, room service, pool, 4 tennis courts, exercise room, windsurfing, boating. MAP. AE, D, DC, MC, V. Closed Nov.–Apr.

$$$–$$$$ ⊡ **Captain's House Inn.** Fine architectural details, superb taste in decorating, opulent home-baked goods, and a feeling of quiet comfort are part of what makes this inn one of the Cape's finest. The rooms, spread over four buildings, have varied personalities—some are lacy and feminine, others refined and elegant. The luxury suites are particularly spacious and have every amenity imaginable. ⊠ *371 Old Harbor Rd., 02633,* ☎ *508/945–0127,* FAX *508/945–0866. 16 rooms, 3 suites. Croquet, bicycles. Full breakfast. No smoking. AE, D, MC, V.*

$$$–$$$$ ⊡ **Moses Nickerson House.** Warm, thoughtful service and fine antiques set the tone at this B&B. Each room in the 1839 house has its own look: one has dark woods, leathers, Ralph Lauren fabrics, and English hunting antiques; another has a high canopy bed and a Nantucket hand-hooked rug. All rooms have queen-size beds and wide-board pine flooring. Bathrooms, however, are small. ⊠ *364 Old Harbor Rd., 02633,* ☎ *508/945–5859 or 800/628–6972. 7 rooms. Full breakfast. No smoking. AE, D, MC, V.*

Nightlife and the Arts

Monomoy Theatre (⊠ 776 Main St., ☎ 508/945–1589) presents summer productions by the Ohio University Players. Chatham's summer **town band concerts** (⊠ Kate Gould Park, Main St., ☎ 508/945–5199) begin at 8 PM on Friday and draw up to 6,000 people.

Shopping

Cape Cod Cooperage (⊠ 1150 Queen Anne Rd., at Rte. 137, ☎ 508/432–0788) sells traditional woodenware made by an on-site cooper. At **Chatham Glass Co.** (⊠ 17 Balfour La., W. Chatham, ☎ 508/945–5547) you can watch glass being blown and buy it, too. **Fancy's Farmhouse in the Cornfield** (⊠ Rte. 28, W. Chatham, ☎ 508/945–1949) sells everything you need for a beach picnic. **Yellow Umbrella Books** (⊠ 501 Main St., ☎ 508/945–0144) has an excellent selection of new and used books.

Orleans

⑫   *4 mi southwest of Eastham, 35 mi east of the Sagamore Bridge.*

Incorporated in 1797, Orleans is part quiet seaside village and part bustling commercial center. A walk along Rock Harbor Road, a winding street lined with gray-shingled houses, white picket fences, and neat gardens, leads to the bay-side **Rock Harbor,** the base of of a small commercial fishing fleet whose catch hits the counters at the fish market here. Sunsets over the harbor are memorable.

Nauset Beach—not to be confused with Nauset Light Beach at the National Seashore—is a 10-mi-long sweep of sandy ocean beach with low dunes and large waves good for bodysurfing or board surfing. There are lifeguards, rest rooms, showers, and a food concession. ⊠ *Beach Rd.,* ☎ *508/240–2229 for a surf report.*

Skaket Beach on Cape Cod Bay is a sandy stretch with calm warm water good for children. There are rest rooms, lifeguards, and a snack bar. ⊠ *Skaket Beach Rd.*

Dining and Lodging

$$$ ✕ **Captain Linnell House.** Grecian columns grace the front of the house; antiques and lace grace the small, cozy dining rooms. The traditional menu is heavy on local seafood, but its meat dishes include an always-perfect rack of lamb. ⊠ *137 Skaket Beach Rd.,* ☎ *508/255–3400. Reservations essential. AE, MC, V.*

\$\$–\$\$\$ ✕ **Kadee's Lobster & Clam Bar.** A summer landmark, Kadee's serves good clams and fish-and-chips that you can grab on the way to the beach from the take-out window. Or sit down in the dining room for steamers and mussels, pasta and seafood stews, or the Portuguese kale soup. There's a miniature golf course out back. ⊠ *Main St.,* ☎ *508/ 255–6184. Reservations not accepted. MC, V. Closed day after Labor Day–week before Memorial Day and weekdays in early June.*

\$\$–\$\$\$ ✕ **Nauset Beach Club.** What was once the unsung local hero has be-
★   come widely known for its fine dining. Except for the wood-fired oven in the dining room, you might feel like you're eating in someone's living room, though the sophisticated, contemporary Italian cuisine is beyond that of the finest home cooks. *Zuppa di pesce* (Italian seafood stew) is one of many menu highlights. ⊠ *222 Main St., E. Orleans,* ☎ *508/255–8547. AE, D, DC, MC, V. Reservations not accepted. No lunch. No dinner Sun. and Mon. mid-Oct.–Memorial Day.*

\$\$\$ 🏨 **Kadee's Gray Elephant.** A mile from Nauset Beach, this 200-year-
★   old house contains small vacation studio and one-bedroom apartments. Unique on the Cape, they are a cheerful riot of color, from wicker painted lavender or green to beds layered in quilts and comforters mixing plaids and florals. The kitchens are fully equipped with stoves, microwaves, attractive glassware, irons and boards—and even lobster crackers. ⊠ *Box 86, 216 Main St., E. Orleans 02643,* ☎ *508/255– 7608,* ℻ *508/240–2976. 6 apartments. Restaurant, air-conditioning, miniature golf, gift shop. MC, V.*

Nightlife and the Arts

The **Academy Playhouse** (⊠ 120 Main St., ☎ 508/255–1963) hosts a dozen or so productions year-round, including original works. The **Cape & Islands Chamber Music Festival** (☎ 508/255–9509) presents three weeks of top-caliber performances in August.

Outdoor Activities and Sports

Arey's Pond Boat Yard (⊠ Off Rte. 28, S. Orleans, ☎ 508/255–0994) has a sailing school where individual and group lessons are taught. **Goose Hummock Shop** (⊠ Rte. 6A off the Rte. 6 rotary, ☎ 508/255–0455) sells licenses, which are required for fishing in Orleans's freshwater ponds. **Rock Harbor Charter Boat Fleet** (⊠ Rock Harbor, ☎ 508/255–9757) goes for bass and blues in the bay from spring to fall. Walk-ons are welcome.

Shopping

Addison Holmes Gallery (⊠ 43 Rte. 28, ☎ 508/255–6200), housed in four rooms of a brick-red Cape, represents area artists. **Hannah** (⊠ 47 Main St., ☎ 508/255–8234) has unique women's fashions. **Tree's Place** (⊠ Rte. 6A, at Rte. 28, ☎ 508/255–1330) displays the works of New England artists.

Eastham

🔞   *6 mi south of Wellfleet.*

The park on Route 6 at Samoset Road has as its centerpiece the **Eastham Windmill,** the oldest windmill on Cape Cod. ⊠ *Rte. 6.* 🎫 *Free.* ☉ *Late June–Labor Day, Mon.–Sat. 10–5, Sun. 1–5.*

A great spot for watching sunsets over the bay, **First Encounter Beach** is drenched in history. Near the parking lot, a bronze marker commemorates the first encounter between local Indians and passengers from the *Mayflower,* who explored the area for five weeks in late 1620.

Along 40 mi of shoreline from Chatham to Provincetown, the 44,000-
★   acre **Cape Cod National Seashore** encompasses superb ocean beaches,

rolling dunes, wetlands, pitch pine and scrub oak forest, wildlife, and several historic structures. Self-guided nature, hiking, biking, and horse trails lace these landscapes. **Salt Pond Visitor Center** has a museum and offers guided tours, boat trips, and lectures, as well as evening beach walks and campfire talks in summer. ⊠ *Off Rte. 6,* ☎ *508/255–3421.* ✑ *Free.* ☉ *Mar.–June and Sept.–Dec., daily 9–4:30; July–Aug., daily 9–5; Jan.–Feb., weekends 9–4:30.*

Roads and bicycle trails lead to Coast Guard and Nauset Light beaches, which begin an unbroken 30-mi stretch of barrier beach extending to Provincetown. This is the beach of Thoreau's 1865 classic, *Cape Cod.* You can still walk its length, as Thoreau did. Tours of the much-photographed red and white **Nauset Light** (☎ 508/240–2612) are given on weekends in season.

Low grass and heathland backs the long **Coast Guard Beach.** It has no parking lot, so park at the Salt Pond Visitor Center and take the free shuttle or walk the 1¾-mi **Nauset Trail** to the beach.

Lodging and Camping

$$$–$$$$ ▥ **Penny House Inn.** Antiques and collectibles decorate the rooms in this rambling inn sheltered by a wave of privet hedge. Deluxe rooms have air-conditioning, minirefrigerators, and phones. ⊠ *Box 238, 4885 County Rd./Rte. 6, Eastham 02651,* ☎ *508/255–6632 or 800/ 554–1751,* ℻ *508/255–4893. 11 rooms. Full breakfast. No smoking. AE, D, MC, V.*

$$$–$$$$ ▥ **Whalewalk Inn.** With windows galore, this 1830 home on 3 acres of rolling lawns and gardens has an airy feeling. Wide-board pine floors, fireplaces, and 19th-century country antiques provide historical appeal. The spacious rooms have floral fabrics and country-cottage furniture. ⊠ *220 Bridge Rd., 02642,* ☎ *508/255–0617,* ℻ *508/240–0017. 11 rooms, 5 suites. Bicycles. Full breakfast. No smoking. MC, V.*

$ ▥ **Hostelling International–Mid Cape.** On 3 wooded acres near the Cape Cod Rail Trail and the bay, this hostel has eight cabins. There is a common area and kitchen. ⊠ *75 Goody Hallet Dr., 02642,* ☎ *508/255– 2785. Ping-Pong, volleyball. Closed mid-Sept.–mid-May.*

$ ⩙ **Atlantic Oaks Campground.** Primarily an RV camp, this campground forest is less than a mile north of the Salt Pond Visitor Center. RV hookups, including cable TV, cost $35 for two people; tent sites are $26 for two people. Showers are free. ⊠ *Rte. 6, 02642,* ☎ *508/ 255–1437 or 800/332–2267. 100 RV sites, 30 tent sites. Bicycles, playground, coin laundry. Closed Nov.–Apr.*

Wellfleet

⓮ *10 mi north of Eastham, 13 mi southeast of Provincetown.*

Less than 2 mi wide, Wellfleet is one of the more tastefully developed Cape resort towns, with fine restaurants, historic houses, and many art galleries.

★ The **Massachusetts Audubon Wellfleet Bay Sanctuary,** a 1,000-acre haven for more than 250 species of birds, is a superb place for walking, birding, and looking west over the salt marsh and bay at wondrous sunsets. The Audubon Society hosts naturalist-led wildlife tours year-round; phone reservations are required. ⊠ *Off Rte. 6, S. Wellfleet,* ☎ *508/ 349–2615.* ✑ *$3.* ☉ *Daily 8 AM–dusk.*

A good stroll around town would take in Commercial and Main streets and end at **Uncle Tim's Bridge.** The short walk across this arcing landmark—with its beautiful, much-photographed view over marshland and a tidal creek—leads to a small wooded island. For a **scenic loop** through a classic Cape landscape near Wellfleet's Atlantic beaches—with scrub and pines on the left, heathland meeting cliffs and the ocean below on the right—take LeCount Hollow Road north of the Marconi Station turnoff. Access to the first and last of four beaches on this stretch, **LeCount Hollow** and **Newcomb Hollow,** is restricted to residents in season. Between the two hollows, the spectacular dune-drop Atlantic beaches **White Crest** and **Cahoon Hollow,** open to the public, charge a $10 parking fee to nonresidents in season. Cahoon Hollow has lifeguards, rest rooms, and a restaurant and music club. Backtrack to Cahoon Hollow Road and turn west for the southernmost entrance to the town of Wellfleet proper, across Route 6.

Dining and Lodging

$$–$$$ ✕ **Aesop's Tables.** Inside this 1805 captain's house are five dining
★ rooms; aim for a table on the porch overlooking the town center. This is a great place to sample various preparations of local seafood; a signature dessert is the death by chocolate. On some nights in summer, the tavern hosts jazz musicians. ⊠ *316 Main St.,* ☎ *508/349–6450. AE, DC, MC, V. Closed Columbus Day–Mother's Day. No lunch Mon.–Tues.*

$$–$$$ ✕ **Finely JP's.** The dining room is noisy, but the Italian-influenced fish
★ and pasta dishes silence all. The appetizers, among them the warm-spinach and scallop salad and the blackened beef with charred-pepper relish, are especially good, and the Wellfleet paella draws raves. ⊠ *Rte. 6, S. Wellfleet,* ☎ *508/349–7500. Reservations not accepted. D, MC, V. Closed Mon.–Wed. Thanksgiving–Memorial Day; Mon.–Tues. Memorial Day–mid-June and Oct.–Thanksgiving; Tues. Labor Day–Sept.*

$–$$ ✕ **Bayside Lobster Hutt.** Diners at long tables break bread with strangers and often as not wind up as neighbors on the beach the next day. Though nothing fancy, the seafood is always fresh. ⊠ *91 Commercial St.,* ☎ *508/349–6333. Reservations not accepted. MC, V. BYOB (beer or wine only). Closed mid-Sept.–Memorial Day.*

$$$–$$$$ ▥ **Surf Side Colony Cottages.** These one- to three-bedroom cottages
★ on the Atlantic shore of the Outer Cape have fireplaces, kitchens, and screened porches. The exteriors are retro-Florida, but the interiors are tastefully decorated. ⊠ *Box 937, Ocean View Dr., S. Wellfleet 02663,* ☎ *508/349–3959,* 𝔽𝔸𝕏 *508/349–3959. 18 cottages. Picnic areas, coin laundry. MC, V. 1-wk minimum in summer. Closed Nov.–Mar.*

$ ▥ **Holden Inn.** If you can deal with the occasional shag carpet, try this old-timey place just out of the town center on the road to the pier. The lodge has shared baths, an outdoor shower, and a screened-in porch with a view of the bay. Rooms are clean and simple. ⊠ *140 Commercial St., 02667,* ☎ *508/349–3450. 27 rooms, 13 with shared bath. No credit cards. Closed mid-Oct.–mid-Apr.*

Nightlife and the Arts

The **Beachcomber** (⊠ Cahoon Hollow Beach, off Rte. 6, ☎ 508/349–6055) has a happy hour with live music and dancing in summer.

The drive-in movie is alive and well at the **Wellfleet Drive-In Theater** (⊠ Rte. 6, ☎ 508/349–7176 or 508/255–9619).

Art galleries host cocktail receptions during the **Wellfleet Gallery Crawl,** on Saturday evening in July and August.

The **Wellfleet Harbor Actors Theater** (⊠ box office on Main St., ☎ 508/349–6835) stages productions of classic and other plays between mid-May and mid-October.

Outdoor Activities and Sports

Jack's Boat Rentals (⊠ Gull Pond, ☎ 508/349–7553) rents canoes, kayaks, sailboats, and sailboards.

Shopping

Blue Heron Gallery (⊠ Bank St., ☎ 508/349–6724), one of the Cape's best galleries, carries contemporary works. **Karol Richardson** (⊠ 3 W. Main St., ☎ 508/349–6378) designs women's wear in luxurious fabrics. **Kendall Art Gallery** (⊠ 40 E. Main St., ☎ 508/349–2482) carries contemporary art and has a serene sculpture garden.

Truro

🔵 *7 mi southeast of Provincetown.*

🔵 Truro, a town of high dunes and rivers fringed by grasses, is a popular retreat for artists, writers, and politicos. Edward Hopper, who summered here from 1930 to 1967, found the Cape light ideal for his austere realism. At **Pamet Harbor,** off Depot Road, you can walk out on the flats at low tide and discover the creatures of the salt marsh.

Truly a breathtaking sight, **Highland Light,** also called Cape Cod Light, is the Cape's oldest lighthouse. Erosion threatened to cut the structure from its 117-ft perch and drop it into the sea, but local citizens raised funds in 1996 to move the lighthouse back 450 ft to safety.

Head of the Meadow Beach, a relatively uncrowded part of the National Seashore off Route 6, has rest rooms. The **Head of the Meadow Trail** is 2 mi of easy cycling between dunes and salt marshes from the beach's parking lot to High Head Road, off Route 6A in North Truro. Bird-watchers love this area.

Lodging

$$–$$$ 🏨 **South Hollow Vineyards Inn.** This elegant inn is decorated in a wine motif, not surprising since it's on the site of a winery that makes chardonnay, cabernet, and other wines. Antique casks and presses stand in the corners, and deep greens and burgundies predominate. Rooms have four-poster beds and modern baths. Homegrown berries often garnish breakfast dishes, and a large sundeck has sweeping views of the vineyard. ⊠ *Rte. 6A, N. Truro 02652, ☎ 508/487–6200, FAX 508/487–4248. 5 rooms. Full breakfast. No smoking. MC, V.*

$ 🏨 **Hostelling International–Truro.** In a former Coast Guard station on the dunes, this handsome facility has 42 beds and kitchen facilities. ⊠ *Box 402, N. Pamet Rd., 02666, ☎ 508/349–3889. Closed Labor Day–mid-June.*

Outdoor Activities and Sports

The **Highland Golf Links** (⊠ Lighthouse Rd., N. Truro, ☎ 508/487–9201), a nine-hole, par-36 course on a cliff overlooking the Atlantic, has a greens fee of $16; an optional cart costs $13.

Provincetown

★ 🔵 *27 mi north of Orleans, 62 mi from the Sagamore Bridge.*

Provincetown's shores form a curled fist at the very tip of the Cape. One of the first of many historically important visitors to anchor in this hospitable natural harbor was Bartholomew Gosnold, who arrived in 1602 and named the area Cape Cod after the abundant codfish he found in the local waters. The Pilgrims arrived on Monday, November 21, 1620, when the *Mayflower* dropped anchor in Provincetown Harbor after a difficult 63-day voyage; while in the Harbor they signed the Mayflower Compact, the first document to declare a democratic form of government in America. Ever practical, one of the first things the Pilgrims did was to come ashore to wash their clothes, thus initiating the age-old New England tradition of Monday washday. They stayed in the area for five weeks before moving on to Plymouth.

Plaques and parks commemorate the landing throughout town. Provincetown was for many decades a bustling seaport, with fishing and whaling as its major industries. Fishing is still an important source of income for many Provincetown natives, and the town is a major whale-watching, rather than hunting, mecca.

During the American Revolution, Provincetown Harbor was controlled by the British, who used it as a port from which to sail to Boston and launch attacks on Colonial and French vessels. In November 1778 the 64-gun British frigate *Somerset* ran aground and was wrecked off Provincetown's Race Point—every 60 years or so the shifting sands uncover her remains.

Provincetown is the nation's oldest continuous arts colony: Painters began coming here in 1899 for the unique Cape Cod light. Eugene O'Neill's first plays were written and produced here, and the Fine Arts Work Center continues to have in its ranks some of the most important writers of our time. In the busy downtown, Portuguese-American fishermen mix with painters, poets, writers, whale-watching families, cruise-ship passengers on brief stopovers, and many lesbian and gay residents and visitors, for whom P-town, as it's almost universally known, is one of the most popular East Coast seashore spots.

In summer, Commercial Street, the town's main thoroughfare, is packed with sightseers and shoppers browsing the treasures of the overwhelming number of galleries and crafts shops. At night, raucous music and people spill out of bars, drag shows, and sing-along lounges. It's a fun, crazy place, with the extra dimension of the fishing fleet unloading their catch at MacMillan Wharf, in the center of the action. On the wharf are a large municipal parking facility and the Chamber of Commerce, so it's a sensible place to start a tour of town.

Commercial Street is 3 mi from end to end. In season, driving from one end of the main street to the other could take forever—walking is definitely the way to go. A broad range of architectural styles—Victorian, Second Empire, Gothic, and Greek Revival, to name a few—was used to build houses for sea captains and merchants. The Provincetown Historical Society publishes walking-tour pamphlets, available for about $1 at many shops in town. Free Provincetown gallery guides are also available.

The quiet East End of town is mostly residential, with some top galleries. The similarly quiet West End has a number of small inns with neat lawns and elaborate gardens.

The first thing you'll see in Provincetown is the incongruous **Pilgrim Monument,** commemorating the first landing of the Pilgrims in the New World and their signing of the Mayflower Compact, America's first rules of self-governance. Climb the 252-ft-high tower (116 steps and 60 ramps) for a panoramic view—dunes on one side, harbor on the other, and the entire bay side of Cape Cod beyond. At the base is a museum of Lower Cape and Provincetown history. ⊠ *High Pole Hill,* ☎ *508/487–1310.* ☞ *$5.* ☉ *Apr.–June and Sept.– Nov., daily 9–5; July and Aug., daily 9–7; last admission 45 mins before closing.*

Founded in 1914 to collect and show the works of Provincetown-associated artists, the **Provincetown Art Association and Museum** (PAAM) houses a 1,650-piece permanent collection; exhibits here combine the works of up-and-comers with established artists of the 20th century. ⊠ *460 Commercial St.,* ☎ *508/487–1750.* ☞ *$3.* ☉ *Nov.–Apr., weekends noon–4 and by appointment; Memorial Day–Labor Day, daily noon–5 and 8–10; May, Sept., and Oct., Fri.–Sun. noon–5.*

Near the Provincetown border, **massive dunes** meet the road in places, turning Route 6 into a sand-swept highway. Scattered among the dunes are primitive cottages, called dune shacks, built from flotsam and other found materials, that have provided atmospheric as well as cheap lodgings to artists and writers over the years—among them Eugene O'Neill, e. e. cummings, Jack Kerouac, and Norman Mailer.

The **Province Lands,** scattered with ponds, cranberry bogs, and scrub, begin at High Head in Truro and stretch to the tip of Provincetown. Bike and walking trails wind through forests of stunted pines, beech, and oak and across desertlike expanses of rolling dunes—these are the "wilds" of the Cape. ⊠ *Visitor center: Race Point Rd.,* ☎ *508/487– 1256.* ◷ *Apr.–Nov., daily 9–5.*

All the **National Seashore beaches** have lifeguards, showers, and rest rooms. Only **Herring Cove Beach,** off Route 6, has food. There is a daily parking fee; an annual passes are more economical if you're staying longer than a week.

Race Point Beach, at the end of Route 6, has a remote feeling, with a wide swath of sand stretching around the point and Coast Guard Station. Because it faces north, the beach gets sun all day long.

Dining and Lodging

$$$ ✕ **Café Edwige.** Delicious contemporary cuisine, friendly service, a
★ homey setting—Café Edwige delivers night after night. Two good starters are the Maine crab cake and the warm goat cheese on crostini; for an entré try lobster and Wellfleet scallops over pasta with a wild mushroom and tomato broth. Don't pass on the wonderful desserts. ⊠ *333 Commercial St.,* ☎ *508/487–2008. AE, DC, MC, V. Closed Nov.–May.*

$$$ ✕ **Martin House.** An island of calm like Martin House right on crazy
★ Commercial Street is rare indeed. Changes in the kitchen have lessened the excitement around the restaurant in recent years, but the contemporary menu is still ambitious. Oysters Claudia matches native Wellfleets-on-the-half-shell with an Asian dipping sauce, wasabi, and pickled ginger. ⊠ *157 Commercial St.,* ☎ *508/487–1327. AE, D, DC, MC, V. Closed Wed. and Thu., Jan.–Mar.*

$$$ ✕ **The Mews.** This P-town favorite is still going strong. Downstairs,
★ the main dining room opens onto magnificent harbor views. The menu focuses on seafood with a cross-cultural flair. One favorite is the rich and spicy Wellfleet scallops, shrimp, and crab mousse in a wonton over grilled filet mignon. Brunch is served daily in season. ⊠ *429 Commercial St.,* ☎ *508/487–1500. AE, D, DC, MC, V.* ◷ *No lunch weekdays off-season or Sat. Columbus Day–Memorial Day.*

$$–$$$ ✕ **Bubala's by the Bay.** Personality abounds at this restaurant inside
★ a building painted bright yellow and adorned with campy carved birds. The kitchen serves three meals, with many vegetarian offerings and lots of local seafood, and the wine list is priced practically at retail. The bar scene picks up in the evening. ⊠ *183 Commercial St.,* ☎ *508/487– 0773. AE, D, MC, V. Closed Nov.–Mar.*

$$–$$$ ✕ **Ciro and Sal's.** From the decor to the pasta-dominated Italian cuisine, this spot would be well at home in Boston's North End. Try the shrimp scampi for a garlicky good time. ⊠ *4 Kiley Ct.,* ☎ *508/487– 0049. DC, MC, V. Closed Mon.–Thurs. Nov.–Memorial Day. No lunch.*

$$–$$$ ✕ **Dancing Lobster Café Trattoria.** Chef and owner Pepe Berg put in
★ some time at Harry's Bar in Venice and brought back rich Italian flavors and stylish whimsy. The wonderfully strange and filling zuppa di pesce with couscous is a highlight of the innovative menu. ⊠ *463 Commercial St.,* ☎ *508/487–0900. MC, V. Closed mid-Nov.–mid-May.*

$$–$$$ ✕ **Front Street.** Many consider this the best restaurant in town. Well
★ versed in classic Italian cooking, chef-owners Donna Aliperti and Kathleen Cotter also venture into other Mediterranean regions. Duck smoked in Chinese black tea is served with a different lusty sauce every day—one of the best is fresh tropical fruit with mixed peppercorns. The wine list is a winner. ⊠ *230 Commercial St.,* ☎ *508/487–9715. Closed Jan.–mid-May. AE, D, MC, V.*

$$–$$$ ✕ **Lobster Pot.** Provincetown's Lobster Pot is fit to do battle with all
★ the Lobster Pots anywhere on the Cape. As you enter you'll pass through one of the hardest-working kitchens on the Cape, which consistently turns out fresh New England classics and some of the best chowder around. ⊠ *321 Commercial St.,* ☎ *508/487–0842. Reservations not accepted. AE, D, DC, MC, V. Closed Jan.*

$$–$$$ ✕ **Napi's.** The zesty meals on Napi's internationally inspired menu in-
★ clude many vegetarian choices and Greco-Roman items like delicious shrimp feta (shrimp flambé in ouzo and Metaxa, served with a tomato, garlic, and onion sauce). The dining room is whimsically tasteful and casual, and the staff is attentive. ⊠ *7 Freeman St.,* ☎ *508/487–1145. Reservations essential. AE, D, DC, MC, V. ☉ No lunch June–mid-Sept.*

$ ✕ **Mojo's.** At Provincetown's fast-food institution, the tiniest of kitchens
★ turns out everything from fresh-cut french fries to fried clams, tacos, and tofu burgers. How they crank it out so fast and so good is anybody's guess. ⊠ *5 Ryder St. Ext.,* ☎ *508/487–3140. Reservations not accepted. No credit cards. Closed at some times mid-Oct.–early May.*

$$$$ 🏨 **Brass Key.** Convenient to Commercial Street's restaurants, shops,
★ galleries, and nightlife, this gay-popular complex is fast becoming Provincetown's most luxurious resort. In season, complimentary cocktails are served in the courtyard; in winter, wine is served before a roaring fire in the common room. The tastefully painted and papered rooms are furnished with country-style antiques, and have Bose stereos, phones, minirefrigerators, and TV/VCRs (there's a videocassette library). Deluxe rooms have gas fireplaces and whirlpools. ⊠ *67 Bradford St., 02657,* ☎ *508/487–9005 or 800/842–9858,* 🖷 *508/487–9020. 33 rooms. Air-conditioning, in-room VCRs, no-smoking rooms, pool, spa. Continental breakfast. AE, D, MC, V.*

$$$–$$$$ 🏨 **Bay Shore.** This apartment complex on the water, ½ mi from the
★ town center, is a great option for longer stays. Many of the units have fireplaces, decks, and large water-view windows; all have full kitchens, modern baths, and phones. Rentals are mostly by the week in season. Pets are welcome. ⊠ *493 Commercial St., 02657–2413,* ☎ 🖷 *508/ 487–9133. 24 apartments. Grills, beach. AE, MC, V.*

$$$–$$$$ 🏨 **Fairbanks Inn.** A block from Commercial Street, this comfortable
★ inn includes a 1776 main house and auxiliary buildings. Many rooms have four-poster or canopy beds, fireplaces, Oriental rugs on wide-board floors, and antique furnishings. The wicker-filled sunporch and the garden are good places to take your afternoon cocktail. ⊠ *90 Bradford St., 02657,* ☎ *508/487–0386. 12 rooms, 1 efficiency. Continental breakfast. AE, MC, V.*

$$–$$$$ 🏨 **The Masthead.** Hidden away in the quiet west end of Commercial Street, the Masthead is a charming cluster of shingled houses that overlook a lush lawn, a 450-ft-long boardwalk, and a private beach. Rooms, efficiencies, apartments, and cottages are among the lodging options. The cottages, which sleep seven, are an ideal choice for families or larger groups and for longer stays. ⊠ *Box 577, 31–41 Commercial St., 02657,* ☎ *508/487–0523 or 800/395–5095,* 🖷 *508/ 487–9251. 7 apartments, 3 cottages, 2 efficiencies, 9 rooms. Beach, dock. AE, D, DC, MC, V.*

$–$$ 🏨 **The Meadows.** At the far west end of Bradford Street, between the town center and the beach, the Meadows is a good value, especially for families. The property is well maintained and nicely landscaped. Rooms are bright and comfortable. ⊠ *Bradford St. Ext., 02657,* ☎ *508/487–0880. 21 rooms. MC, V.*

Nightlife and the Arts

The **Cape Cod National Seashore** (☎ 508/487–1256) sponsors sunset beach walks, sing-alongs, and sunset campfire talks on Provincetown beaches.

The **Provincetown Playhouse Mews Series** (☎ 508/487–0955) presents varied summer concerts. The **Provincetown Repertory Theatre** (☎ 508/487–0600) mounts productions of classic and modern drama in the summer. The **Provincetown Theatre Company** (☎ 508/487–8673) stages classics, modern drama, and new works by local authors year-round.

During the summer the **Boatslip Beach Club** (⊠ 161 Commercial St., ☎ 508/487–1669) holds a mixed gay and lesbian tea dance daily from 3:30 to 6:30 on the outdoor deck. A pianist plays easy-listening tunes weekends in-season at **Napi's** (⊠ 7 Freeman St., ☎ 508/487–1145). The **Pied Piper** (⊠ 193A Commercial St., ☎ 508/487–1527) draws hordes of gay men to its post–tea dance gathering. Later in the evening more women join the crowd.

Outdoor Activities and Sports

BIKING

The **Province Lands Trail** is a 5¼-mi loop off the Beech Forest parking lot on Race Point Road in Provincetown, with spurs to Herring Cove and Race Point beaches and to Bennett Pond.

FISHING

You can go for fluke, bluefish, and striped bass on a walk-on basis from spring to fall with **Cap'n Bill & Cee Jay** (⊠ MacMillan Wharf, ☎ 508/487–4330 or 800/675–6723).

GUIDED TOUR

Art's Dune Tours are hour-long narrated auto tours through the National Seashore and the dunes around Provincetown. ☎ *508/487–1950 or 508/487–1050,* 🖅 *$9 daytime, $10 sunset.* ☉ *Mid-Apr.–late Oct.*

HORSEBACK RIDING

The **Province Lands Horse Trails** lead to the beaches through or past dunes, cranberry bogs, forests, and ponds. **Nelson's Riding Stable** (⊠ 43 Race Point Rd., ☎ 508/487–1112) offers trail rides by reservation.

WHALE-WATCHING

One of the joys of Cape Cod is spotting whales while they're swimming in and around the feeding grounds at Stellwagen Bank, about 6 mi off the tip of Provincetown. Many people also come aboard for birding, especially during spring and fall migration. Several tour operators take whale-watchers out to sea for three- to four-hour morning, afternoon, or sunset trips.

Dolphin Fleet tours are accompanied by scientists from the Center for Coastal Studies in Provincetown who know many of the whales by name and tell you about their habits and histories. Reservations are essential. ⊠ *Tickets: MacMillan Wharf, Chamber of Commerce building,* ☎ *508/349–1900 or 800/826–9300.* 🖅 *$17–$18 (seasonal variations).* ☉ *Late Apr.–Oct.*

The ***Ranger V,*** the largest and fastest whale-watching boat, sails with a naturalist on board. ⊠ *Tickets: Bradford and Standish Sts.,* ☎ *508/487–3322 or 800/992–9333.* 🖅 *$18.* ☉ *Tours Apr.–mid-Oct.*

Shopping

Berta Walker Gallery (⊠ 208 Bradford St., ☎ 508/487–6411) represents Provincetown-affiliated artists working in various media. **Giardelli Antonelli** (⊠ 417 Commercial St., ☎ 508/487–3016) specializes in handmade clothing by local designers. **Long Point Gallery** (⊠ 492 Commercial St., ☎ 508/487–1795) is a cooperative of 17 well-established artists. **Northern Lights Leather** (⊠ 361 Commercial St., ☎ 508/487–9376) has clothing, boots, shoes, and accessories of soft leather, plus silk clothing. **Remembrances of Things Past** (⊠ 376 Commercial St., ☎ 508/487–9443) deals in articles from the 1920s to the 1960s. **West End Antiques** (⊠ 146 Commercial St., ☎ 508/487–6723) specializes in variety: $4 postcards, a $3,000 model ship, handmade dolls, and glassware.

Cape Cod A to Z

Arriving and Departing

BY BOAT

Bay State Cruise Company makes the three-hour trip between Commonwealth Pier in Boston and MacMillan Wharf in Provincetown from Memorial Day to Columbus Day. ☎ 617/457–1428 *in Boston*, ☎ 508/487–9284 *in Provincetown*. ⌑ *One-way/same-day round-trip: $18/$30, $5 additional for bicycles each way.*

BY BUS

Bonanza Bus Lines (☎ 508/548–7588 or 800/556–3815) operates direct service to Bourne, Falmouth, and Woods Hole from Boston and Providence. **Plymouth & Brockton Street Railway** (☎ 508/771–6191 or 508/746–0378) travels to Provincetown from Boston and Logan Airport.

BY CAR

From Boston (60 mi), take Route I–93 South to Route 3 South, across the Sagamore Bridge which becomes Route 6, the Cape's main artery. From western Massachusetts, northern Connecticut, and northeastern New York State, take I–84 East to the Massachusetts Turnpike (I–90 East) and take I–495 south and east to the Bourne Bridge. From New York City, and all other points south and west, take I–95 North toward Providence, where you'll pick up I–195 East (toward Fall River/New Bedford) to Route 25 East to the Bourne Bridge.

BY PLANE

Barnstable Municipal Airport (⊠ 480 Barnstable Rd., Rte. 28 rotary, Hyannis, ☎ 508/775–2020), the Cape's main air gateway, is served by Business Express, Colgan Air, Continental Express, and US Airways Express. **Provincetown Municipal Airport** (⊠ Race Point Rd., ☎ 508/487–0241) has year-round Boston service through Cape Air/Nantucket Airlines. *See* Air Travel *in* the Gold Guide for airline phone numbers.

Getting Around

BY BICYCLE

The Cape's premier bike path, the **Cape Cod Rail Trail,** follows the paved right-of-way of the old Penn Central Railroad. About 30 mi long, the easy-to-moderate trail passes salt marshes, cranberry bogs, ponds, and Nickerson State Park. The trail starts at the parking lot off Route 134 south of Route 6, near Theophilus Smith Road in South Dennis, and it ends at the post office in South Wellfleet. If you want to cover only a segment, there are parking lots in Harwich (across from Pleasant Lake Store on Pleasant Lake Avenue) and in Brewster (at Nickerson State Park).

For bike rentals, try **Bert & Carol's Lawnmower & Bicycle Shop** (⊠ 347 Orleans Rd./Rte. 28, N. Chatham, ☎ 508/945–0137); **Corner Cycle** (⊠ 115 Palmer Ave., Falmouth, ☎ 508/540–4195); **Little Capistrano**

Bike Shop (⊠ Rte. 6, Eastham, ☎ 508/255–6515); the **Rail Trail Bike Shop** (⊠ 302 Underpass Rd., Brewster, ☎ 508/896–8200).

BY BUS

The **Cape Cod Regional Transit Authority** (☎ 508/385–8326; ☎ 800/352–7155 in Massachusetts) operates its SeaLine service along Route 28 daily except Sunday between Hyannis and Woods Hole and connects in Hyannis with the Plymouth & Brockton line. The driver will stop when signaled along the route. The "b-bus" is a fleet of minivans that transports passengers daily door-to-door anywhere on the Cape. Make reservations, which are essential, no later than 11 AM on the day before you want to depart. Reservations are essential. The H2O Line operates scheduled service several times daily, year-round, between Hyannis and Orleans along Route 28.

BY CAR

From the Bourne Bridge, you can take Route 28 south to Falmouth and Woods Hole (about 15 mi), or go around the rotary, following the signs to Route 6; this will take you to the Lower Cape and central towns more quickly. On summer weekends, avoid arriving in the late afternoon. Routes 6, 6A, and 28 are heavily congested eastbound on Friday evening and westbound on Sunday afternoon. When approaching one of the Cape's numerous rotaries (traffic circles), keep in mind that vehicles already in the rotary have the right of way.

BY TAXI

All Village Taxi (Falmouth, ☎ 508/540–7200). **Cape Cab** (Provincetown, ☎ 508/487–2222). **Eldredge Taxi** (Chatham, ☎ 508/945–0068). **Hyannis Taxi** (☎ 508/775–0400 or 800/773–0600).

Contacts and Resources

B&B RESERVATION AGENCIES

Bed and Breakfast Cape Cod (☎ 508/255–3824 or 800/541–6226).

CAMPING

The **Cape Cod Chamber of Commerce** (⊠ Rtes. 6 and 132, Hyannis 02601, ☎ 508/362–3225 or 888/332–2732) maintains a list of private campgrounds.

CAR RENTALS

Budget (☎ 508/771–2744 or 800/527–0700) rents cars at the Barnstable and Provincetown airports.

EMERGENCIES

Cape Cod Hospital (⊠ 27 Park St., Hyannis, ☎ 508/771–1800). **Falmouth Hospital** (⊠ 100 Ter Heun Dr., Falmouth, ☎ 508/548–5300).

GUIDED TOURS

Patriot Boats operates charters and two-hour day and sunset cruises between Falmouth and the Elizabeth Islands on the 68-ft schooner *Liberté*. ⊠ 227 Clinton Ave., Falmouth, ☎ 508/548–2626. ☑ $20.

Cape Cod Tours travels the main streets and back roads of the Mid Cape and gives a good overview of the history of Hyannis and the surrounding areas. Hotel pick-up service is available. ☎ 508/362–1117 or 800/685–9111. ☑ $12; purchase ticket ½ hr before departure.

Cape Cod Scenic Railroad runs several tours between Hyannis and Sagamore. Excursion trains pass ponds, cranberry bogs, and marshes, and stop in Sandwich. The Dinner Train tour begins and ends in Hyannis; a five-course meal is served on board. Reservations are essential for some tours. ⊠ Main and Center Sts., Hyannis, ☎ 508/771–3788 or 800/872–4508. ☉ Call for schedule. ☑ $11.50 (Dinner and Ecology trains: $43.95, Sat. $51.30).

HOUSE RENTALS

Commonwealth Associates (✉ 551 Main St., Harwich Port 02646, ☎ 508/432–2618) can assist in finding rentals in the Harwiches. **Donahue Real Estate** (✉ 850 Main St., Falmouth 02540, ☎ 508/548–5412) lists apartments and houses on the Upper Cape. **Roslyn Garfield Associates** (✉ 115 Bradford St., Provincetown 02657, ☎ 508/487–1308) lists rentals for Wellfleet, Truro, and Provincetown.

LATE-NIGHT PHARMACIES

CVS (✉ 64 Davis Straits, Falmouth, ☎ 508/540–4307). **CVS** (✉ Patriot Square Mall, Rte. 134, Dennis, ☎ 508/398–0724).

OUTDOOR ACTIVITIES AND SPORTS

The Cape Cod Chamber's *Sportsman's Guide* describes fishing regulations and surf-fishing access locations, and contains a map of boat-launching facilities. The Division of Fisheries and Wildlife has a book of maps of Cape ponds. Freshwater fishing licenses are available for a nominal fee at bait and tackle shops.

VISITOR INFORMATION

Army Corps of Engineers 24-hour recreation hot line (☎ 508/759–5991). **Cape Cod Chamber of Commerce** (✉ Rtes. 6 and 132, Hyannis, ☎ 508/362–3225 or 800/332–2732). **Tide, marine, and weather forecast hot line** (☎ 508/771–5522).

MARTHA'S VINEYARD

Updated by
Alan W.
Petrucelli

Far less developed than Cape Cod yet more cosmopolitan than Nantucket, Martha's Vineyard is an island with a double life. From Memorial Day through Labor Day the quieter, some might say real, Vineyard is shaken into a vibrant, star-studded frenzy. The busy main port, Vineyard Haven, welcomes day-trippers fresh off a ferry or private yacht. Oak Bluffs, where pizza and ice-cream emporiums reign supreme, has the air of a boardwalk. Edgartown is flooded with seekers of chic who wander tiny streets that hold boutiques, stately whaling captains' homes, and charming inns. Summer regulars include a host of celebrities, among them William Styron, Walter Cronkite, and Sharon Stone. Things begin to slow down in mid-September, though, and in many ways the Vineyard's off-season persona is even more appealing than its summer self. There's more time to linger over pastoral and ocean vistas, free from the throng of cars, bicycles, and mopeds.

The island is roughly triangular, with maximum distances of about 20 mi east to west and 10 mi north to south. The Down-Island end comprises Vineyard Haven, Oak Bluffs, and Edgartown, the most popular and most populated towns; ferry docks, shops, and centuries-old houses and churches line the main streets. Up-Island, the west end of the Vineyard, is more rural. In Chilmark, West Tisbury, and Gay Head, country roads meander through woods and tranquil farmland.

The Vineyard, except for Oak Bluffs and Edgartown, is dry: There are no liquor stores, and restaurants don't serve liquor. Most restaurants in "dry" towns allow you to bring your own beer or wine.

Vineyard Haven (Tisbury)

❼ *3.3 mi west of Oak Bluffs, 8 mi northwest of Edgartown by the inland route.*

The past and the present blend with a graceful touch of the bohemian in Vineyard Haven (officially named Tisbury), the Island's busiest year-round community.

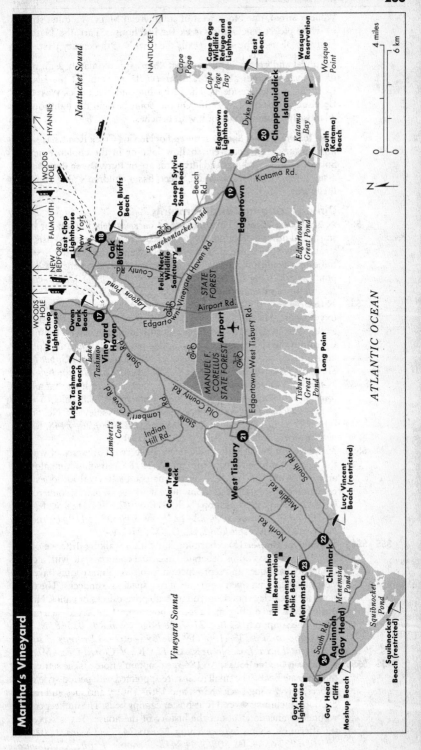

Martha's Vineyard

William Street, one block west of commercial Main, is a quiet stretch of white picket fences and Greek Revival houses. Part of a National Historic District, the street recalls the town's 19th-century past.

Beautiful and green, exclusive **West Chop,** approximately 2 mi north of Vineyard Haven along Main Street, claims some of the island's most distinguished residents. The 52-ft white-and-black brick **West Chop Lighthouse** was built in 1838. On the point beyond the lighthouse is a landscaped scenic overlook with benches.

Lake Tashmoo Town Beach, at the end of Herring Creek Road, has swimming in a warm, relatively shallow lake or in the cooler Vineyard Sound. There is parking, and lifeguards are on duty. **Owen Park Beach,** a small harbor beach off Main Street, has a children's play area and lifeguards.

Dining, Lodging, and Camping

$$$ ✕ **Black Dog Tavern.** This island landmark (widely known for its T-shirts and other merchandise) serves basic chowders, pastas, fish, and steak, as well as more elaborate dishes. Waiting for a table is something of a tradition. Locals love an early breakfast on the glassed-in porch overlooking the harbor. ⊠ *Beach St. Ext.,* ☎ *508/693–9223. Reservations not accepted. AE, D, MC, V. BYOB.*

$$$ ✕ **Le Grenier.** Calling a restaurant French in a dry town verges on being oxymoronic, but the Continental cuisine served here is authentic and expert. For frogs' legs, sweetbreads, tournedos, and calves' brains, Le Grenier is the clear choice. Preparations of veal, scallops, and lobster are sophisticated, but not as inventive as these classics. ⊠ *Upper Main St.,* ☎ *508/693–4906. AE, D, DC, MC, V. BYOB. No lunch.*

$–$$ ✕ **Diodati's Restaurant & Clam Bar.** Just about everything that a food joint should have—from good breakfasts to 10-inch subs to fried clams—can be found at this place on Main Street's sidewalk. Next door is the Get a Life coffee shop. ⊠ *55 Main St.,* ☎ *508/696–7448. Reservations not accepted. No credit cards. BYOB.*

$$$$ ▥ **Thorncroft Inn.** About a mile from the ferry on 3½ acres of woods,
★ the somewhat formal main inn here, a 1918 Craftsman bungalow, is adorned with fine Colonial and Renaissance Revival antiques and tasteful reproductions. Ten rooms have working fireplaces; some rooms have whirlpool baths or canopy beds. ⊠ *Box 1022, 460 Main St., 02568,* ☎ *508/693–3333 or 800/332–1236,* ℻ *508/693–5419. 14 rooms. Full breakfast. No smoking. AE, D, DC, MC, V.*

$$$–$$$$ ▥ **Hanover House.** This charming inn within walking distance of the ferry has spotless rooms decorated in casual country style with a combination of antiques and reproduction furniture. Some rooms have private entrances that open onto one of two spacious sundecks. The three suites in the carriage house are roomy, with private decks or patios. Homemade breads and muffins and a special house cereal are served each morning on the sunporch. ⊠ *Box 2107, 28 Edgartown Rd., 02568,* ☎ *508/ 693–1066 or 800/339–1066,* ℻ *508/696–6099. 12 rooms, 3 suites. Continental breakfast. No pets. AE, D, MC, V. Closed Dec.–Mar.*

$$–$$$$ ▥ **Captain Dexter House.** An 1843 sea captain's house is the setting for this intimate B&B. The small rooms are appointed with period-style wallpapers, velvet wing-back chairs, and 19th-century antiques and reproductions, including several four-poster canopy beds. The innkeepers tell wonderful anecdotes about the history of the house. Tea is served in the afternoon, sherry in the evening. ⊠ *Box 2457, 92 Main St., 02568,* ☎ *508/693–6564,* ℻ *508/693–8448. 7 rooms, 1 suite. Continental breakfast. No pets. No smoking. AE, MC, V. Closed Dec.–Apr.*

$ ⛺ **Martha's Vineyard Family Campground.** Tent-trailer rentals, recre-
★ ational facilities, a camp store, bicycle rentals, and electrical and

water hookups are among the amenities at this campground that also holds three cabins (with electricity, refrigerators, and gas grills). No dogs or motorcycles are allowed. ⊠ *569 Edgartown–Vineyard Haven Rd., 02568,* ☎ *508/693–3772,* ⅏ *508/693–5767. Closed mid-Oct.– mid-May.*

Nightlife and the Arts

Town band concerts take place every other Sunday in summer at 8 PM at Owen Park off Main Street. The **Vineyard Playhouse** (⊠ 24 Church St., ☎ 508/693–6450 or 508/696–6300) presents community theater and Equity productions, including summer programs at a natural amphitheater. **Wintertide Coffeehouse** (⊠ Five Corners, ☎ 508/693– 8830) hosts folk, blues, and jazz performers and holds open-mike nights. Light meals, desserts, and freshly ground coffees are served in this homey alcohol- and smoke-free environment.

Outdoor Activities and Sports

Public tennis courts are on Church Street; they're open in season only, and a fee is charged (reserve with the attendant the previous day). **Martha's Vineyard Scooter and Bike Rental** (⊠ 24 Union St., ☎ 508/ 693–0782) rents scooters and bicycles. **Wind's Up!** (⊠ 199 Beach Rd., ☎ 508/693–4252) rents day sailers, catamarans, surfboards, sea kayaks, canoes, and Sunfish.

Shopping

Bramhall & Dunn (⊠ 19 Main St., ☎ 508/693–6437) carries crafts, linens, hand-knit sweaters, and fine antique country-pine furniture. **Bunch of Grapes Bookstore** (⊠ 44 Main St., ☎ 508/693–2291) carries new books and sponsors book signings. **C. B. Stark Jewelers** (⊠ 126 Main St., ☎ 508/693–2284) creates one-of-a-kind pieces, including island charms. **Paper Tiger** (⊠ 29 Main St., ☎ 508/693–8970) carries handmade paper and gift items, plus works by local artists. **Rainy Day** (⊠ 86 Main St., ☎ 508/693–1830) is the ultimate home store, with highquality cookware and home furnishings.

Oak Bluffs

18 *6 mi northwest of Edgartown, 22 mi northeast of Gay Head.*

Circuit Avenue is the bustling center of the Oak Bluffs action, with most of the town's shops, bars, and restaurants. Colorful gingerbreadtrimmed guest houses and food and souvenir joints enliven Oak Bluffs Harbor, once the setting for several grand hotels (the 1879 Wesley Hotel on Lake Avenue is the last of them).

On the way from Vineyard Haven to Oak Bluffs, **East Chop Lighthouse** stands atop a bluff with spectacular views of Nantucket Sound. The 40-ft tower was built of cast iron in 1876.

The ♻ **Flying Horses Carousel,** a National Historic Landmark, is the nation's oldest continuously operating carousel. The carousel was handcrafted in 1876—the horses have real horse hair and glass eyes. ⊠ *Oak Bluffs Ave.,* ☎ *508/693–9481.* ☜ *Rides: $1; $8 for a book of 10.* ☼ *Mid-June–Labor Day, daily 9:30 AM–10 PM; Easter–mid-June and Labor Day–mid-Oct., weekends only. Closed mid-Oct.–Easter.*

The ★**Oak Bluffs Camp Ground,** a 34-acre warren of streets, contains more than 300 Carpenter Gothic Victorian cottages gaily painted in pastels and with wedding-cake trim. Methodist summer camp meetings have been held here since 1835. Each year on Illumination Night, the end of the season is celebrated with lights, singing, and open houses. Because of the overwhelming crowds of onlookers, the date is not announced until the week before the event.

Joseph A. Sylvia State Beach, between Oak Bluffs and Edgartown, is a 6-mi-long beach with calm water and a view of Cape Cod. Vendors sell food here, and there's parking.

Dining, Lodging, and Camping

$$$-$$$$ ✕ **Sweet Life Café.** An island favorite, this café has a interior that's so
★ subdued you may feel like you've entered someone's home. The main courses include roasted-red-pepper cod served with fresh-corn polenta and sweet peas. The desserts are all homemade, from gingerbread to lemon ice cream. ✉ *63 Upper Circuit Ave., ☎ 508/696–0200. Reservations essential. AE, D, MC, V. Closed Jan.–Mar.*

$$-$$$ ✕ **City, Ale and Oyster.** The beer at the Vineyard's first brew pub is made according to traditional German style; brews include the Oak Bluffberry, made with pure clover honey, and a Hazelnut Porter. As the name suggests, oysters get pride of place, but other local seafood is also on the menu, as are pizzas, burgers, fried chicken, and steaks. ✉ *30 Kennebec Ave., ☎ 508/693–2626. Reservations not accepted. AE, MC, V.*

$$-$$$ ✕ **Zapotec.** Southwest gingerbread describes the decor, with plenty of color, flowerboxes, and Santa Fe funk. The food follows suit: corn tortillas, grilled chicken breast with chili sauce, and nachos and quesadillas. The steamed mussels appetizer with chipotle chili, cilantro, lime, and cream breaks the mold a bit. There's a less expensive children's menu. ✉ *14 Kennebec Ave., ☎ 508/693–6800. Reservations not accepted. AE, MC, V. Closed mid-Oct.–late Apr.*

$ ✕ **Giordano's.** Consistently good, affordable food is what this spot's all about. Portions are notoriously huge and traditionally Italian, with fried fish and other seafood thrown in for good measure. A great place to dine with kids, Giordano's has a sizable children's menu. The summertime wait is long but at least entertaining, thanks to the restaurant's downtown corner location. ✉ *107 Circuit Ave., ☎ 508/693–0184. Reservations not accepted. No credit cards. Closed late-Sept.–early June.*

$ ✕ **Linda Jean's.** Tired of the gourmet world and looking for good diner
★ food, comfortable booths, and friendly waitresses? No problem. Except one: You may have to wait. ✉ *34 Circuit Ave., ☎ 508/693–4093. Reservations not accepted. No credit cards.*

$$$-$$$$ 🏨 **Oak House.** The wraparound veranda of this pastel-painted 1872
★ Victorian looks across a busy street to the beach. The well-preserved wood of the inn's name provides a solid backdrop (in ceilings and wainscoting) for the choice antique furniture and nautical-theme accessories. An elegant afternoon tea is served in a glassed-in sunporch, with cakes and cookies baked by innkeeper Betsi Luce, a Cordon Bleu–trained pastry chef. ✉ *Box 299, Sea View Ave., 02557, ☎ 508/693–4187,* 𝔽𝔸𝕏 *508/696–7385. 8 rooms, 2 suites. Continental breakfast. AE, D, MC, V. Closed late Oct.–early May.*

$$-$$$$ 🏨 **Martha's Vineyard Surfside Motel.** These two buildings are right in the thick of things. Rooms are spacious, bright, and well maintained, with typical motel furnishings. ✉ *Box 2507, Oak Bluffs Ave., 02557, ☎ 508/693–2500 or 800/537–3007,* 𝔽𝔸𝕏 *508/693–7343. 34 rooms, 4 suites. Hot tub. AE, D, MC, V.*

$$ 🏨 **Sea Spray Inn.** Artist Rayeanne King's porch-wrapped Victorian is
★ on an open park that borders an ocean beach; public tennis and golf are within walking distance. The decor is unfettered, and the common living room is large and airy. ✉ *GPO, 2 Nashawena Park, 02557, ☎ 508/693–9388. 7 rooms. Continental breakfast. No smoking. MC, V. Closed mid-Nov.–mid-Apr.*

$ 🏨 **Attleboro House.** This 1874 gingerbread Victorian with wraparound verandas has small, simple rooms, some with sinks, powder-blue walls, lacy white curtains, and a few antiques. Linen exchange but no maid service is provided during a stay. The shared baths are rustic and old but clean. ⊠ *Box 1564, 42 Lake Ave., 02557,* ☎ *508/693–4346. 9 rooms share 5 baths. Continental breakfast. MC, V. Closed Oct.– mid-May.*

$ ⚠ **Webb's Camping Area.** This campground on 84 acres is woodsy and private, with some water-view sites and a store. Swimming is permitted in Lagoon Pond, and there are bathrooms, showers, laundry facilities, playgrounds, and RV hookups. ⊠ *R.F.D. 3, Box 100, Barnes Rd., 02568,* ☎ *508/693–0233. MC, V. Closed day after Labor Day– mid-May.*

Nightlife and the Arts

Atlantic Connection (⊠ 124 Circuit Ave., ☎ 508/693–7129) hosts reggae, R&B, funk, and blues performers and has a strobe-lit dance floor. The **Lamppost** (⊠ 111 Circuit Ave., ☎ 508/696–9352) attracts a young and sometimes rowdy crowd. **Town band concerts** take place every other Sunday in summer at 8 PM at the gazebo in Ocean Park on Beach Road.

Outdoor Activities and Sports

BIKING

DeBettencourt's (⊠ Circuit Ave. Ext., ☎ 508/693–0011) rents bikes, mopeds, scooters, and Jeeps.

BOATING AND FISHING

Dick's Bait and Tackle (⊠ New York Ave., ☎ 508/693–7669) rents gear, sells bait, and has a current list of fishing regulations. The party boat *Skipper* (☎ 508/693–1238) leaves for deep-sea fishing trips out of Oak Bluffs Harbor in summer. **Vineyard Boat Rentals** (⊠ Dockside Marketplace, Oak Bluffs Harbor, ☎ 508/693–8476) rents Boston Whalers, Bayliners, and Jet Skis.

GOLF

Farm Neck Golf Club (⊠ Farm Neck Way, ☎ 508/693–3057), a semiprivate club on marsh-rimmed Sengekontacket Pond, has 18 holes in a par-72 championship layout. The greens fee ranges from $36 to $80; a cart (required at certain times) costs $25. Reservations are required at least 48 hours in advance.

TENNIS

Niantic Park in Oak Bluffs has courts that cost a small fee to use.

Shopping

Book Den East (⊠ New York Ave., ☎ 508/693–3946) stocks 20,000 out-of-print, antiquarian, and paperback books. **Michaela Ltd. Gallery of American Crafts** (⊠ 124 Circuit Ave., ☎ 508/693–8408) carries crafts and gift items.

Edgartown and Chappaquiddick Island

9.3 mi southeast of Vineyard Haven via Beach Rd., 8.6 mi east of West Tisbury.

⑲ Once a well-to-do whaling town, **Edgartown** has preserved some of its elegant past. Sea captains' houses from the 17th and 18th centuries, ensconced in well-manicured gardens and lawns, line the streets, and the many shops here attract see-and-be-seen crowds. The **Old Whaling Church** (☎ 508/627–8619 for tour), built in 1843 as a Methodist church and now a performing-arts center, has a six-column portico, unusual triple-sash windows, and a 92-ft clock tower. The stylish 1840 **Dr. Daniel Fisher House** has a wraparound roof walk, a small front portico with fluted Corinthian columns, and a side portico with thin fluted columns.

Dukes County Historical Society administers a complex of buildings and lawn exhibits. The **Francis Foster Museum** (☎ 508/627–4441) houses the Gale Huntington Reference Library and 19th-century miniature photographs of 110 Edgartown whaling masters. The **Capt. Francis Pease House** (☎ 508/627–4441), an 1850s Greek Revival structure, exhibits Native American, prehistoric, pre-Columbian, and more recent artifacts. ⊠ *Cooke St. at School St.,* ☎ *508/627–4441.* ⊡ *$6.* ☉ *July–Labor Day, daily 10–4:30; Labor Day–June, Wed.–Fri. 1–4, Sat. 10–4.*

★ ☾ The 350-acre **Felix Neck Wildlife Sanctuary,** a Massachusetts Audubon Society preserve 3 mi out of Edgartown toward Oak Bluffs and Vineyard Haven, has 6 mi of hiking trails traversing marshland, fields, woods, seashore, and waterfowl and reptile ponds. Naturalist-led events include sunset hikes, stargazing, snake or bird walks, and canoeing. ⊠ *Off Edgartown–Vineyard Haven Rd.,* ☎ *508/627–4850.* ⊡ *$3.* ☉ *Center: Mid-June–mid-Sept., daily 8–4; mid-Sept.–mid-June, Tues.– Sun. 9–4. Trails: dawn–dusk.*

South Beach, also called Katama Beach, is a 3-mi ribbon of sand on the Atlantic with strong surf and occasional riptides. Check with the lifeguards before swimming here. Parking is limited. ⊠ *Katama Rd.*

㉑ Chappaquiddick Island, a sparsely populated area with many nature preserves, makes for a pleasant day trip or bike ride on a sunny day. The island is actually connected to the Vineyard by a long sand spit that begins in South Beach in Katama—a spectacular 2¾-mi walk, or you can take the On Time ferry from 7 AM to midnight in season.

★ The 200-acre **Wasque Reservation** (pronounced *wayce*-kwee) connects Chappaquiddick Island with the Vineyard and forms Katama Bay. **Wasque Beach** is accessed by a flat boardwalk with benches overlooking the west end of Swan Pond. Beyond that are beach, sky, and boat-dotted sea. From the grove, a long boardwalk leads down amid the grasses to **Wasque Point.** There's plenty of wide beach here to sun on, but swimming is dangerous because of strong currents. *East end of Wasque Rd., 5 mi from Chappaquiddick ferry landing,* ☎ *508/627– 7260.* ⊡ *$3 cars, plus $3 per adult, Memorial Day–mid-Sept.; free rest of year.* ☉ *Property: 24 hrs; gatehouse: Memorial Day–Columbus Day, daily 9–5. Rest rooms, drinking water.*

At the end of Dyke Road is the **Dyke's Bridge,** infamous as the scene of the 1969 accident in which a young woman died in a car driven by Senator Edward M. Kennedy. Across the bridge, the **Cape Poge Wildlife Refuge** is more than 6 mi of wilderness—dunes, woods, cedar thickets, moors, salt marshes, ponds, tidal flats, and barrier beach. The best way to get to the refuge is as part of a naturalist-led Jeep drive (☎ 508/627– 3599). Permits for four-wheel-drive vehicles (the cost ranges from $60 to $110) are available on-site or through Coop's Bait and Tackle. ⊠ *East end of Dyke Rd., 3 mi from the Chappaquiddick ferry landing.*

East Beach on Chappaquiddick Island, one of the area's best beaches, is accessible only by boat or Jeep from the Wasque Reservation. The relatively isolated strand, a good place to bird-watch, has heavy surf.

Dining and Lodging

$$$$ ✕ **L'étoile.** The quiet Edwardian charm and many decorative touches
★   at L'étoile perfectly anticipate French preparations that are at once classic and creative. Not to be missed are the fresh New York State foie gras, lobster etuvée with saffron angel pasta tossed with Little Necks and caviar with champagne cream sauce. The Californian and European wines in L'etoile's cellar are well selected, if a little pricey. The outdoor patio is ideal for brunch ($24 prix fixe). ⊠ *27 S. Summer St.,*

☎ 508/627–5187. *Reservations essential. AE, MC, V. Closed Jan.–mid-Feb. and weekdays spring and fall. No lunch.*

$$$$ ✕ **Savoir Fare.** The Mediterranean sensibility of the chefs at Savoir Fare
★ and their terrific choices of ingredients add up to complex dishes like lobster *en brodo* (in broth), made with corn, roasted peppers, and pancetta, served with spicy Sicilian mashed potatoes and lobster vinaigrette with chive oil. ✉ *14 Church St., in courtyard opposite town hall,* ☎ *508/627–9864. AE, MC, V. Closed Nov.–Mar.; Mon.–Wed. in Apr. and Oct. No lunch.*

$–$$ ✕ **The Sand Bar.** More bar than sand, the Sand Bar is a watering hole for fans of the New England Patriots football team. The food is secondary to the sports on the tube out back, or the breeze on the front porch. The same owners run the downstairs CJ's and send up their award-winning clam chowder. ✉ *Main St.,* ☎ *508/627–9027. Reservations not accepted. AE, D, MC, V.*

$$ ✕⌂ **Daggett House.** The flower-bordered lawn that separates the main
★ house from the harbor makes a great retreat after a day of exploring town, a minute away. All three inn buildings—the main 1660 Colonial house, the Captain Warren house across the street, and a three-room cottage between the main house and the water—are decorated with fine wallpapers, antiques, and reproductions. Breakfast and dinner are served in the 1750 tavern. ✉ *Box 1333, 59 N. Water St., 02539,* ☎ *508/627–4600 or 800/946–3400,* ℻ *508/627–4611. 21 rooms, 6 suites. No smoking. AE, MC, V.*

$$$$ ⌂ **Charlotte Inn.** Tastefully and intelligently decorated inside and out—
★ in parlors, guest rooms, suites, and a maze of garden spaces—the Charlotte consummately realizes the values of a bygone era. Come to the inn for an Edwardian fantasy, an escape in one of the luxurious suites in the Carriage or Coach houses, an utterly tranquil winter holiday with the island nearly to yourself, or a sumptuous meal at L'étoile (☞ *above*). ✉ *27 S. Summer St., 02539,* ☎ *508/627–4751,* ℻ *508/627–4652. 25 rooms and 3 suites in 5 buildings. Restaurant. Continental breakfast. AE, MC, V.*

$$$$ ⌂ **Harbor View Hotel.** This historic hotel, centered in an 1891 gray-shingle main building with wraparound veranda and a gazebo, is part of a complex in a residential neighborhood a few minutes from town. Town houses have cathedral ceilings, decks, kitchens, and large living areas with sofa beds. Rooms in other buildings, however, resemble upscale motel rooms. A good beach for walking stretches ¾ mi from the hotel's dock, from which there's good fishing. ✉ *131 N. Water St., 02539,* ☎ *508/627–7000 or 800/225–6005,* ℻ *508/627–7845. 124 units. Restaurant, room service, pool, golf privileges, 2 tennis courts, volleyball, baby-sitting, laundry service, concierge. AE, DC, MC, V.*

$$$$ ⌂ **Mattakesett.** This community of individually owned three- and four-bedroom homes and condominiums is within walking distance of South Beach. All units are spacious, sleep six to eight, and have phones, full kitchens with dishwashers, washer/dryers, and decks. Usually there's a one-week minimum stay. It's best to book for summer by January 15. ✉ *Katama Rd., 02539,* ☎ *508/627–8920; reservations c/o* ✉ *Stanmar Corp., 130 Boston Post Rd., Sudbury, MA 01776,* ☎ *978/443–1733,* ℻ *508/627–7015. 92 units. Pool, 8 tennis courts, aerobics, bicycles, children's programs. No credit cards. Closed Columbus Day–Memorial Day.*

$$$$ ⌂ **Shiverick Inn.** Rooms in this 1840 house are airy and bright, with
★ high ceilings, lots of windows, American and English antiques, rich fabrics and wallpapers, and antique art. Beds are mostly queen-size—canopies or carved four-posters. Several rooms have fireplaces or woodstoves. Breakfast is served in a summerhouse-style room with a wood-burning fireplace. ✉ *Box 640, Peases Point Way and Pent La.,*

02539, ☎ 508/627–3797 or 800/723–4292, FAX 508/627–8441. 10 rooms. Continental breakfast. No smoking. AE, D, MC, V.

$$–$$$$ 🏠 **Harborside Inn.** The inn—seven two- and three-story buildings around a wide lawn with formal rose beds—offers a central town location, harbor-view decks, and plenty of amenities. ⌂ *Box 67, 3 S. Water St., 02539, ☎ 508/627–4321 or 800/627–4009, FAX 508/627–7566. 89 rooms, 3 suites. Pool, hot tub, sauna. AE, MC, V.*

Outdoor Activities and Sports

Big Eye Charters (☎ 508/627–3649) operates fishing charters that leave from Edgartown Harbor. **Coop's Bait and Tackle** (⌂ 147 W. Tisbury Rd., ☎ 508/627–3909) sells accessories and bait, rents fishing gear, and has a list of fishing regulations. **Wheelhappy** (⌂ 8 S. Water St., ☎ 508/627–5928) rents bicycles and will deliver them to you.

Shopping

Bickerton & Ripley Books (⌂ Main St., ☎ 508/627–8463) carries current and island-related titles. **Edgartown Scrimshaw Gallery** (⌂ 43 Main St. , ☎ 508/627–9439) stocks some antique pieces, as well as Nantucket lightship baskets and nautical paintings and sculpture. The **Gallery Shop** (⌂ 20 S. Summer St., ☎ 508/627–8508) sells 19th- and 20th-century oils and watercolors, plus small English antiques. **Optional Art** (⌂ 35 Winter St., ☎ 508/627–5373) carries handcrafted jewelry.

West Tisbury

㉑ *6.6 mi southwest of Vineyard Haven, 11.9 mi northeast of Gay Head.*

Very much the small New England village, complete with a white steepled church, West Tisbury has a vibrant agricultural life, with several active horse and produce farms. The weekly **West Tisbury Farmers' Market**—Massachusetts's largest—is held on Wednesday and Saturday in summer at the 1859 **Agricultural Hall** (⌂ South Rd.), near the town hall.

★ **Winery at Chicama Vineyards** was started in 1971 by George and Cathy Mathiesen and their six children. From 3 acres of trees and rocks, they created a winery that today produces nearly 100,000 bottles a year from chardonnay, cabernet, and other European grapes. ⌂ *Stoney Hill Rd., ☎ 508/693–0309. 🎫 Free. ☉ Memorial Day–Columbus Day, Mon.–Sat. 11–5, Sun. 1–5; call for off-season hrs and tastings.*

Long Point, a 633-acre preserve, is an open area of grassland and heath bounded on the east by the freshwater Homer's Pond, on the west by the saltwater West Tisbury Great Pond, and on the south by a mile of fantastic South Beach on the Atlantic Ocean. Arrive early on summer days if you're coming by car—the lot fills quickly. *Mid-June–mid-Sept., turn left onto the unmarked dirt road (Waldron's Bottom Rd., look for mailboxes) ⁷⁄₁₀ mi west of airport on Edgartown–W. Tisbury Rd., at end, follow signs to Long Point parking lot. Mid-Sept.–mid-June, follow unpaved Deep Bottom Rd. (1 mi west of airport) 2 mi to lot. ☎ 508/693–3678. 🎫 Mid-June–mid-Sept., $7 per vehicle, $3 per adult; free rest of year. ☉ Daily 10–6.*

★ **Lambert's Cove Beach** (⌂ Lambert's Cove Rd.) has fine sand and very clear water. On the Vineyard Sound side, it has calm waters and views of the Elizabeth Islands. In season the beach is restricted to residents and those staying in West Tisbury.

★ At the center of the island, the **Manuel F. Correllus State Forest** is a 2,000-acre pine and scrub-oak forest crisscrossed with hiking trails and circled with a paved but rough bike trail (mopeds are prohibited). There's a 2-mi nature trail, a 2-mi par course, and horse trails. ⌂ *Headquar-*

ters on Barnes Rd. by the airport, ☎ 508/693–2540. 🌊 Free. ☉ Daily dawn–dusk.

Dining and Lodging

$$$–$$$$
★
✕ **Red Cat.** The works of current and former local and summer-resident artists adorn this small restaurant. Chef Benjamin deForest's eclectic menu changes every three weeks. A recurring favorite is the baked tuna, prepared with white beans, Portobello mushrooms, and a grilled-tomato coulis. ⊠ 688 State Rd., near North Rd., ☎ 508/693–9599. Reservations essential in season. MC, V. BYOB. No smoking. No lunch.

$$–$$$
✕🏨 **Lambert's Cove Country Inn.** A narrow road winds through pine woods to this secluded inn surrounded by gardens and old stone walls. Rooms in the 1790 farmhouse have light floral wallpapers and a country feel. Rooms in outbuildings have screened porches or decks. The soft candlelight and excellent Continental cooking make the restaurant (reservations essential; BYOB) a destination for a special occasion. The chef's delicate creations rely on local produce and seafood. Especially good are the crisp-baked soft-shell crab appetizer and the grilled Muscovy duck breast on caramelized onions. ⊠ Off Lambert's Cove Rd., W. Tisbury; ⊠ mailing address R.R. 1, Box 422, Vineyard Haven 02568, ☎ 508/693–2298, 🗷 508/693–7890. 15 rooms. Restaurant, tennis court, basketball. Full breakfast. AE, MC, V.

$
🏨 **Hostelling International–Martha's Vineyard.** The only budget alternative in season, this hostel is one of the country's best. You'll catch wind of local events from the bulletin board, and there is a large common kitchen. Doing morning chores is required in summer. ⊠ Box 158, Edgartown–W. Tisbury Rd., 02575, ☎ 508/693–2665. 78 dorm-style beds. MC, V. Closed daytime 10–5 and completely Nov.–Apr. 11 PM curfew June–Aug.

Nightlife and the Arts

Hot Tin Roof (⊠ Martha's Vineyard Airport, ☎ 508/693–1137), owned by Carly Simon, is the island's hottest club, with big-name artists—Jimmy Cliff, Jerry Lee Lewis, and sometimes Simon herself.

Outdoor Activities and Sports

Stop at the grammar school on Old County Road to reserve one of its hard-surface **tennis courts. Misty Meadows Horse Farm** (⊠ Old County Rd., ☎ 508/693–1870) conducts trail rides.

Chilmark

㉒ 12 mi southwest of Vineyard Haven, 5.4 mi southwest of West Tisbury.

Chilmark is a rural village whose ocean-view roads, rustic woodlands, and lack of crowds have drawn chic summer visitors and resulted in stratospheric real estate prices. Laced with rough roads and winding stone fences that once separated fields and pastures, Chilmark is a reminder of what the Vineyard was like in an earlier time, before developers took over.

★ A dirt road leads off South Road to beautiful **Lucy Vincent Beach,** which in summer is open only to Chilmark residents and those staying in town.

Dining and Lodging

$$$–$$$$
★
✕ **Feast of Chilmark.** Civilized and calming, the Feast is a welcome break from the Vineyard's busier joints. The seafood entrées, light appetizers, and fresh salads play up summer tastes and flavors, and the whole menu takes advantage of local produce. ⊠ Beetlebung Corner, State Rd., ☎ 508/645–3553. AE, MC, V. BYOB. No smoking. No lunch.

$$$$ ✕🖼 **Inn at Blueberry Hill.** Exclusive and secluded, this unique property comprising 56 acres of former farmland puts you in the heart of the rural Vineyard. The restaurant is relaxed and elegant, and the fresh, innovative, and health-conscious food is superb. A popular four-course Sunday supper, for which reservations are essential, is served in the off season. Guest rooms are simply and sparsely decorated with Shaker-inspired island-made furniture, handmade mattresses with all-cotton sheets and duvets, and fresh flowers. Some of the less expensive rooms are on the small side. Though the restaurant serves only dinner, the cooks will prepare box lunches for guests. ⊠ *R.R. 1, Box 309, 74 North Rd., 02535,* ☎ *508/645–3322 or 800/356–3322,* 🄵🄰🄷 *508/645–3799. 25 rooms. Restaurant, pool, hot tub, massage, tennis court, exercise room, meeting room, airport shuttle. Continental breakfast. AE, MC, V. Closed Dec.–Apr.*

Menemsha

★ ㉓ *1.6 mi northwest of Chilmark, 3.5 mi east of Gay Head.*

Unspoiled by the "progress" of the 20th century, Menemsha is a jumble of weathered fishing shacks, fishing and pleasure boats, drying nets, and lobster pots. If you feel like you've seen this charming town before, you probably have: It was used for location shots in the film *Jaws*.

Menemsha Public Beach, adjacent to Dutcher's Dock, is a pebbly beach with gentle surf on Vineyard Sound. On the western side of the island, it is a great place to catch the sunset. There are rest rooms, food concessions, lifeguards, and parking spaces.

Dining and Lodging

$ ✕ **The Bite.** Fried everything—clams, fish-and-chips, you name it—is on the menu at this roadside shack, where two outdoor picnic tables are the only seating options. The Bite closes at 3 PM on weekdays and 7 PM on weekends. ⊠ *Basin Rd.,* ☎ *no phone. No credit cards.*

$ ✕ **Larson's.** Basically a retail fish store, with reasonable prices and su-
★ perb quality, Larson's will open oysters, stuff quahogs, and cook a lobster to order. The best deal is a dozen littlenecks or cherrystones for $6.50. They taste especially good with a bottle of your own wine, sitting at an outdoor picnic tables or on a blue bench. Larson's closes at 6 PM on weekdays and at 7 PM on weekends. ⊠ *Dutcher's Dock,* ☎ *508/645–2680. MC, V. No seating. BYOB. Closed mid-Oct.–mid-May.*

$$$$ ✕🖼 **Beach Plum Inn.** A woodland setting, a panoramic view of the water, and a romantic restaurant (reservations essential; no lunch; BYOB) are among the attractions of this 10-acre retreat. The smoked bluefish and caper pâté served with crusty bread is excellent, as is the roasted loin of pork with chili, coconut, and basil. Crème brûlée doesn't come too much closer to perfection than it does here. The inn's cottages are decorated in casual beach style. Inn rooms—some with private decks with great views—have modern furnishings. Its casual feel makes the Beach Plum a great place to bring children. ⊠ *Beach Plum La., 02552,* ☎ *508/645–9454,* 🄵🄰🄷 *508/645–2801. 5 rooms, 4 cottages. Restaurant, tennis court, croquet. Full breakfast. No pets. No smoking. AE, D, MC, V. Closed mid-Oct.–mid-May.*

$$$–$$$$ 🖼 **Menemsha Inn and Cottages.** All with screened porches, fireplaces,
★ and full kitchens, the cottages here are spaced on 10 acres; some have more privacy and better water views than others. You can also stay in the 1989 inn building or the pleasant Carriage House, both of which have white walls, plush blue or sea-green carpeting, and Appalachian-pine reproduction furniture. All rooms and suites have private decks, most with fine sunset views. ⊠ *Box 38, North Rd., 02552,* ☎ *508/*

645–2521. 9 rooms, 6 suites, 12 cottages. Continental breakfast (inn and Carriage House only). No pets. No credit cards. Closed Nov.–Apr.

Aquinnah (Gay Head)

㉔ *11.9 mi southwest of West Tisbury, 20 mi west of Edgartown.*

The Wampanoag tribe is the guardian of the 420 acres that constitute the Gay Head Native American Reservation. Also in Gay Head is the 380-acre estate of the late Jacqueline Onassis. In 1997, the town voted to change Gay Head back to its original Native American name, **Aquinnah** (pronounced a-*kwih*-nah), which is Wampanoag for "land under the hill"; the official change will take several years to implement fully.

Quitsa Pond Lookout (⊠ State Rd.) has a good view of the adjoining Menemsha and Nashaquitsa ponds, the woods, and the ocean beyond.

From a roadside iron pipe, **Gay Head spring** (⊠ State Rd.) gushes water cold enough to slake a cyclist's thirst on the hottest day. Feel free to fill a canteen. Locals come from all over the island to fill jugs. The spring is just over the town line.

★ The **Gay Head Cliffs,** a National Historic Landmark, are part of the Wampanoag reservation land. These dramatically striated walls of red clay are the island's major attraction, as evidenced by the tour bus–filled parking lot. Native American crafts and food shops line the short approach to the overlook, from which you can see the Elizabeth Islands to the northeast across Vineyard Sound and Noman's Land Island—part wildlife preserve, part military bombing-practice site—3 mi off the Vineyard's southern coast.

Adjacent to the cliffs overlook is the redbrick **Gay Head Lighthouse,** precariously stationed atop the rapidly eroding cliffs. The lighthouse is open to the public on summer weekends at sunset, weather permitting; private tours can also be arranged. ☎ *508/645–2211.* ☞ *$2.*

Striking **Moshup Beach** provides access to the Gay Head Cliffs. Come early in the day to ensure a quieter experience and finding a parking spot. Climbing the cliffs is against the law—they're eroding much too quickly on their own. It's also illegal to take any of the clay with you. ⊠ *Parking lot: State Rd. and Moshup Dr.* ☞ *$15 parking fee Memorial Day–Labor Day.*

Dining and Lodging

$$$$ ✕⊡ **Outermost Inn.** Standing alone on acres of moorland, the inn is
★ wrapped with windows revealing breathtaking views of sea and sky. The restaurant (reservations required; BYOB; no lunch) seats twice for dinner, at 6 and 8 PM four to six nights a week from spring to fall. Dinners are prix fixe, from about $45 to $60. The overall decor of the inn is clean and contemporary, with white walls, local art, and polished light-wood floors. Each room has a phone, and one has a whirlpool tub. ⊠ *Box 171, Lighthouse Rd., 02535,* ☎ *508/645–3511,* ℻ *508/ 645–3514. 7 rooms. Restaurant. Full breakfast. No pets, no children. AE, D, MC, V. Closed Nov.–May.*

Martha's Vineyard A to Z

Arriving and Departing

BY BUS

Bonanza Bus Lines (☎ *508/548–7588* or *800/556–3815*) travels to the Woods Hole ferry port from Rhode Island, Connecticut, and New York year-round.

Car-and-passenger ferries travel to Vineyard Haven from Woods Hole on Cape Cod year-round. In season, passenger ferries from Falmouth and Hyannis on Cape Cod, and from New Bedford, serve Vineyard Haven and Oak Bluffs. All provide parking where you can leave your car overnight—the fees range from $6 to $10 a night.

FROM FALMOUTH: The *Island Queen* makes the 35-minute trip to Oak Bluffs from late May to Columbus Day. ⊠ *Falmouth Harbor,* ☎ *508/ 548–4800.* ▣ *Round-trip: $10, $6 bicycles; one-way: $6, $3 bicycles.*

Patriot Boats (☎ 508/548–2626) allows passengers on its daily Falmouth Harbor–Oak Bluffs mail run in the off-season ($4 one-way) and operates a year-round 24-hour water taxi. You can also charter a boat for about $300.

FROM HYANNIS: Hy-Line makes the 1¾-hour run to Oak Bluffs between May and October. From June to mid-September, the "Around the Sound" cruise makes a one-day round-trip from Hyannis with stops at Nantucket and Martha's Vineyard ($31). Call to reserve a space in summer because the parking lot often fills up. ⊠ *Ocean St. dock,* ☎ *508/778–2600 or 508/778–2602 for reservations; 508/693–0112 in Oak Bluffs.* ▣ *One-way: $11, $4.50 bicycles.*

FROM NANTUCKET: Hy-Line makes 2¼-hour runs to and from Oak Bluffs from early June to mid-September—the only inter-island passenger service. (To get a car from Nantucket to the Vineyard, you must return to the mainland and drive from Hyannis to Woods Hole.) ☎ *508/778– 2600 in Hyannis; 508/693–0112 in Oak Bluffs; 508/228–3949 on Nantucket.* ▣ *One-way: $11, $4.50 bicycles additional.*

FROM WOODS HOLE: The **Steamship Authority** (☎ 508/477–8600 for information and car reservations; 508/693–9130 on the Vineyard; TTY 508/540–1394 for information and car reservations) runs the only car ferries, which make the 45-minute trip to Vineyard Haven year-round and to Oak Bluffs from late May to September. You'll definitely need a reservation in summer or on weekends in the fall. ▣ *One-way in season (mid-May–mid-Oct.): $5 per adult, $44 cars; one-way off-season: $5 per adult, call for car rates. Bicycles: $3 additional.*

Martha's Vineyard Airport (☎ 508/693–7022) is in West Tisbury, 7½ mi west of Edgartown. **Cape Air/Nantucket Airlines** (☎ 508/790– 3122 or 800/352–0714) connects the Vineyard year-round with Boston (including an hourly summer shuttle), Hyannis, Nantucket, and New Bedford. It offers joint fares and ticketing and baggage agreements with several major carriers. **Direct Flight** (☎ 508/693–6688) is a year-round charter service based on the Vineyard.

Edgartown (☎ 508/627–4746). **Menemsha** (☎ 508/645–2846). **Oak Bluffs** (☎ 508/693–4355). **Vineyard Haven** (☎ 508/696–4249).

Getting Around

Driving on the island is fairly simple (though the few main roads can be crowded in summer). You can book rentals by using the free phone at the Woods Hole ferry terminal.

The three-car **On Time** ferry makes the five-minute run to Chappaquiddick Island. ⊠ *Dock St., Edgartown,* ☎ *508/627–9427.* ▣ *Round-trip: $1 individual, $4.50 car and driver, $2.50 bicycle and rider,*

$3.50 moped or motorcycle and rider.☉ *June–mid-Oct., daily 7 AM– midnight, less frequently off-season.*

BY FOUR-WHEEL-DRIVE

Four-wheel-drive vehicles are allowed from Katama Beach to Wasque Reservation with $50 annual permits ($75 for vehicles not registered on the island) sold on the beach in summer, or anytime at the **Dukes County Courthouse** (⊠ Treasurer's Office, Main St., Edgartown 02539, ☎ 508/627–4250) has information about four-wheel-drive permits. The Wasque Reservation has a separate mandatory permit and requires that vehicles carry certain equipment, such as a shovel, tow chains, and rope; call the rangers before setting out for the dunes.

BY LIMOUSINE

Muzik's Limousine Service (☎ 508/693–2212) provides limousine service on- and off-island.

BY MINIBUS IN EDGARTOWN

The **Martha's Vineyard Transit Authority** (☎ 508/627–9663 or 508/ 627–7448) has three shuttle bus routes, two in Edgartown and one in Tisbury. Weekly, monthly, or seasonal passes are available.

BY SHUTTLE BUS

For the current bus schedule, call the **shuttle hot line** (☎ 508/693–1589).

BY TAXI

All Island Taxi (☎ 508/693–3705). **Martha's Vineyard Taxi** (☎ 508/ 693–8660).

Contacts and Resources

B&B RESERVATION AGENCIES

DestINNations (☎ 508/428–5600 or 800/333–4667). **Martha's Vineyard and Nantucket Reservations** (☎ 508/693–7200; 800/649–5671 in Massachusetts).

CAR RENTALS

Budget (☎ 508/693–1911), **Hertz** (☎ 508/693–2402), and **All Island** (☎ 508/693–6868) arrange rentals from their airport desks.

EMERGENCIES

Dial **911** for the hospital, physicians, ambulance services, police, fire departments, or Coast Guard.

Martha's Vineyard Hospital (⊠ Linton La., Oak Bluffs, ☎ 508/693– 0410).

Vineyard Medical Services (⊠ State Rd., Vineyard Haven, ☎ 508/693– 6399) provides walk-in care; call for days and hours.

GUIDED TOURS

The 50-ft sailing catamaran **Arabella** (☎ 508/645–3511) makes day and sunset sails out of Menemsha to Cuttyhunk and the Elizabeth Islands. The teakwood sailing yacht **Ayuthia** (☎ 508/693–7245) sails to Nantucket or the Elizabeth Islands out of Coastwise Wharf in Vineyard Haven. **Liz Villard** (☎ 508/627–8619) leads walking tours of Edgartown's "history, architecture, ghosts, and gossip."

HOUSE RENTALS

Martha's Vineyard Vacation Rentals (⊠ 107 Beach Rd., Box 1207, Vineyard Haven 02568, ☎ 508/693–7711). **Sandcastle Realty** (⊠ Box 2488, 256 Edgartown Rd., Edgartown 02539, ☎ 508/627–5665).

LATE-NIGHT PHARMACIES

Leslie's Drug Store (⊠ 65 Main St., Vineyard Haven, ☎ 508/693–1010) is open daily and has a pharmacist on 24-hour call for emergencies.

Martha's Vineyard Chamber of Commerce is two blocks from the Vineyard Haven ferry. There are town information booths by the Vineyard Haven Steamship terminal, on Circuit Avenue in Oak Bluffs, and on Church Street in Edgartown. ⊠ *Box 1698, Beach Rd., Vineyard Haven 02568,* ☎ *508/693–0085.* ☉ *Weekdays 9–5; also Sat. 10–2 Memorial Day–Labor Day.*

NANTUCKET

At the height of its prosperity in the early to mid-19th century, the little island of Nantucket was the foremost whaling port in the world. Its harbor bustled with whaling ships and merchant vessels. Ship's chandleries, cooperages, and other shops stood cheek by jowl along the wharves. Barrels of whale oil were off-loaded from ships onto wagons, then wheeled along cobblestone streets to refineries and candle factories. Strong sea breezes carried the smoke and smells of booming industry through town as its inhabitants eagerly took care of business. Shipowners and sea captains built elegant mansions that today remain remarkably unchanged, thanks to a very strict code regulating any changes to structures within the town of Nantucket, an official National Historic District.

Visitors on a day trip usually browse in the art galleries, crafts shops, and boutiques downtown, enjoy the architecture and historical museums, and dine at one of the many gourmet restaurants. Those who stay longer will have time to explore more of the island. Its moors—swept with fresh salt breezes and scented with bayberry, wild roses, and cranberries—and its miles of white-sand beaches make Nantucket a respite from the rush and regimentation of life elsewhere. Most shops stay open until Christmas.

Nantucket Town

㉕ *30 mi southeast of Hyannis, 107 mi southeast of Boston.*

The **Nantucket Historical Association** (☎ 508/228–1894) operates 14 historic properties along Nantucket Town's streets as museums. At any of them you can purchase an NHA Visitor Pass ($10), which entitles you to entry at 24 sites and properties, or you can pay single admission at each (prices vary). Most NHA properties close between Columbus Day and Memorial Day, though some have weekend hours starting in April; hours between Labor Day and Columbus Day vary, so call ahead.

The **Peter Foulger Museum and Nantucket Historical Association Research Center** provide a glimpse into Nantucket's genealogical past. The museum displays portraits, textiles, porcelains, silver, and furniture. The Research Center is open only to researchers. ⊠ *Broad St.,* ☎ *508/228–1655.* 🎫 *$4 or NHA pass. Research permit: $10 (2 days).* ☉ *Weekdays 10–4.*

An 1846 factory built for refining spermaceti and making candles ★ houses the **Whaling Museum.** The exhibits here include a fully rigged whaleboat, harpoons and other implements, portraits of sea captains, a large scrimshaw collection, and the skeleton of a 43-ft finback whale. Lectures on whaling history are given daily. ⊠ *Broad St.,* ☎ *508/228–1894.* 🎫 *$5 or NHA pass. Museum closes after Christmas Stroll and reopens on weekends in Apr.*

Built in 1818, the **Pacific National Bank,** at the corner of Main and Fair streets, is a monument to the Nantucket whaling ships it once fi-

Nantucket

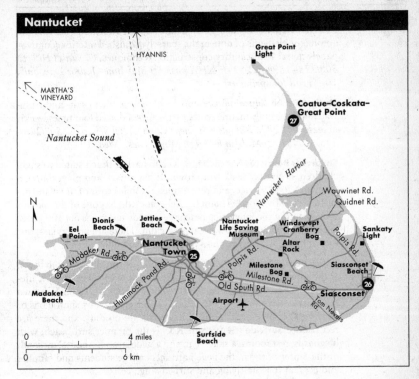

nanced. Above the old-style teller cages, murals show the town as it was in its whaling heyday. At 93–97 Upper Main Street are the **"Three Bricks,"** identical redbrick mansions with columned Greek Revival porches at their front entrances. They were built between 1836 and 1838 by a whaling merchant for his three sons.

Two white porticoed Greek Revival mansions built in 1845–46 stand across the street from the "Three Bricks." One of the buildings, called the **Hadwen House,** is a museum that surveys Nantucket's affluent whaling era. A guided tour points out the grand circular staircase; fine plasterwork; carved Italian marble fireplace mantels; and Regency, Empire, and Victorian furnishings. ⊠ 96 Main St., ☎ $3 or NHA pass. ۞ Mid-June–Labor Day, daily 10–5; spring and fall hrs vary.

The shingles of the 1805 **Old Gaol** (⊠ 15R Vestal St.), which held prisoners until 1933, mask the building's massive square timbers. Walls, ceilings, and floors are bolted with iron.

Several windmills sat on Nantucket hills in the 1700s, but only the **Old Mill,** a 1746 Dutch-style octagonal structure made of lumber from shipwrecks, remains. When the wind is strong enough, corn is ground into meal that is sold here. ⊠ S. Mill St., ☎ 508/228–1894. ☎ $2. ۞ Mid-June–Labor Day, daily 10–5; Memorial Day–mid-June and Labor Day–Columbus Day, daily 11–3. Call for hrs rest of yr.

★ The tower of the **First Congregational Church** provides the best view of Nantucket—for those who climb the 92 steps. Rising 120 ft, the tower is capped by a weather vane that depicts a whale catch. Peek in at the church's 1850 trompe l'oeil ceiling. ⊠ 62 Centre St., ☎ 508/228–0950. ☎ $3. ۞ Mid-June–mid-Oct., Mon.–Sat. 10–4.

The **Oldest House,** a 1686 saltbox also called the Jethro Coffin House, really is the oldest house on the island. The structure's most noteworthy element is the massive central brick chimney with a giant brick horse-shoe adornment. Leaded-glass windows and enormous hearths are among the elements of note in the sparsely furnished interior. Cutaway panels reveal 17th-century construction techniques. ⊠ *Sunset Hill,* ☎ *508/228–1894.* ▢ *$3 or NHA pass.* ☉ *Mid-June–Labor Day, daily 10–5; call for spring hrs.*

Maria Mitchell Aquarium presents local marine life in salt- and fresh-water tanks. Family marine ecology trips are conducted four times weekly in season. ⊠ *28 Washington St., near Commercial Wharf,* ☎ *508/228–5387.* ▢ *$1.* ☉ *Mid-June–Aug., Mon., Tues., Wed. 10–4.*

Children's Beach (⊠ S. Beach St.), a calm harbor beach suited to small children, is an easy walk from town. It has a park and playground, a lifeguard, food service, and rest rooms. Six miles west of town and accessible only by foot, **Eel Point** (⊠ Eel Point Rd.) has one of the island's most beautiful and interesting beaches—a sandbar extends out 100 yards, keeping the water shallow, clear, and calm. There are no services, just lots of birds, wild berries and bushes, and solitude.

Jetties Beach (⊠ Hulbert Ave.), a short bike or shuttle ride from town, is the most popular beach for families because of its calm surf, life-guards, bathhouse, snack bar, water-sports rentals, and tennis. Known for great sunsets and surf, **Madaket Beach** is reached by shuttle bus or the Madaket bike path (6 mi). Lifeguards are on duty, and there are rest rooms. **Surfside** (⊠ Surfside Rd.) is the premier surf beach, with lifeguards, rest rooms, a snack bar, and a wide strand. About 2 mi south of the center of town, the beach attracts college students and families and is great for kite-flying and surf casting.

Dining and Lodging

$$$–$$$$ ✕ **American Seasons.** The culinary context here is geographic: From
★ the four corners of the continental United States, chef and owner Michael Getter gathers specialties. You can mix and match, taking Nan-tucket lobster for an appetizer and then a loin of pork for the main course. Anywhere you travel on the menu, you'll find excellent prepa-rations. ⊠ *80 Centre St.,* ☎ *508/228–7111. No smoking. AE, MC, V. Closed mid-Dec.–early Apr. No lunch.*

$$$–$$$$ ✕ **DeMarco.** Winner of the 1997 award from *Cape Cod Life* as "Best Ethnic Restaurant on Nantucket," it perhaps says more about Nan-tucket than DeMarco that basic northern Italian food is considered "eth-nic" here. The selection of pasta dishes is strong, especially the *maltagliata alla boschaiola* ("badly cut" fresh triangles of pasta in a tangy sauce of pomodoro and wild mushrooms). Among the entrées is *filleto di rombo* (an olive-crusted halibut steak served over a roasted-tomato salsa). ⊠ *9 India St.,* ☎ *508/228–1836. AE, MC, V. Closed Jan.–Apr. No lunch.*

$$$–$$$$ ✕ **India House.** Chefs Michael Caracciolo and Dereck Brewley prepare
★ splendid food, particularly the calamari appetizer with penne and olives and the swordfish entrée with a topping of glazed roasted pecans and cashews. Starting on the Fourth of July, an excellent brunch, usu-ally served outdoors, includes three-berry French toast and poached eggs with smoked salmon and caviar. ⊠ *37 India St.,* ☎ *508/228–9043. Reservations not accepted for brunch. AE, D, MC, V. Closed Jan.–Mar. No lunch.*

$$$–$$$$ ✕ **21 Federal.** The epitome of sophisticated, gentrified island dining,
★ 21 Federal serves some of the island's best new and traditional Amer-ican cuisine. Entrées include Muscovy duck breast and country-grill items like aged sirloin steak and veal chop; a standout dish is the potato-crusted salmon with a lemon beurre-blanc sauce. ⊠ *21 Fed-*

eral St., ☎ *508/228–2121. AE, MC, V. Closed Jan.–Mar., Sun. Apr.–Memorial Day and Columbus Day–Dec.*

$$–$$$ ✕ **Obadiah's Native Seafood.** Bluefish, yellowtail sole, scallops, lobster, swordfish, scrod—fish has been Obadiah's stock in trade for more than 20 years. The patio is especially nice, and you can order children's portions of many of the main dishes at half price plus $2. This is easily the best straight-ahead seafood value on the island. ⊠ *2 India St., at Independence La.,* ☎ *508/228–4430. AE, MC, V.*

$–$$ ✕ **Atlantic Cafe.** The Atlantic has been the island's belly-up-to-the-bar
★ hangout since 1978. Two big, salty codfish cakes with plenty of slaw and fries helps the beer go down. "Mary and the Boys" is a Bloody Mary with six shrimp. ⊠ *15 S. Water St.,* ☎ *508/228–0570. AE, DC, MC, V.*

$–$$ ✕ **Off Centre Café.** Blackboard specials carry the day at this small café, especially the fish chowder or the ratatouille. The owners of Off Centre Café also run a bread and dessert retail and wholesale business. ⊠ *29 Centre St.,* ☎ *508/228–8470. No credit cards. No lunch in season.*

$ ✕ **Espresso Café.** You can get a muffin and a cappuccino here for breakfast; for lunch and early dinner (the café closes at 8 PM) sandwiches, thin-crust pizzas (the feta and black olive is the best), curried lamb stew, veggie quesadillas, and jalapeño corn bread, and other dishes served. ⊠ *40 Main St.,* ☎ *508/228–6930. Reservations not accepted. No credit cards.*

$$$$ ✕🏨 **Harbor House.** This family-oriented complex prides itself on its
★ service. Standard rooms are done in English-country style, with bright floral fabrics and queen-size beds. The 1886 main inn and several "town houses" are set on a flower-filled quadrangle very near the town center. All rooms have phones and TVs. The hotel's restaurant serves simple New England fare—there's a three-course early-bird special between 5 and 6:30. The lavish Sunday brunch buffet (reservations essential) includes a raw bar and a dessert table. ⊠ *Box 1139, S. Beach St., 02554,* ☎ *508/228–1500; 800/475–2637 for reservations,* FAX *508/228–7639. 111 rooms. Restaurant, lounge, room service, concierge, business services. AE, D, DC, MC, V. Closed mid-Dec.–mid-Apr.*

$$$$ 🏨 **Centerboard Guest House.** White walls, blond-wood floors, and natural woodwork create a dreamy atmosphere at this inn a few blocks
★ from the center of town. Stained-glass lamps, antique quilts, and fresh flowers adorn the rooms; the first-floor suite is stunning, with 11-ft ceilings, a Victorian living room with fireplace and bar, inlaid parquet floors, superb furnishings, and a green-marble bath with Jacuzzi. ⊠ *8 Chester St., 02554,* ☎ *508/228–9696. 6 rooms, 1 suite. Continental breakfast. No smoking. AE, MC, V.*

$$$$ 🏨 **White Elephant.** A wide lawn separates this complex from Nantucket Harbor. The rooms have an English country look, with stenciled pine armoires, sponge-painted walls, and floral fabrics. A similar decor characterizes the one- to three-bedroom cottages (some with full kitchens). The main hotel has a formal restaurant with a waterside outdoor café, a lounge with entertainment, and a large harbor-front pool. ⊠ *Box 1139, 50 Easton St., 02554,* ☎ *508/228–2500; 800/475–2637 for room reservations,* FAX *508/325–1195. 48 rooms, 32 cottages. Restaurant, lounge, room service, pool, croquet, concierge, meeting rooms. AE, D, DC, MC, V. Closed late Oct.–early May.*

$$$–$$$$ 🏨 **Westmoor Inn.** The many common areas in this yellow Federal-style
★ mansion include a wide lawn set with Adirondack chairs, a garden patio secluded behind 11-ft hedges, a large living room, and a wicker-filled sunroom. The guest rooms are decorated in country-French style; most have soft florals and stenciled walls. One first-floor suite has a giant bath with extra-large Jacuzzi and French doors opening onto the lawn. ⊠ *Cliff Rd., 02554,* ☎ *508/228–0877,* FAX *508/228–5763. 14 rooms. Bicycles. Continental breakfast. No smoking. AE, MC, V. Closed early Dec.–mid-Apr.*

$$$ ✿ **76 Main Street.** Every room at this 1883 inn has charm and a sim-
★ ple, homespun comfort. Room 3 has wonderful woodwork, a carved-
wood armoire, and twin four-posters; Room 1 has large windows,
massive redwood pocket doors, and an eyelet-dressed canopy bed. The
motel-like annex rooms have low ceilings, but they are spacious enough
for families. ⊠ *76 Main St., Nantucket 02554,* ☎ *508/228–2533. 18
rooms. Refrigerators. Continental breakfast. No smoking. AE, D,
MC, V. Closed Jan.–Apr.*

$$–$$$ ✿ **Cliff Lodge.** Wainscoting, wide-board floors, and other elements lend
★ this 1771 lodge an old-timey feel (as do the decidedly small bath-
rooms in some rooms). The very pleasant apartment has a living room
with a fireplace, a private deck and entrance, and a large eat-in kitchen.
The common areas include a wicker sunporch, a garden patio, and a
roof walk that has a great view of the harbor. ⊠ *9 Cliff Rd., 02554,*
☎ *508/228–9480,* FAX *508/228–6308. 11 rooms, 1 apartment. Con-
tinental breakfast. No smoking. MC, V.*

$ ✿ **Nesbitt Inn.** This family-run guest house in the center of town has
comfortable rooms (including inexpensive singles) done in authenti-
cally Victorian style, with lace curtains, some marble-top and brass an-
tiques, and a sink in each room. Some beds are not as firm as they should
be, but the Nesbitt is a very good buy in this town. Ask for a room
away from the popular bar-restaurant next door. ⊠ *Box 1019, 21 Broad
St., Nantucket 02554,* ☎ *508/228–0156 or 508/228–2446. 9 dou-
bles and 3 singles share 4 baths. Grill, no-smoking rooms, refrigera-
tor. Continental breakfast. No pets. MC, V.*

Nightlife and the Arts

NIGHTLIFE

A pianist at the formal, harbor-view **Brandt Point Grill at the White Ele-
phant** (⊠ Easton St., ☎ 508/228–2500) plays show tunes on most nights
from Memorial Day to mid-September. The **Brotherhood of Thieves** (⊠
23 Broad St., ☎ no phone) presents folk musicians and has a well-stocked
bar. **Hearth at the Harbor House** (⊠ S. Beach St., ☎ 508/228–1500)
hosts dancing to live music (from country to folk) on weekends; on
most nights in season you can also hear Top-40 tunes by a piano-and-
vocal duo. Folks of all ages dance at the **The Muse** (⊠ 44 Surfside Rd.,
☎ 508/228–6873 or 508/228–8801) to rock, reggae, and other music,
live or recorded.

THE ARTS

Actors Theatre of Nantucket (⊠ Methodist Church, 2 Centre St., ☎
508/228–6325) presents Broadway-style plays between Memorial Day
and Columbus Day, children's post-beach matinees in July and August,
comedy nights, and other events. **Band concerts** (☎ 508/228–7213)
take place at 6:30 PM on some summer Sundays at Children's Beach.
The **Nantucket Musical Arts Society** (☎ 508/228–1287) presents Tues-
day-evening concerts in July and August at the First Congregational
Church (⊠ 62 Centre St.). **Theatre Workshop of Nantucket** (⊠ Ben-
nett Hall, 62 Centre St., ☎ 508/228–4305), a community theater, stages
plays, musicals, and readings.

Outdoor Activities and Sports

BIRD-WATCHING

The Maria Mitchell Association (⊠ Vestal St., ☎ 508/228–9198) or-
ganizes wildflower and bird walks from June to Labor Day.

BOATING

Nantucket Harbor Sail (⊠ Swain's Wharf, ☎ 508/228–0424) rents sail-
boats and outboards.

FISHING

Barry Thurston's Fishing Tackle (⊠ Harbor Sq., ☎ 508/228–9595) dispenses fishing tips and rents gear. The **Herbert T.** (⊠ Slip 14, ☎ 508/228–6655) and other boats are available for seasonal charter from Straight Wharf.

ROLLERBLADING

Nantucket Sports Locker (⊠ 14 Cambridge St., ☎ 508/228–6610) rents Rollerblades.

WATER SPORTS

Force 5 Watersports (⊠ Jetties Beach, ☎ 508/228–5358; ⊠ 37 Main St., ☎ 508/228–0700) rents Sunfish, Windsurfers, kayaks, surfboards, and other water gear.

WHALE-WATCHING

Nantucket Whalewatch (⊠ Hy-Line dock, Straight Wharf, ☎ 978/283–0313 or 800/942–5464) operates naturalist-led full-day excursions ($65; reservations essential) on Tuesday from mid-July to August.

Shopping

ANTIQUES

Forager House Collection (⊠ 20 Centre St., ☎ 508/228–5977) specializes in folk art and Americana. **Janis Aldridge** (⊠ 50 Main St., ☎ 508/228–6673) carries home furnishings and beautifully framed antique engravings. **Nina Hellman Antiques** (⊠ 48 Centre St., ☎ 508/228–4677) carries scrimshaw, ship models, nautical instruments, and other marine antiques, plus folk art and Nantucket memorabilia. **Paul La Paglia** (⊠ 38 Centre St., ☎ 508/228–8760) has moderately priced antique prints. **Tonkin of Nantucket** (⊠ 33 Main St., 02584, ☎ 508/228–9697) has two floors of fine English antiques.

BOOKS

The stock at **Mitchell's Book Corner** (⊠ 54 Main St., ☎ 508/228–1080) includes books on Nantucket and whaling and ocean-related children's titles. **Nantucket Bookworks** (⊠ 25 Broad St., ☎ 508/228–4000) carries hardcover and paperback books, with an emphasis on children's books and literary works.

CLOTHING

Cordillera Imports (⊠ 18 Broad St., ☎ 508/228–6140) sells jewelry, affordable clothing in natural fibers, and crafts from Latin America, Asia, and elsewhere. **Murray's Toggery Shop** (⊠ 62 Main St., ☎ 508/228–0437) stocks traditional footwear and clothing—including the famous Nantucket Reds—for men, women, and children. An outlet store (⊠ 7 New St., ☎ 508/228–3584) has discounts of up to 50%.

CRAFTS

Four Winds Craft Guild (⊠ 6 Ray's Ct., ☎ 508/228–9623) carries a antique and new scrimshaw and lightship baskets, as well as ship models, duck decoys, and a kit for making your own lightship basket.

GALLERIES AND GIFTS

The **Museum Shop** (⊠ Broad St. next to the Whaling Museum, ☎ 508/228–5785) has island-related books, antique whaling tools, reproduction furniture, and toys. **Robert Wilson Galleries** (⊠ 34 Main St., ☎ 508/228–6246 or 508/228–2096) carries contemporary American marine, impressionist, and other art. **Seven Seas Gifts** (⊠ 46 Centre St., ☎ 508/228–0958) stocks inexpensive gift and souvenir items, including shells, baskets, toys, and Nantucket jigsaw puzzles.

Siasconset

★ ㉖ *7 mi east of Nantucket Town, 9 mi northeast of Surfside.*

First a whaling town and then an artist's colony, Siasconset (or 'Sconset, as locals call their town) is a charming village of streets with tiny rose-covered cottages and driveways of crushed white shells. At the central square are the post office, a liquor store, a bookstore, a market, and two restaurants. **Siasconset Beach,** at the end of a 7-mi bike path, is an uncrowded beach with sometimes heavy surf and a lifeguard; rest rooms and food are nearby.

★ The **Milestone Bog,** more than 200 acres of working cranberry bogs surrounded by conservation land, is always a beautiful sight to behold, especially during the fall harvest, which begins in September and continues for six weeks. At any time of year, the bog and the moors have a remarkable quiet beauty that's well worth experiencing.

A good spot for bird-watching, **Sesachacha Pond** (pronounced seh-*sah*-kah-cha or, more often here, where long words seem to be too much trouble, just *sah*-kah-cha) is circled by a walking path that leads to an Audubon wildlife area.

An unmarked dirt track off Polpis Road between Wauwinet and Siasconset leads to **Altar Rock,** from which the view is spectacular. The rock sits on a high spot amid open moor and bog land—technically called lowland heath—which is very rare in the United States. The entire area, of which the Milestone Bog is a part, is laced with paths leading in every direction. Keep track of the trails you travel so you'll be able to find your way back.

Dining and Lodging

$$$$ ✕ **Chanticleer.** For more than 20 years, Anne and Jean-Charles Berruet
★ have been serving superb French food in a formal country setting, complete with clematis cascading down the weathered shingles. Their wine cellar is among the best in the country. As for freshness and presentation, the food is unimpeachable and the desserts are profoundly rich. Dining here is a commitment to a classic (stuffy to some) form of elegance—think of it as entering the set of an elaborate play. ⊠ *9 New St.,* ☎ *508/257–6231. Jacket. AE, MC, V. Closed Mon.*

$$$–$$$$ ✕ **'Sconset Café.** If you stop by this café and there is no table (as is often
★ the case), someone will give you a beeper, send you down to the beach or over to the nearby Summer House for a drink, and beep you when your table is ready. On the dinner menu are local fish and a few other items like duck; for lunch are reasonably priced sandwiches and salads. ⊠ *Post Office Sq.,* ☎ *508/257–4008. Reservations essential for first dinner seating at 6 PM and not accepted at other times. . No credit cards. BYOB (liquor store next door).Closed Columbus Day–mid-May.*

$$$$ ✕🏠 **Summer House.** Some find the service at the restaurant here (reservations essential for dinner) overly fussy, but most patrons enjoy the 'Sconset bluff ocean views and live piano music. The seafood specials are often the highlights of the menu. Lunch at the poolside café is very relaxing. Each one- or two-bedroom cottage at Summer House is furnished in romantic English country style: trompe-l'oeil-bordered white walls, Laura Ashley floral accents, white eyelet spreads, and stripped English-pine antique furnishings. ⊠ *Box 800, Ocean Ave., 02564,* ☎ *508/257–4577,* 𝔽𝔸𝕏 *508/257–4590. 8 cottages. 2 restaurants, bar, piano bar, pool. Continental breakfast. AE, MC, V. Closed Nov.–late Apr.*

$$$$ 🏠 **Wade Cottages.** On a bluff overlooking the ocean, this complex of guest rooms, apartments, and cottages in 'Sconset couldn't be better located for beach lovers: The buildings are arranged around a central lawn with a great ocean view. Most inn rooms and cottages have sea

views, and all have phones. Furnishings are generally in somewhat worn beach style, with some antique pieces. ⊠ *Box 211, Shell St., 02564,* ☎ *508/257–6308,* FAX *508/257–4602; 212/989–6423 off-season. 8 rooms (3-night minimum), 4 with private bath; 6 apartments (1-wk minimum); 3 cottages (2-wk minimum). Refrigerator, badminton, Ping-Pong, beach, coin laundry. Continental breakfast. MC, V. Closed mid-Oct.–late May.*

Outdoor Activities and Sports

BIKING

The 8-mi **Polpis Bike Path,** a long trail with gentle hills, winds alongside Polpis Road past the moors, the cranberry bogs, and Sesachacha Pond almost into Siasconset. The 6-mi **'Sconset Bike Path** starts at the rotary east of town and parallels Milestone Road, ending in the village. It is mostly level, with some gentle hills and benches and drinking fountains at strategic locations along the way.

NATURE TOURS

The Trustees of Reservations sponsor naturalist-led **Great Point Natural History Tours** (☎ 508/228–6799).

En Route A scenic drive along Polpis Road takes you past the precariously perched **Sankaty Light,** built in 1849, and large areas of open moorland. The entrance to the 205-acre **Windswept Cranberry Bog,** open to walkers and bike riders, is also on Polpis, between Quidnet and Wauwinet roads.

Coatue–Coskata–Great Point

㉗ *12¾ mi from Nantucket Town to Great Point Light, 11 mi from 'Sconset.*

Wauwinet Road leads to the gateway of Coatue–Coskata–Great Point, an unpopulated spit of sand comprising three cooperatively managed wildlife refuges that can be entered only on foot or by four-wheel-drive over-sand vehicle—phone 508/228–2884 for information. The area's beaches, dunes, salt marshes, and stands of oak and cedar provide a major habitat for marsh hawks, oystercatchers, terns, herring gulls, and other birds. Because of frequent dangerous currents and riptides and the lack of lifeguards, swimming is strongly discouraged, especially around the **Great Point Light.**

The **Nantucket Life Saving Museum,** on the road back to town from Great Point, is housed in a re-creation of an 1874 Life Saving Service station. Exhibits include photos, original rescue equipment and boats, and accounts of daring rescues. ⊠ *Polpis Rd.,* ☎ *508/228–1885.* ☜ *$3.* ☉ *Mid-June–mid-Sept., Tues.–Sun. 9:30–5.*

Dining and Lodging

$$$$ ✕🏠 **Wauwinet.** Some people would say that this historic 19th-century
★ hotel is the only place to stay on Nantucket. The tasteful Topper's restaurant (dinner reservations essential) serves alluring dishes like pan-seared sea scallops with lobster risotto and roasted rack of cervena (venison from a farm-raised New Zealand deer) with creamy polenta and forest-mushroom glaze. Brunch comes highly recommended. The rooms and cottages are decorated in country-beach style, with pine antiques; some have views of the sunset over the water. A wonderful breakfast is included in room rates, as is afternoon port or sherry and cheese. There are also boat shuttles to Coatue beach across the harbor and, perhaps best of all, the innkeeper runs a Land Rover tour of the Great Point reserve—all of which are included in the room rate. Jitney service to and from town 8 mi away, plus Steamship pickup, make the

hotel a convenient place to stay if you don't have a car. ✉ *Box 2580, Wauwinet Rd., 02584,* ☎ *508/228–0145 or 800/426–8718,* FAX *508/ 228–7135. 25 rooms, 5 cottages. Restaurant, bar, room service, 2 tennis courts, croquet, boating, mountain bikes, library, concierge, business services. Full breakfast. AE, DC, MC, V. Closed Nov.–Apr.*

Nantucket A to Z

Arriving and Departing

BY FERRY

Year-round service is available from Hyannis only. Hy-Line has two boats, one of which runs between Nantucket and Martha's Vineyard in summer only. The only way to get a car to Nantucket is on the Steamship Authority. To get a car from the Vineyard to Nantucket, you would have to return to Woods Hole, drive to Hyannis, and take the ferry from there.

The **Steamship Authority** (☎ 508/228–3274 on Nantucket, 508/477–8600 on the Cape) runs car-and-passenger ferries to the island from Hyannis year-round. The trip takes 2¼ hours. ✎ *One-way fare $10; bicycles $5; cars $90 mid-May–mid-Oct., $70 mid-Oct.–Nov. and mid-Mar.–mid-May, $50 Dec.–mid-Mar.*

Hy-Line (☎ 508/228–3949 on Nantucket, 508/778–2600 in Hyannis) departs from Hyannis from early May to October. The trip takes from 1¾ to 2 hours. The cost one-way is $11, plus $4.50 for bicycles. There is also service from Oak Bluffs on Martha's Vineyard (☎ 508/693–0112) from early June to mid-September; that trip takes 2¼ hours and costs the same.

Hy-Line's high-end, high-speed boat, *The Grey Lady,* ferries passengers from Hyannis and back year-round. The trip takes just over an hour. That speed has its downside in rough seas—lots of bouncing and lurching that some find nauseating. ✉ *Ocean St. dock,* ☎ *508/778–0404 or 800/492–8082.* ✎ *One-way fare: $29; bicycles $4.50.*

BY PLANE

Nantucket Memorial Airport (☎ 508/325–5300) is about 3½ mi southeast of town via Old South Road; cars and four-wheel-drive vehicles can be rented at the airport. **Cape Air/Nantucket Air** (☎ 508/771–6944, 508/228–6234, 800/352–0714; 800/635–8787 in Massachusetts) flies from Hyannis year-round and runs charters.

Getting Around

BY BICYCLE AND MOPED

Nantucket Bike Shop (✉ Steamboat Wharf, ☎ 508/228–1999), open between April and October, rents bicycles and mopeds and provides an excellent touring map. Daily rentals typically cost from $15 to $30 for a bicycle and from $30 to $60 for a moped, though half-, full-, and multiple-day rates are available.

BY BUS

From mid-June to Labor Day, **Barrett's Tours** (✉ 20 Federal St., ☎ 508/228–0174 or 800/773–0174), across from the Information Bureau in Nantucket Town, runs beach shuttles to 'Sconset ($5 round-trip, $3 one-way), Surfside ($3 round-trip, $2 one-way), and Jetties ($1 one-way) several times daily. Children pay half fare to 'Sconset and Surfside. The **Nantucket Regional Transit Authority** (☎ 508/228–7025; TDD 508/325–0788) runs shuttle buses around the island between June and September. Most service begins at 7 AM and ends at 11 PM. Fares are 50¢ in town, $1 to 'Sconset and Madaket, $10 for a three-day pass, $15 for a seven-day pass, and $30 for a one-month pass. Seasonal passes are also available.

A-1 Taxi (☎ 508/228–3330). **All Points Taxi** (☎ 508/228–5779). **BG's Taxi** (☎ 508/228–4146).

Contacts and Resources

CAR RENTALS
Budget (☎ 508/228–5666). **Hertz** (☎ 508/228–9421). **Nantucket Windmill** (☎ 508/228–1227 or 800/228–1227).

EMERGENCIES
Nantucket Cottage Hospital (✉ 57 Prospect St., ☎ 508/228–1200).

GUIDED TOURS
The third-generation Nantucketers at **Barrett's Tours** (✉ 20 Federal St., ☎ 508/228–0174) conduct 1½-hour bus tours of the island. **Carried Away** (☎ 508/228–0218) takes people on narrated carriage rides through the Nantucket's historic district in season and on 19th-century-style picnics. Sixth-generation Nantucketer Gail Johnson of **Gail's Scenic Rides** (☎ 508/257–6557) narrates a lively 1½-hour van tour of island highlights. **Nantucket Whalewatch** (✉ Straight Wharf, Hy-Line dock, ☎ 508/283–0313 or 800/942–5464) runs naturalist-led excursions in season. **Roger Young's** historic walking tours (☎ 508/228–1062) of Nantucket's town center are entertaining and leisurely.

HARBOR FACILITIES
The **Boat Basin** (☎ 508/228–1333 or 800/626–2628) operates harbor facilities year-round, with shower and laundry facilities (in season only), electric power, cable TV, phone hookups, a fuel dock, and summer concierge service.

HOUSE RENTALS
Congdon & Coleman (✉ 57 Main St., Nantucket 02554, ☎ 508/325–5000, FAX 508/325–5025). **'Sconset Real Estate** (✉ Box 122, Siasconset 02564, ☎ 508/257–6335; 508/228–1815 in winter).

LATE-NIGHT PHARMACY
Nantucket Pharmacy (✉ 45 Main St., ☎ 508/228–0180) stays open until 10 from Memorial Day to Labor Day.

RESERVATION AGENCIES
DestINNations (☎ 800/333–4667). ☎ 508/257–4000). **Martha's Vineyard and Nantucket Reservations** (☎ 508/693–7200; 800/649–5671 in Massachusetts).

The **Nantucket Information Bureau** (✉ 25 Federal St., ☎ 508/228–0925) monitors room availability in season and at holidays for last-minute bookings. At night, check the lighted board outside for available rooms.

VISITOR INFORMATION
The **Chamber of Commerce** (✉ Pacific Club, 48 Main St., Nantucket 02554, ☎ 508/228–1700). **Nantucket Visitors Service and Information Bureau** (✉ 25 Federal St., ☎ 508/228–0925).

THE NORTH SHORE

Updated by
Kirsten C.
Sadler

The slice of Atlantic coast known as the North Shore extends past grimy docklands, through Boston's well-to-do northern suburbs, to the picturesque Cape Ann region, and beyond Cape Ann to Newburyport, just south of New Hampshire. It encompasses Marblehead, a quintessential New England sea town; historic Salem; Gloucester, the oldest seaport in America; quaint Rockport, crammed with crafts shops and artists' studios; Newburyport and its redbrick center and rows of clapboard

The North Shore

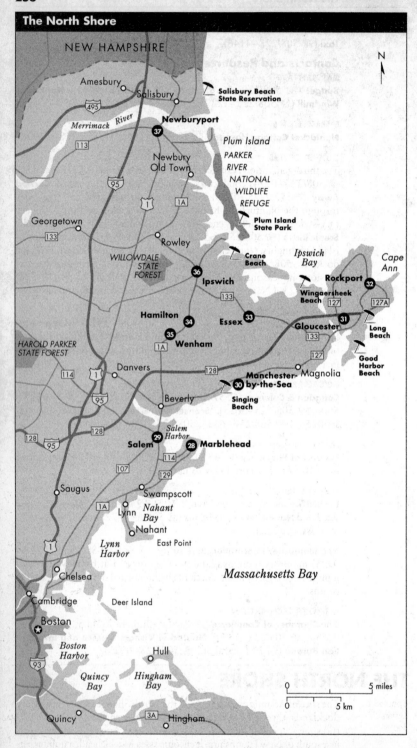

NEW HAMPSHIRE

Amesbury

Salisbury

Salisbury Beach
State Reservation

495

Merrimack River

Newburyport
37

113

Newbury
Old Town

Plum Island

PARKER
RIVER
NATIONAL
WILDLIFE
REFUGE

95

1

1A

Georgetown

Plum Island
State Park

133

Rowley

*Ipswich
Bay*

*Cape
Ann*

Crane
Beach

*WILLOWDALE
STATE
FOREST*

36

Rockport
32

Ipswich

Wingaersheek
Beach

127

127A

133

Hamilton
34

Essex
33

35

Gloucester
31

*HAROLD PARKER
STATE FOREST*

Wenham

1A

Long
Beach

114

1

Danvers

128

133

127

Magnolia

Good
Harbor
Beach

95

Beverly

**Manchester-
by-the-Sea**
30

Singing
Beach

128

128

*Salem
Harbor*

95

Salem
29

Marblehead
28

107

114

Saugus

129

1

Swampscott

1A

Lynn

*Nahant
Bay*

Nahant

*Lynn
Harbor*

East Point

Massachusetts Bay

Chelsea

Cambridge

Boston

Deer Island

93

*Boston
Harbor*

Hull

*Quincy
Bay*

*Hingham
Bay*

0   5 miles

0   5 km

Quincy

3A

Hingham

N

Federal mansions; and miles of beaches. Bright and busy in the short summer season, the North Shore is calmer between November and June.

Marblehead

 15 mi north of Boston.

Marblehead is the gem of the North Shore. Its narrow, winding streets hold ancient clapboard houses and sea captains' mansions whose occupants impress neighbors and visitors with an annual window-box competition. Old Town Marblehead retains much of the character of the village founded in 1629 by fishermen from Cornwall and the Channel Islands. The town's present-day fishing fleet pales, however, in comparison to the armada of pleasure craft that anchors in the harbor: This is the yachting capital of America, and Race Week (usually the last week of July) draws boats from all along the eastern seaboard. Marblehead contains fine restaurants and shops whose owners aren't putting on a show for seasonal tourists but are there to serve year-round residents who won't settle for less than the best. Parking can be difficult; try the 30-car public lot at the end of Front Street, the lot on State Street by the Landing restaurant, or the metered areas on the street.

Plaques on homes tell the date of construction and the original owner. A few mansions are owned and operated by the town historical society and are open to the public. One exquisite example of Marblehead's high society of yore can be seen in the **Jeremiah Lee Mansion.** Colonel Lee was one of the wealthiest people in the colonies in 1768, and although few furnishings original to the house remain, the mahogany paneling, hand-painted wallpaper, and other appointments provide a glimpse into the life of an American gentleman. ⊠ *161 Washington St.,* ☎ *781/ 631–1069.* ◪ *Free.* ☉ *May–mid-Oct., Mon.–Sat. 10–4, Sun. 1–4.*

Marblehead's Victorian municipal building, **Abbott Hall** (built circa 1876), houses A. M. Willard's painting *The Spirit of '76.* One of America's treasured patriotic icons, it depicts three Revolutionary veterans with fife, drum, and flag. The deed used to buy the town from the Nanapashemet Indians and other artifacts of Marblehead's history are also on display. ⊠ *188 Washington St.,* ☎ *781/631–0528.* ☉ *June–Oct., Mon.–Tues. and Thurs. 8–5, Wed. 2:30–8:30, Fri. 8–6.*

Most of exclusive Marblehead Neck, ("the Neck," as it is called by locals), is privately owned, but **Castle Rock** is a spectacular bit of granite where the public can roam. A well-hidden grassy path leads to a small rocky point jutting into the Atlantic. The spot got its name because the closest house is a large stone manor locally known as The Castle. Look for the wrought-iron fence and park on the street. ⊠ *Harbor Ave., Marblehead Neck.*

The Massachusetts Audubon Society operates a section of the Neck as a bird sanctuary, with walking paths and a small pond on which winter skaters glide. Parking is available at the entrances, on Risley Road or Flint Street (off Ocean Avenue). Marblehead is not known for sprawling beaches, but the ones it does have are well maintained and low-profile—mostly used by "'headers" (natives of Marblehead) for family outings or a quick dip in the Atlantic. **Deveraux Beach** (⊠ Ocean Ave. just before the causeway), the most spacious, has some sandy areas and others covered with pebbles. The fee for parking is $5 for nonresidents. The other town beaches are only a few minutes' walk from Old Town. **Grace Oliver's Beach** (⊠ off Beach St.) is small and sandy. **Gashouse Beach** (⊠ Orne St.) is covered with mussel shells. Both are good places to bring kids for a swim or for a picnic lunch.

If the sand and shells aren't for you, continue on Orne Street and take a left on Pond Road to find **Redd's Pond,** named for a Marblehead resident who was convicted and killed during the Salem witch trials. This pond is the site of serious model-sailboat regattas. Every Sunday and some days during the week, you can watch sailors maneuver their boats. In the winter Redd's Pond and **Black Joe's Pond** (⊠ Gingerbread Hill) are fun spots to skate.

Another place for a walk and view of Marblehead harbor is **Crocker Park** (⊠ Front St.). If your timing is good, you'll happen upon one of the many open-air concerts and festivities that occur here in the summer. This park is also the scene of many events in Marblehead's weeklong Fourth of July celebration.

Dining and Lodging

$$ ✕ **King's Rook.** The low ceilings, quaint tablecloths, and working woodstove at this cozy restaurant put you in the mood for a hot toddy or a glass of fine wine. Some of the best items are single-serving pizzas—one has goat cheese, roasted red peppers, and caramelized onions, and another is loaded with veggies. The restaurant also serves quite elegant sandwiches like the curried egg salad with raisins or the overstuffed turkey. The signature dessert, lemonberry-jazz, is a lemon cheesecake drizzled with blueberry sauce. ⊠ *12 State St.,* ☎ *781/631–9838. MC, V. No dinner Mon.*

$ ✕ **Truffles.** This fabulous self-service café has everything you need for a gourmet sunset picnic at Crocker Park or a quick lunch or coffee break. Prepared items include Mediterranean artichoke salad, pad Thai, stuffed baby eggplant, and smoked-turkey calzone. The house-made pastries and desserts complement the strong house coffee. The elephant ears here just might be the best ones this side of Paris. ⊠ *114 Washington St.,* ☎ *781/639–1104. AE, MC, V. No dinner.*

$$$$ 🏨 **Harbor Light Inn.** If you were to describe the ideal New England inn,
★   it might resemble the Harbor Light. Stately antiques are arranged in rooms with floral wallpaper or period-color paint, like Wedgwood blue or Federal red. Fireplaces in the parlor, dining room, and several guest rooms soften the otherwise formal decor. Some rooms have fireplaces, hot tubs, or skylights. Traditional touches are found in the four-poster and canopy beds, carved arched doorways, wide-board floors, and Oriental rugs. These plus afternoon tea and Saturday-night wine and cheese make a stay here special. ⊠ *58 Washington St., 01945,* ☎ *781/631–2186,* FAX *781/631–2216. 21 rooms. Pool, meeting room. Full breakfast. AE, MC, V.*

$$$$ 🏨 **Seagull Inn.** The only B&B in the Neck has decks and wide windows with harbor views. Two of the three rooms are suites; the two-story Lighthouse room has a kitchen. Quilts and feather comforters cover the beds, handcrafted cabinets in each room conceal TVs, VCRs, and minirefrigerators. Many of the artworks and wood furnishings—armoires, Adirondack chairs, pencil-post beds, even the cherry hardwood floors—were created by the innkeeper. ⊠ *106 Harbor Ave., 01945,* ☎ *781/631–1893,* FAX *781/631–3535. 1 room, 2 suites. Continental breakfast. MC, V.*

$$–$$$ 🏨 **Harborside House.** A ship's carpenter built this house, a short drive from Old Town in Marblehead's historic district. Susan Livingston, a considerate and interesting host who whips up delicious breakfasts, has lived here for more than 30 years. The downstairs living room has a working brick fireplace; bedrooms overlook Marblehead harbor's hundreds of sailboats and have polished wide-board floors with Oriental rugs. ⊠ *23 Gregory St., 01945,* ☎ *781/631–1032. 2 rooms. Full breakfast. No credit cards.*

In case you want to be welcomed there.

We're here to see that you're always welcomed at establishments everywhere. That's why millions of people carry the American Express® Card – for peace of mind, confidence, and security, around the world or just around the corner.

do more

Cards

In case you're running low.

We're here to help with more than 118,000 Express Cash locations around the world. In order to enroll, just call American Express before you start your vacation.

do more

Express Cash

And just in case.

We're here with American Express® Travelers Cheques and Cheques *for Two*® They're the safest way to carry money on your vacation and the surest way to get a refund, practically anywhere, anytime.

Another way we help you...

do more

Travelers Cheques

FISHING

From May to November Captain Randy Sigler of **Fly Fishing** (☎ 781/ 639–2577 or 888/359–5163) takes out a few people at a time to fly-fish on the Atlantic for bass and bluefish.

Salem

★ ㉙ *15 mi from Boston, 4 mi from Marblehead.*

Salem unabashedly calls itself "Witch City." Witches astride broomsticks decorate the police cars; witchcraft shops, memorials, and a growing number of resident witches (most of them good ones) commemorate the city's witchcraft trials of 1692, when religious zeal ran out of control and resulted in the hangings of 19 alleged witches. In October the city celebrates its spooky past with Haunted Happenings, starting with a Halloween parade in the beginning of the month. Museums and businesses are converted into haunted houses, graveyards, or dungeons. Most museums have extended hours (events requiring a ticket often sell out, so make reservations as early as possible). By March, most inns are booked solid for October; if you can't find a place, scout around the neighboring towns.

The supernatural intrigue aside, Salem's charms include compelling museums, trendy waterfront stores and restaurants, a traffic-free shopping area, and a wide common with a children's playground and a jogging path. More tourists than ever are coming to this little city, so prepare for crowds in the high season.

One way to take in Salem's sights is to follow the **Heritage Trail** (a red line painted on the sidewalk) around the town, which was settled in 1630. The frigates of Salem opened the Far East trade routes and provided the wealth that produced America's first millionaires. Among Salem's native sons are the author Nathaniel Hawthorne, the navigator Nathaniel Bowditch, and the architect Samuel McIntire.

From April to December, the **Salem Trolley** (✉ Trolley Depot, 191 Essex St., ☎ 978/744–5469) spins around town on one-hour narrated tours ($8).

The figures at the **Salem Wax Museum** tell the town's story, detailing its rich maritime tradition and the witch-related hysterics of 1692. ✉ *288 Derby St.,* ☎ *978/740–2929.* ⌑ *$4; $6.95 for combination ticket with Witch Village (☞ below).* ◷ *Daily 10–5.*

Professional actors reenact a witch trial at the **Witch Dungeon Museum,** which includes a walk through a re-creation of the dungeon where the accused were held. ✉ *16 Lynde St.,* ☎ *978/741–3570.* ⌑ *$4.50.* ◷ *Apr.–Dec., daily 10–5.*

If you want to learn about witchcraft, visit the **Witch Village.** ✉ *282 Derby St.,* ☎ *978/740–9229.* ⌑ *$4; $6.95 for combination ticket with Salem Wax Museum (☞ above).* ◷ *Daily 10–5.*

The **Salem Witch Museum** stages a reenactment of the events of 1692, using 13 sets, life-size models, and a taped narration. The elaborate exterior implies a high-quality presentation, but the show isn't that great. ✉ *19½ Washington Sq. N,* ☎ *978/744–1692.* ⌑ *$4.* ◷ *Daily 10–5 (until 7 July–Aug.).*

No witch ever lived at **Witch House,** but more than 200 accused witches were questioned here. The late-17th-century decor reflects the era when the trials were held. ✉ *310½ Essex St.,* ☎ *978/744–0180.* ⌑ *$5.* ◷ *Mid-Mar.–Nov., daily 10–4:30 (until 6 July–Aug.).*

Putting its macabre past behind it, Salem went on to become a major seaport. At the **Salem Maritime Site** is the famous customs house where Nathaniel Hawthorne wrote the introduction to *The Scarlet Letter*. Also here are an authentic bathhouse, the Government Warehouse, and shipowners' homes. ⊠ *174 Derby St.,* ☎ *978/740–1650.* ☜ *Tours $3, grounds free.* ⊙ *Daily 9–5.*

★ Many exotic spoils brought back by Salem's merchant ships are housed in the **Peabody and Essex Museum,** the oldest continuously operating museum in America. American decorative arts and Korean Art exhibits are among the strengths of the museum, which also has exhibits on New England's whaling and fishing past and documents from the witch trials. You can tour several historic mansions that belonged to shipowners and other wealthy merchants. ⊠ *East India Sq.,* ☎ *978/745–1876.* ☜ *$7.50; good for 2 consecutive days.* ⊙ *May–Nov., Mon.–Thurs. and Sat. 10–5, Fri. 10–8, Sun. noon–5. Closed Mon. Nov.–May.*

★ Tour highlights at the **House of the Seven Gables,** which was immortalized by Nathaniel Hawthorne in his book of the same name, include a secret staircase discovered during 1886 renovations and a garret with a model of the house. This house once belonged to Hawthorne's cousin; the house where Hawthorne was born in 1804 has been moved next door from another location in the city and is included in the tour. ⊠ *54 Turner St.,* ☎ *978/744–0991.* ☜ *$7.* ⊙ *July–Oct., daily until 6. Closed 1st week in Jan.*

☾ **Salem Willows Park,** at the eastern end of Derby Street, has picnic grounds, beaches, food stands, amusements, games, boat rentals, and fishing bait.

The **Rebecca Nurse Homestead** was the home of aged, pious Rebecca, a regular churchgoer whose accusation as a witch shocked townspeople. Her trial was a mockery (she was pronounced innocent, but the jury was urged to change its verdict), and she was hanged in 1692. Her family buried her in secret on the grounds of this house. Furnished in period style, it is gradually being developed as a model 18th-century farm. ⊠ *149 Pine St.,* ☎ *978/774–8799.* ☜ *$3.50.* ⊙ *Mid-June–Labor Day, Tues.–Sun. 1–4:30; Labor Day–Oct., weekends 1–4:30, or by appointment. Closed Nov.–mid-June.*

☾ **Pioneer Village and Forest River Park,** a short drive from downtown, attempts to re-create Salem Village in 1626, then known as Naumkeag, when it was the center of the Puritan colony. Animals roam about, and costumed interpreters lead tours through the small site. The replicas of thatched cottages, dugout homes, and wigwams are bordered by 20th-century homes, so bring your imagination. ⊠ *Rtes. 174 and 129,* ☎ *978/745–0525.* ☜ *$4.50.* ⊙ *Mid-May–Oct., Mon.–Sat. 10–5, Sun. noon–5.*

Dining and Lodging

$$ ✕ **Chase House.** Busy in summer, this restaurant on Pickering Wharf overlooks the harbor. The main dining room has low ceilings and exposed-brick walls. Steak, swordfish, "old-fashioned seafood dinners," and heart-healthy grilled items are on the menu. ⊠ *Pickering Wharf,* ☎ *978/744–0000,* 𝙁𝘼𝙓 *978/744–9651. AE, D, DC, MC, V.*

$ ✕ **Salem Diner.** You can pick out the regulars at this Sterling Streamliner, some of whom have been coming for the entire 50 years the place has been in business—their breakfast is delivered without their saying even a word to the waitress. The food is classic and hearty—omelets, burgers, sandwiches, and daily specials. The diner closes at 7:45 PM. ⊠ *70 Loring Ave.,* ☎ *978/741–7918. No credit cards.*

$$$$ ✕🏨 **Hawthorne's Hotel.** Business travelers patronize the only full-service hotel in Salem, an imposing redbrick structure on the town green. A short walk from the commercial center and most attractions, it has rooms appointed with reproduction antiques, armchairs, and desks. A casual restaurant, Tavern on the Green, serves ordinary pub fare. On the menu at upscale Nathaniel's are steaks, chicken, and fresh seafood dishes like lobster and herb-roasted scrod. ⊠ *On-the-Common, 01970,* ☎ *978/744–4080,* FAX *978/745–9842. 83 rooms, 6 suites. 2 restaurants, bar, exercise room, meeting rooms. AE, D, DC, MC, V.*

$$$$ 🏨 **Inn at Seven Winter St.** Built in 1871 and accurately restored, this conveniently located inn re-creates the Victorian era. Though a little dark, rooms are spacious and well furnished, with heavy mahogany and walnut antiques; Oriental rugs cover the polished hardwood floors. Four rooms have working marble fireplaces; two suites have eat-in kitchens. ⊠ *7 Winter St., 01970,* ☎ *978/745–9520. 7 rooms, 2 suites, 1 studio. Continental breakfast. MC, V.*

$$–$$$ 🏨 **Amelia Payson Guest House.** This Greek Revival house built in 1845 has been converted into a B&B near the common and Salem's historic attractions. Pretty rooms appointed with period or reproduction furnishings have floral-print wallpaper, lace curtains, and shiny, new brass or canopy beds. The downstairs parlor has a grand piano, and breakfast is served family style on fine china. ⊠ *16 Winter St., 01970,* ☎ *978/744–8304. 3 rooms, 1 studio. Continental breakfast. AE, MC, V.*

Shopping

The Broom Closet (⊠ 3 Central St., ☎ 978/741–3669) stocks fresh dried herbs, aromatic oils, candles, tarot cards, and New Age music. At **Crow Haven Corner** (⊠ 125 Essex St., ☎ 978/745–8763), Jodie Cabot, Salem's "official" witch, presides over a fabulous selection of crystal balls, herbs, tarot decks, healing stones, and books about witchcraft. **Pyramid Books** (⊠ 214 Derby St., ☎ 978/745–7171) stocks New Age and metaphysical books.

The **Pickering Wharf Antique Gallery** (☎ 978/741–3113) has five rooms with 40 dealers. The wharf area nearby holds many bars and restaurants.

Manchester-by-the-Sea

㉚ *28 mi from Boston, 9 mi from Salem.*

Established as Manchester in 1645, this tiny town recently increased its quaintness quotient by adding "by-the-sea" to its name. Over the years, wealthy Bostonians have built castlelike "cottages" here. Shopping and dining are limited, but there are some lovely spots for enjoying the landscape.

Many Bostonians take summer day trips to the long and lovely **Singing Beach,** so called because of the noise your feet make on the sand. This fine beach has lifeguards, food stands, and rest rooms but limited parking: Nonresidents must pay $15 on summer weekends or $8 on weekdays to use a private lot. Check behind the town hall for one of the few spaces or try the lot beside Manchester railroad station. Better yet, take the train from Boston: The station is just a ½-mi walk from the sand. **Tuck's Point** (⊠ end of Harbor St.) has a small beach and a park with picnic tables. The **Coolidge Reservation** (⊠ Summer St.) was first owned by Thomas Jefferson Coolidge, a great-grandson of Thomas Jefferson. The old family home and grounds include wetlands, some beachfront, forest, and an expansive "ocean lawn." The park is only open on Saturday.

Lodging

$–$$ ⊡ **Old Corner Inn.** Formerly the summer residence of the Danish Embassy, Manchester's only inn, a house built in 1865, is a mile from the village center and the nearest beach. In 1970, the new doctor in town bought the structure. Ever since, he's been seeing patients in his adjacent office and welcoming guests. And pampering them: Call in advance and the innkeepers might cook you dinner. Ask for a lift and they will drop you off at beaches where only residents can park. The common room has a warm fireplace and a unique couch carved in 1740 by a New England master. Guest rooms vary in size, and have four-poster beds, brass gaslight fixtures, feather mattresses, and claw-foot tubs; some have working fireplaces. All the rooms except the suite are intentionally void of phones, TVs, and modems. ⊠ *2 Harbor St., 01944,* ☎ *978/526–4996. 8 rooms, 5 with bath; 1 suite. Continental breakfast. AE, MC, V.*

Gloucester

③ *37 mi from Boston, 8 mi from Manchester.*

On Gloucester's fine seaside promenade is a famous statue of a man at a ship's wheel, his eyes on the horizon. Dedicated to those "who go down to the sea in ships," the statue was commissioned by residents in 1923 in celebration of the seaport's 300th anniversary. Gloucester is a major fishing port, and home to **Rocky Neck**, the oldest artists' colony in America (the town is loaded with galleries). Several seasonal events in Gloucester are worth attending. During St. Peter's Fiesta, an Italian extravaganza on the last weekend in June, there are religious events, music, and loads of food, a greasy-pole-walking contest, a parade, and the blessing of the fishing fleet. In August, a waterfront festival includes an arts and crafts show and a lobster bake. Labor Day is marked by the schooner festival and Boatlight Parade, for which boat owners drape lights from bow to stern and cruise around the harbor. A fireworks display over the water caps the festivities.

Wingaersheek Beach (⊠ Rte. 128, Exit 13) is a well-protected cove of white sand and dunes. The white Annisquam lighthouse keeps watch over the bay. **Good Harbor Beach** (⊠ signposted from Rte. 127A) is a dune-backed beach with a rocky islet just offshore. Parking on Gloucester beaches costs $10 on weekdays and $15 on weekends, when the lots often fill by 10 AM. Just north of Good Harbor, **Long Beach** (⊠ off Route 127A) is an excellent place to sunbathe; parking here costs only $5 (because half the beach is in Rockport). Gloucester's beaches don't have many tourists.

The **Hammond Castle Museum,** south of Gloucester, is a re-creation of a medieval stone castle, complete with drawbridge, brooding gloomily over the ocean. It was built in 1926 by the inventor John Hays Hammond Jr., who patented, among some 800 inventions, the remote control and the gyroscope. Inside are medieval furnishings and paintings. The Castle houses an organ with 8,600 pipes and 126 stops. Visible from the castle is **Norman's Woe Rock**, made famous by Longfellow's poem "The Wreck of the Hesperus." ⊠ *80 Hesperus Ave.,* ☎ *978/283–2080.* ⊡ *$5.50.* ☉ *May–Oct., Wed.–Sun. 10–5; Nov.–Apr., weekends 10–5.*

Dining and Lodging

$$$ ✕ **Evie's Rudder.** Quaint and quirky, as befits its ramshackle exterior and artists'-colony location, Evie's has been dishing up good food and entertainment under the same ownership for about four decades. The building, which dates from the 1890s, has low ceilings, heavy beams, uneven floors, and shingle walls. You can sit inside in the dimly lighted dining room, which is decorated with Evie's eccentric tchotchkes, or on the deck. Seafood, chicken, and steaks are served. There's a children's menu, and if you have a special request—such as a vegetarian plate— just ask and the chef will concoct something. ⊠ *Rocky Neck,* ☎ *978/ 283–7967. D, MC, V. Closed Nov.–Mar.; Mon.–Wed. Apr. and Oct.*

$$$ ✕ **White Rainbow.** The dining room in this excellent restaurant is in
★ the basement of a west-end store. A fireplace and candlelight set a romantic mood. Specialties include Maui onion soup, lobster bisque, and a fabulous burrito with lobster, spinach, shiitake mushrooms, scallions, and black beans covered with a lobster cream sauce. A cooked-to-order Sunday brunch is served from November to April. More moderately priced fare is available in the the café. ⊠ *65 Main St.,* ☎ *978/281– 0017. AE, D, DC, MC, V. Closed Mon.*

$$$$ 🏨 **Best Western Bass Rocks Ocean Inn.** The inn's main building is an oceanfront manor house, built in 1899 as a wedding present for a bride who subsequently refused to live in such an isolated location. The rooms, each with a patio or deck and a beautiful sea view, are in an adjacent motel-style building decorated with contemporary furnishings. Complimentary breakfast and tea are served in the manor house, which also contains a game room with a billiard table, a library, and a rooftop sundeck. ⊠ *107 Atlantic Rd., 01930,* ☎ *978/283–7600,* ⅎ⅍ *978/ 281–6438. 48 rooms. Pool, bicycles, recreation room. Continental breakfast. AE, D, DC, MC, V. Closed Nov.–Apr.*

$$–$$$ 🏨 **Blue Shutters Inn.** The best thing about this inn is the location—directly across from Good Harbor Beach. The rooms, several of which have ocean views, are small, carpeted with wall-to-wall shag, and contain well-worn department-store-quality American furnishings. Several apartments, some with kitchens and accommodating up to six, are perfect for small groups. Room 1, with a working stone fireplace and white wicker furniture, is the best. ⊠ *1 Nautilus Ave., 01930,* ☎ *978/283–1198. 10 rooms, 7 with bath; 5 apartments. Closed Nov.–May. No credit cards.*

$$–$$$ 🏨 **Cape Ann Motor Inn.** This wood-shingle, three-story motel is as close to the sand as they come, right on Long Beach on the Gloucester-Rockport border. Half the smallish rooms have kitchenettes, and all have balconies and superb views over beach, sea, and the twin lights of Thatcher's Island. ⊠ *33 Rockport Rd., 01930,* ☎ *978/281–2900,* ⅎ⅍ *978/281–1359. 30 rooms, 1 suite. AE, D, MC, V.*

Nightlife and the Arts

NIGHTLIFE

The Rhumb Line (⊠ 40 Railroad Ave., ☎ 978/283–9732) has live entertainment and good food every night but Tuesday, with rock-and-roll on Friday and Saturday and jazz on Sunday.

THE ARTS

The **Gloucester Stage Company** (⊠ 267 E. Main St., ☎ 978/281–4099) is a nonprofit professional group that stages new plays and revivals. The magnificent organ at the **Hammond Castle Museum** (⊠ 80 Hesperus Ave., ☎ 978/283–2080) is used for concerts year-round; in summer pops concerts are added to the schedule.

Outdoor Activities and Sports

FISHING

Captain Bill's Deep Sea Fishing (⊠ 33 Harbor Loop, ☎ 978/283–6995 or 800/339–4253) operates full- and half-day excursions from May to October. **Coastal Fishing Charters** (⊠ Rose Wharf, 415 Main St., ☎ 978/283–5113) operates day and evening fishing trips, kids' trips in Gloucester harbor, and island trips. The **Yankee Fishing Fleet** (⊠ 75 Essex Ave., ☎ 978/283–0313) conducts deep-sea fishing trips.

WHALE-WATCHING

A whale-watching trip is a terrific way to spend the day from May to October, when four breeds of whale feed off the North Shore. You're practically guaranteed to see a half dozen—on ideal days you may see 40. Reputable operations include **Cape Ann Whale Watch** (⊠ 415 Main St., ☎ 978/283–5110 or 800/877–5110), which has whale specialists on board. **Captain Bill's Whale Watch** (⊠ 9 Traverse St., ☎ 978/283–6995) and **Yankee Fleet/Gloucester Whale Watch** (⊠ 75 Essex Ave., ☎ 978/283–0313) sail to Provincetown, where the boats stop for four hours before returning via whale territory.

The *Thomas E. Lannon* (☎ 978/281–6634), a 65-ft fishing schooner, was crafted in Essex in 1996, modeled after the great boats built a century ago. There are two-hour boat cruises and special events, like sunset or Sunday champagne brunch cruises. Reservations are recommended.

Rockport

③ *41 mi from Boston, 4 mi from Gloucester.*

Rockport, at the very tip of Cape Ann, derives its name from its granite formations. Many a Boston-area structure is made of stone from the town's long-gone quarries. Rockport is a mecca for summer tourists attracted by its hilly rows of colorful clapboard houses, historic inns, artists' studios, and small community beaches. (It's also very accessible to Boston—the commuter rail stops in town.)

One of the most exciting events here in the summer is the **Rockport Chamber Music Festival** (⊠ Box 312, 01966, ☎ 978/546–7391). Musicians and music lovers gather from far and wide to play in or enjoy concerts that take place from mid-June to mid-July.

Parking in town during the summer is impossible; leave your car at the Tourist Information Center lot on Route 127 and take the **Cape Ann Trolley,** which leaves roughly once an hour daily in July and August, making 17 stops in and around town. Though it's a tourist haunt, Rockport has not gone overboard on T-shirt shacks and the other accoutrements of a summer economy: Shops sell crafts, folk and fine art, clothing, and cameras, and restaurants serve quiche, seafood, or home-baked cookies rather than fast food.

From downtown walk out to the end of **Bearskin Neck** and climb up one flight to the top of the Old Stone Fort observation tower for a perspective of the open Atlantic. The nearby lobster shack in view is known as "Motif No. 1" because of its popularity as a subject for artists. Thousands of flowers bloom in the springtime, and residents go to great lengths to transform their window boxes and gardens into works of art. Rockport celebrates the year-end holidays with great fanfare—shops and inns all over town hold an open house in mid-December, and Santa arrives by lobster boat for the Christmas pageant.

Rockport has a tremendous concentration of artists' studios and galleries selling work by local painters. *The Rockport Fine Arts Gallery Guide,* available from the Rockport Chamber of Commerce (☞ Visitor Information *in* The North Shore A to Z, *below*), lists about 30 reputable galleries in town, but the best way to find your masterpiece is to stroll for a day from gallery to gallery.

Dining and Lodging

$$–$$$$ ✕ **My Place by the Sea.** The only place to eat outdoors in Rockport is at this restaurant at the end of Bearskin Neck, which provides a 240-degree view of the surrounding seascape. The menu includes New England seafood specialties such as lobster, mussels, and fresh fish as well

as steaks, pasta, salads, and sandwiches. ✉ *Bearskin Neck,* ☎ *978/ 546–9667. AE, D, DC, MC, V. BYOB. Closed Dec.–Mar.*

$$$ ✕ **Brackett's Oceanview Restaurant.** The big bay window of this homey restaurant affords an excellent view across the beach. The menu includes scallop casserole, fish cakes, and other seafood dishes. ✉ *27 Main St.,* ☎ *978/546–2797. AE, D, DC, MC, V. BYOB. Closed Nov.–Mar.*

$$–$$$ ✕ **The Greenery.** For lunch at this airy café try a sproutwich, which is loaded with cheese, mushrooms, sunflower seeds, and sprouts, or an entrée like crab-salad quiche or steamers. Pan-seared citrus salmon, lobster, and grilled swordfish with lime and Dijon mustard are among the seafood offerings at dinner, but you can also order steaks, burgers, and a chef's salad. Breakfast is served between June and October. ✉ *15 Dock Square,* ☎ *978/546–9593. AE, MC, V. Closed Jan.–Apr. and Mon.– Tues. Nov.–Dec.*

$–$$ ✕ **Portside Chowder House.** This great little hole-in-the-wall is one of the few restaurants in Rockport that are open year-round. Chowder is the house specialty; also served are lobster and crab plates, salads, burgers, and sandwiches. ✉ *Bearskin Neck,* ☎ *978/546–7045. No credit cards. No dinner Oct.–Apr.*

$ ✕ **Dock Square Coffee and Tea House.** This little café is a good place to sit outside with coffee and dessert (try the lemon squares or a giant cookie). Inside, classical music plays and the work of local artists hangs on the walls. Pick up a local paper and plan your afternoon adventure over a cup of homemade soup or a rustic pizza. ✉ *25 Dock Square,* ☎ *978/546–2525. No credit cards. No dinner Mon.–Thurs; dinner only until 7 on Sun.*

$$$$ ✕🖬 **Yankee Clipper Inn and Veranda Restaurant.** The imposing Geor-
★ gian mansion that forms the main part of this compound is surrounded by gardens on a rocky point jutting into the sea. Three houses hold guest rooms decorated with impeccable antiques or reproductions and canopy, four-poster, or mahogany beds; several rooms in the main house, which was built in 1930s, have sunporches or decks with ocean views. The 1840 Greek Revival Bulfinch House across the street has tasteful antiques but less of a view. In the attached Veranda restaurant, diners sit on the glass-enclosed porch overlooking the water or in the cozy dining room off the parlor. The menu changes twice a year and includes appetizers like grilled pears on a bed of greens topped with pistachios and chèvre. Among the entrées are the garlic-roasted duck, the pumpkin ravioli in cream sauce with prosciutto, and the Veranda sole, layered with cheese, crab meat, and fresh herbs and poached in a white wine sauce. An elaborate breakfast, served only in summer, is open to the public. For a more economical stay, consider one of the packages, which include a room and dinner. ✉ *96 Granite St., 01966,* ☎ *978/546–3407 or 800/545–3699,* 𝐅𝐀𝐗 *978/546–9730. 26 rooms, 6 suites. Restaurant, pool. Full breakfast; MAP available. AE, D, MC, V. Closed mid-Dec.–Mar.*

$$$–$$$$ 🖬 **Addison Choate Inn.** This lovely white clapboard inn sits incon-
★ spicuously among private homes, a minute's walk from the center of town. The rooms, all with large bathrooms, are beautifully decorated. The navy-and-white captain's room has handmade quilts, Oriental rugs, and a dark-wood four-poster bed with a net canopy. The chimney room is Wedgwood blue with a maple canopy bed. Other rooms have Hitchcock rockers and headboards, spool or filigree brass beds, and local seascape paintings. The two luxuriously appointed duplex carriage-house apartments have skylights, cathedral ceilings, and exposed wood beams. In the afternoon, the innkeepers serve tea or cool drinks and homemade treats. ✉ *49 Broadway, 01966,* ☎ *978/546–7543 or 800/245– 7543,* 𝐅𝐀𝐗 *978/546–7638. 6 rooms, 2 apartments. Pool. Continental breakfast. 2-night minimum summer and holidays. D, MC, V.*

$$$ 📷 **Seacrest Manor.** Staying here feels like visiting a wealthy relative. The inn's motto, "decidedly small, intentionally quiet," aptly describes its atmosphere. Rooms are handsomely and formally decorated with traditional and antique furnishings. Two spacious rooms have large private decks with sea views, and two smaller rooms can be combined as a suite. On a hill overlooking the sea and surrounded by gardens, the inn is maintained by friendly innkeepers as a sanctuary for those escaping a bustling life. The two elegant sitting rooms, one with a fireplace, the other with a picture window facing the ocean, are furnished with antiques and leather chairs. ⊠ *99 Marmion Way, 01966, ☎ 978/546–2211. 6 rooms with bath, 2 share bath. Dining room. 2 night minimum in season. Full breakfast. No credit cards. Closed Dec.–Mar.*

$$–$$$ 📷 **Inn on Cove Hill.** The money to build this 1791 Federal structure
★   just half a block from town reportedly came from a cache of pirates' gold. The very hospitable owners first stayed here on their honeymoon in 1970 and returned to run it themselves in 1977. Some guest rooms are small, but all are cheerfully appointed with bright flower-print paper, patchwork quilts, and old-fashioned beds—some are brass, others are canopy four-posters. Rooms have polished wide-board floors, iron latches, wood bathroom fixtures, and pastel-tone Oriental rugs. ⊠ *37 Mt. Pleasant St., 01966, ☎ 978/546–2701. 9 rooms with bath, 2 rooms share bath. Continental breakfast. MC, V. Closed Nov.–Mar.*

$$–$$$ 📷 **Sally Webster Inn.** Sally Webster was a member of the so-called hatchet
★   gang, which smashed up the town's liquor stores in 1856 and turned Rockport into the dry town it remains today. The Colonial house where Sally lived for most of her life has been converted into this cheery inn. The rooms contain rocking chairs, Oriental rugs, and pineapple four-poster, brass, canopy, or spool beds. Bonnets and wickerwork hang on the walls; most rooms have candle-lanterns that can be lit in the evening. ⊠ *34 Mt. Pleasant St., 01966, ☎ 978/546–9251. 9 rooms. Continental breakfast. D, MC, V. Closed Dec.–Feb.*

Shopping

Half Moon Harry (⊠ 19 South Rd., Bearskin Neck, ☎ 978/546–6601) sells unusual cards, gifts, small photos, and ornaments. The shop is closed in January and February. **Small Fry Shop** (⊠ 18 Bearskin Neck, ☎ 978/546–9354) has been outfitting Rockport's children for almost three decades. **Willoughby's** (⊠ 20 Main St. ☎ 978/546–9820) carries fine contemporary women's clothing. There's a coffee bar in the rear of the shop.

Essex

③③ *31 mi from Boston, 12 mi from Rockport.*

Surrounded by salt marshes, Essex is as picturesque a town as you can find on the New England coast, with a beautiful shoreline drive, three dozen antiques stores, and many seafood restaurants. Lawrence "Chubby" Woodman invented the fried clam here in 1916. The town has been the hub of North Shore shipbuilding for 3½ centuries—more than 4,000 vessels have been produced for fishermen and big shipping companies. A recent example is the **Thomas E. Lannon** schooner now docked in Gloucester (☞ *above*).

The **Essex Shipbuilding Museum** displays artifacts from the 19th century, when the town was an important shipbuilding center; more twin-mast shipping schooners were built here than anywhere else. ⊠ *66 Main St./Rte. 133, ☎ 978/768–7541. 🎟 $3.50. ☉ Thurs.–Sat., Mon. 11–4, Sun. 1–4. Closed Tues.–Wed.*

If you want to experience the waters of the Essex River firsthand or learn how lobster fishermen harvested in the era before motorized lobster boats, join Harold Burnham of **Sloop Boat Charters** (☎ 978/768–2569) for a sail on a restored friendship sloop. He takes up to six people for a few hours out on the water—for a sunset cruise on the ocean, a foliage tour of the river, or a lobstering trip on which you can haul the traps yourself (but not keep the lobsters).

The 1996 movie version of Arthur Miller's *The Crucible* was filmed in Essex and on nearby Hog Island. The **Crane Island Tour** (✉ Argilla Rd., Ipswich, ☎ 978/356–4351) takes you to the island for a look at the movie set. You can also view the island from the deck of the *Essex River Queen,* which is run by **Essex River Cruises** (✉ Essex Marina, 35 Dodge St., ☎ 978/768–6981 or 800/748–3706)—you can see local wildlife and explore the area's extensive salt marshes, which are are accessible only by boat. The company also operates sunset and other cruises.

Dining and Lodging

$$–$$$ ✗ **Periwinkles.** The food at this casual place—garlic and rosemary rotisserie pork, grilled salmon, steak tips and jumbo sandwiches—is prepared for a conservative palate. The restaurant, which overlooks the Essex River, serves summer lunch and dinner on an outdoor deck on the water. ✉ *74 Main St.,* ☎ *978/768–6320. AE, MC, V.*

$$ ✗ **Jerry Pelonzi's Hearthside.** This 250-year-old converted farmhouse is the epitome of coziness. Four small dining rooms have open fireplaces and exposed beams: The first is low-ceilinged with stencils on the walls; the others have cathedral ceilings with rough-panel walls and small windows. Traditional entrées include baked stuffed haddock, seafood casserole, sirloin steak, lobster, and chicken. ✉ *109 Eastern Ave./Rte. 133,* ☎ *978/768–6002 or 978/768–6003. AE, MC, V.*

$ ✗ **Woodman's of Essex.** Run by the family of Chubby Woodman, the
★   inventor of the fried clam, this large wood shack with unpretentious booths is *the* place to come for seafood in the rough. The menu includes fried everything plus lobster, delicacies from the raw bar, clam chowder, and fried clams. ✉ *125 Main St./Rte. 133,* ☎ *978/768–6451. No credit cards.*

$$$–$$$$ ⊞ **George Fuller House.** Built in 1830, this house was the site of the original town store. Cindy Cameron, who runs this B&B with her husband, Bob, inherited many of the antiques in the house from her aunt. Rooms have brass or canopy beds, fireplaces, Boston rockers, TVs, and phones. Ask for one that doesn't face the road—the traffic along Route 133 can be noisy. Cindy prepares a hearty breakfast that's served either in a room overlooking the salt marsh or in the formal dining room. You'll also have a chance to sample Cindy's baking in the afternoon, when tea and snacks are provided. ✉ *148 Main St., 01929,* ☎ *978/768–7766 or 800/768–7766. 7 rooms, 1 suite. Full breakfast. AE, MC, V.*

Shopping

Essex attracts antiques dealers from Europe and bargain hunters from Boston. Most of the shops are along Route 133. Here's a sampling: The **White Elephant** (✉ Rte. 133, ☎ 978/768–6901); **Chebacco Antiques** (✉ Rte. 133, ☎ 978/768–7371); **Howard's Flying Dragon Antiques** (✉ Rte. 133, ☎ 978/768–7282).

Hamilton

㉞   *33 mi from Boston, 3 mi from Ipswich.*

Settled in 1638, incorporated in 1793, and named after Alexander Hamilton, the town of Hamilton is said to have the highest horse-to-person ratio in the Northeast. Most of the property in this small town is owned by a few families who are dedicated to keeping the landscape rural and undeveloped—there are miles of wooded trails. The town center is notable only for its good restaurant, train station, and the eye-catching tank in the middle of the park—a gift from General George S. Patton, a Hamilton native.

Many equestrian events held here are open to the public, among them the polo matches held almost every Sunday by the **Myopia Hunt Club** (✉ Rte. 1A, ☎ 978/887–4026) at Gibney Field, America's oldest polo field. Several weekends a year, jumping, dressage, and other competitions take place. Check the local paper for listings or call the **Hamilton Town Hall** (☎ 978/468–5570).

Dining and Lodging

$$–$$$ ✕ **The Black Cow.** The only restaurant in Hamilton is a comfortable tap and grill. A young professional crowd hangs here—the bar often buzzes on the weekends. The food is similar to what you'd find at an upscale bar in Boston—smoked-chicken ravioli; grilled tuna steak with potatoes, oven-dried tomatoes, roasted onions, and capers; New York strip steak; and seared duck breast with pecan rice. ✉ *16 Bay Rd./Rte. 1A,* ☎ *978/468–1166. AE, MC, V.*

$$$–$$$$ 🏠 **Miles River Country Inn.** This exquisite house had humble beginnings
★   as a farmhouse, and though it has been expanded into an estate, it remains cozy inside, with low ceilings and 12 fireplaces. The guest rooms, living room, and sunporch are beautifully appointed with antiques, and every vase in the house bursts with fresh-cut flowers from one of the 13 gardens on the property. In winter you can cross-country ski for miles, right from the front door. Breakfast often includes eggs from the hens of the gracious innkeepers, Gretel and Peter Clark, and honey from Gretel's beehives. ✉ *823 Bay Rd./Rte. 1A, 01936,* ☎ *978/468–7206. 8 rooms, 6 with bath. MC, V.*

Shopping

The Band Box (✉ 264 Bay Rd., South Hamilton, ☎ 978/468–2740) has tasteful one-of-a-kind housewares.

Wenham

③⑤   *31 mi from Boston, 2 mi from Hamilton.*

The extraordinary **Sedgwick Gardens at Long Hill,** the grounds of the former home of Ellery Sedgwick and his first and second wives, accomplished horticulturists and gardeners Mabel Cabot and Marjorie Russell, include a lotus pool, a Chinese pagoda, a woodland path lined with unusual plants, and a croquet lawn. Garden tours are available by reservation, and during the spring a horticultural lecture series is held in the house. ✉ *Essex St./Rte. 22,* ☎ *978/921–1944.* 🖃 *By donation.* ☉ *Daily 8 AM–dusk.*

☾   At the **Wenham Museum** kids can look at the antique dolls and toys and a model-train exhibit and see how 17th-century New England families lived. ✉ *132 Main St.,* ☎ *978/468–2377.* 🖃 *$4.* ☉ *Weekdays 10–4, weekends 1–4.*

Dining

$ ✕ **Wenham Tea House.** This small tearoom, an adjoining gift shop, and a nearby women's clothing store are run by the Wenham Village Improvement Society. A proper lady would feel quite at home taking tea at the teahouse. The modest menu lists a traditional Club Sandwich, but also one called Healthy Choice that contains turkey and tabouleh rolled in a tortilla. The creamed chicken on toast is a specialty of the house. ✉ *Rte. 1A, Wenham,* ☎ *978/468–1398. AE, MC, V. No dinner.*

Shopping

The **Sport's Stop** (⊠ Rte. 1A, ☎ 978/468–4488) stocks biking and skiing accessories and rents cross-country ski equipment. **The Wenham Exchange** (⊠ Rte. 1A, ☎ 978/468–1235) carries housewares, books, cards, and children's clothes.

Ipswich

36 *36 mi from Boston, 6 mi from Essex.*

Settled in 1633 and famous for its clams, Ipswich has more 17th-century houses standing and occupied than any other place in America; more than 40 homes here were built before 1725.

★ **Crane Beach** (⊠ 290 Argilla Rd., ☎ 978/356–4354) is one of Massachusetts's most beautiful beaches. Parking costs $10 on weekdays and $15 on weekends. The Crane properties span 1,400 acres and include 4 mi of unspoiled beach. An amazing annual event is the sandcastle building contest in early August—simple fun for some and serious business for others.

The small islands that are part of the Crane properties can be explored by taking a **Crane Island Tour** (⊠ Argilla Rd., ☎ 978/356–4351) across the Castle Neck river. You can tour Hog Island, view sets from the film *The Crucible,* and admire the many birds and wildlife protected at this refuge.

Several historic houses in town are open to the public. Walking maps are available at the **Visitor Information Center** (⊠ S. Main St., ☎ 978/356–8540), which is open daily from 10 to 4.

☺ **New England Alive,** a petting farm and nature study center, takes in wild animals, farm animals, and reptiles. ⊠ *189 High St. (Rtes. 1A and 133),* ☎ *978/356–7013.* ⌑ *$6.* ☉ *May–Nov., weekdays 10–5, weekends 9:30–5.*

A short drive from the beach sits an old barn hung with dried flowers and surrounded by apple orchards, raspberry and pumpkin patches, ☺ and a barnyard full of farm animals. **Goodale Orchards** is a local institution that provides all the authentic New England sights and smells you can handle. You can pick-your-own of whatever fruit is in season or sort through the wooden bins and baskets for apples and produce. The small winery here produces hard cider and elderberry and raspberry wine. The regular cider is made with wood presses in the back of the barn—you can watch the smashing of the apples. Kids can buy a bag of grain to feed the friendly animals. ⊠ *123 Argilla Rd.,* ☎ *978/356–5366.* ☉ *May–Dec.*

Dining and Lodging

$$–$$$ ✕ **Stone Soup Cafe.** You may find it hard to believe that a hole-in-the-wall in an industrial park could be this good, but you must make reservations over two months in advance. There are two seatings of six tables a night for a meal of lobster bisque, gnocchi pesto, porcini ravioli, and whatever else the chef finds at the farmstand on a given day. Breakfast and lunch are also served. ⊠ *20 Mitchell Rd.,* ☎ *978/356–4222. Reservations essential for dinner. No credit cards. Closed Sun.–Mon. No dinner Tues.–Wed.*

$ ✕ **Clam Box.** No visit to Ipswich is complete without a sampling of the town's famous clams, and where better than at a restaurant shaped like a box of fried clams? Since 1932, locals and tourists have come here for truly excellent clams and the accompanying fries and onion rings. The dining room is casual, with booths and counter service. If there is a line, order a clam chowder to tide you over during your wait, which could last up to an hour. ⊠ *246 High St./Rte. 1A,* ☎ *978/356–9707. No credit cards.*

$$$–$$$$ ☤ **Town Hill Bed and Breakfast.** This 1850 Colonial sits on the small hill that rises out of downtown Ipswich and is within walking distance of commuter trains into Boston. The interior is part motel and part B&B: All the furnishings are brand new, clean, and unpretentious. The rooms are tiny, so ask for the largest available. Breakfast is served family style. ⊠ *16 N. Main St., 01938,* ☎ *978/356–8000 or 800/457–7799. 9 rooms, 7 with bath; 2 suites. AE, D, MC, V.*

Nightlife and the Arts

From July 4 to mid-August, **Castle Hill** (⊠ Argilla Rd., ☎ 978/356–7774) holds a festival of pop, folk, and classical music.

Outdoor Activities and Sports

The Massachusetts Audubon Society's **Ipswich River Wildlife Sanctuary** (⊠ Rtes. 1 and 97, Topsfield, ☎ 978/887–9264) contains trails through marshland hills with remains of early Colonial settlements and abundant wildlife. Pick up a free self-guiding trail map ($3) from the office, which is open daily except Monday from dawn to dusk.

Newburyport

③⑦   *38 mi from Boston, 12 mi from Ipswich.*

Federal-era mansions line High Street in tiny Newburyport, which was once a leading port and shipbuilding center; the houses were built for prosperous sea captains. An energetic downtown renewal program has brought new life to the town's brick-front center. Renovated buildings house restaurants, taverns, and shops that sell everything from nautical brasses to antique Oriental rugs. The civic improvements have been matched by private restorations of the town's housing stock, much of which dates from the 18th century, with a scattering of 17th-century homes in some neighborhoods.

Newburyport is a good walking city, and there is all-day free parking down by the water. A stroll through the **Waterfront Park and Promenade** yields a good view of the harbor and the fishing and pleasure boats that moor here. Walk to the left as you leave the parking lot to get to the **Custom House Maritime Museum.** Built in 1835 in Classic Revival style, it contains ship models, tools, paintings, and exhibits on maritime history. ⊠ *25 Water St.,* ☎ *978/462–8681.* ☑ *$3.* ⊙ *Apr.–Dec., Mon.–Sat. 10–4, Sun. 1–4.*

A causeway leads from Newburyport to the narrow spit of land known as **Plum Island,** which harbors a summer colony (rapidly becoming year-round) at one end. At the other end is the **Parker River National Wildlife Refuge,** 4,662 acres of salt marsh, freshwater marsh, beaches, and dunes. Bird-watching, surf fishing, plum and cranberry picking, and swimming are among the exhilarating pastimes here. The refuge is so popular in summer, especially on weekends, that cars begin to line up at the gate before 7 AM. Only a limited number of cars are let in, though there's no restriction on the number of people using the beach. ☎ 978/465–5753. ☑ *$5 per car; $2 for bicycles and walk-ins; annual passes available.* ⊙ *Daily dawn–dusk. Beach sometimes closed during endangered-species nesting season in spring and early summer. No pets.*

Dining and Lodging

$$$–$$$$ ✕ **Scandia.** This restaurant is known locally for its fine cuisine; house
★   specialties include rack of lamb and lobster ravioli. The dining room is small, narrow, and dimly lit with candles on the tables and chandeliers with candle bulbs. Hot entrées, cold salads, crêpes, waffles, and

omelets are served for Sunday brunch. ⊠ *25 State St.,* ☎ *978/462–6271. Reservations essential. AE, D, DC, MC, V.*

$$$–$$$$ ✕⬚ **Garrison Inn.** The atmosphere inside this four-story Georgian redbrick hostelry is more mildly shabby hotel than quaint country inn. The rooms vary in size, but all have antique replicas, coffeemakers, phones, and TVs. The best accommodations are the top-floor suites. The two restaurants are under separate management; both provide good food and service. Upstairs in a room with chandeliers and white linen, you can dine on entrées like sautéed lobster with sea scallops and mushrooms in anise cream. Downstairs is less formal, with exposed brick arches, a bar, and a lighter menu of steaks, burgers, and fish. ⊠ *11 Brown Sq., 01950,* ☎ *978/465–0910; 978/462–8077 for restaurants,* 𝖥𝖠𝖷 *978/465–4017. 18 rooms, 6 suites. 2 restaurants, bar. AE, DC, MC, V at inn; AE, D, DC, MC, V at restaurants. No lunch.*

$$–$$$ ⬚ **Clark Currier Inn.** This 1803 Federal mansion has been restored with
★ care, taste, and imagination, making it one of the best inns on the North Shore. The rooms are spacious and partly furnished with antiques, including one with a glorious sleigh bed dating from the late 19th century. ⊠ *45 Green St., 01950,* ☎ *978/465–8363. 8 rooms. Continental breakfast. AE, D, MC, V.*

Nightlife and the Arts

From Thursday to Sunday, blues and rock bands play downstairs at the **Grog** (⊠ 13 Middle St., ☎ 978/465–8008). **Theater in the Open** performs the works of Shakespeare and other classical playwrights at the **Maudsley Arts Center** (⊠ Maudsley State Park, Pine Hill Rd., ☎ 978/499–0050). Musical and other events take place here all summer. Bring a picnic, sit on the lawn, and enjoy the show.

Outdoor Activities and Sports

FISHING

Surf casting is the most popular style of fishing in Newburyport. Bluefish, pollock, and striped bass can be taken from the ocean shores of Plum Island; permits to remain on the beach after dark are free for anyone entering the refuge with fishing equipment in the daylight. You don't need a permit to fish from the public beach at Plum Island. The best spot is around the mouth of the Merrimack River. **Newburyport Whale Watch** (⊠ 54 Merrimac St., ☎ 978/465–9885 or 800/848–1111) operates deep-sea fishing charters and whale-watching and dinner cruises.

HIKING

At the **Parker River National Wildlife Refuge** (⊠ Plum Island, ☎ 978/465–5753), deer and rabbits share space with thousands of migrating and indigenous ducks and geese. The 2-mi Hellcat Swamp Trail cuts through the marshes and sand dunes, taking in the best of the sanctuary. Trail maps are available at the office.

The North Shore A to Z

Getting Around

BY BOAT

A boat leaves Boston for Gloucester daily between May 30 and Labor Day at 10 AM; the return boat leaves Gloucester at 3 PM. The three-hour trip costs $18. Contact **A. C. Cruise Lines** (⊠ 290 Northern Ave., Boston, ☎ 617/261–6633 or 800/422–8419).

BY BUS

The **Coach Company** (☎ 800/874–3377) operates buses along Route 1 and runs express commuter service from Boston to Newburyport. The **Cape Ann Transportation Authority** (CATA, ☎ 978/283–7916) covers the Gloucester/Rockport region with buses and water shuttles. **MBTA** buses leave from Haymarket Station for Marblehead and Salem.

BY CAR

The primary link between Boston and the North Shore is Route 128, which breaks off from I–95 and follows the coast northeast to Gloucester. If you stay on I–95, you'll reach Newburyport. A less direct route, but a scenic one north of Lynn, is Route 1A, which leaves Boston via the Callahan Tunnel. Beyond Beverly, Route 1A travels inland toward Ipswich and Essex; at this point, switch to Route 127, which follows the coast to Gloucester and Rockport.

BY TRAIN

Massachusetts Bay Transportation Authority (MBTA; ☎ 617/722–3200) trains, which run more frequently than buses from Boston, leave Boston's North Station for Salem, Beverly, Gloucester, Rockport, Ipswich, and Newburyport.

Contacts and Resources

EMERGENCIES

Beverly Hospital (⊠ Herrick St., Beverly, ☎ 978/922–3000). **North Shore Medical Center** (⊠ 81 Highland Ave., Salem, ☎ 978/741–1200; emergency 978/744–6000).

LATE-NIGHT PHARMACY

Walgreen's (⊠ 201 Main St., Gloucester, ☎ 978/283–7361) is open until 9 on weeknights, and until 6 on weekends.

VISITOR INFORMATION

National Park Service Visitor Information (⊠ 2 New Liberty St., Salem 02642, ☎ 978/740–1650). **North of Boston Visitors and Convention Bureau** (⊠ Box 642, 248 Cabot St., Beverly 01915, ☎ 978/921–4990 or 800/742–5306). **Rockport Chamber of Commerce** (⊠ Box 67, 3 Main St., Rockport, 01966, ☎ 978/546–6575).

THE PIONEER VALLEY

Updated by
Kirsten Sadler

The Pioneer Valley, a string of historic settlements along the Connecticut River from Springfield in the south up to the Vermont border, formed the western frontier of New England from the early 1600s until the late 18th century. The river and its fertile banks first attracted farmers and traders; later the Connecticut became a source of power and transport for the earliest industrial cities in America. The northern regions of the Pioneer Valley remain rural and tranquil; farms and small towns have typical New England architecture. Farther south, the cities of Holyoke and Springfield are more industrial. Educational pioneers came to this region as well—to form Mount Holyoke College, America's first college for women, and four other major colleges, as well as several well-known prep schools.

Northfield

 97 mi from Boston.

Just south of the Vermont border, this remote country town is known mainly as a center for hikers, campers, and other lovers of the outdoors.

The **Northfield Mountain Recreation Center** has 29 mi of hiking trails. You can rent canoes and rowboats at the large campground at Barton Cove. From here you can paddle to the Munn's Ferry campground, accessible only by canoe. The center also runs sightseeing tours of the Pioneer Valley, along a 12-mi stretch of the Connecticut River between Northfield and Gill, on the *Quinnetukut II* riverboat. Excursions last

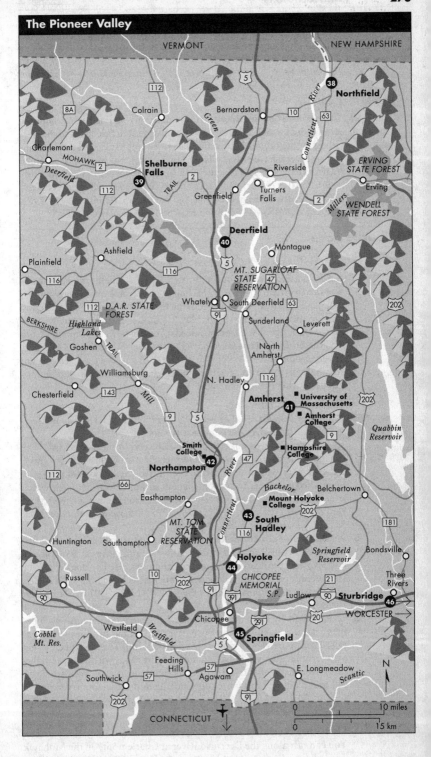

The Pioneer Valley

1½ hours; the commentary covers the geographical, natural, and historical features of the region. Bus tours head up the mountain, where you can see a large underground power station at work. ⊠ *99 Miller's Falls Rd.,* ☎ *413/659–3713.* 🎫 *Bus tour free; riverboat tour $7.* ☉ *Bus tour Sept.–Oct., Wed.–Sun. 10–3, weekends 10–3; riverboat tour June–early Oct., Tues.–Sun. 11–3.*

Lodging

$$ 🏠 **Northfield Country House.** Truly remote, this big English manor house
★ is amid thick woodlands on 16 acres. A wide staircase leads to the bedrooms, some of which have fireplaces. Rooms are decorated with antiques; several have brass beds. The two rooms that were once servants' quarters can be rented together as a suite. The owner has considerably renovated this century-old house and has planted hundreds of tulip and daffodil bulbs in the gardens. ⊠ *181 School St., 01360,* ☎ *413/498–2692 or 800/498–2692. 7 rooms. Pool. Full breakfast. MC, V.*

Shelburne Falls

㊳ *106 mi from Boston.*

A near-perfect example of small-town America, Shelburne Falls straddles the Deerfield River. A sprinkling of quality antiques shops and the Copper Angel restaurant overlooking the river make the village a good place to spend a half day. From May to October an arched, 400-ft abandoned trolley bridge is transformed by Shelburne Falls' Women's Club into the **Bridge of Flowers** (⊠ at Water St., ☎ 413/625–2544), a gardened promenade bursting with colors. In the riverbed just downstream from the town are 50 immense **glacial potholes** ground out of granite during the last ice age.

Dining and Lodging

$$–$$$ ✕ **Copper Angel Café.** Between the Deerfield River and main street, and with a deck over the water for summer dining, the Copper Angel specializes in vegetarian cuisine but also serves poultry and fish. The organic produce–based menu includes lentil cutlets with vegetarian gravy, a tofu stir-fry with peanut sauce, the stuffed chicken breast with garlic mashed potatoes, and orange-pepper shrimp. Hosts of angels watch over diners, and a copper-angel weather vane stands guard on the restaurant roof. ⊠ *2 State St.,* ☎ *413/625–2727. Reservations not accepted. MC, V. Closed Mon.–Tues. Nov.–Mar.*

$ ✕ **Shelburne Falls Coffee Roasters.** A good pit stop inside an old farmhouse, this coffeehouse that opens at 6 AM (and closes at 5 PM) serves coffees, teas, espresso drinks, soups, and focaccia. For dessert try the shortbread, pecan tart, baklava, or chocolate-chip cookies. ⊠ *Rte. 2, 4 mi east of Shelburne Falls village,* ☎ *413/625–0116. No credit cards. No dinner.*

$$ 🏠 **Penfrydd Farm.** In the middle of a 160-acre working farm with lla-
★ mas and horses, this serene B&B in a rejuvenated farmhouse has exposed beams, skylights, and a big whirlpool tub. The ideal place to get away from it all—you travel on miles of dirt roads without streetlights just to get here—Penfrydd Farm has fabulous foliage from spring to fall and plenty of snow for snowshoeing and cross-country skiing in winter. ⊠ *Box 100A, RR1, Colrain 01340,* ☎ *413/624–5516. 4 rooms. Continental breakfast. MC, V.*

Outdoor Activities and Sports

You can raft along the Deerfield River at Charlemont, on the Mohawk Trail. From April to October **Zoar Outdoor** (☎ 413/339–4010 or 800/339–4010) operates one-day raft tours over 10 mi of class II–III rapids daily.

Shopping

The **Salmon Falls Artisans Showroom** (⊠ Ashfield St., ☎ 413/625–9833) carries art, sculpture, pottery, glass, and furniture by 175 local artisans.

Skiing

Berkshire East. This ski area attracts a mostly regional college crowd and loyal families and youngsters interested in the area's racing program. ⊠ Box 727, South River Rd., Charlemont 01339, ☎ 413/339–6617.

DOWNHILL

The 1,200-ft vertical was once considered more difficult than that of neighboring ski areas. Blasting, widening, and sculpting tamed many of the steeper trails, but you can still find steep pitches toward the top. Wide, cruisable intermediate slopes are plentiful, as is beginner terrain. One triple and three double chairlifts and one surface lift serve the 36 trails, which are all covered by snowmaking. There's night skiing on Wednesday, Friday, and Saturday.

CHILD CARE

The nursery takes infants and children up to 8 years old on weekends; children under 6 ski free. Older children can take classes at the ski school. Aspiring racers from age 5 to 18 can train on weekends.

Deerfield

★ ④ *102 mi from Boston, 10 mi from Shelburne Falls.*

Historic Deerfield is the perfect New England village, a Peyton Place without the dark side. A horse pulling a carriage clip-clops past 18th-century homes in perfect condition, neighbors leave their doors unlocked and tip their hats to strangers, kids play ball in fields by the river, and the bell of the impossibly beautiful brick church peals hopefully from a white steeple.

Settled by Native Americans more than 8,000 years ago, Deerfield was originally a Pocumtuck village—deserted after deadly epidemics and a war with the Mohawks that all but wiped out the tribe. Pioneers eagerly settled into this frontier outpost in the 1660s and 1670s, but two bloody massacres at the hands of the Indians and the French caused the village to be abandoned until 1707, when construction began on the buildings that remain today.

Although it has a turbulent past, Historic Deerfield now basks in a genteel aura. **The Street,** a tree-lined avenue of 18th- and 19th-century houses, is protected and maintained as a museum site, with 14 of the preserved buildings open to the public year-round. Some homes contain antique furnishings and decorative arts; other buildings exhibit textiles, silver, pewter, or ceramics. The guides, who are given four to six months of intensive training, are able to converse knowledgeably about the exhibits and Deerfield's history. By the end of your visit you will believe the claim that this is one of the best-documented villages in New England. With 52 buildings on 93 acres, it provides an impressive glimpse into 18th- and 19th-century American life. Start your visit at the information center in Hall Tavern and don't miss the **Wells-Thorn House,** whose rooms depict life as it changed from 1725 to 1850. You could spend several days in Historic Deerfield, but plan on at least one full day here. ⊠ *The Street,* ☎ *413/774–5581.* ☜ *1-wk admission to all houses $10; single-house admission $5.* ☉ *Daily 9:30–4:30.*

The massive store at the landmark **Yankee Candle Company and Car Museum** in South Deerfield holds millions of candles, Christmas decorations, and foodstuffs. The adjacent car museum, a fun stop, exhibits

Lamborghinis, Ferraris, Corvettes, pristine antique classics, novelty drag-sters, funny cars, and even the Batmobile used in the 1989 *Batman* film. ⊠ *Rtes. 5 and 10, S. Deerfield,* ☎ *413/665–2929.*

Dining and Lodging

$$$ ✕ **Sienna.** Off the main street of little South Deerfield is a room with
★ warm lighting, terra-cotta and wrought-iron accents, simple white table settings, and absolutely fabulous food. The atmosphere at Sienna is soothing and the service well mannered, but the food is what really shines. Choices from the ever-changing menu might include an appe-tizer of smoked-salmon samosas on a champagne beurre and entrées like tuna loin on a light stir-fry of zucchini, fennel, and gnocchi with a mustard sauce. After an irresistible dessert, your evening ends with the personal touch of a handwritten check on stationery. ⊠ *6 Elm St., S. Deerfield,* ☎ *413/665–0215. Reservations essential. MC, V. Closed Mon.–Tues. No lunch.*

$$$–$$$$ ✕⚏ **Deerfield Inn.** Period wallpapers decorate the rooms in the main
★ inn, which was built in 1884; the rooms in an outbuilding have iden-tical papers but are newer (1981) and closer to the parking lot. All rooms have antiques and replicas, sofas, and bureaus; some have four-poster or canopy beds. Venison and rack of lamb with Dijon mustard and gar-lic are among the dishes served in the sunny dining room. Save room for the pumpkin crème brûlée. ⊠ *81 Old Main St., 01342,* ☎ *413/774– 5587; 800/926–3865 outside MA,* ℻ *413/773–8712. 23 rooms. Restau-rant, bar, coffee shop. Full breakfast. No smoking. AE, DC, MC, V.*

$$ ✕⚏ **Whately Inn.** Antiques and four-poster beds slope gently on old-wood floors at the Whately. The two rooms over the restaurant (no lunch) can be noisy, so avoid them. The dining room has exposed beams, tables on a raised stage at one end, and some booths; it's dimly lit, with candles on the tables. Cajun shrimp, baked lobster with shrimp stuffing, rack of lamb, and other entrées come with salad, appetizer, and dessert. The restaurant is very busy on weekends; Sunday din-ner begins at 1 PM. ⊠ *Chestnut Plain Rd., Whately Center 01093,* ☎ *413/665–3044 or 800/942–8359. 4 rooms. Restaurant. AE, D, DC, MC, V.*

$$–$$$ ⚏ **Yellow Gabled House.** Edna Stahelek has often been told she reminds guests of their mother or favorite aunt. Her welcoming home, built circa 1800, is as sunny and refined as she is. You enter through the side door into a sunroom, pass a large kitchen, and walk through an elegant din-ing room and a living room with a grandfather clock and other an-tiques. One guest room with a cherry pineapple four-poster bed is downstairs; upstairs are a room with a crocheted canopy bed and couch and a suite. ⊠ *111 N. Main St., South Deerfield 01373,* ☎ *413/ 665–4922. 2 rooms share bath, 1 suite. Full breakfast. No smoking, no children under 12. No credit cards.*

$$ ⚏ **Sunnyside Farm Bed and Breakfast.** Maple antiques and family heir-looms decorate this inn's country-style rooms, all of which are hung with fine-art reproductions and have views across the fields. A full coun-try breakfast, often including strawberries from the farm next door, is served family-style in the dining room. The farm is about 8 mi south of Deerfield, convenient to cross-country skiing, mountain biking, and hiking. ⊠ *21 River Rd., Whately 01093,* ☎ *413/665–3113. 5 rooms share 2 baths. Pool. Full breakfast. No credit cards.*

Amherst

④ *14 mi from Deerfield, 8 mi from Northampton.*

Three of the Pioneer Valley's five major colleges—the University of Massa-chusetts (UMass), Amherst College, and Hampshire College—are in small but lively Amherst, which has a large village green. The area's youthful orientation is reflected in its bookstores, bars, and cafés.

The poet Emily Dickinson was born and died in the **Emily Dickinson Homestead.** She lived her strange and lonely life here; the house, which can only be visited on guided tours, contains some of the poet's belongings, but most of her manuscripts are elsewhere. ⊠ *280 Main St.,* ☏ *413/542–8161.* ⊡ *$3. Reservations essential.* ☉ *Call for hrs.*

The **Amherst History Museum at the Strong House,** built in the mid-1700s, has an extensive collection of household tools, furniture, china, and clothing that reflects the changing styles of interior decoration. Most items are Amherst originals, dating from the 18th to the mid-20th century. ⊠ *67 Amity St.,* ☏ *413/256–0678.* ⊡ *$2.* ☉ *May–Oct., Wed.–Sat. 12:30–3:30; Oct.–May, Thurs.–Sat. 12:30–3:30.*

The **Hitchcock Center for the Environment** is a nonprofit organization in the 27-acre Larch Hill Conservation Area. Self-guided nature trails are wheelchair accessible on a boardwalk, and the resource library focuses on environmental issues. Natural-history programs and workshops are conducted for adults and children. ⊠ *525 S. Pleasant St.,* ☏ *413/256–6006.* ⊡ *Free.* ☉ *Trails: daily dawn–dusk; center: Wed.–Sat. 9–4.*

The effort to save Yiddish books and preserve Jewish culture has become a major movement, and the **National Yiddish Book Center** is its home. The center, modeled after a traditional Eastern European Jewish village, contains more than 1.3 million books, a fireside reading area, a kosher dining area, and a visitors center with interesting exhibits. The work here is performed out in the open: Hundreds of books pour in daily; the workers come across everything from family keepsakes to rare manuscripts. ⊠ *Harry and Jeanette Weinberg Building, Hampshire College, Rte. 116,* ☏ *800/535–3595.* ⊡ *Free.* ☉ *Sun.–Fri. 10–3:30.*

Dining and Lodging

$–$$ ✕ **Judie's.** For 20 years students have crowded around small tables on the glassed-in porch at Judie's, ordering burgers, salads, sandwiches, gourmet pastas, and many dishes served with popovers. You can go health-conscious or decadent (in the form of chocolate cake and other desserts). The atmosphere is casual and artsy—a painting on canvas covers each tabletop. ⊠ *51 N. Pleasant St.,* ☏ *413/253–3491. Reservations not accepted. AE, D, MC, V.*

$ ✕ **Black Sheep.** This student-oriented counter-service café typifies Amherst dining. Newspapers and books are strewn about the tables. A half dozen coffee selections complement excellent desserts and creative, high-quality sandwiches that include the C'est la brie (a baguette smothered with brie, roasted peppers, spinach, and raspberry mustard) and the French Kiss (truffle pâté, Djion mustard, and red onion on a baguette). The Black Sheep opens daily at 7 AM. ⊠ *79 Main St.,* ☏ *413/253–3442. MC, V.*

$$$ ✕▥ **Lord Jeffery Inn.** This gabled brick inn sits on the green between the town center and the Amherst College campus. Many bedrooms have a light floral decor; others have stencils and pastel woodwork. The formal dining room, where traditional dishes are served, is collegiate and Colonial, with old wood panels, heavy drapery, and a large fireplace. Burgers, salads, and the like are served at Boltwood's Tavern, which has a small bar and a wraparound porch. ⊠ *30 Boltwood Ave., 01002,* ☏ *413/253–2576,* ℻ *413/256–6152. 40 rooms, 8 suites. Restaurant, bar. AE, DC, MC, V.*

$$-$$$ 🏠 **Allen House.** A rare find, this inn built in 1886 has been restored
★ with precision: It's a glorious reproduction of the Aesthetic period of
the Victorian era. Busy, colorful wallcoverings reach to the high ceilings. Antiques include a burled walnut bedhead and dresser set, wicker
"steamship" chairs, screens, and carved golden-oak beds. Lace curtains
grace the windows in the rooms, whose supremely comfortable beds
have goose-down comforters. Allen House is a short walk from the center of Amherst. ⊠ 599 Main St., 01002, ☎ 413/253–5000. 7 rooms.
Full breakfast. AE, MC, V.

$$ 🏠 **Campus Center Hotel.** Atop the UMass campus and convenient to
all of Amherst, this modern hotel has spacious rooms with large win-
dows that allow excellent views over campus and countryside. The walls
are made of exposed cinderblock, and the rooms have simple furnish-
ings. Guests can use university exercise facilities with prior reservation,
and because the hotel is at a college, no tax is charged for accommo-
dations. ⊠ *University of Massachusetts, Murray D. Lincoln Tower,
01003,* ☎ *413/549–6000,* 🅵🅰🆇 *413/545–1210. 116 rooms, 6 suites. 2
indoor pools, 3 tennis courts, exercise room. AE, D, DC, MC, V.*

Nightlife and the Arts

Major ballet and modern dance companies appear in season at the **UMass
Fine Arts Center** (☎ 413/545–2511). The **William D. Mullens Memo-
rial Center** (University of Massachusetts; ☎ 413/545–0505) hosts
concerts, theatrical productions, and other entertainment.

Outdoor Activities and Sports

The **Norwottuck Rail Trail** is a paved 9-mi path that links Amherst with
Belchertown. Great for pedaling, Rollerblading, jogging, and cross-coun-
try skiing, it runs along the old Boston & Maine Railroad bed. **Valley
Bicycles** (⊠ 319 Main St., ☎ 413/256–0880) rents bikes and dis-
penses cycling advice.

FISHING

The Connecticut River sustains shad, salmon, and several dozen other
fish species. At **BioShelters** (⊠ 500 Sunderland Rd., ☎ 413/549–
3558) you pay $2 to drop your line, plus an amount that varies de-
pending on what fish you catch and the size.

Shopping

ART AND CRAFTS

The **Leverett Arts Center** (⊠ Montague Rd., Leverett, ☎ 413/548–
9070) houses 20 resident artists who create jewelry, ceramics, glass,
and textiles.

FOOD

Atkins Farms and Fruit Bowl (⊠ Rte. 116, South Amherst, ☎ 413/253–
9528), surrounded by a sea of apple orchards and gorgeous views of
the Holyoke Ridge, is an institution in the Pioneer Valley. Hay rides
take place in the fall, and there are children's events year-round. The
farm sells many varieties of apples and other fresh produce, along with
delicious cider doughnuts.

Northampton

🕹 *19 mi from Springfield.*

Small, bustling Northampton is listed on the National Register of His-
toric Places. Packed with restaurants and activists, the town, which was
first settled in 1654, is most famous as the site of **Smith College,** the
nation's largest liberal arts college for women. The redbrick quadrangles
of this institution founded in 1871 resemble the layouts of the women's
colleges at Cambridge University, England, which were built around

the same period. Worth visiting are the **Lyman Plant House** and the **botanic gardens.** The **College Art Museum** (⊠ Rte. 9, ☎ 413/584–2700), which holds more than 18,000 paintings, is open in the afternoon from Tuesday to Sunday.

The **Historic Northampton,** organization maintains three houses that are open for tours: Parsons House (1730), Shepherd House (1798), and Damon House (1813). ⊠ *46 Bridge St.,* ☎ *413/584–6011.* ☞ *$2.* ☉ *Tours Mar.–Dec., Thurs.–Sun. noon–4.*

The folks who concocted the Teenage Mutant Ninja Turtles operate ᐸ the **Words and Pictures Museum,** a repository of sequential art where you can see the latest comic books and graphic novels and create your own. ⊠ *140 Main St.,* ☎ *413/586–8545.* ☞ *$3.* ☉ *Sun. and Tues.–Thurs. noon–5, Fri. noon–8, Sat. 10–8.*

Northampton was the Massachusetts home of the 30th U.S. president, Calvin Coolidge. He practiced law here and served as mayor from 1910 to 1911. The **Coolidge Room** at the **Forbes Library** (⊠ 20 West St., ☎ 413/587–1011) contains a collection of his papers and memorabilia.

ᐸ Within **Look Memorial Park** (⊠ 300 N. Main St., Florence, ☎ 413/584–5457) are a small zoo, a wading pool, and children's playgrounds.

Dining and Lodging

$$ ✕ **Eastside Grill.** One of the dining rooms here is a glassed-in porch, and the other is wood-paneled with comfortable wood-and-leather booths. The menu includes a large selection of appetizers, great if you've just stopped by for a drink, and entrées such as blackened fish of the day and oysters on the half shell. ⊠ *19 Strong Ave.,* ☎ *413/586–3347. AE, D, DC, MC, V.*

$$ ✕ **Paul and Elizabeth's.** Plants fill this high-ceiling natural-foods restaurant. Among the seasonal specials are butternut-squash soup, home-baked corn muffins and Indian pudding, a large salad platter, Japanese tempura, and innovative fish entrées. ⊠ *150 Main St.,* ☎ *413/584–4832. AE, MC, V.*

$ ✕ **Northampton Brewery.** This microbrewery serves quality pub food—burgers, pizza, porterhouse steak—and exotic home brews. You can sup in warm weather on the roof deck, which also has a bar. Musicians perform on Sunday evening; there's no cover charge. ⊠ *11 Brewster Ct.,* ☎ *413/584–9903. AE, D, MC, V.*

$ ✕ **Sylvester's Restaurant.** Few people have heard of Dr. Sylvester Graham, a 19th-century Northampton resident, but most Americans are familiar with the graham cracker, which was named after him. Graham believed in eating natural foods and exercising, unpopular ideas in the 1830s: Emerson called him "the poet of bran bread and pumpkins." His former home has been converted into this restaurant that serves home-made breads and healthy soups. Sunday brunch is a crowded event. ⊠ *111 Pleasant St.,* ☎ *413/586–5343. MC, V. No lunch May–Sept.*

$$$–$$$$ ✕▥ **Hotel Northampton.** The enclosed porch of this austere brick hotel in the town center has wicker chairs. Room furnishings include Colonial reproductions, heavy curtains, and built-in hair dryers. Some rooms have four-poster beds, balconies overlooking a busy street or the parking lot, whirlpool tubs, and heated towel racks. The inn has been looking a little careworn these days, though comfort has not been compromised. The Wiggins Tavern (no lunch; closed on Monday and Tuesday) serves hearty fare like double-thick pork chops, chateaubriand, and Boston scrod. Fires burn in three dimly lighted dining rooms, where heavy exposed beams support low ceilings and antique kitchen appliances and snowshoes decorate every available space. The Coolidge Park Café serves burgers and sandwiches. ⊠ *36 King St., 01060,* ☎

413/584–3100, FAX *413/584–9455. 77 rooms, 5 suites. Restaurant, bar, café, no-smoking rooms. Continental breakfast. AE, D, DC, MC, V.*

$$$–$$$$ 🏠 **Inn at Northampton.** Country-French prints hang on the walls of this inn's large and tastefully furnished rooms, many of which overlook the parking lot; the more expensive rooms face the indoor pool and solarium and have sliding glass doors that open onto a balcony or a patio. The restaurant is a steak house. ✉ *1 Atwood Dr., 01060,* ☎ *413/586–1211 or 800/582–2929. 122 rooms, 2 suites. Restaurant, bar, indoor and outdoor pools, hot tub, 2 tennis courts, meeting rooms. Continental breakfast weekdays only. AE, D, DC, MC, V.*

$$ 🏠 **Knoll Bed and Breakfast.** This B&B sits well away from the busy road and backs onto steep woodlands. A sweeping staircase whisks you to the upstairs rooms. Oriental rugs grace polished wood floors. The guest rooms are furnished with four-poster beds and a mixture antiques and hand-me-downs. ✉ *230 N. Main St., Florence 01062,* ☎ *413/584–8164. 4 rooms share 2 baths. Library. Full breakfast. No credit cards.*

$$ 🏠 **Twin Maples Bed and Breakfast.** Fields and woods surround this 200-year-old farmhouse that's 7 mi northwest of Northampton near the village of Williamsburg. Colonial-style antiques and reproductions furnish the small rooms, which have restored brass beds. ✉ *106 South St., Williamsburg 01096,* ☎ *413/268–7925 or 413/268–7244,* FAX *413/268–7243. 3 rooms share bath. Full breakfast. AE, MC, V.*

Nightlife and the Arts

NIGHTLIFE

The **Iron Horse** (✉ 20 Center St., ☎ 413/584–0610, FAX 413/586–7488) presents folk, blues, jazz, Celtic, and alternative music nightly. The **Pearl Street Nightclub** (✉ 10 Pearl St., ☎ 413/584–7771) is the area's largest dance club, with frequent dance parties, gay and lesbian events, and live music several nights a week.

THE ARTS

The **Northampton Center for the Arts** (✉ 17 New South St., ☎ 413/584–7327) hosts theater, dance, and musical events and houses two galleries for the visual arts. Some of the ongoing classes—tai chi and swing dance are two of many offerings—are open to walk-ins.

Outdoor Activities and Sports

A 3.3-mi round-trip hike at the **Mt. Tom State Reservation** (✉ Rte. 5, Holyoke) leads to the summit, whose sheer basalt cliffs were formed by volcanic activity 200 million years ago. From the top are excellent views over the Pioneer Valley and the Berkshires.

At the wide place in the Connecticut River known as the Oxbow is the Massachusetts Audubon Society's **Arcadia Nature Center and Wildlife Sanctuary,** where you can enjoy the hiking and nature trails and scheduled canoe trips. ✉ *127 Combs Rd., Easthampton (3 mi from Northampton),* ☎ *413/584–3009.* ✍ *$3 for non-Audubon members.* ⊙ *Tues.–Sun. dawn–dusk; office 9–3.*

The **Quabbin Reservoir,** which provides drinking water for the greater Boston area, was created in 1939 by flooding the Swift River valley. Buildings in four towns were razed, and the bodies in the towns' churchyards were exhumed and reburied elsewhere. The only traces of the settlements are a few cellar holes, stone walls, and overgrown lanes that disappear eerily beneath the water. Today the Quabbin is a quiet spot of beauty, with facilities for fishing, hiking, and picnicking. Two great dams, which hold back 400 billion gallons of water, can be viewed at the south end, near the visitor center. Pictures of the drowned villages are displayed at the center. Fires, alcohol, and dogs are not allowed on the grounds. ✉ *485 Ware Rd., off Rte. 9, Belcher-*

town, ☎ *413/323–7221.* ✉ *Free.* ⊙ *Weekdays 8:30–4:30, week-ends 9–5.*

Shopping

The 8,000-square-ft **Antique Center of Northampton** (✉ 9½ Market St., ☎ 413/584–3600) houses 60 dealers. The **Ferrin Gallery at Pinch Pottery** (✉ 179 Main St., ☎ 413/586–4509) sells contemporary ceramics, jewelry, and glass. **Thorne's Marketplace** (✉ 150 Main St., ☎ 413/584–5582) is a funky four-floor indoor mall in a former department store.

South Hadley

43 *10 mi from Amherst, 6 mi from Holyoke.*

Mount Holyoke College, founded in 1837 as the first women's college in the United States, dominates the small village of South Hadley. Among the college's alumnae are Emily Dickinson and playwright Wendy Wasserstein. The handsome wooded campus, encompassing two lakes and lovely walking or riding trails, was landscaped by Frederick Law Olmsted. The **College Art Museum** has exhibits of Asian, Egyptian, and classical art. ✉ *Rte. 116,* ☎ *413/538–2245.* ✉ *Free.* ⊙ *Tues.–Fri. 11–5, Sat.–Sun. 1–5.*

Lodging

$$$$ 🏠 **Clark Tavern Inn.** Ezra Clark opened the doors of this establishment
★ in 1742. Customers in its early years included travelers crossing on the ferry and minutemen on their way to fight in Concord and Lexington. Two centuries later when the planned route for I–91 ran right through the property, two dedicated conservationists saved the house by moving it to its new site in Hadley. The move saved the house from destruction and made easier the installation of modern plumbing and heating. Braided rugs, canopy beds, and stencils create a genuine New England atmosphere. Fires warm two large common rooms that have comfortable couches; in summer, you can nap in the garden hammock or take a dip in the pool. Breakfast can be enjoyed fireside, on the screened-in porch or in your room. ✉ *98 Bay Rd., Hadley 01035,* ☎ *413/586–1900,* FAX *413/587–9788. 3 rooms. Pool. Full breakfast. AE, D, DC, MC, V.*

Outdoor Activities and Sports

BOATING

Sportsman's Marina Boat Rental Company (✉ Rte. 9, Hadley, ☎ 413/586–2426) rents canoes during summer and early fall.

Shopping

The **Hadley Antique Center** (✉ Rte. 9, ☎ 413/586–4093) contains more than 70 different stores.

The **Village Commons** (✉ College St.), across from Mount Holyoke College, is an outdoor mall with a movie theater, several restaurants, and shops with everything from handmade picture frames to lingerie. **Mona's Lace Place** (✉ Village Commons, 19 College St., ☎ 413/535–2523) stocks gifts, curtains, boxes, Christmas ornaments, bridal accessories, and more. The **Odyssey Bookstore** (✉ Village Commons, 9 College St., ☎ 413/534–7307) has gifts, cards, and more than 50,000 titles. Drop into **Tailgate Picnic** (✉ Village Commons, 7 College St., ☎ 413/532–7597) for specialty bagels, sandwiches, cold pastas, wine, and crackers; you can order the prepared foods to go.

Holyoke

44 *7 mi from Northampton, 8 mi from Springfield.*

A downtrodden town of crumbling redbrick factories and murky canals, Holyoke has little to interest the visitor apart from an imaginatively restored industrial city center and a children's museum.

The **Heritage State Park** tells the story of this papermaking community, the nation's first planned industrial city. The park is the starting point for the **Heritage Park Railroad.** Its antique steam train, which winds for two hours through the valley, runs sporadically, depending on financing and demand. A merry-go-round operates on weekends from 12 to 4. ⊠ *221 Appleton St.,* ☎ *413/534–1723.* 🎫 *Free.* ☉ *Tues.– Sun. noon–4:30.*

The **Children's Museum,** beside Heritage State Park in a converted mill by a canal, is packed with hands-on games and educational toys. Within the museum are a state-of-the-art TV station, a multitiered interactive exhibit on the body, a giant bubblemaker, and a sand pendulum. ⊠ *444 Dwight St.,* ☎ *413/536–5437.* 🎫 *$4.* ☉ *Tues.–Sat. 9:30–4:30, Sun. noon–5.*

The summer amusements at the **Mt. Tom ski area** (⊠ Rte. 5, ☎ 413/ 536–0516), include a wave pool and two water slides. *See* Skiing, *below,* for more information.

Dining and Lodging

$$–$$$$ ✕🏨 **Yankee Pedlar Inn.** This sprawling inn stands at a busy crossroads near I–91. Antiques and four-poster or canopy beds furnish the superb rooms. The elaborate Victorian bridal suite is heavy on lace and curtains; the carriage house has beams, rustic appointments, and simple canopy beds. Duck au poivre and filet mignon are among the dishes served at the elegant Grill Room, which is painted burgundy and accented with stained glass. The upscale Oyster Bar is the type of place where you order a bourbon, not a beer, to go with your black Angus beef burger or sophisticated sandwich. On Friday night the bar hosts local jazz musicians. ⊠ *1866 Northampton St., 01040,* ☎ *413/532– 9494,* 𝙵𝙰𝚇 *413/536–8877. 28 rooms, 11 suites. Restaurant, bar, nightclub, meeting rooms. Continental breakfast. AE, D, DC, MC, V.*

$$ 🏨 **Holiday Inn.** This typical chain property is 5 mi from the Mt. Tom ski area. Samuel's Restaurant and Bar is inside, and the huge Ingleside shopping mall and movie theaters are next door. ⊠ *Whiting Farms Rd. (Exit 15 off I–91), 01040,* ☎ *413/534–3311,* 𝙵𝙰𝚇 *413/533–8443. 219 rooms. Restaurant, bar. AE, D, DC, MC, V.*

Shopping

Holyoke Mall (⊠ Ingleside mall, Exit 15 off I–91) has nearly 200 stores, including JCPenney, Sears, Filene's, and Lord & Taylor.

Skiing

Mt. Tom Ski Area. Minutes from Holyoke, Springfield, and several colleges, Mt. Tom attracts skiers for day and night skiing and offers a five-week series of ski-lesson packages for children and adults. The management begins blasting man-made snow well before fall ends. On the premises are a restaurant, a cafeteria, and a ski shop. ⊠ *Rte. 5,* ☎ *413/536–0516.*

DOWNHILL

Slopes and trails at Mt. Tom tend to be extra wide, if not long, off the vertical of 680 ft. The trails are mostly for intermediates and beginners, with a few steeper pitches. Serving the 15 trails are four double chairlifts and two surface lifts.

In addition to daily group lessons on weekends, day camps provide an entire day of instruction for children from age 6 to 14. During vacation periods in December and February, five-day lesson programs are given. Mt. Tom also has midweek instruction programs for schoolchildren.

Springfield

45 *101 mi from Boston.*

Children's book author Theodore Geisel, also known as Dr. Seuss, was born in Springfield, the largest city in the Pioneer Valley, an industrial town where modern skyscrapers rise between grand historic buildings. Few people vacation in this rough city, but it does have some unusual museums.

Springfield Armory, the country's first arsenal, was established in 1779 and closed in 1968. The armory, which made small arms for the U.S. military, contains an extensive firearms collection. ⊠ *1 Armory Sq., off State St.,* ☎ *413/734–8551.* ⊠ *Free.* ⊙ *Wed.–Sun. 10–4:30.*

Dr. James Naismith invented basketball in Springfield in 1891. The **Naismith Memorial Basketball Hall of Fame** has a cinema, a two-story basketball fountain, and a moving walkway from which visitors can shoot baskets into 20 different-size hoops. ⊠ *W. Columbus Ave. at Union St.,* ☎ *413/781–6500.* ⊠ *$8.* ⊙ *Daily 9–6.*

Four museums have set up shop at the **museum quadrangle** (⊠ State and Chestnut Sts.) near downtown. There's a Dr. Seuss exhibit at the **Connecticut Valley Historical Museum** (☎ 413/263–6895), which commemorates the history of the Pioneer Valley. The **George Walter Vincent Smith Art Museum** (☎ 413/263–6894) contains a private collection of Japanese armor, ceramics, and textiles and a gallery of American paintings. The **Museum of Fine Arts** (☎ 413/263–6800) has paintings by Gauguin, Renoir, Degas, and Monet, as well as 18th-century American paintings and contemporary works. The **Springfield Science Museum** (☎ 413/263–6875) has an "Exploration Center" of touchable displays, a planetarium, a kid-focused eco-center, and dinosaur exhibits. ⊠ *$4 pass valid for all museums.* ⊙ *Wed.–Sun. noon–4.*

Forest Park (⊠ Pecousic Dr., ☎ 413/733–2251) has many recreational facilities, farm animals for feeding, and a children's zoo.

Riverside Park, the largest amusement park in New England, has a giant roller coaster, a water theme park, and picnic facilities. The admission price for children under 4 ft tall is $16.99. ⊠ *1623 Main St./Rte. 159 (south from Rte. 57 west of Springfield), Agawam,* ☎ *413/786–9300 or 800/370–7488.* ⊠ *$24.99.* ⊙ *Memorial Day–Labor Day, Sun.–Thurs. 11–6, weekends 11–11; Apr.–Memorial Day and Labor Day–Oct., weekends 11–11.*

Dining and Lodging

$$ ✕ **Student Prince and Fort Restaurant.** Named after a 1930s operetta, this restaurant established in 1935 in downtown Springfield is known for classic German food—bratwurst, schnitzel, and sauerbraten—and steaks, chops, and seafood. ⊠ *8 Fort St.,* ☎ *413/734–7475. AE, D, DC, MC, V.*

$$ ✕ **Theodore's.** At Theodore's you can dine saloon style in booths near the bar or in a small adjacent dining room. Period furniture and framed advertisements for curious products like foot soap lend the place a 1930s ambience. Burgers, sandwiches, chicken, and seafood are on the menu. Musicians perform on Friday and Saturday evening. ⊠ *201 Worthington St.,* ☎ *413/736–6000. AE, MC, V. Closed Sun. No lunch.*

$$$$ 🏨 **Marriott Hotel.** This downtown hotel opens onto the large Baystate West shopping mall. Rooms in front overlook the river; all are comfortably decorated with oak furniture and Impressionist prints. The business center has modem hook-ups, faxes, and copying machines. ⊠ *1500 Main St., 01115,* ☎ *413/781–7111,* ℻ *413/731–8932. 264 rooms, 3 suites. Restaurant, bar, indoor pool, sauna, exercise room, meeting rooms. AE, D, DC, MC, V.*

$ 🏨 **Cityspace.** The Springfield YMCA offers high-quality motel accommodations. The big advantage over other budget motels is that visitors can use all the sports and fitness facilities at the Y for free. Cityspace is close to I–91, near downtown, and a five-minute walk from the Amtrak station. ⊠ *275 Chestnut St., 01104,* ☎ *413/739–6951. 124 rooms with bath. Restaurant, indoor pool, massage, sauna, steam room, exercise room, racquetball, squash. MC, V.*

Nightlife and the Arts

The **Springfield Symphony Orchestra** (☎ 413/733–2291) performs from October to May at Symphony Hall (⊠ 75 Market Pl.) and mounts a summer program of concerts in the Springfield area. **StageWest** (⊠ 1 Columbus Ctr., ☎ 413/781–2340) presents plays and musicals from October to May. **Theodores'** (⊠ 201 Worthington St., ☎ 413/736–6000) hosts bands and other entertainers on weekend evenings.

Sturbridge

46   *55 mi from Boston, 31 mi from Springfield.*

★   **Old Sturbridge Village,** one of the country's finest period restorations and the star attraction of central Massachusetts, is just east of the Pioneer Valley. The village is a model of an early 1800s New England town, with more than 40 buildings on a 200-acre site. Some of the village houses are furnished with canopy beds and elaborate decoration; in the simpler, single-story cottages interpreters wearing period costumes demonstrate home-based crafts like spinning, weaving, shoe-making, and cooking. On the informative short boat ride along the Quinebaug River, you can learn about river life in 19th-century New England and catch a glimpse of ducks, geese, turtles, and other local wildlife. The village store contains an amazing variety of goods necessary for everyday life in the 19th century. ⊠ *1 Old Sturbridge Village Rd.,* ☎ *978/347–3362.* ☞ *$15, valid for 2 consecutive days.* ☉ *Late Apr.–late Oct., daily 9–5; off-season, Tues.–Sun. 10–4; Jan., weekends 10–4.*

Dining and Lodging

$ ✕ **Rom's.** This 700-seat restaurant is something of a local institution. The six dining rooms have an Early American decor, with wood paneling and beam ceilings. Rom's, which serves Italian and American cuisine—from pizza to roast beef—attracts crowds with a classic formula: good food at low prices. The veal Parmesan is very popular. ⊠ *Rte. 131,* ☎ *978/347–3349. AE, MC, V.*

$$–$$$$ ✕🏨 **Sturbridge Country Inn.** The atmosphere at this one-time farmhouse on Sturbridge's busy Main Street is between that of an inn and a plush business hotel. Guest rooms—all with working gas fireplaces and hot tubs—have reproduction antiques. The best is the top-floor suite; avoid the first-floor rooms—they're comparably priced but small and noisy. The Field Stone Tavern (closed from November to May) is a casual restaurant that serves sandwiches, salads, prime rib, and seafood entrées. The barn adjoining the inn has been converted into a theater where performances are staged year-round. ⊠ *Box 60, 530 Main St., 01566,* ☎ *978/347–5503; 978/347–7603 for restaurant,* ℻ *978/347–5319. 6 rooms, 3 suites. Restaurant, bar, hot tub. Continental breakfast. AE, D, MC, V. No lunch weekdays.*

$$–$$$
★   ✕🏨 **Publick House and Col. Ebenezer Crafts Inn.** Each of these three inns has its own character. The 17 rooms in the Publick House, which dates to 1771, are Colonial in design, with uneven wide-board floors; some have canopy beds. The neighboring Chamberlain House consists of larger suites, and the Country Motor Lodge has more modern rooms. The Crafts Inn, about a mile away, has a library, a lounge, a pool, and eight rooms with four-poster beds and painted wood paneling. The big and bustling restaurant at the Publick House is very busy on weekends. The fare is traditional Yankee food, including lobster pies, double-thick lamb chops, Indian pudding, pecan bread pudding, and apple pie. ✉ *Rte. 131, On-the-Common, 01566,* ☎ *978/347–3313,* 🖷 *978/347–5073. 118 rooms, 12 suites. Restaurant, bar, pool, tennis courts, jogging, shuffleboard, playground, meeting rooms. Continental breakfast at Crafts Inn. AE, DC, MC, V.*

$$$–$$$$ 🏨 **Sturbridge Host.** Across the street from Old Sturbridge Village on Cedar Lake, this hotel has luxuriously appointed bedrooms with Colonial decor and reproduction furnishings. Some rooms have fireplaces, balconies, or patios. ✉ *Rte. 20, 01566,* ☎ *978/347–7393 or 800/582–3232,* 🖷 *978/347–3944. 241 rooms, 9 suites. 2 restaurants, bar, indoor pool, miniature golf, tennis courts, sauna, basketball, exercise room, health club, racquetball, boating, fishing, meeting rooms. AE, D, DC, MC, V.*

Pioneer Valley A to Z

Arriving and Departing

BY BUS

Peter Pan Bus Lines (☎ 413/781–2900 or 800/237–8747) links Boston, Springfield, Holyoke, Northampton, Amherst, and South Hadley.

BY CAR

Interstate 91 runs north–south through the valley, from Greenfield to Springfield. Interstate 90 links Springfield to Boston. Route 2 connects Boston with Greenfield.

BY PLANE

Bradley International Airport (✉ Rte. 20; take Exit 40 off I–91, ☎ 860/627–3000) in Windsor Locks, Connecticut, is the most convenient airport for flying into the Pioneer Valley. American, Continental, Delta, Midway, Northwest, TWA, United, and US Airways serve Bradley. *See* Airline Travel *in* the Gold Guide for airline phone numbers.

BY TRAIN

Amtrak (☎ 800/872–7245) serves Springfield from New York City, stopping in New Haven. The *Lake Shore Limited* between Boston and Chicago calls at Springfield once daily in each direction, and three more trains run between Boston and Springfield every day.

Getting Around

BY BUS

Local bus companies with regular service are the **Pioneer Valley Transit Authority** (☎ 413/781–7882) and **Greenfield Montague Transportation Area** (☎ 413/773–9478).

BY CAR

Interstate 91 passes through or near Springfield, Holyoke, Northampton, Hadley, Deerfield, and Greenfield. Northfield is east (via Route 10) of I–91 on Route 63. Route 2 heads west from Greenfield to Shelburne Falls. Amherst is east of Northampton on Route 9. Sturbridge is east of Springfield, I–90 to I–84.

Contacts and Resources

ANTIQUES

For a list of members of the **Pioneer Valley Antique Dealers Association** write to Maggie Herbert, 201 N. Elm St., Northampton 01060.

EMERGENCIES

Baystate Medical Center (⌧ 759 Chestnut St., Springfield, ☎ 413/784–0000). **Cooley Dickenson Hospital** (⌧ 30 Locust St., Northampton, ☎ 413/582–2000). **Holyoke Hospital** (⌧ 575 Beech St., Holyoke, ☎ 413/534–2500).

RESERVATION SERVICE

Berkshire Bed-and-Breakfast Service (☎ 413/268–7244, ⌶ 413/268–7243) provides information and takes reservations for B&B and other Pioneer Valley accommodations.

VISITOR INFORMATION

The **Amherst Area Chamber of Commerce** (⌧ 11 Spring St., 01002, ☎ 413/253–0700). **Greater Northampton Chamber of Commerce** (⌧ 62 State St., 01060, ☎ 413/584–1900). The **Greater Springfield Convention and Visitors Bureau** (⌧ 34 Boland Way, Springfield 01103, ☎ 413/787–1548).

THE BERKSHIRES

Updated by
Kirsten C.
Sadler

More than a century ago, wealthy families from New York and Boston built "summer cottages" in western Massachusetts's Berkshire hills—great country estates that earned Berkshire County the nickname "inland Newport." Most of those grand houses have been converted into schools or hotels. Occupying the entire far western end of the state, the area is only about a 2½-hour drive directly west from Boston or north from New York City, yet it lives up to the storybook image of rural New England with wooded hills, narrow winding roads, and compact charming villages. Many cultural events take place in summer, among them the renowned Tanglewood classical music festival in Lenox. The foliage blazes brilliantly in fall, skiing is popular in winter, and spring is the time for maple-sugaring.

Picnic tables at the **Mohawk Trail State Forest** (⌧ Rte. 2, Charlemont, ☎ 413/339–5504) are set up under large evergreen trees. A few well-maintained hiking trails of a mile or so lead to a scenic lookouts. A camping area and a few log cabins, which can be rented for under $10 a night, are available.

Bypassing the entrance to the **Hoosac railway tunnel** (which took 24 years to build and at 4.7 mi was the longest in the nation when it was completed in 1875), Route 2 begins a steep ascent to Whitcomb Summit, then continues to the spectacular Western Summit, with excellent views, before dropping through a series of hairpin turns into North Adams.

En Route   Many visitors approach the Berkshires along Route 2 from Boston and the East Coast. The **Mohawk Trail,** a 67-mi stretch, follows the path blazed long ago by Native Americans that ran along the Deerfield River through the Connecticut Valley to the Berkshire hills. Just beyond the town of Charlemont stands *Hail to the Sunrise,* a 900-pound bronze statue of an Indian facing east, with arms uplifted, dedicated to the five Native American nations that lived along the Mohawk Trail. Some mostly tacky "Indian trading posts" on the highway carry out the Mohawk theme. Also along the road are antiques stores, flea markets, and several places to pull off the road, picnic, and photograph.

North Adams

47 *130 mi from Boston.*

Once a railroad boomtown and a thriving industrial city, North Adams is still industrial but no longer thriving. It's not really worth stopping here unless you're intrigued by the ghosts of the Industrial Revolution or are a railway buff.

Exhibits at the restored freight yard that now is the **Western Gateway Heritage State Park** outline the town's past successes, including the construction of the Hoosac tunnel between 1850 and 1875. ⊠ *9 Furnace St., Bldg. 4,* ☎ *413/663–6312.* ⌦ *$1 suggested donation.* ☉ *Daily 10–5.*

The only natural bridge in North America caused by water erosion is the marble arch at **Natural Bridge State Park.** The bridge crosses a narrow 500-ft chasm containing numerous faults and fractures. ⊠ *Rt. 8N,* ☎ *413/663–6392.* ⌦ *$2 per car.* ☉ *Memorial Day–Columbus Day, daily 10–6.*

One sign that things may be on the upswing in North Adams is the **Massachusetts Museum of Contemporary Arts,** or Mass MoCA, set to open in 1999. On 13 acres and consisting of 27 buildings, the complex will contain galleries, studios, performance venues, cafés, and shops. At press time, the admission prices and hours had not been set. ⊠ *87 Marshall St.,* ☎ *413/664–4481.*

Williamstown

48 *140 mi from Boston, 10 mi from North Adams.*

When Colonel Ephraim Williams left money to found a free school in what was then known as West Hoosuck, he stipulated that the name be changed to Williamstown. Williams College opened in 1793, and even today life in this placid town revolves around it. Graceful campus buildings like the Gothic cathedral, built in 1904, line wide Main Street. The collection and exhibits at the **Williams College Museum of Art** focus on American and 20th-century art. ⊠ *Main St.,* ☎ *413/597–2429.* ⌦ *Free.* ☉ *Tues.–Sat. 10–5, Sun. 1–5.*

★ The **Sterling and Francine Clark Art Institute** is one of the nation's notable small art museums. Its famous works include more than 30 paintings by Renoir, as well as canvases by Monet, Pisarro, and Degas. ⊠ *225 South St.,* ☎ *413/458–9545.* ⌦ *Free.* ☉ *Tues.–Sun. 10–5.*

The **Chapin Library of Rare Books and Manuscripts** at Williams College contains the Four Founding Documents of the United States—the Declaration of Independence, the Articles of Confederation, the Constitution, and the Bill of Rights—and 35,000 books, manuscripts, and illustrations dating from as far back as the 9th century. ⊠ *Stetson Hall, Main St.,* ☎ *413/597–2462.* ⌦ *Free.* ☉ *Weekdays 10–noon and 1–5.*

Dining and Lodging

$$$ ✕ **Le Jardin.** On a hillock above the road west of Williamstown, this Continental restaurant has the feel of an inn (there are guest rooms on the upper floor). Candles illuminate the two dining rooms, and a fire burns in the hall in season. The fare includes escargots, Long Island duck, filet mignon, and rack of lamb. ⊠ *777 Cold Spring Rd./Rte. 7,* ☎ *413/458–8032. AE, D, MC, V. Closed Tues. No lunch.*

$$$ ✕ **Wild Amber Grill.** The decor at White Amber may simple, but the food is much more complex. The owner-chef changes his contemporary American menu frequently but always includes a fine cut of beef,

The Berkshires

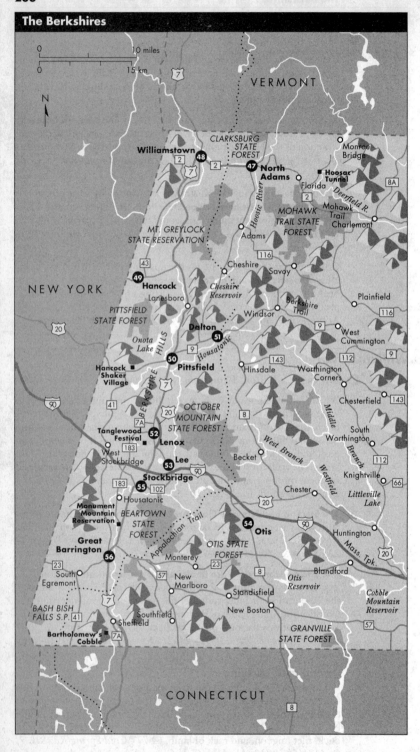

0 ____ 10 miles
0 ____ 15 km

N

VERMONT

NEW YORK

CONNECTICUT

CLARKSBURG STATE FOREST

Williamstown

47 North Adams

Monroe Bridge

Hoosac Tunnel

Florida

MOHAWK TRAIL STATE FOREST

Mohawk Trail Charlemont

MT. GREYLOCK STATE RESERVATION

Hoosic River

Deerfield R.

Adams

Cheshire

Savoy

49 Hancock

Cheshire Reservoir

Berkshire Trail

Plainfield

Lanesboro

PITTSFIELD STATE FOREST

Windsor

West Cummington

Onota Lake

51 Dalton

Housatonic

BERKSHIRE HILLS

50 Pittsfield

Hinsdale

Worthington Corners

Chesterfield

Hancock Shaker Village

Middle Branch

South Worthington

OCTOBER MOUNTAIN STATE FOREST

Westfield

Knightville

Tanglewood Festival

52 Lenox

Becket

West Branch

Chester

Littleville Lake

53 Lee

Huntington

55 Stockbridge

West Stockbridge

Housatonic

Mass. Tpk.

Monument Mountain Reservation

BEARTOWN STATE FOREST

Appalachian Trail

54 Otis

OTIS STATE FOREST

Blandford

Great Barrington

56

Monterey

Otis Reservoir

Cobble Mountain Reservoir

South Egremont

New Marlboro

Standisfield

New Boston

BASH BISH FALLS S.P.

Southfield

GRANVILLE STATE FOREST

Sheffield

Bartholomew's Cobble

a well-prepared poultry dish, and a vegetarian option. The moderately priced wine list has been shrewdly selected. On some weekends, musicians perform next to the fireplace in the lounge. Sunday brunch is served from 11 to 2. ⊠ *101 North St.,* ☎ *413/458–4000. AE, MC, V. Closed Tues.*

$$–$$$ ✕ **Mezze Bistro.** Hip. Happening. Mod. Trendy. Artistic. These are the words that leap to mind when you step inside Mezze. Blond wood covers the walls and simple square tables, and 1950s-style chairs line the walls. Translucent screens section off part of the dining area—perhaps to entice the famous actors and actresses who frequent Mezze after performing at the Williamstown Theater Festival. Veal sweetbreads with artichoke hearts and radicchio, sautéed pork with roasted shallots, prosciutto over soft polenta, and oven-roasted fennel gazpacho are among the zesty offerings. This is the only place in town hopping late into the evening—if you're hankering for a taste of SoHo, drop by for a martini or coffee. ⊠ *84 Water St.,* ☎ *413/458–0123. AE, MC, V. Closed Mon. Sept.–May. No lunch.*

$$$$ ⚑ **Field Farm Guest House.** Built in 1948 on 296 acres, this house, ★ which resembles a modern museum, was donated as part of a land trust by the former owners and is now run as a B&B by a nonprofit organization. The large windows in the guest rooms have expansive views of the grounds. Three rooms have private decks; two rooms have working fireplaces with tiles depicting animals, birds, and butterflies. The grounds, which include a pond, sculptures, a nature center, and 4 mi of trails, are open to the public. ⊠ *554 Sloan Rd., off Rte. 43, 01267,* ☎ *413/458–3135. 5 rooms. Dining room, pool, tennis courts, fishing. D, MC, V.*

$$$$ ⚑ **The Orchards.** It's right on Route 2 and surrounded by parking lots, but this luxury hotel is set around a beautiful central courtyard with fruit trees and a pond stocked with koi. Most of the spacious accommodations are furnished with English antiques. The inner rooms, which have one-way windows looking onto the courtyard, are best for summer stays. The outer rooms have less distinguished views but with their fireplaces are good for winter visits. The restaurant, Yasmine, serves breakfast, lunch, and dinner. ⊠ *222 Adams Rd., 01267,* ☎ *413/458–9611 or 800/225–1517,* ℻ *413/458–3273. 47 rooms, 2 suites. Restaurant, bar, pool, hot tub, sauna, exercise room, meeting rooms. AE, D, DC, MC, V.*

$$$$ ⚑ **Williams Inn.** The large rooms in this modern hotel have good-quality American furnishings and floral-print drapes and bedspreads. The atmosphere is collegiate in the comfortable lounge, which has an open fireplace. The inn allows pets for a $5 fee; children under 14 stay free in their parents' room. ⊠ *On-the-Green, 01267,* ☎ *413/458–9371 or 800/828–0133,* ℻ *413/458–2767. 103 rooms. Bar, coffee shop, dining room, air-conditioning, indoor pool, hot tub, sauna. AE, D, DC, MC, V.*

$$–$$$ ⚑ **Berkshire Hills Motel.** All the rooms at this excellent two-story brick-and-clapboard motel about 3 mi south of Williamstown are furnished in Colonial style. The lounge has an open fireplace, a piano, and a teddy-bear collection. The pool is across a brook amid 2½ acres of woodland and landscaped gardens. ⊠ *Rte. 7, 01267,* ☎ *413/458–3950 or 800/388—9677. 20 rooms. Pool. Continental breakfast. D, MC, V.*

$$–$$$ ⚑ **River Bend Farm.** One of the founders of Williamstown built this farmhouse that has been restored with complete authenticity. The kitchen, through which guests enter, contains an open-range stove and an oven hung with dried herbs. Some bedrooms have wide-plank walls, curtains of unbleached muslin, and four-poster beds with canopies or rope beds with feather mattresses. All rooms are sprinkled with antique pieces—chamberpots, washstands, wing chairs, and spinning wheels. ⊠ *643 Simonds Rd., 01267,* ☎ *413/458–5504. 4 rooms share 2 baths. Full breakfast. No credit cards.*

Nightlife and the Arts

Mezze Bistro (✉ 84 Water St., ☎ 413/458–0123) sometimes has live entertainment on weekends. Jazz and blues musicians perform on weekends at the tavern in the **Williams Inn** (☎ 413/458–9371). The **Williamstown Theatre Festival** (✉ Williams College, Adams Memorial Theatre, ☎ 413/597–3400), which runs from late June to August, presents well-known theatrical works with famous performers on the Main Stage, and contemporary works on the Other Stage.

Outdoor Activities and Sports

Waubeeka Golf Links (✉ Rte. 7, ☎ 413/458–5869) is an 18-hole course, par-72 course. The greens fee is $25 weekdays, $30 weekends; optional golf carts cost $26.

En Route The centerpiece of the 10,327-acre **Mt. Greylock State Reservation** (✉ Rockwell Rd., Lanesboro, ☎ 413/499–4262 or 413/499–4263) is 3,491-ft-high Mt. Greylock, the highest point in Massachusetts. The reservation, which is south of Williamstown, has facilities for cycling, fishing, horseback riding, hunting, camping, and snowmobiling. Walkers can find trail maps for hikes at higher elevations, including a stretch of the Appalachian Trail. Many treks start from the parking lot at the summit of Mt. Greylock. At the top of the mountain is Baskin lodge, where there are accommodations, snacks, and souvenirs from May to October.

Hancock

49 *15 mi from Williamstown.*

Hancock, the closest village to the Jiminy Peak resort, comes into its own during ski season. For summer guests, the resort has an alpine slide, a putting course, tennis courts, swimming facilities, and trout fishing.

Dining and Lodging

$$–$$$ ✕ **The Springs.** This restaurant sits in the shadow of Brodie Mountain and its ski resort. A fireplace in the lobby, exposed-brick walls, and a wood ceiling (from which hang several enormous chandeliers) create a country-lodge atmosphere. On the menu are veal Oscar (veal with lobster, white asparagus, and Newburg sauce), duckling flambé in cherry sauce, and steak Diane. You can choose from a light dinner menu or go for a full dinner, complete with palate-cleansing sherbet between each course. ✉ *Rte. 7, New Ashford,* ☎ *413/458–3465. AE, D, DC, MC, V.*

$$$ ✕▥ **Hancock Inn.** This inn, which dates from the late 1700s, provides
★ cozy Old World accommodations a mile from Jiminy Peak. Two small dining rooms have fireplaces, stained-glass windows, and candles on the tables. The menu changes weekly, but might include duckling in port wine with grapes, honey-mustard lamb chops, and veal and shrimp Dijon. ✉ *Rte. 43, 01237,* ☎ *413/738–5873. 6 rooms. Restaurant, 2 dining rooms. Full breakfast. AE, D, MC, V. No lunch; restaurant closed Nov.–mid-Dec.*

$$$$ ▥ **Country Inn at Jiminy Peak.** The massive stone fireplaces in its lobby and lounge lend this hotel a ski-lodge atmosphere. The modern, condo-style suites accommodate up to four people and have kitchenettes separated from the living area by a bar and high stools; the suites at the rear of the building overlook the slopes. The inn offers lodging-skiing packages. ✉ *Corey Rd., 01237,* ☎ *413/738–5500 or 800/882–8859,* ℻ *413/738–5513. 105 suites. Restaurant, bar, pool, 2 hot tubs, 2 saunas, miniature golf, 6 tennis courts, exercise room, meeting rooms. AE, D, DC, MC, V.*

BONUS MILES MAKE GREAT SOUVENIRS.

MCI Calling Card

123 456 7891 2345
J.D. SMITH

WorldPhone

Earn Miles With Your MCI Card.

Take the MCI Card along on this trip and start earning miles for the next one. You'll earn frequent flyer miles on all your calls and save with the low rates you've come to expect from MCI. Before you know it, you'll be on your way to some other international destination.

Sign up for MCI by calling 1-800-FLY-FREE

Is this a great time, or what? :-)

MCI

Earn Frequent Flyer Miles.

AmericanAirlines'
A**Advantage**®

Continental Airlines
OnePass

▲ Delta Air Lines
SkyMiles®

HAWAIIAN
AIRLINES.

MIDWEST EXPRESS AIRLINES

NORTHWEST AIRLINES
WORLDPERKS®

Rapid Rewards
SOUTHWEST AIRLINES

MILEAGE PLUS.
United Airlines

US AIRWAYS
DIVIDEND MILES

You've read the book. Now book the trip.

For all the best deals on flights, hotels, rental cars, and vacation packages, book them online at www.previewtravel.com. Then click on our Destination Guides featuring content from Fodor's and more. You'll find hotels, restaurants, attractions, and things to do around the globe. There are even interactive maps, videos, and weather forecasts. You'll have everything you need to make your vacation exactly what you want it to be. All it takes is a trip online.

Travel on Your Terms™
www.previewtravel.com
aol keyword: previewtravel

preview travel SM

Nightlife

In winter, the **Blarney Room** (☎ 413/443–4752), on the top floor of the main lodge at the Brodie ski area (☞ *below*), has entertainment nightly and live music on weekends and Sunday afternoon. **Ruby's** (✉ Rte. 8/Cheshire Rd., Lanesboro, ☎ 413/499–3993) has dancing to Top 40 hits spun by a DJ on Thursday, Friday, and Saturday.

Shopping

Amber Springs Antiques (✉ 29 S. Main St./Rte. 7, Lanesboro, ☎ 413/442–1237), in a shop behind an old white-clapboard house, stocks eclectic American furnishings from the 19th to mid-20th century: Tools, pottery, and country-store items are the house specialties.

Skiing

Brodie. The snow can be green, the beer is often green, and the decor is *always* green here. Yet it's more than the Irish ambience that attracts crowds for weekend and night skiing: The base lodge has a restaurant and bar with live entertainment, lodging is within walking distance of the lifts, and RV trailers can be accommodated. ✉ *Rte. 7, New Ashford 01237,* ☎ *413/443–4752, 413/443–4751 for snow conditions.*

DOWNHILL

Almost all the 28 trails at Brodie are beginner and intermediate despite the black diamonds, which designate steeper (but not expert) runs; the vertical is 1,250 ft. Four double chairlifts and two surface lifts serve the trails.

CROSS-COUNTRY

The area's cross-country skiing covers 25 km (16 mi) of trails, half of which are groomed daily.

OTHER ACTIVITIES

A sports center, Brodie Racquet Club (☎ 413/458–4677), 1 mi from the ski area, has five indoor courts for tennis and five for racquetball, an exercise room, and a cocktail lounge.

CHILD CARE

The nursery takes infants through age 8 by the hour, half day, or full day. There are afternoon, weekend, and holiday ski-instruction programs for children.

Jiminy Peak. This area, 2½ hours from New York City and three hours from Boston, has all the amenities of a major mountain resort. Condominiums and an all-suites country inn are within walking distance of the ski lifts; more condominium complexes are nearby; and two restaurants and bars are at the slopes. Rentals are available on a nightly or weekly basis. ✉ *Corey Rd., 01237,* ☎ *413/738–5500; 413/738–7325 for snow conditions.*

DOWNHILL

With a vertical of 1,140 ft, Jiminy has near big-time status. It is mostly a cruising mountain—trails are groomed daily, and only on some are small moguls left to build up along the side of the slope. The steepest black-diamond runs are on the upper headwalls; longer outer runs make for good intermediate terrain. A quad chair—dubbed Q1 because it was the first in Massachusetts—serves Jiminy's shorter left-side slopes. A longer triple chair is on the right. An expansion scheduled to be completed during 1999 will add another peak to the ski area, bringing the number of trails to 40 and lifts to nine. The season runs from late October to early April. There is night skiing from late November to mid-March every day of the week.

OTHER ACTIVITIES

Jiminy has a snowboard park and an old-fashioned ice rink.

CHILD CARE

The nursery takes children from 6 months. Children from age 4 to 12 can take daily SKIwee lessons; those from 6 to 15 can take a series of eight weekends of instruction with the same teacher. The kids' ski area has its own lift.

Pittsfield

㊿ *22 mi from Williamstown.*

Fast-food chains and run-down storefronts dominate Pittsfield, the county seat and geographic center of the Berkshires. But though it isn't particularly pretty, the town has a small-town atmosphere.

A local repository with a bit of everything, the **Berkshire Museum** contains animal exhibits, an aquarium, phosphorescent rocks, historical relics, and works of art. ⊠ *39 South St.,* ☎ *413/443–7171.* ☜ *$3.* ☉ *Tues.–Sat. 10–5, Sun. 1–5.*

The **Herman Melville Memorial Room** (☎ 413/499–9486) at the Berkshire Athenaeum (⊠ Berkshire Public Library, 1 Wendell Ave.) houses books, letters, and memorabilia of the author of *Moby Dick.*

Arrowhead, the house Herman Melville purchased in 1850, is just outside Pittsfield; the underwhelming tour includes the study in which *Moby Dick* was written. ⊠ *780 Holmes Rd.,* ☎ *413/442–1793.* ☜ *$5.* ☉ *Memorial Day–Labor Day, daily 10–5; Labor Day–Oct., Fri.–Mon. 10–5; Nov.–May weekdays only by appt.*

★ **Hancock Shaker Village** was founded in the 1790s, the third Shaker community in America. At its peak in the 1840s, the village had almost 300 inhabitants who made their living farming, selling seeds and herbs, making medicines, and producing crafts. The religious community officially closed in 1960, its 170-year life span a small miracle considering its population's vows of celibacy (they took in orphans to maintain their constituency). Many examples of Shaker ingenuity are visible at Hancock today: The **Round Stone Barn** and the **Laundry and Machine Shop** are two of the most interesting buildings. Also on site are a farm, some period gardens, a museum shop with reproduction Shaker furniture, a picnic area, and a café. ⊠ *Rte. 20, 5 mi west of Pittsfield,* ☎ *413/ 443–0188.* ☜ *$10 (good for 10 consecutive days).* ☉ *Apr.–Memorial Day and late Oct.–Nov., daily 10–3 (guided tours only); Memorial Day–late Oct., daily 9:30–5.*

Dining and Lodging

$$–$$$ ✕ **Dakota.** Moose and elk heads watch over diners at this large, highly acclaimed restaurant decorated like a rustic hunting lodge. A canoe swings overhead, and Native American artifacts hang on the walls. Meals cooked on the mesquite grill include salmon steaks, shrimp, and trout. A hearty brunch buffet is served on Sunday. ⊠ *Rtes. 7 and 20,* ☎ *413/ 499–7900. AE, D, DC, MC, V. No lunch Mon.–Sat.*

$$$$ ☷ **Crowne Plaza Pittsfield.** The upgraded rooms at this former Hilton have good views of the town and mountains. Two tiers of rooms surround the large, glass-dome swimming pool. ⊠ *Berkshire Common, South St., 01201,* ☎ *413/499–2000 or 800/445–8667,* ℻ *413/442– 0449. 173 rooms. 3 restaurants, bar, indoor pool, hot tub, sauna, exercise room, nightclub, meeting rooms. AE, D, DC, MC, V.*

Nightlife and the Arts

The **Berkshire Ballet** (⊠ Koussevitzky Arts Center, Berkshire Community College, West St., ☎ 413/445–5382) performs classical and contemporary works year-round, including *The Nutcracker* at Christmastime. On weekends in winter a DJ at the **Tamarack Lounge** (⊠ Dan Fox Dr., ☎ 413/442–8316), in the Bousquet ski area's base lodge, spins dance tunes.

Outdoor Activities and Sports

BIKING

The gently rolling Berkshire hills are excellent cycling terrain. Mountain bike trails can be found at the **Mt. Greylock State Reservation** (⊠ Rockwell Rd., Lanesboro, ☎ 413/499–4262). You can rent a bike from **Mountain Goat Bicycle Shop** (⊠ 130 Water St., Williamstown, ☎ 413/458–8445), which is about 7 mi west of Mt. Greylock. Making a reservation is advised during the summer.

BOATING

The **Housatonic River** flows south from Pittsfield between the Berkshire hills and the Taconic Range toward Connecticut. You can rent canoes, rowboats, paddleboats, small motorboats, and even pontoon partyboats from the **Onota Boat Livery** (⊠ 463 Pecks Rd., ☎ 413/442–1724), which also provides dock space on Onota Lake and sells fishing tackle and bait.

Skiing

Bousquet Ski Area. Other areas have entered an era of glamour and high prices, but Bousquet remains an economical, no-nonsense place to ski. The inexpensive lift tickets are the same price every day, and there's night skiing except Sunday. You can go tubing when conditions allow. ⊠ *Dan Fox Dr., Pittsfield 01201, ☎ 413/442–8316; 413/442–2436 for snow conditions.*

DOWNHILL

Bousquet, with a 750-ft vertical drop, has 21 trails, but only if you count every change in steepness and every merging slope. Though this is a generous figure, you will find some good beginner and intermediate runs, with a few steeper pitches. There are two double chairlifts and two surface lifts.

OTHER ACTIVITIES

The facilities at the **Berkshire West Athletic Club** (⊠ Dan Fox Dr., ☎ 413/494–4600), directly across the street from Bousquet, include four handball courts, six indoor tennis courts, a sauna and steam room, an indoor pool, a whirlpool, and free weights. Aerobics classes are conducted.

CHILD CARE

Bous-Care Nursery watches children age 6 months and up by the hour; reservations are suggested. Ski instruction classes are offered twice daily on weekends and holidays for children age 5 and up.

Dalton

51 *3 mi from Pittsfield.*

The paper manufacturer Crane and Co., started by Zenas Crane in 1801, is the major employer in working-class Dalton. The **Crane Museum of Paper Making,** housed in the Old Stone Mill (1844), has been beautifully restored with oak beams, Colonial chandeliers, and wide oak floorboards. Exhibits trace the history of American papermaking from Revolutionary times to the present. ⊠ *Off Rte. 9, ☎ 413/684–2600.* ▣ *Free.* ☉ *June–mid-Oct., weekdays 2–5. Closed mid-Oct.–May.*

Lodging

$$–$$$$ ☒ **Dalton House.** Guests in the main house here share a split-level sitting room and a sunny breakfast room. The average-size bedrooms are cheerful, with floral-print wallpaper and white wicker chairs. Two suites in the carriage house have sitting areas, exposed beams, period furnishings, and quilts. ⊠ *955 Main St., 01226,* ☎ *413/684–3854. 9 rooms, 2 suites. Pool. Continental breakfast. AE, MC, V.*

Lenox

🖎 *146 mi from Boston, 5 mi from Pittsfield.*

In the thick of the "summer cottage" region, rich with old inns and majestic buildings, the sophisticated village of Lenox epitomizes the Berkshires.

★ **Tanglewood** (☎ 617/266–1200 to order tickets), the summer home of the Boston Symphony Orchestra, is just outside Lenox. The 200-acre estate attracts thousands every year to concerts by world-famous performers. The 5,000-seat main shed hosts larger concerts; the Seiji Ozawa Hall (named for the BSO conductor) seats approximately 1,200 and is used for recitals, chamber music, and more intimate performances by summer program students and soloists. One of the most rewarding ways to experience Tanglewood is to purchase lawn tickets, arrive early to stroll around the beautiful grounds—don't forget the lawn chairs, because the ground is frequently wet—and enjoy a picnic. In classy Lenox pre-performance picnics often include linen tablecloths, champagne, candelabras, and enthusiastic conversation about the upcoming program.

★ **The Mount,** an American Classical mansion, was the former summer home of novelist Edith Wharton. The house and grounds were designed by Wharton, who is considered by many to have set the standard for 20th-century interior decoration. In designing The Mount, she followed the principles set forth in her book *The Decoration of Houses* (1897), creating a calm and well-ordered home. A "Women of Achievement" lecture series takes place in July and August on Monday. ⊠ *Plunkett St.,* ☎ *413/637–1899.* 🖾 *$6.* ☉ *May, weekends 9–3; June–Oct., daily 9–3.*

🖎 The **Railway Museum,** in a restored 1902 railroad station in central Lenox, contains period exhibits and a large working model railway. It's the starting point for the **Berkshire Scenic Railway,** which travels over a portion of the historic New Haven Railway's Housatonic Valley Line. ⊠ *Willow Creek Rd.,* ☎ *413/637–2210.* 🖾 *$2.* ☉ *Memorial Day weekend–Oct., weekends and holidays 10–4.*

Dining and Lodging

$$$$ ✕ **Blantyre.** Dining at Blantyre is truly an event. A harpist strums
★   softly in the grand parlor music room or on the terrace while you sip cocktails and peruse the prix-fixe menu. The food is a perfect variation on French cuisine—no creams or heavy sauces, light on the butter but fresh and imaginative. Unusual selections include the loin of Texas antelope with white leeks and pink peppercorn. After dinner retire to the music room to enjoy coffee with imported chocolates and marzipan followed by a fine cigar and a cognac. Lunch is served in summer. ⊠ *16 Blantyre Rd., off Rte. 20,* ☎ *413/298–3806,* 𝔽𝔸𝕏 *413/637–4282. Reservations essential. Jacket and tie. AE, DC, MC, V. Closed Nov.–May.*

$$$$ ✕☒ **Wheatleigh.** Wheatleigh was built in 1893, a wedding present for an American heiress who brought nobility into her family by marrying a Spanish count. Set amid 22 wooded acres, the mellow brick building, based on a 16th-century Florentine palazzo, has rooms with high ceilings, intricate plaster moldings, English antiques. and some modern furnishings. The rarefied environment makes this not the best place to bring young children. The main restaurant, a huge room with marble fireplaces and cut-glass chandeliers, has an excellent reputation for its "contemporary classical" cuisine; the prix-fixe menus (with 18% service charge) include roast antelope, pheasant, rabbit, and lobster; the Grill Room serves full meals in a more casual setting. ✉ *Hawthorne Rd., 02140, ☎ 413/637–0610, FAX 413/637–4507. 17 rooms. Restaurant, bar, 2 dining rooms, in-room VCRs, pool, tennis courts, exercise room, meeting rooms. AE, DC, MC, V.*

$$$–$$$$ ✕ **Café Lucia.** *Bistecca alla Fiorentina* (porterhouse steak grilled with olive oil, garlic, and rosemary) and *ravioli basilico e pomodoro* (homemade ravioli with fresh tomatoes, garlic and basil) are among the dishes at this upbeat northern Italian restaurant. The sleek decor includes track lighting and photographs of the owners' Italian ancestors. ✉ *90 Church St., ☎ 413/637–2640. Reservations essential up to 1 month ahead during Tanglewood. AE, MC, V. Closed Sun.–Mon. No lunch.*

$$–$$$ ✕ **Church St. Café.** Original art covers the walls, the tables are surrounded by ficus trees, and classical music wafts through the air at Church St. Café. The menu, which changes with the seasons, might include roast duck with thyme and Madeira sauce, rack of pork with wild mushrooms, and crab cakes. ✉ *69 Church St., ☎ 413/637–2745. MC, V. Closed Sun.–Mon., Nov.–Apr.*

$$–$$$$ ✕🏚 **The Village Inn.** The oldest inn in Lenox has been welcoming guests since 1775. Several of the rooms have fireplaces or whirlpool tubs, and all are appointed with antiques. High tea is served daily in summer and on weekends in the off-season. Breakfast (open to the public) is not included in the room rates during summer. The restaurant serves traditional fare—corn chowder, pecan-breaded breast of chicken, Yankee pot roast, and pan-seared swordfish with a cucumber-yogurt sauce. ✉ *16 Church St., 01240, ☎ 413/637–0527, FAX 413/637–9756. 32 rooms. Restaurant, bar. Continental breakfast Nov.–Apr. 3-night minimum in summer. AE, D, DC, MC, V.*

$$$$ 🏚 **Blantyre.** Modeled after a castle in Scotland, Blantyre is truly awe-★ inspiring, with massive public rooms and 88 acres of beautifully maintained grounds, that include a croquet lawn where professional tournaments take place. Huge and lavishly decorated, the rooms in the main house have hand-carved four-poster beds, overstuffed chaise longues, chintz chairs, boudoirs, walk-in closets, and Victorian bathrooms. The rooms in the carriage house are well appointed but can't compete with the formal grandeur of the main house. The rates include a Continental breakfast served in the dining room or delivered, one course at a time, to your room; a full breakfast is available for an extra charge. ✉ *16 Blantyre Rd., off Rte. 20, 01240, ☎ 413/298–3806, FAX 413/637–4282. 13 rooms, 10 suites. Restaurant, pool, hot tub, sauna, tennis courts, croquet, hiking. Continental breakfast. AE, DC, MC, V. Closed Nov.–May.*

$$$–$$$$ 🏚 **Cliffwood Inn.** Six of the seven guest rooms in this Colonial Revival ★ building have fireplaces, and four more fireplaces glow in the common areas. Much of the inn's furniture comes from Europe; most guest rooms have canopy beds. The patio and pool area are well designed; indoors there's a counter-current pool. ✉ *25 Cliffwood St., 01240, ☎ 413/637–3330 or 800/789–3331, FAX 413/637–0221. 7 rooms. Dining room, pool. Full breakfast. No credit cards.*

$$$–$$$$ 🏚 **Cranwell Resort and Hotel.** The best rooms in this complex are in the century-old Tudor mansion—they're furnished with antiques and have marble bathrooms. Two smaller buildings have 20 rooms each, and there are several small cottages, each with a kitchen. Most of the facilities are open to the public, as are the resort's restaurants, where

you can dine formally or informally. ⊠ *55 Lee Rd., 02140,* ☎ *413/ 637–1364 or 800/272–6935,* ⟨FAX⟩ *413/637–4364. 95 rooms. 3 restaurants, pool, fitness center, driving range, 18-hole golf course, 2 tennis courts, bicycles, cross-country skiing. Continental breakfast. AE, D, DC, MC, V.*

$$$–$$$$ ⬚ **Whistler's Inn.** The antiques decorating the parlor of this English Tudor
★   mansion are ornate with a touch of the exotic. The library, formal parlor, music room, and grand dining room all impress. Designer drapes and bedspreads adorn the rooms, three of which have working fireplaces. The carriage house is only open during warm months; one room in it has an African decor, another is done in southwestern style. ⊠ *5 Greenwood St., 01240,* ☎ *413/637–0975,* ⟨FAX⟩ *413/637–2190. 14 rooms. Badminton, croquet, library. Full breakfast. AE, D, MC, V.*

$$–$$$$ ⬚ **Garden Gables.** On 5 acres of wooded grounds a two-minute walk from the center of Lenox, this 250-year-old "summer cottage" has been an inn since 1947. The three common parlors have fireplaces, and one long narrow room has a unique five-legged Steinway piano. Rooms come in various shapes, sizes, and colors; some have brass beds, and others have pencil four-posters. Some rooms have sloping ceilings, fireplaces, whirlpool baths, or woodland views. Three have private decks. Breakfast is served buffet-style in the airy dining room. ⊠ *Box 52, 135 Main St., 01240,* ☎ *413/637–0193,* ⟨FAX⟩ *413/637–4554. 18 rooms. Dining room, pool. Full breakfast. AE, D, MC, V.*

$$–$$$ ⬚ **Apple Tree Inn.** On a hillside across the street from Tanglewood's main gate, the Apple Tree is perfect for those who are drawn to the concert series. The parlor contains a grand piano, velvet couches, hanging plants, and German nutcracker decorations. Guest rooms in the main inn have four-poster or brass beds, Victorian washstands, and wicker; some have working fireplaces. Avoid Room No. 5—it's hot, noisy, and over the kitchen of the restaurant. The 21 rooms in the motor-lodge style building next door have traditional furnishings with less character. ⊠ *334 West St., 01240,* ☎ *413/637–1477. 30 rooms with bath, 2 rooms share bath, 2 suites. Restaurant, bar, pool. AE, D, MC, V. Closed mid-Nov.–Apr.*

$$ ⬚ **Eastover.** An antidote to the posh atmosphere prevailing in most of Lenox, this resort was opened by an ex-circus roustabout—noisy fun and informality are the order of the day here. The functional rooms range from dormitory- to motel-style; though the period wallpapers are stylish, the rooms with four or more beds resemble hospital wards. A herd of buffalo lives on the huge grounds. The facilities are extensive, and rates include all meals and activities. ⊠ *Box 2160, 430 East St., off Rtes. 20 and 7, 01240,* ☎ *413/637–0625,* ⟨FAX⟩ *413/637–4939. 120 rooms with bath, 75 rooms share baths. Dining room, indoor and outdoor pools, sauna, driving range, 5 tennis courts, badminton, exercise room, horseback riding, volleyball, mountain biking, cross-country skiing, downhill skiing, tobogganing. AP. AE, D, DC, MC, V.*

Nightlife and the Arts

The **Berkshire Performing Arts Theater** (⊠ 70 Kemble St., ☎ 413/637– 1800), on the campus of the National Music Center, attracts top-name artists in jazz, folk, opera, rock, and blues and presents children's shows. **Shakespeare and Company** (⊠ Plunkett St., ☎ 413/637– 1197) performs the works of Shakespeare and Edith Wharton throughout the summer at The Mount. The tavern at the **Village Inn** (⊠ 16 Church St., ☎ 413/637–0527) is a good, dark place to have a drink.

Outdoor Activities and Sports

BIKING

Main Street Sports and Leisure (⊠ 48 Main St., ☎ 413/637–4407) rents mountain and road bikes and provides maps and route suggestions.

CANOEING

Main Street Sports and Leisure (⊠ 48 Main St., ☎ 413/637–4407) rents canoes and leads canoe trips on the Housatonic River and local lakes.

CROSS-COUNTRY SKIING

Cranwell Resort and Hotel (⊠ 55 Lee Rd., ☎ 413/637–1364 or 800/ 272–6935) has miles of skiable golf course and trails. **Kennedy Park** (⊠ Main St. just past the Church on the Hill) has 22 mi of walking trails that are great for skiing, especially if you enjoy some hills. **Main Street Sports and Leisure** (⊠ 48 Main St., ☎ 413/637–4407) rents skis by the day.

HORSEBACK RIDING

Undermountain Farm (⊠ 400 Undermountain Rd., ☎ 413/637–3365) gives lessons and conducts guided trail rides.

Shopping

The **Hand of Man–Craft Gallery** (⊠ 5 Walker St., ☎ 413/637–0631) handles the work of several hundred artists. **Stone's Throw Antiques** (⊠ 51 Church St., ☎ 413/637–2733) carries fine antiques. The **Ute Stubich Gallery** (⊠ 69 Church St., ☎ 413/637–3566) sells folk and contemporary art.

Lee

53 *140 mi from Boston, 6 mi from Lenox.*

Gas stations, convenience stores, and strip motels litter the landscape of Lee, an exit on the Massachusetts Turnpike. Heavy traffic rumbles through town constantly—if you stay here, find lodging away from the main road.

Dining and Lodging

$$$ ✕ **Cork 'n Hearth.** Laurel Lake practically laps against the side of this restaurant that has a large stone fireplace and a picture window. The menu is traditional—steaks, seafood, chicken Kiev, and veal Oscar. Children's plates are available. ⊠ *Rte. 20,* ☎ *413/243–0535. AE, MC, V. Closed Mon. No lunch.*

$$–$$$ 🏨 **Morgan House.** This 1817 inn is in the middle of downtown and accessible to area attractions. The good-size rooms, each with a sitting area, have brightly painted wood furniture, four-poster beds, stenciled walls, and well-worn antiques. The lobby is papered with pages from old guest registers; among the signatures are those of playwright George Bernard Shaw and U.S. president Ulysses S. Grant. ⊠ *33 Main St., 01238,* ☎ *413/243–0181. 6 rooms with bath, 5 rooms share 3 baths. 2 dining rooms, tavern. Full breakfast. AE, D, DC, MC, V.*

Otis

54 *151 mi from Boston, 21 mi from Lenox.*

A change from almost-too-quaint Stockbridge and luxurious Lenox, Otis, with a ski area and 20 lakes and ponds, supplies plenty of what made the Berkshires desirable in the first place—the great outdoors. The dining options here are slim; your best bet is to pack a picnic of goodies from a Lenox gourmet shop.

Route 8, the road into into Otis, follows the Farmington River. The **Otis Reservoir** (⊠ Off Rte. 8, ☎ 413/269–6002), the largest body of fresh water in Massachusetts used exclusively for recreation, has facilities for swimming, boating, and fishing. **J & D Marina** (⊠ 1367 Reservoir Rd., East Otis, ☎ 413/269–4839) rents boats and has a small restaurant. You can hike, bike, or cross-country ski at the 3,800-acre

Otis State Forest (✉ Rte. 23). The 8,000-acre **Tolland State Forest** (✉ Rte. 8, ☎ 413/269–6002) allows swimming in the Otis Reservoir and camping.

Deer Run Maples (✉ Ed Jones Rd., ☎ 413/269–4363) is one of several sugar houses where you can spend the morning tasting freshly tapped maple syrup that's been drizzled onto a dish of snow.

NIGHTLIFE AND THE ARTS

Jacob's Pillow Dance Festival (✉ George Cantor Rd. at Rte. 20, Becket, ☎ 413/637–1322; 413/243–0745 for box office between June and August), the oldest in the nation, happens over 10 weeks each summer. The participants range from well-known contemporary classical ballet companies to Native American dance groups. Before the main events, showings of works-in-progress and even of some of the final productions are staged outdoors, often free of charge. Visitors can picnic on the grounds or eat at the Pillow Café.

Lodging

$$$–$$$$ **Maplewood 1850 House.** This no-nonsense B&B in an old farmhouse is steps from the Farmington River and across a meadow from the ski ridge. The decor of the well-maintained rooms is functional. Hank, the host, knows the Otis area well and is happy to provide tips about outdoor recreation and other activities. ✉ *Main St., 01253,* ☎ *413/269–7351,* FAX *413/269–7276. 6 rooms share 2 baths; 2 suites. MC, V.*

Skiing

Otis Ridge Ski Area (✉ Rte. 23, ☎ 413/269–4446), a family-style ski area with mostly mild terrain, has reasonable rates and night-skiing facilities.

Stockbridge

(55) *149 mi from Boston, 7 mi from Lenox.*

Stockbridge, a major tourist destination, has the look of small-town New England down pat. Its artistic and literary inhabitants have included sculptor Daniel Chester French, writers Norman Mailer and Robert Sherwood, and, fittingly enough, that champion of small-town America, painter Norman Rockwell, who lived here from 1953 until his death in 1978.

The **Norman Rockwell Museum** displays the largest collection of Rockwell originals in the world. The museum also mounts exhibits by other artists. You can stroll along the river walk or picnic on the vast grounds. ✉ *Rte. 183 (2 mi from Stockbridge),* ☎ *413/298–4100.* *$8.* *May–Oct., daily 10–5; Nov.–Apr., weekdays 11–4, weekends 10–5.*

Chesterwood was for 33 years the summer home of the sculptor Daniel Chester French, who created the Minute Man in Concord and the Lincoln Memorial in Washington, D.C. Tours are given of the house, which is maintained in the style of the 1920s, and of the studio, where you can view the casts and models French used to create the Lincoln Memorial. ✉ *Williamsville Rd. off Rte. 183,* ☎ *413/298–3579.* *$6.50.* *May–Oct., daily 10–5.*

The 15-acre **Berkshire Botanical Gardens** contains greenhouses, ponds, nature trails, and perennial, rose, and herb gardens. Picnicking is encouraged. In July, the garden is the site of a well-attended antiques show. ✉ *Rtes. 102 and 183,* ☎ *413/298–3926.* *$5.* *May–late Oct., daily 10–5.*

Naumkeag, a Berkshire cottage once owned by Joseph Choate, an ambassador during the administration of U.S. president William McKinley and a successful New York lawyer, provides a glimpse into the gracious living of the "gilded era" of the Berkshires. Atop Prospect Hill, this 26-room gabled mansion is decorated with many original furnishings and art that spans three centuries; the collection of Chinese export porcelain is also noteworthy. The meticulously kept 8 acres of formal gardens are themselves worth a visit. ⊠ *South Prospect Hill,* ☎ *413/ 298–3239.* 🎟 *$6.50.* ☉ *Memorial Day–Columbus Day, daily 10–4:15.*

Dining and Lodging

$$–$$$ ✕ **Once Upon a Table.** The atmosphere is casual yet vaguely romantic at this little restaurant in a little alley off Stockbridge's main street. Escargots baked in mushroom caps with garlic-tarragon butter and the goat-cheese and red-pepper bruschetta are among the appetizers; entrées include roasted chicken over risotto. ⊠ *36 Main St.,* ☎ *413/298– 3870. Reservations essential. AE, MC, V. Closed Mar. and Sun.–Tues. in Jan.–Feb. No lunch Mon.–Tues.*

$$$$ ✕🏨 **Williamsville Inn.** A couple of miles south of West Stockbridge,
★ this inn re-creates the late 1700s, when it was built. The rooms have wide-board floors, embroidered chairs, and four-poster or canopy beds; several have country furnishings, two have working fireplaces, and four rooms in the converted barn have wood-burning stoves. One of the dining rooms is a cozy library, the other one has a fireplace made of unpolished, locally hewn marble. Entrées include roasted breast of duck with blackberry sauce and potatoes, spicy roasted loin of pork with black-bean chili and corn bread, and vegetarian options. ⊠ *Rte. 41, 01266,* ☎ *413/274–6118,* 🖷 *413/274–3539. 15 rooms, 1 suite. Restaurant, bar, pool, tennis courts, badminton, croquet, horseshoes, volleyball. Full breakfast. AE, MC, V.*

$$$–$$$$ ✕🏨 **Red Lion Inn.** An inn since 1773, the Red Lion has a large main building and seven annexes, each of which is different (one is a converted fire station). Many rooms are small; the ones in the annex houses tend to be more appealing. Rooms have floral-print wallpaper and curtains from the mail-order store Country Curtains, which is owned by the innkeepers and operated out of the inn. All the rooms are furnished with antiques and reproductions and hung with Rockwell prints; some have Oriental rugs. The same menu is served in both of the dining rooms and (in season) in the garden. There is a dress code (jacket and tie) in the formal dining room. New England specialties include clam chowder; broiled scallops prepared with sherry, lemon, and paprika; and steamed or stuffed lobster. ⊠ *Main St., 02162,* ☎ *413/298–5545,* 🖷 *413/298–5130. 96 rooms with bath, 15 rooms share 5 baths, 26 suites. 2 restaurants, bar, pool, massage, exercise room, meeting rooms. AE, D, DC, MC, V.*

$$$$ 🏨 **Inn at Stockbridge.** Antiques and feather comforters are among the accents in the rooms of this inn run by the attentive Alice and Len Shiller. The two serve breakfast in their elegant dining room, and every evening they provide wine and cheese for guests to enjoy while looking through an extensive notebook of area restaurants. There are four new rooms in the adjacent building, each with a decorative theme like Kashmir, St. Andrews, and Provence. ⊠ *Box 618, Rte. 7, 02162,* ☎ *413/298– 3337,* 🖷 *413/298–3406. 8 rooms, 4 suites. Pool. Full breakfast. AE, D, MC, V.*

$$$–$$$$ 🏨 **Golden Goose.** Antiques and bric-a-brac—including dozens of geese in various shapes and sizes—provide cheerful clutter at this inn 5 mi south of Lee. Bedrooms are Victorian in style, with quilts and stenciled walls or floral wallpaper. The two sitting rooms have fireplaces, and there's a deck off the back for summertime relaxing. The studio apartment with a kitchen and a private entrance is perfect for families. ⊠ *Box 336, 123 Main Rd., Tyringham 01264,* ☎ *413/243–3008. 5*

rooms with bath, 2 rooms share bath, 1 studio. Dining room. Full break-fast. AE, D, MC, V.

$$$–$$$$ ⊞ **Historic Merrell Inn.** This inn, which was built more than 200 years
★   ago as a private residence (it was later a stagecoach stopover), has some
good-size rooms, several with working fireplaces. Meticulously main-
tained, the Merrell has an unfussy yet authentic style, with polished wide-
board floors, painted walls, and wood antiques. The breakfast room has
an open fireplace and contains the only intact "birdcage" Colonial bar—
a semicircular bar surrounded by wooden slats—in America. ⊠ *1565
Pleasant St./Rte. 102, South Lee 01260,* ☎ *413/243–1794 or 800/243–
1794,* 𝖥𝖠𝖷 *413/243–2669. 9 rooms, 1 suite. Full breakfast. MC, V.*

Nightlife and the Arts

The **Berkshire Theatre Festival** (☎ 413/298–5536; 413/298–5576 for
box office) stages nightly performances during summer in Stockbridge.
Plays written by local schoolchildren are performed occasionally dur-
ing the summer. The **Lion's Den** (⊠ Red Lion Inn, Main St., ☎ 413/
298–5545) presents live jazz, folk, or blues nightly. From late June to
late August, **Robbins-Zust Family Marionettes** (⊠ East Rd., Richmond,
☎ 413/698–2591) mounts a varied program that always includes
Punch and Judy and classic fairy-tale stories.

Shopping

Downtown Stockbridge's many "country stores" sell New England kitsch
at premium prices—you're better off heading out of town to the smaller,
less crowded shops. **Le Petit Musée** (⊠ 137 Front St., Housatonic, ☎
413/274–1200) is a gallery that exhibits small contemporary and vin-
tage art. **Sawyer Antiques** (⊠ Depot St., West Stockbridge, ☎ 413/
232–7062) sells Early American furniture and accessories in a spare
clapboard structure that was a Shaker mill. **Spazi** (⊠ Barbieri's Lum-
ber Mill, Rte. 183, 3rd floor, ☎ 413/274–3805), near Housatonic, car-
ries contemporary painting, sculpture, and photography.

Great Barrington

 7 mi from Stockbridge.

The largest town in the southern Berkshires was the first place to free
slaves under due process of law and the birthplace of W. E. B. Du Bois,
the civil rights leader, author, and educator. The many ex–New York-
ers who live in Great Barrington expect great food and service, and
the restaurants here deliver complex, tasteful fare. The town is also a
mecca for antiques hunters, as are the nearby villages of South Egre-
mont and Sheffield.

Bartholomew's Cobble, south of Great Barrington, is a natural rock
garden beside the Housatonic River (the Native American name means
"river beyond the mountains"). The 277-acre site is filled with trees,
ferns, wildflowers, and hiking trails. The visitor center has a museum.
⊠ *Rte. 7A,* ☎ *413/229–8600.* 🖾 *$3.50.* ⊙ *Dawn–dusk.*

Mt. Washington State Forest (⊠ Rte. 23, ☎ 413/528–0330) is 16 mi
southwest of Great Barrington on the New York State border. The free
primitive camping area is open year-round, but there's a catch—you
have to hike 1½ mi from the parking lot. The forest's Bash Bish Brook
(say that 10 times, fast) flows through a gorge and over a 50-ft wa-
terfall into a clear natural pool.

The Arts

The **Berkshire Opera Company** (⊠ 314 Main St., ☎ 413/528–4420)
performs two operas in Great Barrington in July and August, one a
classic, the other a 20th-century work in English.

Dining and Lodging

$$$ ✕ **Boiler Room Café.** Whimsical wood sculptures decorate the comfortable rooms of this café. Owner Michèle Miller's eclectic menu might include a light New England seafood stew, mouthwatering grilled baby back ribs, or osso bucco Piedmontese. Fresh salads, tapas, and a chèvre soufflé are among the starters. ⊠ *405 Stockbridge Rd.,* ☎ *413/528–4280. MC, V. Closed Sun.–Mon. except holidays. No lunch.*

$$$ ✕ **Stagecoach Hill Inn.** The 1765 structure that houses this restaurant was a stagecoach stop in the early 1800s. The place has a decidedly English character: Hunting scenes and pictures of the British royal family decorate the walls, and there's British ale on tap. Regional American fare is served in the candlelit dining room; try the popular Stagecoach pizza. ⊠ *Rte. 41, Sheffield,* ☎ *413/229–8585. AE, D, DC, MC, V. Closed Wed. No lunch.*

$$$–$$$$ ✕⊞ **Egremont Inn.** The public rooms in this 1780 inn are enormous, and each has a fireplace. The bedrooms are on the small side, but have four-poster beds, claw-foot baths, and, like the rest of the inn, unpretentious furnishings that will inspire you to kick back and relax. Windows sweep around two sides of the stylish restaurant (reservations essential on weekends in season), where flames flicker in a huge fireplace. The menu changes frequently but always includes salmon or another fresh fish, a homemade pasta, and a hearty meat dish like rib-eye steak with caramelized onions. ⊠ *Box 418, Old Sheffield Rd., South Egremont 01258,* ☎ *413/528–2111, FAX 413/528–3284. 19 rooms, 1 suite. Restaurant, bar, pool, tennis courts. Continental breakfast. AE, D, MC, V. 2-night minimum in season.*

$$$–$$$$ ⊞ **Turning Point Inn.** A mere half-mile east of Butternut Basin, this 200-year-old inn used to be the Pixie Tavern, a stagecoach stop. Guests share a sitting room, a living room with two fireplaces and a piano, and a kitchen made cozy by a Dutch oven. Several of the antiques-filled bedrooms have sloped ceilings. The hosts, natural-foods advocates, serve up robust breakfasts of multigrain hot cereals, frittatas with fresh garden vegetables, buckwheat pancakes, eggs, and home-baked muffins or cakes. The barn has been converted into a two-bedroom cottage, which has modern furnishings, a full kitchen, a living room, and a winterized porch. ⊠ *R.D. 2, Box 140, Rte. 23 and Lake Buel Rd., 01230,* ☎ *413/528–4777. 4 rooms with bath, 2 rooms share bath, 1 cottage. Full breakfast, except in cottage. AE, MC, V.*

$$–$$$$ ⊞ **Ivanhoe Country House.** The Appalachian Trail runs right across the property of this 1780 house, which has been run as a B&B by the current owners for 30 years. The antiques-furnished rooms are generally spacious; four have working fireplaces, several have private porches or balconies, and all have excellent country views. The large sitting room has antique desks, a piano, a fireplace, and comfortable couches. The owners have several golden retrievers; pets are welcome. A Continental breakfast is brought to your door each morning. ⊠ *254 S. Undermountain Rd./Rte. 41, Sheffield, 01257,* ☎ *413/229–2143. 9 rooms, 2 suites. Refrigerators, pool. Continental breakfast. No credit cards.*

$$–$$$$ ⊞ **Mountain View Motel.** This motel 1 mi west of Butternut ski area has pleasant accommodations with coffeemakers; Norman Rockwell prints hang on the walls. ⊠ *304 State Rd./Rte. 23E, 01230,* ☎ *413/ 528–0250, FAX 413/528–0137. 16 rooms, 1 suite, 1 efficiency. AE, MC, V.*

$$–$$$ ⊞ **Weathervane Inn.** The open fireplace and beehive oven in the lounge of this family-run inn date to the 1760s, when the original building was constructed. The formal parlor has striking reproduction wallpaper; guest rooms are decorated with stencils, country curtains, wreaths, Norman Rockwell prints, and rocking chairs. At one point the inn was a dog kennel—one of the guest bathrooms has a dog-size bathtub. ⊠

Box 388, Rte. 23, South Egremont 01258, ☎ 413/528–9580 or 800/ 528–9586, FAX 413/528–1713. 11 rooms. 2 dining rooms, bar, pool. Full breakfast; MAP available. AE, D, MC, V.

Nightlife and the Arts

Jazz musicians perform at the **Egremont Inn** (⊠ Old Sheffield Rd., South Egremont, ☎ 413/528–2111) on Friday and Saturday.

Outdoor Activities and Sports

Three miles north of Great Barrington, you can leave your car in a parking lot beside Route 7 and climb Squaw Peak on **Monument Mountain.** The 2.7-mi circular hike (a trail map is displayed in the parking lot) takes you up 900 ft, past glistening white quartzite cliffs from which Native Americans are said to have leapt to their deaths to placate the gods. The view of the surrounding mountains from the peak is superb. North of Great Barrington is the large and untamed **Beartown State Forest,** which has miles of hiking trails and a small campground where the fee for a site is $4 a night. ⊠ *Blue Hill Rd., Monterey,* ☎ *413/528–0904.*

Shopping

The Great Barrington area, including the small towns of Sheffield and South Egremont, has the greatest concentration of antiques stores in the Berkshires. Some shops are open sporadically, and many are closed on Tuesday. For a list of storekeepers who belong to the **Berkshire County Antiques Dealers Association,** send a self-addressed, stamped envelope to R.D. 1, Box 1, Sheffield 01257. The 100-plus dealers in the three-story **Coffman's Country Antiques Market** (⊠ Jennifer House Commons, Rte. 7, ☎ 413/528–9282) sell furniture, quilts, baskets, and silverware. **Corashire Antiques** (⊠ Rtes. 23 and 7 at Belcher Sq., ☎ 413/528–0014), a shop in a red barn, carries American country furniture and accessories (mostly painted, nothing formal), including the occasional Shaker piece. **Mullin-Jones Antiquities** (⊠ 525 S. Main St./Rte. 7, ☎ 413/528– 4871) has 18th- and 19th-century country-French antiques: armoires, buffets, tables, chairs, and gilded mirrors.

Red Barn Antiques (⊠ Rte. 23, South Egremont, ☎ 413/528–3230) carries antique lamps and 19th-century American furniture, glass, and accessories. The **Splendid Peasant** (⊠ Rte. 23 and Old Sheffield Rd., South Egremont, ☎ 413/528–5755) sells 18th- and 19th-century American and European painted country furniture and has three galleries of museum-quality American folk art.

Bradford Galleries (⊠ Rte. 7, Sheffield, ☎ 413/229–6667) holds monthly auctions of furniture, paintings and prints, china, glass, silver, and Oriental rugs. A tag sale of household items occurs daily. **Darr Antiques and Interiors** (⊠ 28 S. Main St./Rte. 7, Sheffield, ☎ 413/229– 7773) displays elegant 18th- and 19th-century American, English, Continental, and Asian furniture and accessories in an impressive Colonial house. A second building houses another 1,600 square ft of antiques. **Dovetail Antiques** (⊠ Rte. 7, Sheffield, ☎ 413/229–2628) shows American clocks, pottery, and country furniture. **Good & Hutchinson Associates** (⊠ Rte. 7, Sheffield, ☎ 413/229–8832) specializes in American, English, and Continental furniture and paintings, fine pottery, and china. Some of the pottery on display at **Great Barrington Pottery** (⊠ Rte. 41, Housatonic, ☎ 413/274–6259) is crafted on site; there are gallery-style showrooms here, European and Japanese gardens, and a tea room.

Antiques at the Buggy Whip Factory (⊠ Main St./Rte. 272, Southfield, ☎ 413/229–3576) provides space for 75 dealers selling jewelry, glass, china, sterling, books, formal and country furniture, and 19th-century fabrics.

Skiing

Butternut Basin. This friendly resort has good base facilities, pleasant skiing, and an eatery in the base lodge that serves tasty food. Skiers from New York's Long Island and Westchester County and Connecticut's Fairfield County flock to the area. There are three snow parks for snowboarders; ski and snowboard lessons are available for kids and adults. ⊠ *Rte. 23, 01230,* ☎ *413/528–2000 ext. 112; 413/528–4433 for ski school; 800/438–7669 for snow conditions.*

DOWNHILL

Only a steep chute or two interrupt the mellow intermediate terrain on 22 trails. There are slopes for beginners and something for everyone off the area's 1,000-ft vertical. One quad, one triple, and four double chairlifts, plus two surface lifts, keep skier traffic spread out.

CROSS-COUNTRY

Butternut Basin has 8 km (4 mi) of groomed cross-country trails.

CHILD CARE

The nursery takes children from age 2½ to age 6, and younger toddlers or infants by appointment. The ski school's SKIwee program is for children from 4 to 12 years old.

The Berkshires A to Z

Arriving and Departing

BY BUS

Bonanza Bus Lines (☎ 800/556–3815) connects points throughout the Berkshires with Albany, New York City, and Providence. **Peter Pan Bus Lines** (☎ 413/442–4451 or 800/237–8747) serves Lee and Pittsfield from Boston and Albany.

BY CAR

The Massachusetts Turnpike (I–90) connects Boston with Lee and Stockbridge and continues into New York, where it becomes the New York State Thruway. To reach the Berkshires from New York City take either I–87 or the Taconic State Parkway.

BY TRAIN

Amtrak (☎ 800/872–7245) runs the *Lake Shore Limited,* which stops at Pittsfield once daily in each direction on its route between Boston and Chicago.

Getting Around

BY CAR

The main north–south road within the Berkshires is Route 7. The scenic Mohawk Trail (Route 2) runs from the northern Berkshires to Greenfield at the head of the Pioneer Valley and continues across Massachusetts into Boston.

Contacts and Resources

ARTS LISTINGS

The daily *Berkshire Eagle* covers the area's arts festivals; from June to Columbus Day the *Eagle* publishes *Berkshires Week,* the summer bible for events information. The *Williamstown Advocate* prints general arts listings. The Thursday edition of the *Boston Globe* publishes news of major concerts.

CANOEING

Pleasant canoe trips in the Berkshires include Lenox–Dalton (19 mi), Lenox–Stockbridge (12 mi), Stockbridge–Great Barrington (13 mi), and, for experts, Great Barrington–Falls Village (25 mi). Information about these and other trips can be found in *The AMC River Guide to*

Massachusetts, Rhode Island, and Connecticut (AMC, 5 Joy St., Boston, 02198).

EMERGENCIES

Fairview Hospital (⊠ 29 Lewis Ave., Great Barrington, ☎ 413/528–0790). **Hillcrest Hospital** (⊠ 165 Tor Ct., Pittsfield, ☎ 413/443–4761). **North Adams Regional Hospital** (⊠ Hospital Ave., North Adams, ☎ 413/663–3701).

GUIDED TOURS

American Balloon Works, Inc. (☎ 518/766–5111) operates twice-daily balloon trips over the Berkshires. **Berkshire Hiking Holidays** (☎ 413/499–9648) of Lenox conducts guided hiking tours: Less ambitious walkers can combine easy hikes with visits to Tanglewood and Berkshire towns; the more experienced trekker can tackle mountain trails. The company also takes people on combined hiking, biking, and canoe trips; overnight accommodations are provided by Berkshire inns. **New England Hiking Holidays** (☎ 603/356–9696 or 800/869–0949) of North Conway, New Hampshire, organizes guided hiking vacations through the Berkshires, with overnight stays at country inns. Hikes cover from 5 to 9 mi per day.

HIKING

Berkshire Region Headquarters (⊠ 740 South St., Pittsfield, ☎ 413/442–8928) has information about trails and hiking.

LODGING REFERRALS

Lenox Chamber of Commerce (☎ 413/637–3646 or 800/255–3669). **Southern Berkshires Chamber of Commerce** (☎ 413/528–4006).

STATE PARKS

There are 19 state parks and forests in the Berkshires. Those with camping include **Beartown State Forest** (⊠ Blue Hill Rd., Monterey, ☎ 413/528–0904), **Clarksburg State Forest** (⊠ Middle Rd., Clarksburg, ☎ 413/664–8345), **Mt. Greylock State Reservation** (⊠ Rockwell Rd., Lanesboro, ☎ 413/499–4262 or 413/499–4263), **October Mountain State Forest** (⊠ Woodland Rd., Lee, ☎ 413/243–1778), **Otis State Forest** (⊠ Rte. 23, Otis, ☎ 413/528–0904), **Pittsfield State Forest** (⊠ Cascade St., Pittsfield, ☎ 413/442–8992), **Sandisfield State Forest** (⊠ West St., Sandisfield, ☎ 413/229–8212), **Savoy Mountain State Forest** (⊠ 260 Central Shaft Rd., Florida, ☎ 413/663–8469), **Tolland State Forest** (⊠ Rte. 8, Otis, ☎ 413/269–6002), and **Windsor State Forest** (⊠ Windsor, ☎ 413/442–8928).

VISITOR INFORMATION

Berkshire Visitors Bureau (⊠ Berkshire Common, Pittsfield 01201, ☎ 413/443–9186 or 800/237–5747). **Lenox Chamber of Commerce** (⊠ Lenox Academy Building, 75 Main St., 01240, ☎ 413/637–3646). **Mohawk Trail Association** (⊠ Box 722, Charlemont 01339, ☎ 413/664–6256).

MASSACHUSETTS A TO Z

Arriving and Departing

By Bus

Bonanza (☎ 800/556–3815) serves Boston, Cape Cod, and the eastern part of the state from Providence, with connecting service to New York. **Greyhound** (☎ 800/231–2222) buses connect Boston with all major cities in North America. **Peter Pan Bus Lines** (☎ 617/426–7838) connects Boston with cities elsewhere in Massachusetts and in Connecticut, New Hampshire, and New York. **Plymouth & Brockton**

Buses (☎ 508/746–0378) link Boston with the South Shore and Cape Cod. The depot for the bus companies is **South Station** (✉ Atlantic Ave. and Summer St., ☎ 617/345–7451).

By Car

Boston is the traffic hub of New England, with interstate highways approaching it from every direction. New England's chief coastal highway, I–95, skirts Boston; I–90 leads west to the Great Lakes and Chicago. Interstate–91 brings visitors to the Pioneer Valley in western Massachusetts from Vermont and Canada to the north and Connecticut and New York to the south.

By Plane

Boston's **Logan International Airport** (☞ Boston A to Z, *above*) has scheduled flights by most major domestic and foreign carriers. **Bradley International Airport** (☞ Connecticut River Valley A to Z *in* Chapter 2), in Windsor Locks, Connecticut, 18 mi south of Springfield on I–91, has scheduled flights by major U.S. airlines.

By Train

The Northeast Corridor service of **Amtrak** (☎ 800/872–7245) links Boston with the principal cities between it and Washington, D.C. The *Lake Shore Limited,* which stops at Springfield and the Berkshires, carries passengers from Chicago to Boston.

Getting Around

See Arriving and Departing, *above,* or the regional A to Z sections, *above.*

Contacts and Resources

Camping

A list of private campgrounds throughout Massachusetts can be obtained free from the **Massachusetts Office of Travel and Tourism** (☞ *below*).

Visitor Information

Massachusetts Office of Travel and Tourism (✉ 100 Cambridge St., Boston 02202, ☎ 617/727–3201 or 800/447–6277).

5 Vermont

Southern Vermont has farms, freshly starched New England towns, quiet back roads, bustling ski resorts, and strip-mall sprawl. Central Vermont's trademarks include marble quarries north of Rutland and pastures that create the patchwork of the Champlain Valley. The heart of this region is the Green Mountains. The state's largest city (Burlington) and the nation's smallest state capital (Montpelier) are in northern Vermont, as are some of the most remote areas of New England. Logging, dairy farming, and skiing take place here.

Revised and
updated by
Anne Peracca
Bijur

EVERYWHERE YOU LOOK AROUND VERMONT, the evidence is clear: This is not the state it was 25 years ago. That may be true for the rest of New England as well, but the contrasts between the present and recent past seem all the more sharply drawn in the Green Mountain State, if only because an aura of timelessness has always been at the heart of the Vermont image. Vermont was where all the quirks and virtues outsiders associate with up-country New England were supposed to reside. It was where the Yankees were Yankee-est and where there were more cows than people.

Not that you should be alarmed, if you haven't been here in a while; Vermont hasn't become southern California, or even, for that matter, southern New Hampshire. This is still the most rural state in the Union (meaning that it has the smallest percentage of citizens living in statistically defined metropolitan areas), even if there are, finally, more people than cows. It's still a place where cars occasionally have to stop while a dairy farmer walks his herd across a secondary road; and up in Essex County, in what George Aiken dubbed the Northeast Kingdom, there are townships with zero population. And the kind of scrupulous, straightforward, plainspoken politics practiced by Governor (later Senator) Aiken for 50 years has not become outmoded in a state that still turns out on town-meeting day.

How has Vermont changed? In strictly physical terms, the most obvious transformations have taken place in and around the two major cities, Burlington and Rutland, and near the larger ski resorts, such as Stowe, Killington, Stratton, and Mt. Snow. Burlington's Church Street, once a paradigm of all the sleepy redbrick shopping thoroughfares in northern New England, is now a pedestrian mall with chic bistros; outside the city, suburban development has supplanted dairy farms in towns where someone's trip to Burlington might once have been an item in a weekly newspaper. As for the ski areas, it's no longer enough simply to boast the latest in chairlift technology. Stratton has an entire "Austrian village" of restaurants and shops, while a hillside adjacent to Bromley's slopes has sprouted instant replica Victorians for the second-home market. The town of Manchester, convenient to both resorts, is awash in designer-fashion discount outlets.

But the real metamorphosis in the Green Mountains has to do more with style, with the personality of the place, than with development. The past couple of decades have seen a tremendous influx of outsiders—not only skiers and "leaf peepers," but people who have come to stay year-round—and many of them are determined either to freshen the local scene with their own idiosyncrasies or to make Vermont even more like Vermont than they found it. On the one hand, this translates into the fact that one of the biggest draws to the tiny town of Glover each summer is an outdoor pageant that promotes leftist political and social causes; on the other, it means that sheep farming has been reintroduced to the state, largely to provide a high-quality product for the hand-weaving industry.

This ties in with another local phenomenon, one best described as Made in Vermont. Once upon a time, maple syrup and sharp cheddar cheese were the products that carried Vermont's name to the world. The market niche that they created has since been widened by Vermonters—a great many of them refugees from more hectic arenas of commerce—offering a dizzying variety of goods with the ineffable cachet of Vermont manufacture. There are Vermont wood toys, Vermont apple

Vermont

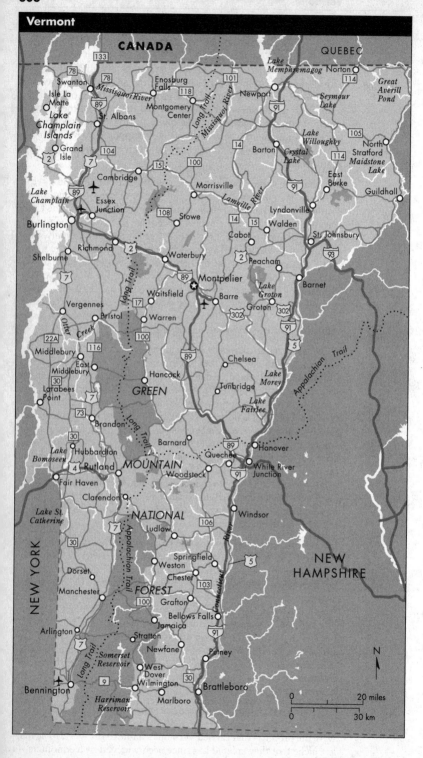

wines, Vermont chocolates, even Vermont gin. All of it is marketed with the tacit suggestion that it was made by Yankee elves in a shed out back on a bright autumn morning.

The most successful Made in Vermont product is Ben & Jerry's ice cream. Neither Ben nor Jerry comes from old Green Mountain stock, but their product has benefited immensely from the magical reputation of the place where it is made. Along the way, the company (which started in Burlington under the most modest circumstances in 1979) has become the largest single purchaser of Vermont's still considerable dairy output.

Pleasures and Pastimes

Biking

Vermont is great bicycle-touring country, especially the often deserted roads of the Northeast Kingdom. Many companies lead weekend tours and weeklong trips throughout the state. If you'd like to go it on your own, most chambers of commerce have brochures highlighting good cycling routes in their area, including *Vermont Life's* "Bicycle Vermont" map and guide, and many bookstores sell *25 Bicycle Tours in Vermont* by John Freidin.

Dining

Vermont restaurants have not escaped common efforts in the Northeast to adapt traditional New England fare to the ways of nouvelle cuisine. The New England Culinary Institute, based in Montpelier, has trained a number of chefs who have turned their attention to native New England foods like fiddlehead ferns (available only for a short time in the spring), maple syrup (Vermont is the largest U.S. producer), dairy products (especially cheese), native fruits and berries that are often transformed into jams and jellies, "new Vermont" products such as salsa and salad dressings, and venison, quail, pheasant, and other game.

Your chances of finding a table for dinner vary with the season: Many restaurants have lengthy waits during peak seasons (when it's always a good idea to make a reservation) and then shut down during the slow months of April and November. Some of the best dining is found at country inns.

CATEGORY	COST*
$$$$	over $35
$$$	$25–$35
$$	$15–$25
$	under $15

*average cost of a three-course dinner, per person, excluding drinks, service, and 7% sales tax

Fishing

Central Vermont is the heart of the state's warm-water lake and pond fishing. Harriman and Somerset reservoirs have both warm- and cold-water species; Harriman has a greater variety. Lake Dunmore produced the state-record rainbow trout; Lakes Bomoseen and St. Catherine are good for rainbows and largemouth bass. In the east, Lakes Fairlee and Morey feature bass, perch, and chain pickerel, while the lower part of the Connecticut River contains smallmouth bass, walleye, and perch; shad are returning via the fish ladders at Vernon and Bellows Falls.

In northern Vermont, rainbow trout inhabit the Missisquoi, Lamoille, Winooski, and Willoughby rivers, and there's warm-water fishing at many smaller lakes and ponds. Lakes Seymour, Willoughby, and Memphremagog and Great Averill Pond in the Northeast Kingdom are good for salmon and lake trout. The Dog River near Montpelier has one of the best wild populations of brown trout in the state. Good news is that landlocked Atlantic salmon are returning to the Clyde River because of a breech in the dam.

Lake Champlain, stocked annually with salmon and lake trout, has become the state's ice-fishing capital; walleye, bass, pike, and channel catfish are also taken. Ice fishing is also popular on Lake Memphremagog.

Lodging

Vermont's largest hotels are in Burlington and near the major ski resorts. There's a dearth of inns and bed-and-breakfasts in Burlington, though chain hotels provide dependable accommodations. Elsewhere you'll find inns, B&Bs, and small motels. Rates are highest during foliage season, from late September to mid-October, and lowest in late spring and November, when many properties close. Many of the larger hotels offer package rates. Some antiques-filled inns discourage bringing children.

The Vermont Chamber of Commerce publishes the *Vermont Travelers' Guidebook,* which is an extensive list of lodgings, and additional guides to country inns and vacation rentals. The Vermont Travel Division has a brochure that lists lodgings at working farms.

CATEGORY	COST*
$$$$	over $150
$$$	$100–$150
$$	$60–$100
$	under $60

All prices are for a standard double room during peak season, with no meals unless noted, and excluding service charge.

National Forests

The 355,000 acres of Green Mountain National Forest extend down the center of the state, providing scenic drives, picnic areas, lakes, and hiking and cross-country ski trails. Grout Pond Recreation Area and Somerset Reservoir are two idyllic boating and hiking destinations—it's worth the wear on your car's struts and shocks driving dirt roads (closed in winter) to get to them. There are also trailheads for the Appalachian and Long trails here, and the trail to the waterfalls at the Lye Brook Wilderness Area is popular.

Skiing

The Green Mountains run through the middle of Vermont like a bumpy spine, visible from almost every point in the state; generous accumulations of snow make the mountains an ideal site for skiing. Increased snowmaking capacity and improved, high-tech computerized equipment at many areas virtually assure a good day on the slopes. Vermont has 21 alpine ski resorts with nearly 900 trails and some 4,000 acres of skiable terrain. Combined, the resorts operate nearly 200 lifts and have the capacity to carry a total of more than 200,000 skiers per hour. Though grooming is sophisticated at all Vermont areas, conditions usually range from hard pack to icy, with powder a rare luxury. The best advice for skiing in Vermont is to keep your skis well tuned.

Route 100 is also known as "Skier's Highway," passing by 13 of the state's ski areas. Vermont's major resorts are Stowe, Jay Peak, Sugarbush, Killington, Okemo, Mt. Snow, and Stratton. Midsize, less hectic areas to consider include Ascutney, Bromley, Bolton Valley, Smugglers' Notch, Pico, Mad River Glen, and Burke Mountain.

Exploring Vermont

Vermont is divided into three regions. The southern part, flanked by Bennington and Brattleboro, played an important role in the formation of

Vermont's statehood. The central part is characterized by its mountains and its marble. Northern Vermont is the site of the state's capital and largest city, yet also is home to its most rural area, the Northeast Kingdom.

Numbers in the text correspond to numbers in the margin and on the Southern Vermont, Central Vermont, and Northern Vermont maps.

Great Itineraries

There are many ways to take advantage of Vermont's beauty—skiing or hiking its mountains, biking or driving its back roads, fishing or sailing its waters, shopping for local products, visiting its museums and sights, or simply finding the perfect inn and never leaving the front porch. Distances in Vermont are relatively short, yet there are mountains and many back roads to contend with, which will slow a traveler's pace.

IF YOU HAVE 3 DAYS

Spend a few hours in historic **Bennington** ⑤, then travel north to see Hildene and stay in 🔝 **Manchester** ⑦. On your second day take Route 100 through Weston, north through the Green Mountains to Route 125, where you turn west to explore 🔝 **Middlebury** ㉕. On day three, enter the Champlain Valley, which has views of the Adirondack Mountains to the west. Stop at Shelburne Farms and carry on to **Burlington** ㉞; catch the sunset from the waterfront and take a walk on Church Street.

IF YOU HAVE 5 TO 7 DAYS

You can make several side trips off Route 100. Visit **Bennington** ⑤ and 🔝 **Manchester** ⑦ on day one. Spend your second day walking around the small towns of **Chester** ⑪ and 🔝 **Grafton** ⑫. On day three head north to explore **Woodstock** ⑲ and 🔝 **Quechee** ⑱, stopping at either the Billings Museum or the Vermont Institute of Natural Science. Head leisurely on your fourth day toward 🔝 **Middlebury** ㉕, along one of Vermont's most inspiring mountain drives, Route 125 west of Route 100. Between Hancock and Middlebury, you'll pass nature trails and the picnic spot at Texas Falls Recreation Area, then traverse a moderately steep mountain pass. Spend day five in 🔝 **Burlington** ㉞. On day six head east to **Waterbury** ㉘ and then north to 🔝 **Stowe** ㉚ and Mount Mansfield for a full day. Begin your last day with a few hours in **Montpelier** ㉗ on your way to **Peacham** ㊴, **St. Johnsbury** ㊳, 🔝 **Lake Willoughby** ㊱, and the serenity and back roads of the Northeast Kingdom. Especially noteworthy are Routes 5, 5A, and 14.

When to Tour Vermont

The number of tourists and the rates for lodging reach their peaks along with the color of the leaves during foliage season, from late September to mid-October. But if you have never seen a kaleidoscope of autumn colors, it is worth braving the slow-moving traffic and paying the extra money. Rates are lowest in late spring and November, although many properties close during these times.

SOUTHERN VERMONT

The Vermont tradition of independence and rebellion began in southern Vermont. Many towns founded in the early 18th century as frontier outposts or fortifications were later important as trading centers. In the western region the Green Mountain Boys fought off both the British and the claims of land-hungry New Yorkers—some say their descendants are still fighting. In the 19th century, as many towns turned to manufacturing, the eastern part of the state preserved much of its farms and orchards.

The first thing you'll notice upon entering the state is the conspicuous lack of billboards along the highways and roads. The foresight back in the 1960s to prohibit them has made for a refreshing absence of aggressive visual clutter that allows travelers unencumbered views of working farmland, freshly starched New England towns, and quiet back roads (but does not hide the reality of abandoned dairy barns, bustling ski resorts, and strip-mall sprawl).

The towns are listed in circular order. We begin in the east, south of the junction of I–91 and Route 9 in Brattleboro, and follow the southern boundary of the state toward Bennington, then north up to Manchester and Weston and south back to Newfane.

Brattleboro

❶ *60 mi south of White River Junction.*

Its downtown bustling with activity, Brattleboro is the center of commerce for southeastern Vermont. At the confluence of the West and Connecticut rivers, this town with about 13,000 inhabitants originated as a frontier scouting post and became a thriving industrial center and resort town in the 1800s. More recently, the area has become a home to political activists and those pursuing alternative lifestyles.

A former railroad station, the **Brattleboro Museum and Art Center** has replaced locomotives with art and historical exhibits. The museum's organs were made in Brattleboro between 1853 to 1961, when the city was home to the Estey Organ Company one of the world's largest organ manufacturers. ⊠ *Vernon and Main Sts.,* ☎ *802/257–0124.* ☑ *$3.* ☉ *Mid-May–early Nov., Tues.–Sun. noon–6.*

Larkin G. Mead, Jr., a Brattleboro resident, stirred 19th-century America's imagination with an 8-ft snow angel he built at the intersection of Routes 30 and 5. **Brooks Memorial Library** has a replica of the angel as well as exhibits of Vermont art. ⊠ *224 Main St.,* ☎ *802/254–5290.* ☉ *Mon.–Wed. 9–9, Thurs.–Fri. 9–6, Sat. 9–5; Memorial Day–Labor Day, Sat. 9–noon.*

Dining and Lodging

$ ✕ **Common Ground.** The political posters and concert fliers that line the staircase at Common Ground attest to Vermont's strong progressive element. The stairs lead to loftlike, rough-hewn dining rooms. Owned cooperatively by the staff, this mostly organic vegetarian restaurant serves cashew burgers, veggie stir-fries, curries, hot soup and stew, and the humble bowl of brown rice. All the desserts, including a chocolate cake with peanut butter frosting, are made without white sugar. ⊠ *25 Elliot St.,* ☎ *802/257–0855. No credit cards. Closed Tues., Wed., and Thurs. in winter.*

$ ✕ **Mole's Eye Cafe.** Built in the 1930s as the tavern for the long-gone Brooks Hotel, the Mole's Eye is an institution. The appeals of this cozy basement gathering place are its convivial atmosphere and the home-baked turkey melts, Mexican munchies, homemade soups, and tasty desserts. ⊠ *High St.,* ☎ *802/257–0771. Reservations not accepted. MC, V.*

$$–$$$ ✕▥ **Latchis Hotel.** Multicolored terrazzo floors animate this 1938 downtown Art Deco landmark run by the current generation of Latchises. Odd-numbered rooms overlook Connecticut River and a New Hampshire mountain beyond. All the rooms have refrigerators, coffeemakers, and original furniture that's comfortable if not high style; muffins arrive outside your door in the morning. You can catch a movie under the Zodiac ceiling of the adjoining Latchis Theater. The Latchis Grille (closed on Monday and Tuesday in winter; no lunch on weekdays) serves pub food—grilled chicken and fish sandwiches, fried calamari, burgers, salads—and more creative fare like chicken and watercress roulade. The Grille is home to the Windham Brewery, which brews rich

Southern Vermont

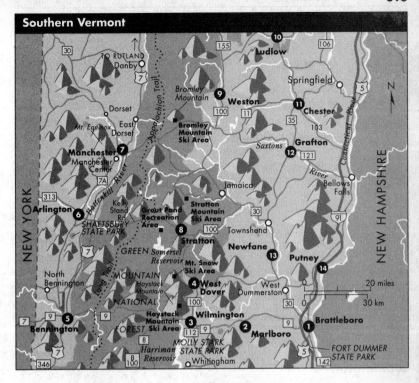

ales and lagers. ⊠ *50 Main St., 05301,* ☎ *802/254–6300,* ⅨX *802/254–6304. 30 rooms. Restaurant. Continental breakfast. AE, MC, V.*

$$$$ ⌂ **Naulakha.** In 1892, Rudyard Kipling came to southern Vermont and was captivated by the area. He bought 11 acres high in a long, thin, protected meadow and built Naulakha (which means "jewel beyond price") so that every room would have a view across woods and farmland to distant hills. Kipling completed *The Jungle Book* here. He had intended to stay permanently but sold the house in 1902. Restored by Britain's Landmark Trust, Naulakha has four bedrooms and sleeps eight comfortably. There's a dishwasher, a washing machine, and a collection of books that would have made Kipling proud. A minimum three-night stay is required in winter; one week is required in summer. Information: ⊠ *The Landmark Trust USA, R.R. 1, Box 510, 05301,* ☎ *802/254–6868.* ⊠ *Reservations: The Landmark Trust, Shottesbrooke, Maidenhead, Berkshire, England SL6 3SW,* ☎ *011/44–1628–825925.*

Nightlife and the Arts

Common Ground (⊠ 25 Elliot St., ☎ 802/257–0855) often presents folk music or performance art on weekends, especially during Sunday brunch. **Mole's Eye Cafe** (⊠ High St., ☎ 802/257–0771) hosts musical performers: acoustic or folk on Wednesday, open mike on Thursday; danceable R&B or blues on weekends; there's a cover charge on Friday and Saturday. The **New England Bach Festival** (⊠ Brattleboro Music Center, ☎ 802/257–4523), with a chorus under the direction of Blanche Moyse, is held in October.

Outdoor Activities and Sports

CANOEING

Connecticut River Safari (⊠ Rte. 5, ☎ 802/257–5008) has guided and self-guided tours as well as canoe rentals.

SKATING

Nelson Withington Skating Rink (⊠ Memorial Park, 4 Guilford St., ☎ 802/257–2311) rents skates.

Shopping

BOOKS

The Book Cellar (⊠ 120 Main St., ☎ 802/254–6026), with two floors of volumes, carries many travel books.

CRAFTS

Vermont Artisan Design (⊠ 106 Main St., ☎ 802/257–7044), one of the state's best crafts shops, displays contemporary ceramics, glass, wood, clothing, jewelry, and furniture.

Marlboro

② *10 mi west of Brattleboro.*

Tiny Marlboro draws musicians and audiences from around the world each summer to the Marlboro Music Festival, founded by Rudolf Serkin and joined for many years by Pablo Casals. **Marlboro College,** high on a hill off Route 9, is the center of musical activity. The college's white-frame buildings have outstanding views of the valley below, and the campus is studded with apple trees.

The **Marlboro Music Festival** (⊠ Marlboro Music Center, ☎ 802/254–2394 or 215/569–4690 Sept.–June) presents chamber music in weekend concerts in July and August.

Wilmington

③ *8 mi west of Marlboro.*

Wilmington is the shopping and dining center for the Mt. Snow ski area to the north. Main Street has a cohesive assemblage of 18th- and 19th-century buildings, many of them listed on the National Register of Historic Places. For a great stroll, pick up a self-guided tour map from the Chamber of Commerce (⊠ Rte. 9, W. Main St., ☎ 802/464–8092).

North River Winery, which occupies a converted farmhouse and barn, produces fruit wines like Green Mountain Apple and Vermont Pear. ⊠ *Rte. 112, 6 mi south of Wilmington,* ☎ *802/368–7557.* ☞ *Free.* ☉ *Memorial Day–Dec., daily 10–5; Jan.–Memorial Day, Fri.–Sun. 11–5.*

OFF THE
BEATEN PATH

SCENIC TOUR – To begin a scenic (though well-traveled) 35-mi circular tour with panoramic views of the region's mountains, farmland, and abundant cow population, drive west on Route 9 to the intersection with Route 8. Turn south and continue to the junction with Route 100; follow Route 100 through Whitingham (the birthplace of the Mormon prophet Brigham Young), and stay with the road as it turns north again and takes you back to Route 9.

Dining and Lodging

$$$–$$$$ ✕☒ **White House of Wilmington.** The grand staircase in this Federal-style mansion leads to rooms with antique bathrooms and brass wall sconces. The newer section has more contemporary plumbing; some rooms have fireplaces, whirlpool tubs, and lofts. The tufted leather wing-back chairs of the public rooms suggest formality, but the atmosphere is casual and comfortable. Although it's a 10-minute drive to Mt. Snow Haystack, the White House is primarily a cross-country ski touring center, with a rental shop and 32 km (19 mi) of groomed trails. ⊠ *Rte. 9, 05363,* ☎ *802/464–2135 or 800/541–2135,* 𝔽𝔸𝕏 *802/464–5222. 23*

rooms. Restaurant, bar, indoor and outdoor pools, sauna, cross-country skiing. Full breakfast; MAP available. AE, D, DC, MC, V.

$$$-$$$$ 🏠 **Trail's End.** A warm, user-friendly, four-season lodge set on 10 acres, Trail's End is 4 mi from Mt. Snow. The inn's centerpiece is its cathedral-ceiling living room with catwalk loft seating and a 21-ft fieldstone fireplace. Guest rooms are comfortable, if simple, though two suites have fireplaces, whirlpool tubs, cable TV, refrigerators, and microwaves; four other rooms also have fireplaces. Breakfast is served at immense round pine tables; dinner is prepared during the holiday season only. There's a stocked trout pond on site and cross-country ski trails are nearby. ⊠ *5 Trail's End La., 05363,* ☎ *802/464–2727 or 800/859–2585,* FAX *802/464–5532. 15 rooms. Pool, pond, tennis court. Full breakfast. AE, D, MC, V.*

Nightlife

The standard fare on weekends at **Poncho's Wreck** (⊠ S. Main St., ☎ 802/464–9320) is acoustic jazz or mellow rock. **Sitzmark** (⊠ Rte. 100, ☎ 802/464–3384) hosts rock bands on weekends.

Outdoor Activities and Sports

SLEIGH RIDES

Adams Farm (⊠ Higley Hill, ☎ 802/464–3762) has three double-traverse sleighs drawn by Belgian draft horses. Rides include a narrated tour and hot chocolate. A petting farm is open during the summer.

WATER SPORTS

Lake Whitingham (Harriman Reservoir) is the largest lake in the state; there are boat launch areas at Wards Cove, Whitingham, Mountain Mills, and the Ox Bow. **Green Mountain Flagship Company** (⊠ about 2 mi west of Wilmington on Rte. 9, ☎ 802/464–2975) runs a cruise boat on the lake and rents canoes, kayaks, surfbikes, and sailboats from May to late October.

Shopping

Wilmington Flea Market (⊠ Rtes. 9 and 100 S, ☎ 802/464–3345) is open on weekends from Memorial Day to mid-October.

West Dover

❹ *6 mi north of Wilmington.*

Many of the churches in small West Dover, a classic New England town, date back to the 1700s. The year-round population of about 1,000 swells on winter weekends as skiers flock to Mt. Snow/Haystack Ski Resort. The many condos, lodges, and inns at the base of the mountain accommodate them.

Dining and Lodging

$$$-$$$$ ✕ **Doveberry Inn.** Rack of venison with a caper-and-fresh-tomato demi-glace served over polenta, wood-grilled veal chop with wild mushrooms, and pan-seared salmon with herbed risotto are among the northern Italian dishes served in the Doveberry's intimate, candlelit dining rooms. ⊠ *Rte. 100,* ☎ *802/464–5652 or 800/722–3204. AE, MC, V.*

$$$-$$$$ ✕🏠 **Deerhill Inn.** The west-facing windows at this English country inn
★ have views of the valley below and the ski slopes across the way. A huge fireplace dominates the living room, and English hand-painted yellow wallpaper, a garden-scene mural, and collections of antique plates accent the dining rooms. One guest room has an Asian bedroom set, several have hand-painted murals on the wall, and many have fireplaces. The four balcony rooms are the largest; they have great views. Long-time Deerhill Valley residents Linda and Michael Anelli enjoy sharing their wealth of information about the area with guests. Michael prepares

upscale comfort food that might include fresh fish, a veal medallion with wild mushrooms in a lemon cream sauce, or a black-pepper sirloin steak. ⊠ *Box 136, Valley View Rd., 05356,* ☎ *802/464–3100 or 800/ 993–3379.* ℻ *802/464–5474. 13 rooms, 2 suites. Restaurant, pool, TV/VCR in common area . Full breakfast; MAP available. AE, MC, V.*

Nightlife

Deacon's Den Tavern (⊠ Rte. 100, ☎ 802/464–9361) books bands on weekends. The **Snow Barn** (⊠ Near the base of Mt. Snow, ☎ 802/ 464–1100, ext. 4693) presents entertainers four days a week during the ski season.

Shopping

Anton of Vermont Quilts (⊠ Rte. 100, 9 mi north of Mt. Snow) has a rich collection of handcrafted fabrics and quilts.

Skiing

Mt. Snow/Haystack Ski Resort. Mt. Snow, established in the 1950s, has come a long way since the 1960s, when its dress-up-and-show-off ski scene earned it the nickname Mascara Mountain. The American Skiing Company, which also owns Sugarbush, Killington, and Pico, purchased Mt. Snow in 1996. A new Grand Summit Hotel and Conference Center and four new lifts are part of the resort's capital improvement plan. You will probably encounter crowds at the ski lifts, but Mt. Snow knows how to handle them. One lift ticket lets you ski at Mt. Snow, Killington, Pico, and Haystack.

At Mt. Snow, both the bustling Main Base Lodge and the Sundance Base Lodge have food service and other amenities. The Carinthia Base Lodge is usually the least crowded and most easily accessible from the parking lot.

Haystack—the southernmost ski area in Vermont—is much smaller than Mt. Snow but has a more personal atmosphere. A modern base lodge is close to the lifts. A free shuttle connects the two ski areas. ⊠ *400 Mountain Rd., Mt. Snow 05356,* ☎ *802/464–3333, 800/245–7669 for lodging, 802/464–2151 for snow conditions.*

DOWNHILL

Mt. Snow is a remarkably well-formed mountain. Most of the trails down its 1,700-ft vertical summit are intermediate, wide, and sunny. Toward the bottom and in the Carinthia section are the beginner slopes; most of the expert terrain is on the North Face, where there's excellent fall-line skiing. Of the 84 trails, about two-thirds are intermediate. The trails are served by two quad, six triple, and eight double chairlifts, plus two surface lifts. The ski school's EXCL instruction program is designed to help advanced and expert skiers.

Most of the 43 trails at Haystack are pleasantly wide with bumps and rolls and straight fall lines—good cruising, intermediate runs. There's also a section with three double-black-diamond trails—very steep but short. A beginner section, safely tucked below the main-mountain trails, provides a haven for lessons and slow skiing. Three triple and two double chairlifts and one T-bar service Haystack's 1,400 vertical ft.

CROSS-COUNTRY

Four cross-country trail areas within 4 mi of the resort provide more than 150 km (90 mi) of varied terrain. **The Hermitage** (⊠ Coldbrook Rd., ☎ 802/464–3511) and the **White House** (⊠ Rtes. 9 and 100, ☎ 802/464–2135) both have 50 km (30 mi) of groomed trails. **Timber Creek** (⊠ Rte. 100, north of the Mt. Snow entrance, ☎ 802/464–0999) is appealingly small with 16 km (10 mi) of thoughtfully groomed trails. **Sitzmark** (⊠ East Dover Rd., Wilmington 05363, ☎ 802/464–3384) has 40 km (24 mi) of trails, with 12 km (7 mi) of them machine tracked.

CHILD CARE

The lively, well-organized child care center (reservations necessary) takes children from age 6 weeks to 12 years in three separate sections: a nursery for those under 18 months, a playroom complex for toddlers up to 30 months, and an adjacent bigger room for older kids. Each has age-appropriate toys and balances indoor play—including arts and crafts—with trips outdoors. Most youngsters sign up for full- or half-day sessions of the ski school–sponsored SKIwee program, designed for those between 4 and 12.

Bennington

❺ *21 mi west of Wilmington.*

Bennington, the state's third-largest city and the commercial focus of Vermont's southwest corner, lies at the edge of the Green Mountain National Forest. It has retained much of the industrial character it developed in the 19th century, when paper mills, grist mills, and potteries formed the city's economic base. It was in Bennington, at the Catamount Tavern, that Ethan Allen organized the Green Mountain Boys, who helped capture Ft. Ticonderoga in 1775. Here also, in 1777, American general John Stark urged his militia to attack the British-paid Hessian troops across the New York border: "There are the Redcoats; they will be ours or tonight Molly Stark sleeps a widow!"

A chamber of commerce brochure describes an interesting self-guided walking tour of **Old Bennington,** a National Register Historic District west of downtown. Impressive white-column Greek Revival and sturdy brick Federal homes stand around the village green. In the graveyard of the **Old First Church,** at Church Street and Monument Avenue, the tombstone of the poet Robert Frost proclaims, "I had a lover's quarrel with the world."

The **Bennington Battle Monument,** a 306-ft stone obelisk with an elevator to the top, commemorates General Stark's victory over the British, who attempted to capture Bennington's stockpile of supplies. The battle, which took place near Walloomsac Heights in New York State, helped bring about the surrender two months later of the British commander "Gentleman Johnny" Burgoyne. ⊠ *15 Monument Ave.,* ☎ *802/447–0550.* ☒ *$1.50.* ☉ *Mid-Apr.–late Oct., daily 9–5.*

The **Bennington Museum**'s rich collections include vestiges of rural life, a good percentage of which are packed into towering glass cases. The decorative arts are well represented; one room is devoted to early Bennington pottery. Two rooms cover the history of American glass and contain fine Tiffany specimens. The museum displays the largest public collection of the work of Grandma Moses, who lived and painted in the area. Among the 30 paintings and assorted memorabilia is her only self-portrait and the famous painted caboose window. Also here are the only surviving automobile of Bennington's Martin company, a 1925 Wasp, and the Bennington Flag, one of the oldest versions of the Stars and Stripes in existence. ⊠ *W. Main St./Rte. 9,* ☎ *802/447–1571.* ☒ *$5.* ☉ *Daily 9–5.*

Contemporary stone sculpture and white-frame neo-Colonial dorms, surrounded by acres of cornfields, punctuate the green meadows of **Bennington College**'s placid campus. The small liberal arts college, one of the most expensive to attend in the country, is noted for its progressive program in the arts. ⊠ *Take Rte. 67A off Rte. 7 and look for stone entrance gate.*

Dining and Lodging

$$–$$$ ✗ **The Brasserie.** Some of the city's most creative fare—classic pâtés, omelets, and sandwiches as well as seasonal salads, hearty stews, and soups that are filling enough to be a meal—is prepared in this contemporary space. The cooks use mostly local produce and organic foods; desserts and bread are always homemade. ⊠ *324 County St. (in the Potters Yard),* ☎ *802/447–7922. MC, V. Closed Tues.*

$ ✗ **Blue Benn Diner.** Breakfast is served all day in this authentic diner, ★ where the eats include turkey hash and breakfast burritos with scrambled eggs, sausage, and chilies. Pancakes of all imaginable varieties are prepared, and there are many vegetarian selections. Especially on weekends, there may be a long wait. ⊠ *Rte. 7N,* ☎ *802/442–5140. No credit cards. No dinner Sat.–Tues.*

$$$–$$$$ ⌂ **South Shire Inn.** Canopy beds in lushly carpeted rooms, ornate plaster moldings, and a dark mahogany fireplace in the South Shire's library re-create the grandeur of yore; fireplaces and hot tubs in some rooms add warmth. The furnishings are antique except for the reproduction beds. The inn is in a quiet residential neighborhood within walking distance of the bus depot and downtown stores. Breakfast is served in the burgundy-and-white wedding cake of a dining room. ⊠ *124 Elm St., 05201,* ☎ *802/447–3839,* FAX *802/442–3547. 9 rooms. Full breakfast. AE, MC, V.*

$$–$$$ ⌂ **Molly Stark Inn.** This gem of a B&B may make you so comfortable ★ you'll feel like you're staying with an old friend. Tidy blue-plaid wallpaper, gleaming hardwood floors, antique furnishings, and a woodburning stove in a brick alcove of the sitting room add country charm to this 1860 Queen Anne Victorian. Molly's Room, at the back of the building, gets less noise from Route 9; the attic suite is most spacious. A secluded cottage with a 16-ft ceiling, a king-size brass bed, and a two-person whirlpool bath surrounded by windows with views of the woods is as romantic as it gets. The innkeeper's genuine hospitality and quirky charisma delight guests, as does the full country breakfast, made with mostly local ingredients, which has been known to include puffed-apple pancakes and freshly baked cinnamon buns. ⊠ *1067 E. Main St./Rte. 9, 05201,* ☎ *802/442–9631 or 800/356–3076,* FAX *802/ 442–5224. 7 rooms. Full breakfast. AE, D, MC, V.*

Nightlife and the Arts

Oldcastle Theatre Co. (⊠ Bennington Center for the Arts, Rte. 9 and Gypsy La., ☎ 802/447–0564) performs from April to October.

Outdoor Activities and Sports

Cutting Edge (⊠ 160 Benmont Ave., ☎ 802/442–8664) has bike rentals and repairs in addition to snowboards and cross-country skis. It also has Vermont's only indoor skateboarding park.

Shopping

The showroom at the **Bennington Potters Yard** (⊠ 324 County St., ☎ 802/447–7531 or 800/205–8033) stocks first-quality pottery and antiques in addition to seconds from the famed Bennington Potters. Prepare to get dusty digging for the almost-perfect piece at a modest discount. On the free walking tour you can follow the clay through production and hear the history of the Potters Yard, which has been in business for five decades. Tours begin at 10 and 2, seven days a week.
Four Corners East (⊠ 307 North St., ☎ 802/442–2612) carries Early American antiques.

Arlington

6 *15 mi north of Bennington.*

Don't be surprised to see familiar-looking faces among the roughly 2,200 people of Arlington. The illustrator Norman Rockwell lived here for 14 years, and many of the models for his portraits of small-town life were his neighbors. Settled first in 1763, Arlington was called Tory Hollow for its Loyalist sympathies—even though a number of the Green Mountain Boys lived here, too. Smaller than Bennington and more down-to-earth than upper-crust Manchester to the north, Arlington exudes a certain Rockwellian folksiness. Dorothy Canfield Fisher, a novelist popular in the 1930s and 1940s, also lived here.

There are no original paintings at the **Norman Rockwell Exhibition.** Instead, the exhibition rooms are crammed with reproductions, arranged in every way conceivable: chronologically, by subject matter, and juxtaposed with photos of the models—several of whom work here. ⊠ *Rte. 7A,* ☎ *802/375–6423.* 🖭 *$2.* ☉ *May–Oct., daily 9–5; Nov.– Dec. and Feb.–Apr., daily 10–4. Closed Jan.*

Dining and Lodging

$$$–$$$$ ✕🏨 **West Mountain Inn.** On 150 acres that include a llama ranch, this
★ romantic inn, a former farmhouse built in the 1840s, has a front lawn with a spectacular view of the countryside. Rooms 2, 3, and 4 overlook the lawn; the three small nooks of Room 11 resemble railroad sleeper berths and are perfect for kids. A new children's room, brightly painted with life-size Disney characters, is stocked with games, stuffed animals, and a TV with VCR. A low-beam candlelit dining room is the setting for six-course prix-fixe dinners that might include Alaskan king crab and forest-mushroom feuilleté with a roasted shallot and tarragon cream sauce. Aunt Min's Swedish rye and other toothsome breads, as well as desserts, are all made on the premises. Try to get a table by the window. ⊠ *Rte. 313, 05250,* ☎ *802/375–6516,* 📠 *802/ 375–6553. 18 rooms, 6 suites. Restaurant, bar, hiking, skiing, meeting rooms. MAP or B&B rates available. AE, D, MC, V.*

$$–$$$$ ✕🏨 **Arlington Inn.** The Greek Revival columns at the entrance to a home
★ built by a railroad magnate in 1848 lend it an imposing presence, but the atmosphere is hardly forbidding. The charm is created by linens that coordinate with the Victorian-style wallpaper, claw-foot tubs in some bathrooms, and the house's original moldings and wainscoting. The carriage house, built a century ago, contains country-French and Queen Anne furnishings. Some rooms have TVs and phones. The restaurant ($$), where local produce and meats are favored, serves French Continental dishes like roast duck and rack of lamb, and the chef also prepares raised game, including antelope from Texas. Polished wood floors, rose walls, and soft candlelight complement the food. ⊠ *Rte. 7A, 05250,* ☎ *802/375–6532 or 800/443–9442,* 📠 *802/375–6534. 16 rooms, 4 suites. Restaurant, bar, air-conditioning, tennis courts. Full breakfast. AE, D, DC, MC, V.*

$$–$$$ 🏨 **Hill Farm Inn.** This homey inn has the feel of the country farmhouse it used to be. The surrounding farmland, deeded to the Hill family by King George in 1775, is protected from development by the Vermont Land Trust. The fireplace in the informal living room, the sturdy antiques, and the spinning wheel in the upstairs hallway all convey a relaxed, friendly atmosphere. Room 7 has a beamed cathedral ceiling, and from its porch you can see Mt. Equinox. The rooms in the 1790 guest house are very private; the cabins are rustic and fun. ⊠ *Box 2015, off Rte. 7A, 05250,* ☎ *802/375–2269 or 800/882–2545,* 📠 *802/375– 9918. 6 rooms with bath, 5 rooms share 3 baths, 2 suites, 4 cabins in summer. Full breakfast; MAP available. AE, D, MC, V.*

Outdoor Activities and Sports

Battenkill Canoe, Ltd. (⊠ Rte. 7A, Arlington, ☎ 802/362–2800 or 800/ 421–5268) has rentals and day trips on the Battenkill and inn-to-inn tours.

Shopping

The shops at **Candle Mill Village** (⊠ Old Mill Rd., between Rtes. 7 and 7A, East Arlington, ☎ 802/375–6068 or 800/772–3759) specialize in community cookbooks from around the country, music boxes, and candles. The mill itself was built in the 1760s by Remember Baker, a cohort of Ethan Allen and one of the Green Mountain Boys. The nearby waterfall makes a pleasant backdrop for a picnic. **Equinox Valley Nursery** (⊠ Rte. 7A, between Arlington and Manchester, ☎ 802/ 362–2610) is known for its perennials (850 varieties) and materials for water gardens but also carries many Vermont-made products (in the fall these include ice cream from a local dairy).

Manchester

★ ❼ *9 mi north of Arlington.*

Manchester, where Ira Allen proposed financing Vermont's participation in the American Revolution by confiscating Tory estates, has been a popular summer retreat since the mid-19th century. Manchester Village's tree-shaded marble sidewalks and stately old homes reflect the luxurious resort lifestyle of a century ago. Manchester Center's upscale factory outlets appeal to the affluent 20th-century ski crowd drawn by nearby Bromley and Stratton mountains. Warning: Shoppers come in droves at times, giving the place the feel of a crowded New Jersey mall on the weekend before Christmas.

★ **Hildene,** the summer home of Abraham Lincoln's son Robert, is a 412-acre estate built by the former chairman of the board of the Pullman Company for his family. With its Georgian Revival symmetry, welcoming central hallway, and grand curved staircase, the 24-room mansion is unusual in that its rooms are not roped off. When the 1,000-pipe Aeolian organ is played, the music reverberates as though from the mansion's very bones. Tours include a short film on the owner's life and a walk through the elaborate formal gardens. When snow conditions permit, you can cross-country ski on the property, which has views of nearby mountains. In December, the house is decorated for special holiday tours, which include horse-drawn sleigh rides. ⊠ *Rte. 7A,* ☎ *802/362–1788.* ☜ *$7.* ◷ *Mid-May–Oct., daily 9:30–5:30 (last tour at 4); Dec. tour hrs vary.*

The **American Museum of Fly Fishing,** which houses the largest collection of fly-fishing equipment in the world, displays more than 1,500 rods, 800 reels, 30,000 flies, and the tackle of celebrities like Bing Crosby, Winslow Homer, and Jimmy Carter. Its library of 2,500 books is open by appointment. ⊠ *Rte. 7A,* ☎ *802/362–3300.* ☜ *$3.* ◷ *Daily 10–4.*

The 10-room **Southern Vermont Art Center** is set on 375 acres dotted with contemporary sculpture. A popular retreat for local patrons of the arts, the nonprofit educational center has a permanent collection and presents changing exhibits. A serene botany trail passes by a 300-year-old maple tree. The graceful Georgian mansion is the frequent site of concerts, performances, and films. In summer a restaurant opens for business. ⊠ *West Rd.,* ☎ *802/362–1405.* ☜ *$3, $2 in winter.* ◷ *Mid-May–late-Oct., Tues.–Sat. 10–5, Sun. noon–5; Dec.–early Apr., Mon.–Sat. 10–5. Closed Nov. and mid-Apr.–mid-May.*

You may want to keep your eye on the temperature gauge of your car as you drive the 5-mi toll road to the top of 3,825-ft **Mt. Equinox.** Looking out the window, you'll see the Battenkill trout stream and the surrounding Vermont countryside. Picnic tables line the drive, and there's an outstanding view down both sides of the mountain from a notch known as the Saddle. ⊠ *Rte. 7A,* ☎ *802/362–1114.* ⊠ *$6 for car and driver, $2 each additional adult.* ☉ *May–Oct., daily 8* AM*–dark.*

Dining and Lodging

$$$$ ✕ **Chantecleer.** Five miles north of Manchester, intimate dining rooms have been created in a former dairy barn with a large fieldstone fireplace. The menu reflects the chef's Swiss background: The appetizers include *Bündnerfleisch* (air-dried Swiss beef) and frogs' legs in garlic butter; among the entrées might be rack of lamb, whole Dover sole filleted tableside, or veal chops. ⊠ *Rte. 7A, East Dorset,* ☎ *802/362–1616. Reservations essential. AE, DC, MC, V. Closed Mon.–Tues. in winter, Tues. in summer. No lunch.*

$$–$$$$ ✕ **Bistro Henry's.** This airy restaurant on the outskirts of town attracts a devoted clientele for authentic Mediterranean fare. Recently on the menu were merlot-braised lamb shank with balsamic-glazed onions and garlic mashed potatoes, eggplant, mushroom, and fontina terrine Provençal, and crispy sweetbreads in Armagnac cream. The award-winning wine list is extensive. ⊠ *Rte. 11/30,* ☎ *802/362–4982. AE, DC, MC, V. Closed Mon.*

$$ ✕ **Quality Restaurant.** Gentrification has reached the down-home neighborhood place that was the model for Norman Rockwell's *War News* painting. Quality has Provençal wallpaper and polished wood booths, and the sturdy New England standbys of grilled meat loaf and hot roast beef or turkey sandwiches have been joined by tortellini Alfredo with shrimp and smoked salmon and grilled swordfish with lemon butter. The breakfasts here are popular. ⊠ *Main St.,* ☎ *802/362–9839. AE, DC, MC, V.*

$$$$ ✕▦ **Barrows House.** Jim and Linda McGinniss's 200-year-old Federal-
★ style inn is a longtime favorite with those who wish to escape the commercial hustle of Manchester (Bromley is about 8 mi away). The deep-red woodwork and library theme of the pub room make it an intimate venue for dining on country fare that might include Chesapeake crab cakes. The greenhouse room, with terra-cotta and deep-blue hues, is a pleasant summer eating spot. The rooms, spread among nine buildings on 12 acres, afford great privacy. All contain country furniture, antiques, and reproductions. ⊠ *Box 98, Rte. 30, Dorset (6 mi north of Manchester), 05251,* ☎ *802/867–4455 or 800/639–1620,* ℻ *802/867–0132. 18 rooms, 10 suites. Restaurant, air-conditioning, pool, sauna, tennis courts, bicycles, cross-country skiing. Full breakfast; MAP available. AE, D, DC, MC, V.*

$$$$ ✕▦ **The Equinox.** This grand white-column resort was a fixture even before Abe Lincoln's family began summering here; it's worth a look around even if you don't stay here. Dining in the Marsh Tavern, you might feel like you're sitting in the middle of a Ralph Lauren Polo ad: Spiral-based floor lamps accompany richly upholstered settees and stuffed arm chairs, high bow-back chairs sit around tables with fluted columns, and several fireplaces create a dreamy glow. The food is equally aesthetically pleasing: Devonshire shepherd's pie and a woodland supper of roast duck, venison sausage, and wild mushrooms are popular. The Colonnade, where men are requested to wear jackets, is as elegant as can be. The resort is often the site of large conferences. ⊠ *Rte. 7A, Manchester Village 05254,* ☎ *802/362–4700 or 800/362–4747,* ℻ *802/362–1595. 119 rooms, 36 suites, 10 3-bedroom town houses. 2 restaurants, bar, indoor and outdoor pools, sauna, steam*

room, golf course, tennis courts, croquet, health club, horseback riding, fishing, mountain bikes, ice-skating, cross-country skiing. AE, D, DC, MC, V.

$$$$ ✕⊞ **Reluctant Panther.** The large bedrooms here have goose-down duvets and Pierre Deux linens. Colored in soft grays and peaches, the rooms are styled with antique, country, and contemporary furnishings. Ten rooms have fireplaces, and some suites have double sunken whirlpools. The best views are from Rooms B and D. In Wildflowers restaurant (reservations essential; closed on Tuesday and Wednesday), known for its sophisticated cuisine, a huge fieldstone fireplace dominates the larger of the two dining rooms; the smaller greenhouse room contains night-blooming flowers. Glasses and silver sparkle in the candlelight, the service is impeccable, and the menu, which changes daily, might include rack of venison with an herbed cornmeal crust or grilled veal chop with ragout of shiitake and wild mushrooms. ⊠ *Box 678, West Rd., 05254,* ☎ *802/362–2568 or 800/822–2331,* ℻ *802/362–2586. 12 rooms, 5 suites. Restaurant, bar, air-conditioning, meeting room. MAP. AE, MC, V.*

$$$–$$$$ ⊞ **1811 House.** The atmosphere of an English country home can be en-
★ joyed without crossing the Atlantic. The pub-style bar serves 58 single-malt Scotches and is decorated with horse brasses, Waterford crystal is used in the dining room, and 3 acres of lawn are landscaped in the English floral style. The rooms contain period antiques; six have fireplaces, and many have four-poster beds. Bathrooms are old-fashioned but serviceable, particularly the Robinson Room's marble-enclosed tub. ⊠ *Box 39, Rte. 7A, 05254,* ☎ *802/362–1811 or 800/432–1811,* ℻ *802/362–2443. 14 rooms. Bar. Full breakfast. AE, D, MC, V.*

$$$–$$$$ ⊞ **Inn at Ormsby Hill.** This 1774 Federal-style building provided refuge
★ during the Revolutionary War for Ethan Allen, who was being pursued by British soldiers, and later for slaves heading north on the Underground Railroad. In renovating the historic building, the inn's gracious hosts, Chris and Ted Sprague, created interesting public spaces and romantic bedrooms. Furnished with antiques and canopied or four-poster beds, many of the rooms have fireplaces that can be viewed from the bed or the whirlpool tub. Some rooms also have views of the Green or Taconic mountains. The Taft room has a vaulted ceiling, a private sitting area, a fireplace, a double whirlpool, and a separate two-person shower. Breakfasts in the conservatory—entrées might include French toast with an apricot brandy sauce—are a sumptuous affair. The meal always ends with a dessert. An optional buffet supper is served on Friday night; on Saturday evening a four-course dinner is served. ⊠ *R.R. 2, Box 3264, Rte. 7A, 05255,* ☎ *802/362–1163 or 800/670–2841,* ℻ *802/362–5176. 10 rooms. Air-conditioning. Full breakfast. D, MC, V.*

$$$ ⊞ **Manchester Highlands Inn.** Almost all the guest rooms in this 1898
★ inn have at least one rocking chair—a detail that reflects innkeepers Patricia and Robert Eichorn's intention to make relaxing their guests' foremost pastime. There are five sitting rooms, including a pub downstairs and a plant-filled sunroom with views of the pool and the mountains beyond. All the rooms have delicate lace curtains, featherbeds, and canopy beds. The Turret and Tower rooms are especially romantic; rooms in the carriage house are good for skiers and families. ⊠ *Highland Ave., 05255,* ☎ *802/362–4565 or 800/743–4565,* ℻ *802/362–4028. 15 rooms. Pool, croquet, recreation room. Full breakfast. AE, MC, V.*

Nightlife and the Arts

The two pre-Revolutionary War barns of the **Dorset Playhouse** (☎ 802/867–5777) host a community group in winter and a resident professional troupe in summer. The **Marsh Tavern** (☎ 802/362–4700) at the

Equinox Hotel has more subdued cabaret music and jazz from Wednesday to Sunday in summer and on weekends in winter. **Mulligan's** (☎ 802/362–3663), which serves American cuisine, is a popular hangout, especially for après-ski; DJs program the music on weekends.

Outdoor Activities and Sports

BIKING

The 20-mi Dorset–Manchester trail runs from Manchester Village north on West Street to Route 30, turns west at the Dorset village green onto West Road, and heads back south to Manchester. **Battenkill Sports** (✉ Exit 4 off Rte. 7, at Rte. 11/30, ☎ 802/362–2734 or 800/340–2734) rents and repairs bikes and provides maps and route suggestions.

FISHING

Battenkill Anglers (☎ 802/362–3184) teaches the art and science of fly-fishing. They have both private and group lessons. **The Orvis Co.** (✉ Manchester Center, ☎ 800/235–9763) hosts a nationally known fly-fishing school on the Battenkill, the state's most famous trout stream, with three-day courses given weekly between April and October. **Strictly Trout** (☎ 802/869–3116) will arrange a fly-fishing trip on any Vermont stream or river.

HIKING

One of the most popular segments of the Long Trail starts at Route 11/30 west of Peru Notch and goes to the top of Bromley Mountain. The trek takes about four hours. About 4 mi east of Bennington, the Long Trail crosses Route 9 and runs south to the summit of Harmon Hill. Allot two or three hours. On Route 30 about 1 mi south of Townshend is Townshend State Park; from here the trail runs to the top of Bald Mountain, passing an alder swamp, a brook, and a hemlock forest. This hike takes two hours.

The **Mountain Goat** (✉ Rte. 7A south of Rte. 11/30, ☎ 802/362–5159) sells hiking, backpacking, and climbing equipment and rents snowshoes and cross-country and telemark skis. The shop also conducts rock and ice-climbing clinics.

Shopping

ART AND ANTIQUES

Carriage Trade (✉ Rte. 7A north of Manchester Center, ☎ 802/362–1125) contains room after room of Early American antiques and has a fine collection of ceramics. **Danby Antiques Center** (✉ ⅛ mi off Rte. 7, 13 mi north of Manchester, ☎ 802/293–5990) has 11 rooms and a barn filled with furniture and accessories, folk art, textiles, and stoneware. **Gallery North Star** (✉ Rte. 7A, ☎ 802/362–4541) shows oils, watercolors, lithographs, and sculptures by Vermont artists. **Tilting at Windmills Gallery** (✉ Rte. 11/30, ☎ 802/362–3022) exhibits the works of well-known artists like Douglas Flackman of the Hudson River school.

BOOKS

Northshire Bookstore (✉ Main St., ☎ 802/362–2200 or 800/437–3700), a community bookstore for more than 20 years, carries many travel and children's books and sponsors readings year-round.

CLOTHING

Orvis Sporting Gifts (✉ Union St., ☎ 802/362–6455), a discount outlet that carries discontinued items from the popular outdoor clothing and home furnishings mail-order company, is housed in what was Orvis's shop in the 1800s. **Anne Klein, Liz Claiborne, Donna Karan, Levi Strauss, Giorgio Armani,** and **Jones New York** are among the shops on Routes 11/30 and 7 South—a center for designer outlet stores.

FISHING GEAR
Orvis Retail Store (⊠ Rte. 7A, ☎ 802/362–3750), an outdoor specialty store that is one of the largest suppliers of fishing gear in the Northeast, also carries clothing, gifts, and hunting supplies.

MALLS AND MARKETPLACES
Manchester Commons (⊠ Rtes. 7 and 11/30, ☎ 802/362–3736 or 800/955–SHOP), the largest and spiffiest of three large factory-direct minimalls, has such big-city names as Joan and David, Baccarat, Coach, Ralph Lauren, Calvin Klein, and Cole-Haan. Not far from the Commons is **Manchester Square** (⊠ Rte. 11/30 and Richville Rd.) with Giorgio Armani, Emporio Armani, Tommy Hilfiger, Brooks Brothers, Levis, and Escada.

Skiing

Bromley Mountain. The first trails at Bromley were cut in 1936. Many families enjoy the resort's convivial atmosphere. The area has a comfortable red-clapboard base lodge, built when the ski area first opened more than 50 years ago, with a large ski shop and a condominium village adjacent to the slopes. A reduced-price, two-day lift pass is available. Kids are still kids (price-wise) up to age 14, but they ski free with a paying adult on nonholiday weekdays. Eighty-four percent of the area is covered by snowmaking. A snowboard park-only lift ticket is available this season. ⊠ *Box 1130, Manchester Center 05255,* ☎ *802/824–5522 for snow conditions, 802/865–4786 or 800/865–4786 for lodging.*

DOWNHILL
Most ski areas are laid out to face the north or east, but Bromley faces south, making it one of the warmer spots to ski in New England. Its 41 trails are equally divided into beginner, intermediate, and advanced terrain; the last is serviced by the Blue Ribbon quad chair on the east side. The vertical drop is 1,334 ft. Four double chairlifts, two quad lifts, a J-bar, and two surface lifts for beginners provide transportation.

CROSS-COUNTRY
With 26 km (16 mi) of marked trails, **Meadowbrook Inn** (⊠ Landgrove, ☎ 802/824–6444 or 800/498–6445), is an intimate, idyllic setting for cross-country skiing, and you can also snowshoe. The inn has rental gear and provides lessons.

OTHER ACTIVITIES
Karl Pfister Sleigh Rides (⊠ Landgrove, ☎ 802/824–6320) has a 12-person Travis sleigh with bench seats.

CHILD CARE
Bromley is one of the region's best places to bring children. Besides a nursery for children from age 6 weeks to 6 years, ski instruction is provided for children from age 3 to 14.

Stratton

⑧ *18 mi southeast of Manchester.*

Stratton, home to the famous Stratton Mountain Resort, has a self-contained town center with an "Austrian village" of shops, restaurants, and lodgings.

Dining and Lodging

$$$$ ✕⊠ **Windham Hill Inn.** Antiques, throw blankets, and cherry pencil-
★ post canopy beds made by a local craftsman decorate the rooms at this exquisite country retreat. Most of them have fireplaces or Vermont Castings stoves, and several have large soaking tubs with gleaming oak handrails and brass fixtures. The barn-loft rooms are the newest and

most luxurious. The Center room has its own private cupola with a 360-degree view of the 160-acre grounds. A floor-to-ceiling bay window is the signature of the South room, which also has a breathtaking view. The restaurant serves nouveau French fare such as grilled mustard-seed-encrusted lamb loin with a rosemary merlot sauce. ✉ *R.R.1, Box 44, West Townshend (10 mi east of Stratton Mountain) 05359,* ☎ *802/874–4080 or 800/944–4080,* FAX *802/874–4702. 21 rooms. Restaurant, bar, air-conditioning, pool, pond, tennis court, hiking, ice-skating, cross-country skiing. MAP. AE, D, MC, V. Closed Apr. and during Christmas holidays.*

$$–$$$$ ✕⬚ **Stratton Mountain Inn and Village Lodge.** The complex includes a 120-room inn—the largest on the mountain—and a 91-room lodge of studio units equipped with microwaves, refrigerators, and small wet bars. The lodge is the only slopeside ski-in, ski-out hotel at Stratton. Ski packages that include lift tickets bring down room rates. ✉ *Stratton Mountain Rd., 05155,* ☎ *802/297–2500 or 800/777–1700,* FAX *802/297–1778. 211 rooms. 2 restaurants, pool, hot tub, sauna, golf course, tennis courts, racquetball. AE, D, DC, MC, V.*

Nightlife and the Arts

Haig's (☎ 802/297–1300) in Bondville, 5 mi from Stratton, has a dance club with a DJ or a band on weekends and holidays. There's also a diverting indoor simulated golf course. Popular **Mulligan's** (☎ 802/297–9293) serves American cuisine. Bands or DJs provide entertainment in the late afternoon and on weekends. The **Red Fox Inn** (☎ 802/297–2488), also 5 mi from Stratton in Bondville, hosts musicians in the tavern on weekends.

Outdoor Activities and Sports

Summertime facilities at **Stratton Mountain** (☎ 800/843–6867) include 15 outdoor tennis courts, 27 holes of golf, horseback riding, and mountain biking (rentals, guided tours, and accessories are available). Instruction programs in tennis and golf are also offered. The area also hosts a summer entertainment series.

Skiing

Stratton Mountain. Owned by Intrawest, the owners of Blackcomb and Mont Tremblant, Stratton has a new master plan that includes the only high-speed six-passenger lift in New England and a 1,000-seat summit lodge complete with cafeteria and five-star restaurant. Since its creation in 1961, Stratton has undergone physical transformations and upgrades, yet the area's sophisticated character has been retained. It has been the special province of well-to-do families and, more recently, young professionals from the New York–southern Connecticut corridor. Since the mid-'80s, an entire village, with a covered parking structure for 700 cars, has arisen at the base of the mountain: Adjacent to the base lodge are a condo-hotel, restaurants, and about 25 shops lining a pedestrian mall. Stratton is 4 mi up its own access road off Route 30 in Bondville, about 30 minutes from Manchester's popular shopping zone. ✉ *R.R. 1, Box 145, Stratton Mountain 05155,* ☎ *802/297–2200 or 800/843–6867, 802/297–4211 for snow conditions, 800/787–2886 for lodging.*

DOWNHILL

Stratton's skiing is in three sectors. The first is the lower mountain directly in front of the base lodge-village-condo complex; several lifts reach mid-mountain from this entry point, and practically all skiing is beginner or low-intermediate. Above that, the upper mountain, with a vertical drop of 2,000 ft, has a high-speed, 12-passenger gondola, Starship XII. Down the face are the expert trails, and on either side are intermediate cruising runs with a smattering of wide beginner slopes. The third sector, the Sun Bowl, is off to one side with two quad chairlifts and two expert trails, a full base lodge, and plenty of intermediate terrain. Stratton hosts the U.S. Open Snowboarding championships; its snowboard park has a 380-ft halfpipe. A Ski Learning Park with 10 trails and five lifts has its own Park Packages available for novice skiers. In all, Stratton has 90 slopes and trails served by the gondola; a six-passenger lift; four quad, one triple, and three double chairlifts; and two surface lifts.

CROSS-COUNTRY

The Stratton area has more than 30 km (18 mi) of cross-country skiing and two Nordic centers: Sun Bowl and Country Club.

OTHER ACTIVITIES

The area's sports center contains two indoor tennis courts, three racquetball courts, a 25-meter indoor swimming pool, a hot tub, a steam room, a fitness facility with Nautilus equipment, and a restaurant.

CHILD CARE

The day-care center takes children from age 6 weeks to 5 years for indoor activities and outdoor excursions. Two options for children from age 4 to 12 are the ski school, and SKIwee instruction programs. A junior racing program and special instruction groups are geared toward more experienced young skiers.

Weston

9 *20 mi northeast of Manchester.*

Weston is perhaps best known for the **Vermont Country Store,** which may be more a way of life than a shop. For years the retail store and its mail-order catalog have carried nearly forgotten items like Lilac Vegetal aftershave, Monkey Brand black tooth powder, Flexible Flyer sleds, and tiny wax bottles of colored syrup. Nostalgia-invoking implements dangle from the store's walls and ceiling. ⊠ *Rte. 100,* ☎ *802/824–3184.* ⊙ *Mon.–Sat. 9–5.*

The **Mill Museum,** down the road from the Vermont Country Store, has numerous hands-on displays depicting the engineering and mechanics of one of the town's mills. The many old tools on view kept towns like Weston running smoothly. ⊠ *Rte. 100,* ☎ *802/824–3119.* ☞ *Donations accepted.* ⊙ *Late May–early Sept., daily 11–4; Sept.–mid-Oct., weekends 11–4.*

Lodging

$$–$$$ ☒ **Highland House.** Skiers find the Highland House convenient: There's cross-country skiing on its 32-acre grounds, Bromley Mountain is 10 minutes away by car, and Stratton and Okemo are also nearby. The common room, which has a fireplace, is a warm place to relax after a day of physical exertion. The simply furnished guest rooms contain antiques and reproduction furniture and quilts. A four-course prix-fixe dinner that emphasizes Vermont-grown products is served by candlelight from Thursday to Sunday. ⊠ *Rte. 100, Londonderry (5 mi south of Weston) 05148,* ☎ *802/824–3019,* ℻ *802/824–3657. 17 rooms. Restaurant, pool, tennis courts, cross-country skiing. Full breakfast. AE, MC, V.*

Nightlife and the Arts

The members of the **Weston Playhouse** (⊠ Village Green, off Rte. 100, ☎ 802/824–5288), the oldest professional theater in Vermont, have produced Broadway plays, musicals, and other works since 1937. Their season runs from late June to mid-October.

Shopping

Vermont Country Store (⊠ Rte. 100, ☎ 802/824–3184) sets aside one room of its old-fashioned emporium for Vermont Common Crackers and bins of fudge and other candy. **Weston Bowl Mill** (⊠ Rte. 100, ☎ 802/824–6219) stocks finely crafted wood products at mill prices.

En Route From Weston you can head south on Route 100 through Jamaica and then down Route 30 through Townshend to Newfane, all pretty hamlets typical of small-town Vermont. South of Townshend, near the Townshend Dam on Route 30, is the state's longest single-span covered bridge, now closed to traffic.

Ludlow

⑩ *9 mi northeast of Weston.*

Ludlow, a former mill town, relies on the popularity of Okemo Mountain Ski Resort to fill its shops and restaurants. A beautiful often-photographed historic church sits on the town green. Calvin Coolidge went to school at Ludlow's Black River Academy.

Dining and Lodging

$$$$ ⊞ **Okemo Mountain Lodge.** Most rooms in this three-story brown-clapboard building have balconies and fireplaces, and the one-bedroom condominiums clustered around the base of the ski lifts are close to restaurants and shops. All have equipped kitchens, fireplaces, decks, and TVs with VCRs. Okemo Mountain Lodging Service also operates the Kettle Brook, Winterplace, and Solitude slopeside condominiums. Ski-and-stay packages are available. ⊠ *77 Okemo Ridge Rd., off Rte. 103, 05149,* ☎ *802/228–5571, 802/228–4041, or 800/786–5366,* FAX *802/228–2079. 76 rooms, 84 condos. Restaurant, bar. AE, MC, V.*

Skiing

Okemo Mountain. An ideal ski area for families with children, Okemo has evolved into a major resort. The main attraction is a long, broad, gentle slope with two beginner lifts just above the base lodge. All the facilities at the bottom of the mountain are close together, so family members can regroup easily during the ski day. The new Solitude Village Area has a triple chairlift, two new trails, and lodging. ⊠ *R.R. 1, Box 106, 05149,* ☎ *802/228–4041, 800/786–5366 for lodging, 802/228–5222 for snow conditions.*

DOWNHILL

Above the broad beginner's slope at the base, the upper part of Okemo has a varied network of trails: long, winding, easy trails for beginners; straight fall-line runs for experts; and curving, cruising slopes for intermediates. The 96 trails are served by an efficient lift system of seven quads, three triple chairlifts, and three surface lifts; 95% are covered by snowmaking. From the summit to the base lodge, the vertical drop is 2,150 ft. The ski school offers a complimentary Ski Tip Station, where intermediate or better skiers can get an evaluation and a free run with an instructor. There are innovative snowboard instructional programs for riders of all ages.

CROSS-COUNTRY

Fox Run (⊠ Fox La., ☎ 802/228–8871) has 26 km (16 mi) of trails, all groomed.

OTHER ACTIVITIES

Cavendish Sleigh Rides (⊠ Proctorsville, ☎ 802/226–7821) operates horse-drawn sleigh rides in snowy weather and wagon rides at other times.

CHILD CARE

The area's nursery, for children from age 6 weeks to 8 years, has many indoor activities and supervised outings. Children ages 3 and up can get brief introduction-to-skiing lessons; those between 4 and 8 can take all-day or half-day SKIwee lessons.

Chester

⑪ *11 mi east of Weston.*

Gingerbread Victorians frame Chester's town green. The **stone village** on North Street on the outskirts of town, two rows of buildings constructed from quarried stone, was built by two brothers and is said to have been used during the Civil War as a station on the Underground Railroad. The **National Survey Charthouse** (✉ Main St., ☎ 802/875–2121) is a map-lover's paradise: It's good for a rainy-day browse even if maps aren't your passion. The local pharmacy down the street has been in continuous operation since the 1860s.

In Chester's restored 1872 train station you can board the *Green Mountain Flyer* for a 26-mi, two-hour round-trip to Bellows Falls, on the Connecticut River at the eastern edge of the state. The journey, in superbly restored cars that date from the golden age of railroading, travels through scenic countryside past covered bridges and along the Brockway Mills gorge. A six-hour tour takes place in the fall. ✉ *Rte. 103,* ☎ *802/463–3069.* 🎫 *2-hr trip $11.* ☉ *Mid-June–early Sept., Tues.–Sun.; early Sept.–mid-Oct., daily. Train departs at 11, 12:10, 2; call to confirm.*

Outdoor Activities and Sports

A 26-mi loop out of Chester follows the Williams River along Route 103 to Pleasant Valley Road north of Bellows Falls. At Saxtons River, turn west onto Route 121 and follow along the river to connect with Route 35. When the two routes separate, follow Route 35 north back to Chester.

Grafton

★ **⑫** *8 mi south of Chester.*

Grafton is the almost-too-picturesque village that got a second lease on life when the Windham Foundation provided funds for its restoration. The town's **Historical Society** documents the change. ✉ *Townshend Rd.,* ☎ *802/843–2255.* 🎫 *$1.* ☉ *Memorial Day–Columbus Day, Sat. 1:30–4; July–Aug., Sun. 1:30–4.*

Dining and Lodging

$$$$ ✕🏨 **Old Tavern at Grafton.** White-column porches on both stories wrap around the main building of this commanding inn, which dates from 1801. Daniel Webster and Nathaniel Hawthorne are among the past guests. The main building holds 14 rooms; the rest are dispersed among two houses across the street and in other buildings in town. Two dining rooms ($$$–$$$$), one with formal Georgian furniture and oil portraits, the other with rustic paneling and low beams, serve New England cuisine—grilled choice sirloin steeped in McNeil's stout and a blend of spices or spinach-and-egg fettuccine tossed with baby shrimp, bay scallops, and littleneck clams in a lightly brandied Parmesan cream sauce. The Phelps Barn Bar, which is filled with authentic English pub furniture, is a popular hangout. ✉ *Rte. 35, 05146,* ☎ *802/843–2231 or 800/843–1801,* 📠 *802/843–2245. 66 rooms. Restaurant, bar, pond, tennis courts, paddle tennis, mountain biking, ice-skating, cross-country skiing, recreation room. Full breakfast. MC, V. Closed Apr.*

Shopping

Gallery North Star (⊠ Townshend Rd., ☎ 802/843–2465) exhibits the oils, watercolors, lithographs, and sculptures of Vermont artists.

Newfane

⑬ *15 mi south of Grafton.*

With a village green surrounded by pristine white buildings, Newfane is sometimes described as the quintessential New England small town. The 1939 **First Congregational Church** and the **Windham County Court House,** with 17 green-shuttered windows and a rounded cupola, are often open. The building with the four-pointed spire is **Union Hall,** built in 1832.

Dining and Lodging

$$$$ ✕🏠 **Four Columns.** The majestic white columns of this Greek Revival mansion, built 150 years ago for a homesick southern bride, are more intimidating than the Colonial-style rooms inside. Room 1 in the older section has an enclosed porch overlooking the town common; three rooms and a suite are annexed. All rooms have antiques, brass beds, and quilts; some have fireplaces and whirlpool or soaking tubs. The third-floor room in the old section is the most private. In the classy restaurant (closed on Tuesdays and for part of April), chef Greg Parks has introduced nouvelle American dishes like roasted young chicken with herbs served in a chardonnay and mushroom sauce and seared tuna with noodles in a ginger lemongrass bouillon. If you're so inclined, you can fish for your dinner in the small trout pond behind the inn. ⊠ *Box 278, West St., 05345,* ☎ *802/365–7713 or 800/787–6633,* FAX *802/365–0022. 15 rooms. Restaurant, hiking. Continental breakfast; MAP in foliage season. AE, D, DC, MC, V.*

Shopping

Twenty dealers operate out of the three-floor **Newfane Antiques Center** (⊠ Rte. 30, south of Newfane, ☎ 802/365–4482). The **Newfane Country Store** (⊠ Rte. 30, ☎ 802/365–7916) carries many quilts (which can also be custom ordered), homemade fudge, and other Vermont foods, gifts, and crafts. Collectibles dealers from across the state sell their wares at the **Newfane Flea Market** (⊠ Rte. 30, ☎ 802/365–7771), which takes place every weekend during summer and fall.

Putney

⑭ *7 mi east of Newfane, 9 mi north of Brattleboro.*

☾ **Harlow's Sugar House** (⊠ Rte. 5, 2 mi north of Putney, ☎ 802/387–5852) has horse-drawn sleigh rides in the winter, wagon rides into the sugar bush to watch the maple sugaring in spring, berry picking in the summer, and apple picking in autumn. You can buy the fruits of these labors in the gift shop. At **Basketville** (⊠ Main St., ☎ 802/387–5509) you can witness the traditional production methods employed in constructing the incredible number of baskets for sale. Tours are given of the **Green Mountain Spinnery,** where you can purchase yarn and items knit from mostly local wool and mohair. ⊠ *Depot Rd. at Exit 4 off I–91,* ☎ *802/387–4528 or 800/321–9665.* 🎟 *Tours $2.* ☺ *Tours of yarn factory at 1:30 on the 1st and 3rd Tues. of each month.*

Dining and Lodging

$$–$$$ ✕🏠 **Putney Inn.** The main building of this inn, part of a farming estate, dates from the 1790s. The building was later part of a seminary—the present-day pub was the chapel. Two fireplaces dominate the lobby, and the guest rooms have Queen Anne mahogany reproductions. The exterior of the adjacent building is not terribly appealing, but the spacious, modern rooms are 100 yards from the banks of the Connecticut River. The massive original beams of a former barn are part of the charm of the dining room, where the regionally inspired cuisine—seafood, New England potpies, a wild-game mixed grill, and burgers with Vermont cheddar—contain innovative flourishes. ⊠ *Depot Rd., 05346,* ☎ *802/387–5517 or 800/653–5517,* ℻ *802/387–5211. 25 rooms. Full breakfast. AE, D, MC, V.*

$$–$$$ 🏠 **Hickory Ridge House.** This stately 1808 Federal mansion, listed on the National Register of Historic Places, holds unusually spacious guest rooms. Their country-farmhouse decor is simple yet comfortable; four have fireplaces. Rag rugs cover pine floors and the walls are done in cheerful pastels; bathrooms have large tubs. The full vegetarian breakfasts might include stuffed pumpkin pancakes or an inspired soufflé. ⊠ *R.D. 3, Box 1410, Hickory Ridge Rd., 05346,* ☎ *802/387–5709 or 800/380–9218,* ℻ *802/387–4051. 5 rooms with bath, 2 rooms share bath. Hiking, cross-country skiing. Full breakfast. MC, V.*

Shopping

FOOD AND DRINK

Allen Bros. (⊠ Rte. 5 north of Putney, ☎ 802/722–3395) bakes apple pies, makes cider doughnuts, and sells Vermont foods and products.

Southern Vermont A to Z

Getting Around

BY BUS

Vermont Transit (☎ 802/864–6811, 800/451–3292, or 800/642–3133 in VT) links Bennington, Manchester, Brattleboro, and Bellows Falls.

BY CAR

In the south the principal east–west highway is Route 9, the Molly Stark Trail, from Brattleboro to Bennington. The most important north–south roads are Route 7; the more scenic Route 7A; Route 100, which runs through the state's center; I–91; and Route 5, which runs along the state's eastern border. Route 30 from Brattleboro to Manchester is a scenic drive.

Contacts and Resources

CANOEING

The Connecticut River between Bellows Falls and the Massachusetts border, interrupted by one dam at Vernon, is a relatively easy paddle. A good resource is "The Complete Boating Guide to the Connecticut River," available from **CRWC Headquarters** (⊠ 125 Combs Rd., Easthampton, MA 01027, ☎ 413/584–0018).

EMERGENCIES

Brattleboro Memorial Hospital (⊠ 9 Belmont Ave., ☎ 802/257–0341).

STATE PARKS

The following state parks have camping sites and facilities. **Emerald Lake State Park** (⊠ Rte. 7, 9 mi north of Manchester, East Dorset, ☎ 802/362–1655) has a marked nature trail, an on-site naturalist, boat and canoe rentals, and a snack bar. The hiking trails at **Fort Dummer State Park** (⊠ S. Main St., 2 mi south of Brattleboro, ☎ 802/254–2610) afford views of the Connecticut River valley. **Lake Shaftsbury State Park** (⊠ Rte. 7A, 10½ mi north of Bennington, ☎ 802/375–9978) is one of a few parks in Vermont with group camping; it has a swimming beach, nature trails, boat and canoe rentals, and a snack bar. **Molly Stark State Park** (⊠ Rte. 9, east of Wilmington, ☎ 802/464–5460) has a hiking trail to a vista from a fire tower on Mt. Olga. **Townshend State Park** (⊠ 3 mi north of Rte. 30, between Newfane and Townshend, ☎ 802/

365–7500), the largest in southern Vermont, is popular for the swimming at Townshend Dam and the stiff hiking trail to the top of Bald Mountain. **Woodford State Park** (⊠ Rte. 9, 10 mi east of Bennington, ☎ 802/447–7169) has an activities center on Adams Reservoir, a playground, boat and canoe rentals, and marked nature trails.

VISITOR INFORMATION
Bennington Area Chamber of Commerce (⊠ Veterans Memorial Dr., Bennington 05201, ☎ 802/447–3311). **Brattleboro Chamber of Commerce** (⊠ 180 Main St., Brattleboro 05301, ☎ 802/254–4565). **Chamber of Commerce, Manchester and the Mountains** (⊠ 2 Main St., Manchester 05255, ☎ 802/362–2100). **Mt. Snow/Haystack Region Chamber of Commerce** (⊠ Box 3, W. Main St., Wilmington 05363, ☎ 802/464–8092).

CENTRAL VERMONT

Jobs in tourism and recreation have increased as those in manufacturing have dwindled in central Vermont. Although some industry is still found, particularly in the west around Rutland, the state's second-largest city, the southern tip of Lake Champlain—as well as many other, smaller lakes—and major ski resorts are what really make the area economically viable. Local trademarks include the state's famed marble quarries, just north of Rutland, and large dairy herds and pastures that create the quilted patchwork of the Champlain Valley. The Green Mountains and the surrounding wilderness of the Green Mountain National Forest, both intensely beautiful areas, provide countless opportunities for outdoor recreation.

The tour below begins in Windsor, on Route 5 near I–91 at the eastern edge of the state, winds westward toward Route 100, up along the spine of the Green Mountains, and crosses over the ridge at two inspiring points.

Windsor

⑮ *50 mi north of Brattleboro, 42 mi east of Rutland, 69 mi south of Montpelier.*

Windsor was the delivery room for the birth of Vermont. An interpretive exhibit on Vermont's constitution, the first in the United States to prohibit slavery and establish a system of public schools, is housed in the **Old Constitution House.** The site, where in 1777 grant holders declared Vermont an independent republic, contains 18th- and 19th-century furnishings, American paintings and prints, and Vermont-made tools, toys, and kitchenware. ⊠ *Rte. 5,* ☎ *802/674–3773.* ▣ *$1.* ☺ *Late May–mid-Oct., Wed.–Sun. 10–4.*

The firm of Robbins & Lawrence became famous for applying the "American system" (the use of interchangeable parts) to the manufacture of rifles. Although the company no longer exists, the **American Precision Museum** extols the Yankee ingenuity that created a major machine-tool industry here in the 19th century. The museum contains the largest collection of historically significant machine tools in the country and presents changing exhibits. ⊠ *196 Main St.,* ☎ *802/674–5781.* ▣ *$5.* ☺ *Memorial Day–Nov. 1, weekdays 9–5, weekends 10–4.*

The mission of the **Vermont State Crafts Center,** in the restored 1846 Windsor House, is to advance the appreciation of Vermont crafts through education and exhibition. The center presents crafts exhibitions and operates a small museum. ⊠ *54 Main St.,* ☎ *802/674–6729.* ☺ *Mon.–Thurs. 10–5, Fri.–Sat. 9–6, Sun. 11–5.*

A British-style pale ale, an American amber ale, a dark porter are among the beers produced at **Catamount Brewery,** one of Vermont's most popular microbreweries. Seasonal specialties include a hearty Christmas ale, oatmeal stout, American wheat, and Octoberfest. You can sample beer at the company store and at the conclusion of the brewery tour. ⊠ *Windsor Industrial Park, Rte. 5S, exit 9 off I-91,* ☎ *802/674–6700 or 800/540–2248.* 🎫 *Free.* ☉ *Mon.–Sat. 9–5, Sun. 1–5; July–Oct., 3 tours Mon.–Sat., 2 tours Sun.; Nov.–June, 3 tours Sat. only.*

At 460 ft, the **covered bridge** off Route 5, which spans the Connecticut River between Windsor and Cornish, New Hampshire, is the longest in the state.

Dining and Lodging

$$ ✕ **Windsor Station.** This converted main-line railroad station serves such main-line entrées as chicken Kiev, filet mignon, and prime rib. The booths, with their curtained brass railings, were created from the high-back railroad benches of the depot. ⊠ *Depot Ave.,* ☎ *802/674–2052. AE, MC, V. Closed Mon. in winter. No lunch.*

$$–$$$ ✕▦ **Juniper Hill Inn.** An expanse of green lawn with Adirondack chairs and a garden of perennials sweeps up to the portico of this Greek Revival mansion, built at the turn of the century and now on the National Register of Historic Places. The central living room, with its hardwood floors, oak paneling, Oriental carpets, and thickly upholstered wing chairs and sofas, has a stately feel. The bedrooms have antiques; 11 have fireplaces. The four-course dinners ($$$) served in the candlelit dining room may include herb-crusted rack of lamb or sautéed scallops with glazed garlic and champagne sauce. The inn is 7 mi from Mt. Ascutney. ⊠ *Juniper Hill Rd. (Box 79), 05089,* ☎ *802/674–5273 or 800/359–2541,* ℻ *802/674–2041. 16 rooms. Restaurant, pool, hiking. Full breakfast. D, MC, V.*

Brownsville

🔞 *5 mi west of Windsor.*

Brownsville is a small village at the foot of Ascutney Mountain. It has everything a village needs: country store, post office, town hall, and historic grange building. The Ascutney Mountain ski area is a self-contained four-season resort.

Dining and Lodging

$$$ ✕▦ **Ascutney Mountain Resort Hotel.** One of the big attractions of this five-building resort hotel–condo complex is the lift outside the main door. The comfortable, well-maintained hotel suites come in different configurations and sizes—some with kitchens, fireplaces, and decks. Slopeside multilevel condos have three bedrooms, three baths, and private entrances. The Ascutney Harvest Inn ($$), which serves Continental and traditional cuisine, is within the complex. ⊠ *Box 699, Rte. 44, 05037,* ☎ *802/484–7711 or 800/243–0011,* ℻ *802/484–3117. 240 suites and condos. 3 restaurants, 2 bars, pool, health club, racquetball, billiards. AE, MC, V.*

$$–$$$ ▦ **Millbrook Bed and Breakfast.** This Victorian farmhouse, built in 1880, is directly across from the Ascutney ski slopes. Making après-ski idleness easy are the four sitting rooms, decorated with antiques and contemporary furnishings. The honeymoon suite has a separate dressing room with a claw-foot bathtub; the other suites are perfect for families. The inn takes some pets with advance notice. ⊠ *Box 410, Rte. 44, 05037,* ☎ *802/484–7283. 2 rooms, 3 suites. Hot tub. Full breakfast. AE, MC, V.*

Central Vermont

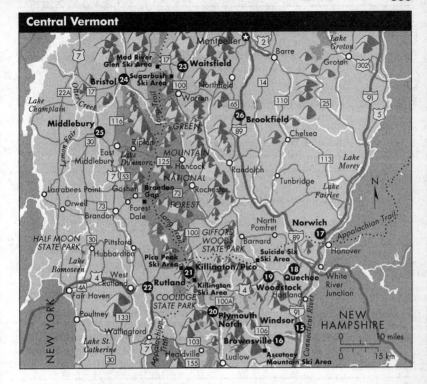

Nightlife and the Arts

Crow's Nest Club (⊠ Ascutney Mountain Resort Hotel, ☎ 802/484–7711) has entertainment on weekends. **Destiny** (☎ 802/674–6671) hosts rock bands most days and has a DJ on Sunday.

Skiing

Ascutney Mountain Resort. The Plausteiner family, whose patriarch, John, was instrumental in operations at Mt. Snow, in Vermont, and White Face Mountain, in Lake Placid, New York, purchased this resort in the mid-1990s and in 1998 launched a five-year expansion that will include new lifts and trails. There's a resort village in five buildings, with hotel suites and condominium units spread throughout. ⊠ *Rte. 44, off I–91 (Box 699, Brownsville 05037),* ☎ *802/484–7711 or 800/243–0011 for lodging.*

DOWNHILL

Forty-six trails with varying terrain are covered by nearly 80% snowmaking. Like a stereotypical ski mountain cutout, this one reaches a wide peak and gently slopes to the bottom. Beginner and novice skiers stay toward the base, while intermediates enjoy the band that wraps the midsection. For experts there are tougher black-diamond runs topping the mountain. One disadvantage to Ascutney, however, is that there is no easy way down from the summit, so novice skiers should not make the trip. Trails are serviced by one double and three triple chairs. Ascutney is popular with families because it offers some of the least expensive junior lift tickets in the region.

CROSS-COUNTRY

There are 32 km (19 mi) of groomed cross-country trails at the resort; lessons, clinics, and rentals are provided.

OTHER ACTIVITIES

Ascutney Mountain Resort Hotel (☞ Dining and Lodging, *above*) has a sports-and-fitness center with full-size indoor and outdoor pools, racquetball, aerobics facilities and classes, weight training, and massage, as well as ice-skating on the pond.

CHILD CARE

Day care is available for children from age 6 months to 12 years, with learn-to-ski options and rental equipment for toddlers and up. There are half- and full-day instruction programs for children from age 3 to 6 and a Young Olympians program for children from age 6 to 14. Evening baby-sitting is available.

Norwich

⑰ *6 mi north of White River Junction.*

Norwich is across the river from Dartmouth College. **King Arthur Flour Baker's Store** (⊠ Rte. 5, ☎ 802/649–3361), a retail outlet for all things baking oriented, sells tools and hard-to-find grains and specialty flours. The company, which has been in business since 1790, displays historic photographs of flour being delivered by horse cart.

ℭ The **Montshire Museum of Science** has numerous hands-on exhibits that explore space, nature, and technology; there are also living habitats, aquariums, and many children's programs. A maze of trails winds through 100 acres of pristine woodland. An ideal destination for a rainy day, this is one of the finest museums in New England. ⊠ *Montshire Rd., Box 770,* ☎ *802/649–2200.* ⊡ *$5.* ⊙ *Daily 10–5.*

Quechee

⑱ *6 mi west of White River Junction.*

Quechee is perched astride the Ottauquechee River. Quechee Gorge, 165 ft deep, is impressive, though overrun by tourists. You can see the mile-long gorge, carved by a glacier, from Route 4, but many visitors picnic nearby or scramble down one of several descents for a closer look. More than a decade ago **Simon Pearce** set up an eponymous glassblowing factory in an old mill by the bank of a waterfall here, using the water power to drive his furnace. The glass studio produces exquisite wares and houses a pottery workshop, a shop, and a restaurant; visitors can watch the artisans at work. ⊠ *Main St.,* ☎ *802/295–2711 or 800/774–5277.* ⊙ *Store daily 9–9, workshop 9–5.*

Dining and Lodging

$$$–$$$$ ✕ **Simon Pearce.** Candlelight, sparkling glassware from the studio downstairs, contemporary dinnerware, exposed brick, and large windows that overlook the roaring Ottauquechee River create an ideal setting for contemporary American cuisine. Sesame-crusted tuna with noodle cakes and wasabi and roast duck with mango chutney sauce are specialties of the house; the wine cellar holds several hundred vintages. ⊠ *Main St.,* ☎ *802/295–1470. AE, D, DC, MC, V.*

$$$ ✕⬚ **Parker House.** The peach-and-blue rooms of this 1857 Victorian mansion are named for former residents: Emily has a marble fireplace, Walter is the smallest room, and Joseph has a view of the Ottauquechee River. All the rooms on the third floor are air-conditioned. Lace window panels, high-back chairs, and traditional wall stenciling contribute to the dining room's elegant atmosphere. American cuisine—loin of venison with a port, balsamic vinegar, and dried cranberry sauce, and Maine crab cakes with a hint of wasabi—is served; in warm weather, you can dine on the terrace, which has a spectacular river view.

Guests have access to the Quechee Country Club's first-rate golf course, tennis courts, indoor and outdoor pool, and cross-country and downhill skiing. ⊠ *Box 0780, 16 Main St., 05059,* ☎ *802/295–6077,* FAX *802/296–6696. 7 rooms. Full breakfast; MAP available. AE, MC, V.*

$$$–$$$$ ★ 🏠 **Quechee Bed and Breakfast.** Dried herbs hang from the beams in the living room of this B&B, where a wood settee sits before a floor-to-ceiling fireplace that was part of the original structure of 1795. Handwoven throws cover the beds in the rooms (ask for one in the back, away from busy Route 4), which are done in pastels. Jessica's Room is the smallest; the Bird Room is one of four that overlook the Ottauquechee River. The wide front porch is adorned with seasonal decorations such as luminarias and cornstalks. The inn is within walking distance of Quechee Gorge. ⊠ *Box 80, Rte. 4 at Waterman Hill, 05059,* ☎ *802/295–1776. 8 rooms. Air-conditioning. Full breakfast. MC, V.*

Outdoor Activities and Sports

FISHING

The **Vermont Fly Fishing School/Wilderness Trails** (⊠ Quechee Inn, Clubhouse Rd., 05059, ☎ 802/295–7620) leads workshops, rents fishing gear and mountain bikes, and arranges canoe and kayak trips. In the winter, the company conducts cross-country and snowshoe treks.

POLO

Quechee Polo Club (⊠ Dewey's Mill Rd., ½ mi north of Rte. 4, ☎ 802/295–7152) draws hundreds of spectators on summer Saturdays to its matches near the Quechee Gorge. Admission is $3 per person or $6 per carload.

Shopping

The 48 dealers at the **Hartland Antiques Center** (⊠ Rte. 4, ☎ 802/457–4745) stock furniture, paper items, china, glass, and collectibles. More than 350 dealers sell their wares at the **Quechee Gorge Village** (⊠ Rte. 4, ☎ 802/295–1550 or 800/438–5565), an antiques and crafts mall in an immense reconstructed barn that also holds a country store. A merry-go-round and a small-scale working railroad operate when weather permits.

Woodstock

★ ⑲ *4 mi east of Quechee.*

Perfectly preserved Federal houses surround Woodstock's tree-lined village green, and streams flow around the town center, which is anchored by a covered bridge. The town owes much of its pristine appearance to the Rockefeller family's interest in historic preservation and land conservation.

The town's history of conservationism dates from the 19th century: Woodstock native George Perkins Marsh, a congressman and diplomat, wrote the pioneering book *Man and Nature* in 1864, and was closely invloved in the creation of the Smithsonian Institution in Washington, D.C. The **Billings Farm and Museum,** on the grounds of Marsh's boyhood home, was founded by Frederick Billings in 1870 as a model of conservation. Billings, a lawyer and businessman, put into practice Marsh's ideas about the long-term effects of farming and grazing. Exhibits in the reconstructed Queen Anne farmhouse, school, general store, workshop, and former Marsh homestead demonstrate the lives and skills of early Vermont settlers. Splitting logs doesn't seem nearly so quaint when you've watched the effort that goes into it! ⊠ *Rte. 12, ½ mi north of Woodstock,* ☎ *802/457–2355.* 🎟 *$7.* ☉ *May–late Oct., daily 10–5; Nov.–Dec., weekends 10–4.*

Period furnishings of the Woodstock Historical Society fill the rooms of the white clapboard **Dana House,** built circa 1807. Exhibits include the town charter, furniture, maps, and locally minted silver. The converted barn houses the Woodstock Works exhibit, an economic portrait of the town. ⊠ *26 Elm St.,* ☎ *802/457–1822.* 🎫 *$1.* ⊙ *May–late Oct., Mon.–Sat. 10–5, Sun. noon–4; tours by appointment in winter.*

Ⓒ The **Raptor Center** of the **Vermont Institute of Natural Science** houses 23 species of birds of prey, among them bald eagles, peregrine falcons, and 3-ounce saw-whet owls. There are also ravens, turkey vultures, and snowy owls. All the caged birds have been found injured and unable to survive in the wild. This nonprofit, environmental research and education center is on a 77-acre nature preserve with walking trails. ⊠ *Church Hill Rd.,* ☎ *802/457–2779.* 🎫 *$6.* ⊙ *May–Oct., daily 10–4; Nov.–Apr., Mon.–Sat. 10–4.*

Dining and Lodging

$$$–$$$$ ✕ **Prince and the Pauper.** Modern French and American fare with a
★ Vermont accent is the specialty of this romantic restaurant in a candlelit Colonial setting. The grilled duck breast might have an Asian five-spice sauce; homemade lamb and pork sausage in puff pastry with a honey-mustard sauce is another possibility. A less expensive bistro menu is available in the lounge. ⊠ *24 Elm St.,* ☎ *802/457–1818. AE, D, MC, V. No lunch.*

$–$$$ ✕ **Bentley's.** Antique silk-fringed lamp shades, long lace curtains, and a life-size carving of a kneeling, winged knight lend a tongue-in-cheek Victorian air to the proceedings here. Burgers, chili, and homemade soups are served; the entrées include roasted Maple Leaf Farm duckling with a sweet mango sauce or maple-mustard chicken coated with chopped pecans. Jazz or blues musicians entertain here on weekends, and there's a popular Sunday brunch. ⊠ *3 Elm St.,* ☎ *802/457–3232. AE, DC, MC, V.*

$$$$ ✕🖼 **Kedron Valley Inn.** Many rooms at this inn have a fireplace or a Franklin stove. Two rooms have decks, another has a veranda, and a fourth has a terrace overlooking the stream that runs through the inn's 15 acres. Exposed-log walls make the motel units in back more rustic than the rooms in the main inn, but they're decorated similarly. The classically trained chef creates French masterpieces like the fillet of Norwegian salmon stuffed with herb seafood mousse in puff pastry and the shrimp, scallops, and lobster with wild mushrooms sautéed in shallots and white wine and served with a Fra Angelico cream sauce. A terrace with views of the grounds is open in summer. ⊠ *Rte. 106, 05071,* ☎ *802/457–1473 or 800/836–1193,* 🖷 *802/457–4469. 26 rooms. Restaurant, bar, pond, beach. MAP. AE, D, MC, V. Closed Apr. and 10 days before Thanksgiving.*

$$$$ ✕🖼 **Woodstock Inn and Resort.** The Rockefeller family owns this inn, whose lobby, which contains a fieldstone fireplace with massive wood-beam mantel, embodies the spirit of New England. Modern ash furnishings are high-quality institutional, enlivened by patchwork quilts: The inoffensive decor is designed to please the large clientele of corporate conference attendees. The dinner fare is nouvelle New England; the menu might include entrées like salmon steak with avocado beurre blanc, beef Wellington, and prime rib. ⊠ *Rte. 4, 05091,* ☎ *802/457–1100 or 800/448–7900,* 🖷 *802/457–6699. 144 rooms. 2 restaurants, bar, indoor and outdoor pools, saunas, golf course, tennis courts, croquet, health club, racquetball, squash, cross-country and downhill skiing, meeting rooms. AE, MC, V.*

$$$$ 🖼 **Twin Farms.** At the center of this exclusive 235-acre resort stands
★ the 1795 farmhouse where writers Sinclair Lewis and Dorothy Thompson lived. Rooms and cottages have original watercolors, ample book-

shelves, fireplaces, and wood-and-stone furniture. One avant-garde studio has huge arched windows, a cathedral-ceiling living room done in spare classical furnishings, and a king-size bed in a loft overhead. Chef Neil Wigglesworth prepares rich contemporary cuisine that draws on local recipes. You can help yourself at the open bar. ✉ *Stage Rd., off Rte. 12, 8 mi north of Woodstock (Box 115, Barnard 05031),* ☎ *802/ 234–9999 or 800/894–6327,* FAX *802/234–9990. 4 rooms, 8 cottages. 2 bars, dining room, Japanese baths, exercise room, boating, bicycles, ice-skating, cross-country and downhill skiing, recreation room, meeting rooms. AP. AE, MC, V.*

$$$–$$$$ 🏠 **The Woodstocker.** A short stroll from the covered bridge and the village green, this 1830s B&B offers the welcome and comfort that you would expect from a friend's living room. The atmosphere is casual, with big leather couches and an an indoor hot tub. The large and light-filled rooms are furnished with a hodgepodge of antiques and reproductions. One large suite has a kitchen. ✉ *61 River St./Rte. 4, 05091,* ☎ *802/457–3896,* FAX *802/457–3897. 7 rooms, 2 suites. Full breakfast. MC, V.*

$$–$$$ 🏠 **Winslow House.** This farmhouse built in 1872 once loomed over a
★ dairy farm that reached down to the banks of the Ottauquechee River. An unpretentious place with great cross-country skiing and golf nearby, Winslow House has only four guest rooms and a small common area, but the two upstairs quarters are uncommonly spacious and have separate sitting rooms: Mahogany furnishings dominate Room 3, and the English oak bed, armoire, and mission desk in Room 4 will transport you to a more luxurious era. ✉ *38 Rte. 4, 05091,* ☎ *802/457–1820,* FAX *802/457–1820. 4 rooms. Air-conditioning, refrigerators. Full breakfast. D, DC, MC, V.*

Nightlife

The popular **Bentleys** (✉ 3 Elm St., ☎ 802/457–3232) restaurant hosts DJs on weekends and has Sunday jazz brunches.

Outdoor Activities and Sports

BIKING

Cyclery Plus (✉ 36 Rte. 4 W, West Woodstock, ☎ 802/457–3377), which rents, sells, and services equipment, has a free touring map of local rides and will help you plan an extended trip in the area.

GOLF

Robert Trent Jones Sr. designed the 18-hole, par-69 course at **Woodstock Country Club** (✉ South St., ☎ 802/457–2112), run by the Woodstock Inn. The greens fee ranges from $41 to $52; an optional cart costs $36.

HORSEBACK RIDING

Kedron Valley Stables (✉ Rte. 106, South Woodstock, ☎ 802/457– 2734 or 800/225–6301) gives lessons and conducts guided trail rides and excursions in a sleigh and a wagon.

RECREATION AREA

Suicide Six (☎ 802/457–6656; ☞ Skiing, *below*) has outdoor tennis courts, lighted paddle courts, croquet, and an 18-hole golf course that are open in the summer.

Shopping

The **Marketplace at Bridgewater Mills** (✉ Rte. 4 west of Woodstock, ☎ 802/672–3332) houses shops and attractions in a three-story converted woolen mill. There's an antiques and crafts center, a bookstore, Miranda Thomas pottery, and Charles Shackleton furniture. Sample Vermont stocks gourmet foods and gifts from all over the state. **North Wind Artisans' Gallery** (✉ 81 Central St., ☎ 802/457–4587) carries contemporary—mostly Vermont-made—crafts with sleek, jazzy designs.

The **Village Butcher** (✉ Elm St., ☎ 802/457–2756) is an emporium of Vermont comestibles. **Who Is Sylvia?** (✉ 26 Central St., ☎ 802/457–1110), in the old firehouse, sells vintage clothing and antique linens, lace, and jewelry.

Skiing

Suicide Six. The site of the first ski tow in the United States (1934), this resort is owned and operated by the Woodstock Inn and Resort (☞ Dining and Lodging, *above*). The inn's package plans are remarkably inexpensive, considering the high quality of the accommodations. ✉ *Woodstock 05091,* ☎ *802/457–6661, 802/457–1100 and 800/448–7900 for lodging, 802/457–6666 for snow conditions.*

DOWNHILL

Despite Suicide Six's short vertical of only 650 ft, the skiing is challenging here: There are steep runs down the mountain's face, intermediate trails that wind around the hill, and glade skiing. Beginner terrain is mostly toward the bottom. Two double chairlifts and one surface lift service the 22 trails.

CROSS-COUNTRY

The ski touring center (☎ 802/457–6674) has 60 km (37 mi) of trails. Equipment and lessons are available.

OTHER ACTIVITIES

There's a snowboard area with a halfpipe. The Woodstock Health and Fitness Center (☎ 802/457–6656) has an indoor lap pool; indoor tennis, squash, and racquetball courts; whirlpool, steam, sauna, and massage rooms; and exercise and aerobics rooms.

CHILD CARE

The ski area has no nursery, but baby-sitting can be arranged through the Woodstock Inn if you're a guest. Lessons for children are given by the ski-school staff, and there's a children's ski-and-play park for those from age 3 to 7.

Plymouth Notch

20 *14 mi southwest of Woodstock.*

U.S. president Calvin Coolidge was born and buried in **Plymouth Notch,** a town that shares his character: low-key and quiet. The perfectly preserved turn-of-the-century buildings look more like a large farm than a town; in addition to the homestead there's the general store once run by Coolidge's father, a visitor center, a cheese factory, and a one-room schoolhouse. Coolidge's grave is in the cemetery across Route 100A. The Aldrich House, which mounts changing historical exhibits, is open on some weekdays during the off-season. ✉ *Rte. 100A, 6 mi south of Rte. 4, east of Rte. 100,* ☎ *802/672–3773.* 🎫 *$5.* ☉ *Late May–mid-Oct., daily 9:30–5.*

Killington/Pico

21 *11 mi (Pico) and 15 mi (Killington) east of Rutland.*

The intersection of Routes 4 and 100 is the heart of central Vermont's ski country, with the Killington, Pico, and Okemo resorts nearby. Strip development characterizes the Killington access road, but the views from the top of the mountain are worth the drive.

Dining and Lodging

$$$$ ✕🏨 **Inn at Long Trail.** This 1938 lodge popular with skiers and hikers is ¼ mi from the Pico ski slopes and even closer to the Appalachian and Long trails. The unusual decor—including massive indoor boulders—has nature as a prevailing theme. Irish music, darts, and Guinness always on tap are all part of the Irish hospitality, which is extended particularly to end-to-end hikers (who get a substantial break in the rates). Meals in the restaurant, open from Thursday to Sunday during peak season, might include roast duckling or mushroom and risotto strudel. The pub ($$) serves food year round. ⊠ *Box 267, Rte. 4, 05751,* ☎ *802/775–7181 or 800/325–2540,* ℻ *802/747–7034. 17 rooms, 5 suites. Restaurant, pub. Full breakfast; MAP on winter weekends. AE, MC, V.*

$$–$$$$ ✕🏨 **Summit Lodge.** Three miles from Killington Peak, this rustic two-story country lodge caters to a varied crowd of ski enthusiasts who are warmly met by the lodge's mascots—a pair of Saint Bernards. Country decor and antiques blend with modern conveniences to create a relaxed atmosphere. Dining ($–$$$) is formal at one of the restaurants and informal at the other. ⊠ *Killington Rd., 05751,* ☎ *802/422–3535 or 800/635–6343,* ℻ *802/422–3536. 45 rooms, 2 suites. 2 restaurants, bar, pool, pond, hot tub, massage, sauna, racquetball, ice-skating, nightclub, recreation room. Full breakfast. AE, DC, MC, V.*

$$$–$$$$ 🏨 **Cortina Inn.** This large lodge and miniresort is comfortable and its location prime. About two-thirds of the rooms have private balconies, though the views from them aren't spectacular. Horseback riding, sleigh rides, ice-skating, and guided snowmobile, fly-fishing, and mountain biking tours are among the off-the-slopes activities. The breakfast buffet is excellent. ⊠ *Rte. 4, Mendon 05751,* ☎ *802/773–3333 or 800/451–6108,* ℻ *802/775–6948. 97 rooms. Restaurant, bar, indoor pool, hot tub, sauna, 8 tennis courts, health club. Full breakfast. AE, D, DC, MC, V.*

Nightlife

The spicy chicken wings at **Casey's Caboose** (⊠ Killington access road, ☎ 802/422–3795) will warm you up after a day on the slopes skiing. The pub at the **Inn at Long Trail** (⊠ Rte. 4, ☎ 802/775–7181) hosts Irish music on weekends. The **Pickle Barrel** (⊠ Killington Rd., ☎ 802/422–3035), a favorite with the après-ski crowd, presents up-and-coming acts and can get pretty rowdy. The **Wobbly Barn** (⊠ Killington Rd., ☎ 802/422–3392), with dancing to blues and rock, is open during ski season.

Outdoor Activities and Sports

Cortina Inn (☎ 802/773–3333) has an ice-skating rink with rentals and offers sleigh rides; you can also skate on Summit Pond.

Skiing

Killington. "Megamountain," "Beast of the East," and plain "huge" are apt descriptions of Killington. The American Skiing Company operates Killington and its neighbor Pico—and a project is underway to join the two mountains by interconnecting trails and lifts. Lines on weekends (especially holiday weekends) at Killington can be downright dreadful—the resort has the longest ski season in the East and some of the best package plans. With a single telephone call, skiers can select the price, date, and type of ski week they want; choose accommodations; book air or railroad transportation; and arrange for rental equipment and ski lessons. ⊠ *400 Killington Rd., 05751,* ☎ *802/422–3333, 802/773–1330 or 800/621–6867 for lodging, 802/422–3261 for snow conditions.*

DOWNHILL

It would probably take a week to test all 212 trails on the six mountains of the Killington complex, even though everything interconnects. About 69% of the more than 1,000 acres of skiing terrain can be covered with machine-made snow. Transporting skiers to the peaks of this complex are three gondolas plus twelve quads, six triples, and four double chairlifts, as well as eight surface lifts. That's a total of 33 ski lifts, a few of which reach the area's highest elevation, at 4,220 ft off Killington Peak, and a vertical drop of 3,150 ft to the base of the gondola. Ride the new Skyeship, the world's fastest and first heated eight-passenger lift, complete with piped-in music. The Skyeship base station has a rotisserie, food court, and a coffee bar. The skiing includes everything from Outer Limits, one of the steepest and most challenging trails anywhere in the country, to the 16-km-long (10-mi-long), super-gentle Juggernaut Trail. The new "Fusion Zones" are the management's attempt to create a backcountry experience by thinning wooded terrain.

CHILD CARE

Nursery care is available for children from 6 weeks to 6 years old. There's a one-hour instruction program for youngsters from age 3 to 8; those from 6 to 12 can join an all-day program.

Pico Ski Resort. Although it's only 5 mi down the road from Killington, Pico has long been a favorite among people looking for uncrowded, wide-open cruiser skiing. When modern lifts were installed and a village square was constructed at the base, some feared a change in atmosphere might occur, but the condo-hotel, restaurants, and shops have not altered the essential nature of the area. Watch for big changes as the American Skiing Company brings Pico up to par with its other major resorts, Sugarbush and Killington. ⊠ *2 Sherburne Pass, Rutland 05701,* ☎ *802/422–3333, 802/775–4345 for snow conditions, 800/848–7325 for lodging.*

DOWNHILL

From the area's 4,000-ft summit, most of the trails are advanced to expert, with two intermediate bail-out trails for the timid. The rest of the mountain's 2,000 ft of vertical terrain is mostly intermediate or easier. The lifts for these slopes and trails are two high-speed quads, two triples, and three double chairs, plus three surface lifts. The area has 85% snowmaking coverage. Snowboarders are welcome and have their own area, Triple Slope. For instruction of any kind, head to the Alpine Learning Center.

CROSS-COUNTRY

Mountain Meadows (⊠ Rte. 4, ☎ 802/775–7077) has 57 km (34½ mi) of groomed trails and 10 km (6 mi) of marked outlying trails. You can also access 500 acres of backcountry skiing; Mountain Top (☎ 802/483–6089) is mammoth with 120 km (72 mi) of trails, 80 km (49 mi) of which are groomed.

OTHER ACTIVITIES

A sports center (☎ 802/773–1786) at the base of the mountain has fitness facilities, a 75-ft pool, whirlpool tub, saunas, and a massage room.

CHILD CARE

The nursery takes children from age 6 months to 6 years and provides indoor activities and outdoor play. The ski school has full- and half-day instruction programs for children from age 3 to 12.

Rutland

㉒ *32 mi south of Middlebury, 31 mi west of Woodstock, 47 mi west of White River Junction.*

In Rutland, there are strips of shopping centers and a seemingly endless row of traffic lights, and the homes of blue-collar workers vastly outnumber the mansions of the marble magnates who made the town famous. Rutland's traditional economic ties to railroading and marble, the latter an industry that became part of such illustrious structures as the central research building of the New York Public Library in New York City, have been rapidly eclipsed by the growth of the Pico and Killington ski areas to the east.

The **Chaffee Center for the Visual Arts** (⊠ 16 S. Main St., ☎ 802/775–0356) exhibits and sells the output of more than 200 Vermont artists who work in various media.

OFF THE
BEATEN PATH

VERMONT MARBLE EXHIBIT – The highlight of the Rutland area is 4 mi north of town. A sculptor-in-residence transforms stone into finished works of art or commerce (you can choose first-hand the marble for a custom-built kitchen counter). The gallery illustrates the many industrial and artistic applications of marble—there's a hall of presidents and a replica of Leonardo da Vinci's *Last Supper* in marble—and depicts the industry's history via exhibits and a video. Factory seconds and foreign and domestic marble items are for sale. ⊠ 62 Main St., Proctor (follow signs off Rte. 3), ☎ 802/459–2300 or 800/427–1396. ⛝ $5. ☉ Memorial Day–Oct., daily 9–5:30.

Dining and Lodging

$$–$$$ ✕ **Royal's 121 Hearthside.** This Rutland institution has an open hearth with hand-painted tiles, behind which the staff prepares prime rib, rack of lamb with strawberry-mint sauce, and pan-roasted salmon with dill hollandaise. ⊠ 37 N. Main St., ☎ 802/775–0856. AE, MC, V.

$–$$ ✕ **Back Home Café.** Wood booths, black-and-white linoleum tile, and
★   exposed brick lend this second-story café the feel of a New York City hole-in-the-wall. Dinner might be chicken breast stuffed with roasted red peppers and goat cheese or tortellini Alfredo primavera. Soup-and-entrée lunch specials can be less than $5. The large bar in the back of the restaurant is occasionally the site of weekend entertainment. ⊠ 21 Center St., ☎ 802/775–9313. AE, MC, V.

$$–$$$$ ⌂ **Inn at Rutland.** One alternative to Rutland's chain motel and hotel accommodations is this renovated Victorian mansion. The ornate oak staircase lined with heavy embossed gold and leather wainscoting leads to rooms that blend modern bathrooms with late-19th-century touches: botanical prints, elaborate ceiling moldings, frosted glass, and pictures of ladies in long white dresses. The two large common rooms, one with a fireplace, have views of surrounding mountains and valleys. ⊠ 70 N. Main St., 05701, ☎ 802/773–0575 or 800/808–0575, FAX 802/775–3506. 12 rooms. Mountain bikes. Full breakfast. AE, D, DC, MC, V.

$$ ⌂ **Comfort Inn.** Rooms at this chain hotel are a cut above the standard, with upholstered wing-back chairs and blond-wood furnishings. ⊠ 19 Allen St., 05701, ☎ 802/775–2200 or 800/432–6788, FAX 802/775–2694. 104 rooms. Restaurant, indoor pool, hot tub, sauna. Continental breakfast. AE, D, DC, MC, V.

Nightlife and the Arts

Crossroads Arts Council (⊠ 39 E. Center St., ☎ 802/775–5413) presents music, opera, dance, jazz, and theater.

Shopping

An anthropologist opened **East Meets West** (⊠ North of Rutland on Rte. 7 at Sangamon Rd., Pittsford, ☎ 802/443–2242 or 800/443–2242), which carries carvings, masks, statues, textiles, pottery, baskets, and other crafts of native peoples from around the world. **Tuttle Antiquarian Books** (⊠ 28 S. Main St., ☎ 802/773–8229) has a large collection of books on Asia, particularly Asian art. The store stocks rare and out-of-print books, genealogies, local histories, and miniature books.

Waitsfield

㉓ *55 mi north of Rutland, 32 mi northeast of Middlebury, 19 mi south-west of Montpelier.*

Although in close proximity to Sugarbush and Mad River Glen ski areas, the Mad River valley towns of Waitsfield and Warren have maintained a decidedly low-key atmosphere. The gently carved ridges cradling the valley and the swell of pastures and fields lining the river seem to keep further notions of ski-resort sprawl at bay. With a map from the Sugarbush Chamber of Commerce you can investigate back roads off Route 100 that have exhilarating valley views.

Dining and Lodging

$$–$$$$ ✕ **Chez Henri.** Tucked in the shadows of Sugarbush ski area, this romantic slopeside bistro has garnered a year-round following with traditional French dishes: onion soup, cheese fondue, rabbit in red-wine sauce, and rack of lamb with rosemary-garlic sauce. Locals frequent the congenial bar and dine alfresco next to a stream. ⊠ *Sugarbush Village,* ☎ *802/583–2600. AE, MC, V.*

$$ ✕ **American Flatbread.** For ideologically and gastronomically sound pizza, you won't find a better place in the Green Mountains than this modest haven on the grounds of the Lareau Farm Country Inn between Waitsfield and Warren. Organic flour and produce fuel mind and body, and Vermont hardwood fuels the earth-and-stone oven. The "punctuated equilibrium flatbread," made with olive-pepper goat cheese and rosemary is a dream, as are more traditional pizzas. There is no table service at lunch, but you can stop by at midday from Monday to Thursday for take-away. ⊠ *Rte. 100,* ☎ *802/496–8856. Reservations not accepted. MC, V. No dinner Sun.–Thurs. July 4–Columbus Day and Christmas–Easter, and Sat.–Thurs. mid-Apr.–July 3 and mid-Oct.–Dec. 24; no take-out lunch Fri.–Sun..*

$$ ✕🛏 **Tucker Hill Lodge.** Pine paneling and otherwise simple furnishings suffice at this 1940s lodge—most guests are more interested in skiing all day than in Victorian frills. Georgio's Café ($$–$$$) occupies two dining rooms: one upstairs, with red tablecloths and a deep blue ceiling; and one downstairs, with a bar, open stone oven, and fireplace. Both have a warm Mediterranean feel. *Pettini alla Veneziana* (stone-seared scallops with raisins and pine nuts), and saltimbocca *alla Valdostana* (roulades of beef with fontina cheese and prosciutto) are two specialties. ⊠ *Rte. 17, 05673,* ☎ *802/496–3983 or 800/543–7841,* 𝔽𝔸𝕏 *802/496–3203. 16 rooms with bath, 6 share bath. Restaurant, bar, pool, tennis court, hiking, game room. Full breakfast; MAP available. AE, MC, V.*

$$$$ 🛏 **Inn at the Round Barn Farm.** Art exhibits have replaced cows in the big round barn here (one of only eight in the state), but the Shaker-style building still dominates the farm's 85 acres. The inn's guest rooms are in the 1806 farmhouse, where books line the walls of the cream-color library. The rooms are sumptuous, with eyelet-trimmed sheets, elaborate four-poster beds, rich-colored wallpapers, and brass wall lamps for easy bedtime reading. Six have fireplaces, three have whirlpool tubs, and four have steam showers. ⊠ *Box 247, E. Warren Rd., R.R. 1, 05673,* ☎ *802/496–2276,* 𝔽𝔸𝕏 *802/496–8832. 11 rooms. Indoor pool, cross-country skiing, recreation room. Full breakfast. AE, D, MC, V.*

$$–$$$ 🛏 **Beaver Pond Farm Inn.** A peaceful drive down a country lane lined
★   with sugar maples leads to this small 1840 farmhouse overlooking rolling meadows, a golf course, and cross-country ski trails. The rooms are decorated simply, and bathrooms are ample. The focal point of the inn is the huge deck, where you can gaze at the mountains and meadows. The full breakfast might include orange-yogurt pancakes. The inn, less than a mile from Sugarbush Ski Area, has a driving range and is next

door to the Sugarbush Golf Course. The innkeeper is building a reputation as a fly-fishing guide. ⊠ *R.D. Box 306, Golf Course Rd., 05674,* ☎ *802/583–2861,* FAX *802/583–2860. 4 rooms with bath, 2 rooms share bath. Dining room. Full breakfast; MAP available Tues., Thurs., Sat. MC, V.*

$$–$$$ 🏠 **Lareau Farm Country Inn.** Surrounded by 67 acres of pastures and woodland, this inn near Mad River is a collection of old farm buildings (the oldest part dates from 1790). Victorian sofas and Oriental rugs decorate the inn, whose owner made the quilts in the bedrooms. You can sit on the covered porch in an Adirondack chair that faces horses grazing in pastures out back, explore the large jazz collection, play with the innkeeper's three dogs, swim in the river, take a horse or sleigh ride, or stroll in the beautiful gardens. American Flatbread, the restaurant in the barn, is a recommended experience for dinner. ⊠ *Box 563, Rte. 100, ,* ☎ *802/496–4949 or 800/833–0766,* FAX *802/496–7979. 11 rooms with bath, 2 rooms share bath. Restaurant. Full breakfast. MC, V.*

Nightlife and the Arts

The **Back Room at Chez Henri** (⊠ Sugarbush Village, ☎ 802/583–2600) has a pool table and is popular with the après-ski and late-night dance crowd. Local bands play danceable music at **Gallaghers** (⊠ Rtes. 100 and 17, ☎ 802/496–8800). **Giorgio's Café** (⊠ Tucker Hill Lodge, Rte. 17, ☎ 802/496–3983) is a cozy spot to warm yourself by the fire to the sounds of soft folk and jazz on weekends.

The **Green Mountain Cultural Center** (⊠ Inn at the Round Barn, E. Warren Rd., ☎ 802/496–7722), a nonprofit organization, brings concerts and art exhibits, as well as educational workshops, to the Mad River valley. The **Valley Players** (⊠ Rte. 100, ☎ 802/496–9612) present musicals, dramas, follies, and holiday shows.

Outdoor Activities and Sports

BIKING
The popular 14-mi Waitsfield–Warren loop begins when you cross the covered bridge in Waitsfield. Keep right on East Warren Road to the four-way intersection in East Warren; continue straight, then bear right, riding down Brook Road to the village of Warren; return by turning right (north) on Route 100 back toward Waitsfield. **Mad River Bike Shop** (⊠ Rte. 100, ☎ 802/496–9500) rents bikes, conducts tours, and sells maps.

GOLF
Great views and challenging play are the trademarks of the Robert Trent Jones–designed 18-hole, par-72 course at **Sugarbush Resort** (⊠ Golf Course Rd., ☎ 802/583–6727). The greens fee runs from $42 to $49; a cart (sometimes mandatory) costs $16.

ICE-SKATING
At **The Skadium** (⊠ Rte. 100, ☎ 802/496–8845 rink, 802/496–9199 recorded message) you can ice-skate in the winter and rollerblade or skateboard in warmer weather.

SLEIGH RIDES
The 100-year-old sleigh of the **Lareau Farm** (⊠ Rte. 100, ☎ 802/496–4949) cruises along the banks of the Mad River.

Shopping
ART AND ANTIQUES
Luminosity Stained Glass Studios (⊠ Rte. 100, ☎ 802/496–2231), inside a converted church, specializes in stained glass, custom lighting, and art glass.

All Things Bright and Beautiful (⌂ Bridge St., ☎ 802/496–3997) is a 12-room Victorian house jammed to the rafters with stuffed animals of all shapes, sizes, and colors as well as folk art, prints, and collectibles. **Warren Village Pottery** (⌂ 5 mi south of Waitsfield, Main St., Warren, ☎ 802/496–4162) sells handcrafted wares from its retail shop and specializes in functional stoneware pottery.

Green Mountain Chocolate Co. (⌂ Rte. 100, Waitsfield, ☎ 802/496–7031) carries hand-rolled truffles, cakes, cookies, and many types of candies.

Skiing

Mad River Glen. In 1995, Mad River Glen became the first ski area to be owned by a cooperative formed by the skiing community. The hundreds of shareholders are dedicated, knowledgeable skiers devoted to keeping skiing what it used to be—a pristine alpine experience. Mad River's unkempt aura attracts rugged individualists looking for less-polished terrain: The area was developed in the late 1940s and has changed relatively little since then. The single chairlift may be the only lift of its vintage still carrying skiers. Most of Mad River's trails (85%) are covered only by natural snow. ⌂ *Rte. 17, Waitsfield 05673, ☎ 802/ 496–355 or 800/850–6742 for cooperative office, 802/496–2001 or 800/696–2001 in VT for snow conditions.*

Mad River is steep, with natural slopes that follow the contours of the mountain. The terrain changes constantly on the 44 interactive trails, of which 35% are beginner, 35% are intermediate, and 30% are expert. Intermediate and novice terrain is regularly groomed. Four chairs service the mountain's 2,037-ft vertical. There is no snowboarding on the mountain, but telemarkers will find many compatriots. Mad River sponsors the North American Telemark Festival in early March.

The nursery (☎ 802/496–2123) takes children from age 6 weeks to 8 years. The ski school has classes for children from age 4 to 12. Junior racing is available weekends and during holiday periods.

Sugarbush. In the early 1960s Sugarbush had the reputation of being an outpost of an affluent crowd from New York. That reputation has faded, but Sugarbush's current owner, the American Ski Company, has spent $28 million to keep the resort on the cutting edge. The new Slide Brook Express quad connects the two mountains, Sugarbush South and Sugarbush North. A computer-controlled system for snowmaking has increased coverage to 80%. At the base of the mountain is a village with condominiums, restaurants, shops, bars, and a sports center. ⌂ *Box 350, Warren 05674, ☎ 802/583–2381, 800/537–8427 for lodging, 802/583–7669 for snow conditions.*

Sugarbush is two distinct, connected, mountain complexes. The Sugarbush South area is what old-timers recall as Sugarbush Mountain: With a vertical of 2,400 ft, it is known for formidable steeps toward the top and in front of the main base lodge. Sugarbush North offers what South has in short supply—beginner runs. North also has steep fall-line pitches and intermediate cruisers off its 2,600 vertical ft. There are 112 trails in all: 23% beginner, 48% intermediate, 29% expert. The resort has 18 lifts: seven quads (including four high-speed versions), three triples, four doubles, and four surface lifts.

CROSS-COUNTRY

More than 25 km (15 mi) of groomed cross-country trails are adjacent to the Sugarbush Inn. **Blueberry Lake cross-country ski area** (✉ Plunkton Rd., Warren, ☎ 802/496–6687) has 30 km (18 mi) of groomed trails through thickly wooded glades. **Ole's** (✉ Airport Rd., Warren, ☎ 802/496–3430) runs a cross-country center and small restaurant out of the tiny Warren airport; it has 50 km (30 mi) of groomed European-style trails that span out into the surrounding woods from the landing strips.

OTHER ACTIVITIES

The **Sugarbush Health and Racquet Club** (☎ 802/583–6700), near the ski lifts, has Nautilus and Universal equipment; tennis, squash, and racquetball courts; a whirlpool, a sauna, and steam rooms; one indoor pool; and a 30-ft-high climbing wall.

CHILD CARE

The Sugarbush Day School accepts children from ages 6 weeks to 6 years; older children have indoor play areas and can go on outdoor excursions. There's half- and full-day instruction available for children from age 4 to 11. Kids have their own magic-carpet lift. Sugarbear Forest, a terrain garden, has fun bumps and jumps.

En Route Route 17 from Waitsfield to Bristol winds westward up and over the Appalachian Gap, one of Vermont's most panoramic mountain passes: The views from the top and on the way down the other side toward the quiet town of Bristol are a just reward for the challenging drive.

Bristol

㉔ *20 mi west of Waitsfield.*

A replica of Benedict Arnold's Revolutionary War gunboat is part of the **Lake Champlain Maritime Museum,** which documents centuries of activity on the historically significant lake. The museum commemorates the days when steamships sailed along the coast of northern Vermont carrying logs, livestock, and merchandise bound for New York City. Among the 11 exhibit buildings is a blacksmith's shop. A one-room stone schoolhouse, built in the late 1810s, houses historic maps, nautical prints, and small crafts. Also on site are a nautical-archaeology center and a conservation laboratory. ✉ *Basin Harbor Rd. (14 mi west of Bristol, 7 mi west of Vergennes),* ☎ *802/475–2022.* ☞ *$7.* ☟ *Early May–late Oct., daily 10–5.*

Dining

$$–$$$$ ✕ **Mary's at Baldwin Creek.** Head to this restaurant in a 1790 farm-
★ house for a truly inspired culinary experience. The "summer kitchen" has a blazing fireplace and rough-hewn barn-board walls, and the main dining room is done in pastels. The innovative, ever-changing fare includes a legendary garlic soup, Vermont rack of lamb with a rosemary-mustard sauce, duck cassis smoked over applewood, and mako shark with a banana salsa. Raspberry gratin is among the many fine desserts. Vermont farmhouse dinners on Mondays in the summer highlight Vermont products—sometimes the farmers who raised them are on hand to discuss them. Sunday brunch is a local ritual. ✉ *Rte. 116, north of Bristol,* ☎ *802/453–2432. AE, MC, V. Closed Mon. in winter. No lunch.*

Outdoor Activities and Sports

A challenging 32-mi bicycle ride starts in Bristol: Take North Street from the traffic light in town and continue north to Monkton Ridge and on to Hinesburg; to return, follow Route 116 south through Starksboro and back to Bristol. The **Bike and Ski Touring Center** (✉ 74 Main St., Middlebury, ☎ 802/388–6666) offers rentals and repairs.

Shopping
Folkheart (✉ 18 Main St., ☎ 802/453–4101) carries unusual jewelry, toys, and crafts from around the world.

Middlebury

★ ㉕ *34 mi south of Burlington.*

In the late 1800s Middlebury was the largest Vermont community west of the Green Mountains: an industrial center of river-powered wool, grain, and marble mills. This is Robert Frost country; Vermont's late poet laureate spent 23 summers at a farm east of Middlebury. Otter Creek, the state's longest river, traverses the town center. Still a cultural and economic hub amid the Champlain Valley's serene pastoral patchwork, the town and countryside beckon a day of exploration.

Smack in the middle of town, **Middlebury College** (☎ 802/443–5000), founded in 1800, was conceived as an accessible alternative to the more worldly University of Vermont—although the two schools have since traded reputations. The early 19th-century stone buildings contrast provocatively with the postmodern architecture of the Center for the Arts and sports center. Music, theater, and dance performances take place throughout the year at the **Wright Memorial Theatre** and **Center for the Arts.** Within the Center, the **Middlebury College Museum of Art** has a permanent collection of paintings, photography, works on paper, and sculpture. ✉ *Center for the Arts, Rte. 30,* ☎ *802/443–5007.* 🖾 *Free.* ☉ *Tues.–Fri. 10–5, weekends noon–5. Closed college holidays and last 2 weeks of Aug.*

The **Vermont Folklife Center** is in the basement of the restored 1801 home of Gamaliel Painter, the founder of Middlebury College. Exhibits of photography, antiques, folk paintings, manuscripts, and other artifacts and contemporary works examine facets of Vermont life. ✉ *2 Court St.,* ☎ *802/388–4964.* 🖾 *Donations accepted.* ☉ *Weekdays 9–5 and, May–Oct., Sat. noon–4.*

The **Sheldon Museum,** an 1829 marble-merchant's house, is the oldest community museum in the country. The period rooms contain Vermont-made textiles, furniture, toys, clothes, kitchen tools, and paintings. ✉ *1 Park St.,* ☎ *802/388–2117.* 🖾 *$2; $4 for guided tour.* ☉ *June–Oct., Mon.–Sat. 10–5; Nov.–May, weekdays 10–5 (but call to make sure museum is open).*

More than a crafts store, the **Vermont State Craft Center at Frog Hollow** displays the work of more than 300 Vermont artisans. The center sponsors classes taught by some of those artists. ✉ *Mill St.,* ☎ *802/388–3177.* ☉ *Jan.–May, Mon.–Sat. 9:30–5; June–Dec., Mon.–Sat. 9:30–5, Sun. noon–5.*

The Morgan horse—the official state animal—has an even temper, good stamina, and slightly truncated legs in proportion to its body. The University of Vermont's **Morgan Horse Farm,** about 2½ mi west of Middlebury, is a breeding and training center where in summer you can tour the stables and paddocks. ✉ *Follow signs off Rte. 23,* ☎ *802/388–2011.* 🖾 *$4.* ☉ *May–Oct., daily 9–4:30.*

About 10 mi east of town on Route 125 (1 mi west of Middlebury College's Breadloaf campus), the easy ¾-mi **Robert Frost Interpretive Trail** winds through quiet woodland. Plaques along the way bear quotations from Frost's poems. There's a picnic area across the road from the trailhead.

Dining and Lodging

$$–$$$ ★ ✕ **Woody's.** In addition to cool jazz, diner-deco light fixtures, and abstract paintings, Woody's has a view of Otter Creek below. Seafood and Vermont lamb are the restaurant's specialties—some folks say the Caesar salad is the best in the state. ⊠ *5 Bakery La.,* ☎ *802/388–4182. AE, MC, V.*

$$$$ ✕⌂ **Blueberry Hill Inn.** If you're looking for total peace and quiet, this is the place. In the Green Mountain National Forest and accessible only by dirt road, Blueberry Hill is an idyllic spot with lush gardens, a stream, an apple orchard, and a pond with a wood-fired sauna on its bank. Many rooms have views of the surrounding mountains; all are furnished with antiques, quilts, and hot-water bottles to warm winter beds. A brick walkway leads through a greenhouse of blooming plants to the rooms in the back of the house. Three rooms have lofts, and the Moosalamoo Room is in a private cottage. The open kitchen, a major gathering spot, always has a jar full of the inn's famous chocolate-chip cookies. Tony Clark, innkeeper for more than 20 years, often joins guests for cocktails by the living room fireplace. Blueberry Hill's ski touring center focuses on mountain biking in the summer. Hikers can take advantage of the 45 mi of marked trails. ⊠ *Rte. 32, Goshen 05733,* ☎ *802/247–6735 or 800/ 448–0707,* FAX *802/247–3983. 12 rooms. Restaurant, sauna, hiking, horseshoes, volleyball, mountain biking, cross-country skiing. MAP; B&B plan available. MC, V. Closed weekdays in Apr.*

$$$ ★ ✕⌂ **Swift House Inn.** The main building at Swift House, the Georgian home of a 19th-century governor and his philanthropist daughter, contains white-panel wainscoting, elaborately carved mahogany and marble fireplaces, and cherry paneling in the dining room. The rooms—each with Oriental rugs and nine with fireplaces—have such antique reproductions as canopy beds, curtains with swags, and claw-foot tubs. Some bathrooms have double whirlpool tubs. Rooms in the gatehouse suffer from street noise but are charming; a carriage house holds six luxury accommodations. Herb-crusted rack of lamb with rosemary and Madeira sauce and creamy risotto with seasonal vegetables and maple syrup are on the menu in the dining room. ⊠ *25 Stewart La., 05753,* ☎ *802/388–9925,* FAX *802/388–9927. 21 rooms. Restaurant, pub, sauna, steam room. Continental breakfast. AE, D, DC, MC, V.*

Outdoor Activities and Sports

BOATING

Otter Creek Canoes (⊠ New Haven, ☎ 802/388–6159) sells maps and guides, rents gear, and will deliver a canoe to the site of your choice. **Chipman Point Marina** (⊠ Rte. 73A, Orwell, ☎ 802/948–2288), where there is dockage for 60 boats, rents houseboats, sailboats, and pontoon fishing boats.

FISHING

Yankee Charters (⊠ 34 North St., Vergennes 05491, ☎ 802/877–3318) rents gear and sets up half- or full-day trips on Lake Champlain from April to October.

HIKING

Several day hikes in the vicinity of Middlebury take in the Green Mountains. About 8 mi east of Brandon on Route 73, a trail that takes an hour to hike starts at Brandon Gap and climbs steeply up **Mt. Horrid.** On Route 116, about 5½ mi north of East Middlebury, a U.S. Forest Service sign marks a dirt road that forks to the right and leads to the start of the hike (about two to three hours) to **Abbey Pond,** which has a fantastic beaver lodge and dam in addition to a view of Robert Frost Mountain.

South of Lake Dunmore on Route 53, a large turnout marks a trail (a hike of about two hours) to the **Falls of Lana** (two hours). Four other trails—two short ones of less than a mile each and two longer ones—lead to the old abandoned Revolutionary War fortifications at **Mt. Independence;** to reach them, take the first left turn off Route 73 west of Orwell and go right at the fork. The road will turn to gravel and once again will fork; take a sharp left-hand turn toward a small marina. The parking lot is on the left at the top of the hill.

Shopping

Historic Marble Works (☎ 802/388–3701), a renovated marble manufacturing facility, is a collection of unique shops set amid quarrying equipment and factory buildings. **Holy Cow** (⊠ 52 Seymour St., ☎ 802/388–6737) is where Woody Jackson creates and sells his infamous Holstein cattle-inspired T-shirts, memorabilia, and paintings.

Brookfield

㉖ *15 mi south of Montpelier.*

The residents of sleepy Brookfield have voted several times to keep its roads unpaved. Crossing the nation's only **floating bridge** (⊠ Rte. 65 off I–89 and follow signs) still afloat feels like driving on water. The bridge, supported by nearly 400 barrels, sits at water level. It's the scene of the annual ice-harvest festival in January. The bridge is closed in winter.

Dining and Lodging

$$–$$$ ✕⚿ **Fogged Inn.** You'll be tempted to spend the whole day on the porch that graces the front of this casual inn that was built in 1790. The inn, atop a knoll, has views of a 46-acre workhorse farm and the surrounding valley. Rooms in the older part of the house have more character; all have phones and TVs with VCRs. Prime rib and veal dishes are among the highlights of the seasonal gourmet country menu at the restaurant ($–$$; no lunch). ⊠ *R.F.D. 1, Clark Rd. (Box 1540), Williamstown 05679,* ☎ *802/433–1355,* ☏ *802/433–5501. 18 rooms. Restaurant, bar, pond, horseback riding, cross-country skiing. MAP and B&B plan available. AE, MC, V.*

$$–$$$ ⚿ **Green Trails Inn.** The enormous fieldstone fireplace that dominates
★   the living and dining area at Green Trails is symbolic of the stalwart hospitality of the innkeepers. Antique clocks fill the common areas, and the comfortably elegant rooms have antiques and Oriental rugs. One two-room suite has a fireplace, and two have whirlpool tubs. Vegetarians are happily accommodated. Taking a walk down a tree-shaded country road was never so pleasant. ⊠ *Main St., 05036,* ☎ *802/276–3412 or 800/243–3412. 14 rooms, 8 with bath. Cross-country skiing, snowshoeing, ski shop, sleigh rides. Full breakfast; MAP available in winter. D, MC, V.*

Central Vermont A to Z

Getting Around

BY BUS

Vermont Transit (☎ 802/864–6811, 800/451–3292, or 800/642–3133 in VT) links Rutland, White River Junction, Burlington, and many smaller towns.

BY CAR

The major east–west road is Route 4, which stretches from White River Junction in the east to Fair Haven in the west. Route 125 connects Middlebury on Route 7 with Hancock on Route 100; Route 100 splits the region in half along the eastern edge of the Green Mountains. Route

17 travels east–west from Waitsfield over the Appalachian Gap through Bristol and down to the shores of Lake Champlain. I–91 and the parallel Route 5 follow the eastern border; Routes 7 and 30 are the north–south highways in the west. I–89 links White River Junction with Montpelier to the north.

Contacts and Resources

EMERGENCIES

Porter Medical Center (⊠ South St., Middlebury, ☎ 802/388–7901). **Rutland Medical Center** (⊠ 160 Allen St., Rutland, ☎ 802/775–7111).

GUIDED TOURS

Country Inn Along the Trail (⊠ R.R. 3, Box 3115, Brandon 05733, ☎ 802/247–3300 or 800/838–3301) leads skiing, hiking, and biking trips from inn to inn in Vermont. The **Vermont Icelandic Horse Farm** (⊠ North Fayston Rd., Waitsfield 05673, ☎ 802/496–7141) conducts year-round guided riding expeditions on easy-to-ride Icelandic horses. Full-day, half-day, and hourly rides, weekend tours, and inn-to-inn treks are available.

LODGING REFERRAL SERVICES

Sugarbush Reservations (☎ 800/537–8427) and the **Woodstock Area Chamber of Commerce** (☎ 802/457–3555) provide lodging referral services.

STATE PARKS

The following state parks have camping and picnicking facilities: **Ascutney State Park** (⊠ Rte. 5, 2 mi north of I–91, Exit 8, ☎ 802/674–2060) has a scenic mountain toll road and snowmobile trails. **Coolidge State Park** (⊠ Near Woodstock, Rte. 100A, 2 mi north of Rte. 100, ☎ 802/672–3612), in Calvin Coolidge National Forest, includes the village where Calvin Coolidge was born and is great for snowmobiling. **Gifford Woods State Park**'s Kent Pond (⊠ Near Rutland, Rte. 100, ½ mi north of Rte. 4, ☎ 802/775–5354) is a terrific fishing hole. **Half Moon State Park**'s principal attraction is Half Moon Pond (⊠ Town Rd., 3½ mi off Rte. 30, west of Hubbardton, ☎ 802/273–2848). The park has approach trails, nature trails, and boat and canoe rentals.

VISITOR INFORMATION

Addison County Chamber of Commerce (⊠ 2 Court St., Middlebury 05753, ☎ 802/388–7951 or 800/733–8376). **Quechee Chamber of Commerce** (⊠ Box 106, Quechee 05059, ☎ 802/295–7900 or 800/295–5451). **Rutland Region Chamber of Commerce** (⊠ 256 N. Main St., Rutland 05701, ☎ 802/773–2747). **Sugarbush Chamber of Commerce** (⊠ Box 173, Rte. 100, Waitsfield 05673, ☎ 802/496–3409 or 800/828–4748). **Woodstock Area Chamber of Commerce** (⊠ Box 486, 4 Central St., Woodstock 05091, ☎ 802/457–3555 or 888/496–6378).

NORTHERN VERMONT

Much of Vermont's logging and dairy farming take place in Northern Vermont, where the state's greatest snowfall is recorded. Cradled between the population centers of Burlington and Montpelier to the south and the border with Canada to the north, the Northeast Kingdom stretches vast and untamed. Moose sightings and the harsh reality of rural life are much more common here than microbreweries and hip cafés (Budweiser and diners are more the norm). With Montréal only an hour's drive from the border, the Canadian influence is strong, and Canadian accents and currency common (the closer you get to the border, the more bilingual signs you'll encounter).

You'll find plenty to do in the region's cities (Burlington, Montpelier, St. Johnsbury, and Barre), in the bustling resort area of Stowe, in the Lake Champlain islands, and in the wilds of the Northeast Kingdom.

The tour below begins in the state capital, Montpelier; moves west towards Waterbury, Stowe, and Burlington; then north through the Champlain Islands; east along the boundary with Canada toward Jay Peak and Newport; and south into the heart of the Northeast Kingdom before completing the circle in Barre.

Montpelier

㉗ *38 mi east of Burlington, 115 mi north of Brattleboro.*

With fewer than 10,000 residents, Montpelier is the country's least populous state capital. The intersection of State and Main streets is the city hub, bustling with the activity of state and city workers during the day. It's an endearing place to spend an afternoon browsing in the local shops; in true, small-town Vermont fashion, the streets become deserted at night.

The **Vermont State House**—with gleaming gold dome and granite columns 6 ft in diameter (plucked from the ground in nearby Barre)—is impressive for a city this size. The interior of the 1859 building had a makeover in 1994, but most of the original furnishings are still in place and continue to reflect the intimacy of the state's citizen legislature. ⊠ *115 State St.,* ☎ *802/828–2228.* ⊠ *Free.* ☉ *Weekdays 8–4; tours July–mid-Oct. every ½ hr 10–3:30, Sat. 11–3.*

Perhaps you're wondering what the last panther shot in Vermont looked like? Why New England bridges are covered? What a niddy-noddy is? Or what Christmas was like for a Bethel boy in 1879? ("I skated on my new skates. In the morning Papa and I set up a stove for Gramper.") The **Vermont Museum,** on the ground floor of the Vermont Historical Society offices in Montpelier, satisfies the curious with intriguing and informative exhibits. ⊠ *109 State St.,* ☎ *802/828–2291.* ⊠ *$3.* ☉ *Tues.–Fri. 9–4:30, Sat. 9–4, Sun. noon–4.*

Dining and Lodging

$$–$$$ ✕ **Chef's Table.** Nearly everyone working here is a student at the New
★ England Culinary Institute. Although this is a training ground, the quality and inventiveness are anything but beginner's luck. The menu changes daily. The atmosphere is more formal than that of the sister operation downstairs, the Main Street Bar and Grill. Tipping is forbidden. ⊠ *118 Main St.,* ☎ *802/229–9202, 802/223–3188 for Grill. AE, D, MC, V. Closed Sun. Grill open 7 days.*

$$ ✕ **Horn of the Moon.** The bulletin board plastered with notices of local events and political gatherings hints at Vermont's prominent progressive contingent. This vegetarian restaurant's cuisine includes a little Mexican, a little Italian, a lot of flavor, and not too much tofu. ⊠ *8 Langdon St.,* ☎ *802/223–2895. No credit cards. Closed Mon.*

$$$–$$$$ 🏨 **Inn at Montpelier.** This inn built in the early 1800s was renovated with the business traveler in mind, but the architectural detailing, antique four-poster beds, Windsor chairs, and the classical guitar on the stereo attract the leisure trade as well. The formal sitting room has a Federal feel to it, and the wide wraparound Colonial Revival porch is perfect for reading a good book or watching the townsfolk stroll by. The rooms in the annex across the street are equally spiffy. ⊠ *147 Main St., 05602,* ☎ *802/223–2727,* 🇫🇦🇽 *802/223–0722. 19 rooms. Meeting rooms. Continental breakfast. AE, D, DC, MC, V.*

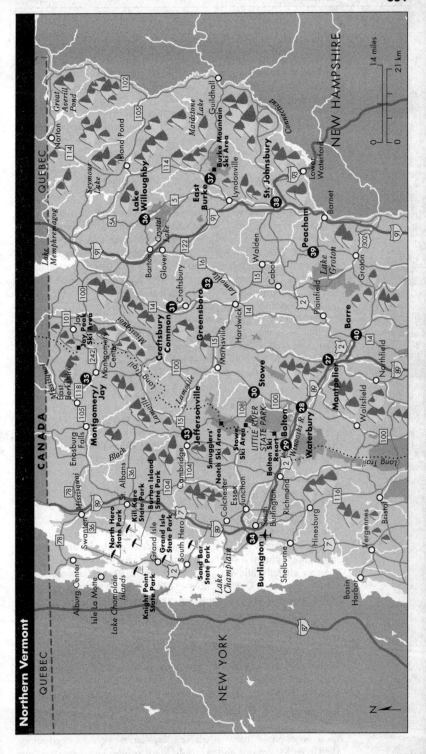

Northern Vermont

Waterbury

28 *12 mi northwest of Montpelier.*

Waterbury holds one of Vermont's best-loved attractions: **Ben & Jerry's Ice Cream Factory,** the mecca, nirvana, and Valhalla for ice-cream lovers. Ben and Jerry began selling ice cream from a renovated gas station in Burlington in the 1970s. Their social and environmental consciousness have made the company a model of corporate responsibility. The tour only skims the surface (pardon the pun) of the behind-the-scenes goings-on at the plant—a flaw forgiven when the free samples are offered. ⊠ *Rte. 100, 1 mi north of I–89,* ☎ *802/244–8687.* ☞ *Tour $2.* ☉ *Daily 9–6 (til 9 in summer and fall); tours every ½ hr in winter, more frequently in summer.*

Dining and Lodging

$$$–$$$$ ✕☲ **Thatcher Brook Inn.** There were once two sawmills across the street from this 1899 mansion, which was the residence for the sawyers and their families. The hub of activity is Ben & Jerry's ice-cream factory next door. Twin gazebos are poised on either end of the front porch, and stands of giant white pines bolster the inn, defining its space on busy Route 100. Comfortable guest rooms have modern bathroom fixtures and Laura Ashley–style floral wallpaper; some have fireplaces and whirlpool tubs. Pine paneling, a fireplace, framed *Life* magazine covers, and tables painted with backgammon boards make the pub a popular socializing spot. Classic French cuisine, which might include pheasant, rack of lamb, or seafood, is served in the dining room. ⊠ *Rte. 100, 05676,* ☎ *802/244–5911 or 800/292–5911,* ℻ *802/244–1294. 24 rooms. Restaurant, pub. Full breakfast; MAP available. AE, D, DC, MC, V.*

Outdoor Activities and Sports

Mount Mansfield State Forest and **Little River State Park** (⊠ Rte. 2, 1½ mi west of Waterbury) have extensive trail systems for hiking, including one that reaches the headquarters of the Civilian Conservation Corps unit that was stationed here in the 1930s.

Shopping

Cabot Creamery Annex (⊠ Rte. 100, 2½ mi north of I–89, ☎ 802/244–6334) is the retail store and tasting center for Vermont's king of cheese. **Cold Hollow Cider Mill** (⊠ Rte. 100, Waterbury Center, ☎ 802/244–8771 or 800/327–7537) sells cider, baked goods, Vermont produce, and specialty foods. The mill owners also produce their own apple butter, apple chutney, and many jams and jellies. Tastes of fresh-pressed cider are offered while you watch how it is made. **Green Mountain Chocolate Co.** (⊠ Rte. 100, ☎ 802/244–1139) greets you with cases of hand-rolled truffles, cakes, cookies, and many candies.

Bolton

29 *20 mi east of Burlington, 20 mi west of Montpelier.*

Bolton attracts cross-country and alpine skiers in the winter and mountain bikers and hikers in the summer. There isn't much to the town itself, but the Bolton Valley Resort is always bustling with activity.

Lodging

$$–$$$ ✕☲ **Black Bear Inn.** Teddy bears in all shapes and sizes decorate this mountaintop inn, many of whose rooms have balconies overlooking the Green Mountains and ski trails. Some rooms have fireplaces, and others have Vermont Castings gas stoves. Grilled Atlantic salmon with a maple-Dijon mustard glaze is a typical dish at the inn's restaurant. ⊠ *Mountain Rd., 05477,* ☎ *802/434–2126 or 800/395–6335,* ℻ *802/*

434–5161. 24 rooms. Restaurant, pool, outdoor hot tub. Full break-fast. MC, V.

$$–$$$ 🏨 **Bolton Resort Hotel and Condominiums.** Like the ski area, this self-contained resort is geared toward families. Hotel units are ski-in, ski-out, and have either fireplaces or kitchenettes; condominium units have as many as four bedrooms. Children under 6 ski for $5, and ski packages are available. Guests have access to the pool, hot tub, and fitness room at the Holiday Inn down the road. ✉ *Mountain Rd., 05477,* ☎ *802/434–3444 or 888/593–2586,* 🖷 *802/434–5282. 143 rooms. 2 restaurants, deli, pub, 9 tennis courts, ice-skating. AE, D, DC, MC, V.*

Skiing

Bolton in Vermont Resort. Although some skiers come for the day, most people who visit this resort stay at one of the hotels or condominium complexes at the base of the mountain. Because of this proximity and the relatively gentle skiing, Bolton attracts more beginners and family groups than singles. The mood is easygoing, the dress and atmosphere casual. On the premises are a ski shop, a country store, a deli, a post office, two restaurants and lounges, a sports club, and meeting and convention space. ✉ *Bolton Access Rd., Bolton 05477,* ☎ *802/434–3444, 888/593–2586 for lodging.*

DOWNHILL

Many of the 52 interconnecting trails on Bolton's two mountains, each with a vertical drop of 1,625 ft, are rated intermediate and novice, but 23% is expert terrain (the DesLauriers brothers of Warren Miller movie fame ski and work here). Timberline Peak trail network, with a vertical of 1,000 ft, is where you'll find some of the wider slopes and more challenging terrain. Serving these trails are one quad chair, four doubles, and one surface lift—enough to prevent long lift lines on all but the most crowded days. Top-to-bottom trails are lit for night skiing 4–10 PM every evening except Sunday. Bolton also has a halfpipe, snowboard park, and 70% snowmaking coverage.

CROSS-COUNTRY

With more than 100 km (62 mi) of cross-country trails, 20 km (12 mi) of which are machine tracked, Bolton Valley is a favorite of Vermonters, especially for backcountry skiing. Lessons and rentals (including telemark) are available.

OTHER ACTIVITIES

The sports center has an indoor pool, whirlpool, sauna, one indoor tennis court, and an exercise room. Weekly events and activities include sleigh rides and races.

CHILD CARE

The child care center has supervised play and games, indoors and outdoors, for infants and children up to 6 years old. Child care is also available three nights per week. There are ski-instruction programs for children from age 5 to 15.

Stowe

★ ㉚ *8 mi north of Waterbury, 22 mi northwest of Montpelier, 36 mi northeast of Burlington.*

To many, Stowe rings a bell as the place the von Trapp family, of *Sound of Music* fame, chose to settle after fleeing Austria. Set amid acres of pastures that fall away and allow for wide-angle panoramas of the mountains beyond, the **Trapp Family Lodge** (✉ Luce Hill Rd., ☎ 802/253–8511) is the site of a popular outdoor music series in summer and an extensive cross-country ski trail network in winter.

For more than a century the history of Stowe has been determined by the town's proximity to **Mt. Mansfield,** the highest elevation in the state. As early as 1858, visitors were trooping to the area to view the mountain whose shape suggests the profile of the face of a man lying on his back. If hiking to the top isn't your idea of a good time, in summer you can take the 4½-mi **toll road** to the top for a short scenic walk and a magnificent view. ⊠ *Mountain Rd., 7 mi from Rte. 100,* ☎ *802/253–3000.* ☞ *$12.* ☉ *Late May–late Oct., daily 10–5.*

An alternative means of reaching Mt. Mansfield's upper reaches is the eight-seat **gondola** that shuttles continuously up to the area of "the Chin," which has a small restaurant (dinner reservations essential). ⊠ *Mountain Rd., 8 mi from Rte. 100,* ☎ *802/253–3000.* ☞ *$9.* ☉ *Mid-June to mid-Oct., daily 10–5; early Dec.–late Apr., daily 8–4 for skiers. Closed mid-Oct.–early Dec. and late-Apr.–mid-June.*

When you tire of shopping on Stowe's Main Street and on Mountain Road (most easily accomplished by car), head for the **recreational path** that begins behind the Community Church in the center of town and meanders for 5⅓ mi along the river valley. There are many entry points along the way; whether you're on foot, ski, bike, or in-line skates, it's a tranquil means of enjoying the outdoors.

Dining and Lodging

$$–$$$ ✕ **Villa Tragara.** Romance reigns in this farmhouse that has been
★   carved into intimate dining nooks. Among the menu highlights are woodland mushrooms sautéed with garlic, shallots, brandy, and cream served over grilled Italian bread, risotto with baby shrimp, mussels, scallops, clams, and squid, and Vermont rack of lamb marinated in herbs, roasted in garlic, and served with a Madeira wine sauce. The tasting menu is a five-course dinner for $40. There is dinner theater year-round, and on Friday, Italian tapas are served to the sounds of live entertainment. ⊠ *Rte. 100, south of Stowe,* ☎ *802/244–5288. AE, MC, V.*

$$ ✕ **Foxfire Inn.** A restored Colonial building might seem an unusual place to find superb Italian delicacies like veal rollatini, steak saltimbocca, and *tartufo* (vanilla and chocolate gelato in a chocolate cup with a raspberry center). But this old farmhouse a couple of miles north of Stowe proper blends the two well, making it worth the short drive from town. ⊠ *Rte. 100,* ☎ *802/253–4887. AE, D, MC, V.*

$$$$ ✕🏨 **Edson Hill Manor.** This French Canadian–style manor built in 1940 sits atop 225 acres of rolling hills. Oriental rugs accent the dark wideboard floors, and a tapestry complements the burgundy-patterned sofas that face the huge stone fireplace in the living room. The guest rooms are pine paneled and have fireplaces, canopy beds, and down comforters. The dining room ($$$–$$$$; no lunch; closed from Sunday to Thursday in April and May) is really the heart of the place: The walls of windows allowing contemplation of the inspiring view compete for diners' attention with paintings of wildflowers, an ivy-covered stone arch, and vines climbing to the ceiling. The highly designed, sculpted food might include rack of lamb or pan-seared salmon. ⊠ *1500 Edson Hill Rd., 05672,* ☎ *802/253–7371 or 800/621–0284,* ℻ *802/253–4036. 25 rooms. Restaurant, pool, hiking, horseback riding, cross-country skiing, sleigh rides. Full breakfast; MAP available. AE, D, MC, V.*

$$$$ ✕🏨 **Topnotch at Stowe Resort and Spa.** This resort on 120 acres 3 mi from the base of the mountain is one of the state's poshest. Floor-to-ceiling windows, a freestanding circular stone fireplace, and cathedral ceilings make the lobby an imposing setting. Rooms have thick carpeting, a small shelf of books, and accents like painted barn-board walls or Italian prints. The minimum stay is two nights. Maxwell's restaurant serves Continental cuisine. ⊠ *Mountain Rd., 05672,* ☎ *802/*

253–8585 or 800/451–8686, FAX *802/253–9263. 77 rooms, 20 1- to 3-bedroom town homes, 13 suites. 2 restaurants, bar, indoor and outdoor pools, 14 tennis courts (4 indoor), health club, horseback riding, cross-country skiing, sleigh rides. Full breakfast; MAP available. AE, D, DC, MC, V.*

$$$–$$$$ ⊞ **Inn at the Brass Lantern.** Home-baked cookies in the afternoon, a basket of logs by your fireplace, and stenciled hearts along the wainscoting reflect the care taken in turning this 18th-century farmhouse into a place of welcome. All rooms have country antiques and locally made quilts; most are oversize and some have fireplaces and whirlpool tubs. This B&B is next door to a Grand Union supermarket, but its breakfast room has a terrific view of Mt. Mansfield, a sight some guest rooms share. ⊠ *Rte. 100, ½ mi north of Stowe, 05672,* ☎ *802/ 253–2229 or 800/729–2980,* FAX *802/253–7425. 9 rooms. Breakfast room. Full breakfast. AE, MC, V.*

$$–$$$ ⊞ **Gables Inn.** The converted farmhouse at the Gables is a rabbit warren of small, charming, antiques-filled rooms. The four larger rooms in the carriage house have cathedral ceilings, fireplaces, TVs, and whirlpool tubs. There is a porch with comfortable chairs on which you can enjoy the view of Mt. Mansfield. The tiny plant-filled sunroom is perfect for lazy mornings, and the breakfasts are generous. Dinner is served during foliage and ski season; lunch is served in the summer. ⊠ *Mountain Rd., 05672,* ☎ *802/253–7730 or 800/422–5371,* FAX *802/ 253–8989. 17 rooms, 2 suites. Dining room, pool, outdoor hot tub. Full breakfast. AE, D, MC, V.*

Nightlife and the Arts

The **Matterhorn Night Club** (☎ 802/253–8198) has live music and dancing on weekends, DJs during the week. Live weekend entertainment takes place at **Stoweflake Inn** (☎ 802/253–7355). Entertainers perform at the **Topnotch at Stowe** (☎ 802/253–8585) lounge on weekends.

Stowe Performing Arts (☎ 802/253–7792) sponsors a series of classical and jazz concerts during July in the Trapp Family Concert meadow. **Stowe Theater Guild** (⊠ Town Hall Theater, Main St., ☎ 802/253– 3961, summer only) performs musicals in July and August.

Outdoor Activities and Sports

BIKING

The junction of Routes 100 and 108 is the start of a 21-mi tour with scenic views of Mt. Mansfield; the course takes you along Route 100 to Stagecoach Road, to Morristown, over to Morrisville, and south on Randolph Road. The **Mountain Bike Shop** (⊠ Mountain Rd., ☎ 802/ 253–7919) supplies equipment and conducts guided tours.

CANOEING

Umiak Outdoor Outfitters (⊠ 849 S. Main St., ☎ 802/253–2317), which specializes in canoes and kayaks, rents them for day trips and leads guided overnight excursions.

FISHING

The **Fly Rod Shop** (⊠ Rte. 100, 3 mi south of Stowe, ☎ 802/253–7346 or 800/535–9763) provides a guiding service, gives fly-tying, casting, and rod-building classes in winter, and rents and sells equipment, including classic and collectible firearms.

HIKING

For the two-hour climb to **Stowe Pinnacle,** go 1½ mi south of Stowe on Route 100 and turn east on Gold Brook Road opposite the Nichols Farm Lodge; turn left at the first intersection, continue straight at an intersection by a covered bridge, turn right after 1.8 mi, and travel 2.3 mi to a parking lot on the left. The trail crosses an abandoned pasture and takes a short, steep climb to views of the Green Mountains and Stowe Valley.

Jackson Arena (☎ 802/253–6148) is a public ice-skating rink that rents skates.

Charlie Horse Sleigh and Carriage Rides (☎ 802/253–2215) operates rides daily from 11 to 7; reservations are suggested for evening rides.

Topnotch at Stowe Resort and Spa (☎ 802/253–8585) has ten outdoor and four indoor courts. Public courts are located at Stowe elementary school.

Shopping

The **Mountain Road** is lined with shops from town up toward the ski area.

Skiing

Stowe Mountain Resort. To be precise, the name of the village is Stowe and the name of the mountain is Mt. Mansfield, but to generations of skiers, the area, the complex, and the region are just plain Stowe. The resort is a classic that dates from the 1930s. Even today the area's mystique attracts more serious skiers than social skiers. In recent years, on-mountain lodging, improved snowmaking, new lifts, and free shuttle buses that gather skiers from lodges, inns, and motels along the Mountain Road have added convenience to the Stowe experience. Yet the traditions remain: the Winter Carnival in January, the Sugar Slalom in April, ski weeks all winter. So committed is the ski school to improvements that even noninstruction package plans include one free ski lesson. Three base lodges provide the essentials, including two on-mountain restaurants. ✉ *5781 Mountain Rd., Stowe 05672,* ☎ *802/253–3000, 800/253–4754 for lodging, 802/253–3600 for snow conditions.*

Mt. Mansfield, with a vertical drop of 2,360 ft, is one of the giants among Eastern ski mountains. It was the only area in the East featured in Warren Miller's 1995 film, *Endless Winter.* Its symmetrical shape allows skiers of all abilities long, satisfying runs from the summit. The famous Front Four runs (National, Liftline, Starr, and Goat) are the intimidating centerpieces for tough, expert runs, yet there is plenty of mellow intermediate skiing and one long beginner trail from the top that ends at the Toll House, where there is easier terrain. Mansfield's satellite sector is a network of intermediate and one expert trail off a basin served by a gondola. Spruce Peak, separate from the main mountain, is a teaching hill and a pleasant experience for intermediates and beginners. In addition to the high-speed, eight-passenger gondola, Stowe has one quad, one triple, and six double chairlifts, plus one handle tow and poma, to service its 47 trails. Night skiing trails are accessed by the gondola. The resort has 73% snowmaking coverage. Plans are underway to create three new halfpipes and four terrain parks that will be open to snowboarders.

The resort has 35 km (22 mi) of groomed cross-country trails and 40 km (24 mi) of backcountry trails. There are four interconnecting cross-country ski areas with more than 150 km (90 mi) of groomed trails within the town of Stowe.

The child-care center takes children from age 2 months to 12 years. A center on Spruce Peak is headquarters for programs for children from age 3 to 12, and there's another program for teenagers 16 and under.

En Route   Northwest of Stowe is an exciting and scenic if indirect route to Burlington: **Smugglers' Notch,** the narrow pass between Mt. Mansfield and Madonna Peak that is said to have sheltered 18th-century outlaws in its rugged, bouldered terrain. Weaving around the huge stones that shoulder the road, you'd hardly know you're on state highway Route 108. There are parking spots and picnic tables at the top. The notch road is closed in winter.

Craftsbury Common

③   *27 mi northeast of Stowe.*

The three villages of Craftsbury—Craftsbury Common, Craftsbury, and East Craftsbury—are among Vermont's finest and oldest towns. Handsome white houses and barns, the requisite common, a classic general store, and the Outdoor Center make them well worth the drive. The rolling farmland hints at the way Vermont used to be: The area's sheer distance from civilization and its rugged weather have kept most of the state's development farther south.

Dining and Lodging

$$$$ ✕🖫 **Inn on the Common.** Craftsbury Common is a perfect hamlet amid remote countryside, and the three white Federal-style buildings of this inn aptly represent the town's civility. All rooms contain antique reproductions and contemporary furnishings; deluxe rooms have generous seating areas and fireplaces. Cocktails and hors d'oeuvres are served in one house's cozy library. Five-course dinners are served at a communal table in the dining room, which overlooks the inn's gardens. Guests have access to the facilities at the Craftsbury Sports Center and Albany's Wellness Barn, which has a lap pool, aerobic machines, a sauna, and a whirlpool. ⊠ *On the common, 05827,* ☎ *802/586–9619 or 800/ 521–2233,* FAX *802/586–2249. 15 rooms, 1 suite. Lounge, pool, tennis court. MAP. AE, MC, V.*

$$$ ✕🖫 **Craftsbury Outdoor Center.** Outside town and surrounded by lakes and hills, this outdoor enthusiasts' haven offers standard accommodations and sporting packages. Because of a long season of snowcover— it's white here when the rest of Vermont is green—the cross-country skiing is terrific on the 160 km (about 100 mi) of trails (96km/60 mi groomed) on the property and through local farmland. During the rest of the year, sculling and running camps take place; other activities include mountain biking and canoeing. Nonguests can ski, mountain bike, and canoe at day-use rates; equipment rental is available. The buffet-style meals include soups, stews, and homemade breads and desserts. ⊠ *Box 31, 05827,* ☎ *802/586–7767 or 800/729–7751,* FAX *802/586–7768. 2 rooms with bath, 40 rooms share baths, 3 cottages, 2 efficiencies. Boating, mountain bikes, cross-country skiing. AP. MC, V.*

Greensboro

③   *10 mi southeast of Craftsbury Common.*

Greensboro is an idyllic small town with a long history as a vacation destination. **Willey's Store** (⊠ Main St., ☎ 802/533–2621), with wooden floors and tin ceilings, warrants exploration; you never know what you'll find—foodstuffs, baskets, candy, kitchen paraphernalia— in this packed-to-the-rafters emporium.

Dining and Lodging

$$$$ ✕🖫 **Highland Lodge.** Tranquility defined: an 1860 house that overlooks a pristine lake, with 120 acres of rambling woods and pastures laced with hiking and skiing trails (ski rentals available). Widely touted as having one of the best front porches in the state, this quiet family

resort is part refined elegance and part casual country of the summer-camp sort. The comfortable guest rooms have Early American furnishings. Most rooms have views of the lake; cottages are more private. The traditional dinner menu ($$), which incorporates Vermont foods, might include entrées such as roasted leg of lamb and grilled Black Angus sirloin. ⊠ *Caspian Lake, 05841,* ☎ *802/533–2647,* FAX *802/533–7494. 11 rooms, 11 cottages. Restaurant, lake, tennis court, hiking, boating, cross-country skiing, recreation room, children's programs. MAP. D, MC, V. Closed mid-Mar.–late May, mid-Oct.–mid-Dec.*

$$ 🏠 **Brick House Guests and Perennial Pleasures Nursery.** Out of a handsome brick home flows an abundance of homespun entrepreneurship. British-born proprietor, Judith Kane, runs an eclectic B&B with large, antiques-filled bedrooms and a cozy library complete with fireplace, sherry, and books on everything from crystal healing to architectural history. The breakfasts, served on charmingly mismatched china, are sumptuous. Judith's daughter Rachel runs the nursery (closed on Monday and from mid-September to April), which specializes in heirloom plants and herbs. Then there is the gift and garden shop, and if that wasn't enough, in summer you can sit for a spell in the gardens and enjoy traditional English cream tea as butterflies dance among the blossoms. Reservations for tea are advised. ⊠ *Box 128, 2 Brick House Rd., East Hardwick 05836,* ☎ *802/472–5512. 1 room with bath, 2 rooms with shared bath. Full breakfast. MC, V.*

Jeffersonville

㉝   *18 mi north of Stowe, 28 mi northeast of Burlington.*

Mt. Mansfield and Madonna Peak tower over Jeffersonville, whose activities are closely linked with those of Smugglers' Notch Ski Resort.

Lodging

$$$$ 🏨 **Smugglers' Notch Resort.** Most of the condos at this large year-round resort have fireplaces and decks. The rates include lift tickets and ski lessons. ⊠ *Rte. 108, 05464,* ☎ *802/644–8851 or 800/451–8752,* FAX *802/644–1230. 375 condos. 3 restaurants, bar, indoor pool, hot tub, sauna, 10 tennis courts (2 indoors), exercise room, ice-skating, recreation room, baby-sitting, children's programs, nursery, playground. AE, DC, MC, V.*

$$ 🏨 **Highlander Motel.** Although most of the rooms are motel-style, the Highlander also has three inn-style, antiques-filled units that have views of the mountain. No matter what configuration you choose, you won't be far from Smugglers' Village, 2½ mi away. You can enjoy breakfast (the only meal the restaurant serves) by the fire. ⊠ *Rte. 108 S, 05464,* ☎ *802/644–2725 or 800/367–6471,* FAX *802/644–2725. 15 rooms. Restaurant, pool, recreation room. MC, V.*

Nightlife

Most après-ski action in the Smugglers' Notch area revolves around the afternoon bonfires and nightly live entertainment in the **Meeting House** (☎ 802/644–8851).

Shopping

ANTIQUES

The Buggy Man (⊠ Rte. 15, 7 mi east of Jeffersonville, ☎ 802/635–2110) and **Mel Siegel** (⊠ Rte. 15, 7 mi east of Jeffersonville, ☎ 802/635–7838) stock affordable, quality antiques.

CLOTHING

Johnson Woolen Mills (⊠ Main St., Johnson, 9 mi east of Jeffersonville, ☎ 802/635–2271) is an authentic factory store with great deals on woolen blankets, yard goods, and the famous Johnson outerwear.

CRAFTS

Vermont Rug Makers (⊠ Route 100C, East Johnson, 10 mi east of Jeffersonville, ☎ 802/635–2434) weaves imaginative rugs and tapestries from fabrics, wools, and exotic materials. **By Vermont Hands** (⊠ Rte. 15, Johnson, 8 mi east of Jeffersonville, ☎ 802/635–7664) displays furniture, paintings, pottery, jewelry, rugs, quilts, and other works by Vermont artisans, in addition to fine antiques, in a farmhouse that dates back to the late 1700s.

Skiing

Smugglers' Notch Resort. Family programs have long been a specialty of this resort, but skiers of all levels come here (in 1996, Smugglers' became the first ski area in the East to designate a triple-black-diamond run—the Black Hole). All the essentials are available at the base of the lifts. The Family Snowmaking Learning Center demonstrates the processes of state-of-the-art computer-controlled snowmaking and teaches about weather and snow crystals. A new snowboard park was added in 1998. ⊠ *Smugglers' Notch 05464,* ☎ *802/644–8851 or 800/451–8752.*

DOWNHILL

Smugglers' has three mountains. The highest, Madonna, with a vertical drop of 2,610 ft, is in the center and connects with a trail network to Sterling (1,500-ft vertical). The third mountain, Morse (1,150-ft vertical), is more remote, but you can visit all three without removing your skis. The wild, craggy landscape lends a pristine, wilderness feel to the skiing experience. The tops of each of the mountains have expert terrain—a couple of double-black diamonds make Madonna memorable. Intermediate trails fill the lower sections. Morse has many beginner trails. Smugglers' 60 trails are served by five double chairlifts, including the Mogul Mouse Magic Lift, and three surface lifts. There is top-to-bottom snowmaking on all three mountains, allowing for 62% coverage.

CROSS-COUNTRY

The area has 37 km (23 mi) of groomed and tracked cross-country trails.

OTHER ACTIVITIES

The self-contained village has ice-skating, sleigh rides, and horseback riding. Vermont Horse Park (☎ 802/644–5347) also conducts rides on authentic horse-drawn sleighs. Indoors are tennis courts, a pool, and a hot tub.

CHILD CARE

The child-care center accepts children from age 6 weeks to 12 years. Children from age 3 to 17 can attend ski camps that have instruction, movies, games, and other activities.

Burlington

★ ㉞ *76 mi south of Montréal, 393 mi north of New York City, 223 mi northwest of Boston.*

Burlington, the largest population center in Vermont, was named one of the country's "Dream Towns" by *Outside* magazine. The city, which was founded in 1763, is growing rapidly—housing complexes heavily outnumber family farms. Burlington had a long history as a trade center following the growth of shipping on Lake Champlain in the 19th century. The town draws an eclectic crew that includes many culture-hungry urban transplants and the roughly 20,000 students from the area's five colleges. For years it was the only city in America with a socialist mayor—now the nation's sole socialist congressional representative. The Church Street Marketplace—a pedestrian mall of funky shops, intriguing boutiques, and an appealing menagerie of sidewalk cafés, food and crafts vendors, and street performers—is an animated downtown focal point. Most people in central and northern Vermont come at least occasionally to the festive town center, if only to run errands or see a show.

Crouched on the shores of Lake Champlain, which shimmers in the shadows of the Adirondacks to the west, Burlington's revitalized **waterfront** teems with outdoor enthusiasts in summer who stroll along its recreation path and ply the waters in sailboats and motorcraft. A replica of an old Champlain paddle wheeler, *The Spirit of Ethan Allen,* takes people on narrated cruises on the lake and, in the evening, dinner and sunset sailings that drift by the Adirondacks and the Green Mountains. ⊠ *Burlington Boat House, College St. at Battery St.,* ☎ *802/862–9685.* ☞ *$8.* ☉ *Cruises late May–mid-Oct., daily 10–9.*

Part of the waterfront's revitalization and still a work-in-progress, the **Lake Champlain Basin Science Center** is in the perfect location to fulfill its mission to educate the public about the ecology, history, and culture of the lake region. The hands-on focus of the "Secrets of the Lake" and "Song of the Wetlands" exhibits will have you looking eye to eye with a turtle, touching fossils, learning how and why a fish moves, and seeing the direct influence on the lake of nonnative species such as the zebra mussel. As part of the "Sea That Used to Be" exhibit you can pick up a live sea star, hermit crab, or sea urchin, descendants of Lake Champlain's ancient past. From looking at plankton through a "kidscope" to dragging a net off UVM's research boat docked on the property, there are activities for the whole family. UVM's Research Lab will open at the Science Center in 1999. ⊠ *One College St.,* ☎ *802/ 864–1848.* ☞ *$2.* ☉ *Mid-June–Labor Day, daily 11–5; fall and winter, weekends and school vacations 12:30–4:30.*

Ethan Allen, Vermont's famous early settler, remains a figure of mystery. Exhibits at the visitor center at the **Ethan Allen Homestead** answer questions about his flamboyant life. The house contains frontier hallmarks like rough saw-cut boards and an open hearth for cooking. A re-created Colonial kitchen garden resembles the one the Allens would have had. After the tour, stretch your legs on scenic trails along the Winooski river. ⊠ *North Ave., off Rte. 127, north of Burlington,* ☎ *802/865–4556.* ☞ *$4.* ☉ *Mid-May–mid-June, Tues.–Sun. 1–5; mid-June–Oct. 19, Mon.–Sat. 10–5, Sun. 1–5.*

A few miles south of Burlington, the Champlain Valley gives way to fertile farmland, affording chin-dropping views of the rugged Adirondacks across the lake. Five miles from the city, one could trace all New England history simply by wandering the 45 acres and 37 buildings of ★ the **Shelburne Museum.** The museum made the headlines because of a controversial decision to sell some of its paintings to raise money for the maintenance of the remainder of its 80,000 objects. The large collection of Americana consists of 18th- and 19th-century period homes and furniture, fine and folk art, farm tools, more than 200 carriages and sleighs, Audubon prints, an old-fashioned jail, even a private railroad car from the days of steam. And an assortment of duck decoys. And an old stone cottage. And a display of early toys. And the *Ticonderoga,* an old side-wheel steamship, grounded amid lawn and trees. ⊠ *Rte. 7, 5 mi south of Burlington,* ☎ *802/985–3346.* ☞ *$17.50 for 2 consecutive days, $7 in winter for 1 day.* ☉ *Mid-May–late-Oct., daily 10–5; call ahead for limited winter hrs.*

★ ☺ **Shelburne Farms** has a history of improving the farmer's lot by developing new agricultural methods. Founded in the 1880s as a private estate, the 1,400-acre property is an educational and cultural resource center. You can see a working dairy farm, milk a cow and get up close to many other farm animals at the Children's Farmyard, watch the making of world-famous cheddar cheese, listen to nature lectures, or simply stroll the immaculate grounds on a scenic stretch of Lake Champlain waterfront. The original landscaping, designed by Frederick Law Olmsted, the creator of New York City's Central Park and Boston's Emerald Necklace, gently channels the eye to expansive vistas and aesthetically satisfying views of such buildings as the five-story, 2-acre Farm Barn. ⊠ *West of Rte. 7 at the junction of Harbor and Bay Rds., 6 mi south of Burlington,* ☎ *802/985–8686.* ⊡ *$5 day pass, tour is an additional $4.* ☉ *Visitor center and shop daily 9–5; tours Memorial Day–mid-Oct., last tour at 3:30.*

☺ On the tour of the **Vermont Teddy Bear Company,** you'll hear more puns than you ever thought possible and learn how a few homemade bears, sold from a cart on Church Street, have turned into a multimillion-dollar business. A children's play tent is set up outdoors in summer, and you can wander the beautiful 57-acre property. ⊠ *2236 Shelburne Rd., Shelburne,* ☎ *802/985–3001.* ⊡ *Tour $1.* ☉ *Tours Mon.–Sat. 10–4, Sun. 11–4; store Mon.–Sat. 9–6, Sun. 10–5.*

At the 6-acre **Vermont Wildflower Farm,** the display along the flowering pathways changes constantly: violets in the spring, daisies and black-eyed Susans for summer, and fall colors that rival the trees' foliage. You can buy wildflower seeds, crafts, and books here. ⊠ *Rte. 7, 5 mi south of the Shelburne Museum,* ☎ *802/425–3500.* ⊡ *$3.* ☉ *Early May–late Oct., daily 10–5.*

OFF THE
BEATEN PATH

GREEN MOUNTAIN AUDUBON NATURE CENTER – Bursting with great things to do, see, and learn, this is a wonderful place to orient yourself to Vermont's outdoor wonders. The center's 300 acres of diverse habitats are a sanctuary for all things wild, and the 5 mi of trails beg you to explore and understand the workings of differing natural communities. Events at the center include dusk walks, wildflower and birding rambles, nature workshops, and educational activities for both kids and adults. ⊠ *18 mi southeast of Burlington, Huntington-Richmond Rd., Richmond,* ☎ *802/434-3068.* ⊡ *Donations accepted.* ☉ *Grounds dawn–dusk, center weekdays 9-4:30.*

LAKE CHAMPLAIN ISLANDS – Samuel de Champlain's claim on the islands dotting the northern expanses of Lake Champlain is represented on Isle La Motte by a granite statue that looks south toward the site of the first French settlement and its shrine to St. Anne. Today the Lake Champlain Islands are a center of water recreation in summer, and ice fishing in winter. North of Burlington, the scenic drive through the islands on Route 2 begins at I–89 and travels north through South Hero, Grand Isle, and Isle La Motte to Alburg Center, 5 mi from the Canadian border. Here Route 78 will take you east to the mainland.

MISSISQUOI NATIONAL WILDLIFE REFUGE – The 6,300 acres of federally protected wetlands, meadows, and woods provide a beautiful setting for bird-watching, canoeing, or walking nature trails. ⊠ *Swanton, 36 mi north of Burlington,* ☎ *802/868-4781.*

Dining and Lodging

$$–$$$ ✕ **Daily Planet.** A solarium, a century-old bar, and a more formal din-
★ ing room compose one of Burlington's hippest restaurants. This is Marco Polo cuisine—basically Mediterranean with Asian influences:

Korean vegetable pancakes, roasted rack of lamb with country mashed potatoes, and a Moroccan vegetable sauté. ⊠ *15 Center St.,* ☎ *802/ 862–9647. AE, D, DC, MC, V.*

$$–$$$ ✕ **Isabel's.** An old lumber mill on Lake Champlain houses this restaurant that has high ceilings, exposed-brick walls, and knockout views. The menu is seasonal; past dishes, all presented with an artistic flair, have included Thai seafood pasta and vegetable Wellington. Lunch and weekend brunch are popular; you can dine on the outdoor patio on warm days. ⊠ *112 Lake St.,* ☎ *802/865–2522. AE, D, DC, MC, V.*

$$ ✕ **Sweet Tomatoes.** The wood-fired oven of this bright and boister-
★   ous trattoria sends off a mouthwatering aroma. With hand-painted ceramic pitchers, bottles of dark olive oil perched against a backdrop of exposed brick, and crusty bread that comes with a bowl of oil and garlic for dunking, this soulful eatery beckons you to Italy's countryside. The menu includes pizzas and *caponata* (roasted eggplant with onions, capers, olives, parsley, celery, and tomatoes), and farfalle with sweet sausage, roasted red peppers, onions, tomatoes, black olives, and rosemary in a tomato basil sauce. ⊠ *83 Church St.,* ☎ *802/660–9533. AE, MC, V.*

$ ✕ **Richard's Special Vermont Pizza (RSVP).** Walk through the door of RSVP and you'll immediately be transported through time (to the 1950s) and space (to anywhere but Vermont). The pizza, with paper-thin crust and toppings like cilantro pesto, cob-smoked bacon, and pineapple, has become known for transport as well: Richard will send a pie almost anywhere in the world by overnight delivery. Salads, soups, and sandwiches are also on the menu. ⊠ *79 Mechanics La., off Church St. across from City Hall,* ☎ *802/658–7787 or 800/682–7787. MC, V.*

$$$–$$$$ ✕⊞ **Inn at Essex.** About 10 mi from downtown Burlington is a state-of-the-art conference center dressed in country-inn clothing. Rooms with flowered wallpaper and library books on the reproduction desks lend the place some character, and the staff is attentive. The two restaurants ($$$)—the refined Butler's and the more casual Tavern—are run by the New England Culinary Institute. Students, coached by an executive chef, rotate through each position, from sous-chef to waiter. The gourmet American cuisine at Butler's includes dishes like the sweet dumpling squash with ginger-garlic basmati rice and the lobster in yellow-corn sauce with spinach pasta. Five-onion soup, burgers, and daily flatbread pizza specials are among the highlights at the Tavern. ⊠ *70 Essex Way, off Rte. 15, Essex Junction 05452,* ☎ *802/878–1100 or 800/288–7613,* ℻ *802/878–0063. 94 rooms. 2 restaurants, bar, pool, billiards, library. Continental breakfast. AE, D, DC, MC, V.*

$$$–$$$$ ✕⊞ **Inn at Shelburne Farms.** This is storybook land: Built at the turn
★   of the century as the home of William Seward and Lila Vanderbilt Webb, the Tudor-style inn perches on Saxton's Point overlooking Lake Champlain, the distant Adirondacks, and the sea of pastures that make up this 1,400-acre working farm. Each room is different, from the wallpaper to the period antiques. The two dining rooms define elegance. The seasonal contemporary menu makes clever use of local ingredients. The inn's profits help support the farm's environmental education programs for local schools. ⊠ *Harbor Rd., Shelburne 05482,* ☎ *802/985–8498,* ℻ *802/985–8123. 24 rooms, 17 rooms with bath. Restaurant, lake, tennis court, hiking, boating, fishing, billiards, recreation room. AE, D, DC, MC, V. Closed mid-Oct.–mid-May.*

$$$ ✕⊞ **Radisson Hotel–Burlington.** This sleek corporate giant, which faces the lakefront, is the hotel closest to downtown shopping. Some rooms have incredible views of the Adirondack Mountains. The hotel's restaurant serves traditional but inspired Continental fare. ⊠ *60 Battery St., 05401,* ☎ *802/658–6500 or 800/333–3333,* ℻ *802/658–*

4659. 255 rooms. 2 restaurants, bar, indoor pool, exercise room, airport shuttle. AE, D, DC, MC, V.

$$–$$$$ 🏨 **Willard Street Inn.** High in the historic hill section of Burlington, this grand house with an exterior marble staircase and English gardens incorporates elements of Queen Anne and Colonial–Georgian Revival styles. The stately foyer, paneled in cherry, leads to a more formal sitting room with velvet drapes. The solarium is bright and sunny with marble floors, many plants, and big velvet couches to relax in while contemplating views of Lake Champlain. All the rooms have down comforters and phones; some have lake views and canopied beds. Orange French toast is among the breakfast favorites. ⊠ *349 S. Willard St., 05401,* ☎ *802/651–8710 or 800/577–8712,* FAX *802/651–8714. 15 rooms, 5 with shared bath. Full breakfast. AE, D, DC, MC, V.*

Nightlife and the Arts

NIGHTLIFE

Name and local musicians come to **Club Toast** (⊠ 165 Church St., ☎ 802/660–2088). The music at the **Metronome** (⊠ 188 Main St., ☎ 802/865–4563) ranges from cutting-edge sounds to funk, blues, and reggae. The band Phish got its start at **Nectar's** (⊠ 188 Main St., ☎ 802/658–4771). This place is always jumping to the sounds of local bands and never charges a cover. **Vermont Pub and Brewery** (⊠ College and St. Paul Sts., ☎ 802/865–0500) makes its own beer and fruit seltzers and is arguably the most popular spot in town. Folk musicians play regularly.

THE ARTS

Burlington City Arts (☎ 802/865–7166 or 802/865–9163 for 24-hr Artsline) has up-to-date arts-related information. **Flynn Theatre for the Performing Arts** (⊠ 153 Main St., ☎ 802/863–8778 for information, 802/863–5966 for tickets), a grandiose old structure, is the cultural heart of Burlington; it schedules the Vermont Symphony Orchestra, theater, dance, big-name musicians, and lectures. The **Lyric Theater** (☎ 802/658–1484) puts on musical productions in the fall and spring at the Flynn Theatre. **St. Michael's Playhouse** (☎ 802/654–2281 box office, 802/654–2617 administrative office) performs in the McCarthy Arts Center Theater. The **UVM Lane Series** (☎ 802/656–4455 for programs and times, 802/656–3085 for box office) sponsors classical as well as folk music concerts in the Flynn Theatre, Ira Allen Chapel, and the UVM Recital Hall.

Outdoor Activities and Sports

BIKING

A recreational path runs 9 mi along Burlington's waterfront. South of Burlington, a moderately easy 18½-mi trail begins at the blinker on Rte. 7 in Shelburne and follows Mt. Philo Road, Hinesburg Road, Route 116, and Irish Hill Road. **North Star Cyclery** (⊠ 100 Main St., ☎ 802/863–3832) and **Ski Rack** (⊠ 81 Main St., ☎ 802/658–3313) rent equipment and provide maps.

WATER SPORTS

Marina services are available north and south of Burlington. **Malletts Bay Marina** (⊠ 228 Lakeshore Dr., Colchester, ☎ 802/862–4072) and **Point Bay Marina** (⊠ 1401 Thompson's Point Rd., Charlotte, ☎ 802/425–2431) provide full service and repairs.

Burlington Community Boathouse (⊠ Foot of College St., Burlington Harbor, ☎ 802/865–3377) has sailboard and boat rentals (some captained) and lessons. **Chiott Marine** (⊠ 67 Main St., ☎ 802/862–8383) caters to water-sports enthusiasts, with two floors of hardware, apparel, and accessories. **Marble Island Resort** (⊠ Colchester, ☎ 802/864–6800) has a marina and a nine-hole golf course.

Shopping

ANTIQUES

Architectural Salvage Warehouse (✉ 212 Battery St., ☎ 802/658–5011) has claw-foot tubs, stained-glass windows, mantels, andirons, and the like. The large rhinoceros head bursting out of the **Conant Custom Brass** (✉ 270 Pine St., ☎ 802/658–4482) storefront will lure you in to see the custom work; the store specializes in decorative lighting and bathroom fixtures.

BOOKS

Chassman & Bem Booksellers (✉ 1 Church St., ☎ 802/862–4332), probably the best bookstore in Vermont, has more than 40,000 titles and a large magazine rack.

COUNTRY STORE

Shelburne Country Store (✉ Village Green, Shelburne, ☎ 802/985–3657) offers a step back in time as you walk past the potbellied stove and take in the aroma emanating from the fudge neatly piled behind huge antique glass cases. Candles, weather vanes, glassware, and Vermont food products are its specialties.

CRAFTS

Bennington Potters North (✉ 127 College St., ☎ 802/863–2221) has, in addition to its popular pottery, interesting gifts, glassware, furniture, and other housewares. **Vermont State Craft Center** (✉ 85 Church St., ☎ 802/863–6458) displays contemporary and traditional crafts by more than 200 Vermont artisans. **Yankee Pride** (✉ Champlain Mill, Winooski, ☎ 802/655–0500) has a large inventory of quilting fabrics and supplies as well as Vermont-made quilts.

MALLS AND MARKETPLACES

Burlington Square Mall (✉ Church St., ☎ 802/658–2545) contains Porteous (the city's major department store) and a few dozen shops. The **Champlain Mill** (✉ Rte. 2/7, northeast of Burlington, ☎ 802/655–9477), a former woolen mill on the banks of the Winooski River, holds three floors of stores. **Church Street Marketplace** (✉ Main St.–Pearl St., ☎ 802/863–1648), a pedestrian thoroughfare, is lined with boutiques, cafés, and street vendors. Built to resemble a ship, the funky **Wing Building** (✉ Next to ferry dock on waterfront) houses boutiques, a café, and an art gallery.

En Route   The top of the mountain pass on Route 242 in Montgomery Center and the Jay Peak area affords vast views of Canada to the north and of Vermont's rugged Northeast Kingdom to the east.

Montgomery/Jay

③⑤   *51 mi northeast of Burlington.*

Montgomery is a small village near the Canadian border and Jay Peak ski resort. Amid the surrounding countryside are seven historic covered bridges.

Dining and Lodging

$$$ ✕▥ **Inn on Trout River.** The large stove is often the center of attention in the two-tiered living and dining area of this 100-year-old inn, though the piano, the library, the pub with a U-shape bar, and the pool table down in the recreation room might also draw your attention. Guest rooms are decorated in either English country cottage style or country Victorian, and all have down quilts and flannel sheets in winter; the largest room has a Franklin potbellied stove, a dressing area, and a claw-foot tub. The back lawn rambles down to the river, and llama treks are conducted in warm months. The restaurant ($$–$$$) serves

American and Continental fare. ✉ *Main St., Montgomery Center 05471,* ☎ *802/326–4391 or 800/338–7049,* 𝖥𝖠𝖷 *802/326–3194. 10 rooms. Restaurant, pub, recreation room, library. Full breakfast; MAP available. AE, D, MC, V.*

$$ ╳🖾 **Black Lantern.** Built in 1803 as a hotel for mill workers, the inn has been providing bed and board ever since. Though the feeling is country, little touches of sophistication abound: Provençal-print wallpaper in the dining room, a subtle rag-roll finish in the rooms in the renovated building next door. All the suites have whirlpools, and most have fireplaces. The menu at the restaurant ($$–$$$) includes pan-seared salmon served with a red pepper sauce and grilled lamb Margarite. ✉ *Rte. 118, Montgomery Village 05470,* ☎ *802/326–4507 or 800/255–8661,* 𝖥𝖠𝖷 *802/326–4077. 10 rooms, 6 suites. Restaurant. Full breakfast. AE, D, MC, V.*

$$$–$$$$ 🖾 **Hotel Jay & Jay Peak Condominiums.** Ski-lodge simplicity was the decorating goal at the hotel, with wood paneling in the rooms, built-in headboards, and vinyl wallpaper in the bathroom. Right at the lifts, the hotel is convenient for people who plan to spend most of their time on the slopes. Rooms on the southwest side have a view of Jay Peak, those on the north overlook the valley; upper floors have balconies. The 120 condominiums (most slopeside) have fireplaces, one to three bedrooms, modern kitchens, and washers and dryers. In winter, a minimum two-night stay is required, and lift tickets and some meals are included in the rates. The summer rates are low. ✉ *Rte. 242, 05859,* ☎ *802/988–2611 or 800/451–4449,* 𝖥𝖠𝖷 *802/988–4049. 48 rooms, 120 condos. Restaurant, bar, pool, hot tub, sauna, tennis courts, recreation room. Continental breakfast in summer, MAP in winter. AE, D, DC, MC, V.*

Skiing

Jay Peak. Sticking up out of the flat farmland, Jay catches an abundance of precipitation from the maritime provinces of Canada. Its proximity to Québec attracts Montréalers and discourages Eastern seaboarders; hence, there are some bargain packages. Lifestyles Resorts, a Canadian group that also owns Horseshoe Mountain, purchased Jay in 1998. ✉ *Rte. 242, Jay 05859,* ☎ *802/988–2611 or 800/451–4449.*

DOWNHILL

Jay Peak is in fact two mountains with 64 trails, the highest reaching nearly 4,000 ft with a vertical drop of 2,153 ft, served by a 60-passenger tram (the only one in Vermont). The area also has a quad, a triple, two double chairlifts, and two T-bars. The smaller mountain has more straight-fall-line, expert terrain, and the tram-side peak has many curving and meandering trails perfectly suited for intermediate and beginning skiers. Jay, known for its glade skiing, has 19 gladed trails. Every morning at 9 AM the ski school offers a free tour, from the tram down one trail. The area has 80% snowmaking coverage.

CROSS-COUNTRY

A touring center at the base of the mountain has 20 km (12 mi) of groomed cross-country trails. A network of 200 km (124 mi) of trails is in the vicinity.

CHILD CARE

The child care center for youngsters age 2 and older is open from 9 to 4. Guests of the Hotel Jay or the Jay Peak Condominiums receive this nursery care free, as well as free skiing for children ages 6 and under, evening care, and supervised dining at the hotel. Children from age 5 to 12 can participate in an all-day SKIwee program, which includes lunch.

En Route The descent from Jay Peak on Route 101 leads to Route 100, which can be the beginning of a scenic loop tour of Routes 14, 5, 58, and back to

100, or take you east to the city of **Newport** on Lake Memphremagog. The waterfront is the dominant view of the city, which is built on a peninsula. The grand hotels of the last century are gone, yet the buildings still drape dramatically along the lake's edge and climb the hills behind.

You will encounter some of the most unspoiled areas in all Vermont on the drive south from Newport on either Route 5 or I–91 (I–91 is faster, Route 5 is prettier). This region, the Northeast Kingdom, is named for the remoteness and stalwart independence that have helped to preserve its rural nature.

Lake Willoughby

36 *7 mi northeast of Barton, 28 mi north of St. Johnsbury.*

On the northern shore of Lake Willoughby, the cliffs of surrounding Mts. Pisgah and Hor drop to water's edge, making this glacially carved, 500-ft-deep lake bear a striking resemblance to a Norwegian fjord. Some also compare the landscape to Lucerne's or Scotland's. In any case, Lake Willoughby is stunning. The lake is popular for summer and winter recreation, and the trails to the top of Mt. Pisgah reward hikers with glorious views.

The **Bread and Puppet Museum** is an unassuming, ramshackle barn that houses a surrealistic collection of props used in past performances by the world-renowned Bread and Puppet Theater. The troupe, whose members live communally on the surrounding farm, have been performing social and political commentary with the towering (they're supported by people on stilts), eerily expressive puppets for about 30 years. ⊠ *South of Lake Willoughby, Rte. 122, Glover, 1 mi east of Rte. 16,* ☎ *802/525–3031.* ☞ *Donations accepted.* ☉ *Call for hrs.*

Lodging

$$–$$$ ★ 🏨 **Fox Hall Inn.** Moose miscellany embellishes the furnishings and rooms at this 1890 Cottage Revival structure that's listed on the National Register of Historic Places—a response to northern Vermont's passionate interest in these once-scarce creatures. The generous wraparound veranda overlooking Lake Willoughby, dotted with swinging seats and comfortable chairs, is perfect for a summer evening spent listening to loons while gazing over the 82-acre property. The two corner turret rooms, which have lake views, are the most distinctive; the other rooms, also bright, are furnished with wicker and quilts. An inspired guest returns every summer to give a chamber music concert and piano workshops. The innkeepers conduct guided nature and bird walks on adjacent state lands. ⊠ *Willoughby Lake Rd. off Rte. 16, 05822,* ☎ *802/525–6930,* 🏮 *802/525–1185. 9 rooms, 4 with bath. Hiking, horseshoes, Ping Pong, volleyball, boating, bicycles, cross-country skiing, snowmobiling. Full breakfast. MC, V.*

En Route If it's a moose sighting you're after, head north on Route 114 toward **Island Pond.**

East Burke and West Burke

37 *17 mi south of Lake Willoughby.*

A jam-packed general store, a post office, and a couple of great places to eat are about all you'll find in the twin towns of East Burke and West Burke.

Dining and Lodging

$$–$$$ ✕ **River Garden Café.** You can eat outdoors on the enclosed porch or the patio and enjoy the perennial gardens that rim the grounds; the

café is bright and cheerful on the inside as well. The healthful fare includes roasted rack of lamb, warm artichoke dip, bruschetta, pastas, and fresh fish. ⊠ *Rte. 114,* ☎ *802/626–3514. AE, D, MC, V. Closed Mon., and Apr., Nov.*

$–$$ ✕🏨 **Old Cutter Inn.** Only ½ mi from the Burke Mountain base lodge is this small converted farmhouse that will fulfill your quest for the quaint-inn experience. The restaurant ($$–$$$$) serves fare that reflects the Swiss chef-owner's heritage, as well as superb Continental cuisine including osso buco and veal piccata. ⊠ *R.R. 1 Box 62, Old Pinkham Rd., 05832,* ☎ *802/626–5152 or 800/295–1943. 9 rooms, 5 with bath, 1 suite. Restaurant, bar, pool, hiking, biking, cross-country skiing. EP, MAP available. D, MC, V. Closed Wed. and Apr., Nov.*

$$$ 🏨 **Burke Mountain Resort.** The modern accommodations at this resort range from economical digs to luxurious slopeside town houses and condominiums with kitchens and TVs. Some rooms have fireplaces, and others have wood-burning stoves. A two-night minimum stay is required, and ski and lodging packages are available. ⊠ *Box 247, 05832,* ☎ *802/626–3305 or 800/541–5480,* ℻ *802/626–3364. 150 condos. Restaurant. AE, MC, V.*

Outdoor Activities and Sports

The **Wildflower Inn** (⊠ Darling Hill Rd., ☎ 800/627–8310) has 15-passenger sleighs drawn by Belgian draft horses.

Shopping

Baily's Country Store (⊠ Rte. 114, East Burke, ☎ 802/626–3666), a veritable institution, sells baked goods, wine, clothing, and other sundries.

Skiing

Burke Mountain. This low-key resort draws many families from Massachusetts and Connecticut. There's plenty of terrain for tenderfeet, but intermediate skiers, experts, racers, telemarkers, and snowboarders will find time-honored New England narrow trails. Many packages at Burke are significantly less expensive than those at other Vermont areas, and the resort has the lowest midweek prices in Vermont. Burke Mt. Academy has contributed a number of notable racers to the U.S. Ski Team. ⊠ *Mountain Rd., East Burke 05832,* ☎ *802/626–3305, 800/ 541–5480 for lodging, 800/922–2875 for snow conditions.*

DOWNHILL

With a 2,000-ft vertical drop, Burke is something of a sleeper among the larger eastern ski areas. It has greatly increased its snowmaking capability (70%), which is enhanced by the mountain's northern location and exposure, assuring plenty of natural snow. An expansion plan including a 20% increase in skiable terrain and a new snowboard park is underway. Burke has one quad, one double chairlift, and two surface lifts. Lift lines, even on weekends and holidays, are light to nonexistent.

CROSS-COUNTRY

Burke Ski Touring Center has more than 95 km (57 mi) of trails (65 km/39 mi groomed); some lead to high points with scenic views. There's a snack bar at the center.

CHILD CARE

In the newly constructed Children's Center, the nursery takes children from age 6 months to 6 years. SKIwee and MINIriders lessons through the ski school are available to children from age 4 to 16.

St. Johnsbury

🟤 *39 mi east of Montpelier.*

St. Johnsbury is the southern gateway to the Northeast Kingdom. Though the town was chartered in 1786, its identity was not firmly established until 1830, when Thaddeus Fairbanks invented the platform scale, a device that revolutionized weighing methods that had been in use since the beginning of recorded history. Because of the Fairbanks family's philanthropic bent, this city with a distinctly 19th-century industrial feel has a strong cultural and architectural imprint.

Opened in 1891, the **Fairbanks Museum and Planetarium** attests to the Fairbanks family's inquisitiveness about all things scientific. The red-brick building in the squat Romanesque architectural style of H. H. Richardson houses Vermont plants and animals and an intimate 50-seat planetarium. Especially bizarre are the intricate paintings of insects by an amateur entomologist and inventor who worked with Thomas Edison. On the third Saturday in September, the museum sponsors the annual Festival of Traditional Crafts, with demonstrations of early American household and farm skills such as candle and soap making. ⊠ *Main and Prospect Sts.,* ☎ *802/748–2372.* 🎟 *$4.* ☉ *July–Aug., Mon.–Sat. 10–6, Sun. 1–5; Sept.–June, Mon.–Sat. 10–4, Sun. 1–5. Planetarium shows July–Aug., daily at 11 and 1:30; Sept.–June, weekends at 1:30.*

The **St. Johnsbury Athenaeum,** with its dark rich paneling, polished Victorian woodwork, and ornate circular staircases that rise to the gallery around the perimeter, is one of the oldest art galleries in the country. The gallery at the back of the building specializes in Hudson River School paintings and has the overwhelming *Domes of Yosemite* by Albert Bierstadt. ⊠ *30 Main St.,* ☎ *802/748–8291.* 🎟 *Free.* ☉ *Mon. and Wed. 10–8, Tues. and Thurs.–Fri. 10–5:30, Sat. 9:30–4.*

OFF THE BEATEN PATH	**CABOT CREAMERY COOPERATIVE –** The biggest cheese producer in the state has a visitor center with an audiovisual presentation about the state's dairy and cheese industry. You can taste samples and tour the plant. ⊠ *3 mi north of Rte. 2, midway between Barre and St. Johnsbury, Cabot,* ☎ *802/563–2231 or 800/639–4031 for orders only.* 🎟 *$1.* ☉ *June–Oct., daily 9–5; Nov.–Dec. and mid-Feb–May, Mon.–Sat. 9–4. Closed Jan.–mid-Feb.*

Dining and Lodging

$$$$ ✕🏨 **Rabbit Hill Inn.** The rooms at Rabbit Hill all have different styles: The Loft, with an 8-ft Palladian window, a king canopy bed, a double whirlpool bath, and a corner fireplace, is one of the most requested. Rooms toward the front of the inn have views of the Connecticut River and New Hampshire's White Mountains. The low wooden beams of the Irish pub next door are a casual contrast to the rest of the inn. Regional cuisine is served in the low-ceiling dining room—perhaps grilled sausage of Vermont pheasant with pistachios or smoked chicken and red lentil dumplings nestled in red-pepper linguine. Meat and fish are smoked on the premises, and the herbs and vegetables often come from gardens out back. A two-night minimum stay is required on weekends. ⊠ *Rte. 18, Lower Waterford 05848,* ☎ *802/748–5168 or 800/762–8669,* 🖷 *802/748–8342. 16 rooms, 5 suites. Restaurant, pub, hiking, cross-country skiing. MAP. AE, MC, V. Closed 1st 3 wks of Apr., 1st 2 wks of Nov., and Dec. 24, 25.*

$$$–$$$$ ✕🏨 **Wildflower Inn.** This rambling complex of old farm buildings on
★   500 acres was a working dairy farm until 1985. The rooms in the restored Federal-style main house and the carriage houses are decorated

simply with reproductions and contemporary furnishings. A former blacksmith's shop holds the suites. In warm weather, the inn is family-oriented in every respect: There's a petting barn, planned children's activities in the summer, and a kid's swimming pool. The inn quiets down in winter when it caters more to cross-country skiers. At the restaurant ($–$$$), homemade breads and vegetables grown in the garden accompany the country-style entrées. ⊠ *North of St. Johnsbury on Darling Hill Rd., Lyndonville 05851,* ☎ *802/626–8310 or 800/627–8310,* ℻ *802/626–3039. 12 rooms, 10 suites. Restaurant, pool, hot tub, sauna, tennis court, soccer, fishing, ice-skating, cross-country skiing, sleigh rides, sledding, recreation room. Full breakfast. MC, V. Closed Apr., Nov.*

Nightlife and the Arts

Catamount Arts (⊠ 60 Eastern Ave., ☎ 802/748–2600) brings avant-garde theater and dance performances to the Northeast Kingdom as well as films and classical music.

Outdoor Activities and Sports

Village Sport Shop (⊠ 4 Broad St., Lyndonville, north of St. Johnsbury, ☎ 802/626–8448) rents canoes, kayaks, bikes, rollerblades, paddleboats, snowshoes, and skis.

Groton Pond (⊠ Rte. 302, off I–91, 20 mi south of St. Johnsbury, near Peacham, ☎ 802/584–3829) is a popular spot for trout fishing; boat rentals are available.

Peacham

39 *10 mi southwest of St. Johnsbury.*

Tiny Peacham's stunning scenery and 18th-century charm have made it a favorite with urban refugees, artists seeking solitude and inspiration, and movie directors looking for the quintessential New England village. *Ethan Frome,* starring Liam Neeson, was filmed here.

Transylvanian goulash, stuffed peppers, and lamb-and-barley soup are among the take-out specialties at the **Peacham Store** (⊠ Main St., ☎ 802/592–3310). You can browse through the locally made crafts while waiting for your order.

Barre

40 *7 mi east of Montpelier, 35 mi south of St. Johnsbury.*

Barre has been famous as the source of Vermont granite ever since two men began working the quarries in the early 1800s; the large number of immigrant laborers attracted to the industry made the city prominent in the early years of the American labor movement.

You might recognize the sheer walls of the **Rock of Ages granite quarry** from the *Batman* film that starred George Clooney and Arnold Schwarzenegger. The attractions of the site range from the awe-inspiring (the quarry resembles the Grand Canyon in miniature) to the mildly ghoulish (the company invites you to consult a directory of tombstone dealers throughout the United States). The view from the craftsman center, which you pass on the drive to the visitor center, seems like a scene out of Dante's *Inferno:* A dusty, smoky haze hangs above the acres of people at work, with machines screaming as they bite into the rock. The process that transfers designs to the smooth stone and etches them into it is fascinating. ⊠ *Exit 6 off I–89, follow Rte. 63,* ☎ *802/476–3119.* 🖭 *$4 tour of active quarry, craftsman center and self-guided tour free.* ☉ *Quarry and visitor center June–mid-Oct., Mon.–Sat. 8:30–*

5, Sun. 12–5; craftsman center weekdays 8–3:30. Quarry shuttle bus tour weekdays 9:15–3.

The Arts

Barre Opera House (⌧ City Hall, Main St., ☎ 802/476–8188) hosts music, opera, theater, and dance performances.

Northern Vermont A to Z

Getting Around

BY BOAT

Lake Champlain Ferries (☎ 802/864–9804), in operation since 1826, operates three ferry crossings during the summer months and one in winter through thick lake ice. Ferries leave from the King Street Dock in Burlington, Charlotte, and Grand Isle. This is a convenient means of getting to and from New York, as well as a pleasant way to spend an afternoon.

BY BUS

Vermont Transit (☎ 802/864–6811 or 800/451–3292; 800/642–3133 in VT) links Burlington, Waterbury, Montpelier, St. Johnsbury, and Newport.

BY CAR

In north-central Vermont, I–89 heads west from Montpelier to Burlington and continues north to Canada. Interstate 91 is the principal north–south route in the east, and Route 100 runs north–south through the center of the state. North of I–89, Routes 104 and 15 provide a major east–west transverse. From Barton, Routes 5 and 122 south are beautiful drives. Strip-mall drudge bogs down the section of Route 5 around Lyndonville.

BY TRAIN

The **Sugarbush Express** runs between Middlebury and Burlington with stops in Vergennes and Shelburne. Relax in coach cars, dating from 1917, as you contemplate the views of Lake Champlain, the valley farmlands, and surrounding mountains. ☎ 802/388–0193 or 800/707–3530. ⌧ $12 round trip. ☉ Mid-June–Columbus Day.

Contacts and Resources

BEACHES

Some of the most scenic Lake Champlain beaches are on the Champlain islands. **Knight Point State Park** (⌧ North Hero, ☎ 802/372–8389) is the reputed home of "Champ," Lake Champlain's answer to the Loch Ness monster. **North Hero State Park** (☎ 802/372–8727) has a children's play area nearby. **Sand Bar State Park** (⌧ Milton, ☎ 802/893–2825) is near a waterfowl preserve. Arrive early to beat the summer crowds. Admission is $1; the park is open from mid-May to October.

The **North Beaches** are on the northern edge of Burlington: North Beach Park (⌧ North Ave., ☎ 802/864–0123), Bayside Beach (⌧ Rte. 127 near Malletts Bay); and Leddy Beach, which is popular for sailboarding. **North Beach Campground** (☎ 802/862–0942) is open from May to mid-October and has 130 sites, including 16 that are full hookup.

EMERGENCIES

Fletcher Allen Health Care (⌧ Colchester Ave., Burlington, ☎ 802/656–2345). For 24-hour medical health care information, call 802/656–2439.

GUIDED TOURS

Two foresters run **Cold Hollow Llamas** (⌧ Belvedere, ☎ 802/644–5846); they lead trips through the countryside and answer questions about

Vermont's natural history. The gourmet picnic lunches and sunset tours are highlights.

P.O.M.G. Bike Tours of Vermont (⊠ Richmond, ☎ 802/434–2270) leads weekend and five-day adult camping–bike tours.

There's nothing quite like floating on a sea kayak and catching the dreamy sunsets over the Adirondack Mountains. **True North Kayak Tours** (⊠ Burlington, ☎ 802/860–1910) operates a guided tour of Lake Champlain, a natural-history tour, and will arrange a custom multiday trip.

HIKING

Stop into the headquarters of the **Green Mountain Club** (⊠ 1 mi north of Waterbury Center, ☎ 802/244–7037), which maintains the Long Trail—the north–south border-to-border footpath that runs the length of the spine of the Green Mountains—as well as other trails nearby. The club sells maps and guides, and experts dispense advice.

LODGING REFERRAL SERVICE

A lodging referral service can be reached at 800/247–8693.

STATE PARKS

The following have camping and picnicking facilities. **Burton Island State Park** (⊠ Follow directions to Kill Kare Park, St. Albans, ☎ 802/524–6353) is accessible only by ferry or boat; at the nature center a naturalist discusses the island habitat. There's a 100-slip marina with hookups and 20 moorings, and a snack bar. **Grand Isle State Park** (⊠ Rte. 2, 1 mi south of Grand Isle, ☎ 802/372–4300) has a fitness trail, hiking, and boat rentals. **Kill Kare State Park** (⊠ Rte. 36, 4½ mi west of St. Albans Bay, then south on town road 3½ mi, ☎ 802/524–6021) is popular for sailboarding and hiking and also has boat rentals; there is ferry service to Burton Island. **Little River State Park** (⊠ Little River Rd., 3½ mi north of Rte. 2, 2 mi east of Rte. 100, ☎ 802/244–7103) has boat rentals, a ramp, and marked nature trails for hiking on Mt. Mansfield and Camel's Hump. **Smugglers' Notch State Park** (⊠ Rte. 108, 10 mi north of Mt. Mansfield, ☎ 802/253–4014) is good for picnicking and hiking on wild terrain among large boulders.

VISITOR INFORMATION

Greater Newport Area Chamber of Commerce (⊠ The Causeway, Newport 05855, ☎ 802/334–7782 or 800/635–4643). **Lake Champlain Regional Chamber of Commerce** (⊠ 60 Main St., Suite 100, Burlington 05401, ☎ 802/863–3489). **St. Johnsbury Chamber of Commerce** (⊠ 30 Western Ave., St. Johnsbury 05819, ☎ 802/748–3678 or 800/639–6379). **Smugglers' Notch Area Chamber of Commerce** (⊠ Box 364, Jeffersonville 05464, ☎ 802/644–2239). The **Stowe Area Association** (⊠ Main St., Box 1320, Stowe 05672, ☎ 802/253–7321 or 800/247–8693).

VERMONT A TO Z

Arriving and Departing

By Bus

Bonanza (☎ 800/556–3815) connects New York City and Providence with Bennington. **Vermont Transit** (☎ 802/864–6811 or 800/552–8737) connects Bennington, Brattleboro, Burlington, Rutland, and other Vermont cities and towns with Boston, Springfield, Albany, New York, Montréal, and cities in New Hampshire.

By Car

Interstate–91, which stretches from Connecticut and Massachusetts in the south to Québec in the north, reaches most points along Vermont's eastern border. I–89, from New Hampshire to the east and Québec to the north, crosses central Vermont from White River Junction to Burlington. Southwestern Vermont can be reached by Route 7 from Massachusetts and Route 4 from New York.

By Plane

Continental, Delta, United, and US Airways fly into **Burlington International Airport** (⊠ Airport Dr., 4 mi east of Burlington off Rte. 2). *See* Airline Travel *in* the Gold Guide for airline numbers. West of Bennington and convenient to southern Vermont, **Albany–Schenectady County Airport** in New York State is served by 10 major U.S. carriers.

By Train

Amtrak's (☎ 800/872–7245) *Vermonter* is a daytime service linking Washington, D.C., with Brattleboro, Bellows Falls, White River Junction, Montpelier, Waterbury, Essex Junction, and St. Albans. The *Adirondack,* which runs from Washington, D.C., to Montréal, serves Albany, Ft. Edward (near Glens Falls), Ft. Ticonderoga, and Plattsburgh, allowing relatively convenient access to western Vermont. The *Ethan Allen Express* connects New York City with Fair Haven and Rutland.

Getting Around

By Car

The official speed limit in Vermont is 50 mph, unless otherwise posted; on the interstates it's still 65 mph. You can get a state map, which has mileage charts and enlarged maps of major downtown areas, free from the Vermont Travel Division. The *Vermont Atlas and Gazetteer,* sold in many bookstores, shows nearly every road in the state and is great for driving on the back roads.

By Plane

Aircraft charters are available at Burlington International Airport from **Valet Air Services** (☎ 802/863–3626). **Southern Vermont Helicopter** (⊠ West Brattleboro, ☎ 802/257–4354) provides helicopter transportation throughout New England.

Contacts and Resources

The Arts

Vermont Symphony Orchestra (☎ 802/864–5741) performs throughout Vermont.

B&B Reservation Agencies

American Country Collection of Bed and Breakfasts (⊠ 1353 Union St., Schenectady, NY 12308, ☎ 518/370–4948 or 800/810–4948) and **American–Vermont Bed and Breakfast Reservation Service** will help you find lodging (⊠ Box 1, East Fairfield 05448, ☎ 802/827–3827).You can also try calling the chambers of commerce in many ski areas.

Emergencies

Medical Health Care Information Center (☎ 802/864–0454). **Vermont State Police** (☎ 800/525–5555).

Foliage and Snow Hot Line

Call 802/828–3239 for tips on peak viewing locations and times and up-to-date snow conditions.

Guided Tours

BIKING

Bicycle Holidays (⊠ Middlebury, ☎ 802/388–2453) creates custom-designed bike trips and will help you put together your own inn-to-inn tour by providing route directions and booking your accommodations. **Vermont Bicycle Touring** (⊠ Bristol, ☎ 802/453–4811 or 800/245–3868), the nation's first bike-tour operator, leads numerous tours throughout the state.

CANOEING

Umiak Outdoor Outfitters (⊠ 849 S. Main St., Stowe, ☎ 802/253–2317) has shuttles to nearby rivers for day excursions and customized overnight trips. **Vermont Canoe Trippers/Battenkill Canoe, Ltd.** (⊠ Arlington, ☎ 802/362–2800) organizes canoe tours (some are inn-to-inn) and fishing trips.

HIKING

New England Hiking Holidays (⊠ North Conway, NH, ☎ 603/356–9696 or 800/869–0949) leads guided walks with lodging in country inns. **North Wind Touring** (⊠ Waitsfield, ☎ 802/496–5771 or 800/496–5771) conducts guided walking tours through Vermont's countryside. **Walking Tours of Southern Vermont** (⊠ Arlington, ☎ 802/375–1141 or 800/588–9255) specializes in inn-to-inn tours, some of which include yoga and massage. Canoe tours are also organized.

HORSEBACK RIDING

Kedron Valley Stables (⊠ South Woodstock, ☎ 802/457–1480 or 800/225–6301) has one- to six-day riding tours with lodging in country inns.

Hiking and Camping

The **Green Mountain Club** (⊠ Rte. 100, Waterbury Center, ☎ 802/244–7037) publishes hiking maps and guides. The club also manages the Long Trail, the north–south trail that traverses the entire state.

Call Vermont's **Department of Forests, Parks, and Recreation** (☎ 802/241–3655) for a copy of the Vermont Campground Guide, which lists state parks and other public and private camping facilities.

Visitor Information

Forest Supervisor, Green Mountain National Forest (⊠ 231 N. Main St., Rutland 05701, ☎ 802/747–6700). **Vermont Chamber of Commerce** (⊠ Box 37, Montpelier 05602, ☎ 802/223–3443). **Vermont Travel Division** (⊠ 134 State St., Montpelier 05602, ☎ 802/828–3237 or 800/837–6668).

There are **state information centers** on the Massachusetts border at I–91, the New Hampshire border at I–89, the New York border at Route 4A, and the Canadian border at I–89.

6 New Hampshire

When General John Stark coined the expression "Live Free or Die," he spoke from experience. Stark had been through the Revolutionary War battles of Bunker Hill and Bennington. But the general could never have imagined that hundreds of thousands of New Hampshirites would display the same fierce sentiment as they traveled the roads of the state: Live Free or Die is the legend of the New Hampshire license plate, the only state license plate in the Union to adopt a sociopolitical ultimatum instead of a tribute to scenic beauty or native produce.

Revised and
updated by
Paula J.
Flanders

THE CITIZENS OF NEW HAMPSHIRE are a diverse lot. The state's strong civic tradition has variously been described as individualistic, mistrustful of government, even libertarian. This tradition manifests itself most prominently in a long-standing aversion to any form of broad-based tax: There is no earned-income tax, nor is there a retail sales tax. Instead, the government relies for its revenue on property taxes, sales of liquor and lottery tickets, and levies on restaurant meals and lodgings.

Another aspect of New Hampshire's suspiciousness of government is its limitation of the gubernatorial term of service to two years: With a campaign for reelection ever imminent, no incumbent is likely to risk being identified as the proponent of an income or a sales tax—or any other unpopular measure.

And then there's the New Hampshire House of Representatives. With 400 members, it is the most populous state assembly in the nation and one of the largest deliberative bodies in the world. Each town with sufficient population sends at least one representative to the House, and he or she had better be able to give straight answers on being greeted— on a first-name basis—at the town hardware store on Saturday.

Yankee individualism, a regional cliché, may or may not be the appropriate description here, but New Hampshire does adhere to a quirky, flinty interpretation of the Jeffersonian credo that the government governs best that governs least. Meanwhile, visitors to New Hampshire see all those license plates and wonder whether they're being told that they've betrayed General Stark's maxim by paying an income tax or a deposit on soda bottles—still another indignity the folks in the Granite State have spared themselves.

Pleasures and Pastimes

Beaches

New Hampshire makes the most of its 18-mi coastline with several good beaches, among them Hampton Beach, Hampton, and Rye. Those who prefer warm lake waters to the bracing Atlantic can choose among some of the finest lakes in New England, such as Lake Winnipesaukee, Lake Sunapee, and Newfound Lake.

Biking

A safe and scenic route along New Hampshire's seacoast is the bike path along Route 1A, for which you can park at Odiorne Point and follow the road 14 mi south to Seabrook. Some bikers begin at Prescott Park and take Route 1B into New Castle, but beware of the traffic. Another pretty route is from Newington Town Hall to the Great Bay Estuary. The volume of traffic on the major roads on the seacoast makes cycling difficult and dangerous for people unfamiliar with the area: Avoid Routes 1, 4, and 101. You'll find excellent routes in the White Mountains detailed in the mountain-bike guide map "20 Off Road and Back Road Routes in Mt. Washington Valley," sold at area sports shops. There's also a bike path in Franconia Notch State Park at the Lafayette Campground, and a mountain-biking center, Great Glen Trails, at the base of Mt. Washington. Many of the ski areas permit summer mountain biking on some trails.

Dining

New Hampshire is home to some of the best seafood in the country, not just lobster but also salmon pie, steamed mussels, fried clams, and

New Hampshire

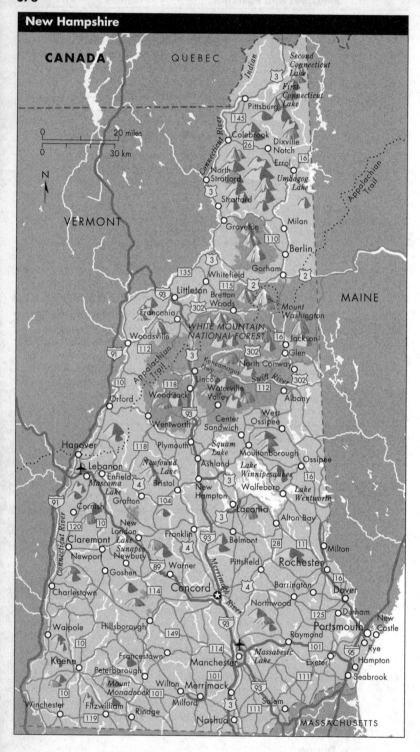

seared tuna steak. Each region has its share of country-French dining rooms and nouvelle American kitchens, but the best advice is to eat where the locals do. That can be anywhere from a local greasy-spoon diner to an out-of-the-way inn whose chef builds everything—including the butter—from scratch. Roadside farm stands and small gourmet groceries—stocking cranberry chutneys, hot-pepper jellies, and other delicacies—are growing in popularity. Restaurants around the lakes and along the seacoast serve throngs of visitors in summer, so always make reservations.

CATEGORY	COST*
$$$$	over $35
$$$	$25–$35
$$	$15–$25
$	under $15

per person for a three-course meal, excluding drinks, service, and 8% tax

Fishing

Lake trout and salmon swim in Lake Winnipesaukee, trout and bass in smaller lakes, and trout in streams all around the Lakes region. Alton Bay has an "Ice Out" salmon derby in spring. In winter, ice fishers fish on all the lakes from huts known as "ice bobs." In the Sunapee region, you can fish for brook, rainbow, and lake trout; smallmouth bass; pickerel; and horned pout. In the Monadnock region are more than 200 lakes and ponds, most with good fishing for rainbow trout, brown trout, smallmouth and largemouth bass, northern pike, white perch, golden trout, pickerel, and horned pout.

Hiking

Some of the East's most scenic hiking trails, including several that lead to Mt. Washington's summit, are in the White Mountains. Mt. Monadnock, in the southwestern part of the state, is the chief draw at Monadnock State Park. Other state parks and privately maintained recreation areas have trails along lake shores, through forests, and within sight and sound of the crashing Atlantic Ocean.

Lodging

In the mid-19th century, wealthy Bostonians would pack up and move to their grand summer homes in the countryside for two- or three-month stretches. Many of these homes have been restored and converted into country inns. The smallest have only a couple of rooms; typically, they're done in period style. The largest contain 30 or more rooms, with private baths, fireplaces, and even hot tubs. A few of the grand old resorts still stand, with their world-class cooking staffs and tradition of top-notch service. In Manchester and Concord, as well as along major highways, chain hotels and motels dominate the lodging scene.

CATEGORY	COST*
$$$$	over $190
$$$	$145–$190
$$	$100–$145
$	under $100

All prices are for a standard double room during peak season, with no meals unless noted, and excluding service charge and 8% tax.

National and State Parks and Forests

Parklands vary widely, even within a region. The White Mountain National Forest covers 770,000 acres in northern New Hampshire. Major recreation parks are at Franconia Notch, Crawford Notch, and Mt. Sunapee. Rhododendron State Park, in Monadnock, has a singular collection of wild rhododendrons. Mt. Washington Park is on top of the highest mountain in the Northeast. Twenty-three state recreation areas provide vacation facilities that include camping, picnicking, hiking, boating, fishing, swimming, biking, and winter sports.

Shopping

ANTIQUES AND CRAFTS

Outside the state's outlet meccas, shopping revolves around antiques and local crafts. In the southern end of the lakes region, crafts shops, galleries, and boutiques are all geared to summer tourists—the wares tend toward T-shirts and tacky trinkets. Many close from late-October to mid-April. Summertime fairs, such as the one operated by the League of New Hampshire Craftsmen at Mt. Sunapee State Park, showcase some of the state's best arts and crafts. On roads throughout the state, signs mark the locations of galleries and open studios.

The densest clusters of antiques shops are along Route 4, between Route 125 and Concord; along Route 119, from Fitzwilliam to Hinsdale; along Route 101, from Marlborough to Wilton; and in the towns of North Conway, North Hampton, Hopkinton, Hollis, and Amherst. In the lakes region, most shops are along the eastern side of Winnipesaukee, near Wolfeboro and around Ossipee. Particularly in the Monadnock region, stores in barns and homes along back roads are "open by chance or by appointment." And don't ignore the summer flea markets and yard sales—deals are just waiting to happen.

MALLS AND OUTLET STORES

Because New Hampshire steadfastly refuses to institute a sales tax, border towns like Salem and Nashua have become meccas for shoppers from neighboring states. Malls and strips of chain specialty stores abound in these locations. North Conway's more than 150 outlet stores lure droves of bargain hunters. Other outlet concentrations are in North Hampton and Lincoln.

Skiing

Scandinavian settlers who came to New Hampshire's high, handsome, rugged peaks in the late 1800s brought their skis with them. Skiing got its modern start in the Granite State in the 1920s, with the cutting of trails on Cannon Mountain; there are now nearly 20 ski areas, from the old, established slopes (Cannon, Cranmore, Wildcat) to more contemporary ones (Attitash, Loon, Waterville Valley). Promotional packages assembled by the ski areas allow you to sample different resorts. There's Ski 93 (referring to resorts along I–93), Ski the Mt. Washington Valley, and more.

Exploring New Hampshire

The main attraction of the New Hampshire coast is historic Portsmouth. Inland a bit is Exeter, home of the eponymous prep school. The lakes region has good restaurants, hiking trails, and antiques shops. People come to the White Mountains to hike, ski, and photograph vistas and vibrant foliage. Western and central New Hampshire are the unspoiled heart of the state.

Numbers in the text and in the margin correspond to numbers on the maps: New Hampshire Coast, New Hampshire Lakes, The White Mountains, Dartmouth–Lake Sunapee, and Monadnock Region and Central New Hampshire.

Great Itineraries

IF YOU HAVE 3 DAYS

Drive along Route 1A to see the coastline or take a boat tour of the Isles of Shoals before exploring ☷ **Portsmouth** ⑦. On the next day, visit Lake Winnipesaukee. ☷ **Wolfeboro** ㉒, on the edge of the lake, makes a good overnight stop. On the following day, drive across the scenic Kancamagus Highway from **Conway** to **Lincoln** ㉖ to see the granite ledges and mountain streams for which the White Mountains are famous. Interstate 93 will take you to Route 101, on which you can return to Portsmouth or straight south to Massachusetts.

IF YOU HAVE 5 DAYS

After visiting ⌖ **Portsmouth** ⑦ and ⌖ **Wolfeboro** ㉒, explore **Squam** and **Ossipee** lakes and the charming towns that surround them: **Moultonborough** ⑳, **Center Harbor** ⑰, and **Tamworth** ㉑. Spend your third night in the White Mountain town of ⌖ **Jackson** ㉙, which is equally beautiful in the winter, when cross-country skiing is popular, and in the summer, when hiking is the main activity. After crossing the Kancamagus Highway to **Lincoln** ㉖, tour the western part of the White Mountain National Forest by following Route 112 to Route 110. Take Route 25 to 25B and follow Route 10 south through the upper Connecticut River valley. ⌖ **Hanover** ㊷, home of Dartmouth College, is a good overnight stop. Interstate 89 will bring you back to Interstate 93 via **Newbury** ㊵ and the Lake Sunapee region.

IF YOU HAVE 8 DAYS

If you spend two nights in ⌖ **Portsmouth** ⑦, you'll have time to visit Strawbery Banke Museum and soak up more of the city's restaurant and cultural scene. After exploring ⌖ **Wolfeboro** ㉒ and ⌖ **Jackson** ㉙, continue north on Route 16 through Pinkham Notch to Mt. Washington, where you can hike or drive to the top. Return via Route 302 and Route 3 to ⌖ **Franconia** ㉟ and Franconia Notch State Park. Drive along Route 112 to Route 110 and take Route 25 to 25B; follow Route 10 south through the upper Connecticut River valley, where the scenery is straight out of Currier & Ives. Stop by ⌖ **Hanover** ㊷ and the Shaker Community at **Enfield** ㊶; then take either Route 12A along the Connecticut River or Route 10 south to ⌖ **Keene** ㊻. Route 119 East leads to Rhododendron State Park in **Fitzwilliam** ㊼. Nearby is **Mt. Monadnock**; take the trail in Jaffrey to the top. Dawdle along back roads on your way to the preserved villages of **Harrisville, Dublin,** and **Hancock.** Continue east along Route 101 to return to the coast.

When to Tour New Hampshire

New Hampshire is a year-round destination. In summer, visitors flock to seaside beaches, mountain hiking trails, and lake boat ramps. In the cities, festivals bring music and theater to the forefront. Fall brings leaf-peepers, especially to the White Mountains and along the Kancamagus Highway. Skiers take to the slopes and the cross-country trails in winter, when Christmas lights and carnivals brighten the long, dark nights. April's mud season, the black fly season in late May, and unpredictable weather keep visitor numbers low in spring, but the season has its joys, not the least of which is the appearance of New Hampshire's state flower, the purple lilac, from mid-May to early June.

THE COAST

The first VIP to vacation on the New Hampshire coast was George Washington, in 1789. By all accounts he had a good time, though a bizarre fishing accident left him with a nasty black eye. Accompanied as he was by 14 generals (all in full dress uniform), he probably didn't have time to walk barefoot along the area's sandy beaches or picnic at Odiorne Point, though he may have visited the homes of John Paul Jones and John Langdon, both of which still stand.

A tour of the coast can take a Sunday afternoon or last for several days. This section begins with Seabrook, the town closest to the Massachu-

setts border; follows the coast to Portsmouth; and circles inland to Newington, Durham, and Exeter.

Seabrook

❶ *2 mi north of the Massachusetts border, 16 mi south of Portsmouth,
55 mi southeast of Concord.*

Once known mainly as the inspiration for Al Capp's *Li'l Abner* comic
strip, Seabrook has become synonymous with Seabrook Station, one
of New England's few remaining nuclear power plants, which looms
large on the Atlantic.

☝ At the **Seabrook Science & Nature Center,** adjacent to the Seabrook
Station nuclear power plant, you can tour exhibits on the science of
power, see control-room operators in training, walk through a replica
of a cooling tunnel, pedal a bike to create electricity, and use interactive computer games that further explain nuclear power. The center
maintains the ¾-mi Owascoag nature trail, a touch pool for kids, and
several large aquariums of local sea life. ⊠ *Lafayette Rd.,* ☎ *800/338–
7482.* 🎟 *Free.* ☉ *Weekdays 10–4.*

Lodging

$$ 🏨 **Hampshire Inn.** This modern motel has one- and two-room suites
with microwaves and refrigerators. Though small, the lobby is light
and airy; breakfast is served here in the morning, hot drinks and cook-
ies in the evening. ⊠ *Rte. 107, 03874,* ☎ *603/474–5700 or 800/932–
8520,* FAX *603/474–2886. 35 rooms. In-room modem lines, indoor pool,
hot tub, exercise room. Continental breakfast. AE, D, DC, MC, V.*

Hampton

❷ *4 mi north of Seabrook, 12 mi south of Portsmouth.*

One of New Hampshire's first towns, Hampton was settled in 1638.
Its name in the 17th century was Winnacunnet, which means "beau-
tiful place of pines." The center of the early town was **Meeting House
Green,** where 42 stones represent the founding families.

Tuck Museum, across from Meeting House Green, contains displays on
the town's early history. ⊠ *40 Park Ave.,* ☎ *603/929–0781, 603/926–
2543 for appointments.* 🎟 *Free.* ☉ *June–Sept., Wed.–Fri. and Sun.
1–4 PM; and by appointment.*

At **Applecrest Farm Orchards,** you can pick your own apples and
berries or buy fresh fruit pies and cookies from the bakery. Fall brings
cider pressing, hay rides, pumpkins, and music on weekends. In win-
ter you can follow a cross-country ski trail through the orchard. ⊠
Rte. 88, Hampton Falls, ☎ *603/926–3721.* ☉ *Daily 8 AM–dusk.*

The **Raspberry Farm** has pick-your-own raspberries, strawberries,
blueberries, blackberries, and other berries. The shop sells fresh baked
goods, jams, and sauces. ⊠ *3 mi inland on Rte. 84, Hampton Falls,*
☎ *603/926–6604.* ☉ *Early June–late Oct., weekdays noon–5, week-
ends 9–5. Call for picking conditions.*

From July to September, the **Hampton Playhouse** brings familiar Hol-
lywood movie and New York theater actors to the coast. Regular per-
formances are held in the evening except on Monday, with matinees
on Wednesday and Friday; children's shows take place on Saturday at
11 and 2. Schedules and tickets are available at the box office or at
the Chamber of Commerce Seashell on Ocean Boulevard in Hampton
Beach. ⊠ *357 Winnacunnet Rd./Rte. 101E, 03842,* ☎ *603/926–3073.*

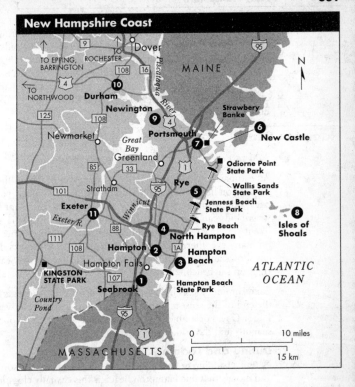

New Hampshire Coast

Lodging and Camping

$$ 🏠 **Victoria Inn.** Built as a carriage house in 1875, this romantic bed-and-breakfast is done in the style Victorians loved best: wicker, chandeliers, and lace. One room is completely lilac; the honeymoon suite has white eyelet coverlets and a private sunroom. Innkeepers Tara and Nicholas DiTullio have named one room in honor of President Franklin Pierce, who for years summered in the home next door. ☒ *430 High St. (½ mi from Hampton Beach), 03842,* ☏ *603/929–1437. 6 rooms, 3 with bath. MC, V. Full breakfast.*

$ 🏠 **Curtis Field House.** On 10 acres between Exeter and Hampton, this Cape-style B&B is decorated with Federal-era antiques and some reproductions. Guest rooms have four-poster beds, comfortable chairs, and private baths. Relaxing on the sundeck with a good book and enjoying the fragrant gardens are favorite pastimes at this quiet property that's a short drive from Portsmouth and the beaches. ☒ *735 Exeter Rd., 03842,* ☏ *603/929–0082. 3 rooms. Full breakfast. No credit cards. Closed Nov.–May.*

$ 🏠 **Hampton Falls Motor Inn.** Intricate Burmese wall hangings and leather furniture decorate the lobby of this modern motel. The rooms are typical of those found in chain motels, but many have a view of the neighboring farm. An enclosed porch by the indoor pool looks out over the woods and fields. The restaurant does not serve dinner. ☒ *11 Lafayette Rd./Rte. 1, 03844,* ☏ *603/926–9545,* ☒ *603/926–4155. 33 rooms, 15 suites. Restaurant, indoor pool, meeting rooms. AE, D, DC, MC, V.*

$ ⛺ **Tidewater Campground.** This camping area has 200 sites, a large playground, a pool, a game room, and a basketball court. ☒ *160 Lafayette Rd., 03842,* ☏ *603/926–5474. MC, V. Closed mid-Oct.–mid-May.*

Shopping

Antiques shops line Route 1 in Hampton and neighboring Hampton Falls. **Antiques at Hampton Falls** (☎ 603/926–1971) sells silver, jewelry, and collectibles. **Antiques New Hampshire** (☎ 603/926–9603) is a group shop with 35 dealers. **Antiques One** (☎ 603/926–5332) carries everything but furniture, including many books and maps. The **Barn at Hampton Falls** (☎ 603/926–9003) is known for its American and European furniture.

Hampton Beach

❸ *2 mi east of Hampton, 14 mi south of Portsmouth.*

An estimated 150,000 people visit Hampton Beach on the Fourth of July. If you like fried dough, loud music, arcade games, palm readers, parasailing, and bronzed bodies, don't miss it. The 3-mi boardwalk, where kids can play games and see how saltwater taffy is made, looks like it was snatched out of the 1940s. Free outdoor concerts are held on many evenings, and once a week there's a fireworks display. Talent shows and karaoke performances take place in the Seashell Stage, right on the beach.

Each summer locals hold a children's festival in August and celebrate the end of the season with a huge seafood feast on the weekend after Labor Day. For a quieter time, stop by for a sunrise stroll, when only seagulls and the odd jogger interrupt the serenity.

Dining and Lodging

$$–$$$$ ✕ **Ron's Landing at Rocky Point.** Nestled in among the souvenir shops and motels that line Hampton Beach is this casually elegant restaurant that serves fresh seafood, pasta, beef, and veal dishes. Specialties include smoked Virginia oysters and filet mignon topped with fresh horseradish sauce and served with Alaskan king crab legs. The second-floor screened porch, which has a sweeping view of the Atlantic, is open for dining in summer. ⊠ *379 Ocean Blvd.,* ☎ *603/929–2122. AE, D, DC, MC, V.*

$$–$$$$ ✕🏨 **Ashworth by the Sea.** This family-owned, hotel was built across the street from Hampton Beach in 1912; most rooms have private decks, and the furnishings vary from period to contemporary. The beachside rooms have breathtaking ocean views. The others look out onto the pool or the quiet street. The Ashworth Dining Room ($$–$$$) serves steaks, poultry, and fresh seafood. ⊠ *295 Ocean Blvd., 03842,* ☎ *603/ 926–6762 or 800/345–6736, ℻ 603/926–2002. 105 rooms. 3 restaurants, in-room modem lines, pool, gift shop. AE, D, DC, MC, V.*

$–$$ 🏨 **Oceanside Inn.** The square front and simple awnings of this oceanfront inn look much the same as those on all the other buildings lining Hampton Beach's Ocean Boulevard. Inside, though, is a hidden treasure. Carefully selected antiques and collectibles, individually decorated rooms, a cozy living room and library with a fireplace, and a second-floor veranda for watching the waves give the Oceanside the feel of a late-19th-century home. Should the beach resort's crush of people and noise begin to overwhelm, you'll appreciate the soundproofing that makes this inn seem like a calm port in a storm. ⊠ *365 Ocean Blvd., 03842,* ☎ *603/926–3542, ℻ 603/926–3549. 10 rooms. Refrigerators, in-room safes, in-room VCRs. Full breakfast. AE, D, MC, V. Closed mid-Oct.–mid-May.*

Nightlife

The **Hampton Beach Casino Ballroom** (⊠ 169 Ocean Beach Blvd., ☎ 603/926–4541, 603/929–4201 for event hot line) books name entertainment from April to October. Tina Turner, the Monkees, Jay Leno, and Loretta Lynn have all played here.

North Hampton

❹ *3 mi north of Hampton, 11 mi southwest of Portsmouth.*

Factory outlets along Route 1 coexist in North Hampton with mansions lining Route 1A.

Fuller Gardens, designed in the 1920s with an addition by the Olmsted brothers in the 1930s, bloom all summer long with 2,000 rosebushes of every shade and type, a hosta display garden, and a serenity-inspiring groomed Japanese garden. ⊠ *10 Willow Ave.,* ☎ *603/ 964–5414.* ➹ *$4.* ☉ *Early May–mid-Oct., daily 10–6.*

Shopping

The **North Hampton Factory Outlet Center** (⊠ Lafayette Rd./Rte. 1, ☎ 603/964–9050) has tax-free goods and discounts on brand names like Famous Footwear and American Tourister. The center's stores include the Paper Factory, the Sports Outpost, and Bass.

En Route On Route 1A as it winds through North Hampton and Rye sits a group of mansions known as **Millionaires' Row.** Because of the way the road curves, the drive south along this route is even more breathtaking than the drive north.

Rye

❺ *5 mi north of North Hampton, 6 mi south of Portsmouth.*

In 1623 the first European settlers landed at Odiorne Point in what is now Rye, making it the birthplace of New Hampshire. The main reasons for visiting the area are its beaches—there are two oceanfront state parks in Rye—and the view from Route 1A.

☙ **Odiorne Point State Park** and the **Seacoast Science Center** encompass more than 350 acres of protected land. You can pick up an interpretive brochure on any of the nature trails or simply stroll and enjoy the vistas of the nearby Isles of Shoals. The tidal pools, considered the best in New England, shelter crabs, periwinkles, and sea anemones. The Science Center conducts guided nature walks and interpretive programs, has exhibits on the area's natural history, and traces the social history of Odiorne Point back to the Ice Age. Kids love the tide-pool touch tank and the 1,000-gallon Gulf of Maine deepwater aquarium. ⊠ *Rte. 1A north of Wallis Sands State Park,* ☎ *603/436–8043.* ➹ *$1 for Science Center, $2.50 for park in summer, fall, and on weekends.* ☉ *Daily 10–5.*

Good for swimming and sunning, **Jenness Beach,** on Route 1A, is a favorite with locals. The facilities include a bathhouse, lifeguards, and parking. **Wallis Sands State Park,** also on 1A, is another swimmers' beach with bright white sand, a bathhouse, and ample parking.

Lodging

$ ⊞ **Rock Ledge Manor.** Built out on a point, this mid-19th-century mansion with a wraparound porch was part of a resort colony and predates the houses along Millionaires' Row. All rooms have water views. Owners Stan and Sandi Smith serve breakfast each morning in the sunny dining room overlooking the Atlantic. ⊠ *1413 Ocean Blvd./Rte. 1A, 03870,* ☎ *603/431–1413. 2 rooms with bath, 2 rooms with half bath and shared shower. Full breakfast. No smoking. 2-night minimum on weekends and holidays. No credit cards.*

New Castle

6 *5 mi north of Rye, 1 mi south of Portsmouth.*

Though it consists of a single square mile of land, the small island of New Castle was once known as Great Island. The narrow roads lined with pre-Revolutionary houses make the island perfect for a stroll.

Wentworth by the Sea, the last of the great seaside resorts, is impossible to miss as you approach New Castle. Empty these days, it was the site of the signing of the Russo-Japanese Treaty in 1905, a fact that attracts many Japanese tourists. Because the current owners and the town have been unable to come to agreement on a restoration and redevelopment plan, this grand old hotel may be torn down.

Ft. Constitution was originally Ft. William and Mary, a British stronghold overlooking Portsmouth Harbor. Rebel patriots raided the fort in 1774 in one of revolutionary America's first overt acts of defiance against the King of England. The rebels later used the captured munitions against the British at the Battle of Bunker Hill. Panels throughout the fort explain its history. ⊠ *Great Island,* ☎ *no phone.* ⚃ *$2.50.* ☉ *Mid-June–Labor Day, daily 9–5; Labor Day–mid-June, weekends 9–5.*

Lodging

$–$$ 🏠 **Great Islander Bed & Breakfast.** This charming 1740 Colonial faces New Castle's Main Street and has a view of the water from the deck by the lap pool in back. Wide pine floors and exposed beams recall the pre-Revolutionary era. Antiques, quilts, and reproduction floral-patterned wallpapers decorate the rooms. ⊠ *Box 135, 62 Main St., 03854-0135,* ☎ *603/436–8536. 3 rooms, 1 with bath. Fans, lap pool. Continental breakfast. No smoking. MC, V.*

Portsmouth

★ **7** *1 mi north of New Castle, 45 mi southeast of Concord.*

Originally settled in 1623 as Strawbery Banke, Portsmouth became a prosperous port before the Revolutionary War. The cultural epicenter of the coast, it contains restaurants of every stripe, plus theater, music, and art galleries.

The **Portsmouth Trail** passes many pre–Revolutionary War homes in the Historic District. The trail breaks the city into three sections that can be explored separately or together. The walking trail can be enjoyed year-round; six houses along the way are open to visitors in summer and fall. Purchase a tour map at the information kiosk on Market Square, the Chamber of Commerce, or any of the houses.

The yellow, hip-roof **John Paul Jones House** was a boardinghouse when Jones lived there while supervising the outfitting of two ships for the Continental Navy. The 1758 structure, the headquarters of the **Portsmouth Historical Society,** contains costumes, glass, guns, portraits, and documents of the late 18th century. ⊠ *43 Middle St.,* ☎ *603/436–8420.* ⚃ *$4.* ☉ *June–Oct., Mon.–Sat. 10–4, Sun. noon–4.*

Lining the hall staircase of the 1716 **Warner House** are the oldest-known wall murals still in place in the United States. ⊠ *150 Daniel St.,* ☎ *603/436–5909.* ⚃ *$5.* ☉ *June–Oct., Tues.–Sat. 10–4, Sun. 1–4.*

Also on the Portsmouth Trail, the **Moffatt-Ladd House,** built in 1763, tells the story of Portsmouth's merchant class through portraits, letters, and fine furnishings. ⊠ *154 Market St.,* ☎ *603/436–8221.* ⚃ *$4.* ☉ *June–mid-Oct., Mon.–Sat. 10–4, Sun. 2–5.*

The first English settlers named the area around what's now called Portsmouth for the abundant wild strawberries they found along the shore of the Piscataqua River. **Strawbery Banke,** a 10-acre outdoor museum with period gardens, holds more than 40 buildings that date from 1695 to 1820. Ten furnished homes here represent several different time periods. The **Drisco House,** built in 1795, was first used as a dry-goods store, and one room still depicts this history; the living room, on the other hand, is decorated just as it was in the 1950s. The boyhood home of Thomas Bailey Aldrich (author of *The Story of a Bad Boy*) is still called **Nutter House,** the name he gave it in that novel—it's been restored to look like it did when he wrote about it. The **Shapiro House** has been restored to reflect the life of the Russian immigrant family who lived in the home in the early 1900s. *Strawbery Banke:* ⊠ *Marcy St.,* ☎ *603/433–1100 or 603/433–1101.* ▣ *$12 pass for 2 consecutive days.* ◷ *Mid-Apr.–Oct., daily 10–5; weekend after Thanksgiving, 10–4; 1st 2 weekends in Dec., 4:30–9:30.*

Picnicking is popular in **Prescott Park,** which is on the waterfront between Strawbery Banke and the Piscataqua River. A large formal garden with fountains is the perfect place to while away an afternoon. The park also contains **Point of Graves,** Portsmouth's oldest burial ground, and two warehouses that date from the early 17th century. The **Sheafe Museum** was the warehouse where John Paul Jones outfitted the USS *Ranger,* one of the U.S. Navy's earliest ships. The Strawbery Banke Museum (☞ *above*) gives boatbuilding demonstrations here. ⊠ *Prescott Park, Marcy St.,* ☎ *603/431–1101.* ◷ *Call for hrs and events.*

☾ Hands-on exhibits at the **Children's Museum of Portsmouth** explore lobstering, earthquakes, sound and music, computers, outer space, and other subjects. Some programs require reservations. ⊠ *280 Marcy St.,* ☎ *603/436–3853.* ▣ *$4.* ◷ *Tues.–Sat. 10–5, Sun. 1–5; also Mon. 10–5 in summer and during school vacations.*

The **Wentworth-Coolidge Mansion** was originally the residence of Benning Wentworth, New Hampshire's first Royal Governor. Notable among the period furnishings in the house is the carved pine mantelpiece in the council chamber. Wentworth's imported lilac trees bloom each May. ⊠ *Little Harbor Rd. at South St. Cemetery,* ☎ *603/436–6607.* ▣ *$2.50.* ◷ *Mid-June–Sept., Tues. and Thurs.–Sat. 10–3, Sun. 1–6; Oct–mid-June, tours by appointment.*

Docked at the **Port of Portsmouth Maritime Museum,** in Albacore Park, is the USS *Albacore,* which was built here in 1953. A prototype submarine, it was a floating laboratory assigned to test a new hull design, dive brakes, and sonar systems for the navy. The nearby **Memorial Garden** and its reflecting pool are dedicated to those who lost their lives in submarine service. ⊠ *600 Market St.,* ☎ *603/436–3680.* ▣ *$4.* ◷ *May–Columbus Day, daily 9:30–5:30; Columbus Day–Apr., daily 9:30–4.*

The **Redhook Ale Brewery,** visible from Route 4, conducts tours that end with a beer tasting. If you don't have time to tour, you can drop in the pub to sample a brew. ⊠ *Pease International Tradeport, 35 Corporate Dr.,* ☎ *603/430–8600.* ▣ *$1.* ◷ *Call for tour times.*

Dining and Lodging

$$$–$$$$ ✕ **Dunfey's Aboard the** *John Wanamaker.* Portsmouth's floating restaurant, aboard a restored tugboat, prepares delicacies like shiitake-encrusted halibut with wild-mushroom ravioli and Black Angus beef with garlic mashed potatoes. You can watch the river from the bar, enjoy the bistrolike atmosphere of the main dining room, or relax in the romantic Captain's Room. The upper-level deck is a favorite on starry summer nights for light meals, a glass of wine, or dessert and

cappuccino. ⊠ *1 Harbour Pl., Ste. 10.,* ☎ *603/433–3111. Reservations essential on weekends. AE, MC, V.*

$$–$$$$ ✕ **Library at the Rockingham House.** This Portsmouth landmark was a luxury hotel, but most of the building has been converted to condominiums. The restaurant retains the original atmosphere, though, with hand-carved mahogany paneling and bookcases on every wall. The food also seems to belong in a social club of another century: Don't miss the grilled rack of lamb with a port wine and rosemary demi-glace or the filet mignon with béarnaise sauce. The waitstaff presents the check between the pages of a vintage best-seller. ⊠ *401 State St.,* ☎ *603/431–5202. Reservations essential. AE, DC, MC, V.*

$$–$$$ ✕ **Blue Mermaid World Grill.** The chefs at Blue Mermaid prepare hot Jamaican-style dishes on a wood-burning grill. Specialties include smoked-scallop chowder and grilled Maine lobster with mango butter. In summer you can eat on a deck that overlooks the 13 historic houses collectively known as The Hill. Entertainers perform (outdoors in summer) on Friday and Saturday. ⊠ *409 Hanover St.,,* ☎ *603/427–2583. AE, D, DC, MC, V.*

$$–$$$ ✕ **Muddy River Smokehouse.** Red-checker tablecloths and wall murals of trees and meadows make this restaurant look like an outdoor summer barbecue joint—even when the weather turns cold, you can roll up your sleeves and dig into platters of ribs, homemade corn bread, and molasses baked beans. Chicken, steak, and other dishes are on the menu, but the signature dish is hickory-smoked St. Louis ribs. ⊠ *21 Congress St.,* ☎ *603/430–9582. AE, MC, V.*

$$–$$$ ✕ **Porto Bello Ristorante Italiano.** This family-run restaurant has ★   brought the tastes of Naples to downtown Portsmouth. In the second-story dining room overlooking the harbor, you can enjoy daily antipasto specials ranging from grilled calamari to stuffed baby eggplant. Pastas include spinach gnocchi and homemade ravioli. A house specialty is veal *carciofi*—a 6-ounce cutlet served with artichokes. The tastes are so simple and the ingredients so fresh that you won't have trouble finishing four courses. ⊠ *67 Bow St., 2nd floor,* ☎ *603/431–2989. Reservations essential. AE, D, MC, V. Closed Mon.–Tues.*

$$–$$$ ✕🏨 **Sheraton Harborside Portsmouth Hotel.** Portsmouth's only luxury hotel, this five-story redbrick building is within easy walking distance of shops and attractions. Suites have full kitchens and living rooms. The main restaurant, Harbor's Edge ($$$–$$$$), serves fresh seafood and American cuisine. The Krewe Orleans restaurant and bar dishes up Cajun specialties. ⊠ *250 Market St., 03801,* ☎ *603/431–2300 or 800/325–3535,* FAX *603/433–5649. 181 rooms, 24 suites. 2 restaurants, bar, indoor pool, spa, exercise room, nightclub, meeting rooms. AE, D, DC, MC, V.*

$$$ 🏨 **Sise Inn.** Each room at this Queen Anne town house in Portsmouth's ★   historic district is decorated in a Victorian and postmodern mélange, with special fabrics and antique reproductions. Some rooms have whirlpool baths. The inn is close to the Market Square area and within walking distance of the theater district and several restaurants. ⊠ *40 Court St., 03801,* ☎ FAX *603/433–1200 or* ☎ *800/267–0525. 26 rooms, 8 suites. Air-conditioning, in-room VCRs, meeting rooms. Continental breakfast. No smoking. AE, DC, MC, V.*

$–$$ 🏨 **Martin Hill Inn.** Two buildings downtown hold this charming inn that's within walking distance of the historic district and the waterfront. The quiet rooms, comfortably furnished with antiques, are decorated in formal Colonial or country-Victorian style. The Greenhouse suite has a private solarium facing the water garden. ⊠ *404 Islington St.,* ☎ *603/436–2287. 4 rooms, 3 suites. Air-conditioning. Full breakfast. No smoking. MC, V.*

Nightlife and the Arts

NIGHTLIFE

The **Portsmouth Gas Light Co.** (⊠ 64 Market St., ☎ 603/430–9122) is a popular brick-oven pizzeria and restaurant by day. But on summer nights, the management opens up the back courtyard, brings in local rock bands, and serves a special punch in plastic sandpails. By midnight, not only is the courtyard full, but the three-story parking garage next door has become a makeshift auditorium. People come from as far away as Boston and Portland to hang out at the **Press Room** (⊠ 77 Daniel St., ☎ 603/431–5186), which presents folk, jazz, blues, and bluegrass performers.

THE ARTS

Music in Market Square (⊠ North Church, Market Square, ☎ 603/436–9109), a summer series of free classical concerts, takes place on Friday at noon. The **Prescott Park Arts Festival** (⊠ 105 Marcy St., ☎ 603/436–2848) kicks off with the Independence Day Pops concert and continues for eight weeks with the works of more than 100 regional artists, as well as music, dance, and theater productions.

Beloved for its acoustics, the **Music Hall** (⊠ 28 Chestnut St., ☎ 603/436–2400) brings the best touring events to the seacoast—from classical and pop concerts to dance and theater. The hall also hosts an ongoing art-house film series. The Portsmouth Academy of Performing Arts and the Portsmouth Youth Theatre fill the calendar of the **Seacoast Repertory Theatre** (⊠ 125 Bow St., ☎ 603/433–4472 or 800/639–7650) with musicals, classic dramas, and works by up-and-coming playwrights. The **Player's Ring** (⊠ 105 Marcy St., ☎ 603/436–8123) presents touring theatrical groups. The **Pontine Movement Theater** (⊠ 135 McDonough St., ☎ 603/436–6660) presents dance performances in a renovated warehouse.

Outdoor Activities and Sports

Portsmouth doesn't have any beaches, but the **Seacoast Trolley** departs from Market Square on the hour, servicing a continuous loop between Portsmouth sights and area beaches (☞ Odiorne Point State Park *and* Wallis Sands State Park *in* Rye, *above*). You can get a schedule for the trolley, which operates from mid-June to Labor Day, at the information kiosk in Market Square. The **Urban Forestry Center** (⊠ 45 Elwyn Rd., ☎ 603/431–6774) has marked trails appropriate for short hikes.

Shopping

Market Square, in the center of town, has gift and clothing boutiques, book and card shops, and exquisite crafts stores.

Kumminz Gallery (⊠ 65 Daniel St., ☎ 603/433–6488) carries pottery, jewelry, and fiber art by New Hampshire artisans. Look for classic and vintage clothing at **Mad Lydia's Waltz** (⊠ 20 Market St., 2nd floor, ☎ 603/433–7231). The **Museum Shop at the Dunaway Store** (⊠ 66 Marcy St., ☎ 603/433–1114) stocks quilts, crafts, candy, gifts, postcards, reproduction and contemporary furniture, and books about the area's history. **N. W. Barrett** (⊠ 53 Market St., ☎ 603/431–4262) specializes in leather, jewelry, pottery, and fiber and other art and crafts and sells furniture, including affordable steam-bent oak pieces and one-of-a-kind lamps and rocking chairs. **Pierce Gallery** (⊠ 105 Market St., ☎ 603/436–1988) has prints and paintings of the Maine and New Hampshire coasts. The **Portsmouth Bookshop** (⊠ 1 Islington St., ☎ 603/433–4406) carries old and rare books and maps. At **Salamandra Glass Studios** (⊠ 7 Commercial Alley, ☎ 603/436–1038), you'll find hand-blown glass vases, bowls, and other items. **Tulips** (⊠ 19 Market St., ☎ 603/431–9445) specializes in wood crafts and quilts.

Isles of Shoals

❽ *10 mi off the coast.*

The Isles of Shoals are nine small islands (eight at high tide). Many, like Hog Island, Smuttynose, and Star Island, retain the earthy names given them by the transient fishermen who visited them in the early 17th century. A colorful history of piracy, murder, and ghosts surrounds the archipelago, long populated by an independent lot who, according to one writer, hadn't the sense to winter on the mainland. Not all the islands lie within the New Hampshire border: After an ownership dispute between Maine and New Hampshire, they were divvied up between the two states (five went to Maine, four to New Hampshire).

Celia Thaxter, a native islander, romanticized these islands with her poetry in *Among the Isles of Shoals* (1873). In the late 19th century, **Appledore Island** became an offshore retreat for her coterie of writers, musicians, and artists. The island is now used by the Marine Laboratory of Cornell University. **Star Island** contains a nondenominational conference center and is open to those on guided tours. For information about visiting the Isles of Shoals, *see* Guided Tours *in* The Coast A to Z, *below.*

Newington

❾ *2 mi northwest of Portsmouth.*

With the closing of Pease Air Force Base and the conversion of that space to public lands and private industry, Newington is undergoing a transformation. The region's only malls are here, and from the highway this seems like simply a commercial town. But the original town center, hidden away from the traffic and the malls, retains an old-time New England feel.

Great Bay National Wildlife Refuge preserves one of Newington's greatest assets: its shoreline on the Great Bay Estuary (☞ Off the Beaten Path, *below*). Two trails loop through more than 1,000 acres that are home to eagles in the winter and herons, loons, deer, and harbor seals year-round. ⊠ *336 Nimble Hill Rd.,* ☎ *603/431–7511.* ⌨ *Free.* ☉ *Daily, dawn–dusk.*

Dining

$–$$$ ✕ **Newick's Seafood Restaurant.** Newick's might serve the best lobster roll on the New England coast, but regulars cherish the onion rings, too. This oversize shack serves seafood and atmosphere in heaping portions. Picture windows allow terrific views over Great Bay. ⊠ *431 Dover Point Rd., Dover,* ☎ *603/742–3205. AE, D, MC, V.*

Shopping

Country Curtains (⊠ Old Beane Farm, 2299 Woodbury Ave., ☎ 603/431–2315) sells curtains, bedding, furniture, and folk art. The huge and generic **Fox Run Mall** (⊠ Fox Run Rd., ☎ 603/431–5911) houses Filene's, Macy's, JC Penney, Sears, and 100 other stores.

OFF THE BEATEN PATH   **GREAT BAY ESTUARY –** Great blue heron, osprey, and the snowy egret, all of which are especially conspicuous during their spring and fall migrations, can be found among the 4,471 acres of tidal waters, mud flats, and about 48 mi of inland shoreline that compose the Great Bay Estuary. New Hampshire's largest concentration of winter eagles also lives here. Access to the estuary can be tricky and parking is limited, but the Fish and Game Department's Sandy Point Discovery Center (⊠ Depot Rd. off Rte. 101, Greenland, ☎ 603/778–0015) distributes maps and information. Nearby towns have recreation areas along the bay. Hikers will find trails at Adam's Point (in Durham), Great Bay National Wildlife Refuge (☞ Newington, *above*), and at Sandy Point (in Greenland). Canoeists can put in at Chapman's Landing (⊠ Rte. 108, Stratham) on the Squamscott River.

Durham

⑩ *7 mi northwest of Newington, 9 mi northwest of Portsmouth.*

Settled in 1635 and home of General John Sullivan, a Revolutionary War hero and three-time New Hampshire governor, Durham was where Sullivan and his band of rebel patriots stored the gunpowder they captured from Fort William and Mary (☞ Ft. Constitution *in* New Castle, *above*). Easy access to Great Bay via the Oyster River made Durham a center of maritime activity in the 19th century. Among the lures today are the water, farms that welcome visitors, and the University of New Hampshire, which occupies much of the town's center.

The **University of New Hampshire Art Gallery** occasionally exhibits items from a permanent collection of about 1,100 pieces but generally uses its space to host traveling exhibits of contemporary and historic art. Noted items in the collection include 19th-century Japanese woodblock prints and American landscape paintings. ⊠ *Paul Creative Arts building, 30 College Rd.,* ☎ *603/862–3712.* ▨ *Free.* ☉ *Sept.–May, Mon.–Wed. 10–4, Thurs. 10–8, weekends 1–5.*

Emery Farm sells fruits and vegetables in summer (including pick-your-own raspberries, strawberries, and blueberries), pumpkins in fall, and Christmas trees in December. The farm shop carries breads and pies, as well as local crafts. Children enjoy petting the resident goats, sheep, and other furry critters. ⊠ *Rte. 4,* ☎ *603/742–8495.* ☉ *May–Dec., call for hrs.*

Several dozen American bison roam the **Little Bay Buffalo Farm.** The on-site Drowned Valley Trading Post sells bison-related gifts and top-quality bison meat. ⊠ *50 Langley Rd., 03824,* ☎ *603/868–3300.*☉ *Trading Post daily 10–5, observation area daily 9–dusk.*

Dining and Lodging

$$–$$$ ✕▥ **Three Chimneys Inn.** This stately yellow Georgian house on 3.5 acres has graced a hill overlooking the Oyster River since 1649. Together, the house and the barn hold 25 rooms, named after plants from the extensive gardens and decorated with Georgian and Federal period antiques and reproductions, canopy or four-poster beds, and Oriental rugs. Specialties in the Maples dining room ($$$) include the grilled lobster with lo mein noodles and a spicy Thai ginger sauce and the venison tenderloin with herbed sweet potatoes. ⊠ *17 Newmarket Rd., 03824,* ☎ *603/868–7800 or 888/399–9777,* FAX *603/868–5011. 25 rooms. 2 restaurants, air-conditioning, in-room modem lines, meeting rooms. Full breakfast. No smoking. No children under age 6. D, MC, V.*

$–$$ ✕▥ **New England Center Hotel.** In a lush wooded area on the campus of the University of New Hampshire, this hotel is large enough to be a full-service conference center but quiet enough to feel like a retreat. The new wing holds the largest rooms, each with two queen-size beds. ⊠ *15 Strafford Ave., 03824,* ☎ *603/862–2801,* FAX *603/862–4897. 115 rooms. 2 restaurants, bar, meeting rooms. AE, DC, MC, V.*

$ ▥ **Hickory Pond Inn.** The rooms at this inn have fresh, flowered wallpaper and individualized color schemes. The common areas, spiffy as well, include a charming breakfast room and a reading nook with a woodstove. ⊠ *One Stagecoach Rd., 03824,* ☎ *603/659–2227 or 800/*

658–0065, ℻ 603/659–7910. 14 rooms with bath, 2 rooms share bath. 9-hole golf course. Continental breakfast. No smoking. AE, MC, V.

$ 🏠 **Moody Parsonage Bed and Breakfast.** The first things guests notice about this red-clapboard Colonial are the original paneling, old staircases, and wide pine floors. With a fire crackling on chilly evenings and a spinning wheel on the stair landing, some think they've stepped back in time. The house was built in 1730 for John Moody, the first minister of Newmarket—if he came back today, he'd recognize it inside and out. Innkeeper Debbie Reed serves summer breakfasts on the front porch, which has a golf-course view. ⊠ *15 Ash Swamp Rd., Newmarket 03857, ☎ 603/659–6675. 1 room with bath, 3 rooms share bath. Continental breakfast. No smoking. No children under 8. No credit cards.*

Nightlife and the Arts

The **Celebrity Series** (☎ 603/862–3227) at the University of New Hampshire brings music, theater, and dance to Durham. The **UNH Department of Theater and Dance** (☎ 603/862–2919) produces shows. UNH's **Whittemore Center** hosts everything from Boston Pops concerts to home shows.

Outdoor Activities and Sports

HIKING

Take a picnic to **Wagon Hill Farm** (⊠ Rte. 4 across from Emery Farm), overlooking the Oyster River. The old farm wagon, sitting by itself on the top of a hill, is one of the most photographed spots in New England. Park next to the farmhouse and follow walking trails to the wagon and through the woods to the picnic area by the water. Sledding and cross-country skiing are popular winter activities.

Shopping

Calef's Country Store (⊠ Rte. 9, Barrington, ☎ 603/664–2231 or 800/462–2118) stocks gifts and farm products. **Salmon Falls Pottery & Stoneware** (⊠ Oak St. Engine House, Dover, ☎ 603/749–1467 or 800/621–2030) produces handmade, salt-glaze stoneware using a method that was favored by early American potters. Potters are on hand should you want to place a special order or watch them work. **Tuttle's Red Barn** (⊠ Dover Point Rd., Dover, ☎ 603/742–4313) carries homemade jams, pickles, and other farm products.

Exeter

❶ *13 mi south of Durham, 8 mi west of Hampton Beach, 11 mi southwest of Portsmouth.*

Exeter's first settlers built their homes in 1638 around the falls where the freshwater Exeter River meets the salty Squamscott. During the Revolutionary War, Exeter was the state capital, and it was here that the first state constitution and the first Declaration of Independence from Great Britain were put to paper. Phillips Exeter Academy, which opened its doors in 1783, is still one of the nation's most esteemed prep schools.

The **American Independence Museum,** adjacent to Phillips Exeter Academy in the Ladd-Gilman House, celebrates the birth of our nation. The story of the Revolution unfolds during each guided tour, on which you'll see drafts of the U.S. Constitution and the first Purple Heart. ⊠ *1 Governor's La.,* ☎ *603/772–2622.* 🎟 *$4.* ☉ *May–Oct., Wed.– Sun. noon–5 (last tour at 4).*

Dining, Lodging, and Camping

$$ ✕ **Vincent's String Bridge Cafe.** In the heart of Exeter, Vincent's prepares veal scallopini, chicken marsala, and other Italian dishes. Many

specials, like the shrimp in a garlic sherry sauce, incorporate fresh local ingredients. For lunch, try soup or a salad, served with a loaf of bread still warm from the oven. ⊠ *69 Water St., ☎ 603/778–8219. AE, D, MC, V.*

$ ✕ **Loaf and Ladle.** Hearty chowders, soups, and stews and huge sandwiches on homemade bread are served cafeteria-style at this understated eatery. Check the blackboard for the ever-changing rotation of chef's specials, breads, and desserts. And don't miss the fresh salad bar. Overlooking the river, the café is handy to the shops, galleries, and historic houses along Water Street. ⊠ *9 Water St., ☎ 603/778–8955. Reservations not accepted. AE, D, DC, MC, V.*

$–$$$ ✕🏨 **Exeter Inn.** This brick Georgian-style inn on the campus of Phillips Exeter Academy is furnished with antique and reproduction pieces and possesses every modern amenity. It's been the choice of visiting parents for the past half century. The specialty at the Terrace Restaurant is chateaubriand served on an oak plank with duchess potatoes and a béarnaise sauce, though the chef also concocts a showstopping veal culinaire. On Sunday, the line forms early for a brunch with more than 40 options. ⊠ *90 Front St., 03833, ☎ 603/772–5901 or 800/782–8444, FAX 603/778–8757. 47 rooms. Restaurant, air-conditioning, meeting rooms. AE, D, DC, MC, V.*

$$ 🏨 **Inn by the Bandstand.** Owners George and Muriel Simmons lovingly restored this 1809 Federal town house, which is listed on the National Register of Historic Places. Seven rooms have working fireplaces. After a day of sightseeing, relax with a glass of the complimentary sherry found in each room. ⊠ *4 Front St., 03833, ☎ 603/772–6352, FAX 603/778–0212. 7 rooms, 2 suites. Air-conditioning. Continental breakfast. AE, D, MC, V.*

$ 🏕 **Exeter Elms Family Campground.** This campground has 200 sites (some riverfront), a swimming pool, a playground, and canoes for rent. ⊠ *188 Court St., 03833, ☎ 603/778–7631. MC, V. Closed mid-Sept.–mid-May.*

Shopping

The shop of the **Exeter League of New Hampshire Craftsmen** (⊠ 61 Water St., ☎ 603/778–8282) carries original jewelry, woodworking, and pottery. **A Picture's Worth a Thousand Words** (⊠ 65 Water St., ☎ 603/778–1991) stocks antique and contemporary prints, old maps, town histories, and rare books. **Starlight Express** (⊠ 103 Water St., ☎ 603/772–9477) sells clocks with elaborate hand-painted faces, picture frames, candles, and other accessories for the house. **Water Street Artisans** (⊠ 20 Water St., ☎ 603/778–6178) carries fine crafts.

The Coast A to Z

Arriving and Departing

BY BUS

C&J (☎ 603/431–2424), **Concord Trailways** (☎ 800/639–3317) and **Vermont Transit** (☎ 603/436–0163 or 800/451–3292) provide bus service to New Hampshire's coast from other regions.

BY CAR

The main route to New Hampshire's coast from other states is I–95, which travels from the border with Maine to the border with Massachusetts.

BY PLANE

Manchester Airport (☞ Arriving and Departing *in* New Hampshire A to Z, at the end of this chapter) is a one-hour drive from the Seacoast Region.

Getting Around

BY BUS

Coast (☎ 603/862–2328) provides limited access to towns in New Hampshire's coastal section.

BY CAR

Coastal Route 1A has breathtaking views of water, beaches, and summer estates. The more convenient Route 1 travels inland. Route 1B tours the island of New Castle. Route 4 connects Portsmouth with Dover, Durham, and Rochester. Route 108 links Durham and Exeter. The quick route along the coast is I–95.

Contacts and Resources

BOATING

Between April and October, deep-sea fishermen head out for cod, mackerel, and bluefish. There are rentals and charters aplenty, offering half- and full-day cruises, as well as some night fishing at the Hampton, Portsmouth, Rye, and Seabrook piers. Try **Al Gauron Deep Sea Fishing** (⊠ Hampton Beach, ☎ 603/926–2469), **Atlantic Fishing Fleet** (⊠ Rye Harbor, ☎ 603/964–5220), **Eastman Fishing & Marine** (⊠ Seabrook, ☎ 603/474–3461), and **Smith & Gilmore** (⊠ Hampton Beach, ☎ 603/926–3503).

EMERGENCIES

New Hampshire State Police (☎ 603/679–3333 or 800/852–3411). **Columbia Portsmouth Regional Hospital** (⊠ 333 Borthwick Ave., ☎ 603/436–5110 or 603/433–4042). **Exeter Hospital** (⊠ 10 Buzzell Ave., ☎ 603/778–7311).

FISHING

For information about fishing and licenses, call the **New Hampshire Fish and Game Office** (☎ 603/868–1095).

GUIDED TOURS

Clip-clop your way through Colonial Portsmouth and Strawbery Banke with **Portsmouth Livery Company** (☎ 603/427–0044), which gives narrated horse-and-carriage tours. Look for carriages in Market Square.

The **Isles of Shoals Steamship Company** (⊠ Barker Wharf, 315 Market St., Portsmouth, ☎ 603/431–5500 or 800/441–4620) runs island cruises, river trips, and whale-watching expeditions from May to October. Trips on Great Bay may include foliage excursions and tours of the Little Bay Buffalo Farm in Durham. Captain Bob Whittaker hosts these voyages aboard the M/V *Thomas Laighton,* a replica of a Victorian steamship, on which he regales passengers with tall tales and genuine history. Breakfast, lunch, and light snacks are available on board, or you can bring your own. Some trips include a stopover and historic walking tour on Star Island.

New Hampshire Seacoast Cruises (⊠ Rte. 1B, Rye 03870, ☎ 603/964–5545 or 800/734–6488) conducts narrated tours of the Isles of Shoals and whale-watching expeditions from June to Labor Day out of Rye Harbor State Marina. From May to October, **Portsmouth Harbor Cruises** (⊠ Ceres Street Dock, ☎ 603/436–8084 or 800/776–0915) operates tours of Portsmouth Harbor, trips to the Isles of Shoals, foliage trips on the Cocheco River, and sunset cruises aboard the M/V *Heritage.*

HIKING

An excellent 1-mi trail reaches the summit of **Blue Job Mountain** (⊠ Crown Point Rd. off Rte. 202A, 1 mi from Rochester), where a fire tower has a good view. The **New Hampshire Division of Parks and Recreation** (☎ 603/271–3254) maintains the Rockingham Recreation Trail, which wends 27 mi from Newfields to Manchester and is open to hikers, bikers, snowmobilers, and cross-country skiers.

VISITOR INFORMATION

Exeter Area Chamber of Commerce (⊠ 120 Water St., Exeter 03833, ☎ 603/772–2411). **Greater Dover Chamber of Commerce** (⊠ 299 Central Ave., Dover 03820, ☎ 603/742–2218). **Greater Portsmouth Chamber of Commerce** (⊠ 500 Market St. Ext., Portsmouth 03801, ☎ 603/436–1118). **Hampton Beach Area Chamber of Commerce** (⊠ 836 Lafayette Rd., Hampton 03842, ☎ 603/926–8717).

LAKES REGION

Lake Winnipesaukee, a Native American name for "Smile of the Great Spirit," is the largest of the dozens of lakes scattered across the eastern half of central New Hampshire. With 283 mi of shoreline, it's the largest in the state. Some claim Winnipesaukee has an island for each day of the year, but the total actually falls a tad short: 274.

Unlike Winnipesaukee, which hums with activity all summer long, the more secluded Squam Lake has a dearth of public-access points. Its tranquillity no doubt attracted the producers of *On Golden Pond;* several scenes of the Oscar-winning film were shot here. Nearby Lake Wentworth is named for the first Royal Governor of the state, who, in building his country manor here, established North America's first summer resort.

Well-preserved Colonial and 19th-century villages are among the region's many landmarks, and you'll find hiking trails, good antiques shops, dozens of good restaurants, several golf courses, and myriad water-oriented activities. The towns in this section begin with Alton Bay, at Lake Winnipesaukee's southernmost tip, and move clockwise around the lakes, starting on Route 11.

Alton Bay

⑫ *35 mi northeast of Concord, 41 mi northwest of Portsmouth.*

Neither quiet nor secluded, Lake Winnipesaukee's southern shore is alive with tourists from the moment the first flower blooms until the last maple has shed its leaves. Two mountain ridges hold 7 mi of Winnipesaukee in Alton Bay, the name of both the inlet and the town at its tip. The lake's cruise boats dock here. There's a dance pavilion, along with miniature golf, a public beach, and a Victorian-style bandstand.

Mount Major, 5 mi north of Alton Bay on Rte. 11, has a 2½-mi trail with views of Lake Winnipesaukee. At the top is a four-sided stone shelter built by George Phippen in 1925.

Dining

$$$$ ✕ **Crystal Quail.** Inside an 18th-century farmhouse, the tiny (12 seats) Crystal Quail is worth the drive even if you don't like quail. The prix-fixe menu might include saffron-garlic soup, a house pâté, quenelle-stuffed sole, or duck in crisp potato shreds. ⊠ *Pitman Rd., Center Barnstead (12 mi south of Alton Bay),* ☎ *603/269–4151. Reservations essential. No credit cards. BYOB. Closed Mon.–Tues. No lunch.*

Gilford

⑬ *18½ mi northwest of Alton Bay, 30 mi northeast of Concord.*

One of the larger public beaches on Lake Winnipesaukee is in Gilford, a resort community. When it was incorporated in 1812, the town

New Hampshire Lakes

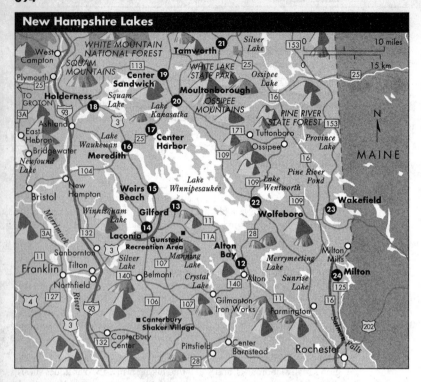

asked its oldest resident to name it. A veteran of the Battle of the Guilford Courthouse, in North Carolina, he borrowed that town's name—though apparently he didn't know how to spell it. As quiet and peaceful as it must have been then, Gilford remains decidedly uncommercial. The **New Hampshire Music Festival** (⊠ 88 Belknap Mountain Rd., ☎ 603/524–1000) presents award-winning orchestras from early July to mid-August.

The **Gunstock Recreation Area** has an Olympic-size pool, a children's playground, hiking trails, mountain-bike rentals and trails, horses, paddleboats, and a campground. A major downhill-skiing center (☞ Skiing, *below*), it once claimed the longest tow rope in the country—an advantage that helped local downhill skier and Olympic silver medalist Penny Pitou perfect her craft. ⊠ *Rte. 11A,* ☎ *603/293–4341 or 800/486–7862.*

Ellacoya State Beach, on Route 11, covers just 600 ft along the southwestern shore of Lake Winnipesaukee, with views of the Ossipee and Sandwich mountain ranges.

Lodging and Camping

$$–$$$ 🏨 **Gunstock Country Inn.** This country-style resort and motor inn is about a minute's drive from the Gunstock Recreation Area. The rooms, of various sizes, have views of the mountains and Lake Winnipesaukee and are furnished with American antiques. ⊠ *580 Cherry Valley Rd./Rte. 11A, 03246,* ☎ *603/293–2021 or 800/654–0180,* 🗺 *603/293–2050. 27 rooms. Restaurant, indoor pool, health club. AE, MC, V.*

$ 🏨 **B. Mae's Resort Inn.** All the rooms in this resort and conference center are large; some are suites with kitchens. Close to Gunstock Ski Area and Lake Winnipesaukee, B. Mae's is popular with skiers in the winter and boaters in the summer. ⊠ *Rtes. 11 and 11B, 03246,* ☎ *603/ 293–7526 or 800/458–3877,* 🗺 *603/293–4340. 82 rooms. 2 restau-*

rants, bar, indoor pool, outdoor pool, whirlpool, exercise room, recreation room. AE, D, DC, MC, V.

$ ⚕ **Gunstock Campground.** The campground at the Gunstock Recreation Area (☞ *above*) has a pool and 300 tent and trailer sites. ⊠ *Rte. 11A (Box 1307, Laconia 03247),* ☎ *603/293–4341 or 800/486–7862. AE, D, MC, V.* ☺ *Year-round.*

Shopping
Pepi Hermann Crystal (⊠ 3 Waterford Pl., ☎ 603/528–1020) sells hand-cut crystal chandeliers and stemware. You can take a tour and watch the artists at work.

Skiing
Gunstock. High above Lake Winnipesaukee, this all-purpose area that dates from the 1930s attracts some skiers for overnight stays and others for day skiing. Gunstock allows skiers to return lift tickets for a cash refund for any reason—weather, snow conditions, health, equipment problems—within an hour and 15 minutes of purchase. Thrill Hill, a tubing park, has three runs and lift service. ⊠ *Rte. 11A (Box 1307, Laconia 03247) 03246,* ☎ *603/293–4341 or 800/486–7862.*

DOWNHILL
Clever trail cutting along with grooming and surface sculpting three times daily have made this otherwise pedestrian mountain good for intermediates. That's how most of the 44 trails are rated, with a few more challenging runs and designated sections for slow skiers and learners. Lower Ramrod trail is set up for snowboarding. Gunstock, which has one quad, two triple, and two double chairlifts and two surface tows, has the largest night-skiing facility in New Hampshire, with 15 lighted trails and five lifts operating.

CROSS-COUNTRY
Gunstock has 50 km (30 mi) of cross-country trails. Fifteen kilometers (9⅓ miles) are for advanced skiers, and there are backcountry trails as well.

CHILD CARE
The nursery takes children ages 6 months and up; the ski school teaches the SKIwee system to children from age 3 to 12.

Laconia
⑭ *4 mi southwest of Gilford, 26 mi north of Concord.*

When the railroad reached Laconia—then called Meredith Bridge—in 1848, the formerly sleepy community became a manufacturing and trading center. The town's **Belknap Mill** (⊠ Mill Plaza, ☎ 603/524–8813), the oldest unaltered, brick-built textile mill in the United States, contains a knitting museum devoted to the textile industry and a year-round cultural center that sponsors concerts, exhibits, a lecture series, and workshops. Area beaches include **Bartlett Beach** (⊠ Winnisquam Ave.) and **Opechee Park** (⊠ N. Main St.).

Dining and Lodging
$$–$$$ ✕ **Le Chalet Rouge.** This yellow house with a modestly decorated dining room recalls a country-French bistro. To start, try the house pâté, escargots, or steamed mussels. The steak au poivre is tender and well spiced, and the duckling is prepared with seasonal sauces: rhubarb in spring, raspberry in summer, orange in fall, creamy mustard in winter. ⊠ *385 W. Main St., Tilton (10 mi west of Laconia),* ☎ *603/286–4035. Reservations essential. MC, V.*

$ ╳⊞ **Hickory Stick Farm.** The 200-year-old Cape-style inn has two
★ large, old-fashioned rooms with cannonball beds, stenciled wallpaper,
and lace curtains. Breakfast, served on the sunporch, might include
French toast stuffed with peaches and cream cheese. Roast duckling
with country-herb stuffing and orange-sherry sauce is the specialty of
the nearly half-century-old restaurant ($$–$$$; no lunch). Also con-
sider the beef tenderloin, rack of lamb, or vegetarian casserole. ⊠ *60
Bean Hill Rd., Belmont (4 mi from Laconia) 03220, ☎ 603/524–3333.
2 rooms. Restaurant. Full breakfast. AE, D, MC, V. Closed Mon. Call
for winter restaurant hrs.*

$ ⊞ **Ferry Point House.** Built in the 1800s as a summer retreat for the
Pillsbury family, this red Victorian farmhouse has superb views of
Lake Winnisquam. The white wicker furniture and hanging baskets of
flowers that decorate the 60-ft veranda and the gazebo by the water's
edge will make you want to spend your whole vacation lounging and
listening for loons. A paddle boat, a row boat, and inner tubes await
those anxious to get in the water. The pretty rooms have Oriental-style
rugs and Victorian furniture. ⊠ *100 Lower Bay Rd., Sanbornton, 03269,
☎ 603/524–0087. 6 rooms. Beach, boating, fishing. Full breakfast.
No credit cards. Closed Nov.–Apr.*

Shopping

The **Belknap Mall** (⊠ Rte. 3 , ☎ 603/524–5651) has boutiques, crafts
stores, and a New Hampshire state liquor store. **The Bending Birch** (⊠
569 Main St., ☎ 603/524–7589) sells local crafts including Laconia
pottery, birdhouses made in Meredith, and lap robes in New Hampshire's official tartan. The **Lakes Region Factory Stores** (⊠ 120 Laconia Rd., Tilton, ☎ 603/286–7880) center includes Brooks Brothers,
Eddie Bauer, and Black & Decker.

OFF THE   **CANTERBURY SHAKER VILLAGE –** This outdoor museum and National His-
BEATEN PATH toric Landmark has a large shop with fine Shaker reproductions. A religious community, the Canterbury village, which was founded in 1792,
flourished in the 1800s and practiced equality of the sexes and races,
common ownership, celibacy, and pacifism. Members lived here until
1992. Shakers invented household items such as the clothespin and the
flat broom, and were known for the simplicity and integrity of their designs, especially furniture. Ninety-minute tours pass through some of the
694-acre property's 24 restored buildings, and crafts demonstrations
often take place. The Creamery Restaurant serves lunch daily and candlelight dinners before the tour on Friday and Saturday. ⊠ *288 Shaker
Rd., 7 mi from Exit 18 off I-93, Canterbury, ☎ 603/783-9511. ⊠ $9
for 2 consecutive days. ⊙ May–Oct., daily 10-5; Apr. and Nov.–Dec.,
Fri.–Sun. 10-5; Fri.–Sat. 6:45 dinner and tour (reservations essential).*

Weirs Beach

⑮ *7½ mi north of Laconia, 33½ mi north of Concord.*

Weirs Beach is Lake Winnipesaukee's center for arcade activity. Anyone who loves souvenir shops, fireworks, bumper cars, and hordes of
children will feel right at home. Several cruise boats (☞ Guided Tours
in Lakes Region A to Z, *below*) depart from the town dock for tours
of the lake.

The period cars of the **Winnipesaukee Railroad** carry passengers along
the lake's shore on one- or two-hour rides; boarding is at Weirs Beach
or Meredith. ⊠ *Rte. 3, Meredith, ☎ 603/279–5253 or 603/745–2135.
⊠ 1-hr trip $7.50, 2-hr trip $8.50. ⊙ July–mid-Sept., daily; weekends*

only Memorial Day–late June and late Sept.–mid-Oct. Call for hrs for special Santa trains in Dec.

from mere 10:30/12:30/2:30/.4:30/ dinner train/6:30. every hour on the hour 11-5 A giant **Water Slide** (☎ 603/366–5161) overlooks the lake. For a more extensive aquatic experience, visit **Surf Coaster** (☎ 603/366–4991), which has seven slides, a wave pool, and a large area for young children. Day or night you can work your way through the miniature golf course, 20 lanes of bowling, and more than 500 games at **Funspot** (☎ 603/366–4377).

Nightlife

Moonlight dinner-and-dance cruises take place on the **M/S Mount Washington** (☎ 603/366–5531) from Tuesday to Saturday, with two bands and a different menu each night.

Outdoor Activities and Sports

Thurston's Marina (☎ 603/366–4811) rents pontoon boats, power boats, and personal watercraft.

Meredith

16 *6 mi north of Weirs Beach, 42 mi north of Concord.*

Meredith, on Route 3 at the western end of Lake Winnipesaukee, has a fine collection of crafts shops and art galleries. An information center is across from the Town Docks. Admission is free to **Annalee's Doll Museum** (⊠ Hemlock Dr. off Rte. 104, ☎ 603/279–3333), where you can view—daily from 9:30 to 5:30 except on Monday—a collection of the famous felt dolls and learn about the woman who created them. The **Lakes Region Summer Theatre** (⊠ Interlakes Auditorium, Rte. 25, 03253, ☎ 603/279–9933) presents Broadway musicals.

At the **Children's Museum and Shop** kids can make bubbles and play musical instruments. ⊠ *28 Lang St.,* ☎ *603/279–1007.* ☜ *Free.* ☉ *Wed.–Sat. 9:30–5, Sun. noon–5.*

Wellington State Beach (⊠ Off Rte. 3A, Bristol), on the western shore of Newfound Lake, is one of the most beautiful area beaches. You can swim or picnic along the ½-mi shoreline or take the scenic walking trail.

Lodging and Camping

$ 🏠 **Nutmeg Inn.** A sea captain dismantled his ship to provide the timber for this 1763 Cape-style house. An 18th-century ox yoke is bolted to the wall over a walk-in-size fireplace, and the wide-board floors are original. All the rooms, two of which have fireplaces, are named after spices and are decorated accordingly. The inn is on a rural side street off Route 104, the main link between I–93 and Lake Winnipesaukee. ⊠ *80 Pease Rd., 03253,* ☎ *603/279–8811,* ℻ *603/279–7703. 7 rooms with bath, 2 rooms share bath, 1 suite. Pool. Full breakfast. No smoking. MC, V. Closed Nov.–mid-May.*

$ ⚠ **Clearwater Campground.** This wooded tent and RV campground on Lake Pemigewasset has 153 shady sites, a large sandy beach, a recreation building, a playground, basketball and volleyball courts, and boat rentals and slips. ⊠ *26 Campground Rd., off Rte. 104, 03253,* ☎ *603/ 279–7761. Closed mid-Oct.–mid-May.*

$ ⚠ **Meredith Woods.** An indoor heated pool, a hot tub, and a game room are among the amenities at this campground, whose patrons have full use of the waterfront facilities across the road at Clearwater Campground (☞ *above*). ⊠ *26 Campground Rd./Rte. 104, 03253,* ☎ *603/ 279–5449 or 800/848–0328.* ☉ *Year-round.*

Outdoor Activities and Sports

BOATING

Meredith Marina and Boating Center (✉ Bay Shore Dr., ☎ 603/279–7921) rents power boats. **Wild Meadow Canoes & Kayaks** (✉ Rte. 25 between Center Harbor and Meredith, ☎ 603/253–7536 or 800/427–7536) rents canoes and kayaks.

GOLF

Waukewan Golf Course (✉ Off Rtes. 3 and 25, ☎ 603/279–6661) is an 18-hole, par-71 course. The greens fee ranges from $22 to $28; an optional cart costs $24.

Shopping

About 170 dealers operate out of the three-floor **Burlwood Antique Center** (✉ Rte. 3, ☎ 603/279–6387), which is open daily from May to October. The **Meredith League of New Hampshire Craftsmen** (✉ Rte. 3, ½ mi north of Rte. 104, ☎ 603/279–7920) sells the works of area artisans. **Mill Falls Marketplace** (✉ Rte. 3, ☎ 603/279–7006, on the bay in Meredith, contains nearly two dozen shops. The **Old Print Barn** (✉ Winona Rd.; look for LANE on the mailbox, ☎ 603/279–6479), the largest print gallery in northern New England, carries rare prints from around the world.

Center Harbor

⓱ *6 mi northeast of Meredith, 45 mi northwest of Concord.*

In the middle of three bays at the northern end of Winnipesaukee, the town of Center Harbor also borders Lakes Squam, Waukewan, and Winona.

Dining and Lodging

$$–$$$ ✕🏠 **Red Hill Inn.** The large bay window in the common room of this rambling inn overlooks "Golden Pond." Furnished with Victorian pieces and country furniture, many rooms have fireplaces, and some have whirlpool baths; one has a mural of nursery-rhyme characters. For dinner, try the ravioli Golden Pond, stuffed with spinach, tomatoes, mushrooms, and garlic, followed by the rack of Vermont lamb served with a stuffing of feta cheese, Dijon mustard, and breadcrumbs. ✉ *R.D. 1, Box 99M, Rte. 25B, 03226, ☎ 603/279–7001 or 800/573–3445, FAX 603/279–7003. 24 rooms. Restaurant, bar, outdoor hot tub, cross-country skiing. Full breakfast. AE, D, DC, MC, V.*

Outdoor Activities and Sports

HIKING

Red Hill, a trail on Bean Road off Route 25, northeast of Center Harbor, really does turn red in autumn. The reward at the end of the trail in any season is a view of Squam Lake and the mountains.

Shopping

Keepsake Quilting & Country Pleasures (✉ Senter's Marketplace, Rte. 25B, ☎ 603/253–4026), reputedly America's largest quilt shop, contains 5,000 bolts of fabric, hundreds of quilting books, and countless supplies.

Holderness

⓲ *15 mi northwest of Center Harbor, 10 mi north of Meredith, 44 mi north of Concord.*

Routes 25B and 25 lead to the town of Holderness, perched between Squam and Little Squam lakes. *On Golden Pond,* starring Katharine

Hepburn and Henry Fonda, was filmed on Squam, whose quiet beauty attracts nature lovers.

☾ The several trails at the 200-acre **Science Center of New Hampshire** include one of ¾ mi, on which you will encounter black bears, bobcats, otters, and other native wildlife in trailside enclosures. Educational events at the center include the Up Close to Animals series in July and August, at which you can study species like the red-shouldered hawk. The Children's Activity Center has interactive exhibits. ⊠ *Rtes. 113 and 25,* ☎ *603/968–7194.* ⊡ *$8.* ☉ *May–Oct., daily 9:30–4:30.*

Dining, Lodging, and Camping

$$$$ ✕⌂ **Manor on Golden Pond.** Built in 1903, this dignified inn has well-★ groomed grounds, clay tennis courts, a swimming pool, and a private dock with canoes, paddle boats, and a boathouse. You can stay in the main inn, the carriage-house suites, or housekeeping cottages. Many rooms have wood-burning fireplaces; four have two-person whirlpool baths. Five-course prix-fixe dinners include rack of lamb, filet mignon, and apple pie. ⊠ *Rte. 3, 03245,* ☎ *603/968–3348 or 800/545–2141,* FAX *603/968–2116. 21 rooms, 4 cottages. Restaurant, pub, pool, tennis court, beach, boating. MAP. No smoking. AE, MC, V.*

$$ ⌂ **Inn on Golden Pond.** This informal country home, built in 1879 and set on 50 wooded acres, is just across the road from Squam Lake. Rooms have a traditional country decor of hardwood floors, braided rugs, easy chairs, and calico-print bedspreads and curtains; the quietest rooms are in the rear on the third floor. The homemade jam at breakfast is made from rhubarb grown on the property. ⊠ *Box 680, Rte. 3, 03245,* ☎ *603/968–7269,* FAX *603/968–9226. 7 rooms, 1 suite. Hiking, gift shop. Full breakfast. AE, MC, V.*

$–$$ ⌂ **Glynn House Inn.** Innkeepers Karol and Betsy Paterman restored the elegance of this three-story 1890s Queen Anne–style home but added modern touches like whirlpool baths. The two-level honeymoon suite, with a large whirlpool tub and fireplace downstairs and a four-poster bed and skylights above, is a favorite. Breakfast, served in the oval dining room, always includes fresh-baked strudel. ⊠ *Box 179, 43 Highland St., Ashland 03217,* ☎ *603/968–3775 or 800/637–9599,* FAX *603/ 968–3129. 7 rooms, 1 suite. Full breakfast. No smoking. AE, MC, V.*

$ ⚠ **Squam Lakes Camp Resort and Marina.** The 119 sites at this campground have full hookups and there's cable TV, a heated pool, a hot tub, lake frontage, a playground, and hiking trails. ⊠ *R.F.D. 1, Box 42, Rte. 3, Ashland, 03217,* ☎ *603/968–7227.* ☉ *Year-round.*

$ ⚠ **Yogi Bear's Jellystone Park.** Geared toward families, this campground with 261 wooded, open, and riverfront sites has a pool, a hot tub, planned activities, miniature golf, a basketball court, river swimming, canoe and kayak rentals, and daily movies. Among the many special events are country-western-jamboree weekends and ice-cream socials. ⊠ *R.R. 1, Box 396, Rte. 132N, Ashland 03217,* ☎ *603/968–9000.*

Outdoor Activities and Sports

White Mountain Country Club (⊠ N. Ashland Rd., Ashland, ☎ 603/ 536–2227) has an 18-hole, par-71 golf course. The greens fee ranges from $26 to $32; an optional cart costs $22.

Center Sandwich

⑲ *12 mi northeast of Holderness, 56 mi northeast of Concord.*

With Squam Lake to the west and the Sandwich Mountains to the north, Center Sandwich enjoys one of the prettiest settings of any town in the Lakes Region. So inspiring are the town and its views that John Greenleaf Whittier used the Bearcamp River as the inspiration for his poem "Sunset on the Bearcamp." The town attracts artisans—crafts shops abound. The village center holds charming 18th- and 19th-century buildings.

The **Historical Society Museum** traces the history of Center Sandwich largely through the faces of its inhabitants. Works by mid-19th-century portraitist and town son Albert Gallatin Hoit hang alongside a local photographer's exhibit portraying the town's mothers and daughters. The museum also houses a replica country store and furniture and other items belonging to or made by Sandwich natives. ⊠ *4 Maple St.,* ☎ *603/284–6269.* ☜ *Free.* ☉ *June–Sept., Tues.–Sat. 11–5; closed rest of year.*

Dining and Lodging

$ ✕⛉ **Corner House Inn.** The comfortable rooms in this quaint Victorian inn have cannonball beds and display original paintings and quilted wall hangings. The inn's restaurant, in a converted barn decorated with whimsical local arts and crafts, serves standard American cuisine. Before you get to the white-chocolate cheesecake with key-lime filling, try the chef's lobster-and-mushroom bisque or mouthwatering crab cakes. On Thursday, storytellers perform in the glow of the woodstove. ⊠ *Rtes. 109 and 113, 03227,* ☎ *603/284–6219 or 800/501–6219,* ☒ *603/284–6220. 3 rooms. Restaurant. Full breakfast. AE, D, MC, V. Closed Mon. Nov.–May.*

$ ⛉ **Blanchard House.** In 1822, when the Blanchard House was built, Sandwich was still very much the frontier. The Indian shutters and large fireplace in the parlor and the wide floor boards reflect the lifestyle of that period. Innkeeper Catherine Hope is a descendant of Augustus Blanchard, who built the house; many of the quilts, linens, and other items in the large rooms are family heirlooms. ⊠ *Box 389, 55 Main St., 03227,* ☎ *603/284–6540. 2 rooms share 1 bath. Full breakfast. No smoking. MC, V.*

Shopping

Sandwich Home Industries (⊠ Rte. 109, ☎ 603/284–6831) presents crafts demonstrations in July and August and sells home furnishings and accessories from mid-May to October. **Ayottes' Designery** (⊠ Rte. 113, ☎ 603/284–6915), open from Tuesday to Saturday between 10 and 5, sells weaving supplies, rugs, wall hangings, and place mats.

Moultonborough

⓴ *5 mi south of Center Sandwich, 48 mi northeast of Concord.*

Moultonborough claims 6½ mi of shoreline on Lake Kanasatka, as well as a small piece of Squam. The highly browsable store that's part of the **Old Country Store and Museum** (⊠ Moultonborough Corner, ☎ 603/476–5750) has been selling handmade soaps, antiques, maple products, aged cheeses, penny candy, and other items since 1781. The museum displays antique farming and forging tools.

Construction on the **Castle in the Clouds,** the town's best-known attraction, began in 1911 and continued for three years. The odd, elaborate stone mansion, which was built without nails, has 16 rooms, eight bathrooms, and doors made of lead. Owner Thomas Gustave Plant spent $7 million, the bulk of his fortune, on this project and died penniless in 1946. Castle Springs water is bottled on the property. ⊠ *Rte. 171,* ☎ *603/476–2352 or 800/729–2468.* ☜ *$10 with tour, $4 without tour.* ☉ *Mid-June–mid-Oct., daily 9–5; mid-May–mid-June, weekends 10–4.*

The **Loon Center** at the Frederick and Paula Anna Markus Wildlife Sanctuary is the headquarters of the Loon Preservation Committee, an

Audubon Society project. The loon, one of New Hampshire's most popular birds, is threatened by lake traffic, poor water quality, and habitat loss. At the center, you can learn about the black-and-white birds, whose calls haunt New Hampshire lakes. Two nature trails wind through the 200-acre property; vantage points on the Loon Nest Trail overlook the spot that resident loons sometimes occupy in June. ⊠ *Lees Mills Rd. (follow signs from Rte. 25 to Blake Rd. to Lees Mills Rd.), 03254,* ☎ *603/476–5666.* ⚑ *Free.* ☉ *July 4–Columbus Day, daily 9–5; rest of yr, Mon.–Sat. 9–5.*

Dining

$$–$$$ ✕ **The Woodshed.** Farm implements and antiques hang on the walls of this former barn, built in 1860. Make your way through the raw bar or try the New England section of the menu, which includes clam chowder, scrod, and Indian pudding. For dessert there's Denver chocolate pudding, a dense pudding-cake served warm with vanilla ice cream. ⊠ *Lee's Mill Rd.,* ☎ *603/476–2311. AE, D, DC, MC, V. Closed Mon.*

Tamworth

㉑ *11 mi northeast of Moultonborough, 59 mi northeast of Concord.*

President Grover Cleveland summered here. His son, Francis, returned to stay and founded the Barnstormers Theater. Tamworth has a clutch of villages within its borders. At one of them—Chocorua—the view through the birches of Chocorua Lake has been so often photographed that you may feel like you've been here before. The tiny South Tamworth post office looks like a children's playhouse.

Dining and Lodging

$$ ✕▥ **Tamworth Inn.** Every room at this inn 15 mi from Hemenway State
★   Forest has 19th-century American pieces and handmade quilts. Among the menu highlights in the dining room (closed on Sunday and Monday in summer, and from Sunday to Tuesday in winter) are the provolone-and-pesto terrine and the pork tenderloin with apple-walnut cornbread stuffing and an apple-cider sauce. The profiterole Tamworth is big enough for two. Sunday brunch is a summer favorite. ⊠ *Main St., 03886,* ☎ *603/323–7721 or 800/642–7352,* ℻ *603/323–2026. 16 rooms. Restaurant, pub, pool. Full breakfast; MAP available. MC, V.*

Nightlife and the Arts

The **Arts Council of Tamworth** (☎ 603/323–7793) produces concerts—soloists, string quartets, revues, children's programs—from September to June, and a summer arts show on the last weekend in July. **Barnstormers** (⊠ Main St., ☎ 603/323–8500), New Hampshire's oldest professional theater, performs in July and August. The box office opens in June; before June, call the Tamworth Inn (☞ *above*) for information.

Outdoor Activities and Sports

The 72-acre stand of native pitch pine at **White Lake State Park** (⊠ Rte. 16, 03886, ☎ 603/323–7350) is a National Natural Landmark. The park has hiking trails, a sandy beach, trout fishing, canoe rentals, two separate camping areas, a picnic area, and swimming.

Shopping

The many themed rooms—a Christmas room, a bride's room, a children's room, among them—at the **Country Handcrafters & Chocorua Dam Ice Cream Shop** (⊠ Rte. 16, Chocorua 03817, ☎ 603/323–8745) contain handcrafted items. When you're done shopping, enjoy ice cream, coffee, or tea and scones.

En Route Route 16 between Ossipee and West Ossipee passes sparkling Lake Ossipee, known for fine fishing and swimming. Among these hamlets you'll
find several antiques shops and galleries. Local craftspeople create
much of the jewelry, turned wooden bowls, pewter goblets, glassware,
and other items sold at **Tramway Artisans** (⊠ Rte. 16, West Ossipee
03890–0748, ☎ 603/539–5700).

Wolfeboro

㉒ *28 mi south of Tamworth, 15 mi southeast of Moultonborough, 41
mi northwest of Portsmouth.*

Downtown Wolfeboro is right on Lake Winnipesaukee. The Chamber
of Commerce estimates that the town's population increases tenfold
each June, as throngs of tourists descend upon the lake. Wolfeboro has
been a resort since John Wentworth, the first Royal Governor of the
state, built his summer home on the shores of Lake Wentworth in 1763.

Uniforms, vehicles, and other artifacts at the **Wright Museum** illustrate
the contributions of those on the home front to America's World War
II effort. ⊠ *77 Center St.,* ☎ *603/569–1212.* ⊡ *$5.* ☉ *May–Oct.,
daily 10–4; rest of yr, call for hrs.*

The artisans at the **Hampshire Pewter Company** (⊠ 43 Mill St., ☎ 603/
569–4944) use 17th-century techniques to make pewter hollowware
and accessories. Free tours are conducted at 10, 11, 1, 2, and 3 between Memorial Day and Labor Day and at 10, 11, 2, and 3 from Labor
Day to Columbus Day.

Beach

Wentworth State Beach (⊠ Rte. 109, ☎ 603/569–3699) has good swimming and picnicking areas and a bathhouse.

Dining and Lodging

$$–$$$ ✕ **The Bittersweet.** This converted barn with an eclectic display of old
quilts, pottery, sheet music, and china has the feel of a cozy crafts shop,
but it's really a restaurant that locals love for the nightly specials that
range from seafood to chateaubriand. The upper level has antique tables and chairs and dining by candlelight. The lower-level lounge, decorated with Victorian wicker furniture, serves lighter fare. ⊠ *Rte. 28,*
☎ *603/569–3636. AE, D, MC, V.*

$$ ✕🏨 **Wolfeboro Inn.** Built 200 years ago, this white clapboard house
has 19th- and 20th-century additions that extend to the waterfront of
Wolfeboro Bay. The rooms have polished cherry and pine furnishings,
armoires (to hide the TVs), stenciled borders, and country quilts. More
than 45 brands of beer are available at Wolfe's Tavern, where food is
cooked in a fireplace. Veal Wolfeboro is a combination of sautéed veal,
lobster, and shrimp topped with a cream sauce. The main dining room
serves a very popular twin-lobster special. ⊠ *Box 1270, 90 N. Main
St., 03894,* ☎ *603/569–3016 or 800/451–2389,* 𝖥𝖠𝖷 *603/569–5375.
41 rooms, 3 suites, 1 1-bedroom apartment. 2 restaurants, bar, air-con-
ditioning, beach, boating, meeting rooms. Continental breakfast. AE,
MC, V.*

Outdoor Activities and Sports

BOATING

Winnipesaukee Kayak Company (⊠ 1 Bay St., ☎ 603/569–9926) gives
kayak lessons and leads group excursions on the lake.

GOLF

Kingswood Golf Course (⊠ Rte. 28, ☎ 603/569–3569) has an 18-hole,
par-72 course. The greens fee ranges from $35 to $48, and in the sum-
mer includes an optional cart. At other times, a cart costs $25.

HIKING

A few miles north of town on Route 109 is the trailhead to **Abenaki Tower.** A short (¼-mi) hike to the 100-ft post-and-beam tower, followed by a more rigorous climb to the top, rewards you with a vast view of Winnipesaukee and the Ossipee mountain range.

WATER SPORTS

Look for waterskiing regulations at every marina. Scuba divers can explore a 130-ft-long cruise ship that sunk in 30 ft of water off Glendale in 1895. **Dive Winnipesaukee Corp.** (⊠ 4 N. Main St., ☎ 603/569–2120) runs charters out to this and other wrecks and offers rentals, repairs, scuba sales, and lessons in waterskiing and windsurfing.

Shopping

Dow's Corner Shop (⊠ Rte. 171, Tuftonboro Corner, ☎ 603/539–4790) is so crowded with memorabilia it could pass for a museum.

Wakefield

❷❸ *18 mi east of Wolfeboro, 26 mi southeast of Tamworth, 40 mi north of Portsmouth.*

East of Winnipesaukee lie several laid-back villages that combine to form Wakefield, a town with 10 lakes. **Wakefield Corner,** on the Maine border, is a registered historic district, with a church, houses, and an inn that look just as they did in the 18th century.

☻ The **Museum of Childhood** displays a one-room schoolhouse, a child's room from 1890, model trains, antique sleds, teddy bears, 3,000 dolls, and 44 furnished dollhouses.⊠ *Wakefield Corner, off Rte. 16, ☎ 603/522–8073. ☜ $3. ☉ Memorial Day–Labor Day, Mon. and Wed.–Sat. 11–4, Sun. 1–4.*

Lodging

$ **🏠 Wakefield Inn.** The restoration of this 1804 stagecoach inn, a high-★ light of Wakefield's historic district, has been handled with an eye for detail. The dining-room windows retain the original panes and Indian shutters, but the centerpiece of the building is the freestanding spiral staircase that rises three stories. The large rooms, named for famous guests or past owners, have wide-board pine floors, big sofas, and handmade quilts. In late fall and early spring, you can learn how to quilt as part of the weekend Quilting Package. ⊠ *2723 Wakefield Rd., 03872, ☎ 603/522–8272 or 800/245–0841. 7 rooms. Full breakfast. MC, V.*

Milton

❷❹ *15½ mi south of Wakefield, 25 mi north of Portsmouth.*

Milton stretches alongside the Salmon Falls River, Town House Pond, Milton Pond, and Northeast Pond, all of which flow together to create a seemingly endless body of water.

The **New Hampshire Farm Museum** houses more than 60,000 artifacts recalling New Hampshire farm life from 1700 to the early 1900s. Take a guided tour through the Jones Farmhouse, and then explore the Grand Barn—filled with vehicles, farm implements, and tools—the gardens, and the nature trails at your leisure. Special events demonstrating farm-related crafts take place throughout the season. ⊠ *Rte. 125, ☎ 603/652–7840. ☜ $5. ☉ Mid-May–mid-Oct., Mon. and Wed.–Sat. 10–4, Sun. 1–4.*

Lakes Region A to Z

Arriving and Departing

BY BUS

Concord Trailways (☎ 800/639–3317) stops daily in Tilton, Laconia, Meredith, Center Harbor, Moultonborough, and Conway.

BY CAR

Most people driving into this region arrive via I–93 to Route 3 in the west or by the Spaulding Turnpike to Route 11 in the east.

BY PLANE

Manchester Airport (☞ Arriving and Departing *in* New Hampshire A to Z, at the end of this chapter) is about an hour's drive from the Lakes Region.

Getting Around

BY BUS

See Arriving and Departing, *above.*

BY CAR

On the western side of the Lakes Region, I–93 is the principal north–south artery. Exit 20 leads to Route 11 and the southwestern side of Lake Winnipesaukee. Take Exit 23 to Route 104 to Route 25 and the northwestern corner of the region. From the coast, Route 16 heads to the White Mountains, with roads leading to the lakeside towns.

BY PLANE

Moultonborough Airport (✉ Rte. 25, Moultonborough, ☎ 603/476–8801) operates chartered flights and tours.

Contacts and Resources

BOATING

The **Lakes Region Association** (☎ 603/253–8555 or 800/605–2537) provides boating advice.

EMERGENCIES

Lakes Region General Hospital (✉ 80 Highland St., Laconia, ☎ 603/524–3211).

FISHING

The **New Hampshire Fish and Game** office (☎ 603/744–5470) has information about fishing and licenses.

GUIDED TOURS

The 230-ft **M/S Mount Washington** (✉ Box 5367, 03247, ☎ 603/366–5531) makes 2½-hour cruises of Lake Winnipesaukee between mid-May and mid-October from Weirs Beach, Wolfeboro, Center Harbor, and Alton Bay.

The **M/V Sophie C.** (☎ 603/366–2628) has been the area's floating post office for more than a century. The boat departs Weirs Beach with mail and passengers daily except Sunday from mid-June until the Saturday following Labor Day.

Sky Bright (✉ Laconia Airport, ☎ 603/528–6818) operates airplane and helicopter tours and instruction on aerial photography.

From Memorial Day to late October, **Golden Pond Boat Tour** (✉ Manor Resort, ☎ 603/279–4405) visits filming sites of the movie *On Golden Pond* on Squam Lake, aboard the *Lady of the Manor,* a 28-ft pontoon craft.

From late May to October, **Squam Lake Tours** (☎ 603/968–7577) takes up to 20 passengers on a two-hour pontoon tour of "Golden Pond." The company also operates guided fishing trips and private charters.

HIKING
Contact the Alexandria headquarters of the **Appalachian Mountain Club** (☎ 603/744–8011) or the **Laconia Office of the U.S. Forest Service** (☎ 603/528–8721) for trail advice and information.

VISITOR INFORMATION
Greater Laconia Chamber of Commerce (✉ 11 Veterans Sq., Laconia 03246-3485, ☎ 603/524–5531 or 800/531–2347). **Lakes Region Association** (✉ Box 589, Center Harbor 03226, ☎ 603/253–8555 or 800/605–2557). **Squam Lakes Area Chamber of Commerce** (✉ Box 65, Ashland 03217, ☎ 603/968–4494). **Wolfeboro Chamber of Commerce** (✉ Box 547-WT7, Railroad Ave., Wolfeboro 03894, ☎ 603/569–2200 or 800/516–5324).

THE WHITE MOUNTAINS

Sailors approaching East Coast harbors frequently mistake the pale peaks of the White Mountains—the highest range in the northeastern United States—for clouds. It was 1642 when explorer Darby Field could no longer contain his curiosity about one mountain in particular. He set off from his Exeter homestead and became the first man to climb what would eventually be called Mt. Washington, the king of the Presidential Range. More than a mile high, Mt. Washington must have presented Field with a slew of formidable obstacles—its peak claims the highest wind velocity ever recorded and it usually sees snow every month of the year.

A few hundred years after Field's climb, curiosity about the mountains has not abated. People come here by the tens of thousands to hike and climb in spring and summer, to photograph the vistas and the vibrant foliage in autumn, and to ski in winter. In this four-season vacation hub, many resorts (some of which have been in business since the mid-1800s) are destinations in themselves, with golf, tennis, swimming, hiking, cross-country skiing, and renowned restaurants.

The tour covered in this section begins in Waterville Valley, off I–93, continues to Lincoln, across the Kancamagus Highway to North Conway, and circles north on Routes 16 and 302 back to the northern reaches of I–93. There is some backtracking involved because of the mountains.

Waterville Valley

㉕ *63 mi north of Concord.*

In 1835, visitors began arriving in Waterville Valley, a 10-mi-long cul-de-sac cut by one of New England's Mad Rivers and circled by mountains. They have come in increasing numbers ever since. First a summer resort, then more of a ski area, and now a year-round resort, Waterville Valley retains a small-town feel. There are inns, lodges, and condominiums; restaurants, cafés, and taverns; shops, conference facilities, a grocery store, and a post office.

In winter, those who don't ski can ice-skate, snowboard, or snowshoe or amuse themselves in the sports center, which has tennis, racquetball, and squash courts; a 25-meter indoor pool, a jogging track, exercise equipment, whirlpools, saunas, steam rooms, and a games room. Hiking and mountain biking are the popular summer sports.

Dining and Lodging

$$–$$$ ✕ **William Tell.** Seven miles west of Waterville, this small wood-beam and stucco restaurant has four quiet and romantic dining rooms. The traditional Swiss dishes served here include schnitzel, sauerbraten,

The White Mountains

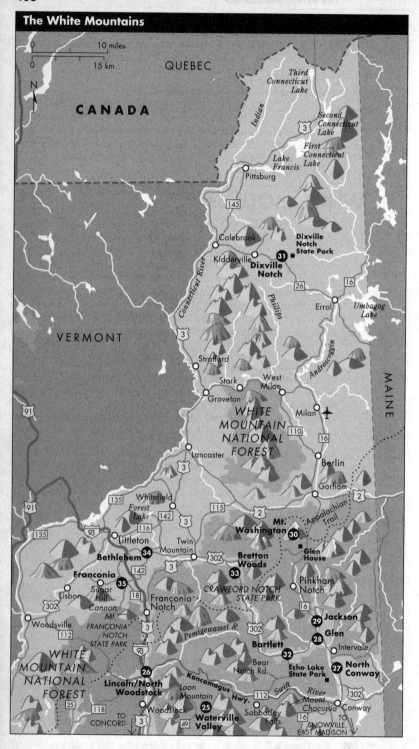

QUEBEC

CANADA

VERMONT

MAINE

Third Connecticut Lake

Second Connecticut Lake

First Connecticut Lake

Lake Francis

Indian

Pittsburg

Colebrook

Kidderville

Dixville Notch

Dixville Notch State Park

31

26

16

Errol

Umbagog Lake

Phillips

Connecticut River

Strafford

Stark

Groveton

West Milan

Milan

Androscoggin

WHITE MOUNTAIN NATIONAL FOREST

110

16

Lancaster

Berlin

Gorham

2

Whitefield

Forest Lake

Littleton

Bethlehem 34

Franconia 35

Lisbon

Sugar Hill

Cannon Mt.

FRANCONIA NOTCH STATE PARK

Franconia Notch

Twin Mountain

Mt. Washington 30

Appalachian Trail

Glen House

Bretton Woods 33

CRAWFORD NOTCH STATE PARK

Pinkham Notch

Jackson 29

Glen 28

Intervale

North Conway 27

Woodsville

Pemigewasset R.

Bartlett 32

Echo Lake State Park

WHITE MOUNTAIN NATIONAL FOREST

Lincoln/North Woodstock 26

Woodstock

Kancamagus Hwy.

Loon Mountain

Bear Notch Rd.

Sabbaday Falls

Waterville Valley 25

Swift

Mount Chocorua

River

Conway

TO SNOWVILLE, EAST MADISON

TO CONCORD

10 miles

15 km

N

fondue, and fresh venison. ⊠ *Rte. 49, Thornton,* ☎ *603/726–3618. AE, D, MC, V. Closed late Apr.–late May, late Oct.–late Nov..*

$–$$ ✕ **Chile Peppers.** Southwest-inspired Chile Peppers caters to skiers with fajitas, tacos, enchiladas, and other Tex-Mex staples. The food here may not be authentic Mexican, but it's well priced and filling. If you're solely into Tex, the lineup includes ribs, steak, seafood, and chicken. ⊠ *Town Square,* ☎ *603/236–4646. AE, DC, MC, V.*

$$$–$$$$ ⊞ **Golden Eagle Lodge.** Waterville's premier condominium property recalls the grand hotels of an earlier era. The full-service complex, which opened in 1989, has a two-story lobby and a very capable front-desk staff. ⊠ *Snow's Brook Rd., 03215,* ☎ *603/236–4600 or 800/910– 4499,* ℻ *603/236–4947. 139 suites. Indoor pool, sauna, recreation room. AE, D, DC, MC, V.*

$–$$$$ ⊞ **Black Bear Lodge.** This family-oriented all-suites hotel has one- and two-bedroom units with full kitchens. Each unit is individually owned and decorated. Children's movies are shown at night in season, and there's bus service to the slopes. ⊠ *Box 357, Village Rd., 03215,* ☎ *603/236–4501 or 800/349–2327,* ℻ *603/236–4114. 107 suites. Indoor-outdoor pool, hot tub, sauna, steam room, exercise room, recreation room. AE, D, DC, MC, V.*

$–$$$ ⊞ **Snowy Owl Inn.** The fourth-floor bunk-bed lofts at this intimate inn are ideal for families; first-floor rooms, some with whirlpool tubs, are suitable for couples seeking a quiet getaway. The atrium lobby, where guests are treated to afternoon wine and cheese, contains a three-story fieldstone fireplace and many prints and watercolors of snowy owls. Four restaurants are within walking distance. ⊠ *Box 407, Village Rd., 03215,* ☎ *603/236–8383 or 800/766–9969,* ℻ *603/236–4890. 84 rooms. Indoor pool, hot tub. Continental breakfast. AE, D, DC, MC, V.*

Nightlife

Chile Peppers (⊠ Town Square, ☎ 603/236–4646) is an après-ski gathering spot.

Skiing

Waterville Valley. Former U.S. ski-team star Tom Corcoran designed this family-oriented resort. It's about a mile from the slopes, but a shuttle makes a car unnecessary. ⊠ *Box 540, 03215,* ☎ *603/236–8311, 603/236–4144 for snow conditions, 800/468–2553 for lodging.*

DOWNHILL

Mt. Tecumseh, a short shuttle ride from the Town Square and accommodations, has been laid out with great care. This ski area has hosted more World Cup races than any other in the East, so most advanced skiers will be adequately challenged. Most of the 50 trails are intermediate: straight down the fall line, wide, and agreeably long. A 7-acre tree-skiing area adds variety. Snowmaking coverage of 100% ensures good skiing even when nature doesn't cooperate. The lifts serving the 2,020 ft of vertical rise include two high-speed detachable quad, two triple, three double, and four surface lifts.

CROSS-COUNTRY

The Waterville Valley cross-country network, with the ski center in the Town Square, has 101 km (63 mi) of trails. About two-thirds of the trails are groomed; the rest are backcountry.

CHILD CARE

The nursery takes children from age 6 months to 4 years. There are SKIwee lessons and other instruction for children ages 3 to 12. The Kinderpark, a children's slope, has a slow-running lift.

Lincoln/North Woodstock

26 *Exit 32 off I–93; 26 mi from Waterville Valley, 65 mi from Concord.*

Lincoln and North Woodstock, at the western end of the Kancamagus Highway, combine to make one of the state's liveliest ski-resort areas. Festivals, like the New Hampshire Scottish Highland Games in mid-September, keep Lincoln swarming with visitors year-round, while North Woodstock maintains more of a village feel.

A ride on the **Hobo Railroad** yields scenic views of the Pemigewasset River and the White Mountain National Forest. The narrated excursions take 1 hour and 20 minutes. ⊠ *Rte. 112, Lincoln,* ☎ *603/745–2135.* ☞ *$8.* ☼ *June–Labor Day, daily 11, 1, 3 (sometimes 5), and 7 (dinner train); May and Sept.–Oct., weekends 11, 1, 3 (sometimes 5), and 7 (dinner train).*

In summer and fall at **Loon Mountain Park,** you can ride the gondola ($10) to the summit for a panoramic view of the White Mountain National Forest. Daily activities at the summit include lumberjack shows, storytelling by a mountain man, and nature tours. You can also take self-guided walks to glacial caves. Other recreational opportunities include horseback riding, mountain biking, and in-line skating. ⊠ *Kancamagus Hwy., Lincoln,* ☎ *603/745–8111.*

At the **Whale's Tale Water Park,** you can float on an inner tube along a gentle river, careen down giant water slides, or body surf in the large wave pool. ⊠ *Rte. 3, North Lincoln,* ☎ *603/745–8810.* ☞ *$16.50.* ☼ *Mid-June–Labor Day., daily 10–6; call for early and late season hrs.*

Dining and Lodging

$ ✕🏨 **Woodstock Inn.** The inn's 21 rooms, spread over three buildings, are named after local geographic features. The romantic Ellsworth room comes with a whirlpool tub, a king-size canopy bed, and complimentary champagne. The Notchview, great for families, has two double beds; a ladder leads to a cozy tower with a daybed. The restaurants include the elegant Clement Room Grill ($$–$$$); Woodstock Station ($–$$), where everything from meat loaf to fajitas is prepared; and the Woodstock Inn Brewery. ⊠ *Box 118, Rte. 3, North Woodstock 03262,* ☎ *603/745–3951 or 800/321–3985,* FAX *603/745–3701. 13 rooms with bath, 8 rooms share bath. 2 restaurants, bar, air-conditioning, refrigerators, outdoor hot tub. Full breakfast. AE, D, MC, V.*

$$–$$$$ 🏨 **Mountain Club on Loon.** This first-rate slopeside resort hotel has an assortment of accommodations: suites that sleep as many as eight, studios with Murphy beds, and 117 units with kitchens. All rooms are within walking distance of the lifts, and condominiums are on-slope and nearby. Entertainers perform in the lounge on most winter weekends. ⊠ *Rte. 112 (take Exit 32 from I–93), Lincoln, 03251,* ☎ *603/745–2244 or 800/229–7829,* FAX *603/745–2317. 234 rooms. Restaurant, bar, indoor pool, massage, sauna, aerobics, health club, racquetball, squash. AE, D, MC, V.*

$$–$$$ 🏨 **Indian Head Resort.** Views across the 180 acres of this resort motel near the Loon and Cannon Mountain ski areas are of Indian Head Rock, the Great Stone Face, and the Franconia Mountains. Cross-country ski trails and a mountain-bike trail from the resort connect to the Franconia Notch trail system. ⊠ *Rte. 3, North Lincoln 03251,* ☎ *603/745–8000 or 800/343–8000,* FAX *603/745–8414. 98 rooms. Restaurant, indoor and outdoor pools, indoor and outdoor hot tubs, lake, sauna, tennis court, fishing, ice-skating, cross-country skiing, recreation room. AE, D, DC, MC, V.*

$–$$ ▣ **Mill House Inn.** This country inn–style hotel on the western edge of the Kancamagus Highway offers free transportation to Loon Mountain during ski season. Nearby are shopping, restaurants, a cinema, and the North Country Center for the Performing Arts. ✉ *Box 696, Rte. 112, Lincoln 03251,* ☎ *603/745–6261 or 800/654–6183,* FAX *603/745–6896. 74 rooms, 21 suites. Restaurant, indoor and outdoor pools, indoor and outdoor hot tubs, sauna, tennis court, exercise room, nightclub. AE, D, DC, MC, V.*

Nightlife and the Arts

The **North Country Center for the Performing Arts** (✉ Mill at Loon Mountain, ☎ 603/745–6032) presents theater for children and adults and art exhibitions from July to September. Skiers head to the **Granite Bar** at the Mountain Club at the Loon Mountain Resort (☎ 603/745–8111). You can also dance at the **Loon Saloon** at the ski area. **Thunderbird Lounge** (✉ Indian Head Resort, North Lincoln, ☎ 603/745–8000) has nightly entertainment year-round and one of the largest dance floors in the area. The **Timbermill Pub** (✉ Mill at Loon Mountain, ☎ 603/745–3603) hosts bands on weekends year-round.

Outdoor Activities and Sports

HIKING

A couple of short hiking trails off the Kancamagus Highway (☞ En Route, *below*) yield great rewards for relatively little effort. The **Lincoln Woods Trail** starts from a large parking lot 4 mi east of Lincoln. The trail crosses a suspension bridge over the Pemigewasset River and follows an old railroad bed for 3 mi along the river. The parking and picnic area for **Sabbaday Falls,** about 20 mi east of Lincoln, is the trailhead for an easy ½-mi trail to the falls, a multilevel cascade that plunges through two potholes and a flume. **Russell Colbath Historic House** (circa 1831), 2 mi east of Sabbaday Falls, is now a U.S. Forest Service information center where you can purchase the recreation pass ($5 per vehicle, good for seven consecutive days) needed to park in any of the White Mountain National Forest lots or overlooks (stopping for photos or to use the rest rooms is permitted without a pass). At **Lost River Reservation** (✉ North Woodstock, ☎ 603/745–8031), open from mid-May to mid-October, you can tour the river gorge and view geological wonders like the Guillotine Rock and the Lemon Squeezer.

Shopping

CRAFTS

The Curious Cow (✉ Main St., N. Woodstock, ☎ 603/745–9230) is a multidealer shop selling country crafts. The **Russell Craig Gallery of Fine Crafts** (✉ 99 Main St., N. Woodstock, ☎ 603/745–8664) carries pottery, jewelry, miniatures, and other items by New Hampshire artisans. **Sunburst Fashions** (✉ 108 Main St., N. Woodstock, ☎ 603/745–8745) stocks handcrafted gemstone jewelry and imported gift items.

MALLS

The **Lincoln Square Outlet Stores** (✉ Rte. 112, ☎ 603/745–3883) stock predominantly factory seconds, including London Fog and Bass. **Millfront Marketplace, Mill at Loon Mountain** (✉ I–93 and the Kancamagus Hwy., ☎ 603/745–6261), a former paper factory, contains restaurants, boutiques, a bookstore, a pharmacy, and a post office.

Skiing

Loon Mountain. A modern resort on the Kancamagus Highway and the Pemigewasset River, Loon Mountain opened in the 1960s and underwent serious development in the 1980s. In the base lodge and around the mountain are many food-service and lounge facilities. At night, you can enjoy lift-serviced tubing on the lower slopes. ✉ *Kancamagus*

Hwy., 03251, ☎ *603/745–8111, 603/745–8100 for snow conditions,*
800/227–4191 for lodging.

DOWNHILL

Wide, straight, and consistent intermediate trails prevail at Loon. Beginner trails and slopes are set apart. Most advanced runs are grouped on the North Peak section farther from the main mountain. Snowboarders enjoy a halfpipe and their own snowboard park, and an alpine garden with bumps and jumps provides thrills for skiers. The vertical is 2,100 ft; a four-passenger gondola, one high-speed detachable quad, two triple and three double chairlifts, and one surface lift serve the 43 trails and slopes.

CROSS-COUNTRY

The touring center at Loon Mountain has 35 km (22 mi) of cross-country trails.

CHILD CARE

The day-care center takes children as young as 6 weeks old. The ski school runs several programs for children of different age groups. Children 5 and under ski free.

En Route Interstate 93 is the fastest way to the White Mountains, but it's hardly the most scenic. From Lincoln, take the **Kancamagus Highway** for classic vistas and follow it nearly all the way to North Conway. This 34½-mi stretch, punctuated by scenic overlooks and picnic areas, erupts into fiery color each fall, when photo-snapping drivers can really slow things down. Prepare yourself for a leisurely pace.

North Conway

㉗ *72 mi northeast of Concord, 42 mi east of Lincoln.*

North Conway is a shopper's paradise, with more than 150 outlet stores ranging from Anne Klein to Joan & David. Most of them stretch along Route 16.

☺ The **Conway Scenic Railroad** operates trips of varying durations in vintage trains pulled by steam or diesel engines. The 5½-hour trip through Crawford Notch winds past some of the finest scenery in the Northeast. Lunch is served in the dining car on the Valley train to Conway and Bartlett. The Victorian train station has displays of railroad artifacts, lanterns, and old tickets and timetables. ⊠ *Rtes. 16 and 302 (38 Norcross Circle),* ☎ *603/356–5251 or 800/232–5251.* ☞ *$8.50–$42, depending on trip.* ☉ *Mid-May–late Oct., daily 9–6; Apr.–mid-May and Nov.–late Dec., weekends 9–6. Call for departure times. Reserve early during foliage season for Crawford Notch or Valley dining car.*

At **Echo Lake State Park,** you needn't be a rock climber to glimpse views from the 1,000-ft **White Horse** and **Cathedral** ledges. From the top you'll see the entire valley in which Echo Lake shines like a diamond. An unmarked trailhead another ⁷⁄₁₀-mi on West Side Road leads to **Diana's Baths,** a spectacular series of waterfalls. ⊠ *Off Rte. 302,* ☎ *603/ 356–2672.* ☞ *$2.50.* ☉ *Mid-June–mid-Oct., daily dawn–dusk.*

The **Hartmann Model Railroad Museum** houses 14 operating layouts (from G to Z scales), approximately 2,000 engines, and more than 5,000 cars and coaches. A café, a crafts store, and a hobby shop are also on site. ⊠ *Rte. 302 and Town Hall Rd., Intervale,* ☎ *603/356–9922 or 603/356–9933.* ☞ *$5.* ☉ *Open daily 10–5.*

Dining and Lodging

$–$$$ ✕ **Delaney's Hole in the Wall.** Perfect after a long day on the slopes or out shopping, this casual restaurant has an eclectic decor of sports and other memorabilia that includes autographed baseballs and an early photo of skiing at Tuckerman's Ravine. The menu is varied as well, with entrées that range from fish tacos to medallions of sirloin fillet with steamed broccoli, sautéed baby shrimp, and hollandaise sauce. ⊠ ¼ mi north of North Conway on Rte. 16, ☎ 603/356–7776. D, MC, V.

$$–$$$ ✕ **Scottish Lion.** Scotch is the specialty at this restaurant-pub—you can choose from 60 varieties. In the tartan-carpeted dining rooms, scones and Devonshire cream are served at breakfast, and Scottish Highland game pie at lunch and dinner. The "rumpldethump" potatoes (mashed and mixed with cabbage and chives, then baked au gratin) are deservedly famous. Chef Michael Procopio has spent time in the Pacific Rim, so don't be surprised to find Thai pork loin or Bali chicken on the menu. ⊠ Rte. 16, ☎ 603/356–6381. AE, D, DC, MC, V.

$$–$$$ ✕▦ **Darby Field Inn.** After a day of outdoor activity in the adjacent White Mountain National Forest, you can warm yourself by the field-stone fireplace in the Darby Inn's living room or by the woodstove in the bar. Most of the rooms in this unpretentious 1826 converted farmhouse have mountain views. The menu at the restaurant ($$$) usually includes roast duckling with a raspberry Chambord sauce, rack of lamb with a burgundy-wine sauce, and daily specials like Jamaican jerk pork with a mango puree. For dessert try the dark-chocolate pâté with white-chocolate sauce or the famous Darby cream pie. ⊠ Bald Hill Rd., Conway 03818, ☎ 603/447–2181 or 800/426–4147, FAX 603/447–5726. 13 rooms with bath, 2 rooms share bath, 1 suite. Restaurant, bar, pool, cross-country skiing. MAP available, required during foliage season and Christmas wk. AE, MC, V. Closed Apr.

$–$$$ ✕▦ **Snowvillage Inn.** Journalist Frank Simonds built the main gam-
★ brel-roof house in 1916. To complement the inn's tome-jammed bookshelves, guest rooms are named for famous authors. The nicest of the rooms, with 12 windows that look out over the Presidential Range, is a tribute to native son Robert Frost. Two additional buildings—the carriage house and the chimney house—also have libraries. Menu highlights in the candlelit dining room ($$$; reservations essential) include roasted rack of lamb with herbes de Provence. Among the dessert treats are a cranberry walnut tart and a chocolate truffle cake. ⊠ Box 68, Stuart Rd. (5 mi southeast of Conway) Snowville 03849, ☎ 603/447–2818 or 800/447–4345, FAX 603/447–4345. 18 rooms. Restaurant, sauna, cross-country skiing. Full breakfast; MAP available. AE, D, DC, MC, V.

$ ✕▦ **Eastern Slope Inn Resort and Conference Center.** This National Historic Site on 40 acres in the heart of North Conway near Mt. Cranmore has been an operating inn for more than a century. The Ledges restaurant ($$–$$$) serves creative American fare in a glassed-in courtyard and has nightly entertainment. ⊠ Main St., 03860, ☎ 603/356–6321 or 800/258–4708, FAX 603/356–8732. 145 rooms. Restaurant, pub, indoor pool, hot tub, sauna, tennis courts, recreation room. AE, D, MC, V.

$$$ ▦ **Purity Spring Resort.** In the late 1800s, Purity Spring was a farm and sawmill on a private lake. Since 1944 it's been a four-season resort with two Colonial inns, lakeside cottages, and a ski lodge. The King Pine Ski Area is right on the property. ⊠ HC 63 Box 40, Rte. 153, East Madison 03849, ☎ 603/367–8896 or 800/373–3754, FAX 603/367–8664. 61 rooms with bath, 13 rooms share baths. Restaurant, indoor pool, lake, hot tub, tennis court, hiking, volleyball, fishing. AP, MAP. AE, D, MC, V.

$$–$$$ ▦ **Hale's White Mountain Hotel and Resort.** The rooms at this hotel at the base of Whitehorse Ledge have mountain views. Proximity to the White Mountain National Forest and Echo Lake State Park makes guests feel farther away from civilization (and the nearby outlet malls)

than they actually are. ⊠ *Box 1828, West Side Rd., 03860,* ☎ FAX *603/356–7100 or* ☎ *800/533–6301. 80 rooms, 13 suites. Restaurant, bar, pool, saunas, 9-hole golf course, tennis court, health club, hiking, cross-country skiing. AE, D, MC, V.*

$$ ⊞ **Best Western Red Jacket Mountain View.** A motor inn–cum–resort, the Best Western has many of the amenities of a fine hotel. Most rooms are spacious and have balconies or decks overlooking the White Mountains. The cozy public rooms have deep chairs and plants, and the 40-acre grounds are neatly landscaped. ⊠ *Box 2000, Rte. 16, 03860,* ☎ *603/356–5411 or 800/752–2538,* FAX *603/356–3842. 152 rooms, 12 town houses. Restaurant, refrigerators, indoor and outdoor pools, sauna, 2 tennis courts, exercise room, sleigh rides, recreation room, playground, meeting rooms. AE, D, DC, MC, V.*

$ ⊞ **Cranmore Inn.** This authentic country inn opened in 1863, and many of its furnishings date from the mid-1800s. A mere ⅓ mi from the base of Mt. Cranmore, the inn is within easy walking distance of North Conway Village. ⊠ *Kearsarge St., 03860,* ☎ *603/356–5502 or 800/526–5502. 18 rooms. Pool. Full breakfast. AE, MC, V.*

Nightlife and the Arts

The **Best Western Red Jacket Mountain View** (⊠ Rte. 16, ☎ 603/356–5411) has weekend and holiday entertainment. **Horsefeather's** (⊠ Main St., ☎ 603/356–6862) hops on weekends. **Mt. Washington Valley Theater Company** (⊠ Eastern Slope Playhouse, ☎ 603/356–5776) presents musicals and summer theater from July to September. The Resort Players, a local group, give pre- and post-season performances.

Shopping

ANTIQUES

The **Antiques & Collectibles Barn** (⊠ Rte. 16/302, 3425 Main St., ☎ 603/356–7118), 1½ mi north of the village, is a 35-dealer colony with everything from furniture and jewelry to coins and other collectibles. **North Country Fair Jewelers** (⊠ Main and Seavy Sts., ☎ 603/356–5819) carries diamonds, antique and estate jewelry, silver, watches, coins, and accessories. **Richard M. Plusch Fine Antiques** (⊠ Rte. 16/302, ☎ 603/356–3333) deals in period furniture and accessories, including glass, sterling silver, Oriental porcelains, rugs, and paintings. **Sleigh Mill Antiques** (⊠ Snowville, off Rte. 153, ☎ 603/447–6791), an old sleigh and carriage mill 6 mi south of Conway, specializes in 19th-century oil lighting and early gas and electric lamps.

CRAFTS

The **Basket & Handcrafters Outlet** (⊠ Kearsarge St., ☎ 603/356–5332) sells gift baskets, dried-flower arrangements, and country furniture. **Handcrafters Barn** (⊠ Rte. 16, ☎ 603/356–8996) stocks the work of 350 area artists and artisans. **League of New Hampshire Craftsmen** (⊠ Main St., ☎ 603/356–2441) carries the works of the area's best artisans.

FACTORY OUTLETS

More than 150 factory outlets—Timberland, Pfaltzgraff, London Fog, Anne Klein, and Reebok—can be found around Route 16. The Mount Washington Valley Chamber of Commerce (☎ 603/356–3171) has guides to the outlets.

SPORTSWEAR

Popular stores for skiwear include **Chuck Roast** (⊠ Rte. 16, ☎ 603/356–5589), **Joe Jones** (⊠ Rte. 16, ☎ 603/356–6848), and **Tuckerman's Outfitters** (⊠ Norcross Circle, ☎ 603/356–3121). You'll wait about a year for made-to-order **Limmer Boots** (⊠ Intervale, ☎ 603/356–5378), but believers say they're worth the wait and the price.

Skiing

King Pine Ski Area at Purity Spring Resort. King Pine, a little more than 9 mi from Conway, has been a family-run ski area for more than 100 years. Some ski-and-stay packages include free skiing for midweek resort guests. Among the facilities and activities are an indoor pool and fitness complex, ice-skating, and dogsledding. ✉ *Rte. 153, East Madison 03849,* ☎ *603/367–8896 or 800/367–8897; 800/373–3754 for ski information.*

DOWNHILL

King Pine's gentle slopes make it an ideal area for those learning to ski. Because most of the terrain is geared for beginner and intermediate skiers, experts won't be challenged here except for a brief pitch on the Pitch Pine trail. Sixteen trails are serviced by two triple chairs and a double chair. There's tubing on Tuesday, Saturday, and Sunday afternoon, and tubing and night skiing on Tuesday, Friday, and Saturday.

CROSS-COUNTRY

King Pine has 28 km (17 mi) of cross-country skiing. Sixty-four kilometers (40 miles) of groomed cross-country trails weave through North Conway and the countryside along the Mt. Washington Valley Ski Touring Association Network (✉ Rte. 16, Intervale, ☎ 603/356–9920 or 800/282–5220).

CHILD CARE

Children up to 6 years old are welcome (from 8:30 to 4) at the nursery on the second floor of the base lodge. Children ages 4 and up can take lessons.

Mt. Cranmore. This ski area on the outskirts of North Conway opened in 1938. Two new glades, one for beginners and intermediates, one for intermediates and experts, have opened more skiable terrain. The fitness center has an indoor climbing wall, tennis courts, exercise equipment, and a pool. ✉ *Box 1640, Snowmobile Rd., 03860,* ☎ *603/356–5543, 603/356–8516 for snow conditions, 800/786–6754 for lodging.*

DOWNHILL

The mountain's 40 trails are well laid out and fun to ski. Most runs are naturally formed intermediates that weave in and out of glades. Beginners have several slopes and routes from the summit, but experts must be content with a few short but steep pitches. One high-speed quad, one triple, and three double chairlifts carry skiers to the top. There are also two surface lifts. There is night skiing from Thursday to Saturday and during holiday periods. There's also outdoor skating and a halfpipe for snowboarders.

CHILD CARE

The nursery takes children 1 year old and up. There's instruction for children from age 4 to 12.

Glen

28 *6 mi north of North Conway, 78 mi northeast of Concord.*

Glen is hardly more than a crossroads between North Conway and Jackson, but its central location has made it the home of a few noteworthy attractions and dining and lodging options.

That cluster of fluorescent buildings on Route 16 is **Story Land,** a theme park with life-size storybook and nursery-rhyme characters, a flume ride, Cinderella's Castle, a Victorian-theme river-raft ride, a farm-family variety show, and a simulated voyage to the moon. ✉ *Rte. 16,* ☎

603/383–4186. ☎ *$17.* ☉ *Mid-June–Labor Day, daily 9–6; Labor Day–Columbus Day, weekends 10–5.*

A trip to **Heritage New Hampshire,** next door to Story Land, is as close as you may ever come to experiencing time travel. Theatrical sets, sound effects, and animation usher you aboard the *Reliance* and carry you from a village in 1634 England over tossing seas to the New World. You will saunter along Portsmouth's streets in the late 1700s and hear a speech by George Washington. ⊠ *Rte. 16,* ☎ *603/383–9776.* ☎ *$10.* ☉ *Mid-May–mid-Oct., daily 9–5.*

Dining and Lodging

$–$$$ ✕ **Red Parka Pub.** Practically an institution, the Red Parka Pub has been in downtown Glen for more than 25 years. The menu has everything a family could want, from an all-you-can-eat salad bar to scallop pie. The barbecued ribs are local favorites, and there are always many specials on the board. ⊠ *Rte. 302,* ☎ *603/383–4344. Reservations not accepted. AE, D, MC, V.*

$–$$ ✕☒ **Bernerhof.** This Old World–style hotel is right at home in its alpine setting. The rooms have hardwood floors with hooked rugs, antiques, and reproductions. The fanciest four rooms have brass beds and spa-size bathtubs; one suite has a Finnish sauna. Stay four days, and you'll be served a champagne breakfast in bed. The menu at the Prince Palace restaurant ($$$–$$$$) includes Swiss specialties like fondue and Wiener schnitzel, along with New American and classic French dishes. The Black Bear pub pours many microbrewery beers. Ask the hosts about the Taste of the Mountains cooking school. ⊠ *Box 240, Rte. 302, 03838,* ☎ *603/383–9132 or 800/548–8007,* FAX *603/383–0809. 9 rooms. Restaurant, pub. Full breakfast. AE, D, MC, V.*

$–$$ ☒ **Best Western Storybook Resort Inn.** On a hillside near Attitash, this motor inn with large rooms is well suited to families. Copperfield's Restaurant has gingerbread, sticky buns, omelets, and a children's menu. ⊠ *Box 129, Glen Junction 03838,* ☎ *603/383–6800,* FAX *603/ 383–4678. 78 rooms. Restaurant, bar, refrigerators, indoor and outdoor pools, indoor and outdoor hot tubs, sauna, tennis courts, playground. AE, DC, MC, V.*

Nightlife

The **Bernerhof Inn** (☎ 603/383–9132) is the setting for an evening of fondue and soft music by the fireside. **Red Parka Pub** (☎ 603/383–4344) is a hangout for barbecue and steak lovers. The crowd swells to capacity in the Pub Downstairs on weekends, when musical entertainers perform.

Jackson

★ ㉙   *4 mi north of Glen, 82 mi northeast of Concord.*

The village of Jackson, north of Glen on Route 16, has retained its storybook New England character. Art and antiques shopping, tennis, golf, fishing, and hiking to waterfalls are among the draws. When the snow falls, Jackson becomes the state's cross-country skiing capital. The village's proximity to four downhill areas makes it popular with alpine skiers, too.

Dining and Lodging

$$$–$$$$ ✕☒ **Christmas Farm Inn.** Despite its winter-inspired name, this 200-year-old village inn is an all-season retreat. Rooms in the main inn and the saltbox next door, five with whirlpool baths, are done in Laura Ashley prints. The suites, in the cottages, log cabin, and dairy barn, have beam-ceilings, fireplaces, and rustic Colonial furnishings. These accommodations are better suited to families. Some standbys in the

restaurant ($$–$$$) include vegetable-stuffed chicken, shrimp scampi, and New York sirloin; the list of homemade soups and desserts varies nightly. "Heart-healthy" dishes are also on the menu. ⊠ *Box CC, Rte. 16B, 03846,* ☎ *603/383–4313 or 800/443–5837,* ℻ *603/383–6495. 34 rooms. Restaurant, pub, pool, sauna, hot tub, volleyball, cross-country ski trails, recreation room. MAP. AE, MC, V.*

$$–$$$$ ✕🏠 **Inn at Thorn Hill.** Architect Stanford White designed this 1895 Vic-
★ torian house that's a few steps from cross-country trails and Jackson Village. Romantic touches include rose-motif papers and antiques like a blue-velvet fainting couch. The restaurant ($$$; reservations essential; closed mid-week in April) serves new American dishes like the roasted citrus-marinated pork loin with sesame-crusted sweet potatoes and the brook trout brushed with a chipotle-lemon glaze and dusted with ground pecans. Leave room for the cappuccino crème brûlée or the sour-cherry chocolate torte. ⊠ *Box A, Thorn Hill Rd., 03846,* ☎ *603/383–4242 or 800/289–8990,* ℻ *603/383–8062. 14 rooms, 5 suites. Restaurant, pub, air-conditioning, pool, hot tub, cross-country skiing. MAP. No smoking. AE, D, DC, MC, V.*

$$$ ✕🏠 **Wentworth.** Though this resort built in 1869 retains a Victorian look, the European accents include French-provincial antiques. All rooms have TVs and telephones; some have working fireplaces and whirl-pool tubs. The dining room serves innovative New England regional cuisine; in the more casual lounge you can order raclette and Swiss-cheese fondue. ⊠ *Rte. 16A, 03846,* ☎ *603/383–9700 or 800/637–0013,* ℻ *603/383–4265. 60 rooms in summer, 45 in winter. Restaurant, bar, air-conditioning, pool, golf course, tennis, ice-skating, cross-country skiing, sleigh rides. MAP. AE, D, DC, MC, V.*

$–$$ ✕🏠 **Eagle Mountain House.** This country estate, which dates from 1879, is close to downhill ski slopes and even closer to cross-country trails, which leave right from the property. The public rooms of this show-place have a tycoon-roughing-it feel, and the bedrooms are large and furnished with period pieces. On a warm day, you can nurse a drink in a rocking chair on the wraparound deck. ⊠ *Carter Notch Rd., 03846,* ☎ *603/383–9111 or 800/966–5779,* ℻ *603/383–0854. 93 rooms. Restaurant, pool, hot tub, sauna, 9-hole golf course, 2 tennis courts, health club, playground. AE, D, DC, MC, V.*

$–$$$$ 🏠 **Nordic Village Resort.** The light wood and white walls of these deluxe condos near several ski areas are as Scandinavian as the snowy views. The Club House has pools and a spa, and there is a nightly bonfire at Nordic Falls. Larger units have fireplaces, full kitchens, and whirlpool baths. ⊠ *Rte. 16, Jackson 03846,* ☎ *603/383–9101 or 800/472–5207,* ℻ *603/383–9823. 140 condominiums. Indoor and outdoor pools, hot tub, steam room, ice-skating, cross-country skiing, hiking, sleigh rides. D, MC, V.*

$$–$$$ 🏠 **Ellis River House.** Most of the period-decorated rooms in this con-
★ verted Colonial farmhouse on the Ellis River have fireplaces, and some have two-person whirlpool baths or private balconies. In winter, a snow bridge across the river connects you with the Ellis River Trail and Jackson's renowned cross-country trail system. Inn guests can enjoy a romantic candlelit dinner in the elegant dining room. ⊠ *Box 656, Rte. 16, 03846,* ☎ *603/383–9339 or 800/233–8309,* ℻ *603/383–4142. 13 rooms, 3 suites, 1 cottage. Air-conditioning, dining room, pool, hot tub, sauna. Full breakfast. No smoking. AE, D, DC, MC, V.*

$–$$$ 🏠 **Inn at Jackson.** The builders of this 1902 Victorian followed a de-sign by Stanford White. The inn has spacious rooms—six with fireplaces—with oversize windows and an airy feel. Other than an imposing grand staircase in the front foyer, the house is unpretentious: The hardwood floors, braided rugs, smattering of antiques, and mountain views are sure to make you feel at home. The hearty breakfast will fill you up for the entire day. ✉ *Box 807, Thornhill Rd., 03846,* ☎ *603/383–4321 or 800/289–8600,* ℻ *603/383–4085. 14 rooms. Air-conditioning, hot tub, cross-country skiing. Full breakfast. AE, D, DC, MC, V.*

$ ▦ **Wildcat Inn & Tavern.** After a day of skiing, collapse on a comfy sofa by the fire in this small 19th-century tavern in the center of Jackson Village. The fragrance of home-baking permeates into suite-style guest rooms, which are full of interesting furniture and knickknacks. The tavern, where bands often perform, attracts many skiers. In summer, dining is available in the landscaped garden. ✉ *Rte. 16A, 03846,* ☎ *603/383–4245 or 800/228–4245,* ℻ *603/383–6456. 13 rooms with bath, 2 share bath, 1 cottage. Restaurant, bar, air-conditioning. Full breakfast; MAP available. AE, DC, MC, V.*

Nightlife

The **Shovel Handle Pub** in Whitneys' Village Inn (☎ 603/383–8916) is the après-ski bar adjacent to Black Mountain's slopes.

Outdoor Activities and Sports

ICE SKATING

Nestlenook Farm (✉ Dinsmore Rd., ☎ 603/383–0845) maintains an outdoor ice-skating rink complete with music and a bonfire. You can rent skates here or get yours sharpened. Going snowshoeing or taking a romantic sleigh ride are two other winter options; in summer you can fly-fish in Emerald Lake or ride in a horse-drawn carriage.

Skiing

Black Mountain. The atmosphere at Black Mountain is fun, friendly, and informal—perfect for families and singles who want a low-key skiing holiday. The Family Passport, which allows two adults and two juniors to ski at discounted rates, is a good value. Midweek rates here are usually the lowest in Mt. Washington Valley. Lift-serviced tubing takes place on weekends and holidays and during vacation periods. ✉ *Box B, Rte. 16B, 03846,* ☎ *603/383–4490 or 800/475–4669.*

DOWNHILL

The 35 trails and two glades on the 1,100-vertical-ft mountain are evenly divided among beginner, intermediate, and expert. There are a triple and a double chairlift and two surface tows. Most of the skiing is user-friendly, particularly for beginners, and the southern exposure keeps skiers warm. In addition to trails, snowboarders can use two terrain parks and the halfpipe.

CHILD CARE

The nursery takes children from age 6 months to 5 years. Children from 3 to 12 can take classes at the ski school.

Jackson Ski Touring Foundation. Rated as one of the top four cross-country skiing areas in the country and by far the largest in the New Hampshire, Jackson offers 157.6 km (98 mi) of trails. Ninety-six kilometers (60 miles) are track groomed, 85 km (53 mi) are skate groomed, and there are 63 km (38½ mi) of marked and mapped backcountry trails. ✉ *Main St., 03846,* ☎ *800/927–6697.*

Mt. Washington

③⓪ *15 mi north of Jackson, 91 mi north of Concord.*

You can drive to the top of **Mt. Washington,** the highest mountain (6,288 ft) in the northeastern United States and the spot where weather observers have recorded 231-mph winds (the strongest in the world). But you'll have to endure the **Mt. Washington Auto Road** to get here. This toll road opened in 1861 and is said to be the nation's first manufactured tourist attraction. Closed in inclement weather, the road begins at **Glen House**, a gift shop and rest stop 15 mi north of Glen. Allow two hours round-trip and check your brakes first. Cars with automatic transmissions that can't shift down into first gear aren't allowed on the road. A better option is to hop into one of the vans at Glen House for a 1½-hour guided tour (two hours if you purchase your ticket before 9:30 AM). Up top, visit the **Sherman Adams Summit Building,** which contains a museum of memorabilia from each of the three hotels that have stood on this spot and a display of native plant life and alpine flowers. Stand in the glassed-in viewing area to hear the roar of that record-breaking wind. ☎ 603/466–3988. ⌚ *$15 per car and driver plus $6 for each adult passenger; van fare $20.* ☉ *Mid-May–late Oct., daily (weather permitting).*

Although not a town per se, scenic **Pinkham Notch** covers the eastern side of Mt. Washington and includes several ravines, including **Tuckerman's Ravine,** famous for spring skiing. The Appalachian Mountain Club maintains a visitor center here.

Great Glen Trails (*see* Cross-country *in* Skiing, *below*) has an extensive trail network for hiking and mountain biking, as well as full- or half-day programs in canoeing, kayaking, and fly-fishing.

Skiing
Wildcat. Glade skiers head to Wildcat, which has official glade trails with 28 acres of tree skiing. Wildcat's runs include some stunning double-black-diamond trails. The 4-km-long (2¾-mi-long) Polecat is where skiers who can hold a wedge should head. Experts can be found zipping down the Lynx, a run constantly voted by patrons of a local bar as the most popular in the Mt. Washington Valley. On a clear day, the views of Mt. Washington and Tuckerman's Ravine are superb. The trails are classic New England—narrow and winding. ⊠ *Pinkham Notch (Rte. 16, Jackson 03846),* ☎ *603/466–3326, 800/643–4521 for snow conditions, 800/255–6439 for lodging.*

DOWNHILL
Wildcat's expert runs deserve their designations and then some. Intermediates have mid-mountain-to-base trails, and beginners will find gentle terrain and a broad teaching slope. The 40 runs, with a 2,100-ft vertical drop, are served by a two-passenger gondola and one double and four triple chairlifts.

CHILD CARE
The child-care center takes children ages 6 months and up. All-day SKIwee instruction is offered to children from age 5 to 12. Ski instruction for children takes place on a separate slope.

CROSS-COUNTRY
Great Glen Trails. There are 40 km (24 mi) of cross-country trails here and access to more than 50 acres of backcountry. You can even ski the lower half of the Mt. Washington Auto Road. Trees shelter most of the trails, so Mt. Washington's famous weather shouldn't be a concern. Evenings of cross-country skiing and snowshoeing by moonlight are scheduled throughout the winter. ⊠ *Box 300, Rte. 16, Pinkham Notch, Gorham 03581,* ☎ *603/466–2333.*

Dixville Notch
③ *60 mi north of Mt. Washington, 166 mi north of Concord.*

Not everyone likes to venture this far north, but if you want to really get away from it all, Dixville Notch is the place to go. Just 12 mi from the Canadian border, this tiny community is known for two things. It's the home of the Balsams Grand Resort Hotel, one of the oldest and most celebrated resorts in New Hampshire. And Dixville Notch and Harts Location are the first election districts in the nation to vote in the presidential elections. Long before the sun rises on election day, the 30 or so Dixville Notch voters gather in the little meeting room beside the hotel bar to cast their ballots and make national news.

Dining and Lodging

$$$$ ✕⊞ **Balsams Grand Resort Hotel.** At this resort founded in 1866,
★   guests will find many nice touches: valet parking, dancing and entertainment, cooking demonstrations, wine tastings, and organized activities. Families particularly enjoy magic shows and late-night games of broomball. The Tower Suite, with its 20-ft conical ceiling, is in a Victorian-style turret and offers 360-degree views. Standard rooms, furnished with overstuffed chairs and soft queen-size beds, have views of the 15,000-acre estate and the mountains beyond. In the restaurant (reservations essential, jacket and tie), the summer buffet lunch is heaped upon a 100-ft-long table. Given the awesome amount of food, it's amazing that anyone has room left for the stunning dinners. A starter might be chilled strawberry soup spiked with Grand Marnier, followed by poached salmon with golden caviar sauce and chocolate hazelnut cake. ⊠ *Rte. 26, 03576,* ☎ *603/255–3400 or 800/255–0600; 800/255–0800 in NH,* ℻ *603/255–4221. 212 rooms. Restaurant, pool, golf, tennis courts, hiking, boating, fishing, mountain bikes, ice-skating, cross-country skiing, downhill skiing, children's programs. Rates are AP in summer, MAP in winter, and include sports and entertainment. AE, D, MC, V. Closed late Mar.–mid-May and mid-Oct.–mid-Dec.*

$$–$$$ ⊞ **The Glen.** This rustic lodge with stick furniture, fieldstone, and cedar is on First Connecticut Lake, surrounded by log cabins, seven of which are right on the water. The cabins come equipped with efficiency kitchens and minirefrigerators—not that you'll need either, because rates include meals in the lodge restaurant. ⊠ *77 Glen Rd., 1 mi off Rte. 3, 03592,* ☎ *603/538–6500 or 800/445–4536. 8 rooms, 10 cabins. Restaurant, dock. AP. No credit cards. Closed mid-Oct.–mid-May.*

Outdoor Activities and Sports

Dixville Notch State Park (⊠ Rte. 26, ☎ 603/788–3155), the northernmost notch in the White Mountains, has picnic areas, a waterfall, many hiking trails, and a moose-observation platform.

Skiing

Balsams. Skiing was originally provided as an amenity for hotel guests at the Balsams, but the area has become popular with day-trippers as well. ⊠ *Rte. 26, 03576,* ☎ *603/255–3400 or 800/255–0600; 800/255–0800 in NH; 603/255–3951 for snow conditions,* ℻ *603/255–4221.*

DOWNHILL

Slopes with names like Sanguinary, Umbagog, Magalloway may sound tough, but they're only moderately difficult, leaning toward intermediate. There are 12 trails and four glades from the top of the 1,000-ft vertical for every skill level. One double chairlift and two T-bars carry skiers up the mountain. There is a halfpipe for snowboarders.

CROSS-COUNTRY

Balsams has 76 km (47 mi) of cross-country skiing, tracked and groomed for skating (a cross-country ski technique), with natural-history markers annotating some trails; there's also telemark and backcountry skiing.

CHILD CARE

The nursery takes children up to age 6 at no charge to hotel guests. There are lessons for children 3 and up.

OFF THE
BEATEN PATH

PITTSBURG – Just north of the White Mountains, Pittsburg contains the four Connecticut Lakes and the springs that form the Connecticut River. The entire northern tip of the state—a chunk of about 250 square mi—lies within the town's borders, the result of a dispute between the United States and Canada. The two countries could not decide on a border, so the inhabitants of this region declared themselves independent of both countries in 1832 and wrote a constitution providing for an assembly, a council, courts, and a militia. They named their nation the Indian Stream Republic, after the river that passes through the territory—the capital of which was Pittsburg. In 1835 the feisty, 40-man Indian Stream militia invaded Canada—with only limited success. The Indian Stream war ended more by common consent than surrender; in 1842 the Webster-Ashburton Treaty fixed the international boundary. Indian Stream was incorporated as Pittsburg, making it the largest township in New Hampshire. Canoeing and taking photographs are the favorite pastimes up here; the pristine wilderness teems with moose. Contact the **North Country Chamber of Commerce** (✉ Box 1, Colebrook 03576, ☎ 603/237–8939) for information about the region.

Bartlett

32 *7 mi southwest of Glen, 85 mi north of Concord.*

Bear Mountain to the south, Mount Parker to the north, Mount Cardigan to the west, and the Saco River to the east combine to create an unforgettable setting for the village of Bartlett, incorporated in 1790. Bear Notch Road in Bartlett has the only midpoint access to the Kancamagus (closed winter).

From Glen, Route 302 follows the Saco River to Bartlett and the **Attitash Ski Area** (✉ Rte. 302, ☎ 603/374–2368), which has a dry alpine slide, a water slide, a children's area, and a driving range. A chairlift whisks passengers to the White Mountain Observation Tower, which delivers 270-degree views of the Whites.

Dining and Lodging

$$–$$$ ✕▦ **Grand Summit Hotel & Conference Center.** The gables and curves of this resort hotel at the base of Attitash Bear Peak mimic the peaks and slopes of the mountain that rises behind it. The luxurious contemporary-style rooms have kitchenettes, VCRs, and stereo systems. ✉ *Box 429, Rte. 302, 03812,* ☎ *603/374–0869 or 800/554–1900,* ℻ *603/374–3040. 143 rooms. 2 restaurants, bar, heated pool, hot tubs, sauna, steam room, exercise room, gift shop. AE, D, MC, V.*

$$$–$$$$ ▦ **Attitash Mountain Village.** The style at this condo-motel complex—across the street from the mountain via a tunnel—is alpine contemporary, and the staff is young and enthusiastic. The many amenities include indoor and outdoor pools and whirlpools. Units, some with fireplaces and kitchenettes, accommodate from two to 14 people. The restaurant has unrestricted views of the mountain. ✉ *Rte. 302, 03812-0358,* ☎ *603/374–6501 or 800/862–1600,* ℻ *603/374–6509. 250 rooms. Restaurant, pub, indoor pool, sauna, recreation room. AE, D, MC, V.*

Skiing

Attitash Bear Peak. This high-profile resort, which hosts many special events and ski races, continues to expand. Lodgings at the base of the mountain is in condominiums and motel-style units are away from the hustle of North Conway. Attitash Bear Peak has a computerized lift-ticket system that in essence allows skiers to pay by the run. Skiers can share the ticket, which is good for two years. ✉ *Rte. 302, 03812,* ☎ *603/374–2368, 603/374–0946 or 800/223–7669 for snow conditions, 800/223–7669 for lodging.*

DOWNHILL

Enhanced with massive snowmaking (93%), the trails now number 60 on two peaks, both with full-service base lodges. The bulk of the skiing is geared to intermediates and experts, with some steep pitches, glades, and good use of terrain. Beginners have a share of good terrain on the lower mountain and some runs from the top. Serving the 30 km (18 mi) of trails and the 1,750-ft vertical drop are one high-speed quad, one fixed-grip quad, three triples, four double chairlifts, and two surface tows.

CROSS-COUNTRY

Bear Notch Ski Touring Center (☎ 603/374–2277) has more than 60 km (36 mi) of groomed cross-country trails, with over 20 km (12 mi) skate groomed and 50 km (30 mi) tracked. There's also unlimited backcountry skiing. Guests staying at the Grand Summit Hotel can connect to the trail system from the hotel door.

CHILD CARE

Attitots Clubhouse takes children from age 6 months to 5 years. Other programs accommodate children up to 16 years of age.

En Route   Route 302 passes through **Crawford Notch State Park** (⊠ Rte. 302, Harts Location, ☎ 603/374–2272), where you can stop for a picnic and a short hike to Arethusa Falls or the Silver and Flume cascades.

Bretton Woods

㉝   *20 mi northwest of Bartlett, 95 mi north of Concord.*

Early in this century, as many as 50 private trains a day brought the rich and famous from New York and Philadelphia to the Mount Washington Hotel, the jewel of Bretton Woods.

In 1858, when Sylvester Marsh asked the state legislature for permission to build a steam railway up Mt. Washington, one legislator responded that he'd have better luck building a railroad to the moon.

★   Despite such skepticism, the **Mt. Washington Cog Railway** opened in 1869 and has since provided tourists a thrilling alternative to driving or climbing to the top. Allow three hours round-trip. ⊠ *Rte. 302, 6 mi northeast of Bretton Woods,* ☎ *603/846–5404; 800/922–8825 outside NH.* ☎ *$39 round-trip.* ☉ *Mid-June–mid-Oct., daily 8–5, weather permitting; May–mid-June and mid-Oct.–early Nov., limited schedule.*

Dining, Lodging, and Camping

$$$$ ✕☰ **Mount Washington Hotel.** The 1902 construction of this leviathan was one of the most ambitious projects of its day. It quickly became one of the nation's favorite grand resorts, most notable for its 900-ft-long veranda, which affords a full view of the Presidential Range. With its stately public rooms and large, Victorian-style bedrooms and suites, the hotel retains a turn-of-the-century formality; jacket and tie are required in the dining room. This 2,600-acre property has an extensive recreation center. ⊠ *Rte. 302, 03575,* ☎ *603/278–1000 or 800/258–0330,* ﬀ *603/278–8838. 200 rooms. 2 restaurants, indoor and outdoor pools, sauna, golf, tennis courts, hiking, horseback riding, bicycles, children's programs. MAP. AE, MC, V. Closed mid-Oct.–mid-May.*

$–$$ ✕☰ **Bretton Arms Country Inn.** Built in 1896, this restored inn predates the Mount Washington Hotel across the way. Reservations are required in the dining room ($$$–$$$$) and should be made on arrival. Guests are invited to use the facilities of the Mount Washington Hotel during the summer and of the Bretton Woods Motor Inn year-round.

⊠ *Rte. 302, 03575,* ☎ *603/278–1000 or 800/258–0330,* ⒻⅩ *603/278–8838. 31 rooms, 3 suites. Restaurant, lounge. AE, D, MC, V.*

$–$$ 🏨 **Bretton Woods Motor Inn.** Rooms here have contemporary furnishings, a balcony or patio, and views of the Presidential Range. The Continental cuisine prepared at Darby's Restaurant is served around a circular fireplace. The bar is a hangout for skiers. The motor inn, across the road from the Mount Washington Hotel, shares its facilities in summer. ⊠ *Rte. 302, 03575,* ☎ *603/278–1000 or 800/258–0330,* ⒻⅩ *603/278–8838. 50 rooms. Restaurant, bar, indoor pool, sauna, recreation room. AE, D, MC, V.*

$ ⛺ **Dry River Campground.** This rustic campground in Crawford Notch State Park has 30 tent sites and is a popular base for hiking the White Mountain National Forest. ⊠ *Rte. 302 (Box 177, Twin Mountain 03595), Harts Location,* ☎ *603/374–2272. Closed mid-Dec.–mid-May.*

Skiing

Bretton Woods. This area has a three-level, open-space base lodge, a convenient drop-off area, easy parking, and an uncrowded setting. On-mountain town houses are available as part of reasonably priced packages. The views of Mt. Washington alone are worth the visit; the scenery is especially beautiful from the Top o' Quad restaurant. ⊠ *Rte. 302, 03575,* ☎ *603/278–5000, 800/232–2972 for information, 603/278–1000 or 800/258–0330 for lodging.*

DOWNHILL

The skiing on the 32 trails is novice and intermediate, with steeper pitches near the top of the 1,500-ft vertical and glade skiing to satisfy expert skiers. Skiers and snowboarders enjoy a terrain park with jumps and halfpipes. One detachable quad, one triple, and two double chairlifts service the trails. The area has night skiing and snowboarding on Friday, Saturday, and holidays. A limited lift-ticket policy helps keep lines short.

CROSS-COUNTRY

The large full-service cross-country ski center at Bretton Woods has 90 km (54 mi) of groomed and double-track trails and also rents snowshoes.

CHILD CARE

The nursery takes children from age 2 months to 5 years. The ski school has an all-day program for children ages 3 to 12, using progressive instructional techniques. Rates include lifts, lessons, equipment, lunch, and supervised play.

Bethlehem

③④ *25 mi west of Bretton Woods, 84 mi north of Concord.*

In the days before antihistamines, hay-fever sufferers came by the busload to the town of Bethlehem, whose crisp air has a blissfully low pollen count. The town, elevation 1,462 ft, was also home to a group of Hasidic Jews who established kosher resorts in the Arlington and Alpine hotels.

Lodging

$$–$$$$ 🏨 **Adair.** In 1927 attorney Frank Hogan built this three-story Geor-
★ gian Revival home as a wedding present for his daughter Dorothy Adair. Walking paths on this luxurious country inn's 200 acres wind through gardens and offer magnificent mountain views. The rooms, which have garden or mountain views, are decorated with period antiques and antique reproductions. One of the suites has a large two-person hot tub, a fireplace, a balcony, and a king-size sleigh bed. ⊠ *80 Guider*

La., 03574, ☎ *603/444–2600 or 888/444–2600,* FAX *603/444–4823. 7 rooms, 2 suites. Tennis court, billiards. Full breakfast. No smoking. AE, MC, V.*

Outdoor Activities and Sports

Bretzfelder Park, a 77-acre nature and wildlife park, has a picnic shelter (☎ 603/869–5688). The **Rocks Estate** (☎ 603/444–6228), owned by the Society for the Protection of New Hampshire Forests, is a working Christmas-tree farm with walking trails, historic buildings, and educational programs.

Franconia

㉟ *10 mi south of Bethlehem, 74 mi north of Concord.*

Travelers first came to Franconia because the notch of the same name provided a north–south route through the mountains. The town, which is north of the notch, and the notch itself are worth a look. Famous literary visitors include Washington Irving, Henry Wadsworth Longfellow, and Nathaniel Hawthorne, who wrote a short story about the Old Man of the Mountain.

The **Frost Place,** Robert Frost's home from 1915 to 1920, is where the poet wrote his most-remembered poem, "Stopping by Woods on a Snowy Evening." The mountain views from this house would inspire any writer. Two rooms contain memorabilia and signed editions of his books. Outside, you can follow short trails marked with lines from Frost's poetry. Occasional poetry readings take place at the house. ⊠ *Ridge Rd. (off Rte. 116; follow signs),* ☎ *603/823–5510.* ☜ *$3.* ☉ *Memorial Day–June, weekends 1–5; July–Columbus Day, Wed.–Mon. 1–5.*

Franconia Notch State Park, south of Franconia, contains a few of New Hampshire's best-loved attractions. **Cannon Mountain Aerial Tramway** will lift you 2,022 ft for one more sweeping mountain vista. It's a five-minute ride to the top, where marked hiking trails lead from the observation platform. ⊠ *Cannon Mountain Ski Area,* ☎ *603/823–5563.* ☜ *$9.* ☉ *Memorial Day–3rd weekend in Oct., daily 9–4.*

The **New England Ski Museum,** north of Cannon Mountain at the foot of the tramway, has photographs and old trophies, skis and bindings, boots, and ski apparel dating from the late 1800s. ☎ *603/823–7177.* ☜ *Free.* ☉ *Dec.–Mar., Thurs.–Tues. noon–5; Memorial Day–Columbus Day, daily noon–5; closed rest of year.*

It would be a shame to come to the White Mountains and leave without seeing the granite profile of the **Old Man of the Mountain,** the icon of New Hampshire. Nathaniel Hawthorne wrote about it, New Hampshire resident Daniel Webster bragged about it, and P. T. Barnum wanted to buy it. The two best places to view the giant stone face are the highway parking area on Route 3 or along the shores of Profile Lake.

The **Flume** is an 800-ft-long natural chasm discovered by a local woman en route to her favorite fishing hole. The narrow walls give the gorge's running water a deeply eerie echo. The route through the flume has been built up with a series of boardwalks and stairways. ⊠ *Exit 1 off I–93,* ☎ *603/745–8391.* ☜ *$6.* ☉ *May–Oct., daily 9–5.*

Dining, Lodging, and Camping

$–$$$ ✕▥ **Franconia Inn.** This resort has recreations for all seasons. You can golf next door at Sunset Hill's nine-hole course, play tennis, ride horseback, swim in the pool or sit in the hot tub, order your lunch to go for a day of hiking—even try soaring from the inn's airstrip. Movies are shown in the evening in the lounge. Rooms have designer chintzes, canopy beds, and country furnishings; some have whirlpool baths or fireplaces. At meals ($$–$$$), children choose from a separate menu. Among the fare for adults are the medallions of veal with apple-mustard sauce and the filet mignon with green-chili butter and Madeira sauce. ⊠ *1300 Easton Rd., 03580,* ☎ *603/823–5542 or 800/473–5299,* FAX *603/823–8078. 34 rooms. Restaurant, pool, hot tub, tennis, croquet, horseback riding, bicycles, ice-skating, cross-country skiing, sleigh rides. Full breakfast; MAP available. AE, MC, V. Closed Apr.–mid-May.*

$–$$ ✕⊞ **Sugar Hill Inn.** The old carriage on the lawn and wicker chairs on the wraparound porch set a Colonial mood before you even enter this converted 1789 farmhouse. Many rooms have hand-stenciled walls, a view of Franconia Notch, and rippled antique windows; all contain antiques. The late film star Bette Davis used to visit friends in this house before she bought her own farm nearby—the room with the best view is named after her. Afternoon refreshments include scones and tea breads. The restaurant ($$$) serves meat, fish, and poultry dishes and delicious desserts. There are 10 rooms in the inn and six (some with fireplaces) in three country cottages. ⊠ *Rte. 117, Sugar Hill 03585 (Box 954, Franconia 03580-0954),* ☎ *603/823–5621 or 800/548–4748,* FAX *603/823–5639. 16 rooms. Restaurant, pub, cross-country skiing. Full breakfast; MAP available (required during foliage season). No smoking. AE, MC, V.*

$–$$ ⊞ **Hilltop** Staying with innkeepers Mike and Meri Hern is just like dropping by Grandma's—they even welcome pets. The rooms in their 1895 country farmhouse are done in a quirky mix of antiques with handmade quilts, Victorian ceiling fans, piles of pillows, and big, fluffy towels. The TV room has hundreds of movies on tape. Rockers on the porch are perfect for watching the sun set behind the mountains. The large country breakfast includes homemade jams, pancakes made with homegrown berries, soufflés, and smoked ham, bacon, or salmon. ⊠ *Rte. 117/Main St., Sugar Hill 03585,* ☎ *603/823–5695 or 800/770–5695,* FAX *603/823–5518. 3 rooms, 3 suites, 1 2-bedroom cottage. Restaurant, bar, library. Full breakfast. 2-night minimum during foliage season; no smoking. D, MC, V.*

$ ⊞ **Horse and Hound Inn.** Off the beaten path yet convenient to the Cannon Mountain tram, this inn is on 8 acres surrounded by the White Mountain National Forest. Antiques and assorted collectibles provide a cheery atmosphere, and on the grounds are 65 km (39 mi) of cross-country ski trails. Pets are welcome ($8.50 per stay). ⊠ *205 Wells Rd., 03580,* ☎ *603/823–5501 or 800/450–5501. 8 rooms with bath, 2 rooms share bath. Restaurant, bar, cross-country skiing. Full breakfast. AE, D, DC, MC, V. Closed Apr. and Nov.*

$ ⚠ **Lafayette Campground.** This campground has hiking and biking trails, 97 tent sites, showers, a camp store, a bike trail, and easy access to the Appalachian Trail. ⊠ *Franconia Notch State Park, 03580,* ☎ *603/823–9513 for information, 603/271–3628 for reservations. No pets. MC, V.*

Nightlife

Hillwinds (⊠ Main St., ☎ 603/823–5551) has live entertainment on weekends.

Shopping

The **Franconia Marketplace** (⊠ Main St., ☎ 603/823–5368) sells only products made in Franconia. Stores in the complex include the **Grateful Bread Quality Bakery** and **Tiffany Workshop,** which stocks clothing and crystal jewelry.

Skiing

Cannon Mountain. Nowhere is the granite of the Granite State more pronounced than here. One of the first ski areas in the United States, Cannon, which is owned and run by the state, gives strong attention to skier services, family programs, snowmaking, and grooming. The New England Ski Museum (☞ Franconia Notch State Park, *above*) is adjacent to the base of the tramway. ⊠ *Franconia Notch State Park, 03580,* ☎ *603/823–5563, 603/823–7771 or 800/552–1234 for snow conditions, 800/237–9007 for lodging.*

DOWNHILL

The tone of this mountain's skiing is reflected in the narrow, steep pitches off the peak of the 2,146 ft of vertical rise. Some trails marked intermediate may seem more difficult because of the sidehill slant of the slopes (rather than the steepness). Under a new fall of snow, Cannon's 38 trails have challenges not often found at modern ski areas. For additional fun, try the two glade-skiing trails, Turnpike and Banshee. There is a 70-passenger tramway to the top, one quad, one triple, and two double chairlifts, and one surface lift.

CHILD CARE

Cannon's Peabody Base Lodge takes children ages 1 year and older. All-day and half-day SKIwee programs are available for children from age 4 to 12, and season-long instruction can be arranged.

CROSS-COUNTRY

Franconia Village Cross-Country Ski Center (☎ 603/823–5542 or 800/473–5299) has 65 km (39 mi) of groomed trails and 40 km (24 mi) of backcountry trails. One popular trail leads to Bridal Veil Falls, a great spot for a picnic lunch. Nordic skiing is also available on a 13-km (8-mi) bicycle path through Franconia Notch State Park.

The White Mountains A to Z

Arriving and Departing

BY BUS

Concord Trailways (☎ 800/639–3317) stops in Chocorua, Conway, Franconia, Glen, and Jackson.

BY CAR

Access to the White Mountains is from I–93 via the Kancamagus Highway or Route 302. From the seacoast, Route 16 is the popular choice.

BY PLANE

Manchester Airport (☞ Arriving and Departing *in* New Hampshire A to Z, at the end of this chapter) is about an hour's drive from the White Mountains region.

Getting Around

BY BUS

See Arriving and Departing, *above.*

BY CAR

I–93 and Route 3 bisect the White Mountain National Forest, running north from Massachusetts to Québec. Route 16 brings visitors north from the New Hampshire coast. The Kancamagus Highway (Route 112), the east–west thoroughfare through the White Mountain National Forest, is a scenic drive but is often impassable in winter. Route 302, a longer, more leisurely east–west path, connects I–93 to North Conway.

Charters and private planes land at **Franconia Airport & Soaring Center** (⊠ Easton Rd., Franconia, ☎ 603/823–8881) and **Mt. Washington Regional Airport** (⊠ Airport Rd., Whitefield, ☎ 603/837–9532).

Contacts and Resources

CAMPING

White Mountain National Forest (⊠ U.S. Forest Service, 719 N. Main St., Laconia 03246, ☎ 603/528–8721 or 800/283–2267) has 20 campgrounds with more than 900 campsites spread across the region; only some take reservations. All sites are subject to a 14-day limit.

CANOEING

River outfitter **Saco Bound Canoe & Kayak** (⊠ Box 119, Center Conway 03813, ☎ 603/447–2177) leads gentle canoeing expeditions, guided kayak trips, white-water rafting on seven rivers, and provides lessons, equipment, and transportation.

EMERGENCIES

Memorial Hospital (⊠ 3073 Main St., North Conway, ☎ 603/356–5461).

FISHING

For trout and salmon fishing, try the **Connecticut Lakes,** though any clear stream in the White Mountains will do. Many are stocked, and there are 650 mi of them in the national forest alone. **Conway Lake** is the largest of the area's 45 lakes and ponds; it's noted for smallmouth bass and—early and late in the season—good salmon fishing. The **New Hampshire Fish and Game Office** (☎ 603/788–3164) has up-to-date information on fishing conditions.

The **North Country Angler** (⊠ N. Main St., ☎ 603/356–6000) schedules intensive guided fly-fishing weekends.

HIKING

With 86 major mountains in the area, the hiking possibilities are endless. Innkeepers can usually point you toward the better nearby trails; some inns schedule guided day-trips for their guests. The **White Mountain National Forest** (⊠ U.S. Forest Service, 719 N. Main St., Laconia 03246, ☎ 603/528–8721 or 800/283–2267) has hiking information.

The **Appalachian Mountain Club** (⊠ Box 298, Gorham 03581, ☎ 603/466–2721, 603/466–2725 for trail information, 603/466–2727 for reservations or a free guide to huts and lodges) headquarters at Pinkham Notch offers lectures, workshops, slide shows, and movies from June to October. Accommodations include a 100-bunk main lodge and eight rustic cabins. The club's hut system provides reasonably priced meals and dorm-style lodging on several trails throughout the Whites.

New England Hiking Holidays (⊠ Box 1648, North Conway 03860, ☎ 603/356–9696 or 800/869–0949) conducts guided hiking tours for as few as two nights or as many as eight.

LLAMA TREKKING

Snowvillage Inn (⊠ Snowville 03849, ☎ 603/447–2818 or 800/447–4345) conducts a guided trip up Foss Mountain. Your elegant picnic will include champagne and gourmet food from the inn's kitchen. Reservations are essential.

RESERVATION SERVICES

Country Inns in the White Mountains (☎ 603/356–9460 or 800/562–1300). **Jackson Resort Association** (☎ 800/866–3334).

VISITOR INFORMATION

Mt. Washington Valley Chamber of Commerce (☎ 603/356–3171 or 800/367–3364). **Mt. Washington Valley Visitors Bureau** (✉ Box 2300, North Conway 03860, ☎ 603/356–5701 or 800/367–3364). **White Mountain Attractions Association** (✉ Kancamagus Highway, Lincoln 03251, ☎ 603/745–8720 or 800/346–3687).

WESTERN AND CENTRAL NEW HAMPSHIRE

Here is the unspoiled heart of New Hampshire. The beaches to the east attract sun worshipers, and the resort towns to the north keep the skiers and hikers beating a well-worn path up I–93, but western and central New Hampshire have managed to keep the water slides and the outlet malls at bay. In the center of New Hampshire you'll see one pristine town green after another. Each village has its own historical society and tiny museum filled with odd bits of memorabilia: a cup from which George Washington took tea, a piano that belonged to the Alcott family, whose Louisa May wrote *Little Women.*

Two other lures in this area are the shining waters of Lake Sunapee and the looming presence of Mt. Monadnock. When you're done climbing and swimming and visiting the past, look for the wares and small studios of area artists. The region has long been an informal artists' colony where people come to write, paint, and weave in solitude.

The towns in this region, beginning with Concord, are listed in counterclockwise order. From Concord, you can take I–89 through the Lake Sunapee region to Hanover, follow the Connecticut River south to Keene, and then meander through the Monadnock region to Manchester.

Concord

36 *40 mi north of the Massachusetts border via I–93, 20 mi north of Manchester, 45 mi northwest of Portsmouth.*

New Hampshire's capital is a quiet, conservative town (population 38,000) that tends to the state's business but little else. The residents joke that the sidewalks roll up promptly at 6. The **Concord on Foot** walking trail winds through the historic district. Maps are available from the Chamber of Commerce (✉ 244 N. Main St.) or stores along the trail. The trail includes the **Pierce Manse,** the Greek Revival home in which Franklin Pierce lived before moving to Washington to become the 14th U.S. president. ✉ *14 Penacook St.,* ☎ *603/224–9620 or 603/224–7668.* 🎟 *$3.* ☉ *Mid-June–Labor Day, weekdays 11–3.*

At the gilt-domed **State House,** New Hampshire's legislature still meets in its original chambers. ✉ *107 N. Main St.,* ☎ *603/271–1110.* ☉ *Weekdays 8–4:30.*

Among the artifacts at the **Museum of New Hampshire History** is an original Concord Coach. During the 19th century, when more than 3,000 of them were built in Concord, this was about as technologically perfect a vehicle as you could find—many say it's the coach that won the West. Other exhibits provide an overview of New Hampshire's history, from the Abenaki Indians to the settlers of Portsmouth up to current residents. ✉ *6 Eagle Sq.,* ☎ *603/226–3189.* 🎟 *$5.* ☉ *Mon. in Dec. and July–mid-Oct., Tues.–Wed. and Sat. year-round 9:30–5, Thurs.–Fri. 9:30–8:30, Sun. noon–5.*

The high-tech **Christa McAuliffe Planetarium** was named for the Concord teacher and first civilian in space, who was killed in the *Challenger*

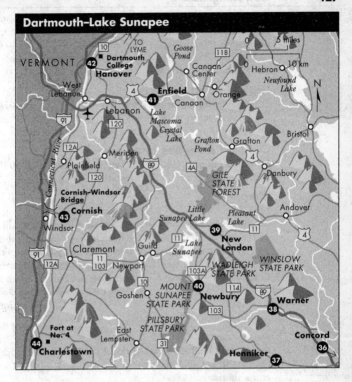

Dartmouth–Lake Sunapee

space-shuttle explosion in 1986. Shows on the solar system, constellations, and space exploration incorporate computer graphics, sound equipment, and views through the 40-ft dome telescope. Children especially love seeing the tornado tubes, magnetic marbles, and other hands-on exhibits. Outside, explore the scale-model planet walk and the human sundial. ⊠ *New Hampshire Technical Institute, 3 Institute Dr.,* ☎ *603/271–7827.* ☞ *Exhibit area free, shows $6.* ☉ *Tues.–Thurs. 9–5, Fri. 9–7, Sat. and Sun. 10–5. Call for show times.*

Guided tours of the 1765 high Gothic **Kimball-Jenkins Estate** focus on the craftsmanship of the mansion, its furnishings—including the woodwork and frescoed ceilings—and stories of more than 200 years of life in Concord. The formal gardens are the perfect spot for a summer picnic. ⊠ *266 N. Main St.,* ☎ *603/225–3932.* ☞ *$4.* ☉ *Memorial Day–Oct., Tues.–Sun. 11–4.*

Dining

$$–$$$ ✕ **Endicott Grill.** Chef Graham Gifford changes the Endicott's menu each month. Past dishes have included smoked-salmon napoleons with caper-dill aioli, roasted free-range half-chicken with pecan wild rice and a mushroom-wine sauce, and a raspberry-chocolate pecan cheesecake. ⊠ *6 Pleasant St. Ext.,* ☎ *603/224–0582. MC, V. Closed Sun.–Mon.*

$–$$ ✕ **Hermanos Cocina Mexicana.** The food at this popular two-level restau-
★ rant is standard Mexican, but with fresher ingredients and more subtle sauces than one might expect. Everything on the menu is available à la carte, so you can mix and match to build a meal. ⊠ *11 Hills Ave.,* ☎ *603/224–5669. Reservations not accepted. MC, V.*

$$–$$$ ⌂ **Centennial Inn.** Built in 1896 for widows of Civil War veterans, this brick and stone building is set back from busy Pleasant Street. Much of the original woodwork has been preserved. Each room is decorated with antiques and reproductions, and all have ceiling fans, VCRs, and

dedicated modem lines. In the Franklin Pierce dining room, where the menu changes seasonally, try the shredded-duck pizza and the roast medallions of venison. ⊠ *96 Pleasant St., 03301,* ☎ *603/225–7102 or 800/267–0525,* FAX *603/225–5031. 27 rooms, 5 suites. Restaurant, bar. AE, D, DC, MC, V.*

Nightlife and the Arts

The **Capitol Center for the Arts** (⊠ 46 S. Main St., ☎ 603/225–1111) has been restored to reflect its Roaring '20s origins. It hosts touring Broadway shows, dance companies, and musical acts.

Outdoor Activities and Sports

Hannah's Paddles, Inc. (⊠ 15 Hannah Dustin Dr., ☎ 603/753–6695) rents canoes for use on the Merrimack River.

Shopping

CRAFTS

Capitol Craftsman and **Romance Jewelers** (⊠ 16 N. Main St., ☎ 603/ 224–6166 or 603/228–5683), which share adjoining shops, sell fine jewelry and handicrafts. The **Den of Antiquity** (⊠ 2 Capital Plaza, ☎ 603/225–4505) carries handcrafted country gifts and accessories. The **League of New Hampshire Craftsmen** (⊠ 205 N. Main St., ☎ 603/ 224–1471) exhibits crafts in many media. **Mark Knipe Goldsmiths** (⊠ 2 Capitol Plaza, Main St., ☎ 603/224–2920) sets antique stones in rings, earrings, and pendants.

MALLS

Steeplegate Mall (⊠ 270 Loudon Rd., ☎ 603/224–1523) has more than 70 stores, including chain department stores and some smaller crafts shops.

Henniker

㊲ *20 mi west of Concord via Rte. 202 or I–89 and Rte. 202.*

Governor Wentworth named this town in honor of his friend John Henniker, a London merchant and member of the British Parliament (residents delight in their town's status as "the only Henniker in the world"). Once a mill town producing bicycle rims and other light-industrial items, Henniker reinvented itself after a 1936 flood damaged the factories. New England College was established in the following decade. One of the area's covered bridges can be found on campus.

Dining and Lodging

$-$$$ ✕☱ **Colby Hill Inn.** The cookie jar is always full in this Federal Colonial farmhouse, where guests are greeted by a pair of Great Danes. There is no shortage of relaxing activities: You can curl up with a book by the parlor fireplace, stroll through the gardens and 5 acres of meadow, ice-skate out back in winter, or play badminton in summer. Rooms in the main house contain antiques, Colonial reproductions, and frills like lace curtains and Laura Ashley prints. In the carriage-house rooms, plain country furnishings, white walls, and exposed beams are the norm. The dining menu ($$–$$$) is excellent: Try the chicken Colby Hill (breast of chicken stuffed with lobster, leeks, and Boursin) or the New England seafood pie. ⊠ *Box 779, 3 The Oaks, 03242,* ☎ *603/428–3281,* FAX *603/428–9218. 16 rooms. Restaurant, air-conditioning, in-room modem lines, pool, ice-skating, recreation room. Full breakfast. AE, D, DC, MC, V.*

$-$$ ✕☱ **Meeting House Inn & Restaurant.** The owners of this 200-year-old farmhouse at the base of Pat's Peak, who tout the complex as a lovers' getaway, start guests' days off with breakfast in bed. The old barn has become a restaurant ($$–$$$$) that specializes in leisurely, romantic dining. Items like lobster pepito are served in a heart-shape puff pastry, and the chocolate-raspberry frozen mousse is also heart-shape. ⊠ *Rte. 114/Flanders Rd., 03242,* ☎ *603/428–3228,* FAX *603/ 428–6334. 6 rooms. Restaurant, hot tub, sauna. Full breakfast. AE, D, MC, V.*

Shopping
The **Fiber Studio** (⊠ 9 Foster Hill Rd., ☎ 603/428–7830) sells beads, hand-spun natural-fiber yarns, spinning equipment, and looms.

Skiing
Pats Peak. Convenient for Bostonians, Pats Peak is geared to families. Base facilities are rustic, and friendly personal attention is the rule. ⊠ *Rte. 114, 03242,* ☎ *603/428–3245, 800/742–7287 for snow conditions.*

DOWNHILL

Despite its size of only 710 vertical ft, with 19 trails and slopes, Pats Peak has something for everyone: New skiers can take advantage of a wide slope and several short trails; intermediates have wider trails from the top; and advanced skiers have a couple of real thrillers. Night skiing takes place in January and February. One triple and two double chairlifts, one T-bar, and three surface lifts serve the runs.

CHILD CARE

The nursery takes children from age 6 months to 5 years. Special nursery ski programs operate on weekends and during vacations for children from 4 to 12; all-day lessons for self-sufficient skiers in this age range are scheduled throughout the season.

Warner

38 *18 mi north of Henniker, 22 mi west of Concord.*

Three New Hampshire governors were born in this quiet agricultural town just off I–89. Buildings dating from the late 1700s and early 1800s and a charming library give the town's main street a welcoming feel.

Mount Kearsarge Indian Museum contains examples of the incomparable artistry of Native Americans, including moose-hair embroidery, a tepee, quillwork, and basketry. Signs on the self-guided Medicine Woods trail identify plants and explain how Native American peoples used them as foods, medicines, and dyes. ⊠ *Kearsarge Mountain Rd., 03278,* ☎ *603/456–2600.* ⊡ *$6.* ⊙ *May–mid-Dec., Mon.–Sat. 10–5, Sun. noon–5.*

A scenic auto road at **Rollins State Park** (⊠ off Rte. 103) snakes nearly 3,000 ft up the southern slope of Mt. Kearsarge, where you can then tackle on foot the ½-mi trail to the summit.

New London

39 *12 mi northwest of Warner, 10 mi west of Andover, 34 mi west of Concord.*

New London, the home of Colby-Sawyer College (1837), is a good base for exploring the Lake Sunapee region. Be sure to visit the 10,000-year-old **Cricenti's Bog,** off Business Route 11 (Business Route 11 goes right through town; Route 11 goes around town). A short trail, maintained by the local conservation commission, shows off the shaggy mosses and fragile ecosystem of this ancient pond.

Dining, Lodging, and Camping

$–$$ ✕ **Peter Christian's Tavern.** Exposed beams, wooden tables, a smattering of antiques, and half shutters on the windows make Peter Christian's a cool oasis in the summer and a cozy haven in winter. Tavern fare like beef stew and shepherd's pie has been updated for this century. ⊠ *186 Main St., 03257,* ☎ *603/526–4042. AE, D, MC, V.*

$$–$$$ ✕⬚ **Inn at Pleasant Lake.** This family-run property is aptly named for its location and ambience. The original farmhouse dates from 1790, and that early country look has been maintained by keeping frills to a minimum. Five acres of woods, fields, and gardens surround the inn. Candlelight and classical music accompany the restaurant's five-course prix-fixe dinner. ⊠ *Box 1030, 125 Pleasant St., 03257,* ☎ *603/526–6271 or 800/626–4907,* ℻ *603/525–4111. 12 rooms. Restaurant. Full breakfast. MC, V.*

$$ ✕⬚ **New London Inn.** The two porches of this rambling 1792 country inn overlook Main Street. Rooms have a Victorian decor; those in the front of the house overlook the pretty campus of Colby-Sawyer College. The nouvelle-inspired menu in the restaurant ($$–$$$; no lunch; closed on Sunday and Monday) starts with items like butternut squash with a sun-dried cranberry pesto and includes entrées like grilled cilantro shrimp with a saffron risotto. ⊠ *Box 8, 140 Main St., 03257,* ☎ *603/526–2791 or 800/526–2791,* ℻ *603/526–2749. 28 rooms. Restaurant. Full breakfast. No smoking. AE, MC, V.*

$–$$ ⬚ **Follansbee Inn.** Built in 1840, this quintessential country inn on the shore of Kezar Lake is a perfect fit in the 19th-century village of North Sutton, about 4 mi south of New London. The common rooms and bedrooms are loaded with collectibles and antiques. You can ice-fish on the lake and ski across it in the winter and swim or boat from the inn's pier in the summer. ⊠ *Rte. 114, North Sutton 03260,* ☎ *603/927–4221 or 800/626–4221. 23 rooms, 11 with bath. Lake, boating, fishing, ice-skating, cross-country skiing. Full breakfast. No smoking. No children under 8. MC, V.*

$ ⬠ **Otter Lake Camping Area.** The 28 sites on Otter Lake have plenty of shade and there are numerous activities. Facilities include a beach, boating, fishing, a recreation hall, a playground, and canoe and paddleboat rentals. ⊠ *55 Otterville Rd., 03257,* ☎ *603/763–5600.*

Nightlife and the Arts

The **New London Barn Playhouse** (⊠ Main St., ☎ 603/526–4631) presents on Broadway-style and children's plays every summer in New Hampshire's oldest continuously operating theater.

Outdoor Activities and Sports

Pleasant Lake, off Route 11 in Elkins, has salmon, brook trout, and bass.

Shopping

Artisan's Workshop (⊠ Peter Christian's Tavern, 186 Main St., ☎ 603/526–4227) carries jewelry, hand-blown glass, and other local handicrafts.

Skiing

Norsk Cross Country Ski Center. The 75 km (46½ mi) of scenic cross-country ski trails here are perfect for hiking in the warmer months. ⊠ *Rte. 11,* ☎ *603/526–4685 or 800/426–6775.*

Newbury

🔟 *10 mi south of New London, on the edge of Mt. Sunapee State Park; 38 mi west of Concord.*

Mt. Sunapee, which rises to an elevation of nearly 3,000 ft, and sparkling Lake Sunapee are the region's outdoor recreation center. **Mt. Sunapee State Park** (⊠ Rte. 103, ☎ 603/763–2356) has 130 acres of hiking and picnic areas, a beach, and a bathhouse. You can rent canoes at the beach or take a chairlift to the summit. In winter the mountain becomes a downhill ski area and host to national ski competitions. In summer the park holds the League of New Hampshire Craftsmen's Fair, a Fourth of July flea market, and the Gem and Mineral Festival. The **Lake Sunapee Association** (✉ Box 400, Sunapee 03782, ☎ 603/763–2495) has information about local events.

The narrated cruises aboard *MV Mt. Sunapee* (✉ Sunapee Harbor, ☎ 603/763–4030) provide a closer look at Lake Sunapee.

Camping

$ ⚠ **Crow's Nest Campground.** This year-round campground on the Sugar River has 100 sites, some on the river. The facilities include a recreation hall, a swimming pool, a children's wading pool, miniature golf in summer, and a warm-up room with fireplace for winter use. River swimming and fishing are summer pastimes; you can skate or sled in the winter, and area snowmobile trails connect to the campground. ✉ *Rte. 10, Newport 03773, ☎ 603/863–6170.*

Outdoor Activities and Sports

Lake Sunapee has brook and lake trout, salmon, smallmouth bass, and pickerel.

Shopping

Dorr Mill Store (✉ Rte. 11/103, Guild, ☎ 603/863–1197), the yarn and fabric center of the Sunapee area, has a huge selection of fiber.

Skiing

Sunapee. The state-run Sunapee may lack glitz and glamour, but its low-key atmosphere and easy skiing make it popular with locals and skiers from Boston, Hartford, and the coast. Black-diamond slopes now number six—including Goosebumps, a double-black diamond—so experts have some challenges. Two base lodges and a summit lodge supply the essentials. ✉ *Mt. Sunapee State Park, Rte. 103, 03772, ☎ 603/763–2356, 800/552–1234 for snow conditions, 800/258–3530 for lodging.*

DOWNHILL

This mountain is 1,510 vertical ft, the highest in southern New Hampshire, and has 31 km (19 mi) of gentle-to-moderate terrain with a couple of pitches that could be called steep. A nice beginner's section is beyond the base facilities, well away and well protected from other trails. Three triple and three double chairlifts and two surface lifts transport skiers.

CHILD CARE

The Duckling Nursery takes children from age 1 to 5. The Little Indians children's program gives ages 3 and 4 a taste of skiing, and SKIwee lessons are available for kids ages 5 to 12.

Enfield

④ *35 mi north of Newbury, 55 mi northwest of Concord.*

In 1782, two Shaker brothers from Mount Lebanon, New York, arrived at a community on the northeastern side of Mascoma Lake. Eventually, they formed Enfield, the ninth of 18 Shaker communities in this country, and moved it to the lake's southern shore, where they built more than 200 buildings. The Great Stone Dwelling is the largest Shaker structure ever built.

The **Enfield Shaker Museum** preserves the legacy of the Enfield Shakers. A self-guided walking tour takes you through 13 of the buildings that remain. The museum preserves and explains Shaker artifacts, and skilled craftspeople demonstrate Shaker techniques. Numerous special events take place each year. ⊠ *2 Lower Shaker Village Rd., 03748,* ☎ *603/632–4346.* ⛫ *$5.* ⊙ *Memorial Day–mid-Oct., Mon.–Sat. 10–5, Sun. noon–5; mid-Oct.–Memorial Day, Sat. 10–4, Sun. noon–4.*

Outdoor Activities and Sports

Rainbow trout, pickerel, and horned pout swim in **Lake Mascoma.**

Shopping

West Lebanon, just west of Enfield on the Vermont border, has a busy commercial section. The owners of the **Mouse Menagerie of Fine Crafts** (⊠ Rte. 12A, West Lebanon, ☎ 603/298–7090) have created a collector's series of toy mice and also sell furniture, wind chimes, and other gifts. The **Powerhouse Mall** (⊠ Rte. 12A, 1 mi north of Exit 20 off I-89, West Lebanon, ☎ 603/298–5236), a onetime power station, comprises three adjacent buildings of specialty stores, boutiques, and restaurants.

Hanover

42   *12 mi west of Enfield via Rte. 120 from Lebanon, 60 mi from Concord.*

Eleazer Wheelock founded Hanover's **Dartmouth College** in 1769 to educate Native American youth. Daniel Webster graduated in 1801. Robert Frost spent part of a brooding freshman semester on this campus before giving up on college altogether. Dartmouth is the northernmost Ivy League school and the cultural center of the region. The buildings that cluster around the green include the **Baker Memorial Library,** which houses literary treasures that include 17th-century editions of Shakespeare's works. If the towering arcade at the entrance to the **Hopkins Center** (☎ 603/646–2422) appears familiar, it's probably because it resembles the project that architect Wallace K. Harrison completed just after designing it: New York City's Metropolitan Opera House at Lincoln Center. The complex includes a 900-seat theater for film and music, a 400-seat theater for plays, and a black-box theater for new plays. The Dartmouth Symphony Orchestra performs here, as does the Big Apple Circus (in summer). In addition to the exhibits on African, Asian, European, and American art, the **Hood Museum of Art** owns the Picasso painting *Guitar on a Table,* silver by Paul Revere, and a set of Assyrian reliefs from the 9th century BC. Rivaling the collection is the museum's architecture: a series of austere redbrick buildings with copper roofs arranged around a small courtyard. Free guided tours are given on some weekend afternoons. ⊠ *Museum: Wheelock St.,* ☎ *603/646–2808.* ⊙ *Tues.–Sat. 10–5 (Wed. until 9), Sun. noon–5.*

Dining and Lodging

$$$$ ✕▥ **Hanover Inn.** Owned and operated by Dartmouth College, this
★   Georgian brick house rises four white-trimmed stories. The building was converted to a tavern in 1780 and has been open ever since. Rooms have Colonial reproductions, pastels, Audubon prints, and large sitting areas. The formal Daniel Webster Room ($$–$$$$) serves regional American dishes like soy-seared tuna steak with shrimp dumplings. The contemporary Ivy Grill prepares lighter meals. ⊠ *Box 151, The Green, 03755,* ☎ *603/643–4300 or 800/443–7024,* ℻ *603/646–3744. 92 rooms. 2 restaurants. AE, D, DC, MC, V.*

Outdoor Activities and Sports

The Connecticut River is generally considered safe after June 15, but canoeists should always exercise caution. This river is not for beginners. **Ledyard Canoe Club of Dartmouth** (☎ 603/643–6709) provides canoe and kayak rentals and classes.

Shopping

Goldsmith Paul Gross of **Designer Gold** (⊠ 3 Lebanon St., ☎ 603/643–3864) designs settings for color gemstones and opals—all one-of-a-kind or limited-edition. He also carries some silver jewelry by other American artisans.

Cornish

43 *18 mi south of Hanover on Rte. 12A, 70 mi northwest of Concord.*

The village of Cornish is best known for its four covered bridges, one of which is the longest in the United States: The **Cornish-Windsor Bridge** was built in 1866. It spans the Connecticut River, connecting New Hampshire with Vermont.

At the turn of the century Cornish was known primarily as the home of the country's then most popular novelist, Winston Churchill (no relation to the British prime minister). His novel *Richard Carvell* sold more than a million copies. Churchill was such a celebrity that he hosted Teddy Roosevelt during the president's 1902 visit. At that time the town was an enclave of artistic talent. Painter Maxfield Parrish lived and worked here, and sculptor Augustus Saint-Gaudens set up his studio and created the heroic bronzes for which he is known. The **Saint-Gaudens National Historic Site** contains the sculptor's house, studio, gallery, and 150 acres of grounds and gardens. Scattered throughout are full-size replicas of his works. There are two hiking trails on the property, the longer of which is the 2.5 mi Blow-me-down trail. ⊠ *Off Rte. 12A,* ☎ *603/675–2175.* ⊡ *$2.* ☉ *Memorial Day weekend–Oct., daily 9–4:30; grounds open until dusk year-round.*

Lodging

$$–$$$ ✕⌂ **Home Hill Country Inn.** This restored 1800 mansion set back from the river on 25 acres of meadow and woods is a tranquil place. The owners, from Provence, have given the inn a French influence with 19th-century antiques and collectibles. A suite in the guest house is a romantic hideaway. The dining room serves classic and nouvelle French cuisine like Vermont rabbit with prune Armagnac sauce or gulf prawns grilled and served with a saffron sauce. An extensive wine list complements the menu. ⊠ *River Rd., Plainfield 03781,* ☎ *603/675–6165. 6 rooms, 2 suites, 1 seasonal cottage. Pool, 9-hole golf course, tennis court, cross-country skiing. Continental breakfast. No children under 12. MC, V.*

$–$$ ⌂ **Chase House Bed & Breakfast Inn.** This 1775 Federal-style house
★ is the birthplace of Salmon P. Chase, who was Abraham Lincoln's secretary of the treasury, a chief justice of the United States, and a founder of the Republican Party. It's been restored to 19th-century elegance with Colonial furnishings and Waverly fabrics throughout. Ask for a room with a canopy bed or one with a view of the Connecticut River valley and Mt. Ascutney. The innkeeper will give you the history of the house and can point out all of the area's landmarks. ⊠ *R.R. 2, Box 909, Rte. 12A (1½ mi south of Cornish-Windsor covered bridge), 03745,* ☎ *603/675–5391 or 800/401–9450,* ℻ *603/675–5010. 4 rooms with baths, 2 doubles share bath, 2 suites. Exercise room, boating, snowshoeing. Full breakfast. No smoking. No children under 12. MC, V. Closed Nov.*

Nightlife and the Arts

The beautifully restored 19th-century **Claremont Opera House** (⊠ Tremont Sq., Claremont, ☎ 603/542–4433) hosts plays and musicals from September to May.

Outdoor Activities and Sports

Northstar Canoe Livery (⊠ Rte. 12A, Balloch's Crossing, ☎ 603/542–5802) rents canoes for half- or full-day trips on the Connecticut River.

Charlestown

44 *20 mi south of Cornish, 32 mi north of Keene.*

Charlestown has the state's largest historic district: 63 homes of Federal, Greek Revival, and Gothic Revival architecture are clustered about the center of town; 10 of them were built before 1800. Several merchants on Main Street distribute brochures that contain an interesting walking tour of the district.

The **Fort at No. 4,** which in 1747 was an outpost on the lonely periphery of Colonial civilization, is 1½ mi north of Charlestown. That year it withstood an attack by 400 French soldiers, which changed the course of New England history. Costumed interpreters at the only living-history museum from the era of the French and Indian War cook dinner over an open hearth and demonstrate weaving, gardening, and candlemaking. Each year the museum holds full reenactments of militia musters and battles of the French and Indian War. ⊠ *Rte. 11/Springfield Rd.,* ☎ *603/826–5700.* ⊇ *$6.* ☉ *Late May–mid-Oct., Wed.–Mon. 10–4 (weekends only 1st 2 wks of Sept.).*

On a bright, breezy day you might want to detour to the **Morningside Flight Park** (⊠ Rte. 12/11, ☎ 603/542–4416), not necessarily to take hang-gliding lessons, although you could. It's safer to watch the bright colors of the gliders as they swoop over the school's 450-ft peak.

Walpole

45 *12 mi south of Charlestown, 20 mi north of Keene.*

Walpole possesses yet another perfect town green. This one is surrounded by homes built about 1790, when the townsfolk constructed a canal around the Great Falls of the Connecticut River and brought commerce and wealth to the area. The town now has 3,200 inhabitants, more than a dozen of whom are millionaires.

The **Old Academy Museum** contains the original piano mentioned in Louisa May Alcott's *Little Women*; it had been a gift to the Alcott sisters. A printing plant operated in Walpole from 1793 to the 1820s. The museum has a large collection of books printed there and a genealogical section for people interested in researching ancestors from the area. ⊠ *Main St.,* ☎ *603/756–3449.* ☉ *Mid-June–mid-Sept. Wed., Sat., and Sun. 2–4 and by appointment.*

OFF THE
BEATEN PATH

SUGARHOUSES – Maple-sugar season is a harbinger of spring, occurring about the first week in March. The days become warmer but the nights are still frigid; this is when a drive along maple-lined backroads reveals thousands of taps and buckets catching the fresh but labored flow of unrefined sap. Plumes of smoke rise from nearby sugarhouses—where sugaring off, the process of boiling down this precious liquid, takes place. Many sugarhouses are open to the public; after a short tour and demonstration, you can sample the syrup with traditional unsweetened doughnuts and maybe a pickle—or taste hot syrup over fresh snow, a favorite confection. Open to the public are **Bacon's Sugar House** (⊠ 243 Dublin Rd., Jaffrey, ☎ 603/532–8836); **Bascom's** (⊠ Mt. Kingsbury, off Rte. 123A, Alstead, ☎ 603/835–2230), which serves maple pecan pie and maple milk shakes; and **Stuart & John's Sugar House & Pancake Restaurant** (⊠ Rtes. 12 and 63, Westmoreland, ☎ 603/399–4486), which offers a tour and pancake breakfast.

Keene

46 *20 mi southeast of Walpole, 53 mi west of Manchester.*

Keene is the largest city in the southwest corner, and the proud locus of the widest main street in America. **Keene State College,** hub of the local arts community, is on the tree-lined main street. The college's **Arts Center on Brickyard Pond** (☎ 603/358–2167) has three theaters and eight art studios. The **Thorne-Sagendorph Art Gallery** (☎ 603/358–2720) houses George Ridci's *Landscape* and presents traveling exhibitions. The **Putnam Art Lecture Hall** (☎ 603/358–2160) shows art films and international films.

Dining, Lodging, and Camping

$–$$$ ✕ **Mangos.** Paintings of fruits and vegetables on the wall and fruit-motif tablecloths adorn this restaurant that serves vegetarian dishes—try the grilled eggplant sandwich or the mixed grilled vegetables with a side of spicy pepper jelly—along with nonveggie fare like New Zealand rack of lamb and grilled Atlantic salmon. ⊠ *81 Main St.,* ☎ *603/358–5440. D, MC, V.*

$–$$ ✕ **One Seventy Six Main.** This restaurant in the heart of Keene has a relaxed atmosphere and a varied menu that runs the gamut from steak fajitas to blackened catfish. The bar stocks a an equally wide selection of domestic and imported beers. ⊠ *176 Main St.,* ☎ *603/357–3100. AE, D, MC, V.*

$$–$$$ ✕🏠 **Chesterfield Inn.** Surrounded by gardens, the Chesterfield sits
★ above Route 9, the main Brattleboro–Keene road. The spacious rooms, decorated with armoires, fine antiques, and period-style fabrics, have telephones in the bathroom and refrigerators. The views from the dining room (\$\$\$–\$\$\$\$) are of the gardens and the Vermont hills. Crab cakes with rémoulade and salmon with a mustard-mango glaze are among the menu highlights. ⊠ *Box 155, Rte. 9, Chesterfield 03443,* ☎ *603/256–3211 or 800/365–5515,* 📠 *603/256–6131. 11 rooms, 2 suites. Restaurant. Full breakfast. AE, D, DC, MC, V.*

$ 🏠 **Carriage Barn.** Antiques and wide pine floors lend this inn across from Keene State College a cozy charm. An expansive buffet is served each morning in the breakfast room, but many guests like to enjoy a second cup of coffee in the summer house under the lilacs. ⊠ *358 Main St., 03431,* ☎ *603/357–3812. 4 rooms. Continental breakfast. No credit cards.*

$ 🏕 **Swanzey Lake Camping Area.** This 82-site campground has a sandy beach, a dock, a ball field, a recreation area, and boat rentals. ⊠ *88 E. Shore Rd. (Box 115, W. Swanzey), 03469,* ☎ *603/352–9880.*

Nightlife and the Arts

The **Apple Hill Chamber Players** (⊠ E. Sullivan, ☎ 603/847–3371) produce summer concert series. The **Arts Center at Brickyard Pond** (☎ 603/358–2167) has year-round music, theater, and dance performances. The **Colonial Theatre** (⊠ 95 Main St., ☎ 603/352–2033) opened in 1924 as a vaudeville stage. It still hosts some folk and jazz concerts and has the largest movie screen in town.

Outdoor Activities and Sports

In the Monadnock region there are more than 200 lakes and ponds, most of which offer good fishing. Rainbow trout, smallmouth and largemouth bass, and some northern pike swim in **Spofford Lake** in Chesterfield. **Goose Pond** in West Canaan, just north of Keene, holds smallmouth bass and white perch.

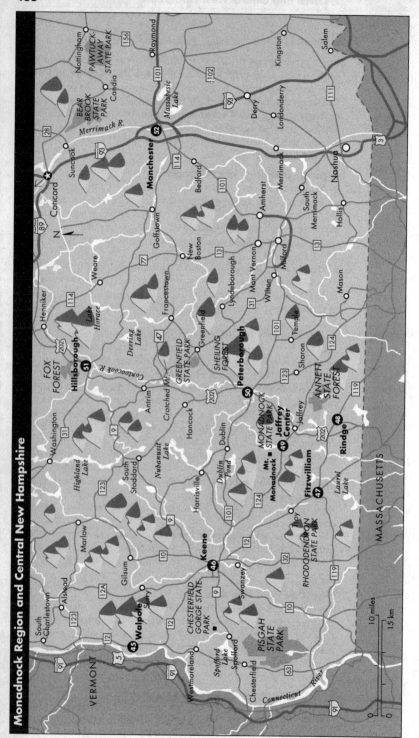

Monadnock Region and Central New Hampshire

Shopping

ANTIQUES

The more than 240 dealers at **Antiques at Colony Mill** (⊠ 222 West St., ☎ 603/358–6343) sell everything from furniture to dolls.

BOOKS

The extraordinary collection of used books at the **Homestead Bookshop** (⊠ Rtes. 101 and 124, Marlborough, ☎ 603/876–4213) includes biographies, cookbooks, and town histories.

MARKETPLACE

Colony Mill Marketplace (⊠ 222 West St., ☎ 603/357–1240), an old mill building, was converted into a shopping center whose stores and boutiques include **Autumn Woods** (☎ 603/352–5023), which sells fine Shaker-style furniture and Colonial reproductions; **Country Artisans** (☎ 603/352–6980), which showcases the stoneware, textiles, prints, and glassware of regional artists; the **Toadstool Bookshop** (☎ 603/352–8815), which carries many children's and regional travel and history books; and **Ye Goodie Shoppe** (☎ 603/352–0326), whose specialty is handmade chocolates and confections.

Fitzwilliam

47 *12 mi south of Keene, 50 mi southwest of Manchester.*

A well-preserved historic district of Colonial and Federal houses has made the town of Fitzwilliam, on Route 119, the subject of thousands of postcards—particularly views of its landscape in winter, when a fine white snow settles on the oval common. Town business is still conducted in the 1817 meeting house. The **Amos J. Blake House,** maintained by the Fitzwilliam Historical Society, contains a museum with period antiques and artifacts and the law office of its namesake. ⊠ *Village Green,* ☎ *603/585–7742.* ☉ *Late May–mid-Oct., Sat. and Sun. 1–4 or by appointment.*

More than 16 acres of wild rhododendrons burst into bloom in mid-July at **Rhododendron State Park.** This is the largest concentration of *Rhododendron maximum* north of the Allegheny Mountains. Bring a picnic lunch and sit in a nearby pine grove, or follow the marked footpaths through the flowers. ⊠ *Off Rte. 12, 2½ mi northwest of the common.* ☎ *603/532–8862.* ☞ *$2.50 weekends and holidays; free at other times.* ☉ *Daily 8–sunset.*

Dining and Lodging

$$–$$$ 🏨 **Inn at East Hill Farm.** At this 1830 farmhouse resort at the base of Mt. Monadnock, children are not only allowed, they are expected. In fact, if you don't have kids, you might be happier elsewhere. Children collect the eggs for the next day's breakfast, milk the cows, feed the animals, and participate in arts and crafts, storytelling, hiking, and games. Three meals, all served family-style, are included in the room rate. The innkeepers schedule weekly sleigh rides or hay rides and can whip up a picnic lunch for families who want to spend the day away from the resort. ⊠ *Monadnock St., Troy 03465,* ☎ *603/242–6495 or 800/242–6495,* FAX *603/242–7709. 65 rooms. Restaurant, indoor pool, 2 outdoor pools, indoor and outdoor whirlpools, wading pool, sauna, tennis, horseback riding, boating, waterskiing, fishing, baby-sitting. AP required. D, MC, V.*

$ 🏨 **Amos Parker House.** The garden of this old Colonial B&B is the
★ town's most stunning, complete with lily ponds, Asian stone benches, and Dutch waterstones. Two rooms have garden views. ⊠ *Box 202, Rte. 119, 03447,* ☎ *603/585–6540. 4 rooms. Full breakfast. No credit cards.*

$ ☒ **Hannah Davis House.** This 1820 Federal house has retained its el-
★   egance. The original beehive oven still sits in the kitchen, and one suite
has two Count Rumford fireplaces. The inn is just off the village
green—your host has the scoop on area antiquing. ☒ *186 Depot Rd.,*
03447, ☎ *603/585–3344. 6 rooms. Full breakfast. D, MC, V.*

Outdoor Activities and Sports

You can find rainbow and golden trout, pickerel, and horned pout in
Laurel Lake (Fitzwilliam). Rainbow and brown trout line the **Ashuelot
River.**

Rindge

🔵 *8 mi east of Fitzwilliam on Rte. 119, 42 mi southeast of Manchester.*

Cathedral of the Pines is an outdoor memorial to American men and
women, both civilian and military, who have sacrificed their lives in
service to their country. There's an inspiring view of Mt. Monadnock
and Mt. Kearsarge from the **Altar of the Nation,** which is composed
of rock from every U.S. state and territory. All faiths are welcome to
hold services here; there are organ meditations at midday from Monday to Thursday in July and August. The **Memorial Bell Tower,** with
a carillon of bells from around the world, is built of native stone; Norman Rockwell designed the bronze tablets over the four arches. Flower
gardens, an indoor chapel, and a museum of military memorabilia share
the hilltop. ☒ *75 Cathedral Entrance Rd., off Rte. 119,* ☎ *603/899–*
3300. ☉ *May–Oct., daily 9–5.*

Lodging

$–$$ ☒ **Woodbound Inn.** This rustic inn was built as a farmhouse in 1819
and became an inn in 1892. On 200 acres on the shores of Con-
toocook Lake, it is a favorite with families and people who fish. Accommodations are basic and range from traditional rooms in the main
inn to modern hotel-style rooms in the Edgewood building to cabins
by the water. ☒ *62 Woodbound Rd., 03461,* ☎ *603/532–8341 or 800/*
688–7770, ☏ *603/532–8341, ext. 213. 29 rooms with bath, 4 rooms*
share bath, 11 cottages. Restaurant, bar, lake, 9-hole golf course, ten-
nis court, croquet, hiking, horseshoes, shuffleboard, volleyball, fish-
ing, ice-skating, cross-country skiing, tobogganing, recreation room.
Full breakfast; MAP available. AE, MC, V.

$ ☒ **Cathedral House Bed and Breakfast.** This 1850s farmhouse on the
edge of the Cathedral of the Pines was the home of the memorial's
founder. Innkeepers Don and Shirley Mahoney are well versed in area
history. Rooms have high ceilings, flowered wallpapers, quilts, and
braided rugs, all of which combine to create the feeling that you've just
arrived at grandmother's house. ☒ *63 Cathedral Entrance Rd. 03461,*
☎ *603/899–6790. 1 room with bath, 4 rooms share 2 baths. Full break-*
fast. MC, V.

Jaffrey Center

🔵 *7 mi north of Rindge, 46 mi west of Manchester.*

Novelist Willa Cather came to the historic village of Jaffrey Center in
1919 and stayed in the Shattuck Inn, which now stands empty on Old
Meeting House Road. She pitched a tent not far from here in which
she wrote several chapters of *My Antonia.* She returned here nearly
every summer thereafter until her death, and was buried in the Old Burying Ground. **Amos Fortune Forum,** near the Old Burying Ground,
brings nationally known speakers to the 1773 meeting house on summer evenings.

The chief draw at **Monadnock State Park** is Mt. Monadnock. The oft-quoted statistic about the mountain is that it's the most-climbed mountain in America—second in the world to Japan's Mt. Fuji. Whether this is true or not, locals agree that it's never lonely at the top. Some days more than 400 people crowd its bald peak. Monadnock rises to 3,165 ft, and on a clear day the hazy Boston skyline is visible from its summit. The park maintains picnic grounds and some tent campsites and sells a trail map for $2. Five trailheads branch into more than two dozen trails of varying difficulty that wend their way to the top. Some are considerably shorter than others, but you should allow between three and four hours for any round-trip hike. A visitor center has a small museum documenting the mountain's history. ⊠ *2½ mi north of Jaffrey Center off Rte. 124, 03452,* ☎ *603/532–8862.* ☜ *$2.50.* ☉ *Year-round.*

OFF THE BEATEN PATH	**HARRISVILLE** – This perfectly preserved mill town was founded in 1774 by Abel Twitchell. The **Harris Mill,** an old woolen mill, still stands in the heart of town. The combination of red brick and blue sky reflecting off **Harrisville Pond** is worth at least one picture. **Harrisville Designs** (⊠ Mill Alley, ☎ 603/827–3996) operates out of a historic building and sells hand-spun and hand-dyed yarn sheared from local sheep, as well as looms for the serious weaver. The shop also hosts classes in knitting and weaving.

Lodging

$–$$ 🏠 **Benjamin Prescott Inn.** The working dairy farm surrounding this 1853 Colonial farmhouse makes guests feel as though they are miles out in the country rather than just minutes from Jaffrey Center. Stenciling, quilts handmade by innkeeper Jan Miller, and wide pine floors add to the country feel. A full breakfast of Welsh miner's cakes, baked French toast with apple or peach slices, and Jaffrey maple syrup prepares you for a day of antiquing or climbing Mt. Monadnock. ⊠ *Rte. 124, 03452,* ☎ *603/532–6637. 9 rooms, 3 suites. Full breakfast. No children under 10. AE, MC, V.*

Outdoor Activities and Sports

Gilmore Pond in Jaffrey has several types of trout.

Shopping

Sharon Arts Center (⊠ Rte. 123, Sharon, ☎ 603/924–7256) has a gallery that exhibits locally made pottery, fabric, and woodwork, and also houses a school with classes in everything from photography to paper marbling.

Peterborough

🔵 *8 mi north of Jaffrey, 40 mi west of Manchester.*

The nation's first free public library opened in Peterborough in 1833. The town, which was the first in the region to be incorporated (1760), is still a commercial and cultural hub. The **MacDowell Colony** (⊠ 100 High St., ☎ 603/924–3886) was founded by the composer Edward MacDowell in 1907 as an artists' retreat. Willa Cather wrote part of *Death Comes for the Archbishop* here. Thornton Wilder was in residence when he wrote *Our Town;* Peterborough's resemblance to the play's Grover's Corners is no coincidence. Only a small portion of the colony is open to visitors.

Dining and Lodging

$$–$$$ ✕ **Latacarta.** The innovative menu at Latacarta relies heavily on fresh, organic products. Start with gyoza, the pan-grilled Japanese dumplings filled with vegetables and tofu, and then try the Mongolian lamb mar-

inated in wine and served with a fresh ginger sauce. Dessert might be a mocha custard or wonderful hot pear crunch. ✉ *Noone Falls, Rte. 202,* ☎ *603/924–6878. AE, D, MC, V. Closed Sun. No lunch Sat.*

$$–$$$ ✕🏠 **Hancock Inn.** This Federal inn dates from 1789 and is the pride of the historically preserved town for which it's named. Common areas possess the warmth of a tavern, with fireplaces, big wing-back chairs, couches, dark-wood paneling, and Rufus Porter murals. Rooms, done in traditional Colonial style, have high four-poster antique beds. Updated Yankee fare is served by candlelight in the dining room. ✉ *Box 96, 33 Main St., Hancock 03449,* ☎ *603/525–3318,* FAX *603/525– 9301. 11 rooms. Restaurant, bar, air-conditioning. Full breakfast. AE, D, DC, MC, V.*

$$ ✕🏠 **Inn at Crotched Mountain.** This 1822 Colonial inn has nine fireplaces, four of which are in private rooms. The other five spread cheer among several common areas. The inn, whose rooms are furnished with early Colonial reproductions, is a particularly romantic place to stay when snow is falling on Crotched Mountain. The restaurant's multicultural menu includes Eastern specialties like Indonesian charbroiled swordfish with a sauce of ginger, green pepper, onion, and lemon; cranberry-port pot roast is one of the regional entrées. ✉ *Mountain Rd., Francestown 03043,* ☎ *603/588–6840. 21 rooms. Restaurant, bar, pool, tennis court, cross-country skiing. Full breakfast; MAP required weekends. No credit cards.*

$ ✕🏠 **Birchwood Inn.** Thoreau slept here, probably on his way to climb Monadnock or to visit Jaffrey or Peterborough. Country furniture and handmade quilts outfit the bedrooms, as they did in 1775 when the house was new and no one dreamed it would someday be listed on the National Register of Historic Places. In the dining room ($$; reservations essential; BYOB; no lunch; closed Sunday and Monday), she-crab soup, roast duckling, and fresh-fruit cobblers are often on the menu. Allow time for lingering. ✉ *Box 197, Rte. 45, Temple 03084,* ☎ *603/878–3285,* FAX *603/878–2159. 5 rooms with bath, 2 rooms share bath. Restaurant. Full breakfast. No smoking. No credit cards.*

$ 🏠 **Apple Gate Bed and Breakfast.** With 90 acres of apple orchards across the street, this B&B is appropriately named. The four rooms and even the yellow labrador, Macintosh, are named for types of apples. Some rooms are small, but Laura Ashley prints and stenciling make them cheery and cozy. The house dates from 1832, and the original beams and fireplace still grace the dining room. A music and reading room has a piano and a television with VCR tucked in the corner. From June to October, there's a two-night minimum on weekends. ✉ *199 Upland Farm Rd., 03458,* ☎ *603/924–6543. 4 rooms. Full breakfast. MC, V.*

Nightlife and the Arts

Monadnock Music (☎ 603/924–7610 or 800/868–9613) produces a summer series of concerts from mid-July to late August, with solo recitals, chamber music, and orchestra and opera performances by renowned musicians. At locations throughout the region, the concerts usually take place in the evening at 8 and on Sunday at 4; many are free. The **New England Marionette Theatre** (☎ 603/924–4022) is America's largest marionette theater devoted to opera. There are four performances a week from May to December. The **Peterborough Players** (✉ Stearns Farm, off Middle Hancock Rd., ☎ 603/924–7585) have performed for more than 60 seasons. Their plays are staged in a converted barn. The **Temple Town Band** (☎ 603/924–3478) was founded in 1799. Members range from teenagers to septuagenarians. The band plays a selection of patriotic songs, traditional marches, and show tunes at the Jaffrey Bandstand, the Sharon Arts Center, and local festivals and events.

Outdoor Activities and Sports

Several types of trout swim in **Dublin Pond.**

Shopping

The corporate headquarters and retail outlet of **Eastern Mountain Sports** (⊠ 1 Vose Farm Rd., ☎ 603/924–7231) sells everything from tents to skis to hiking boots, gives hiking and camping classes, and conducts kayaking and canoeing demonstrations. **North Gallery at Tewksbury's** (⊠ Rte. 101, ☎ 603/924–3224) stocks thrown pots, sconces, candlestick holders, and woodworkings.

En Route   If you travel from Peterborough to Amherst via Route 101, you'll pass **Miller State Park** (☎ 603/924–3672), where an auto road that takes you almost 2,300 ft up Mt. Pack Monadnock.

Hillsborough

51   *20 mi north of Peterborough via Rte. 202, 25 mi west of Manchester.*

The four villages that make up Hillsborough include Hillsborough Center, where 18th-century houses surround the town green. Many of the houses are still occupied by descendants of the original settlers who founded the town in 1769.

Franklin Pierce was born in Hillsborough and lived here until he married. The **Pierce Homestead,** operated by the Hillsborough Historical Society, welcomes visitors for guided tours. The house is decorated much as it was during Pierce's life. ⊠ *Box 896, Rte. 31, 03244,* ☎ *603/478–3165.* ☜ *$3.* ☉ *June and Sept.–Columbus Day, Sat. 10–4, Sun. 1–4; Jul. and Aug., Mon.–Sat. 10–4, Sun. 1–4.*

Lodging

$–$$ 🏠 **Inn at Maplewood Farm.** The white-clapboard 1794 farmhouse on the side of Peaked Hill beside a quiet country road may make you feel like you've been transported back in time. The rooms, three with fireplaces, have antiques and quilts but contain modern bathrooms. The luxurious Garden suite has a queen-sized canopy bed, a fireplace, a skylight over the bathtub, and a sitting area. All rooms have vintage radios so that guests can listen to the old-time radio shows broadcast nightly on the inn's transmitter. Breakfast here is a three-course event. You might be served chilled cantaloupe and strawberry soup with candied violets, lemon-blueberry scones, and cream-basil shirred eggs with maple-glazed ham. ⊠ *Box 1478, 447 Center Rd., 03244,* ☎ *603/464–4242,* ℻ *603/464–5401. 2 rooms, 2 suites. Guest kitchen with refrigerator and coffeemaker. Full breakfast. No smoking. AE, D, DC, MC, V. Closed Apr.*

Shopping

At **Gibson Pewter** (⊠ 18 East Washington Rd., ☎ 603/464–3410), the father and son team of Raymond and Jonathan Gibson create and sell museum-quality, lead-free pewter in contemporary and traditional designs. Visitors are welcome to watch them work. **William Thomas, Master Cabinetmaker** (⊠ 217 Saw Mill Rd., ☎ 603/478–3488), a founding member of the New Hampshire Furniture Masters Association, creates well-crafted wood furniture.

Manchester

52   *25 mi east of Hillsborough, 23 mi north of the Massachusetts border via Rte. 3 or I–93.*

Manchester, with just over 100,000 residents, is New Hampshire's largest city. The town grew around the power of the Amoskeag Falls on the

Merrimack River, which fueled small textile mills through the 1700s. By 1828, a group of investors from Boston had bought the rights to the river's water power and built on its eastern bank the **Amoskeag Textile Mills.** In 1906, the mills employed 17,000 people and churned out more than 4 million yards of cloth per week. The enterprise formed the entire economic base of Manchester—when it closed in 1936, the town was devastated. As part of an economic recovery plan, the mill buildings have been converted into warehouses, classrooms, restaurants, and office space. You can wander among these huge blood-red buildings; contact the **Manchester Historic Association** (⌂ 129 Amherst St., ☎ 603/622–7531) for a map.

The **Currier Gallery of Art,** in a 1929 Beaux Arts Italianate building downtown, has a permanent collection of European and American paintings, sculpture, and decorative arts from the 13th to the 20th century. Frank Lloyd Wright designed the Zimmerman House, built in 1950. Wright called this sparse, utterly functional living space "Usonian." The house is New England's only Wright-designed residence open to the public. ⌂ *201 Myrtle Way, 03104,* ☎ *603/669–6144, 603/626–4158 for Zimmerman House tours.* ☞ *$5; free Sat. 10–1; Zimmerman House $7 (reservations required).* ⊙ *Call for tour times.*

⌘ Children and adults enjoy watching the salmon, shad, and herring "climb" the **Amoskeag Fishways** fish ladder at the Amoskeag Dam during the migration period, from May to June. The visitor center has an underwater viewing window, interactive exhibits, and a hydroelectric-station viewing area. ⌂ *Fletcher St.,* ☎ *603/626–3474.* ⊙ *Call for hrs.*

Dining and Lodging

$$$–$$$$ ✕⊞ **Bedford Village Inn.** This luxurious Federal-style inn, just minutes from Manchester, was once a working farm and still shows horse-nuzzle marks on its old beams. Gone, however, are the hayloft and the old milking room, which have been converted into lavish suites containing king-size beds, imported marble in the whirlpool baths, and three telephones. The tavern has seven intimate dining rooms, each with original wide pine floors and huge fireplaces. The menu, which often includes New England favorites like lobster and Atlantic salmon with a chardonnay beurre blanc, changes every two weeks. ⌂ *2 Village Inn La., Bedford 03110,* ☎ *603/472–2001 or 800/852–1166,* ℻ *603/472–2379. 12 suites, 2 apartments. Restaurant, meeting rooms. AE, DC, MC, V.*

Nightlife and the Arts

American Stage Festival (⌂ 14 Court St., Nashua, ☎ 603/886–7000) is the state's largest professional theater. The season runs from early June to Labor Day and includes five Broadway plays, one new work, and a children's-theater series.

Shopping

Try **Bell Hill Antiques** (⌂ Rte. 101 at Bell Hill Rd., Bedford, ☎ 603/472–5580) for country furniture, glass, and china. The enormous **Mall of New Hampshire** (⌂ 1500 S. Willow St., ☎ 603/622–7833) has every conceivable store and is anchored by Sears and Filene's.

Western and Central New Hampshire A to Z

Arriving and Departing

BY BUS

Concord Trailways (☎ 800/639–3317) runs from Concord to Boston. **Vermont Transit** (☎ 603/351–1331 or 800/451–3293) links the cities of western New Hampshire with major cities in the eastern United States.

Most people who travel up from Massachusetts do so on I–93, which passes through Manchester and Concord before cutting a path through the White Mountains. I–89 connects Concord, in the Merrimack Valley, with Vermont. Route 12 runs north–south along the Connecticut River. Farther south, Route 101 connects Keene and Manchester, then continues to the seacoast.

BY PLANE

Manchester Airport (☞ Arriving and Departing *in* New Hampshire A to Z, at the end of this chapter) is the main airport in western and central New Hampshire. Colgan Air offers flights to Rutland, Vermont, and Newark, New Jersey, from **Keene Airport** (⊠ Rte. 32 off Rte. 12, North Swanzey, ☎ 603/355–4883). **Lebanon Municipal Airport** (☎ 603/298–8878), near Dartmouth College, is served by US Airways. *See* Air Travel *in* The Gold Guide for airline phone numbers.

Getting Around

BY BUS

Advance Transit (☎ 802/295–1824) stops in Enfield and Hanover.

Keene City Express (☎ 603/352–8494) buses run from 9 AM to 4 PM.

Manchester Transit Authority (☎ 603/623–8801) has hourly local bus service around town and to Bedford from 6 AM to 6 PM.

BY CAR

Routes 12 and 12A are picturesque but slow-moving. Route 4 crosses the region, winding between Lebanon and the seacoast. Other pretty routes include 101, 202, and 11.

Contacts and Resources

BIKING

For information on organized bike rides in southern New Hampshire contact the **Granite State Wheelmen** (⊠ 16 Clinton St., Salem 03079, ☎ no phone). Eastern Mountain Sports (☞ Shopping *in* Peterborough, *above*) and the **Greater Keene Chamber of Commerce** (⊠ 8 Central Sq., Keene 03431, ☎ 603/352–1303) have maps of and information about local bike routes.

EMERGENCIES

Cheshire Medical Center (⊠ 580 Court St., Keene, ☎ 603/352–4111). **Concord Hospital** (⊠ 250 Pleasant St., Concord, ☎ 603/225–2711). **Dartmouth Hitchcock Medical Center** (⊠ 1 Medical Center Dr., Lebanon, ☎ 603/650–5000). **Elliot Hospital** (⊠ 1 Elliot Way, Manchester, ☎ 603/669–5300 or 800/235–5468). **Monadnock Community Hospital** (⊠ 452 Old Street Rd., Peterborough, ☎ 603/924–7191). **Nashua Memorial Hospital** (⊠ 8 Prospect St., Nashua, ☎ 603/883–5521).

Monadnock Mutual Aid (☎ 603/352–1100) responds to any emergency, from a medical problem to a car fire.

FISHING

For word on what's biting where, contact the **Department of Fish and Game** (☎ 603/352–9669) in Keene.

RESERVATION SERVICE

The **Sunapee Area Lodging and Information Service** (☎ 800/258–3530) can help with reservations.

STATE PARKS

In addition to the state parks described above, **Bear Den Geological Park** (⊠ Gilsum) is a 19th-century mining town surrounded by more than 50 abandoned mines; **Curtiss Dogwood State Reservation** (⊠

Lyndeborough, off Rte. 31) shimmers with dogwood blossoms in early May; and the 13,000-acre **Pisgah State Park** (⊠ Off Rte. 63 or Rte. 119), the largest wilderness area in the state, lures hikers, bikers, fisherfolk, and skiers.

VISITOR INFORMATION

Concord Chamber of Commerce (⊠ 244 N. Main St., Concord 03301, ☎ 603/224–2508). **Hanover Chamber of Commerce** (⊠ Box A-105, Hanover 03755, ☎ 603/643–3115). **Keene Chamber of Commerce** (⊠ 48 Central Sq., Keene 03431, ☎ 603/352–1308). **Lake Sunapee Business Association** (⊠ Box 400, Sunapee 03782, ☎ 603/763–2495; 800/258–3530 in New England). **Manchester Chamber of Commerce** (⊠ 889 Elm St., Manchester 03101, ☎ 603/666–6600). **Monadnock Travel Council** (⊠ 8 Central Sq., Keene 03431, ☎ 603/355–8155). **Peterborough Chamber of Commerce** (⊠ Box 401, Peterborough 03458, ☎ 603/924–7234). **Southern New Hampshire Visitor & Convention Bureau** (⊠ 1 Airport Rd., Suite 198, Manchester 03103, ☎ 603/645–9889).

NEW HAMPSHIRE A TO Z

Arriving and Departing

By Bus
C&J (☎ 603/431–2424) serves the seacoast area of New Hampshire. **Concord Trailways** (☎ 603/228–3300) links the capital with other parts of the state. **Vermont Transit** (☎ 603/228–3300 or 800/451–3292) links the cities of western New Hampshire with major cities in the eastern United States.

By Car
Interstate 93 is the principal north–south route through Manchester, Concord, and central New Hampshire. To the west, I–91 traces the Vermont–New Hampshire border. To the east, I–95, which is a toll road, passes through the coastal area of southern New Hampshire on its way from Massachusetts to Maine. Interstate 89 travels from Concord to Montpelier and Burlington, Vermont.

By Plane
Manchester Airport (☎ 603/624–6539), the state's largest airport, has scheduled flights by Continental, Delta, United, and US Airways. *See* Air Travel *in* the Gold Guide for airline phone numbers.

Getting Around

By Bus
See Arriving and Departing, *above,* and the A to Z sections of the New Hampshire regions covered in this chapter.

By Car
The official state map, available free from the Office of Travel and Tourism Development (☞ Visitor Information, *below*), has directories for each of the tourist areas.

By Plane
Small local airports that handle charters and private planes are **Berlin Airport** (☎ 603/449–7383) in Milan, **Concord Airport** (☎ 603/229–1760), **Jaffrey Municipal Airport** (☎ 603/532–7763), **Laconia Airport** (☎ 603/524–5003), **Nashua Municipal Airport** (☎ 603/882–0661), and, in Rochester, **Sky Haven Airport** (☎ 603/332–0005).

Contacts and Resources

Biking

Bike & Hike New Hampshire's Lakes (☎ 603/968–3775), **Bike the Whites** (☎ 800/933–3902), **Great Outdoors Hiking & Biking Tours** (☎ 603/356–3271 or 800/525–9100), **Monadnock Bicycle Touring** (⊠ Box 19, Harrisville 03450, ☎ 603/827–3925), **New England Hiking Holidays** (☎ 603/356–9696 or 800/869–0949), and **Sunapee Inns Hike & Bike Tours** (☎ 800/662–6005) organize bike tours.

Bird-Watching

Audubon Society of New Hampshire (⊠ 3 Silk Farm Rd., Concord 03301, ☎ 603/224–9909) schedules monthly field trips throughout the state and a fall bird-watching tour to Star Isle and other parts of the Isles of Shoals.

Camping

New Hampshire Campground Owners Association (⊠ Box 320, Twin Mountain 03595, ☎ 603/846–5511 or 800/822–6764, FAX 603/846–2151) publishes a guide to private, state, and national-forest campgrounds.

Visitor Information

New Hampshire Office of Travel and Tourism Development (⊠ Box 1856, Concord 03302, ☎ 603/271–2343; 800/386–4664 for a free vacation packett). **Events, foliage, and ski conditions** (☎ 800/258–3608 or 800/262–6660). **New Hampshire Parks Department** (☎ 603/271–3556). **New Hampshire State Council on the Arts** (⊠ 40 N. Main St., Concord 03301, ☎ 603/271–2789).

7 Maine

At its extremes Maine measures 300 miles by 200 miles; all the other states in New England could fit within its perimeters. The Kennebunks hold classic townscapes, rocky shorelines, sandy beaches, and quaint downtown districts. Portland has the state's best selection of restaurants, shops, and culture. Freeport is a mecca for outlet shoppers. North of Portland, sandy beaches give way to rocky coast. Acadia National Park is Maine's principal tourist attraction. Outdoors enthusiasts head to inland Maine's lakes and mountains and the vast North Woods.

Revised and
updated by
Hilary M.
Nangle

ON THE MAINE–NEW HAMPSHIRE BORDER is a sign that plainly announces the philosophy of the region: WELCOME TO MAINE: THE WAY LIFE SHOULD BE. Local folk say too many cars are on the road when you can't make it through the traffic signal on the first try. Romantics luxuriate upon the feeling of a down comforter on an old, yellowed pine bed or in the sensation of the wind and salt spray on their faces while cruising in a historic windjammer. Families love the unspoiled beaches and safe inlets dotting the shoreline and the clear inland lakes. Hikers and campers are revived by the exalting and exhausting climb to the top of Mt. Katahdin, and adventure seekers get their thrills rafting the Kennebec or Penobscot River.

There is an expansiveness to Maine, a sense of distance between places that hardly exists elsewhere in New England, and along with the sheer size and spread of the place there is a tremendous variety of terrain. One speaks of "coastal" Maine and "inland" Maine, as though the state could be summed up under the twin emblems of lobsters and pine trees. Yet the topography and character in this state are a good deal more complicated.

Even the coast is several places in one. Portland may be Maine's largest city, but its attitude is decidedly more big town than small city. South of this rapidly gentrifying city, Ogunquit, Kennebunkport, Old Orchard Beach (sometimes called the Québec Riviera because of its popularity with French Canadians), and other resort towns predominate along a reasonably smooth shoreline. North of Portland and Casco Bay, secondary roads turn south off Route 1 onto so many oddly chiseled peninsulas that it's possible to drive for days without retracing your route. Slow down to explore the museums, galleries, and shops in the larger towns, and the antiques and curio shops and harborside lobster shacks in the smaller fishing villages found on the peninsulas. Freeport is an entity unto itself, a place where a bewildering assortment of off-price, name-brand outlets has sprung up around the famous outfitter L. L. Bean.

Inland Maine likewise defies characterization. For one thing, a lot of it is virtually uninhabited. This is the land Henry David Thoreau wrote about in *The Maine Woods* more than 150 years ago; aside from having been logged over several times, much of it hasn't changed since Thoreau and his Native American guides passed through. Ownership of vast portions of northern Maine by forest-products corporations has kept out subdivision and development; many of the roads here are private, open to travel only by permit.

Wealthy summer visitors, or "sports," came to Maine beginning in the late 1800s to hunt, fish, and play in the clean air and clean water. The state's more than 6,000 lakes and more than 3,000 mi of rivers and streams still attract such folks, and more and more families, for the same reasons. Sporting camps still thrive around Greenville, Rangeley, and in the Great North Woods.

Logging in the north created the culture of the mill towns, the Rumfords, Skowhegans, Millinockets, and Bangors that lie at the end of the old river drives. The logs arrive by truck today, but Maine's harvested wilderness still feeds the mills and the nation's hunger for paper.

Our hunger for potatoes has given rise to an entirely different Maine culture, in one of the most isolated agricultural regions of the country. Northeastern Aroostook County is where the Maine potatoes come from. This place is also changing. In what was once called the

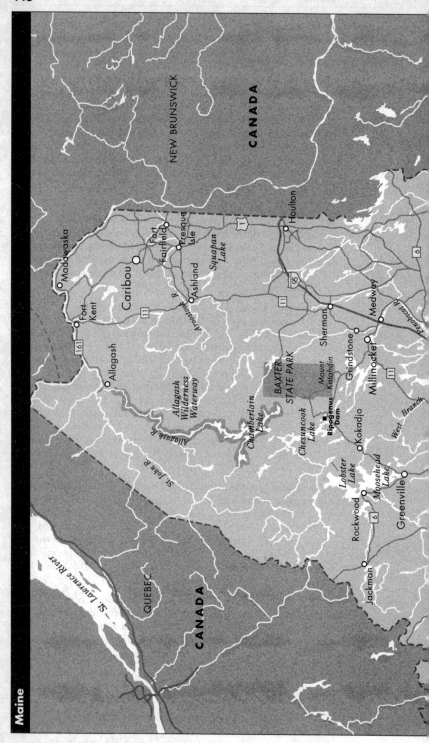

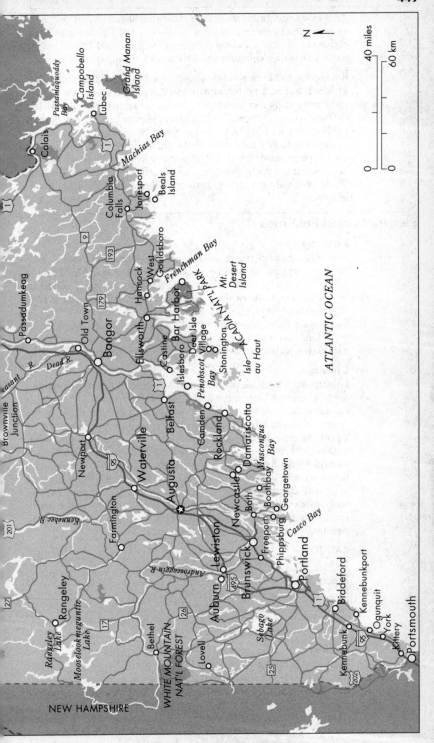

Potato Empire, farmers are as pressed between high costs and low prices as any of their counterparts in the Midwest, and a growing national preference for Idaho baking potatoes to small, round Maine boiling potatoes has only compounded Aroostook's troubles.

If you come to Maine seeking an untouched fishing village with locals gathered around a potbellied stove in the general store, you'll likely come away sadly disappointed; that innocent age has passed in all but the most remote villages. Tourism has supplanted fishing, logging, and potato farming as Maine's number one industry; most areas are well equipped to receive the annual onslaught of visitors. But whether you are stepping outside a motel room for an evening walk or watching a boat rock at its anchor, you can sense the infinity of the natural world. Wilderness is always nearby, growing to the edges of the most urbanized spots.

Pleasures and Pastimes

Boating

Maine's long coastline is justifiably famous: All visitors should get on the water, whether on a mail boat headed for Monhegan Island for the day or on a windjammer for a relaxing weeklong vacation. Windjammers, traditional two- or three-masted tall ships, sail past long, craggy fingers of land that jut into a sea dotted with more than 2,000 islands. Sail among these islands and you'll see hidden coves, lighthouses, boat-filled harbors, and quiet fishing villages. Most windjammers depart from Rockland, Rockport, or Camden, all ports on Penobscot Bay.

Dining

Lobster and Maine are synonymous. As a general rule, the closer you are to a working harbor, the fresher your lobster will be. Aficionados eschew ordering lobster in restaurants, preferring to eat them "in the rough" at classic lobster pounds, where you select your dinner out of a pool and enjoy it at a waterside picnic table. Shrimp, scallops, clams, mussels, and crab are also caught in the cold waters off Maine. Restaurants in Portland and in resort towns prepare shellfish in creative combinations with lobster, haddock, salmon, and swordfish. Blueberries are grown commercially in Maine, and Maine cooks use them generously in pancakes, muffins, jams, pies, and cobblers. Full country breakfasts of fruit, eggs, breakfast meats, pancakes, and muffins are commonly served at inns and bed-and-breakfasts.

CATEGORY	COST*
$$$$	over $45
$$$	$30–$45
$$	$15–$30
$	under $15

average cost of a three-course dinner, per person, excluding drinks, service, and 7% restaurant sales tax

Hiking

From seaside rambles to backwoods hiking, Maine has a walk for everyone. This state's beaches are mostly hard packed and good for walking. Many coastal communities, such as York, Ogunquit, and Bar Harbor, have shoreside paths for people who want to keep sand out of their shoes yet enjoy the sound of the crashing surf and the cliff-top views of inlets and coves. And those who like to walk in the woods will not be disappointed: Ninety percent of the state is forested land. Acadia National Park has more than 150 mi of hiking trails, and within Baxter State Park are the northern end of the Appalachian Trail and Mt. Katahdin, at nearly 1 mi high the tallest mountain in the state.

Lodging

The beach communities in the south beckon visitors with their weathered look. Stately digs can be found in the classic inns of Kennebunkport. Bed-and-breakfasts and Victorian inns furnished with lace, chintz, and mahogany have joined the family-oriented motels of Ogunquit, Boothbay Harbor, Bar Harbor, and the Camden–Rockport region. Although accommodations tend to be less luxurious away from the coast, Bethel, Carrabassett Valley, and Rangeley have sophisticated hotels and inns. Greenville and Rockwood have the largest selection of restaurants and accommodations in the North Woods region. Lakeside sporting camps, which range from the primitive to the upscale, are popular around Rangeley and the North Woods. Many have cozy cabins heated with woodstoves and serve three hearty meals a day (American Plan, or AP). At some of Maine's larger hotels and inns with restaurants, the Modified American Plan (MAP; rates include breakfast and dinner) is either an option or required during the peak summer season. B&Bs generally prepare full breakfasts, though some serve only a Continental breakfast, pastries and coffee.

CATEGORY	COST*
$$$$	over $150
$$$	$110–$150
$$	$70–$110
$	under $70

Prices are for a standard double room during peak season, excluding 7% lodging sales tax.

Skiing

Weather patterns that create snow cover for Maine ski areas may come from the Atlantic or from Canada, and Maine may have snow when other New England states do not—and vice versa. Thanks to Sunday River's owner, Les Otten, Maine is moving to the forefront of the regional skiing scene. Otten developed Sunday River from a small operation into one of New England's largest and best-managed ski resorts. Since acquiring Sugarloaf in 1996, he's focused much-needed attention there, upgrading lifts and snowmaking. It's worth the effort to get to Sugarloaf, which provides the only above-tree-line skiing in New England and also has a lively base village. Ski Mt. Abram, which sits in Sunday River's shadow, has also blossomed under new ownership, becoming a true family area with reliable skiing day and night as well as snow tubing.

Saddleback, in Rangeley, has big-mountain skiing at little-mountain prices. Its lift system is sorely out of date, but many would have it no other way, preferring its down-home, wilderness atmosphere. New ownership at Squaw Mountain in Greenville is making improvements. Its remote location ensures few crowds, and its low prices make it an attractive alternative to other big mountains. Shawnee Peak remains popular with families and for night skiing; by day the resort has awesome views of Mt. Washington. The Maine coast isn't known for skiing, but winter visitors to Camden will find a small, lively park, Camden Snowbowl, that has downhill skiing, tobogganing, and snow tubing as well as magnificent views over Penobscot Bay.

Exploring Maine

Numbers in the text and in the margin correspond to numbers and on the maps: Southern Main Coast, Portland, Penobscot Bay, Mount Desert Island, and Western Maine.

Great Itineraries

IF YOU HAVE 2 DAYS

Begin in **Ogunquit** ③ with a morning walk along the Marginal Way. Then head north to **Kennebunkport** ⑥, allowing at least two hours to wander through the shops and historic homes around Dock Square. Relax on the beach for an hour or so before heading to 🖼 **Portland** ⑧–⑬. If you thrive on arts and entertainment, spend the night here. Otherwise, continue north to 🖼 **Freeport** ⑯, where you can shop all night at L. L. Bean. On day two, head north, stopping in **Bath** ⑱ to tour the Maine Maritime Museum and finishing up with a lobster dinner on **Pemaquid Point** ㉑.

IF YOU HAVE 4 DAYS

From New Harbor on **Pemaquid Point** ㉑, take the boat to 🖼 **Monhegan Island** ㉓ for a day of walking the trails and exploring the artists' studios and galleries. The next day, continue northeast to **Rockland** ㉔ and 🖼 **Camden** ㉕. On day three, visit the Farnsworth Museum in Rockland, hike or drive to the top of Mt. Battie in Camden, and meander around Camden's boat-filled harbor. Or, bypass midcoast Maine in favor of 🖼 **Mt. Desert Island** ㉜–㊵ and Acadia National Park. To avoid sluggish traffic on Route 1, from Freeport, stay on I–95 to Augusta and the Maine Turnpike; then take Route 3 to Belfast and pick up Route 1 north there.

IF YOU HAVE 8 DAYS

Spend two days wandering through the gentrified towns and weather-beaten fishing villages from 🖼 **Kittery** ① to 🖼 **Portland** ⑧–⑮. On your third day explore Portland and environs, including a boat ride to **Eagle Island** ⑮ or one of the other Casco Bay islands and a visit to **Portland Headlight and Two Lights** in Cape Elizabeth. Continue working your way up the coast, letting your interests dictate your stops: outlet shopping in **Freeport** ⑯, Maine Maritime Museum in 🖼 **Bath** ⑱, antique shops in **Wiscasset** ⑲, fishing villages and a much-photographed lighthouse on **Pemaquid Point** ㉑. Allow at least one day in the **Rockland** ㉔ and 🖼 **Camden** ㉕ region before taking the leisurely route to **Bar Harbor** ㉜ via the **Blue Hill** ㉘ peninsula and 🖼 **Deer Isle Village** ㉙. Finish up with two days on 🖼 **Mt. Desert Island** ㉜–㊵.

When to Tour Maine

From July to September is the choice time for a vacation in Maine. The weather is warmest in July and August, though September is less crowded. In warm weather, the arteries along the coast and lakeside communities inland are clogged with out-of-state license plates, campgrounds are filled to capacity, and hotel rates are high. It's less busy midweek, and lodging rates are often lower then than on weekends.

Fall foliage can be brilliant in Maine and made ever more so by its reflection in inland lakes or streams or off the ocean. Late September is peak season in the north country, while in southern Maine the prime viewing dates are usually from October 5 to 10. In September and October the days are sunny and the nights crisp.

In winter, the coastal towns almost completely close down. If the sidewalks could be rolled up, they probably would be. Maine's largest ski areas usually open in mid-November and, thanks to excellent snowmaking facilities, provide good skiing often into April.

Springtime is mud season here, as in most other rural areas of New England. Mud season is followed by spring flowers and the start of wildflowers in meadows along the roadsides.

YORK COUNTY COAST

Maine's southernmost coastal towns, most of them in York County, won't give you the rugged, wind-bitten "down-east" experience, but they are easily reached from the south, and most have the sand beaches that all but vanish beyond Portland.

These towns are highly popular in summer, an all-too-brief period. Crowds converge and gobble up rooms and dinner reservations at prime restaurants. You'll have to work a little harder to find solitude and vestiges of the "real" Maine here. Still, even day-trippers who come for a few fleeting hours to southern Maine will appreciate the magical warmth of the sand along this coast.

North of Kittery, the Maine coast has long stretches of hard-packed white-sand beach, closely crowded by nearly unbroken ranks of beach cottages, motels, and oceanfront restaurants. The summer colonies of York Beach, Ogunquit, and Wells Beach have the crowds and ticky-tacky shorefront overdevelopment. Farther inland, York's historic district is on the National Register.

More than any other region south of Portland, the Kennebunks—and especially Kennebunkport—provides the complete Maine-coast experience: classic townscapes where white clapboard houses rise from manicured lawns and gardens; rocky shorelines punctuated by sandy beaches; quaint downtown districts packed with gift shops, ice-cream stands, and tourists; harbors where lobster boats bob alongside yachts; lobster pounds and well-appointed dining rooms.

These towns are best explored on a leisurely holiday of two days—more if one requires a fix of solid beach time. Route 1 travels along the coast. Inland, the Maine Turnpike (I–95) is the fastest route if you want to skip some towns.

Kittery

❶ *55 mi north of Boston, 5 mi north of Portsmouth, New Hampshire.*

Kittery, which lacks a large sand beach of its own, hosts a complex of factory outlets that makes it more popular, or at least better known with tourists, than the summer beach communities.

As an alternative to shopping, drive north of the outlets and go east on Route 103 for a peek at the hidden Kittery most tourists miss. Along this winding stretch are two forts. **Ft. Foster** (1872) was an active military installation until 1949. **Ft. McClary** (1690) was staffed during five wars. There are also hiking and biking trails, and, best of all, great views of the water.

Dining and Lodging

$$ ✕ **Warren's Lobster House.** A local institution, this waterfront restaurant specializes in lobster and seafood but also serves steak and chicken and has a huge salad bar. In season, you can dine outdoors overlooking the water in season. ⊠ *Rte. 1,* ☎ *207/439–1630. AE, MC, V.*

$$$ 🏨 **Gundalow Inn.** This brick Victorian built in 1889 on the old Kittery town green overlooks the Piscataqua River and Portsmouth Harbor. The rooms, some with water views, are named after gundalows, the sailing barges that worked the river for 250 years. Allow at least an hour for the sumptuous breakfast, served on antique china to the tune of classical music. ⊠ *6 Water St., 03904,* ☎ 🖶 *207/439–4040. 6 rooms. Full breakfast. D, MC, V.*

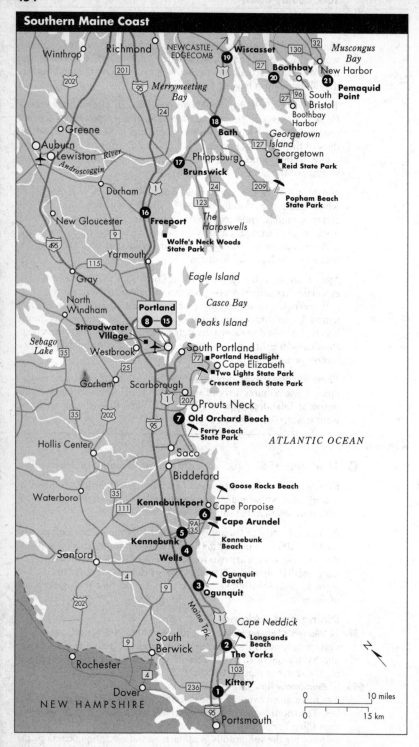

Nightlife and the Arts

Hamilton House (✉ Vaughan's La., South Berwick, ☎ 603/436–3205), the Georgian home featured in Sarah Orne Jewett's historical romance novel *The Tory Lover*, presents Sundays in the Garden, six summer concerts ranging from classical to folk music in July and August. Concerts ($5) begin at 4; the grounds are open from noon until 5 for picnicking.

Shopping

Kittery has more than 120 outlet stores. Along a several-mile stretch of Route 1 you can find just about anything you want, from hardware to underwear. Among the stores you'll encounter are Crate & Barrel, Eddie Bauer, Jones New York, Esprit, Waterford/Wedgwood, Lenox, Ralph Lauren, Tommy Hilfiger, DKNY, and J. Crew.

The Yorks

❷ *4 mi north of Kittery.*

The Yorks are typical of small-town coastal communities found in New England and are smaller than most. Many of their nooks and crannies can be explored in a few hours.

Most of the 18th- and 19th-century buildings within the **York Village Historic District** are clustered along York Street and Lindsay Road; some charge admission. You can buy an admission ticket for all the buildings at the **Jefferds Tavern** (✉ Rte. 1A at Lindsay Rd.), a restored late-18th-century inn. The **Old York Gaol** (1720) was once the King's Prison for the Province of Maine; inside are dungeons, cells, and the jailer's quarters. The 1731 **Elizabeth Perkins House** reflects the Victorian style of its last occupants, the prominent Perkins family. Members of the Old York Historical Society lead tours. ☎ 207/363–4974. ✒ *$6 for all buildings.* ☉ *Mid-June–Sept., Tues.–Sat. 10–5, Sun. 1–5.*

Get your camera ready for a photo of the essence of Maine. If you drive down Nubble Road from Route 1A and go to the end of Cape Neddick, you can park and gaze out at the **Nubble Light** (1879), which sits on a tiny island just offshore. The keeper's house is a tidy Victorian cottage with gingerbread woodwork and a red roof.

Route 1A runs right behind **Long Sands Beach,** which has free parking. The smaller **Short Sands Beach** has meter parking.

Dining and Lodging

$$–$$$ ✗ **Cape Neddick Inn.** The American bistro-style menu at this restaurant and art gallery changes with the seasons. Past offerings have included a pâté Duval appetizer and entrées like sage-roasted quail and poached Atlantic salmon on lobster succotash. ✉ *Rte. 1, Cape Neddick,* ☎ *207/363–2899. D, MC, V. Closed Mon. and mid-Oct.–May. No lunch.*

$$–$$$$ ✗▥ **York Harbor Inn.** A mid-17th-century fishing cabin with dark tim-
★ bers and a fieldstone fireplace forms the heart of this inn, to which various wings and outbuildings have been added over the years. The rooms are furnished with antiques and country pieces; many have decks overlooking the water, and a few have whirlpool tubs or fireplaces. The dining room has country charm and great ocean views. For dinner, start with Maine crab cakes, a classic Caesar salad, or a creamy seafood chowder, and then try the lobster-stuffed chicken breast or the angel-hair pasta with shrimp and scallops. ✉ *Box 573, Rte. 1A, York Harbor 03911,* ☎ *207/363–5119 or 800/343–3869,* ℻ *207/963–7151. 35 rooms, 1 suite. Continental breakfast. AE, MC, V. No lunch off-season.*

$$-$$$$ ☒ **Edward's Harborside.** This turn-of-the-century B&B sits on the harbor's edge and is just a two-minute walk from the beach. Rooms are spacious, with big windows to take in the water views. One room has a whirlpool tub. ⊠ *Box 866, Stage Neck Rd., York Harbor 03911, ☎ 207/363–3037. 4 rooms share 2 baths, 3 suites. Dock. Continental breakfast. MC, V.*

$$-$$$$ ☒ **Union Bluff.** This fortresslike white structure, with balconies across the front and turrets on the ends, sits right across from Short Sands Beach with views to forever. The best rooms are in the front, but many on the north side, which cost less, also have ocean views. ⊠ *Box 1860, 8 Beach St., York Beach 03910, ☎ 207/363–1333 or 800/833–0721, ℻ 207/363–1381. 36 rooms, 4 suites. Restaurant, pub. AE, D, MC, V. .*

$$$ ☒ **Cutty Sark Motel.** The rooms are standard motel fare, but you can't beat the oceanfront location, right on the edge of Long Sands Beach. Every room has an ocean view, and a light breakfast is included in the rate. ⊠ *58 Long Beach Ave., York Beach 03910, ☎ 207/363–5131 or 800/543–5131, ℻ 207/351–1335. 42 rooms. Continental breakfast. D, MC, V.*

Ogunquit

❸ *68 mi north of Boston, 39 mi southwest of Portland.*

Probably more than any other south-coast community, Ogunquit combines coastal ambience, style, and good eating. Shore Road passes the 100-ft **Bald Head Cliff,** which has views up and down the coast. On a stormy day the surf can be quite wild here. Shore Road will take you right into downtown Ogunquit. This coastal village became a resort in the 1880s and gained fame as an artists' colony. A mini Provincetown, Ogunquit has a gay population that swells in summer; many inns and small clubs cater to a primarily gay and lesbian clientele. Families love the protected beach area and friendly environment.

Perkins Cove, a neck of land connected to the mainland by Oarweed Road and a pedestrian drawbridge, draws visitors to its jumble of sea-beaten fish houses. These have largely been transformed by the tide of tourism to shops and restaurants. When you've had your fill of browsing and jostling the crowds at Perkins Cove, stroll out along the **Marginal Way,** a mile-long footpath that hugs the shore of a rocky promontory known as Israel's Head. Benches along the route give walkers an opportunity to stop and appreciate the open sea vistas, flowering bushes, and million-dollar homes.

Ogunquit Museum of American Art, in a low-lying concrete building overlooking the ocean, is set amid a 3-acre sculpture garden. Inside are works by Henry Strater, Marsden Hartley, Winslow Homer, Edward Hopper, Gaston Lachaise, Marguerite Zorach, and Louise Nevelson. The huge windows of the sculpture court command a view of cliffs and ocean. ⊠ *Shore Rd., ☎ 207/646–4909. ☜ $3. ☉ July–Sept., Mon.–Sat. 10:30–5, Sun. 2–5.*

Ogunquit Beach, a 3-mi wide stretch of sand at the mouth of the Ogunquit River, has snack bars, a boardwalk, rest rooms, and, at the Beach Street entrance, changing areas. Families gravitate to the ends; gay visitors camp at the beach's middle. The less-crowded section to the north is accessible by footbridge and has portable rest rooms, all-day paid parking, and trolley service.

Dining and Lodging

$$$$ ✗ **Arrows.** Elegant simplicity is the hallmark of this 18th-century farmhouse, 2 mi up a back road. Fillet of beef glistening in red and

yellow sauces, grilled salmon and radicchio with marinated fennel and baked polenta, and Chinese-style duck glazed with molasses are typical entrées on the daily-changing menu. Maine crabmeat mousse and lobster risotto appetizers and desserts like strawberry shortcake with Chantilly cream and steamed chocolate pudding are also beautifully executed. ⊠ *Berwick Rd.,* ☎ *207/361–1100. Reservations essential. MC, V. Closed Mon. and Dec.–late Apr. No lunch.*

$$–$$$ ✕ **Hurricane.** Don't let the weather-beaten exterior deter you—this small
★ seafood bar and grill with spectacular views of the crashing surf turns out first-rate dishes. Start with lobster chowder, a chilled fresh-shrimp spring roll, or the house salad (assorted greens with pistachio nuts and roasted shallots). Entrées include lobster cioppino, rack of lamb, and grilled venison loin. Save room for the classic crème brûlée. ⊠ *Perkins Cove,* ☎ *207/646–6348. AE, D, DC, MC, V. Closed late Dec.–mid-Jan.*

$$$–$$$$ 🏨 **Cliff House.** Elsie Jane Weare opened the Cliff House in 1872. Her granddaughter Kathryn now presides over this sprawling oceanfront resort comprising three buildings atop of Bald Head Cliff. Every room has a view of the water, which makes up for the unremarkable decor. ⊠ *Box 2274, Shore Rd., 03907,* ☎ *207/361–1000,* FAX *207/361–2122. 162 rooms. Restaurant, indoor and outdoor pools, hot tub, sauna, 2 tennis courts, exercise room. AE, D, MC, V. Closed mid-Dec.–late Mar.*

$$–$$$ 🏨 **The Rockmere.** Midway along Ogunquit's Marginal Way, this shingle-style Victorian cottage is an ideal retreat from the hustle and bustle of Perkins Cove. All the rooms have prized corner locations and are large and airy, and all but one have ocean views. You'll find it easy to laze the day away on the wraparound porch or in the gardens. ⊠ *Box 278, 40 Stearns Rd., 03907,* ☎ *207/646–2985. 8 rooms. Continental breakfast. AE, D, MC, V.*

Nightlife and the Arts

Much of the nightlife in Ogunquit revolves around the precincts of Ogunquit Square and Perkins Cove, where visitors stroll, often enjoying an after-dinner ice cream cone or espresso. Ogunquit is popular with gay and lesbian tourists, and its club scene reflects this.

The Club (⊠ 13 Main St., ☎ 207/646–6655) is Ogunquit's main gay disco. **Ogunquit Playhouse** (⊠ Rte. 1, ☎ 207/646–5511), one of America's oldest summer theaters, mounts plays and musicals with name entertainment from late June to Labor Day.

Outdoor Activities and Sports

Finestkind (⊠ Perkins Cove, ☎ 207/646–5227) operates cocktail cruises, lobstering trips, and cruises to Nubble Light.

Wells

❹ *5 mi north of Ogunquit, 35 mi southwest of Portland.*

This family-oriented beach community consists of several densely populated miles of shoreline interspersed with trailers and summer and year-round homes.

Wells Reserve sprawls over 1,600 acres of meadows, orchards, fields, salt marshes, and extensive trails, as well as two estuaries and 9 mi of seashore. The visitor center screens an introductory slide show and holds five rooms of exhibits. In winter, cross-country skiing is permitted. ⊠ *Laudholm Farm Rd.,* ☎ *207/646–1555.* 🎫 *Free; parking $7.* 🕙 *Grounds daily 8–5; visitor center May–Oct., Mon.–Sat. 10–4, Sun. noon–4; open sporadically in winter.*

A must for motor fanatics and youngsters, the 🐣 **Wells Auto Museum** has 70 vintage cars, antique coin games, and a restored Model T you can ride in. ⊠ *Rte. 1,* ☎ *207/646–9064.* ⊡ *$3.50.* ☯ *Mid-June–Sept., daily 10–5; Labor Day–Columbus Day, weekends 10–5.*

Dining and Lodging

$–$$ ✕ **Billy's Chowder House.** Tourists and locals head to the simple restaurant in a salt marsh for the generous lobster rolls, haddock sandwiches, and chowders. ⊠ *216 Mile Rd.,* ☎ *207/646–7558. AE, D, MC, V. Closed mid-Dec.–mid-Jan.*

$$ ✕🛏 **Grey Gull.** A century-old Victorian inn, the Grey Gull has views of the open sea and rocks on which seals like to sun themselves. The unpretentious rooms, most with ocean views, have shared or private baths. The restaurant ($$–$$$) serves excellent seafood dishes like softshell crabs almondine and regional fare such as Yankee pot roast or chicken breast rolled in walnuts and baked with maple syrup. Breakfast is popular here in summer: Blueberry pancakes, ham-and-cheese strata, or eggs McGull served on crab cakes with hollandaise sauce are good choices. ⊠ *475 Webhannet Dr., at Moody Point,* ☎ *207/646–7501,* ☏ *207/646–0938. 6 rooms, 2 with shared bath. Restaurant. Continental breakfast; MAP available. AE, D, MC, V.*

Outdoor Activities and Sports

Rachel Carson National Wildlife Refuge (⊠ Rte. 9) is a mile-long loop through a salt marsh bordering the Little River and a white-pine forest where migrating birds and waterfowl of many varieties are regularly spotted.

Shopping

Factory outlet stores along Route 1 from Kittery to Wells sell clothing, shoes, glassware, and other products from top-of-the-line manufacturers.

Kenneth & Ida Manko (⊠ Seabreeze Dr., ☎ 207/646–2595) sells folk art, rustic furniture, paintings, and 19th-century weather vanes. From Route 1 head east on Eldridge Road for a half mile, then turn left on Seabreeze Drive. **R. Jorgensen** (⊠ Rte. 1, ☎ 207/646–9444) stocks 18th- and 19th-century formal and country antiques from the British Isles, Europe, and the United States. **Douglas N. Harding Rare Books** (⊠ Rte. 1, ☎ 207/646–8785) has many old books, maps, and prints.

Kennebunk

❺ *5 mi north of Wells, 27 mi southwest of Portland.*

Large white clapboard homes with shutters lend Kennebunk a look that's quintessentially New England. The historic town is a fine place for a stroll. The cornerstone of the **Brick Store Museum,** a block-long preservation of early-19th-century commercial buildings, is **William Lord's Brick Store.** Built as a dry-goods store in 1825 in the Federal style, the building has an open-work balustrade across the roof line, granite lintels over the windows, and paired chimneys. Walking tours of Kennebunk's National Historic Register District depart from the museum on Friday at 1 and Wednesday at 10 from June to October. ⊠ *117 Main St.,* ☎ *207/985–4802.* ⊡ *$3.* ☯ *Tues.–Sat. 10–4:30.*

Kennebunk Beach has three parts: Gooch's Beach, Mother's Beach, and Kennebunk Beach. Beach Road, with its cottages and old Victorian boardinghouses, runs right behind them. Gooch's and Kennebunk attract teenagers; Mother's Beach, which has a small playground and tidal puddles for splashing, is popular with families. For parking permits (a fee is charged in summer), go to the Kennebunk Town Office (⊠ 1 Summer St., ☎ 207/985–2102).

Dining

$–$$ ✕ **The Impastable Dream.** If it's pasta you crave, head to this restaurant in an old Cape Cod cottage on Main Street. Tables are small and close together and the decor is simple, but the food is reasonably priced, plentiful, and very good. ⊠ *17 Main St.,* ☎ *207/985–6039. Reservations not accepted. D, MC, V.*

Shopping

J. J. Keating (⊠ Rte. 1, ☎ 207/985–2097) deals in antiques, reproductions, and estate furnishings. **Marlow's Artisans Gallery** (⊠ 39 Main St., ☎ 207/985–2931) carries a large and eclectic collection of crafts.

Kennebunkport

❻ *27 mi southwest of Portland, 10 mi northeast of Ogunquit.*

When George Bush was president, Kennebunkport was his summer White House. But long before Bush came into the public eye, tourists were coming to Kennebunkport to soak up the salt air, seafood, and sunshine. This is a picture-perfect town with manicured lawns, elaborate flower beds, freshly painted homes, and a small-town wholesomeness. Tourists flock to Kennebunkport mostly in summer; some come in early December when the **Christmas Prelude** is celebrated on two weekends. Santa arrives by fishing boat and the Christmas trees are lighted as carolers stroll the sidewalks.

The **Wedding Cake House,** on Summer Street (Route 35), has long been a local landmark. The legend behind this confection in fancy wood fretwork is that its builder, a sea captain, was forced to set sail in the middle of his wedding, and the house was his bride's consolation for the lack of wedding cake. The home, built in 1826, is not open to the public, but in the attached carriage house is a gallery and studio.

Route 35 merges with Route 9 in Kennebunk and takes you right into Kennebunkport's **Dock Square,** the busy town center. Boutiques, T-shirt shops, a Christmas store, a decoy shop, and restaurants encircle the square. Although many businesses close in winter, the best bargains often are had in December. Walk onto the drawbridge to admire the tidal Kennebunk River.

The very grand **Nott House,** known also as White Columns, is an imposing Greek Revival mansion with Doric columns that rise the height of the house. It is a gathering place for village walking tours, which are given on Wednesday and Friday in July and August. ⊠ *Maine St.,* ☎ *207/967–2751.* 🎟 *$3.* ☉ *June–late Oct., Wed.–Sat. 1–4.*

Ocean Avenue follows the Kennebunk River from Dock Square to the sea and winds around the peninsula of **Cape Arundel.** Parson's Way, a small and tranquil stretch of rocky shoreline, is open to all. As you round Cape Arundel, look to the right for the entrance to George Bush's summer home at Walker's Point.

♻ The **Seashore Trolley Museum** displays streetcars built from 1872 to 1972 and includes trolleys from major metropolitan areas and world capitals—Boston to Budapest, New York to Nagasaki, and San Francisco to Sydney, Australia—all beautifully restored. Best of all, you can take a trolley ride for nearly 4 mi over the tracks of the former Atlantic Shoreline trolley line, with a stop along the way at the museum restoration shop, where trolleys are transformed from junk into gems. ⊠ *Log Cabin Rd.,* ☎ *207/967–2800.* 🎟 *$8.* ☉ *May–mid-Oct., daily 10–5:30; reduced hrs in spring and fall.*

Goose Rocks, a few minutes' drive north of town, is the largest beach in the Kennebunk area and the favorite of families with small children. You can pick up a parking permit ($5 a day, $15 a week), at the Kennebunkport Town Office (⌧ Elm St., ☎ 207/967–4244) or the police department (⌧ Rte. 9, ☎ 207/967–2454).

Dining and Lodging

$$–$$$ ✕ **Windows on the Water.** This restaurant overlooks Dock Square and the working harbor of Kennebunkport. Lobster ravioli and rack of lamb are two noteworthy entrées. The special five-course dinner for two, including wine, tax, and gratuity (total: $82), is a good value if you have a healthy appetite. ⌧ *12 Chase Hill Rd.,* ☎ *207/967–3313. Reservations essential. AE, D, DC, MC, V.*

$–$$ ✕ **Alisson's.** A year-round favorite, this restaurant in the heart of Dock Square serves reliable salads, burgers, sandwiches, and dinner fare. ⌧ *5 Dock Square,* ☎ *207/967–4841,* FAX *207/967–2532. MC, V.*

$$$$ ✕🖬 **White Barn Inn.** For a romantic overnight stay or a superb meal,
★   you need look no further than the exclusive White Barn Inn, known for its attentive service. The meticulously appointed rooms have luxurious baths and are decorated with a blend of hand-painted pieces and period furniture; some rooms have fireplaces and whirlpool baths. Regional New England fare is served at the rustic but elegant dining room. The fixed-price menu, which changes weekly, might include steamed Maine lobster nestled on fresh fettuccine with carrots, ginger, and snow peas. ⌧ *Box 560C, 37 Beach St., 04046,* ☎ *207/967–2321,* FAX *207/967–1100. 18 rooms, 7 suites. Restaurant, pool, bicycles. Continental breakfast. Jacket required for dinner. AE, MC, V.*

$$$–$$$$ ✕🖬 **Cape Arundel Inn.** A new owner is updating this cottage-style inn and motel. The rooms are furnished with country-style furniture and antiques, and most have sitting areas with ocean views. Relax on the wraparound porch, furnished with antique white wicker, or in front of the living-room fireplace. In the candlelit dining room, open to the public for dinner, every table has a view of the surf. The entrées include seafood, lamb, duckling, and steak. ⌧ *Ocean Ave., 04046,* ☎ *207/967–2125,* FAX *207/967–1199. 13 rooms, 1 apartment. Restaurant. AE, D, MC, V. Closed early Dec.–early May.*

$$$$ 🖬 **Captain Lord Mansion.** Of all the mansions in Kennebunkport's historic district that have been converted to inns, the 1812 Captain Lord Mansion is the most stately and sumptuously appointed. The three-story Federal inn is topped with a widow's walk, from which guests can peer out over the town and harbor, just three blocks away. Distinctive architecture, including a suspended elliptical staircase, gas fireplaces in 14 rooms, and decorating of near museum quality, makes for a formal but not stuffy atmosphere. The most extravagant suite has fireplaces in the bathroom and the sleeping area, a double whirlpool, a hydro-massage body spa, a TV/VCR and stereo system, exercise equipment, and a king-size canopy bed. ⌧ *Box 800, Pleasant and Green Sts., 04046,* ☎ *207/967–3141,* FAX *207/967–3172. 16 rooms, 1 suite. Full breakfast. D, MC, V.*

$$$–$$$$ 🖬 **Bufflehead Cove.** On the Kennebunk River at the end of a winding dirt road, this gray-shingle B&B amid quiet country fields and apple trees is only five minutes from Dock Square. Rooms in the main house have white wicker and flowers handpainted on the walls. The Hideaway Suite, with a two-sided gas fireplace, king-size bed, and large whirlpool tub, overlooks the river. The Garden Studio has a fireplace and the most privacy. ⌧ *Box 499, Gornitz La., 04046,* ☎ *207/967–3879. 2 rooms, 3 suites. Dock. D, MC, V.*

$$$-$$$$ 🖬 **Maine Stay Inn and Cottages.** On a quiet residential street a short walk from Dock Square is the circa 1860 Maine Stay Inn. Two of the accommodations in the Italianate main house have fireplaces. Families often stay in the cottages, some with fireplaces and kitchens, behind the inn. ⊠ *Box 500A, 34 Maine St., 04046,* ☎ *207/967–2117 or 800/950–2117,* 🖾 *207/967–8757. 4 rooms, 2 suites, 11 cottages. Full breakfast. AE, MC, V.*

$$$-$$$$ 🖬 **The Seaside.** This handsome seaside property has been in the hands of the Severance family for 12 generations. The modern motel units, all with cable TVs and sliding-glass doors that open onto private decks or patios (half with ocean views), are appropriate for families; so are the cottages, which have from one to four bedrooms. The four bedrooms in the 1756 inn, furnished with antiques, are more suitable for adults. ⊠ *Gooch's Beach, 04046,* ☎ *207/967–4461. 26 rooms, 10 cottages. Beach, playground, laundry service. Continental breakfast for inn and motel guests. AE, MC, V. Inn rooms closed Labor Day–June; cottages closed Nov.–Apr.*

Outdoor Activities and Sports

Cape-Able Bike Shop (⊠ Townhouse Corners, ☎ 207/967–4382) rents bicycles. **Chick's Marina** (⊠ 75 Ocean Ave., ☎ 207/967–2782) conducts sightseeing and fishing cruises for up to six people. **First Chance** (⊠ Arundel Wharf, Lower Village, ☎ 207/967–5912) guarantees whale sightings. The **Indian** (⊠ Ocean Ave., ☎ 207/967–5912) runs trips to view the whale migrations.

Old Orchard Beach

❼ *18 mi south of Portland, 25 mi northeast of Portsmouth.*

Old Orchard Beach, a 7-mi strip of sand beach with an amusement park that's like a small Coney Island, is only a few miles north of Biddeford on Route 9. Despite the summertime crowds and fried-food odors, the atmosphere can be captivating. During the 1940s and '50s, in the heyday of the Big Band era, the pier had a dance hall where stars of the era performed. Fire claimed the end of the pier, but booths with games and candy concessions still line both sides. In summer the town sponsors fireworks (usually on Thursday night). The many places to stay run the gamut from cheap motels to cottage colonies to full-service seasonal hotels. The area is popular from July 4 to Labor Day with the Québecois. You won't find free parking anywhere in town, but there are ample lots.

☺ **Palace Playland** (⊠ Old Orchard St., ☎ 207/934–2001), which is open from Memorial Day to Labor Day, has rides, booths, and a roller coaster that drops almost 50 ft.

Lodging

$$$$ 🖬 **Black Point Inn.** Toward the top of the peninsula that juts into the ocean at Prouts Neck, 12 mi south of Portland and about 10 mi north of Old Orchard by road, stands a stylish, tastefully updated old-time resort with views up and down the Maine coast. Mahogany bedsteads, Martha Washington bedspreads, and white-ruffle priscilla curtains decorate the rooms. The extensive grounds contain beaches, trails, a bird sanctuary, and sports facilities. Seafood is the star attraction at the inn's restaurant. ⊠ *510 Black Point Rd., Scarborough 04074,* ☎ *207/883–4126 or 800/258–0003,* 🖾 *207/883–9976. 74 rooms, 20 suites. Restaurant, bar, indoor and outdoor pools, hot tub, golf, tennis courts, croquet, volleyball, boating, bicycles. AE, D, MC, V. Closed Dec.–Apr.*

Outdoor Activities and Sports

Shorebirds congregate at the **Biddeford Pool East Sanctuary** (⊠ Rte. 9, Biddeford). The **Maine Audubon Society** (⊠ Rte. 9, Scarborough, ☎ 207/781–2330 or 207/883–5100, from mid-June to Labor Day) operates guided canoe trips and rents canoes in Scarborough Marsh, the largest salt marsh in Maine. Programs at Maine Audubon's Falmouth headquarters include nature walks and a discovery room for children.

York County Coast A to Z

Arriving and Departing

BY CAR

Route 1 from Kittery is the shopper's route north; other roads hug the coastline. Interstate 95 is usually faster for travelers headed to towns north of Ogunquit. The exit numbers can be confusing: As you go north from Portsmouth, Exits 1–3 lead to Kittery and Exit 4 leads to the Yorks. After the tollbooth in York, the Maine Turnpike begins, and the numbers start over again, with Exit 2 for Wells and Ogunquit and Exit 3 (and Route 35) for Kennebunk and Kennebunkport. Route 9 goes from Kennebunkport to Cape Porpoise and Goose Rocks.

BY PLANE

The closest airport is the Portland International Jetport (☞ Arriving and Departing *in* Maine A to Z, *at the end of this chapter*), 35 mi northeast of Kennebunk.

Getting Around

BY CAR

Parking is tight in Kennebunkport in peak season. Possibilities include the municipal lot next to the Congregational Church ($2 an hour from May to October), the Consolidated School on School Street (free from late June to Labor Day), and, except on Sunday morning, St. Martha's Church (free year-round) on North Street.

BY TROLLEY

A **trolley** circulates among the Yorks from June to Labor Day. Eight trolleys serve the major tourist areas and beaches of Ogunquit, including four that connect with Wells from mid-May to mid-October. The trolley from Dock Square in Kennebunkport to Kennebunk Beach runs from late June to Labor Day. ☏ *$1–$3.*

Contacts and Resources

EMERGENCIES

Maine State Police (⊠ Gray, ☎ 207/793–4500 or 800/482–0730). **Kennebunk Walk-in Clinic** (⊠ Rte. 1 N, ☎ 207/985–6027). **Southern Maine Medical Center** (⊠ Rte. 111, Biddeford, ☎ 207/283–7000 or 207/283–7100 for emergency room).

VISITOR INFORMATION

Kennebunk-Kennebunkport Chamber of Commerce (⊠ 17 Western Ave., Kennebunk 04043, ☎ 207/967–0857). **Kittery-Eliot Chamber of Commerce** (⊠ 191 State Rd., Kittery 03904, ☎ 207/384–3338). **Maine Publicity Bureau** (⊠ Rte. 1 and I–95, Kittery 03904, ☎ 207/439–1319). **Ogunquit Chamber of Commerce** (⊠ Box 2289, Ogunquit 03907, ☎ 207/646–2939). **Wells Chamber of Commerce** (⊠ Box 356, Wells 04090, ☎ 207/646–2451). The **Yorks Chamber of Commerce** (⊠ Box 417, York, ☎ 207/363–4422).

PORTLAND TO PEMAQUID POINT

Maine's largest city, Portland, is small enough to be explored in a day or two. The Old Port Exchange, among the finest urban renovation projects on the East Coast, balances modern commercial enterprise and salty waterfront character in an area bustling with restaurants, shops, and galleries. Water tours of the harbor and excursions to the Calendar Islands depart from the piers of Commercial Street. Downtown Portland, in a funk for years, is now a burgeoning arts district connected to the Old Port by a revitalized Congress Street, where L. L. Bean operates a factory store.

Freeport, north of Portland, was made famous by its L. L. Bean store, whose success led to the opening of scores of other clothing stores and outlets. Brunswick is best known for Bowdoin College. Bath has been a shipbuilding center since 1607; the Maine Maritime Museum preserves its history. Wiscasset contains many antiques shops and galleries.

The Boothbays—the coastal areas of Boothbay Harbor, East Boothbay, Linekin Neck, Southport Island, and the inland town of Boothbay—attract hordes of vacationing families and flotillas of pleasure craft. The Pemaquid peninsula juts into the Atlantic south of Damariscotta and just east of the Boothbays. Near Pemaquid Beach one can view the objects unearthed at the Colonial Pemaquid Restoration.

This south mid-coast area provides an overview of Maine: a little bit of city, a little more coastline, and a nice dollop of history and architecture.

Portland

105 mi northeast of Boston, 320 mi northeast of New York City, 215 mi southwest of St. Stephen, New Brunswick.

Portland's first home was built on the peninsula now known as Munjoy Hill in 1632. When the Civil War broke out in 1861, Maine was asked to raise only a single regiment to fight, but the state raised 10 and sent the 5th Maine Regiment into the war's first battle at Bull Run. Much of Portland was destroyed on July 4 in the Great Fire of 1866, when a boy threw a celebration firecracker into a pile of wood shavings; 1,500 buildings burned to the ground. Poet Henry Wadsworth Longfellow said at the time that his city reminded him of the ruins of Pompeii. The Great Fire started not far from where tourists now wander the streets of the Old Port Exchange.

Congress Street runs the length of the peninsular city from alongside the Western Promenade in the southwest to the Eastern Promenade on Munjoy Hill in the northeast, passing through the small downtown area. A few blocks southeast of downtown, the bustling Old Port Exchange sprawls along the waterfront. Below Munjoy Hill is India Street, where the Great Fire of 1866 started.

❽ One of the notable homes on Congress Street is the **Neal Dow Memorial,** a brick mansion built in 1829 in the late Federal style by General Neal Dow, an abolitionist and prohibitionist. The library has fine ornamental ironwork, and the furnishings include the family china, silver, and portraits. Don't miss the grandfather clocks. ⊠ *714 Congress St.,* ☎ *207/773–7773.* 🎫 *Free.* ◷ *Tours weekdays 11–4.*

For well more than a century, the tower of the Morse-Libby House, **❾** better known as the **Victoria Mansion,** has been a landmark visible from Casco Bay and Portland's harbor. A National Historic Landmark, the Italianate-style villa, built between 1858 and 1860, is widely regarded

464

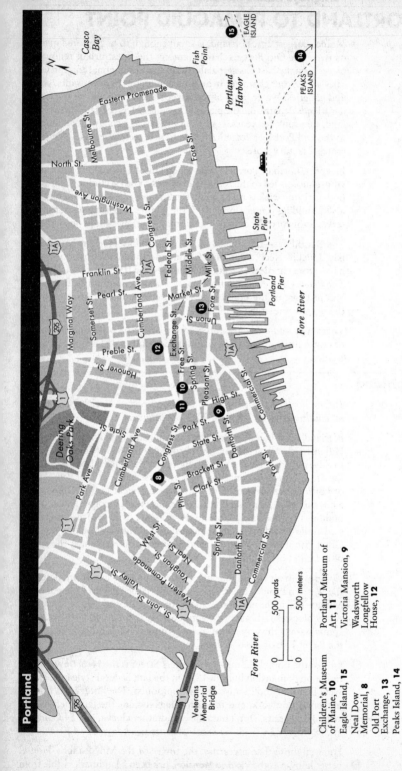

Portland

Casco Bay

Fish Point

Portland Harbor

EAGLE ISLAND

PEAKS ISLAND

Eastern Promenade

State Pier

Melbourne St.

North St.

Washington Ave.

Congress St.

Fore St.

Portland Pier

Fore River

Franklin St.

1A

Federal St.

Middle St.

Milk St.

Pearl St.

Cumberland Ave.

Market St.

Fore St.

Somerset St.

Exchange St.

Union St.

⑬

Marginal Way

Preble St.

⑫

Free St.

Hanover St.

Spring St.

⑩

Pleasant St.

1A

11

⑪

Park St.

High St.

Commercial St.

⑨

Deering Oaks Park

State St.

State St.

Danforth St.

York St.

Congress St.

Cumberland Ave.

⑧

Brackett St.

Park Ave.

Pine St.

Clark St.

11

11

West St.

Spring St.

Vaughan St.

Neal St.

Danforth St.

Western Promenade

St. John St.

Valley St.

Commercial St.

11

1A

95

Fore River

Veterans Memorial Bridge

11

0   500 yards

0   500 meters

as the most sumptuously ornamented dwelling of its period remaining in the country. The lavish exterior is understated compared to the interior, which has colorful frescoed walls and ceilings, ornate marble mantelpieces, gilded gas chandeliers, stained-glass windows, and a mahogany flying staircase. ⊠ *109 Danforth St.,* ☎ *207/772–4841.* ☑ *$5.* ☉ *May–Oct., Tues.–Sat. 1–4, Sun. 1–5.*

🖐 ❿ Touching is okay at the **Children's Museum of Maine,** where kids can pretend they are fishing for lobster or are shopkeepers or computer experts. Camera Obscura, on the third floor, charges a separate admission fee ($2). ⊠ *142 Free St.,* ☎ *207/828–1234.* ☑ *$4.* ☉ *Summer and school vacations, Mon.–Sat. 10–5, Sun. noon–5; during school yr., Wed.–Sat. 10–5, Sun. noon–5.*

⓫ The **Portland Museum of Art** has a strong collection of seascapes and landscapes by Winslow Homer, John Marin, Andrew Wyeth, Marsden Hartley, and other painters. Homer's *Pulling the Dory* and *Weatherbeaten,* two quintessential Maine coast images, are here. The Joan Whitney Payson Collection includes works by Monet, Picasso, and Renoir. Harry N. Cobb, an associate of I. M. Pei, designed the strikingly modern Charles Shipman Payson building. ⊠ *7 Congress Sq.,* ☎ *207/775– 6148.* ☑ *$6; free Fri. evenings 5–9.* ☉ *Tues.–Wed. and Sat. 10–5, Thurs.– Fri. 10–9, Sun. noon–5; also Mon. July–Columbus Day 10–5.*

⓬ The **Wadsworth Longfellow House,** the boyhood home of the poet and the first brick house in Portland, is worth a stop. The late Colonial–style structure, built in 1785, sits back from the street and has a small portico over its entrance and four chimneys surmounting the hip roof. Most of the furnishings are original to the house. Christmas is celebrated with special tours of the house that highlight a particular period in the history of the poet. ⊠ *485 Congress St.,* ☎ *207/879–0427.* ☑ *$4.* ☉ *June–Oct., Tues.–Sun. 10–4.*

★ ⓭ The **Old Port Exchange** bridges the gap between yesterday and today. Allow a couple of hours to wander at leisure on Market, Exchange, Middle, and Fore streets. Like the Customs House, the brick buildings and warehouses of the Old Port Exchange were built following the Great Fire of 1866 and were intended to last for ages. When the city's economy slumped in the middle of the present century, however, the Old Port declined and seemed slated for demolition. Then artists and craftspeople began opening shops in the late 1960s, and restaurants, chic boutiques, bookstores, and gift shops followed. You can park your car either at the city garage on Fore Street (between Exchange and Union streets) or opposite the U.S. Customs House at the corner of Fore and Pearl streets.

Crescent Beach State Park (⊠ Rte. 77, Cape Elizabeth, ☎ 207/767–3625), about 8 mi south of Portland, has a sand beach, picnic tables, a seasonal snack bar, and a bathhouse. Popular with families with young children, it charges a nominal fee for admittance. **Scarborough Beach Park** (⊠ Rte. 207, Scarborough, ☎ 207/283–0067) is a long sand beach on open ocean with primitive facilities; admission is charged in season.

OFF THE BEATEN PATH

CAPE ELIZABETH – This upscale Portland suburb juts out into the Atlantic. Take Route 77 south and east from Portland and follow signs to Two Lights State Park, home to one of the Cape's three lighthouses, where you can wander through old World War II bunkers and picnic on the rocky coast. Stay on Two Lights Road to the end, where you'll find another lighthouse, privately owned, and the Lobster Shack, a seafood-in-the-rough restaurant where you can dine inside or out. Return to the center of Cape Elizabeth and turn right on Shore Road, which winds along the coast to Portland. About 2 mi from town center is Fort Williams, a town-owned park where you'll find Portland Head Light, commissioned by George Washington in 1791. The keeper's house is now the **Museum at Portland Head Light.** ⊠ *Museum: 1000 Shore Rd.,* ☎ *207/799–2661.* ☞ *$2.* ☉ *June–Oct., daily 10–4.*

Dining and Lodging

$$–$$$ ✕ **Fore Street.** Two of Maine's best chefs, Sam Hayward and Dana Street,
★ opened this restaurant in an old warehouse on the edge of the Old Port Exchange. Every table in the two-level main dining room has a view of the enormous brick oven and hearth and the open kitchen, where entrées such as roasted Maine lobster, applewood-grilled Atlantic swordfish loin, or wood-oven braised cassoulet are prepared. ⊠ *288 Fore St.,* ☎ *207/775–2717. AE, D, MC, V.*

$$–$$$ ✕ **Street and Co.** You enter through the kitchen, with all its wonder-
★ ful aromas, and dine, amid dried herbs and shelves of staples, on one of a dozen copper-topped tables (so your waiter can place a skillet of steaming seafood directly in front of you). In one dining room is a beer and wine bar. Fish and seafood are the specialties here, and you won't find any better or fresher. The entrées include lobster diavolo for two, scallops in Pernod and cream, and sole Française. A vegetarian dish is the only alternative to seafood. ⊠ *33 Wharf St.,* ☎ *207/775–0887. AE, MC, V. No lunch.*

$$–$$$ ✕ **Wharf Street Café & Café Club.** Tucked away on cobblestoned Wharf Street, an alley that runs parallel to Fore Street between Moulton and Union, this place is really two finds in one. The small, informal restaurant has a partially exposed kitchen, brick walls, and a painted floor. The menus changes seasonally, but the house specialty, lobster and Brie ravioli with roasted grapes and caramelized onion sauce, is a mainstay. After dinner, head upstairs to the Café Club for dessert, wine, espresso, and drinks. ⊠ *38 Wharf St.,* ☎ *207/773–6667 for restaurant, 207/772–6976 for wine bar. Reservations essential. AE, D, MC, V. No lunch.*

$$ ✕ **Aubergine.** This bistro and wine bar has staked out a prime downtown location, across the street from L. L. Bean and just down the street from the Portland Museum of Art. The atmosphere is casual and the food is very good. The menu changes daily, but might include appetizers such as Swiss onion soup with fresh tarragon or fried Pemaquid oysters and entrées like spiced duck breast with fennel sauce or crispy salmon with spinach and Pernod. Wines by the glass are chosen to complement the dishes. ⊠ *555 Congress St.,* ☎ *207/874–0680.* ☉ *Open Tues.–Sat.; Sun. brunch. No lunch. MC, V.*

$$ ✕ **Katahdin.** Painted tables, a flea-market decor, mismatched dinnerware, and a log-pile bar provide a fun and unpretentious setting for dining on large portions of home-cooked New England fare. Try the chicken potpie, fried trout, crab cakes, or the nightly blue-plate special, and save room for the fruit cobbler. ⊠ *106 High St.,* ☎ *207/774–1740. D, MC, V. No lunch.*

$$$$ ✕🏨 **Inn by the Sea.** On greater Portland's most prime real estate, this all-suites inn is set back from the shoreline and has views of the ocean—Crescent Beach and Kettle Cove in particular. The dining room ($$–$$$$), open to nonguests, serves fine seafood and regional dishes. The architecture throughout is typical New England. ⊠ *40 Bowery Beach Rd., Cape Elizabeth (7 mi south of Portland) 04107,* ☎ *207/799–3134 or 800/888–4287,* ☎ *207/799–4779. 25 suites, 18 cottage condominiums. Restaurant, pool, tennis, croquet, bicycles. AE, D, MC, V.*

$$$$ 🏨 **Portland Regency Hotel.** The only major hotel in the center of the Old Port Exchange, the Regency building was Portland's armory in the late 19th century. Rooms have four-poster beds, tall standing mirrors,

floral curtains, and love seats. ✉ *20 Milk St., 04101,* ☎ *207/774–4200 or 800/727–3436,* FAX *207/775–2150. 95 rooms, 8 suites. Restaurant, massage, sauna, steam room, health club, nightclub, meeting rooms. AE, D, DC, MC, V.*

$$–$$$$ 🏨 **Radisson Eastland.** This 1927 hotel is in Portland's arts district. Rooms in the tower section have floor-to-ceiling windows; higher floors have harbor views. ✉ *157 High St., 04101,* ☎ *207/775–5411 or 800/ 777–6246,* FAX *207/775–2872. 201 rooms, 3 suites. Restaurant, 2 bars, sauna, exercise room, meeting rooms. AE, D, DC, MC, V.*

Nightlife and the Arts

NIGHTLIFE

Brian Boru (✉ 57 Center St., ☎ 207/780–1506) is an Irish pub with occasional entertainment and an outside deck. The **Café Club** (✉ 38 Wharf St., ☎ 207/772–6976) has comfortable chairs, couches, and a fireplace. A dozen of the 250 wines by the bottle can be ordered by the glass. Espresso, light meals, and desserts are served. **Comedy Connection** (✉ 6 Custom House Wharf, ☎ 207/774–5554) hosts stand-up comedians from Wednesday to Sunday.

Gritty McDuff's—Portland's Original Brew Pub (✉ 396 Fore St., ☎ 207/ 772–2739) brews fine ales and serves British pub fare and seafood dishes. **Stone Coast Brewery** (✉ 14 York St., ☎ 207/773–2337) is a brew pub with entertainment. **Three Dollar Dewey's** (✉ 241 Commercial St., ☎ 207/772–3310), long a popular night spot, is an English-style ale house. **Top of the East** (✉ Radisson Eastland, 157 High St., ☎ 207/ 775–5411) has a view of the city and live entertainment—jazz, piano, and comedy.

THE ARTS

Portland Performing Arts Center (✉ 25A Forest Ave., ☎ 207/761–0591) presents music, dance, and theater performances. **Cumberland County Civic Center** (✉ 1 Civic Center Sq., ☎ 207/775–3458) hosts concerts, sporting events, and family shows.

Portland City Hall's Merrill Auditorium (✉ 20 Myrtle St., ☎ 207/874–8200) is home to the Portland Symphony Orchestra and Portland Concert Association and the site of numerous theatrical and musical events. **Portland Symphony Orchestra** (✉ 30 Myrtle St., ☎ 207/773–8191) concerts take place from October to August. **Mad Horse Theatre Company** (✉ 92 Oak St., ☎ 207/797–3338) performs classic, contemporary, and original works. **Portland Stage Company** (✉ 25A Forest Ave., ☎ 207/774–0465) mounts productions year-round at the Portland Performing Arts Center.

Outdoor Activities and Sports

BALLOON RIDES

Balloon Rides (✉ 17 Freeman St., ☎ 207/772–4730) operates scenic flights over southern Maine.

BASEBALL

The Class AA **Portland Sea Dogs** (☎ 207/879–9500), a farm team of the Florida Marlins, play at Hadlock Field (✉ 271 Park Ave.). Tickets cost from $4 to $6.

BOAT TRIPS

For tours of the harbor, Casco Bay, and the nearby islands, try **Bay View Cruises** (✉ Fisherman's Wharf, ☎ 207/761–0496), **Casco Bay Lines** (✉ Maine State Pier, ☎ 207/774–7871), **Eagle Tours** (✉ Long Wharf, ☎ 207/774–6498), **Old Port Mariner Fleet** (✉ Long Wharf, ☎ 207/ 775–0727), or **Palawan Sailing** (✉ Old Port, ☎ 207/774–2163).

HOCKEY

The **Portland Pirates,** the farm team of the Washington Capitals, play home games at the Cumberland County Civic Center (⊠ 85 Free St., ☎ 207/828–4665). Tickets cost from $8 to $13.

Shopping

ART AND ANTIQUES

Abacus (⊠ 44 Exchange St., ☎ 207/772–4880) has unusual gift items in glass, wood, and textiles, plus fine modern jewelry. **F. O. Bailey Antiquarians** (⊠ 141 Middle St., ☎ 207/774–1479), Portland's largest retail showroom, carries antique and reproduction furniture and jewelry, paintings, rugs, and china.

Greenhut Galleries (⊠ 146 Middle St., ☎ 207/772–2693) carries contemporary Maine art. The **Pine Tree Shop & Bayview Gallery** (⊠ 75 Market St., ☎ 207/773–3007 or 800/244–3007) has original art and prints by prominent Maine painters. **Stein Glass Gallery** (⊠ 20 Milk St., ☎ 207/772–9072) specializes in decorative and utilitarian contemporary glass.

BOOKS

Carlson and Turner (⊠ 241 Congress St., ☎ 207/773–4200) is an antiquarian book dealer with an estimated 50,000 titles.

MALL

Maine Mall (⊠ 364 Maine Mall Rd., South Portland, ☎ 207/774–0303), 5 mi south of Portland, has 145 stores, including Sears, Filene's, JCPenney, and Macy's.

Casco Bay Islands

The islands of Casco Bay are also known as the Calendar Islands because an early explorer mistakenly thought there was one for each day of the year (in reality there are only 140). The brightly painted ferries of Casco Bay Lines are the islands' lifeline. There is frequent service to the most populated ones, including Peaks, Long, Little Diamond, and Great Diamond.

⑭ **Peaks Island,** nearest to Portland, is the most developed, but you can still commune with the wind and the sea, explore an old fort, and ramble along the alternately rocky and sandy shore. The trip to the island by boat is particularly enjoyable at or near sunset. Order a lobster sandwich or cold beer on the outdoor deck of **Jones' Landing** restaurant, steps from the dock. A circle trip without stops takes about 90 minutes. On the far side of the island you can stop on the rugged shoreline and have lunch. A small museum with Civil War artifacts is maintained in the **Fifth Maine Regiment** building.

⑮ The 17-acre **Eagle Island,** owned by the state and open to the public for day trips in summer, was the home of Admiral Robert E. Peary, the American explorer of the North Pole. Peary built a stone-and-wood house on the island as a summer retreat in 1904, but made it his permanent residence. With his stuffed Arctic birds, the quartz he brought home and set into the fieldstone fireplace, and other objects, the house remains as it was when Peary lived here. The *Kristy K.,* departing from Long Wharf, makes a four-hour narrated tour; there are also tours of Portland Headlight and seal-watching cruises on the *Fish Hawk.* ⊠ *Long Wharf,* ☎ *207/774–6498.* ⌑ *$8–$15, depending on tour.* ☉ *Departures mid-June–Labor Day, daily beginning 10 AM.*

Chebeague Island measures about 5 mi long and is less than 2 mi across at its widest. Service to the island is via **Casco Bay Lines** (☎ 207/774–7871) from Portland or the **Chebeague Transportation Company** (☎

207/846–3700) from the dock on Cousins Island, north of Portland and accessible by car. You can stay overnight at the **Chebeague Island Inn** (☎ 207/846–5155), open from mid-May–mid-October, or the **Chebeague Orchard B&B** (☎ 207/846–9488).

Dining and Lodging

$$$$ ✕🖼 **Diamond Cove.** In 1900, nearly 700 soldiers were stationed at Fort McKinley on Great Diamond Island, which was created to protect Portland's harbor. By mid-century, though, the fort was obsolete. Now it's a gem of a resort, with an art gallery, a summer theater, a general store, beaches, and walking trails. Accommodations are in town houses with living rooms and kitchens; in season there's a six-night minimum stay. The menu in the top-notch restaurant changes regularly, but entrées might include brochette made with Maine lobster tails, jumbo shrimp, scallops, tuna, and vegetables over basmati rice. ⊠ *Great Diamond Island (mailing address: Box 3572, Portland 04101),* ☎ *207/766–5804,* FAX *207/766–2973. 17 3-bedroom town homes. Restaurant, bar, pool, 5 beaches, health club, tennis courts. MC, V.*

Outdoor Activities and Sports

Maine Island Kayak Co. (⊠ 70 Luther St., Peak's Island, ☎ 800/796–2373) provides sea-kayaking instruction and conducts expeditions and tours along the Maine coast.

Freeport

16 *17 mi northeast of Portland, 10 mi southwest of Brunswick.*

Freeport, on Route 1, northeast of Portland, has charming back streets lined with historic buildings and old clapboard houses, and there's a small harbor on the Harraseeket River, but most people come here to shop—L. L. Bean is the store that put Freeport on the map.

Wolfe's Neck Woods State Park has 5 mi of hiking trails along Casco Bay, the Harraseeket River, and a fringe salt marsh. Naturalists lead walks. There are picnic tables and grills, but no camping. ⊠ *Wolfe's Neck Rd. (follow Bow St. opposite L. L. Bean off Rte. 1),* ☎ *207/865–4465.* 🔳 *$2 Memorial Day–Labor Day, $1 off-season.*

Bradbury Mountain State Park has moderate trails to the top of Bradbury Mountain, which has views of the sea. A picnic area and shelter, a ball field, a playground, and 41 campsites are among the facilities. ⊠ *Pownal (5 mi from Freeport-Durham exit off I–95),* ☎ *207/688–4712.* 🔳 *$2 Memorial Day–Labor Day, $1 off-season.*

Dining and Lodging

$–$$ ✕ **Freeport Café.** South of Freeport's shopping district, this small restaurant serves creative homemade food, including soups, salads, sandwiches, and dinner entrées. Breakfast is available all day, and there's a children's menu. You can sit on the outdoor deck in good weather. ⊠ *Rte. 1,* ☎ *207/865–3106. AE, D, MC, V.*

$ ✕ **Harraseeket Lunch & Lobster Co.** Seafood baskets and lobster dinners are what this bare-bones place beside the town landing in South Freeport is all about. You can eat outside on picnic tables in good weather. ⊠ *Main St., South Freeport,* ☎ *207/865–4888. Reservations not accepted. No credit cards. Closed mid-Oct.–Apr.*

$$$$ 🖼 **Harraseeket Inn.** Despite modern appointments such as elevators, whirlpools, and an indoor pool, this 1850 Greek Revival home gives its visitors an old-fashioned country-inn experience. Afternoon tea is served in the mahogany drawing room, and guest rooms have reproductions of Federal canopy beds. The formal dining room, which serves New England–influenced Continental cuisine, is a simply decorated space with picture windows facing a garden courtyard. The casual Broad Arrow Tavern, with an open kitchen and a wood-fired oven and grill, serves heartier fare. ⊠ *162 Main St., 04032,* ☎ *207/865–9377 or 800/342–6423,* ℻ *207/865–1684. 82 rooms, 2 suites. Restaurant, bar, indoor pool, croquet. Full breakfast. AE, D, DC, MC, V.*

$$–$$$ ⌕ **Isaac Randall House.** On a 5-acre lot outside town, this circa-1829 inn is a quiet retreat. Rooms are furnished with Victorian antiques and country pieces. A red caboose in the backyard has been turned into a room that's ideal for families. ⊠ *Independence Dr., 04032,* ☎ *207/865–9295. 8 rooms, 1 suite. Playground. D, MC, V.*

Outdoor Activities and Sports

Atlantic Seal Cruises (⊠ South Freeport, ☎ 207/865–6112) operates day trips to Eagle Island and evening seal and osprey watches.

Shopping

The *Freeport Visitors Guide* (☎ 207/865–1212 or 800/865–1994 for a copy) lists the many shops and factory outlet stores that can be found on Main Street, Bow Street, and elsewhere. Try **Fashion Outlet Mall** (⊠ 2 Depot St.) for clothing. **Freeport Crossing** (⊠ 200 Lower Main St.) has a wider array of merchandise.

Founded in 1912 as a mail-order merchandiser of products for hunters, guides, and fisherfolk, **L. L. Bean** (⊠ Rte. 1, ☎ 800/341–4341) attracts 3.5 million shoppers a year to its giant store (open 24 hours a day) in the heart of Freeport's shopping district. You can still find the original hunting boots, along with cotton, wool, and silk sweaters; camping and ski equipment; comforters; and hundreds of other items for the home, car, boat, or campsite. Across from the main store, a Bean factory outlet has seconds and discontinued merchandise at discount prices.

Harrington House Museum Store (⊠ 45 Main St., ☎ 207/865–0477) is a restored 19th-century merchant's home owned by the Freeport Historical Society; all the period reproductions that furnish the rooms are for sale. You can also buy books, rugs, jewelry, crafts, Shaker items, toys, and kitchen utensils.

Brunswick

⑰ *10 mi north of Freeport, 11 mi west of Bath.*

Harriet Beecher Stowe wrote *Uncle Tom's Cabin* while living in Brunswick. Lovely brick and clapboard homes and structures are the highlights of the town's **Federal Street Historic District,** which includes Federal Street and Park Row and the stately campus of Bowdoin College. Pleasant Street, in the center of town, is the business district.

Maine Street, which is at the east end of Pleasant Street, leads to the 110-acre campus of **Bowdoin College,** an enclave of distinguished architecture, gardens, and grassy quadrangles. Campus tours (☎ 207/725–3000) depart daily except Sunday from the admissions office in Chamberlain Hall. Among the historic buildings are Massachusetts Hall, a stout, sober, hip-roofed brick structure dating from 1802 that once housed the entire college. Hubbard Hall, an imposing 1902 neo-Gothic building, is home to Maine's only gargoyle and the **Peary-MacMillan Arctic Museum.** The museum contains photographs, navigational instruments, and artifacts from the first successful expedition to the North Pole, in 1909, by two of Bowdoin's most famous alumni, Admiral Robert E. Peary and Donald B. MacMillan. The poet Henry Wadsworth Longfellow attended the college. *Museum:* ☎ *207/725–3416.* ⌑ *Free.* ☉ *Tues.–Sat. 10–5, Sun. 2–5.*

The **Bowdoin College Museum of Art,** in a splendid Renaissance Revival–style building, has seven galleries radiating from a rotunda. Designed in 1894 by Charles F. McKim, the building stands on a rise, its facade adorned with classical statues and the entrance set off by a triumphal arch. The collections encompass Assyrian and classical art and works by Dutch, Italian, French, and Flemish old masters; a superb gathering of Colonial and Federal paintings, notably Gilbert Stuart portraits of Madison and Jefferson; and a Winslow Homer Gallery of engravings, etchings, and memorabilia (open in summer only). The museum's collection also includes 19th- and 20th-century American painting and sculpture, with works by Mary Cassatt, Andrew Wyeth, and Robert Rauschenberg. ⊠ *Walker Art Bldg.,* ☎ *207/725–3275.* 🎟 *Free.* ⏱ *Tues.–Sat. 10–5, Sun. 2–5.*

The **General Joshua L. Chamberlain Museum** displays memorabilia and documents the life of Maine's most celebrated Civil War hero. The general, who played an instrumental role in the Union army's victory at Gettysburg, was elected governor in 1867, and from 1871 to 1883 served as president of Bowdoin College. ⊠ *226 Main St.,* ☎ *207/729–6606.* 🎟 *$3.* ⏱ *Tues.–Sat. 10–4.*

OFF THE BEATEN PATH	**THE HARPSWELLS –** A side trip from Bath or Brunswick on Route 123 or Route 24 takes you to the peninsulas and islands known collectively as the Harpswells. Small coves along Harpswell Neck shelter the boats of lobstermen, and summer cottages are tucked away amid the birch and spruce trees.

Dining and Lodging

$–$$ ✕ **The Great Impasta.** You can match your favorite pasta and sauce to create your own dish at this storefront restaurant that's a great choice for lunch, tea, or dinner. Or try the tasty seafood lasagna. ⊠ *42 Maine St.,* ☎ *207/729–5858. Reservations not accepted. D, DC, MC, V.*

$$$–$$$$ 🏨 **Captain Daniel Stone Inn.** This Federal inn overlooks the Androscoggin River. No two rooms are furnished identically, but all contain executive-style comforts and many have whirlpool baths, queen-size beds, and pullout sofas. A guest parlor, a breakfast room, and excellent service in the Narcissa Stone Restaurant (no lunch on Saturday) make this an upscale escape from college-town funkiness. ⊠ *10 Water St., 04011,* ☎ FAX *207/725–9898. 30 rooms, 4 suites. Restaurant. Continental breakfast. AE, DC, MC, V.*

$–$$$$ 🏨 **Harpswell Inn.** Spacious lawns and neatly pruned shrubs surround the stately white clapboard Harpswell Inn, built in 1761. The living room has a view of Middle Bay and Birch Island from its position on Lookout Point. Half the rooms also have water views. The carriage house in back has two luxury suites, one with a whirlpool. Children over 10 are welcome at the inn. ⊠ *141 Lookout Point Rd., S. Harpswell 04079,* ☎ *207/833–5509 or 800/843–5509. 11 rooms, 6 with bath; 3 suites. Full breakfast. No smoking. MC, V.*

Nightlife and the Arts

Bowdoin Summer Music Festival (⊠ Bowdoin College, ☎ 207/725–3322 for information or 207/725–3895 for tickets) is a six-week concert series featuring performances by students, faculty, and prestigious guest artists. **Maine State Music Theater** (⊠ Pickard Theater, Bowdoin College, ☎ 207/725–8769) stages musicals from mid-June to August. **Theater Project of Brunswick** (⊠ 14 School St., ☎ 207/729–8584) performs semiprofessional, children's, and community theater.

Outdoor Activities and Sports

H2Outfitters (⊠ Orr's Island, ☎ 207/833–5257) provides sea-kayaking instruction and rentals and conducts day or overnight trips.

Shopping

ICON Contemporary Art (⊠ 19 Mason St., ☎ 207/725–8157) specializes in modern art. Nearby **O'Farrell Gallery** (⊠ 58 Maine St., ☎ 207/729–8228) represents artists such as Neil Welliver, Marguerite Robichaux, and Sheila Geoffrion. **Tontine Fine Candies** (⊠ Tontine Mall, 149 Maine St., ☎ 207/729–4462) has many chocolates and other goodies.

A **farmers' market** takes place on Tuesday and Friday from May to October, on the town mall between Maine Street and Park Row.

Bath

⓲ *11 mi east of Brunswick, 38 mi northeast of Portland.*

Bath, east of Brunswick on Route 1, has been a shipbuilding center since 1607. These days the Bath Iron Works turns out guided-missile frigates for the U.S. Navy and merchant container ships. It's a good idea to avoid Bath and Route 1 on weekdays between 3:15 and 4:30 PM, when BIW's major shift change occurs. The massive exodus can tie up traffic for miles.

The **Maine Maritime Museum and Shipyard** contains ship models, journals, photographs, and other artifacts. The 142-ft Grand Banks fishing schooner *Sherman Zwicker,* one of the last of its kind, is on display when in port. You can watch boatbuilders wield their tools on classic Maine boats at the restored Percy & Small Shipyard and Boat Shop. The outdoor shipyard is open from May to November; during these months the *Linekin II* sails the scenic Kennebec River. During the off-season, the Maritime History Building has indoor exhibits, videos, and activities. ⊠ *243 Washington St.,* ☎ *207/443–1316.* ⊡ *$7.75.* ⊙ *Daily 9:30–5.*

Reid State Park (☎ 207/371–2303), on Georgetown Island, off Route 127, has 1½ mi of sand on three beaches. Facilities include bathhouses, picnic tables, fireplaces, and snack bar. Parking lots fill by 11 AM on summer Sundays and holidays; admission is charged.

OFF THE
BEATEN PATH

POPHAM – Follow Route 209 south from Bath to Popham, the site of the short-lived 1607 Popham Colony, where the *Virginia,* the first European ship built in the New World, was launched. Benedict Arnold set off from Popham on his ill-fated march against the British in Québec. Here also are granite-walled **Ft. Popham** (⊠ Phippsburg, ☎ 207/389–1335), built in 1607, and **Popham State Park.** The park, at the end of Route 209, has a good sand beach, a marsh area, bathhouses, and picnic tables; admission is charged.

Dining and Lodging

$$–$$$$ ✕ **Robinhood Free Meetinghouse.** Chef Michael Gagne, one of Maine's
★ best, finally has a restaurant that complements his classic and creative multi-ethnic cuisine. The 1855 Greek Revival–style meeting house has large-pane windows and is decorated simply: cream-color walls, pine floorboards, cherry Shaker-style chairs, white table linen. Begin with the artichoke strudel, segue to veal saltimbocca or confit of duck, and finish up with Gagne's signature Obsession in Three Chocolates. Jazz and theme nights take place in the off-season. ⊠ *Robinhood Rd., Georgetown,* ☎ *207/371–2188. AE, D, MC, V. Closed some weeknights mid-Oct.–mid-May. No lunch.*

$$ ✕ **Kristina's Restaurant & Bakery.** This restaurant in a frame house with a front deck built around a huge maple tree prepares some of the finest pies, pastries, and cakes on the coast. The satisfying new American cuisine served for dinner usually includes fresh seafood and grilled meats. All meals can be packed to go. ⊠ *160 Centre St.,* ☎ *207/442–8577. D, MC, V. Closed Jan. No dinner Sun. Call ahead in winter.*

$$$–$$$$ ⌂ **The 1774 Inn.** On the National Register of Historic Places, the 1774 Inn is a pre-Revolutionary mansion. Architecture buffs will savor the interior detailing and antiques lovers will covet the magnificent pieces in the house. The inn, on a bend in the Kennebec river, has large corner guest rooms, two with fireplaces, two with river views. ⊠ *Parker Head Rd., Phippsburg Center 04562,* ☎ *207/389–1774. 4 rooms. Full breakfast. No credit cards.*

Nightlife and the Arts

Chocolate Church Arts Center (⊠ 804 Washington St., ☎ 207/442–8455) hosts folk, jazz, and classical concerts, theater productions, and performances for children. The gallery presents exhibits of works in various media by Maine artists.

Shopping

The **Montsweag Flea Market** (⊠ Rte. 1 between Bath and Wiscasset, ☎ 207/443–2809) is a roadside attraction with trash and treasures. It takes place on weekends from May to October and also on Wednesday (for antiques) and Friday during the summer.

Wiscasset

19 *10 mi northeast of Bath, 21 mi east of Brunswick, 46 mi northeast of Portland.*

Settled in 1663 on the banks of the Sheepscot River, Wiscasset fittingly bills itself as Maine's Prettiest Village. Stroll through town and you'll pass by elegant sea captains' homes (many now antiques shops or galleries), old cemeteries, churches, and public buildings.

The **Nickels-Sortwell House,** maintained by the Society for the Preservation of New England Antiquities, is an outstanding example of Federal architecture. ⊠ *Main St.,* ☎ *207/882–6218.* ☞ *$4.* ☉ *June–Sept., Wed.–Sun. 11–5; tours on the hr, 11–4.*

The 1807 **Castle Tucker,** also maintained by the Society for the Preservation of New England Antiquities, is known for its extravagant architecture, Victorian decor, and freestanding elliptical staircase. ⊠ *Lee and High Sts.,* ☎ *207/882–7364.* ☞ *$4.* ☉ *July–Aug., Thurs.–Sat. noon–5; tours on the hr 12–4.*

The **Musical Wonder House** contains a vast collection of antique music boxes from around the world. ⊠ *18 High St.,* ☎ *207/882–7163.* ☞ *1-hr presentation on main floor $10; 3-hr tour of entire house $30 or $50 for 2 people.* ☉ *Mid-May–mid-Oct., daily 10–6; last tour usually at 4; call ahead for 3-hr tours.*

☾ The restored 1930s coaches of the **Maine Coast Railroad** travel from Wiscasset to Bath. ⊠ *Box 614, Rte. 1,* ☎ *207/882–8000 or 800/795–5404.* ☞ *$10.* ☉ *Daily late June–early Sept., weekends only late May–late June and early Sept.–mid-Oct.*

Dining and Lodging

$$$$ ✕⌂ **Squire Tarbox.** The Federal-style Squire Tarbox is equal parts inn, restaurant, and working goat farm. Its country setting toward the end of Westport Island, midway between Bath and Wiscasset, is far removed from the rushing traffic of Route 1, yet area attractions are eas-

ily accessible. Rooms are simply furnished with antiques and country pieces; four have fireplaces. The menu at the dining room ($$$; reservations essential for dinner) changes nightly, but always includes a vegetarian entrée and a sampling of the inn's own goat cheese. ⊠ *R.R. 2, Box 620, Rte. 144, Westport 04578),* ☎ *207/882–7693,* FAX *207/ 882–7107. 11 rooms. Restaurant. Full breakfast; MAP available. AE, D, MC, V. Closed late Oct.–mid-May.*

Shopping

The Wiscasset area rivals Searsport as a destination for antiquing. Shops line Wiscasset's main and side streets and spew over the bridge into Edgecomb.

The **Butterstamp Workshop** (⊠ Middle St., ☎ 207/882–7825) carries handcrafted folk-art designs from antique molds. The **Maine Art Gallery** (⊠ Warren St., ☎ 207/882–7511) carries the works of local artists. The **Wiscasset Bay Gallery** (⊠ Main St., ☎ 207/882–7682) specializes in the works of 19th- and 20th-century American and European artists.

Boothbay

⓴ *60 mi northeast of Portland, 50 mi southwest of Camden.*

When Portlanders want a respite from what they know as city life, many come north to the Boothbay region, which comprises Boothbay proper, East Boothbay, and Boothbay Harbor. This part of the shoreline is a craggy stretch of inlets where pleasure craft anchor alongside trawlers and lobster boats. Commercial Street, Wharf Street, the By-Way, and Townsend Avenue are filled with shops, galleries, and ice-cream parlors. Excursion boats (☞ Outdoor Activities and Sports, *below*) leave from the piers off Commercial Street. From the harbor, you can catch a boat to Monhegan Island.

At the **Boothbay Railway Village,** about a mile north of Boothbay, you can ride 1½ mi on a narrow-gauge steam train through a re-creation of a century-old New England village. Among the 24 buildings is a museum with more than 50 antique automobiles and trucks. ⊠ *Rte. 27,* ☎ *207/633–4727.* 🖼 *$7.* ☉ *Memorial Day–mid-Oct., weekends 9:30–5; early-June–Columbus Day, daily 9:30–5; special Halloween schedule. Closed Columbus Day–Memorial Day.*

Dining and Lodging

$$–$$$ ✕ **Christopher's 1820 House.** This restaurant in quiet East Boothbay serves breakfast, lunch, and dinner in an oceanfront dining room. Choose from appetizers such as pan-seared Maine crab cakes or lobster-and-cheese quesadillas, and then move on to entrées like roasted rack of New Zealand lamb, Asian flavored duck confit, or lobster succotash. ⊠ *Rte. 96, East Boothbay,* ☎ *207/633–6565,* FAX *207/633– 6178. MC, V. Closed Nov.–Memorial Day.*

$ ✕ **Lobstermen's Coop.** Crustacean lovers and landlubbers will find something to like at this dockside working lobster pound. Lobster, steamers, hot dogs, hamburgers, sandwiches, and desserts are on the menu. Eat indoors or outside and watch the lobstermen at work. ⊠ *Atlantic Ave., Boothbay Harbor,* ☎ *207/633–4900. Closed mid-Oct.–mid-May.*

$$$$ ✕🖬 **Spruce Point Inn.** Escape the hubbub of Boothbay Harbor at this sprawling resort, which is a short shuttle ride to town yet a world away. Guest rooms are in the main inn, family cottages, and condominiums. Most rooms are comfortable but not fancy and have ocean views. Lobster cioppino made with local shellfish and served over cappellini is the signature dish at the dining room ($$$), which has an unparalleled view of the outer harbor and open ocean. ⊠ *Box 237, Atlantic Ave.,*

Boothbay Harbor 04538, ☎ 207/633–4152 or 800/553–0289, FAX 207/633–7138. 37 rooms, 24 suites, 7 family cottages, 4 condominiums. Lounge, freshwater pool, saltwater pool, tennis, health club, dock. MAP. AE, D, MC, V. Closed mid-Oct.–mid-May.

$–$$$ 🖫 **Admiral's Quarters Inn.** This renovated 1830 sea captain's house is ideally situated for those wanting to explore Boothbay Harbor by foot, a good thing since in-town parking is limited and expensive. The rooms have private decks, many overlooking the harbor, and on rainy days you can relax by the woodstove in the solarium. ⊠ *Commercial St., Boothbay Harbor 04538, ☎ 207/633–2474, FAX 207/633–5904. 2 rooms, 4 suites. Full breakfast. D, MC, V.*

Outdoor Activities and Sports

Balmy Day Cruises (☎ 207/633–2284 or 800/298–2284) operates day boat trips to Monhegan Island and tours of the harbor and nearby lighthouses. **Cap'n Fish's Boat Trips** (⊠ Pier 1 for departures, ☎ 207/633–3244) operates sightseeing cruises throughout the region, including puffin-watching cruises, lobster-hauling and whale-watching rides, and trips to Damariscove Harbor, Pemaquid Point, and up the Kennebec River to Bath.

Shopping

BOOTHBAY HARBOR

Gleason Fine Art (⊠ 15 Oak St., ☎ 207/633–6849) carries fine art, regional and national, early 19th century and contemporary. **House of Logan** (⊠ Townsend Ave., ☎ 207/633–2293) stocks clothing for men and women; children's clothes can be found next door at the Village Store. **Maine Trading Post** (⊠ 80 Commercial St., ☎ 207/633–2760) sells antiques, fine reproductions, gifts, and decorative accessories.

EDGECOMB

Edgecomb Potters (⊠ Rte. 27, ☎ 207/882–6802) sells glazed porcelain pottery and other crafts at rather high prices; some discontinued items or seconds are discounted. These potters have an excellent reputation. There's a store in Freeport if you miss this one. The **Gil Whitman Gallery** (⊠ Rte. 1, Edgecomb, ☎ 207/882–7705) exhibits the work of bronze sculptor Gil Whitman in a barn gallery and an outdoor sculpture garden, where giant metal flowers bloom amid real ones. The studio and workshop areas are open to visitors. **Sheepscot River Pottery** (⊠ Rte. 1, ☎ 207/882–9410) has original hand-painted pottery as well as a large collection of American-made crafts, including jewelry, kitchenware, furniture, and home accessories.

Pemaquid Point

㉑ *8 mi southeast of Wiscasset.*

You may find yourself checking your map as you travel through this region of river outlets, rocky inlets, and peninsulas. Not that getting to Pemaquid Point is so difficult—it's just nice to have confirmation that the circuitous route you're taking really is getting you somewhere. Navigation is a breeze coming from Boothbay or Wiscasset. Follow Route 27 out of Boothbay or Route 1 north from Wiscasset into Damariscotta, then head south on Route 129 and 130 into Pemaquid Point. Return to Route 1 via Route 32 through the fishing villages of New Harbor and Round Pond.

At the **Colonial Pemaquid Restoration,** on a small peninsula jutting into the Pemaquid River, English mariners established a fishing and trading settlement in the early 17th century. The excavations at **Ft. William Henry,** begun in the mid-1960s, have turned up thousands of artifacts from the Colonial settlement, including the remains of an old customs house, a tavern, a jail, a forge, and homes. Some of the items are from even earlier Native American settlements. The state operates a museum displaying many of the artifacts. ⊠ *Rte. 130,* ☎ *207/677–2423.* ☒ *$2.* ☉ *Memorial Day–Labor Day, daily 9:30–5.*

Route 130 terminates at the **Pemaquid Point Light,** which looks as though it sprouted from the ragged, tilted chunk of granite that it commands. The former lighthouse-keeper's cottage is now the **Fishermen's Museum,** with photographs, models, and artifacts that explore commercial fishing in Maine. Here, too, is the **Pemaquid Art Gallery,** which mounts exhibitions from July to Labor Day. ⊠ *Rte. 130,* ☎ *207/677–2494.* ☒ *Donation requested.* ☉ *Memorial Day–Columbus Day, Mon.–Sat. 10–5, Sun. 11–5.*

Pemaquid Beach Park (⊠ Off Rte. 130, New Harbor, ☎ 207/677–2754) has a good sand beach, a snack bar, changing facilities, and picnic tables overlooking John's Bay; admission is charged.

Dining and Lodging

$ ╳ **Round Pond Lobstermen's Co-op.** Lobster doesn't get much rougher, any fresher, or any cheaper than that served at this no-frills dockside takeout. The best deal is the dinner special: a 1-pound lobster, steamers, and corn-on-the-cob, with a bag of chips. Regulars often bring beer, wine, bread, and/or salads. Settle in at a picnic table and breathe in the fresh salt air while you drink in the view over dreamy Round Pond Harbor. ⊠ *Round Pond Harbor, off Rte. 32, Round Pond,* ☎ *207/529–5725. MC, V.*

$$–$$$$ ╳▥ **Newcastle Inn.** This classic country inn with a riverside location and an excellent dining room attracts guests year-round. All the rooms are filled with country pieces and antiques; some rooms have fireplaces and whirlpool tubs. Guests spread out in the cozy pub, comfortable living room, and sunporch overlooking the river. Breakfast is served on the back deck in fine weather. Three- or five-course dinners, open to the public by reservation, emphasize Pemaquid oysters, lobster, Atlantic salmon, and other Maine seafood. ⊠ *River Rd., Newcastle 04553,* ☎ *207/563–5685 or 800/832–8669,* ℻ *207/563–6877. 13 rooms, 2 suites. 2 dining rooms, pub, TV room. Full breakfast. AE, MC, V.*

$$ ▥ **Mill Pond Inn.** A quiet residential street holds this circa 1780 inn that's on a mill pond across the street from Damariscotta Lake. Loons, otters, and bald eagles reside on the lake, and you can arrange a trip with the owner, a Registered Maine Guide, on the inn's 17-ft antique lapstrake boat. The rooms are warm and inviting and there's a pub for guests, though you may find it hard to tear yourself away from the hammocks-for-two overlooking the pond. ⊠ *50 Main St. off Rte. 215 N, Nobleboro 04555,* ☎ *207/563–8014. 5 rooms, 1 suite. Horseshoes, boating, bicycles. Full breakfast. No credit cards.*

$–$$ ▥ **Briar Rose.** Round Pond is a sleepy harborside village with a old-fashioned country store, two lobster co-ops, a nice restaurant, and a handful of antiques and craft shops. The mansard-roof Briar Rose commands a ship-captain's view over it all. Antiques and whimsies decorate the airy rooms. ⊠ *Box 27, Rte. 32, Round Pond 04556,* ☎ *207/529–5478. 2 rooms, 1 suite. Full breakfast. MC, V.*

Portland to Pemaquid Point A to Z

Arriving and Departing

See Arriving and Departing *in* Maine A to Z, at the end of this chapter.

Getting Around

BY BUS

Greater Portland's **Metro** (☎ 207/774–0351) runs seven bus routes in Portland, South Portland, and Westbrook. The fare is $1; exact change ($1 bills accepted) is required. Buses run from 5:30 AM to 11:45 PM.

BY CAR

Congress Street leads from I–295 into the heart of Portland; the Gateway Garage on High Street, off Congress, is a convenient place to leave your car while exploring downtown. North of Portland, I–95 takes you to Exit 20 and Route 1, Freeport's Main Street, which continues on to Brunswick and Bath. East of Wiscasset you can take Route 27 south to the Boothbays, where Route 96 is a good choice for further exploration.

Contacts and Resources

CAR RENTAL

See Contacts and Resources *in* Maine A to Z.

EMERGENCIES

Maine Medical Center (⊠ 22 Bramhall St., Portland, ☎ 207/871–0111). **Mid Coast Hospital** (⊠ 1356 Washington St., Bath, ☎ 207/443–5524; ⊠ 58 Baribeau Dr., Brunswick, ☎ 207/729–0181). **St. Andrews Hospital** (⊠ 3 St. Andrews La., Boothbay Harbor, ☎ 207/633–2121). **Miles Memorial Hospital** (⊠ Bristol Rd., Damariscotta, ☎ 207/563–1234).

VISITOR INFORMATION

Boothbay Harbor Region Chamber of Commerce (⊠ Box 356, Boothbay Harbor 04538, ☎ 207/633–2353). **Chamber of Commerce of the Bath Brunswick Region** (⊠ 45 Front St., Bath 04530, ☎ 207/443–9751; ⊠ 59 Pleasant St., Brunswick 04011, ☎ 207/725–8797) . **Convention and Visitors Bureau of Greater Portland** (⊠ 305 Commercial St. 04101, ☎ 207/772–5800). **Freeport Merchants Association** (⊠ Box 452, Freeport 04032, ☎ 207/865–1212). **Greater Portland Chamber of Commerce** (⊠ 145 Middle St., Portland 04101, ☎ 207/772–2811). **Maine Publicity Bureau** (⊠ Rte. 1, Exit 17 off I–95, Yarmouth 04347, ☎ 207/846–0833).

PENOBSCOT BAY

Purists hold that the Maine coast begins at Penobscot Bay, where the vistas over the water are wider and bluer; the shore a jumble of broken granite boulders, cobblestones, and gravel punctuated by small sand beaches; and the water numbingly cold. Port Clyde in the southwest and Stonington in the southeast are the outer limits of Maine's largest bay, 35 mi apart across the bay waters but separated by a drive of almost 100 mi on scenic but slow two-lane highways. From Pemaquid Point at the western extremity of Muscongus Bay to Port Clyde at its eastern extent, it's less than 15 mi across the water, but it's 50 mi for the motorist, who must return north to Route 1 to reach the far shore.

Rockland, the largest town on the bay, is Maine's major lobster distribution center and the port of departure for trips to Vinalhaven, North Haven, and Matinicus islands. The Camden Hills, looming green over Camden's fashionable waterfront, turn bluer and fainter as you head toward Castine, the small town across the bay. In between Camden and Castine is the flea-market mecca of Searsport. Deer Isle is connected to the mainland by a slender, high-arching bridge, but Isle au Haut, accessible from Deer Isle's fishing town of Stonington, can be reached by passenger ferry only: More than half of this steep, wooded island is wilderness, the most remote section of Acadia National Park.

The most promising shopping areas are Main Street in Rockland, Main and Bay View streets in Camden, Main Street in Blue Hill, and Main Street in Stonington. Antiques shops are clustered in Searsport and scattered around the outskirts of villages, in farmhouses and barns. Yard sales abound in summertime.

Tenants Harbor

22 *13 mi south of Thomaston.*

Tenants Harbor is a quintessential Maine fishing town, its harbor dominated by lobster boats, its shores rocky and slippery, its center a scattering of clapboard houses, a church, a general store. The fictional Dunnet Landing of Sarah Orne Jewett's classic book *The Country of the Pointed Firs* is based on this region.

Dining and Lodging

$$–$$$$ ✕🔲 **East Wind Inn & Meeting House.** Overlooking the harbor and the islands, the East Wind has unadorned but comfortable rooms, suites, and apartments in three buildings; some accommodations have fireplaces. The inn is open to the public for dinner, breakfast, and Sunday brunch. Dinner options include prime rib, boiled lobster, and baked stuffed haddock. ⊠ *Box 149, Rte. 131 (10 mi off Rte. 1), 04860,* ☎ *207/372–6366 or 800/241–8439 ,* 🅵🅰🆇 *207/372–6320. 23 rooms, 9 with bath; 3 suites; 4 apartments. Restaurant. Continental breakfast. AE, D, MC, V. Closed Dec.–Apr. No lunch.*

Monhegan Island

23 *East of Pemaquid Point, south of Port Clyde.*

Remote Monhegan Island, with its high cliffs fronting the open sea, was known to Basque, Portuguese, and Breton fishermen well before Columbus "discovered" America. About a century ago Monhegan was discovered again by some of America's finest painters, including Rockwell Kent, Robert Henri, A. J. Hammond, and Edward Hopper, who sailed out to paint its meadows, savage cliffs, wild ocean views, and fishermen's shacks. Tourists followed, and Monhegan is now overrun with visitors in summer. Seventeen miles of paths crisscross the island, leading from the village to the lighthouse, through the woods and to the cliffs.

Port Clyde, a fishing village at the end of Route 131, is the point of departure for the *Laura B.* (☎ 207/372–8848 for schedules), the mail boat that serves Monhegan Island. The *Balmy Days* (☎ 207/633–2284 or 800/298–2284) sails from Boothbay Harbor to Monhegan on daily trips in summer, and Hardy Boat Cruises (☎ 207/677–2026 or 800/278–3346) leaves daily from Shaw's Wharf in New Harbor. Day visitors should bring a picnic lunch, as restaurants can have long waits at lunchtime.

The **Monhegan Museum,** in an 1824 lighthouse and an adjacent, newly built assistant-keeper's house, has wonderful views of Manana Island and the Camden Hills in the distance. Inside are artworks and displays depicting island life and local flora and birds. ⊠ *White Head Rd.,* ☎ *no phone.* 🆓 *Donations accepted.* ☉ *July–mid-Sept., daily 11:30–3:30.*

Swim Beach, a five-minute walk from the ferry, is rocky but rarely has more than a few sun worshipers.

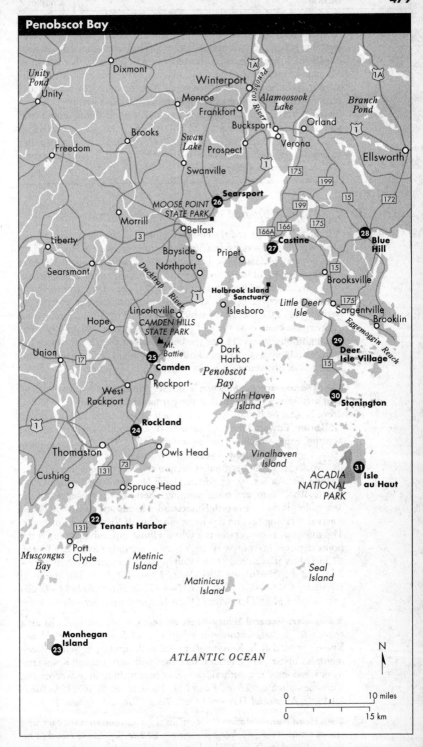

Lodging

$$$–$$$$ ⊠ **Island Inn.** This three-story inn, which dates from 1807, has a commanding presence on Monhegan's harbor. The waterside rooms, though mostly small, are the nicest, with sunset views over the harbor and stark Manana Island. Some of the meadow-view rooms have the distinct disadvantage of being over kitchen vents. New owners are updating and redecorating the property, which includes the main inn, the adjacent Pierce Cottage, a small bakery café, and a good dining room that serves breakfast, lunch, and dinner. ⊠ *Box 128, Monhegan Island 04852,* ☎ *207/596–0371,* FAX *207/594–5517. 32 rooms, 3 with bath; 4 suites in 2 buildings. Restaurant, café. Full breakfast. MC, V. Closed Columbus Day–Memorial Day.*

Rockland

㉔ *27 mi south of Belfast, 53 mi northeast of Brunswick.*

A large fishing port and the commercial hub of the coast, with working boats moored alongside a flotilla of cruise schooners, Rockland retains a working-class flavor. The expansion of the Farnsworth Museum and the opening of more boutiques, restaurants, and bed-and-breakfasts have increased its appeal to coastal travelers. Day trips to Vinalhaven and North Haven islands and distant Matinicus depart from the harbor, the outer portion of which is bisected by a nearly mile-long granite breakwater. At the end of the breakwater is a late-19th-century lighthouse that is one of the best places in the area to watch the many windjammers sail in and out of Rockland Harbor. Owl's Head Lighthouse, off Route 73, is also a good vantage point.

The ★**Farnsworth Art Museum** is an excellent small museum of American art. Artists represented in the permanent collection include Andrew, N. C., and Jamie Wyeth, Fitz Hugh Lane, George Bellows, Frank W. Benson, Edward Hopper, Louise Nevelson, and Fairfield Porter. The Wyeth Center, which opened in summer 1998, is devoted to Maine-related works of Andrew Wyeth and other members of the Wyeth family. Works from the personal collection of Andrew and Betsy Wyeth include *The Patriot, Adrift, Maiden Hair, Dr. Syn, The Clearing, Geraniums, Watch Cap,* and other paintings. Between the museum and the new gallery is the **Farnsworth Homestead,** a handsome circa 1852 Greek Revival dwelling that retains its original lavish Victorian furnishings. The museum also operates the **Olson House** in Cushing. This is the house depicted in Andrew Wyeth's famous painting *Christina's World.* ⊠ *356 Main St., Cushing (14 mi southwest of Rockland),* ☎ *207/596–6457.* ☞ *$9.* ☉ *Museum May–Sept., Mon.–Sat. 9–5, Sun. noon–5; Homestead Mon.–Sat. 10–5, Sun. 1–5; Olson House daily 11–4. Museum closed Mon. Oct.–Apr.; Olson House closed Oct.–Apr.*

Montpelier: General Henry Knox Museum was built in 1930 as a replica of the late-18th-century mansion of Major General Henry Knox, a general in the Revolutionary War and Secretary of War in Washington's Cabinet. The interior is furnished with antiques and Knox family possessions. Architectural features of note include an oval room and a double staircase. ⊠ *Rtes. 1 and 131, Thomaston,* ☎ *207/354–8062.* ☞ *$3.* ☉ *Memorial Day–mid-Oct., Tues.–Sat., 10–4; Sun. 1–4.*

☯ **Owls Head Transportation Museum** displays antique aircraft, cars, and engines and stages weekend air shows. ⊠ *Rte. 73, Owls Head (2 mi south of Rockland),* ☎ *207/594–4418.* ☞ *$6.* ☉ *May–Oct., daily 10–5; Nov.–Apr., weekdays 10–4, weekends 10–3.*

★ ☯ The **Shore Village Museum** displays many lighthouse and Coast Guard artifacts and has exhibits of maritime and Civil War memorabilia. ⊠

104 Limerock St., ☎ 207/594–0311. ☒ Donation suggested. ☉ June–mid-Oct., daily 10–4; rest of yr "by chance and appointment."

Dining and Lodging

$$ ★ ✕ **Jessica's.** On a hill at the southern end of Rockland, Jessica's occupies four cozy rooms in a renovated Victorian home. Billed as a European bistro, the restaurant lives up to its Continental label with creative entrées that include veal Zurich, paella, and pork Portofino; other specialties of the Swiss chef are risottos, pastas, and focaccia. ☒ *2 S. Main St./Rte. 73,* ☎ *207/596–0770. D, MC, V. Closed Tues. in winter.*

$–$$ ✕ **Water Works.** This restaurant in a brick building off Main Street serves light pub-style fare, including soups and home-style suppers like turkey and meat loaf. Maine microbrewery beers are on tap, and the selection of single-malt Scotches is excellent. A wall of water decorates the small dining room, and a stone fireplace dominates the pub. A children's menu is available. ☒ *Lindsey St.,* ☎ *207/596–7950. MC, V.*

$$$$ ⊞ **Samoset Resort.** On the Rockland–Rockport town line next to the breakwater, this sprawling oceanside resort has excellent facilities. Ask about special packages. ☒ *220 Warrenton St., Rockport,* ☎ *207/594–2511 or 800/341–1650 outside ME,* FAX *207/594–0722. 132 rooms, 18 suites. Restaurant, indoor and outdoor pools, golf, tennis, exercise room, racquetball, children's programs. AE, D, DC, MC, V.*

$$–$$$$ ★ ⊞ **Limerock Inn.** You can walk to the Farnsworth and the Shore Village museums from this magnificent Queen Anne–style Victorian on a quiet residential street. The meticulously decorated rooms include Island Cottage, with a whirlpool tub and doors that open onto a private deck overlooking the backyard garden, and Grand Manan, which has a fireplace, a whirlpool tub, and a four-poster king-size bed. ☒ *96 Limerock St., 04841,* ☎ *207/594–2257 or 800/546–3762. 8 rooms. Croquet, bicycles. Full breakfast. MC, V.*

Outdoor Activities and Sports

BOAT TRIPS

North End Shipyard Schooners (☎ 800/648–4544) operates three- and six-day cruises on the schooners *American Eagle, Isaac H. Evans,* and *Heritage.* **Vessels of Windjammer Wharf** (☎ 207/236–3520 or 800/999–7352) organizes three- and six-day cruises on the *Pauline,* a 12-passenger motor yacht, and the *Stephen Taber,* a windjammer. *Victory Chimes* is a 132-ft, three-masted schooner, the largest in Maine's windjammer fleet, that takes three- and six-day trips. **Bay Island Yacht Charters** (☒ 120 Tillison Ave., ☎ 207/236–2776 or 800/421–2492) operates bareboats and charters and rents boats. **Three Cheers** (☒ Rockland Landing, Marina Park Dr., ☎ 207/594–0900) operates lobster-fishing and lighthouse cruises.

Shopping

Many galleries are clustered around the Farnsworth Art Museum. Maine authors frequently sign books at the **Personal Bookstore** (☒ 78 Main St, Thomaston, ☎ 207/354–8058 or 800/391–8058). The **Reading Corner** (☒ 408 Main St., ☎ 207/596–6651) carries many cookbooks, children's books, and Maine-related titles, and has good newspaper and magazine selections. The **Store** (☒ 435 Main St., ☎ 207/594–9246) stocks top-of-the-line cookware and table accessories and has an outstanding card selection.

Camden

㉕ *8 mi north of Rockland, 19 mi south of Belfast.*

"Where the mountains meet the sea" is an apt description of Camden, as you will discover when you step out of your car and look up from the harbor. Camden is famous not only for geography but for its large fleet of windjammers—relics and replicas from the age of sail. At just about any hour during warm months you're likely to see at least one windjammer tied up in the harbor. The best shopping in the region can be found downtown. The district's compact size makes it perfect for exploring on foot: Shops, restaurants, and galleries line Main and Bayview streets and side streets and alleys around the harbor.

The entrance to 5,500-acre **Camden Hills State Park** is 2 mi north of Camden. If you're accustomed to the Rockies or the Alps, you may not be impressed with heights of not much more than 1,000 ft, yet the Camden Hills are landmarks for miles along the low, rolling reaches of the Maine coast. The park contains 20 mi of trails, including the easy Nature Trail up Mount Battie. Hike or drive to the top for a magnificent view over Camden and island-studded Penobscot Bay. The 112-site camping area, open from mid-May to mid-October, has flush toilets and hot showers. ⊠ *Rte. 1,* ☎ *207–236–3109.* ⌗ *Trails and auto road up Mount Battie $2.*

☪ **Kelmscott Farm** is a rare-breed animal farm (sheep, pigs, horses, poultry, goats, and cows) with displays, a nature trail, children's activities, a picnic area, heirloom gardens, and special events on most weekends. ⊠ *Rte. 52, Lincolnville,* ☎ *207/763–4088.* ⌗ *$5.* ⊙ *Memorial Day–Labor Day, Thurs.–Sun. 11–4.*

Dining and Lodging

$$–$$$ ✕ **Waterfront Restaurant.** A ringside seat on Camden Harbor can be had here; the best view is from the outdoor deck, open in warm weather. The fare is primarily seafood: boiled lobster, scallops, bouillabaisse, seafood risotto. Lunchtime highlights include lobster and crabmeat rolls. ⊠ *Bay View St.,* ☎ *207/236–3747. Reservations not accepted. AE, MC, V.*

$$ ✕ **Chez Michel.** Chef Michel Hetuin, the mastermind behind unassuming Chez Michel, prepares fine rabbit pâté, mussels marinière, steak au poivre, and boeuf bourguignon—his restaurant could just as easily be on the Riviera as in Lincolnville Beach. Hetuin, who creates bouillabaisse that's as deft as his New England fisherman chowder, welcomes special requests. ⊠ *Rte. 1, Lincolnville Beach,* ☎ *207/789–5600. AE, D, MC, V. Closed Nov.–mid-Apr.*

$$$–$$$$ ✕⊞ **Whitehall Inn.** One of Camden's best-known inns, just north of town, is an 1843 white clapboard sea captain's home with a wide porch and a turn-of-the-century wing. The Millay Room, off the lobby, preserves memorabilia of the poet Edna St. Vincent Millay, who grew up in the area. The sparsely furnished rooms have dark-wood bedsteads, white bedspreads, and claw-foot tubs. The dining room ($$), which serves traditional and creative American cuisine, is open to the public for dinner. ⊠ *Box 558, 52 High St., 04843,* ☎ *207/236–3391 or 800/789–6565,* ℻ *207/236–4427. 44 rooms, 40 with baths. Restaurant, golf privileges, tennis courts, shuffleboard. MAP. AE, MC, V. Closed mid-Oct.–mid-May.*

$$–$$$ ✕⊞ **Youngtown Inn** Inside this white Federal farmhouse are a French-inspired country retreat and a well-respected French restaurant. The country location guarantees quiet, and the inn is a short walk to the Fernald Neck Preserve on Lake Megunticook. Simple, airy rooms open to decks with views of the rolling countryside. Two have fireplaces. The restaurant, open to the public for dinner, serves entrées such as lobster ravioli and pan-seared breast of pheasant with foie gras mousse. ⊠ *Rte. 52 at Youngtown Rd., Lincolnville 04849,* ☎ *207/763–4290 or 800/291–8438,* ℻ *207/763–4078. 5 rooms, 1 suite. Full breakfast. AE, MC, V. Closed Jan.*

$$$–$$$$ ⭐ 🏠 **Victorian Inn.** It's less than 10 minutes from downtown Camden, but with a quiet, waterside location well off Route 1 the Victorian Inn feels a world away. Most rooms and the wraparound porch have magnificent views over island-studded Penobscot Bay. Romantic touches include canopy and brass beds, braided rugs, white wicker furniture, and floral wallpapers. Five guest rooms have fireplaces, and there are four more in common rooms, including the glass-enclosed breakfast room in the turret, where a full breakfast is served. ✉ *Box 258, Sea View Dr., Lincolnville 04849*, ☎ *207/236–3785 or 800/382–9817. 4 rooms, 2 suites. Full breakfast. AE, MC, V.*

$$–$$$ ⭐ 🏠 **Camden Maine Stay.** Within walking distance of shops and restaurants, this 1802 clapboard inn is on the National Register of Historic Places. The grounds are classic and inviting, from the colorful flowers lining the granite walk in summer to the snow-laden bushes in winter. The equally fresh and colorful rooms contain many pieces of Eastlake furniture. ✉ *22 High St., 04842*, ☎ *207/236–9636*, 𝖥𝖠𝖷 *207/236–0621. 7 rooms, 1 suite. Restaurant, pub. Full breakfast. AE, MC, V.*

Nightlife and the Arts

Bay Chamber Concerts (✉ Rockport Opera House, 6 Central St., Rockport, ☎ 207/236–2823) presents chamber music on Thursday and Friday night during July and August; concerts are given once a month from September to May. **Gilbert's Public House** (✉ 12 Bay View St., ☎ 207/236–4320) has dancing and live entertainment. **Sea Dog Tavern & Brewery** (✉ 43 Mechanic St., ☎ 207/236–6863), a popular brew pub in a converted woolen mill, has live entertainment in season. The **Whale's Tooth Pub** (✉ Rte. 1, Lincolnville Beach., ☎ 207/236–3747) has with low-key entertainment on weekends.

Outdoor Activities and Sports

Maine Sport (✉ Rte. 1, Rockport, ☎ 207/236–8797), the best sports outfitter north of Freeport, rents bikes, camping and fishing gear, canoes, kayaks, cross-country skis, ice skates, and snowshoes. It also conducts skiing and kayaking clinics and trips.

Windjammers create a stir whenever they sail into Camden harbor, and a voyage around the bay on one of them, whether for an afternoon or a week, is unforgettable. The season for the excursions is from June to September. Excursion boats also provide an opportunity for getting afloat on the waters of Penobscot Bay. Eggemoggin Reach is a famous cruising ground for yachts, as are the coves and inlets around Deer Isle and the Penobscot Bay waters between Castine and Camden.

Appledore (✉ 0 Lily Pond Dr., ☎ 207/236–8353 or 800/233–7437) operates two-hour sails and private charters on an 86-ft schooner. The **Maine Windjammer Association** (✉ Box 1144, Blue Hill 04614, ☎ 800/807–9463) represents the Camden-based windjammers *Angelique, Grace Bailey, J & E Riggin, Lewis R. French, Mary Day, Mercantile, Nathaniel Bowditch, Roseway,* and *Timberwind,* which sail on cruises that last from three to eight days.

Shopping

Shops and galleries line Camden's Bay View and Main streets and the alleys that lead to the harbor. **Maine's Massachusetts House Galleries** (✉ Rte. 1, Lincolnville, ☎ 207/789–5705) display regional art, including bronzes, carvings, sculptures, and landscapes and seascapes in pencil, oil, and watercolor. The **Owl and Turtle Bookshop** (✉ 8 Bay View St., ☎ 207/236–4769) sells books, CDs, cassettes, and cards. The two-story shop has rooms devoted to marine and children's books. The **Pine Tree Shop & Bayview Gallery** (✉ 33 Bay View St., ☎ 207/236–4534) specializes in original art, prints, and posters, almost all with Maine themes. The **Windsor Chairmakers** (⊠ Rte. 1, Lincolnville, ☎ 207/789–5188 or 800/789–5188) sells custom-made, handcrafted beds, chests, china cabinets, dining tables, highboys, and chairs.

Skiing

Camden Snow Bowl. This ski area has views over Penobscot Bay. ⊠ *Box 1207, Hosmer Pond Rd., 04843,* ☎ *207/236–3438.*

DOWNHILL

In a Currier & Ives setting there's a 950-ft-vertical mountain, a small lodge with cafeteria, a ski school, and ski and toboggan rentals. Camden Snow Bowl has 11 trails accessed by one double chair and two T-bars. It also has night skiing and a toboggan chute.

CROSS-COUNTRY

There are 16 km (10 mi) of cross-country skiing trails at **Camden Hills State Park** (☎ 207/236–9849) and 20 km (12½ mi) at **Tanglewood 4-H Camp** (☎ 207/789–5868), about 5 mi away in Lincolnville.

OTHER ACTIVITIES

Camden Snowbowl has a small lake that is cleared for ice-skating, a snow-tubing park, and a 400-ft toboggan run that shoots sledders out onto the lake.

En Route   Queen Anne cottages with freshly painted porches and exquisite architectural details dot the community of **Bayside,** a section of Northport off Route 1 on the way to Belfast. Some of these homes line the main one-lane thoroughfare, George Street; others are on bluffs with water views around town greens complete with flagpoles and swings; and yet others are on the shore. **Belfast** has a lively waterfront and a charming Main Street lined with shops and galleries. A 1-mi self-guided walking tour passes many sea captains' homes—Belfast was once home to more sea captains than any other port in the world. A ride on the **Belfast & Moosehead Lake Railroad** (⊠ One Depot Sq., Unity 04988, ☎ 207/948–5500 or 800/392–5500), which operates from mid-June to December ($14), is especially enjoyable in the fall after the leaves begin to change colors. The sailing schedules of two **cruise boats** (☎ 800/392–5500) coordinate with the railroad's timetable; a discount applies if you travel on the train and one of the boats.

Searsport

㉖   *38 mi north of Rockland, 57 mi east of Augusta.*

Searsport, Maine's second-largest deepwater port (after Portland)—bills itself as the antiques capital of Maine. The town's stretch of Route 1 has many antiques shops and a large weekend flea market in summer.

The holdings within the nine historic and two modern buildings of the **Penobscot Marine Museum** document the region's seafaring way of life. Included are display photos of 284 sea captains, artifacts of the whaling industry (lots of scrimshaw), navigational instruments, treasures collected by seafarers, and paintings and models of famous ships. ⊠ *Church St.,* ☎ *207/548–2529.* ⌷ *$5.* ☉ *Memorial Day weekend–mid-Oct., Mon.–Sat. 10–5, Sun. noon–5.*

Moose Point State Park (⊠ Rte. 1 between Belfast and Searsport, ☎ 207/548–2882) is ideal for easy hikes and picnics overlooking Penobscot Bay.

Dining and Lodging

$$–$$$ ✕ **Nickerson Tavern.** A sea captain built the 1838 structure that holds this restaurant. Its three dining rooms are decorated in a nautical motif; the Searsport Room is the most intimate. The menu changes sea-

sonally—crab cakes or shrimp satay are potential appetizers; raspberry-hazelnut chicken or veal piccata Milanese might show up as entrées. ⊠ *Rte. 1,* ☎ *207/548–2220. D, MC, V.* ☉ *Mid-June–Labor Day, daily; reduced hrs off-season. Closed Jan.–Apr. No lunch.*

$$ ✕ **90 Main.** Young chef-owner Sheila Costello helms this family-run restaurant that has an outdoor patio. Using Pemaquid oysters, Maine blueberries, organic vegetables grown on a nearby farm, and other local ingredients, Costello creates flavorful dishes that delight the senses. Choose from a chalkboard full of specials that always includes a macrobiotic option, or start with the smoked seafood and pâté sampler or the spinach salad topped with sautéed chicken, sweet peppers, hazelnuts, and a warm raspberry vinaigrette. Entrées include rib-eye steak and seafood linguine fra Diablo. ⊠ *90 Main St., Belfast,* ☎ *207/338–1106. AE, MC, V.*

$–$$ 🏨 **Homeport Inn.** This 1861 inn, a former sea captain's home, provides an opulent Victorian environment that might put you in the mood to rummage through the nearby antiques and treasure shops. The back rooms downstairs have private decks and views of the bay. Families often stay in the two-bedroom housekeeping cottage. ⊠ *Rte. 1,* ☎ *207/548–2259 or 800/742–5814. 7 rooms with bath, 3 rooms share bath, 1 2-bedroom cottage. Full breakfast. AE, D, MC, V.*

$–$$ 🏨 **Inn on Primrose Hill.** Built in 1812 and once the home of a navy admiral, this inn near the waterfront is the most elegant in the area. The 2 acres that surround it have formal gardens and a brick terrace with wrought-iron furniture. Owners Pat and Linus Heinz have restored authentic details such as the ornate Waterford chandeliers, a mahogany dining set, and a black-marble fireplace. The spacious public rooms include double parlors, a library with a large-screen TV, and a sunny conservatory with wicker and plump upholstered furniture. Guest rooms, which are less elaborate than the public spaces, have either partial bay views or garden views. ⊠ *212 High St.,* ☎ *207/338–6982 or 888/338–6982. 3 rooms with bath, 1 room shares bath. Croquet. Full breakfast. No credit cards.*

Castine

27 *16 mi south of Bucksport.*

The French, the British, the Dutch, and the Americans fought over Castine from the 17th century to the War of 1812. Present-day Castine's many attributes include its lively landing, Federal and Greek Revival houses, and town common; there are two museums and the ruins of a British fort to explore. For a nice stroll, park your car at the landing and walk up Main Street past the two inns and on toward the white Trinitarian Federated Church, which has a tapering spire.

Among the white clapboard buildings that ring the town common are the Ives House (once the summer home of the poet Robert Lowell), the Abbott School, and the Unitarian Church, capped by a whimsical belfry.

Dining and Lodging

$$–$$$ ✕🏨 **Castine Inn.** Upholstered easy chairs and fine prints and paintings are typical of the furnishings in this inn's airy rooms. The third ★ floor has the best views: the harbor over the handsome formal gardens on one side, the village on the other. The dining room, decorated with a wraparound mural of Castine and its harbor, is open to the public for breakfast and dinner; the creative menu includes New England fare and entrées such as Kalamata-olive-crusted salmon with a yellow-pepper–grapefruit sauce. There's a snug, English-style pub off the lobby. ⊠ *Box 41, Main St., 04421,* ☎ *207/326–4365,* 𝔽𝕏 *207/*

*326–4570. 17 rooms, 3 suites. Restaurant, pub, sauna. Full break-
fast. MC, V. Closed Nov.–Apr.*

Shopping
Chris Murray Waterfowl Carver (✉ Upper Main St., ☎ 207/326–9033)
sells award-winning wildfowl carvings. **H.O.M.E.** (✉ Rte. 1, Orland,
☎ 207/469–7961) is a cooperative crafts village. **McGrath-Dunham
Gallery** (✉ Main St., ☎ 207/326–9938) carries fine art.

Blue Hill

28   *19 mi southeast of Bucksport.*

With a more dramatic perch over its harbor and a Main Street that's
not a major thoroughfare, Castine probably has the edge over Blue Hill
in the charm department. But Blue Hill is by no means unappealing,
and the town, renowned for its pottery, has better shops and galleries.

Dining and Lodging

$$–$$$ ✕ **Jonathan's.** The downstairs room at nautically minded Jonathan's
has captain's chairs, linen tablecloths, and local art; in the post-and-
beam upstairs, there's wood everywhere, plus candles with hurricane
globes and high-back chairs. Fresh fish and meat entrées are always
on the menu. French, Italian, Californian, and Maine-produced vin-
tages are on the lengthy wine list. ✉ *Main St.,* ☎ *207/374–5226. MC,
V. Closed Mar. No lunch.*

$$ ✕ **The Landing.** There's a great view over boat-filled Bucks Harbor from
★   this second-floor restaurant in sleepy South Brooksville. Tasty starters
include the roasted corn and crab cakes and the rabbit and shiitake
ravioli, which you can follow with grilled medallions of halibut, pan-
seared breast of Long Island duckling, or penne with grilled tiger
shrimp. ✉ *Steamboat Wharf Rd.,* ☎ FAX *207/326–8483. MC, V. Closed
mid-Sept.–mid-June.*

$$$$ ✕▣ **Blue Hill Inn.** Rambling and antiques-filled, this inn is a comfort-
★   ing place to relax after exploring nearby shops and galleries; four
rooms have fireplaces. The multicourse, candlelit dinners at Blue Hill's
renowned dining room ($$$; reservations essential) are prepared with
organically raised produce and herbs, local meats, and seafood. An hors
d'oeuvres hour in the garden, or by the living-room fireplace, precedes
dinner. ✉ *Box 403, Union St., 04614,* ☎ *207/374–2844 or 800/826–
7415,* FAX *207/374–2829. 11 rooms, 1 apartment. Restaurant. MAP.
MC, V. Closed early Dec., Jan.–Mar.*

$$–$$$$ ▣ **John Peters Inn.** The John Peters is unsurpassed for the privacy of
★   its location and the good taste in the decor of its guest rooms. The liv-
ing room has two fireplaces and a baby grand piano. Huge breakfasts
include a lobster omelet. The Surry Room has a king-size bed, a fire-
place, a curly-maple chest, and six windows. The large rooms in the
carriage house have dining areas, cherry floors and woodwork, and
wicker and brass accents. ✉ *Box 916, Peters Point 04614,* ☎ *207/
374–2116. 6 rooms and 1 suite in inn; 6 suites in carriage house. Pool,
boating. Full breakfast. MC, V. Closed Nov.–Apr.*

$–$$ ▣ **Bucks Harbor Inn.** The spirit and decor here are like those of a tra-
★   ditional B&B, but owners Peter and Anne Eberling, unlike many
innkeepers, welcome children. Breezes off the water cool the large
corner rooms. A full cooked-to-order breakfast is served on the porch.
✉ *Box 268, Rte. 176, South Brooksville 04617,* ☎ *207/326–8660,*
FAX *207/326–0730. 6 rooms share 2 1/2 baths. Full breakfast; dinner
available Sat. in winter. MC, V.*

Nightlife and the Arts

Kneisel Hall Chamber Music Festival (✉ Kneisel Hall, Rte. 15, ☎ 207/374–2811) has concerts on Sunday and Friday in summer. **Left Bank Bakery and Café** (✉ Rte. 172, ☎ 207/374–2201) presents musical talent from across the nation. **Surry Opera Co.** (✉ Morgan Bay Road, Surry, ☎ 207/667–2629) stages operas throughout the area in summer.

Outdoor Activities and Sports

Holbrook Island Sanctuary (✉ Penobscot Bay, Brooksville, ☎ 207/326–4012) has a gravelly beach with a splendid view, a picnic area, and hiking trails. The **Phoenix Centre** (✉ Rte. 175, Blue Hill Falls, ☎ 207/374–2113) operates sea-kayaking tours of Blue Hill Bay and Eggemoggin Reach.

Shopping

Big Chicken Barn (✉ Rte. 1, Ellsworth., ☎ 207/374–2715) has three floors filled with books, antiques, and collectibles. **Handworks Gallery** (✉ Main St., ☎ 207/374–5613) carries unusual crafts, jewelry, and clothing. **Leighton Gallery** (✉ Parker Point Rd., ☎ 207/374–5001) shows oil paintings, lithographs, watercolors, and other contemporary art in the gallery, and sculpture in its garden. **North Country Textiles** (✉ Main St., ☎ 207/374–2715) specializes in fine woven shawls, place mats, throws, baby blankets, and pillows in subtle patterns and color schemes. **Old Cove Antiques** (✉ Rte. 15, Sargentville, ☎ 207/359–2031) has folk art, quilts, and hooked rugs.

Rackliffe Pottery (✉ Rte. 172, ☎ 207/374–2297) is famous for its vivid blue pottery, including plates, tea and coffee sets, pitchers, casseroles, and canisters. **Rowantrees Pottery** (✉ Union St., ☎ 207/374–5535) has an extensive selection of styles and patterns in dinnerware, tea sets, vases, and decorative items.

En Route Scenic Route 15 south from Blue Hill passes through Brooksville and on through the graceful suspension bridge that crosses Eggemoggin Reach to Deer Isle. The turnout and picnic area at Caterpillar Hill, 1 mi south of the junction of Routes 15 and 175, commands a fabulous view of Penobscot Bay, hundreds of dark green islands, and the Camden Hills across the bay, which from this perspective look like a faraway mountain range, although they are less than 25 mi away.

Deer Isle Village

29 *16 mi south of Blue Hill.*

In Deer Isle Village, thick woods give way to tidal coves. Stacks of lobster traps populate the backyards of shingled houses and dirt roads lead to summer cottages.

Haystack Mountain School of Crafts attracts internationally renowned glassblowers, potters, sculptors, jewelers, blacksmiths, printmakers, and weavers to its summer institute. You can attend evening lectures or visit artists' studios (by appointment only). ✉ *South of Deer Isle Village on Rte. 15, turn left at Gulf gas station and follow signs for 6 mi,* ☎ *207/348–2306.* ⊡ *Free.* ☉ *June–Sept.*

Dining and Lodging

$$$$ ✕🏨 **Goose Cove Lodge.** This heavily wooded property at the end of a back road has a fine stretch of ocean frontage, a sandy beach, and a long sandbar that leads to a nature preserve. Cottages and suites are in secluded woodlands and on the shore. Some are attached, some have a single large room, and still others have one or two bedrooms. All but three units have fireplaces. The prix-fixe four-course dinner at the

restaurant ($$$; reservations essential) is always superb and always includes at least one vegetarian entrée; dinner is preceded by complimentary hors d'oeuvres. On Friday night, there's a lobster feast on the inn's private beach. ⊠ *Box 40, Goose Cove Rd., Sunset 04683,* ☎ *207/348–2508 or 800/728–1963,* 𝔽𝔸𝕏 *207/348–2624. 6 rooms, 7 suites, 13 cottages. Restaurant, hiking, volleyball, beach, boating. MAP. MC, V. Closed mid-Oct.–mid-May.*

$$$–$$$$ ✕🏠 **Pilgrim's Inn.** A deep-red, four-story gambrel-roof house, the Pil-
★ grim's Inn, which dates from about 1793, overlooks a mill pond and harbor in Deer Isle Village. The library has wing chairs and Oriental rugs; a downstairs taproom has a huge brick fireplace and pine furniture. Guest rooms have English fabrics and carefully selected antiques. The dining room ($$$; reservations essential; no lunch) is in the attached barn, a rustic and yet elegant space with farm implements, French oil lamps, and tiny windows. The five-course, single-entrée menu changes nightly; it might include rack of lamb or fresh seafood. ⊠ *Rte. 15A, 04627,* ☎ 𝔽𝔸𝕏 *207/348–6615. 13 rooms, 10 with bath; 2 seaside cottages. Restaurant, bicycles. Full breakfast; MAP available. MC, V. Closed mid-Oct.–mid-May.*

Shopping

Blue Heron Gallery & Studio (⊠ Church St., ☎ 207/348–6051) sells the work of the Haystack Mountain School of Crafts faculty. **Harbor Farm** (⊠ Rte. 15, Deer Isle, ☎ 207/348–7737) carries wonderful products for the home, such as pottery, artworks, furniture, dinnerware, linens, and folk art. **Old Deer Isle Parish House Antiques** (⊠ Rte. 15, Deer Isle Village, ☎ 207/348–9964) is a place for poking around in jumbles of old kitchenware, glassware, books, and linen. **Turtle Gallery** (⊠ Rte. 15, ☎ 207/348–9977) shows contemporary fine art and crafts.

Stonington

30 *7 mi south of Deer Isle.*

Stonington is an emphatically ungentrified community that tolerates summer visitors but makes no effort to cater to them. Main Street holds gift shops and galleries, but this is a working port town—the principal activity is at the waterfront, where fishing boats arrive with the day's catch. At night, the town can be rowdy. The high, sloped island that rises beyond the archipelago of Merchants Row is Isle au Haut (accessible by mail boat from Stonington), which contains a remote section of Acadia National Park.

Lodging

$$–$$$ 🏠 **Inn on the Harbor.** From the front, this inn composed of four 100-year-old Victorian buildings is as plain and unadorned as Stonington itself. But out back it opens up, with an expansive deck over the harbor. Many guests take breakfast here in the morning. Rooms on the harbor side have views, and some have fireplaces and private decks. Those on the street side lack the views and can be noisy at night. ⊠ *Box 69, Main St., 04681,* ☎ *207/367–2420 or 800/942–2420,* 𝔽𝔸𝕏 *207/367–5165. 13 rooms, 1 suite. Espresso bar. Continental breakfast. AE, D, MC, V. Closed Jan.–Mar.*

Shopping

Dockside Books & Gifts (⊠ W. Main St., Stonington, ☎ 207/367–2652) stocks an eclectic selection of books, crafts, and gifts in a harborfront shop. **Eastern Bay Gallery** (⊠ Main St., Stonington, ☎ 207/367–5006) carries contemporary Maine crafts; summer exhibits highlight the works of specific artists.

Isle au Haut

③ *14 mi south of Stonington.*

Isle au Haut thrusts its steeply ridged back out of the sea south of Stonington. Accessible only by passenger mail boat (☎ 207/367–5193), the island is worth visiting for the ferry ride itself, a half-hour cruise amid the tiny, pink-shore islands of Merchants Row, where you might see terns, guillemots, and harbor seals. More than half the island is part of **Acadia National Park**: 17½ mi of trails extend through quiet spruce and birch woods, along beaches and seaside cliffs, and over the spine of the central mountain ridge. (For more information on Acadia National Park, *see* Bar Harbor and Acadia, *below*.) From late June to mid-September, the mail boat docks at **Duck Harbor** within the park. The small campground here, with five Adirondack-type lean-tos, is open from mid-May to mid-October and fills up quickly. Reservations, which are essential, can be made after April 1 by writing to Acadia National Park (⊠ Box 177, Bar Harbor 04609).

Dining and Lodging

$$$$ 🏨 **The Keeper's House.** This converted lighthouse-keeper's house is on a rock ledge surrounded by thick spruce forest. There is no electricity, but every guest receives a flashlight upon registering; guests dine by candlelight on seafood or chicken and read in the evening by kerosene lantern. Trails link the inn with Acadia National Park's Isle au Haut trail network, and you can walk to the village. The spacious rooms contain simple, painted-wood furniture and local crafts. A separate cottage, the Oil House, has no indoor plumbing. Access to the island is via the daily (except Sunday and holidays) mail boat from Stonington. ⊠ Box 26, Lighthouse Rd., 04645, ☎ 207/367–2261. *4 rooms share 2 baths, 1 cottage. Dock, bicycles. AP. No credit cards. BYOB. Closed Nov.–Apr.*

Penobscot Bay A to Z

Getting Around

BY CAR

Route 1 follows the west coast of Penobscot Bay, linking Rockland, Rockport, Camden, Belfast, and Searsport. On the east side of the bay, Route 175 (south from Route 1) takes you to Route 166A (for Castine) and Route 15 (for Blue Hill, Deer Isle, and Stonington). A car is essential for exploring the bay area.

Contacts and Resources

B&B RESERVATION AGENCY

Camden Accommodations (☎ 207/236–6090 or 800/236–1920, ℻ 207/236–6091) provides assistance for reservations in and around Camden.

EMERGENCIES

Blue Hill Memorial Hospital (⊠ Water St., Blue Hill, ☎ 207/374–2836). **Island Medical Center** (⊠ Airport Rd., Stonington, ☎ 207/367–2311). **Penobscot Bay Medical Center** (⊠ Rte. 1, Rockport, ☎ 207/596–8000). **Waldo County General Hospital** (⊠ 56 Northport Ave., Belfast, ☎ 207/338–2500).

VISITOR INFORMATION

Belfast Area Chamber of Commerce (⊠ Box 58, Belfast 04915, ☎ 207/338–5900). **Blue Hill Chamber of Commerce** (⊠ Box 520, Blue Hill 04614, ☎ no phone). **Castine Town Office** (⊠ Emerson Hall, Court St., Castine 04421, ☎ 207/326–4502). **Rockland–Thomaston Area Chamber of Commerce** (⊠ Harbor Park, Box 508, Rockland 04841, ☎ 207/596–0376 or 800/562–2529). **Rockport-Camden-Lincolnville**

Chamber of Commerce (⊠ Public Landing, Box 919, Camden 04843, ☎ 207/236–4404 or 800/223–5459). **Waldo County Regional Chamber of Commerce** (⊠ School St., Unity 04988,☎ 207/948–5050 or 800/870–9934).

MOUNT DESERT ISLAND

East of Penobscot Bay, Acadia is the informal name for the area that includes Mount Desert Island (pronounced "dessert") and its surroundings: Blue Hill Bay; Frenchman Bay; and Ellsworth, Hancock, and other mainland towns. Mount Desert, 13 mi across, is Maine's largest island, and it encompasses most of Acadia National Park, Maine's principal tourist attraction, with more than 4 million visitors a year. The 40,000 acres of woods and mountains, lake and shore, footpaths, carriage roads, and hiking trails that make up the park extend to other islands and some of the mainland. Outside the park, on Mount Desert's east shore, Bar Harbor has become a busy tourist town. An upper-class resort town of the 19th century, Bar Harbor inns, motels, and restaurants.

Bar Harbor

③ *160 mi northeast of Portland, 22 mi southeast of Ellsworth. Coastal Rte. 1 passes through Ellsworth, where Rte. 3 turns south to Mount Desert Island and heads into Bar Harbor.*

Most of Bar Harbor's grand mansions were destroyed in a fire that devastated the island in 1947, but many of the surviving estates have been converted into inns and restaurants. Motels abound, yet the town retains the beauty of a commanding location on Frenchman Bay. Shops, restaurants, and hotels are clustered along Main, Mt. Desert, and Cottage streets.

The **Bar Harbor Historical Society Museum,** on the lower level of the Jesup Memorial Library, displays photographs of Bar Harbor from the days when it catered to the very rich. Other exhibits document the fire of 1947. ⊠ *34 Mt. Desert St.,* ☎ *207/288–4245.* ⛳ *Free.* ☉ *Mid-June–mid-Oct., Mon.–Sat. 1–4 or by appointment.*

☙ **Acadia Zoo** has pastures, streams, and woods that shelter about 40 species of wild and domestic animals, including reindeer, wolves, monkeys, and a moose. A barn has been converted into a rain-forest habitat for monkeys, birds, reptiles, and other Amazon creatures. ⊠ *Rte. 3, Trenton, north of Bar Harbor,* ☎ *207/667–3244.* ⛳ *$6.* ☉ *May–Dec., daily 9:30–dusk.*

On Frenchman Bay but off Mount Desert Island, the 55-acre **Lamoine State Park** (⊠ Rte. 184, Lamoine, ☎ 207/667–4778) has a boat-launching ramp, a fishing pier, a children's playground, and a 61-site campground that's open from mid-May to mid-October.

Arcady Music Festival (☎ 207/288–3151) schedules concerts (primarily classical) at locations around Mount Desert Island and at some off-island sites, year-round. **Bar Harbor Music Festival** (⊠ 59 Cottage St., ☎ 207/288–5744) programs recitals, jazz, chamber music, string-orchestra, and pop concerts by young professionals from July to early August.

Dining and Lodging

$$$ ✕ **George's.** Candles, flowers, and linens grace the tables of the four
★ small dining rooms in this old house. The menu's Mediterranean influences can be tasted in the phyllo-wrapped lobster; the lamb and wild-

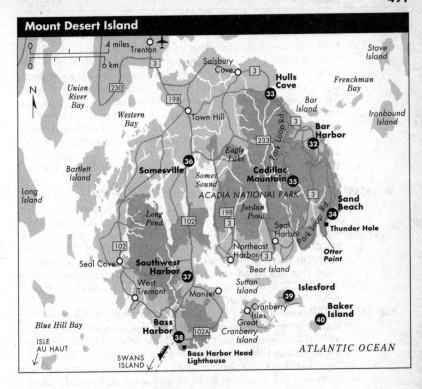

Mount Desert Island

game entrées are superb. The prix-fixe menu includes an appetizer, an entrée, and dessert. ⊠ *7 Stephen's La.,* ☎ *207/288–4505. AE, D, DC, MC, V. Closed Nov.–mid-June. No lunch.*

$$–$$$ ✕ **Porcupine Grill.** Named for a cluster of islets in Frenchman Bay, this restaurant has a menu that changes regularly but might include starters such as pan-roasted mussels or citrus barbecued quail and main courses like grilled lobster, twin Portobello fillets, or filet mignon. Soft green walls, antique furnishings, and Villeroy & Boch porcelain create an ambience that complements the cuisine. At the Thrumcap wine bar, you can unwind by the fire, sip any of 20 wines by the glass, and order from a lighter menu. ⊠ *123 Cottage St.,* ☎ *207/288–3884. AE, DC, MC, V. Closed Mon.–Thurs. Nov.–June. No lunch.*

$–$$$ ✕ **Galyn's.** The upstairs dining rooms at this casual restaurant have a
★ limited view of the harbor, but most people come here for the well-crafted dishes and affordable prices. The dinner menu includes fish, chicken, lobster, seafood, beef, and vegetarian dishes. Sandwiches, salads, and entrées like quiche, jambalaya, ribs, and stir-fries are served at lunch. ⊠ *17 Main St.,* ☎ *207/288–9706. AE, D, MC, V.*

$$$–$$$$ ✕🔲 **Bar Harbor Inn.** The roots of this genteel inn date from the 1880s. The large yet cozy lobby, where breakfast and tea are served daily, has a fireplace and wing-back chairs. Rooms in the Oceanfront Lodge are larger than those in the main building and have balconies with ocean views. The formal waterfront dining room, the Reading Room ($$), serves mostly Continental fare but has some Maine specialties like lobster pie and a scrumptious Indian pudding. ⊠ *Newport Dr., 04609,* ☎ *207/288–3351 or 800/248–3351,* ℻ *207/288–5296. 153 rooms. 2 restaurants, no-smoking rooms, pool, business services. Continental breakfast. AE, D, DC, MC, V.*

$$$–$$$$ 🏠 **Balance Rock Inn.** This grand summer cottage built in 1903 commands a prime, secluded location on the water but is only two blocks from downtown. The atmosphere is a bit stuffy, but the service is thorough and thoughtful. Rooms are spacious and meticulously furnished with reproduction pieces—four-poster and canopy beds in guest rooms, crystal chandeliers and a grand piano in common rooms. Some rooms have fireplaces, saunas, steam rooms, whirlpool tubs, or private porches, and most have views of the pool and well-tended gardens on the front lawn and to the water beyond. From the bar on the veranda, you can watch the activity in the harbor. ⊠ *21 Albert Meadow 04609,* ☎ *207/288–2610 or 800/753–0494,* 𝔽𝔸𝕏 *207/288–2005. 15 rooms, 1 suite. Bar, pool, exercise room, concierge. Full breakfast. AE, D, MC, V. Closed late Oct.–early May.*

$$$–$$$$ 🏠 **Inn at Canoe Point.** Seclusion and privacy are the main attributes
★   of this snug, 100-year-old Tudor-style house on the water at Hulls Cove, 2 mi from Bar Harbor and ¼ mi from Acadia National Park's Hulls Cove Visitor Center. The Master Suite, a large room with a gas fireplace, has French doors that open onto a waterside deck. The inn's living room has huge windows that look out on the water, a granite fireplace, and a waterfront deck where breakfast is served on summer mornings. ⊠ *Box 216, Rte. 3, 04609,* ☎ *207/288–9511. 3 rooms, 2 suites. Full breakfast. D, MC, V.*

$$$–$$$$ 🏠 **Ullikana.** Inside the stucco and timber walls of this traditional Tudor cottage is a riotous decor that juxtaposes traditional antiques with contemporary country pieces, vibrant color with French country wallpapers, and abstract art with folk art. It not only works, it shines. Rooms are large, most have at least a glimpse of the water, many have fireplaces, and some have decks. Breakfast is a multicourse, gourmet affair. Ullikana is a short walk to downtown shops, yet it's a private location with pretty gardens. ⊠ *16 The Field, 04609,* ☎ *207/288–9552,* 𝔽𝔸𝕏 *207/288–3682. 10 rooms. Full breakfast. MC, V. Closed Nov.–May.*

$–$$ 🏠 **Bass Cottage in the Field.** What a bargain! Anna Jean Turner began welcoming guests to this former summer estate when she came here as a young girl in 1928. She continues to operate the inn with the help of her niece. Behind Bar Harbor's Main Street and a short walk from the Marginal Way, Bass Cottage is a step back in time in both decor and price. The rooms could use a face-lift, but most likely you'll spend your time on the glassed-in wraparound porch, which is furnished with antique white wicker. ⊠ *In the Field, 04609,* ☎ *207/288–3705,* 𝔽𝔸𝕏 *207/288–2005. 10 rooms, 6 with private baths. No credit cards. Closed mid-Oct.–late May.*

Nightlife

For dancing, try **Carmen Verandah** (⊠ 119 Main St., upstairs, ☎ 207/288–2766). **Geddy's Pub** (⊠ 19 Main St., ☎ 207/288–5077) has live entertainment early in the evening followed by a DJ spinning discs.

Outdoor Activities and Sports

BICYCLING

Acadia Bike & Canoe (⊠ 48 Cottage St., ☎ 207/288–9605) and **Bar Harbor Bicycle Shop** (⊠ 141 Cottage St., ☎ 207/288–3886) rent bicycles.

BOATING

For canoe rentals try **Acadia Bike & Canoe** (☞ Bicycling, *above*). For guided kayak tours, try **National Park Kayak Tours** (⊠ 137 Cottage St., ☎ 207/288–0342) or **Coastal Kayaking Tours** (⊠ 48 Cottage St., ☎ 207/288–9605).

Acadian Whale Watcher (⊠ Golden Anchor Pier, West St., ☎ 207/288–9794 or 800/421–3307) runs 3½-hour whale-watching cruises from June to mid-October. ***Chippewa*** (⊠ Bar Harbor Inn Pier, ☎ 207/288–4585 or 207/288–2373) is a 65-ft classic motor vessel that cruises past islands and lighthouses three times a day (including sunset) in summer. ***Natalie Todd*** (⊠ Bar Harbor Inn Pier, ☎ 207/288–4585 or 207/288–2373) operates two-hour cruises on a three-masted windjammer between mid-May and mid-October. **Whale Watcher Inc.** (⊠ 1 West St., ☎ 207/288–3322 or 800/508–1499) operates the windjammer *Bay Lady,* the nature-sightseeing cruise vessel *Acadian,* and the 300-passenger *Atlantis* in summer.

CARRIAGE RIDES

Wildwood Stables (⊠ Park Loop Rd., near Jordan Pond House, ☎ 207/276–3622) gives romantic tours in horse-drawn carriages on the 51-mi network of carriage roads designed and built by philanthropist John D. Rockefeller, Jr. There are three two-hour trips and three one-hour trips daily, including a "tea-and-popover ride" that stops at Jordan Pond House (☞ Dining, Lodging, and Camping *in* Acadia National Park, *below*) and a sunset ride to the summit of Day Mountain.

Shopping

Bar Harbor in summer is prime territory for browsing for gifts, T-shirts, and novelty items; for bargains, head for the outlets that line Route 3 in Ellsworth, which have good discounts on shoes, sportswear, cookware, and more.

Birdsnest Gallery (⊠ 12 Mt. Desert St., ☎ 207/288–4054) sells fine art, paintings, and sculpture. The **Eclipse Gallery** (⊠ 12 Mt. Desert St., ☎ 207/288–9048) carries handblown glass, ceramics, art photography, and wood furniture. **Island Artisans** (⊠ 99 Main St., ☎ 207/288–4214) is a crafts cooperative. The **Lone Moose–Fine Crafts** (⊠ 78 West St., ☎ 207/288–4229) has art glass and works in clay, pottery, wood, and fiberglass.

Acadia National Park

4 mi northwest of Bar Harbor (to Hulls Cove).

❸❸ The **Hulls Cove** approach to Acadia National Park is northwest of Bar Harbor on Route 3. Even though it is often clogged with traffic in summer, the **Park Loop Road** provides the best introduction to the park. At the start of the loop at Hulls Cove, the **visitor center** shows a free 15-minute orientation film. Also available at the center are books, maps of hiking trails and carriage roads, the schedule for naturalist-led tours, and cassettes for drive-it-yourself tours. Traveling south on the Park Loop Road, you'll reach a small ticket booth where you pay the $5-per-vehicle entrance fee. Take the next left to the parking area for Sand Beach. ⊠ *Visitor center, Park Loop Rd. off Rte. 3,* ☎ *207/288–3338.* ⊙ *June–Aug., daily 8–6; mid-Apr.–June and Sept.–Oct., daily 8–4:30. Closed Nov.–mid-Apr.*

❸❹ **Sand Beach** is a small stretch of pink sand backed by the mountains of Acadia and the odd lump of rock known as the Beehive. The **Ocean Trail,** which runs alongside the Park Loop Road from Sand Beach to the Otter Point parking area, is an easily accessible walk with some of the most spectacular scenery in Maine: huge slabs of pink granite heaped at the ocean's edge, ocean views unobstructed to the horizon, and **Thunder Hole,** a natural seaside cave into which the ocean rushes and roars.

35 **Cadillac Mountain,** at 1,532 ft, is the highest point on the eastern seaboard. From the smooth, bald summit you have a 360-degree view of the ocean, islands, jagged coastline, and woods and lakes of Acadia and its surroundings. You can drive or hike to the summit.

The **Abbe Museum** surveys the culture, history, and art of Maine Indians from prehistoric times to the present. ⊠ *Sieur de Mont Spring exit from Rte. 3 or Acadia National Park Loop Rd.,* ☎ *207/288–3519.* ⊡ *$2.* ⊙ *July–Aug., 9–5; mid-May–June and Sept–mid-Oct., 10–4. Closed mid-Oct.–mid-May.*

The Wild Gardens of Acadia present a miniature view of the plants that grow on Mt. Desert Island. ⊠ *Rte. 3 at the Sieur de Mont Spring exit,* ☎ *207/288–3400.* ⊡ *Free.* ⊙ *Paths open 24 hrs.*

Dining, Lodging, and Camping

$$ ✕ **Jordan Pond House.** Oversize popovers with homemade strawberry jam and tea are a century-old tradition at this rustic restaurant, where in fine weather you can sit on the terrace or the lawn and admire the views of Jordan Pond and the mountains. Lobster stew and other seafood dishes are on the dinner menu. ⊠ *Park Loop Rd.,* ☎ *207/276–3316. AE, D, MC, V. Closed late Oct.–mid-May.*

$ ⛺ **Blackwoods and Seawall.** These two campgrounds with a total of 530 campsites fill up quickly during the summer. Space at Seawall is allocated on a first-come, first-served basis, starting at 8 AM. Between mid-June and mid-September, reserve a Blackwoods site within eight weeks of a visit. No reservations are required in the off-season. *Blackwoods:* ⊠ *Rte. 3, Northeast Harbor,* ☎ *800/365–2267.* ⊙ *Year-round. Seawall:* ⊠ *Rte. 102A, Northeast Harbor,* ☎ *207/244–3600. Closed late Sept.–late May.*

Outdoor Activities and Sports

BIKING

The carriage roads that wind through the woods and fields of Acadia National Park are ideal for biking and jogging when the ground is dry and for cross-country skiing in winter. The Hulls Cove visitor center has maps.

HIKING

Acadia National Park maintains nearly 200 mi of foot and carriage paths, from easy strolls along flatlands to rigorous climbs that involve ladders and handholds on rock faces. Among the more rewarding hikes are the Precipice Trail to Champlain Mountain, the Great Head Loop, the Gorham Mountain Trail, and the path around Eagle Lake. The Hulls Cove visitor center has trail guides and maps.

Around Acadia

On completing the 27-mi Park Loop Road, you can continue your auto tour of the island by heading west on Route 233 for the villages on Somes Sound, a true fjord—the only one on the East Coast—which **36** almost bisects Mount Desert Island. **Somesville,** the oldest settlement on the island (1621), is a carefully preserved New England village of white clapboard houses and churches, neat green lawns, and bits of blue water visible behind them.

37 Route 102 south from Somesville takes you to **Southwest Harbor,** which combines the salty character of a working port with the refinements of a summer resort community. From the town's Main Street (Route 102), turn left onto Clark Point Road to reach the harbor.

♻ **Mount Desert Oceanarium** has exhibits in two locations on the fishing and sea life of the Gulf of Maine, a live-seal program, a lobster hatchery, and hands-on exhibits such as a touch tank. ✉ *Clark Point Rd., Southwest Harbor,* ☎ *207/244–7330;* ✉ *Rte. 3, Thomas Bay, Bar Harbor,* ☎ *207/288–5005.* ☎ *Call for admission fees (combination tickets available for both sites).* ⊙ *Mid-May–mid-Oct., Mon.–Sat. 9–5.*

Wendell Gilley Museum of Bird Carving showcases bird carvings by Gilley, presents carving demonstrations and workshops and natural-history programs, and exhibits wildlife art. ✉ *4 Herrick Rd., Southwest Harbor,* ☎ *207/244–7555.* ☎ *$3.25.* ⊙ *July–Aug., Tues.–Sun. 10–5; June and Sept.–Oct., Tues.–Sun. 10–4; May and Nov.–Dec., Fri.–Sun. 10–4. Closed Jan.–Apr.*

㊳ In **Bass Harbor,** 4 mi south of Southwest Harbor (follow Route 102A when Route 102 forks), visit the **Bass Harbor Head lighthouse,** which clings to a cliff at the eastern entrance to Blue Hill Bay. It was built in 1858. The tiny lobstering village has cottages for rent, inns, a restaurant, a gift shop, and the **Maine State Ferry Service**'s car-and-passenger ferry to Swans Island. ☎ *207/244–3254.* ⊙ *6 daily runs June–mid-Oct.; fewer trips rest of yr.*

Dining and Lodging

$$$–$$$$ ✕🏨 **Claremont Hotel.** Built in 1884 and operated continuously as an inn, the Claremont calls up memories of the long, leisurely vacations of days gone by. The yellow clapboard structure commands a view of Somes Sound. Croquet is played on the lawn, and cocktails and lunch are served at the Boat House in summer. The cottages have not been updated as much as the inn's rooms; some guests complain about the facilities in them. The old-style dining room ($$–$$$), open to the public for breakfast and dinner, has picture windows. The menu changes weekly and always includes fresh fish and at least one vegetarian entrée; reservations are essential, and a jacket is required for dinner. ✉ *Box 137; off Clark Point Rd., Southwest Harbor 04679,* ☎ *207/244–5036 or 800/244–5036,* ℻ *207/244–3512. 29 rooms, 1 suite, 12 cottages. Restaurant, tennis court, croquet, dock, boating, bicycles. Full breakfast; MAP available. No credit cards. Hotel and restaurant closed mid-Oct.–mid-June; cottages closed Nov.–mid-May.*

$$ 🏨 **Island House.** This sweet B&B on the quiet side of the island has no-nonsense rooms in the main house. The carriage-house suite comes complete with a sleeping loft and a kitchenette. ✉ *Box 1006, 121 Clark Point Rd., Southwest Harbor 04679,* ☎ *207/244–5180. 4 rooms share 3 baths, 1 suite. Full breakfast. MC, V.*

Nightlife

A lively boating crowd frequents the lounge at the **Moorings Restaurant** (✉ Shore Rd., Manset, ☎ 207/244–7070), which is accessible by boat and car. The lounge stays open until after midnight from mid-May to October.

Outdoor Activities and Sports

BICYCLING

Southwest Cycle (✉ Main St., Southwest Harbor, ☎ 207/244–5856) rents bicycles.

BOATING

Manset Yacht Service (✉ Shore Rd., ☎ 207/244–4040) rents sailboats. **National Park Canoe Rentals** (✉ Pretty Marsh Rd., Somesville, at the head of Long Pond, ☎ 207/244–5854) rents canoes.

Blackjack (✉ Town Dock, Northeast Harbor, ☎ 207/276–5043 or 207/288–3056), a 33-ft Friendship sloop, makes four trips daily from mid-June to mid-October. The **Rachel B. Jackson Schooner** (✉ Manset Town Wharf, Manset, ☎ 207/244–7813), a Maine-built windjammer, takes passengers on 2 ½-hour sails around Somes Sound and the Cranberry Isles.

Shopping

Marianne Clark Fine Antiques (⊠ Main St., Southwest Harbor, ☏ 207/244–9247) has formal and country furniture, American paintings, and accessories from the 18th and 19th centuries. **Port in a Storm Bookstore** (⊠ Main St., Somesville, ☏ 207/244–4114) is a book-lover's nirvana.

Island Excursions

Off the southeast shore of Mount Desert Island at the entrance to Somes Sound, the five **Cranberry Isles**—Great Cranberry, Islesford (or Little Cranberry), Baker Island, Sutton Island, and Bear Island—escape the hubbub that engulfs Acadia National Park in summer. Great Cranberry and Islesford are served by the **Beal & Bunker passenger ferry** (☏ 207/244–3575) from Northeast Harbor and by **Cranberry Cove Boating Company** (☏ 207/244–5882) from Southwest Harbor. Baker Island is reached by the summer cruise boats of the **Islesford Ferry Company** (☏ 207/276–3717) from Northeast Harbor; Sutton and Bear islands are privately owned.

㊴ **Islesford** comes closest to having a village: a collection of houses, a church, a fishermen's co-op, a market, and a post office near the ferry dock.

The **Islesford Historical Museum,** run by Acadia National Park, has displays of tools, documents relating to the island's history, and books and manuscripts of the poet Rachel Field (1894–1942), who summered on Sutton Island. ⊠ *Islesford Historical Museum,* ☏ *207/288–3338.* ▧ *Free.* ⊙ *Mid-June–Sept., daily 10:30–noon and 12:30–4:30.*

㊵ The 123-acre **Baker Island,** the most remote of the Cranberry Isles, looks almost black from a distance because of its thick spruce forest. The Islesford Ferry cruise boat from Northeast Harbor conducts a 4½-hour narrated tour, during which you are likely to see ospreys nesting on a sea stack off Sutton Island, harbor seals basking on ledges, and cormorants flying low over the water. Because Baker Island has no natural harbor, the boat ties up offshore, and you take a fishing dory to get to shore.

Mount Desert Island A to Z

Getting Around

BY CAR

North of Bar Harbor, the scenic 27-mi Park Loop Road takes leave of Route 3 to circle the eastern quarter of Mount Desert Island, with one-way traffic from Sieur de Monts Spring to Seal Harbor and two-way traffic between Seal Harbor and Hulls Cove. Route 102, which serves the western half of Mount Desert, is reached from Route 3 just after it enters the island or from Route 233 west from Bar Harbor. All these island roads pass in, out, and through the precincts of Acadia National Park.

Contacts and Resources

CAR RENTAL

Avis (⊠ Bangor International Airport, 299 Godfrey Blvd., ☏ 207/947–8383 or 800/331–1212). **Budget** (⊠ Hancock County Airport, ☏ 207/667–1200 or 800/527–0700). **Hertz** (⊠ Bangor International Airport, 299 Godfrey Blvd., ☏ 207/942–5519 or 800/654–3131). **Thrifty** (⊠ Bangor International Airport, 357 Odlin Rd., ☏ 207/942–6400 or 800/367–2277).

EMERGENCIES
Mount Desert Island Hospital (✉ 10 Wayman La., Bar Harbor, ☎ 207/
288–5081). **Maine Coast Memorial Hospital** (✉ 50 Union St., Ellsworth,
☎ 207/667–5311). **Southwest Harbor Medical Center** (✉ Herrick
Rd., Southwest Harbor, ☎ 207/244–5513).

GUIDED TOURS
Bar Harbor Taxi and Tours (☎ 207/288–4020) conducts half-day historic and scenic tours of the area.

National Park Tours (☎ 207/288–3327) operates a 2½-hour bus tour
of Acadia National Park, narrated by a naturalist. The bus departs twice
daily, from May to October, across from Testa's Restaurant at Bayside
Landing on Main Street in Bar Harbor.

Acadia Air (☎ 207/667–5534), on Route 3 in Trenton, between
Ellsworth and Bar Harbor at Hancock County Airport, rents aircraft
and flies seven aerial sightseeing routes, from spring to fall.

VISITOR INFORMATION
Acadia National Park (✉ Box 177, Bar Harbor 04609, ☎ 207/288–
3338). **Bar Harbor Chamber of Commerce** (✉ 93 Cottage St., Box 158,
Bar Harbor 04609, ☎ 207/288–3393, 207/288–5103, or 800/288–
5103).

WAY DOWNEAST

East of Ellsworth on Route 1 is a different Maine, one that seduces
with its rugged, simple beauty. Red-hued blueberry barrens dot the landscape, and scraggly jack pines hug the highly accessible shoreline. The
quiet pleasures here include hiking, birding, and going on whale-
watching and puffin cruises. Many artists live in the region; you can
often purchase works directly from them.

Hancock

41 *9 mi east of Ellsworth.*

As you approach the small town of Hancock and the summer colony
at Hancock Point, stunning views await, especially at sunset, over
Frenchman Bay toward Mt. Desert.

Dining and Lodging

$$$ ✕🏠 **Le Domaine.** Owner-chef Nicole L. Purslow whips up classic haute
cuisine, the perfect accompaniments to which can be found amid the
more than 40,000 bottles of French wine in the restaurant's cellar. Le
Domaine is known primarily for its food, but its small French-coun-
try-style guest rooms are also inviting. Ask for a room in the rear, over-
looking the lawns and gardens and away from the noise of Route 1.
✉ *Box 496, Rte. 1, 04640,* ☎ *207/422–3395 or 800/554–8495,* ℻
207/422–2316. 7 rooms. Restaurant. Full breakfast; MAP available.
AE, D, MC, V. Closed late Oct.–mid-May.

$$–$$$ ✕🏠 **Crocker House Inn.** Amid tall fir trees and a mere 200 yards from
the water, this century-old shingle-style cottage holds comfortable
rooms decorated with antiques and country furnishings. The accom-
modations in the Carriage House, which also has a TV room and a
hot tub, are best for families. The inn's dining room draws Maine res-
idents from as far away as Bar Harbor for meals that might include
poached salmon or rack of lamb. ✉ *Hancock Point Rd., 04640,* ☎
207/422–6806, ℻ *207/422–3105. 13 rooms. Restaurant, hot tub, boat-
ing, bicycles. Full breakfast; MAP available. AE, D, MC, V.*

Way Downeast

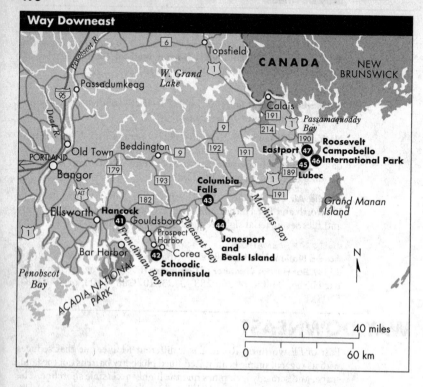

$–$$ 🏠 **Island View Inn.** John Calvin Stevens is rumored to have designed this waterfront shingle-style cottage, which has a wraparound porch and views of Frenchman's Bay and Cadillac Mountain. All the rooms have decks, but the nicest (and quietest) accommodations are in the rear. ⊠ *HCR 32 Box 24, Rte. 1, Sullivan Harbor, 04664,* ☎ *207/422–3031. 6 rooms. Beach, boating. Full breakfast. D, MC, V. Closed mid-Oct.–late May.*

Nightlife and the Arts

Pierre Monteux School for Conductors (⊠ Off Rte. 1, ☎ 207/422–3931) presents orchestral and chamber concerts from mid-June through July. The **Monteux Opera Festival** (⊠ Off Rte. 1, ☎ 207/422–3931) stages works in the Forest Studio of the Pierre Monteux Memorial Foundation from mid-July to mid-August.

Schoodic Peninsula

㊷ *23 mi southeast of Hancock; 32 mi east of Ellsworth.*

It's easy to understand why the overflow from Bar Harbor's wealthy summer population settled in Winter Harbor: the views over Frenchman's Bay to Mt. Desert, the craggy coastline, and the towering evergreens. Drive through the community of Grindstone Neck for a glimpse of what Bar Harbor might have been like before the Great Fire of 1947. Artists and craftspeople have opened galleries in and around Winter Harbor, to which no visit would be complete without a stop at **Gerrish's Store** (⊠ Main St. ☎ 207/963–5575), an old-fashioned ice-cream counter with a marble top, chrome stools, and penny candy that still costs a penny.

The Schoodic Section of **Acadia National Park** (☎ 207/288–3338) is 2 mi east of Winter Harbor. A 6½-mi one-way loop that edges around the tip of the Schoodic Peninsula yields views of Winter Harbor, Grindstone Neck, and Winter Harbor Lighthouse. At the tip of the point, you'll get a sense of how unforgiving the sea can be: Huge slabs of pink granite lie jumbled along the shore, thrashed unmercifully by the crashing surf, and jack pines cling to life amid the rocks. The Fraser Point Day-Use Area at the beginning of the loop is an ideal place for a picnic. Work off your lunch with a hike up Schoodic Head for the panoramic views up and down the coast.

Prospect Harbor, on Route 186 northeast of Winter Harbor is a small fishing village nearly untouched by tourism. There's little to do in **Corea,** at the tip of Route 195, other than watch the fishermen at work, pick your way over stone beaches, or gaze out to sea—and that's what makes it so special.

The wines at the **Bartlett Maine Estate Winery** are produced from locally grown apples, pears, blueberries, and other fruit. You can tour the facility and sample the wines. ⊠ *Rte. 1, Gouldsboro,* ☎ *207/ 546–2408.* ⊙ *June–mid-Oct., Mon.–Sat. 10–5.*

Dining and Lodging

$$–$$$ ✕ **Fisherman's Inn.** The wide-ranging menu at the two pine-panel dining rooms here includes straightforward seafood, Italian, and beef dishes. ⊠ *7 Newman St.,* ☎ *207/963–5585. AE, D, MC, V. Closed Nov.–Mar.*

$$ ✕ **Olde Post Office Restaurant.** Winter Harbor's former post office is now an intimate, candlelit dining room where the menu focuses on home-style foods like pot roast, lobster, and roast chicken and pork. ⊠ *Rte. 186, South Gouldsboro,* ☎ *207/963–5900. Reservations essential. MC, V. Closed Mon.–Tues. No lunch.*

$–$$ ✕ **West Bay Lobsters in the Rough.** Lobsters, steamers, corn-on-the-cob, coleslaw, baked beans, and homemade blueberry pie are among the offerings here. Eat at picnic tables on the shore or picnic on nearby Schoodic Point. ⊠ *Rte. 186, Prospect Harbor,* ☎ *207/963–7021. AE, D, DC, MC, V. Closed Nov.–May.*

$$ 🏠 **Black Duck.** This small bed-and-breakfast has comfortable public areas and guest rooms. Two tiny cottages perch on the harbor. ⊠ *Crowley Island Rd., Corea 04624,* ☎ *207/963–2689,* 🖷 *207/963–7495. 4 rooms, 2 with bath, 2 cottages. MC, V.*

$$ 🏠 **Oceanside Meadows.** With the ocean out the front door; fields, woods, and a salt marsh out back; and moose, eagles and other wildlife, it should come as no surprise that the owners want to create an environmental center here. Rooms, furnished with antiques, country pieces, and family treasures, are spread out among two white clapboard buildings. Many have ocean views. Classical music plays softly in the background during breakfast, an extravagant multicourse affair served on china. In the off-season, the inn is open by special arrangement. ⊠ *Box 90, Rte. 195/ Corea Rd., Prospect Harbor 04669,* ☎ *207/963–5557,* 🖷 *207/963– 5928. 13 rooms, 1 suite. No-smoking rooms, croquet, horseshoes, beach. Full breakfast. AE, MC, V. Closed Nov.–Apr.*

$ 🏠 **The Pines.** The rooms may be small and undistinguished, but this motel's location, right at the beginning of the Schoodic Point Loop, makes it a good value. ⊠ *430 Main St., 04693,* ☎ *207/963–2296. 2 rooms, 4 suites, 3 cabins. Snack bar. MC, V.*

Outdoor Activities and Sports

Moose Look Guide Service (⊠ HC 35 Box 246, Gouldsboro 04607, ☎ 207/963–7720) provides kayak tours and rentals, rowboat and canoe rentals, and bike rentals and conducts guided fishing trips.

Shopping

Pyramid Glass (✉ Rte. 186, South Gouldsboro, ☎ 207/963–2027) sells stained-glass artwork and mosaics. The **Harbor Shop** (✉ Newman St., ☎ 207/963–4117) has handmade gifts by American artisans. **Lee Art Glass Studio** (✉ Main St., ☎ 207/963–7004) carries fused-glass tableware and other items. Whimsical and serious metal sculptures can be found at **McDavid Sculpture** (✉ 177 Main St., ☎ 207/963–5990). **U.S. Bells** (✉ Rte. 186, Prospect Harbor, ☎ 207/963–7184) carries hand-cast bronze wind and door bells.

Columbia Falls

43 *41 mi east of Ellsworth, 78 mi west of Calais.*

Judge Thomas Ruggles, a wealthy lumber dealer, store owner, postmaster, and Justice of the Court of Sessions, among other duties, built **Ruggles House** in 1818. The house's distinctive Federal architecture, flying staircase, Palladian window, and woodwork—supposedly crafted over a period of three years by one man with a penknife—are worth making the ¼-mi detour off Route 1. ✉ *Main St.,* ☎ *no phone.* 🎟 *Donation requested.* ☉ *June 1–Oct. 15, Mon.–Fri. 9:30–4:30, Sun. 11–4:30.*

Lodging

$–$$ 🏠 **Pleasant Bay Inn and Llama Keep.** This Cape-style inn takes advantage of its riverfront location. You can stroll the nature paths on the property, which winds around a peninsula and out to Pleasant Bay, and you can even take a llama with you for company. The rooms, all with water views, are decorated with antiques and have country touches. ✉ *Box 222, West Side Rd., Addison 04606,* ☎ *207/483–4490. 3 rooms, 1 with bath. Full breakfast. MC, V.*

Shopping

Columbia Falls Pottery (✉ Main St., ☎ 207/483–4075) stocks stoneware and a sampling of Maine foods.

Jonesport and Beals Island

44 *12 mi south of Columbia Falls, 20 mi southwest of Machias.*

Jonesport and Beals Island, two fishing communities joined by a bridge over the harbor, are less polished than the towns on the Schoodic Peninsula. The birding here is superb. Puffin-watching cruises (☞ Outdoor Activities and Sports, *below*) to Machias Seal Island depart from Jonesport.

Great Wass Island Preserve (☎ 207/729–5181) a 1,540-acre nature conservancy at the tip of Beals Island, is home to rare plants, stunted pines, and raised peat bogs. Trails lead through the woods and emerge onto the undeveloped, raw coast, where you can make your way along the rocks and boulders before retreating into the forest. To get to the preserve from Jonesport, cross the bridge over Moosabec Reach to Beals Island. Go through Beals to Great Wass Island. Follow the road, which eventually becomes unpaved, to Black Duck Cove, about 3 mi from Beals, where there is a marked parking area on the left.

Dining and Lodging

$$ ✕ **Seafarer's Wife/Old Salt Room.** Allow at least a couple of hours to dine at the Seafarer's Wife, where a five-course meal (hors d'oeuvres, soup, salad, entrée, and dessert) is presented at a leisurely pace in a candlelit dining room. The casual Old Salt Room specializes in fresh fish and seafood. Bring your own wine—the restaurant hasn't a liquor license. ✉ *Rte. 187,* ☎ *207/497–2365. MC, V. No lunch at the Seafarer's Wife.*

$$ ×⛫ **Harbor House.** The first floor of this three-story waterfront building houses an antiques shop and a lobster-in-the-rough restaurant. You can eat on the porch overlooking the water or on picnic tables on the lawn. Upstairs are two rooms with private baths. ⊠ *Sawyer Square, Jonesport 04649,* ☎ *207/497–5417,* 🗏 *207/497–3211. 2 rooms. Restaurant, air-conditioning, no-smoking rooms. Full breakfast. MC, V. Café closed Nov.–Apr.*

$ ⛫ **Raspberry Shores.** Comfortably furnished, this Victorian sits right on Main Street, but its backyard slopes down to a small beach on Jonesport Harbor. Rooms in the back of the house share the view, but the nicest room is in the turret and right on the road, which can be noisy. ⊠ *Box 217, Rte. 187, Jonesport 04649,* ☎ *207/497–2463. 3 rooms with shared bath. Beach. Full breakfast. MC, V. Closed Nov.–Apr.*

Outdoor Activities and Sports
Norton of Jonesport (☎ 207/497–5933) takes passengers on day trips to Machias Seal Island, where there's a large puffin colony.

Lubec

🔵 *28 mi east of Machias.*

Lubec is the first town in the United States to see the sunrise. Once a thriving shipbuilding and sardine packing site, it now attracts residents and visitors with its rural beauty.

Quoddy Head State Park, the easternmost point of land in the United States, is marked by candy-striped West Quoddy Head Light. The mystical, magical, 2-mi path along the cliffs here yields magnificent views of Grand Manan island. Whales can often be sighted offshore. The 483-acre park has a picnic area. ⊠ *S. Lubec Rd. off Rte. 189,* ☎ *no phone.* 🗏 *$1 donation requested.* ⊙ *Memorial Day–mid-Oct., daily 8 AM–sunset; Apr.–early May and mid-Oct.–Dec., weekends 9 AM–sunset.*

🔵 **Roosevelt Campobello International Park** The only way to get to this Canadian park by land is by crossing the International Bridge from Lubec. Stop at the information booth for information on tides—specifically, when you will be able to walk out to East Quoddy Head Lighthouse—as well as details on walking and hiking trails. The **Roosevelt Cottage,** which is open for touring, was presented to Eleanor and Franklin as a wedding gift. ⊠ *Rte. 774, Welshpool, Campobello Island, New Brunswick, Canada,* ☎ *506/752–2922.* 🗏 *Free.* ⊙ *Mid-May–mid-Oct., daily 10–6.*

Dining and Lodging
$–$$ ×⛫ **Home Port Inn.** The grandest accommodations in Lubec are in this 1880 Colonial atop a hill. The spacious rooms, some with water views, are furnished with antiques and family pieces. The large living room has a fireplace and a television, and there are two sitting areas. The dining room ($$), the best in town, is open to the public for dinner. The menu emphasizes seafood. ⊠ *45 Main St., 04652,* ☎ *207/733–2077 or 800/457–2077. 7 rooms. Restaurant. Continental breakfast. D, MC, V.*

$$ ⛫ **Peacock House.** Four generations of the Peacock family lived in this 1860 Victorian before it was converted into an inn. The Downeast hospitality of owners Chet and Veda Childs comes with a southern accent. A few of the simply furnished rooms have water views through lace-curtained windows; rooms on the first floor have air-conditioning. ⊠ *27 Summer St., 04652,* ☎ 🗏 *207/733–2403. 5 rooms. Full breakfast. MC, V. Closed mid-Oct.–mid-May.*

$–$$ 🏠 **Bayviews.** This unfussy waterfront B&B welcomes families and musicians; there are pianos in the living room and one guest room. Some rooms have water views. ⊠ *6 Monument St., 04652,* ☎ *207/733–2181. 4 rooms, 1 with bath, 1 suite. Continental breakfast. No credit cards. Closed Oct.–June.*

Outdoor Activities and Sports

East Coast Charters (⊠ Lubec Marina, ☎ 800/853–3999) operates whale-watching trips and sea-kayaking tours.

En Route   The road to Eastport leads through the Pleasant Point Indian Reservation, where the **Waponahki Museum and Resource Center** explains the culture of the Passamaquoddy or People of the Dawn. Tools, baskets, beaded artifacts, historic photos, and arts and crafts are displayed. ⊠ *Rte. 190, Perry,* ☎ *207/853–4001.* 🎟 *Free.* ☉ *Mon.–Fri., 8:30 AM–11 AM, noon–4 PM.*

Eastport

🔴 *102 mi east of Ellsworth, 28 mi south of Calais.*

The town of Eastport is actually a small island, connected to the mainland by a granite causeway. In the late 18th century, 14 sardine canneries operated in Eastport. The decline of that industry in the 20th century has left the city economically depressed, though a new port facility, growing aquaculture, and an increase in tourism bode well for the future.

The **National Historic Waterfront District** extends from the Customs House, down Water Street to Bank Square and the Peavey Library. Pick up a walking map at the **Chamber of Commerce** (⊠ 78 Water St., ☎ 207/853–4644) and wander through streets lined with historic homes and buildings. Or take the waterfront walkway to watch the fishing boats and freighters. The tides fluctuate as much as 28 ft, which explains the ladders and steep gangways necessary to access boats.

Raye's Mustard Mill is the only remaining mill in the U.S. producing stone-ground mustard. Historically, this mill served the sardine-packing industry. You can purchase mustards made on the premises at the mill's Pantry Store. ⊠ *85 Washington St.,* ☎ *207/853–4451 or 800/ 853–1903.* 🎟 *Free.* ☉ *Year-round, Mon.–Fri. 8–5; Apr.–Dec., Sat. and Sun. 10–5. Tours on the hr Memorial Day–Labor Day; rest of year subject to guide availability.*

The short hike to **Shakford Head** affords views over Passamaquoddy Bay to Campobello. From here you can see the pens for Eastport's growing salmon-farming industry as well as the construction site of the new port facility. From the waterfront, you can take a ferry to Deer Island and Campobello.

Cobscook Bay State Park is one of Maine's prettiest and least crowded parks. More than 200 species of birds, including the American bald eagle, have been identified in and around the park, which has picnic grounds, a playground, a nature trail, and campsites ($12–$16) with showers. ⊠ *RR1 off Rte. 1, Dennysville,* ☎ *207/726–4412.* 🎟 *$1.* ☉ *Mid-May–mid-Oct.*

Dining and Lodging

$$–$$$ ✕ **Eastport Lobster and Fish.** Fish and seafood don't come much fresher than they do at this restaurant, where the lobsters weigh as much as 2½ pounds. You can eat in the dining room, the downstairs pub, or out on the dock. ⊠ *167 Water St.,* ☎ *207/853–6006. MC, V. Closed Oct.–mid-May.*

$–$$ ✕ **La Sardina Loca.** Bright lights and Christmas decorations are among the festive touches at the easternmost Mexican restaurant in the U.S. ✉ *28 Water St.,* ☎ *207/853–2739. MC, V. Closed Mon. No lunch.*

$$ ▥ **Motel East.** Rooms at this waterfront motel are spacious; many have kitchenettes, and most have private balconies overlooking the water. ✉ *23A Water St., 04631,* ☎ FAX *207/853–4747. 14 rooms. AE, D, MC, V.*

$–$$ ▥ **Brewer House.** In 1827, Captain John Nehemiah Marks Brewer built an ornate Greek Revival house across from one of his shipyards. Now a B&B, the house, which is on the National Register of Historic Places, is distinguished by architectural details like carved Grecian moldings, Ionic pilasters, marble fireplaces, silver doorknobs, and an elliptical staircase. ✉ *Box 98, Rte. 1, Robbinston 04671,* ☎ *207/454–2385. 4 rooms, 2 with bath, 1 apartment. Full breakfast. MC, V.*

$–$$ ▥ **Lincoln House.** Built in 1787 by Judge Theodore Lincoln and on the National Register of Historic Places, this classic Colonial captures the feel of the late 18th century. Bald eagles and osprey are frequently seen on the 95 wooded, riverfront acres that surround the inn. Rooms in the front of the house are spacious, and two have working fireplaces. All rooms are decorated with antiques such as four-poster beds and braided rugs. ✉ *Main St., Dennysville 04628,* ☎ *207/726–3953 or 888/726–3953,* FAX *207/726–0654. 6 rooms, 4 with shared bath. Full breakfast. No credit cards.*

$ ▥ **Weston House.** A Federal-style home built in 1810, the antiques-filled Weston House overlooks Eastport and Passamaquoddy Bay from a prime in-town location. Breakfast, served in the formal dining room, is accompanied by classical music. The family room, with a fireplace and a TV, is a casual place to plan the day's activities. Naturalist John J. Audubon stayed here in 1833. ✉ *26 Boynton St., 04631,* ☎ *207/ 853–2907 or 800/853–2907. 5 rooms share 2½ baths. Full breakfast. No credit cards.*

Outdoor Activities and Sports

East Coast Ferries, Ltd. (☎ 506/747–2159) provides ferry service between Eastport and Deer Island and Deer Island and Campobello. **Harris Whale Watching** (✉ Harris Point Rd., Eastport, ☎ 207/853–2940 or 207/853–4303) operates three-hour tours. **Tidal Trails** (✉ Leighton Point, Pembroke, ☎ 207/726–4799) operates boat charters, natural-history tours, and guided bird-watching, canoeing, sea-kayaking, and saltwater-fishing trips.

Shopping

Dog Island Pottery (✉ 224 Water St., ☎ 207/853–4775) stocks stoneware pottery and local crafts. The **Eastport Gallery** (✉ 69 Water St., ☎ 207/853–4166) displays works by area artists. **Jim's Smoked Salmon** (✉ 37 Washington St., ☎ 207/853–4831) sells Atlantic salmon, mussels, and roe hot-smoked in apple wood.

Way Downeast A to Z

Guided Tours

Quoddy Air (✉ Eastport Municipal Airport, County Rd., ☎ 207/ 853–0997) operates scenic flights.

Visitor Information

Eastport Area Chamber of Commerce (✉ Box 254, Water St., 04631, ☎ 207/853–4644). **Machias Bay Area Chamber of Commerce** (✉ Box 606, Rte. 1, Machias 04654, ☎ 207/255–4402). **Schoodic Peninsula Chamber of Commerce** (✉ Box 381, Winter Harbor 04693, ☎ no phone).

WESTERN LAKES AND MOUNTAINS

Fewer than 20 mi northwest of Portland and the coast, the sparsely populated lake and mountain areas of western Maine stretch north along the New Hampshire border to Québec. In winter this is ski country; in summer the woods and waters draw vacationers.

The Sebago–Long Lake region has antiques stores and lake cruises on a 42-mi waterway. Kezar Lake, tucked away in a fold of the White Mountains, has long been a hideaway of the wealthy. Children's summer camps dot the region. Bethel, in the Androscoggin River valley, is a classic New England town, its town common lined with historic homes. The far more rural Rangeley Lake area brings long stretches of pine, beech, spruce, and sky—and stylish inns and bed-and-breakfasts with easy access to golf, boating, fishing, and hiking.

Sebago Lake

48 *17 mi northwest of Portland.*

Sebago Lake, which provides all the drinking water for Greater Portland, is Maine's best-known lake after Moosehead. Many camps and year-round homes surround Sebago, which is popular with water-sports enthusiasts. At the north end of the lake, the **Songo Lock** (☎ 207/693–6231), which permits the passage of watercraft from Sebago Lake to Long Lake, is the one surviving lock of the Cumberland and Oxford Canal. Built of wood and masonry, the original lock dates from 1830 and was expanded in 1911; today it sees heavy traffic in summer.

The 1,300-acre **Sebago Lake State Park** on the north shore of the lake provides opportunities for swimming, picnicking, camping (250 sites), boating, and fishing (salmon and togue). ☎ *207/693–6615 May–mid-Oct.; 207/693–6231 at other times.*

The **Jones Museum of Glass & Ceramics** houses more than 7,000 objects of glass, pottery, stoneware, and porcelain from around the world; also on the premises are a research library and gift shop. ⊠ *Douglas Mountain Rd. off Rte. 107,* ☎ *207/787–3370.* 🎟 *$5.* ☉ *Mid-May–mid-Nov., Mon.–Sat. 10–5, Sun. 1–5.*

OFF THE BEATEN PATH | **SABBATHDAY LAKE SHAKER MUSEUM** – Established in the late 18th century, this is the last active Shaker community in the United States. Members continue to farm crops and herbs, and visitors are shown the meetinghouse of 1794—a paradigm of Shaker design—and the ministry shop with 14 rooms of Shaker furniture, folk art, tools, farm implements, and crafts from the 18th to early 20th centuries. There is a small gift shop on the premises, but don't expect to find furniture or other large Shaker items. On the busy road out front, a farmer usually has summer and fall vegetables for sale. In autumn, he sells cider and apples and pumpkins. On Sunday, the Shaker day of prayer, the community is closed to visitors. ⊠ *Rte. 26, New Gloucester (20 mi north of Portland, 12 mi east of Naples),* ☎ *207/926–4597.* 🎟 *Tour $5, extended tour $6.50.* ☉ *Memorial Day–Columbus Day, Mon.–Sat. 10–4:30.*

Naples

49 *16 mi northwest of North Windham, 32 mi northwest of Portland.*

Naples swells with seasonal residents and visitors in summer. The town enjoys an enviable location between Long Lake and Sebago Lake.

Western Maine

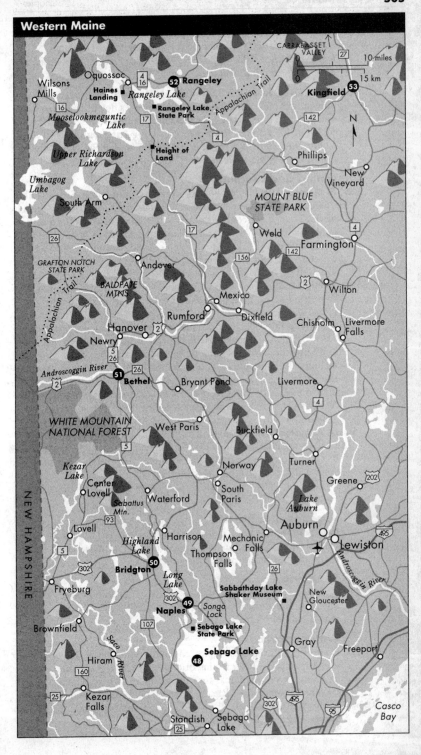

Carrabasset Valley
27
10 miles
0
15 km

Wilsons Mills
Oquossoc
4
16
52 Rangeley
Kingfield 53
Haines Landing
Rangeley Lake
142
16
Mooselookmeguntic Lake
Rangeley Lake State Park
17
Appalachian Trail
Phillips
New Vineyard
Upper Richardson Lake
Height of Land
4
MOUNT BLUE STATE PARK
Umbagog Lake
South Arm
Weld
4
26
17
156
142
Farmington
GRAFTON NOTCH STATE PARK
Andover
Mexico
Wilton
2
BALDPATE MTNS.
Rumford
Dixfield
Chisholm
Livermore Falls
Hanover
2
Newry
5
26
Androscoggin River
Bryant Pond
Livermore
51 Bethel
26
4
WHITE MOUNTAIN NATIONAL FOREST
West Paris
Buckfield
5
Kezar Lake
Norway
Turner
Center Lovell
Greene
202
Sabattus Mtn.
Waterford
South Paris
Lake Auburn
Lovell
93
Auburn
5
Harrison
Mechanic Falls
Lewiston
302
Highland Lake
Bridgton 50
Thompson Falls
26
495
Fryeburg
Long Lake
Sabbathday Lake Shaker Museum
New Gloucester
302
49
Songo Lock
Naples
Brownfield
107
Sebago Lake State Park
Gray
Freeport
Saco River
48 Sebago Lake
Hiram
160
95
25
Kezar Falls
Standish
Sebago Lake
Casco Bay
25
302
495

NEW HAMPSHIRE

N

The **Naples Historical Society Museum** has a jailhouse, a bandstand, a Dodge 1938 fire truck, a coach, and information about the Cumberland and Oxford Canal and the Sebago–Long Lake steamboats. ⊠ *Village Green, Rte. 302,* ☏ *207/693–4297.* ☞ *Free.* ☉ *July–Aug., Fri. 10–3; call for additional hrs.*

☻ **Songo River Queen II,** a 92-ft stern-wheeler, takes passengers on hour-long cruises on Long Lake and longer voyages down the Songo River and through Songo Lock. ⊠ *Rte. 302, Naples Causeway,* ☏ *207/ 693–6861.* ☞ *Songo River ride $10, Long Lake cruise $7.* ☉ *July– Labor Day, daily at 9:45, 1, 2:30, 3:45, 7; Memorial Day–July and Labor Day–Sept., weekends 9:45. Closed rest of yr.*

Dining and Lodging

$$$ ✕ **Bistro du Lac.** Inside a big red farmhouse across from Sebago Lake, this casual restaurant has a perhaps-too-ambitious country-French menu. Though entrées like salmon with caramelized leeks and rack of lamb don't quite live up to their potential, the food is good and the prix-fixe menu ($45) most reasonable. Sunday brunch is also served. ⊠ *Rtes. 302 and 85, Raymond,* ☏ *207/655–4100. MC, V. Closed Tues.–Wed. No lunch.*

$$$$ ▥ **Migis Lodge.** The lodge's pine-panel cottages, scattered among 100 shorefront acres, have fieldstone fireplaces and are handsomely furnished with braided rugs and handmade quilts. The main inn has a warm, woodsy feeling. The deck has views (marvelous at sunset) of Sebago Lake. Though you may be tempted just to gaze out on the lake, the lodge provides plenty of outdoor and indoor activities, all of which are included in the room rate. Guests gather in the main dining room for three fancy meals daily. ⊠ *Box 40, Rte. 302, South Casco 04077,* ☏ *207/655–4524,* ☎ *207/655–2054. 17 cottages, 5 rooms. Restaurant, tennis court, exercise room, beach, boating, waterskiing, fishing, playground. AP. No credit cards.*

$$ ▥ **Augustus Bove House.** Built as the Hotel Naples in 1850, this brick B&B at the intersection of Routes 302 and 114 has lake views from its front rooms and is convenient to shops. Each room has a different color wallpaper and is furnished with antiques and a television. ⊠ *Box 501, R.R. 1, 04055,* ☏ *207/693–6365. 6 rooms, 2 with bath. Hot tub. Full breakfast. D, MC, V.*

Nightlife and the Arts

Deertrees Theater and Cultural Center (⊠ Deertrees Rd. off Rte. 117, Harrison, ☏ 207/583–6747), hosts musicals, dramas, dance, shows for children, concerts and other events.

Shopping

The **Shops of South Casco Village** (⊠ Rte. 302, South Casco, ☏ 207/ 655–5060) include a gift shop, an antiques shop, and an art gallery with a sculpture garden.

Water Sports

Route 302 cuts through Naples, and in the center at the Naples Causeway are rental craft for fishing or cruising. Sebago, Long, and Rangeley lakes are popular areas for sailing and motorboating. For rentals, try **Mardon Marine** (⊠ Rte. 302, ☏ 207/693–6264), **Naples Marina** (⊠ Rtes. 302 and 114, ☏ 207/693–6254; motorboats only), or **Sun Sports Plus** (⊠ Rte. 302, ☏ 207/693–3867).

Bridgton

⑤ *8 mi north of Naples, 16 mi east of Fryeburg, 30 mi south of Bethel.*

In and around the drab town of Bridgton, between Long and Highland Lakes, are antiques shops, a museum, and the Shawnee Peak ski resort.

The **Bridgton Historical Society Museum** is in a former fire station that was built in 1902. On display are artifacts of the area's history and materials on the local narrow-gauge railroad. ⊠ *Gibbs Ave.,* ☎ *207/647–3699.* ⊠ *$2 admission.* ⊙ *July–Aug., Tues.–Fri. 10–4.*

Dining and Lodging

$–$$$ ✕ **Black Horse Tavern.** A Cape Cod cottage more than 200 years old houses this country-style restaurant with a shiny bar, horse blankets and stirrups for decor, and a menu of steaks, seafood, soups, salads, and burgers. ⊠ *8 Portland St.,* ☎ *207/647–5300. Reservations not accepted. D, MC, V.*

$$ ✕ **Tom's Homestead.** An 1821 house holds two quiet dining rooms and a spacious bar. The international-style menu includes a wide selection of choices, from Louisiana frog legs Provençale to Wiener schnitzel. ⊠ *Rte. 302,* ☎ *207/647–5726. D, MC, V. Closed Mon.*

$$$$ ✕🖭 **Quisisana.** Music lovers may think they've found heaven on earth at this delightful resort on Kezar Lake, about 14 mi northwest of Bridgton. After dinner, the staff, students, and graduates of some of the finest music schools in the country perform at the music hall—everything from Broadway tunes to concert piano pieces. White cottages have pine interiors and cheerful decor. One night you might have a typical New England dinner of clam chowder, lobster, and blueberry pie; the next night you might have a choice of saddle of lamb with a black-olive tapenade or salmon-and-leek roulade with a roasted-red-pepper sauce. All meals and activities are included in the rates (except for a nominal fee for the use of the motorboats). For most of the resort's season, a one-week stay beginning Saturday is required. ⊠ *Pleasant Point Rd., Center Lovell 04016,* ☎ *207/925–3500,* ℻ *207/925–1004 in season. 11 rooms in 2 lodges, 32 cottages. Restaurant, 3 tennis courts, windsurfing, boating, waterskiing. AP. Closed Sept.–mid-June.*

$$–$$$$ 🖭 **Bear Mountain Inn.** After swimming at the private beach on Bear Lake or hiking up Bear Mountain, which is across the street, it's nice to return to this rambling farmhouse inn, which has been meticulously decorated in a woodsy theme by the owner. A country breakfast with an emphasis on organic ingredients is served in the dining room, which has a fieldstone fireplace and views over the lake. ⊠ *Rte. 35, South Waterford 04081,* ☎ *207/583–4404. 6 rooms, 4 share 2 baths; 1 suite. Badminton, croquet, horseshoes, volleyball, beach, ice-skating, cross-country skiing, snowmobiling. Full breakfast. MC, V.*

$$ 🖭 **Bridgton House.** An easy walk to village shops and restaurants or to Highland Lake, this white clapboard cottage has a fine wraparound porch, on which breakfast is served when the weather's nice. The rooms in the back of the house are quieter than those on the Route 302 side of the house. ⊠ *2 Main St./Rte. 302, 04009,* ☎ *207/647–0979. 6 rooms, 3 rooms share 2 baths. Full breakfast. No credit cards. Closed Nov.–Apr.*

$$ 🖭 **Waterford Inne.** This gold-painted house on a hilltop provides a good home base for trips to lakes, ski trails, and antiques shops. The bedrooms have lots of nooks and crannies. The Nantucket, with a whale motif, and the Chesapeake, with a private porch and a fireplace, are the nicest. A converted woodshed has five additional rooms, and though they have less character than the rooms in the inn, four have sunny decks. ⊠ *Box 149, Chadbourne Rd., Waterford, 04088,* ☎ ℻

207/583–4037. 9 rooms, 6 with bath; 1 suite. Badminton, ice-skating, cross-country skiing. Full breakfast. AE. Closed Apr.

Outdoor Activities and Sports

Two scenic canoeing routes on the Saco River (near Fryeburg) are the gentle stretch from Swan's Falls to East Brownfield (19 mi) and from East Brownfield to Hiram (14 mi). For rentals, try **Canal Bridge Canoes** (⌧ Rte. 302, Fryeburg Village, ☎ 207/935–2605) or **Saco River Canoe and Kayak** (⌧ Rte. 5, Fryeburg, ☎ 207/935–2369).

Shopping

Craftworks (⌧ Main St., ☎ 207/647–5436) carries American crafts, Maine foods, women's clothing, and gifts. **The Maine Theme** (⌧ Main St., ☎ 207/647–2161) specializes in handcrafted wares from throughout New England.

Skiing

Shawnee Peak. On the New Hampshire border, Shawnee Peak draws many skiers from the North Conway, New Hampshire (18 mi), area and from Portland (45 mi). Popular with families, this facility is being upgraded. ⌧ *Box 734, Rte. 302, Bridgton 04009,* ☎ *207/647–8444.*

DOWNHILL

Shawnee Peak has a 1,300-ft vertical and perhaps the most night-skiing terrain in New England. Most of the 31 runs are pleasant cruisers for intermediates, with some beginner slopes, a few pitches suitable for advanced skiers, and a few gladed runs. Lifts include one quad, two triple, and one double chairs and one surface lift. There's also snow tubing and snowshoeing.

CHILD CARE

The area's nursery takes children from age 6 months to 6 years. The SKIwee program is for children between ages 4 and 6; those between 7 and 12 also have a program. Children under 6 ski free when accompanied by a parent. The Youth Ski League has instruction for aspiring racers.

En Route   From Bridgton, the most scenic route to Bethel is along Route 302 west, across Moose Pond to Knight's Hill Road, turning north to Lovell and Route 5, which will take you on to Bethel. It's a drive that lets you admire the jagged crests of the White Mountains outlined against the sky to the west and the rolling hills that alternate with brooding forests at roadside. At Center Lovell you can barely glimpse the secluded Kezar Lake to the west, the retreat of wealthy and very private people; Sabattus Mountain, which rises behind Center Lovell, has a public hiking trail and stupendous views of the Presidential Range from the summit.

Bethel

51 *66 mi north of Portland, 22 mi east of Gorham, NH.*

Bethel is pure New England, a town with white clapboard houses and white-steeple churches and a mountain vista at the end of every street. In winter this is ski country: Bethel is midway between Sunday River in Newry and Ski Mt. Abram in Locke Mills.

A stroll in Bethel should begin at the **Moses Mason House and Museum,** a Federal home of 1813. On the town common, across from the Bethel Inn and Country Club, the Mason Museum has nine period rooms and a front hall and stairway wall decorated with murals by Rufus Porter. You can pick up materials here for a walking tour of Bethel Hill Village, most of which is on the National Register of Historic Places. ⌧

14 Broad St., ☎ 207/824–2908. ☒ $2. ⊙ July–Labor Day, Tues.–
Sun. 1–4; Labor Day–June, by appointment.

The **architecture** of Bethel is something to behold. The **Major Gideon Hastings House** on Broad Street has a columned-front portico typical of the Greek Revival style. The severe white **West Parish Congregational Church** (1847), with an unadorned triangular pediment and a steeple supported on open columns, is on Church Street, around the common from the Major Gideon Hastings House. The campus of **Gould Academy** (☒ Church St., ☎ 207/824–7777), a preparatory school, opened its doors in 1835; the dominant style of the school buildings is Georgian.

White Mountain National Forest straddles New Hampshire and Maine. Although the highest peaks are on the New Hampshire side, the Maine section has magnificent rugged terrain, camping and picnic areas, and hiking opportunities from hour-long nature loops to a 5½-hour scramble up Speckled Mountain. ☒ *Evans Notch Visitation Center, 18 Mayville Rd., 04217, ☎ 207/824–2134. ⊙ Weekdays 8–4:30.*

At **Grafton Notch State Park** (☒ Rte. 26, 14 mi north of Bethel, ☎ 207/824–2912) you can take an easy nature walk to Mother Walker Falls or Moose Cave and see the spectacular Screw Auger Falls, or you can hike to the summit of Old Speck Mountain, the state's third-highest peak. If you have the stamina and the equipment, you can pick up the Appalachian Trail here, hike over Saddleback Mountain, and continue on to Katahdin. The **Maine Appalachian Trail Club** (☒ Box 283, Augusta 04330) publishes a map and trail guide.

Dining and Lodging

$$–$$$ ✕ **Mother's Restaurant.** This gingerbread house furnished with woodstoves and bookshelves is a cozy place to enjoy Maine crab cakes, steaks, and pastas. There's outside dining in summer. ☒ *Upper Main St., ☎ 207/824–2589. MC, V.*

$$$$ ✕▦ **Bethel Inn and Country Club.** Bethel's grandest accommodation is a full-service resort with extensive facilities, including 36 km (22 mi) of cross-country skiing. Although not very large, the rooms in the main inn, sparsely furnished with Colonial reproductions, are the most desirable: The choice rooms have fireplaces and face the mountains that rise over the golf course. All 40 two-bedroom condos on the fairway face the mountains; they are clean, even a bit sterile. A formal dining room ($$–$$$; reservations essential) serves elaborate dinners of roast duck, prime rib, lobster, and swordfish. The room rates include a full breakfast and dinner. ☒ *Box 49, Village Common, 04217, ☎ 207/824–2175 or 800/654–0125, 𝖥𝖠𝖷 207/824–2233. 57 rooms, 40 condo units. Restaurant, bar, pool, golf, tennis, health club, cross-country skiing, conference center. MAP. AE, D, DC, MC, V.*

$$–$$$$ ✕▦ **Sudbury Inn.** Value and location are the chief attributes of this white clapboard inn, whose guest rooms and dining room have country charm. Prime rib, sirloin au poivre, broiled haddock, lasagna, and other standards are on the menu. The pub, with a large-screen TV and a larger selection of microbrews, is a popular hangout. The huge breakfast includes omelets, eggs Benedict, pancakes, and homemade granola. ☒ *Box 369, 151 Main St., 04217, ☎ 207/824–2174 or 800/395–7837, 𝖥𝖠𝖷 207/824–2329. 10 rooms, 7 suites. Restaurant, pub. Full breakfast. AE, MC, V.*

$$$–$$$$ ▦ **Summit Hotel and Conference Center.** This condominium hotel, a hit with Sunday River skiers, has 700 slopeside units, most with kitchenettes. An 800-seat ballroom and conference facilities give a great excuse to combine business and skiing for groups of up to 400. ☒ *Box 450, Sunday River Rd. off Rte. 2, 04217, ☎ 207/824–3000 or 800/*

543–2754, ⍐ *207/824–2111. 230 units. Restaurant, pool, tennis, health club, baby-sitting, meeting rooms. AE, D, MC, V.*

$$$–$$$$ 🏠 **Sunday River Inn.** On the Sunday River ski-area access road, this modern chalet has private rooms for families and dorm rooms (bring your sleeping bag) for groups and students, all within easy access of the slopes. A hearty breakfast and dinner are served buffet-style, and the comfy living room is dominated by a stone hearth. The inn operates an excellent ski-touring center. ⊠ *R.R. 3 Box 1688, Sunday River Rd., 04217,* ☎ *207/824–2410,* ⍐ *207/824–3181. 3 rooms with bath, 12 rooms share 2 baths, 5 dorms share 2 baths, 4 rooms in separate building share 2 baths. Hot tub, sauna, cross-country skiing. MAP. AE, MC, V. Closed Apr.–late-Nov.*

$$ 🏠 **Chapman Inn.** Many rooms at this circa 1865 Colonial inn on Bethel's town green can be joined together as family suites; there are dorm accommodations in the barn; and guests have use of a game room, a kitchen, saunas, and a washer and dryer. The rooms are nice but not fancy. The huge country-style breakfast will fuel skiers and others for an active morning. There is a private beach (boats available) 6 mi from the inn. ⊠ *Box 206, Bethel Common, 04217,* ☎ *207/824–2657,* ⍐ *207/824–7152. 2 rooms with bath, 4 rooms share 2 baths, 3 efficiencies, 24-bed dormitory. Saunas, ice-skating. Full breakfast. AE, D, MC, V.*

Nightlife

Sunday River nightlife is spread out between the mountain and downtown Bethel. At the mountain, try **Bumps Pub** (⊠ Whitecap Lodge, ☎ 207/824–5269) for après-ski and evening entertainment—Tuesday night is comedy night, ski movies are shown on Wednesday, and bands play on weekends and holidays. **Sunday River Brewing Company** (⊠ Rte. 2, ☎ 207/824–4253) has pub fare and live entertainment—usually progressive rock bands—on weekends. The **Sudbury Inn** (⊠ 151 Main St., ☎ 207/824–2174) also is popular for après-ski and has music that tends toward the blues. For a quiet evening, head to the piano bar at the **Bethel Inn** (⊠ The Common, ☎ 207/824–2175).

Outdoor Activities and Sports

Mahoosuc Guide Service (⊠ Bear River Rd., Newry, ☎ 207/824–2073) leads day and multiday dog-sledding expeditions on the Maine–New Hampshire border. Lifts at **Sunday River Mountain Bike Park** (⊠ Sunday River Rd., Newry, ☎ 207/824–3000) bring cyclists to the trails. **Telemark Inn & Llama Treks** (⊠ King's Hwy., Mason Township, ☎ 207/836–2703) operates one- to six-day llama-supported hiking trips in the White Mountain National Forest.

Shopping

Bonnema Potters (⊠ 146 Lower Main St., ☎ 207/824–2821) sells plates, lamps, tiles, and vases in colorful modern designs. The **Lyons' Den** (⊠ Rte. 2, Hanover, ☎ 207/364–8634), a great barn of a place just near Bethel, stocks glass, china, tools, prints, rugs, hand-wrought iron, and some furniture. **Mt. Mann Jewelers** (⊠ 57 Main St. Pl., ☎ 207/824–3030) carries contemporary jewelry with unusual gems.

Skiing

Ski Mt. Abram. This ski area has a rustic Maine feeling and is known for its snow grooming, home-style cooking, and family atmosphere. Skiers here prefer the low-key attitude and wallet-friendly rates. Night skiing and snow tubing are available. Many skiers stay in the reasonably priced condominiums on the mountain road. ⊠ *Box 120, Rte. 26, Locke Mills 04255,* ☎ *207/875–5003.*

DOWNHILL

The mountain reaches just over 1,000 vertical ft. The majority of the terrain is intermediate, with fall-line steep runs and two areas for beginning and novice skiers. The area has two double chairlifts and three T-bars. In addition to learn-to-ski classes, there are improvement clinics for all ability levels and age groups. Facilities include two base lodges, a children's terrain garden, a halfpipe for snowboarders, a snowboard park, and a snow-tubing park.

CHILD CARE

The Ski Mt. Abram's Day Care Center takes children from age 6 months to 6 years. Children between ages 3 and 6 who are enrolled in the center can take lessons on weekends and during vacation weeks. For juniors from age 6 to 16 there are individual classes plus a series of 10 two-hour lessons on weekends.

Sunday River. In the 1980s, Sunday River was a sleepy little ski area with minimal facilities. Today it is among the best-managed ski areas in the East and the flagship of the owner Les Otten's American Skiing Company empire. Spread throughout the valley are three base areas, two condominium hotels, trailside condominiums, town houses, and a ski dorm. Sunday River is home to the Maine Handicapped Skiing program, which provides lessons and services for skiers with disabilities. ⊠ *Box 450, Sunday River Rd. off Rte. 2, Bethel 04217,* ☎ *207/ 824–3000, 207/824–5200 for snow conditions, 800/543–2754 for reservations.*

DOWNHILL

White Heat has gained fame as the steepest, longest, widest lift-served trail in the East; but skiers of all abilities will find plenty of suitable terrain, from a 5-km (3-mi) beginner run to steep glades and in-your-face bumps. The area has 126 trails, the majority of them in the intermediate range. Expert and advanced runs are grouped from the peaks, and most beginner slopes are near the base. Trails spreading down from eight peaks have a total vertical descent of 2,340 ft and are served by nine quads, four triples, and two double chairlifts and two surface lifts.

OTHER ACTIVITIES

Within the housing complexes are indoor pools, outdoor heated pools, saunas, and hot tubs. Sunday River also has a snowboard park. The Entertainment Center at White Cap has a lighted halfpipe, a lighted ice-skating rink, a teen center, and a nightclub with live music.

CHILD CARE

Sunday River operates three licensed day-care centers for children from ages 6 weeks to 6 years. Coaching for children from ages 3 to 18 is available in the Children's Center at the South Ridge base area.

En Route The routes north from Bethel to the Rangeley district are all scenic, particularly in the autumn when the maples are aflame with color. In the town of Newry, make a short detour to the **Artist's Bridge** (turn off Route 26 onto Sunday River Road and drive about 3 mi), the most painted and photographed of Maine's eight covered bridges. Route 26 continues on to **Grafton Notch State Park,** about 12 mi from Bethel. Here you can hike to stunning gorges and waterfalls and into the Baldpate Mountains. Past the park, Route 26 continues to Errol, New Hampshire, where Route 16 will return you east around the north shore of Mooselookmeguntic Lake, through Oquossoc, and into Rangeley. A more direct route (if marginally less scenic) from Bethel to Rangeley still allows a stop in Newry. Follow Route 2 north and east from Bethel to the twin towns of Rumford and Mexico, where Route 17 continues north to Oquossoc, about an hour's drive. When you've driven for about 20 minutes beyond Rumford, the signs of civilization all but vanish and you pass through what seems like untouched territory— though the lumber companies have long since tackled the virgin forests—and sporting camps and cottages are tucked away here and there. The high point of this route is **Height of Land,** about 30 mi north of Rumford, with its unforgettable views of range after range of mountains and the island-studded blue mass of Mooselookmeguntic Lake directly below. Turnouts on both sides of the highway allow you to pull over for a long look. **Haines Landing** on Mooselookmeguntic Lake lies 7 mi west of Rangeley. Here you can stand at 1,400 ft above sea level and face the same magnificent scenery you admired at 2,400 ft from Height of Land on Route 17. Boat and canoe rentals are available at Mooselookmeguntic House.

Rangeley

52 *39 mi northwest of Farmington, 67 mi from Bethel.*

Rangeley, north of Rangeley Lake on Route 4/16, has lured fisherfolk, hunters, and winter-sports enthusiasts for a century to its more than 40 lakes and ponds and 450 square mi of woodlands. Equally popular in summer or winter, Rangeley has a rough, wilderness feel to it. Lodgings are in the woods, around the lake, and along the golf course.

On the south shore of Rangeley Lake, **Rangeley Lake State Park** (☎ 207/864–3858) has superb lakeside scenery, swimming, picnic tables, a boat ramp, showers, and 50 campsites.

OFF THE BEATEN PATH

SANDY RIVER & RANGELEY LAKES RAILROAD – Ride a mile through the woods along a restored narrow-gauge railroad on a century-old train drawn by a replica of the *Sandy River No. 4* locomotive. ⊠ *Bridge Hill Rd., Phillips (20 mi southeast of Rangeley),* ☎ *207/639-3352.* ✉ *$3.* ☉ *June–Oct., 1st and 3rd Sun. each month; rides at 11, 1, and 3.*

Dining and Lodging

$$ ✕ **Gingerbread House.** A big fieldstone fireplace, well-spaced tables, and an antique marble soda fountain, all with views to the woods beyond, make for a comfortable atmosphere at this gingerbread-trim house that's open for breakfast, lunch, and dinner. For dinner, you might begin with crab cakes or bruschetta, and then move on to seafood fettuccine alfredo, lamb kabobs, or veal marsala. ⊠ *Rtes. 17 and 4, Oquossoc,* ☎ *207/864–3602. Reservations essential on summer weekends. AE, D, DC, MC, V. Closed Mon.–Tues. No dinner Sun.*

$–$$ ✕ **Porter House Restaurant.** This popular restaurant, seemingly in the middle of nowhere, draws diners from Rangeley, Kingfield, and Canada with its good service, excellent food, and casual atmosphere. Of the 1908 farmhouse's four dining rooms, the front one downstairs, which has a fireplace, is the most intimate and elegant. The broad Continental-style menu includes entrées for diners with light appetites. On the heavier side are porterhouse steak and roast duckling. Try the boneless lamb loin and lobster Brittany casserole if they're on the menu. ⊠ *Rte. 27, Eustis,* ☎ *207/246–7932. Reservations essential on weekends. AE, D, MC, V.*

$$ ✕▥ **Country Club Inn.** Built in the 1920s on the Mingo Springs Golf Course, this retreat enjoys a secluded hilltop location and sweeping lake and mountain views. The inn's baronial living room has a cathedral ceiling, a fieldstone fireplace at each end, and game trophies. The rooms downstairs in the main building and in the motel-style wing added in the 1950s are cheerfully if minimally decorated. The glassed-in dining room—open to nonguests by reservation only—has linen-draped

tables set well apart. The menu includes roast duck, veal, fresh fish, and filet mignon. ⊠ *Box 680, Mingo Loop Rd., 04970,* ☎ *207/864–3831. 19 rooms. Restaurant, outdoor pool. Full breakfast; MAP available. AE, MC, V. Closed Apr.–mid-May, mid-Oct.–late-Dec.*

$$$$ 🏠 **Grant's Kennebago Camps.** Rough it in comfort at this traditional Maine sporting camp on Kennebago Lake. "Sports" and families have been coming here for more than 85 years, lured by the fresh water, mountain views, excellent fly-fishing, and hearty home-cooked meals. The wilderness setting, between the Kennebago Mountains, is nothing less than spectacular. The cabins, whose screened porches overlook the lake, have woodstoves and are finished in knotty pine. Motorboats, canoes, sailboats, Windsurfers, and mountain bikes are available. Float-plane rides and fly-fishing instruction can be arranged. ⊠ *Box 786, off Rte. 16, 04970,* ☎ *207/864–3608 in summer, 207/282–5264 in winter, or 800/644–4817. 19 cabins. Lake, hiking, boating, fishing, mountain bikes, baby-sitting, playground. No credit cards. Closed Oct.–late May.*

$$$–$$$$ 🏠 **Hunter Cove on Rangeley Lake.** These lakeside cabins, which sleep from two to six people, provide all the comforts of home in a rustic setting. The interiors are unfinished knotty pine and include kitchens, full baths, and comfortable, if plain, living rooms. Cabin No. 1 has a fieldstone fireplace, and others have wood-burning stoves. Cabins No. 5 and No. 8 have hot tubs. Summer guests can take advantage of a sand swimming beach, boat rentals, and a nearby golf course. In winter, snowmobile right to your door or ski nearby (cross-country and downhill). ⊠ *Mingo Loop Rd.,* ☎ *207/864–3383. 8 cabins. Beach, boating. AE.*

$$–$$$ 🏠 **Rangeley Inn and Motor Lodge.** From Main Street you see only the three-story, blue inn building (circa 1907), but behind it is a newer motel wing with views of Haley Pond, a lawn, and a garden. Some of the inn's sizable rooms have iron-and-brass beds and subdued wallpaper, some have claw-foot tubs, and others have whirlpool tubs. The motel units contain Queen Anne reproduction furniture and velvet chairs. ⊠ *Box 160, 51 Main St., 04970,* ☎ *207/864–3341 or 800/666–3687,* FAX *207/864–3634. 36 inn rooms, 15 motel rooms, 2 cabins. Restaurant, bar, meeting room. MAP available. AE, D, MC, V.*

Nightlife and the Arts

Rangeley Friends of the Arts (⊠ Box 333, ☎ 207/864–5364) sponsors musical theater, fiddlers' contests, rock and jazz, classical, and other summer fare, mostly at Lakeside Park.

Outdoor Activities and Sports

BOATING

Rangeley and Mooselookmeguntic lakes are good for canoeing, sailing, and motorboating. For rentals call **Oquossoc Cove Marina** (⊠ Oquossoc, ☎ 207/864–3463), **Dockside Sports Center** (⊠ Town Cove, ☎ 207/864–2424), or **River's Edge Sports** (⊠ Rte. 4, Oquossoc, ☎ 207/864–5582).

FISHING

Fishing for brook trout and salmon is at its best in May, June, and September; the Rangeley area is especially popular with fly-fishers. Nonresident anglers over the age of 12 must have a fishing license. The **Department of Inland Fisheries and Wildlife** (⊠ 284 State St., Augusta 04333, ☎ 207/287–2871) can provide further information.

If you'd like a fishing guide, try **Clayton (Cy) Eastlack** (☎ 207/864–3416) or **Westwind Charters and Guide Service** (☎ 207/864–5437).

SNOWMOBILING

This is a popular mode of winter transportation in the Rangeley area, with more than 100 mi of maintained trails linking lakes and towns to wilderness camps. The **Maine Snowmobile Association** (⌧ Box 77, Augusta 04330) has information about Maine's nearly 8,000-mi Interconnecting Trail System.

Skiing

Saddleback Ski and Summer Lake Preserve. A down-home atmosphere prevails at Saddleback, where the quiet and the absence of crowds, even on holiday weekends, draw return visitors—many of them families. The base area has the feeling of a small community. ⌧ *Box 490, Saddleback Rd. off Rte. 4, 04970,* ☎ *207/864–5671, 207/864–3380 for snow conditions, 207/864–5364 for reservations.*

DOWNHILL

The expert terrain is short and concentrated at the top of the mountain; an upper lift makes the trails easily accessible. The middle of the mountain is mainly intermediate, with a few meandering easy trails; the beginner or novice slopes are toward the bottom. Two double chairlifts and three T-bars carry skiers to the 40 trails on the 1,830 ft of vertical.

CROSS-COUNTRY

Forty km (25 mi) of groomed cross-country trails spread out from the base area and circle Saddleback Lake and several ponds and rivers.

CHILD CARE

The nursery takes children from age 6 weeks to 8 years. There are ski classes and programs for children of different levels and ages.

Kingfield

53 *33 mi east of Rangeley, 15 mi west of Phillips, 21 mi north of Farmington.*

In the shadows of Mt. Abraham and Sugarloaf Mountain, Kingfield has everything a "real" New England town should have: a general store, historic inns, and a white clapboard church. Don't ignore Sugarloaf in summer: The resort has an 18-hole golf course and six tennis courts for public use in warmer months.

The **Stanley Museum** houses a collection of original Stanley Steamer cars built by the Stanley twins, Kingfield's most famous natives. ⌧ *School St.,* ☎ *207/265–2729.* ⌧ *$2.* ☉ *May–Oct., Tues.–Sun. 1–4; Nov.–Apr. by appointment.*

Dining and Lodging

$$$$ ✕⊡ **Sugarloaf Inn Resort.** This lodge provides ski-on access to Sugarloaf/USA, a complete health club, and rooms that range from king-size on the fourth floor to dorm-style (bunk beds) on the ground floor. A greenhouse section of the Seasons Restaurant ($$–$$$) affords views of the slopes; "ski-in" lunches are served here. At breakfast the sunlight pours into the dining room, and at dinner you can watch the snow-grooming machines prepare your favorite run. Winter rates include skiing lessons. ⌧ *R.R. 1 Box 5000, 04947,* ☎ *207/237–6814 or 800/843–5623,* ⅋Ⅹ *207/237–3773. 38 rooms, 4 dorm-style rooms. Restaurant, health club, meeting rooms. AE, D, MC, V.*

$$$$ ⊡ **Sugarloaf Mountain Hotel.** This six-story brick structure at the base of the lifts on Sugarloaf combines a New England ambience with European-style service. Oak and redwood paneling in the main rooms is enhanced by contemporary furnishings. Valet parking, ski tuning, lockers, and mountain guides are available through the concierge.

There's a lively après-ski scene at the Double Diamond Pub. ⊠ *R.R. 1, Box 2299, Carrabassett Valley 04947,* ☎ *207/237–2222 or 800/ 527–9879,* ℻ *207/237–2874. 100 rooms, 19 suites. Restaurant, pub, hot tub, massage, sauna, spa. AE, D, DC, MC, V.*

$ ⌂ **Three Stanley Avenue.** This simple Victorian B&B is in a quiet neighborhood a few-minutes' walk from downtown Kingfield and about a 20-minute drive from Sugarloaf Ski Resort. The rooms are decorated with antiques and country pieces. Next door is the expensive, gourmet restaurant One Stanley Avenue, under the same ownership. ⊠ *Box 169, 3 Stanley Ave., 04947,* ☎ *207/265–5541. 6 rooms, 3 share 2 baths. Full breakfast. MC, V.*

Nightlife

At Sugarloaf, nightlife is concentrated at the mountain's base village. Monday is blues night at the **Bag & Kettle** (☎ 207/237–2451), which is the best choice for pizza and burgers. In the base village you'll find **Gepetto's** (☎ 207/237–2953), a popular après-ski hangout that serves American-style food. A microbrewery on the access road called the **Sugarloaf Brewing Company** (☎ 207/237–2211) pulls in revelers who come for après-ski brewskies. **Widowmaker Lounge** (☎ 207/237–6845) frequently presents live entertainment in the base lodge.

Outdoor Activities and Sports

DOG-SLEDDING

T.A.D. Dog Sled Services (⊠ Rte. 27, Carrabassett Valley, ☎ 207/246–4461) conducts short 1½-mi rides near Sugarloaf/USA. Sleds accommodate up to two adults and two children.

Skiing

Sugarloaf/USA. Abundant natural snow, a huge mountain, and the only above-tree-line skiing in the East have made Sugarloaf one of Maine's best-known ski areas. Improvements by the American Skiing Company have resulted in increased snowmaking, new lifts, and new trails. Sugarloaf skiers like the nontrendy Maine atmosphere and the base village, which has restaurants and shops. Two slopeside hotels and hundreds of slopeside condominiums provide ski-in/ski-out access. Once you are here, a car is unnecessary—a shuttle connects all mountain operations. Summer is much quieter than in winter, but you can bike, hike, golf, and fish. ⊠ *R.R. 1 Box 5000, 04947,* ☎ *207/237–2000, 207/237–6808 for snow conditions, or 800/843–5623.*

DOWNHILL

With a vertical of 2,820 ft, Sugarloaf is taller than any other New England ski peak except Killington in Vermont. The advanced terrain begins with the steep snowfields on top, wide open and treeless. Coming down the face of the mountain, there are black-diamond runs everywhere, often blending into easier terrain. Many intermediate trails can be found down the front face, and a couple more come off the summit. Easier runs are predominantly toward the bottom, with a few long, winding runs that twist and turn from higher elevations. Serving the resort's 122 trails are two high-speed quad, two quad, one triple, and eight double chairlifts and one T-bar.

CROSS-COUNTRY

The Sugarloaf Ski Outdoor Center has 95 km (62 mi) of cross-country trails that loop and wind through the valley. Trails connect to the resort.

OTHER ACTIVITIES

Snowboarders will find two snowboard parks and a halfpipe, the largest in the Northeast. The **Sugarloaf Sports and Fitness Club** (☎ 207/ 237–6946) has an indoor pool, six indoor and outdoor hot tubs, racquetball courts, full fitness and spa facilities, and a beauty salon. Use of club facilities is included in all lodging packages. Snowshoeing and ice skating are available at the Outdoor Center.

CHILD CARE

A nursery takes children from age 6 weeks to 6 years. Children's ski programs begin at age 3. A night nursery is open on Thursday and Saturday from 6 to 10 PM by reservation. Instruction is provided on a half-day or full-day basis for children from age 4 to 14. Nightly children's activities are free. The teen club, Avalanche, is located in the base lodge.

Western Lakes and Mountains A to Z

Getting Around

BY CAR

A car is essential to a tour of the western lakes and mountains. Of the variety of routes available, the itinerary in Exploring, *above,* takes Route 302 to Route 26 to Route 2 to Route 17 to Route 4/16 to Route 142.

BY PLANE

Mountain Air Service (⊠ Rangeley, ☎ 207/864–5307) provides air access to remote areas, scenic flights, and charter fishing trips.

Naples Flying Service (⊠ Naples Causeway, ☎ 207/693–6591) operates sightseeing flights over the lakes in summer.

Contacts and Resources

EMERGENCIES

Bethel Area Health Center (⊠ Railroad St., Bethel, ☎ 207/824–2193). **Mt. Abram Regional Health Center** (⊠ Depot St., Kingfield, ☎ 207/265–4555). **Rangeley Regional Health Center** (⊠ Main St., Rangeley, ☎ 207/864–3303).

RESERVATION SERVICES

Condominium lodging at Shawnee Peak is available through the **Bridgton Group** (☎ 207/647–2591). Bethel's **Chamber of Commerce** (☎ 207/824–3585 or 800/442–5826) has a reservations service. For reservations at Sugarloaf/USA, contact **Sugarloaf Area Reservations Service** (☎ 800/843–2732).

VISITOR INFORMATION

Bethel Area Chamber of Commerce (⊠ Box 439, Bethel 04217, ☎ 207/824–2282 or 800/442–5526). **Bridgton–Lakes Region Chamber of Commerce** (⊠ Box 236, Bridgton 04009, ☎ 207/647–3472). **Rangeley Lakes Region Chamber of Commerce** (⊠ Box 317, Rangeley 04970, ☎ 207/864–5571 or 800/685–2537).

THE NORTH WOODS

Maine's North Woods, the vast area in the north-central section of the state, is best experienced by canoe or raft, hiking trail, or on a fishing or hunting trip. The driving tour below takes in three great theaters for these activities—Moosehead Lake, Baxter State Park, and the Allagash Wilderness Waterway—as well as the summer resort town of Greenville, dramatically situated Rockwood, and the no-frills outposts that connect them. For much of what to see and do in this region consult the Outdoor Activities and Sports section, *below;* for outfitters, *see* Contacts and Resources *in* North Woods A to Z, *below.*

Rockwood

 180 mi north of Portland, 91 mi northwest of Bangor, 20 mi north of Greenville.

The North Woods

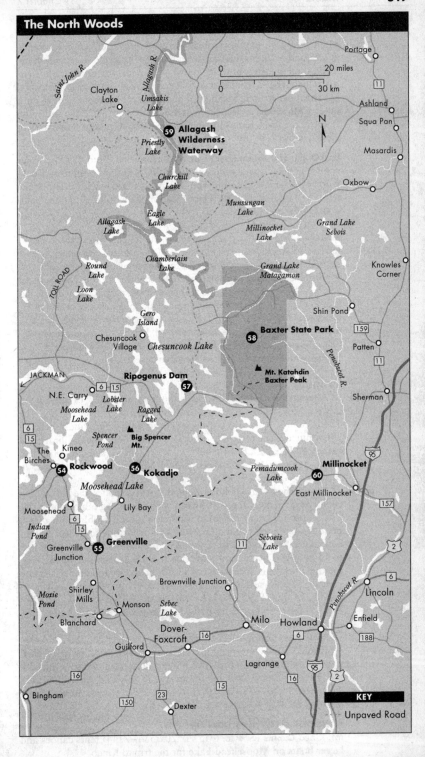

Portage

Saint John R.

Allagash R.

Clayton Lake

Umsakis Lake

Ashland

11

Squa Pan

59 Allagash Wilderness Waterway

Priestly Lake

Masardis

Churchill Lake

Munsungan Lake

Oxbow

Eagle Lake

Millinocket Lake

Grand Lake Seboeis

Allagash Lake

Chamberlain Lake

Knowles Corner

Round Lake

Grand Lake Matagamon

TOLL ROAD

Loon Lake

Shin Pond

159

Gero Island

Chesuncook Village

Baxter State Park

58

Patten

11

Chesuncook Lake

Penobscot R.

JACKMAN

Ripogenus Dam

57

Mt. Katahdin Baxter Peak

Sherman

N.E. Carry

6 15

Lobster Lake

Ragged Lake

Moosehead Lake

Spencer Pond

Big Spencer Mt.

6 15

Kineo

The Birches

54 Rockwood

56 Kokadjo

Pemadumcook Lake

Millinocket

60

95

Moosehead Lake

Lily Bay

East Millinocket

157

Moosehead

6 15

Indian Pond

Seboeis Lake

55 Greenville

Greenville Junction

11

2

Moxie Pond

Shirley Mills

Brownville Junction

Lincoln

6

Monson

Sebec Lake

Blanchard

Dover-Foxcroft

Milo

Howland

Enfield

16

188

Guilford

6

16

95

Bingham

16

150

23

15

Lagrange

16

2

Dexter

KEY

Unpaved Road

0   20 miles

0   30 km

N

Rockwood, on Moosehead Lake's western shore, is a good starting point for a wilderness trip or a family vacation on the lake. Moosehead Lake, Maine's largest, supplies more in the way of rustic camps, restaurants, guides, and outfitters than any other northern locale. Its 420 mi of shorefront, three-quarters of which is owned by paper manufacturers, is virtually uninhabited. Though it doesn't possess many amenities, Rockwood has the most striking location of any town on Moosehead: The dark mass of **Mt. Kineo,** a sheer cliff that rises 789 ft above the lake and 1,789 ft above sea level, looms just across the narrows (you get an excellent view just north of town on Route 6/15).

East Outlet of the Kennebec River, a popular Class II and III white-water run for canoeists and white-water rafters, is about 10 mi from Rockwood on Route 6/15 south. You'll come to a bridge with a dam to the left. The outlet ends at the Harris Station Dam at Indian Pond, headwaters of the Kennebec.

OFF THE BEATEN PATH

KINEO – Once a thriving summer resort, the original Mount Kineo Hotel (built in 1830 and torn down in the 1940s) was accessed primarily by steamship. An effort to renovate the remaining buildings in the early 1990s failed, but Kineo still makes a pleasant day trip from Rockwood. You can rent a motorboat in Rockwood and make the journey across the lake in about 15 minutes. There's a small marina on the shore, in the shadow of Mt. Kineo, and a half dozen buildings dot the land—some are for sale and others are being restored, but there is no real town here. A tavern sells cold libations to drink there or take with you. A walkway laces the perimeter of the mountain.

Lodging

$$$$ 🏨 **Attean Lake Lodge.** This lodge about an hour west of Rockwood has been owned and operated by the Holden family since 1900. The 18 log cabins, which sleep from two to six people, provide a secluded environment. The tastefully decorated central lodge has a library and games. ☒ *Box 457, Birch Island, Jackman 04945,* ☎ *207/668–3792,* 🆁🅰🆇 *207/668–4016. 18 cabins. Beach, boating, recreation room, library. AP. AE, MC, V. Closed Oct.–May.*

$–$$ 🏨 **The Birches.** This family-oriented resort supplies the full north-country experience: Moosehead Lake, birch woods, log cabins, and boats. The century-old main lodge has four guest rooms, a lobby with a trout pond, and a living room dominated by a fieldstone fireplace. The 15 cottages have wood-burning stoves or fireplaces and sleep from two to 15 people. The dining room (closed in December and April) overlooking the lake is open to the public for breakfast and dinner; the fare at dinner is pasta, seafood, and steak. ☒ *Box 41, off Rte. 6/15, on Moosehead Lake, 04478,* ☎ *207/534–7305 or 800/825–9453,* 🆁🅰🆇 *207/534–8835. 4 lodge rooms share bath, 15 cottages. Dining room, hot tub, sauna, boating. AE, D, MC, V.*

$ 🏨 **Rockwood Cottages.** These eight white cottages Moosehead Lake, off Route 15 and convenient to the center of Rockwood, have screened porches and fully equipped kitchens and sleep from two to seven people. There is a one-week minimum stay in July and August. ☒ *Box 176, Rte. 15, 04478,* ☎ *207/534–7725. 8 cottages. Sauna, dock, boating. D, MC, V.*

Outdoor Activities and Sports

Mt. Kineo Cabins (☒ *Rte. 6/15,* ☎ *207/534–7744*) rents canoes and larger boats on Moosehead Lake for the trip to Kineo.

Rent a boat or take a shuttle operated by **Rockwood Cottages** (☎ *207/ 534–7725*) or **Old Mill Campground** (☎ *207/534–7333*) and hike one of the trails to the summit of Mt. Kineo for a picnic lunch and panoramic views of the region.

Greenville

55   *160 mi northeast of Portland, 70 mi northwest of Bangor.*

Greenville has a smattering of shops, restaurants, and hotels. The largest town on Moosehead Lake, it is home to the Squaw Mountain ski area, which in summer runs a recreation program for children and has two tennis courts, hiking, and lawn games.

Moosehead Marine Museum has exhibits on the local logging industry and the steamship era on Moosehead Lake, plus photographs of the Mount Kineo Hotel. ⊠ *Main St.,* ☎ *207/695–2716.* 🎫 *Free.* ☉ *Late May–early Oct., daily 10–4.*

The Moosehead Marine Museum offers three-hour and six-hour trips on Moosehead Lake aboard the **Katahdin**, a 1914 steamship (now diesel). The 115-ft *Katahdin* (fondly called *The Kate*) carried passengers to Kineo until 1942 and then was used in the logging industry until 1975. ⊠ *Main St. (boarding is on the shoreline by the museum),* ☎ *207/695–2716.* 🎫 *$9–$24.* ☉ *Late May–Columbus Day.*

Lily Bay State Park (⊠ Lily Bay Rd., ☎ 207/695–2700), 8 mi northeast of Greenville, has a good swimming beach, two boat-launching ramps, and a 93-site campground.

Dining and Lodging

$–$$ ✕ **Road Kill Cafe.** The motto here is "Where the food used to speak for itself." It's not for everyone, but if you don't mind a menu with items such as the Chicken That Didn't Make It Across the Road, Bye-Bye Bambi Burgers, Brake and Scrape sandwiches, and Mooseballs, this fun-loving spot is for you. The staff takes pride in its borderline-rude attitude, but it's all in jest. Tables on the rear deck have views of the water. ⊠ *Rte. 15, Greenville Junction,* ☎ *207/695–2230. D, MC, V.*

$ ✕ **Kelly's Landing.** This family-oriented restaurant on the Moosehead shorefront has indoor and outdoor seating, excellent views, and a dock for boaters. The fare includes sandwiches, burgers, lasagna, seafood dinners, and prime rib. ⊠ *Rte. 6/15, Greenville Junction,* ☎ *207/695–4438. MC, V.*

$$$–$$$$ ✕🏨 **Greenville Inn.** Built more than a century ago, this rambling structure is a block from town on a rise over Moosehead Lake. The ornate cherry and mahogany paneling, Oriental rugs, and leaded glass create an aura of masculine ease. Cottages have mountain and lake views, and some have decks. The restaurant ($$; reservations essential; no lunch) has water views. The menu, revised daily, reflects the owners' Austrian background: shrimp with mustard-dill sauce, salmon marinated in olive oil and basil, a veal cutlet with a mushroom cream sauce. ⊠ *Box 1194, Norris St., 04441,* ☎ FAX *207/695–2206 or* ☎ *888/695–6000. 4 rooms and 1 suite in main inn, 1 suite in carriage house, 6 cottages. Restaurant. Full breakfast. D, MC, V.*

$$$$ 🏨 **Lodge at Moosehead Lake.** This mansion overlooking Moosehead ★ Lake is about as close as things get to luxury in the North Woods. All rooms have whirlpool baths, fireplaces, and hand-carved four-poster beds; most have lake views. The restaurant, where breakfast is served year-round and dinner is served in the off-season, has a spectacular view of the water. ⊠ *Lily Bay Rd., 04441,* ☎ *207/695–4400,* FAX *207/ 695–2281. 5 rooms, 3 suites. D, MC, V.*

$–$$ 🏨 **Chalet Moosehead.** Fifty yards off Route 6/15 and right on Moosehead Lake, this accommodation holds efficiencies (which have two double beds, a living room, and a kitchenette), motel rooms, and cabins, all with picture windows to capture the view. The attractive grounds include a private beach and dock. ⊠ *Box 327, Rte. 6/15, Greenville Junction 04442,* ☏ *207/695–2950 or 800/290–3645. 8 efficiencies, 7 motel rooms, 2 cabins. Horseshoes, beach, dock, boating. AE, D, MC, V.*

$–$$ ☑ **Sawyer House Bed & Breakfast.** The convenient in-town location across the street from the lake makes it easy to tour Greenville on foot from this comfortable B&B. The two upstairs rooms are on the small-ish side, but the room on the first floor is huge. ⊠ *Box 521, Lakeview St., 04441,* ☏ *207/695–2369. 3 rooms. Full breakfast. AE, D, MC, V.*

Outdoor Activities and Sports

FISHING

Togue, landlocked salmon, and brook and lake trout lure thousands of fisherfolk to the region from ice-out in mid-May until September; the hardiest return in winter to ice fish. For up-to-date information on water levels, call 207/695–3756.

RAFTING

The Kennebec and Dead rivers and the West Branch of the Penobscot River offer thrilling white-water rafting (guides are strongly recommended). These rivers are dam-controlled, so trips run rain or shine daily from May to October (day and multiday trips are conducted). Most guided raft trips on the Kennebec and Dead rivers leave from the Forks, southwest of Moosehead Lake, on Route 201; Penobscot River trips leave from either Greenville or Millinocket. Many rafting outfitters operate resort facilities in their base towns. **Raft Maine** (☏ 800/723–8633) has lodging and rafting packages and information about outfitters.

Shopping

Indian Hill Trading Post (⊠ Rte. 6/15, ☏ 207/695–2104) stocks just about anything you might need for a North Woods vacation, including sporting and camping equipment, canoes, and hunting and fishing licenses; there's even an adjacent grocery store.

Skiing

Big Squaw Mountain Resort. The management is modernizing this remote but pretty resort overlooking Moosehead Lake. The emphasis is on affordable family skiing—prices are downright cheap compared with other in-state areas. New snowmaking, new grooming equipment, and a new attitude make this a wonderful place for skiers longing to escape crowds. ⊠ *Box D, 04441,* ☏ *207/695–1000.*

DOWNHILL

Trails are laid out according to difficulty, with the easy slopes toward the bottom, intermediate trails weaving from midpoint, and steeper runs high up off the 1,750-vertical-ft peak. The 22 trails are served by one triple and one double chairlift and two surface lifts.

CHILD CARE

The nursery takes children from infants through age 6. The ski school has daily lessons and racing classes for children of all ages.

Kokadjo

56   *22 mi northeast of Greenville.*

Kokadjo, population "not many," has a sign that reads "Keep Maine green. This is God's country. Why set it on fire and make it look like hell?" This is last outpost before you enter the North Woods. As you leave Kokadjo, bear left at the fork and follow signs to Baxter State Park. A drive of 5 mi along this road (now dirt) brings you to the Bowater/Great Northern Paper Company's Sias Hill checkpoint, where from

June to November you must sign in and pay a user fee ($8 per car for nonresidents, valid for 24 hours) to travel the next 40 mi. Access is through a forest where you're likely to encounter logging trucks (which have the right of way), logging equipment, and work in progress. At the bottom of the hill after you pass the checkpoint, look to your right—there's a good chance you'll spot a moose.

Lodging

$$ 🏠 **Northern Pride Lodge.** North Woods–quaint with basic creature comforts is the best way to describe this lakefront lodge decorated with Victorian-era antiques and fishing and hunting trophies. Rooms are small, but the big porch is likely where you'll be spending much of your time. A huge country breakfast is served to all guests; lunch and dinner are available, too. ⊠ *HC 76 Box 588, Greenville Rd., 04441,* ☎ *207/695–2890. 5 rooms share 2 baths. Full breakfast; MAP and AP available. MC, V.*

Ripogenus Dam

57 *20 mi northeast of Kokadjo, 25 min southeast of Chesuncook Village by floatplane.*

Ripogenus Dam and the granite-walled Ripogenus Gorge are on Ripogenus Lake, east of Chesuncook Lake. The gorge is the jumping-off point for the famous 12-mi West Branch of the Penobscot River whitewater rafting trip and the most popular put-in point for Allagash canoe trips. The Penobscot River drops more than 70 ft per mile through the gorge, giving rafters a hold-on-for-your-life ride. The best spot to watch the Penobscot rafters is from Pray's Big Eddy Wilderness Campground, overlooking the rock-choked **Crib Works Rapid** (a Class V rapid). To get here, follow the main road northeast and turn left on Telos Road; the campground is about 10 yards after the bridge.

En Route From the Pray's Big Eddy Wilderness Campground, take the main road (here called the Golden Road for the amount of money it took the Great Northern Paper Company to build it) southeast toward Millinocket. The road soon becomes paved. After you drive over the one-lane Abol Bridge and pass through the Bowater/Great Northern Paper Company's Debsconeag checkpoint, bear left to reach Togue Pond Gatehouse, the southern entrance to Baxter State Park.

Baxter State Park

58 *24 mi northwest of Millinocket.*

Few places in Maine are as remote, or as beautiful some will say, as **Baxter State Park** and the Allagash. Baxter State Park (☎ 207/723–5140), a gift from Governor Percival Baxter, is the jewel in the crown of northern Maine, a 204,733-acre wilderness area that surrounds **Katahdin,** Maine's highest mountain (5,267 ft at Baxter Peak) and the terminus of the Appalachian Trail. There are 46 mountain peaks and ridges, 18 of which exceed an elevation of 3,000 ft. The park is intersected by about 175 mi of trails. No pets, domestic animals, oversize vehicles, or motorcycles are allowed in the park.

OFF THE
BEATEN PATH

LUMBERMAN'S MUSEUM – This museum comprises 10 buildings filled with exhibits depicting the history of logging, including models, dioramas, and equipment. ⊠ *Shin Pond Rd./Rte. 159, Patten (22 mi southeast of Baxter State Park),* ☎ *207/528-2650.* 🎫 *$2.50.* ☉ *Memorial Day–Sept., Tues.–Sat. 9–4, Sun. 11–4.*

Camping

$ ⚠ **Baxter State Park.** Camping spaces here can only be reserved by mail (phone reservations not accepted). Reservations can be made beginning January 1—some sites are fully booked for midsummer weekends soon after that. The state also maintains primitive backcountry sites that are available without charge on a first-come, first-served basis. ✉ *Baxter State Park Authority, 64 Balsam Dr., Millinocket 04462.* ⊙ *Mid-may–mid–Oct.*

Outdoor Activities and Sports

Katahdin, in Baxter State Park, draws thousands of hikers every year for the daylong climb to the summit and the stunning views of woods, mountains, and lakes from the hair-raising Knife Edge Trail along its ridge. The crowds can be formidable on clear summer days, so if you crave solitude, tackle one of the 45 other mountains in the park, all of which are accessible from a 150-mi network of trails. South Turner can be climbed in a morning (if you're fit)—it affords a great view of Katahdin across the valley. On the way you'll pass Sandy Stream Pond, where moose are often seen at dusk. The Owl, the Brothers, and Doubletop Mountain are good day hikes.

The Allagash Wilderness Waterway

59 *22 mi north of Ripogenus Dam.*

The Allagash is a 92-mi corridor of lakes and rivers that cuts across 170,000 acres of wilderness, beginning at the northwest corner of Baxter and running north to the town of Allagash, 10 mi from the Canadian border. ✉ *Allagash Wilderness Waterway, 106 Hogan Rd., Bangor 04401,* ☎ *207/941–4014.*

Outdoor Activities and Sports

The Allagash rapids are ranked Class I and Class II (very easy and easy), but that doesn't mean the river is a piece of cake; river conditions vary greatly with the depth and volume of water, and even a Class I rapid can hang your canoe up on a rock, capsize you, or spin you around. On the lakes, strong winds can halt your progress for days. The Allagash should not be undertaken lightly or without planning; the complete 92-mi course requires 7 to 10 days. The canoeing season along the Allagash is from mid-May to October, although it's wise to remember that the black-fly season ends about July 1. The best bet for a novice is to go with a guide; a good outfitter will help plan your route and provide your craft and transportation.

The Mt. Everest of Maine canoe trips is the 110-mi route on the St. John River from Baker Lake to Allagash Village, with a swift current all the way and two stretches of Class III rapids. The best time to canoe the St. John is between mid-May and mid-June, when the river level is high.

Those with their own canoe who want to go it alone can take Telos Road north from Ripogenus Dam, putting in at Chamberlain Thoroughfare Bridge at the southern tip of Chamberlain Lake, or at Allagash Lake, Churchill Dam, Bissonnette Bridge, or Umsaskis Bridge. One popular and easy route follows the Upper West Branch of the Penobscot River from Lobster Lake (just east of Moosehead Lake) to Chesuncook Lake. From Chesuncook Village you can paddle to Ripogenus Dam in a day.

The Aroostook River from Little Munsungan Lake to Fort Fairfield (100 mi) is best run in late spring. More-challenging routes include the Passadumkeag River from Grand Falls to Passadumkeag (25 mi with Class I–III rapids); the East Branch of the Penobscot River from Matagamon Wilderness Campground to Grindstone (38 mi with Class I–III rapids); and the West Branch of the Pleasant River from Katahdin Iron Works to Brownville Junction (10 mi with Class II–III rapids).

Millinocket

60 *90 mi northwest of Greenville, 19 mi southeast of Baxter State Park, 70 mi north of Bangor.*

Millinocket, with a population of 7,000, is a gateway to Baxter State Park.

OFF THE
BEATEN PATH

KATAHDIN IRON WORKS – For a worthwhile day trip from Millinocket, take Route 11 west to a trailhead 5 mi north of Brownville Junction. Follow the gravel road 6 mi to Katahdin Iron Works, the site of a mining operation that employed nearly 200 workers in the mid-1800s; a deteriorated kiln, a stone furnace, and a charcoal-storage building are all that remain. The trail continues over fairly rugged terrain into **Gulf Hagas,** the Grand Canyon of the East, with natural chasms, cliffs, a 3-mi gorge, waterfalls, pools, exotic flora, and rock formations.

Dining and Lodging

$–$$ ✕ **Scootic Inn and Penobscot Room.** This informal restaurant and lounge has a varied menu of steak, seafood, pizza, and sandwiches. The large-screen TV is usually tuned to sports. ⊠ *70 Penobscot Ave.,* ☎ *207/723–4566. AE, D, MC, V.*

$ ☷ **Atrium Motel.** Off Route 157 next to a shopping center, this motor inn has a large central atrium with facilities that make up for its unappealing location and standard motel furnishings. ⊠ *740 Central St., 04462,* ☎ ℻ *207/723–4555. 72 rooms, 10 suites. Indoor pool, hot tub, health club. Continental breakfast. AE, D, DC, MC, V.*

North Woods A to Z

Getting Around

BY CAR

A car is essential to negotiate this vast region but may not be useful to someone spending a vacation entirely at a wilderness camp. Public roads are scarce in the north country, but lumber companies maintain private roads that are often open to the public (sometimes by permit only). When driving on a logging road, always give lumber company trucks the right of way. Be aware that loggers often take the middle of the road and will neither move over nor slow down for you.

BY PLANE

Charter flights, usually by seaplane, from Bangor, Greenville, or Millinocket to smaller towns and remote lake and forest areas can be arranged with the following flying services, which will transport you and your gear and help you find a guide: **Currier's Flying Service** (⊠ Greenville Junction, ☎ 207/695–2778), **Folsom's Air Service** (⊠ Greenville, ☎ 207/695–2821), **Katahdin Air Service** (⊠ Millinocket, ☎ 207/723–8378), **Scotty's Flying Service** (⊠ Shin Pond, ☎ 207/528–2626).

Contacts and Resources

CAMPING

Reservations for state park campsites (excluding Baxter State Park) can be made from January until August 23 through the **Bureau of Parks and Lands** (☎ 207/287–3824 or 800/332–1501 in ME). Make reservations as far ahead as possible (at least seven days in advance), because sites go quickly. **Maine Sporting Camp Association** (⊠ Box 89,

Jay 04239, ☎ no phone) publishes a list of its members, with details on the facilities available at each camp.

Camping and fire permits are required for many areas outside state parks. The **Bureau of Parks and Lands** (⊠ State House Station 22, Augusta 04333, ☎ 207/287–3821) will tell you if you need a camping permit and where to obtain one. The **Maine Forest Service, Department of Conservation** (⊠ State House Station 22, Augusta 04333, ☎ 207/287–2791) will direct you to the nearest ranger station, where you can get a fire permit (⊠ Greenville Ranger Station, Box 1107, Lakeview St., Greenville 04441, ☎ 207/695–3721). The **Maine Campground Owners Association** (⊠ 655 Main St., Lewiston 04240, ☎ 207/782–5874) publishes a helpful annual directory of its members; 18 are in the Katahdin/Moosehead area, and 25 are in the Kennebec and Moose River valleys. **Maine Publicity Bureau** (⊠ Box 2300, 325B Water St., Hallowell 04347, ☎ 207/623–0363; 800/533–9595 outside ME) publishes a listing of private campsites and cottage rentals. **North Maine Woods** (⊠ Box 421, Ashland 04732, ☎ 207/435–6213) maintains 500 primitive campsites on commercial forest land and takes reservations for 20 of them; early reservations are recommended.

CANOEING

Most canoe rental operations will arrange transportation, help plan your route, and provide a guide. Transport to wilderness lakes can be arranged through the flying services listed under Getting Around by Plane, *above.*

The **Bureau of Parks and Lands** (State House Station 22, Augusta 04333, ☎ 207/287–3821) provides information on independent Allagash canoeing and camping. The following are:

Allagash Canoe Trips (⊠ Box 713, Greenville 04441, ☎ 207/695–3668) operates guided trips on the Allagash Waterway, plus the Moose, Penobscot, and St. John rivers. **Allagash Wilderness Outfitters/Frost Pond Camps** (⊠ Box 620, Greenville 04441, ☎ 207/695–2821) provides equipment, transportation, and information for canoe trips on the Allagash and the Penobscot rivers. **Mahoosuc Guide Service** (⊠ Bear River Rd., Newry 04261, ☎ 207/824–2073) conducts guided trips on the Penobscot, Allagash, and Moose rivers. **North Country Outfitters** (⊠ Box 41, Rockwood 04478, ☎ 207/534–2242 or 207/534–7305) operates a white-water canoeing and kayaking school, rents equipment, and sponsors guided canoe trips on the Allagash Waterway and the Moose, Penobscot, and St. John rivers. **North Woods Ways** (⊠ R.R. 2 Box 159-A, Guilford 04443, ☎ 207/997–3723) organizes wilderness canoeing trips on the Allagash, as well as on the Penobscot and St. John rivers. **Willard Jalbert Camps** (⊠ 6 Winchester St., Presque Isle 04769, ☎ 207/764–0494) has been sponsoring guided Allagash trips since the late 1800s.

EMERGENCIES

Charles A. Dean Memorial Hospital (⊠ Pritham Ave., Greenville, ☎ 207/695–2223 or 800/260–4000). **Mayo Regional Hospital** (⊠ 75 W. Main St., Dover-Foxcroft, ☎ 207/564–8401). **Millinocket Regional Hospital** (⊠ 200 Somerset St., Millinocket, ☎ 207/723–5161).

GUIDES

Hunting and fishing guides are available through most wilderness camps, sporting goods stores, and canoe outfitters. For assistance in finding a guide, contact **North Maine Woods** (☞ Visitor Information, *below*). A few well-established guides are **Gilpatrick's Guide Service** (⊠ Box 461, Skowhegan 04976, ☎ 207/453–6959), **Maine Guide Fly Shop and Guide Service** (⊠ Box 1202, Main St., Greenville 04441, ☎

207/695–2266), and **Professional Guide Service** (⊠ Box 346, Sheridan 04775, ☎ 207/435–8044).

HORSEBACK RIDING

Northern Maine Riding Adventures (⊠ 64 Garland Line Rd., Dover-Foxcroft 04426, ☎ 207/564–3451), owned by registered Maine guides Judy Cross-Strehlke and Bob Strehlke, conducts one-day, two-day, and weeklong pack trips (10 people maximum) through various parts of Piscataquis County. A popular two-day trip explores the Whitecap–Barren Mountain Range, near Katahdin Iron Works (☞ Millinocket, *above*).

RAFTING

Raft Maine (☎ 800/723–8633) is an association of white-water outfitters that are licensed to lead trips down the Kennebec and Dead rivers and the West Branch of the Penobscot River. Rafting season begins May 1 and continues through mid-October.

VISITOR INFORMATION

Baxter State Park Authority (⊠ 64 Balsam Dr., Millinocket 04462, ☎ 207/723–5140). **Millinocket Area Chamber of Commerce** (⊠ 1029 Central St., Millinocket 04462, ☎ 207/723–4443). **Moosehead Lake Region Chamber of Commerce** (⊠ Box 581, Rtes. 6 and 15, Greenville 04441, ☎ 207/695–2702). **North Maine Woods** (⊠ Box 421, Ashland 04732, ☎ 207/435–6213; for maps, a canoeing guide for the St. John River, and lists of outfitters, camps, and campsites).

MAINE A TO Z

Arriving and Departing

By Boat

Bay Ferries (☎ 888/249–7245) operates car-ferry service between Yarmouth, Nova Scotia, and Bar Harbor from mid-May to mid-October. **Prince of Fundy Cruises** (☎ 800/341–7540; 800/482–0955 in Maine) operates a car ferry from May to October between Portland and Yarmouth, Nova Scotia.

By Bus

Concord Trailways (☎ 800/639–3317) provides service between Boston and Bangor (via Portland); a coastal route connects towns between Brunswick and Searsport. **Vermont Transit** (☎ 207/772–6587), connects towns in southwestern Maine with cities in New England and throughout the United States. Vermont Transit is a subsidiary of **Greyhound** (☎ 800/231–2222).

By Car

Interstate 95 is the fastest route to and through the state from coastal New Hampshire and points south, turning inland at Brunswick and going on to Bangor and the Canadian border. Route 1, more leisurely and scenic, is the principal coastal highway from New Hampshire to Canada.

By Plane

Portland International Jetport (⊠ Westbrook St. off Rte. 9, ☎ 207/774–7301) is served by Continental Express, Delta, United, and US-Airways.

Bangor International Airport (⊠ Godfrey Blvd., Exit 47 off I–95, ☎ 207/947–0384) is served by Continental, Delta, Northwest Airlink, and USAirways Express. **Hancock County Airport** (⊠ Rte. 3, ☎ 207/667–7329), in Trenton, 8 mi northwest of Bar Harbor, is served by

Continental Connection/Colgan Air. **Knox County Regional Airport** (⊠ Off Rte. 73, ☎ 207/594–4131), in Owls Head, 3 mi south of Rockland, has flights to Boston and Bar Harbor on Continental Connection/Colgan Air.

See Air Travel *in* the Gold Guide for airline phone numbers.

Getting Around

By Boat

Casco Bay Lines (☎ 207/774–7871) provides ferry service from Portland to the islands of Casco Bay. **Maine State Ferry Service** (☎ 207/596–2202 or 800/491–4883) provides service from Rockland, Lincolnville, and Bass Harbor to islands in Penobscot and Blue Hill bays.

By Car

In many areas a car is the only practical means of travel. The *Maine Map and Travel Guide,* available for a small fee from the Maine Publicity Bureau, is useful for driving throughout the state; it has directories, mileage charts, and enlarged maps of city areas.

By Plane

Regional flying services, operating from regional and municipal airports (☞ Arriving and Departing, *above*), provide access to remote lakes and wilderness areas as well as to Penobscot Bay islands.

Contacts and Resources

Camping

The **Maine Campground Owners Association** (⊠ 655 Main St., Lewiston 04240, ☎ 207/782–5874, FAX 207/782–4497) has a statewide listing of private campgrounds.

Car Rental

Alamo (⊠ Rear 9 Johnson St., ☎ 207/775–0855 or 800/327–9633 in Portland). **Avis** (⊠ Portland International Jetport, ☎ 207/874–7501 or 800/331–1212). **Budget** (⊠ Portland International Jetport, ☎ 207/772–6789 or 800/527–0700). **Hertz** (⊠ 1049 Westbrook St., Portland International Jetport, ☎ 207/774–4544 or 800/654–3131). **Thrifty** (⊠ 1000 Westbrook St., Portland International Jetport, ☎ 207/772–4628 or 800/367–2277).

Guided Tours

Golden Age Festival (⊠ 5501 New Jersey Ave., Wildwood Crest, NJ 08260, ☎ 609/522–6316 or 800/257–8920) operates a four-night bus tour geared to senior citizens, with shopping at Kittery outlets and L. L. Bean, a Boothbay Harbor boat cruise, and stops at Kennebunkport, Mt. Battie in Camden, and Acadia National Park. Tours run from May to mid-October.

Visitor Information

Maine Innkeepers Association (⊠ 305 Commercial St., Portland 04101, ☎ 207/773–7670. **Maine Publicity Bureau** (⊠ Box 2300, 325B Water St., Hallowell 04347, ☎ 207/623–0363; 800/533–9595 outside ME).

8 Portraits of New England

"A Solo Sojourn on Cape Cod's Beaches," by Anthony Chase

Books and Videos

A SOLO SOJOURN
ON CAPE COD'S BEACHES

WHEN YOU RIDE a motorcycle slowly across the Newport Bridge on a fair, windless Saturday morning in early May, it comes as a bit of a shock to realize that there are seagulls at your elbows. They glide without moving their wings, a few feet from the handlebars. Several hundred yards below, the sea is a silent blue-green diamond field, full of sparkling whitecap flaws. If you are on your way north, to the outer dunes of Cape Cod, the gulls will stay there, like feather guides, wild and discrete, nearby, in the bright droning of the north Atlantic surf.

I am spending the better part of a week walking the lower Cape, from Chatham to Provincetown, staying the night at different inns in different towns along the way, relishing the clean sheets and hot showers, setting off again early the next morning. A small rucksack reduces my worldly possessions to about seven pounds. The landscape is the journey's rationale: forest, wetlands, ponds, and ocean a movable spa. I want to swim in the surf and the kettle holes, eat seafood caught nearby, hang my shabby body out in the wind to dry, like a threadbare rug after a long winter.

Even during the late spring or early fall, when mild breezes and empty beaches make walking a delight, spending a week outdoors in New England invites a tormented relationship with the weather, and so I plan on constantly changing plans. If long stretches of beach walking become too grueling, I'm prepared to find a road that winds along the coast; a storm could restrict me to the same town for three days; head winds might send me into the forest for shelter. I will rely on that fascinating state of mind we tend to abandon as we fumble through middle age: serendipity.

Henry David Thoreau made three trips to Cape Cod in the middle of the 19th century and published his journal descriptions in book form in 1865. In a piece called "Walking," originally published in *The Atlantic* in 1862, he remarks: "I have met with but one or two persons in the course of my life who understood the art of Walking, that is, of taking walks—who had a genius, so to speak, for *sauntering*: which word is beautifully derived 'from idle people who roved about the country, in the middle Ages . . . under pretense of going *à la Sainte Terre,*' to the Holy Land, till the children exclaimed, 'There goes a *Sainte-Terrer,*' a Saunterer, a Holy-Lander . . . Some . . . would derive the word from *sans terre,* without land or home, which . . . will mean, having no particular home, but equally at home everywhere. For this is the secret of successful sauntering . . . no more vagrant than the meandering river, which is all the while sedulously seeking the shortest course to the sea."

Thoreau is known for his eccentricities: living as a hermit in a cabin at Walden Pond, paddling down Concord rivers in a rowboat, or exploring the remote forests of northern Maine in the company of Native American guides. But in fact, he was as sane, and almost as suburban, as anyone. He taught in a secondary school, he worked as a surveyor, and he took an active interest in his family's pencil-manufacturing business. One legacy of Thoreau's life and work is his understanding that there can be no appreciation of solitude without society's presence; there can be no healthy arrangement of human affairs without the surrounding energies of the natural world.

The year's first contact with the ocean is always startling. In the fading afternoon light the water shines more brightly than the sky, in Caribbean shades, with lime-green shallows and blue depths offshore, as if lit by an underwater sun: The sand is free of people, but there are a dozen terns out fishing. They lift off and fly upstream, land, settle their feathers, and drift gently past again.

At low tide, a beach walk is a pleasant stroll on hard sand, with playful surf cooling your ankles. At high tide, the same walk becomes a grueling trudge through ankle-deep, shifting grains. T. E. Lawrence knew. Tide is everything. It is a short climb up to the summit of the Chatham Bar itself. Turning back, I can see the shingled homes and white steeples, the New England Thoreau knew.

Ten yards down the beach's outer slope, every trace of human presence disappears. It is not being on the beach by myself that is so exhilarating; it is being in the company of the shorebirds, the horseshoe crabs, and the striped bass swimming in schools offshore. The spring waves crumble and boom. Long hollow green-and-yellow tunnels rise, slide, tower, and fall along the scalloped ridges at the bottom of the tier of dunes. The sky is cloudless and blue, without any trace of high summer's humid haze. It is low tide and the gulls are fishing.

Every mile or so I stop to remove a piece of clothing. Long pants, sweater, T-shirt, socks, and sneakers all end up in the rucksack, and, after a three-hour walk up the Nauset beaches, I arrive at the green lawn, the oasis of the Nauset Knoll, with a sunburn on the back of my knees.

I sit watching the light easing, the cool gray mists rolling in. I fall asleep when my breathing synchronizes with the waves arriving from the ocean, the water snoring.

I study the wrinkled map. A route runs through Orleans to the old Cape Cod railroad bed, which the astute citizens have transformed into a bike trail. It leads quietly through an enormous marsh, through a pine wood, and past freshwater kettle ponds with beautiful names.

As I walk out into the marsh, the wind begins veering from the north. A mackerel sky appears. Everything seethes: water and grasses, even last year's unraked oak leaves. The railroad bed passes straight through the marsh in a way a road never would. I head out onto the cattail territory, the nesting red-winged blackbirds watching me go. Turtles are basking, but as the clouds send shadows like wind gusts across the water, I watch them one by one plop and swim down. As I reach the edge of the black kettle pond, a marsh hawk begins to wheel and cry. Something about the bird screaming and the haunting impression made by the visible sky is simultaneously startling and reassuring; a brief experience of the world, a Zen telephone call.

Hours pass. As the features of the world glide by, I can identify them on the map.

This is satisfying; just reading off the names tells a traveler what the inhabitants thought about the place he's in: Ireland Land, Mean Tide Way, Winterberry Road.

OUT HERE the boundaries dissolve: bird/human, man/nature, mudflat/bay. This is "land" because there are acres and acres of cattails waving, but it is sea as well, because the water fumes a few feet from the trail. And the misty atmosphere clings to the fibers of your sweater, drips gently from your eyebrows, mingling with the sweat above your eyes.

After a 3-mile crossing of the marsh, in the shelter of the first woods on the northern side, I notice a tiny sand crescent at the edge of Herring Pond. I settle under a young maple and spread a cloth for a picnic lunch. Testing the shallow, transparent water, I think, why not, and quickly wade in. Standing waist deep, just about to plunge, I notice a fur head paddling a few yards offshore: A muskrat is diving and reappearing after long fishing trips to the bottom. The raw wind and the May chill of the pond quickly transform my idea of a leisurely swim into a quick splash and a sprint back to shore for a towel.

After I cross the lowlands and have my picnic and my swim, I stop briefly in an ancient cemetery and browse among the gravestones the way you'd wander the aisles of a bookstore, looking for titles, other lives. Bright orange and yellow lichen stand out on the wet black tilted graves. Some of the stones are so old the writing has been worn to an illegible carved wrinkle, haiku epitaphs faded like the bones they identify.

Cold water and the shadows of the pine trees on the gold needles at their feet make me think of the first Pilgrim expeditions to this territory. By walking through a landscape and stopping to swim the waters, a traveler can sense the world in a way earlier generations did. I can trace the roots of our current ecological crises back to the First Encounter Beach, a mile from where I am hiking along and musing. That "first encounter" between European and native civilizations was an exchange of weapons fire. The European conception of land as property displaced a native understanding of the natural realm as common bounty. If you cannot own an ocean, or a cloud, or the sunlight, how can you own a hill, a meadow, a salt marsh, a beach?

In the imagination of everyone who grew up in New England, there is a kind of Ur-Town, and I was convinced that no such place remained. Wellfleet changes my mind. There is a forested bay and an estuary ringed by the hardwoods and the quiet town. The white steeple leans away into the changing clouds. The few streets wind among the watermen's houses, and the children still run barefoot in the picket fence backyards. A dog yelps, a slow car putters by, the ships in the harbor ride their algae moorings, and a walker sidles effortlessly in.

I eat a plate of pasta with oyster sauce and drink a glass of wine at a place called Aesop's Tables, and for the only time in my week outdoors the sky pours, and just as the world grows absolutely black, the lightning bolts of the passing squall make the candles on every table tremble and fade. Ancient Taoist philosophers in China said that hunger makes the best sauce; it's also true that a thunderstorm makes a room cozy and a dinner by a ship captain's hearth even more delightful.

THE NEXT MORNING, after an hour spent winding among small hardwood thickets and low watery ferns, for the first time out of earshot of the sea, I get that little uh-oh feeling that usually means, "You are completely lost."

The world and the map no longer coincide. I choose the world. I make the week's most valuable mistake, turning left at an unsigned intersection. The road gives way to a sandy trail, and I find myself in one of those beautiful lost valleys where the wealthy hide. A woman mowing in a pasture explains a different route to the water, and in half an hour I reach a dune paradise—long, deep, surging ridges, grassy bowls, sheltered valleys entirely without footprints. It is only the swarm of hungry mosquitoes that starts me sprinting toward the coast, where the onshore wind will keep them away. The bay is a different body of water altogether; it is pacific, with transparent green and blue gradations, quite shallow, with visible stones and randomly

strewn kelp drawings on the bottom. I wade in and swim. The ocean here is warmer and as quiet as a pond. No matter how hot I am, the cool is instant, total, and as I sit eating my market picnic, alone in all directions, even my thoughts are clean.

The next few miles of walking are effortless. Here along Ryder Beach the heather rolls up toward the forest and the land itself begins to swell. It is bare without being barren, somewhat wistfully austere. Edward Hopper built himself a house in Truro in the 1930s, and the clear light he gave his life to is still here. Up in the warm meadows, there is toe-soft loam producing flowers, twitching gently in the early afternoon; coiled streams and estuaries are set in beside the land. I'm trying not to exaggerate, but you can't tell if what you're seeing is a painting or a dream.

The morning of the final day, I wake to a room full of chilly fog. Having left both windows open, I am literally wrapped in weather. On the Highland Road to the Cape Cod Lighthouse for the final leg, my footsteps have a new reluctance.

One of the most remarkable aspects of this week outdoors is the experience of the ocean on its own terms; what seems recreational and tame among the tilted umbrellas and radios and Frisbee-chasing dogs becomes altogether unfamiliar after a few hours alone. Water rises and falls, wrapping an entire globe as it rockets through outer space, centrifugally whirling as it goes. The water speaks in tongues, and after several days you begin to listen.

My hands are actually cold, my knuckles frozen. I'm playing Guess the Season. In a world of sand and water and wind, there are fewer clues. The wind booms, the ocean's humming, and the loud waves build and fall and shake the gravel I'm on as the last wave hisses and recedes into the next.

After several days of steady traveling up the coast, walking and thinking fuse, the ordinary divisions of mind and body lose their boundaries. The easygoing motion of my limbs seems to belong to the Cape dunes and riverbeds, the way the ebbing and flooding tides, the piled clouds, the crying birds do. Toward the end of his life Thoreau made an unobtrusive entry in his journal: "All I can say is that I live and breathe and have my thoughts." Out here that short list of attributes seems plenty.

The harbor side streets are empty as I go searching for a room. It is strange to have touched a long stretch of geography with your feet. You feel a friendship toward the roaming world out there; contact has given you calm.

A lighthouse blinks every four seconds. A white lobster boat is mooring in the last light. I find a room in a house by the water. As New England weather will, the sky changes while I'm at the front desk checking in. Up on the third floor, I can look off into the sunset's afterglow. The sky clears, turning cheddar gold.

— Anthony Chase

BOOKS AND VIDEOS

NEW ENGLAND has been home to some of America's classic authors, among them Herman Melville, Edith Wharton, Mark Twain, Robert Frost, and Emily Dickinson. Henry David Thoreau wrote about New England in *Cape Cod, The Maine Woods,* and his masterpiece, *Walden* (which is also available on audiotape).

Melville's *Moby-Dick,* set on a 19th-century Nantucket whaler, captures the spirit of the whaling era; Gregory Peck starred in the 1956 screen version under John Huston's direction. Nathaniel Hawthorne portrayed early New England life in his novels *The Scarlet Letter* (the 1995 movie stars Demi Moore) and *The House of the Seven Gables* (the actual house, in Salem, is open to the public). Newburyport native Henry James's books include *The Bostonians, Daisy Miller,* and *Portrait of a Lady.* The beautiful 1994 screen adaptation of Louisa May Alcott's classic, *Little Women,* casts Winona Ryder as Jo and Susan Sarandon as Marmee. Visitors are welcome at Alcott's house (look for shots of it in the movie) in Concord, Massachusetts. Some scenes were also filmed in Historic Deerfield in the Pioneer Valley. Hog Island, near Essex, was a 1995 location for the filming of *The Crucible,* Arthur Miller's 1953 play about the Salem witch trials. It stars Daniel Day-Lewis and Winona Ryder.

Among books written about the Maine islands are Philip Conkling's *Islands in Time,* Bill Caldwell's *Islands of Maine,* and Charlotte Fardelmann's *Islands Down East.* Kenneth Roberts set a series of historical novels, beginning with *Arundel,* in the coastal Kennebunk region during the Revolutionary War. Ruth Moore's *Candalmas Bay, Speak to the Winds,* and *The Weir* and Elisabeth Ogilvie's "Tide Trilogy" books capture both the romanticism and hardships of coastal life. Carolyn Chute's 1985 best-seller, *The Beans of Egypt, Maine,* offers a fictional glimpse of the hardships of contemporary rural life.

After a limited theatrical release in 1994, the movie version of the book, starring Martha Plimpton, is in video stores with the title *Forbidden Choices.*

Charles Morrissey's *Vermont: A History* delivers just what the title promises. *Without a Farmhouse Near,* by Deborah Rawson, describes the impact of change on small Vermont communities. *Real Vermonters Don't Milk Goats,* by Frank Bryan and Bill Mares, looks at the lighter side of life in the Green Mountain state. Both books and movies, *Peyton Place* and *Ethan Frome* have links to Vermont.

Visitors to New Hampshire may enjoy *The White Mountains: Their Legends, Landscape, and Poetry,* by Starr King, and *The Great Stone Face and Other Tales of the White Mountains,* by Nathaniel Hawthorne. New Hampshire was also blessed with the poet Robert Frost, whose first books, *A Boy's Way* and *North of Boston,* are set here. It's commonly accepted that the Grover's Corners of Thornton Wilder's *Our Town* is the real-life Peterborough; Willa Cather wrote part of *Death Comes for the Archbishop* while residing in Peterborough. The 1981 movie *On Golden Pond* was partially filmed on Squam Lake.

Sloan Wilson's novel *The Man in the Gray Flannel Suit* renders the life of a Connecticut commuter (Cary Grant in the movie version) in the 1950s. Julia Roberts's first movie, the charming *Mystic Pizza,* focuses on a group of young Mystic women and their romances. In *Theophilus North,* Thornton Wilder portrays Newport, Rhode Island, in its social heyday.

Also published by Fodor's, *New England's Best Bed & Breakfasts* has more than 300 reviews; *National Parks and Seashores of the East* covers many New England destinations; and *Where Should We Take the Kids? The Northeast* provides ideas on what to do with the little ones while in New England.

INDEX

Looking for a different kind of vacation?

Fodor's makes it easy with a full line of guidebooks to suit a variety of interests—from sports and adventure to romance to family fun.

WHEREVER YOU TRAVEL, *H*ELP IS NEVER FAR AWAY.

From planning your trip to providing travel assistance
along the way, American Express® Travel Service Offices
are always there to help.

New England

CONNECTICUT
American Express Travel Service
Stamford
203/359-4244

NEW HAMPSHIRE
Griffin Travel Service (R)
Manchester
603/668-3730

MAINE
American Express Travel Service
Portland
207/772-8450

RHODE ISLAND
American Express Travel Service
Cranston
401/943-4545

MASSACHUSETTS
American Express Travel Service
Boston
617/439-4400

VERMONT
Milne Travel (R)
Brattleboro
802/254-8844

American Express Travel Service
Cambridge
617/868-2600

American-International Travel (R)
Burlington
802/864-9827

Travel

http://www.americanexpress.com/travel

American Express Travel Service Offices are located throughout
New England. For the office nearest you, call 1-800-AXP-3429.